Discovering the Mystery of the Unity of God

Discovering the Mystery of the Unity of God

A Theological Study
on the Plurality and Tri-unity
of God in the Hebrew Scriptures

by
John B. Metzger, M.A.

Discovering the Mystery of the Unity of God
Copyright © 2010 by John B. Metzger

www.PromisesToIsrael.org
PO Box 1996
Matthews, NC 28106

ISBN: 978-1-935174-04-2

Library of Congress Control Number: 2010908277

REL 067040 RELIGION - Christian Theology - Christology
REL 006210 RELIGION - Biblical Studies - Old Testament
REL 067030 RELIGION - Christian Theology - Apologetics

Permission to publish from SPCK Publishing & Sheldon Press was granted to print an extract (pages 262-296) from Jakob Jocz's book "The Jewish People and Jesus Christ: A Study in the controversy between Church and Synagogue" which was printed in 1954 by S.P.C.K. publishing in London (appendix # 6).

Printed in the United States of America

Art work by Amy Sheetreet
www.AmysDesignsOfIsrael.com

Design by Dolores Testerman
www.GladTidingsStudio.com

Published by:

11926 Radium Street
P.O. Box 792507
San Antonio, TX
www.Ariel.org

Special Acknowledgement

To my Wife
Sharon
For her patience as I studied and wrote,
under a mountain of books, for the past nine years.
Also for her proofreading and help in preparing this book for
publication.

We have celebrated our 42nd wedding anniversary.

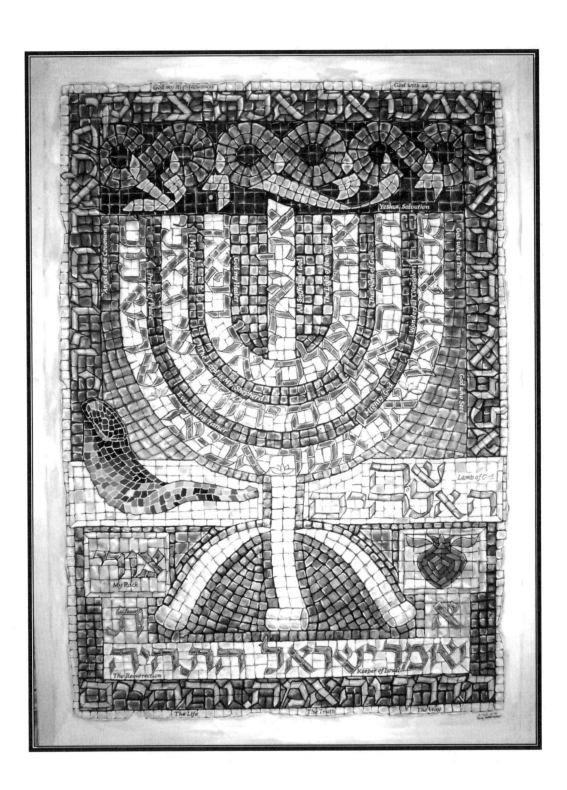

A translation
of the Hebrew words
from the front cover of this book

The border at the top moving to the right
Top: God my Righteousness, God with us,
Right: God who is there, God who Sees
Bottom: The Way, The Truth, The Life
Left: Angel of the Covenant

Second from the bottom
Keeper of Israel, The Resurrection

Third from the bottom
My Rock

Fourth from the bottom
Lamb of God

Menorah
Servant branch: All Sufficient God
Right side first: The Light of the World
Right side second: The Word of God
Right side third: Wonderful Counselor
Left side first: God my Helper
Left side second: My Redeemer
Left side third: Prince of Peace

Above the Menorah and below the lights
Yeshua, Salvation

Other acknowledgements to the following people
who were an indispensable help in editing and
proofreading this book.

Dr. Thomas Figart
Retired
Professor of Bible and Theology
at Lancaster Bible College

Dr. Henry Heijermans
Biblical Ministries Worldwide
Executive General Director Emeritus

Mr. Kenneth Martin
Retired
Pastor and Real Estate Broker

Miss Sandra Achenbach
Eastern Mennonite Missions
For her volunteer services in editing

Mrs. Linda Young
For her help in causing me to look at the text
of the book from the viewpoint of a person who is not necessarily
familiar with biblical terms and phrases.

Dr. Robert Spender
Chairman of the Biblical Studies Department
Lancaster Bible College and Graduate School
Much gratitude and appreciation goes to Dr. Spender
for taking the time to proofread the Hebrew in this book.

I would like to dedicate this book to
the four following individuals:

Mabel Metzger
My 102-year-old mother for her godly example and
for all her encouragement over the years.

Rev. J. Albert Ford (Deceased)
the first pastor of
McLean Bible Church
McLean, VA
who preached the whole Scripture:
doctrine, book studies, and prophecy.
Because of his ministry,
a love of the Word of God
and a love for Jewish people and Israel
took root in my life and gave me direction
as a teenager and for the rest of my life.

Dr. Willis Bishop (Retired)
Professor of Old Testament Studies
at
Washington Bible College
Lanham, MD
For his faithfulness in teaching over the years
and for giving me the foundation
for my Old Testament understanding.

Dr. Arnold G. Fruchtenbaum
Founder & Director of Ariel Ministries
San Antonio, TX
and
Camp Shoshannah
Keeseville, NY
For the understanding of the Scriptures
from a Jewish perspective.
God has used him to change my
life and ministry.

Table of Contents

FOREWORD

by

Dr. Arnold G. Fruchtenbaum

The concept of the triune nature of the God of Israel, as taught even by the Hebrew Scriptures, has traditionally been the hardest thing for Jewish people to believe and accept. Often, no matter how well it is explained, Jewish people still tend to conclude that "Christianity" actually teaches the concept of three different gods. Even among some circles of Messianic Jews, this is a difficult teaching to accept and is also denied by some who affirm to believe in the Messiahship of *Yeshua* (Jesus).

While the New Testament does present the concept of the Trinity in a clearer manner, yet even many New Testament believers have a difficulty in explaining the concept in a way that does not cross the line from monotheism to tritheism. New Testament believers certainly affirm the concept but have a difficult time explaining it.

So how does one explain the inexplicable? This is what John Metzger has zealously endeavored to do in this volume, and he has done a superb job in both expounding what both testaments teach on the subject and explaining it in a way that communicates to the uninitiated. While a complete understanding of the Three in One would not be possible this side of eternity, this work is one of the best I have seen in bringing out the clarity of Scripture on the subject.

Dr. Arnold G. Fruchtenbaum

PREFACE

Words from the Author

Why is there a need for another book on the Trinity? There are so many books already published on that subject, so why do we need another one? The purpose of this book is twofold: first, all other books written today are written from a New Testament perspective; this one will be written from an Old Testament perspective exclusively. Secondly, in addressing the subject of the Trinity (tri-unity) we will interact with the Jewish belief that God is an absolute one and not a tri-unity. This book will show Christian and Jewish people alike that God did reveal Himself to mankind as a tri-unity, more accurately as a plural unity of one.

In writing this book I realize that many people will understand the terms used, but also some readers will not. So if you come across a word that you are not familiar with, please look to the footnotes at the bottom of that page. There will also be a complete word glossary at the end of this book. It is my desire to have this theological study on the tri-unity from the Old Testament written in a way that the average Christian and Jewish individual can read it with understanding.

This book is written to two audiences and neither one is completely familiar with the religious terms that the other uses. All of the terms will be given from the belief of a true New Testament believer first. Terms such as Christ (Messiah), and then the Jewish term Messiah will follow from that point on throughout the book. Two other examples will illustrate: New Testament believers use the term Old Testament to denote the first 39 books of the Bible. However, the words Old Testament which are used to describe the Jewish Bible is offensive to the Jewish reader. It is not only offensive but is also an inaccurate title for that part of the Bible. So we will use two alternating expressions to describe the Old Testament for the Jewish reader, first *Tanakh* and secondly Hebrew Scriptures. The Hebrew word *Tanakh* is an acronym derived from the threefold division of the Jewish Scriptures; the Law (Torah), the Prophets (*Nevi'im*) and the Writings (*Kethuvim*). The second example is the word Jesus. Because that name is also offensive to our Jewish audience, His Hebrew name *Yeshua* will be used in its place.

These two great faiths, Judaism and true New Testament Faith, have many things in common and also many things that are diverse. The central issue that divides these faiths is the New Testament teachings concerning the person of God known as the Trinity (tri-unity) and Judaism's teaching that God is an absolute one. This doctrine impacts many other doctrines where the New Testament believers and Judaism are at opposite ends of their respective belief systems.

There is much confusion and lack of knowledge on both sides. Christianity does not understand Judaism and Judaism's belief that God is an absolute one and what has led them to that position. Nor does Judaism understand Christianity and its belief in the Trinity. There is much ignorance on both sides and the problem is made worse by their different respective teachings. Consequently the bias on both sides has added dramatically to the confusion and misunderstanding. That division has been greatly magnified by the historic persecution of the Jewish people by the "Christian Church." So there is a great need to sit down and study the Scriptures as God wrote them through Moses, the Prophets and the New Testament writers such as Paul. Within Judaism the teachings of the rabbis hold great authority in understanding the Jewish Bible. Christianity equally has given great importance to the writings of the church fathers. It is my position that both give too much authority to their rabbis, priests or pastors and scholars. While some of their insights help us to understand Scripture better, these men are fallible. The written word of God is God's Word and He alone should hold complete authority. We should not revere the interpretations of men. In this book while many rabbinic and New Testament and Christian scholars are referenced, it is God's Word alone that is lifted up. I have only used references to other authors because I am unknown in the academic community.

I write this with great love and respect for the Jewish people, who are the most blessed nation on earth with some of the world's greatest intellects that are consistently rising to the top in almost every field of endeavor whether collectively or individually. My prayer is that each person individually will carefully investigate the Hebrew Scriptures as God (*HaShem*[1]) wrote them, for He longs to reveal Himself to you. It is clear that Jewish people have had little historical and theological incentive to personally investigate the Christian "Jesus." Unbiblical atrocities that have been committed against Jewish people, in the name of Jesus, for centuries is the cause of their lack of incentive.

Much to my dismay many evangelical and fundamental Christians do not see the tri-unity of God clearly in the Hebrew Scriptures. They often perform biblical and secular "gymnastics" and discount the inspiration of God's Word. They too have often been influenced by humanistic higher criticism that came out of Germany in the 18th century. I equally discovered that many popular Christian commentaries ineffectively handle the Scriptures as related to the nature of God as well as other doctrinal issues, but especially the tri-unity of God in the Hebrew Scriptures.

Lastly, I acknowledge my limitations with the Hebrew language. With the available contemporary Hebrew helps and computer technologies, I believe that I am completely accurate in this book. I am not a novice in the Scriptures. I have greatly appreciated

---

[1] *HaShem*: This is a common expression by Jewish people who do not wish to speak God's name; it simply means 'the name.' *HaShem* would be inserted instead of Yahweh, the personal name of God.

Dr. Robert Spender of Lancaster Bible College and Dr. Arnold Fruchtenbaum for looking over all my Hebrew words to make sure that I have written them correctly. I am deeply passionate that this book will be an encouragement to evangelical and fundamental Bible believers to maintain their faith. The pressures of Christian marketing create more interest in the dollar than in presenting doctrinal purity to the hearts and minds of believers. I am equally passionate that Jewish people who read this book will discover the God of Israel and that His authority is above all human authority.

I trust that your study of this issue will be edifying and that it will dispel the lack of knowledge on both sides. I know this is not a novel, which means that it is not a quick read. But I believe that the insights of the person of God in the *Tanakh* will be of great benefit to both New Testament believers and Jewish persons who take the time to learn about their God. May the God of Abraham, Isaac and Jacob richly bless you in your study.

Hebrew Alphabet

Letter	Final Form	Name	Transliteration	Pronunciation
א		Alef		Silent Letter
בּ		Bet	b	B as in Boy
ב			v	V as in Vine
גּ		Gimel	g	G as in Go
ג			g	G as in Go
דּ	ד	Dalet	d	D as in Dare
ה		Heh	h	H as in His
ו		Vav	v	V as in Vine
ז		Zayin	z	Z as in Zion
ח		Chet	h	CH as in BaCH
ט		Tet	t	T as in Tall
י		Yod	y	Y as in Yes
כּ		Kaf	k	K as in Keep
כ	ך		kh	CH as in BaCH
ל		Lamed	l	L as in Let
מ	ם	Mem	m	M as in Met
נ	ן	Nun	n	N as in Net
ס		Samech	s	S as in Set
ע		Ayin		Silent Letter
פּ		Peh	p	P as in Pet
פ	ף		f	F as in Fat
צ	ץ	Tzadi	s	TS as in NeTS
ק		Kof	q	K as in Keep
ר		Reyshr		R as in Rule
שׁ		Shin	s	S as in Set
שׂ			s	SH as in SHine
תּ	ת	Tav	t	T as in Tall

Books of the Hebrew Scriptures

Jewish Hebrew Bible		Christian Old Testament	
Torah		Pentateuch	
Genesis	- Bere'shit	Genesis	(Gen)
Exodus	- Shemot	Exodus	(Exod)
Leviticus	- Vayikra	Leviticus	(Lev)
Numbers	- Bemidbar	Numbers	(Num)
Deuteronomy	- Devarim	Deuteronomy	(Deut)
Prophets – Nevi'im		Historical	
Joshua		Joshua	(Josh)
Judges		Judges	(Judg)
1 & 2 Samuel		Ruth	(Ruth)
1 & 2 Kings		1 & 2 Samuel	(Sam)
Isaiah		1 & 2 Kings	(Kgs)
Jeremiah		1 & 2 Chronicles	(Chr)
Ezekiel		Ezra	(Ezra)
(The Twelve)		Nehemiah	(Neh)
Hosea		Esther	(Esth)
Joel		Poetical	
Amos		Job	(Job)
Obadiah		Psalms	(Psa)
Jonah		Proverbs	(Prov)
Micah		Ecclesiastes	(Eccl)
Nahum		Song of Solomon	
Habakkuk		Lamentations	(Lam)
Zephaniah		Major Prophets	
Haggai		Isaiah	(Isa)
Zechariah		Jeremiah	(Jer)
Malachi		Ezekiel	(Ezek)
Writings - *Kethuvim*		Daniel	(Dan)
Psalms		Minor Prophets	
Proverbs		Hosea	(Hos)
Job		Joel	(Joel)
(The Scrolls - Megillah)		Amos	(Amos)
The Song of Songs		Obadiah	(Obad)
Ruth		Jonah	(Jon)
Lamentations		Micah	(Mic)
Ecclesiastes		Nahum	(Nah)
Esther		Habakkuk	(Hab)
Daniel		Zephaniah	(Zeph)
Ezra		Haggai	(Hag)
Nehemiah		Zechariah	(Zech)
1 & 2 Chronicles		Malachi	(Mal)

DEFINING OF TERMS

Before going any further, each side needs to understand what is meant by the terms Judaism and Christianity and the alternate terms that this author uses. First, as it relates to Judaism: The most common term that this author will use is Rabbinic Judaism. Rabbinic Judaism has controlled the Jewish people spiritually and physically basically from the beginning of the second temple period to this present day with the zenith of its influence between the destruction of the temple in 70 C.E. and the period called the enlightenment when Jewish people began to leave Rabbinic Judaism for a much more secular appearance and lifestyle. Religious Judaism is embraced by the following groupings: Ultra-Orthodox, Modern Orthodox, Conservative Judaism, Reform Judaism, as well as Reconstructionist Judaism, leaving nearly 50% of the Jewish people in the United States as secular (80% in Israel). This means they are ethnically Jewish but do not practice Judaism as a faith. If a Jewish person is religious, he has been impacted in his beliefs by Rabbinic Judaism regardless of what grouping he belongs too. This will be spelled out later. Occasionally I will use the term biblical Judaism, which means the Scriptures are interpreted literally as God gave them, pure and not influenced by rabbinic thought.

Next we need to understand the term Christianity and the terms that I will use in place of it. In Judaism you are born ethnically Jewish or as a Hebrew. A Christian is not born ethnically a Christian because ethnicity is not a religion. A Gentile makes a conscious decision to become a Christian. Being baptized as a baby does not make a Gentile a Christian any more than a Gentile baby being circumcised makes him Jewish. Being a true New Testament believer in Jesus is a conscious decision that I made when I was 14 years old on July 23, 1960. That is when I understood that I was a sinner in need of a Saviour, and I consciously prayed to God confessing my sinfulness and accepting Jesus Christ as my personal Saviour from sin. That made me a Christian, a follower of Christ. The problem with much of Christianity today, and historically, is that it has abandoned, or has become apostate from the true teachings of the Scriptures, and as a result Jewish people have seen the worst of Christianity. I also abhor what so-called Christianity did in the name of Jesus Christ to the Jewish people. So being a Roman Catholic, Greek or Russian Orthodox or Protestant does not make a person a Christian. They may have been christianized, but are not Christian. They may use the language and dress piously with their religious robes, collars, and suits decorated with religious things, but that does not make them Christian. Again a Christian is one who has consciously confessed his sins and has accepted the substitutionary sacrifice that Jesus Christ made for him/her on the cross of Calvary and lives according to the teachings of the Jewish authors of the New Covenant. However, most Jewish people have not read the New Covenant, so they do not know what it teaches as to how the Christian is to be living out his faith before God and his fellowman. What Jewish people have experienced at the hands of Christians is erroneous teaching from the New Covenant.

Under Christianity there is another group who has consciously accepted Jesus Christ as their personal Saviour and have organized themselves into another Christian group, but they most often will not use that name. These are Jewish people who are still ethnically Jewish, and will always be Jewish, but have accepted Jesus as the Messiah of Israel and have come to Jesus Christ the same way a Gentile does when he becomes a believer. Many within this group choose to call themselves Messianic Believers or Messianic Jews belonging to Messianic Judaism. However, many others of them belong to Bible-believing churches that are faithful to the Scriptures. I have chosen not to use Messianic Believers or Messianic Jews because they are one in the body of Messiah, with the Gentile believers, while still remaining ethnically, and many of them, culturally Jewish. Instead of Christianity all the time, I have chosen to use terms that better express what a true Christian is, such as biblical Christianity, True Believers, biblical Faith, or New Testament Faith or a combination of these words. I will be predominantly using these terms in reference to true believers to distinguish their faith in Jesus Christ from the rest of Christianity that is not genuinely Christian.

I trust this will help both Jewish and Christian readers understand why I am using the terms Rabbinic Judaism instead of Judaism and true biblical Bible believers instead of the term Christianity. I also trust that this brief treatment of these terms will serve to clarify and not confuse the reader. Those of us who are true Bible believing Christians, Christian Zionists, love and wholly support the Jewish people whether in Israel or in the Diaspora.

THE DIVIDING POINT

The dividing point is clearly and unquestionably a theological issue. Notice that this issue is being introduced in the singular and not as plural issues. There are many issues that revolve around this one theological dividing point which are secondary but linked very closely to that central issue. The central issue to be discussed is the Trinity (hereafter called the plurality or tri-unity of God). However, the word "trinity" is an inadequate term to describe God because it emphasizes the three persons and not the unity within the Trinity. Hence the term "tri-unity" or "plural unity" of God (*Elohim*) will be used as a better way to unite the oneness or unity of God with the plurality of God.[2] But even tri-unity is not palatable in the minds of Jewish people. The best term available for us to describe the person of God are the words "plural unity." So the latter expression (plural unity) will be used more frequently than the first (tri-unity). To understand the tri-unity of God one needs to first understand what both Rabbinic Judaism and true biblical New Testament believers teach in relation to the nature and person of God. First I will give the position of Rabbinic Judaism and then biblical New Testament faith as taught from a Jewish perspective to the nature and person of God.

---

[2] Paul Enns, *The Moody Handbook of Theology* (Chicago: Moody, 1989), 199.

Belief of Judaism

Within Judaism and Christianity today the foundational belief that both hold in common is that God is one and there are no gods besides Him (Deuteronomy 6:4; Isaiah 44:6; 1 Corinthians 8:6). However, Rabbinic Judaism and the biblical New Testament faith part company after that point. Rabbinic Judaism has an unmovable belief in monotheism, which is that God is one alone. Rabbi Stanley Greenberg of Temple Sinai of Philadelphia and Rabbi Dan Cohn-Sherbok clearly contrast the following statements of the Jewish belief in the oneness of God with the Christian belief of the tri-unity of God:

> Christians are, of course, entitled to believe in a Trinitarian conception of God, but their effort to base this conception on the Hebrew Bible must fly in the face of the overwhelming testimony of that Bible. Hebrew Scriptures are clear and unequivocal on the oneness of God...The Hebrew Bible affirms the one God with unmistakable clarity. Monotheism, an uncompromising belief in one God, is the hallmark of the Hebrew Bible, the unwavering affirmation of Judaism and the unshakable Faith of the Jew. Under no circumstances can a concept of a plurality of the Godhead or a trinity of the Godhead ever be based upon the Hebrew Bible.[3]

> ... all Jewish thinkers reject trinitarianism as incompatible with monotheism. Modern Jewish thought is equally critical of any attempt to harmonize the belief in God's unity with the concept of a triune God. Contemporary Jewish theologians of all degrees of observance affirm that Judaism is fundamentally incompatible with what they perceive as the polytheistic character of Trinitarian belief.[4]

Keep these two statements in mind as we proceed through the evidence that is laid out before us in this book. The contrast between the absolute monotheism[5] of Rabbinic Judaism and the monotheism true New Testament believers expressed in the tri-unity of God is the central issue which divides these two faiths. There are two other articles of faith that are closely tied to the New Testament belief in the tri-unity of God. In fact they are inseparably connected together, which further divides these two great faiths. The two other articles of faith are the Incarnation and the need of a Mediator.

---

[3] Rabbi Stanley Greenberg, "Jewishness and the Trinity," n.p. [cited 18 November 2003]. Online: http://*www.JewsForJesus.org/library.issue8* & [cited 19 July 2003] *www.Messiahnj.org/ af-tri-unity.htm*. It is also cited in a booklet called *Jewishness and the Trinity*, written by Jews for Jesus.

[4] Rabbi Dan Cohn-Sherbok, *The Jewish Messiah* (Edinburgh, Scotland: T & T Clark, 1997), 75-76.

[5] *Monotheism* is the belief in one God and that no other gods exist.

According to Rabbi Aryeh Kaplan, there are three major obstacles for Rabbinic Judaism: (1) the Trinity: the "Christian belief that G-d[6] consists of three persons, the Father, the Son and the Holy Spirit;" (2) the Incarnation: "according to this doctrine, G-d in the person of the Son assumed human form in the person of Jesus;" (3) the need of a Mediator: "that man cannot approach G-d except through Jesus."[7] Here lies the heart of the division between Rabbinic Judaism and biblical Christianity. That is not to say that there are no other differences, but these are paramount.

Even though the Incarnation and the need of a Mediator are very important issues, the tri-unity of God is central. Rabbinic Judaism believes not only in the oneness of God but that He is an absolute one, which leaves no room for a plurality of God that New Testament believers hold. That sets the stage for this book and the understanding of "The Mystery of the Unity of God." Who is right according to the Old Testament (called hereafter the Hebrew Scriptures or *Tanakh*)? Does God present Himself in the Hebrew Scriptures as an absolute one, a unity, or as a plurality (tri-unity) of God who is a unity of one? That will be the quest of this book.

Belief of True New Testament Faith

First, before going on, the term Christianity needs again to be defined biblically. The word Christendom is the umbrella word for anything that is called Christian. This is to help our Jewish readers to understand the different branches of Christianity. All branches of Christianity whether Roman Catholic, Greek Orthodox, Russian Orthodox or the Protestant Church today is largely an apostate church; meaning by apostate, they have abandoned the faith that was given by the prophets and the apostles. So who is a true New Testament believer within Christianity? True believers believe that we are sinners and that we as humans cannot obtain merit from God by good works or sacraments. Salvation is by faith alone, not by any works. Within all branches of Christianity there are true believers in Jesus, but they are in the minority. Even within Protestant Christianity most denominations have left the faith by denying the Scriptures as God's Word, that Jesus is the only way of salvation. They have rejected creation in favor of evolution; they have rejected the miracles of the Bible by trying to explain them strictly by natural means. They have reinterpreted Scripture to suit their own human biases. True New Testament believers believe that salvation is by faith alone, and they hold to the inerrancy (without error) of Scripture, and that the Scripture is the inspired Word of God. Within the true believers one of the biggest differences is how to

---

[6] It is necessary to interject the reason for the hyphen placed in the word for God. It is not to show disrespect for the person of God as some Christians believe, but rather it is showing Jewish sensitivity in writing and/or speaking the name for God. Many orthodox Jews will not pronounce the name of God out of respect to Him, so they use the term *HaShem* (meaning the name) when speaking of God. In writing the name of God, they will often hyphenate the word God as G-d, and Lord as L-rd.

[7] Aryeh Kaplan, *The Real Messiah? A Jewish Response to Missionaries* (New York: National Conference of Synagogues, 1985), 14-19.

deal with Israel. Do Israel and the Jewish people have a future in God's plan or has Israel been replaced by the Church? These two views are called Dispensational Theology and Reform Covenant (replacement) Theology. I approach the Scriptures as a Dispensationalist, a lover of Israel and the Jewish people with full support for the Jewish People and the Nation of Israel. The covenants made to Abraham, to Israel (Land), the Davidic Covenant and New Covenants must be literally fulfilled.

Christianity views God as a Trinity, meaning that God is one but that He expresses Himself to mankind in a plurality of persons, God the Father, God the Son and God the Holy Spirit who are one and indivisible. The fallacy of Christianity is that through history in their effort to prove the Trinity against heretics within the Church, their emphasis on the three persons of God has given the appearance to Judaism that Christianity worships three gods or Tri-theism, thus making them idolatrous in the minds of Jewish people. However, Christianity and true believers declare emphatically that God is one and that He expresses Himself in three persons. True biblical Christianity does not in any way believe that there are three gods, nor does true biblical Christianity venerate and exalt the Virgin Mary to co-redemptrix as does the Roman Catholic Church, nor is Mary part of the Trinity as adherents to Islam are taught. True biblical Christianity believes, as Judaism, that God is one, that He is an indivisible, incorporeal Spirit being. Biblical Christianity does believe that God appeared to mankind by taking on flesh in the person called Jesus (hereafter His Hebrew name *Yeshua* will be used), who was God incarnate (Isaiah 9:6-7; John 1:14). Because of this, Rabbinic Judaism emphatically rejects the teaching of New Testament believers that *Yeshua* is God and that He is the Saviour of the world from sin. So the theological stage is set as both Rabbinic Judaism and biblical Christianity or as true New Testament faith lay out their beliefs. Even though there is only one main theological issue, there is the need to understand the historical issue that has arisen between Judaism and Christianity from the Church's belief in the Trinity. Christianity took that belief of the "trinity" and used it as a club to beat the Jewish people, because of their rejection of the *Yeshua* who is the expression of God's plurality. The church has become guilty themselves of disobeying God and His Word.

History of Rejection by the Jewish People of Christianity

In Old Testament times unbelief in the oneness of God was demonstrated by turning to other gods and not being obedient to the Written Law of God found in the Torah or the five books of Moses. Both Israel in 722 BCE[8] and later Judah in 586 BCE suffered two great defeats, which resulted in the people being carried away into Assyria (Amos 7:10-17; Hosea 4:1-6; 9:1-9)[9] and Babylon (2 Chronicles 34:14-28; Jeremiah 2:5–3:10)[10]

---

[8] *Common Era and Before the Common Era*: These are alternate terms used as synonyms for the Latin adopted by the Church after the birth of Christ. So BC and AD are the exact equivalent of BCE and CE.

[9] Andrew E. Hill and John H. Walton. *A Survey of the Old Testament*, (Grand Rapids: Zondervan, 1991), 359.

respectively. The beginning of the Diaspora,[11] the "scattering around the world" as spoken of by Moses in Deuteronomy 28:15-68 (with Deuteronomy 30:1-10; Jeremiah 11:8) had begun. These great defeats were a direct result of the Jewish people's unbelief and apostasy in relation to their God and to His law given through Moses. They forsook God, and the Mosaic Law, which is also known as the Written Law, and worshipped false gods.

Upon returning from Babylonian captivity Israel wanted to make absolutely sure that they never again break God's Written Law and that they would never again worship pagan gods. So their focus, and rightfully so, was on teaching the oneness of God, and that He alone was to be worshiped. That ancient belief in the oneness of God, however, became the major reason Jewish people later rejected *Yeshua* as their Messiah, because in the *Tanakh* God presented Himself as a plural unity of one God, which made the understanding of "The Mystery of the Unity of God" more complex. That concept they refused to believe because of God's judgment against their idolatry. Thus, not recognizing the plurality of God in the *Tanakh* by focusing only on the oneness of God, they missed all that Moses and the Prophets said about the Messiah being not just a man but also the God/man. Consequently they have resisted the advancement of the Gospel of Christ (hereafter called Messiah or *Moshiach*) for over twenty centuries. They rejected *Yeshua* the Messiah,[12] the promised Messiah of Israel as God incarnate.

Because of that rejection (Matthew 12:22-45) *Yeshua* pronounced a judgment on "*that generation*" (Luke21:5-6; 20-24 cf. Daniel 9:26). This brought about a second set of Jewish defeats (70 and 135 CE) forty and one hundred five years later which further contributed to the Diaspora. This dispersion occurred not because they denied the oneness of God through idolatry as they had previously done, but because they had rejected their Messiah who, as this book will show, was the God of Israel whom they worshiped. This denial and rejection were primarily a result of their belief in the absolute oneness of God which was compounded by the rabbinic teaching also known as the Oral Law (Daniel 9:26; Zechariah 11:1-17; 12:10; Matthew 24:1-2; Mark 13:1-2; Luke 21:5-6; 20-24).[13] The Oral Law made an even greater division between the

---

[10] Hill and Walton, *A Survey of the Old Testament*, 329.

[11] *Diaspora*: *The dispersion of Jews throughout the world beginning with Israel* (722 BCE) and Judah (586 BCE) through the fall of the Second Temple (70 CE) and the defeat in the revolt in 135 CE. Diaspora also known as the "Exile" refers to all Jews living outside the land of Israel.

[12] *Messiah*: Messiah comes from the Hebrew word *Mashiach*, meaning "anointed." When translated into New Testament Greek, Messiah is *Christos* which becomes "Christ" in English.

[13] *Oral Law*: Oral instruction beyond the written *Torah*, which was written down in the *Mishnah* around 220 CE (core of the Talmud) and is considered by Jewish people as authoritative, equal to the Scriptures. Rabbinic authorities use this argument to substantiate the Oral Law being as weighty as Scripture. They teach that Moses received more from God than the written Torah on Mount Sinai, that he received the Oral Law, also known as the fence around the Law, which was transmitted to Joshua, who taught it to the Judges, who then taught it to the Prophets and finally to the men of the Great Synagogue or the *Sopherim* (David Klinghoffer,

Hebrew text and what first-century Pharisees taught about the Jewish concept of Messiah. That subject will not be addressed here, but it is dealt with in Appendix 3. For an informative study on the development of the Oral Law read chapter 7 in Arthur Kac's book to receive an insight as to the Jewish reasoning behind the Jewish people leaving the Written Law to obey the Oral Law.[14]

The New Covenant book of The Acts of the Apostles documents Rabbinic Judaism's persecution of the early church for its belief that *Yeshua* was not only the Messiah of Israel but the God of Israel. Also early church history, after the close of the canon of Scripture, continues to describe that persecution. Because of the rejection of *Yeshua*, which was fueled by the teaching of the absolute oneness of God and the Oral Law, the Church responded unbiblically and unjustly persecuting the Jewish people for more than seventeen centuries in "Christian Europe." Also Islam has persecuted Israel for other reasons since the 7th century CE.[15] Today Jewish bias against Christianity is understandable because of the centuries of both verbal and violent persecution that the "Christian Church" has committed against the Jewish people in the name of Jesus. Although I understand this bias, I also realize that the horrific acts done against the Jewish people are not what the New Covenant teaches! The Church accepted erroneous teaching about the Jewish people that cannot be supported by the New Covenant. Some of the best known persecutions against the Jewish people were the Crusades, Inquisition, Pogroms, and the Holocaust. The Jewish people were also falsely accused of blood libel, host desecration, black plague only to name a few.[16] True New Testament believers should be in mourning with a broken heart because of the acts of anti-Semitism done in the name of Jesus against His own flesh and blood, the Jewish

---

Why The Jews Rejected Jesus, New York: Three Leaves Press: Doubleday, 2005, pg. 25). This Oral Law is one of the two central reasons why *Yeshua* and the Pharisees were at odds and is equally the central issue that prevents Jewish people from studying the Written Law because the rabbis have replaced the Written Law with their authority, the Oral Law.

[14] Arthur W. Kac, *The Spiritual Dilemma of the Jewish People* (2nd ed. Grand Rapids: Baker, 1983), 62-82.

[15] To understand the significance of the Christian persecution of the Jewish people over the centuries, I recommend reading *Jews, God and History* by Max I. Dimont.

[16] *Blood Libel, Host Desecration and the Black Plague:* Blood libel was when Jewish people were accused of killing a Christian child to use their blood in the Passover rites. This is an absolutely ludicrous accusation and it shows the complete ignorance on the part of Christians in understanding the adherence of the Jewish people to the Law concerning the use of blood (Leviticus 3:17; 7:26-27; 17:10-12, 14; 19:26; Deuteronomy 12:16, 23; 15:23). Host desecration was the supposed act of Jewish people of stealing the Host wafer used in the Catholic Mass to stab it till it would bleed so they could inflict more pain on Jesus. This belief comes from the erroneous teaching of the Catholic Church on the wafer used in the communion (Eucharist) becoming the very body of Christ. (*Catechism of the Catholic Church*, 2nd Edition, New York: Doubleday, 1995, page 376.) The death of one-third of Europe due to the Black Plague was also blamed on the Jews. They were accused of poisoning springs and wells throughout Europe to kill their Christian overlords. History now tells us that fleas on rats spread the plague throughout Europe. Jewish people were not dying as much because of the Jewish kosher laws. Because the Kosher laws kept their home cleaner, they did not attract the rats.

people, and should be confessing their sins to God and to Jewish people for all the acts done against them.

THE QUESTION

The question that Jewish people and biblical Christians alike should be investigating is, did or did not God reveal Himself as a plurality in unity to Israel in the pages of the *Tanakh*? Milton Lindberg, a Jewish believer in Messiah, has stated that unless true believers can find the plurality of God in the Hebrew Bible, they should cease claiming that they believe and worship the God of Abraham:

> Although it may be granted that the Christian's New Testament teaches that the term God may be applied to God the Father, to God the Son, and to God the Holy Spirit, the Christian should cease to claim that he worships the God of Abraham, Isaac, and Jacob, the God of Moses and the prophets, the God of the Torah, the Nevi'im, and the Kethuvim, unless there is found in the Tanakh, indisputable evidence that God exists in more than one personality.[17]

That is a very real and forthright question to be asked and is the quest of this book. Can the mystery of the unity of God be found in the pages of the Hebrew Scriptures as a tri-unity or the plural unity of God? Rabbinic Judaism responds with an emphatic "no" concerning this doctrine. They view Christianity as tri-theism, the worship of three gods, as reflected by the following statements:

> Worship of any three-part god by a Jew is nothing less than a form of idolatry. The three-part God of Christianity is not the G-d of Judaism. Therefore, in the Jewish view, Christianity may very well be a variation of idolatry.

> Although Christianity began among Jews, it was rapidly adopted by the pagans of the ancient world. These pagans believed in an entire pantheon of gods. It was just too much for them to give up all these gods in favor of the One True G-d. So early Christian missionaries compromised with these pagans by introducing the Trinity, a sort of three-in-one god. Even many contemporary Christian scholars see the Trinity as the result of pagan influence on Christianity.[18]

The problem with the second statement is that Kaplan is partially correct. Many pagan practices were adopted by the Church, especially after Constantine in 325 CE declared Christianity the state religion. However, long before corruption came into the fourth-century Church, the plural unity or the tri-unity of God was already well established in the first-century Church (Matthew 28:19; Acts 2:14-41). Thus Kaplan's claim of paganism is a false charge. He also draws his conclusions from "Christian"

---

[17] Milton B. Lindberg, *In the Light of the Tenach: The Trinity* (Brochure, Lansing, MI: AMF International, 1992), 1-2.

[18] Aryeh Kaplan, *The Real Messiah? A Jewish Response to Missionaries*, 15.

scholars, but most of the scholars come from a liberal background. They do not represent genuine believers in the Scriptures for they have already denied the faith, making themselves apostates.

Jacob Jocz, a Jewish believer in Messiah, identifies that the difference between Rabbinic Judaism and biblical Christianity revolves around the identity of the Person of Messiah. The Messiah of Judaism is a human Messiah, whereas the Messiah of biblical Christianity is God taking on flesh becoming the God/Man. Jocz states:

> At the center of the controversy between Church and Synagogue stands the Christological question. This is not a question whether Jesus is the Messiah, but whether the Christian understanding of the Messiah is admissible in view of the Jewish concept of God. Here lies the dividing line between Judaism and the Church. On this point neither can afford to compromise.[19]

At the heart of this book lay three controversies: (1) Who is Jesus (*Yeshua*)? (2) How do the Scriptures present God? and (3) How does Rabbinic Judaism and biblical Christianity interpret those Scriptures? This book on "Discovering the Mystery of the Unity of God" will answer these three controversies from the perspective that the Bible will interpret itself. I was very interested in reading the book entitled "Why The Jews Rejected Jesus" by David Klinghoffer,[20] but I came away from it very disappointed. In this book I found a lack of biblical scholarship, as well as a pre-set bias against the person and message of *Yeshua* and of true biblical faith. I freely admit to my own bias. The foundation of my bias is rooted in what the Hebrew Scripture and the New Covenant teach. The Scriptures are the only secure source of authority concerning the knowledge of God's truth of Himself. The truth is not found in the bias of rabbis who have added to and often contradict the Written Law (Mosaic Law) by means of their Oral Law (interpretation of rabbis), which was and is their authoritative source. Nor is truth found in the bias of priests who value the tradition of the Church to be equal in authority to the Scriptures. Nor is truth found in Protestantism when the Scriptures is reinterpreted to suit their pre-conceived bias whether it be from higher criticism or by inconsistent hermeneutic beliefs.[21] The true source of authority for the two different belief systems is another point of division between Rabbinic Judaism and true believers in Messiah *Yeshua*.

In the first century, as well as today, the core belief of Rabbinic Judaism teaches that God is one and not a unity of plurality. People need to have a good understanding of why Rabbinic Judaism believes that God is one (Deuteronomy 6:4), not two or three, as Jewish people understand the teachings of Christianity. The true believers of the

---

[19] Jacob Jocz, "The Invisibility of God and the Incarnation," *CJT 4*, no. 3 (July 1958): 179-186.

[20] David Klinghoffer, *Why the Jews Rejected Jesus* (New York: Three Leaves Press: Doubleday, 2005).

[21] *Hermeneutics* is the method of interpretation that the reader uses to determine the intent of the author.

Scriptures believe in the tri-unity of the Godhead and can substantiate that from the Hebrew Scriptures. But the rabbis equally believe, from the same Scriptures (and the Oral Law), that God is one and cannot allow for a God/man as is understood by New Testament believers. How can both get two different readings from the same Scriptures? *Yeshua* was very precise on who He was, and that was understood by the rabbinic leadership of Israel in the days of *Yeshua. Yeshua* received a strong negative and aggressive response from the Pharisees and Sadducees because of who He said He was (Jn 8:54-59; 10:30-31).

True New Testament believers have two other biblical positions which underlie all discussions of the plurality and tri-unity of God in the Hebrew Scriptures and throughout this study. First, fundamentalist and conservative evangelical believers affirm the inspiration of Scripture, which is the "breathing out of God" (God-breathed) through the Holy Spirit into men (2 Timothy 3:16; 2 Peter 1:20-21). This enabled them to receive and communicate divine truth, without error, making the speaker and/or writer infallible in the communication of God's truth. The Scriptures are God-breathed.[22] There are two other terms tied very closely to the doctrine of inspiration: They are verbal and plenary inspiration. By verbal is meant that every word of the original manuscripts of the Bible was given by inspiration of God. By plenary it means that it is full, complete and entire, extending to every part. So, every part of the Hebrew Scriptures and New Covenant are inspired equally by God.[23] *Yeshua* went one step further when He stated that every letter is eternal and inspired (Matthew 5:18).

Since verbal plenary inspiration is completely valid, the words of Jesus from the Prophets as He taught regarding the subject of His divinity and the plurality of God should be highly regarded. *Yeshua* clearly stated that Moses and the Prophets spoke of Him:

Search the [Hebrew] scriptures; for in them ye think ye have eternal life: and *they are they which testify of me* (John 5:39).

For had ye believed Moses, ye would have believed me; *for he wrote of me* (John 5:46).

Then he said unto them, O fools, and slow of heart to believe all that the prophets have spoken: Ought not Christ to have suffered these things, and to enter into his glory? *And beginning at Moses and all the prophets, he expounded unto them in all the scriptures* [Hebrew] *the things concerning himself* (Luke 24:25-27).

And he said unto them, these are the words which I spake unto you, while I was yet with you, that all things must be fulfilled, *which were written in the law of*

---

[22] H. S. Miller, *General Biblical Introduction* (Houghton, N.Y: Word-Bearer, 1960), 17.
[23] Miller, *General Biblical Introduction*, 24.

11

Moses, and in the prophets, and in the psalms, concerning me. Then opened he their understanding, that they might understand the scriptures[24] (Luke 24:44-45).

Was *Yeshua* speaking irresponsibly by telling His disciples that Moses and the Prophets bore witness of Him? Did He really mean that He, as the Son of God, was revealed in the Hebrew Scriptures? In order for that to be so, He as the Messiah would have to be presented as God in the *Tanakh*, meaning that God would then have to be clearly presented in the Hebrew Scriptures in a plural form. Notice one final thought provoking reference of *Yeshua* from the Gospels in John 5:37:

The Father himself, which hath sent me, hath borne witness of me. **Ye have neither heard his voice at any time, nor seen his shape.**

The Pharisees would have had every right to reject *Yeshua* if He and the New Covenant taught that He was divine if the plurality of God, that great mystery of the unity of God, was not taught in the Hebrew Scriptures. But if He was taught and proclaimed in the Hebrew Scriptures as He said, then the Pharisees rejected Him for reasons beyond the claim of being divine, and they misinterpreted some very important Scriptures that God intended them to understand and believe. God would not have presented His Son in a vacuum, but the *Tanakh* would have had to give clear and ample evidence of His divine nature. If the Father had not given ample witness of His plurality in the *Tanakh*, the Father would have been setting up the Pharisees to reject *Yeshua*. All that Israel has suffered over the centuries would have been a direct result of God's silence or deception on the subject of His plurality in the Hebrew Scriptures. The words of *Yeshua* should not have been considered blasphemous as they were by the Sanhedrin (John 10:33; Matthew 26:63-66; Luke 5:21), or belittled by Christian scholars when teaching the doctrine of the tri-unity of God from the *Tanakh*. An interesting fact develops when the plurality of God is shown through the names of God, the theophanies,[25] the plural descriptions and the *Shema* of Deuteronomy 6:4 which contradict Rabbinic Judaism. Christian theologians far too often have abandoned or abdicated the doctrine of the tri-unity of God in the *Tanakh* for Rabbinic Judaism.

The second biblical position coupled with a belief in verbal plenary inspiration is the belief in the literal method of interpretation. If the Scriptures are God-breathed, then God meant what He said without man's attempt to reinterpret what He said. David Cooper gives the following definition of this literal method of interpretation:

When the plain sense of Scripture makes common sense, seek no other sense; therefore, take every word at its primary, ordinary, usual, literal meaning unless

---

[24] *The Holy Bible*, King James Version (New York: Oxford University, 1996), 1281. All New Testament references are cited from the King James Version unless otherwise stated. For all Old Testament references see footnote 207. The italics are added for emphasis.

[25] *Theophany*: Is the appearance of God to man in a physical form that man can either saw Him or hear Him audibly or both.

the facts of the immediate context, studied in the light of related passages and axiomatic and fundamental truths, indicate clearly otherwise.[26]

So when coming to the names of God, like *Elohim*, why do Christian and Jewish scholars want to argue against what God says about Himself? If verbal plenary inspiration of the Scripture, as believed by fundamentalists and conservative evangelicals, why do some of them try to make it "plural of majesty"?

Over forty years ago, the professors at Washington Bible College impressed upon their students that when looking at Scripture always look at context, context, context! If a passage is not viewed within the context that God gave it, one's study is vulnerable merely to the thoughts and intellect of man. That principle applies to our study of the relationship of *Elohim* to the plurality or tri-unity of God. Scholars and translators allow the context to determine whether it refers to pagan gods or the true God. Why are false gods recognized in the plurality (Isaiah 36:18-20), but when the identical word is used of the true God as in Exodus 20:2-3, the plurality of God is explained away by calling it a "plural of majesty"? Is it because there were no singular words for God available in the Hebrew language that they want to view it in the singular? There were three words in the singular to be exact!

There are two other terms that need to be understood because they relate to the subject matter that is addressed throughout this book. They are the term Oral Law and the plurality of God. These two terms have a significant bearing that interacts with the theme of this book: Did God reveal Himself as an absolute one or as a plural unity in one?

THE ORAL LAW

Rabbinic Judaism teaches and believes it is the Oral Law which makes it unique from Christianity, because both reference the Hebrew Scriptures as their authoritative source. They teach, as is explained in footnote 13, that the Written and Oral Law were given to Moses at Mt. Sinai and they explain their position in the following statement:

> The important *tannatic* text called *Sifra*, a *Midrash* on the book of Leviticus taught that all the commandments were revealed from Sinai, in every detail, whether in written or oral form. Not only that, but God spoke to Moses *every word* that would be recorded in the ancient rabbinic sources, no matter when it happened to be first written down. Oral Torah was a special bond between God and the Jewish people, a secret link untrammeled by outsiders.[27]

What is critical to understand is that the reference from the *Sifra* that Klinghoffer quotes equates the Oral Torah (Oral Law) as God inspired, making it equal to the Hebrew Bible. There is no biblical evidence in all of the *Tanakh* to substantiate the rabbinic

---

[26] David L Cooper, *The God of Israel* (Los Angeles: Biblical Research Society, 1945), 34-35.
[27] David Klinghoffer, *Why the Jews Rejected Jesus*, 25.

teaching that the Oral Law was also given to Moses, none whatsoever, but it does make it very convenient for the rabbis to insert their own oral laws. Because of this position, Rabbinic Judaism has diverted the biblical intent from the Written Law to a man-made authority. By doing so they are violating the Law in Deuteronomy 12:32 [13:1][28] which states: "*Be careful to observe only that which I enjoin upon you: neither add to it nor take away from it*" (Deuteronomy 4:2; Exodus 24:3-4; Joshua 1:8).

The core belief today in Judaism, or more precisely Rabbinic Judaism,[29] is this one primary underlying point: God is "one" (Deuteronomy 6:4). A related point is the fact that the Pharisees[30] believed the Messiah would be a Pharisee and he would help them build up the Oral Law[31] which served as a fence around the Written Law.[32] The fence was constructed of man-made rules and regulations beginning with the generation after Ezra to protect the Written Law from being broken and to prevent the Jewish people from ever going into captivity again. It was between the years of the first generation of scribes which followed Ezra the Scribe, to Judah Ha-Nasi in 220 CE that the memorized laws were written down into what is called the *Mishnah*.[33] The *Mishnah*, known as the fence the rabbis built around the Written Law,[34] also was known as the Oral Law which became equal to Scripture.[35] Rabbinic Judaism's teaching in regard to the Messiah was that he would be a great man, a gifted leader[36] and warrior, but he would not be God,[37] contradicting the very *Tanakh*[38] they said they believed. So when

---

[28] The brackets after a reference with a verse inside like [13:1] mean that in the English Bible the reference is found in 12:32 and in the Hebrew Bible it is found in 13:1.

[29] *Rabbinic Judaism:* There are two Judaism's: First, biblical Judaism which is given in the Hebrew Scriptures without the Talmud, Oral Law and rabbinic commentaries; secondly, Rabbinic Judaism with the Oral Law, which is the heart of the *Mishnah*, and is the core of the Talmud. Rabbinic Judaism follows the interpretations of the rabbis to the neglect of the Scriptures.

[30] *Pharisees:* Pharisees were the most well known of several sects in Judaism in the first century. They are the ones primarily responsible for the Oral Law, which are man-made rules and regulations on how to keep the law of Moses.

[31] Marc H. Tanenbaum and Marvin R. Wilson, eds., *Evangelicals and Jews in Conversation on Scripture, Theology, and History* (Grand Rapids: Baker Book House, 1978), 60-61.

[32] J. Julius Scott, *Jewish Backgrounds of the New Testament* (Grand Rapids: Baker, 1995), 172-173.

[33] George Robinson, *Essential Judaism, a Complete Guide to Beliefs, Customs, and Rituals* (New York: Pocket Books, 2000), 341.

[34] A growing belief within Messianic Judaism is that in order to be a good Christian, many Messianic Jews (and Gentile believers) believe that the observance of the Written Law or the Mosaic Law consisting of 613 laws is necessary. This is a dangerous position of mixing Law and Grace. These positions are expressed in *Torah Rediscovered* (a book) and *First Fruits of Zion* (a magazine published by Ariel and D'vorah Berkowitz). These are very dangerous publications and not for a theological novice or person ungrounded in the faith.

[35] Jacob Neusner, *An Introduction to Judaism* (Louisville, Kent: Westminster/John Knox, 1991), 168.

[36] Louis Goldberg, *Our Jewish Friends* (Neptune, NJ: Loizeaux, 1983), 92-93.

[37] Emil Schurer, *A History of the Jewish People in the Time of Jesus Christ* (Peabody, Mass: Hendrickson, Division Two, 1890), 2:160-162.

14

Yeshua came on the scene and tore down the fence, the rabbis were incensed.[39] They could have considered *Yeshua* as the Messiah, except for two things: He tore down the fence of the Oral Law and He made Himself to be God and for that the Pharisees wanted Him dead by any means (see Appendix 8). Their theological position was based on the reinterpretation of the Law and Prophets in conjunction with Oral Law and their reaction to His claim of deity is clearly seen in John 10:32-33. The Messiah could not be God from their Pharisaic perspective.

PLURAL UNITY

This study of the unity (oneness) and plurality of God is based on the way Hebrew Scriptures treat the subject. The understanding of the unity and plurality of God is the heart of the issue and must be dealt with before an "*uncircumcised heart*" of unbelief becomes a "*circumcised*" heart (Deuteronomy 30:6; Jeremiah 9:25-26; Acts 3:11-19; Acts 8:26-37). The unity and plurality of God is foundational to what Moses and the Prophets wrote. Before the Jewish mind can embrace *Yeshua* as the Messiah, he must acknowledge God as one (a unity in plurality) and the Messiah as the God/man promised by the Hebrew Scriptures.

To help you understand what the plural unity of God means, Robert Morey has made a very basic statement which is at the heart of this book. If God wanted to show that He was "multi-personal," the student of the Word would be expected to find His plurality in the Hebrew Scriptures. The same would be true if God wanted to show that He was "only one person," that is what He would have written. Morey makes this statement:

> If the authors of the Bible believed that God was multi-personal, then we would expect to find that they would write about God in such a way as to indicate this idea to their readers. Thus, we must ask, "What would we expect to find in the Bible, if its authors believed that God was multi-personal?"

> On the other hand, if the authors of the Bible believed that God was only one person, i.e., they were classic Unitarians, then they would write about God in

---

[38] Robert Schoen, *What I Wish My Christian Friends Knew About Judaism* (Chicago: Loyola Press, 2004), 34. The Hebrew term for *Tanakh* is an acronym derived from the three divisions of the Jewish Scriptures. Taking the first letters from the words Torah (Law), Nevi'im (Prophets) and Ketuvim (Writings) you arrive at the acronym TNK, pronounced "*Tanakh*," which makes up the Jewish Bible or the Hebrew Scriptures.

[39] This whole subject is beyond the scope of the treatise at hand, but it does have a direct connection to why the Jewish leadership in Jesus' day rejected Him as the long awaited promised Messiah of Israel. There is a direct relationship between the Oral Law (fence) and its teaching with their rejection of Jesus.

such a way as to indicate that idea. Thus, we are also warranted to ask, "What would we expect to find in the Bible, if Unitarians wrote it?" [40]

We will not be using the term "Unitarian" in this work, but it includes anyone who denies the plural unity of God because he believes that God is only one person. This would include Jews, Muslims, Modalists and "Christian" cults such as the Jehovah Witnesses.

A clear understanding of the phrase "unity of God" is important to comprehend and needs to be defined so both Jewish and Christian readers of this book understand one another. True believers of the biblical faith understand that God is a unity expressed in three persons, usually referred to as the trinity: God the Father, God the Son and God the Holy Spirit. The persons of the Godhead are indivisible (undivided) and equal in character and essence, for they are one. However, the Jewish people understand that God is one, a unity both numerically and qualitatively indivisible, and therefore they hold only to God the Father. The following author defines the usage of the unity of God as understood by Rabbinic Judaism:

> When Judaism proclaims that God is one, it means that He is not simply a numerical unity, but also a qualitative unity. That is the second major aspect of monotheism in Judaism. God is not only one; He is unique as the Source and Sustainer of all moral values. He is not only one unto Himself; He is the only one of His kind in the universe. [41]

Next the term "indivisible" is used because in the history of the Hebrew Scriptures the pagan gods were able to be divided into multiple gods and locations. The multiplicity of deities is explained well by Jacobs:

> There is only one God and there are no others. Allied to this is the idea that God in His essence is indivisible. A deity like Baal could be split up, as it were, into various local deities, hence the plural form Baalim and Ashterot found in the Bible when speaking of the pagan gods. God is one and indivisible. He is Lord of all. He cannot be united syncretistically with other gods. [42]

The term "indivisible" accentuates the fact that God is not divided and is outside His creation, not part of it, nor is He divided into different locations competing with Himself. True believers would agree with the Jewish people in their understanding of God, except that Rabbinic Judaism does not recognize the plural unity of God that will be demonstrated in this book as well as in the New Covenant. Nor do they recognize the multitude of references in the Hebrew Scriptures, which gives the foundation of the

---

[40] Robert Morey, *The Trinity: Evidence and Issues* (Grand Rapids: World Publishing, 1996), 87.

[41] Howard R. Greenstein, *Judaism: An Eternal Covenant* (Philadelphia: Fortress Press, 1983), 6-7.

[42] Louis Jacobs, *A Jewish Theology* (West Orange, N.J: Behrman House, 1973), 21.

Christian teaching of the tri-unity. In this study, I will affirm the unity of God from a biblical perspective with the plural concept of the tri-unity of God.

The perspective of the plural unity of God is not acceptable to the Jewish people because of their strong absolute monotheistic heritage. Jewish believers in Messiah *Yeshua* uphold the tri-unity, but it is not their term of preference. The problem is how to define a doctrine that has no biblical term. Sam Nadler of the Hope of Israel Congregation in Charlotte, NC, told me in a personal conversation that he has been dialoguing with Messianic pastors in Israel. He asked them if they have a term to define Trinity or tri-unity and they do not. However since talking with Sam, Arnold Fruchtenbaum has stated in correspondence with me that there is a word used for Trinity by Jewish believers in *Yeshua* in Israel. That word is *"Shilush,"* and in checking with a Jewish believer in Israel whom I know I asked the question and she responded that they use the word *"Shilush"* to denote trinity in their congregation. In checking further I found the following usage, הקדוש השילוש meaning "the Holy Trinity." The Hebrew is *HaShilush Hakadosh,* which means "the Holy, the Three." This still gives me a problem for it appears that *"Shilush"* would be just as troubling a term as trinity because it emphasizes three rather than a unity of three. As seen in the following verses it clearly speaks of three but not a unity of three in one:

Genesis 6:10 - Noah had three sons

Exodus 23:14 - Jewish men were to present themselves before the LORD three times a year

1 Kings 17:21 - Elijah stretches out three times on the dead boy

2 Kings 13:18 - King Joash strikes the ground three times

Esther 4:16 - Esther calls for a three-day fast

Daniel 6:11 - Daniel prays three times a day

It does not seem to be a good word for it appears to be no better than the term Trinity with its emphasis on the three members of the Godhead. We need a Hebrew word or words that expresses the tri-unity or triune nature of God. Also it is quite clear that the *Tanakh* does not use the Hebrew *"Shilush"* in reference to God. I would like to propose two possibilities: one being *"Hakadosh Shilush-Echad"* (The Holy Three in One) or secondly *"Hakadosh Echad* (the Holy One)." You may wonder why I chose to use *echad* (one) in both phrases because of how Judaism today understands the term in reference to the *Shema* in Deuteronomy 6:4. This will be clearly seen when you get to chapter 9 on the *Shema* and see the biblical use of *echad.*

"Trinity" and "tri-unity" are not biblical terms. However, the concept of the tri-unity of God is clearly seen in the *Tanakh*. God is so overwhelming that He overflows or transcends our human notions of personhood. Anything beyond "one" or the "unity of God" is a problem for Jewish people. Jewish believers in Messiah *Yeshua*

17

accept the tri-unity because they have examined the historical and biblical materials and concluded that it is correct, even though the term is an inadequate concept to the Jewish mind. Michael Schiffman has a chapter in his book called *Messianic Jews & the Tri-unity of God* that would be very beneficial for Jewish and Gentile believers to read. This work would help Gentile believers understand the frame of reference that Jewish people have.[43] Jewish people do not use creeds or councils like the Nicene Council in 325 CE or the Westminster Catechism of today. Instead of creeds, they use "testimonials" or "the quotation of Scriptures that supported their views."[44] Dwight Pryor further illustrates that there was no creedal usage of this doctrine when first-century believers spoke of *Yeshua*:

> How do they explain theologically this devotion to a man and their veneration of him with God? They don't – to the frustration of our western minds! These Jewish believers expressed their monotheism in the same manner Israel had done from the beginning – in their worship. Not abstractly with theological speculations, but with actions demonstrating loyalty, veneration and service; not with propositional truths so much as with liturgical exclamations. For them the relationship of Jesus and God focused more on identity than divinity, and the truth was framed in textual associations more than theological affirmations. For example, scriptures that apply to *YHVH* are now, in the light of the resurrection, applied to the Lord Jesus. The exclusive prerogatives of *Adonai*, such as creation and kingship are now extended to Jesus – not as some external, albeit divine agent, but as someone within the very identity and oneness of God himself. This is a crucial point. This veneration of *Yeshua* with and connected to *YHVH* is permissible only if he in some way is within the *echad* of God. Otherwise such attributions of scriptures, functions, authority, power, and identity to him that apply exclusively to the God of Israel would violate the *Shema's* monotheism.[45]

That gives some idea of the Jewish frame of reference to the plurality or tri-unity of God and also how the early believers affirmed their belief in *Yeshua ha Mashiach*.[46] Now how is the plurality of God understood today among various Messianic groups?

Today there is no indication that the Jewish people have changed their view relative to *Yeshua* being the Messiah of Israel, the promised God/man who is one with the Father. However, Jewish people are coming to faith in Messiah *Yeshua*, but the percentages are quite small, even in Israel. Among some fringe Messianic groups there is no belief that *Yeshua* is God, as is reflected in this quote from Uri Marcus:

---

[43] Michael Schiffman, *Return of the Remnant* (Baltimore: Lederer Publications, 1992), 93-103.

[44] John Fischer, "Yeshua: The Deity Debate." *Mishkan* (issue 39, 2003), 20.

[45] Dwight A. Pryor, "One God and Lord," *Mishkan* (issue 39, 2003), 56.

[46] *Yeshua Ha Mashiach*: These are the Hebrew words meaning Jesus the Messiah. When it goes from Hebrew to Greek to English, it becomes Jesus the Christ.

Myself as well as our entire congregation of Believers in *Ma'aleh Adumim*, [the name of a Messianic Congregation in Israel] completely reject the Trinitarian notions of plural unity, and will not acquiesce to any theology which challenges the ONEness of HaShem[47] in any fashion…. *Yeshua* is the Son of the living G-d, never G-d the son, in our view.[48]

I have come across some "Messianic" individuals who share the above view. First the term Messianic believer needs to be clarified. Throughout this book that term will refer specifically to believers in *Yeshua* who have accepted Him as the God of Israel, their Messiah, their personal Saviour from sin.[49] I question the salvation of "Messianic" Jewish people who reflect the view given by Uri Marcus. Joe Good reveals, according to his definition of Messianic believers, that some Messianic believers in Israel and America do not accept the plural unity of God:

> *Yeshua* was an attribute of the Father that was made flesh. But in being flesh, he was a man, totally man…*Yeshua* we do not see as being God when he walked here on earth. We see him as a man, a man anointed by God, sent by God to perform a function. Now in his resurrection, we do not see him as God. We see him as a man appointed by God and that has been restored back to what man was intended to be…. I once believed in the Trinity; now I obviously don't.[50]

According to the Hebrew Scriptures, as it will be laid out in the coming chapters of this book, they without question substantiate the deity of *Yeshua* as the Second Person of the plural unity of God (*Elohim*). In Rabbinic Judaism, without question, the issue of the plural unity of God is not embraced, and it also has spilled over to some Jewish "believers." New Testament believers treat this topic by either affirming the tri-unity of God in the Hebrew Scriptures or by affirming that this doctrine is foreshadowed in the Hebrew Scriptures.

The pharisaic teaching on the Oral Law has resulted in the unwarranted suffering at the hands of Rome and later Christianity since the third-century CE. It was not in Judaism's failure to believe in the unity and oneness of God that caused their suffering. It was their failure to believe in God as He presented Himself as a plurality of one God who could and did appear as a man in the Hebrew Scriptures (Genesis 18). However, because of their disbelief in the plurality of the oneness God, they would not believe that *Yeshua* was one with the Father, and consequently they could not believe that

---

[47] *HaShem*: literally means "the name." Jewish people will refer to God as HaShem rather than mentioning the name of God.

[48] Richard Harvey, "Jesus the Messiah in Messianic Jewish Thought: Emerging Christologies," *Mishkan* (issue 39, 2003): 7.

[49] *Messianic Believer*: is better understood as Hebrew-Christian which unifies ethnicity and faith together. The confusion can come in relationship to ultra-orthodox Jews who also consider themselves Messianic, but they are not believers in *Yeshua* as Messiah and saviour from sin.

[50] John Fischer, "Yeshua: The Deity Debate," *Mishkan* (issue 39, 2003): 23.

Yeshua was the long awaited promised Messiah of Israel. The foundation for the plural unity of the Godhead was laid out in the Hebrew Scriptures. [51] The leadership of Israel did not recognize that fact and consequently they rejected *Yeshua*, who clearly presented Himself as one with the Father (John 10:30; 14:9-10).

David Dockery probably expresses the best way to view the tri-unity in the Hebrew Scriptures:

> God did not reveal Himself in clearly defined trinitarian terms in the Old Testament. However, the Old Testament prepared the faithful for the doctrine of the Trinity. [52]

The New Covenant truths are not intended to be understood in a vacuum. The plurality of God taught in the New Covenant merely confirms what has already been taught in the *Tanakh*. The plurality and tri-unity of God are clearly rooted in the teachings of the Hebrew Scriptures. The *Tanakh* will not necessarily prove in dogmatic terms the tri-unity of the Godhead until the prophet Isaiah. But it will lay a strong foundation for the teaching of the plural unity of God. Benjamin Warfield presents the concept of the tri-unity in the Hebrew Scriptures in the following statement:

> The Mystery of the Trinity is not revealed in the Old Testament; but the mystery of the Trinity underlies the Old Testament revelation, and here and there almost comes into view. Thus the Old Testament revelation of God is not corrected by the fuller revelation which follows it, but only perfected, extended and enlarged. [53]

Dockery and Warfield express the fact that the tri-unity is in the Hebrew Scriptures although not clearly seen as in the New Covenant. Erickson makes the comment that the *Tanakh* will lead us to a monotheistic belief, but as he said, what led the Church to move beyond the monotheistic belief was additional biblical witness (New Covenant). [54] This book validates the *Tanakh* that it did not need additional New Covenant revelation to substantiate the plurality or tri-unity of God. It is the intent of this book to go one step further, demonstrating that the plurality and/or tri-unity of God was revealed but

---

[51] *Hebrew Scriptures*: The first 39 books of the Bible called the Old Testament. The term "Hebrew Scriptures" is used so as not to alienate Jewish people by saying Old Testament, which equates to them as being old, out of date or no longer in force. "... the word 'old' is used to connote that which is replaceable, or that which was replaced. That is what Christians mean when they say 'the Old Testament.' And that is why Jews resent that term." Samuel Levine, *You Take Jesus, I'll Take God: How To Refute Christian Missionaries* (Los Angeles: Hamoroh Press, 1980), 11.

[52] David S. Dockery, *Biblical Illustrator* (Nashville: Sunday School Board of the Southern Baptist Convention, Vol. 17 No 4, Summer 1991), 27-30.

[53] Benjamin Breckinridge Warfield, *Biblical and Theological Studies* (Philadelphia: The Presbyterian and Reformed, 1968), 30-31.

[54] Millard J. Erickson, *Introducing Christian Doctrine* (Grand Rapids: Baker Book House, 1992), 98.

Chapter 1
Are Judaism and New Testament
Faith Compatible With the
Mystery of the Unity of God?

The complexities of the mysteries of God will never be comprehended on this side of life, neither by Jewish or Christian scholars. Clearly as human beings we are at a disadvantage in trying to understand His Person. The title of this book is a mere statement concerning a subject we have little knowledge about. What is recorded in the Scripture tells us only what God wants us to know and perhaps all that our human minds can grasp. The question is, do we even grasp the knowledge of the person of God that has been revealed to us? We can say yes and no to that question. There are some things that we can know about God, but we are sadly mistaken if we think that we can comprehend all of God. In writing this book it has become crystal clear in my mind, that as much as I learned about God in writing this book, I still do not grasp the fullness of His nature, character and essence. What I do know is that God is a person, an indivisible spirit who has revealed to all of us that He is a holy, righteous, and a just God who does not tolerate sin. He is also loving, compassionate and longsuffering. These are some things that you and I can understand through our earthly experience about God. One of those very difficult areas relates to God's person: Is He an absolute unity of one as Rabbinic Judaism states or is He a plural unity of one as true New Testament Faith states? That is the quest of this book, to understand just how God did reveal Himself to mankind in relation to the mystery of His unity.

These two great faiths, Judaism and Christianity, have co-existed over the centuries often with either subtle or open hostilities which for the most part came from the Christian side. In the first 200 years of Christianity it was Rabbinic Judaism that was hostile to Christianity. However, the next 1800 years those hostilities have usually been created by Christianity against the Jewish people. The central issue of those hostilities is how both Judaism and Christianity understand "the Mystery of the Unity of God." There are many issues that divide these two faiths, but there is a core issue that is at the heart of the matter. That core issue will not be studied from a New Testament (New Covenant) perspective, but rather from the evidence that lies in the text of the Hebrew Scriptures.

Unless otherwise noted, Scripture quotes are taken from the Jewish Tanakh, and New Testament quotations are from the King James Version (KJV).

not as fully developed as it is in the New Covenant. Would Abraham, Moses and David, to name a few, see the tri-unity and understand it? Probably not. Would they have understood the plural unity of God? Yes! The Pharisees and Sadducees in Jesus' day should have minimally understood the fact of the plural unity of God.

It has been the observation of this writer during the last forty years, that two things have led to a tremendous ignorance on the part of New Testament believers on the plurality and tri-unity of God in the Hebrew Scriptures. First, historically Christian Bible colleges and seminaries have taught the Old Testament on one side and the New Testament on the other side and unconsciously divorced each from the other. Second, pastors have used the Pauline Epistles; it seems almost exclusively, as the fuel for most of the messages in the Church today, only going to the *Tanakh* for a little prophetic study and to do character studies of biblical characters. They did not connect both testaments together in teaching the whole counsel of God's truth. Paul makes mention of only one mystery which the *Tanakh* did not teach, the mystery of the Church (Romans 16:25-27; 1 Corinthians 2:7, 10; Ephesians 3:4-10; Colossians 1:26-27).[55] Because of the Jewish insistence on the oneness of God to the exclusion of the plural unity of God, Rabbinic Judaism has missed their Messiah and has fallen prey to 46 false messiahs over the centuries.[56] A current example of a false messiah is seen within the ultra-orthodox Lubavitch Hasidic community, which believes that the late Rebbe Menachem Mendel Schneerson[57] was the Messiah.[58]

NEED FOR STUDY

This most critical study cannot be separated from the eternal destiny of both Jewish and Gentile people. One cannot separate the salvation provided through the Messiah from his or her belief, or lack of, in the plural unity and oneness of God. Jewish belief is only in the oneness of God. Therefore, their belief in absolute monotheism rules out the whole redemptive plan of God presented in the *Tanakh*, which is provided through the Messiah and must include the acceptance of the plural unity of God. The Jewish people

---

[55] Robert L. Saucy, *The Church in God's Program* (Chicago: Moody, 1972), 59-60.

[56] James E. Smith, *The Promised Messiah*, (Nashville: Thomas Nelson, 1993), 470-474.

[57] *Messianic Scriptures:* (a) These tell us the Messiah will be of Abraham (Gen 12:1-3), (b) the scepter will not depart from Judah until He is revealed (Gen 49:10), (c) He would be a prophet like Moses (Deut 18:15-19 with Num 12:5-8), (d) He would be of the house of David (1 Chr 17:10-14), (e) He would be born in Bethlehem (Isa 9:6-7: Mic 5:2), (f) He would have to come before the destruction of the second temple (Dan 9:24-27; Gen 49:10), (g) He would die (Isa 53:10; Ps 22), (h) and would be resurrected (Isa 53:10). Menachem Mendel Schneerson has failed to meet biblical criteria except for one: He was Jewish. He was born in Nikolaev, Ukraine on April 18, 1902, not in Bethlehem as Micah prophesied. He escaped Europe and came to New York City in March 1940. Since he had no idea what tribe he descended from, he could not lay claim to the tribe of Judah and the house of David. Not only was he not born in Bethlehem, but he was born 19 centuries after the destruction of the temple according to Daniel the prophet.

[58] David Berger, *The Rebbe, the Messiah and the Scandal of the Orthodox Indifference* (Portland: Littman Library of Jewish Civilization, 2001), 20-25.

reject *Yeshua ha Mashiach* as their Messiah. Contrary to rabbinic teaching,[59] there is no biblical way to address the question of sin and its separation from God, except by the substitutionary sacrifice of the Servant of the LORD,[60] the Messiah of Israel, on the Tree.

The Purpose of the Law

Jewish rabbis and liberal Christian theologians would have us believe that the Jewish people[61] are saved through the Abrahamic[62] and Mosaic Covenants (the Law).[63] These covenants were not intended by God as saving covenants for the Jewish people. Contrary to modern liberalism and some evangelical leaders, the Scriptures do not teach Inclusivism (see Appendix 5).[64] The testimony of the *Tanakh* says, "*The just shall live by his faith*" (Habakkuk 2:4 – Harkavy Version), and in relationship to Abraham the *Tanakh* states "*and he believed in the LORD; and he counted it to him for righteousness*" (Genesis 15:6). That faith was in the God of Israel alone. Peter in his statement before the Sanhedrin in the New Covenant book of Acts is so clear you wonder how it could be missed (or ignored). Look carefully at Peter's words as he responded to the High Priest:

---

[59] Rabbinic Judaism teaches that salvation is obtained through repentance, charity and good works, because man is not inherently sinful. Man is made in the "image of God," he alone is responsible to give heed to his "good inclination" and not his "evil inclination" for in Jewish theology man is not born in sin, thus he does not need the Incarnation of God through "the Virgin Birth" or a mediator to act on his behalf.

[60] Because Jewish people are very sensitive about writing or speaking the name of G-d, they will often refer to Him by using the terms *Adonai* (Lord) or *HaShem* (the name). Because of the variety of names that the *Tanakh* uses for G-d, it is important to be correct when referring to the Hebrew Scriptures. This is done to be precise, not to be insensitive to Jewish people.

[61] G. Jeffrey MacDonald, "Christian Scholars: Jews Don't Need Jesus." *Press Republican* (Plattsburgh, N.Y; September 13, 2002), A7. The lead statement in the article states "Proclaim that members of Judaism can be saved without coming to faith in Jesus Christ."

[62] *Abrahamic Covenant*: The election of Israel under the Abrahamic Covenant was an eternal, unconditional covenant which promised the nation of Israel that God would fulfill His promises to Abraham, Isaac and Jacob. It was not a covenant of salvation but rather it promised a national identity through time into eternity and the fulfillment of the promises personally to Abraham, Isaac and Jacob as well as the Nation of Israel. See Arnold Fruchtenbaum's book *Israelology* on pages 567-581 and in particular page 569.

[63] *Mosaic Covenant*: God made five covenants with Israel. These covenants were divided into two groupings: one conditional and four unconditional. Unconditional means that the Abrahamic, Land, Davidic and New Covenants were made by God and cannot be broken by man. By conditional we mean that Israel had a responsibility to keep their part of the covenant to receive the blessing of God. If Israel disobeyed, God would not keep His part until they repented. This covenant is called the Mosaic Covenant, which is known as the law of Moses given in the books of Exodus through Deuteronomy.

[64] *Inclusivism* teaches that if one responds to the light that one has, even though that person has never seen a Bible, heard of Jesus Christ, or heard that Jesus died on the cross for one's sins, God will save that person.

[10] Be it known unto you all, and to all the people of Israel, that by the name of Jesus Christ of Nazareth, whom ye crucified, whom God raised from the dead, even by him doth this man stand here before you whole. [11] This is the stone which was set at nought of your builders, which is become the head of the corner (Psalm 118:22; Isaiah 8:14). [12] Neither is there salvation in any other: for there is none other name under heaven given among men, whereby we must be saved. Acts 4:10-12

Peter is clear and precise: Only in the name of *Yeshua* can anyone, Jew or Gentile, be saved. God does not have a Plan 'B.'

There have been no offerings or sacrifices for sin in over 1940 years since 70 CE when the temple was destroyed in Jerusalem by the Romans. The possible exception was between the years of 132-135 CE, during the second revolt against Rome led by Bar Kokhba.[65] If the Law was intended to be a saving covenant, then God has made it completely impossible for the Jewish people to bring sacrifices, in reference to their sin, to Him in Jerusalem on the Temple Mount. John Johnson expresses in a very clear and understandable way the development and belief of Dual Covenant Theology.[66] The basic belief came out of the Holocaust and teaches that Jewish people are saved by observance of the Law, while Gentiles are saved by their belief in Jesus. In other words, Jewish people have the Abrahamic Covenant and the Mosaic Law while Gentiles have Jesus.[67]

The purpose of the Law was to provide a redeemed people (Old Testament saints) with a rule of life in three areas; civil, religious and moral.[68] Its purpose was not to secure salvation, but the sacrifices were a provision by God for the time when they would fail to keep His Law. Fruchtenbaum states, "Sacrifices were accepted as a means to restoration just as confession is for the believer today."[69] Fruchtenbaum has made two other observations. First, the 613 commandments derived from the Mosaic Law were issued as conditional. The conditional nature of the covenant is given in Exodus 15:26[70] as well as in Deuteronomy 28:15. It states in Deuteronomy 28 that if the

---

[65] Rabbi Leibel Reznick, *The Holy Temple Revisited* (Northvale, N.J: Jason Aronson, 1993), 155-159.

[66] *Dual Covenant Theology*: This teaches that God's covenant (Mosaic Law) with the Jews has not been revoked and they are still in a saving covenant with God. In other words, a good Christian is saved by being obedient to the New Testament and the Jew is saved by being obedient to the Mosaic Law. However, the Mosaic Law was never a saving covenant, no one was saved by obedience to the Law but by faith alone.

[67] John J. Johnson, "A New Testament Understanding of the Jewish Rejection of Jesus: Four Theologians on the Salvation of Israel," *JETS* 43, no. 2 (2000): 229-246.

[68] Lewis Sperry Chafer, *Systematic Theology* (8 vols. Dallas: Dallas Seminary Press, 1948) 4:159-160.

[69] Arnold G. Fruchtenbaum, *Israelology, the Missing Link in Systematic Theology* (Tustin, CA: Ariel Ministries, 1989), 376.

[70] Fruchtenbaum, *Israelology, the Missing Link in Systematic Theology*, 588.

commandments were obeyed, abundant blessing was promised (verses 1-14). But if they were disobeyed, even more abundant cursing (verses 16-68) would befall them. The second, the offering on the Day of Atonement, did not remove sin (New Covenant book of Hebrews 8-10). The Day of Atonement had its shortcomings because it was a temporary answer, not the permanent answer for sin.[71] If it was a permanent answer, no further sacrifice on the Day of Atonement would have been necessary (Hebrews 9:1-15). Instead, the atonement provided only a covering for sin and restoration of fellowship but not the removal of the sin.[72] This Mosaic Law was fulfilled in the person of *Yeshua ha Mashiach* for He became the sin bearer (Isaiah 53 – See Appendix 4).

The primary focus of this study is the oneness or unity and plurality of God and how the Hebrew Scriptures treat the subject. Therefore, it will not be the main purpose of this book to deal with the New Covenant[73] proofs of the tri-unity. Areas such as the Oral Law or rabbinic interpretation of the law of Moses will only be dealt with in a limited scope to help the reader understand the belief system of Rabbinic Judaism and to understand the purpose of this book (See Appendix 3).

The desire of this author was to interact with anti-missionaries and their arguments against the biblical teachings of those who hold to the biblical faith when dealing with the plural unity of God and the deity of *Yeshua* as He is presented in the *Tanakh*. But after reading numerous anti-missionary books, it was decided to interact only directly on a few issues. The argument of this book will interact automatically with most of their arguments because all their issues revolve around a few key points which are the core issues being presented. A list of these and other belief issues will be given in Appendix 7.

Neglected Issue

Many Christian authors give little attention to the tremendous weight of Scripture in the *Tanakh* concerning the unity and plurality of God. Clearly, there is a need to synthesize and clarify in one book the foundations of the plural unity of God. I will identify how the plural unity of God is anchored in the *Torah*,[74] *Nevi'im*,[75] and

---

[71] Daniel Fuchs, *Israel's Holy Days* (Neptune, N.J: Loizeaux, 1985), 64-68.

[72] Fruchtenbaum, *Israelology, the Missing Link in Systematic Theology*, 588-589.

[73] *New Covenant*: This is another name for the New Testament.

[74] *The Torah*: Also known as the Pentateuch, the first five books of the Bible. Meaning literally "teaching" or "instruction" or "guidance." Often translated as "the Law" in English Bibles, as in "the Law of the LORD is perfect" (Psa 19:7 [v. 8 in Hebrew]). Torah in Judaism is an elastic term which can also mean a single point of teaching to the whole of the Hebrew Bible, and the Oral Law.

[75] *Nevi'im*: This is the second division of the Hebrew Scriptures called the Prophets (Joshua, Judges, 1 & 2 Samuel, 1 & 2 Kings, Isaiah, Jeremiah, Ezekiel, Hosea, Joel, Amos, Obadiah, Jonah, Micah, Nahum, Habakkuk, Zephaniah, Haggai, Zechariah, and Malachi).

Kethuvim[76] just as the oneness of God is anchored in the Hebrew Scriptures. Authors such as Hodge[77] and Berkhof[78] add nothing or very little to the subject at hand. One reason is because they have not made it the emphasis or premise of their books or articles. Paul House in his *Old Testament Theology* "summarizes its content and shows its theological significance in relationship to the whole of Old Testament Canon."[79] His theme is God and how He expresses Himself to Israel through the Hebrew Scriptures. Even though there are places where he speaks about the plural form for God, it is not the thrust of his book.[80] David Hinson's book, *Theology of the Old Testament*, addresses the oneness of God and quotes the *Shema* of Deuteronomy 6:4 without an adequate explanation of the word "one" or *echad*.[81] In fact, he says:

> It is the ordinary word used in counting, and fails to provide any single explanation of what the Jews meant when they said that "the LORD our God is one LORD."[82]

Later in chapter 9 that will be shown to be a false statement. He later speaks of *"the angel of the LORD"* (*Yahweh*) with no reference to the fact that the angel of *Yahweh* is *Yahweh* and yet distinct from the LORD (*Yahweh*). He does reference Genesis 16:7-14 in connection with Hagar that "the angel is the LORD himself,"[83] but he makes no use of examples to illustrate this from Genesis 19:24 or Judges 2:1, which show that the angel of *Yahweh* is the LORD, yet distinct from God. Walter Brueggemann's *Theology of the Old Testament* deals with Israel's relationship to *Yahweh*. He makes good observations and statements on the Hebrew Scriptures but says little about the oneness or plural unity of the person of God. Thus, he and the others do not address the formidable weight of evidence on how God is revealed in the Hebrew Scriptures.[84]

Books such as *Theological Wordbook of the Old Testament*,[85] *All the Divine Names and Titles in the Bible*,[86] *The Names of God*,[87] *Dictionary of Old Testament Theology &*

---

[76] *Kethuvim*: This is the third division of the Hebrew Scriptures called the Writings (Psalms, Proverbs, Job, Song of Songs, Ruth, Lamentations, Ecclesiastes, Esther, Daniel, Ezra, Nehemiah, and 1 & 2 Chronicles).

[77] Charles Hodge, *Systematic Theology* (4 vols. Grand Rapids: Eerdmans, 1970), 1:442-482.

[78] L. Berkhof, *Systematic Theology* (Grand Rapids: Eerdmans, 1941), 82-99.

[79] Paul House, *Old Testament Theology* (Downers Grove, IL: InterVarsity, 1998), front cover.

[80] House, *Old Testament Theology*, 61-62.

[81] One [*echad*]: Throughout this book this combination "one [*echad*]" will be used to show that the Hebrew word for one, *echad*, is used in Scripture to point to the plurality of people and things as well as God being a plural unity of one [*echad*]. This will be explained in depth in chapter 9 and in Appendix 2.

[82] David Hinson, *Theology of the Old Testament* (London: Society for Promoting Christian Knowledge, 2001), 23-24.

[83] Hinson, *Theology of the Old Testament*, 60-61.

[84] Walter Brueggemann, *Theology of the Old Testament* (Minneapolis: Fortress, 1997).

[85] Laird R. Harris, Gleason L. Archer, Jr. and Bruce K. Waltke, eds., *Theological Wordbook of the Old Testament* (2 vols; Chicago: Moody, 1980).

25

Exegesis[88] and *Names of God*[89] do reference the oneness or unity of God and the plurality of God. They speak of the origin and meaning of such terms as *El, Eloah, Elohim, YHVH, Adonai, echad* versus *yachid,*[90] plus the plural descriptions of God. However, most of these books only lay out the basic facts of the unity and plurality of God and do not draw them together to enable the reader to get a full perspective of these plural terms of God in the Hebrew Scriptures and their weight as they stand together. It is my goal to draw the references together and enable Jewish people and true believers in Messiah to understand the full weight of the evidence.

Another example is J. Barton Payne.[91] He touches on the names, titles and plurality of God but he does not offer the depth of study that would be beneficial to the Jewish audience. Payne discusses how the term *Elohim* developed during the time of Abraham to Moses rather than how it is used and understood throughout the Hebrew Scriptures. His understanding is that Abraham was a monolatrist rather than a monotheist.[92] His example of Abraham before Abimelech is lacking because nothing else in the Genesis text gives any reason to believe that Abraham was a monolatrist. Yet when coupling the biblical text with archaeology, a better candidate for monolatry is Balaam (Numbers 22:7-13). *Bible and Spade,* a magazine of Associates for Biblical Research, gives the discovery of Balaam's name and prophecy on a pagan temple in present day Jordan.[93] Another possible candidate for monolatry would be Jethro, Moses' father-in-law (Exodus 18:11). Baker, in the *Dictionary of the Old Testament Pentateuch,*[94] spends a considerable part of an article on the etymology of the names of God without showing how the names of God relate to each other or how the text of Scripture uses them in relation to one other. It is disappointing to see his short treatment of the plural noun *Elohim*. He does not present the possibility of *Elohim* being anything beyond "a plurality of majesty, or royal plurals, as an intensification or claim to exclusivity, or as an honorific."[95]

---

[86] Herbert Lockyer, *All the Divine Names and Titles in the Bible* (Grand Rapids: Zondervan, 1975).

[87] Andrew Jukes, *The Names of God* (Grand Rapids: Kregel, 1888).

[88] William VanGemeren, *Dictionary of Old Testament Theology & Exegesis* (Grand Rapids: Zondervan, 1997).

[89] Nathan Stone, *Names of God* (Chicago: Moody, 1944).

[90] *Yachid* is the Hebrew word to designate one and only.

[91] J. Barton Payne, *The Theology of the Older Testament* (Grand Rapids: Zondervan, 1962), 125-127, 144-151.

[92] Monolatry is the worship of one god while recognizing there are other gods that can be worshiped. Monotheism is the belief in one God and that no other gods exist.

[93] B. G. Wood, "Prophecy of Balaam Found in Jordan," *Bible and Spade* 6 (Autumn 1977): 121-124.

[94] Desmond Alexander and David Baker, *Dictionary of the Old Testament Pentateuch* (Downers Grove, IL: InterVarsity, 2003).

[95] Alexander and Baker, *Dictionary of Old Testament Pentateuch,* (Downers Grove, IL: InterVarsity Press, 2003), 362.

The "plural of majesty," when referring to *Elohim,* means that when God addresses someone, He uses the plural "we" or "royal we," much as the Queen of England would use when addressing others in her presence. Baker's thoughts on the subject indicate a presupposition that the plurality of God does not play a part in his thinking.

This lack of attention to the plural unity and the tri-unity in the Hebrew Scriptures is also evident in evangelical theological journals. In 210 years of *Bib Sac, Westminster Theological Journal, JETS, Canadian Theological Journal, Grace Theological Journal* and *Master's Theological Journal*s, almost nothing can be found on the tri-unity in the *Tanakh* unless it is embedded within another subject.[96]

It is not that Payne, Alexander and others, as mentioned above, do not speak of the issues of the names of God used in a singular and plural context, but they are scattered throughout their books. The purpose of this study is to put the references and insights on the unity and plurality of God together and study them in more depth, in one place, so that a reader can get a fuller and unhindered view of the subject.

ORGANIZATION OF STUDY

This book will address what God meant in making mankind in His "image" and "likeness." The study addresses the names for God, such as God, Lord, LORD, and how they are used throughout the Hebrew Scriptures and how the authors of Scripture revealed God to the reader. This study will also state how Christians view the core statement of Judaism (Deuteronomy 6:4) and how the word for "one" and the plurality of God is used throughout the Law, Prophets and Writings. Plural descriptions of God will then be discussed (such as Joshua 24:19; Psalm 149:2; Ecclesiastes 12:1; Isaiah 54:5) followed by a study on the Holy Spirit and passages in the *Tanakh* that speak of the Messiah being divine. This book will continue to show from the *Tanakh* that God has a Son, that the Branch passages present the divinity of Messiah and that the "*Word of the LORD*" is God, separate and distinct from the Father yet one in essence with the Father.

Image and Likeness of God – Chapter 2

Chapter 2 deals with a question that many people have desired to know over the centuries: What is the meaning of the "image" and "likeness" of God? Many have tried to understand just how mankind was created in His image. Countless authors have made good observations on how mankind is like God and also how mankind is not like God. The complete answer to this subject is probably unknowable. However, God did give man some parameters to work within. This chapter is focused on how mankind was

---

[96] *Bib Sac* from 1945 to present, *Westminster Theological Journal* from 1960 to present, *JETS* from 1969 to present, *Canadian Theological Journal* from 1955 to 1970, *Grace Theological Journal* from 1960 to present, and *Master's Theological Journal* from 1990 to present.

created in the "image" and "likeness" of God in relationship to the plural unity of His person.

Names of God – Chapter 3

Chapter 3 addresses the understanding and usage of the terms *El, Elim, Elohim* and *Eloah* and that *Elohim* is applied to two divine beings as in Psalm 45:6-7. Some of these names are singular and some are plural: It is incumbent on the student to see and understand just how these words are used in the Hebrew Scriptures. What does Hebrew grammar say in relation to *Elohim*, which is a plural term for one God? Consideration is also given to the usage of the term Lord, as *Adonai* and *Yahweh* (LORD) or *YHVH*, and why it is also applied to two divine beings in Genesis 19:24 and Zechariah 2:8-9. Christian theologians and scholars have abandoned the plural unity or tri-unity of God in the Hebrew Scriptures it seems for Rabbinic Judaism's interpretation of God. The rabbis have had complete authority and control over the Jewish people for 2000 years. The difference is as great as day and night between biblical Judaism and Rabbinic Judaism. One leads to truth and one to falsehood in relation to how the subject of the plurality of God is treated and understood. God, who is one, chose to reveal Himself with a multitude of plural references to Himself. Why, if God chose that course to reveal Himself, do some New Covenant Bible believing scholars who believe in the tri-unity in the New Covenant constantly force those plural references into singular interpretation in the Hebrew Scriptures? The outcome of how this subject is treated and understood by men who are usually very faithful to the text of the Hebrew Scriptures can determine the eternal fate of Jewish lives.

Theophanies of God – Chapters 4 - 8

Chapters 4 through 8 pertain to the understanding of the term "theophany" in the Hebrew Scriptures and how it is used. Rabbinic Judaism insists that God will not, has not, and did not appear as a man in human history. Yet throughout the *Tanakh*, God did appear to Abraham, Isaac, Jacob, Moses, Joshua and others in the form of a man. Jewish rabbis have a narrow unbiblical view because the incarnation of God cannot be entertained at all or Rabbinic Judaism is finished. The term "theophany" involves such terms as "*the angel of the Lord*," "*Captain of the host of the Lord*," or *Metatron*[97] where God appeared in the form of a man with those first two of these names and the last one made up by Rabbinic Judaism. *Yahweh* also said that He would send "*My angel*" (Exodus 23:23) to lead them as they traveled through the wilderness. The second part of theophany is the *Shechinah* of God, which designates God's presence.[98] The presence of God, which appeared to Moses and Israel as the Glory of God, dwelt with Israel on

---

[97] *Metatron*: This is the ancient Jewish word for the one Christians call the Angel of the LORD.

[98] Jacob Neusner and William Scott Green, *Dictionary of Judaism in the Biblical Period* (Peabody, Mass: Hendrickson, 1999), 577.

Mount Sinai, then in the Holy of Holies of the tabernacle and later in the temple. If the theophanies of God are God Himself, God is a plurality and the whole of Jewish understanding is at odds with the *Tanakh*, because in those theophanies God has chosen to show Himself distinct from God and yet the same as God, as one God and yet as a plurality within His oneness.

Shema – *Chapter 9*

Chapter 9 deals with the cornerstone and affirmation of the Jewish faith, the *Shema* of Deuteronomy 6:4. As far as Rabbinic Judaism today is concerned, this verse puts to rest, forever, the whole subject of the plurality or tri-unity of God. It specifically puts to rest the whole subject of the incarnation of the Messiah in the Jewish mind because "*Yahweh* is one." This chapter focuses particularly on the words *echad* and *yachid* and the meaning of both. Rabbi Maimonides, who is called the second Moses and who lived in the eleventh-century CE, changed the reading of the *Shema* in his second of Thirteen Articles from *echad* to *yachid*. It is necessary to understand why these two Hebrew words in his Thirteen Articles are so very important to the Jewish understanding of the *Shema* of Deuteronomy 6:4. Once again, Christian theologians and scholars bypass studies on exactly how that word is used throughout the Hebrew Scriptures. Is God making a statement beyond His desire for Israel to love Him and commit to Him alone? Jewish rabbis say no. But in this statement of belief, the *Shema* on the oneness of God, the LORD also had His unity or plurality in mind.

Plural Terms – Chapter 10

Chapter 10 addresses the plural pronouns used of God as well as other plural descriptions, with the intention of showing how they apply to the unity and plurality of God. God, in numerous places, used both plural and singular terms to describe Himself. God used the plural personal pronoun "us," seven times in the Hebrew Scripture (Genesis 1:26; 3:22; 11:7; Isaiah 6:8). There are four references in the *Tanakh* where the personal pronouns are found. They make a strong statement toward understanding plurality of His person.

There are other descriptive terms that God used to further strengthen His plurality, such as the plural attribute of "Creator" in Ecclesiastes 12:1. Other descriptive plural words for God (*Elohim*) are located in Genesis 20:13; Genesis 35:7; 2 Samuel 7:23 and Psalm 58:11.

Holy Spirit – Chapter 11

Chapter 11 pertains to the neglected area concerning the "*spirit of the LORD*" in the Hebrew Scriptures. While there are many references to His personal character in the New Covenant, the same is not true in the *Tanakh*. God did not just become a tri-unity in the New Covenant; He always was a tri-unity. But how is the "*spirit of the LORD*" and the fact that God is spirit distinct in the *Tanakh*? The purpose of this chapter will be to substantiate that the Holy Spirit is active in the *Tanakh* and that He is represented often by His deeds or actions rather than by always showing His personhood as is usually presented in the New Covenant.

Christian cults and the Jewish people reject His personhood. To them He is merely the extension of God or the presence of God, but not a separate and distinct person. In Rabbinic Judaism there is no belief in the tri-unity of God. The person of Messiah usually takes center stage on the discussion of the plurality or tri-unity of God and not the person of the *Ruach HaKodesh* (Holy Spirit). The absence of the argument of the Holy Spirit does not remove the importance of the ministry of the Holy Spirit in the Hebrew Scriptures.

Messiah is Divine – Chapters 12 - 15

The purpose of chapters 12 through 15, along with the rest of this study, is to show that the Messiah is God in the Law, Prophets and the Writings. This is contrary to everything that Rabbinic Judaism stands for. Here the specific purpose is to show the eternality of the Messiah. The term for "eternity" or "everlasting" in the Hebrew Scriptures is not the same as currently understood in the English language. A complete understanding of the terms and how they were used is the first area to be discussed in chapter 12. The second area is to show how the term "eternal" relates to the Messiah in chapters 13 through 15. Passages like 1 Chronicles 17:11-14; 2 Samuel 7:10-14; Isaiah 9:6-7; Micah 5:2 and Jeremiah 23:5-6 will be used to prove His divinity. Also, there are other verses where the main speaker is God or *Yahweh*, who describes in His own words what happened to Him. Those descriptions of Himself can only point to one person, the incarnation of God in the person of *Yeshua*.

God Has A Son! – Chapter 16

Chapter 16 deals with a subject that the New Covenant speaks about often, *Yeshua*, the Son of God. However, can that same concept be found in the Hebrew Scriptures? Does God have a son? The answer to that issue is present in the *Tanakh*. While the actual wording is used in the Hebrew Scriptures on a very limited basis, it is used. That brings the natural question of how can God have a son, if indeed He has one? It is the goal of this chapter to point out that God does claim to have a son and explain how that is possible since God is understood to be a unity of one by Rabbinic Judaism.

The Branch – Chapter 17

In chapter 17 the prophets use the term "Branch" four times primarily to reference the relationship between two comings of the same individual, which are separated by a lengthy period of time. First it is used in reference to the successor to David's throne as in Jeremiah 23:5 "*I will raise unto David a righteous Branch, and a King shall reign and prosper, and shall execute judgment and justice in the earth.*" Secondly, it is used to identify that person as the Messiah of Israel, the God/man. In verse 6 of Jeremiah 23

His eternal attribute of holiness is given, "*... and this is his name whereby he shall be called, THE LORD OUR RIGHTEOUSNESS.*" The other verses for the Branch will also show the divinity of the Messiah.

The Word of the LORD – Chapter 18

Chapter 18 deals with a phrase that appears in the prophetic writings often, "*the word of the LORD came to....*" It appears in the book of 1 Samuel 3:21 where the text states that "*the LORD continued to appear at Shiloh: The LORD revealed Himself to Samuel at Shiloh by the word of the LORD.*" It is an unusual phrase: Could the Word of the LORD be a person? The rabbis of old referred to the "*word of the LORD*" as the *Memra* (Aramaic for *word*), and at times equated it with *Metatron* (the angel of the LORD) as well as with the Messiah. What is interesting is that in the New Covenant in the Gospel of John, the apostle opens his gospel with this sentence in John 1:1-2; "*In the beginning was the Word, and the Word was with God, and the Word was God. The same was in the beginning with God.*" That is a New Covenant verse. The goal of this chapter is to investigate and show from the Hebrew Scriptures the personification of the "*Word of the LORD.*"

Summary and Conclusion – Chapter 19

Chapter 19 provides a summary and conclusion. God revealed Himself to man through His Word in a progressive manner. Beginning in Genesis 1, He makes statements of Himself throughout the pages, chapters, and books of the Scripture and unfolds His plurality before the reader, until the final revelation is given in the incarnation of the Messiah to Israel. Both the plurality and the tri-unity of God can be proven in the Hebrew Scriptures. However, the tri-unity is not as well developed in the *Tanakh* as it is in the New Covenant. The *Tanakh*, as it adds one teaching point upon another throughout the Law, Prophets and Writings,[99] becomes a very formidable weight of evidence to prove the plurality of God. It is not just a plurality but the tri-unity that is in view when all is compiled.

The knowledge and understanding of this subject is very important in reaching Jewish people as well as the various "Christian" cults. I also have been told that this information on the tri-unity and deity of Jesus is a valuable resource for those ministering to Muslims. Understanding how God presented Himself in the Hebrew Scriptures as well as in the New Covenant will also be helpful in showing Muslims that God is one, but a plurality in one. Today, the Jewish people are listed as one of the least reached people groups in the United States of America.[100] Less than one percent of

---

[99] *Law, Prophets and Writings*: This is the Jewish designation for the three divisions of the *Tanakh*, or the Hebrew Scriptures.

[100] Patrick Johnstone and Jason Mandryk. *Operation World* (Waynesboro, GA: Paternoster USA, 2001), 662.

Jewish people embrace *Yeshua ha Mashiach* as their Redeemer, Saviour and Lord.[101] This study is devoted to understanding the oneness of God as well as understanding the plural unity of God as set forth in the Hebrew Scriptures by biblical, not rabbinic interpretation.

---

[101] Jews For Jesus. "How many Jews of Jesus are there?" No pages. [Cited 12, January 2004]. Online: http://*www.jfjonline.org/about/howmany.htm.*

Chapter 2
In the Image and Likeness of God

The topic of how man is created in reference to the image and likeness of *Elohim* could fill a book. The focus of this chapter is to show how the "image" and "likeness" model of man reflects the plurality of the person of *Elohim*. This is a limited subject in relation to the doctrine of God, but a much needed one to help mankind understand this aspect of the person, nature, and essence of *Elohim*. There is a need to first study these two words "image" and "likeness" which first appear in Genesis 1:26.

צֶלֶם – *Tzelem* - IMAGE

The Hebrew word צֶלֶם (tzelem), meaning "image," is used in numerous places throughout the *Tanakh*.[102] Defined from a strictly human perspective, the word "image" refers to an image as a representation of a deity, such as an idol.[103] The ordinary use of "*selem*," (image) indicates a three dimensional figure or relief like a statue, whether resembling a man or a god.[104] An "image" is a "likeness" or model of something. Examples of idols which illustrate this are the pagan gods found in 2 Kings 11:18 and Amos 5:26. Ezekiel 16:17 and 23:14 speak of images of humans, while 1 Samuel 6:5 makes reference to images of mice. The truth of that fact is that God calls them idols, and we are commanded not to make graven images of God (Exodus 20:3-4). Even when Moses, Aaron and the 70 elders of Israel saw God, there was no description given of what they saw (Exodus 24:9-11). The following author describes God as being spirit, which is beyond our ability to completely comprehend, for He is not a physical being:

> Theologically, when the OT [Old Testament] forbids making images of God, speaks of God's mediated appearance or formlessness, or declares that humans cannot see God and live, its language communicates the transcendence and incomparability of God. In himself God is beyond human comprehension and

---

[102] *Selem* is used 17 times: Gen 1:26; 5:1-3; 9:6; Num 33:52; 1 Sam 6:5, 11; 2 Kgs 11:18; 2 Chron 23:17; Ezek 7:20; 16:17; 23:14; (used in Aramaic 17 times in Dan 2:31, 32, 34, 35; 3:1-3, 5, 7, 10, 12, 14, 15, 18, 19); Amos 5:26.

[103] R. Laird Harris, Gleason L. Archer, Jr. and Bruce K. Waltke, *Theological Wordbook of the Old Testament*, 2:767.

[104] VanGemeren, *New International Dictionary of Old Testament Theology & Exegesis*, 4:645-646.

depiction. He is known only as he makes himself known, and that necessarily occurs in mediated fashion.[105]

If God is formless and beyond human comprehension and depiction, how are we made in His image? Christianity and Judaism stand in stark contrast to Mormonism that believes and teaches that their gods have a physical body.[106] However, the word "image" as used by *Elohim* of Himself reflects His person but does not reflect a physical image of Himself. What is obviously seen is that God's image does not consist of, nor is it representative of man's body which was formed from the earth. What becomes obvious is that *Elohim* is speaking of His person and character. Man is spiritual, intellectual, and moral in his likeness of God, but only so because of the breath of life that God breathed (Genesis 2:7) into him.[107] When man became a living soul by the breath of God, he was made in the "image" of *Elohim*, and that fact can be difficult to comprehend. We are completely dependent on God for our understanding of this great truth. Our understanding only occurs when we study the complete revelation God gave to man so that we could comprehend Him and how we are created in His "image."

The conclusion is that mankind being made in the "image" of God is a hard concept to comprehend. We only know God by the revelation He makes about Himself through the Scriptures, and some of His revelations are beyond our comprehension. Yes, we are created in the "image" of God's person and character, but only in a limited respect.

דְּמוּת - Demut - LIKENESS

The Hebrew word דְּמוּת (*demut*) or "likeness" comes from the root word דָּמָה (*damah*) and has been defined as a pattern, form, shape, or image[108] and is used in

---

105 VanGemeren, *New International Dictionary of Old Testament Theology & Exegesis*, 4:647.

[106] Anthony A. Hoekema, *The Four Major Cults* (Grand Rapids: Eerdmans, 1965), 34-53. In the Mormon book "The Articles of Faith" it states that the Trinity is "three separate individuals, physically distinct from each other." It states further that "the Father is a personal being, possessing a definite form, with bodily parts and spiritual passions." They state later in the paragraph concerning Christ that He "was in the express image of His Father, after which image man also has been created." (James E. Talmage, A Study of the Articles of Faith, Salt Lake City: The Church of Jesus Christ of Latter-day Saints, 1982, pgs 39, 41-42.) The following is stated in the Doctrines of Covenants concerning the Mormon belief of God being a corporeal physical being, "The Father has a body of flesh and bones as tangible as man's; the Son also; but the Holy Ghost has not a body of flesh and bones, but is a personage of Spirit. Were it not so, the Holy Ghost could not dwell in us." (Doctrines and Covenants, 130:22, published by The Church of Jesus Christ of Latter-day Saints in Salt Lake City, UT.

[107] R. Laird Harris, Gleason L. Archer, Jr. and Bruce K. Waltke, *Theological Wordbook of the Old Testament*, 2:768.

[108] VanGemeren, *New International Dictionary of Old Testament Theology & Exegesis*, 1:967.

numerous places within the pages of the *Tanakh*.[109] The technical information on the usage of the word "likeness" is as follows:

> *Damah* appears 13 times in the *qal*, where it is intransitive and should be rendered "to be like, look like" (Isa 1:9; 46:5; Ezek 31:2, 8 [twice], 18; Psa 89:7[6]; 102:7[6]; 144:4). We may add to this two occurrences in the Aramaic *piel* in Dan 3:25; 7:5. LXX usually translates the *qal* by *homoioun*, "to be like" (9 times), and rarely also by *homoios*, "like," or *homoios einai*, "to be like." *Damah* also occurs 13 times in the *piel* (Num 33:56; Judg 20:5; 2 Sam 21:5; Isa 10:7; 14:24; 40:18, 25; 46:5; Psa 48:10 [9]; 50:21; Lam 2:13). It has in this case a "declarative-estimative" meaning (to declare or consider something or someone to be in the condition suggested by the verb), i.e., the *piel* of *damah* should be translated "to compare, to consider suitable or appropriate."[110]

John Phillips expresses the relationship between *selem* (image) and *demut* (likeness) in Genesis 1:26 by giving a more practical expression of these two words:

> Nowhere else in the OT do these two nouns appear in parallelism or in connection with each other. The more important word of the two is "image" but to avoid the implication that man is a precise copy of God, albeit in miniature. *Demut* [or likeness] then defines and limits the meaning of *selem* [image]. No distinction is to be sought between these two words. They are totally interchangeable. The word "likeness" rather than diminishing the word "image" actually amplifies it and specifies its meaning. Man is not just an image but a likeness-image. He is not simply representative but representational. Man is the visible, corporeal representative of the invisible, bodiless God. *Demut* guarantees that man is an adequate and faithful representative of God on earth.[111]

In speaking personally with Dr. Arnold Fruchtenbaum on this issue, he also agrees that "image" and "likeness" are the same in meaning and that "likeness" simply qualifies the first term, "image."[112] Charles Feinberg states the same thing in Bib Sac (a theological journal) when he writes:

> In short, use reveals the words [*selem* and *demuth* – literally image and likeness] are used interchangeably.[113]

---

[109] Gen 1:26; 5:1-3; Ex 20:4; 25:9; Deut 5:8; 2 Kgs 16:10; 2 Chron 4:3; Psa 58:4; Isa 13:4; 40:18; Ezek 1:5, 10, 13, 16, 22, 26, 28; 8:2; 10:1, 21, 22; 23:15; Dan 10:16.

[110] G. Johannes Botterweck, Helmer Ringgren and Heinz-Josef Fabry, *Theological Dictionary of the Old Testament* (14 vols. Grand Rapids: Eerdmans, 1978), 3:250-251.

[111] R. Laird Harris, Gleason L. Archer, Jr., and Bruce K. Waltke, *Theological Wordbook of the Old Testament*, 1:192.

[112] Arnold Fruchtenbaum, *Personal Communication*, July 2006.

[113] Charles L. Feinberg, "The Image of God," *Bib Sac* 129:515 (July 1972): 237.

Distinctions Between Man and Animals

Even though many authors say much about how mankind is in the "image" and "likeness" of *Elohim*, they still do not give a complete answer. Perhaps there is not a complete answer. But there is a distinct uniqueness in man that some authors capture in writing as they reference man who stands between the animal creation of *Elohim* and *Elohim* Himself. Phillips' insights into the differences between man and the animal kingdom are outstanding, yet the creation of mankind reflects man's likeness to *Elohim* and not animals':

> Man is in no way related to the beasts. What animal can transmit accumulated achievements from one generation to another? What animal experiences a true sense of guilt when it does wrong or has a developed consciousness of judgment to come? What animal shows any desire to worship? What animal has hope of immortality beyond the grave? What beast can exercise abstract moral judgment or show appreciation of the beauties of nature? (When did we ever see a dog admiring a sunset or a horse standing breathless before the rugged grandeur of a mountain range?) What animal ever learned to read and write, to act with deliberate purpose, and set goals and achieve long-range objectives? What animal ever learned to cook its food, to cut cloth and make clothes, or invent elaborate tools? What animal ever enjoyed a hearty laugh? What animal has the gift for speech? Even the most primitive human tribe possesses linguistics of a subtle, complex and eloquent nature. Man stands alone. *Physically*, he alone of all the creatures on the globe walks upright; *mentally*, he alone has the ability to communicate in a sophisticated manner; *spiritually*, he alone has the capacity to know the mind and will of God.[114]

Phillips expresses the chasm between man and animal. The qualities of man are the same as those of *Elohim*. *Elohim* gave these qualities to man uniquely as the image bearer of Himself. Another aspect of mankind's uniqueness in the creation account of Genesis 1 is to see the formula that God used. The formula that *Elohim* gives shows a complete uniqueness in God's created order. On the creative days one through five and on the beginning of the sixth day, in Genesis 1, verses 3, 6, 9, 11, 14, 20, and 24, *Elohim* states "*let there be.*" In verse 26 the formula for the creation of mankind is unique to the other days because He states "*let us*" rather than "*let there be.*" When *Elohim* created living things He used the word מִין (*min*) meaning "kind" or "species." The word *min* would be similar to the modern taxonomical idea of species, making certain that all living creatures must be understood in terms of categories, or species. The creation of mankind is clearly distinct from the animal kingdom or of any other form of life that precedes it, because the human race does not belong to a category called *min*. So mankind is a unique creation and cannot be compared to creatures of any other kind, which is what evolution has taught. Evolution is a destructive doctrine

---

[114] John Phillips, *Exploring Genesis* (Chicago: Moody, 1980), 45.

because it teaches mankind to compare themselves to the animal kingdom, rather than to *Elohim* his Creator. Mankind's humanity is in the "image" and "likeness" of *Elohim*, not an evolutionary process from lower life forms.

Comparisons of God in Man

Mankind is not connected to the animal kingdom, but is representative of *Elohim*, for mankind is made in His "image" and "likeness" and not like animals. The difficulty with comparing God and man in relationship to God's "image" and "likeness" in Genesis 1:26-27 is that there is no description of the likeness of *Elohim* provided.[115] What is learned comes from the progressive revelation of Scripture. That is how mankind learns of the meaning of "image" and "likeness" and how mankind represents the presence of *Elohim* on this earth:

> The likeness does not consist of the physical form at all; rather, the likeness is in the function of that form to represent the presence of God in the world; the divine presence is represented through the creation of humans, who exercise dominion (Psa 8:5-8 [6-9]).[116]

One of the keys to understanding the "image" and "likeness" in the person of *Elohim* that mankind represents is to grasp the meaning of Genesis 1:26-27. But this may not be completely possible. God is unknowable except as He revealed Himself to mankind in the *Tanakh*. The likelihood is that what *Elohim* revealed of Himself through His Word is only a fraction of His person, essence and nature, although He has revealed what man needs to know about Him, or perhaps what mankind can grasp of His person. Moses stated that mankind is made in the "image" and "likeness" of *Elohim* in Genesis 1:26-27. Moses does not state what *Elohim* means by "image" and "likeness." Mankind has no way of making an absolute examination of what is intended in the Genesis account. In the revelation that man has been given through the Scriptures, he learns that he is not part of the animal kingdom. Mankind can learn dimly through the same Scriptures how God created him in His (*Elohim*'s) likeness. Mankind is somewhat at a disadvantage because God does not give an explanation in this verse; He just makes the statement or declaration. This much can be observed: Genesis 1:26-27 gives the only credible evidence of who *Elohim* is, and mankind is that evidence. All other passages where the terms "image" and "likeness" are used, with the exception of Genesis 5:1-3 and 9:6, are in connection with idols and other likenesses of man or animals.[117] One author has given a brief observation on the difficulty of grasping this concept:

---

[115] VanGemeren, *New International Dictionary of Old Testament Theology & Exegesis*, 1:969.

[116] VanGemeren, *New International Dictionary of Old Testament Theology & Exegesis*, 1:969.

[117] *Image*: In the New Covenant the word "image" is used in connection with Messiah. Paul states in Col. 1:15 that Messiah "*is the image of the invisible God*" which has a direct relationship to the tri-unity of God in the *Tanakh*. What is clearly recognized is that God created

> The passage is unique in the OT, if one disregards echoes in Gen 5 and 9, ...
> Precisely because Gen 1:26 stands in such isolation, it has given free rein to
> theological speculation.[118]

Indeed, this passage from the Scripture is unique. Understanding just how the "image" and "likeness" of *Elohim* are revealed through mankind is difficult, but it is this image that mankind bears. All of man's life is taken up with getting to know *Elohim* well enough to understand what His "image" and "likeness" are. There is no shortage of writings on the subject of how mankind is in the "image" and "likeness" of *Elohim*. In order to continue in the quest to understand *Elohim* and the words "image" and "likeness," we will continue to analyze them.

The words "image" and "likeness" as stated earlier are used synonymously and interchangeably, and do not refer to two different things.[119] These two words reflect in mankind the plural (triune) personhood of an indivisible *Elohim*. Mankind is unique, a personal entity that at conception is created by God (Malachi 2:10)[120] and is immediately and forever joined to one's propagated human nature (body, soul and spirit).[121] In contrast to the lower animals, which are made each after its kind or type, man is made in the "image of God."[122] That distinction must not be missed. The following author reflects his understanding of being in the "image of God" by saying:

> To be made in the image of God thus means that man is a creative, rational, moral being. He has creative emotions, a rational intellect, and a moral volition. These three correspond to what under the great commandment are called his soul, his mind and his heart respectively.[123]

Mankind is a spiritual being that in some way reflects the image of *Elohim*. Mankind's bodily nature does not reflect the person of God, but mankind does reflect the person of God through his spiritual nature. As has been stated, mankind is a reflection of *Elohim*'s invisible, incorporeal person. Mankind is unique in all of God's creation in that he

---

mankind in His image, and mankind is male and female as well as being individually made up of body, soul and spirit, a tri-unity. God in His wisdom created mankind to reflect who He is in mankind, and in that wisdom God chose the Messiah to be the very image of the invisible God. As will be clearly seen in the *Tanakh*, the second member of the tri-unity of God became visible in the theophanies of the Hebrew Scriptures, but in the New Covenant, through the Incarnation of God, the invisible God became visible.

[118] Ernst Jenni and Claus Westermann, *Theological Lexicon of the Old Testament* (Peabody, MA: Hendrickson, 1997), 3:1082.

[119] Louis Berkhof, *Systematic Theology*, 203.

[120] In the Hebrew it is אֵל or *El*, which just happens to be in the singular.

[121] Floyd H. Barackman, *Practical Christian Theology: Examining the Great Doctrines of the Faith* (4th Ed. Grand Rapids: Kregel, 2001), 256.

[122] John Skinner, *The International Critical Commentary: A Critical and Exegetical Commentary on Genesis* (Edinburgh: T & T Clark, 1969), 30.

[123] Basil R. C. Atkinson, *The Pocket Commentary of the Bible: Genesis* (Chicago: Moody, 1957), 22.

reflects the "image of God" in a way that mankind finds hard to grasp. It also needs to be clearly understood that mankind is not like *Elohim* in every dimension; he only reflects certain aspects of God's "image" and "likeness." To illustrate, man is not immutable (changeless), nor is he omnipresent (everywhere present), nor is he omniscient (all knowing), nor is he omnipotent (all powerful), nor did mankind exist in eternity past. What mankind shares with *Elohim* are qualities such as personality, will, and sensibility. That is, humanity's resemblance to *Elohim* is analogous[124] but not ontologically[125] identical. To be like *Elohim* is to be patterned after Him while inferior to Him. This "image" and "likeness" are further supported by understanding that image exists in the creation narratives by the use of the first person pronouns (I, we, us) that God used of Himself. In Genesis chapters 1 and 2 the personality and rulership of God are observed, but there are differences that quickly become apparent as the following author expresses:

> [When] both God and humans speak, [they] are referred to by personal pronouns, [they] exercise authority over lesser beings and have the capacity to make choices (Gen 2:17). On the other hand, God has always existed (Gen 1:1), whereas humanity was created (Gen 1:27); humankind is under the dominion of God and is therefore not equal to him (Gen 2:16); human-kind is physical and corporeal (Gen 2:7), but God is spirit (Ex 33:17-23; cf. Jn 4:24); humans are mortal (Gen 2:17), but God is eternal. To be in the image of God cannot mean equivalence between deity and humanity, then, but only an analogous [likeness] or corresponding relationship between the two.[126]

Elohim and mankind share some things in common, namely *Elohim*'s "image" and "likeness." At the same time however, that "image" and "likeness" have limitations. Mankind is created in the "image" and "likeness" of *Elohim*, not everything in mankind is equal with Him. It is in the personhood of God that we are created in His "image" and "likeness."

How Mankind Is Like Elohim in His Person

Pastors and teachers offer to explain the tri-unity and the "image" and "likeness" of *Elohim* in order to help their congregations and students by stating that the tri-unity is like an egg with three parts, or the three components of water, or even using a tree with its roots, trunk and branches. But all of these are inadequate to explain the tri-unity, as one author expresses:

> …common analogies of the Trinity – the egg (yoke [sic], albumen, shell), a man (employee, husband, citizen), and water (liquid, ice, vapor) – have serious

---

[124] *Analogous*: Showing an analogy or a likeness, permitting one to draw an analogy.

[125] *Ontology*: A study of conceptions of reality and the nature of being. It is the study of being or existence and forms the basic subject matter of metaphysics.

[126] Alexander and Baker, *Dictionary of the Old Testament Pentateuch*, 443.

shortcomings which do more to hinder and mislead than to aid understanding.[127]

Heinze is exactly correct in his observation. However, he goes on to say that the three aspects of "space" (height, width and length) come closer to explaining the tri-unity of God. I, even though viewing Heinze's statement with interest, still believe that none of the above symbolisms define the triune nature of a personal God. God intended people to understand something very special about His person. What was it that He wanted readers of Scripture to understand?

Elohim is a plural noun for the word "God" which has given rise to many statements, both positive and negative, by Jewish and Christian scholars as to its precise meaning. The difficulty lies in the fact that *Elohim* is a plural noun. Jewish scholars reject the tri-unity of *Elohim* because in Hebrew grammar, as in English, you would have a plural noun following a plural verb. The word "created" in Genesis 1:1 is a singular verb, not a plural verb which is the case in most instances throughout the *Tanakh*. So Jewish scholars interpret *Elohim* as one (*echad*) or as a "plural of majesty."[128] It is odd that Moses had two other Hebrew words to express the absolute oneness of *Elohim*; however, he did not use them often. The two words are אֵל or *El* and אֱלוֹהַ or *Eloah*, which are singular expressions for God and not plural as is *Elohim*. This subject will be dealt with in depth in chapter 3.

After extensive research on this subject I have found that most authors do have some good insights pertaining to the "image" and "likeness" of *Elohim*. They adequately describe the character and attributes of God; however they miss the personal nature of Him. Gordon Talbot defines the differences between man who is made in the "image" and "likeness" of God and animals that are not. He states:

> Human beings were to be different from all other creatures in two distinct ways. First, they were to be made in God's image or likeness. Man would have an intelligence superior to that of animals, the ability to communicate freely by language, sensitive emotional capacities, sophisticated social relationships with others, personal consciences, and immortal souls designed to have fellowship with God. Second, they were to have dominion over all the earth's resources.[129]

As man has an "intelligence superior to that of animals," God has an intelligence superior to that of man. God and man have "the ability to communicate freely by language, sensitive emotional capacities, sophisticated social relationships with others,

---

[127] E. Charles Heinze, *Trinity & Triunity* (Dale City, VA: Epaphras Press, 1995), 6.

[128] *Plural of Majesty*: This term is used to represent God speaking in the plural as referencing Himself with the heavenly hosts (angels). Many state that a plural of majesty does not represent a true plural, or that it is an abstract plural and is not meant to represent a numeric plural. It is also referred to as a "royal we" as the Queen of England would use. This will be dealt with in detail in chapter 3.

[129] Gordon Talbot, *A Study of the Book of Genesis* (Harrisburg, PA: Christian Publications, 1981), 18.

and personal consciences." God designed us with immortal souls to have fellowship with Him. God gave man dominion over the earth's resources and the animal kingdom in reflection of God's dominion over the heavens and earth. Talbot expresses how man reflects the "image" and "likeness" of *Elohim*, yet he does not fully express the essence of the personal nature of God as is described in the tri-unity of God.

While I was attending the 2006 Messianic Jewish Alliance of America (MJAA), Messianic Rabbi David Rosenberg presented a workshop called "The Mystery of the Godhead & the Divinity of *Yeshua*." Some of the insights he presented will be reflected in the next section on the plurality of God in its relationship to mankind.

Background for the Plurality of God that Mankind Reflects

One can ask how God can be a plurality in one. How can monotheism and the triune concept of God be harmonized? The answer lies in Genesis 1:26 and within humanity. When *Elohim* and man are introduced in Genesis one, they are both introduced in the singular and plural forms as the following author describes:

> One feature of the text which seems to have been completely overlooked in the discussion of the divine plural is that as soon as Elohim is associated with a plurality, humankind is presented in the same way. Throughout the creation account, third person singular verbs describe God's actions, clearly presenting him in the singular. But when the divine plural appears, thereby introducing the idea of plurality, it occurs along with the presentation of humanity as both singular and plural ("Let us create man...so that they...." [v. 26], and "God created man in his own image, in the image of God created he him, male and female created he them" [v. 27]). Thus both Deity and humanity are simultaneously presented as both singular and plural.[130]

Genesis 1:26-27 gives the only credible evidence of who *Elohim* is.[131] We are that evidence. So the focus is placed on Genesis 1:26-27. There are only two other related passages found in Genesis 5:1-3; 9:6. To aid in our understanding of the use of the

---

[130] Thomas A. Keiser, *The Divine Plural Contextual Presentation of Plurality in the Godhead* (A paper presented March 24, 2006 to Evangelical Theological Society, Southwest Region), 2.

[131] Only two other passages use the terms "image" and "likeness" in the *Tanakh*: Genesis 5:1-3 and 9:6. All other times those two terms are used in connection with idols and other likenesses of man or animals. In the New Covenant the word "image" is used in connection with Messiah. Paul states in Colossians 1:15 that Messiah "*is the image of the invisible God*" which has a direct relationship to the tri-unity of God in the *Tanakh*. What is clearly recognized is that God created mankind in His image, God in His wisdom created mankind to reflect who He is in mankind, and in that wisdom God chose the Messiah to be the very image of the invisible God. As will be clearly seen in the *Tanakh*, the second member of the tri-unity of God became visible in the theophanies of the Hebrew Scriptures, but in the New Covenant, through the Incarnation of God, the invisible God became visible.

41

plural and singular words as they relate to *Elohim*, the Creator, and to man, the created, I will quote Genesis 1:26-27 with the plural and singular words pointed out:

> 26 And God (*Elohim* – **Pl**ural) said, "Let us make man (**s**ingular) in our (pl) image (s), after our (pl) likeness (s). They (pl) shall rule the fish of the sea, the birds of the sky, the cattle, the whole earth, and all the creeping things that creep on earth." 27 And God (*Elohim* – pl) created man (s) in His (s) image, in the image (s) of God (*Elohim* – pl) He (s) created him (s); male (s) and female (s) He created them (pl) (Emphasis mine)[132] (Jewish Tanakh).

In verse 27, twice God stresses that man (mankind – singular) was "created" in His image, using singular pronouns for Himself. Then a third time He states that He "created" them (mankind – plural) male and female. Sailhamer points to the plurality of God in whose image man, both singular and plural, were made:

> Verse 27 stated twice that humankind was created in God's image and a third time that humankind was created "male and female." The same pattern is found in Genesis 5:1-2a: When God created humankind…"male and female he created them." The singular, "human being," is created as a plurality, "male and female." In a similar way, the one God created humanity through an expression of his plurality.[133]

Throughout chapter 1 of Genesis, Sailhamer states that God is speaking and acting in the singular while using *Elohim* a plural noun. But in verses 26 and 27 God or *Elohim* presents Himself in the plural when He is about to create mankind (singular). In verse 27 *Elohim* again returns to the singular with the act of creating mankind, showing unity, but now in that creative act He creates mankind singular as plural male and female. You need to review Sailhamer's statement because it is so important to understand. Now let me finish Sailhamer's quote:

> Following this clue, one may see the divine plurality expressed in verse 26 as an anticipation of the human plurality of man and woman, thus casting the human relationship between man and woman in the role of reflecting God's own personal relationship with himself.[134]

Re-read Sailhamer's full quotation thoughtfully and slowly to grasp his statement concerning the singular-plurality of mankind, man and woman, and how we reflect "God's own personal relationship with himself." Something that has been missed by most scholars is the fact that *Elohim* speaks in the plural and creates in the singular only in verses 26-27; He generates life, and in that generation of life He creates (singular) mankind and in particular that life is presented as male and female, plural. Thus when

---

[132] All **bold** passages in this book indicate my emphasis unless otherwise indicated.

[133] John H. Sailhamer, *The Pentateuch as Narrative: A Biblical-Theological Commentary* (Grand Rapids: Zondervan, 1992), 95-96.

[134] Sailhamer, *The Pentateuch as Narrative: A Biblical-Theological Commentary,* 95-96.

man and woman generate life, they give birth to male and female images or likenesses of themselves (Genesis 5:1-3). The picture becomes clear that *Elohim* in the context of plurality creates singular a plural being known as humanity, male and female. Mankind then procreates and gives birth to sons and daughters, plural in the image and likenesses of humanity. Yet in their procreation, male and female act as one (singular) to procreate that life (Genesis 2:24; 4:1), even as *Elohim* in the plural creates life acting in the singular. God does not procreate or have a wife as in Mormon theology.[135] This concept is completely foreign to the Scripture, both in the *Tanakh* and New Covenant. There is a very strong parallel in what God is saying about Himself, His personhood (plural), and about mankind (plural). Thomas Keiser presents this picture but in a more technical way in the following statement, which is only a portion of his total argument:

> A review of the expression זָכָר וּנְקֵבָה ("male and female"), occurring only in Gen 1:27; 5:2; 6:19; 7:3, 9, 16, reveals that the context is always one of generation of life.... It is notable that the divine plural is introduced with a similar nuance to that of humankind. That is, the transition from singular to plural with reference to God is also made in the context of the generation of life ("let us make man"). Thus, not only are both the divine and human singular-plurals introduced together, they are both presented in connection with the same concept, namely, generation of life. Perhaps one can say that in both cases the text presents a cooperation of a plurality of individuals, who are simultaneously seen as a unity, in the production of life.[136]

Elohim in the plural creates in the singular, mankind, who then procreates and produces images of themselves by acting together as a plural with a singular act. In order to understand just how mankind is created in His "image" and "likeness" there needs to be a clearer and more practical, understandable presentation as to how mankind is like God.

Man and Woman, a Plurality and Tri-unity in One

How is this possible? Now observe two known but unused examples of just how mankind is in the "image" and "likeness" of God. **First**, *Elohim*, who is a plural unity, stated, *"let us make man."* The Hebrew word אָדָם or *aw-dawm`* (adam) means mankind. *Elohim* made mankind, according to Genesis 1:27, by splitting mankind into "male and female." Sailhamer states that *Elohim* created mankind as a plural

---

[135] Hoekema, *The Four Major Cults*, 36. Mormonism also teaches that God is a corporeal being having flesh and bones as stated in the Doctrine and Covenants: "The Father has a body of flesh and bones as tangible as man's; the Son also; but the Holy Ghost has not a body of flesh and bones, but is a personage of Spirit." *The Book of Mormon; The Doctrine and Covenants; The Pearl of Great Price*, (Salt Lake City: The Church of Jesus Christ of Latter-day Saints, 1982), 130:22.

[136] Thomas A. Keiser, *The Divine Plural Contextual Presentation of Plurality in the Godhead*, 3.

representation of Himself, not as a single representation. *Elohim*, who said *"let us,"* created mankind as a plural reflection of His "image" and "likeness:"

> The singular man (Adam) is created as a plurality, "male and female." In a similar way the one God created man through an expression of his plurality. Following this clue the divine plurality expressed in v. 26 is seen as an anticipation of the human plurality of the man and woman, thus casting the human relationship between man and woman in the role of reflecting God's own personal relationship with himself.[137]

The plural relationship is a significant insight and should not be missed. Man and woman were created to reflect the personal relationship that the plural unity of *Elohim* experienced from eternity past. That relationship was to be pictured as a harmonious relationship that the first man and woman were to have with each other. Man and woman were equals, yet *Elohim* gave the man headship. Woman was to submit to man as a reflection of the Son and the Holy Spirit in voluntary submission to the Father.[138] Man and woman were to reflect the harmonious relationship that existed between the members of the Godhead. So, both man and woman were created to function in the "image" and "likeness" of God:

> It is as both male and female that humankind is to function as the image of God (Gen 1:28). Animals thus relate to one another within their own subhuman category, but in some grand and mysterious sense humankind resembles God.[139]

Together both man and woman would be responsible to have dominion over the earth and the animal world just as *Elohim* in His plural unity has dominion over the heavens and the earth as stated below:

> Male and female human members are image-bearers who both are responsible for governing the world.[140]

Here is a good picture of man and woman who bear the "image" and "likeness" of *Elohim* together. *Elohim* is a triune unity of one (*echad*). Each member of that unity has different responsibilities and functions as they relate to human experience. In their

---

[137] John H. Sailhamer, *The Expositor's Bible Commentary: Genesis* (12 vol. Grand Rapids: Zondervan, 1990), 2:38.

[138] The harmonious relationship that man and woman were to exhibit as a reflection of *Elohim* was marred by the fall of mankind into sin. What is interesting is that in the New Testament, that relationship is re-instated because we are a "new creation" (2 Cor 5:17) in Messiah. That which was lost in the fall to a large degree has been reinstated through the indwelling of the Holy Spirit. For once again the man has the headship and is to be a servant leader in the home where the wife who, as his equal, submits to his leadership (Eph 5:18-6:4; Col 3:1-4:6). It can be a reality IF both the husband and the wife actively walk in Messiah and do not serve selfish interests.

[139] Alexander and Baker, *Dictionary of the Old Testament Pentateuch*, 443.

[140] Kenneth A. Mathews, *The New American Commentary: Genesis 1-11:26* (Nashville: Broadman & Holman, 2002), 173.

unity, *Elohim* the Father has taken the leadership role; whereas, *Elohim* the Son and *Elohim* the Holy Spirit have taken subordinate roles and responsibilities to the Father, yet they are equal in all respects. The Son and the Holy Spirit voluntarily submit to the Father as they carry out their responsibilities in their interaction with humans on earth. When *Elohim* created mankind and split them into male and female, they were to reflect the image of *Elohim*, who harmoniously worked together in relationship to one another in the universe. In the same way mankind was to work harmoniously together in their relationship to one another as they exercised dominion over the earth together. As two of the equal triune members of the unity of *Elohim* submit to the Father, so woman is to submit to man, working harmoniously together as equals. I use the word "triune" which relates to three; however in the Genesis 1 account only a plurality is referenced. We know from the rest of the *Tanakh* that that plurality is a tri-unity. Male and female are equals on earth as the triune members of *Elohim* are equal in the universe, but each, whether mankind or *Elohim*, carries out different responsibilities and functions. Male and female were created in the very "image" and "likeness" of *Elohim* as reflected in this statement by Grudem:

> Just as the Father and the Son are equal in deity and equal in all their attributes, but different in role, so husband and wife are equal in personhood and value, but they are different in the roles God has given to them. Just as God the Son is eternally subject to the authority of God the Father, so God has planned that wives be subject to the authority of their husbands.[141]

In his summary statement Keiser gives a brief statement on the picture that *Elohim* gives in His creative act:

> In summary, a contextual analysis of the divine plural in Genesis 1 reveals that it is directly associated with a human plural, resulting in both Deity and humanity simultaneously presented as both singular and plural. Additionally, the presentation of each singular-plural is associated with the generation of life which, in some respect, is related to those who generate life. A comparison of the common interpretations of the divine plural with this contextual review reveals that it is best understood as plurality in the Godhead.[142]

Before we move on to the second point, it is extremely important to clarify another fact to men and women in the 21st century. Historically men have frequently been abusive, domineering, and have suppressed and belittled women as though they are inferior to them. Today women have reacted to the male dominance and abuse in the feminist movement. Two wrongs do not make a right. The feminist movement is as unbiblical as the male dominance of the past and present. They both ignore God's design and plan in creating male and female in His image and likeness. A quote from

---

[141] Wayne Grudem, *Evangelical Feminism & Biblical Truth* (Sisters, OR: Multnomah Publishers, 2004), 46.

[142] Thomas A. Keiser, *The Divine Plural Contextual Presentation of Plurality in the Godhead,* 5.

Wayne Grudem will illustrate the unbiblical problem and the unwillingness to recognize God's purpose and plan:

> The Bible thus corrects the errors of male dominance and male superiority that have come as the result of sin and that have been seen in nearly all cultures in the history of the world. Wherever men are thought to be better than women, wherever husbands act as selfish "dictators," wherever wives are forbidden to have their own jobs outside the home or to vote or to own property or to be educated, wherever women are treated as inferior, wherever there is abuse or violence against women or rape or female infanticide or polygamy or harems, the biblical truth of equality in the image of God is being denied. To all societies and cultures where these things occur, we must proclaim that the very first page of God's Word bears a fundamental and irrefutable witness against these evils.[143]

Lay down this book for a minute and pick up your Bible and read Proverbs 31:10-31 about the virtuous woman. In this passage women are not presented as inferior, but as intelligent, wise, thrifty, hard-working, industrious, and equal partners with man. But because of sin man's attitude toward women is sin and the feminist movement today is equally sin. Men and women are equals serving together, both with differing functions and responsibilities, but equals. Two other brief quotes by Grudem re-emphasize the point:

> Every time we talk to each other as men and women, we should remember that the person we are talking to is a creature of God who is more like God than anything else in the universe, and men and women share that status equally. Therefore we should treat men and women with equal dignity and we should think of men and women as having equal value. If men and women are equally in the image of God, then we are equally important and equally valuable to God. We have equal worth before Him for all eternity, for this is how we were created.[144]

This biblical truth is absent from Islam which treats women as being created inferior, deficient in intelligence, described as animals or toys for the pleasure of men. Women in Islam are a thing to be ashamed of, which is one of the reasons for the veil, forcing them to stay or remain in their homes and on it goes.[145] The concept of equality is easier to understand theologically than it is for men and women to live and practice. Why? Because humanity willfully became a fallen creation of God in overt rebellion to the Creator whose image and likeness mankind still bears. Thus, there is a need to restore that which was lost to mankind. Thus you have the allusion to the first sacrifice for sin

---

[143] Grudem, *Evangelical Feminism & Biblical Truth,* 26.

[144] Grudem, *Evangelical Feminism & Biblical Truth,* 26-27.

[145] John Ankerberg and John Weldon, *Fast Facts on Islam* (Eugene, OR: Harvest House Publishers, 2001), 55-61.

in Genesis 3:21 and the need for a future Redeemer to mediate between fallen sinful mankind and their Creator.

Second, not only did God create man and woman to reflect His plurality, but He further reflected His plurality and tri-unity by creating man and woman in three dimensions: body, soul, and spirit. Men and women in themselves are a tri-unity made up in one (*echad*) person, each of us individually are body, soul, and spirit. That designation of body, soul, and spirit is completely different from the created animal world. Of those three dimensions in the "image" and "likeness" of *Elohim*, one is visible, the body. The remaining two dimensions, being soul and spirit, are invisible. Who has seen man's soul or spirit? No one! Who has seen man's body? Everyone! Equally so, *Elohim*, in His plurality in unity, has three dimensions or persons. One of those dimensions or Persons of the plural unity of *Elohim*, became visible when He chose to reveal Himself to mankind, while the other two persons of the plural unity of *Elohim* have remained invisible. These two points on the image and likeness of *Elohim* that mankind bears give us the best insight and picture to begin to understand the mystery of the unity of God.

As will be demonstrated throughout this book, *Elohim* revealed Himself to mankind as an indivisible plurality in unity. One person of the plural unity of *Elohim* would become visible and use physical or auditory revelations of Himself to mankind. He did so through what is known theologically as a theophany, where He revealed Himself as the "*angel of the LORD*" or the *Shechinah* glory of God. This member of the plural unity of *Elohim* became visible on a consistent basis while the other two persons of the tri-unity of *Elohim* remained invisible. Yet when the triune *Elohim* spoke, He almost always spoke in the first person to avoid confusing mankind. The whole concept as to why *Elohim* spoke in the singular becomes very clear and why He did not speak in a plurality is also very apparent. Mankind, after they fell in sin, worshipped many gods in their pantheon of gods. *Elohim* spoke as one (*echad*) so that mankind would not be confused as to His nature, character and essence. It was a critical issue for *Elohim* to reveal Himself as one (*echad*) God, yet it was also necessary to be true to His plurality of persons within Himself that He revealed Himself as a plural unity.

ANTHROPOMORPHISM

The Bible often speaks of God with anthropomorphisms as if comparing Him with man, not only by using images that describe Him as a king, a shepherd, a father, and a judge, but also by speaking of *Yahweh* and/or *Elohim* as engaging in such human actions as walking (Genesis 3:8), smelling an aroma (Genesis 8:21), etc. Scripture also through anthropomorphisms ascribes body parts to God, including arms (Numbers 11:23), hands (Psalm111:7), a mouth (Deuteronomy 8:3), and eyes (Deuteronomy 11:12).

Rabbinic Judaism, however, had problems with Moses and the prophets of God using these terms to describe God. The prophets sometimes describe something that God does, or God Himself used human terms that correspond to God having human body parts such as arms, hands, mouth and eyes. So Judaism "softens" the Scriptures to reflect their sensitivity to God being equated with humanity by the use of anthropomorphic terms. The Jewish sages of the past have removed the wording from the translated biblical text or have substituted other words to get away from God having any identity with man as the following statements from Goldberg clearly express:

> In personal references to God, all anthropomorphic expressions are avoided and other expressions are substituted. All human traits ascribed to deity are toned down or avoided so as not to create false impressions among the unlearned, namely, that Yahweh was not like any pagan deity. The expressions of Memra and Shekinah are used freely in substitutions.[146]

Goldberg expresses that the Jewish translators of both the Greek LXX (Septuagint) and the Aramaic Targums (paraphrase) did not like the anthropomorphism of the *Tanakh* and thus would change the words to reflect God's glory or presence rather than allow the biblical text to stand as written with terms like *"the hand of God"* or *"The LORD stood by* [Abraham]." One of the reasons they did not like the language was and is that God is a pure spirit and does not have arms, legs, feet, etc., whereas the pagans made images of gods that Israel worshipped before the captivity, images which had those human characteristics. Another author references Maimonides who correctly viewed that for God to have a body or form was irrational but also deadly heresy.[147] With that biblical Christianity would have to be in complete agreement. The confusion comes because biblical Christianity without hesitation stands on the fact that God is spirit, indivisible and does not have a body, period. But in biblical Christianity it also embraces the fact that God can and did take on human form for the benefit of communicating with human beings by the use of theophanies. Biblical faith also believes that God, who is spirit, can and did take on flesh to be the sin bearer to fulfill in the future, as the Messiah, the promises to Abraham and David. In the process God also fulfills these promises to Israel through Himself by first taking on a physical body to deal with sin and then returning to fulfill His promises to the fathers (Abraham, Isaac and Jacob). But Rabbinic Judaism has misunderstood biblical faith and Goldberg continues to state just how they attempted to get away from the literal meaning of these anthropomorphisms:

> Anthropomorphisms are rendered in such a way in translation as to avoid any possible misconception. Thus God does not smell an offering but accepts it; He does not go before the people but He leads them. Instead of God hearing or

---

[146] Louis Goldberg, *The Deviation of Jewish Thought from an Old Testament Theology in the Intertestamental Period* (Doctor of Theology Thesis, Grace Theological Seminary, 1963), 53.

[147] George Foot Moore, "Intermediaries in Jewish Theology: Memra, Shekinah, Metatron." *Harvard Theological Review*, vol. 15 (1922), 41.

seeing, it is said it was revealed or heard before Him. God's feet are His glorious throne (Targum Isaiah 38:5; 60:13).… Shekinah is another word used as a substitute for personal references to God. In this instance, anthropomorphic references to God in the Isaiah text are attributed in the Targum to the Shekinah or the glory of the Shekinah, e.g., hiding the eyes is removing the presence of His Shekinah, to see the King is to see the glory of the Shekinah (1:15; 6:5).[148]

What is interesting is that God, as He revealed Himself to mankind, had no problem with anthropomorphic terms in describing Himself. God chose language, human language, to help man understand Him in terms that mankind could identify with:

> All Scripture is written in human language, not some divine language. God's revelation is "accommodated," as Calvin liked to say, to human understanding. Scripture takes abstract attributes of God, no less than concrete images of him, from human life – words that have uses in our conversation about earthly things. This is the only kind of revelation there is. The purpose of revelation is communication, and so the very purpose of revelation is to get God's message into human terms. Granted that God is not a physical being, we are rightly inclined to say that he does not really have hands, though human hands appropriately symbolize the means of God's workmanship. [149]

God not only chose to use anthropomorphic terms to relate to mankind in a manner that mankind would understand, but He also used many word pictures to describe Himself. A partial list follows:

- God is pictured as the Father.
- God is also related to His people as a husband (Isaiah 54:5).
- The image of God as a shepherd (Numbers 27:17; Psalm 77:20).
- God the potter (Isaiah 64:8; Jeremiah 18-19).
- God a farmer (Isaiah 5).
- God a refiner (Psalm 12:6; Proverbs 17:3; Malachi 3:2).
- God a landowner (Matthew 20:1-16).
- God is like a lion, a leopard, or a bear, who will devour His wicked people (Hosea 13:7-8).
- God is the Rock (Deuteronomy 32; I Samuel 2:2; 2 Samuel 22:2-3, 32, 47).[150]

These anthropomorphic word pictures present a further interesting facet of how God chose to reveal Himself. It does need to be clearly and emphatically stated that God is

---

[148] Goldberg, *The Deviation of Jewish Thought from an Old Testament Theology in the Intertestamental Period,* 20-21.

[149] John M. Frame, *The Doctrine of God* (Phillipsburg, NJ: P & R Publishers, 2002), 367.

[150] John M. Frame, *The Doctrine of God,* 366-377.

spirit and not human. God does not have body parts as humans, He is pure spirit. The rabbis, in attempting to "protect" God by using alternate terms, have over-reacted to God's using human terms of Himself in speaking to men and have distorted the Word of God. God in His Word is completely capable of protecting His own person and character without the help of well intentioned rabbis.

To move beyond this God throughout the pages of the *Tanakh*, used multiple male images, and He always spoke in the masculine. God in His wisdom also chose, at times, to use feminine references to Himself, a practice which bothers some people. As previously stated however, when *Elohim* created mankind, He created both male and female to reflect His "image" and "likeness." He reflected His plural person; there is nothing in Scripture to indicate that God is sexually a male. However, the female characteristics of woman came from the creative mind and hand of *Elohim*. He created the female as an equal partner for man. Below is the first of three rare references that illustrates God referring to Himself in the feminine:

> You neglected the Rock that begot you, Forgot the God [*El*] who brought you forth (Deuteronomy 32:18).

In Deuteronomy 32:18, Moses gives both the masculine and the feminine as he speaks to Israel about their God. Kohlenberger translates the Hebrew word יְלָדְךָ in the masculine as "he fathered you,"[151] which corresponds with the English word "begot you" in Jewish Tanakh quoted above. Then Gramcord referenced Brown, Driver, and Briggs, who identify מְחֹלְלֶךָ as "in pain as childbirth" which is a feminine characteristic.[152] Kohlenberger translates the phrase as "one bearing you," or as in the King James, the one that "formed thee." Moses, in speaking of God, uses feminine characteristics to illustrate His relationship with Israel. Moses is speaking to God about the burden of Israel that he (Moses) is carrying:

> Did I conceive all this people, did I bear them, that You should say to me, Carry them in your bosom as a nurse carries an infant (Numbers 11:12).

Does Moses' use of feminine language to describe his relationship to Israel mean that Moses was feminine? Hardly. The following author expresses this issue well:

> In this image, God plays both male and female roles in Israel's origin. In Numbers 11:12, Moses, frustrated by the grumbling of the Israelites, denies before God that he (Moses) conceived these people and brought them forth. So he asks, 'Why do you tell me to carry them in my arms, as a nurse carries an infant?'[153]

---

[151] John Kohlenberger, *The Interlinear NIV Hebrew-English Old Testament* (Grand Rapids: Zondervan, 1987), 579.

[152] Paul A. Miller, The Gramcord Institute, (Vancouver, WA: Gramcord, n.d.), *www.Gramcord.org.*

[153] Frame, *The Doctrine of God,* 380.

Moses, as he speaks to God, says in paraphrase: "Did I conceive or become pregnant? Did I give birth? Am I to carry them as a nurse carries an infant?" Jewish translators clearly saw and translated the female references that Moses was comparing to God in relation to the people. Another reference of God given by Isaiah where *Yahweh* uses feminine characteristics of childbirth in connection to Himself in Isaiah 42:14:

> I have kept silent for too long, kept still and restrained Myself; Now I will scream like a woman in labor, I will pant and I will gasp.

The King James Version states, "*now will I cry like a travailing woman.*" They both say the same thing using different words. The travailing woman or the woman in labor is in the feminine as *Yahweh* refers to Himself in relation to Israel. As Frame states:

> But "now, like a woman in childbirth, I cry out, I gasp and pant." Feminine nouns do not necessarily denote female persons.[154]

Frame is absolutely correct. The usage of feminine characteristics does not necessarily denote female persons. God used the expression to illustrate to Israel the agony and pain that He experienced as Israel served and worshipped other gods.

In these three examples, the Scriptures refer to God in the feminine. The purpose of recording all this is to get a better understanding of God's attitude toward woman. God created woman as co-equal with man, each having their individual responsibilities, with *Elohim* giving the headship to man. All of these feminine and masculine anthropomorphisms were to be an earthly reflection of a heavenly reality. *Elohim*, in His plural unity, chose to reflect this aspect of His image to mankind in the creation of mankind, male and female.

Elohim further expresses His plural unity in making mankind a tri-unity, having a body, soul, and spirit. Mankind, being of a triune nature, reflects *Elohim*, even as each member of the tri-unity of *Elohim* is co-equal yet voluntarily submitted to one member in the plural unity of *Elohim* for the purpose of ministering to mankind. God created mankind in His "image" and "likeness." But that does not make mankind divine nor does it give him a "spark of divinity:"

> While both "image" and "likeness" express correspondence to God, "likeness" indicates that this correspondence is one of similarity, not identicalness. That the image of God in humans is not one of identical correspondence is supported by the fact that this image was created while God Himself is uncreated. Also, it is very likely that God's image has unrevealed features that the divine image in people does not have. Keep in mind that this divine image in humans is not essentially their having God's divine nature. This would make them to be God. To my mind, it means that humans have a created feature, apart from their propagated human nature, that is like something that belongs to God's makeup

---

[154] Frame, *The Doctrine of God*, 380-382.

and distinguishes them from lower creatures. This correspondence gives humans a sacredness, dignity, and value that animals do not have (Gen 9:6; James 3:9; cp 2 Pet 2:12).[155]

Man was created in the "image" and "likeness" of God. The writers of Scripture as well as God Himself used anthropomorphisms to help humanity understand His person, nature, character, and essence. However, in the use of these anthropomorphisms, let it be understood that God DOES NOT have a wife and God is NOT feminine! Nothing in Scripture supports that conclusion. But God created the sexes so men and women could share companionship and propagate the earth. In other words, God is not anti-woman; He created her as co-equal with man but with different responsibilities and functions than He gave to man. In this 21st-century liberal Jewish and Christian scholars attempt to feminize God or to make Him gender neutral. This is absolutely ludicrous and shows the complete depravity of mankind in trying to bring God down to their level, as in Mormon theology. That concept of God cannot, in any way, be supported by the Scriptures. God was not made in man's image and likeness, for then God would not be God at all. It is sin in the world that obscures the "image" and "likeness" that mankind is made in, and it is sin that has given birth to the suppression of woman by the physically stronger male. Man, in his sin, has distorted the "image" and "likeness" of *Elohim* that male and female are to model.

It is a common teaching among rabbis that Christianity took on the teachings of the Trinity, which was accepted officially at the Council of Nicea in 325 CE. But they add that it was to accommodate the pagans who had been worshipping Greek and Roman gods, as the following states:

> If belief in the Trinity is idolatry, then from the Jewish point of view, this concept is perhaps even more objectionable. The pagan gods came down in human form, copulated with mortals, and bore human children. Many Christian historians attribute it to the early Christians who were attempting to win over pagans to their new religion, and therefore adopted this pagan concept.[156]

> Jews could make a counter-charge that the Christian Scripture, with their pagan doctrines of Incarnation and a god co-habiting with a human, are an unwarranted addition to Scripture.[157]

Rabbinic Judaism wants to charge biblical faith with incorporating the pagan Greek and Roman world where the gods co-habited with woman and had offspring. They attempt to place the incarnation in this category. One thing even biblical believers will agree with Judaism on is that Christianity after Constantine, which later became the Roman

---

[155] Barackman, *Practical Christian Theology: Examining the Great Doctrines of the Faith,* 256.

[156] Kaplan, *The Real Messiah? A Jewish Response to Missionaries,* 17.

[157] Chaim Picker, "Make Us A God!" *A Jewish Response to Hebrew Christianity; A Survival Manual for Jews* (New York: iUniverse Press, 2005), 12.

Catholic Church, did compromise their faith to entice pagans to Christianity. However, one very big point is purposely overlooked by Rabbinic Judaism. The doctrine of the incarnation was well established in the Jerusalem Church long before the pagans were even evangelized. Remember that all the books of the New Testament were written before the fall of Jerusalem in 70 CE, except the writings of the Apostle John.

In summary, the purpose of this section was not to try to explain every facet of how mankind was created in the "image" and "likeness" of *Elohim*. The purpose was to get a better understanding of the triune nature of *Elohim* and to realize that He created mankind to reflect Himself. God created mankind as male and female with the intent to lessen the natural doubt that *Elohim* Himself is a plural unity. He created mankind with a body which is visible, and a soul and spirit which are invisible. Because mankind reflects His "image" and "likeness," it is not so hard to believe that He Himself chose to have one person of His plural unity reveal Himself visibly, while the other two persons remain invisible. *Elohim* gave to male and female total equality but with different functions and responsibilities with man given headship. Because of the way He created man and woman, it is not hard to believe that the persons of the triune *Elohim*, being completely equal, chose within Themselves to voluntarily submit Themselves to the First Person of the plural unity as the head. As the following chapters in this book unfold, the plurality and tri-unity of God will be clearly seen and understood. Throughout the *Tanakh* God did present Himself as a plural unity of one (*echad*). When the Messiah came as the visible person of the invisible plural unity of *Elohim*, He came as Moses and the Prophets said He would: He was and is God, indivisible in the fullest sense of the word.

In reading through this book, keep this discussion on the "image" and "likeness" of God at the center of your thinking. In Genesis 1:26 with *Elohim* making man and woman in His image, as a reflection of His plurality, He has chosen to make Himself, the invisible indivisible God, visible in revealing His person, essence and attributes through the revelation of Himself through His written Word to mankind.

Chapter 3
Names for God

The nature and essence of God, as they relate to the revelation of the plural unity of God in the Hebrew Scriptures, is an area of controversy between liberal theologians and Jewish rabbis[158] on one side and fundamental and conservative evangelical theologians on the other. Even among conservative theologians there seems to be a tendency not to follow through on their beliefs from the New Covenant to the Hebrew Scriptures. The primary, authoritative source material that the New Covenant writers used was the Hebrew Scriptures. God did not just reveal Himself out of a vacuum as the triune God in the New Covenant. Nor did the church fathers invent the tri-unity of God in the Nicene Council as others proclaim. Rather, God started in Genesis 1 using clear statements of Himself in such terms as *Elohim* and "us." Geisler makes the following statements on these two terms:

It is true that the very word for God in the Old Testament (*Elohim*) is plural in form; indeed, it can be translated "gods" (Ps 82:6). However, when used of God, it is plural grammatically, not ontologically. It is plural in literary form, but not in actual reality.

The use of "we" or "us" of God is another literary form known as a royal or regal plural. It is used of royalty and of God in Semitic cultures.[159]

Geisler is a much respected apologetic writer and former President of Southern Evangelical Seminary in Charlotte, NC. But this author, with great respect, could not disagree with him more on his characterization of *Elohim* and plural pronouns. Geisler, though not seeing the plurality of God in the term *Elohim*, does see the tri-unity of God throughout the *Tanakh*. However, many of his references look back from the New Covenant to the *Tanakh*.[160] That is a questionable practice and yet an easy thing to do. Scholars must not read New Covenant truth back into the Hebrew Scriptures. The Scriptures are inspired by God; every word, in every part of Scripture, is equally inspired. Man's logic and wisdom cannot reinterpret what God Himself said. The New Covenant was not written in a vacuum. The theological foundations and principles of all church doctrines are rooted and anchored in the Hebrew Scriptures. The difficulty in dealing with the plurality or tri-unity of God in the Hebrew Scriptures is determining

---

[158] *Jewish rabbis:* By placing rabbis together with liberals, this does not mean to imply that rabbis are liberal. Liberals and rabbis may have the same conclusions, but they arrive at them from totally different perspectives.

[159] Norman Geisler, *Systematic Theology* (Minneapolis: Bethany House, 2003), 2:277.

[160] Geisler, *Systematic Theology*, 278-290.

how much, or if there is anything found in the *Tanakh*. There is seemingly endless insistence by Jewish rabbis that the plurality of God in the *Tanakh* does not exist, as expressed below:

> The doctrine of God's having three identities appears incomprehensible: the Jewish biblical record does not speak of God in a way that allows us to characterize His nature as a relation among Father, Son, and Holy Spirit.... we must, instead find a way to reason Jewishly about them.[161]

Rabbis must insist that the plurality of God is non-existent or Rabbinic Judaism will collapse around them. The difficulty lies with Christian scholars who appear to follow their lead. Their logic demonstrates the same basic argument as the rabbis' which minimizes the impact that the doctrine of the plurality or tri-unity of God could have in the *Tanakh*. The Hebrew Scriptures are more than just the foundation of Judaism. They are also the foundation for all doctrines that the Apostles taught in the New Covenant. Corroboration of this lies in the statements made by the Apostles Paul and Peter in 2 Timothy 3:16 and 2 Peter 1:20-21 respectively:

> All scripture is given by inspiration of God, and is profitable for doctrine, for reproof, for correction, for instruction in righteousness.

> Knowing this first, that no prophecy of the scripture is of any private interpretation. For the prophecy came not in old time by the will of man: but holy men of God spake as they were moved by the Holy Ghost [Spirit].

These verses are directly referencing the Hebrew Scriptures. Paul and Peter, under the guidance and inspiration of the Holy Spirit (*Ruach haKodesh*), penned these words (2 Timothy 3:16; 2 Peter 1:21) to express the fact that the Hebrew Scriptures were the foundational documents for themselves, as well as for Luke, John, Paul and the other authors of the New Covenant.

This argument being expressed now is based on the New Covenant and not strictly the *Tanakh*. This is for the true biblical student and scholar. If the plurality and tri-unity of God was not presented in the *Tanakh*, then God is unjust and cannot hold the Jewish people and leadership in *Yeshua*'s day responsible for rejecting Jesus as the Messiah and the God/man. If God did not reveal Himself in the Hebrew Scriptures as a plurality, there is no way that the Jewish people and leadership of the first century could have interpreted the words of *Yeshua* recorded in John 10:30, "*I and my father are one*" as anything other than blasphemy. If God did not present His plurality in the *Tanakh*, then the Jewish leadership was absolutely correct in rejecting *Yeshua* as the Messiah and they should be praised and exonerated by the church for being faithful to the Word of *HaShem*. God would have hit the Jewish people broadside, without warning, and the Jewish people would be a victim of a teaching that they could not have possibly known.

---

[161] Tikva Frymer-Kensky, David Novak, Peter Ochs, David Fox Sandmel and Michael A. Signer, *Christianity in Jewish Terms* (Boulder, CO: Westview Press, 2000), 59.

However, the reality of this doctrine is that God did reveal Himself as a plurality throughout the *Tanakh*, so they are responsible for rejecting Him and they are, at this present time, in the state of unbelief in their own Scriptures. Look at the plural and singular words for God, Lord and LORD as related in the Hebrew text of Scripture.

אֵל *EL*

El is used in the Hebrew Scriptures as a singular form for God about 238 times and is a very ancient Semitic term that was widely used.[162] In fact, it is said by Friedrich Oehler to be the oldest Semitic name for God.[163] In the Ugaritic Canaanite culture[164] "*El*, the pagan god, was the proper name of the titulary head of the hierarchy of deities."[165] Preuss explains that *El* was "connected with the conception of a heavenly council. His titles include bull, ancient one, hero, king, and creator."[166] Although a particular definition of *El* may not be derived from Hebrew Scriptures, they contain material aids in understanding and have a direct relationship to Israel:

> *El* was considered the chief among the Canaanitic deities. Likened to a bull in a herd of cows, the people referred to him as "father bull" and regarded him as creator. *Asherah* was the wife of *El*.

> Chief among the seventy gods and goddesses that were considered offspring of *El* and *Asherah* was *Hadad*, more commonly known as *Baal*, meaning Lord.[167]

The etymology of *El*, when tracing all known historical information, makes it very difficult to come up with an original meaning. David Baker gives the following: (1) "The derivation or etymology of *El* and its related forms is unclear." He further adds that the term has to do with power.[168] James Smith also concurs with Baker in saying that (2) "Most frequently mentioned suggestions for the original meaning are 'power' or 'fear,' but these are widely challenged and much disputed."[169]

---

[162] Harris, Archer, and Waltke, *Theological Wordbook of the Old Testament*, 1:42.

[163] Gustave Friedrich Oehler, *Theology of the Old Testament*, (Grand Rapids: Zondervan, 1883), 87.

[164] The name "Ugaritic" is taken from the name of a Canaanite city state located on the Mediterranean Coast of present day Lebanon called Ugarit from around the 14th and 13th century BCE. As an archaeological site it became very important because it has survived as the principle source for direct knowledge of Canaanite religion at the time when the Children of Israel entered the land of Canaan. Geoffrey W. Bromiley, *The International Standard Bible Encyclopedia* (Grand Rapids: Eerdmans, 1988), 4:937-941.

[165] Alexander and Baker, *Dictionary of the Old Testament Pentateuch,* 360.

[166] Horst Dietrich Preuss, *Old Testament Theology* (Trans. Leo G. Perdue: 2 vols.; Louisville: Westminster John Knox, 1996), 1:149.

[167] Samuel J. Schultz, *The Old Testament Speaks* (New York: Harper & Row, 1970), 92.

[168] Alexander and Baker, *Dictionary of the Old Testament Pentateuch*, 360.

[169] Harris, Archer, and Waltke, *Theological Wordbook of the Old Testament*, 1:42.

The Hebrew Scriptures predominantly use *El* as a generic term for God.[170] *El* is rarely used by itself but it can be used by itself. More often, it is used in combination with other words that further describe Him. An example would be Genesis 16:13 where Hagar spoke of God as "*El* who sees."[171] Throughout the Torah (Law), Prophets and Writings of the Hebrew Scriptures, in prose and poetry,[172] writers used *El* in at least three different ways. The following are some samples of how the authors of Scripture used this term.

El is used as a designation for *Elohim*. *El* is personal, showing His character of holiness, justice, might and that He is to be feared. The term *El* can be used by itself, without being combined with other terms, as is illustrated in the following examples. First, *El* is not a man (Numbers 23:19). Secondly, *El* brought Israel out of Egypt (Numbers 23:22). Thirdly, *El* made covenant promises to Abraham (Genesis 17:1) and to Jacob (Genesis 35:11). Fourthly, Moses pleads with *El,* who is also identified as *Yahweh,* for Miriam's healing from leprosy (Numbers 12:13). Fifthly, according to Deuteronomy 32:18, *El* is the one who birthed Israel. Lastly, when Jesus cried out to the Father on the cross, "*My El, my El, why hast Thou forsaken me?*" He was quoting from Psalm 22:1.

The following combination of names shows *El* to be the same God as *Elohim* or *Yahweh*. *El* is combined with other terms to represent God in His various attributes such as *El Elyon*, the Highest God that Melchizedek refers to in Genesis 14:18. *El Gibbor* or "Mighty God" is used as one of the names of the Messiah in Isaiah 9:6-7. *El Roe* means "the Lord that sees" in Genesis 16:13-14. Moses refers to *El Olam* in Psalm 90:2 meaning "God of Eternity." When speaking to Abraham, God refers to Himself as *El Shaddai* or "God Almighty," the All Sufficient God, as in Genesis 17:1.

The Hebrew Scriptures use numerous adjectives with *El*, showing the personal character of God, such as *El* of heaven (Psalm 136:26) and the Most High *El* used by both Abraham and Melchizedek in Genesis 14:18-20, 22. *El* is faithful in all that He says (Deuteronomy 7:9) and He also hides Himself (Isaiah 45:15). Jonah refers to God as a gracious *El* (Jonah 4:2) who can also be a great and dreadful *El* as is referenced in Daniel 11:36. *El* is the God of Jacob (Psalm 146:5) and the *El* of Israel (Psalm 68:35). *El*, which is used with LORD (*Yahweh*) and God (*Elohim*), shows that *El* in the Scriptures is the God of Israel and the God of the Bible (Deuteronomy 4:31; Joshua 22:22).

This word for God (*El*) is always used in the singular form. Most often it is used of the true God of Israel and is used of God by itself and with other descriptive words. The different words for God relate to each other. This word for God reveals a personal God,

---

[170] Harris, Archer, and Waltke, *Theological Wordbook of the Old Testament*, 1:41.

[171] Payne, *The Theology of the Older Testament,* 145.

[172] John R. Kohlenberger III and James A Swanson, *The Hebrew English Concordance to the Old Testament* (Grand Rapids: Zondervan, 1998), 95-96.

a mighty God, a God to be feared, and a covenant making God.[173] Liddon observes that God used the words for Himself, with the singular verbs and plural nouns and pronouns. He says the following:

> When Moses is describing the primal creative act of God, he joins a singular verb to a plural noun. Language, it would seem, thus submits to a violent anomaly, that she may the better hint at the mystery of several Powers or Persons who not merely act together but who constitute a single Agent. The Hebrew language could have described God by singular forms, such as *El*, *Eloah*, and no question would have been raised as to the strictly Monotheistic force of those words. The Hebrew language might have amplified the idea of God thus conveyed by less dangerous processes than the employment of a plural form. Would it not have done so unless the plural form had been really necessary, in order to hint at the complex mystery of God's inner life, until that mystery should be more clearly unveiled by the explicit Revelations of a later day?[174]

This statement could be repeated under the sections on *Eloah* and *Elohim* a little later in this chapter. God, through the pen of Moses, wanted to teach monotheism to Israel as an absolute truth, but He also wanted to give reference to His plurality. Moses had the words for God available to express the oneness of God only, but he did not choose to use them often. This can be seen with two examples in the Torah as God carefully reveals His unity of one, monotheism, as well as His plurality:

> He [Jacob] set up an altar there, and called it *El-elohe-yisrael* (Gen 33:20). You shall not bow down to them or serve them. For I the LORD [Yahweh] your God [Elohim] am an impassioned God [El], visiting the guilt of the parents upon the children, upon the third and upon the fourth generations of those who reject Me (Exod 20:5).

In these two passages God carefully reveals His monotheism as well as the fact that in His oneness, there is a plurality. In Genesis 33:20 the word אֵל (*El*) is in the singular number and means God; whereas, the word אֱלֹהֵי (*elohim*) is in the plural number. Thus it affirms the plural unity of God at the same time. In Exodus 20:5 in the English text, God is used twice, but they are two different words. In the phrase "*the LORD your God*," God is used as a plural, meaning Gods. Whereas, the second word in Exodus 20:5 for God, אֵל קַנָּא, means a jealous or impassioned God, which is in the singular rather than plural. If this is the inspired Word of God and He has revealed Himself to man, then what Moses wrote down was the presenting of the plural unity of God, which

---

[173] Harris, Archer and Waltke, *Theological Wordbook of the Old Testament*, 1:42-43.

[174] J. Glentworth Butler, *Butler's Bible Work* (6 vols. New York: Funk & Wagnalls, 1889), 1:92.

can be seen even in the Second Commandment. [175] Cooper, as he adds to his presentation, illustrates by using Joshua 22:22 and states the following:

> In one word אֱלֹהֶיךָ, thy Gods, the Lord speaks of His plurality and at the same time of His unity in His use of the word אֵל. The plurality and the unity of God's nature is seen in a wonderful statement made by the Israelites who settled on the East side of the Jordan and who were upbraided by their kinsmen on the West side for having set up a memorial altar, in the following quotation (Josh 22:22): וְאִם־בְּמַעַל בַּיהוָה אֵל אֱלֹהִים יְהוָה אֵל אֱלֹהִים יְהוָה הוּא יֹדֵעַ וְיִשְׂרָאֵל הוּא יֵדָע אִם־בְּמֶרֶד "God, Gods, the Lord, God, Gods, the Lord, He knoweth, and Israel he shall know; if it be in rebellion, or in treachery against the LORD." The word אֵל declares God's unity, but אֱלֹהִים, which is in the apposition with it affirms the plurality of the Divine Being, while יְהוָה identifies this unity of Divine Personalities as the Covenant God of Israel (Exod 6:2-3).[176]

What becomes clear as the words for God are studied is that these singular and plural words are used by God to show that *El* as a singular and *Elohim* as a plural are used interchangeably by the great law-giver, Moses.

אֵלִים *ELIM*

Elim is the plural form of *El* but is used only four times in the Hebrew Scriptures (Exodus 15:11; Psalm 29:1; 89:6[7];[177] Daniel 11:36).[178] This word seems to bear no special significance. In fact, most books referred to do not even acknowledge the word. One text refers to the Exodus 15:11 passage as it relates to pagan gods.[179] *Elim* is called, along with *Elohim*, a plural form of *El*.[180] However, others have taken the Psalm references of *Elim* and applied them to angels and sons of God or to heavenly beings.[181] Keil and Delitzsch also use the Psalm references and render them as sons of God or angelic beings.[182]

Elim seems to have no bearing on the subject of this study. Even though *Elim* is the plural of *El*, it is never used of the true God, thus making it a mute issue for the subject.

---

[175] David L. Cooper, *The Shepherd of Israel Seeking His Own* (Los Angeles: Biblical Research Society, 1962), 38.

[176] Cooper, *The Shepherd of Israel Seeking His Own,* 38-39.

[177] When a Scripture reference appears as in Psalm 89:6[7], putting verse 7 in parentheses means that in English translations it is found in v. 6 but in Hebrew Scriptures it would be found in verse 7.

[178] Botterweck, Ringgren and Fabry, *Theological Dictionary of the Old Testament*, 1:254.

[179] Alexander and Baker, *Dictionary of the Old Testament Pentateuch*, 361.

[180] Jenni and Westermann, *Theological Lexicon of the Old Testament,* 1:115.

[181] H. C. Leupold, *Exposition of Psalms* (Grand Rapids: Baker, 1959), 250.

[182] C. F. Keil and F. Delitzsch, *Commentary on the Old Testament* (trans. James Martin; 10 vols.; Grand Rapids: Eerdmans, 1973). 5:368.

אֱלָהּ *ELAH*

Elah is used 89 times in the Hebrew Scriptures. All but one of them (Jeremiah) are used during the time of the exile (Daniel) or post-exilic period (Ezra). Of those 89 references, at least 15 of them refer to false gods.[183] *Elah* is the Aramaic form of *Eloah*, which is known as a verbal noun, "and is associated with the Hebrew verb *alah*, meaning to fear, to worship, to adore."[184] *Elah* indicates that the living and true God is identified with His people in captivity. It also carries a meaning of an oak, a tree symbolizing durability, a virtue characteristic of Him as being the Everlasting God.[185] It is also a singular word for God, and it is used in the same context as *Yahweh* (Ezra 6:18, 21-22).[186]

Elah is the same God as *El, Eloah, Elohim* and *Yahweh*. This word was used exclusively during the exile and post-exilic periods, when the oneness of God needed to be taught and reaffirmed to Israel, after their displacement from the land by God for worshipping other gods. As Israel was once again being instructed under the leadership of Ezra and then Nehemiah, the concept of monotheism was of utmost importance. The following questions must be asked even though the answers cannot be known this side of human life. The observations and questions remain, and draw the student of the Scriptures to these unanswerable questions.

1. First the rabbis say, God is one alone with no plurality. How is it that an all-knowing God could not see down through the corridor of time and prevent this problem in the beginning?

2. Second, why isn't the singular form of God, *Elah*, used exclusively by Haggai, Malachi, Zephaniah, Zechariah or Ezekiel, exile or post-exilic writers, and not just in Ezra and Daniel? What should be noted is that the Jewish people of this era had largely lost their Hebrew language (Nehemiah 8:8) and were speaking in Aramaic. So it would have been very easy in retraining the Jewish people in monotheism to have only used *Elah*. But those prophets did not go in that direction. Israel's worship of other gods was one of the major reasons for their displacement. If the urgency of teaching monotheism was so important, the observation once again is present.

3. Third, since *Elah* is used to affirm monotheism to exiled and post-exilic Israel, why did Daniel and Ezra also use *Elohim*?

---

[183] George V. Wigram, *The Englishman's Hebrew Concordance of the Old Testament* (Peabody, Mass: Hendrickson, 1996), 78-79.

[184] Lockyer, *All the Divine Names and Titles in the Bible,* 8.

[185] Lockyer, *All the Divine Names and Titles in the Bible,* 8-9.

[186] Samuel Prideaux Tregelles, *Gesenius' Hebrew and Chaldee Lexicon to the Old Testament Scriptures* (Grand Rapids: Eerdmans, 1957), 48.

61

4. The fourth question is, if God is one alone, a unity, why didn't the writers of Scripture, during that era, only use singular terms to remove all doubt and prevent future controversy?

These questions are an argument from silence, to be sure, yet why the Hebrews used these words still remains a haunting question.

אֱלוֹהַ ELOAH

Eloah occurs 57 times in the Hebrew Scriptures and may be the singular form of plural *Elohim*. Most of those references (41) occur in the book of Job.[187] The others are scattered mostly in the other poetic portions of the Scriptures as well as in a few other books. *Eloah* first appears in Deuteronomy 32:15-17, then 2 Kings, 2 Chronicles, Nehemiah, Psalms, Proverbs, Isaiah, Daniel, and Habakkuk. Its use stretches from Job, believed by some to be the oldest book in the Hebrew Scriptures, to the post-exilic time of Nehemiah. In Job there are two references where God uses the term *Eloah* of Himself: in 39:17 He relates to His providence and in 40:2 as the Almighty.[188] *Eloah* is unique in that it does not occur in combination with other divine names. *Eloah* is reaffirmed as God, in the singular, by this following observation:

> This term for God was usually clearly used for Israel's God, the true God. This is evident from the fact that the Levites in the post-exilic period used the term in quoting the descriptive revelation of God given in Exodus 34:6-7, where the original revelation to Moses had used *El* and *Yahweh* (Neh 9:17).[189]

VanGemeren says that the terms *Eloah, El* and *Yahweh* are all singular and interchangeable names of God.[190]

Eloah is used throughout the time period of the Hebrew Scriptures, along with *El*, as being singular for the name of God. But the writers of the Scriptures chose to use *El* and *Eloah* sparingly in relation to the term *Elohim*. Noam Hendren speaks to the point when he says:

> The first hints of plurality are found in the terms used to designate God – "*Elohim*" and "*Adonai*" – both of which are plural forms of existing singular nouns. Had the biblical authors intended to assert the absolute (rather than compound) unity of the Godhead, they had readily available singular terms (*Eloah, Adoni,* as well as *El*) which would have avoided any confusion on this crucial point.[191]

---

[187] VanGemeren, *Dictionary of Old Testament Theology & Exegesis,* 1:405.

[188] Harris, Archer, and Waltke, *Theological Wordbook of the Old Testament,* 1:43.

[189] Harris, Archer, and Waltke, *Theological Wordbook of the Old Testament,* 1:43.

[190] VanGemeren, *Dictionary of Old Testament Theology and Exegesis,* 1:405.

[191] Noam Hendren, "The Divine Unity and the Deity of Messiah," *Mishkan* (issue 39, 2003), 38.

62

Hendren points out that if the Hebrew writers had wanted to show monotheism throughout the Scriptures, thus leaving no doors open for a plurality of God, they could have used *El, Elah* or *Eloah* in the place of *Elohim*, but they chose not to do that. Instead they chose to use a plural word for God the vast majority of the time rather than the singular form of God (*El, Elah, Eloah*), thereby showing the plural nature of God. This reality is brought out by Barackman when he specifically says that "*Elohim*, the plural form indicates the plurality of Persons within the divine Trinity."[192] The authors of Hebrew Scripture left the door wide open for the New Covenant's teaching of the tri-unity.

אֱלֹהִים *ELOHIM*

What is true of singular words for God (*El, Elah, Eloah*) is also true of the plural word *Elohim*. The etymology is, at best, uncertain.[193] Jack Scott presents three possibilities on the root of *Elohim*. First, he takes for granted that *'lh* is the assumed root of *El, Eloah* and *Elohim*, which means "gods" or "God." Next, he says, "The view that the three Hebrew words come from one root is much disputed, and a final verdict is lacking." His third statement is, "More probable is the view that *Elohim* comes from *Eloah* as a unique development of the Hebrew Scriptures."[194] Yet Payne makes further statements:

> *El*, seems to have arisen from the root *ūl,* the probable meaning of which is to be strong (cf. Gen 31:29 "power").[195]

There is just no solid consistent information as to the etymology of *Elohim*. The words being used: "assumed," "much disputed," "lacking," and "probable" indicate that there is nothing much here that is solid. There are words such as *Elohim* that scholars do not have enough information about to draw a strong conclusion. Since there is no consensus on the etymology of *Elohim*, the only alternative to help in understanding *El, Eloah,* and *Elohim* is to see how the Hebrew Scriptures use them and in what context they are used. But that is beyond the scope of this book. What is known and recognized is that *El, Elah, Eloah,* and *Elohim* are all nouns translated as "God." But when *Elohim* is translated as singular in the English text, there ought to be a note stating that *Elohim*, though used as a singular when translated, is in fact a plural noun representing the plurality of *Elohim*.

It is very important to see how *Elohim*, in particular, is used within the Hebrew text in relationship to *El, Eloah, Yahweh* and the Angel of *Yahweh*. First, *Elohim* is used 2600 times and is the second most frequent substantive in the Hebrew Scriptures

---

[192] Barackman. *Practical Christian Theology*, 66.

[193] Alexander and Baker, *Dictionary of the Old Testament Pentateuch*, 360.

[194] Harris, Archer, and Waltke, *Theological Wordbook of the Old Testament*, 1:41.

[195] Payne, *The Theology of the Older Testament*, 145.

following *ben* (son).[196] *Elohim* is introduced exclusively throughout the creation account of Genesis 1:1-2:3 as the God of creation. *Elohim* is not a personal name but the general Hebrew word for deity.[197] Also, *Elohim* is often accompanied with *Yahweh* (יְהֹוָה) as in Genesis 2:4-5; Exodus 34:23; Psalm 68:18 [19].[198] In fact, *Elohim* and *Yahweh* are combined together 930 times throughout the Hebrew Scriptures in one of the following translated forms: "LORD thy God," "LORD God," "LORD our God," "LORD my God," "LORD your God," "LORD their God," "LORD his God."[199] Richard DeHaan in referencing the combination of LORD God in Psalm 88:1 speaks to the issue of these two words reflecting both the plurality and unity of God in this following statement:

> The word "LORD" in this verse is a singular name for God. The word "God" [*Elohim*] in this verse is plural. This in itself strongly suggests the idea of plurality of persons within the unity of the Godhead. The plural name for God suggests the plurality of persons, while the singular verb form and the singular word for God which is often compounded (used side by side) with the plural name, definitely indicates His unity.[200]

God, through the writers of Scripture, chose to combine the plural and singular form of Himself to safeguard and protect His nature, essence and person while at the same time revealing Himself as a plural-singular unity. God chose to combine His name *Yahweh* (LORD) and God (*Elohim*) 930 times instead of using the singular form exclusively. He was teaching that He was a plural unity. However, Rabbinic Judaism wants to substantiate monotheism without plurality by trying to ignore the fact that God chose to use a plural description of Himself for one particular reason: He is a plurality (tri-unity).

God was revealing Himself to Israel by showing His indivisible oneness and at the same time showing His complex unity, being also a plurality. There is a uniqueness with God in Genesis 1:1; rather than showing absolute oneness as Rabbinic Judaism prescribes, God is presenting Himself as a plural-singular unity as the following author expresses:

> … the Scriptures reveal that in that plural-singular unity, interaction takes place between what we often refer to as 'the members of the Godhead.'[201]

Hayford's statement speaks volumes on two accounts: First he states that Genesis 1:1, and 26 with the use of the plural word shows *Elohim* creating in the singular, a plural-

---

[196] Jenni and Westermann, *Theological Lexicon of the Old Testament,* 1:116.

[197] Nahum M Sarna, *The JPS Torah Commentary, Genesis* (Philadelphia: The Jewish Publication Society, 1989), 5.

[198] Harris, Archer, and Waltke, *Theological Wordbook of the Old Testament*, 1:44.

[199] Robert Young, *Analytical Concordance to the Bible* (Grand Rapids: Eerdmans, 1955), 411-418.

[200] Richard W. DeHaan, *The Living God* (Grand Rapids: Zondervan, 1967), 83.

[201] Jack Hayford, *The Trinity* (Grand Rapids: Chosen Books, 2003), 15.

singular unity and not an absolute unity. Secondly, it removes all need for statements such as "plural of majesty" that are commonly used by many scholars.

This is not acceptable to the Jewish mind because it is an antithesis and appears to go against the strict monotheism of Rabbinic Judaism.[202] *Yahweh* is combined with *El*, which is the singular form, only 21 times out of 258.[203] *Elah*, the singular form, is never once used with *Yahweh* out of a possible 95 times.[204] *Eloah* is used only once with *Yahweh* in Psalm 68:31 out of 58 times.[205] All of these combinations are in the singular, which would show absolute monotheism. But the fact that *Elohim* is used in combination with *Yahweh* over 930 times is a significant amount more than the aforementioned group. God is showing to Israel that indeed He is one and that *Elohim* is a plural-singular unity. Also in seeing the plural and singular usages, it should be clearly noted that when God spoke, He only spoke in the first person singular. There are only four exceptions to that rule, which will be seen later in this chapter.

Elohim as a plurality is a person involved in the lives of His created beings. *Elohim* shows His personhood in a plural context. He was not distant, unconcerned or detached from human need. *Elohim* was used of God as the Creator (Genesis 1:1, 27; 2:3-4; 5:1). He interacts with humans (Genesis 18; Deuteronomy 34:10 with Numbers 12:6-8) and walks with man (Genesis 3:8; 5:24). He spoke to them (Genesis 8:15; 9:8, 12, 17; 17:3, 23; 21:2; 35:15; 46:2) and listened to them (Genesis 21:17; 30:17, 22; Exodus 2:24). He provided for them (Genesis 1:29, 2:8-9, 15; 4:25; 9:27; 22:8; 28:4; 30:18, 20) and protected them (Genesis 31:7, 9, 16; 45:5, 7). He also made covenants (Genesis 9:16) and promises with man (Genesis 17:9). *Elohim* was gracious and did good (Genesis 50:20; Exodus 1:20), but at the same time, He obligated man to keep certain responsibilities and commandments (Genesis 2:16; 3:1, 3; 6:22; 7:9, 16; 17:9, 16; 21:4, 12; 31:16, 24; 35:1, 11; Exodus 18:23).[206] According to Scott, titles are attached to the noun *Elohim* that pertain to His work of Creation (Isaiah 45:18) and His sovereignty (Isaiah 54:5), as well as focusing around His majesty or glory. But a far more frequent title is found in those passages that pertain to the Saviour God.[207] In *Elohim*, the plurality of God is expressed in ways which would minimally show the activity of God the Father and God the Son. He is also mighty, terrible and executes judgment as Deuteronomy 10:17-18 speaks of Him:

For the Lord your God is God supreme, and Lord supreme, the great, the mighty, and the awesome God, who shows no favor and takes no bribes, but

---

[202] Schiffman, Return *of the Remnant,* 95.
[203] Young, *Analytical Concordance to the Bible,* 411.
[204] Young, *Analytical Concordance to the Bible,* 411.
[205] Young, *Analytical Concordance to the Bible,* 418.
[206] Alexander and Baker, *Dictionary of the Old Testament Pentateuch,* 362.
[207] Harris, Archer, and Waltke, *Theological Wordbook of the Old Testament,* 1:44.

upholds the cause of the fatherless and the widow, and befriends the stranger, providing him with food and clothing.[208]

Elohim shows Himself in a multitude of ways. Unlike *El, Elah,* or *Eloah, Elohim* always appears in the plural, not in the singular, in the Hebrew Scriptures. This word for God is used predominantly of the true God, and of the false pagan gods of the lands around Israel. Although *Elohim* is a plural noun, associated verbs and descriptive terms are usually in the singular.[209] Since *Elohim* is plural, the term presents a paradox and attracts attention because the monotheistic God of Israel is representing Himself as a plurality. *Elohim* is used in the Hebrew text over 2600 times as a plural (2350 of them are in reference to the God of Israel), which is many more times than the singular usages of *El* (238), *Elah* (89), and *Eloah* (57) combined. *Elohim,* with singular nouns, verbs and descriptive terms, definitely shows monotheism, but it also can argue in favor of plurality, rather than against it.[210]

Arguments Against a Literal Understanding of Elohim

Jewish and/or Christian scholars do not object to the scriptural term *Elohim* that is used for God. The problem lays with how biblical scholars interpret *Elohim* in the context where *Elohim* is used by God Himself or where others refer to Him as God in His revealed Word. There is no conscious effort, on the part of conservative Christian scholars, to undermine a doctrine of Scripture. In respect to Jewish scholars, Paul says in Romans there is a spiritual blindness upon the hearts of Jewish people resulting in not being able to see the plurality of God (Amos 8:11-12). Paul, in Romans 11:10, is very clear as he quotes David in Psalm 69:23: "Let their eyes be darkened, that they may not see, and bend down their back always."

Most of the authors (Jewish and Christian) cited agree that *Elohim* is plural and that it should be looked upon as a "plural of majesty" or an intensified form of the word. They, for the most part, do not think there is enough contextual evidence to warrant *Elohim* as a plural reference to God. However, they say that it is a foundation from which the New Covenant builds its doctrine of the trinity or tri-unity. Mathews states the following:

---

[208] Adele Berlin and Marc Zvi Brettler, *The Jewish Study Bible* (New York: Jewish Publication Society, 2004), 388. (All Old Testament references are cited from this translation unless otherwise noted.) Three other translations are also used but not cited (1) Alexander Harkavy, *The Twenty-Four Books of the Old Testament* (2 vols., New York, N.Y: Hebrew Publishing, 1916), (2) Isaac Leeser, *The Twenty-Four Books of the Holy Bible* (New York: Hebrew Publishing, n.d.), (3) The Holy Bible, *The Orthodox Jewish Bible* (3rd edition, New York: Artists For Israel International, 2002).

[209] Sarna, *The Jewish Publication Society Torah Commentary: Genesis,* 5.

[210] Arnold G. Fruchtenbaum, *Messianic Christology* (Tustin, CA: Ariel Ministries, 1998), 103.

Why the plural was also used of the one God of Israel is uncertain, though most ascribe it to the use of the Hebrew plural that indicates honor or majesty. As a plural it is a literary convention that reflects special reverence.[211]

In my judgment, this statement does not reflect a verbal plenary view of inspiration. Mathews states that its interpretation is uncertain and most scholars ascribe or agree that there is not enough biblical evidence to support plurality. He continues:

Since its plurality does not designate more than one entity, its morphological shape does not necessarily refer to the plurality of the Godhead. It is unreasonable to burden this one word *Elohim* with a developed view of the Christian Trinity. It is fair to say, however, that the creation account (Gen 1:2, 26-27) implies that there is a plurality within God (cf. 3:22; 11:7; 18:1ff.). But it is not until the era of the church that the Trinity is clearly articulated. New Testament tradition ascribes to Christ a role in creation (Jn 1:1-3; Col 1:15-17; Heb 1:2), but it is less clear about the role of the Spirit.[212]

Mathews hedges on the implications of *Elohim*'s plurality and in the process explains away what God was intending readers to understand about Himself in the *Tanakh*. This researcher sees three things: First, the "burden" of a full blown development of the tri-unity is not being laid on one word. However, something is going on throughout the pages of the *Tanakh*. God, by His choice of terms, is saying that He, *Elohim*, is a plurality. Secondly, to say that the New Testament tradition ascribes to Messiah the full role in creation is a totally inadequate and misleading statement. But it will be clearly seen in chapter 14 of this book that Isaiah 48:12-16 and Zechariah 12:1, 10 ascribe creation to Messiah the Second Person of the plural unity of God. Thirdly, this whole argument has given this author a strong impression that Christian theologians have conceded the subject to Rabbinic Judaism.

Statements have been made by various authors on the plural aspect of *Elohim*. Louis Jacobs, a Jewish author, makes an honest statement when he says that the plural form of God has long been a puzzle to the rabbis. They are obliged by Rabbinic Judaism to defend it against "sectarians" (Christians) who say that the plural form is proof of more than one god.[213] Arnold Fruchtenbaum, a Jewish believer in Messiah *Yeshua*, says that the Hebrew grammar requires that when the plural form is used, as is the case with *Elohim*, the verbs are to agree with the associated nouns in both gender and number.[214] *Elohim* is plural and is used of the true God and the false gods, as seen in Exodus 20:2-3. When it is used of false gods, the verbs will also be plural, which is correct Hebrew grammar. When *Elohim* is used of the true God, the verbs, as in Genesis 1:1 (*Elohim* created), are singular, which shows the plural unity and oneness of

[211] Kenneth A. Mathews, *The New American Commentary: Genesis 1-11:26* (vol. 1a. Nashville: Broadman & Holman, 2002), 1a:127.

[212] Mathews, *The New American Commentary,* 1a:127.

[213] Louis Jacobs, *A Jewish Theology*, 138.

[214] Fruchtenbaum, *Messianic Christology,* 103.

God. But that singular construction can also imply that, even though *Elohim* is one, He is also a plurality in that oneness. Youngblood identifies the oneness and plurality of God in Genesis 1.

> The first verse of Genesis itself provides us with a helpful cue. It tells us that "God created" (Gen 1:1). The noun "God" is plural in the Hebrew text, but the verb "created" is singular in the Hebrew text. The Bible clearly teaches that God is one being, a unity (Deut 6:4; 1 Cor 8:4). At the same time, the Bible just as clearly teaches that the one God exists in three persons and is therefore also a trinity.[215]

Youngblood clearly sees and understands that God in His omniscience chose to reveal Himself as one being and yet at the same time a unity of three persons. In reference to the oneness of *Elohim*, Hebrew grammar also demonstrates the plurality of *Elohim* as in Exodus 20:3 and Deuteronomy 13:2. In both cases, when referring to *elohim* as false gods, it is correctly translated as "gods" by both Jewish and Christian scholars.

Plural of Majesty

Because this issue is used so frequently by authors, it needs to be dealt with before proceeding further. "Plural of majesty" needs to be simply defined so that everyone understands the term. This term incorporates all the attributes of God into one statement. A few of His attributes include being the Creator of the universe, an incorporeal spirit being, and indivisible living outside of time and space as man understands it. He is eternal, immutable, omnipresent, omnipotent, and omniscient. Other terms that are more familiar to the reader such as the love, mercy, grace, and longsuffering of God as well as His holiness, righteousness and justice are incorporated within the statement "plural of majesty." The attributes of this majestic being called God are plural. But to say that when God is speaking of Himself or to other individuals such as angels in heaven, He is speaking of His Majesty is abusing the biblical text. God in the Scriptures is revealing Himself to mankind, including all that He is as well as His plural unity. The *Tanakh* insists on a monotheistic God who is a plural unity of persons which historically has been called Trinity, which this book chooses to call the plural unity or tri-unity of God.

All of these attributes are automatically included when He speaks, but He speaks because He is also a plurality of persons in the plural unity of *Elohim*. He speaks in reference to His person and not just to all that is involved in the complex being humans call God. Higher criticism, as well as Rabbinic Judaism, likes to use the term "plural of majesty" as a decoy from the reality that even though God is majestic, incomprehensible to the human mind, He is a plural unity of persons in *Elohim*.

---

[215] Ronald Youngblood, *The Book of Genesis* (2nd ed. Eugene, OR: Wipf and Stock Publishers, 1991), 23.

What does Rabbinic Judaism mean, or what does it intend to picture in the human mind when it uses the term "unity of God?" It is grouping together all the attributes of God in the statement "unity of God." As is shown throughout this book God is a unity, and true biblical faith completely affirms that absolute truth. Judaism reflects all the attributes of God in this term and biblical believers completely affirms that position. But God has also revealed, in abundance, that He is also a plural unity of persons within that unity of *Elohim*. This truth Rabbinic Judaism vigorously rejects with every ounce of strength. To fit God only behind the mask of "plural of majesty" or the Jewish "unity of God" is to divert the plurality of persons within the plural unity of God from man's understanding of *Elohim* as He Himself intended it to be revealed. Understand what authors are implying when they interpret these plural references to God as "plural of majesty."

Numerous authors affirm the view that *Elohim* is to be understood as a "plural of majesty" and not as a reference to the plurality of God:

> The plural ending is usually described as a plural of majesty and not intended as a true plural when used of God. This is seen in the fact that the noun *Elohim* is consistently used with singular verb forms and with adjectives and pronouns in the singular.[216]

> The grammatical form of *Elohim* is that of an abstract plural of greatness or majesty, and not a true numeric plural.[217]

> The divine name, *Elohim* probably describes a plural of intensity or plural of majesty (simply "God" – an abstract plural).[218]

> The plural form may signify majesty or serve to intensify the basic idea. The preference for the use of *Elohim* in this chapter, rather than the sacred divine name *YHVH*, may well be conditioned by theological considerations; the term *Elohim*, connoting universalism and abstraction, is most appropriate for the transcendent God of creation.[219]

> Though morphologically plural, the word is regularly used as a singular when referring to Israel's God. This is shown by the regular use of singular verbs and adjectives in conjunction with the term. The purpose and meaning of the plural form is debated, with some seeing it as a plural of majesty, or royal plural as an intensification or claim to exclusivity, or as an honorific.[220]

> Some scholars have held that the plural represents an intensified form for the supreme God; others believe it describes the supreme God and His heavenly

---

[216] Harris, Archer, and Waltke, *Theological Wordbook of the Old Testament*, 1:44.

[217] Payne, The *Theology of the Older Testament*, 145.

[218] Preuss, *Old Testament Theology*, 1:149.

[219] Sarna, *The Jewish Publication Society Torah Commentary: Genesis*, 5.

[220] Alexander and Baker, *Dictionary of the Old Testament Pentateuch*, 362.

court of created beings. Still others hold that the plural form refers to the triune God of Genesis 1:1-3, who works through Word and Spirit in the creation of the world. In any event, *Elohim* conveys the idea that the one Supreme Being, who is the only true God, is in some sense plural.[221]

Collectively, the consensus of these scholars is that the term *Elohim* is not a true plural, and that it does not represent the plurality of God in the *Tanakh*. Their arguments are centered around these thoughts: *Elohim* is a "plural of Majesty," and secondly, Hebrew grammar of the plural noun is followed by a singular verb when speaking of the true God, showing that God is one alone. They are reaffirming that belief, by the use of Hebrew grammar, that false gods, which always have plural verbs, show only the plural concept of pagan gods such as Baal. This is a Jewish rabbinic argument whose views differ on revelation and inspiration[222] from that which is held by fundamental and evangelical scholars. Also, they generally do not use the literal interpretation of the Scriptures, or as Renald Showers calls it, the historical-grammatical method.[223]

Preview of Revelation and Inspiration Held by Rabbinic Judaism

A short pause on the names of God will be given to help the readers understand how Rabbinic Judaism holds to revelation and inspiration. It is very important in this study to understand the doctrine of revelation and inspiration, and it is imperative for the student of Scripture to understand the Jewish approach to Scripture. Rabbinic Judaism has, as this author refers to them, levels of revelation and inspiration. In the first level, God spoke to Moses *"face to face"* in the Torah (Law), which makes it the most inspired because it was direct revelation communicated personally to Moses. In the second level, God spoke to prophets in visions and dreams, making them less inspired than the Law. The third level contains the Writings which are the least inspired of the Scriptures. This concept is reflected by Stenning in *The Targum of Isaiah* where he states:

> There it is laid down that the reader should first recite a verse from the Law, and be followed by the meturgeman [an individual who translated or interpreted] who translated it into Aramaic. In reading from the Prophets three verses might be read at a time, partly because these readings were considered less sacred than those taken from the Torah.[224]

---

[221] Ronald F. Youngblood, *New Illustrated Bible Dictionary* (Nashville: Thomas Nelson, 1995), 504.

[222] *Jewish Inspiration*: Based on Numbers 12:5-8 you have three tiers of Inspiration. First because God spoke to Moses face to face in the Torah (Law), that is the most inspired. Secondly, God spoke to prophets in visions and dreams, so they are less inspired than the Law. Thirdly, the least inspired are the Writings.

[223] Renald E. Showers, *There Really Is a Difference!* (Bellmawr, NJ: Friends of Israel Gospel Ministry, 1990), 53.

[224] J. F. Stenning, *The Targum of Isaiah* (London: Oxford University Press, 1953), viii.

Stenning did not say that the Prophets and Writings were not sacred, only less sacred or inspired than the Torah. This teaching is based on Jewish interpretation of Numbers 12:5-8 where they see levels of revelation and inspiration. That is not the expression that rabbis would use and it could cause some misunderstanding as to Jewish belief. This is not usually stated directly by rabbis as in the quote above, for they do believe in the revelation and inspiration of all portions of the *Tanakh,* just to greater or lesser degrees.

Arguments for a Literal Understanding of Elohim

In the preceding section, no flexibility was shown toward the proposition that God could be revealing Himself by using the same Hebrew grammar to show exceptions in the language. God was affirming His oneness and plurality while protecting the teaching of the Hebrew Scriptures against polytheism. Israel was surrounded by polytheistic Canaanite nations as well as by the Amorites, Moabites and the Egyptians.

When *Elohim* is modified by a singular word, both Jewish and Christian translators want it to be understood as God, whereas God meant it to be understood as a plural representation of Himself with the singular modifier to show His oneness. Cooper expresses the same thing when he asks:

> Why should the grammar be ignored and the word be translated as if it were a singular noun when it refers to Israel's God, since the facts are that it is a plural noun and means more than one?[225]

According to Hebrew grammar, if *Elohim*, a noun, is plural, it is not grammatically correct for singular verbs to follow. So the Hebrew construction is in conflict with itself according to the pattern of Hebrew grammar. However, there are several instances where plural verbs follow *Elohim*, the true God, which is grammatically correct. Note, for example 2 Samuel 7:23:

> And who is like Your people Israel, a unique nation on earth, whom God went and redeemed as His people, winning renown for Himself.

Literally it says:

> And what one nation on the earth is like Thy people Israel, whom God [*Elohim*] **they** went to redeem for themselves.[226]

Robert Morris, a Jewish believer in *Yeshua*, speaks to the fact that Jews for Judaism[227] teaches that the doctrine of the Trinity is a pagan concept.[228] Yet 2 Samuel 7:23 says that more than one *Elohim* redeemed Israel.

---

[225] Cooper, *The God of Israel*, 24-25.
[226] Fruchtenbaum, *Messianic Christology*, 104.

In dealing with arguments for *Elohim* being a unity, the first concept to consider is a complex unity. God did introduce Himself as a plural unity in the *Tanakh*. An example can be given in Genesis 2:24 of a complex unity when God took two separate identities (man and woman) and put them together as a complex unity of one. This concept is difficult for Jewish people to comprehend in relation to *Elohim*. Stan Rosenthal, a Jewish believer in Messiah *Yeshua*, tells how they view it:

> Jewish people often object to the tri-unity of God because of what they believe is taught in the *Shema*.... The accepted premise among Jewish people views this as saying that God is indivisibly one. Consequently, the objection is raised: I cannot believe in this person, Jesus, whom Christians claim to be God. For them the *Shema* appears to have silenced forever the argument which embraces the historic Christian belief in the deity of Jesus.[229]

Rosenthal is simply saying that the *Shema*, to the Jewish people, teaches that God is indivisible, and because of that, Jesus is another god. Hence, they reject Jesus as God, as well as God's substitutionary sacrifice for sin. The *Shema* has become the watch word in Rabbinic Judaism, and they use it to show that *Elohim* (God) is indivisible, one. In this section, the object is to show that God is indivisible, one, and yet plural. The argument that *Elohim* represents a "plural of majesty" is a foreign concept in the *Tanakh*. The Hebrew kings never spoke of themselves as a "plural of majesty," so there is no background for this concept in the Hebrew Scriptures, which the following statement expresses:

> But that is to read into Hebrew speech a modern mode of address. So far as our biblical records can help us, the kings of Judah and Israel are all addressed in the singular.[230]

So in the Hebrew text the kings of Judah and Israel never used a "plural of majesty" in speaking of themselves. This is echoed by Grudem when he says:

> In Old Testament Hebrew there are no other examples of a monarch using plural verbs or plural pronouns of himself in such a "plural of majesty," so this suggestion has no evidence to support it.[231]

---

[227] *Jews for Judaism*: Jews for Judaism is an anti-missionary organization against Christian missionaries to Jewish people which strongly tries to reconvert new Jewish believers in Messiah back to Rabbinic Judaism.

[228] Robert Morris, *Anti-Missionary Argument: The Trinity* (Irvine, CA: HaDavar Messianic Ministries, n.d.), 1.

[229] Stanley Rosenthal, *One God or Three?* (Bellmawr, NJ: Friends of Israel Gospel Ministry, 1978), 17-18.

[230] George A. F. Knight, A *Christian Theology of the Old Testament* (Carlisle, UK: Paternoster Publishing, 1998), 54.

[231] Wayne Grudem, *Systematic Theology* (Grand Rapids: Zondervan, 1994), 227.

The closest thing to the idea of "plural of majesty" is in Isaiah 7:13-14 when God speaks of the house of David. However, that is a collective statement about the house of David, not a "plural of majesty." Nathan Stone echoes the fact that the term "plural of majesty" is an expression unknown to the kings of Israel:

> They say that the plural is only a plural of majesty such as used by rulers and kings. But such use of the plural was not known then. We find no king of Israel speaking of himself as "we" and "us."[232]

Although the Queen of England uses the "plural of majesty," England is a western Gentile nation, whereas Israel was a Middle Eastern Semitic nation, then 20 centuries removed from modern England. This has been observed and answered by Stuart Briscoe:

> Some commentators suggest that the plural words are used to give a sense of intensity and majesty to God (in much the same way that the Queen in her official pronouncements uses the "royal we"). But a clear statement about the Trinity becomes apparent when the "Us" and "Our" and the plural *Elohim* are considered alongside the statement about the "Spirit of God" being active in creation.[233]

Another author adds his voice to the chorus of others mentioned, affirming that "plural of majesty" was not the style of writing in the Hebrew Scriptures:

> … the style of royalty was adopted, which is refuted by two considerations that almighty God in other instances speaks in the singular and not in the plural number; and that this was not the style of the sovereigns of the earth when Moses or any of the sacred penmen composed their writings; no instance of it being found in any of the inspired books.[234]

Henry Smith says that the "plural of majesty" cannot be accepted today because "such plurals of majesty are without parallel in Hebrew."[235] Then he draws an inaccurate conclusion by saying that the only plausible view is that the word originally was narrowed down to apply to One and that vestiges of a belief in a group of divine beings have survived even in our present Bible. He then cites Genesis 1:26: *"Let us make man in our image"* and 3:22 where God takes counsel with His associates, or as in 6:2 with the *"sons of God."* Smith uses human logic instead of letting Scripture interpret Scripture. It appears that since he does not accept a high view of Scripture, he attempts to find some natural human answer rather than accepting the plurality of God. Towner

---

[232] Stone, *Names of God*, 16.

[233] Stuart Briscoe, *The Communicator's Commentary: Genesis* (vol. 1. Waco, Tex: Word, 1987), 34.

[234] Richard Watson, Theological Institutes: Or, a View of the Evidences, Doctrines, Morals, and Institutions of Christianity (New York: Phillips & Hunt, 1850), 1:468-469.

[235] Henry Preserved Smith, *The Religion of Israel* (New York: Charles Scribner's Sons, 1914), 14.

uses similar logic by stating that "plural of majesty" is not likely, but then goes on to state that because the plural personal pronoun is used rarely by God, it must be a heavenly council:

> Is God using the "plural of majesty," and speaking in the manner of the queen of England or the pope? Not likely! If anyone has the right to make self-references in the plural (especially considering that God is, at least from a Christian point of view, a Holy Trinity), it would surely be God. However, this plural usage happens again only very rarely (Gen 3:22; 11:7; Isa 6:8). Surely, if God were thinking majestically, the plural would be used more consistently than that. We are left, then, with the heavenly council as the only likely way of explaining this use of the plural in verse 1:26.[236]

The fact is that God did use first person plural pronouns only in four passages. But to conclude that it must be a heavenly council merely on that basis ignores the abundance of other plural references that not only show Him to be a plurality but a tri-unity. In a sense there was a heavenly council that was not made up by the angelic hosts but by the third members of the plural unity of *Elohim* as They conferred among Themselves.

Interpreting Scripture must always be done within its immediate and distant context, whether in the *Tanakh* or the New Covenant. If the Hebrew Scriptures do not use a "plural of majesty," why do scholars force that reading into the text? The Scriptures, as a whole, are the writings of God Himself to reveal Himself to mankind. The only viable way to develop that concept, when studying the Scriptures, is to let God reveal Himself rather than reading into the text what God never intended. God is intending man to understand from Genesis 1 that He is a plural compound of one. This concept of a complex unity is not "plural of majesty" or intensity but a complex plural unity of the tri-unity of God. Complex unity is expressed well by Robert Morris, a Jewish believer in Messiah *Yeshua*:

> Philosophically, the idea of a complex, indivisible unity is not foreign to the Bible. The nation of Israel is a complex indivisible unity (one nation made up of 12 tribes), the Law of Moses is a complex, indivisible unity (one law made up of 613 commandments), and marriage is a complex, indivisible unity (a one flesh relationship consisting of man and woman). Is it inconsistent if the God of the Universe is a complex, indivisible unity as well?[237]

Is God a complex unity? Yes. Can He reveal Himself in a tri-unity? Yes. To force the fully developed doctrine of the tri-unity from the New Covenant into Genesis 1 or the word *Elohim* is exegetically improper. What can be seen is that God is a plurality, not a "plural of majesty," which is a foreign term to the *Tanakh*. It can also be seen that God

---

[236] W. Sibley Towner, *Westminster Bible Companion: Genesis* (Louisville, KY: Westminster John Knox Press, 2001), 24-25.

[237] Morris, *Anti-Missionary Arguments – The Trinity*, 3.

is a complex compound unity. It is the strong opinion of this author that God has given ample evidences of His unity, as well as His plurality.

It is not that Israelite people did not know how to use the word "we," they did use it. But kings did not use it when they were functioning as kings. There is only one consistent use of the "we" that so many scholars want to see as "plural of majesty." But it is just not present in the Hebrew text in relation to the kings of Judah or Israel. Prayers of confession before God were the predominant way that the word "we" was used in the *Tanakh*. Some of the great men of God confessed their sins and the sins of the nation before God using "we." They used the plural "we" but not as a "plural of majesty" as seen in the following references from Isaiah Daniel and Nehemiah:

Isaiah:

53:2   He had no form or beauty that **we** should look at him:

53:3   No charm, that **we** should find him pleasing.

53:4   Yet it was our sickness that he was bearing, Our suffering that he endured. **We** accounted him plagued, smitten and afflicted by God;

53:5   But he was wounded because of our sins, crushed because of our iniquities. He bore the chastisement that made us whole, and by his bruises **we** were healed.

Daniel:

9:5   **We** have sinned; **we** have gone astray; **we** have acted wickedly; **we** have been rebellious and have deviated from Your commandments and Your rules,

9:8   The shame, O LORD, is on us, on our kings, our officers, and our fathers, because **we** have sinned against You.

9:9   To the Lord our God belong mercy and forgiveness, for **we** rebelled against Him,

9:11   All Israel has violated Your teaching and gone astray, disobeying You; so the curse and the oath written in the Teaching of Moses, the servant of God, have been poured down upon us, for **we** have sinned against Him.

9:13   All that calamity, just as is written in the Teaching of Moses, came upon us, yet **we** did not supplicate the LORD our God, did not repent of our iniquity or become wise through Your truth.

9:14   Hence the LORD was intent upon bringing calamity upon us, for the LORD our God is in the right in all that He has done, but **we** have not obeyed Him.

9:15   Now, O Lord our God, You who brought Your people out of the land of Egypt with a mighty hand, winning fame for Yourself to this very day, **we** have sinned, **we** have acted wickedly.

9:18   Not because of any merit of ours do **we** lay our plea before You but because of Your abundant mercies.

Nehemiah:

1:6   Let Your ear be attentive and Your eyes open to receive the prayer of Your servant that I am praying to You now, day and night, on behalf of the Israelites, Your servants, confessing the sins that **we** Israelites have committed against You, sins that I and my father's house have committed.

1:7   **We** have offended You by not keeping the commandments, the laws, and the rules that You gave to Your servant Moses.

"We" is used in the confession of sin but it is never used in the context of a king speaking in reference to himself and his court. Nor do you find the king speaking of himself and the people as "we." When he speaks it is within the context of "I am the king."

Getting back to the plural word *Elohim*, Cooper states that the regular ending for a plural noun in the masculine gender and plural number is ם׳ (*im*) and that with this grammatical structure no one would disagree.

> Since this word has the plural ending and is listed by all lexicographers and grammarians as a noun in the plural number, we must accept this connotation in every instance unless there are facts in the context showing a departure from the ordinary, usual literal meaning.[238]

Previously cited authors say that *Elohim* is not a true plural word. Yet when the plural Hebrew ending is present, it is consistently treated as a plural until God describes Himself. This is an observation anyone can make. Observe in either the *Tanakh* or Hebrew/English interlinear, אֱלֹהִים (*Elohim*) is consistently translated as God in the singular. The plural Hebrew ending is ם׳ ('*im*'), as in *cherubim*, *seraphim* or *shedhim* (demons). Whenever the ending '*im*,' is used, it is translated in the plural, except for *Elohim*.[239] It is the view of this author that many of the previously cited authors want to explain away the plural '*im*' ending rather than accept it for what it is, a plural.

---

[238] Cooper, *The God of Israel*, 34.

[239] There are two other words that have a plural '*im*' ending that are used to show unity without plurality. There are the words "heavens" and "waters." However, only a casual study will show that both of these words are a plurality in unity. Both of these words clearly have a multiplicity about them. Water is made of many units of water making the word "waters" plural. The same is true of the heavens.

The plural personal pronouns of God, which will be covered in more detail in chapter 10, are relevant here. What does God say about Himself? *Elohim* is making a statement early in human history (3 of the 4 times in Genesis) that He is a plural unity by using the plural personal pronoun "us" before the time of Abraham. The references are: "*Let US make man*" (Genesis 1:26); when Adam and Eve sinned, God said, "*They have become one of US*" (Genesis 3:22); and at the tower of Babel God said, "*Let US go down*" (Genesis 11:7). The other plural pronoun reference is found in the call of Isaiah when God said, "*Who will I send, Who will go for US?*" (Isaiah 6:8). Isaiah hears pronouns in the singular and plural, simultaneously, from the very "lips" of God.[240]

The argument of what God has written cannot be expressed too strongly. He was revealing Himself to His people. Why do scholars explain the plurality of *Elohim* in ways that are not in harmony with the context of how God has chosen to reveal Himself to His people? An example of that denial is reflected by Jack Scott in *Theological Wordbook of the Old Testament* where he states that the word *Elohim* is not to be understood as a true plural:

> The plural ending is usually described as a plural of majesty and not intended as a true plural when used of God. This is seen in the fact that the noun *Elohim* is consistently used with singular verb forms and with adjectives and pronouns in the singular.[241]

In agreement with Scott, Page Kelley, in his book on Hebrew grammar, continues to reinterpret what God has purposely written down in the following statement "that אֱלֹהִים (*Elohim*) is plural in form but normally functions as a singular noun."[242] Contrary to Scott's and Kelley's statements, if they would base their view on verbal plenary inspiration and the literal method of interpretation of the Scriptures, it is impossible to arrive at that conclusion. This author believes that if *Elohim* is viewed by verbal plenary inspiration, using the literal method of interpretation, the conclusion must be that God is using the term *Elohim* of Himself to strongly state that He, as God, is presenting Himself in a plural context. Not only must scholars be consistent in their view of inspiration, but they must also be consistent in using the literal method of interpretation. Otherwise scholars become the authority and God is reduced to just a point of argument.

Jesus (*Yeshua*) expected the Pharisees to know and understand the plurality of *Elohim* when He equated Himself with God, the Father, as in John 10:30. The fact that Hebrew grammar is broken, when a singular verb is used with the plural noun (*Elohim*), should immediately attract the attention of the reader. It can be argued that God is revealing Himself as a plural God who is, in essence, one (*echad*). Why turn and explain away the conclusion that *Yeshua* expected the Pharisees to see?

---

[240] Knight, *A Christian Theology of the Old Testament*, 55.

[241] Harris, Archer, and Waltke, *Theological Wordbook of the Old Testament*, 1:44.

[242] Page H. Kelley, *Biblical Hebrew: An Introductory Grammar* (Grand Rapids: Eerdmans, 1992), 32.

Another important observation is that often *Elohim* and *Yahweh* are used together to denote the same God, as was previously mentioned at the beginning of the section entitled *Elohim*. *Yahweh* and *Elohim* are combined showing unity and plurality, and *Elohim* and *Yahweh* are both individually applied to two divine personalities, distinct and separate from each other, yet a unity of one, a compound unity. *Yahweh* in Hosea 1:2, 7 is applied to two separate and distinct *Yahweh*s and one of them is their *Elohim*.

It is pointed out by Fruchtenbaum that Hosea is saying there are two *Elohims* which are separate and distinct from each other, yet a unity:

> When the LORD first spoke to Hosea, and the LORD said to Hosea, Go, get yourself a wife of whoredom.... But I will have compassion on the house of Judah. And I will give them victory through the LORD their God [*Elohim*], I will not give them victory with bow, and sword and battle, by horses and riders.[243]

Fruchtenbaum says that the speaker is *Elohim* who will save them by *Yahweh*, their *Elohim*. Fruchtenbaum is correct, except for the fact that *Elohim* is not the speaker. *Yahweh* is the speaker. Here the speaker is the LORD, or *Yahweh*, communicating to Hosea, rather than *Elohim*, saying that He will send another LORD, or *Yahweh* who is their *Elohim*, to save them. So *Yahweh*, the speaker, the personal God of Israel, is going to send another *Yahweh*, who is their *Elohim*, to save them.[244] Here the text is dealing with two *Yahweh*s rather than two *Elohims*, and the one being sent is their *Elohim*. A second example of two *Elohims*[245] is found in Psalm 45:6-7[7-8] where *Elohim* is applied to two separate and distinct *Elohims*:

> Thy throne, O God, is for ever and ever: the scepter of thy kingdom is a right scepter. Thou lovest righteousness, and hatest wickedness: therefore God, thy God, hath anointed thee with the oil of gladness above thy fellows (KJV).

Dr. Arnold Fruchtenbaum has noted that in Psalm 45:6-7 the first *Elohim* is being addressed, and the second *Elohim* is the God of the first *Elohim*. Here are two distinct *Elohims*. *Elohim's Elohim* has set *Elohim* above His fellows and has anointed Him with the oil of joy or gladness.[246]

Another source of evidence to show the plurality of *Elohim* is the plural verbs and modifiers that follow *Elohim*. Normal Hebrew grammar says that following the plural *Elohim*, a noun, with a plural verb or modifier is correct grammar.

---

[243] Fruchtenbaum, *Messianic Christology*, 105.

[244] In a personal conversion with Dr. Fruchtenbaum in July of 2008 at Camp Shoshanah, he said that my observation was correct. It was an editorial error and would be corrected in future printings.

[245] Grudem, *Systematic Theology*, 227.

[246] Fruchtenbaum, *Messianic Christology*, 104.

78

אֱלֹהִים [*Elohim*] is plural in form, but normally functions as a singular noun. However, it may also function as a plural noun, accompanied by plural modifiers and plural verb forms. This usually occurs when reference is being made to the "gods" of the nations.[247]

In most places throughout Scripture *Elohim* is followed by a singular verb or modifier, which breaks the Hebrew grammatical construction. But there are four verses with *Elohim* and four plural verbs, or modifiers that apply to the true *Elohim*. This coincides with normal Hebrew grammatical construction. The impact of this is that *Elohim* is a true plurality of God, and these four examples help to show further that plurality. First, in Genesis 20:13 Abraham says, "*When God (Elohim) caused me to wander from my father's house.*" Literally it says, "God (*Elohim*) **They** caused me to wander." Second, in Genesis 35:7, Jacob says, "*And he built there an altar and called the place El-beth-el: because there God appeared unto him, when he fled from the face of his brother.*" Again, it literally says that God (*Elohim*) revealed **Themselves**. Third, in 2 Samuel 7:23, David said, "*And what one nation in the earth is like thy people, even like Israel, whom God went to redeem for a people to himself?*" Literally, again David said, "whom God [*Elohim*] **They** went to redeem for Themselves." Lastly, in Psalm 58:11[12], the psalmist says, "*So that a man shall say, verily there is a reward for the righteous: verily there is a God that judgeth in the earth.*" Literally it means, "God (*Elohim*) **They** judge on earth!" So here the testimony of Abraham, Jacob, David and the psalmist refer to God in the plural.

Sadly, the systematic theologies of Hodge,[248] Bancroft,[249] Buswell,[250] Barackman,[251] Grudem,[252] Berkhof,[253] and Erickson[254] do not cover or recognize these four verses (Genesis 20:13, 35:7, 2 Samuel 7:23, and Psalm 58:11). Only *Strong's Systematic Theology* refers to Genesis 20:13 and 35:7 as plural descriptions of *Elohim* the true God.[255] These systematic theologies referred to by pastors, theological students and lay people, are found to give a completely inadequate treatment of the plurality and tri-unity of *Elohim* in the Hebrew Scriptures.

Lastly, all of the preceding arguments for the plurality or tri-unity of *Elohim* in the Hebrew Scriptures are not new to the New Covenant, and the Church is not witnessing the birth of something new. Plurality has been firmly established and reflected

---

[247] Kelley, *Biblical Hebrew: An Introductory Grammar*, 32.

[248] Hodge, *Systematic Theology*, 1:442-482.

[249] Emery H. Bancroft, *Christian Theology* (Grand Rapids: Zondervan, 1964), 71-73, 83-85.

[250] James Oliver Buswell, *A Systematic Theology of the Christian Religion* (Grand Rapids: Zondervan, 1962), 1:102-129.

[251] Barackman, *Practical Christian Theology*, 60-68.

[252] Grudem, *Systematic Theology*, 226-261.

[253] Berkhof, *Systematic Theology*, 82-99.

[254] Erickson, *Introducing Christian Doctrine*, 96-105.

[255] Augustus H. Strong, *Systematic Theology* (Westwood, N.J: Fleming H. Revell, 1965), 318.

throughout the pages of the *Tanakh*. The *Tanakh* and New Covenant are Trinitarian to the very heart. This tri-unity of *Elohim* in the New Covenant has its foundations clearly grounded in the *Tanakh*. This doctrine does not appear in the making in the New Covenant, it has already been made.[256] Warfield gives a very logical argument for the foundation of the tri-unity in the word *Elohim* as he introduces it to us in the following statement:

> It was the task of the Old Testament revelation to fix firmly in the minds and hearts of the people of God the great fundamental truth of the unity of the God-head; and it would have been dangerous to speak to them of the plurality within this unity until this task had been fully accomplished. The real reason for the delay in the revelation of the Trinity, however, is grounded in the secular development of the redemptive purpose of God: the times were not ripe for the revelation of the Trinity in the unity of the Godhead until the fullness of the time had come for God to send forth His Son unto redemption, and his Spirit unto sanctification."[257]

Warfield is saying that in Genesis 1, or even in the *Torah*, God did not present a full-blown revelation of Himself because of the rampant polytheism in the ancient world. He was a triune God from the beginning, but He used progressive revelation to unfold His tri-unity until the full revelation was given in the New Covenant. That does not eradicate the fact that His plurality (and tri-unity) are presented in the *Tanakh* through numerous avenues. David L. Cooper also expresses why God revealed Himself, both as a unity (one) and as a plurality:

> What is the reason for the use of this plural noun referring to the Divine Being with the verb in the singular number? There can be but one true explanation which is that, while emphasizing the distinct personalities of the God-head, the ancient writers were anxious to refute polytheism and to assert the unity and the oneness of these divine personalities. Thus this peculiar grammatical usage is an affirmation of both the unity and plurality of the Divine Being.[258]

A Jewish believer expresses why the tri-unity of God is not fully revealed in the Hebrew Scriptures:

> The reason a formal Trinitarian concept does not exist in the Old Testament is not because it is borrowed from Hellenism, as some suggest, but because as the revelation of God is progressive, so as with the nature of the Messiah Himself, a full enough revelation did not exist in Jewish scripture until the New Covenant.[259]

---

[256] Warfield, *Biblical and Theological Studies*, 32.

[257] Warfield, *Biblical and Theological Studies*, 33-34.

[258] David L. Cooper, *God's Gracious Provision for Man* (Los Angeles: Biblical Research Society, 1953), 114.

[259] Schiffman, *Return of the Remnant,* 94.

This statement is a little vague, but the revelation of God was full enough, although they did have to put all the Scripture together, which Rabbinic Judaism failed to do. Due to the fact that the singular verbs or modifiers follow *Elohim*, God was showing the Jewish people the plurality of Himself and the fact that the combination of the plural and singular lends support to the plural unity of God. In the Soncino Commentaries rabbis try to say the opposite, that it can only mean the unity of *Elohim*:

> The Hebrew has the plural form, the plural of majesty; but no idea of plurality is to be read into the word, because the verb created is in the singular (E).[260]

As illustrated, *Elohim* denotes the oneness of God, the fact that He is indivisible, but is at the same time plural. "Plural of majesty" does not apply because "plural of majesty" is not used by Hebrew kings as the leadership in Israel, within the *Tanakh*. Contrary to Abraham Ibn Ezra's quote above, the plurality can be read into *Elohim* because God used it in revealing Himself. Cooper further states that writers of the *Tanakh* used all three names of God: *El, Elah, Eloah* in the singular and *Elohim* in the plural. Cooper demonstrates that the writers of the *Tanakh* had ample words to express the singular, absolute oneness of God but, in the majority of cases, chose the plural *Elohim* instead:

> The English word which is translated 'God' in the Hebrew Scriptures in the majority of cases is אֱלֹהִים *Elohim*. This term is in the plural number, as everyone who knows Hebrew admits. Moses and the prophets referring to — idols in the plural — invariably used this same form. Since it connoted a plurality of idols, it certainly indicates a plurality of the divine personalities subsisting in the one divine essence when applied to the true God. Frequently, however, Moses and the prophets used אֵל *El*, in referring to the Divine Being, which is in the singular number and means only one. Occasionally they used אֱלוֹהַּ *Eloah*. Beyond controversy this also is in the singular number. If the Divine Being were simply a single personality, the sacred writers could have used either of these words in the singular to convey that idea. In Joshua 22:22 however appear both the singular and plural forms, which combination amounts to an affirmation regarding the unity of the divine personalities constituting the one God: אֵל אֱלֹהִים יְהוָה אֵל אֱלֹהִים יְהוָה "God, Gods, Jehovah, God Gods, Jehovah ...."[261]

Cooper's argument on the names of God is well done, and his reference to Joshua 22:22 is quite convincing. In this text Joshua repeats, twice for emphasis, that *El* (singular), *Elohim* (plural) and *Yahweh* (singular) are both singular and plural terms for God. In this verse the God of Israel is called by all three names, and one of them is in

---

[260] A. Cohen, *The Soncino Chumash, the Five Books of Moses* with Haphtaroth (London: Soncino, 1993), 1.

[261] David L. Cooper, *What Men Must Believe* (Los Angeles: Biblical Research Society, 1943), 105.

the plural. When the *Ruach haKodesh* (Holy Spirit) of God wrote the Scriptures, every word was inspired (verbal plenary), because He knew exactly what He wanted to say.

The authors of Scripture use the plural forms of *Elohim* to denote pagan gods only in the context that Israel did not worship plural gods as the heathen do. They worshipped a plural God who is a complete complex unity, indivisibly one and completely equal in nature, character and essence. The greater portion of the 2600 uses of *Elohim* refers to the God of Israel; only about 250 of them refer to pagan gods. The writers of Scripture use the term as a contrast between plural pagan gods and the plural indivisible God of Israel.

Moses, from Genesis through Deuteronomy, was God's human author who composed the whole of the Pentateuch. Moses used the term *Elohim* throughout his writings of the true God. *Elohim* met with Abraham, Isaac, Jacob, Moses and was the one who guided the children of Israel through the wilderness to the Promised Land.[262] The Creator God of Genesis 1 is the same God throughout the *Torah* who does refer to Himself in the plural. Throughout the *Torah* God is identified as not just *Elohim*, but *Yahweh*, *Adonai*, the Messenger (Angel) of the LORD, and the *Shechinah* of God. Psalm 96:5, in reference to the Creator God, calls Him LORD. Sailhamer and Watson make two appropriate statements that reflect the fact that *Elohim* is the God of the *Torah*:

> The Creator identified in [Genesis] 1:1 as God, that is, Elohim. Although God is not further identified here, the author appears confident that his reader will identify this God with the God of the fathers and the God of the covenant Sinai. In other words, the proper context for understanding [Genesis] 1:1 is the whole of the book of Genesis and the Pentateuch. Already in Genesis 2:4b God (Elohim) is identified with the Lord (Yahweh), the God who called Abraham (Gen 12:1) and delivered Israel from Egypt (Exod 3:15). The God of Genesis 1:1, then, is far from a faceless deity. From the perspective of the Pentateuch as a whole he is the God who has called the fathers into his good land, redeemed his people from Egypt, and led them again to the borders of the land, a land which he provided and now calls on them to enter and possess. He is the "Redeemer-Shepherd" of Jacob's blessing in 48:15. The purpose of [Genesis] 1:1 is not to identify this God in a general way but to identify him as the Creator of the universe.[263]

The very first name in the Scriptures under which the Divine Being is introduced to us as the Creator of heaven and earth is a plural one, אלהים, *Aleim* (Elohim); and to connect in the same singular manner as in the foregoing instance, plurality with unity, it is the nominative case to a verb singular. "In the beginning, Gods created the heavens and the earth." Of this form innumerable instances occur in the Old Testament. That the word is plural, is

---

[262] Sailhamer, *The Expositor's Bible Commentary: Genesis*, 2:20.
[263] Sailhamer, *The Pentateuch as Narrative: A Biblical-Theological Commentary*, 82.

made certain by its being often joined with adjectives, pronouns, and verbs plural; and yet when it can mean nothing else than the true God, it is generally joined in its plural form with verbs singular. To render this still more striking, the *Aleim* (Elohim) are said to be Jehovah, and Jehovah, he, the *Aleim* (Elohim): thus in Psalm 100:3, "Know ye, that Jehovah, he, the *Aleim* (Elohim), he hath made us and not we ourselves."[264]

Jewish scholars typically put more emphasis on the *Torah* because it was written by the great law-giver Moses. The Prophets and the Writings are typically understood to be a calling of the people back to the law of Moses given in the *Torah*. The *Torah* is central to Judaism. Yet throughout the *Torah*, Moses presents *Elohim* as a plural unity of one (*echad*) and the same *Elohim* as *Yahweh*.

DUAL PLURALITY

Hebrew nouns have another quality that impacts the study, and that quality is number. Number is the singular and plural aspect as it relates to nouns. Another number used in Hebrew is the "dual," which indicates plurality, but only in the sense of "a pair or two." Ross, in his Hebrew grammar, clarifies that "Hebrew nouns have three numbers, singular, plural and dual. Dual is a special kind of plural ending used to indicate a pair, or two of something."[265] Examples of dual nouns are: two ears (אָזְנַיִם), two days (יוֹמַיִם), two horses (סוּסַיִם), two mares (סוּסָתַיִם), two hands (יָדַיִם), two feet (רַגְלַיִם), and two horns (קַרְנַיִם). Rendsburg states that dual forms are not as rare as would be expected when he says:

> Although most grammars have not recognized them, dual forms are not as rare in Hebrew as one might expect.[266]

He goes on in his article to illustrate that the dual is used more often than normally seen, such as in Ruth 1:22 when the text says concerning Ruth and Naomi "and they (c. dual) came to Bethlehem."[267] D. L. Cooper adds insight that dual is never used of God, which would simply mean that if *Elohim* is a plurality, He must be more than two.

> Usually this form of noun was employed when a pair of objects was mentioned. When, for instance, a Hebrew wished to speak of a person's hands, he put the noun in the dual number. The same thing was true with reference to eyes and feet. By the use of this form the writer indicated that there were but two. If there had been only two personalities in the Divine Being and the prophets had

---

[264] Watson, *Theological Institutes: Or, a View of the Evidences, Doctrines, Morals and Institutions of Christianity*, 1:467.

[265] Allen P. Ross, *Introducing Biblical Hebrew* (Grand Rapids: Baker Academic, 2001), 71.

[266] Gary Rendsburg, "Dual Personal Pronouns and Dual Verbs in Hebrew," *JQR* 73, no. 1 (1982): 38-58.

[267] Rendsburg, "Dual Personal Pronouns and Dual Verbs in Hebrew," *Jewish Quarterly Review,* 40.

wished to emphasize that fact, they could have put the word for God in the dual number. But not one time did they resort to any such method. On the contrary, as we have already seen, they used a word for God in the singular and another in the plural number, which facts show that there were at least three personalities constituting the Divine Being. The noun in the singular number doubtless stressed the unity of God, whereas the one in the plural laid emphasis upon the plurality of the Almighty. In the original the plural word for God is used with a verb in the plural number in Genesis 20:13 and 35:7. Evidently, since the Scriptures are infallibly inspired, there was a very definite reason why the noun for God, *Elohim*, is used here with a plural verb."[268]

Observations and insights such as these should not be ignored and minimized because the *Tanakh* is God's book, and He is revealing Himself to Israel and mankind. A Christian Arab originally from the West Bank area of Israel draws a parallel between Arabic and Hebrew in relation to dual plurality:

Our Arabic verbs and pronouns are very different from many other languages. The Old Testament, written in Hebrew, has similar verbs and pronouns. Arabic has a singular, a dual, and then a plural verb. "He ate" would be *Akal*. "They (two) ate" would be *Akalou*. In the Semitic language, the verb frequently identifies the number of persons involved in the action. "You" in English can refer to one, two, or a million, but not so in Arabic or Hebrew.[269]

Shorrosh affirms that the tri-unity is assumed in the very first chapter in Genesis (1:26) and in 3:22 in the Hebrew Scriptures. Barackman states that God is one (Deuteronomy 6:4) but that *Elohim* indicates a plurality of persons (Genesis 1:1) coupled with the "us" passages (Genesis 1:26).[270] *Elohim* clearly indicates more than two because it always has a plural ending and never has a dual ending. Barackman also says that God is a tri-unity because of passages such as Isaiah 48:16, which is a representation of three persons.[271]

Special uses of *Elohim*, in a plural sense, serve as a powerful argument for His plurality. In Genesis 3:5 Satan says to Eve, "*You shall be as Elohim* (plural), *knowing good and evil*." Why would Satan be using that plural descriptive word so early in human history? There were no other gods or idols at that point to be worshipped. There was nothing! Adam and Eve were in innocence in paradise at that stage of history; no sin was yet in the world. Could it be that Satan used *Elohim* because, as one of the anointed *cherubim*, he had served in the immediate presence of God and knew God to be a plurality? Charles Baker expressed the impact of *Elohim* in relation to Adam and Eve:

---

[268] Cooper, *What Men Must Believe*, 105-106.

[269] Anis A. Shorrosh, *Islam Revealed: A Christian Arab's View of Islam* (Nashville: Nelson, 1988), 239.

[270] Barackman, *Practical Christian Theology*, 63.

[271] Barackman, *Practical Christian Theology*, 66.

… Satan told Eve that she and her husband would be as gods, knowing good and evil, it would appear that Eve at this time could not have known of any false gods or others who could be called gods, and it would therefore make better sense to make *Elohim* here refer to the one true God. There is nothing in this verse to make the first occurrence of *Elohim* (translated *God* – vv. 1 and 3) to be a different person from the *Elohim* at the end of the v. 5 (translated *gods*).[272]

Baker's observation has merit and insight into understanding the probable situation in the temptation scene of Genesis 3.

In Psalm 138:1 David says that before the gods he will sing praise unto you (God). David was not a polytheist, and yet David praised God before the *Elohims*, and *Elohim* is translated from the Hebrew Scripture as "gods"![273] Why do all these translations (ASV 1901, NASV, KJV, NKJV, NIV, RSV) use "gods"? How is this to be understood? Did David praise *Elohim* because he understood something about the plural nature of *Elohim*? Or is David praising *Elohim* before the judges in Israel (Exodus 21:6; 22:8, 9, 28)? Both are real possibilities, but the second one is more likely. *Elohim* is translated as "God" with a marginal note saying "to the judges" in the Jewish Tanakh.[274] Obviously, David was praising *Elohim* in the "holy temple," not before false gods, but before the judges. Baker makes the following observation:

Of course, David could have had in mind praising God before some great ones in the earth, but it is unlikely that he was thinking about standing in an idol temple to praise God. It seems more likely that he was simply reiterating what he had said in the first part of the verse; "I will praise thee with my whole heart: before *Elohim* will I sing praise unto thee."[275]

Since Adam and Eve knew nothing of polytheism, understanding the Genesis 3:5 reference as a plurality of God would fit into their frame of reference. David was a monotheist in his worship of God, and the Psalms reference that he was worshipping God in His holy temple "before the judges" makes more sense. It is hard to believe that God would move the writers of the *Tanakh* to select a name for God from polytheistic terminology, since that same Hebrew Scripture completely condemns polytheism. If God did breathe His Word through Moses, David and the prophets, it seems more logical to believe that He led them to use the plural noun with singular verbs and plural adjectives to reveal something of His true nature as a tri-unity. This truth would only be fully revealed after the incarnation of His Son, the Messiah of Israel.[276]

---

[272] Charles F. Baker, *A Dispensational Theology* (Grand Rapids: Grace Bible College, 1971), 143.

[273] The following translations all use gods: ASV 1901, NASV, KJV, NKJV, NIV, RSV.

[274] *Tanakh: The Holy Scriptures*, (Philadelphia: The Jewish Publication Society, 1985), 117.

[275] Baker, *A Dispensational Theology*, 143.

[276] Baker, *A Dispensational Theology*, 142.

Exodus 21:5-6 illustrates the scriptural text translated correctly to reflect the context of the passage:

And if the servant shall plainly say, I love my master, my wife, and my children; I will not go out free: Then his master shall bring him unto the judges, ...[277]

The NASB (New American Standard Bible) uses the word "God," but in the footnotes it says "or judges." Clearly *Elohim* is translated in the plural when it refers to God's representatives, the judges, but not when it is translated for the true God. In Psalm 97:7 *Elohim* is used again and translated "gods," but the text is referring to angels who are called to worship God.[278] So *Elohim* is made plural when the text demands it, but when it is used of God, authors switch to "plural of majesty." Attempting to change the meaning by interpreting plural as singular, is not *"rightly dividing the word of truth"* (2 Timothy 2:15). Have Christian theologians conceded or abdicated the plural unity of God to Rabbinic Judaism? As this study has progressed this author came to realize that Christian theologians have conceded to "higher criticism" and not Rabbinic Judaism.

Clearly, scriptural usages of *Elohim* indicate that the plurality of *Elohim*, as well as the tri-unity of *Elohim*, was present in the beginning of *Elohim*'s revelation of Himself. Over the years of interacting with this world's liberal religious perspective, there seems to be the consensus that religion evolved from polytheism to monotheism. Some authors, like Jacobs,[279] allude to the fact that monotheism developed in an evolutionary manner from polytheism[280] over the centuries, to henotheism,[281] and then to monotheism,[282] which Israel embraced. He further states that this is a matter for biblical scholarship. Payne follows the lead of Jacobs by saying the following:

Historically, however, this truth was only progressively revealed by God and grasped by fallen man. Before the fall Adam knew God, but most of his descendants became polytheists (Josh 24:2).[283]

Dyrness references Payne's statement that Israel had no clear understanding of monotheism. In fact, he continues to state that Abraham and the other patriarchs were only practical monotheists, because there is no indication of the denial of other gods.[284] Both Payne and Dyrness once again use higher criticism to twist the Scripture to fulfill their own unbelief in the Word of God. Some of Israel may have lost that concept of

---

[277] Alexander Harkavy, *The Twenty-Four Books of the Old Testament* (2 vols., New York, N.Y: Hebrew Publishing, 1916), 123.

[278] Cooper, *The God of Israel*, 35.

[279] Jacobs, *A Jewish Theology,* 22.

[280] *Polytheism*: The belief in many gods.

[281] *Henotheism*: The worship of one god without denying the existence of other gods.

[282] *Monotheism*: The belief that there is but one God.

[283] Payne, *The Theology of the Older Testament*, 125.

[284] William Dyrness, *Themes in Old Testament Theology* (Downers Grove, IL: InterVarsity, 1977), 48.

monotheism because of the idolatry in Egypt, but not everyone in Israel lost monotheism. Niehaus in his book, *God At Sinai*, reflects on the Apostle Paul's statement (Romans 1:18-32), which is the reverse of Jacob's premise. God had revealed Himself to mankind from the beginning. But man chose, from the beginning, to turn his back on God and worship images of mortal man, birds, animals and reptiles:

> Those pagan religions-characterized by polytheism (or Henotheism at best) and idolatry-represent a *Weltanschauung* (world view) that is degraded from the truth. The apostle Paul put pagan religion in perspective when he portrayed it as a result of the Fall. According to Paul, humanity knew God from the beginning but chose not to glorify him or give thanks to him, and as a result, "their foolish hearts were darkened" and "they became fools and exchanged the glory of the immortal God for images made to look like mortal man and birds and animals and reptiles (Rom 1:21-23)."[285]

The concept that *Elohim* revealed Himself from the beginning is continued by Henry Thiessen: "We assert that monotheism was the original religion of mankind."[286] That concept of God did not evolve from polytheism to monotheism but rather degenerated from monotheism to polytheism. What better reason and convincing proof can be given than these scriptural uses of *Elohim* where God revealed Himself to Adam and Eve as one God in a plurality of unity? This is further suggested by Jack Scott:

> However, a better reason can be seen in Scripture itself where, in the very first chapter of Genesis, the necessity of a term conveying both the unity of the one God and yet allowing for a plurality of persons is found (Gen 1:2, 26).[287]

So *Elohim* opens the door for God's revelation of Himself in a plural manner. He is one God. He has revealed Himself to mankind as a plurality of unity, indivisible. He is revealed as a tri-unity, which the Hebrew word *Elohim* represents by being translated as a plurality. The Rabbinic argument affirms the absolute oneness of God, which preserves their rejection of Jesus as the God/man, Who is equal, in essence, with the Father, Who is *Elohim*, a plurality, yet one.

From the time of Moses through the exile, Israel struggled with worshipping *Elohim*, alone, as God. Joshua, at the end of his life, challenged Israel to choose whom they were going to serve (Joshua 24:14-15). He told them to put away the gods (*elohim*) which their fathers served. In Judges 2, where the cycle of sin is given, the first step to bondage was the worship of Baalim (v. 11). The worship of other gods (*elohim*) was Israel's stumbling block throughout the pages of the *Tanakh*, but Israel knew that their God was *Elohim*, *Yahweh*, and that He demanded complete, exclusive worship. As Isaiah 44 points out so clearly, the other gods (*elohim*) were not gods (*elohim*) at all but

---

[285] Jeffrey J. Niehaus, *God At Sinai* (Grand Rapids: Zondervan, 1995), 82.

[286] Henry C. Thiessen, *Lectures in Systematic Theology* (Grand Rapids: Eerdmans, 1979), 38.

[287] Harris, Archer, and Waltke, *Theological Wordbook of the Old Testament*, 1:44.

mere objects of wood and stone or heavenly bodies, all lifeless, created by the imagination of man's fallen mind and with his hands.

אֲדֹנִי *ADONAI*

The word *adonai*, translated "Lord," is plural of *adon* (lord) in the Hebrew Scriptures and is consistently in the plural when used of God.[288] The word is used by itself 134 times and connected to *Yahweh* 315 times.[289] That is an additional 449 plural references of *Adonai*, and *Adonai* linked together with *Elohim*, as well as the other plural descriptions (discussed in chapter 10), to show the plurality of *Elohim*. However, Jenni calls *adonai* a majestic plural as seen with *Elohim*.[290] Alden affirms *adonai* as a plural usage as is true with *Elohim*, but also equates it with "plural of majesty" as is often done with *Elohim*.[291] This is the same argument used with *Elohim* in trying to make it a "plural of majesty" instead of accepting it as God used it. The Scripture, God's revelation of Himself, speaks for itself. If He chose to use the plural *adonai* for Lord as He spoke of Himself, who are scholars to say that He cannot speak of Himself in that manner? In contrast Barackman says of *Adonai* that "the plural form indicates the plurality of Persons."[292] Even more significant is the statement from a Jewish dictionary:

> *Adon* means lord, master when applied to persons in authority (Gen 45:8-9; Deut 10:17; Judg 19:26-27; I Sam 29:8), and is occasionally used for God (Exod 23:17; 34:23; Josh 3:11, 13). *Adonai*, on the other hand, is a plural form based on *Adon*, but is used exclusively for God and is often used as a parallel to *YHVH* (Gen 15:2, 8; Josh 7:7; Isa 25:8) or as a substitute for it (Isa 13:17; Amos 7:7-8, 9:1; Ezek 18:25).[293]

The plural usage of *adonai* in connection with, or in place of, *Yahweh*, further makes the point that *Yahweh*, is "one," and within that oneness is plurality. This adds even more weight for the plurality of *Elohim* in the *Tanakh*.

Adonai and *Yahweh* were equally used of God as divine names before 300 BCE. After that period of time, *adonai* gradually came into use more than *Yahweh*. Finally, around the time of Christ, *adonai* completely replaced *Yahweh* in the spoken language.

---

[288] Fruchtenbaum, *Messianic Christology*, 105.

[289] Botterweck, Ringgren, and Fabry, *Theological Dictionary of the Old Testament*, 1:62.

[290] Jenni and Westermann, *Theological Lexicon of the Old Testament*, 1:24.

[291] Harris, Archer, and Waltke, *Theological Wordbook of the Old Testament*, 1:13.

[292] Barackman, *Practical Christian Theology*, 66.

[293] Neusner and Green, *Dictionary of Judaism in the Biblical Period*, 389.

יְהֹוָה *YAHWEH*

Although *Yahweh* is Israel's personal name for God, the correct pronunciation was lost sometime during the Middle Ages. During the late second temple period, this name was regarded as unspeakably holy and therefore unsuitable for use in public. However, although it was used privately in the synagogue and temple,[294] by the Middle Ages its pronunciation was lost.[295] *Yahweh* was replaced by the word *adonai* for Lord sometime before the end of the second temple period.

Yahweh is made up of the Hebrew consonants יהוה or [*yhwh*], which are called the Tetragrammaton.[296] No consensus exists in relation to the structure and etymology of *Yahweh*. The name is generally thought to be a verbal form derived from the root *hwy*, later *hyh*. The meaning of the word is not completely certain, but the general consensus is that it means "to be, happen, become" or "be at hand, exist, come to pass."[297] *Yahweh* seems to be native to Hebrew, since there seem to be no references to the word among the other nations before the time of Moses.[298] The primary explanation of *Yahweh* occurs in Exodus 3:13-15, where God reveals His name to Moses. Those verses state that He is the one who exists (Exodus 3:14); He is with His people; (verse 12), and He wants to be known by them (verse 15).[299] In Exodus 6:3, God told Moses that Abraham, Isaac and Jacob knew Him as *El Shaddai* (God Almighty), but *Yahweh* was His name even in the times of the patriarchs. Moses, as he records the history of man, the call of Abraham and his descendants in Genesis, starts using God's name (*Yahweh*) in 2:4. Moses was the compiler of the ancient history that *Yahweh* wished to have recorded. Moses compiled what is known as Toledots,[300] ten of them. Moses gave the background

---

[294] Neusner and Green, *Dictionary of Judaism in the Biblical Period,* 259.

[295] Stone, *Names of God,* 25.

[296] Botterweck, Ringgren, and Fabry, *Theological Dictionary of the Old Testament,* 1:71.

[297] Botterweck, Ringgren, and Fabry, *Theological Dictionary of the Old Testament,* 5:500.

[298] Alexander and Baker, *Dictionary of the Old Testament Pentateuch,* 363.

[299] Alexander and Baker, *Dictionary of the Old Testament Pentateuch,* 363.

[300] The Toledots are ten natural divisions in the text for the book of Genesis and most of them begin with the words "These are the generations of ...." After the creation account in Genesis 1:1-2:3, the ten are as follows: (1) The generations of heaven and earth; 2:4-4:26. (2) The generations of Adam; 5:1-6:8. (3) The generation of Noah; 6:9-9:29. (4) The generations of the sons of Noah; 10:1-11:9. (5) The generations of Shem; 11:10-26. (6) The generations of Terah; 11:27-25:11. (7) The generations of Ishmael; 25:12-18. (8) The generations of Isaac; 25:19-35:39. (9) The generations of Esau; 36:1-43. (10) The generations of Jacob; 37-50 [William Smith, *Old Testament History* (Joplin, MO: College Press, 1970), 7]. David L. Cooper deals with Toledots extensively [David L. Cooper, *Messiah: His First Coming Scheduled* (Los Angeles: Biblical Research Society, 1939), 25-48. Also see Gordon Talbot, *A Study of the Book of Genesis* (Harrisburg, PA: Christian Publications, 1981), 8-9; and T. Desmond Alexander and David W. Baker, *Dictionary of the Old Testament Pentateuch* (Downers Grove, IL: IVP, 2003), 350-352. This is in stark contrast to scholars of the higher criticism theory which is called Documentary Hypothesis – also called the Graff-Wellhausen Hypothesis, which divides the Pentateuch (Genesis) into four major documentary sources. The four sources are usually dated much later than the Biblical text itself gives and they are called the (1) J source for Jehovah

material to Israel in the wilderness so that they would understand that the LORD, who led them through the wilderness and into the Land of Promise, was the *El Shaddai* that communed with Abraham, Isaac, and Jacob. Also it strongly appears that Moses understood clearly the plurality of God because of what he wrote about God and how he wrote it. Once again if the literal method of interpretation of the verbal and plenary inspiration is held, this concept of Moses' understanding cannot be avoided. *Yahweh*, which is used 6,828 times, is the second most used word in the Hebrew Scriptures[301] in the singular form,[302] which lays a very strong foundation for monotheism in the Scriptures.

Genesis 21:33 clearly identifies *Yahweh*, who is called upon and is connected with *El* of eternity or everlasting. *Yahweh* is identified with *Elohim* in Leviticus 19:2, where the people are to be *"holy, for I, the LORD (Yahweh) your God (Elohim) am holy."* *Yahweh*, in combination with *Elohim*, is significant because the two are equated with each other. The difference in meaning, with the combination of these names, is that *Yahweh* is their personal God and *Elohim* is more removed from the creation as expressed here:

> In the Pentateuch … the name *Yahweh* is employed when God is presented to us in His personal character and in direct relationship to people or nature; and *Elohim*, when the Deity is alluded to as a Transcendental Being who exists completely outside and above the physical universe.[303]

While *Yahweh* and *Elohim* are called holy in Leviticus 19:2, holy is a very special statement which only applies to *Yahweh*. In Isaiah 6:3 *Yahweh* is addressed as *"Holy, Holy, Holy is LORD [Yahweh] of hosts."* In Deuteronomy 5:9 Moses also spells out that *Yahweh*, *El* and *Elohim* is a jealous God. *"For I, the LORD [Yahweh] your God [Elohim], am a jealous God [El]."* These three words are used as synonyms for the same God.

Yahweh's name is also combined with other words, making compound forms of His name to describe certain aspects of His person. Such as *Yahweh-jireh*: "The LORD will provide" (Genesis 22:14) and *Yahweh-Nissi* "The LORD our banner" (Exodus 17:15). Other compound forms are *Yahweh-Shalom*: "The LORD is peace" (Judges 6:24) and *Yahweh-Sabbaoth*: "The LORD of hosts" (1 Samuel 1:3). The last compound form is *Yahweh-M'Kaddesh* and it means "The LORD thy sanctifier" (Exodus 31:13), a reference to the Messiah, *Yahweh-Tsidkenu*: *"The LORD our righteousness"* (Jeremiah 23:6). The only discussion or question with *Yahweh* is the root word for the

---

[approx. date 950 BCE], (2) E source for Elohist [approx date 850], (3) D source for Deuteronomist [approx. date 650-621 BCE] and (4) P source for Priestly [550-400 BCE]. Stephen L. Harris, *Understanding the Bible* (2nd Ed. Palo Alto, CA: Mayfield Publishing, 1985), 46-50.

[301] Enns, *The Moody Handbook of Theology,* 197.

[302] Chafer, *Chafer's Systematic Theology,* 6:17.

[303] Walter A. Elwell, *Evangelical Dictionary of Theology* (Grand Rapids: Baker, 1986), 466.

name of God. Everything else seems to be in agreement in relationship to His singularity and oneness.

Yahweh is singular in the Hebrew text, yet plural terms of God are connected with His name. *Yahweh, El* and *Elohim* are used together as the same God, a plural and singular designation of God. There are plural references to *Yahweh* (LORD) in the English text which are not always seen by the casual reader of the Scriptures.

Two Yahwehs in the Tanakh

Yahweh is the name of Israel's personal God, and the word substantiates that God is one. His oneness is borne out in many passages of the Hebrew text (Genesis 21:33; Exodus 20:2; Leviticus 19:2; 20:26; 21:8; Deuteronomy 4:24; 5:9, 6:4; Isaiah 41:4, 44:6, 45:5, 14, 18, 21; 48:12; Jeremiah 2:5, 11). Yet God, in His revelation of Himself, continues to identify Himself (*Yahweh*) with plurality, as presented in the following Scriptures:

The LORD … from the LORD … Genesis 19:24

In Genesis 18-19 three men visited Abraham, and he recognized them simply as men, but Abraham also recognized one of them from previous appearances of God to him such as in Genesis 17. The promise of Isaac's birth was given in verse 9, but the text did not begin to identify the men until verse 13, where the one man identified Himself as *Yahweh*. The other two men were identified as angels going to Sodom (Genesis 19:1). The focus of this section of Scripture is not the two men who left but the one who identified Himself to Abraham as *Yahweh*. In Genesis 18:17-33 Abraham was having a dialogue with *Yahweh*, the LORD. Rabbis say that God cannot become a man in human form. Yet, here *Yahweh* appeared in human form, and He even had a meal with Abraham. This passage of Scripture goes against what Rabbinic Judaism teaches about the nature of God as seen in this quote by Weiss-Rosmarin:

> The Unity of God, sacred to Judaism beyond all else, is utterly irreconcilable with the Christian idea of the divisibility of the Divine Being and, above all, with the belief in incarnation. According to Jewish belief God is pure spirit, eternally transcendent and divorced from even the slightest vestige of corporeality. Christianity, on the other hand, asserts that God became man in Jesus, a teaching which is contrary to the very spirit of Judaism.[304]

Weiss-Rosmarin says that Judaism is "irreconcilable" to what New Covenant believers believe about two key issues: the divisibility of God and *Yeshua* being the incarnation of God. First of all true biblical faith does not and has not taught the divisibility of God. True believers would also consider the divisibility of God as irreconcilable. On the issue of the incarnation Rabbinic Judaism says that God is pure spirit and in no way can

---

[304] Trude Weiss-Rosmarin, *Judaism and Christianity, the Differences* (Middle Village, NY: Jonathan David, 1997), 21.

He be placed in a corporal body. Yet in Genesis 18, God did appear in a "corporal body" and even ate a meal with Abraham. Weiss-Rosmarin's statement is in complete conflict with the statements of Moses, who records what Abraham saw and heard. Weiss-Rosmarin continues his argument with the following statement:

> Is not this contrary to all Jewish teachings of God which emphasize and stress that God is not like man and can never become man or even resemble man? Judaism has always fought, and with all weapons at its disposal, against the Christian idea of incarnation, that is to say, of God's coming into human life. The thought that "God was made man" is shocking beyond words to the Jew who believes that God is One and Unique, and that this Uniqueness consists also in His utter difference from anything and everything in existence and anything and everything man can possibly fashion in his mind to label "God." How, then, can the Jewish and Christian ideas of God be reconciled, or how can it be said that the "two religions are truly, basically one"? Is the One and Unique God, the absolute Unity – unknowable, indefinable – really the same as the Christian Trinity which *divides* the Unity of God into three, namely, God the Father, Jesus the Son and the Holy Spirit?[305]

Where, in the *Tanakh*, does God say He cannot appear (or become) as a man or even resemble man? It does say that *"God is not a man,"* (Numbers 23:19). That is absolutely correct. But that statement does not say that God cannot take on the appearance of man to communicate with man. Nor does it say that God, who is Spirit, cannot become a man! True biblical faith does not teach that God can be divided into three. Nor does it teach tri-theism, which is what Rabbinic Judaism teaches concerning Christianity, but not biblical Judaism. Weiss-Rosmarin continues:

> Jewish monotheism is not only the negation of the many gods but also the rejection of the personification of God on the one hand and of the deification of human beings on the other. Judaism's refusal to worship Jesus is therefore not only due to its repudiation of the doctrine of incarnation, the belief that God became a person, but equally so to its defiant resistance to all and any attempts of according Divine qualities and honors to mere mortals.[306]

Weiss-Rosmarin's perspective is tainted by the writings of Rabbinic Judaism as well as Roman Catholicism which to Judaism has deified man with their statues (idols) and prayers to "saints" (worship). However, if Rabbinic Judaism were to acknowledge even the possibility of the plurality of God, then Rabbinic Judaism would fall like a sandcastle on the seashore. Yet, contradictory to what Weiss-Rosmarin said, *Yahweh* did appear in human form as a man to Abraham, the Father of the Jewish people, and to Jacob as he wrestled with the Angel of *Yahweh* (Genesis 32:24-30; Hosea 12:3-5) and to Joshua before the attack of Jericho (Joshua 5:13-15). In Genesis 18, the one man who

---

[305] Weiss-Rosmarin, *Judaism and Christianity, the Differences*, 21-22.
[306] Weiss-Rosmarin, *Judaism and Christianity, the Differences*, 21-23.

identifies Himself eight times between verses 13-33 is *Yahweh*. In this section of Scripture *Yahweh* is in human form and eating a meal with Abraham after he had washed the visitors' feet. Fruchtenbaum comments on Genesis 19:24 by saying that *Yahweh,* the one who was talking with Abraham, rains down fire from *Yahweh* in heaven. Clearly there are two distinct *Yahwehs* showing plurality:

> The first *YHVH* is on earth and is said to be raining down fire from a second *YHVH* who is in heaven. Two distinct persons are called *YHVH* in the same text.[307]

So not only are there two *Yahwehs*, but one of them appeared in a human form and was called the Angel of the LORD. If rabbis would study the *Tanakh* as well as the Targums, perhaps they would see the plurality of *Elohim* as the following rabbi relates his study of the *Tanakh* and also adds a dimension that will be covered in chapter 18 of this study. This one is also called the Word of the LORD.

> Our God has declared by the Prophet Isaiah (42:8), "I am the Lord: that is my name: and my glory will I not give to another." What a stream of light was poured into my mind, when investigating the mystery contained in these words, "Then the Lord rained upon Sodom and upon Gomorrah brimstone and fire from the Lord out of heaven" (Gen 19:24). My teacher, Jonathan ben Uziel, taught me, by his Jerusalem [Targum] Paraphrase, that the Lord (יהוה) mentioned in this passage of Scripture, is the Word of the Lord. "And the Word of the Lord caused to descend upon the people of Sodom and Gomorrah, brimstone and fire from the Lord from heaven."[308]

What this rabbi saw came from his personal study of the Scriptures and not from the Oral Torah rabbis in vain try to uphold. It is the prayer of this author that rabbis and Jewish people would open the pages of the *Tanakh* and find within its pages the Word of Life.

YHVH # 1 and YHVH # 2 ... Zechariah 2:8-9

In this passage one *Yahweh* will be sent to Israel, and Israel will recognize that He was sent by another *Yahweh*. Bob Morris, a Jewish believer in Messiah, says *Yahweh* is presented as two distinct *Yahwehs*, one sending the other:

> In verse 12 of the *Tanakh* (verse 8 in English), *YHVH* #1 is the speaker. He speaks about the value of Israel using the word picture of the pupil of the eye. Israel is personal and valuable and protected by God as the eye of a man is personal, valuable and protected by him. He is extremely personal here using the term "My eye." Then in verse 9, *YHVH* #1 says that He is being sent to

---

[307] Fruchtenbaum, *Messianic Christology*, 105.

[308] Rabbi Tzvi Nassi, *The Great Mystery: or How Can Three Be One?* (Jerusalem: Yanetz, 1970), 31.

accomplish a task by *YHVH* #2. One *YHVH* is sending another *YHVH* to perform a task.[309]

Walter Kaiser, also referring to this passage of Scripture, sees the same thing as Morris noted above: "Mystery of mysteries, *Yahweh* is Lord, yet He was also sent."[310]

YHVH will deliver by another YHVH ... Hosea 1:1-7

In Hosea 1:1-7 not only are there two *Yahwehs*,[311] but an additional factor is added in verse 7. *Yahweh*, who spoke in verses 2, 4, and 6, will deliver Israel by sending another *Yahweh* who is Israel's *Elohim*. This passage is even more interesting because of that additional factor.[312] Not only are there two *Yahwehs*, but the second *Yahweh* that is being sent is their *Elohim*, plural God.

Yahweh the King and His Redeemer ... Isaiah 44:6

In this passage of Isaiah there is another reference to two distinct *Yahwehs*. One called Himself "*Yahweh* the King of Israel," and then referred to a second as "His Redeemer, the *Yahweh* of hosts." It can be clearly seen in this verse that there are two distinct *Yahwehs*. God throughout the *Tanakh* shows His plurality, but it is especially seen in the book of Isaiah.

What is clearly seen in Isaiah 44:6 is that *Yahweh* speaks of Himself and then of another *Yahweh*, but at the end of the verse He states: "*and beside me there is no God*" (KJV) or *Elohim*. *Yahweh* refers to two *Yahwehs* and then states there is no other *Elohim*. *Yahweh* emphasizes His oneness and unity, and *Elohim* emphasizes His plurality in unity. There is one additional point concerning the Angel of *Yahweh*, which also shows His plurality, but this will be developed under the topic of theophanies in chapters 4 through 8. Those chapters will be dedicated to showing God's plurality through two kinds of theophanies, the Angel of *Yahweh* and the *Shechinah* glory of God.

This complex nature of God is assumed in the Scripture, rather than explained. That is why a portion like the following one in Genesis can only make sense in light of this assumption.[313] Sam Nadler, a Jewish believer in Messiah, gives logical and biblical reasons for all of these passages in the Hebrew Scriptures that express plurality and tri-unity in the unity or oneness of God:

---

[309] Morris, *Anti-Missionary Arguments - The Trinity*, 6.

[310] Walter C. Kaiser, Jr. *The Communicator's Commentary: Micah - Malachi* (21 vols. Waco, Tex: Word, 1992), 21:315.

[311] Grudem, *Systematic Theology*, 228.

[312] Cooper, *The God of Israel*, 27.

[313] Sam Nadler, *The Messianic Answer Book*, (Charlotte, NC: Word of Messiah Ministries, 2005), 50.

In light of the many polytheistic religions surrounding Israel at that time, the Tanakh emphasized the oneness of God, while remaining faithful to the subtle teaching of His complex and triune nature. The tri-unity is not a contradiction of the oneness of God, but the best explanation of His oneness. (1) The tri-unity of God best explains the *Tanakh*'s grammatical use of plural nouns and pronouns in identifying God, (Gen. 1:26; Isa. 6:8, Eccl. 12:1). (2) The tri-unity best explains the various manifested appearances of God, (Gen. 19:24). (3) The tri-unity best explains the use of Echad for 'one' instead of other words for God, (Gen. 2:24). (4) The tri-unity best explains the enigmatic and paradoxical divine nature of God (Isa. 48:16). (5) The tri-unity best explains the Jewish mystical view of God: Kabbalah.

a. Shimon Ben Yohai (2nd century): "Come and see the mystery of the word Elohim: that there are three degrees, and each degree is by itself alone, and yet they are all one, and joined together in one, and are not divided from each other."

b. Zohar (the 10-11th century book on Jewish mysticism; on Deuteronomy 6:4): " 'Hear, O Israel: Jehovah our God, Jehovah is one.' Why is there need of mentioning the name of God three times in this verse? ... The first Jehovah is the Father above. The second is the stem of Jesse, the Messiah who is to come from the family of Jesse through David. And the third one is the Way which is below (meaning the Holy Spirit who shows us the way) and these three are one."

(6) The tri-unity best explains our own "triune nature" and response to God as alluded to in Deuteronomy 6:5 – "You shall love the LORD your God with all your heart and with all your soul and with all your might."[314]

The names of God, whether *Elohim*, *El*, *Elah*, *Eloah*, *Yahweh*, or *Adonai,* are best reflected in the plural unity of a triune God who speaks as one (echad) God, yet has revealed Himself as plurality in unity.

Finally, in Scripture, *Yahweh*, though singular, is also seen as a plurality, but in that plurality He is never combined with a female counterpart, such as *Asherah* (1 Kings 15:13; 2 Kings 17:10; 2 Chronicles 19:3; Micah 5:14), a female counterpart of *Baal*, the pagan gods of Canaan. One author says:

The fact that *Yahweh* never had a female counterpart is of great fundamental value. The Hebrew language does not even have a native word for goddess![315]

---

[314] Nadler, *The Messianic Answer Book,* 52-53.
[315] Th. C. Vriezen, *An Outline of Old Testament Theology* (Newton, Mass: Charles T. Branford Company, 1970), 327.

Yahweh expresses God's oneness and plural unity as well as two equal beings called *Yahweh*. Even the plural unity of *Yahweh* is evident as it is clearly presented from the above mentioned Scriptures.

SUMMARY

This chapter examined the names of God (*El*, *Elah*, *Eloah*, *Elohim*, Lord and LORD), and concluded that God used both singular and plural names for Himself. God also used singular verbs and plural adjectives with the plural noun *Elohim* to draw attention to Himself as the monotheistic God who in essence is a plural unity. Particular attention was given to *Elohim* and *Yahweh* (LORD), which shows that God did reveal Himself as a plurality in unity.

One final comment in relation to rabbinic explanation of the plural usage of *Elohim* in the *Tanakh*. They try to pass off the word as a pagan Canaanite and Phoenician word retained by the Israelites for God. The purpose is to reduce the significance of the word *Elohim* to a Jewish reader:

> Why is the plural Elohim used for the one God? Hebrew was spoken by the polytheistic pagans before Israelite monotheism. The plural form for a god was common in Canaan and Phoenicia.... The Israelites retained the pagan term for God, while adding the name YHVH to make God exclusive. The plural form, Elohim, is termed by grammarians, *pluralis majestatis*, "majestic plural," or *pluralis amplitudinus*, "quantitative plural," suggesting infinite fullness.... To suggest that it implies a plural God betrays ignorance of the Hebrew idiom. No reputable Hebrew scholar would concur with the Trinitarian argument based on the grammar of Gen. 1:1.[316]

If the Israelites retained or borrowed a Canaanite word for God, it was not Israel's choice, but the sovereign will of *Yahweh* to retain a word that when used in the context of the monotheistic God of Israel it would be used to help show Israel His identity, both His oneness as well as His plurality in unity. *HaShem* is the author of His own word which is settled in heaven (Psalm 119:89). He used Moses and the prophets, while they expressed their own language style and gifts, to record exactly what *HaShem* wished for them to record without error. The subject of "plural of majesty" has been clearly shown to be an invention of liberal Christian scholars (Higher Criticism) who already reject the Hebrew Scriptures as God's infallible word, which falls right in line with Rabbinic Judaism.

It is regrettable that some conservative evangelicals and fundamentalist authors have bowed the knee in this instance to higher criticism and to faithless hermeneutics in relation to "plural of majesty," and siding instead against the divine authority of God on

---

[316] Chaim Picker, "Make Us A God!" *A Jewish Response to Hebrew Christianity: A Survival Manual For Jews*, 22.

the issue of singular verbs with the plural noun *elohim* representing the plurality in unity of the Godhead.

As to the argument that no Hebrew scholar would see a "Trinitarian" concept of God, let them be reminded that there have been many Jewish scholars who recognize Messiah as their personal Saviour from sin, and embraced the view of the plural unity of God. These are men such as Arnold Fruchtenbaum, Louis Goldberg, Charles Feinberg, Michael Rydelnik, David Baron, Alfred Edersheim, Steve Herzig, David Levy, Rachmiel Frydland, Ernest Hengstenberg, Jacob Jocz, Arthur Kac, Stan and Marvin Rosenthal, Jacob Gartenhaus, Mitch Glaser, Mark Robinson, Moshe Rosen, Sam Nadler and Michael Brown to name only a few.

In reading through this book keep in the center of your thinking the discussion laid out in chapter 2 on the image of God as well as this discussion on the names of God. Keep in mind throughout this book the interaction between the persons of the Godhead as they act within the plural unity of *Elohim*, whose name is *Yahweh*, Who is one (*echad*) as they act individually. This author knows that this is a complex issue for New Covenant believers to comprehend as well as Jewish people who only see God in terms of *yachid* (chapter 9).

Chapter 4
Theophanies

Chapter 4 affirms the plurality of *Elohim* by validating that theophanies show the unity and plurality of *Yahweh*. This chapter affirms two points: first, theophanies were the appearances of God; second, many of these references show a distinction between the Theophany Himself and God.[317] A theophany is the appearance of God in three manifestations: a human form, an audible voice, or both, and by the appearance of His glory, better known as the *Shechinah*. Theophany is not a biblical term.[318] It is a theological term used to refer to the visible or auditory manifestations of God.[319] In other words, a theophany is a manifestation of God to the physical senses.[320] God becomes visible so that man can actually interact with Him. It should also be noted that theophanies are completely different from visions and dreams. God did use visions and dreams to communicate His will to man, but they were not visible, auditory appearances of God, as He clearly states in Numbers 12:6-8. The word theophany (Θεοφάνεια) is derived from two Greek terms, θεόσ (*theos*) meaning God and φαίνω (*phaino*) a verb in the passive, meaning "to appear or to be revealed (shine, give light)."[321] Hence, the appearance of "*the captain of the host of the LORD*" before Joshua, the audible voice of God heard by Abraham (Genesis 22) or the glory (*Shechinah*) of God that appeared before all Israel on Mount Sinai were theophanies of God. However, the brief appearances to Abraham, Joshua and Gideon were very different from the abiding presence in the *Shechinah* that appeared before all of Israel. For this reason the physical and auditory theophanies and the *Shechinah* appearances will be divided and dealt with separately.[322]

God always took the initiative. He never revealed Himself completely, only in a temporary way. There was only one permanent manifestation of God, and that was the incarnation of Messiah when He dwelt on the earth for approximately 36 years.[323] Borland expresses this but also adds considerable material by giving eight basic facts

---

[317] James Borland, *Christ in the Old Testament* (Ross-shire, Great Britain: Christian Focus Publications, 1999), 13.

[318] Merrill C. Tenney, *The Zondervan Pictorial Encyclopedia of the Bible*, (Grand Rapids: Zondervan, 1975), 5:388.

[319] Elwell, *Evangelical Dictionary of Theology*, 1087.

[320] Enns, *The Moody Handbook of Theology,* 258.

[321] Geoffrey W. Bromiley, *The International Standard Bible Encyclopedia*, (Grand Rapids: Eerdmans, 1988), 4:827.

[322] Borland, *Christ in the Old Testament,* 15.

[323] Elwell, *Evangelical Dictionary of Theology,* 1087.

that need to be understood concerning physical and/or auditory appearances. They are as follows: first (1), theophanies were actual appearances and not imaginary; second (2) they were initiated by God; third (3) they were revelatory, meaning that God's primary purpose was to reveal, at least in a partial manner, something about Himself, or His will, to the recipient; fourth (4) they were for individuals; fifth (5) they were intermittent in appearance; sixth (6) they were also temporary; seventh (7) they were audible and visible, and last (8) they did vary in form.[324]

These theophanies will be dealt with in four chapters: the pre-Sinai appearances in chapter 5, the Sinai and wilderness appearances in chapter 6; the *Shechinah* appearances in chapter 7, and the post-Sinai-wilderness appearances in chapter 8.

In Exodus 24:9-11 there was a unique appearance of *Yahweh* before Moses, Aaron and his two sons, as well as the 70 elders of Israel. At that point, 74 men literally "saw" the God of Israel in a human form. Morey points out that not only did they see the God of Israel (verse 10), but they also stared at God (verse 11). Morey makes the following observations:

> That the men saw God in human form is clear from the fact that, in verse 10, the form had "[his] feet" (Heb. רַגְלָיו and Gk. πόδας) and God was "standing before them as opposed to "sitting" on the throne before them (cf. Isa 6:1)."

> It is impossible to escape the fact that the appearance which they saw had feet. And, if God had feet, then He had legs. And if He had legs, then He had a torso, etc.

> This passage cannot be dismissed on the basis that it was a dream. What happened to these seventy-four men was not a dream because, (1) the men were not asleep and, (2) dreams are never group events. Throughout the Bible, only individuals had dreams (Gen 20:3; 31:10; 37:5; Judg 7:13; Dan 2:3).

> Neither can we dismiss this passage as a vision. The Biblical authors had no problem identifying when visions took place (Gen 15:1; Num 12:6; Ezek 1:1).[325]

What the 74 men saw and stared at was God standing before them identified both as the God of Israel and *Yahweh*. What they saw was a theophany of God.

Theophanies are important and their significance must be understood. First of all, Jewish rabbis reject the concept that God, a spirit being, who is holy and far above His creation, would ever take on the appearance of a man. Second, in the appearances of *"the angel of the LORD,"* He is presented as being equal with God and yet distinct from God. However, Jewish rabbis would reject this as well. But if it is true that *"the angel of the LORD"* and God are equal, then who is *"the angel of the LORD"* and does the

---

[324] Borland, *Christ in the Old Testament,* 21-30.
[325] Morey, *The Trinity: Evidence and Issues,* 123.

Tanakh then present God as being in the plural or what true believers call the tri-unity? It is noteworthy and of great interest that ancient Jewish leaders did see "*the angel of the LORD*" as unique but came short of calling Him God. What they did recognize was that this angel was no ordinary angel for He was the only mediator between God and man; He was the author of all revelations, the Word of God, or the *Memra*. They gave Him the name *Metatron*.[326]

THEOPHANY – THE ANGEL OF *YAHWEH*

Theophanies, in the Hebrew Scriptures, did appear to men in one of four forms so that God could magnify and authenticate His revelation of Himself to His servants.[327] The term is used to indicate how God appeared in these four different forms for four basic purposes.

1. He appeared in human form to Abraham (Genesis 18) and to Joshua (Joshua 5).
2. He appeared in a non-human form to Moses in Exodus 3.
3. He appeared as an angel in Exodus 23:20-23 [which could be any one of the other three].
4. He spoke audibly in Genesis 3:8; 22:1-2; 1 Kings 19:12.

Theophanies had four basic purposes:

1. God appeared to initiate/ratify a covenant with Abraham (Genesis 15) and later with Moses and the Israelite nation at large (Exodus).
2. God appeared to instruct, or correct, His covenant partner, Israel (Joshua 5:13-15; 1 Kings 18:20-40).
3. God appeared to commission or encourage His prophets (Isaiah 6; Ezekiel 1; 1 Kings 18:9-18).
4. God appeared to the nation to bring covenantal judgment on his rebellious subjects (Leviticus 9:23-10:2; Numbers 11:1-2; 12:2).[328]

Theophanies are viewed by New Covenant believers differently than by Jewish people. What is quite clear, according to Morey, is that:

As a man, God walked, talked, ate and fellowshipped with other men. During these times God could be seen by the human eye, touched by the human hand, and heard by the human ear. God was literally manifested in the flesh and dwelt

---

[326] A. C. Gaebelein, *The Angels of God* (Grand Rapids, MI: Baker Book House, 1969), 20.
[327] Tenney, *Zondervan Pictorial Encyclopedia of the Bible,* 5:720.
[328] Alexander and Baker, *Dictionary of the Old Testament Pentateuch*, 860.

among us. The Invisible became Visible and the Immaterial became Material without ceasing, at any time, to be true deity.[329]

Sometimes true biblical believers look only at the passages that deal only with the Angel of *Yahweh*. For example, Chafer seems to focus on a narrow view of theophany:

> Theophany usually is limited to appearances of God in the form of man or angels, other phenomena such as *shekinah* glory not being considered a theophany.[330]

Chafer is unclear and leaves the wrong impression when he speaks of God's appearances in the form of angels. A theophany was the appearance of God as one particular angel (the Angel [Messenger] of the LORD), not angels plural. Also the Scriptures indicate a broader view than does Chafer, as is mentioned in the first grouping in the above four categories. For the purpose of this study theophanies will be divided into two groupings: the Angel of the LORD, who speaks audibly and/or appears in human form, and the appearance of the glory (*Shechinah*) of God where He appears in His glory, with fire, cloud and smoke, as on Mount Sinai or as in the dedication of the Solomonic temple. It will be shown that all of these appearances are the same person who is equal to and yet distinct from God the Father.

There was a common thought throughout the *Tanakh* that if you saw God you would die, for it was written "*you cannot see My face, for man may not see Me and live*" (Exodus 33:20). Yet consistently individuals and one group of 74 men saw God. How can it be explained? One writer has expressed it well in the following statement:

> If it is written that "no man can see God and live," why were choice individuals privileged to see God and remain alive? The explanation is simple. God, in His essence, cannot be seen by any human being; however, these human beings who did see God saw not the very essence of God but only the veil with which God covered Himself.

> God used various veils according to the necessity and situation. Look at the Bible panorama of the various veils which God used. To Adam, the first man, it was "the Voice;" to Job, it was the "Whirlwind." To our patriarch Abraham it was "One of three men;" to Jacob it was "a Man." To Moses our teacher it was "the Burning Bush;" to the generation of the wilderness days, it was "a Pillar of Cloud and a Pillar of Fire." To the High Priest it was the "Shekinah;" to Daniel it was "the Ancient of Days."[331]

---

[329] Morey, *The Trinity: Evidence and Issues,* 106.

[330] Chafer, *Chafer Systematic Theology,* 5:31.

[331] M. Gitlin, "The Divine Veil," *Message to Israel* (Vol. LXV – May-August, 2000) Brooklyn: Immanuel Ministries Int'l.

The Angel of Yahweh

Numerous times in the Hebrew Scriptures *Yahweh* is associated with, yet is distinguished from, the Angel of *Yahweh* (LORD – *YHVH*). A careful study of the Hebrew Scriptures clearly shows that God or the LORD, and "*the angel of the LORD*" are two different persons and that they differentiate Themselves from each other, as Reymond expresses:

> A careful analysis of the relevant passages will disclose that God differentiates himself from this Angel by the very title itself as by the fact that he refers to him in the third person and may even address him in the second person in 2 Sam 24:16, and yet the Angel in his speeches, while also often distinguishing himself from God, lays claim to divine attributes and prerogatives, indeed, to identify with God.[332]

These distinctions between the Angel of *Yahweh* and the LORD are examined in this chapter as well as in chapters 5 through 8, but before these distinctions are viewed, another matter in the *Tanakh* needs to be cleared up.

Authors like Payne are more precise with the usage of the term *malakh Yahwe* or "*the angel of the LORD*." Payne freely admits that "*the angel of the LORD*" is more than just an angel and can only be a person of the unity of *Elohim*:

> The Hebrew noun *malakh* means "messenger" or "angel," from which comes the phrase *malakh Yahwe*, "the angel of Yahweh." *Malakh Yahwe* may refer to any of God's angels (1Kings 19:7; cf. v. 5). But at certain points, though the Angel of Yahweh may seem initially to be no more than any other angel (as Judges 6:11), He soon transcends the angelic category and is described in terms that are suitable only to a distinct Person of the Godhead (Judg 6:12, 14).[333]

Payne is correct; what will be demonstrated throughout these chapters is that the term "*the angel of the LORD*" is used consistently throughout the biblical text as a person distinct from God and yet God Himself. Yes, there are passages such as 1 Kings 19:7 that do not give enough descriptive information to say with complete dogmatism to the divine character of "*the angel of the LORD*." However, because it is used by Moses in his writings concerning Hagar, Abraham, Isaac, Jacob, Moses, Aaron, Elders of Israel, the nation of Israel, Joshua, Gideon, Manoah and so on through the pages of the *Tanakh*, this Angel is always a member of the plural unity of *Elohim*. The name by itself refers to one particular messenger, and many times that Angel is unquestionably a divine being who is God Almighty. The fact that "*the angel of the LORD*" and *Yahweh* are the same and also distinct is seen throughout the *Tanakh*; whether the theophany is "*the angel of the LORD*" or the *Shechinah* of God, He is distinctly God.

---

[332] Robert L. Reymond, *Jesus: Divine Messiah* (Ross-shire, Scotland: Mentor Imprint, 2003), 72.

[333] J. Barton Payne, *The Theology of the Older Testament,* 167.

103

Understanding the appearances of *"the angel of the LORD"* in these four chapters requires that the term "angel" be clarified. Clarification is due to the unbiblical imagery that has been attached to the term "angel" from the Middle Ages to the present time. Today when people think of angels, they visualize created beings with wings, wearing halos, who happen to be both male and female sitting on clouds playing harps. These mental pictures are not biblical and give an incorrect picture of angels, and in particular, of *"the angel of the LORD."*

The word מַלְאָךְ in the Hebrew when translated correctly, is "messenger" and not "angel." Anyone who took a message to someone else and delivered that message was called an מַלְאָךְ or messenger. The term messenger would include a human messenger, such as a prophet who delivered a message from God, or a government representative, or an ambassador for an earthly king. This also would include a heavenly messenger (angel), sent by God to bear messages to His earthly servants. There are both human and heavenly messengers, but each is distinct from each other. Man is man, and heavenly spirits (angels) are not human beings. Angel or messenger is used hundreds of times in the Hebrew Scriptures and is understood to mean "messenger." There is nothing mystical or magical about the word.[334]

How did the Hebrew word "messenger" become "angel" in our Bibles today, or how is it that translators chose to use the word "angel" rather than "messenger?" Morey gives a brief history or evolution of the word:

> If the word מַלְאָךְ simply meant "messenger," then where did we get the word "angel?" The mistake was made during the Middle Ages. The Greek word ἄγγελος was used in the Septuagint (LXX) for מַלְאָךְ because it also meant messenger. It was a real and proper translation from Hebrew to Greek.

> This is in contrast to the Latin Bible where the Greek word ἄγγελος is merely transliterated into Latin and becomes *angelus*. Thus, instead of translating the word ἄγγελος as "messenger," the Latin Bible transliterated the Greek word ἄγγελος into the Latin word *angelus*.

> This error was further compounded when the Latin Bible was translated into English. Instead of translating the Latin word *angelus* as "messengers," it was transliterated into the English word "angel." They did not translate it most of the time, but simply retained the Latin transliteration.[335]

Morey continues by referencing Matthew 11:10 where the Greek word ἄγγελος is translated "messenger" and not "angel." This meant that the English translators knew the difference but most of the time chose to transliterate instead of translate the Hebrew (מַלְאָךְ) and Greek (ἄγγελος) words.[336] In order to be consistent with the Scriptures

---

[334] Morey, *The Trinity: Evidence and Issues,* 138.
[335] Morey, *The Trinity: Evidence and Issues,* 139.
[336] Morey, *The Trinity: Evidence and Issues,* 139.

throughout the rest of this book, the term "messenger" will be used instead of "angel" unless it is part of a quotation.

This study on "*the angel of the LORD*" is important, for it confirms the pre-existence of Messiah. It is the teaching of both testaments, but in particular the teaching from the *Tanakh*, which shows with unmistakable clarity that this One is God and yet He is distinct from God. There are three lines of evidence that substantiate this claim. First, Messiah as "*the angel of the LORD*" is identified as *Yahweh* in numerous *Tanakh* passages. Second, "*the angel of the LORD*" is also revealed to be a distinct Person from *Yahweh*, who is a Person of the plural unity of *Elohim*. Last, "*the angel of the LORD*" is the second Person of the plural unity. It is imperative to demonstrate that the Messenger (Angel) of the LORD is the Second Person of the plural unity of *Elohim*. In fact, if that cannot be demonstrated as the solution, the whole picture becomes blurred and confusing as to the possibilities of the plural unity of *Elohim*. The question to be asked is whether a Person in the unity of *Elohim* can be God and at the same time be addressed as God. The answer lies in the personal distinctions of the plural unity of *Elohim* as addressed by John Walvoord who shows that there are at least four lines of evidence which identify the Messenger (Angel) of the LORD as the second Person of the plural unity of *Elohim* in the following comments:

1. The second Person is the visible God of the New Testament. Neither the Father nor the Spirit is characteristically revealed in a bodily and visible form. While the Father's voice is heard from heaven, and the Holy Spirit is seen descending in the form of a dove, but only in the New Covenant, Messiah the second Person, is the full manifestation of God in visible form.

2. Confirming this induction is the fact that the Angel of the LORD of the Hebrew Scriptures no longer appears after the incarnation.

3. The similarity of function between the Angel of the LORD and Messiah can be observed in the fact that Both are sent by the Father. In the Old Testament, the Angel of the LORD is sent by Yahweh to reveal truth, to lead Israel and to defend and judge them. In the New Covenant, Messiah is sent by God the Father to reveal God in the flesh, to reveal truth and to become the Saviour. It is characteristic for the Father to send and the Son to be the sent One (Isa 48:16; Zech 2:8-9; also see the Gospel of John in the New Covenant where *Yeshua* states 43 times that He is sent by the Father[337]). These facts again point to the identification of the Angel of the LORD with Messiah.

4. By process of elimination, it can be demonstrated that the Angel of the LORD could not be either the first Person or the third Person. As the Angel

---

[337] Gospel of John records the words of *Yeshua* who stated 44 times that He was sent by the Father: John 3:17, 34; 4:34; 5:23-24, 30, 36-38; 6:29, 38-40, 44, 57; 7:16, 18, 28-29, 33; 8:16, 18, 26, 29, 42; 9:4; 10:36; 11:42; 12:44-45, 49; 13:16, 20; 14:24; 15:21; 16:5; 17:3, 8, 18, 21, 23, 25; 20:21. This extra footnote was added by the author.

of the LORD is the sent One, He could not be the Father for the Father is the Sender. As the Angel of the LORD characteristically appears in bodily, usually human form, He could not be the Holy Spirit who does not appear bodily in the *Tanakh*. It may, therefore, be concluded that the Angel of the LORD is the second Person of the Triune God.[338]

These four points are straightforward and do show how the Person of the Messenger (Angel) of the LORD can only be the second Person of the plural unity of *Elohim*.

There are two interesting observations made on the identity of the Messenger (Angel) of the LORD: One comes from a Jewish perspective and the other from some Christian perspectives. Neither example recognizes *"the angel of the LORD"* as deity; however, in reading the quote below it is surprising that the Jewish rabbis do not:

It is noteworthy and of great interest that the ancient Jews in their traditions regarded the Angel of the Lord, in every instance, not as an ordinary angel, but as the only mediator between God and the world, the author of all revelations, to whom they gave the name *Metatron*. They called him "the angel of the countenance" (Isa 63:9), because he always sees and beholds God's countenance, and they speak of him as the highest revelation of the unseen God, a partaker of His nature and of His majesty. They speak of him as the Shechinah. A Talmudic statement declares "the *Metatron*, the Angel of the Lord, is united with the most high God by oneness of nature," while another source speaks of him as "having dominion over all created things." The very ancient Midrash known as *Otiot de Rabbi Akiba* makes the following declaration about the Angel of the Lord, "The *Metatron* is the angel, the prince of the face, the prince of the law, the prince of wisdom, the prince of strength, the prince of glory, the prince of the temple, the prince of the kings, the prince of the rulers and of the high and exalted." These ancient Jewish sources identify, therefore, the Angel of the Lord, whom they call Metatron, with the Messiah and as one with God. This was also the view of later Jews. Malachi 3:1 sanctions such an interpretation, the angel of the covenant is Jehovah, and the Messiah is the Angel of the Lord.[339]

This is a very interesting observation (see page 113 in this chapter) on *Metatron* made by early Jewish religious leaders concerning the person of *"the angel of the LORD."* Below Youngblood's comment is on the Messenger (Angel) of the LORD as not being God, based on his view of Hebrews 1 where Youngblood asks:

"Who was the angel of the Lord? Many answers have been given to this question. In Genesis 16:13 he seems to be equated with the Lord himself. Thus some students of Scripture have taught that the angel of the Lord was really Jesus Christ in a pre-incarnation form. I would observe, however, that in

---

[338] John Walvoord, *Jesus Christ Our Lord* (Chicago: Moody, 1969), 45-46.

[339] Arno Clemens Gaebelein, *The Angels of God* (Grand Rapids: Baker, 1969), 20.

Hebrews 1 the author goes to great lengths to point out that Jesus is far superior to all of God's angels. Also, if the angel of the Lord were Jesus, the uniqueness of the incarnation would be severely weakened.[340]

Even though *Yeshua*, a member of the plural unity of *Elohim*, is far superior to all of His created messengers (angels) who are *Elohim*'s servants and messengers, it destroys nothing if one member of the plural unity of *Elohim* becomes the Messenger for *Elohim* Himself. That does not make Him a created being and it does nothing to severely weaken the uniqueness of the incarnation! There is obviously a mix-up of understanding between what a "messenger" is and the fictitious term "angel." "Angels" are not fictitious, so a better name for them could be "heavenly messengers." An appearance of the Messenger (Angel) of the LORD is not an incarnation, but a temporary appearance of a member of the plural unity of *Elohim* for a very short duration of time, as a theophany. Next Youngblood's statement speaks inconsistently and shows an inadequate understanding of the Person, the Messenger (Angel) of the LORD:

> Since the Hebrew word for "angel" also means "messenger," it is perhaps best to explain the angel of the Lord as a special messenger from the court of heaven who bears the credentials of the King of heaven and can therefore speak on his behalf. This was the case with other messengers in ancient times. They had the right and the authority to speak on behalf of the one who had sent them. On some occasions such a messenger would use the first-person pronoun, as though he were in fact the sender himself. At other times he used the third-person pronoun in reference to the sender (Judges 6:12 with 6:16). In either case he symbolized the presence of the king who had given him his mission.[341]

Yes, the Messenger of the LORD is a special Messenger, but not from the courts of heaven, for He is not a created being. He is personally from the very throne of God Himself. To illustrate, a king is a man, and a messenger is a man. The difference between the two is not that they are not men, but as men they have differing responsibilities. Likewise, God is God. God being a plurality can send a messenger through another member of the plural unity of *Elohim*. What is their difference? They are still both God, but voluntarily the members of the plurality of *Elohim* have chosen different responsibilities as they relate to mankind. Some scholars make the issue of the Messenger of the LORD more difficult than it has to be.

It seems strange that Youngblood states that he clearly sees the tri-unity in the creation account in Genesis 1:1 and 26 but does not see it here in Genesis 16:13. But instead he reverts to Hebrews 1 in an effort to prove his point. There is a misunderstanding by Youngblood, who confuses the Messenger of the LORD with a

---

[340] Youngblood, *The Book of Genesis*, 166-67.

[341] Youngblood, *The Book of Genesis*, 166-67. Youngblood also supports his view from Oehler: Gustav Friedrich Oehler, *Theology of the Old Testament*, 129-134.

created messenger and servant of *Elohim*. Also, Youngblood does not give a convincing biblical reason when referencing Hebrews 1. Youngblood's argument is flawed because in his reference of Genesis 17:1 (and 15:7) he clearly stated that "the Lord again appeared to Abram in a covenant context, just as he had to Abram in 15:7."[342] However, Genesis 15:1 tells the reader that this was a vision. Genesis 12:7, 17:1 and 18:1 clearly state that the LORD appeared to Abram. If God cannot become a messenger and take on a human form, then Youngblood is not consistent when he states in 16:13 that it is not a Theophany of God, the second Person of the tri-unity. From this author's understanding, Youngblood is contradicting himself.

Some say that the Messenger (Angel) of the LORD speaks as *Yahweh* because he has been commissioned by God to perform a task in the name of God as a present-day ambassador might do. However, Watson and Leupold state very clearly that even ambassadors do not apply the title of the one they are representing to themselves, but the Messenger of the LORD does:

> The answer to this is, that though ambassadors speak in the name of their masters, they do not apply the names and titles of their masters to themselves. Created angels, mentioned in Scripture as appearing to men, declare that they were sent by God, and never [im]personate Him, that the prophets uniformly declare their commission to be from God, that God himself declares, "Jehovah is my name, and my glory will I not give to another," and yet that the appearing Angel calls himself, as we have seen by this incommunicable name in almost innumerable instances, and that though the object of the Mosaic dispensation was to preserve men from idolatry, yet this Angel claims and receives the exclusive worship both of the patriarchs to whom he occasionally appeared, and the Jews among whom he visibly resided for ages. It is therefore a proposition too monstrous to be for a moment sustained, that a created being of any kind should thus allure men into idolatry, by acting the Deity, assuming his name, and attributing to himself God's peculiar and incommunicable perfections and honour.[343]

Watson clearly presents the argument that ambassadors do not take on the name of the one sending them. Yet the Messenger (Angel) of the LORD clearly does, meaning that He is not a created Messenger (angel), but God Himself. If the Messenger of the LORD is not God Himself, then He is acting in complete rebellion against *Elohim* by accepting worship (Ezekiel 28:1-19). That would be completely repugnant to *Elohim*. Leupold continues the argument that *Elohim* would not allow such presumption on the part of a created messenger:

---

[342] Youngblood, *The Book of Genesis*, 168.

[343] Richard Watson, *Theological Institutes: Or, a View of the Evidences, Doctrines, Morals and Institutions of Christianity*, 1:488-489.

Attempts to dispose of all such arguments by the too simple explanation that an ambassador most readily makes a transition into the words of the one who commissioned him. Granting that such a thing might be done by ordinary human ambassadors – a thing of which we personally are still very doubtful – we feel that the Almighty stands too far above the creature, even an angel, to allow for such a piece of presumption on the part of His representatives.[344]

Youngblood raised the question: "Who was the angel of the LORD?" He then proceeded to show that the angel of the LORD could not be God, based on Hebrews 1. However, Leupold discusses the issue of the identity of the Messenger (Angel) of the LORD by saying that Genesis 16:13 fully establishes the identity of the Messenger (Angel) of the LORD, and then gives five clear points to substantiate that fact:

But the angel of the Lord (mal'akh Yahweh), who was He? We believe Hengstenberg and Keil demonstrate adequately both that He was divine and that He is to be regarded as a kind of pre-incarnation of the Messiah – using the term "preincarnation" as indeed open to criticism if pressed too close. For our passage His identity with Yahweh is fully established by v. 13 (Gen 16:13). For the present we offer Whitelaw's five arguments (condensed from Pulpit Commentary – Genesis for this position. The Angel of the Lord is not a created being but the Divine Being Himself; for (1) He explicitly identifies Himself with Yahweh on various occasions. (2) Those to whom He makes His presence known recognize Him as divine. (3) The Biblical writers call Him Yahweh. (4) The doctrine here implied of a plurality of persons in the Godhead is in complete accordance with earlier foreshadowing. (5) The organic unity of Scripture would be broken if it could be proved that the central point in the OT revelation was a created angel, while that of the New is the incarnation of the God-Man.[345]

Almost every passage that will be opened and studied on *"the angel of the Lord"* will continue to advance the teaching that He is God and yet distinct from God in each of the following four chapters.

Yahweh – *Distinct from the Messenger (Angel) of the LORD*

Yahweh is the personal God of Israel. However, when He communicated with Israel in person, He did so through the Messenger (Angel) of the LORD (*Yahweh*), also called the Messenger of God (*Elohim*). This will be clearly shown in the following four chapters. *Yahweh* and the Messenger of the LORD (*Yahweh*) spoke as God, even though both are distinct personalities (Genesis 32:24-30; Exodus 3:4-5; Joshua 5:14-15; Judges 2:1; 6:11-24; 13:2-24).[346]

---

[344] H. C. Leupold, *Exposition of Genesis* (Grand Rapids: Baker, 1942), 1:501.

[345] Leupold, *Exposition of Genesis,* 1:501.

[346] Buswell, *A Systematic Theology of the Christian Religion,* 122.

Hengstenberg meticulously demonstrates that *Yahweh* and the Messenger (Angel) of the LORD (*Yahweh*) are two distinct personalities.

> Sound Christian Theology has discovered the outlines of such a distinction betwixt the hidden and the revealed God, in many passages of the Old Testament, in which mention is made of the Angel or Messenger of God.[347]

> There is no substantial difference betwixt the passages in which Jehovah Himself is mentioned, and those in which the Angel of Jehovah is spoken of.[348]

Like Hengstenberg, Payne expresses the point that the Messenger (Angel) of the LORD (*Yahweh*) is distinct from God and yet is God.[349] He also maintains that in Exodus 14:9 and Numbers 20:16 the Messenger leads, while other passages say God leads.[350] In fact, Payne even lays out the possibility that there may be other appearances that have not yet been seen.

> It is indeed possible that when visible appearances of God occur elsewhere in the Scriptures the actual subject may again be the *Malakh Yahwe*,[351] even though the term itself may not be used.[352]

Notice in the above statement that Payne said it was possible that *Elohim* or *Yahweh* have revealed Themselves in other passages not yet known or understood at this point. It is his personal belief that the more the person and work of *Yeshua* is known in relationship to His activities in the *Tanakh*, the more passages will come to light. Payne sums up his argument about the Messenger (Angel) of the LORD (*Yahweh*) by saying that:

> Old Testament revelations of the unique angel of the Testament can be appreciated only when understood as pre-incarnate appearances of Jesus Christ the Second Person of the Trinity and the one Savior of mankind.[353]

Chafer argues for two distinct personalities since God, at times, spoke as the Messenger (Angel) of *Yahweh* and at other times as *Yahweh* Himself:

> The fact is that the Angel of Jehovah is at times One other than Jehovah, and at other times He is Jehovah Himself.[354]

---

[347] E. W. Hengstenberg, *Christology of the Old Testament* (Grand Rapids: Kregel, 1956), 1:116.

[348] Hengstenberg, *Christology of the Old Testament,* 1:119.

[349] Payne, *The Theology of the Older Testament,* 167-168.

[350] Payne, *The Theology of the Older Testament,* 168.

[351] The Hebrew noun *malakh* means "messenger" or "angel."

[352] Payne, The *Theology of the Older Testament,* 168.

[353] Payne, *The Theology of the Older Testament,* 170.

[354] Chafer, *Chafer's Systematic Theology,* 1:299.

Clearly, the Messenger (Angel) of the LORD (*Yahweh*) is recognized as the Second Person of the plural unity of *Elohim*. He is distinct from the Father and yet one in unity with Him. Two distinctive Hebrew terms, the Messenger (Angel) of the LORD (*Yahweh*) and *Elohim*, give strong evidence or support that the plurality, or tri-unity of *Elohim*, is indeed in the Hebrew Scriptures. In other words, the Messenger (Angel) of the LORD (*Yahweh*) was clearly God Himself.[355]

Throughout the *Tanakh*, both *Yahweh* and the Messenger (Angel) of *Yahweh* are in the singular form for God. The Messenger (Angel) of *Yahweh* and *Yahweh* both, without question, teach the oneness of God because they are always in the singular form. What must be identified is that the Messenger (Angel) of *Yahweh*, who is distinct from *Yahweh*, spoke as *Yahweh*. This is an inescapable fact when these passages are studied. These facts also show plurality within *Yahweh*, because the Messenger (Angel) of *Yahweh* is distinct from *Yahweh*. The Messenger (Angel) of *Yahweh* and *Yahweh* relate to Israel as a monotheist God. Yet in the revelation of Themselves, they did sometimes reveal Themselves in a compound or complex unity as the *Shema* in Deuteronomy 6:4 confirms in chapter 9 of this book.

Usually the Messenger (Angel) of the LORD revealed Himself in giving instructions to His people. However, there are other times when He was revealed as a judge, as reflected in the following quotation:

> The Angel of the LORD as the righteous Judge is revealed also in His judgment upon sin, as in the case of David's sin in numbering Israel (2 Sam 24:14-17; 1 Chron 21:11-30), and the slaying of 185,000 Assyrians (2 Kgs 19:35; Isa 37:36). The thoughtful care of the Angel of the LORD is shown in His treatment of Elijah (1 Kgs 19:5-7). He instructs Elijah in his controversy with Ahaziah and the judgment of the messengers (1 Kgs 1:1-16). He is also the revealer of secrets to Zechariah in his prophecy (Zech 1:9).[356]

So the Messenger (Angel) of the LORD also judged, but predominantly He was a provider to those in need. He guided His people in the path of God's will as well as protected His people from their enemies. He did in general execute the providence of God.[357] This is important for numerous reasons because it confirms the preexistence of Messiah and it shows that He was actively revealing to men the ministry of God in the *Tanakh*, as John Walvoord's statement unfolds:

> It is the teaching of Scripture that the Angel of the LORD is specifically the second person of the Tri-unity. At least three lines of evidence substantiate this claim:

---

[355] Merrill C. Tenney, *The Zondervan Pictorial Encyclopedia of the Bible,* 5:389.
[356] Walvoord, *Jesus Christ Our Lord*, 53.
[357] Walvoord, *Jesus Christ Our Lord*, 53.

1. Christ as the Angel of the LORD is identified as Yahweh in numerous Old Testament passages. When the Angel of the LORD spoke to Hagar (Gen 16:7-13), He was identified as Yahweh in v. 13. The account of the sacrifice of Isaac (Gen 22:15-18), affords the same identification. In some instances the expression "Angel of God" is used as a synonym for Yahweh. The Hebrew for God in these instances is Elohim. In either case the deity of the Angel is confirmed by many passages (Gen 31:11-13; 48:15-16; "angel of the LORD," "God" and "Yahweh" used interchangeably, "Yahweh," Exodus 13:21; "angel of God," Exodus 14:19; both "angel of the LORD," and "angel of God," Judges 6:11-23; both "angel of God" and "angel of Yahweh," Judges 13:9-20).

2. The Angel of the LORD is also revealed to be a distinct Person from Yahweh, that is, a Person of the Tri-unity. In Genesis 24:7 (ASV), for instance, Yahweh is described as sending "his angel." The servant of Abraham testifies to the reality of this in Genesis 24:40. Moses speaks of Yahweh sending an angel to lead Israel (Num 20:16). An instance which is clearly found in Zechariah 1:12-13, where the Angel of the LORD addressed Yahweh. Many other similar passages occur (Exodus 23:20; 11:10; 1 Chron 21:15-18; Isa 63:9).

3. The Angel of the LORD is the second Person of the unity of God. Having determined the deity of the Angel of the LORD and that He is a Person of the Tri-unity, it remains to demonstrate that He is the second Person. That is, in fact, the only solution of an otherwise confused picture. How can a Person be God and at the same time address God? The answer lies in the personal distinctions of the Triune God.[358]

All of this material clearly presents the Messenger (Angel) of the LORD as God, and yet He is distinct from God. He is the visible member of the plural unity of *Elohim*, commonly known as the Godhead, who communicated and interacted with individuals in biblical history. While Jewish rabbis reject this, they are faced with insurmountable evidence from the Hebrew Scriptures. However, most Jewish scholars spend their years in a "Talmudic school of higher education" know as a *Yeshiva*[359] and then as rabbis, studying the sages rather than *HaShem* whom they say they worship. But because of their premise that God is an absolute one, they miss the fact of Scripture that *Elohim* presented Himself as a plurality in unity. This is a challenge to them to study *HaShem* and His Word, which is what they committed themselves to obey in the first place (Exod 24:4-7), rather than the Oral Law which has no biblical justification. Their fathers who stood before Moses and *HaShem* committed themselves to every "word" that the LORD gave to Moses and that he "wrote" down. The Jewish people have been

---

[358] Walvoord, *Jesus Christ Our Lord*, 44-46.

[359] Dagobert D. Runes, *Concise Dictionary of Judaism* (New York: Philosophical Library, 1966), 122. There are traditional Jewish seminaries where Jewish men go to be trained for being a rabbi in a local synagogue.

known as the "People of the Book." That book was not the collection of the sages that was handed down, but the "written" Word of *HaShem*. One of the more fascinating things that this author has found, or observations that Jewish rabbis in the past have made concerning the Messenger (Angel) of the LORD, whom they named *Metatron*, will be reviewed next.

METATRON

Rabbinic Judaism states that *Metatron,* is a name given to one particular messenger (angel) who stands before the face of God. This name was given to this angel because he has many of the same characteristics of God Himself. The term *Metatron* is not a biblical word; it was a word given to a specific angel in rabbinic sources. Following are several quotations from Jewish literature that give some pertinent information concerning this tradition:

> The story in tractate Sanhedrin [38:b] also confers on Metatron a supernatural status. He is the angel of the Lord mentioned in Exodus 23:21 of whom it is said, "… and hearken to his voice; be not rebellious against him … for My name is in him."[360]

Metatron is equated with the Angel of the LORD in Exodus 23:21. But as the tractate Sanhedrin goes on, it is clear that *Metatron* is not to be worshipped and equated as being equal to God. As to where the term *Metatron* came from, Andrei Orlov will help supply that answer:

> The substantial part of 2 Enoch's narrative is dedicated to Enoch's ascent into the celestial realm and to his heavenly metamorphosis near the Throne of Glory. In these lengthy and elaborated descriptions of Enoch's transformation into a celestial being, on a level with the arch-angels, one may find the origin of another image of Enoch which was developed later in Merkabah mysticism, that is the image of the angel Metatron, The Prince of Presence.[361]

In other words when Enoch walked with God and was not because God took him (Gen 5:24), he was promoted into being an angel who the rabbis say was given a throne next to God, as referenced by Black:

> In the Metatron figure of Talmud, Targum Midrashim, and the writing of later Jewish mysticism, the conception of a mediator or intermediary between God and man reaches its most developed form in Judaism. According to one view of this peculiar deviation in Judaism, the patriarch Enoch, after his translation and a kind of heavenly transformation, was raised to the rank of the first of angels or 'prince of the Presence' (sar ha-pannim). He received the name Metatron,

[360] Isidore Singer, *The Jewish Encyclopedia* (New York: Funk and Wagnalls, 1904), 8:1443.
[361] Andrei A. Orlov, "Titles of Enoch-Metatron in 2 Enoch," *Journal for the Study of the Pseudepigrapha*, vol. 18 (1998), 74.

and occupied a throne next to the throne of glory, exercising both judicial and intercessory functions. Like the earlier Enoch, Enoch-Metatron was the heavenly scribe and the revealer of divine secrets, but with his quasi-apotheosis, Metatron assumed divine status. He is the angel of whom it is said in Exod 23:20, 'Take ye heed of him ... for my name is in him.' ... At any rate the idea that Metatron should become an object of worship is repudiated (Sanhedrin 1c).[362]

One important thing needs to be understood quickly and clearly. The book of Enoch is not the Word of God and should not be equated as such. There are numerous other rabbinic traditions concerning *Metatron*, but they are also merely traditions or legends and not fact. There are two other references in the Talmud to *Metatron* which will be mentioned next, first from the Babylonian Talmud in Chagigah 15a and Abodah Zarah 3b (10)[363] of which the first will be quoted:

> Aher mutilated the shoots. Of him Scripture says: Suffer not thy mouth to bring Thy flesh into guilt. What does it refer to? He saw that permission was granted to Metatron (4) to sit and write down the merits of Israel. Said he: It is taught as a tradition that on high there is no sitting and no emulation, and no back, and no weariness. Perhaps – God forfend [a verb meaning "to forbid"]! There are two divinities! [Thereupon] they led Metatron forth, and punished him with sixty fiery lashes, saying to him: Why didst thou not rise before him when thou didst see him? Permission was [then] given to him to strike out the merits of Aher.[364]

Nowhere in Scripture is there any such statement; this comes from the creative imagination of rabbinic teachers. In Sanhedrin 38b one final reference is made to *Metatron*:

> Once a Min [believer] said to R. Idith: It is written, And unto Moses He said, Come up to the Lord. But surely it should have stated, Come up to me! – It was Metatron [who said that], he replied, whose name is similar to that of his Master, for it is written, For my name is in him. But if so [he retorted,' we should worship him!

Metatron is unique in that He bears the Tetragrammaton; for Exodus 23:21 says, "*My name is in him.*"[365] Following are a few statements from Rabbinic Judaism concerning *Metatron*:

---

[362] M. Black, "The Origin of the Name Metatron," *Vetus Testamentum*, vol. 1 (1951), 217.

[363] Rabbi I. Epstein, *The Babylonian Talmud* (London: The Soncino Press, 1938), Abodah Zarah 3b (10). Foot note in Abodah Zarah: Metatron: Name of an angel, who is also called הַפָּנִי שַׂר Metatron is probably derived from Metator, meaning guide, precursor, he being regarded as the angel who went before the Israelites in the wilderness.

[364] Rabbi I. Epstein, *The Babylonian Talmud* , Hag 15a (93).

[365] Singer, *The Jewish Encyclopedia,* 8:519.

Metatron may derive from the Greek *metathronos*, the one enthroned with God, or from the Latin *metator*, the title of the officer who went ahead of the Roman army to prepare the camp, hence, more generally, a forerunner.... 3 Enoch designates him "the lesser YHWH," in contrast to God himself, "the greater YHWH," who withdraws from the world, leaving Metatron in charge.... He is sometimes identified with the archangel Michael (Israel's celestial representative). He also functions as the Prince of Torah, the Heavenly Scribe and the Heavenly High Priest, serving in the celestial tabernacle, the Tabernacle of Metatron.[366]

The Metatron of the Jew, the supreme revealer of the invisible God,...is the medium of all intercourse between the invisible God and the creation.... The Metatron is not infrequently identified with the Shechinah....For if the Messiah was to be divine according to the Old Testament system of religion, he must necessarily stand in the same relation to God in which the angel of the LORD is said to have stood.[367]

Notice that the information given above has absolutely no foundation in the Hebrew text; it is mere tradition and legend which has driven the people of God away from the Scriptures. Also, where in the Hebrew Scriptures does it say or even allude to the fact that God has withdrawn from His creation and put *Metatron* in charge? What the Hebrew Scriptures do clearly present is that *Elohim* is a plurality in a unity of one (echad), meaning that the Second Person of the plural unity of *Elohim* is the one interacting with Israel and His creation.

A close friend of this writer, who is a Jewish believer in Messiah, shared that he has heard very little on the subject of *Metatron* from the Jewish community. However, the following quotation from the Talmud, Sanhedrin 38b, speaks to the point that *Metatron* was an issue between the rabbis and early messianic believers in Messiah during the first few centuries of the Common Era as rabbis interacted concerning the identity of the messenger they have called *Metatron*:

אָמַר לֵיהּ Rav Idit said to the heretic: It was not God who said, "Come up to the Lord," but the Archangel Metatron, whose name is like that of his master, for he bears God's name, as the Torah states (Exod 23:20-21): "Behold, I send an angel before you...Take heed of him and obey his voice, provoke him not, for he will not pardon your transgressions; for My name is in him." Thus, it was Metatron who, speaking for God, said to Moses: "Come up to the Lord." אִי הָכִי The heretic said to him: If so, then Israel should serve Metatron, for he bears God's name and the Torah commands that they "take heed of him and obey his voice." כְּתִיב Rav Idit answered: The verse also states: "Provoke him not," אַל תַּמֵּר בּוֹ. While Metatron bears the name of God and must be listened to, he is only a messenger and is not to be taken as His substitute, nor

[366] Neusner and Green, *Dictionary of Judaism in the Biblical Period,* 427-428.
[367] Hengstenberg, *Christology of the Old Testament,* 4:288-292.

should he be regarded as the object of divine service. כָּ אִם The heretic then asked: If so, why does the verse state: "He, Metatron, will not pardon your transgressions?" If Metatron has the power to pardon transgressions, but will not do so, he is certainly a power worthy of worship. But if the verse teaches that he is unable to pardon transgressions, what good is he then to lead the people of Israel in the wilderness, when they are likely not to heed him? לֵיהּ אָמַר Rav Idit said to the heretic: Indeed, he has no power to pardon. And by the faith in our hands we refused to accept him even as a guide to lead us through the wilderness, as the verse states (Exod 33:15): "And Moses said to Him, If Your presence go not with me, carry us not up from here." We will not accept an angel in Your place.

NOTES: שֶׁשְּׁמוֹ כְּשֵׁם רַבּוֹ Whose name is like that of his master. The matter of Metatron can only be understood in the context of other Rabbinic teachings regarding related esoteric issues. The few allusions in the Talmud imply that this special Angel through whom God reveals Himself is also called by God's name (and so it would appear from various Biblical verses), for it is through that Angel that the divine glory becomes manifest. The rabbis stress in many places that this in no way implies a dual deity, for the Angel merely serves as God's messenger.[368]

Here in the Talmud is a reference to *Metatron* and comments of Rabbi Idit as he answers the questions of a heretic. The heretic most likely is a Jewish believer in *Yeshua*. Louis Goldberg, a Jewish believer in Messiah *Yeshua*, gives a good descriptive accounting of who *Metatron* is according to Rabbinic Judaism:

The name of the angel peculiar to the Talmud is that of Metatron or precursor; he was regarded as the angel who went before the Israelites in the wilderness and that he was held in high reverence for some have thought they ought to pray to him inasmuch as he stood so close to God (Sanhedrin 38b). He is the only one who sits in the presence of God (Hagigah 15a). There seems to be some hint, in the presentation of this being, of a mystery of this one's relation to God. The Talmud did not want to equate this angel with God, and yet this angel was considered to have many of His attributes; even God's Name is in him, and he was declared to be able to pardon transgression (Sanhedrin 38b). Did not the Talmudists recognize here in the passage of Exodus 23:20-25 a reference to the peculiar nature of the Godhead and that there could have been some multiplicity of persons of personality in the nature of God? At any rate, it would seem that there was here something of this presentation set forth in the Exodus passage.[369]

---

[368] Rabbi Adin Steinsaltz, *The Talmud: The Steinsaltz Edition* (21 Vols. Trans. Rabbi David Strauss. New York: Random House, 1998), San 38b, 17:88-89.

[369] Goldberg, *The Deviation of Jewish Thought from an Old Testament Theology in the Intertestamental Period,* 89-90.

One interesting feature of the Targumim and Talmud is the presentation of personalities known as Memra and Metatron, respectively. These terms express more than just the avoidance of the anthropomorphic expressions of God. In the contexts of the literature mentioned, there comes an almost hypostatic union with God, or in other words, expressions that almost speak of personalities within the complex nature of God. Yet, the literature stops short of actually ascribing deity to these expressions. It is to be noted also that the concept of wisdom in the Apocrypha also expressed a near hypostasis with God.[370]

The rabbis of old did see the uniqueness of this particular angel or messenger, but because of the pre-conceived belief in absolute monotheism they were, and are, unable to see the multi-persons in the plural unity of *Elohim*. Also within the *Tanakh "the angel* (Messenger) *of the LORD"* is never called an archangel. That is a rabbinic invention to categorize Him as different from who He is and to disconnect Him from the plural unity of the *echad* (one) *Elohim*. Therefore, the next section will be dedicated to help Jewish people and true believers come to an understanding of the uniqueness of this angel or messenger and just how he relates to *"the angel of the LORD"* with his distinctiveness and oneness with *Yahweh*.

Rather than seeing *"the angel* [Messenger] *of the LORD"* as the Second Person of the plural unity of *Elohim*, the rabbis have taken those references and in a fanciful manner have projected them to the translated Enoch. What is astonishing is that the rabbis have used great imagination to "create" in their minds this *Metatron* who has the very character of God and name of God into a created angel or exalted human being to avoid the testimony of the *Tanakh* itself concerning the identity of *"the angel* [Messenger] *of the LORD."* They bristle at biblical believers when they say that God became a man in the incarnation, yet within Rabbinic Judaism the rabbis have with great imagination taken a man (Enoch) and have bestowed upon him the very character and name of the Almighty God. In reading rabbinic materials on the *Metatron* and His identity it is amazing how much Scripture they have ignored or have used out of context, with great imagination, to build a teaching with no biblical foundation in attributing to a man, God like character.[371] They actually have done what they accused Christianity of; they have taken a man and made him a god. This is truly tradition, legend and myth, for most of this material goes back to the second temple period into the Common Era up into the Middle Ages which is from 2000 to 4000 years removed from Enoch. In reading rabbinic literature there is one thing which is glaringly absent; there are no *"thus saith the LORD"* statements, only rabbi so and so speaking in the

---

[370] Goldberg, *The Deviation of Jewish Thought from an Old Testament Theology in the Intertestamental Period,* 329-330.

[371] Andrei A. Orlov, *The Enoch-Metatron Tradition: Texts and Studies in Ancient Judaism 107* (Tubingen, Germany: Gulde-Druck, 2005), 86-147. Orlov references another author numerous times, Gershom G. Scholem, *Major Trends in Jewish Mysticism* (London: Thames and Hudson, 1954), 67-72

name of rabbi so and so. The reality is the rabbis speak with the mere authority of men and not as spokesmen for *HaShem*.

The Hebrew word for "angel" is מַלְאָךְ and actually means "messenger" as noted earlier in this chapter. This term "angel" never should have been used because of the confused image that it gives in the minds of people. Liberal Christian and Jewish scholars, along with some evangelical Christians, do not want to see the Second Person of the plural unity of *Elohim* in the terms "*the angel of God*" or "*the angel of the LORD*." Two questions will be explored: First, just how is the word translated "angel" or "messenger" used in the Hebrew text? Secondly, can the identity of the angel or messenger be determined?

Following is a general breakdown of the usage of the term "angel" or more accurately, "messenger," in the Hebrew text to clearly show just how it is used. A total of 110 times in the Hebrew Scriptures it relates to a heavenly messenger:

1. Used as "*the angel of the LORD*" 49 times in the text. However, in addition to those 49 contexts of "*the angel of the LORD*" it is used another 28 times within those same texts. That is a total of 77 times in direct reference to "*the angel of the LORD*."

2. Used as "*the angel of God*" 11 times in the text, but four of them refer to David.

3. Used as a plurality of angels 9 times in the text.

4. Assorted questionable usages: 13 times.

"Messenger" is also used of human agents 97 times, which is well recorded in the Hebrew Scriptures. Two examples of human agents come from the books of Hosea and Malachi. In Hosea 1:13 a supernatural being is not seen, for in this passage it is very specific who the messenger of the LORD is: the human servant of the LORD, Hosea. The second example is found in Malachi 2:7 where the priests of the LORD act as the messengers of the LORD as they teach the Law of God to the people.[372]

What is amazing is the number of times this phrase "*angel of the LORD*" appears and is identified as a particular heavenly being. Following is a sample table of the passages of Scripture that pertain to this particular person as well as a list of ordinary angels and references that are questionable.

---

[372] Hengstenberg, *Christology of the Old Testament*, 254.

REFERENCES

The Angel of the Lord

Passages:	Times used: 82	Context used:
Genesis 16:7, 9-11	4	Hagar
Genesis 22:11, 15	2	Abraham
Exodus 3:2	1	Moses
Exodus 23:20, 23 (see Judg 2:1)	2	To accompany Israel
Exodus 32:34; 33:2 (see Judg 2:1)	2	To accompany Israel
Numbers 22:23-27, 31-32, 34-35	8	Balaam
Joshua 5:13-15 (see Exod 3:5-6)	1	Joshua
Judges 2:1, 4	2	Israel
Judges 5:23	1	Joshua
Judges 6:11-12, 21 (2), 22 (2)	6	Gideon
Judges 13:3, 13, 15-18, 20-21	8	Manoah
2 Samuel 24:16 (3), 17	4	David's sin-numbering
1 Kings 19:5, 7	2	Elijah
2 Kings 1:3, 15	2	Elijah
2 Kings 19:35; 2 Chronicles 32:21	2	Slaughter of 185,000 Assyrians
1 Chronicles 21:12, 15-16, 18, 20, 27, 30	7	David's sin in numbering
Psalm 34:7; 35:5-6	3	Psalms of David
Isaiah 37:36	1	Camp of Assyrians
Isaiah 63:9	1	The Exodus
Hosea 12:4 (Genesis 32:24-30)	1	Man wrestling with Jacob
Zechariah 1:9, 11-14, 19; 2:3 (2); 3:1, 3, 5-6; 4:1, 4-5 (2); 5:5, 10; 6:4-5; 12:8	21	Zechariah
Malachi 3:1	1	Messenger of the Covenant

The Angel of God

Genesis 21:17	1	Hagar
Genesis 31:11	1	Jacob
Genesis 48:16	1	Jacob
Exodus 14:19	1	Exodus from Egypt
Numbers 20:16	1	sent angel
Judges 6:20	1	Gideon
Judges 13:6, 9	1	Manoah

Ordinary Angels

Genesis 19:1, 15	2	Lot
Genesis 28:12	1	Jacob's ladder
Genesis 32:1	1	Jacob

Questionable References

Genesis 24:7, 40	2	Probably Eliezer – Abraham's servant
I Samuel 29:9	1	Referring to David
II Samuel 14:17, 20	1	Referring to David
II Samuel 19:27	1	Referring to David
1 Kings 13:18	1	Prophet lied
Job 4:18	1	Spoken by Eliphaz to Job
Psalm 78:49	1	Evil angels
Psalm 91:11	1	
Psalm 103:20	1	His angels
Psalm 104:4	1	Angels' spirits
Psalm 148:2	1	His angels
Ecclesiastes 5:6	1	The Angel
Daniel 3:28	1	Spoken by Nebuchadnezzar
Daniel 6:22	1	Spoken by Daniel

There are other messengers (angels) that the Scriptures speak about but only two are given names: Gabriel and Michael. These messengers (angels) are called, in groupings, by several different names: "Sons of the Mighty," "Sons of God," and "holy ones." Symbolically, they are called "stars," and there are two special classes of messengers (angels) called *cherubim* and *seraphim*.[373] The Septuagint (LXX) has an interesting verse that will only be mentioned in passing:

> Rejoice, ye heavens, with him, and let all the angels of God worship him.[374]

The question is in the context of the Song of Moses (Deuteronomy 32), the messengers (angels) of *Elohim* are to worship "him." Hebrews 1:6 states that the "him" is *Yeshua*. However, even if a Jewish person does not accept a New Covenant interpretation, one thing is very clear; angels do not worship angels! Messengers (angels) will not bow to any other angel or they would not be messengers (angels) but fallen messengers (angels), better known as demons. Messengers (angels) play an active part in the affairs of the world, nations, rulers and individuals. But there is one particular messenger (angel) that is mentioned by name many times in the *Tanakh*, "*the angel of the LORD*," who completely overshadows all the other messengers (angels) including the two mentioned by name in the book of Daniel; Gabriel and Michael.

---

[373] C. Fred Dickason, *Angels: Elect and Evil* (Chicago: Moody, 1975), 58-71.
[374] Sir Lancelot C. L. Brenton, *The Septuagint with the Apocrypha: Greek and English*, (Grand Rapids: Zondervan, 1980), 277.

Other Angels

Daniel 8:15-16	1	Gabriel
Daniel 9:21	1	Gabriel
Daniel 10:13, 21	2	Michael
Daniel 12:1	1	Michael

Gabriel also appears in the New Covenant to Mary (Luke 1:26) and Zacharias (Luke 1:19).

Michael also appears in the New Covenant in Jude 9 and Revelation 12:7. It becomes obvious even to a casual eye that the Messenger (Angel) of the LORD is more than an ordinary messenger (angel) but He is the LORD. מַלְאַךְ יְהֹוָה, the Hebrew term for "*the angel of the LORD*," relates specifically to one person and is not to be understood as general usage. The word messenger (angel) (מַלְאַךְ) is used to designate both a heavenly being and a human messenger. This is best shown in Genesis 32:1, 3. Verse 1 uses מַלְאֲכֵי for "angels of" who met Jacob and verse 3 uses מַלְאָכִים for "messengers" that Jacob sent to Esau. This word is used for both human and celestial beings who bear messages. The order of the celestial beings to which the terms belong needs to be determined. It is known that there are *cherubim*, *seraphim*, archangels, and ordinary messengers (angels) who are ministering spirits before the LORD. However, there seems to be a special connection between the one called "*the angel of the LORD*" and the LORD Himself, even as the rabbis acknowledge with *Metatron* but come up short in acknowledging His deity. The Messenger (Angel) of the LORD and *HaShem* share the same character, nature and essence but are separate persons within the plural unity of *Elohim*. D. L. Cooper further defines the term in this statement:

> If יְהֹוָה [LORD] is to be understood as being in apposition with מַלְאַךְ [angel], without regard to the Masoretic pointing, the phrase must be rendered "an angel or messenger, the LORD." Furthermore, if מַלְאַךְ is in the absolute state, we should expect יְהֹוָה to have the article and to be written הַיְהֹוָה [the LORD] as is always the case with אָדוֹן *Lord*. In such instances it is always written הָאָדוֹן [the Lord]. Whenever this form is used, reference is made to the Lord and never to a created being. Upon the same principle we would expect to see the article prefixed in יְהֹוָה. But it never is.[375]

In Malachi 2:7 there is an interesting insight that may help to determine the solution of how to understand these words or phrases. The passage is as follows:

> For the lips of a priest's guard knowledge, and men seek rulings from his mouth; for he is **the messenger** of the LORD of hosts.

---

[375] David L. Cooper, *Messiah: His Nature and Person* (Los Angeles: Biblical Research Society, 1933), 16.

Here it is seen that "angel" (מַלְאָךְ) is followed by LORD (יְהֹוָה). The priest is a human messenger of the law, and there is no definite article with LORD, because it is not needed; there is only one LORD. Jewish versions, such as Isaac Leeser's and Alexander Harkavy's versions, translate the phrase in Judges 6:11 as "*an angel of the LORD.*" The point is that this phrase can be equally translated "the angel of the LORD," for the same construction is found in the above passage in Malachi 2:7. To continue quoting Cooper:

> Against this translation it cannot be urged that מַלְאָךְ [angel] is used without the definite article, for nouns in the construct state never have the article. According to Hebrew grammar, the article is attached to the following noun to make the phrase definite.... To this rule, however, there are few exceptions. For instance, the phrase אֱלֹהֵי יִשְׂרָאֵל "the God of Israel" is indeed specific. In this case no article is needed to make the phrase definite. But the phrase הֵיכַל יְהֹוָה "the temple of the LORD" is also by all scholars recognized as definite, though the article does not occur in the expression. The sacred name of God יְהֹוָה is considered throughout the Tenach sufficiently definite so that the article is never used with it. No Hebrew scholar will call this statement into question. Consequently the phrase is rendered definite by the specific nature of God's memorial Name.[376]

The definite article is used within a text to make the phrase definite, yet there are some phrases that the writers of Scripture use that are definite statements but without the definite article.

One of the most interesting points is that a person will absolutely never read in the Hebrew Scriptures "the angels of the LORD." It just does not occur. It is with great uniformity that the writers of the *Tanakh* only used "*the angel of the LORD,*" singular in reference to one individual who was the LORD. The point is that this title belongs to only one heavenly being. It is also interesting to note that twice in the *Tanakh* the phrase "angels of God" are recorded (Genesis 28:12; 32:1). Granted the term for God (*Elohim*) is a general term for God; it applies to the true God as well as to false gods (*elohims*), whereas *Yahweh* is a specific proper name for the one God (*Elohim*), the God of Israel. It is borne out in Genesis 31:11 with the statement מַלְאָךְ הָאֱלֹהִים (the angel of God). אלהים (angel) of God is made definite by prefixing the article ה to angel, making it "the angel of God," hence a specific angel or messenger. To give another example, Exodus 14:19 states that מַלְאָךְ הָאֱלֹהִים (the angel of God), who went before the camp of Israel, removed and went behind them. So by putting the article before "angel," the writers of Scripture could, by prefixing it, make a phrase definite. Cooper summarizes his argument by saying:

> In view of the facts which we have thus far seen, there is but one conclusion to be reached, namely, that the phrase מַלְאָךְ הָאֱלֹהִים "the angel of God" was used to designate a special heavenly being, whereas the expression מַלְאֲכֵי אֱלֹהִים

---

[376] Cooper, *Messiah: His Nature and Person,* 17.

"angels of God" was employed as a comprehensive term to indicate the angels of God in general.[377]

Lastly, there is an association between the phrases "*the angel of God*" and "*the angel of the LORD.*" What has been seen is that the phrase "*the angel of God*" is a specific term referring to a single heavenly being, strongly implying that these two expressions refer to the same person. In Judges 6:20-21 the two phrases are synonymous. In these two verses both phrases "*the angel of God*" and "*the angel of the LORD*" are used interchangeably, showing the same person. The same conclusion is seen in Judges 13:3, which uses "*the angel of the LORD*" and verse 9, which uses "*the angel of God,*" once again showing that both phrases are used of one person; the phrases are interchangeable and apply to the same heavenly being.

Since "*the angel of God*" and "*the angel of the LORD*" are the same person, the next point is whether that person can be identified. The first reference to "*the angel of the LORD*" is found in Genesis 16 in relation to Hagar, Sarah's servant. In this passage "*the angel of the LORD*" is clearly presented by Moses as the LORD speaking directly to Hagar. In the following statement, Rabbi Isaac Abravanel[378] speaks of the frustration that Genesis 16 gives to Jewish scholars:

> Because the peculiar name of God is employed, 'she [Hagar] called the name of the Lord who spake with her;' and how can it possibly be, that the First Cause, blessed be He, should speak with Hagar; when the law itself testifies and says, that it was the angel of the Lord who appeared unto her, and not the Lord himself?[379]

That frustration for serious Jewish scholars will continue to exist until they recognize that within the unity of *Elohim* there is a plural unity. Exodus 3 causes the same frustration, because the "*angel of the LORD,*" the *Shechinah* glory of God, and LORD are interchangeably used to express one person. Judges 6 causes the same problem for in verse 12 "*the angel of the LORD*" appeared to Gideon, and the LORD looked upon Gideon in verse 14, and finally in verse 16 the LORD spoke to Gideon, once again showing that the "angel of the LORD" is the LORD. Also in Zechariah 3:1-6 "*the angel of the LORD*" is identified as the LORD Himself. This is a unique name and also carries with it a characteristic that is unique to God alone. But others just want to identify Him as a messenger sent by the LORD. If the angel is merely a created heavenly messenger, then the evidence should support that conclusion. However, when ordinary angels appear in the context they are never named, with the exception of Michael and Gabriel

---

[377] Cooper, *Messiah: His Nature and Person,* 18-19.

[378] Singer, *The Jewish Encyclopedia,* 1:126-127. Rabbi Isaac Abravanel was born in Lisbon, Portugal in 1437 and died in Venice, Italy in 1508. His family was one of the oldest and most distinguished Spanish families and traced their origin from King David. Two things of interest about Rabbi Abravanel, first he wrote a commentary on the *Tanakh* and second he was an apologetic, defending the Jewish doctrine of the Messiah.

[379] Cooper, *Messiah: His Nature and Person,* 20.

123

in the book of Daniel, and they never speak as the LORD. There is a clear distinction made. Here are three examples:

1. In Daniel chapters 8 and 9 the angel Gabriel appeared to Daniel, but is not called by the name of Him that sends him.

2. In the vision of Zechariah in 1:7-11, many angels were commissioned to execute the Lord's will but none of these were called by the LORD who sent them.

3. In Isaiah 6:6-7 the one who was sent to Isaiah was not called by the name of Him that sent him, but on the contrary was described as one of the seraphim.

So the answer to this whole discussion is that one particular Angel or Messenger was given the memorial name of YHVH because He was Himself God. As has already been covered, the name *"the angel of the LORD"* was only given to one particular Angel or more precisely, Messenger. There is a clear statement recorded by the prophet Isaiah to help further draw the net (42:8):

I am the LORD, that is my name; and my glory I will not give to another, neither my praise unto graven images.

Rabbi David Kimchi gives a clear response to the statement of Isaiah when he says:

That is my name which is appropriate to myself alone, not like the name of the graven images; for although worshippers associate them with me in the application of the name, God, they cannot associate them with me in this name; for I am Lord over all....but in this name He is associated with none but himself.[380]

Isaiah's statement is clear and Rabbi David Kimchi's statement is equally as clear; the Lord God has no partner in the name יְהָיָה. Cooper mentions Maimonides in reference to Numbers 6:27, which states: "And they shall put my name" in Sotah. Fol. 3.1:

All the names of God which occur in Scripture are all derived from the works, as is well known, except one name, and that is, יהיָ, which is the name appropriated to God alone.... not one of the creatures has a share in the teaching of this name, as our rabbis of blessed memory have said: 'My name, the name that is appropriated to me alone'.[381]

Rabbi Kimchi is absolutely correct in his observation. The ultimate question then is, how could a mere created messenger (angel) ever assume that name of *Yahweh*, which is ascribed to Him alone, unless, that Angel or Messenger is the LORD Himself, an equal member of the plural unity of *Elohim*?

---

[380] Cooper, *Messiah: His Nature and Person*, 22.
[381] Cooper, *Messiah: His Nature and Person*, 23.

SHECHINAH

Earlier in the introduction, theophanies were divided into two sections, the Messenger (Angel) of the *Yahweh* and now the second, the *Shechinah* or glory of God's presence. The Hebrew word for *Shechinah* is שָׁכַן [skn], literally meaning "to dwell," as in Numbers 5:3.[382] The definition is "the majestic presence or manifestation of God which has descended to 'dwell' among men."[383] Rabbi Nahmanides (1194-1270) considered it the essence of God as manifested in a distinct form.[384] The *Shechinah* as a theophany includes the non-human appearances of God through fire, cloud, and smoke. The Jewish people called that revelation of *HaShem* the *Shechinah* of G-d or the glory of G-d.

According to VanGemeren, the word *Shechinah* does not occur in the *Tanakh*. VanGemeren continues by stating that:

> The root *skn* occurs not only in the verb ("dwell"), but also in the noun *miskan* ("dwelling place," "tabernacle") and the name Shecaniah ("*Yahweh* dwells"; e.g., 1 Chron 3:21f.).[385]

Fruchtenbaum concurs with VanGemeren and adds some additional information to help understand more clearly the above statement:

> The usual title found in the Scriptures for the *Shechinah* Glory is the glory of Jehovah, or the glory of the Lord. The Hebrew form is *Kvod Adonai*, which means "the glory of Jehovah" and describes what the *Shechinah* Glory is.

> Other titles give it the sense of "dwelling," which portrays what the *Shechinah* Glory does. The Hebrew word *Shechinah*, from the root *shachan*, means "to dwell." The Greek word *Skeinei*, which is similar in sound as the Hebrew *Shechinah* (Greek has no "sh" sound), means "to tabernacle."[386]

The Hebrew word for glory, כָּבוֹד (*kavod*), as in the *"glory of the LORD filled the tabernacle"* in Exodus 40:34, is not the term *Shechinah*, but glory. Over the years through Israel's contact with Hellenism, the glory of the LORD was equated with *Shechinah*. Post-exilic Jews, and later Christians,[387] understood the term *Shechinah* as *"to dwell"* or "to reside."[388] The apostle John picked this up in John 1:14 where he said,

---

[382] Jenni and Westermann, *Theological Lexicon of the Old Testament,* 3:1328.

[383] Singer, *The Jewish Encyclopedia,* 11:258.

[384] Singer, *The Jewish Encyclopedia,* 11:259.

[385] Bromiley, *The International Standard Bible Encyclopedia,* 4:466. VanGemeren is a contributing author in ISBE.

[386] Arnold G. Fruchtenbaum, *The Footsteps of the Messiah: A Study of the Sequence of Prophetic Events* (Tustin, CA: Ariel Ministries, 2003), 599.

[387] Merrill F. Unger, *Unger's Bible Dictionary* (Chicago: Moody Press, 1961), 1009.

[388] James Orr, *The International Standard Bible Encyclopedia,* (Grand Rapids: Eerdmans, 1939), 4:2758.

"The Word was made flesh, and dwelt (tabernacled or *shekhinah*) *among us."* Shechinah first appeared in the *Targums*[389] and rabbinic literature.

This term is most predominant in the Torah, when God came and dwelt in the tabernacle in the wilderness. God's glory resided in the Holy of Holies in the tabernacle and later the temple until just prior to the captivity in 586 BCE. As far as references outside of the Torah, the *Shechinah* is referenced at the dedication of the Solomonic temple (1 Kings 8:4-11; 2 Chronicles 5:2-14) and at the departure of the *Shechinah* from the temple in Ezekiel 9-11. So most of the focus on this topic will come from the Torah because that is where the abundance of references lay.

What will be seen in relation to the *Shechinah* of God is that God revealed Himself to Moses and Aaron as well as to the Children of Israel in the form of fire, cloud and smoke. But also it will be seen in chapter 7, that the Messenger (Angel) of the LORD is the *Shechinah* of God. Connect this with the background of the Messenger (Angel) of the LORD who revealed Himself to individuals, as is laid out in this chapter. That same person of the plural unity of *Elohim* who revealed Himself to Moses and Israel in the wilderness as the visible representative of *Elohim* is also the *Shechinah* of God.

In summary, the name, *"the angel of the LORD"* of the *Tanakh* presents Him as a member of the plural unity of *Elohim*, the LORD. In this chapter it has been shown that the Messenger of the LORD is a unique member of the plural unity of *Elohim*. In the next four chapters each theophany of *Elohim* will be discussed, with a special emphasis given to the *Shechinah* or Glory of God. With some of the theophanies there is not much evidence, but with other passages evidence abounds that unites the Messenger of the LORD as an equal member or partner with *HaShem* in His nature, character and essence. This will be shown as three periods of history unfold, the Pre-Sinai theophanies, the Sinai/Wilderness theophanies and the Post-Sinai/Wilderness theophanies.

---

[389] *Targum*: This is an Aramaic paraphrase of the Hebrew Scriptures from the first century BCE into the first century of the CE. The *"Targums* regarded the *Shechinah* as God himself." It was first used in the *Targums* to avoid the anthropomorphic references to God as in Gen 9:27 - "let him [God] dwell in the tents of Shem" to "may the Glory of his shekhinah dwell in the midst of the tents of Shem."

Chapter 5
Pre-Sinai Theophanies

Among the early pre-Sinai theophanies there were five recorded times when God interacted with mankind. The first is recorded in Genesis 3:8, when "*the LORD God came walking in the garden in the cool of the day*" after Adam and Eve sinned. The second time God interacted with man was with Cain in the context of murdering his brother Abel (Genesis 4:9-15). The third was in relation to Enoch who "*walked with God*" (Genesis 5:24). The fourth was during the life of Noah, when God gave the details in relation to the building of the Ark and the flood in four speeches (Genesis 6:8-9, 13-21; 7:1-3; 8:15-17; 9:1-17). The fifth and last theophany was the call of Abraham in Genesis 12:1. These theophanies present quite a challenge because there was so little information given in the texts about how God revealed Himself when He gave His revelation to these individuals. There were other pre-Sinai appearances of God to Abraham, Hagar, Isaac, and Jacob, but these are dealt with in more detail a little later in this chapter.

In each of the five references above, God communicated with Adam and Eve, Satan, Cain, Enoch, Noah, and Abraham. What He said is not in question as much as how He communicated His word to them. Did God take on a form of some kind, or was it that they just heard Him audibly? The answer may never be completely discerned. However, scholars attempt to find the answer by what has been called "reading into the text" or speculating by using pagan or extra-biblical sources from that period of time to ascertain the answer. This author personally believes that such a practice stretches the limits for the purpose of achieving "biblical" answers. The fact is that God did not give Moses sufficient details, or Moses knowing the details simply did not give the details for students to arrive at any concrete answers. What is evident, God did communicate His word to those early individuals and they understood His words.

Scholars, in their attempt to find an answer, put too much weight on uniting the pagan culture of the day and ancient languages, other than Hebrew, to help find an answer. Consequently, they force upon the Hebrew text unnatural meanings that are alluded to through the interpretation of words from ancient pagan cultures and languages. Look at several quotes related to Genesis 3:8 to help understand what authors are doing:

> However, **some Akkadian evidence sheds light on the Meaning**[390] of the Hebrew. It has been known for some time that the Akkadian word *umu(m)*

---

[390] All bold typeface used in passages is my emphasis unless otherwise indicated.

corresponds to the Hebrew יוֹם, "day." But a second *umu* in Akkadian means "storm" and appears often in divine epithets. The god Ninurta is referred to as "the great storm" [*umu rabu*], the god Assur is called "the angry storm" [*umu nanduru,*] and the god Bel (Enlil) is identified as the storm in a Babylonian text that reads: "Mighty Bel whose utterance is unchangeable, He, the storm [*umu*] destroys the stable, tears up the fold." This Akkadian *umu* also *appears* to have a Hebrew cognate, a second יוֹם that also means "storm." On the basis of Akkadian, Koehler and Baumgartner have noted this second יוֹם, "Wind, Storm," in the Old Testament.

Akkadian *umu* is often used with theophanic overtones. **What if the same were true in Hebrew יוֹם, "storm"?** Such an interpretation understands the enigmatic phrase לְרוּחַ הַיּוֹם to mean not "in the cool of the day," but "in the wind of the storm." The storm wind is the advancing presence of Yahweh. He advances in terrible Theophany, in judgment, *just like* the gods Ninurta, Assur, or Bel in the Akkadian literature.... This understanding of יוֹם affects the translation of other terms in the passage. For example, in the context of such a Theophany, the קוֹל [voice] of Yahweh that the man and woman hear is no longer merely Yahweh's "voice." It is the "thunder" of his stormy presence. These Hebrew terms come together to describe the awesome Theophany of Yahweh in Gen. 3:8: 'Then the man and his wife heard the thunder [קוֹל] of Yahweh God going back and forth [מִתְהַלֵּךְ] in the garden in the wind of the storm [לְרוּחַ הַיּוֹם], and they hid from Yahweh God among the trees of the garden (Niehaus trans.).[391]

This author believes that such thinking is dangerous. The authors who agree with the above quote are looking to uninspired pagan or extra-biblical literature to attempt to prove the presence of God beyond what the Hebrew text gives. Using pagan or extra-biblical literature[392] to push a meaning on the Hebrew text has also been done with the Noahic flood. This method cannot be substantiated within the immediate or related biblical texts. Following are a few quotations from one author: notice the words "perhaps," "evidently perceived" and "Gilgamesh Epic declares," along with the other places in bold typeface. They draw too heavily on extra-biblical source materials.

The Old Testament does teach, however, that Yahweh was gloriously present at the Flood. The storm clouds that play such an important role in that judgment event carry connotations of theophany. Mendenhall has said of the Flood story at Genesis 9:14, "The translation, 'When I bring cloud over the earth,...' is completely inadequate, since it does not convey the sense that the *anan* is first and foremost a theophany in the form of a storm-cloud."

---

[391] Niehaus, *God at Sinai*, 156-159. Niehaus references numerous other authors in his work on this section. Jeffrey J. Niehaus, "In the Wind of the Storm: Another Look at Genesis 3:8," *Vetus Testamentum* (v. 44 no. 2, 1994), 263-268.

[392] *Extra-biblical* means to be outside scope of the biblical text.

The most dramatic expression of Yahweh's storm presence at the Flood is **perhaps** to be found in Psalm 29. Kline comments, "The psalmist **evidently perceived** the royal Glory-presence in the phenomena of the flood."

The **Gilgamesh Epic declares** that "the gods decided to make the Deluge [*abubu*]" to eliminate humanity. **Naram-Sin** (2249-2213 B.C.) boasts that he "made the land of Akkad [look] like [after] the Deluge of water that happened at an early time of mankind." A fascinating echo of Yahweh's presence at the Flood **may occur in the Enuma Elish.** Tablet IV portrays Marduk as he arms himself for combat against Tiamat the sea dragon goddess: …. **The parallels to Yahweh theophany are remarkable. Like** Yahweh, Marduk came with "lightning" and "winds" (a perfect number of them – seven). He mounts a "storm chariot," and has "a frightful halo."

Psalm 29 holds an unusual place in the Psalter, not least because of the history of criticism regarding it. H. L Ginsberg first **suggested** in 1935 that the hymn might be Phoenician…. F. M. Cross, in an article on the psalm three years later, believed that Ginsberg had presented "**conclusive evidence that Psalm 29 was a Canaanite Baal hymn.**[393]

Attempting to show by the use of pagan [extra-biblical] culture and literature that the theophanies of God were in the presence of the cloud cover over the earth during the flood is just too much of a stretch upon the biblical text. Rather, in this book the biblical text will be the source to determine the context, and if there is enough biblical evidence, it is within the realm of possibility that God did appear to the pre-flood inhabitants, as Borland presents:

God appeared at various times solely to individuals such as Adam and Eve (Gen 3:8-19), Cain (Gen 4:9-15), and Enoch (Gen 5:22, 24). It is a reasonable thesis that God also appeared visibly to Noah (Gen 6-9).[394]

Clearly, the biblical text allows the student of Scripture to go only so far in determining if God did or did not appear in some form before Adam, Cain, Enoch and Noah. But this author will leave the pre-Abraham theophanies open for discussion, as it cannot be definitely determined that there was a physical manifestation, for the text does not give adequate information to draw a definite conclusion. Even though it cannot be established with any certainty, this author's impression is that a physical appearance was likely or possible.

Now observe the first five theophanies up to and including the time of Abram in Genesis up through chapter 12:1.

---

[393] Niehaus, *God at Sinai*, 160-163.
[394] Borland, *Christ in the Old Testament,* 25.

The Voice of the LORD God Walking … Genesis 3:8

> And they heard the voice of the LORD God walking in the garden in the cool of the day: and Adam and his wife hid themselves from the presence of the LORD God amongst the trees of the garden (KJV).

Niehaus takes the theophanies of God back to the Genesis 1 creation account, as well as to the fall of man in Genesis 3, including the judgment account of Genesis 6, and labels them pre-Sinai theophanies.[395] The fact is that God did communicate with Adam and Eve by His voice, but the *Tanakh* does not indicate how He walked and communicated with man in the garden. The phrase that is under discussion is *"heard the voice of the LORD God walking in the garden in the cool of the day."* Morris suggests that this phrase was a common event for God in His relationship with Adam and Eve:

> God was "walking in the garden in the cool of the day." The more or less off hand way in which this is stated indicates that this was a normal event, perhaps a daily appointment time at which the Lord met with them for communion and fellowship. This is no crude anthropomorphism, but a repeated, or even continual, Theophany, in which the Word of God, Christ preincarnate, clothed Himself in human form in order to communicate with those whom He had created in His own image.[396]

Although this may indeed have been a normal and common event for God as He entered the garden, the latter part of the statement is an assumption. Morris' assumption of Messiah would be correct based on what will be shown through progressive revelation as it is detailed with specific theophanies, but the text in Genesis 3:8 did not give the reader that kind of understanding. Currid, for example, notes that the phrase *"heard the voice of the LORD God walking in the garden in the cool of the day"* can be taken several ways:

> The opening phrase of this verse has been interpreted in a variety of ways. Many commentators give the readings, 'the sound' instead of 'the voice,' and 'walking' in place of 'going forth'; thus they would view the scene as an anthropomorphic one in which God's feet are making a noise as he strolls through the garden. Others argue for a less symbolic translation, such as the one I have given above, which reflects God's speaking in the garden, calling out to the creatures he has made. Still others assert that it is a Theophany – the voice is accompanying the divine presence. All these interpretations are linguistically possible.[397]

Even though Currid has said that these are all linguistically possible, the reader is often left in a quandary as to how to proceed with the meaning. There is one point that is safe

---

[395] Niehaus, *God At Sinai*, 142-171.

[396] Henry M. Morris, *The Genesis Record* (Grand Rapids: Baker, 1976), 116.

[397] John D. Currid, *Genesis 1:1-25:18* (2 vols. Webster, NY: Evangelical Press, 2003), 1:122.

to say; before the fall there was no sin to separate man from God, so God could appear to man in a human form for communion and fellowship. There would not be a prohibition of sin to separate or to prohibit God from communicating with man on a very personal level. Keil and Delitzsch express this without hesitation in the following statement:

> God conversed with the first man in visible shape, as the Father and Instructor of His children. He did not adopt this mode for the first time after the fall, but employed it as far back as the period when He brought the beasts to Adam, and gave him the woman to be his wife.[398]

Keil and Delitzsch do not see God walking in the garden as a first time event. The language used in Genesis 3:8 and the use of the "walking" expresses fellowship as man and God walked together on a regular basis, as expressed by Mathews and Leupold:

> The anthropomorphic description of God "walking" (*mithallek*) in the garden suggests the enjoyment of fellowship between him and our first parents. The adverbial phrase "in the cool of the day" (NIV, NASB, NJB) or "the breezy time of the day" (NJPS, NAB) translates the Hebrew phrase "wind (*ruah*) of the day."

> The NRSV's rendering makes the time more explicit, "at the time of the evening breeze."[399]

> Besides, there is extreme likelihood that the Almighty assumed some form analogous to the human form which was made in His image. Nor is there anything farfetched about the further supposition that previously our first parents had freely met with and conversed with their heavenly Father. In this instance they again hear His "voice." Though *qol* does often mean "sound" (2 Sam 5:24; 1 Kgs 14:6) and now by almost common consent is quite regularly translated thus in this verse, yet v. 10 [Genesis 3:10] definitely points to the use of the word in the more common meaning of "voice," and this must be a reference to the word *qol* used in our verse.[400]

> [Bible versions mentioned above: NIV, New International Version; NASB, New American Standard Bible; NJB, New Jerusalem Bible; NJPS, New Jewish Publication Society; NAB, New American Bible]

Mathews deals with the word "walking" but he does not deal with the word "voice," whereas Leupold deals with the word "voice." In Kohlenberger's Hebrew-English Concordance, the word for "walking" (הָלַךְ - halak) that is used in Genesis 3:8, most frequently denotes or implies physical walking or it is translated with the idea of

---

[398] Keil and Delitzsch, *Commentary on the Old Testament: Genesis*, 1:97.
[399] Mathews, *The New American Commentary: Genesis 1:1 – 11:26*, 239.
[400] Leupold, *Exposition of Genesis*, 1:155.

walking in mind.[401] It is also a Hithpael verb (Genesis 5:24); "here it has a durative force, signifying its continuous nature"[402] or God is continuously walking in the garden and this time He is calling for Adam.

Also as indicated in Kohlenberger's Hebrew-English Concordance, there are two basic uses of the word translated "sound" or "voice" (קוֹל - qol) as is seen in the following references:

Sound:

1 Sam 12:17:	"I will call upon the LORD to send **thunder** and rain"
Jer 4:19:	"O my soul, the **sound** of the trumpet, the alarm of war"
Jer 48:34:	"The **sound** of their cry rises from Heshbon to Elealeh"
Jer 50:22:	"The noise of battle is in the land"
Joel 2:5:	"With a **noise** like that of chariots they leap over the mountains"
Zech 11:3:	"**Listen** to the wail of the shepherds. **Listen** to the roar of the lions"

Voice:

Gen 27:22	"The **voice** is the **voice** of Jacob"
Num 7:89	"He heard the **voice** speaking to him from between the two cherubim"
Deut 5:24	"and we have heard his **voice** from the fire"
Deut 5:25	"we will die if we hear the **voice** of the LORD our God any longer"
1 Sam 1:13	"in her heart, and her lips were moving but her **voice** was not heard"
2 Sam 22:7	"From his temple he heard my **voice**"
Psa 64:1	"Hear me, O God, as I **voice** my complaint"
Psa 116:1	"I love the LORD, for he heard my **voice**"
Daniel 8:16	"And I heard a man's **voice** from the Ulai calling, Gabriel"
Nahum 2:13	"The **voices** of your messengers will no longer be heard"[403]

---

[401] Kohlenberger and Swanson, *The Hebrew English Concordance of the Old Testament,* 456-466.

[402] Currid, *Genesis 1:1-25:18*. 1:164. Footnote in Currid book, 1:458.

[403] Kohlenberger and Swanson, *The Hebrew English Concordance of the Old Testament,* 1395-1398.

However, the greatest usage is given over to "sounds" with a few of the references pertaining to "voices." There is disagreement between just how this word is used as either "sound" or "voice." According to Sailhamer, Genesis 3:8 is the introduction to the beginning of the judgment of God upon Adam and Eve. This drama opens with the "voice" or "sound" of the Lord walking in the garden.[404] Sailhamer states that the word "sound" is a common expression for the Hebrew word קוֹל for voice and references several verses out of Deuteronomy.

This author respectfully disagrees with Sailhamer's interpretation of the word in reviewing the first three references in Deuteronomy 5:25; 8:20 and 13:18. There is a difference between "voice" and "sound." Inanimate objects make sounds but people have a voice to speak words, though being sounds, are verbal. Each one of the three passages cited above uses the Hebrew word קוֹל as "voice." The word "sound" would make no sense in the context. In Deuteronomy 5:25 קוֹל is translated "voice" by the KJV, NIV, NAS, and even the Jewish Tanakh (verse 22), as well as by the Hebrew text in Kohlenberger's Hebrew Interlinear.[405] In both Deuteronomy 8:20 and 13:18 all the above versions use "voice" except the NIV, which is a mistranslation because בְּקוֹל means "voice of." There are places like Exodus 19:19 where קוֹל is correctly translated the "sound" of the trumpet, but most of the time the word demands the use of "voice" because words are spoken. Thus, in Genesis 3:8 קוֹל is not a sound but the voice of the Lord walking in the garden. For the immediate context there is a conversation among God, Satan and Adam and Eve, but קוֹל does not answer whether or not the form of God was visible.

Another view is that the ancient Akkadian language has evidence that sheds some light on the phrase "*in the cool of the day,*" which Niehaus suggests should be rendered "in the wind of the storm." The Akkadian word *umu* corresponds to the Hebrew "*ywm,*" or "day" that corresponds with the Hebrew (Genesis 3:8) phrase "*in the cool of the day*" as stated by Niehaus:

> It has been known for some time that the Akkadian word, *umu*, corresponds to the Hebrew, *ywm*, "day." But there is a second *umu* in Akkadian, which means "storm," and which appears often in divine epithets. For instance, the god Ninurta is referred to as "the great storm" (*umu rabu*). The god Assur is called "the angry storm" (*umu nanduru*). And the god Bel (Enlil) is identified as the storm in a Babylonian text....[406]

Niehaus notes that the second Akkadian word, which corresponds to the "breeze" or "cool of the day," should be rendered "storm." As God in judgment comes to the garden, He also compares this "storm-wind" as the presence of *Yahweh* in judgment, to the gods Ninurta, Assur, or Bel in the Akkadian literature. However, as this author

---

[404] Sailhamer, *The Pentateuch as Narrative: The Biblical-Theological Commentary,* 105.

[405] Kohlenberger, *The Interlinear NIV Hebrew-English Old Testament,* 500.

[406] Jeffrey Niehaus, "In the Wind of the Storm: Another look at Genesis 3:8," *Vetus Testamentum* (44, no 2, 1994), 263-267.

stated before, it is dangerous to interpret biblical truth through the lens of pagan or extra-biblical culture and literature. Also, even though judgment is evident in Genesis 3, the immediate context does not reflect God coming in a threatening, terrifying way. It does strongly reflect that the reaction of hiding and the covering themselves on the part of Adam and Eve was from their immediate knowledge that they had disobeyed God. They were reacting to the coming presence of God, not to a "storm-wind."

As stated before, this author feels very uneasy about using pagan or extra-biblical language to try to decipher the meaning of Hebrew words that are more difficult to interpret than others. Niehaus uses words or phrases that assume in his writings three different times: "perhaps," "what if," and "if" in his interpretative process. It could be that the best interpretation is "wind-storm," but when the answer is not readily apparent in the immediate or the broader content of the biblical text, the conclusion is on uncertain ground.

Ancient Judaism had some interesting observations as to how the early Targums referred to Genesis 3:8. This becomes even more interesting in the light of the New Covenant passage in John 1:1 which is dealt with in chapter 18 of this book. Both the Targums of Onkelos and Jonathan say that the voice which humanity's first parents heard walking in the garden was the *Memra* Jehovah, i.e., the Word of the Lord, or the Messiah, as the expression *Memra* always means. The Jerusalem Targum commences the verse thus: "And the *Memra* of the Lord God called unto Adam." The rabbis called the Messiah *Memra* Jehovah because after man had sinned, God refused to have any further interaction with him, but made known His mind and will by the Messiah, either through speaking or writing.[407] If the word קוֹל is best translated as "sound" then how, in the context of Genesis 3:8, does sound walk? Voice and walking identify a person who makes sounds. Also in the immediate context is the dialogue among God, Satan and Adam and Eve. Sounds do not communicate, but voices of people do!

קוֹל primarily signifies a sound produced by the vocal cords (actual or figurative).[408] According to Kohlenberger and Swanson, there are 505 usages of קוֹל and the most predominant use is to indicate some kind of "sound" (400 times). However, there are over 101 other usages to indicate the sound as a "voice."[409] It appears that the context where the word is found has to determine its meaning.

Kohlenberger translates Genesis 3:8 and 10 as the "sound" of God[410] whereas Young interprets it as "voice."[411] He states "the fact that the Hebrew word which

[407] Joseph Samuel C. F. Frey, *The Messiahship of Jesus* (Philadelphia: American Baptist Publication Society, 1850), 36.

[408] Harris, Archer and Waltke, *Theological Wordbook of the Old Testament*, 2:792.

[409] Kohlenberger and Swanson, *The Hebrew-English Concordance*, 1395-1398.

[410] Kohlenberger, *The Interlinear NIV Hebrew-English Old Testament,* 6-7.

[411] Edward J. Young, *Genesis 3* (London: The Banner of Truth, 1966), 72.

appears here normally means voice."[412] Here are two respected scholars who obviously take opposite views on its usage in these verses.

> We are compelled to recognize that it presents a conversation between God and man. How could this conversation have occurred, if God was not actually present in the garden in a form in which man could converse with Him?...God is the infinite One; He is a spirit. In order to reveal Himself to man in an intimate way He appeared during Old Testament times in human form. Such appearances were called theophanies and these theophanies found their culmination in the incarnation of the second Person of the Trinity....Man however, cannot speak face to face with a spirit; hence, God graciously appeared in human form so that man could speak directly to Him and receive from Him His commands.[413]

A summary of Genesis 3:8 is that God on a regular basis met with Adam and Eve for communion and fellowship. But after they sinned against Him, they were afraid to meet with Him because they knew they had disobeyed His Word. God came walking in the garden calling them; Adam and Eve heard His voice coming towards them. What is not clear is the exact manner in which God came to them. Was it in a physical form as He would later appear to Abraham, Moses, Joshua, and Gideon? The assumption is that it was, but again it is an assumption.

The LORD and Cain ... Genesis 4:6-16

(6) And the LORD **said** to Cain, "Why are you distressed, and why is your face fallen? (7) Surely, if you do right, there is uplift. But if you do not do right sin couches at the door; its urge is toward you, yet you can be its master." (8) Cain **said** to his brother Abel...and when they were in the field, Cain set upon his brother Abel and killed him. (9) The LORD **said** to Cain, "Where is your brother Abel?" and he **said**, "I do not know. Am I my brother's keeper?" (10) Then He **said**, "What have you done? Hark, your brother's blood cries out to Me from the ground! (11) Therefore, you shall be more cursed than the ground, which opened its mouth to receive your brother's blood from your hand. (12) If you till the soil, it shall no longer yield its strength to you. You shall become a ceaseless wanderer on earth." (13) Cain **said** to the LORD, "My punishment is too great to bear! (14) Since You have banished me this day from the soil, and I must avoid Your presence and become a restless wanderer on earth – anyone who meets me may kill me!" (15) The LORD **said** to him, "I promise, if anyone kills Cain, seven-fold vengeance shall be taken on him." And the LORD put a mark on Cain, lest anyone who met him should kill him. (16) Cain left the presence of the LORD and settled in the land of Nod, east of Eden.

---

[412] Young, *Genesis 3*, 72.
[413] Young, *Genesis 3*, 73-74.

In this passage of Scripture from the *Tanakh*, the word "said" becomes very interesting as the dialogue between Cain and the LORD progresses. It is the Hebrew word וַיֹּאמֶר which is translated "and he said."[414] It is used four times by the LORD (verses 6, 9-10, 15) and twice by Cain (verses 8, 13). It is rather obvious that God and Cain are interacting verbally. Did the LORD in this theophany take on a visible form that Cain could see or was it only audible?

The answer to this issue lies in verse 16, if it can be discerned. There the text says, וַיֵּצֵא קַיִן מִלִּפְנֵי יְהוָה or it is literally translated "so he went out – Cain – from – presence-of-*Yahweh*."[415] This leans strongly to the possibility that the LORD's presence was more than just audible, but a physical appearance. It is difficult to discern in what way God manifested Himself to Cain. In more than a dozen commentaries examined, much is said about the conversations between God and Cain but nothing on the possible theophany.

In the Genesis 3 account, Adam and Eve were driven from the garden of Eden, probably into the area immediately east of the garden (3:24). There Adam and Eve raised their first two sons, Cain and Abel. It appears that God did have communication with them, for God approached Cain in relationship to his offering and the hatred that was burning in his heart toward God but was carried out violently against Abel. God may have had a constant presence in the garden of Eden area. This may be the context of Cain going out from the presence of the LORD, to wander in Nod, a more eastern location, which is what Nod means in the Hebrew.

Several scholars make incomplete observations on the dialogue in Genesis chapter 4. They speak as if this account was a theophany, but none of them actually refer to this passage as being a theophany of God:

> We do not know how the Lord manifested Himself to the two brothers....The natural implication of the text is that He spoke in some outward way, as He had done to Adam and Eve in the garden, rather than in the conscience or heart.[416]

> The clear assumption made throughout Genesis 4 is that God and Cain are bodily present in their setting, which is somewhere east of the Garden of Eden.[417]

> There is nothing said here about God appearing visibly; but this does not warrant us in interpreting either this or the following conversation as a simple process that took place in the heart and conscience of Cain.[418]

---

[414] Kohlenberger, *The Interlinear NIV Hebrew-English Old Testament*, 9.

[415] Kohlenberger, *The Interlinear NIV Hebrew-English Old Testament*, 9.

[416] Atkinson, *The Pocket Commentary on the Bible: Genesis*, 58.

[417] Victor P. Hamilton, *The New International Commentary on the Old Testament. Genesis Chapters 1-17*, (XX vols. Grand Rapids: Eerdmans, 1990), 1:235.

[418] Keil and Delitzsch, *Commentary on the Old Testament: Genesis*, 1:112.

Immediately after the deed God's voice is heard, see also 3:9. Cain replies: You ask as if I had to be his keeper. In Hebrew the word "I" emphatically used at the end of the sentence is the classical speech of egotism.[419]

He [God] engaged Cain in a gentle conversation to give him the opportunity to confess and repent.[420]

Proposing that these verses are a theophany seems to be sailing uncharted waters. Once again, Moses did not give enough information to make a strong statement on the passage. However, one thing is clear; *Yahweh* and Cain did have dialogue together. Whether or not *Yahweh* appeared in some form cannot be known, but it still can be clearly called a pre-Sinai theophany. The least definite of the five quotes above is the third one on the conscience of Cain. What is quite evident from the Hebrew text is that God and Cain had an audible dialogue.

Enoch Walked with God ... Genesis 5:22-24

(22) After the birth of Methuselah, Enoch walked with God 300 years; and he begot sons and daughters. (23) All the days of Enoch came to 365 years. (24) Enoch walked with God; then he was no more, for God took him.

Enoch's walk with God was probably not literal in the sense in which Adam may have walked with Him in the garden before the fall. Since Enoch had inherited the fallen nature of all men, he could not even "look upon God and live," unless God chose to veil His glory in theophanic revelation, as He later did on occasion to Abraham and Moses.[421]

The normal description of the recorded individuals in Genesis 5 is that they lived a certain number of years, after which they became fathers and died a certain number of years later, as seen in verses 5, 8, 11, 14, 17, 20, 27, and 31. But in connection with Enoch the text simply reads that he "*walked with God*" (verse 24). This verb is often employed idiomatically to mean "to commune" – that is, it is a habit and a manner of life. Further insight from the Hebrew language in relation to Enoch and his walk is given by Currid, who indicates that Enoch and God communed and walked continuously:

The stem of the Hebrew verb is a Hithpael, and here it has a durative force, signifying its continuous nature. Thus the point is that Enoch constantly communed with the Creator.[422]

---

[419] Rabbi Ernest I. Jacob, *The First Book of the Bible: Genesis,* (New York, Ktav Publishing, 1974), 34.

[420] Scherman, *The Chumash: The Stone Edition*, 21.

[421] Morris, *The Genesis Record*, 157-158.

[422] Currid, *Genesis 1:1-25:18*, 1:164.

The use of the Hithpael with that verb is reminiscent of God's "walking" in the garden in 3:8. According to Genesis 5:22, Enoch maintained his walk and lifestyle with God for 300 years, as is stated below:

> The special formula "walked with God," is used only of Enoch and Noah (6:9) though Abraham walked "before God" (17:1; 24:40).[423]

> "Walked with God" is metaphorical and indicates that Enoch had a lifestyle characterized by his devotion to God. The sense of "walk" (halak) in its verbal stem indicates a communion or intimacy with God.[424]

> The phrase "walked with God," which is only applied to Enoch and Noah (Gen 6:9), denotes the most confidential intercourse, the closest communion with the personal God, a walking as it were by the side of God, who still continued His visible intercourse with men.[425]

The net result from the biblical text is that there is simply not enough information given by Moses to make any definitive statement as to whether Enoch's walk with God was lived out on a daily basis in a physical communion with God or a metaphorical walk with God.

Noah Walked with God ... Genesis 6:8-9, 13-21; 7:1-3; 8:15-17; 9:1-17

> (8) But Noah found grace in the eyes of the LORD. (9) These are the generations of Noah: Noah was a just man and perfect in his generations, and Noah walked with God.

Within these four passages or messages to Noah, God gave to him instructions for building the ark, taking animals on the ark, and receiving the Noahic Covenant. In these passages are four references of God speaking to Noah, in Genesis 6:13; 7:1; 8:15; and 9:1. All four times the same Hebrew word אָמַר - amar is translated as "said," "say," "spake". This is the same word used in Genesis 16:11 where "the angel of the LORD" said to her (Hagar); in Genesis 18:12-13 where Yahweh in Abraham's presence made the promises of Isaac's birth; and in Genesis 22:2, 11-12 where Elohim told Abraham to offer his only son, and then "the angel of the LORD" called Abraham and told him not to take his son's life.

Regarding Noah, it simply says in Genesis 6:13 that God spoke to him, but it does not say how He communicated the information. The biblical text does not give the mode of how God spoke to Noah. There is not enough evidence to say, with authority,

---

[423] Walter Brueggemann, *Interpretation, A Bible Commentary for Teaching and Preaching: Genesis,* (Atlanta: John Knox Press, 1982), 68.

[424] Mathews, *The New American Commentary: Genesis 1:-11:26*, 313.

[425] Keil & Delitzsch, *Commentary on the Old Testament: Genesis*, 1:125.

how God communicated to Noah, but one thing is known: Noah knew exactly what God had said.[426]

The four texts from Genesis do not indicate whether or not God appeared to Noah in a physical form. What is understood is that Noah was righteous in his moral relationship to God and was blameless (τέλελο) in his character and conduct. His righteousness and integrity were manifested in his walking with God, a walk which resembled Enoch's (5:22).[427] Not only is Noah's walk seen as communion with God, but the expression is also used of Enoch. In this text, the Hithpael verb "walking" again verifies that Noah regularly had communion and fellowship with God; he indeed walked with God. What is clearly understood by comparing them with the earlier Genesis texts and latter texts of Hagar (Genesis 16) and Abraham (Genesis 17, 18, 22) is unmistakable that God spoke in an audible voice to Noah, but as to a physical theophany of some kind, the text is silent.

The Call of Abram … Genesis 12:1 with Acts 7:2-4

The LORD said to Abram, "Go forth from your native land and from your father's house to the land that I will show you."

Genesis 12:1 states God's call to Abram. The verse repeats the word "and he said" (וַיֹּאמֶר), the same word discussed in relation to Cain, Noah and related verses to Hagar and Abraham. Genesis chapters 16, 18 and 22 give the accounts of God speaking to Hagar and Abraham by appearing visibly, as a theophany. However, in the Noahic passages, the personal appearing part is absent. Yet in all the related passages of God speaking or appearing, when the Lord came to Abraham, He appeared personally in the form of a theophany:

Now if the individual instances of the appearing of God to Abram be listed as well as the instances where the word of the Lord came unto Abram, it will be found that these experiences make a total of eight, or, counting the original word in Ur of Chaldees according to Acts 7:2, nine. But the distinction between the mere coming of the Word to Abram (12:1; 13:14; 21:12; 22:1) and the vision (15:1) or the appearance of the Lord (12:7; 17:1; 18:1), is largely artificial. Even when the word of the Lord came to Abram, the Lord may have appeared to Abram even where there is no specific mention made of His appearing.[428]

The key element in Genesis 12:1 is the use of the word "said," which would seem to indicate the possibility that there was an appearance of God, but once again the text of the *Tanakh* does not give the answer. However, there is one other passage that is

---

[426] Leupold, *Exposition of Genesis*, 1:287.
[427] Keil & Delitzsch, *Commentary on the Old Testament: Genesis*, 141.
[428] Leupold, *Exposition of Genesis*, 1:403.

outside the *Tanakh*, coming from the New Covenant book of Acts 7:2-4 where Stephen states that the Lord did appear to Abram while in Ur of the Chaldaeans, as stated below:

> And he (Stephen) said, Men, brethren, and fathers, hearken; The God of glory appeared unto our father Abraham, when he was in Mesopotamia, before he dwelt in Haran, and said unto him, Get thee out of thy country, and from thy kindred, and come into the land which I shall show thee. Then came he out of the land of the Chaldacans, and dwelt in Haran: and from thence, when his father was dead, he removed him into this land, wherein ye now dwell.

Stephen understood that the God of glory appeared to Abraham in Ur of the Chaldees. For Jewish people the Acts 7 passage would not be a valid point because they do not accept the testimony of the New Covenant. But to New Covenant believers the Acts 7 passage is significant, for God then would have appeared to Abraham in Genesis 12:1 as well as in Genesis 12:7; 17:1; 18:1. So the internal evidence from the *Tanakh* leads one toward seeing God appearing to Abraham, and with the evidences from the New Covenant, this confirms that this was Abraham's first experience of meeting God in person.

Up to this point in the biblical text, to prove the form that a theophany took on would be impossible. The fact that a theophany did take place is very apparent as the texts are studied. Since Adam directly spoke to God, a theophany of some kind is probable. However, the text does not reveal the form that God took. The text on Enoch is very weak in that it does not reveal just how Enoch walked with God. Noah clearly understood the instructions of the Lord in preparation of the ark, the flood, the animals, and the Noahic Covenant. But once again the text does not reveal any form of the theophany. It is not until Abram comes on the scene that a clear picture of the theophany of God in a visible form begins to develop. The first reference to Abram in Genesis 12:1 is not very helpful in determining the nature of theophanies. But when coupled with Acts 7:2-4 and the picture that Moses paints throughout the Torah (Law) concerning the theophanies of God, the visible nature of those theophanies begins to unfold. Before the theophanies are discussed further, anthropomorphic references of God need to be understood (also see chapter 2). This is especially true as it pertains to the Jewish understanding of the theophanies and how they responded in regard to the physical characteristics of these theophanies.

As the history of the *Tanakh* unfolds, from the time of the golden calf episode (Exodus 32:7-10), at the beginning of the exodus at Mt. Sinai, to the destruction of the northern and southern kingdoms of Israel and Judah, idolatry was a major stumbling block to Israel. As a result of Israel's long history in the *Tanakh* with idols and the ensuing captivities, the Jewish people became sensitized as a result of the Assyrian and Babylonian captivities to the teaching of one God. Idolatry, after the return of Israel and Judah from captivity, was no longer a major problem.

Because the pagan nations around Israel worshipped gods made in images of man which had arms, hands, feet and legs which were representations of human characteristics, the Jewish rabbis began to change words to avoid the depiction that God has these physical characteristics. This was done because of their sensitivity to their own past idolatry. The ancient rabbis who translated the Greek Septuagint (LXX) and the Aramaic Targums began to modify these texts to remove the language in the *Tanakh* of God having physical human-like parts. The rabbis did not like the anthropomorphism of God in the *Tanakh* and thus would change the words to reflect God's glory or presence rather than the "hand of God" or "the Lord stood by [Abraham]." The Scripture presents the LORD as pure spirit, an incorporeal indivisible being having no human likeness. They softened the terms used to reflect God as pure spirit rather than having human characteristics. Louis Goldberg illustrates some of this in the following statements:

> In personal references to God, all anthropomorphic expressions are avoided and other expressions are substituted. All human traits ascribed to deity are toned down or avoided so as not to create false impressions among the unlearned, namely, that Yahweh was not like any pagan deity. The expressions of Memra and Shekinah are used freely in substitutions.[429]

> Anthropomorphisms are rendered in such a way in translation as to avoid any possible misconception. Thus God does not smell an offering but accepts it; He does not go before the people but He leads them. Instead of God hearing or seeing, it is said it was revealed or heard before Him. God's feet are His glorious throne (Targum Isaiah 38:5; 60:13).... Shekinah is another word used as a substitute for personal references to God. In this instance, anthropomorphic references to God in the Isaiah text are attributed in the Targum to the Shekinah or the glory of the Shekinah, e.g., hiding the eyes is removing the presence of His Shekinah, to see the King is to see the glory of the Shekinah (1:15; 6:5).[430]

The rabbis who soften the anthropomorphism were not covering up to erode the future God/man aspect of the Messiah by Jewish scholars. This was simply done as a reaction to Israel's previous failings with other gods, to protect them from ever again worshipping other gods. However, in their concern to protect the Scripture and their revelation of God, rabbis have detracted from the Scripture as God Himself saw fit to have it written by Moses and the other authors of Scripture.

---

[429] Goldberg, *The Deviation of Jewish Thought from an Old Testament Theology in the Intertestamental Period*, 53.

[430] Goldberg, *The Deviation of Jewish Thought from an Old Testament Theology in the Intertestamental Period*, 20-21.

The LORD Appeared to Abram … Genesis 12:7

The LORD appeared to Abram and said, "I will assign this land to your offspring." And he built an altar there to the LORD who had appeared to him.

The first five theophanies that do not indicate directly a physical form of God before Adam, Cain, Enoch and Noah have been discussed. From this point on, theophanies are much more frequent and there is definitely a physical manifestation. So not only are the words of God expressed, but God appears to man in a form that man can see with his natural eyes. This starts a whole new level of appearances and communication as stated below:

> This is the first time that any appearance of the Deity is mentioned. Always previously the communications between God and man had been direct, without the intervention of any visible medium. Thus, God commanded Adam: Adam and Eve heard His voice, and He called them: He said unto Cain: unto Noah … this visible manifestation is subsequently connected with the phrase "an angel of Jehovah" and less frequently "an angel of God."[431]

> At this point, God "appeared unto him." This is the first time in Scripture where we read of an actual appearance of God. God had "walked" and spoken with Adam, Enoch, and Noah, and perhaps He also had been visible in some way to them, but Scripture does not say so. Here, however, there must have been an actual visible manifestation – a Theophany – and, therefore, we must understand this as a pre-incarnate appearance of Christ (Jn 1:18).[432]

For the first time Genesis 12:7 in the *Tanakh* states that *Yahweh* appeared to Abram. The Hebrew word is וַיֵּרָא [but he appeared] from the root word רָאָי meaning "to appear," a third person masculine *nifal* verb. In many of the other references in the Torah where Moses used this word, it becomes very obvious that "appear" means to be seen. So *Yahweh*, who was seen by Abram, gives him a message. This is definitely a theophany, but once again the form by which, or the manner *Yahweh* was seen by Abram is not given. What the word "appear" strongly conveys is the idea that *Yahweh* literally appeared in some physical or bodily form as is reflected below:

> It is at this point that 'Yahweh appeared to Abram.' This is the language of Theophany – that is, God appearing before the patriarch in a physical form. That same verb is used of other theophanies in Genesis (to Isaac in 26:2, 24; to Jacob in 35:9). The verb is in the Niphal pattern, reflecting a passive state: this is a construction signifying God's self-disclosure to Abram.[433]

---

[431]Payne Smith, *The Handy Commentary: Genesis, ed. Charles John Ellicott,,* (London, Cassell & Co, n.d.), 173.

[432] Morris, *The Genesis Record*, 296.

[433] Currid, *A Study Commentary: Genesis 1:1 – 25:18,* 1:255.

Genesis 12:7 is the first instance in the *Tanakh* of the self-disclosure of God to Abram in visible form. As has been stated earlier, Rabbinic Judaism today emphatically states that God has never appeared to man in a physical way, for God is pure spirit and is above His creation. However, in a copy of Chumash—the Torah, Haftaros and five Megillos[434] with a commentary—occurs the following interesting statement that the LORD appeared to Abram in Genesis 12:7:

> HaShem[435] appeared. God is not physical, so the means by which He "speaks" and makes Himself "visible" to people is an eternal mystery. Nevertheless, the Torah tells us that He appeared in a way that was tangible to Abraham.[436]

The conclusion that comes from this verse is that *Yahweh* first appeared to Abram in some kind of physical form to give him the promise of the land. Atkinson concludes that:

> This was an appearance of the Word of God, the pre-incarnate Christ, often called in the OT the Angel of the Lord.[437]

This is a premature statement by Atkinson at this point, but his conclusion is correct. This conclusion about Messiah being the theophany will be borne out as the rest of Scripture unfolds. To summarize this verse on theophany, Mathews states that the LORD did appear and made promises to Abram:

> This theophany reassured Abram of the Lord's presence; the patriarch responded by building an altar, the first of many (v. 7b; cp. Jacob, 18:10-19; 35:1; 48:3 and Moses, Exod 3:2, 12, 16), second, the Lord reassured Abram by reiterating the two signal promises; children and land (v. 7a.).[438]

Hagar and the El [God] Who Sees … Genesis 16:7-13

> (7) An angel of the LORD found her by a spring of water in the wilderness, the spring on the road to Shur, (8) and said, Hagar, slave of Sarai, where have you come from, and where are you going?" And she said, "I am running away from

---

[434] *Torah*: is the first five books of the *Tanakh* also known as the Pentateuch or the five books of Moses. *Haftaros*: This Hebrew term meaning "conclusion" refers to the reading from the Prophets that supple-ments and follows the Torah portion read in the synagogue on the Sabbath and holidays (Alfred J. Kolatch, *Inside Judaism* [Middle Village, NY: Jonathan David Publishers, 2006], 225). *Five Megillos*: Five books of the Bible – Esther, Lamentations, Song of Songs, Ruth, and Ecclesiastes – are designated *Megillot*, meaning "scrolls." The word *Megillah*, when used without specification, refers to the Scroll of Esther (Alfred J. Kolatch, *Inside Judaism*, 332).

[435] *HaShem*: This is a common epression by Jewish people who do not wish to speak God's name; it simply means "the Name." *HaShem* would be inserted instead of Yahweh, the personal name of God.

[436] Scherman, *The Chumash: The Stone Edition*, 57.

[437] Atkinson, *The Pocket Commentary of the Bible: Genesis*, 118.

[438] Mathews, The New American Commentary: Genesis 11:27-50:26, 119.

my mistress Sarai." (9) And the angel of the LORD said to her, "Go back to your mistress, and submit to her harsh treatment." (10) And the angel of the LORD said to her, "I will greatly increase your offspring, And they shall be too many to count." (11) The angel of the LORD said to her further, "Behold, you are with child and shall bear a Son; You shall call him Ishmael, for the LORD has paid heed to your suffering. (12) He shall be a wild ass of a man; His hand against everyone, and everyone's hand against him; He shall dwell alongside of all his kinsmen." (13) And she called the LORD who spoke to her, "You are El-roi," by which she meant, "Have I not gone on seeing after He saw me!"

In this passage from Genesis, two personages are presented, first Hagar and then "*the angel of the LORD*." This is the first recorded instance of "*the angel of the LORD*" as both Atkinson and Morris recognize:

> This is the first time that this expression occurs in the Bible.... The angel of the Lord was recognized in the OT to be Jahweh Himself....[439]

> This is the first occurrence of this phrase in the Bible, and the context indicates (v. 13) that this "angel" was indeed God Himself, that is, another pre-incarnate appearance of the Messiah.[440]

The translation of "angel" is misleading because in the Hebrew, it designates a human or heavenly "messenger," as was shown in the previous chapter. Although the first reference to the person of "*the angel of the LORD*" in Genesis 16:7 clearly shows a distinction between *Yahweh* and the Messenger (Angel) of the LORD, Von Rad acknowledges that the Messenger of the LORD and the LORD are one and the same in the following statement:

> The patriarchal narratives are very strange; for here there is no clear distinction between the angel of the LORD and Yahweh himself. The one who speaks, now Yahweh (16:10, 13; 21:17, 19; 22:11), now the messenger (who then speaks of God in the third person), is obviously one and the same person. The angel of the LORD is therefore a form in which Yahweh appears. He is God himself in human form.[441]

Even though Von Rad recognizes the Messenger (Angel) of the LORD as God, it is unclear whether or not he sees a distinction between the two. What he does recognize is that the "Messenger" and *Yahweh* are the same. To the contrary, Currid sees the distinction between *Yahweh* and the Messenger (Angel) of the LORD:

> This Angel is identified with God later in the passage (16:13), and he speaks as if he is God (16:10-12). That identification is made elsewhere in the Bible

---

[439] Atkinson, *The Pocket Commentary of the Bible: Genesis,* 150.

[440] Morris, *The Genesis Record*, 330.

[441] Gerhard Von Rad, *The Old Testament Library: Genesis* (Philadelphia: Westminster, 1961), 188.

(Ex 3:2; Judg 13:17-22). To put it simply, the Angel of Yahweh is a manifestation of Yahweh himself – he is God in human form. A strong argument can be made that the Angel of Yahweh is the Second Person of the Trinity, a pre-incarnate Christ.[442]

Others, such as Westermann, do see this as a theophany, and he adds that one person (God) is meeting another person:

> This is saying something decisive for the meaning of יהוה מַלְאַךְ: it is a messenger of God who in the form of a person meets a person on earth who is on route or about his work (Judg 13).[443]

Westermann does not commit himself as to whether or not this "messenger" is just a heavenly being or God Himself. But other authors, such as Talbot, say that Moses presents a member of the plural unity of *Elohim* who took on a physical form. God in His unity is plural, as was discussed in chapter 3. God who is pure spirit is represented by another member of the plural unity of *Elohim* who reveals Himself to Hagar with a message that only God would know:

> The language in verse 10 supports the interpretation that the divine visitant here was an appearance of Christ in a human form, for the angel said that He would give Hagar many descendants. He had supernatural knowledge for He knew she was pregnant, that she would bear a son, and that the child was to be named Ishmael (Hebrew for 'God hears'). Ishmael's character according to the "angel of the Lord" would be that of a fiercely independent person, roaming the deserts.[444]

Gordon Wenham's remark is short but to the point, for he clearly, without hesitation, sees the Messenger (Angel) of the LORD as God when stating, "This must be understood as God himself appearing in human form."[445]

In these verses the Messenger (Angel) of the LORD (מַלְאַךְ יְהוָה or mal'ak *Yahweh*) is mentioned four times in verses 7 and 9-11 and referred to by Hagar once in verse 13 as "the God who sees" (אֵל רֳאִי). Hagar used the word for God that is in the singular אֵל or *El*. This Messenger (Angel) speaks as God and in the name of God when He makes the following statements to Hagar. The emphasis is to draw attention to the phrases that point out that the Messenger of the LORD is more than just any ordinary messenger:

v. 8: Hagar, **slave of Sarai**,....

v. 9: Go back to your mistress, and **submit to her harsh treatment**.

[442] Currid, *A Study Commentary: Genesis 1:1-25:18*, 1:305.

[443] Claus Westermann, *Genesis 1-11: A Continental Commentary* (Translated by John J. Scullion. Minneapolis: Fortress Press, 1994), 242.

[444] Talbot, *A Study of the Book of Genesis*, 110-111.

[445] Gordon Wenham, *Word Biblical Commentary: Genesis 16-50* (Waco: Word, 1994), 9.

v. 10: **I will greatly increase your offspring**, And they shall be too many to count.

v. 11: Behold, you **are with child** and shall **bear a son**; You shall call him Ishmael, for the LORD has paid heed to your suffering.

v. 12: He shall be a wild ass of a man; His hand against everyone, and **everyone's hand against him**; He shall dwell alongside of all his kinsmen.

First, the Messenger (Angel) of the LORD knew her situation in Genesis 16:8-9. He knew who she was and to whom she belonged. He told her to submit to the harshness of Sarai. Second, the Angel (Messenger) of the LORD said, "I will" multiply your descendants exceedingly (verse 10) and will make a great nation from her son (Genesis 21:18). The "I will" is the same language in Genesis 12:2-3 where *Yahweh* gives Abram three "I wills." Third, the Messenger (Angel) of the LORD proceeds to tell Hagar that she is pregnant and will have a son (verse (11), and there was no ultrasound in those days. Lastly, He tells Hagar the character of her son (verse (12). Notice never once does the Messenger speak for God, but He speaks with the authority of God. But also notice the response of Hagar after it is over. She calls him *El Roi*, "the God who sees." Lastly, Moses, who recorded the occasion, distinctly called the Angel, the LORD (Genesis 16:13), and Moses would never have applied the sacred name of *Yahweh* to anyone who was not divine or God Himself.[446]

Even Von Rad states that "she saw the one who saw her."[447] Morris notes that Hagar called the well where all this occurred Beer-lahai-roi meaning, "the well of the Living One who seeth me."[448] This was a far different conclusion on her part, who had been raised in Egypt with all the gods that the Egyptians worshipped (Genesis 16:2-3).

This Theophany of God, the Messenger (Angel) of the LORD, who appeared to Hagar was God. Hagar knew that the Messenger (Angel) of the LORD had heard her affliction and then with the authority of God Himself, speaking as God, fulfilled these promises in the power of God on her behalf. Hagar's response indicated that she understood who had seen her and had spoken to her.

The LORD Appears to Abraham … Genesis 17:1, 22

(1) When Abram was ninety-nine years old, the LORD appeared to Abram and said to him, "I am El Shaddai. Walk in My ways and be blameless."

(22) And when He was done speaking with him, God was gone from Abraham.

---

[446] Renald Showers, *Those Invisible Spirits Called Angels* (Bellmawr, NJ: Friends of Israel Gospel Ministry, 1997), 158.

[447] Von Rad, *The Old Testament Library: Genesis*, 189.

[448] Morris, *The Genesis Record*, 331.

Genesis 17:1 is the first of five narratives where Moses explicitly states that the LORD "appeared" (וַיֵּרָא יְהֹוָה) to Abraham, Isaac and Jacob (Genesis 12:7; 18:1; 26:2, 24; 35:9). Unlike the similar statement in chapter 18 (וַיֵּרָא אֵלָיו יְהֹוָה verse 1), where the author devotes special attention to the actual nature of the Lord's appearance, here the interest of the author seems to lie solely in what the Lord said, not in the nature of the appearance itself.

Moses had immediately identified God as the LORD (יְהֹוָה verse 1b), the God of the covenant at Sinai (Exodus 3:15). Within the narrative, however, God identified Himself to Abram as "God Almighty" (*El Shaddai*). In so doing, Moses removed all doubt regarding the faith of Abram at that stage in the narrative. Abram worshipped the covenant making God, *Yahweh* (יְהֹוָה), but he knew Him only as בְּאֵל שַׁדָּי or as "God Almighty" (Exodus 6:3).[449] Sailhamer ties together some interesting facts, one of which needs to be expanded. Moses in Exodus 6:3 states that Abram did not know God by the name *Yahweh*, but by "God Almighty." Yet in Genesis 17:1 Moses referred to *Yahweh*. It would seem strange that Moses throughout the Genesis narrative uses God's name as *Yahweh* when He was not known by that name. There are several explanations given by the following authors:

> When the establishment of the covenant commenced, as described in Gen 15, with the institution of the covenant sign of circumcision and the promise of the birth of Isaac, Jehovah said to Abram, "I am EL SHADDAI, God Almighty," and from that time forward manifested Himself to Abram and his wife as the Almighty, in the birth of Isaac, which took place apart altogether from the powers of nature, and also in the preservation, guidance, and multiplication of his seed. It was in His attribute as El Shaddai that God had revealed His nature to the patriarchs; but now He was about to reveal Himself to Israel as JEHOVAH, as the absolute Being working with unbounded freedom in the performance of His promises. For not only had He established His covenant with the fathers (v. 4), but He had also heard the groaning of the children of Israel, and remembered His covenant (verse 5; וְגַם , not only – but also). The divine promise not only commences in verse 2, but concludes at verse 8, with the emphatic expression, "I Jehovah," to show that the work of Israel's redemption resided in the power of the name Jehovah.[450]

George Bush adds some additional insight in the first view:

> Others, and we think for better reasons, understand the words as implying, not that the literal name 'Jehovah' was unknown to the ancient fathers who preceded Moses, but that its true, full, and complete import – its force, burden, and pregnant significancy, was not before known; whereas now hereafter, the chosen people should come to understand this august name, not in the letter

---

[449] Sailhamer, *The Expositor's Bible Commentary: Genesis,* 137.
[450] Keil and Delitzsch*, Commentary on the Old Testament: Genesis*, 1:467-468.

merely, but in the actual realization of all which it implied. The name 'Jehovah,' as before remarked, natively denotes not only God's eternal existence, but also his unchangeable truth and omnipotent power, which give being to his promises by the actual performance of them.[451]

Their argument definitely has many plausible points and makes it worth studying Exodus 3:3-8, which does have a larger immediate context than just verse 3. So it is not that the patriarchs did not know the name, but that their concept of God was best described as *El Shaddai*:

> The meaning is, not that the name Jehovah was never used by them or given of God to them; but that its special significance had not been manifested to them as he was now about to make it manifest. His power God had revealed – His power to protect them in their perils, his power to fulfill to Abraham [the] promise of a son; but such a glorious testimony to his faithfulness in fulfilling promise as was now to be given, the patriarchs had never seen.[452]

> It was not the name, but the true depth of its significance which was unknown to and uncomprehended by the patriarchs. They had known God as the omnipotent, El Shaddai (Gen 17:1; 28:3), the ruler of the physical universe, and of man as one of his creatures; as a God eternal, immutable, and true to his promises he was yet to be revealed.[453]

Therefore, the best understanding of Exodus 6:3 is that the patriarchs knew the name *Yahweh* (Jehovah), but did not fully comprehend the name *Yahweh* as they understood the name *El Shaddai*.

These above interpretations of Exodus 6:3 raise an issue in relation to the *El Shaddai* passage of Genesis 17:1. If God was known by both names, LORD and *El Shaddai*, by the patriarchs in the Genesis narrative, why does the text only use *El Shaddai* six times (Genesis 17:1; 28:3; 35:11; 43:14; 48:3; 49:3),[454] but uses *Yahweh* 165 times?[455] It must be conceded that the previous question when compared to the book of Job which used *El Shaddai* 30 times (*Yahweh* 32, *Eloah* 41, *Elohim* 17, and *El* 47 times), raises even more questions. For Job has been viewed as being written during the patriarchal period, yet Job uses *El Shaddai* 24 more times than does the book of Genesis. There is a predominant usage of *El Shaddai* in Job and not in Genesis where God specifically says that the patriarchs knew Him by that name.

This author also suggests Moses was writing history for the nation of Israel for his own generation and for future generations. To account for the repeated usage of God's

---

[451] George Bush, *Exodus* (Minneapolis: Klock & Klock Christian Publishers, 1981), 83.

[452] Butler, *Butler's Bible Work*, 1:598. Contributing author Henry Cowles.

[453] William Smith, *Dictionary of the Bible* (Boston: Little, Brown, and Company, 1863), 1:958.

[454] Sailhamer, *The Expositor's Bible Commentary: Genesis,* 1:340.

[455] Jenni and Westermann, *Theological Lexicon of the Old Testament,* 2:523.

148

name (165 times) in Genesis was to connect the patriarchs to the generation of Moses' day so that Israel understood that the God who made the promises to the patriarchs (*El Shaddai*) is the same LORD (*Yahweh*) who gave them deliverance from Egypt.

In the text of Genesis 17:1 *El Shaddai* and *Yahweh* are the same personalities and the verse distinctly states that *Yahweh* "appeared" to Abram. That is the same word used in Genesis 12:7. "To appear" means to see things that were unable to be seen until they appeared visibly so that they could be seen by the human eye. In Genesis 15:1, *Yahweh* uses the medium of a vision to make the covenant with Abram. But vision and actual appearances are two totally different things. Genesis 17 gives a further elaboration of the promise in chapter 12 and of the covenant in chapter 15. Verse 22 of chapter 17 is very critical in understanding the word "appeared" for it specifically states *"and he left off talking with him, and God went up from Abraham."* As Mathews states, "God went up," indicating a visible ascension; it is the language of Theophany (35:13; cp. 18:33; Exodus 21:18).[456] The Jewish Tanakh states, as quoted at the beginning of this section, that God was simply gone from Abraham. That reduces the impact of what verse 22 implies. Literally, God ascended, or "went up" (וַיַּעַל) before Abraham's eyes, even as Targum of Onkelos on the Torah states "the Glory of the Lord ascended up from Abraham."

The LORD Appears Again to Abraham
... Genesis 18:1-22, 33

(1) The LORD appeared to him by the terebinths (plains) of Mamre; he was sitting at the entrance of the tent as the day grew hot. (2) Looking up, he saw three men standing near him. As soon as he saw them, he ran from the entrance of the tent to greet them and, bowing to the ground, (3) he said, "My lords, if it please you, do not go on past your servant. (4) Let a little water be brought; bathe your feet and recline under the tree. (5) And let me fetch a morsel of bread that you may refresh yourselves; then go on – seeing that you have come your servant's way." They replied, "Do as you have said."

(6) Abraham hastened into the tent to Sarah, and said, "Quick, three seahs (measures) of choice flour! Knead and make cakes!" (7) Then Abraham ran to the herd, took a calf, tender and choice, and gave it to a servant-boy, who hastened to prepare it. (8) He took curds and milk and the calf that had been prepared and set these before them; and he waited on them under the tree as they ate. (9) They said to him, "Where is your wife Sarah?" And he replied, "There, in the tent." (10) Then one said, "I will return to you next year, and your wife Sarah shall have a son!" Sarah was listening at the entrance of the tent, which was behind him.

---

[456] Mathews, *The New American Commentary: Genesis 11:27-50:26*, 207.

(11) Now Abraham and Sarah were old, advanced in years; Sarah had stopped having the periods of women. (12) And Sarah laughed to herself, saying, "Now that I am withered, am I to have enjoyment – with my husband so old?" (13) Then the LORD said to Abraham, "Why did Sarah laugh, saying, 'shall I in truth bear a child, old as I am?' (14) Is anything too wondrous for the LORD? I will return to you at the same season next year, and Sarah shall have a son." (15) Sarah lied, saying, "I did not laugh," for she was frightened. But he replied, "You did laugh."

(16) The men set out from there and looked down toward Sodom, Abraham walking with them to see them off. (17) Now the LORD had said, "Shall I hide from Abraham what I am about to do, (18) since Abraham is to become a great and populous nation and all the nations of the earth are to bless themselves by him? (19) For I have singled him out, that he may instruct his children and his posterity to keep the way of the LORD by doing what is just and right, in order that the LORD may bring about for Abraham what He has promised him." (20) Then the LORD said, "The outrage of Sodom and Gomorrah is so great, and their sin so grave! (21) I will go down to see whether they have acted altogether according to the outcry that has reached Me; if not, I will take note." (22) The men went on from there to Sodom, while Abraham remained standing before the LORD.

(33) When the LORD had finished speaking to Abraham, He departed; and Abraham returned to his place.

In Genesis 18:1-17 there are five personalities in the context, of which two were human beings (Abraham and Sarah) and the other three were messengers from heaven. Those three personalities need to be investigated. The identities of these three men or heavenly representatives, one of them in particular, must be determined by careful study of strategic verses in this section of Scripture. Also there are key words and phrases such as "appeared" and "*Abraham stood yet before the LORD*" and "*the LORD went his way ... and Abraham returned to his place*" that need to be understood. As will be shown in Genesis 18, God can make Himself known by using whatever mode He chooses as Sailhamer states:

> The biblical God is one who makes himself known intimately and concretely to his covenant people. He can make himself known through "speaking" (1:3), "in a vision" (15:1), or through his "angel" (16:7) who speaks for him. He can even "appear" to individuals, as in 12:7; 17:1; and 18:1.[457]

The verb "appeared" signifies a physical appearance of God.[458] God is not limited as mankind is; He can choose to appear in a human form. Since God created human beings, flesh is not evil. Only sin is evil. Most scholars will agree that the three men are

---

[457] Sailhamer, *The Pentateuch as Narrative: A Biblical-Theological Commentary,* 163.
[458] Currid, *A Study Commentary: Genesis 1:1-25:18,* 1:323.

minimally angelic beings who appeared as men. Because three men appear before Abraham, scholars like Ellicott refer to the Church of England (Anglican) teaching that this is the trinity:[459]

> The number three pointed also to the Trinity of Persons in the Godhead, and is therefore read by our Church as one of the lessons for Trinity Sunday.[460]

Genesis 18 is the only occurrence in the Scriptures where the biblical text has "three men," a trio of heavenly guests, one of which is presented as a theophany.[461] Any general study of Genesis 18-19 draws nearly everyone to the same conclusion, that this is not an example of the Trinity in the *Tanakh* as the Anglican Church has taught.

Like Genesis 17:1 this passage begins with *Yahweh* appearing before Abram. However, Genesis 18:1 includes two other individuals that appeared with the LORD. These three persons are very important to identify, so that the personages can be clarified as they appear in Genesis chapters 18 and 19. Sailhamer states:

> The narrative begins, in the same way as chapter 17, with the author's report that "the LORD [יְהוָה] appeared [וַיֵּרָא] to Abraham." The importance of this comment at the beginning of the narrative should not be overlooked. Its effect is to help clarify one of the most puzzling features of that narrative, namely, who were the three men who visited Abraham and what was their mission?[462]

As Genesis 18-19 are observed these three persons will be distinguished. When the LORD and the two other men appear before Abraham in verse 2, he immediately acknowledges them and runs to meet them. In the ancient Near East, hospitality was extended to visitors, but Abraham's reaction to their appearance was not mere hospitality. There is another explanation for his quick and decisive response. The following proposal has biblical backing: Abraham recognized the LORD who had appeared unto him on at least two other occasions (12:7; 17:1). His quick and immediate response is reflected in the text by words that show Abraham acted quickly; he "*ran*" and he "*bowed himself*" in verse 2. In verse 6 Abraham "*hastened*" to instruct Sarah to "*make ready quickly*," then in verse 7 Abraham "*ran to the herd*," and "*hastened to dress it*." These words all give the sense of urgency about waiting on his guests and more so than normal. Normal hospitality was common, but Abraham responded with an unusual sense of urgency in action and word. This urgency suggests that Abraham was aware, or minimally sensed, that these visitors are extraordinary and special. Keil and Delitzsch also point out this perspective:

---

[459] Victor P. Hamilton, *The New International Commentary on the Old Testament: Genesis 18-50* (Grand Rapids: Eerdmans, 1995), 8.

[460] Payne Smith, *The Handy Commentary: Genesis,* ed. Charles John Ellicott, 206.

[461] Mathews, *The New American Commentary: Genesis 11:27-50:26,* 2:216.

[462] Sailhamer, *The Expositor's Bible Commentary: Genesis,* 2:142.

Perceiving at once that one of them was the Lord, he prostrated himself reverentially before them, and entreated them not to pass him by, but to suffer him to entertain them as his guests.[463]

Abraham's urgency is clearly seen, because he did recognize the LORD. On another occasion, in Judges 13, the LORD appeared multiple times to Manoah's wife, and the text specifically states that she recognized "*the angel of the LORD*" when He returned the second time (Judges 13:9-10). Now the biblical texts from Genesis 12:7 and Genesis 17:1 give good evidence that Abraham recognized the LORD when He and the other two stood by him. This event may be what *Yeshua* was referring to in John 8:56-59.

When the scene opens in Genesis 18:3 Abraham is addressing only one of the three men before him, because he probably recognized him from prior appearances. Currid states that this encounter is in the singular form between Abraham and the LORD:

> Abraham addresses the visitors with the Hebrew name *Adonai*, which literally means 'my Lord.' It is a singular appellation, and it is followed by three singular forms in the verse. Abraham is thus speaking directly to one person. The term *Adonai* is reserved for God in the Scriptures. Then in verses 4-5 Abraham includes all three of the travelers as he speaks to them in the second person plural.[464]

Sailhamer continues with the same thought:

> There appears to be a conscious shift in the verbal forms between v. 3 and vv. 4-9. In v. 3 the verbs and pronouns are all singular masculine, whereas in vv. 4-9 the forms are plural masculine.[465]

Currid and Sailhamer concur that in Genesis 18:3, Abraham addresses only *Yahweh*. Yet in verses 4-9 he is speaking in the plural to all three. Careful analysis of the text clarifies that not only does Abraham address the LORD, but the LORD is the spokesman for the group, as can be seen in verses 1, 13, 17, 20, 22, 26, and 33.[466]

At this point it is needful to address the Jewish tradition and interpretation as to who the three men were that appeared suddenly before Abraham in the heat of the day. Some Jewish scholars teach that the three men were simply heavenly messengers (angels) and they suggest names of the messengers (angels) and give reasons why there were three of them. See the following comments:

> In response, God sent him three angels in the guise of people.... Three men, as is apparent from the rest of the narrative, they were actually angels in the "guise" of men. God sent three different angels because, by definition, an angel

---

[463] Keil & Delitzsch, *Commentary on the Old Testament: Genesis*, 1:228.
[464] Currid, *A Study Commentary: Genesis 1:1-25\:18*, 1:324.
[465] Sailhamer, *The Expositor's Bible Commentary: Genesis,* 2:143.
[466] Talbot, *A Study of the Book of Genesis*, 118.

is a function that God wishes to have performed. Thus, each function is a new angel, and since there were three missions to be accomplished in connection with Abraham and Sarah at this time, there were three angels to carry them out. In the words of the Midrash, "one angel does not perform two missions." In this case the three angels *were* Michael, who informed Abraham that Sarah would have a son [v. 14]; Gabriel, who overturned Sodom [19:25]; and Raphael, who healed Abraham and saved Lot (Rashi as explained by Gur Aryeh). The last two tasks, healing Abraham and saving Lot, constituted a single mission because they were for the sake of rescue.[467]

There is absolutely nothing that would even hint at these Jewish interpretations. In none of the biblical accounts, let alone Genesis, are the three men (messengers or angels) ever given names. Second, rabbinic sources said that God sent three messengers who looked like men because they can only function with one task at a time, meaning that one was to heal Abraham (circumcision), another was to overturn Sodom and Gomorrah, and the last one was to tell Abraham and Sarah of the future birth of their son. Does this mean that angels cannot multi-task and human beings who are created lower than angels can? To repeat, there is nothing in the Genesis account to substantiate that kind of interpretation. The second observation includes the need for Abraham to be healed from circumcision. Since when did Abraham need to be healed from his circumcision? He surely had no problems moving about with his running here and there and he did it all with haste in making provision of the meal for his three guests. Now notice how other Jewish rabbis interpret the meaning of the three men:

> The angels Michael, Gabriel, and Raphael disguised as Arab wayfarers. Michael came to announce to Sarah that she would give birth to a son, Raphael came to heal Abraham from his circumcision; and Gabriel's mission was to overturn Sodom (Bava Metzia 86b).[468]

Nowhere in the Genesis 18 text does it state that the three men were disguised as "Arab wayfarers." Ishmael was only 12 years old at this time and not married and had no sons. It would be impossible to have Arabs coming to Abraham, for at this point in history there were no Arabs, just lonely Ishmael himself who would be the father of the Arabs. Once again Jewish rabbis are diverting the Jewish people away from the reality of the passage that one of those messengers was the LORD Himself. Notice how the diversion continues from the point that God is making in the text:

> My Lord. According to most interpretations, the word אֲדֹנָי in this passage is sacred, referring to God. In taking leave from God, Abraham implored Him to pass not away from Your servant, but wait while he attended to his guests. Abraham's action shows that "hospitality to wayfarers is greater than receiving the Divine Presence" (Shevuos 35b; Shabbos 127a). Abraham's departure from

---

[467] Scherman, *The Stone Edition: The Chumash, The Torah: Haftoros and Five Megillos,* 79.
[468] Avraham Yaakov Finkel, *The Torah Revealed* (San Francisco: Jossey-Bass, 2004), 39.

God was not disrespectful, however, because he knew that by hurrying to serve God's creatures, he was serving God Himself (Tanchuma Yashan).[469]

"And they ate." Angels do not eat in the human sense; they only appeared to eat. This teaches that one should not deviate from the local custom (Rashi). In the Kabbalistic sense, angels, as spiritual beings, receive their sustenance from holiness.[470]

There is no reference in the *Tanakh* that says angels only appear to eat. The Scriptures do not address that subject at all. It is absolutely amazing that rabbinic scholars of old could make up such stories just to get away from the inevitable, that *Yahweh* and two of His messengers (angels) came and met and dialoged and shared a meal with Abraham.

In reading the statements that come out of rabbinic literature, people may say that they do not remember reading anything in Scripture that even suggests this kind of interpretation. That is because in all of the biblical texts there is absolutely nothing that would even hint at the above Jewish interpretations.

One further point that the rabbis did not bring up was that Abraham fed *Yahweh* the LORD and two messengers (angels) a rabbinic [rather than biblical] non-kosher meal. This was a meat and dairy meal, which is strictly forbidden by Orthodox Judaism. What rabbis claim to be a law of God is not biblical, but only man made rules and regulations. In summary to the Jewish responses, their comments are a disguise to distract Jewish people from seeing that God did appear in human form and that *Elohim* is a plurality in unity.

Many people chafe at the virgin birth of the Messiah, yet the promise that is given here to Sarah (Genesis 18:12-14) and Abraham (Genesis 17:15-17) and its fulfillment (Genesis 21:1-8) was also a miracle. The context of those passages strongly indicates that since Sarah had stopped having her menstrual cycle, getting pregnant was not possible, and both of them knew it (Romans 4:17-22; Hebrews 11:11). Yet the LORD questions Sarah as to whether anything would be "too hard" for Him. The Hebrew word הֲיִפָּלֵא translated as "is he too hard" [a verb form] from the root word פלא [too hard] is the same word used in Isaiah 9:6-7 as a noun, where it is translated "wonderful" and speaks to the character of the Messiah. This word פלא ("too hard") is used only of God.

The identity of one of the three men that visited with Abraham is *Yahweh* (LORD) as has already been seen. In Genesis 18:16 Abraham walks together with the LORD and the other two messengers (angels). The other two men (messengers or angels) are separated from the LORD in Genesis 18:22 when they turn and leave Abraham (Genesis 19:1, 15). The text states that they were messengers (angels) who went to

[469] Scherman, *The Stone Edition: The Chumash, The Torah: Haftoros and Five Megillos*, 79.

[470] Scherman, *The Stone Edition: The Chumash, The Torah: Haftoros and Five Megillos*, 79-80.

Sodom to destroy it. The word "stood" reflects the idea of continuance, Abraham remained standing before the LORD who had been speaking to him (Genesis 18:22).

After the two angels left the presence of the LORD and Abraham, Abraham pled for the righteous that might be in the city (Lot's family) in Genesis 18:23-32. However, notice in verse 22 it clearly says, "*but Abraham stood yet before the LORD.*" Then when Abraham got down to ten possible righteous ones in Sodom, he stopped and verse 33 states, "*And the LORD went his way, as soon as he had left communing with Abraham: and Abraham returned unto his place.*" Genesis 18 shows with clear unmistakable language that *Yahweh* appeared to Abraham as a theophany, in a physical form. He ate with Abraham, told Sarah about getting pregnant, and shared with Abraham about what He was going to do with Sodom and Gomorrah. After they finished talking, the LORD departed and Abraham returned to his tent.

The LORD Rained Fire … from the LORD … Genesis 19:24

The LORD rained upon Sodom and Gomorrah sulfurous fire from the LORD out of heaven.

The literal method of interpretation and using God's Word just as He gave it through Moses documents that there are two LORDs present in the text. One of them is undoubtedly the LORD who met with Abraham in chapter 18 and another LORD who is in heaven. *Yahweh* is a singular noun, therefore this verse indicates two *Yahwehs* involved in the destructive action against Sodom and Gomorrah. The Jewish statement on this verse admits to only one LORD doing the action against the two cities. It does not interact with the usage of two *Yahwehs* or *HaShems*. Notice the rabbinic explanation:

> Now HaShem had caused…to rain. The Torah uses the Name that denotes mercy, and it speaks of rain, although what descended from heaven was hardly rain in the usual sense of the word. This is because nothing evil descends directly from Heaven. First it descended as beneficent rain; only when it approached earth did it become sulfur and fire (*Tanchuma*). [471]

The rabbinic explanation does not interact at all with the two *Yahwehs* in the *Tanakh*; their answer avoids the obvious and just does not coincide with other passages in the *Tanakh*. In 2 Kings 1:3 "*the angel* (Messenger) *of the LORD*" gives Elijah a message and then in verse 4 tells Elijah to speak in the name of the LORD, who then sent down fire from heaven to destroy three groups of fifty soldiers on two different successive occasions. Also, in 1 Kings 18:38 God sent down fire upon the altar that Elijah built on Mt. Carmel. So God does send fire from heaven. Also in Genesis 7:10-12 God sent rain to destroy the earth with a flood. The rabbinic argument that nothing evil comes from

---

[471] Scherman, *The Stone Edition: The Chumash, The Torah: Haftoros and Five Megillos*, 89.

heaven simply is not logical. Another rabbinic argument against the passage having two LORDs is related in the Talmud as follows:

> אָמַר לֵיהּ It was further related that a certain heretic said to Rabbi Yishmael the son of Rabbi Yose: The verse states (Gen 19:24): "Then the Lord rained upon Sodom and upon Gomorrah brimstone and fire from the Lord out of heaven." Surely, the verse should have read: "Then the Lord rained upon Sodom and Gomorrah brimstone and fire from Him," for the Torah's formulation implies that there is more than one God! A certain launderer who heard the heretic's argument said to Rabbi Yishmael: Leave him to me, for I will answer him. The verse dealing with Sodom and Gomorrah is similar to the verse that states (Gen 4:23): "And Lemech said unto his wives, Adah and Zillah, Hear my voice, wives of Lemech." There, too, it might be argued that the verse should have read: "And Lemech said to his wives, Adah and Zillah, Hear my voice, my wives," rather than "wives of Lemech," for it is Lemech himself talking. Rather, you must say that this is the way that the Torah speaks, repeating the subject's name even though a pronoun would have sufficed. Here, too, then, regarding Sodom and Gomorrah, you can say that is the way the Torah speaks, repeating the subject's name even though a pronoun would have sufficed.[472]

The launderer's argument reveals two things: First, Lemech is only one person with two wives and regardless of how the Genesis 4:23 passage reads, even a casual reader of the text understands that Lemech is speaking to his two wives. The problem is that in the text the wives are named and whether or not Lemech used the expression "wives of Lemech" or "my wives," it is still one Lemech and two wives. The fact remains that the Torah, which is the inspired Word of *HaShem*, in Genesis 19:24 clearly implies two *HaShem*'s. So it is of little significance whether Lemech is mentioned twice, or by name once with a pronoun. It does nothing for the rabbi's argument concerning Genesis 19:24. The text in Genesis 19:24 clearly indicates that the LORD Who was standing with Abraham called "down" fire from the LORD in heaven. Genesis 19:24 is God's inspired Word and He wrote exactly how He wanted mankind to understand it.

Currid in his commentary on Genesis misses the point of two *Yahwehs* and even goes to great lengths to argue that the use of two *Yahwehs* "appears redundant and unnecessary."[473] As elsewhere in His Word, God does not use redundant and unnecessary language in Genesis 19:24. Saying that His inspired Word is "redundant and unnecessary" is an affront to God. *Yahweh*, the LORD, appeared to Abraham, interacted with him, fellowshipped with him, ate with him, made a promise to him (Sarah), and discussed the plight of Sodom and Gomorrah with him. Then this same LORD or *Yahweh* called down fire and brimstone from the LORD in heaven. The uniqueness of this is that *Yahweh* is a singular noun, referring to the one and only God of Israel. Yet in Genesis 19:24 two *Yahwehs* are present in the Torah. The pre-incarnate

---

[472] Steinsaltz, *The Talmud: The Steinsaltz Edition,* San 38b, 17:89.
[473] Currid, *A Study Commentary: Genesis 1:1-25:18,* 1:350

Messiah and the Father are both *Yahweh*. They are a plurality in unity, thus showing the plural unity of *Elohim*. This will be laid out in more detail in later chapters.

Westermann, as well as Keil and Delitzsch do not see the plurality of God in Genesis 19:24. Westermann incorrectly says that "the only explanation of the text is that two different descriptions of God's judgment have merged."[474] Keil and Delitzsch also do not see the plurality of God as revealed in the following quote:

> In the words 'Jehovah caused it to rain from Jehovah' there is no distinction implied between the hidden and the manifested God, between the Jehovah present upon earth in His angels who called down the judgment, and the Jehovah enthroned in heaven who sent it down.[475]

Once again, it needs to be repeated that Genesis 19:24 is the inspired Word of God and what He described through the pen of Moses was that two persons were involved in this passage — the LORD and the LORD, not angels of the LORD as Keil and Delitzsch imply. The language of Genesis 19:24 is too precise to derive anything else from it. There are also those who do not recognize in this passage two separate persons involved in the destruction of Sodom and Gomorrah. They would attempt to say that the second *Yahweh* is used instead of a pronoun; that is the rabbinic argument. They ask how Moses could have written: *Yahweh* rained from Himself (pronoun). This statement involving two *Yahwehs* is meant to be an emphatic statement as to who was involved in the destruction. If Moses had wanted to express one *Yahweh*, he could have used the expression, "God, or *Yahweh*, rained from heaven," and that would have served very adequately to convey such an emphatic statement. Here the LORD was physically present with Abraham and the other two angels were sent ahead to rescue Lot. When the destruction was to occur, "God the Son brought down the rain from God the Father in heaven."[476]

Morris clearly expresses what Genesis 19:24 stated: that the judgment on Sodom and Gomorrah involved two members of the Godhead:

> As Lot and his family fled the city and reached Zoar, "the Lord rained upon Sodom and upon Gomorrah brimstone and fire from the Lord out of heaven." This verse seems to note that two persons of the Godhead were participating. "The LORD" (evidently the one manifested to Abraham) called down the judgment, but it came from "the LORD" out of heaven.[477]

Many commentaries deal only with the judgment motif rather than the most important revelation of the text. God had Moses write His Word in a certain way (verbal, plenary inspiration), because the *Tanakh* is His revelation of Himself to

---

[474] Claus Westermann, *A Continental Commentary: Genesis 12 – 36* (trans. John J. Scullion. Minneapolis: Fortress Press, 1995), 306.

[475] Keil & Delitzsch, *Commentary on the Old Testament: Genesis*, 235.

[476] Leupold, *Exposition of Genesis*, 1:569-570.

[477] Morris, *The Genesis Record*, 353.

mankind. So when God opens the illumination of the mind by direct references to Himself in the Word, the student needs to hear, to listen (*shema*), to take note of the pen of the authors of Scripture.

Three scholars, when dealing with Genesis 19:24, without hesitation, see the plurality of God in the two *Yahwehs* that are involved with the destruction of Sodom and Gomorrah. Arnold Fruchtenbaum clearly refers to the plurality of God in this passage of Scripture. He draws the attention of the student to the plurality in the text.[478] The second author, David L. Cooper, also quickly draws the attention of the reader as seen in the following statement:

> I ask the reader to note the fact that there was one Jehovah who was upon earth and another Jehovah who was in heaven and from whom the Jehovah upon earth caused fire and brimstone to rain down upon the cities of Sodom and Gomorrah. When the record is allowed to give its message untrammeled, we see that there are two divine personalities who are called Jehovah in this instance.[479]

Like Fruchtenbaum and Cooper, Borland also draws attention to the plurality of *Elohim* in this verse. He quotes Genesis 19:24 by inserting comments to again draw attention to it:

> Then the LORD [who appeared and spoke to Abraham] rained brimstone and fire on Sodom and Gomorrah, from the LORD [notice the distinction of persons] out of the heavens.[480]

The conclusion is that the LORD has revealed Himself to mankind once again as God who is one in unity. He is God alone who is also a plurality in unity.

Hagar and the Angel of God … Genesis 21:17-21

> (17) God heard the cry of the boy, and an angel of God called to Hagar from heaven and said to her, "What troubles you, Hagar? Fear not, for God has heeded the cry of the boy where he is. (18) Come, lift up the boy and hold him by the hand, for I will make a great nation of him." (19) Then God opened her eyes and she saw a well of water. She went and filled the skin with water, and let the boy drink. (20) God was with the boy and he grew up; he dwelt in the wilderness and became a bowman. (21) He lived in the wilderness of Paran; and his mother got a wife for him from the land of Egypt.

The difference between this passage (Genesis 21:15-21) and 16:7 is not the name "*angel of God*" and "*the angel of the Lord*," but that He called to Hagar from heaven as He also did to Abraham in Genesis 22:11-12, meaning that this was not a physical

---

[478] Arnold G. Fruchtenbaum, *Genesis* (Tustin, CA: Ariel Press, n.d.), tape series.
[479] Cooper, *What Men Must Believe or God's Gracious Provision for Man,* 106.
[480] Borland, *Christ in the Old Testament,* 152.

appearance as in Genesis 16.[481] Once again, there is a clear distinction between "*the Angel of God*" and "God" in verse 17. God saw and rescued them by His Messenger or Angel who is God. Notice that the "angel" did not act in the name of God but as God. This would also be classified as a theophany, but there is no hint of a personal appearance as in Genesis 16.

God Tested Abraham … Genesis 22:1-2, 11-12, 15-16

(1) And it came to pass after these things, that God did tempt Abraham, and said unto him, Abraham: and he said, Behold, here I am. (2) And he said, Take now thy son, thine only son Isaac, whom thou lovest, and get thee into the land of Moriah; and offer him there for a burnt-offering upon one of the mountains which I will tell thee of.

(11) And the angel of the LORD called unto him out of heaven, and said, Abraham, Abraham: and he said, Here am I. (12) And he said, lay not thine hand upon the lad, neither do thou any thing unto him: for now I know that thou fearest God, seeing thou hast not withheld thy son, thine only son from me.

(15) And the angel of the LORD called unto Abraham out of heaven the second time, (16) and said, By myself have I sworn, saith the LORD, for because thou hast done this thing, and hast not withheld thy son, thine only son: (KJV)…

In verse 1 *Elohim* gave Abraham instructions for offering his son as a sacrifice to Him. When Abraham was about to offer his son, the Messenger (Angel) of *Yahweh* stopped him in verses 11-12. Then the Messenger of *Yahweh* said, "*for now I know that you fear God.*" The Messenger spoke as *Elohim* who initially instructed Abraham. But here in verse 12 the Messenger of *Yahweh* used the personal pronoun "Me," which refers back to verse 1 as *Elohim*. The Messenger (Angel) of *Yahweh* equated Himself equally with *Elohim* by using the personal pronoun "Me."

In this section of Scripture God identifies Himself in four ways: first, as *Elohim* (Genesis 22:1), second, as the Messenger (Angel) of *Yahweh* (verse 11), third as Me (verse 12), referring back to the first two terms for God, and fourth, as *Yahweh* (verse 16).

In this text (Genesis 22), *Elohim* (plural), is speaking and then one of the persons of the plural unity God speaks separately as the Messenger (Angel) of *Yahweh*, who also represents Himself as *Yahweh* in verse 16. This Messenger (Angel) of *Yahweh* identifies Himself as the one who swore to Abraham earlier, which reflects back on the Abrahamic Covenant of Genesis 12 and 15 (also see Judges 2:1). In Genesis 22:11-12, the Messenger (Angel) of *Yahweh* identified Himself with *Elohim* and He also spoke as *Yahweh* in verses 15-16, yet He is distinct from *Elohim*. There are scholars who just do not want to see what God is obviously conveying – that He is one in plurality. Both

---

[481] Leupold, *Exposition of Genesis,* 2:67.

159

Currid and Van Rad seem to make the distinctions obscure as to be "almost completely removed":

> At the critical moment of decision, as Abraham is about to deal the death-blow, the 'Angel of Yahweh' intervenes. This angel speaks as if he is God; in fact, the distinction between the two is almost completely removed.[482]

> Here too the angel of God calls from heaven, and here too the angel of God is only the form in which God makes himself known to man. In fact, the distinction here between the angel and Yahweh seems to be almost completely removed, for in everything it is God's voice that comes to Abraham and solemnly tells him he "fears God."[483]

Currid and Von Rad speak of the distinction but attempt to discount it. Distinct lines are drawn between two distinct personalities that are reflected in this passage. First *Elohim* is a reference to the plural unity of God, and then one of the persons of *Elohim* spoke, the Messenger (Angel) of *Yahweh*, and He identified Himself as *Yahweh*. Remember as well that God created mankind in His "image" and "likeness," and they reflect the plurality of *Elohim* (see chapter 2). Atkinson and Morris clearly reflect the differences and distinction of *Elohim*:

> Notice the change of the Divine Name in the middle of the narrative, a fact that cannot be reconciled with the theories of the liberal critics, who suppose the differentiation of names to indicate a difference of origin for the narratives.[484]

> Note that the "angel of the Lord" commended Abraham because "thou hast not withheld thy son, thine only son, from me" (verse 12). It is evident here that this "angel of the Lord" is claiming to be none other than the Lord himself.[485]

Genesis 22 is different from Genesis 21:17 only in that it is the Messenger (Angel) of the LORD calling to Abraham from heaven and not the Messenger (Angel) of God calling to Hagar. The Messenger (Angel) of the LORD confirms His deity by telling Abraham that he has not withheld his own son from Him.

Clearly, it is seen from the *Tanakh* and from other authors that the Messenger (Angel) of the LORD is distinct from God and yet the same as God, thus expressing the plurality in unity of *Elohim*.

The Jewish Tanakh in Genesis 22:2 and 16 uses the term "favored one" in reference to Isaac. For two reasons they miss the point of what Moses is recording. First of all, the word "favored one" is not the best translation. The Hebrew word is יָחִיד [*yachid*],

---

[482] Currid, *A Study Commentary: Genesis 1:1-25:18*, 1:393.
[483] Von Rad, *The Old Testament Library: Genesis*, 236.
[484] Atkinson, *The Pocket Commentary of the Bible: Genesis*, 199.
[485] Morris, *The Genesis Record*, 381.

translated by Kohlenberger as "only of you" [יְחִידְךָ].[486] Isaac was his favored one, but Abraham also had a great love for Ishmael. This leads to the second point, for Genesis 22:2, 16 is referencing the "only one," the son of promise (Genesis 18:10-15). Ishmael was not the son of promise. Abraham's great love for Ishmael is reflected in his passionate statement to God in Genesis 17:18, *"O that Ishmael might live before thee."*

There is another point related to the resurrection that is not part of the discussion on the tri-unity of God. The New Covenant states that the Sadducees of *Yeshua*'s day did not believe in the resurrection because it could not be found in the Torah of the law of Moses. *Yeshua* answered their unbelief in the resurrection (Matthew 22:23-33; Mark 12:18-27; Luke 20:27-38), but another reference which occurs in Genesis 22:5. Notice that Abraham tells his servants traveling with him and Isaac to wait while he and Isaac go to sacrifice and return. See Abraham's statement of belief in the resurrection when he responds to his servants, *"I and the lad will go yonder and worship, and come again to you."* Because Isaac was the son of promise, Abraham believed that God would have to resurrect Isaac, because of the promises that God had made to him concerning Isaac and his posterity in Genesis 12, 13, 15, 17.

Eliezer and the Angel of the LORD ... Genesis 24:40

This is not as clear a passage with respect to the Messenger (Angel) of the LORD, but it still deserves attention because of its reference to the "angel" that would go before Abraham's servant in Genesis 24:7, 40. In Genesis 24:2-9 Abraham commissioned and sent his servant [probably Eliezer of Damascus] to the house of Bethuel, the nephew of Abraham. As Abraham's servant told the story of why he came and how the LORD led him, in verse 40 he told Bethuel, Laban and those present at the dinner what Abraham had said to him: "The LORD, before whom I walk, will send his angel with thee, and prosper thy way." Walvoord clearly connects this angel with the angel of the Exodus (Exodus 23:20; 32:34; Numbers 20:16):

> The Angel of Jehovah is also revealed to be a distinct person from Jehovah, that is a Person of the Trinity. In Genesis 24:7 (ASV), for instance, Jehovah is described as sending "his angel." The servant of Abraham testifies to the reality of this in Genesis 24:40 (ASV). Moses speaks of Jehovah sending an angel to lead Israel (Num 20:16, ASV).[487]

Walvoord clearly presents the pre-incarnate Messiah as the "angel" that led Abraham's servant in finding Isaac a wife from his kin. In the New Covenant, the author of Hebrews (1:6) quotes Deuteronomy 32:43 in the Greek Septuagint (LXX) and applies

---

[486] Kohlenberger, *The Interlinear NIV Hebrew-English Old Testament,* 50.
[487] Walvoord, *Jesus Christ Our Lord,* 45.

the passage to the Messiah, the Son of God.[488] Notice that in the LXX the angels of heaven are to worship one particular Angel (Hebrews 1:6). If that Angel/Messenger was not God, then the angels of heaven were to worship another created being as God. That has only happened once in eternity and God removed that "anointed Cherub" from His presence; and today he is called Satan (Ezekiel 28:11-19). Is the "angel" of Genesis 24:7, 40 the Messenger (Angel) of the LORD, the "angel" of the Exodus in Exodus 23:20 and 32:34 and the Messenger (Angel) of the LORD who spoke to Israel in Judges 2:1? It cannot be stated dogmatically, but it is very probable.

Rebekah and the LORD's Answer … Genesis 25:23

And the LORD answered her, "Two nations are in your womb, two separate peoples shall issue from your body; One people shall be mightier than the other, and the older shall serve the younger."

This passage is not commonly recognized as a theophany. The following research on this verse as to whether or not others consider this brief passage a theophany turned up little to no comments. Most commentaries do not even raise the issue of a possible theophany. So this author was forced back to the biblical text to see what information Moses gave concerning the words, "*and the LORD answered her*." In verse 21, Isaac as the patriarchal head of the family entreated the LORD on Rebekah's behalf, for she was barren. Then in verse 22, because of the struggle going on within her womb, Rebekah "*went to enquire of the LORD*." This is an open ended statement, for the text does not say where, or even to whom she went to inquire of the LORD. Mathews gives a very disappointing explanation of this phrase:

That Rebekah sought out a prophet or cult functionary who could explain her condition is suggested by "she went to inquire" [daras].[489]

It is not the prophetic part that is troubling, but the implication that she went to a pagan cult site to inquire of the LORD is not probable. In the Genesis account, prophets are not mentioned in the context. Some say that Rebekah appealed to Abraham, Shem and Melchizedek,[490] while others say she did not go to Abraham, Shem or to Melchizedek.[491] To take the Scripture at face value, "*she went to enquire of the LORD*," could be in the privacy of her tent or a special place of solitude near their encampment. The fact is the text does not tell the student where or to whom she might have gone, but it does say she inquired of the LORD.

---

[488] Brenton, *The Septuagint with Apocrypha: Greek and English*, 277. "Rejoice, ye heavens, with him, and let all the angels of God worship him; rejoice ye Gentiles, with his people, and let all the sons of God strengthen themselves in him… ."

[489] Kenneth A. Mathews, *The New American Commentary: Genesis 11:27-50:26* (Nashville: Broadman, 2005), 387.

[490] Keil and Delitzsch, *Commentary on the Old Testament in Ten Volumes: Genesis,* 1:267.

[491] Ellicott, *The Handy Commentary: Genesis*, 262.

The *Tanakh* says, "*And the LORD said unto her.*" The text gives no other information on the issue. This much can be determined from the text. The word "said" is a word that has been discussed before. *Yahweh* said to her; it does not say that He spoke to her through Isaac or Abraham, nor is a dream or vision even hinted at. What students are left with is that *Yahweh* spoke to her audibly, but did not appear to her. This passage also is a theophany. The word "said" means to respond to someone's question or to ask a question with the anticipation that a verbal answer is coming; that is the context of the word "said." In Genesis 4 both God and Cain "said" things back and forth to each other. God also used the word "*said*" when He spoke to Abraham in Genesis 17:1; 18:1; 22:2. In Genesis 22 there is a dialogue between Abraham, Isaac and the servants of Abraham. There is plenty of narration in that chapter. In 1 Samuel 3 there is the dialogue first between Samuel and Eli and then between Samuel and the LORD and the word "said" is used to describe what is communicated to the different parties. So in Genesis 25:23 *Yahweh* "said" to Rebekah and gave the answer to her inquiry of the LORD. Morris has given the best answer of any author that has been consulted:

> Marvelously, the Lord did give her an answer! Whether through a prophet [not likely], or dream [not in the context], or theophany, we are not told, but in some way God spoke to her so clearly that she could never forget the remarkable revelation which she received.[492]

Even though little is said about this passage by other authors, it becomes clear that the LORD spoke to her personally, a theophany, through the Second Person of the plural unity of *Elohim*.

The LORD Appeared to Isaac ... Genesis 26:2-4, 24-25

(2) The LORD had appeared to him and said, "Do not go down to Egypt; stay in the land which I point out to you. (3) Reside in this land, and I will be with you and bless you; I will assign all these lands to you and to your heirs, fulfilling the oath that I swore to your father Abraham. (4) I will make your heirs as numerous as the stars of heaven, and assign to your heirs all these lands, so that all the nations of the earth shall bless themselves by your heirs."

(24) That night the LORD appeared to him and said, "I am the God of your father Abraham. Fear not, for I am with you, and I will bless you and increase your offspring for the sake of My servant Abraham." (25) So he built an altar there and invoked the LORD by name. Isaac pitched his tent there and his servants started digging a well.

In Genesis 26 "*Yahweh* appeared" to Isaac twice in verses 2 and 24 and Moses used the language of theophany. *Yahweh* appeared in a physical manifestation, and God

---

[492] Morris, *The Genesis Record*, 312.

renewed the covenant promises to Isaac that He had made with Abraham his father.[493] The Hebrew word וַיֵּרָא translated "*and he appeared*" is the same word used in Genesis 12:7; 17:1; 18:1. This is the first time that *Yahweh* appeared to Isaac personally. Rebekah heard the LORD speak to her in relation to the question of the struggling within her womb. Isaac heard the words of the LORD when he and Abraham were on Mt. Moriah, when he was delivered from being a sacrifice. But Isaac had never heard the LORD speak to or appear to him as He had done to Rebekah and Abraham.[494]

Yahweh appeared to Isaac in a physical form, just as he had to his father Abraham on several occasions. So when God chose to appear on these two occasions, He did so in human form. He did not appear as the Father, but as the Second Person of the plural unity of *Elohim*, the Son, the pre-incarnation of the Messiah of Israel.

Jacob's Ladder ... Genesis 28:12-15

(12) He had a dream; a stairway was set on the ground and its top reached to the sky, and angels of God were going up and down on it. (13) And the LORD was standing beside him and He said, "I am the LORD, the God of your father Abraham and the God of Isaac: the ground on which you are lying I will assign to you and to your offspring. (14) Your descendants shall be as the dust of the earth; you shall spread out to the west and to the east, to the north and to the south. All the families of the earth shall bless themselves by you and your descendants. (15) Remember, I am with you: I will protect you wherever you go and will bring you back to this land. I will not leave you until I have done what I have promised you."

Genesis 28:12-15 and Genesis 31:11-13 are closely connected. Here the LORD, standing at the top of a heavenly staircase, identifies Himself and confirms the promises given to Abraham and Isaac. This reference is different in that it is a dream that Jacob had, whereas the others were heard audibly and seen physically. But the question that can be asked is which member of the unity of *Elohim* spoke, for the speaker is referenced by the term *Yahweh* and simply as God. This passage relates God confirming to Jacob the promise that was previously made to Abraham and Isaac, what is commonly called the Abrahamic Covenant. The speaker was referenced as "*the LORD stood*" who called Himself "*the LORD God*" and "*the God of your father Abraham and the God of Isaac*" and said that He would keep His promises. This reference does not identify which member of the Godhead He is, but notice He uses the above terms of Himself interchangeably. In the next passage the speaker identifies Himself clearly.

---

[493] Currid, *A Study Commentary: Genesis 25:19-50:26*, 2:33.

[494] Hamilton, *The New International Commentary on the Old Testament. Genesis,* Chapters 18-50, 2:204.

The Angel of God's Provision For Jacob ... Genesis 31:11-13

(11) And in the dream an angel of God said to me, 'Jacob!' 'Here' I answered. (12) And he said, 'Note well that all the he-goats which are mating with the flock are streaked, speckled, and mottled; for I have noted all that Laban has been doing to you. (13) I am the God of Beth-el, where you anointed a pillar and where you made a vow to Me. Now, arise and leave this land and return to your native land.'

Once again a message came to Jacob in the form of a dream which is different from that of Abraham and Isaac, where God met them in a personal appearance. In Jacob's dream the "*angel* (Messenger) *of God*" spoke in verse 11 and then in verse 13 the Messenger (Angel) identified Himself as the God of Beth-el. This passage and Genesis 28:10-17 must be looked at together. The question that was raised in the previous section as to the identity of the person in the Genesis 28 passage is answered in the Genesis 31 passage. Leupold gives a very clear and concise statement as to the identity of the one who spoke to Jacob:

> The one who addresses Jacob is "the angel of God." Yet in verse 13 this person identifies himself with God and so cannot [could not] have been a created angel but must have been divine.[495]

When both passages (Genesis 28:12-15 and 31:11-13) are compared, it is abundantly clear that the speaker was the Messenger (Angel) of *Elohim*, who in turn referred to Himself as the Messenger of *Elohim* and *Yahweh* Himself.

Jacob Wrestled with God ... Genesis 32:24-31

(24) After taking them across the stream, he sent across all his possessions. (25) Jacob was left alone. And a man wrestled with him until the break of dawn. (26) When he saw that he had not prevailed against him, he wrenched Jacob's hip at its socket. So that the socket of his hip was strained as he wrestled with him. (27) Then he said, "Let me go, for dawn is breaking." But he answered, "I will not let you go, unless you bless me." (28) Said the other, "What is your name?" He replied, "Jacob." (29) Said he, "Your name shall no longer be Jacob, but Israel, for you have striven with beings divine and human, and have prevailed." (30) Jacob asked, "Pray tell me your name." But he said, "You must not ask my name!" And he took leave of him there. (31) So Jacob named the place Peniel, meaning, "I have seen a divine being face to face, yet my life has been preserved."

Genesis 32:24-31 (verses 23-30 in the KJV) yields Jacob's first personal biblical encounter with God in human form. In this passage it is an assailant who is identified

---

[495] Leupold, *Exposition of Genesis,* 2:834.

simply as a "man." Jacob in verse 30 identified the man as *Elohim* and Hosea 12:4-5 identified Him as the LORD God.[496] The rabbis explain it as Jacob's guardian angel (Genesis Rabba, pg 77), but that explanation is insufficient because Jacob said in verse 30, "I have seen God face to face." In *The Jewish Study Bible* quoted above it states, "I have seen a divine being face to face." To use the term "divine being" is misleading for the Hebrew word is אֱלֹהִים meaning God (*Elohim*). Another interesting point is that Jacob did not let go until he was blessed. When he was blessed it involved a name change; Jacob would now be called Israel. Jacob, now Israel, had a divine encounter with a man who was none other than the Angel or Messenger of the LORD, God Himself. His identity is clearly expressed by the following authors:

> The wrestler is referred to as 'a man.' Later He is called God by Jacob himself (30), and He is called God by the prophet Hosea (12:3), who also calls Him 'the angel' (12:4). There can be little doubt of His identity. He was the Angel of the Lord, the pre-incarnate Christ, the second Person of the Blessed Trinity, Who is the exact image of the Father's Person (Heb 1:3).[497]

> Apparently in Jacob's evaluation, his combatant was more than even an angel. It was none other than the Angel, the preincarnate Christ, because, according to Jacob's testimony, he had "seen God face to face."[498]

> God had met him in the form of a man: God in the angel, according to Hos. 12:4-5, not in a created angel, but in the Angel of Jehovah, the visible manifestation of the invisible God.[499]

Genesis 32:24-30, when connected to Hosea 12:4-5, clearly showed Him as a plurality in unity. The Messenger (Angel) is God, and yet distinct from God, yet one in essence with *Elohim*.

El Shaddai Appeared Again to Jacob at Luz …
Genesis 35:6-7, 9-13

(6) Thus Jacob came to Luz – that is, Bethel – in the land of Canaan, he and all the people who were with him. (7) There he built an altar and named the site El-bethel, for it was there that God had revealed Himself to him when he was fleeing from his brother.

(9) God appeared again to Jacob on his arrival from Paddan-aram, and He blessed him. (10) God said to him, "You whose name is Jacob, you shall be called Jacob no more." Thus He named him Israel. (11) And God said to him,

---

[496] Hamilton, *The New International Commentary on the Old Testament: Genesis 18-50,* 329-330.

[497] Atkinson, *The Pocket Commentary of the Bible: Genesis*, 310.

[498] Morris, *The Genesis Record*, 499.

[499] Keil & Delitzsch, *Commentary on the Old Testament in Ten Volumes: Genesis,* 1:304.

"I am El Shaddai. Be fertile and increase; A nation, yea an assembly of nations, Shall descend from you. Kings shall issue from your loins. (12) The land that I assigned to Abraham and Isaac I assign to you; And to your offspring to come will I assign the land." (13) God parted from him at the spot where He had spoken to him.

On the surface Genesis 35:6-7 appears to have nothing to do with the plurality of *Elohim*, the subject of this book. However, there is a phrase that is dealt with in two different ways depending on a person's theological viewpoint. The phrase at the center of controversy is *"God had revealed Himself to him."* In the Hebrew text, God or *Elohim* is plural, and is normally followed by a singular verb which is an abnormal grammatical pattern in Hebrew. In Hebrew as in English when the noun is plural the verb will also be plural. So throughout Scripture God is violating grammar with the plural noun *Elohim* and singular verb. Here the plural noun, *Elohim*, is followed by a plural verb which is actually correct grammatical pattern. So the verse, if translated literally, would read, "God had revealed Themselves to him" (see chapter 9 in this book for a fuller discussion, under the section Plural Verbs Used With *Elohim*). Some liberal Christian scholars say that this is a polytheistic form of expression that was mistakenly carried over into the biblical text. That statement violates the inspiration of Scripture and destroys the integrity and authority of Moses and God.

If the literal method of interpretation is believed and practiced, and verbal plenary inspiration is accepted, then what is written in Scripture must be taken as given in the text and must be accepted. Writers like Currid avoid the issue and miss the point of the context; it is not a polytheistic form of expression as he presents. He does throw out the possibility that Genesis 35:6 is a reference to divine beings or multiple gods, but he says nothing about it being a plural reference to *Elohim*.[500] Others like Ellicott simply do not adhere to the plural aspect of the verse.[501] But Leupold identifies the verb *nighlu* (revealed) as plural with *Elohim*.[502] Kohlenberger translates נִגְלוּ as "they were revealed."[503] So this verse, which on the surface seems to have nothing to do with the subject of the plurality of *Elohim* in the *Tanakh*, becomes a very important verse to show the plurality of *Elohim* in the Hebrew Scriptures.

In Genesis 35:9 and 13 God introduces another theophany to Jacob. Special attention will be given to verses 9 and 13, which give the facts that relate to this theophany of God. In verse 9 two things draw attention. First, the familiar word וַיֵּרָא (appear) is used of *Elohim* again, which is the same word that was used in Genesis 12:7; 17:1; 18:1 in reference to God appearing to Abraham. The word "appear" was used of a physical manifestation of God before Abraham, and now *Elohim* appears before Jacob on his return to Bethel. The second word is the word "again;" this is the second time

---

[500] Currid, *A Study Commentary: Genesis 25:19-50:26,* 2:163.

[501] Payne Smith, *The Handy Commentary:* Genesis, ed. Charles John Ellicott, 331-332.

[502] Leupold, *Exposition of Genesis,* 2:918.

[503] Kohlenberger, *The Interlinear NIV Hebrew-English Old Testament,* 96.

God has appeared to Jacob in a short period of time. In Genesis 32:34-40 Jacob wrestled with God for a blessing.

This is the second appearance of God to Jacob as a theophany since the patriarch left Haran, where the wrestling match took place at the Jabbok River (32:30).[504] Now that Jacob is back in the land *Elohim* renews with him the covenant (verses 10-11) that *El Shaddai* made with Abraham, which also makes *El Shaddai* and *Elohim* the same God.

In Genesis 35:13 there is another familiar phrase, "*And God went up from him.*" This is the same expression that was used in connection to Abraham in Genesis 17:22 (Judges 13:20). Without a doubt this was another theophany wherein *Elohim* appeared in some form and spoke to Jacob.[505] What is also interesting about this theophany is that it is *Elohim* throughout the chapter who spoke and appeared to Jacob. Once again it was the Second Person of the plural unity of *Elohim* that appeared and revealed the nature, character and essence of *Elohim* as He guided and directed His people.

The net result of this passage is not only that God presents Himself as a theophany but, also, it is one of the unique places in Scripture where the plural noun *Elohim* is followed by a plural verb in relation to the true God of Israel in the context of a theophany.

Jacob and the Angel Who Redeemed ... Genesis 48:15-16

(15) And he blessed Joseph, saying, "The God in whose ways my fathers Abraham and Isaac walked, The God who has been my shepherd from my birth to this day – (16) The Angel who has redeemed me from all harm – Bless the lads. In them may my name be recalled, and the names of my fathers Abraham and Isaac, and may they be teeming multitudes upon the earth."

In Genesis 48:15-16 Jacob was expressing his delight in not only seeing Joseph again, whom he thought was dead, but he was about to bless Joseph's seed, Ephraim and Manasseh. In these verses Jacob gave his blessing and made the following reference: "*The Angel who has redeemed me from all harm.*" The immediate question comes to mind, who is this angel who redeemed him from all harm?

Jacob speaks of God in three different ways: First, that his fathers had walked before God; second, that God fed him all his life, which spoke of God's provision; third, on the same level as the other two, he stated that "*the angel*" redeemed him from all harm or evil. Because this Angel is placed on equal status with *Elohim*, He is God. This angel then is none other than the Messenger (Angel) of the LORD, the Second Person of the plural unity of *Elohim*. Several authors reflect this perspective concerning the "Angel:"

---

[504] Currid, *A Study Commentary: Genesis 25:19-50:26*, 2:164.
[505] Wenham, *Word Biblical Commentary: Genesis 16-50*, 2:326.

This is clearly the Angel of Yahweh who is one and the same as Yahweh himself.[506]

The third statement, however, is the most important theologically. When Jacob here no longer speaks of God but rather of "the angel," that does not mean that he is here speaking of a being subordinate to God; on the contrary, his speech now prepares for its final and most concentrated statement about God's rule. The "angel of the Lord" is of course God himself as he appears on earth; in him Israel experienced Yahweh's special supporting and redeeming activity.[507]

Notice first that God and the Angel are identical, just as they were at Penuel (32:30; Hos 12:4). The Angel is the second Person of the Holy Trinity, the pre-incarnate Christ.[508]

Jacob described the Lord in three ways – the God of his fathers Abraham and Isaac, the God who fed him all of his life, and the "Angel" who redeemed him from all harm. The angel of the Lord is generally considered to be a reference of Jehovah himself.[509]

God is also described in Jacob's blessing as the "God who has been my shepherd all my life to this day" (v. 15) and as the "Angel who has delivered me from all harm" (v. 16). It is unusual that God himself should be described as "the angel" since earlier in the book it is said that God sent "his angel" or simply that one of the patriarchs was visited by "the angel of the LORD."[510]

Jacob's statement is indeed unusual, but clearly shows that *Elohim* is a plural reference to God. The Angel who is sent by *Elohim* is also *Elohim* because He speaks and acts as *Elohim*. So indeed the Angel did keep him from all harm.

"The God (*Elohim*) before whom my fathers Abraham and Isaac did walk, the God (*Elohim*) which fed me all my life long unto this day, the angel which redeemed me from all evil, bless the lads," he places the angel of God on a perfect equality with God, not only regarding Him as the Being to whom he has been indebted for protection all his life long, but entreating from Him a blessing upon his descendants.[511]

This triple reference to God, in which the Angel who is placed on an equality with *Ha-Elohim* cannot possibly be a created angel, but must be the "Angel of God," God manifested in the form of the Angel of Jehovah, or the "Angel of

---

[506] Currid, *A Study Commentary: Genesis 25:19-50:26*, 2: 367.

[507] Von Rad, *The Old Testament Library: Genesis*, 412.

[508] Atkinson, *The Pocket Commentary of the Bible: Genesis*, 422-423.

[509] Talbot, *A Study of the Book of Genesis*, 276.

[510] Sailhamer, *The Expositor's Bible Commentary: Genesis*, 2:272.

[511] Keil & Delitzsch, *Commentary on the Old Testament in Ten Volumes: Genesis*, 1:184-185.

His face" (Isa 63:9), contains a foreshadowing of the Trinity, though only God and the Angel are distinguished, not three persons of the divine nature.[512]

There seems to be no doubt that this Angel that Jacob references is "*the Angel* (Messenger) *of the LORD*" that has also appeared to Abraham and Isaac. He is not a created being, for no created being could be placed with equality on the same level with *Elohim*. The word הַגֹּאֵל translated as "the one delivering" from the root word גָּאַל means "redeemed." This is the first time that this word appears in the Hebrew Scripture. The Angel of the LORD, who is the pre-incarnate Messiah, was to be the redeemer of mankind. That is not only in the New Covenant but is pictured in the *Tanakh* as well. The meaning of the word "redeem" — to redeem or to act as a kinsman redeemer[513] — is expressed in the following statement:

> The primary meaning of this root is to do the part of a kinsman and thus to redeem his kin from difficulty or danger. It is used with its derivatives 118 times. One difference between this root and the very similar root *pada* "redeem," is that there is usually an emphasis in *ga'al* on the redemption being the privilege or duty of a near relative.[514]

"Redeem" is used 118 times, but the majority of uses are found in Leviticus 25-27 in the context of a kinsman. The word "redeem" also appears heavily in the book of Ruth, which is the story of a kinsman redeemer. "Redeem" is also used frequently in the second section of Isaiah that is connected to the Servant of the Lord Who redeems Israel.[515] This Servant of the LORD is a kinsman, because God became a man and He was a Jewish man, of the tribe of Judah, or the line of David who indeed was their kinsman. The relationship of the words "redeem" and "kinsman" is more than a coincidence. The Messenger (Angel) of the LORD is God the Son, the Messiah, and the Son of David, He is the Kinsman Redeemer of both the Jew and the Gentile. The one just described was the one who redeemed Jacob from all harm, as Morris expresses in his statement:

> Also, the word "redeem" (Hebrew *goel*) is used here for the first time in the Bible, and it is significant that it occurs as a description of the work of the great Angel of Jehovah, none other than the pre-incarnate Christ.[516]

Jacob did recognize the "angel" as the one Who redeemed him from all harm. What Jacob recognized as the delivering hand of the "Angel," the biblical text refers to as

---

[512] Keil & Delitzsch, *Commentary on the Old Testament in Ten Volumes*: *Genesis*, 1:383-384.

[513] Francis Brown, S.R. Driver and C. A. Briggs, *A Hebrew and English Lexicon of the Old Testament* (London: Oxford, n.d.),145.

[514] Harris, Archer and Waltke, *Theological Wordbook of the Old Testament*, 1:144.

[515] Kohlenberger and Swanson, *The Hebrew-English Concordance to the Old Testament*, 342.

[516] Morris, *The Genesis Record*, 648.

God's provision and protection of Jacob. See the following examples from Genesis of God redeeming Jacob from all harm:

> God's provision for Jacob by Isaac and Rebekah by sending him off to Haran to marry a daughter of Laban (27:42-28:7). God's promise to Jacob in a dream and confirming of the Abrahamic Covenant to Jacob (28:12-15). God's provision for Jacob, even when Laban had been deceitful (31:1-10). God's protection of Jacob when Laban caught up with him (31:25-55). God's pacifying Esau's anger toward Jacob by the use of time (33:1-17). God's plan to safeguard Jacob and family through Joseph in Egypt, where Israel was made into a nation.

SUMMARY

These pre-Sinai theophanies yield some very fruitful information in understanding God and His plural unity of persons. What the New Covenant clearly teaches is that God became a Jewish man to fulfill the Law and the Prophets (Luke 24:25-27, 44-45). The foundation that God laid out for Himself in revealing His essence, character and person in the book of Genesis is phenomenal. The Genesis account written by Moses, the author of the other four books of the Torah, gives a clear picture of His person. God had to stress His oneness through Moses to be faithful to Who He is, for He is God alone, the indivisible God of Israel. He had to protect His character and essence from a polytheistic world view which would cause Israel trouble in the following centuries.

These pre-Sinai theophanies were divided into two groupings. First, God did communicate His will and word to Adam (Eve), Cain, Enoch, Noah and Abraham. However, there is no definitive information to project that God appeared to His human creatures in a visible form. There are some hints that He did appear, but that cannot be dogmatically taught. But this much can be substantiated: God did talk, interacting verbally, enabling mankind to completely understand that communication. God did not speak through a heart conscience.

In the second grouping, God not only communicated, but He also physically appeared to Abraham, Hagar, Isaac, and Jacob. It was clearly seen that God appeared as a man before His people, but there is also another important point that cannot be missed. That appearance of God which often took place as *"the Angel* (Messenger) *of the LORD"* had an even greater dimension. In these appearances as a Messenger (Angel) of God, He spoke as God and not for God. These passages clearly show that the word *Elohim* speaks of the plurality of God, and *Yahweh* and/or *"the angel* (Messenger) *of the LORD"* speaks to the individuality of a member of the Godhead, which is encompassed in the Hebrew word *Elohim*.

Thus, God is beginning to lay the groundwork that He can, does and will reveal Himself to man in a visible form. Even though these appearances, called theophanies, cannot be called incarnations, they lay the foundation for that time when God will

171

permanently reside on the earth, as the Second Person of the plural unity of *Elohim*, the Godhead. Even though this is very difficult for Jewish people to accept, they need to look at what *HaShem* did and said to their people centuries ago.

Chapter 6
Sinai and Wilderness Theophanies

In the previous chapter it was shown that God revealed Himself to individuals and, in particular, He revealed Himself to Abraham in the form of the Messenger (Angel) of the LORD and other audio and physical appearances called theophanies. In the wilderness wandering of Israel, God would continue to reveal Himself through the Messenger (Angel) of the Lord and the *Shechinah* glory of God. This chapter will discuss a multitude of appearances of God as He journeyed with Israel for 40 years (Exodus – Deuteronomy).

As discussed in the last chapter, many of the theophanies of God revealed Him as God and yet He was distinct from God. That pattern of revealing Himself will continue throughout this chapter.

Liberal Christianity and Rabbinic Judaism do not want to acknowledge that *Yeshua* revealed Himself to mankind throughout the *Tanakh* as a member of the plural unity of *Elohim* in the Hebrew Scriptures. Yet when the literal Scriptures are coupled with a belief in verbal/plenary inspiration, the plural unity of *Elohim* is clearly seen. However, some authors, usually those of a liberal persuasion, treat the Messenger (Angel) of the LORD as a created being who spoke in the name of God. They leave the impression that God Himself was not present and speaking in the biblical text, but that the one who was sent represented God. Their position simply does not conform to the abundance of Scriptures which will be clearly seen. Here are several points from their liberal bias:

The OT regularly refers to messengers whose task is to bridge the spatial distance between the sender and the person or group one wishes to reach. A very close relationship exists between them and their sender: they speak/act in his name, that is, the sender speaks/acts through them. So messengers can be addressed as if they were the sender himself....As earthly princes have their messengers so YHWH has his emissaries. Human beings can function in this capacity, but ordinarily it is celestial beings for whom the designation 'messenger of YHWH' is used. Enthroned in heaven, a king is surrounded by his heavenly court through a member of his entourage. By means of a messenger he can bridge the distance between himself and the people, communicate with them and help them....In the early church it was widely held that 'the messenger of YHWH' was the Logos. Few today subscribe to that kind of theological interpretation. A view that is somewhat popular is that one particular figure, the Grand Vizier, the prime minister of YHWH, is meant.... There is no careful distinction between YHWH and his messenger. The passages in which a messenger of YHWH/God appears more than once give the impression that YHWH/God himself is present and speaks. In [Exodus] 3:2 we read of a messenger of YHWH, while in 3:4ff. YHWH/God is the one who speaks. The sender is present in the one sent. What is said is that YHWH, the exalted Lord, nevertheless wishes to bridge the distance separating him from his human creatures. Referring to YHWH as doing the speaking himself is a way of underscoring his personal involvement. The image of the messenger, who represents his Lord, without being identical with him, safeguards the distance between YHWH and man.[517]

It can be clearly seen that many "Christians" reject the idea that the Messenger (Angel) of the LORD is God Himself, in person. The Exodus 3 passage will be used to refute the argument that there is a need for any celestial created being to speak in God's name. God Himself is fully capable of speaking for Himself by sending the Messenger (Angel) of the LORD, who is God Himself and yet distinct from God the Father. He is the second person of the plural unity of *Elohim*.

One Jewish author wrote an extensive work on Exodus and when dealing with Exodus 3:2-15, says absolutely nothing about the Messenger (Angel) of the LORD. Rather, he spends considerable time on the nature of the burning bush.[518] Instead of the burning bush being the vehicle God chose to use to reveal Himself, it became the distraction from who actually spoke from the burning bush. This very passage has a tremendous amount of material to show the distinction of the members of the plural unity of *Elohim*. In the following passage, those distinctive portions are shown in bold:

Moses and the Burning Bush ... Exodus 3:2-15

(2) **An angel of the LORD appeared** to him in a blazing fire out of a bush. He gazed, and there was a bush all aflame, yet the bush was not consumed. (3) Moses said, "I must turn aside to look at this marvelous sight; why doesn't the bush burn up?" (4) When the **LORD** saw that he had turned aside to look, **God** called to him out of the bush: "Moses! Moses!" He answered, "Here I am." (5) And He said, "Do not come closer. **Remove your sandals from your feet, for the place on which you stand is holy ground**. (6) "**I am**," He said, "the God of your fathers, the God of Abraham, the God of Isaac, and the God of Jacob." And Moses hid his face, for he was afraid to look at God.

(7) And the **LORD** continued, "I have marked well the plight of My people in Egypt and have heeded their outcry because of their taskmasters; yes, **I** am mindful of their sufferings. (8) **I** have come down to rescue them from the

---

[517] Cornelis Houtman, *Historical Commentary on the Old Testament: Exodus* (3 Vols. Kampen, Netherlands: Kok Publishing House, 1993), 1:335-336.
[518] Benno Jacob, *The Second Book of the Bible: Exodus* (trans. Walter Jacob; Hoboken, NJ: Ktav Publishing, 1992), 49-57.

Egyptians and to bring them out of that land to a good and spacious land, a land flowing with milk and honey, the region of the Canaanites, the Hittites, the Amorites, the Perizzites, the Hivites, and the Jebusites. (9) Now the cry of the Israelites has reached **Me**; moreover, **I** have seen how the Egyptians oppress them. (10) Come, therefore, **I** will send you to Pharaoh, and you shall free **My** people, the Israelites, from Egypt." (11) But Moses said to God, "Who am I that I should go to Pharaoh and free the Israelites from Egypt?"

(12) And He said, "**I** will be with you; that shall be your sign that it was **I** who sent you. And when you have freed the people from Egypt, you shall worship God at this mountain."(13) Moses said to God, "When I come to the Israelites and say to them, 'The God of your fathers has sent me to you,' and they ask me, 'What is His name?' what shall I say to them?" (14) And God said to Moses, "*ehyeh-Asher-ehyeh* [I AM that I AM]." He continued, "Thus shall you say to the Israelites '*Ehyeh* [I AM] sent me to you.'" (15) And God said further to Moses, "Thus shall you speak to the Israelites: The **LORD** the God of your fathers, the **God of Abraham**, the **God of Isaac**, and the **God of Jacob**, has sent me to you: This shall be My name forever, This is My appellation for all eternity."

In an immediate response to the above Scripture is the same response that was dealt with in Genesis 1:26 in relation to "plural of majesty" back in chapter 3 of this book, as will also be seen in chapter 10. God can use messengers [angels] to communicate with mankind. However, in the early part of the *Tanakh*, created beings known as angels were not predominantly part of the biblical text until the time of the exile, as Cole quotes Driver in the following statement:

Advanced angelology does not occur until the apocalyptic books of the Old Testament (Ezekiel, Daniel, Zechariah). Throughout the whole of the earlier period, it would be better to translate the word 'angel' as 'messenger' and leave it to the context to decide whether this emissary is human, superhuman, or simply a reverential way of referring to God Himself, as apparently here.[519]

In Exodus 3, the Messenger (Angel) of the LORD made Himself quite clear as to who He was. This phrase "*the angel of the LORD*" refers to a phenomenon that was associated with the presence of God Himself and here there was a visible manifestation of deity.[520] God did use messengers (angels) to communicate with man, but as Cole pointed out, this generally did not occur until the period of the exile. The context of the Messenger (Angel) of the LORD is the audible and/or physical communication of God Himself through the One Who is God yet distinct from God. Davidson points out that the people to whom the Messenger (Angel) of the LORD appeared may not all have

---

[519] R. Alan Cole, *Tyndale Old Testament Commentaries: Exodus* (Downers Grove, IL: InterVarsity, 1973), 64.
[520] John L. Mackay, *A Mentor Commentary: Exodus* (Fearn, Ross-shire, Great Britain: Mentor, 2001), 66-67.

known the complete ramifications of what they saw and heard. But this much they did understand:

> These passages indicate that in the minds of those to whom this angel appeared, it was an appearance of Jehovah in person. Jehovah's face was seen. His name was revealed. The Angel of the LORD is Jehovah present in definite time and particular place. What is emphatic is that Jehovah here is fully present.[521]

All of the forthcoming passages throughout the *Tanakh* strongly indicate that in the minds of those to whom the Messenger (Angel) of the LORD appeared and spoke, to them it was the appearance of *Elohim* and/or *Yahweh* in person. What is emphatic here in Exodus 3:2-15 is that *Yahweh* was fully present. Observe several of the verses in Exodus 3:2-15 and see the distinction of the Messenger (Angel) of the LORD and how He uses pronouns and interchanges titles that refer to Himself distinctly in this passage.

In Exodus 3:2 the *"the angel of the LORD"* appeared to Moses *"in a flame of fire out of the midst of the bush."* There are two observations from this verse: First *"the angel of the LORD"* is the same person that appeared to Hagar (Genesis 16:7; 21:17), Abraham (Genesis 22:11, 15), and Jacob (Genesis 31:11-13; 48:16) who now is appearing to Moses. Second the word "appear" denotes a physical appearance of some kind as it did in Genesis 12:7 and 17:1. So the reader is introduced to *"the angel of the LORD"* who has been seen previously to be God, yet distinct from God, and the same in His nature, essence and character. Another author states the method that God used to reveal Himself to His servants:

> For many years theologians have discussed and debated the identity of the "Angel of the Lord" that appeared to Moses "in a flame of fire from the midst of a bush." In some passages of Scripture, the angel seems to be different from God (Exod 23:20-23; Num 22:22; Judg 5:23; 2 Sam 24:16; Zech 1:12-13). In other places God and the Angel are identical and interchangeable (Gen 16:7-13; 22:11-22; 48:15-16; Judg 2:1; 6:11-24; 13:3-22). It seems most appropriate to perceive the Angel of the Lord as a visible manifestation of God. Such visible manifestations of God in the Old Testament are called theophanies, from a word that means "an appearance of God." They often occur in the midst of natural phenomena: in fire, Exodus 3:2; in a cloud, Exodus 13:21; in a whirlwind, Job 38:1; in an earthquake, 1 Kings 19:11. They also appear in human form: Exodus 33:21-23; Isaiah 6:1; Genesis 18; Ezekiel 1:26-27.[522]

In this instance the Messenger (Angel) of the LORD chose to appear in a fire or "flame" in the burning bush in His call of Moses. To borrow a phrase, Edward Young states that if Scripture is accepted at face value, "God spoke to Moses personally through the

---

[521] A. B. Davidson, *The Theology of the Old Testament* (Edinburgh: T & T Clark, 1955), 297-298.

[522] Maxie D. Dunnam, *The Communicator's Commentary: Exodus* (Waco: Word, 1967), 64.

distinct person of the Messenger (Angel) of the LORD who is God Himself."[523] Davis states that the call of Moses for his upcoming leadership came by the Messenger (Angel) of the LORD, who is also *Yahweh* and *Elohim*, according to the text of Exodus 3:2-15:

> The special call of Moses to the task of leadership came by means of "the angel of the Lord" (v. 2), which, in fact, was an appearance of the Lord himself, the second Person of the God-head. The manner in which the angel of the Lord appeared to him was quite unique.[524]

Exodus 3:4 identifies the Messenger (Angel) of the LORD as God by calling Him *Yahweh* or LORD. There is absolutely nothing in the text that would indicate that the Messenger (Angel) of the LORD is a mere celestial created being who is speaking or acting for God. The text simply does not reflect that kind of interpretation. When the literal language of the text speaks for itself, it presents the Messenger (Angel) of the LORD as *Yahweh*. Then the text moves on to identify *"the Angel of the LORD"* not only as *Yahweh* but also as *Elohim*. The one who spoke to Moses was not God the Father but an equal member of the plural unity of *Elohim*. There is no mistake: He is God. Walter Kaiser reflects the same idea:

> The easy movement from the title (mal'ak yhwh, "Messenger or 'angel'] of the LORD") to LORD and Elohim in v. 4 shows that this person was a real being who was at once identified with God yet also was sent by him and was therefore distinct from the father.[525]

Another author expresses what Kaiser says — that the Messenger (Angel) of the LORD is a unique being sent from God but at the same time He is still God:

> As the text stands, however, it clearly identifies the Angel with God. The Angel appeared unto Moses in a flame of fire from the midst of the bush, and God called to Moses from the midst of the bush. Furthermore, the manner in which the LORD is introduced as one who sees that Moses had turned aside suggests that the LORD and the Angel are one.
>
> The Angel is a real Being, and He is to be identified with God. Inasmuch as He is sent from the Lord, He is not God the Father Himself but distinct from the Father. If we would do justice to the scriptural data, we must insist therefore both upon the distinguishableness of the Angel from the Father and also upon the identity of essence with the Father. Christian theologians have rightly seen in this strange figure a pre-incarnate appearance of the One who in the days of

---

[523] Edward J. Young, "The Call of Moses," *WTJ* 30, (1967-68), 117.

[524] John J. Davis, *Moses and the Gods of Egypt: Studies in Exodus* (Winona Lake, IN: BMH Books, 2003), 68-69.

[525] Walter Kaiser, *The Expositor's Bible Commentary: Exodus* (Grand Rapids: Zondervan, 1990), 317.

His flesh could say, "And the Father who sent me has himself borne witness of me" (John 5:37).[526]

So if the Messenger (Angel) of the LORD is just an ordinary angel, he could not possibly have spoken as the Eternal One who is the *Elohim* of Abraham, Isaac and Jacob. In verse 2 the Messenger (Angel) of the LORD "*appeared unto him in a flame of fire out of the midst of a bush,*" and in verse 4, "*God [Elohim] called unto him out of the midst of the bush.*" The literal rendering of Exodus 3:2 clearly leads the reader to understand that the Messenger (Angel) of the LORD is the same person as *Yahweh* and *Elohim* in verse 4! Greenberg, reflecting on this passage from a Jewish background, states:

> Malak [angel] YHWH here, as everywhere, refers to a visible manifestation of YHWH, essentially indistinguishable from YHWH himself, except that here the manifestation is not anthropomorphic but fiery. There is, then, no especial difficulty in the shift from "angel" to YHWH in verses 2 and 4.[527]

This Jewish scholar refers to this passage in Exodus 3:2-15 as a theophany of God to Moses in the form of fire to prepare him for his future encounter with God's glory on Mt. Sinai. However, later in the paragraph, although Greenberg tries to soften the obvious in relationship to the term *Elohim*, he sees the Messenger (Angel) of the LORD and *Yahweh* as the same. But he does not reference the fact that they are also distinct from each other. Greenberg does call this appearance of God recorded in Exodus 3 a theophany.

Hengstenberg clearly presents the fact that all these names show that even in verses 6 and 14-16, the Messenger (Angel) of the LORD of verse 2, *Yahweh* in verse 4 and God in verse 4 are one and the same person:

> In addition to those already noticed in the five books of Moses, there is a passage in Exodus 3 which deserves special consideration. In verse 2, the angel of Jehovah is said to have appeared to Moses in the fiery flame of a thorn-bush. In verse 4, we read, "Jehovah saw that he drew near to look, and Elohim called to him out of the thorn-bush." In verse 6 and 14-16, the angel of Jehovah assumes to himself all the attributes of the true God, calls himself the Eternal One, the God of the fathers, Abraham, Isaac, and Jacob, and promises to deliver the children of Israel out of Egypt, and inflict severe punishment on the Egyptians. In verse 5, Moses is commanded to take off his shoes from off his feet, because the place where he stands is holy ground. And in verse 6, he is said to have hidden his face, because he was afraid to look upon God.[528]

---

[526] Edward J. Young, "The Call of Moses," *WTJ* 30, (1967-68), 3-5.

[527] Moshe Greenberg, *The Heritage of Biblical Israel: Understanding Exodus* (New York: Behrman House, 1969), 70.

[528] Hengstenberg, *Christology of the Old Testament,* 4:255.

Therefore, if the literal sense of the text means anything at all, it clearly and unquestionably refers to the Messenger (Angel) of the LORD as being equal to and yet distinct from God.

Yahweh, the name that God was now to be called, reflects the eternal aspect and timelessness of God, Who in this instance, was introduced in the text as the Messenger (Angel) of the LORD. A rabbi speaks of the significance of *Yahweh*, the personal name of God in the following statement:

> This Name also represents the eternity of God, for it is composed of the letters that spell הָיָה הֹוֶה יִהְיֶה, He was, He is, and He will be, meaning that God's Being is timeless....However, יְ־הֹ־וָ־ה [*HaShem*] is more than a descriptive Name; it is a proper noun, for it is the actual Name of God, and is known as Shem HaMeforash, or the "Ineffable Name." In respect for its great sanctity, it is not pronounced as it is written. Instead, it is pronounced Adonoy during prayer or when reading from the Torah; in ordinary speech, the word HaShem [the Name] is substituted for it.[529]

This name is greatly revered in Rabbinic Judaism and Scherman uses the term *HaShem*, meaning The Name in place of *Yahweh*.

In Exodus 3:5 another strong factor is presented by the first words that the Messenger (Angel) of the LORD utters to Moses. Moses is told to stop and not come any further because he is in the presence of God, so this Messenger (Angel) of the LORD is not just a celestial being. Moses was to remove his shoes for he was standing on holy ground, before God. When Davis references this passage, he points out strongly that "Moses recognized the fact that he was in the presence of deity and feared to look upon the face of God."[530] Not only was Moses told not to approach the burning bush any further because of it being holy ground, but also Moses, now was fully aware that God had spoken directly to him, and he hid his face before God as Exodus 3:6 states. The Messenger (Angel) of the LORD was unapproachable at this time because Moses had to learn about the holiness of *Yahweh*. Sailhamer states:

> The fact that God is a holy God should not be understood to mean that he is an impersonal force – God is holy yet intensely personal.[531]

Before this combination of the fire and/or the glory of God at the burning bush, the Messenger (Angel) of the LORD appeared to Hagar, Abraham and Jacob in human form. So at this point in biblical history He chose to communicate to Moses from His holiness and not in a human form. Later in biblical history, Joshua would encounter the "*Captain of the Host of the LORD*" but without the fire or glory of God. Yet, He also told Joshua to remove his shoes for it was also holy ground (Joshua 5:14-15). These are

---

[529] Scherman, The Chumash: The Stone Edition, 304-305.

[530] Davis, *Moses and the Gods of Egypt: Studies in Exodus,* 71.

[531] Sailhamer, *The Pentateuch as Narrative: A Biblical-Theological Commentary*, 245.

179

the only two times that a theophany of God gave such instructions to the individual to whom He revealed Himself.

In Exodus 3:6 the Messenger (Angel) of the LORD, who has now been called *Yahweh* and *Elohim*, tells Moses that He is the God of Abraham, Isaac and Jacob, the covenant making God:

> "The Angel of Jehovah" (v. 2), who is immediately afterwards Himself called "Jehovah" and "God" (vv. 4-5), spake to him "out of the midst of the bush." His first words warned Moses to put his shoes from off his feet, as standing on holy ground; the next revealed Him as the same Angel of the Covenant, who had appeared unto the fathers as "the God of Abraham, the God of Isaac, and the God of Jacob."[532]

In the following verses of Exodus 3 the Messenger (Angel) of the LORD, who is also *Yahweh*, makes the following statements that show His sovereignty and omniscience over Israel and Egypt:

Verse 7	[*Yahweh*] said, I have surely seen the affliction and cry because of the taskmaster and I know their sorrows.
Verse 8	I [*Yahweh*] am come to deliver them from Egypt and to bring them into the land that I promised their fathers. This should be tied together with Genesis 15:1, 4; Joshua 1:6 and Judges 2:1 as to the identity of God that claims to be the originator of the promise.
Verse 9	because [I – *Yahweh*] He has seen and heard the cry of the people.
Verse 10	I [*Yahweh*] will send you Moses.
Verse 12	I [*Yahweh*] will be with you Moses.
Verse 14	I [*Yahweh*] AM that I AM.
Verse 15	[*Elohim*] said for Moses to tell the people that the *Yahweh Elohim* of your fathers (Abraham, Isaac and Jacob), this is my name.

As all these verses in Exodus 3 reveal, *Elohim, Yahweh*, and the Messenger (Angel) of the LORD all had spoken to Moses as an *echad* (one) individual. The speaker uses these names interchangeably throughout this passage. Exodus 3:2-15 presents the Messenger (Angel) of the LORD, who is also *Yahweh* and *Elohim*, who spoke to Moses from the burning bush about the mission He was sending him to do.

---

[532] Alfred Edersheim, *The Exodus and the Wanderings in the Wilderness* (London: The Religious Tract Society, 1876), 46.

In summary, "*the angel of the LORD*" not only declared that He is the Messenger of *Yahweh* but that He is *Yahweh* and *Elohim*. He then stopped Moses in his tracks by stating that the ground on which Moses was standing was holy ground, and no mere angel was going to make that kind of a statement about himself. Moses' reaction was to cover his face so that he did not look on God. Then the Messenger (Angel) of the LORD told Moses that He was the *Elohim* of Abraham, Isaac and Jacob, the covenant making God, and that He saw Israel's affliction and heard their cry. He instructed Moses to go and deliver them for He would be with him and would deliver them and bring them into the Land promised to the fathers four centuries before, for the Messenger (Angel) of the LORD is the great I AM. An interesting point is that when this passage is tied in with Judges 2:1 — the end of the story — it is once again the Messenger (Angel) of the LORD who spoke to the next generation that eventually entered the Land for their possession.

LORD Smites the First Born ... Exodus 12:12, 23

(12) For that night I will go through the land of Egypt and strike down every first-born in the land of Egypt, both man and beast; and I will mete out punishments to all the gods of Egypt, I the LORD.

(23) For when the LORD goes through to smite the Egyptians, He will see the blood on the lintel and the two doorposts, and the LORD will pass over the door and not let the Destroyer enter and smite your home.

These two verses are not commonly recognized as theophanies, so an investigation of these passages needs to be done. An obvious observation is that in verse 12 the LORD states that He will punish the land of Egypt and then in verse 23 *Yahweh* is called the Destroyer. Who is the Destroyer? The LORD, true. But again, who is the person called the Destroyer? *The Jewish Study Bible* capitalizes "destroyer," so it recognizes the Destroyer as God. When God acts in judgment or in revelation of Himself it has been seen consistently that it is the Second Person of the plural unity of *Elohim*. Keil and Delitzsch give an identity to the Destroyer:

Jehovah effected the destruction of the first-born through הַמַּשְׁחִית, the destroyer, or destroying angel, ὁ ὀλοθρεύων (Heb 11:28), i.e. not a fallen angel, but the angel of Jehovah, in whom Jehovah revealed Himself to the patriarchs and Moses.[533]

Keil and Delitzsch confirm how *The Jewish Study Bible* handles the verse. It becomes clear that the Destroyer was the Messenger (Angel) of the LORD who punished the land of Egypt as the Destroyer. Not all conservative authors, such as Kaiser, see the Destroyer as the Messenger of the LORD. However, Kaiser does state that this term "Destroyer" is used in the Hebrew Scriptures 35 times but only here is it used as a

---

[533]Keil and Delitzsch, *Commentary on the Old Testament in Ten Volumes: Exodus,* 1:23.

technical term.[534] Because of the destruction that this "Destroyer" produces, some want to identify him as a demon who is allowed to act within God's limits. However, a better fit is the Messenger (Angel) of the LORD who on two other occasions brought about great destruction of human life. Once after David's sin of numbering the people, 70,000 died (1 Chronicles 21:9-17), and the second time when the Messenger of the LORD acted against the Assyrian army of Sennacherib (2 Kings 19:35; 2 Chronicles 32:21), He destroyed 185,000 soldiers in one night. Currid also identifies the Destroyer as the Messenger of *Yahweh*,[535] a theophany, the Second Person of the plural unity of *Elohim*.

This is the first reference of *Yahweh* moving in a destructive manner to punish the Egyptians and to show Egypt and Israel His great power and that the gods of Egypt are nothing. There are two other places where the person that brings great loss of life is described as the Messenger (Angel) of the LORD. The most obvious answer to the identity of the Destroyer is that He is the Messenger of the LORD.

The Angel of God in the Pillar of Fire ... Exodus 14:19-31

(19) The angel of God, who had been going ahead of the Israelite army, now moved and followed behind them; and the pillar of cloud shifted from in front of them and took up a place behind them,

(24) At the morning watch, the LORD looked down upon the Egyptian army from a pillar of fire and cloud, and threw the Egyptian army into panic.

This passage describes the pursuit and destruction of the Egyptian army as the Israelites camped unprotected on the beach of the Red Sea.[536] The Israelites were trapped with the sea on one side and the mountains on the other side. With the Egyptians in hot pursuit, God was about to perform a great miracle for them. Israel was camped on the beach and the pillar of cloud was their covering from the heat of the sun but it also would hold the heat of the day so that the nights were not so cold. In Exodus 14:19-31 two significant verses are found. First verse 19 equates the pillar of cloud with the Messenger (Angel) of the LORD. The pillar of cloud moved from before Israel to block the advancing Egyptian army while the waters of the Red Sea were separated. The key is that the Messenger (Angel) of the LORD is identified with the pillar of cloud. The second factor is in verse 24 where the LORD looked at the Egyptian army through the pillar of fire and cloud. Verse 19 identifies the Messenger (Angel) of the LORD with the pillar of the cloud, and verse 24 equally identifies the LORD from the same cloud as looking down at the Egyptian army:

---

[534] Kaiser, *The Expositor's Bible Commentary: Exodus,* 1:376.

[535] John D. Currid, *A Study Commentary on Exodus 19-40* (2 vols. Auburn, MA: Evangelical Press, 2000), 2:251.

[536] *Red Sea*: Sea of Aquaba, also known as the Gulf of Eilat. This body of water was the probable site and crossing of the Red Sea. For more information see the video: Campus Crusade for Christ. *The Exodus Revealed, Search for the Red Sea Crossing.* (Irvine CA: Discovery Media Productions, 2001), videotape sold by Friends of Israel Gospel Ministry at www.foi.org.

The angel of the Lord was clearly God Himself. Exod 13:21 took note of God's going before Israel, and later the statement was recorded that "the angel of God who went before the host of Israel moved and went behind them; and the pillar of cloud moved from before them and stood behind them" (Ex 14:19) which obviously equated the angel with God.[537]

Once again, the plain sense of Scripture equates the Messenger (Angel) of the LORD with *Yahweh* the One who moves the pillar of cloud. He is the One who looked upon the Egyptian army from the pillar of fire and cloud. But the Angel (Messenger) of the LORD is not God the Father. In Exodus 3 the Angel (Messenger) of the LORD is God and yet distinct from God (as well as in Genesis 16:7-13; 22:11-12; 31:11-13; 32:24-30; 16:7-13). Mackay is clear in his understanding of this passage that the Messenger (Angel) of the LORD is God and yet distinct from the Father, as he reveals in this statement:

> Then the angel of God, who had been traveling in front of Israel's army, withdrew and went behind them. It is evident that 'the angel of God' is to be identified with 'the angel of the LORD' who had appeared earlier (3:2). Although 'angel' means simply a 'messenger' or 'courier,' it is clear that the angel of the LORD is not merely human. In the plural the word is frequently used of heavenly beings, but this angel is more than that. The angel is a specific manifestation of the divine presence, usually understood to be a pre-incarnate appearance of the second person of the Trinity.[538]

Mackay elaborates by saying that this "*angel of God*" in Exodus 14:19 is directly tied to the LORD in verse 24 and he continues to place them together in Exodus 23:21 and 33:14:

> In verse 24 it is said that "the LORD looked down from the pillar of fire and cloud;" in chapter 23 mention is made of an angel in whom the divine Name is (23:21); and in 33:14 the LORD talks of his Presence going with Moses. The personality of the angel is further brought out in Isaiah 63:9, which, referring to these events, says "The angel of his presence saved them."[539]

Although Mackay places these names or titles together, LORD, angel, and the angel of His Presence, they are not the same as the person of God the Father. Currid also makes the same observation:

> *Yahweh* now acts to protect his people. First, the angel of God, who had been leading the Israelites in their escape, moves between God's people and the Egyptians. It may be that the angel of God poses in a military stance, as he does

---

[537] Tenney, *The Zondervan Pictorial Encyclopedia of the Bible*, 5:389.
[538] Mackay, *A Mentor Commentary: Exodus*, 254-255.
[539] Mackay, *A Mentor Commentary: Exodus*, 255.

in Numbers 22:22-23, 31-32. This is the same figure who appeared in the burning bush in Exodus 3:2. There he spoke and acted as if he was God.[540]

The pillar of cloud was not removed at night because of the Egyptians and it became a pillar of fire for Israel (Exodus 13:21-22). New Covenant scholars, such as Kaiser, have also seen the connection and are specific as to the identity of the "cloud" and the *angel of God:*"

> The identity of the angel of God is clarified in the second part of v. 19: the pillar of cloud and fire (see comments on 13:22). The reality of God's promised presence may be stated in the symbol of his presence (the pillar of cloud and fire), in his messenger (the angel of the Lord), or as the Lord himself who "went ahead of them" (13:21; 14:24). But when the presence of God "withdrew" (*ns'*), he went behind them to protect Israel's rear guard.[541]

So clearly were the Messenger (Angel) of the LORD and the pillar of cloud connected together that Moses, in verse 24, proceeds to tie together all of this with *Yahweh*, as is seen by Edersheim making "*the angel of the LORD*" and *Yahweh* equal:

> "Jehovah looked unto" them "through the pillar of fire and of the cloud, and troubled the host of the Egyptians."[542]

In summary, the *Tanakh* made the Messenger (Angel) of the LORD equal to *Yahweh*. Yet throughout the biblical text it has been clearly demonstrated that the Messenger (Angel) of the LORD is distinct from the Father. In Exodus 3 it was demonstrated that a theophany of God was the second person of the plural unity of *Elohim*, who has been recognized as the Messiah of Israel, the Son of David, the God/man. In Exodus 14:19-31, the Messenger (Angel) of the LORD spoke as *Yahweh* and as *Elohim*, and He was visibly present for the Israelites to see His glory in the pillar of cloud by day and the pillar of fire by night. This one was the pre-incarnate Messiah.

The LORD Spoke to Israel at Mt. Sinai ... Exodus 20:22

> The LORD said to Moses: Thus shall you say to the Israelites: You yourselves saw that I spoke to you from the very heavens:

This passage in Exodus 20:22 has a much larger context than verses 18-21, because its context begins back in 19:9 where the LORD told them to prepare themselves for His talk with them. The immediate reference in this context (Exodus 20:18-21) gives the people's response to what they had just experienced. This passage will be dealt with more fully in chapter 7 under the subject of the *Shechinah* of God. The purpose for referencing this verse now is to see the relationship between Exodus chapters 3 and 14,

---

[540] John D. Currid, *A Study Commentary on Exodus 1-18,* 1:300.
[541] Kaiser, *The Expositor's Bible Commentary: Exodus,* 389.
[542] Edersheim, *The Exodus and the Wanderings in the Wilderness,* 87.

where the Messenger (Angel) of the LORD, appearing as the *Shechinah* of God spoke to Moses, and His activity at the Red Sea crossing. Now that the glory of the LORD, the *Shechinah* of God, has been equated in the immediate past with the Messenger (Angel) of the LORD, He would also be the One who spoke at the giving of the 10 commandments. This passage also shows Him to be a theophany of God. What the people saw and heard literally put the fear of God in them and they trembled (Exodus 19:16). When the people experienced this personal revelation of *Yahweh* on Mt. Sinai, they requested of Moses that God would speak to him and said they would listen to Moses because God was too terrifying to hear and see. Samuel Frey, in his commentary on Exodus 20:18-22, states that the LORD would speak to Moses who would speak to them, and some day a prophet like Moses (Deuteronomy 18:15-18) would speak to His people:

> The people said, "let not God speak to us, lest we die." And Jehovah, who not only can do what we ask, but always exceeds our requests, not only answered their petition to speak to them by Moses, but graciously promised to raise up another prophet like unto him.[543]

In chapter 7 this passage, in connection with the *Shechinah*, is dealt with in more detail.

God and the Sent One ... Exodus 23:20-23

> (20) I am sending an angel before you to guard you on the way and to bring you to the place that I have made ready. (21) Pay heed to him and obey him. Do not defy him, for he will not pardon your offenses, since My Name is in him; (22) but if you obey him and do all that I say, I will be an enemy to your enemies and a foe to your foes. (23) When My angel goes before you and brings you to the Amorites, the Hittites, the Perizzites, the Canaanites, the Hivites, and the Jebusites, and I annihilate them,

Exodus 23:20-23 reads that Israel had not yet made the "golden calf" (Exodus 32) and broken the law just given to them. Exodus 23 follows the passage of Scripture where God gave the Decalogue (Ten Commandments) to Moses (in chapter 20) with other laws and judgments. Yet in this passage God chooses to send His Angel as His representative to lead the vassal nation of Israel through the wilderness. The coming of "My angel" was a covenant representative from *Yahweh* to the vassal Israel. This covenant between God and Israel is important to understand, as Mackay relates the significance of "My angel" being sent:

> The angel as the LORD's covenant emissary is going to convey instructions to the people and these must not be disregarded. The route to covenant blessing is by obedience to the LORD and the one he has sent to represent him.[544]

---

[543] Frey, *The Messiahship of Jesus,* 44.
[544] Mackay, *A Mentor Commentary: Exodus,* 408.

The identity of the Angel or Messenger must be known. Three views are prevalent: (1) the Messenger is Moses, but Moses does not fit the description given in Exodus 23:21-23; (2) the Messenger is a created celestial being who will lead them, but that also does not fit the text description in verse 21; (3) the Messenger is the Angel of the LORD, a theophany of God, who has been appearing since the time of Abraham; this does fit the description in verses 20-23. Walter Kaiser and John Davis express the same sentiments respectively about the identity of the Messenger (Angel) of the LORD:

> The angel mentioned here cannot be Moses, God's messenger, or an ordinary angel; for the expressions are too high for any of these: "he will not forgive your rebellion" (who can forgive sin but God alone?) and "my Name is in him" (v. 22). This must be the Angel of the covenant (cf. Isa 63:9; Mal 3:1), the Second Person of the Trinity. (See our discussion in Exod 33 and in Old Testament Theology, p. 120, for four forms of Yahweh's divine presence.) Just as Yahweh's name resided in his temple (Deut 12:5, 11; 1 Kgs 8:29), so this Angel with the authority and prestige of the name of God was evidence enough that God himself was present in his son. Obedience to the Angel would result in all the blessings listed in the text. Israel was commanded: "Do not rebel against him" (v. 21); yet they did just that (Num 14:11; Psa 78:17, 40, 56).[545]

> The angel mentioned in verse 20 has been identified three different ways. Some consider (1) Moses to have been that angel while others see it as one of the (2) created angelic beings. More popular, however, is the (3) view that this angel was indeed the Angel of Jehovah or the second person of the trinity. In the light of the context and other evidence the last view appears to be preferable. Since this is Jehovah himself who leads, He demands absolute obedience (v. 21). Those who disobeyed were regarded as enemies and treated as such (v. 22). This angel would also lead them in the land as they confronted the major enemies and it would be He who would provide the key to victory (v. 23).[546]

In Exodus 23:20-23 there is a specific description of this Angel or Messenger that needs to be noted carefully. First, the LORD states that He will send His Messenger (Angel) who will keep them and lead them into the Land. Second, in verse 21, Israel is told to obey Him and not to provoke Him for He will not pardon their transgressions. Third, this Messenger (Angel) bears the very name of God in Him, and that is most important to observe. In Exodus 13:21, 14:19 and 24 it is simply the LORD, the Messenger (Angel) of the LORD who has spoken. Under the second point this Messenger (Angel) has the power to forgive sins, and the Pharisees in Luke 5:21 understood that to be blasphemy for only God could forgive sins. The Pharisees were correct; so who was seated before them was the very one who was the Messenger (Angel) of God who led

---

[545] Kaiser, *The Expositor's Bible Commentary: Exodus,* 446.
[546] Davis, *Moses and the Gods of Egypt: Studies in Exodus,* 247.

Israel through the wilderness. Mackay makes this statement in relation to the Messenger who had the power to forgive sin:

> It is the angel who has the power to forgive rebellion. In light of Mark 2:7-10 ("Who can forgive sins but God alone?"), the angel is divine. This is what is in effect said in the phrase "my name is in him." 'Name' represents the revelation of the character and attributes of God (Exod 6:3; 34:5). It is virtually a synonym for God's effective presence. The alternation between the angel and 'I' suggests an identity between the angel and Yahweh.[547]

This "Angel" is unique and as will be seen in the following quote, this Messenger (Angel) spoke and acted as God and not for God:

> Exodus 23:20-23 is a key text in this regard, since it shows how this angel carries the Lord's character and authority. Exodus 23:21 shows that the angel has the authority to forgive sins and that the Lord's name is "in him"; vv. 21-22 both specify the angel's authority to speak for God. On the other hand, in Exodus 32:34 – 33:17 we see more of a distinction between the Lord and his angel: the Lord pledges to send his angel before Israel, despite their sin (32:24; 33:2), but he himself will not go with them (33:3). This seems to distinguish this "angel" from God himself. When the passage speaks in 33:14 of God's presence with Israel, it does not refer to his "angel" but rather his "face" (panay: lit. "my face") that goes with them.[548]

Exodus 33:14-15 adds that the presence of God also means the very face of God. Some commentators, like Cassuto, have tried to say that the messenger (angel) simply stands for God's presence with Israel when he states "the angel stands only for the guidance and help of the Lord."[549] Currid correctly points out that the Messenger (Angel) has already been present since His introduction to Moses in Exodus 3:2 and then at the Red Sea crossing in Exodus 14:19. Currid sees this Messenger (Angel) as equivalent to *Yahweh* Himself as seen in the following statement:

> There is no reason to think that God would not continue to supply such protection until Israel entered the land of Canaan. This angel appears to be an extension of God's person and word, an equivalent of Yahweh himself. The identity of God with an angel has already been witnessed in Exod 3:2-6. It would seem likely that, as in chapter 3, this angelic being is a pre-incarnate appearance of the Messiah.[550]

---

[547] Mackay, *A Mentor Commentary: Exodus,* 408.

[548] David M. Howard, Jr. *The New American Commentary: Joshua* (Nashville: Broadman, 1998), 160.

[549] U. Cassuto, *A Commentary on the Book of Exodus* (Jerusalem: Magnes Press, 1967), 148.

[550] Currid, *Exodus 19-40*, 2:124-125.

Currid's observation is correct. The *Tanakh* states that the Messenger (Angel) will not only be with Israel to lead them but will continue to do so until the Promised Land is settled as seen in Exodus 23:20-23 and Judges 2:1.

This Messenger (Angel), then, is a very special individual, not an ordinary messenger (angel) as Edersheim brings out in the following statement:

> First and foremost, assurance is given them of the personal presence of Jehovah in that Angel, in Whom is the Name of the Lord (v. 20) [Exodus 25:20]. This was no common angel, however exalted, but a manifestation of Jehovah Himself, prefigurative of, and preparatory to His manifestation in the flesh in the Person of our Lord and Saviour Jesus Christ. For all that is here said of Him is attributed to the Lord Himself in Exodus 33:21; while in Exodus 33:14-15, He is expressly designated as "the Face" of Jehovah ("My Face" – in the authorized Version "My presence").[551]

Keil and Delitzsch affirm the same basic idea as Edersheim when they see the Messenger (Angel) as God Himself:

> The name of Jehovah was in this angel (v. 21), that is to say, Jehovah revealed Himself in him; and hence he is called in chapter 23:15-16, the face of Jehovah, because the essential nature of Jehovah was manifested in him. This angel was not a created spirit, therefore, but the manifestation of Jehovah Himself, who went before them in the pillar of cloud and fire, to guide and to defend them (23:21). But because it was Jehovah who was guiding His people in the person of the angel, He demanded unconditional obedience (v. 21), and if they provoked Him (תַּמֵּר for תָּמַר see chapter 13:18) by disobedience, He would not pardon their transgression; but if they followed Him and hearkened to His voice, He would be an enemy to their enemies, and an adversary to their adversaries (v. 22). And when the angel of the Lord had brought them to the Canaanites and exterminated the latter, Israel was still to yield the same obedience, by not serving the gods of the Canaanites, or doing after their works, by not making any idolatrous images, but destroying them (these works), and smiting to pieces the pillars of their idolatrous worship (מַצֵּבֹה does not mean statues erected as idols, but memorial stones or columns dedicated to idols: see my commentary on 1 Kings 14:23), and serving Jehovah alone.[552]

Even Jacob in Genesis 48:16 refers to the angel that delivered him from all harm, which is the exact act of God here, sending His Angel to protect and lead Israel into the Promised Land.[553] Jewish scholars struggle to deal with the obvious language of the Messenger (Angel) of the LORD having the name of the LORD, the authority to forgive sins and trespasses. Some use the argument that the Angel speaks for the LORD

---

[551] Edersheim, *The Exodus and the Wanderings in the Wilderness,* 119.

[552] Keil & Delitzsch, *Commentary on the Old Testament: Exodus,* 1:152-153.

[553] Sailhamer, *The Pentateuch as Narrative: A Biblical-Theological Commentary,* 294.

and that makes the LORD present. But others in Rabbinic Judaism speak of *Metatron* (*the angel of the LORD*), who is recognized by them as one who stands very close to the LORD. Goldberg states that *Metatron* (see chapter 4) was the Angel who provided, guided, and protected, as well as judged the Israelites in the wilderness:

> The name of the angel peculiar to the Talmud is that of Metatron or precursor; he was regarded as the angel who went before the Israelites in the wilderness and that he was held in high reverence for some have thought they ought to pray to him inasmuch as he stood so close to God (Sanhedrin 38b). He is the only one who sits in the presence of God (Hagigah 15a). There seems to be some hint, in the presentation of this being, of a mystery of this one's relation to God. The Talmud did not want to equate this angel with God, and yet this angel was considered to have many of His attributes; even God's Name is in him, and he was declared to be able to pardon transgression (Sanhedrin 38b). Did not the Talmudists recognize here in the passage of Exodus 23:20-25 a reference to the peculiar nature of the Godhead and that there could have been some multiplicity of persons or personality in the nature of God? At any rate, it would seem that there was here something of this presentation set forth in the Exodus passage.[554]

The Jewish sages of old did recognize the Messenger (Angel) of the LORD as a very special person who had the very attributes of God, but they did not want to call Him God because of their insistence on the absolute oneness of God as they understood the *Tanakh*. This Jewish belief can be clearly seen by the comments of Scherman on the Angel who went up with Israel:

> God told Moses (33:2) that He would withdraw His Presence from them and send an angel to lead them to the Land (Rashi). There, Moses protested the decree and begged that God Himself accompany the people, and God relented. Here, however, Moses accepted it because God did not convey the news to him as a punishment. Rather, in the context of our verse, it was presented as the triumphant manner of Israel's entry into Eretz Yisrael (Be'er BaSadeh). Ramban notes that this prophecy was not fulfilled in Moses' lifetime, for Moses pleaded with God not to withdraw from the people, and God acceded to his request (33:15-17). After Moses' death, however, an angel appeared to Joshua and identified himself as the head of HaShem's legion (Joshua 5:13-15). That was the angel announced in this verse, who had been held in abeyance during Moses' lifetime, but was dispatched to lead Israel after his death.[555]

Joshua 5:13-15 refers to the same one who brought Israel through the wilderness, but one item is neglected. The messenger (angel) that Scherman refers to in Joshua as "*the*

---

[554] Goldberg, *The Deviation of Jewish Thought from an Old Testament Theology in the Intertestamental Period*, 89-90.

[555] Scherman, *The Chumash: The Stone Edition, The Torah, Haftoros and Five Megillos*, 437-438.

Captain of the LORD's host" was the same messenger (angel) of the Exodus text, but one important point is missing in their statement. Jewish rabbis state that He is called the head of *HaShem*'s legion, yet this *"Captain of the LORD's host"* tells Joshua that the ground on which he stood is holy ground, reflecting the point that *"the Captain of the LORD's host"* is God present in the form of a theophany.

So whether God appeared as the Messenger (Angel) of the LORD in human form or in a fiery bush, or in a pillar of cloud and fire, this Messenger (Angel) is God Himself, the second member of the plural unity of *Elohim*. It is clearly seen that God is one; He is monotheistic, but that oneness is revealed in a plurality, as this book discerns from Genesis to Chronicles in the Jewish Scriptures.[556]

In summary, Exodus 23:20-23 from the Torah clearly presents the Messenger (Angel) of the LORD as the LORD and presents this "sent one" by God as distinct from God, yet God as well.

The God of Israel Appears to 74 Men … Exodus 24:9-11

(9) Then Moses and Aaron, Nadab and Abihu, and seventy elders of Israel ascended; (10) and they saw the God of Israel: under His feet there was the likeness of a pavement of sapphire, like the very sky for purity. (11) Yet He did not raise His hand against the leaders of the Israelites; they beheld God, and they ate and drank.

This is one of the most unusual theophanies in all of the *Tanakh*. Here God appeared to not just one person, which is the usual way, but appeared in a physical form to 74 men at the same time. To set the background for what happened, verses 1-8 need to be understood as well. God had just given His law to Moses who gave it to the people in Exodus 24:3:

Moses went and repeated to the people all the commands of the LORD and all the rules;

First, Moses repeated or recounted to the people all the commands or words of the LORD. The phrase כָּל־דִּבְרֵי means "the whole" or "all" of the words. דָּבָר is *dabar*, a noun that is translated "word" or "words" as in speech. Here Moses recounted all the "words" of the LORD before the people. Exodus 24:3, along with verse 4, states that *"Moses then wrote down all the commands of the LORD."* Once again the word "commands" is דָּבָר (*dabar*) or "words" וַיִּכְתֹּב (*katab*) or "written down," that is "all" the "words" of the LORD. That leaves absolutely no room for the oral law that

---

[556] *Genesis to Chronicles.* This is used by Jewish people to reference the whole of the *Tanakh*; it is like Christians saying Genesis to Malachi. It all has to do with the order of the books. Christianity uses the same books found in the Hebrew Scriptures but places them in a different order.

Rabbinic Judaism clutches on to so they can have spiritual dominance over the Jewish people.

In the latter part of Exodus 24:3, the people respond to "all" the "words" that Moses had spoken and "written down" with אֶחָד (*echad*) or with "one voice." Here is an instance where *echad* (Deuteronomy 6:4) is used as a compound unity, many as one. The people of God were committing themselves to keep "all" of the "words" of the law that Moses had "written" down. They never committed themselves to keep an oral law that was not written down and that the *Tanakh* itself does not support.

The morning after the people made their commitment to obey all the "words" of the law that were written down by Moses, he erected an altar and placed on it a burnt-offering and peace-offering unto the LORD. Then the covenant agreement between Israel and *Yahweh* was made. Understand this as a covenant agreement: *Yahweh* is the new King and the people are His vassals, or His servants. In a covenant agreement in biblical times a victorious king laid down the conditions to the defeated vassal kingdom; he had laws, commandments, and rules that needed to be observed to maintain the king's protection over the vassal kingdom. So it is here that *Yahweh* gave His laws and commandments for Israel to obey. Moses ratified that covenant by taking the blood from the offerings and by dividing it in half. Half was sprinkled on the altar and the other half was sprinkled on the people. Then in Exodus 24:8 Moses committed Israel to the covenant by his action and the following statement:

> Moses took the blood and dashed (sprinkled) it on the people and said, "This is the blood of the covenant that the LORD now makes with you concerning all these commands."

In this covenant agreement between Israel and the LORD, Israel's part was to be obedient to all the words that Moses gave to the people and had written down. In Exodus 24:7, Moses took the book of the covenant and read it in Israel's presence and they responded by saying *"all that the LORD has spoken we will faithfully do."* Israel made a covenant-binding commitment to keep the written law of the LORD (no reference to an oral law). The next step for the leaders of Israel was to meet their new King!

Moses, Aaron and two of his four sons, Nadab and Abihu, with 70 of the elders of Israel, were asked by God to attend the final stage of the covenant ratification ceremony. They were permitted an audience with the covenant King, to come and worship and have a fellowship meal (Exodus 24:9-12), ratifying the covenant in the presence of *Yahweh*.[557] In Exodus 19 the Israelites were banned from approaching Mt. Sinai, but not so here. In this covenant ratification (in verse 10) *"they saw the God of Israel"* but Moses only described that the feet of God were standing on a pavement that had the likeness of sapphire. רָאָה is Hebrew for "to see" or "saw" and the text says וַיִּרְאוּ or *"they saw"* the LORD. This was not a dream or vision; the text makes no

---

[557] Mackay, *A Mentor Commentary: Exodus,* 420.

reference to either. This was a literal theophany of *Yahweh* as He appeared to all 74 leaders of Israel. This is a very unique passage of Scripture. However, some scholars refuse to see the visual manifestation of God in this passage, as reflected by the following author:

> This was not, of course, a visible representation of God, but the glory they saw was compared to a paved work of sapphire having the brilliance of the heavens.[558]

It is biblically irresponsible to look at a passage of Scripture and deny what is clearly in the text. Look at Exodus 24:10 which describes *Yahweh* in the following manner: *"under His feet there was the likeness of a pavement of sapphire."* Nothing is given as to the form of God that the 74 men saw. God did manifest Himself to them, but what He looked like was purposely not given so as not to give encouragement to a people who would, in the near future and later history, make a likeness of the gods, thus preventing them from doing so of *Yahweh*. Exodus 24:11 says that *Yahweh* did not raise His hand upon them. Also, verse 11 seems to repeat the statement that they saw the LORD. However, this verse uses a different Hebrew word, וַיֶּחֱזוּ, with the root verb being חָזָה meaning to "see" or "behold" with the eye.[559] To behold something is different from just seeing it, for this is an intensified form.[560] Verse 11 is saying that these 74 men stared at the LORD; they could not take their eyes off what they were seeing. They were actually seeing God and living to tell about it. Then in Exodus 24:11 it states that *"they ate and drank"* which was the completion of the covenant agreement with *Yahweh*. What an awesome experience these men had! God is holy and God, in all His glory, is unapproachable. Yet *Yahweh* allowed them to see Him or behold Him and still live. This is perhaps the most outstanding theophany in the *Tanakh*. Clearly, the second member of the plural unity of *Elohim* is the one who reveals the Father. All the other passages have served as a precedent – the passages concerning the Messenger (Angel) of the LORD, the appearing of the glory of the LORD, and all the other passages that point back to the same member of the plural unity of *Elohim*. Nothing has been changed in relation to the person speaking and acting. Sailhamer gives a great summary statement of what transpired that day:

> When the people heard Moses, they consented to the covenant and ratified it by means of a covenant ceremony (24:4-8). After this ceremony, Moses and Aaron "went up" (v. 9) to feast with Nadab and Abihu and the seventy elders (vv. 10-11).[561]

The understanding of the people was that anyone who saw God would die. Kaiser deals with what appears to be a contradiction by the following statement:

---

[558] Tom Julien, *Studies in Exodus : Spiritual Greatness* (Winona Lake, IN: BMH Books, 1979), 134.

[559] Brown, Driver, and Briggs, *A Hebrew and English Lexicon of the Old Testament,* 302.

[560] Currid, *Exodus 19-40,* 2:139.

[561] Sailhamer, *The Pentateuch as Narrative: A Biblical-Theological Commentary,* 295.

That Moses and his company "saw the God of Israel" at first appears to contradict [Exod] 33:20; John 1:18; and 1 Tim 6:16; but what they saw was a "form ['similitude'] of the LORD" (Num 12:8), just as Ezekiel (Ezek 1:26) and Isaiah (Isa 6:1) saw an approximation, a faint resemblance and a sensible adumbration of the incarnate Christ who was to come. There is a deliberate obscurity in the form and details of the one who produced such a splendid, dazzling effect on these observers of God's presence.[562]

This physical appearance of God is not described. What they saw, except for feet and the platform on which God stood, will become very important. For in less than 40 days Israel would attempt to make a graven image of God.

What is so remarkable about this section in Exodus is that in 24:12 the LORD calls Moses up to Mt. Sinai and from chapter 25 through 31, He gave to Moses the plans for the tabernacle, the priesthood, and the offerings. Moses spends 40 days on the mountain with *Yahweh*. Yet in chapter 32 the people get Aaron to make a golden calf to worship as *Yahweh*. The LORD says to Moses that they have "acted basely" or have "corrupted themselves." He proceeds to call them a stiff-necked people and says to Moses "*let Me be, that My anger may blaze forth against them and that I may destroy them.*" Only 40 days after seeing the LORD and making a commitment to observe the law given to them, Israel departed so quickly from the LORD and His words or commandments.

Now that the text has been studied, some comments by rabbis are appropriate. Two great rabbis quoted by Scherman in The Chumash, Rashi and Ramban, are quoted in connection with this passage. Rashi has a very negative interpretation while Ramban has a positive interpretation. The negative interpretation gives evidence of a lack of biblical accuracy:

> According to Rashi, citing *Tanchuma*, the onlookers – with the exception of Moses, of course – sinned grievously in that they gazed at the sacred vision while irreverently indulging in food and drink. For that, they deserved to die immediately, but God did not stretch out His hand to harm them, in order not to mar the Joy of the giving of the Torah. Therefore the punishments of Nadab, Abihu, and the elders were deferred until later on. In line with this view, *Tur* comments that God purposely did not send Elazar and Issamar, Aaron's younger sons, with the group so that they would not incur the death penalty, like their brothers. Had they, too, died, Aaron would have been left childless.

> According to Onkelos and Ramban that they did not sin, the verse speaks in their praise, saying that they suffered no harm even though they had a

---

[562] Kaiser, *The Expositor's Bible Commentary: Exodus,* 449.

profoundly holy prophetic vision that would ordinarily have been far beyond a human being's capacity to endure.[563]

The statements of Rashi simply do not have any relevance to the context of Exodus 24:9-12. A quotation from Avraham Finkel distorts what actually happened in this passage:

> Rav used to say the following: The world to come is not like this world. In the world to come, there is no eating or drinking or begetting of children or business; there is no jealousy, hatred, or competition; the righteous will sit with their crowns on their heads and delight in the radiance of the Shechinah, as it says "They – the seventy elders of Israel – had a vision of the Divine, yet they ate and drank." Not in a physical sense, but the spiritual delight they derived from the radiance of the Shechinah is compared to the pleasure of eating and drinking (Berachot 17a).[564]

In the first part of the quotation, Finkel deals with the world to come, while in the second half he references the 70 elders having a vision. However, nowhere in the whole context is there any reference to a vision. In fact, the word "see" or "behold" with the eyes in Exodus 24:11 mitigates against a vision. Finkel states that the 74 leaders in Exodus 24:9-11 did not physically experience what they saw and ate, but had a spiritual experience, yet the language of the text does not support such a view.

The rabbis have had trouble with this passage because God, who is pure spirit, an incorporeal being, takes on a physical form for the benefit of the 74 men present. Here is another example of a principle of translation used in Exodus 24:10 by Stenning as the rabbis have attempted to get away from the obvious:

> The nearest approach to a general principle is the dictum ascribed to Jehuda b. Ilai (2nd cent. A.D.): 'He who translates a verse quite literally is a liar, while he who adds anything thereto is a blasphemer.' Thus Exodus 24:10 'and they saw the God of Israel' must not be rendered literally since no man can be said to have seen God: on the other hand, to insert the word 'angel'....would be blasphemous, since an angel would be substituted for God. The correct rendering is 'and they saw the glory...of the God of Israel.'[565]

As can be clearly seen, this argument by Stenning is an obvious attempt on the part of rabbis to get away from the obvious meaning that Exodus 24:10 in the *Tanakh* has given. Stenning is condemning himself because he himself is mistranslating the very words that *Yahweh* gave to Moses, which Moses then wrote down.

---

[563] Scherman, *The Chumash: The Stone Edition: The Torah, Haftoros and Five Megillos,* 442-443.

[564] Finkel, *The Torah Revealed,* 128.

[565] Stenning, *The Targum of Isaiah,* ix.

Exodus 24 is one of the most unusual theophanies in the *Tanakh*. Any teaching that rabbis might possibly give that God cannot be seen and is busy in heaven, separated from His creation because of His holiness, is untrue. It is completely refuted by the person of God meeting with the leaders of Israel in Exodus 24:9-11. The holy God of Israel does not just visit with Moses and Israel through the pillar of cloud and fire; He becomes very friendly and personable. God initiated this manifestation in a clear and unquestionable manner. This personal revelation of the eternal God is a theophany, the revealing of the second person of the plural unity of God, the future Son of David and Messiah of Israel.

My Angel Shall go Before You … Exodus 32:34 – 33:3

(34) "Go now, lead the people where I told you. See, My angel shall go before you. But when I make an accounting, I will bring them to account for their sins." (35) Then the LORD sent a plague upon the people, for what they did with the calf that Aaron made. (33:1) Then the LORD said to Moses, "Set out from here, you and the people that you have brought up from the land of Egypt, to the land of which I swore to Abraham, Isaac, and Jacob, saying, 'To your offspring will I give it' – (2) I will send an angel before you, and I will drive out the Canaanites, the Amorites, the Hittites, the Perizzites, the Hivites, and the Jebusites – (3) a land flowing with milk and honey. But I will not go in your midst, since you are a stiff-necked people, lest I destroy you on the way."

This passage contains some interesting and comparative statements made by God to Moses concerning Israel. First, in 32:34-35 God tells Moses to lead "the" people instead of "my" people. Because of Israel's sin *Yahweh* in His anger is distancing Himself from Israel, yet He will fulfill His promise to Abraham, Isaac and Jacob. God will judge them for their sin according to Exodus 32:34 where He says, "*in that day when I visit I will visit their sin upon them.*" What does God mean by this statement? Is He referencing the messages of the later prophets? It is as if this sin is being stored up for future judgment. One author has an interesting and somewhat lengthy explanation as to the meaning of this statement:

What is meant by the time when God will call Israel to account? According to rabbinic exegesis, whenever YHWH visits Israel for their sins, they are at the same time also punished for the sin with the golden calf (b. Sanh 102a; ExR., XLIII, 2; Rashi). Keil, for one is quite specific: Israel has filled up the measure of its guilt, when at the border of Canaan it again betrays distrust in YHWH and wants to return to Egypt (Num. 14:4ff.); YHWH condemns the people to perish in the wilderness (14:26; Deut. 1:35) (for other ideas see in Hahn, 97f.). It could be that that is what the writer was thinking of. At the same time, however, he will have had in mind the fate of Northern Israel: Jeroboam I failed to take to heart the lesson of the stay in the desert, breathed new life into the bull worship, and so struck out in a direction which, historically speaking, had to lead to the downfall of the nation; perhaps he also thought of the fall of Judah.[566]

Secondly, in Exodus 32:34 and 33:2 *Yahweh* uses two interesting phrases to speak of the Messenger (Angel) that will go up with them. Verse 34 refers to "My angel," directly referencing Exodus 23:20-23, but then in verse 2 the LORD spoke of "an angel." It is obvious that *Yahweh* was distancing Himself from the people. This angel would fulfill the covenant made to Abraham, Isaac and Jacob and drive out all the nations in the land of Canaan (Exodus 3:8). Minimally, this "an angel" is an impersonal statement concerning the angel of Exodus 23:20-23 and 32:34, who is recognized as part of the plural unity of *Elohim*. Authors such as Kaiser and Mackay[567] state that this angel "is altogether different from the angel of His presence in Isaiah 63:9, since God declared that his "Name is in him" (23:2-23).[568] With great respect for Dr. Kaiser, it could first of all be proposed that even though God distanced Himself with His use of language, the angel is still the same angel of the Exodus 23 account. Secondly, it can be verified by the testimony of the "*angel* [Messenger] *of the LORD*" in Judges 2:1 where He clearly states that He took Israel from Egypt, through the wilderness and into the Promised Land.

There are two words used by the LORD to describe the distance that He puts between Himself and Israel as He tells Moses to go up to the land. He uses impersonal words as they are to start traveling, you and "the" people which "thou" or "you" have brought up out of Egypt. Three times *Yahweh* uses statements that show that He is distancing Himself from them: from "my" angel to "an" angel; from "my" people to "the" people; and from the people that "I" brought up out of Egypt to the people "you" brought up out of Egypt.

The LORD Came Down in a Cloud … Exodus 34:5

The LORD came down in a cloud; He stood with him there, and proclaimed the name LORD.

In Exodus 34:5 Moses and *Yahweh* came together again. In verse 4 Moses ascended the mountain and *Yahweh* descended in the cloud. So God, who is above all creation, and Moses, whom *Yahweh* knows by name (Exodus 33:17), met again on the mountain separated from the people below. The text says that *Yahweh* stood with Moses, but what the LORD said is correctly evaluated by Keil and Delitzsch:

---

[566] Houtman, *Historical Commentary on the Old Testament: Exodus,* 3:674.

[567] Mackay, *A Mentor Commentary: Exodus,* 295.

[568] Kaiser, *The Expositor's Bible Commentary: Exodus,* 482.

What Moses saw we are not told, but simply the words in which Jehovah proclaimed all the glory of His being; whilst it is recorded of Moses, that he bowed his head toward the earth and worshipped.[569]

The question to be raised here is, to whom was Moses speaking: God the Father or the Second Person of the plural unity of *Elohim*? There are two interesting points in relation to this Messenger (Angel) or *Shechinah* that met with Moses. First, in Exodus 6 "*the angel* [Messenger] *of the LORD*" appeared to Moses. At the end of 47 years with Israel in the land, it is "*the angel* [Messenger] *of the LORD*" who said He did all that happened to Israel while they were wandering in the wilderness. Second, in understanding the nature of theophanies, it is apparent that any appearance of God has to be the Second Person in the plural unity of *Elohim*. As has been observed previously, the Messenger (Angel) of the LORD and the *Shechinah* of God were distinct from the Father and yet God. Coupled with that, the "*My angel*" in whom the name of *Yahweh* is, Who will lead Israel through the wilderness, is also linked to theophanies of God. Then continually *Yahweh* spoke personally to Moses which also was a theophany. By testimony of the *Tanakh* itself, in all of these theophanies of *Yahweh* where He appeared, spoke and acted, He is the Second Person of the plural unity of *Elohim*. This connection may not be given in a dogmatic statement, but the relationship of all these points cannot be ignored. Although Exodus 34:5 is not a Messenger (Angel) of the LORD passage, it is brought up because of its relation to the Messenger (Angel) of the LORD, the cloud over Mt. Sinai.

Balaam and the Talking Donkey … Numbers 22:22-35

(22) But **God** was incensed at his going; so an **angel of the LORD** placed himself in his way as an adversary. He was riding on his she-ass, with his two servants alongside, (23) when the ass caught sight of **the angel of the LORD** standing in the way, with his **drawn sword** in his hand. The ass swerved from the road and went into the fields; and Balaam beat the ass to turn her back onto the road. (24) The **angel of the Lord** then stationed himself in a lane between the vineyards, with a fence on either side. (25) The ass, seeing **the angel of the LORD**, pressed herself against the wall and squeezed Balaam's foot against the wall; so he beat her again.

(26) Once more **the angel of the LORD** moved forward and stationed himself on a spot so narrow that there was no room to swerve right or left. (27) When the ass now saw **the angel of the LORD**, she lay down under Balaam; and Balaam was furious and beat the ass with his stick. (28) The **LORD** opened the ass's mouth, and she said to Balaam, "What have I done to you that you have beaten me these three times?" (29) Balaam said to the ass, "You have made a mockery of me! If I had a sword with me, I'd kill you." (30) The ass said to

---

[569] Keil & Delitzsch, *Commentary on the Old Testament: Exodus,* 240.

Balaam, "Look, I am the ass that you have been riding all along until this day! Have I been in the habit of doing thus to you?" And he answered, "No."

(31) Then the **LORD** uncovered Balaam's eyes, and he saw **the angel of the LORD** standing in the way, his **drawn sword** in his hand; thereupon he bowed "right down to the ground." (32) **The angel of the LORD** said to him, "Why have you beaten your ass these three times? It is I who came out as an adversary, for the errand is obnoxious to me. (33) And when the ass saw me, she shied away because of me those three times. If she had not shied away from me, you are the one I should have killed, while sparing her." (34) Balaam said to **the angel of the LORD**, "I erred because I did not know that you were standing in my way. If you still disapprove, I will turn back." (35) But **the angel of the LORD** said to Balaam, "Go with the men. But you must say nothing except what I tell you." So Balaam went on with Balak's dignitaries.

Balaam was a false prophet from Mesopotamia (Numbers 22:5) who evidently knew who God was but did not worship Him alone. Balaam had a reputation that whomever he blessed was blessed and whomever he cursed was cursed (Numbers 22:6). So the king of Moab wanted Balaam to curse Israel so that he could defeat them. The popularity and work of Balaam can be seen at tel Dir Alla in present day Jordan on the plain near where the Jabbok River flows into the Jordan River Valley. A Dutch excavation team uncovered an inscription recounting the activities of a Balaam, son of Beor (Numbers 22:5).[570] So archaeology has unearthed secular evidence for the biblical person called Balaam.

So Balaam who was from Mesopotamia was well known to the king of Moab. Balaam received the emissaries from the king of Moab and Balaam inquired of the LORD as to whether he could go with them. The end result was that he finally departed with them and *Elohim* was angry with him. In Numbers 22:22-35 *"the angel of the LORD"* is mentioned 10 times in these 14 verses, with the LORD mentioned twice. Once again, the Messenger (Angel) of the LORD is not just an ordinary angel or messenger but a theophany of God who is the Second Person of the plural unity of *Elohim*. This Messenger (Angel) of the LORD stood against Balaam with His sword drawn, which reminds the reader of two other occasions when the *"Captain of the LORD's host"* stood before Joshua (Joshua 5:13-15), and when the Messenger (Angel) of the LORD slew 70,000 Israelites because of David's sin in numbering the people (1 Chronicles 21:16-27 cf 2 Samuel 24:18-25).

Numerous authors such as Lange, Jamieson, and Keil and Delitzsch all recognize the Messenger (Angel) of the LORD as divine. Lange states, "He [Balaam] encounters the divine opposition in the definite form of the Angel of Jehovah," and when Balaam is confronted with the Angel (Messenger) of the LORD, *"he bowed right down to the*

---

[570] R. Dennis Cole, *The New American Commentary: Numbers* (Nashville: Broadman, 2000), 367.

ground" before "*the Angel* (Messenger) *of the LORD.*"[571] Jamieson states that "*the angel of the Lord*" is the old formula for the covenant God of Israel (see Genesis 16:7), which occurs in this narrative not less than nine times interchanged with 'the Lord' twice."[572] Keil and Delitzsch also see "*the angel of the LORD*" as God; they state, "this visible manifestation of God (on "*the angel of the LORD,*" see vol. 1. pp 185) was seen by the ass; but Balaam the seer was so blinded…Jehovah…opened his eyes."[573] This is another in a long list of references in the Torah of "*the Angel* [Messenger] *of the LORD*" appearing to man to reveal something from God or to protect someone from harm or judgment. Here, too, He speaks as God as referenced by Cole:

> Clearly this messenger speaks the words of God as echoed in the familiar refrain in v. 35, "That which I speak to you, it shall you speak."[574]

Four couplets given by God in Numbers 22:22-35 deserve attention: (1) Moab sends emissaries to Balaam and God sends His emissary to Balaam, the Messenger (Angel) of the LORD. (2) Balaam, because of the behavior of the donkey, becomes angry and *Elohim* becomes angry with Balaam. (3) Balaam, out of his anger, said that if he had a sword, he would kill the donkey; the Messenger (Angel) of the LORD appeared to the donkey with a sword drawn to kill Balaam. (4) The LORD opens the mouth of the donkey to speak, and the LORD controls the mouth of Balaam so that he can only speak blessing. God uses these four couplets to compare and contrast the behavior of Balaam with His own will.

In summary, this much has been observed concerning theophanies and the Messenger (Angel) of the LORD in particular. In chapter 5 of this book, theophanies in the pre-flood world did occur but with little or no description as to form. Then during the patriarchal period, the LORD appeared in some form to Hagar and frequently appeared to Abraham as well as to Isaac and Jacob. The appearances of the Messenger (Angel) of the LORD were, without question, appearances of someone Who is God and yet distinct from God. He is the Second Person of the plural unity of *Elohim*.

In chapter 6 of this book, the Messenger (Angel) of the LORD starts out with Moses at the burning bush and concludes with the pillar of cloud and fire. God stated to Israel after the ratification of the Written Law that He would send His Messenger (Angel) to go up to the land with them. The Messengers' [Angels] was described, that He would not forgive their sin and God's name was in Him. Through these passages runs the thread of the appearances throughout the Exodus and Wilderness journey of the *Shechinah* glory of God guiding, protecting and judging Israel as the covenant partner

---

[571] John Peter Lange, *Lange's Commentary on the Holy Scriptures: Numbers – Ruth* (12 Vols. Grand Rapids: Zondervan, 1960), 2:127-128.

[572] Robert Jamieson, A. R. Fausset and David Brown, *A Commentary: Critical, Experimental and Practical on the Old and New Testaments: Genesis – Deuteronomy* (Grand Rapids: Eerdmans, 1945), 575.

[573] Keil & Delitzsch, *Commentary on the Old Testament: Numbers,* 1:169.

[574] Cole, *The New American Commentary: Numbers*, 390.

with the LORD. These references are seen in abundance during the Exodus and Wilderness journey of Israel. Once again, these passages of the theophanies of God show that the Angel (Messenger) of the LORD, "My angel," are all connected with the *Shechinah* glory of God. The Second Person of the plural unity of *Elohim* is very clear.

Chapter 7
Shechinah

Shechinah is a theophany of God, but this appearance is different from other theophanies in the *Tanakh*. For a fuller understanding of the term "theophany" of which the *Shechinah* is a part, see chapter 4. Whether God revealed His presence as a plurality to the nation of Israel as *Yahweh*, the Messenger (Angel) of *Yahweh* or as the *Shechinah* glory of God, that presence was the Second Person of the plural unity of *Elohim*. That is rarely disputed among fundamental and conservative evangelical scholars. *Shechinah*, meaning to dwell among or to dwell in the midst, has carried numerous implications, a reality discussed by Neusner and Green in referencing the dwelling aspect but who go on to say:

> But it means more than that, for wherever it appears, shekhinah designates the attribute of God's presence, often to specify his presence in the Temple or the Tabernacle.[575]

Louis Jacobs adds a little more information on the *Shechinah* as seen from a rabbinic perspective in his following statement:

> The indwelling presence of God, from the root *shakhan*, 'to dwell'. The verbal form is found in Scripture, for example, in the verse: 'And let them make Me a sanctuary, that I may dwell [*ve-shekhanti*] among them' (Exodus 25:8) but Shekhinah as a noun is a Rabbinic coinage, used in the Talmudic literature and the Targum both for the abiding of God in a particular spot and as a divine name irrespective of spatial location.[576]

This visible presence of the glory of God is important to understand. When the *Shechinah* of God or the glory of God appears, God's personal presence is there as it was in the case with Moses and the burning bush encounter, or before all of Israel at Mt. Sinai and in the Holy of Holies of the tabernacle. Tenney states that the Targums (Aramaic paraphrases) also show the *Shechinah* equal with *Yahweh*:

> … the Targum regarded the Shekinah as God Himself and not as a mediator who stood between God and Israel. It became a name for God.[577]

---

[575] Neusner and Green, *Dictionary of Judaism in the Biblical Period,* 577.

[576] Louis Jacobs, *A Concise Companion to the Jewish Religion* (Oxford, England: Oxford University Press, 1999), 226.

[577] Tenney, *The Zondervan Pictorial Encyclopedia of the Bible,* 5:389.

What the exodus account does in relation to the *Shechinah* of God is to unquestionably connect the very glory of God with the Messenger (Angel) of the LORD. In His presence with Moses, the Messenger (Angel) of *Yahweh* spoke as *Yahweh* the LORD, not just in Exodus 6 but throughout the Exodus and Wilderness accounts. This not only connects the *Shechinah* glory of God to the Second Person of the plural unity of God, but it also makes Him *Elohim*.

The revelation of God Himself is nothing that can be induced by man; it is totally at the discretion of God Himself as to how, when and in what form He chooses to communicate with man, as the following statement by Frame reflects:

> God is essentially invisible. This means, not that he can never be seen under any circumstances, but rather that, as Lord, he sovereignly chooses when, where, and to whom to make himself visible.[578]

God is Spirit, an indivisible incorporeal or immaterial being whose glory and majesty are totally beyond anything that mankind could ever dream of, as is reflected by the accounts of Isaiah and Ezekiel who saw God's throne in a vision. They could not find words or points of reference to anything on earth to compare His glory to what they saw.

There is a noticeable absence of the word *Elohim* in Deuteronomy. *Elohim*, when used by itself, only occurs 15 times. In Exodus *Elohim* is used quite frequently alone to speak of the God of Israel. *Elohim* in Deuteronomy is used primarily in connection with *Yahweh* (270 times) as in the LORD God (*Elohim*) or LORD thy God (*Elohim*), throughout the restatement of the Law by Moses to the next generation about to enter the Promised Land. It becomes very obvious that Moses was emphasizing monotheism as he repeated the law to the generation who would be the ones tempted with the polytheism of the nations that surrounded them.

Before looking at the references on the *Shechinah* glory of God in the wilderness wandering, a picture needs to be given as to just how the text flows in relationship to the Messenger (Angel) of the LORD to this subject:

1. The Messenger (Angel) of the LORD appears in the burning bush as the glory (*Shechinah* glory) of the LORD appeared to Moses in Exodus 3 as seen in chapter 6 of this book. This Messenger (Angel) of the LORD spoke as the LORD and yet was distinct from the LORD. These two (LORD and the *Shechinah*) are tied together throughout the exodus account. This passage shows a plurality in the unity of *Elohim*.

2. In Exodus 23 the LORD, who gave the Law to Moses, is also the *Shechinah* of God, distinct from the Father. The LORD stated that He was going to send a Messenger (Angel) who had the nature and character of the LORD. Then in Exodus 32 the LORD, who again is the *Shechinah* of God,

---

[578] Frame, *The Doctrine of God*, 590.

stated that He would not go up with the people, but that His Messenger (Angel) would go up. This passage also shows a plurality in the unity of *Elohim*.

3. Throughout the wilderness account the LORD spoke directly to Moses,[579] as well as to Aaron. The LORD, Who is by deduction the same Messenger (Angel) going up with them, was identified with the pillar of cloud, the glory of the LORD. He spoke to Moses, giving him instructions, and judged sin in Israel whether on Mt. Sinai (Exodus 24:15-18) or at the Tent of Meeting (Exodus 33:7-11).

4. At the end of the exodus, wilderness wandering, and conquest of the Promised Land, it is once again the Messenger (Angel) of the LORD who connects His activity from the time of Abraham to Moses to the plagues in Egypt to *Shechinah* appearances and other theophanies throughout the Exodus and Wilderness wanderings (Judges 2:1-5).

5. The One who had been speaking to Moses showed no indication that He was different from the One who was speaking from Exodus 3 to Judges 2. All the references of the LORD speaking directly to Moses, as in the theophany of the *Shechinah* glory and the pillar of cloud at the tent door, had the LORD speaking audibly to Moses.[580]

6. The time table of the books of the Law:

   a) Exodus was the time from Moses' calling and Israel's leaving Egypt, to their arrival and stay at Mt. Sinai in the second year, first day of the second month (Leviticus 1:1).

   b) Leviticus dealt with the priesthood, sacrificial system and the feasts of the LORD which *Yahweh* gave to Israel. This took place during the stay at Mt. Sinai.

   c) Numbers took up where the book of Exodus left off chronologically. Chapters 1 through 14 dealt with additional instructions or commandments,

---

[579] The following passages are the passages that state the activity of the LORD: Exod 3:2-6; 19:16-19; 23:20-23; 24:16-18; 32:34-33:2, 9, 14, 18; 34:5; 40:34-38; Lev 9:23-10:2; Num 9:15; 11:1, 25; 12:5-10; 14:10; 16:19, 35, 42; 20:6; 22:23-35; Deut 4:11-12, 15, 36; 5:4, 22, 25-26; 31:15.

[580] References of the LORD speaking: **Exodus** 3:7; 4:2-3, 6, 11, 19, 21, 27; 6:1-2, 10, 13, 26, 28-29; 7:1, 8, 13-14, 19; 8:1, 5, 16, 20; 9:1, 8, 13, 22; 10:1, 12, 21; 11:1, 9; 12:1, 43; 13:1, 21; 14:1, 15, 26; 16:4, 11, 28; 17:5; 19:9-10, 21, 24; 20:1, 22; 24:12; 30:11, 17, 22, 34; 31:1, 12; 32:7, 9, 33; 33:1, 21; 34:1, 5-6, 27; 40:1 **Leviticus** 1:1; 3:1; 6:1, 8, 19, 24; 7:22, 28; 8:1; 10:2, 8; 11:1; 12:1; 13:1; 14:1, 33; 15:1; 16:1-2; 17:1; 18:1; 19:1; 20:1; 21:1, 16; 22:1, 17, 26; 23:1, 9, 23, 26, 33; 24:1, 13; 25:1; 27:1 **Numbers** 1:1; 2:1; 3:5, 11, 14, 40, 44; 4:1, 21; 5:1, 5, 11; 6:1, 22; 7:4, 11; 8:1, 5, 23; 9:1, 9; 10:1; 11:16, 25; 12:5-6, 14; 13:1; 14:11, 20, 26, 28, 35; 15:1, 17, 35, 37; 16:20, 23, 36, 44; 17:1, 10; 18:1, 8, 20; 19:1; 20:7, 12, 23; 21:8, 34; 22:32, 35; 25:4, 10, 16; 26:1, 52; 27:6, 12, 18; 28:1; 31:1, 25; 33:50; 34:1, 16; 35:1, 9; **Deuteronomy** 1:42; 2:2, 9, 17; 3:2; 4:12; 31:14-16, 48; 34:1-4.

Israel's unbelief and murmuring and the sin of unbelief of the people at Kadesh-barnea, which resulted in God's judgment for the balance of the 38 years of wandering, which involves Numbers 15-36.

d) In Deuteronomy Moses restated the Law for the new generation that was about to go into the land (Deuteronomy 1:1-3). The time period was from the end of the wilderness wandering to Moses' death (Deuteronomy 34:1-8).

The importance of how the Torah fits together is critical to the understanding of the writings of Moses. Exodus and Leviticus occurred at Mt. Sinai. The book of Numbers deals with the balance of the wilderness journey. Deuteronomy is a restatement of the Law for a new generation about to enter the Promised Land under Joshua's leadership. The significance is that from the beginning of Exodus to the possession of the inheritance of the Land, God used theophanies to communicate with Moses, Aaron, and the nation at large. Those theophanies started (Exodus 3) and finished (Judges 2:1-5) the exodus context with the Messenger (Angel) of the LORD who spoke to Moses from Mt. Sinai, to the glory of the LORD which appeared to him at the Tent of Meeting, to His meeting with Israel at Bochim. The Torah is largely the interaction between Moses and this theophany of God who is God, yet is distinct from God. Yet the *Shechinah* and the Messenger (Angel) of the LORD are a plural unity, *echad* (one) in the unity of *Elohim*.

TEN APPEARANCES OF SHECHINAH

First Appearance … Genesis 15:9-18

There are ten important appearances of the *Shechinah* of God in the biblical text. The **first** undisputed *Shechinah* is recorded in the vision of Genesis 15:9-18[581] who is also identified in verse 1 and 4 as the Word of the LORD. In these verses God made a covenant with Abraham by walking between the carcasses of slaughtered animals.

When the sun was set and it was very dark, there appeared a smoking oven, and a flaming torch which passed between these pieces (Gen 15:17-18).

This was a vision to Abraham of something that God was literally and physically doing in the presence of Abraham, for God used the animals that Abraham physically cut in two in making His covenant with Abraham. This pre-Sinai theophany introduced smoke (smoking oven) and fire (flaming torch), two non-human elements that were part of the Mt. Sinai theophanies. These are characteristic of the *Shechinah* of God that appeared to Israel and to some of the prophets. In Judges 2:1 the Messenger (Angel) of *Yahweh* identified Himself as the "*word of the LORD,*" the covenant maker with Abraham (and with Israel in Exodus 24:9-12): This fact was confirmed in the pre-Sinai theophany of Genesis 15. This is the same Messenger of the Covenant spoken of in Malachi 3:1.

---

[581] Niehaus, *God at Sinai*, 172-180.

There is little doubt that the *Shechinah* of God and the Messenger (Angel) of *Yahweh* were the same person.

Second Appearance ... Exodus 3

The **second** notable *Shechinah* was the burning bush experience recorded in Exodus 3; here God attracted Moses' attention when he was shepherding sheep on Mt. Sinai. Exodus 3:2 made it clear that the Person who spoke was the Messenger (Angel) of *Yahweh* Who appeared to Moses in a blazing fire from a bush that was not consumed. This Messenger (Angel) told Moses to remove his shoes because he was standing on holy ground in the presence of God. Then He referred to the Abrahamic Covenant (Genesis 15:12-18) and the predicted deliverance that was going to take place. Moses was to be the deliverer. When asked His name, the Messenger (Angel) of *Yahweh* responded, "I AM WHO I AM" (Exodus 3:14). This "I AM" was undoubtedly the same person that had spoken to Abraham, Isaac, and Jacob throughout the patriarchal period, and who was then speaking to Moses from the burning bush. The phrase, "I AM" is also used by *Yeshua* in the New Covenant book of John ten times.[582] This appearance to Moses led to a personal relationship between Israel and their God.

Third Appearance ... Exodus 13:21-22

In the **third** notable *Shechinah*, God traveled with Israel and gave them a pillar of cloud by day and a pillar of fire by night (Exodus 13:21-22). As the Egyptian army advanced against Israel at the shore of the Red Sea (Sea of Aquaba),[583] the evidence of God's glory became a wall between Israel and the pursuing Egyptian army. According to Exodus 40:36-38, it was this cloud and fire that led them throughout the wilderness wanderings. Up to this point, God had appeared only to individual patriarchs and Moses. Now He was about to appear before the nation of Israel at large (Exodus 19:9-25; 24:3-11). However, God could not reveal Himself completely because the holiness of His very nature required that He conceal Himself from the presence of man in the form of a thick, dark cloud.[584]

In this appearance of the *Shechinah* of God, the pillar of cloud and fire moved between the Egyptian army and the Israelites. Exodus 14:19 says, "*The angel*

---

[582] (1) John 6:35, 48 "I am the bread of life" (2) John 8:12 "I am the light of the world" (3) John 8:24 "That ye shall die in your sins; for if ye believe not that I am, ye shall die in your sins" (4) John 8:58 "Before Abraham was, I am" (5) John 10:7, 9 "I am the door" (6) John 10:11 "I am the good shepherd" (7) John 11:25 "I am the resurrection, and the life" (8) John 14:6 "I am the way, the truth, and the life" (9) John 15:1 "I am the true vine, and my Father is the husbandman" (10) John 18:6 "As soon then as he had said unto them, I am, they went backward, and fell to the ground."

[583] Campus Crusade for Christ. *The Exodus Revealed, Search for the Red Sea Crossing.* (Irvine CA: Discovery Media Productions, 2001), DVD. Sold by Friends of Israel Gospel Ministry at www.foigm.org.

[584] Alexander and Baker, *Dictionary of the Old Testament Pentateuch*, 861.

(Messenger) *of God had been going ahead of the Israelite army.*" Here the *Shechinah* is identified as the Messenger of *Elohim*.[585] The use of *Elohim* is significant in that it identified the *Shechinah* of God, or the theophany of God, within a plural context. It did so in the plural form of *Elohim* rather than as *El, Elah* or *Eloah* in the singular. Then, as if such proofs were insufficient, Exodus 14:24 declared that this Messenger (Angel) of *Elohim* was *Yahweh* looking down from the pillar of cloud and fire. Clearly, the plural *Elohim* and the singular *Yahweh* were the same person. It is also noted that the phrase "*angel* (Messenger*) of God*" is used (seven times) alternately with "*the angel* (Messenger) *of Yahweh.*"[586]

Fourth Appearance … Exodus 19:16-20

The **fourth** notable *Shechinah* was God's appearance before the whole nation of Israel at the foot of Mt. Sinai. The human reaction to the *Shechinah* of God that appeared before Israel was one of fear and terror.[587] Deuteronomy 18:16 expresses the fear and terror of the people as they heard and saw His glory or *Shechinah*. The *Shechinah* of God rested on Mt. Sinai, and a cloud covered it (Exodus 24:16) to conceal His full glory. As *Yahweh* spoke from the midst of the fire and cloud, Israel "*heard the sound of words, but saw no form, only a voice*" (Deuteronomy 4:12). Deuteronomy 5:22 added that the Lord spoke "*from the midst of the fire, of the cloud and of the thick gloom, with a great voice.*" Exodus 19:16-20 adds more descriptive words: "*thunder and lightning flashes,*" "*thick cloud,*" "*very loud trumpet sound,*" "*so that all the people…trembled,*" "*smoke because Yahweh descended upon it in fire,*" "*its smoke ascended like the smoke of a furnace, and the whole mountain quaked violently,*" "*…sound of the trumpet grew louder and louder.*" The *Shechinah* of God, the Second Person of the plural unity of *Elohim*, was the pre-incarnate Messiah as He established the Mosaic Covenant with Israel.

Fifth Appearance … Exodus 33:17-23

The **fifth** notable *Shechinah* appearance occurred when Moses asked the LORD "*let me know Your ways, that I may know you*" (Exodus 33:13) and then Moses asked *Yahweh* to "*let me behold Your Presence!*" or to see His glory (Exodus 33:18). The complete scriptural text is Exodus 33:17-23:

> (17) And the LORD said to Moses, "I will also do this thing that you have asked; for you have truly gained My favor and I have singled you out by name." (18) He said, "Oh, let me behold Your Presence!" (19) And He answered, "I will make all My goodness pass before you, and I will proclaim before you the name LORD, and the grace that I grant and the compassion that I show." (20) But, He said, "you cannot see My face, for man may not

---

[585] Arthur W. Kac, *The Messiahship of Jesus* (Grand Rapids: Baker, 1986), 200-201.
[586] Botterweck, Ringgren, and Fabry, *Theological Dictionary of the Old Testament*, 1:281.
[587] Alexander and Baker, *Dictionary of the Old Testament Pentateuch*, 863.

see Me and live." (21) And the LORD said, "See, there is a place near Me. Station yourself on the rock, (22) and, as My Presence passes by, I will put you in a cleft of the rock and shield you with My hand until I have passed by. (23) Then I will take My hand away and you will see My back; but My face must not be seen."

Keil and Delitzsch bring out the absolute uniqueness of Moses' request and just what his request involved. For it was common knowledge that to physically see God meant death, and Moses requested to see Him and live:

> What Moses desired to see, as the answer of God clearly shows, must have been something surpassing all former revelations of the glory of Jehovah (Exod 16:7, 10, 24:16-17), and even going beyond Jehovah's talking with him face to face (v. 11) [Exodus 33:11]. When God talked with him face to face, or mouth to mouth, he merely saw a "similitude of Jehovah" (Num. 12:8), a form which rendered the invisible being of God visible to the human eye, a manifestation of the divine glory in a certain form, and not the direct or essential glory of Jehovah, whilst the people saw this glory under the veil of a dark cloud, rendered luminous by fire, that is to say, they only saw its splendour as it shone through the cloud;.... What Moses desired, therefore, was a sight of the glory or essential being of God, without any figure, and without a veil.[588]

Yahweh stated that Moses had found grace (favor) in His sight and that *Yahweh* knew Moses' name; from a biblical perspective that is impressive. Although *Yahweh* said that Moses could not see His face and live (Exodus 33:20), God did show as much of Himself as was humanly possible to accept. So God put Moses in the cleft of the rock and covered Moses with His hand and after that *Yahweh* passed by. He removed His hand and allowed Moses to see His back, or as some have translated it, His afterglow. Moses' request to see *Yahweh's* face was impossible to grant, but God would accommodate Moses as much as was possible for Moses to receive:

> God responded that there were limits to what even the greatest of all prophets could perceive of God's ways. Even the angels, which are purely spiritual beings, cannot approach the fullness of God's essence; surely it is beyond the capacity of human beings. However, God agreed to show Moses the highest degree of revelation and understanding that man is capable of assimilating.

> My face. This simile refers to a complete and unadulterated perception of God. To achieve this was impossible, but God would allow Moses to see Him from the back (v. 23), meaning a vague degree of perception. The distinction

---

[588] Keil & Delitzsch, *Commentary on the Old Testament in Ten Volumes: Exodus,* 2:236.

between these degrees of vision is like the difference between seeing a person's face clearly and merely glimpsing him from behind.[589]

This is a very unusual account, for only Moses was granted such a request. Later God referred to their relationship together as, "*I speak mouth to mouth*" (Numbers 12:8) with Moses, which is a Hebrew idiom meaning face to face. However, *Yahweh* did not say face to face, but mouth to mouth, for God's face no one can see. The editor's statement at the end of Deuteronomy concerning Moses was that "*there arose not a prophet since in Israel like unto Moses, whom the LORD knew face to face*" (Deuteronomy 34:10 KJV). Moses was one of the most privileged men in Scripture to have a "*face to face*" or personal relationship with *Yahweh* even though Moses never saw God's face in His full essence, for they spoke "*mouth to mouth*." What an epitaph on Moses' life and relation to *Yahweh*! Moses had the most privileged opportunity and statement made on his life as recorded in Deuteronomy 34:10. Moses had a personal relationship with *Yahweh*, in this theophany of God, this One who is the Second Person of the plural unity of *Elohim*.

Sixth Appearance ... Exodus 40:34-35

The **sixth** notable *Shechinah* appearance occurred when God took His place in the Holy of Holies in the tabernacle. Since the glory of God cannot be seen by man, God covered His glory, or *Shechinah*, with a thick dark cloud that filled the tabernacle as He took up residence (Exodus 40:34-35).[590]

Seventh Appearance ... 40 Years in the Wilderness

The **seventh** notable *Shechinah* appearance was the pillar of fire by night and the cloud by day that followed Israel as they traveled for 40 years through the area of the Sinai Peninsula and part of western Arabia. The *Shechinah* of God appeared at numerous times as He met with Moses, but He also appeared to judge individuals or the nation. Following are six examples of individual and corporate judgments that were given to Israel for their rebellion in the wilderness. These judgments (Exodus 23:23; 32:34; 33:3) were not carried out by *Yahweh* because He did not go with them. Rather, the Messenger carried out these judgments as He took Israel through the wilderness and into the Land. So all of the following examples are the Messenger (Angel) of *Yahweh*, equal, yet distinct from *Yahweh*, showing plurality:

1. Nadab and Abihu offered strange fire before the Lord[591] in Leviticus 10:1-2, and fire came from the presence of *Yahweh* and consumed them.

---

[589] Scherman, *The Chumash: The Stone Edition: The Torah, Haftoros and Five Megillos,* 506-507.

[590] Elwell, *Evangelical Dictionary of Theology,* 1010.

[591] Niehaus, *God at Sinai*, 208.

Leviticus 9:23-24 shows that it was the glory of *Yahweh* that was present and that fire proceeded from *Yahweh*.

2. In Numbers 11:1-2, at Taberah, Israel murmured before God, and He responded to their sin: "The fire of the LORD burned among them and consumed some at the outskirts of the camp."[592]

3. In Numbers 12:2-5 the *Shechinah* of God appeared at the "d*oorway of the tent of meeting*" in judgment of Aaron and Miriam for their sin against Moses, their brother, and condemned their sin and caused Miriam to be leprous.[593]

4. Numbers 14:10 says that the *Shechinah* of God appeared before Israel "*in the tent of meeting*" to quell the riot against Moses after the report of the ten unbelieving spies. Verse 23 gave the verdict that Israel would not "*see the land which I swore to their fathers*." The Shechinah who spoke is the same person that spoke to Moses at the burning bush in Exodus 3:8 and it was *Yahweh* that spoke to Joshua concerning the same promises in Joshua 1:6 and it also includes the Messenger (Angel) of the LORD which spoke to all Israel in Judges 2:1. This act of rebellion, their refusal to believe "*by faith*" in Him, was an unpardonable sin (Numbers 14:11). This was an "*evil congregation*," (Numbers 14:27, 35; cf. Matthew 12:31-45) and as a result, He condemned them to wander in the wilderness for 38 years until they all died.

5. Later Korah, from a Levitical family, not of the family of Aaron, rebelled against Moses and Aaron and gathered the congregation against Moses and Aaron at the door of the tent of meeting. There the glory of *Yahweh* appeared to the congregation. He opened the earth and swallowed up all the families of Korah, Dathan, and Abiram and sent fire to consume 250 men offering incense (Numbers 16:1-40). The responsibility that they wanted to assume belonged to Aaron and his sons, not to Korah, who was attempting to usurp Aaron's God-given responsibility that was reserved by God for the Aaronic priesthood.[594]

6. Even after such a devastating judgment, Israel grumbled against Moses and Aaron, saying that they were the cause of the death of these men. Again, the *Shechinah* of God appeared with a plague upon the people so that 14,700 died (Numbers 16:42, 49). As mentioned earlier in this section, the *Shechinah* of God is the pre-incarnate Messiah of Israel.

Each one of these six examples of judgment by the *Shechinah* glory of God continues to show that this Person, the *Shechinah* glory, is united in the plural unity of *Elohim* are *echad* (one), yet distinct from the other members of the plural unity of

---

[592] Niehaus, *God at Sinai*, 210.
[593] Niehaus, *God at Sinai*, 211.
[594] Niehaus, *God at Sinai*, 214-215.

Elohim. Exodus 33:3 clearly states that *Yahweh* would not go with Israel, but that He would send His Messenger (Angel), establishing the fact that *Yahweh* and His Messenger in these *Shechinah* glory references are equal and distinct. Clearly, these *Shechinah* references establish the plural unity of *Elohim*.

Eighth Appearance ... 1 Kings 8:10-12

The **eighth** notable *Shechinah* appearance occurred when the presence of God filled the new Solomonic temple in Jerusalem.[595] In 1 Kings 8:10-11; 9:3 and 2 Chronicles 7:1 the *Shechinah* of God, the glory of *Yahweh*, filled the temple, and as in the Mt. Sinai appearance (Exodus 40:34-38), this also was with a cloud. Solomon (1 Kings 8:12) referred to the cloud as a thick cloud. Not only did the *Shechinah* of God fill the temple, but also fire came down from heaven and consumed the burnt offerings and sacrifices.

Ninth Appearance ... Isaiah 6:1-8 and Ezekiel 1

The **ninth** notable *Shechinah* appearance that could be called a post-Sinai appearance occurred when Isaiah and Ezekiel received their commissions as prophets.[596] In Isaiah 6, Isaiah in a vision saw the Lord seated on His throne. Verses 1-3 give a description of God that very few have seen. Verse 4 has two examples of a theophany: *"The foundations of the thresholds trembled at the voice of him...the temple was filling with smoke."* This theophany marks the call of Isaiah by God into his prophetic ministry, calling to memory Israel's Mt. Sinai experience and the consecration of Solomon's temple.[597]

Isaiah's vision was awesome, but Ezekiel's vision was indescribable. Certain theophanic pictures are seen in Ezekiel 1, such as *"a great cloud with fire flashing continually"* (verse 4). Ezekiel 1 is filled with things that Ezekiel tried to express but he had nothing on earth to compare with what he saw as he attempted to describe it in the Hebrew Scriptures. This theophany is also associated with Ezekiel's call, found in Ezekiel 2:3.[598]

Tenth Appearance ... Ezekiel 8 – 11

The last notable appearance of the *Shechinah* of God occurred in vision form to Ezekiel who was in Babylon in Ezekiel chapters 8-11. Here the sin of the religious and political leaders of Israel is described in their worship of pagan deities in the temple. Not only was Israel's sin described in these chapters, but the *Shechinah* of God was in the process of leaving the temple of God to return to heaven (Hosea 5:15;

---

[595] Niehaus, *God at Sinai*, 243.
[596] Singer, *The Jewish Encyclopedia,* 12:137.
[597] Niehaus, *God at Sinai*, 249-254.
[598] Niehaus, *God at Sinai*, 254-279.

Matthew 23:37-39). Neusner, in giving a rabbinic Jewish response, says that in 70 AD the *Shechinah* of God went into exile with the captives.[599] Passages in Ezekiel document that the *Shechinah* of God left the temple in 592 BCE (Ezekiel 8:1) in several stages (Ezekiel 9:3; 10:18; 11:23). Singer states that the *Shechinah* of God was one of five things missing in the second temple.[600] Also, according to Josephus, neither the Ark of God nor the *Shechinah* was present in 63 BCE when Pompey, the conquering Roman general, entered the temple and the Holy of Holies.[601] So the *Shechinah* did not go into exile with the captives but had left the temple and the nation over 600 years earlier and returned to heaven. Proof of the absence of God's tangible glory from the temple is that Pompey was not struck dead upon penetrating the veil, as Jewish authors like Singer[602] and Schurer[603] attest. Christian authors such as Pfeiffer,[604] Moeller,[605] Sloan,[606] and Sacchi[607] also validate those Jewish authors.

SUMMARY

In summary, all of the aforementioned references of the *Shechinah* glory of God reflect the conclusion that the *Shechinah* and the Messenger (Angel) of *Yahweh* are equal to and yet distinct from *Yahweh*. God appeared as a man (Genesis 18) and in the burning bush (Exodus 3) as the Messenger (Angel) of *Yahweh*. These two points are important, but the main emphasis is that God's personal presence was revealed. In other words, as the passages are examined, the terms for *Yahweh* and the theophanies of God are distinct from each other and yet united in a plural unity of *Elohim* who is *echad* (one). The main point to ponder is who the Angel (Messenger) of *Yahweh* is. If God appeared in a localized place, then who was He? Scholars of biblical faith maintain that the Messenger (Angel) of *Yahweh* and other disclosures of God were the Second Person of the plural unity of *Elohim*, God the Son, *Yeshua ha Mashiach*. For example, Walvoord points out four reasons why the Messenger (Angel) of *Yahweh* is Messiah *Yeshua* and not the Father or the Holy Spirit:

1. The Second person is the visible God of the New Covenant (John 10:30).

---

[599] Neusner, *God at Sinai*, 577.

[600] Singer, *The Jewish Encyclopedia,* 11:260.

[601] Flavius Josephus, *Josephus Complete Works* (trans. William Whiston. Grand Rapids: Kregel, 1978), 436.

[602] Singer, *The Jewish Encyclopedia,* 10:123.

[603] Schurer, *A History of the Jewish People in the Time of Jesus Christ,* 1:322.

[604] Charles F. Pfeiffer, *Old Testament History* (Grand Rapids: Baker Books), 586.

[605] Henry Moeller, *The Legacy of Zion: Intertestamental Texts related to the New Testament* (Grand Rapids: Baker, 1977), 126.

[606] W. W. Sloan, *Between the Testaments* (Paterson, NJ: Littlefield, Adams & Co. n.d.), 58.

[607] Paolo Sacchi, *The History of the Second Temple Period* (Sheffield, England: Sheffield Academic Press, 2000), 270.

2. The Angel of *Yahweh* no longer appears after the incarnation (John 5:36-38).[608]

3. Both the Angel of *Yahweh* and Messiah are sent by the Father.

4. In the process of elimination it could not be the Father, for the Father is the sender. Angel of *Yahweh* appears in a bodily form usually in human form: the Holy Spirit never has appeared in human or bodily form.[609]

In the context of the theophanies of God, John the Baptist in John 1:18 clearly tells the student of Scripture that *Yeshua* is the exact image of the Father and He has declared Him:

No man hath seen God at any time; the only begotten Son, which is in the bosom of the Father, he hath declared him.

The words of *Yeshua* in John 14:9-11 declare that He is the exact representation of the Father, which parallels the author of Hebrews 1:1-3, who stated that God has spoken through His Son. Chapter 2 of this book shows that mankind was made in the "image" and "likeness" of God, but here *Yeshua* is saying that He is the very image of God (Philippians 2:5-11). Because Messiah was the Son, He was equal to the Father, and on the Mt. of Transfiguration, His glory, which was veiled in flesh at the time of His incarnation (Matthew 17:1-8), briefly shone through the veil of His flesh. The *Tanakh*, through the theophanies, is a rich source of information on the plurality of *Elohim*.

At this point this author needs to clear up an erroneous teaching by many in the church today. Having read and heard the statement, "You have read the trinity back into the Old Testament," the response to this is threefold. First, (1) the foundational document of the New Covenant readers was the *Tanakh*. It was the Hebrew Scriptures that they used on a daily basis in their ministry after the resurrection of *Yeshua*, showing their physical brethren (Jewish people) that *Yeshua* was the Messiah of Israel promised by the prophets. Second, (2) there are those who say that the doctrine of the trinity was not developed until the early church councils. That is a statement which shows lack of knowledge of the New Covenant (Testament), for the apostles and early disciples of that first century spoke freely of the tri-unity of God throughout the gospels and epistles, as well as in the book of Revelation. They understood that doctrine. Third, (3) suppose that they are right in stating that the *Tanakh* did not reveal the doctrine of the trinity. If that were the case — and this is said with much reservation on this author's part — if God had not revealed ample testimony of His person in the Hebrew Scriptures, then He is an unjust God. To hold the Jewish people responsible for

---

[608] Isaiah 48:16 and Zechariah 2:8-9 say that the Angel [Messenger] of *Yahweh* was sent by *Yahweh*. In John's gospel *Yeshua* clarified that the Father sent Him; 3:34; 4:34; 5:23-24, 30, 36-38; 6:29, 38-39, 44, 57; 7:16, 18, 28-29, 33; 8:16, 18, 26, 29, 42; 9:4; 10:36; 11:42; 12:44-45, 49; 13:20; 14:24; 15:21; 16:5, 27; 17:3, 8, 18, 21, 23, 25. These 40 references document that the Father sent the Messiah into the world.

[609] Walvoord, *Jesus Christ Our Lord,* 44-46.

something that they could not have possibly known would be completely unjust on God's part. Rejecting *Yeshua* the Messiah because He presented Himself as one with the Father would have been a logical outgrowth of that teaching. So God, being just and righteous, could not hold the Jewish people accountable for a teaching of His Messiah if His Word, His very own Scriptures, said nothing about the plural unity of *Elohim*! If that were the case, then the Pharisees and the Sadducees were absolutely correct in rejecting *Yeshua* as Messiah, the God/man. They would have been faithful to the Scriptures and *Yeshua* would have been a deceiver who tried to pawn Himself off as a god, a Roman/Greek religious concept. Not only that, *Yeshua* would have been a false prophet (Deuteronomy 18), guilty and deserving of the crucifixion by equating Himself with God, by insisting that He and the Father were one (*echad*). The whole doctrine of the atonement of *Yeshua* would be erroneous.

If that is true, what is called the believing church today worships a false god and it is still lost in its sins. Please understand that the enemy of the faith in relation to this aspect of the Doctrine of God is higher criticism that came out of Germany in the 19th and 20th centuries. That movement of "enlightenment" destroyed much of the Protestant movement after the reformation that had taken place 200-300 years previously. Higher criticism is responsible more than anything else for the humanistic teachings on the Scriptures today.

Minimally, with this rich source of biblical information from the *Tanakh*, the rabbis should have recognized the plurality of *Yahweh* as He presented Himself as different persons, equal, indivisible, yet a plurality.

When the nature, character and essence of God are examined from the *Tanakh*, the words of *Yeshua* in Luke 24:25-27, 44-48 and John 5:39, 46-47, spoken to the two disciples on the Emmaus Road and the Jewish leadership, becomes one of the most astounding statements made by *Yeshua*. In the Luke and John passages *Yeshua* very simply said that the Law, Prophets and Writings (which is the Jewish division of the Hebrew Scriptures) all referred to Himself:

> And beginning at Moses and all the Prophets, he expounded unto them in all the scriptures the things concerning himself (Luke 24:27). These are the words which I spake unto you, while I was yet with you, that all things must be fulfilled, which were written in the law of Moses, and in the prophets, and in the psalms, concerning me. Then opened he their understanding, that they might understand the scriptures (Luke 24:44-45).

> Search the scriptures; for in them ye think ye have eternal life: and they are they which testify of me.... For had ye believed Moses, ye would have believed me: for he wrote of me. But if ye believe not his writings, how shall ye believe my words? (John 5:39, 46-47).

Perhaps today, in this intellectual age, scholars have retreated from what *Yeshua* taught to His disciples on that eventful day. These verses apply to all that was said of *Yeshua* in the Law, Prophets, and Writings. One of the many things that *Yeshua* would have related from the *Tanakh* was to show the disciples that He was the Messenger (Angel) of *Yahweh*, the *Shechinah* of God, as well as *Yahweh* and *Elohim*, the Creator and covenant-making God with Israel. What an awesome view of *Yeshua* in the Hebrew Scriptures that must have been! Based on the New Covenant, this person Who revealed Himself in the theophanies of the *Tanakh* in the form of man, Messenger (Angel) of *Yahweh*, *Shechinah* of God, was the pre-incarnate Messiah of Israel.[610]

All of the references of the *Shechinah* Glory of God, with the Messenger (Angel) of *Yahweh* references, amount to a heavy weight in substantiating the plurality or tri-unity of *Elohim*. The Father and the Holy Spirit are never revealed in a physical form. Only the Second Person of the tri-unity appeared in human form as a theophany or as the *Shechinah* glory of God.

---

[610] Enns, *The Moody Handbook of Theology,* 216.

Chapter 8
Post-Sinai, Wilderness Theophanies

In the previous three chapters (chapters 5, 6, 7) theophanies have been viewed from pre-Sinai, Sinai, and wilderness accounts, including the *Shechinah* glory of the LORD. What has been seen is a unique relationship between the invisible God of Israel Who has revealed Himself to them. This God of Israel has stressed throughout His Word that He is *echad* (one) and that there are no other gods besides Him; He constitutes monotheism. It should be clear to the careful reader of the *Tanakh* that although He stresses oneness in the *Shema* (Deuteronomy 6:4), He has also chosen to reveal the fact that in His oneness, there is a plurality in unity. This chapter will continue to follow up on the theme that He also revealed Himself in the lives of Joshua, Gideon, Manoah, Samuel, David, Elijah, Isaiah, Ezekiel, Hosea, and Zechariah.

Joshua and the Captain of the LORD's Host ... Joshua 5:13 - 6:2

(13) Once, when Joshua was near Jericho, he looked up and saw a man standing before him, drawn sword in hand. Joshua went up to him and asked him, "Are you one of us or of our enemies?" (14) He replied, "No, I am captain of the LORD's host. Now I have come!" Joshua threw himself face down to the ground and, prostrating himself, said to him, "What does my lord command his servant?" The captain of the LORD's host answered Joshua, "Remove your sandals from your feet, for the place where you stand is holy." And Joshua did so.

(1) Now Jericho was shut up tight because of the Israelites; no one could leave or enter. (2) The LORD said to Joshua, "See, I will deliver Jericho and her king [and her] warrior into your hands."

In Joshua 5:13 – 6:2 there is a unique manifestation of God before Joshua, this One who identified Himself as "*the captain of the LORD's host.*" Although the Joshua 5 text does not use the phrase "*the angel of the LORD,*" scholars identify Him as the Messenger (Angel) of the LORD who sometimes is not distinguished from the LORD Himself,[611] because He is *echad* (one) with *Yahweh*, and as this book is in the process of showing, is also distinct from *Yahweh*. There are several comparisons between "*the angel of the Lord*" and "*the captain of the LORD's host.*"

---

[611] Donald H. Madvig, *The Expositor's Bible Commentary: Joshua* (12 Vols. Grand Rapids: Zondervan, 1992), 3:276.

1. His sword was drawn as it was with Balaam (Numbers 22:23-35) and when the Messenger (Angel) of the LORD judged David for his sin of numbering the people (1 Chronicles 21:12-30).

2. He told Joshua to remove his shoes, which is exactly what happened to Moses in Exodus 3.

3. His presence was unique for He made the surrounding ground holy, which also happened to Moses in the burning bush episode.

4. In chapter 6 of the book of Joshua which is a continuation of the appearance of *"the captain of the LORD's Host,"* He clearly speaks as *Yahweh* in verse 2, *"and the LORD said to Joshua,"* which also happened to Moses.[612]

5. When He and Joshua become formally introduced, Joshua falls on his face in worship, as did Moses.

After Israel had celebrated the Passover, Joshua was doing reconnaissance near the city of Jericho. He was surprised to see a man with his sword drawn, a sign of being in combat readiness. Joshua asked him if he was for or against Israel. The man who answered did not directly address Joshua's question; He simply identified himself as *"the captain of the LORD's host."* The word translated captain (Heb. *sar*) is used of princes (Genesis 12:15; Numbers 22:13) and of prominent officers of a royal court. In Genesis 21:22 it is used in the sense of a military captain.[613] Woudstra points out that this passage is obviously a theophany of God Who entered into human events at critical junctures of history.

> The commander is a self-manifestation of God. A number of such theophanies occur in the Bible, often at critical junctures in the life of the individual or the life of the nation. God appears to Moses in the burning bush to give him his commission (Exod 3); the angel of the Lord finds Gideon hovering in a winepress to call him to lead his people in a fight for freedom (Judg 6:11-18). That a divine being appears to Joshua just before he leads Israel in their battle against Jericho, their first military action in Canaan, is not unexpected.[614]

God entered history at a critical point to aid Joshua with the conquest of the Land as he approached Jericho. A Jewish author has an interesting observation concerning the person identified in Scripture as *"the captain of the LORD's host."* He references the Talmud, which calls Him *Metatron*:

> Here we had the heavenly messenger who appeared to Joshua before Jericho and who introduced himself as leader of the hosts from HIM (Josh 5:13). He

---

[612] Showers, *Those Invisible Spirits Called Angels,* 164.

[613] M. H. Woudstra, *The New International Commentary on the Old Testament: The Book of Joshua* (Grand Rapids: Eerdmans, 1981), 105.

[614] Carolyn Pressler, *Joshua, Judges and Ruth* (Louisville, KY: Westminster John Knox Press, 2002), 41-42.

bore a drawn sword in his hand, as the struggle for the land was about to begin and Jericho would fall first. The sword was also a warning against disobedience. Here, too, the *mal-akh* gave advice about their wanderings and the conquest of the land. The Talmud identified this angel (San 38b) as "Metatron," who stood nearest the throne of God and whose name sounded like that of his master (she-sh'mo k'shem ra-vo). Maimonides (Moreh II, 34) and many who followed his explanation identified him with the prophet announced in Deut 18:18, whom God would send after Moses.[615]

He does not recognize Him as God, but he clearly ties together the Captain of the LORD's Host with the Angel that aided Israel in their wanderings. He also identifies Him with *Metatron* who is recognized by Jewish scholars as the Angel (Messenger) of the LORD throughout the *Tanakh*. What is even more interesting and so unexpected by a Jewish scholar is his reference to Maimonides who identified this Captain of the LORD's Host with Deuteronomy 18:18 as the promised prophet that would be like Moses. This passage is commonly recognized by believers in *Yeshua* as Messiah as a first coming Messianic appearance of the God/man, Son of David, the Messiah of Israel. But for Maimonides to equate Him on a human level as the "Prophet" foretold in Deuteronomy 18:15-18 is not warranted. Deuteronomy 18:18 distinctly states that the "Prophet" would be a man and from his brethren. The Captain of the LORD's host does not qualify; He is not human, thus He cannot be the fulfillment of that passage. Later in the biblical record this Person who appeared to Joshua would take on flesh in the incarnation, which would then qualify Him as the "Prophet" spoken of by Moses. He would not only fulfill this passage but fulfill all of the future prophets' messages who would describe His future earthly ministry, nature, character, attributes and essence of this individual, the Messiah of Israel.

The Deliverer and Covenant Maker ... Judges 2:1-5

(1) An angel of the LORD came up from Gilgal to Bochim and said, "I brought you up from Egypt and I took you into the land which I had promised on oath to your fathers. And I said, 'I will never break My covenant with you. (2) And you, for your part, must make no covenant with the inhabitants of this land; you must tear down their altars.' But you have not obeyed Me – look what you have done! (3) Therefore, I have resolved not to drive them out before you; they shall become your oppressors, and their gods shall be a snare to you." (4) As the angel of the LORD spoke these words to all the Israelites, the people broke into weeping. (5) So they named that place Bochim, and they offered sacrifices there to the LORD.

This passage is one of the most unique references to the Messenger (Angel) of the LORD in the *Tanakh*. In Judges 2:1 He states that He was not only involved in the

---

[615] Jacob, *The Second Book of the Bible: Exodus,* 732.

exodus of Israel into the Promised Land, but He also was the covenant maker with Abraham in Genesis 15. Notice in the passage that He uses the first personal pronoun "I" and spoke as God Himself as the following author states:

> This "angel of the Lord" was mentioned once before in Judges (2:1-3). Because in the verses given both there and here this Person uses the first person references while speaking in behalf of God, it is clear that He is God Himself, specifically the second Person of the Godhead, here in Theophany.[616]

The second example is found in Judges 2:1, which is a fascinating reflection of the distinctiveness on the Messenger (Angel) of *Yahweh* from *Yahweh*. The Messenger does not introduce His speech to the nation of Israel by "Thus says *Yahweh*," which was the practice of the prophets as in Judges 6:8. Here the Messenger (Angel) of *Yahweh* spoke in the first person as God Himself, the One who brought them out of Egypt into the land that was promised to their fathers.[617] According to Morey, some Jewish paraphrases, such as "*Targum of Jonathan*," have the words, "Thus says *Yahweh*," but the phrase does not appear in any Hebrew manuscripts or the Septuagint.[618] George Moore also makes a very clear statement as to the identity of the Messenger (Angel) of the LORD:

> Yahweh himself as he appears to men in human form or otherwise sensibly manifests his presence (Exodus 3:2; 23:20; 32:34; Numbers 20:16; Joshua 5:13-16).[619]

The LORD who spoke in verse 1 is the Messenger (Angel) of *Yahweh* who makes reference to four things. First (1), He says that He brought Israel out of Egypt. There is a clear connection with *Yahweh* and His reference to this Messenger:

> I am sending an angel before you to guard you on the way and to bring you to the place that I have made ready. Pay heed to him and obey him. Do not defy him, for he will not pardon your offenses, since My Name is in him; but if you obey him and do all that I say, I will be an enemy to your enemies and a foe to your foes. When My Angel goes before you and brings you to the Amorites, the Hittites, the Perizzites, and Canaanites, the Hivites and the Jebusites, and I will annihilate them, (Exodus 23:20-23).

In Exodus 23:20-23 *Yahweh* spoke of "*an angel* [Messenger]" in verse 20 and "*My angel*" (Messenger) in verse 23, and He equates Him as *echad* (one) with Him when He says, "*My Name is in him*." In Isaiah 42:8 and 48:11 *Yahweh* makes these statements:

---

[616] Leon J. Wood, *Distressing Days of the Judges* (Grand Rapids: Zondervan, 1975), 231.

[617] Morey, *The Trinity: Evidence and Issues,* 156.

[618] Morey, The *Trinity: Evidence and Issues,* 157.

[619] George F. Moore, *International Critical Commentary: Judges* (New York: Charles Scribner's, 1903), 57.

I am the LORD, that is My name; I will not yield My glory to another, nor My renown to idols. For My sake, My own sake, do I act – lest My name be dishonored! I will not give My glory to another.

Vine connects God's glory with the name of God (*Yahweh*):

This is a ratification of the significance of His Name. His glory is the manifestation of His nature, attributes and power.[620]

Yahweh makes this connection. He, *Yahweh*, will not give or yield His glory (*Shechinah*) to another. Yet in Exodus 23:20-23 *Yahweh* says that His name is in the Messenger. The Messenger of *Yahweh* appears numerous times as He leads them to the Promised Land as the *Shechinah* of God. So who is the Messenger? In Exodus 32:34 and 33:2-3, *Yahweh* adds more information on the Messenger:

Go now, lead the people where I told you. See, My angel shall go before you. But when I make an accounting, I will bring them to account for their sins. I will send an angel before you, and I will drive out the Canaanites, the Amorites, the Hittites, the Perizzites, the Hivites, and the Jebusites: unto a land flowing with milk and honey. But I will not go in your midst, since you are a stiff-necked people, lest I destroy you on the way.

Twice *Yahweh* says that He will send "*My* [messenger] *angel*" or "*a* [messenger] *angel*" before Israel to lead them. *Yahweh* clearly states that He will not go up with them. So who is that Messenger? Exodus 33:14-16 seems to contradict the other passages that say He did not go with them. In this dialogue between Moses and the LORD (*Yahweh*), Moses requested that *Yahweh's* presence go with them, and *Yahweh* consented because Moses had found favor and knew His name. The word "presence" in the Hebrew is פָּנִים (*panim*) meaning "face," which is always a plural.[621] It is my view that the Messenger (Angel) of *Yahweh* (Judges 2:1) is also called the "*messenger of His Presence*" or face in Isaiah 63:9. It is the Second Person of the plural unity of *Elohim* rather than God the Father who went up with them. It is also interesting to note that *The Jewish Study Bible* recognizes the Messenger as divine. Judges 2:1 clearly answers that question by stating that "*the Angel* [Messenger] *of Yahweh*" brought them up from Egypt. In Judges 2:4-5 notice the response of the people: "*The people broke into weeping. So they named that place Bochim, and they offered sacrifices there to the LORD.*" Their response was that the Messenger of *Yahweh* was equal to *Yahweh*.

The second (2) point of reference that the Messenger of *Yahweh* makes is that He brought them into the Promised Land. Exodus 33:2-3 expresses the same thing as Judges 2:1. The third (3) point of reference of Judges 2:1 is that the Messenger (Angel) of *Yahweh* says, "*I had promised an oath to your fathers.*" That is a direct reference to the Abrahamic Covenant in Genesis 15; He is "*the word of the LORD*" the same one

---

[620] V. E. Vine, *Isaiah* (Grand Rapids: Zondervan, 1946), 108.
[621] Harris, Archer, and Waltke, *Theological Wordbook of the Old Testament*, 2:727.

that walked between the cut animals. The Messenger (Angel) of *Yahweh* also known as *"the word of the LORD"* in Genesis 15 made the Covenant with Abraham and that is no small detail. Jewish and Christian scholars are united in agreement that the Lord God is the one who walked between the cut animals. The fourth (4) point of reference is that He says, *"I will never break My covenant with you."* So in Judges 2:1 the Messenger (Angel) of *Yahweh* is clearly distinct from *Yahweh*, yet He is equal to Him and He speaks as God.

It is my heart's prayer that rabbis who attempt to put the Almighty God, *HaShem,* into a prescribed rabbinic box in their thinking will realize the futility of that act. How can a finite creature confine *HaShem* in a box when the entire universe is measured by the span of His hand (Isaiah 40:12)? Isaiah 40:12 is so descriptive of the overwhelming power and strength of *HaShem*:

> Who hath measured the waters in the hollow of his hand, and meted out heaven with the span, and comprehended the dust of the earth in a measure, and weighed the mountains in scales, and the hills in a balance? (KJV)

HaShem is beyond comprehension and if He wishes to take on the appearance of man and then do it later by the incarnation, by His great omnipotence, that is nothing to Him. *HaShem* does not fit into the confining box of restrictive rabbinic thought when He Himself has expressed clearly otherwise.

Which I Sware unto Their Fathers to Give Them ... Joshua 1:1, 6

(1) Now after the death of Moses the servant of the LORD it came to pass, that the LORD spake unto Joshua the son of Nun, Moses' minister, saying,

(6) Be strong and of a good courage: for unto this people shalt thou divide for an inheritance the land, which I sware unto their fathers to give them.

I want to take this opportunity to retrace our steps through the Torah as we have looked at the God of Israel who swore unto the fathers, Abraham, Isaac and Jacob to give this generation, the generation of Joshua, the land of Canaan. We want to look at the passages that deal with the Abrahamic Covenant and the promise of the Land to Israel so that we once again identify Who made that covenant. In the Joshua 1:6 passage we need to observe first of all verse 1. After the death of Moses, the *Tanakh* distinctly states that *Yahweh* spoke to Joshua. What the text does is to clearly lead the student of Scripture to the conclusion that the LORD did this without the aid of a prophet, vision or dream, but personally spoke to Joshua with His message of encouragement.

In verse 6 The LORD stated that He swore unto the fathers that He was going to give this Land. Who is speaking to Joshua? It is obviously the LORD or *Yahweh*, but who? As we have already discovered in the previous chapters the theophanies of God can be none other than the second personal of the plural unity of *Elohim*. Let us go back and reference certain passages to help us see it more clearly:

Genesis 15:1, 4	The **word of the LORD** spoke to Abraham.
Genesis 22:16	The **angel of the LORD** spoke who is identified as Yahweh.
Genesis 26:3	Confirmation of the Covenant to Isaac by **Yahweh** who swore to Abraham
Genesis 28:13	Confirmation of the Covenant to Jacob by **Yahweh**
Genesis 50:24	Joseph repeats the promise given to Abraham, Isaac and Jacob.
Exodus 3:2-6	The **Angel of the LORD, Yahweh, and Elohim** at the burning bush identifies Himself of the God of Abraham, Isaac and Jacob.
Exodus 13:5	**Yahweh** to Moses **identifies Himself of the covenant maker**
Exodus 32:13	Moses reminds **Yahweh** of His covenant promise
Exodus 33:1	**Yahweh identifies Himself as the covenant maker**
Numbers 11:12	Moses again reminds the **LORD** of the covenant **He made** with the fathers
Numbers 14:23	**LORD's** judgment on the exodus generation
Numbers 32:11	**LORD references** His covenant to Abraham, Isaac and Jacob
Deuteronomy 1:8	**Moses speaking for God** as he references the Abrahamic Covenant
Deuteronomy 6:10	**The author of the Shema** stated that He made the covenant with Abraham, Isaac and Jacob.
Deuteronomy 6:13	Israel is to **swear by His Name**
Deuteronomy 7:8	**Yahweh** who loved them, redeemed them has taken an oath and **has sworn** to the fathers
Deuteronomy 30:20	**LORD thy God swore unto the fathers**
Judges 2:1	The **Angel of the LORD** made the Covenant.

There is a common denominator between these verses. As we have been going through the Torah, the LORD, "*the angel* [Messenger] *of the LORD*," the *Shechinah* glory of the LORD has been interacting with Moses. What becomes increasingly clear is that when

Elohim or *Yahweh* communicated to mankind He did so through the Second Person of the plural unity of *Elohim*.

Let me use two verses as book ends. First in Genesis 15:1 and 4 it is the *"word of the LORD"* who communicated to Abraham making the blood covenant, He is Second Person of the plural unity of *Elohim*. This will be covered in more detail in chapter 18. The second verse is Judges 2:1 where the *"angel of the LORD"* distinctly stated that He not only made the covenant, but He also led Israel through the wilderness, from Egypt to Canaan. It was not God the Father who made the Covenant, but *"the word of the LORD"* and *"the angel of the LORD"* who made and accomplished the covenant from the promises to Abraham into reality in Joshua's day. Now in between those verses you have numerous verses already discussed in the previous three chapters that point to only one individual, the Second Person of the Godhead, the theophany of God that appeared to Abraham, Isaac and Jacob as well as to Moses as the God of Israel. This member of the plurality of *Elohim* is the One who constantly referred to Himself, that it was He who swore unto the fathers, Abraham, Isaac and Jacob as the God of Israel. Look briefly at a couple of these verses.

In Exodus 3:2-12 it is the Angel (Messenger) of the LORD who interacted with Moses, told Moses to take off his shoes because he was standing on holy ground, the Angel (Messenger) of the LORD was the Shechinah of God before Moses. Moses then refers to Him as *Yahweh*, the LORD who said to Moses, *"I am the God of thy father, the God of Abraham, the God of Isaac, and the God of Jacob."* Notice that the Angel (Messenger) of the LORD who spoke to Moses uses the personal pronoun "I" 9 times, "my" twice, and "me" once, no possibility of Him only representing the Father. Observe as well in verses 4 and 12, the Angel (Messenger) of the LORD is referred to as *Elohim*.

In Exodus 13:1-5 it is the LORD who spoke to Moses and in verse 5 He stated that He had sworn to the fathers. Here the *"word of the LORD"* and *"the angel* [Messenger] *of the LORD"* is *Yahweh* who made the covenant. These names all reference to the Second Person of the plural unity of *Elohim*.

Exodus 32:11 and 33:1 reference to when Moses was on Mt. Sinai in the presence of the *Shechinah* of God, who is also referred to as *Yahweh* or the LORD. In fact in Exodus 33:1 the LORD stated *"unto the land which I sware unto Abraham, to Isaac, and to Jacob,"* He is the covenant signer, the *"word of the LORD,"* *"the angel* [Messenger] *of the LORD."* The Second Person of the Godhead is *echad* (see chapter 9), a plurality, He is one LORD, and the *"word of the LORD"* and *"the angel of the LORD"* is that member of the plural *Elohim*, distinct from and yet equal in character and essence, who interacted with Moses and Israel on behalf of God the Father.

At Kadesh-barnea in Numbers 14 it states in verse 10 that *"the glory of the LORD appeared in the tabernacle,"* then in verse 11 the *Shechinah* of God is called *Yahweh* as He spoke to Israel. Here once again we are dealing with a theophany that communicated with Israel and Moses. Then on top of that in verse 23 *Yahweh*, the *Shechinah* of God said that "*I swore unto their fathers.*" Here the one who intervened and saved the lives of Moses, Joshua and Caleb claims to be the one who made the covenant to Abraham, the "*word of the LORD*" and "*the angel* [Messenger] *of the LORD*," two descriptive names for the same person, the Second Person of the plural unity of *Elohim*.

Who is the one being referenced in Deuteronomy 6:10 and the verses immediately preceding it known as the *Shema* (verses 4-9)? Who is it that says in verse 4 "*Hear O Israel*"? Moses in verse 10 identifies the speaker when he says:

> And it shall be, when the LORD thy God shall have brought thee into the land which **he sware** unto thy fathers, to Abraham, to Isaac, and to Jacob, to give thee great and goodly cities which thou buildedst not, ….

Who is the covenant maker? It is the LORD thy God, who is described in Genesis 15 and Judges 2 as the "*word of the LORD*" and "*the angel* [Messenger] *of the LORD*" respectively. So in reality, who gave the *Shema* to Israel that they clutch to with their belief in the absolute oneness of God? Rather than showing absolute oneness, it shows plurality in unity. Once again, if verbal plenary inspiration means anything it is God the Son, the Messiah, the Son of David, Immanuel, the Branch who made this covenant with the fathers. It was none other than the Second Person of the plural unity of *Elohim* who made the covenant. It becomes a very significant point to show the plurality of *Elohim* as Moses the Law giver wrote it down at the direction of *Yahweh* the Son.

Finally, remember that Joshua was no stranger to the Shechinah glory of God nor was Joshua unknown by *Yahweh*. He was never far away from Moses and the appearances of the *Shechinah* at the tabernacle. See the following references:

Exodus 17:14	God directly references Joshua
Exodus 24:13-14 (32:17)	Joshua goes part way up Mt. Sinai with Moses
Exodus 33:11	Joshua stays in the tabernacle where God spoke to Moses
Numbers 27:18	Joshua anointed at the word of the LORD
Deut 1:38	Joshua again referenced by the LORD
Deut 31:14	The LORD gives a charge to Joshua

The main differences this time is that *Yahweh* spoke to Joshua personally to encourage and strengthen him for the big task in front of him. This time the covenant maker spoke to Joshua directly for Moses had died.

Gideon and the Angel of the LORD … Judges 6:11-24

(11) An **angel of the LORD** came and sat under the terebinths at Ophrah, which belongeth to Joash the Abiezrite. His son Gideon was then beating out

wheat inside a winepress in order to keep it safe from the Midianites. (12) The **angel of the LORD appeared to him** and said to him, "The LORD is with you, valiant warrior!" (13) Gideon said to him, "Please, my lord, if the LORD is with us, why has all this befallen us? Where are all His **wondrous** deeds about which our fathers told us, saying, 'Truly the LORD brought us up from Egypt'? Now the LORD has abandoned us and delivered us into the hands of Midian!" (14) **The LORD turned to him and said**, "Go in this strength of yours and deliver Israel from the Midianites. I herewith make you My messenger." (15) He said to Him, "Please, my lord, how can I deliver Israel? Why, my clan is the humblest in Manasseh, and I am the youngest in my father's household."

(16) The **LORD replied**, "I will be with you, and you shall defeat Midian to a man." (17) And he said to Him, "If I have gained Your favor, give me a sign that it is You who are speaking to me: (18) Do not leave this place until I come back to You and bring out my offering and place it before You." And He answered, "I will stay until you return." (19) So Gideon went in and prepared a kid, and [baked] unleavened bread from an ephah of flour. He put the meat in a basket and poured the broth into a pot, and he brought them out to Him under the terebinths. As he presented them, (20) the **angel of God** said to him, "Take the meat and the unleavened bread, put them on yonder rock, and spill out the broth." (21) **The angel of the LORD** held out the staff that he carried, and touched the meat and the unleavened bread with its tip. A fire sprang up from the rock and consumed the meat and the unleavened bread. **And the angel of the LORD** vanished from his sight.

(22) Then Gideon realized that it was an **angel of the LORD**; and Gideon said, "Alas, O Lord God! For **I have seen an angel of the LORD face to face**. (23) But the LORD said to him, "All is well; have no fear, **you shall not die**." (24) So Gideon built there an altar to the LORD and called it Adonai-Shalom. To this day it stands in Ophrah of the Abiezrites.

Gideon, for fear of the Midianites, was harvesting some grain in a winepress when the Messenger (Angel) of the LORD appeared to him. Gideon only recognized this visitor as a human being. So "*the angel* [Messenger] *of the LORD*" that appeared to him did so in a human form. After the introduction Gideon asked a question of the visitor: "*Where be all his miracles* [wondrous deeds] *which our fathers told us of?*" The word פֶּלֶא (pele'), meaning wondrous deeds, has a particular meaning. It is used as a verb [פָּלָא] and as a noun [פֶּלֶא] and minimally it refers to the acts of God, sometimes beyond human capabilities.[622] The noun form of פֶּלֶא is used in Isaiah 9:6 as one of the descriptive names of the child that would be born, "wonderful," which is only used of God Himself. So Gideon asked the man where were all the miracles [נִפְלְאֹתָיו] that God had done for them, that their fathers had spoken of? It was a question and accusation of

---

[622] Harris, Archer and Waltke, *Theological Wordbook of the Old Testament*, 2:723.

God at the same time. What Gideon did not know at that moment was that this visitor was the LORD that had performed all those miracles for his fathers.

This passage on Gideon shows by the following dialog that the visitor was the LORD Himself. In Judges 6:12 "*the angel* [Messenger] *of the LORD*" spoke to Gideon, then in verses 14 and 16 the writer of the book of Judges stated, "*and the LORD looked upon him, and said.*" The conclusion of these two verses is that "*the angel* [Messenger] *of the LORD*" was *Yahweh* Who was currently speaking with him. In verse 20 this "*angel* [Messenger] *of the LORD*" who spoke to Gideon was now called "*the angel* [Messenger] *of God.*" Verse 21 speaks again of the visitor as "*the angel* [Messenger] *of the LORD*" Who touched the food which Gideon prepared with the end of His staff. Then fire came out of the rock on which the food had been set and the Messenger (Angel) of the LORD disappeared or vanished. At that point in time Gideon's response was: "*I have seen an angel of the LORD face to face*" and in verse 23 he was fearful of death until he was reassured by the LORD. [623] Wood and Wilcock point out in this passage an obvious theophany of God that appeared to Gideon in human form:

Because Gideon did not recognize his visitor as supernatural until after the miracle of the burning food, it is clear that He did not look other than human. Gideon clearly thought that he was talking merely to another man, though probably an unusual one, since He spoke the way He did. That this person was the Angel of the LORD is evident, however, because He is referred to as the LORD (Yahweh) in Judges 6:14, 16, that He uses the first personal pronoun "I" (vv. 14, 16) in speaking as God to Gideon, and that He finally performs the miracle and disappears thus causing Gideon to recognize Him. There is no question but what this was a true Theophany.[624]

> This time there is no question but that the 'angel of the Lord' is supernatural, and is to be identified with the Lord himself (6:14, 16), although Gideon does not recognize it at first.[625]

Once again it is clearly presented by the author of Judges that the one whom Gideon met in the winepress, as he was harvesting, was the Messenger (Angel) of the LORD presenting Himself as *Yahweh*:

In all the old accounts of such appearances the mal'ak is, first or last, identified with deity; see Gen 16:7-14; 21:17-19; 22:11-18; 31:11-13; Exod 3:2 … further in Gen 18:19, in which Yahweh appears precisely as elsewhere the Mal'ak Yahweh. In the Yahwistic narratives in the Pentateuch, as in Judges ch[apter] 6 and 13, the Messenger of Yahweh appears in human form and converses freely with men.[626]

---

[623] Showers, *Those invisible Spirits Called Angels,* 164.

[624] Wood, *Distressing Days of the Judges,* 205.

[625] Michael Wilcock, *The Bible Speaks Today: The Message of Judges* (Downers Grove: IVP, 1992), 78.

[626] Moore, *International Critical Commentary: Judges,* 183-184.

What is becoming increasingly clear is that from the time of creation throughout the *Tanakh*, the LORD God has appeared many times and in many ways to mankind in revealing His nature, character and essence to fallen sinful man. From the beginning of history — from the very first chapter in Genesis — He has also presented Himself as a plurality in unity.

Manoah and his Wife with the Angel of the LORD ... Judges 13:2-25

(2) There was a certain man from Zorah, of the stock of Dan, whose name was Manoah. His wife was barren and had borne no children. (3) **An angel of the LORD appeared** to the woman and said to her, "You are barren and have borne no children; but you shall conceive and bear a son. (4) Now be careful not to drink wine or other intoxicant, or to eat anything unclean. (5) For you are going to conceive and bear a son; let no razor touch his head, for the boy is to be a nazirite to God from the womb on. He shall be the first to deliver Israel from the Philistines." (6) The woman went and told her husband, "**A man of God** came to me; he **looked like an angel of God, very frightening**. I did not ask him where he was from, nor did he tell me his name."

(7) He said to me, 'You are going to conceive and bear a son. Drink no wine or other intoxicant, and eat nothing unclean, for the boy is to be a nazirite to God from the womb to the day of his death!' (8) Manoah pleaded with the LORD. "Oh, my Lord!" he said, "please let the man of God that You sent come to us again, and let him instruct us how to act with the child that is to be born." (9) **God** heeded Manoah's plea, and **the angel of God** came to the woman again. She was sitting in the field and her husband Manoah was not with her. (10) The woman ran in haste to tell her husband. She said to him, "The man who came to me before has just appeared to me." (11) Manoah promptly followed his wife. He came to the man and asked him: "Are you the man who spoke to my wife?" "Yes," he answered. (12) Then Manoah said, "May your words soon come true! What rules shall be observed for the boy?"

(13) **The angel of the LORD** said to Manoah, "The woman must abstain from all the things against which I warned her. (14) She must not eat anything that comes from the grapevine, or drink wine or other intoxicant, or eat anything unclean. She must observe all that I commanded her." (15) Manoah said to **the angel of the LORD**, "Let us detain you and **prepare a kid** for you." (16) But **the angel of the LORD** said to Manoah, "If you detain me, I shall not eat your food; and if you **present a burnt offering, offer it to LORD**." For Manoah did not know that he was an **angel of the LORD**. (17) So Manoah said to **the angel of the LORD**, "What is your name? We should like to honor you when your words come true."

(18) The angel said to him, "You must not ask for my name; it is unknowable!" (19) Manoah took the kid and the meal offering and offered them up on the rock to the LORD; and a **marvelous** thing happened while Manoah and his wife looked on. (20) As the flames leaped up from the altar toward the sky, **the angel of the LORD ascended** in the flames of the altar, while Manoah and his wife looked on; and they flung themselves on their faces to the ground. (21) **The angel of the LORD** never appeared again to Manoah and his wife. Manoah then realized that it had been an **angel of the LORD**. (22) And Manoah said to his wife, "We shall surely die, for we have seen a divine being (Elohim)."

(23) But his wife said to him, "Had the LORD meant to take our lives, He would not have accepted a burnt offering and meal offering from us, nor let us see all these things; and He would not have made such an announcement to us." (24) The woman bore a son, and she named him Samson. The boy grew up, and the LORD blessed him. (25) The spirit of the LORD first moved him in the encampment of Dan, between Zorah and Eshtaol.

Manoah's wife was barren, and in the Jewish culture of that day this was generally taken to mean divine disfavor (Psalm 127:3-5), because having children was regarded as a reward. The Messenger (Angel) of the LORD appeared to her and told her that she would have a son and that he was to be a Nazirite from birth (Numbers 6:12). The Messenger (Angel) of the LORD appeared in a human form, but there was something frightening about Him to her, for according to her description, He was like an angel, as she told her husband Manoah. Manoah asked God to send the "*man of God*" to them again for more instruction, which the LORD did later. In Judges 13:3 the writer of Judges stated that the Messenger (Angel) of the LORD appeared and spoke to the wife of Manoah. In verse 9 the same Messenger came again but was identified this time as the Messenger (Angel) of God, equating the two as the same,[627] and spoke as the Messenger (Angel) of the LORD again in verses 13 and 16. Manoah asked his questions and he also asked the Messenger for His name so he could honor Him when the birth of the child occurred. But the Messenger would not give His name. He did give them two things to confirm who He was. First, in reference to His name, He gave an indirect answer, and second He ascended in the flames of the sacrifice that Manoah prepared for Him. Also notice that Manoah's wife recognized Him, even as this author believes that Abraham in Genesis 18 recognized one of the three visitors from at least two other appearances before him.

Names in the Hebrew Scriptures were often designed to reveal the nature of the bearer of that name.[628] Wood states that the term the Messenger used was "wonderful":

---

[627] Keil and Delitzsch, *Commentary on the Old Testament: Judges,* 2:406.
[628] Showers, *Those Invisible Spirits Called Angels,* 165.

This one had appeared earlier to Abraham and Sarah at Mamre to announce the birth of Isaac, and had appeared last in the biblical account to extend the call to Gideon. That this was the same Angel here is indicated both by the authority with which He spoke, even using the first person form of reference in speaking as God, and by the fact that He referred to His name as "wonderful" (pele' translated unusually in KJV as "secret"; Judg 13:18).[629]

As the Messenger (Angel) of the LORD used this word "wonderful" with Gideon, so it is used twice in the passage concerning Manoah and his wife. In Judges 13:18 it has been translated as "unknowable," "secret," or as "wonderful." In this verse "wonderful" (פֶּלִאי) is an adjective describing the nature of the name. Keil and Delitzsch connect the word "wonderful" with Isaiah 9:6 in the following statement:

> The word [פֶּלִאי] therefore is not a proper name of the angel of the LORD, but expresses the character of his name; and as the name simply denotes the nature, it expresses the peculiarity of his nature also. It is to be understood in an absolute sense – "absolutely and supremely wonderful" as a predicate belonging to God alone (compare the term "Wonderful" in Isa 9:6).[630]

Then "wonderful" is used again in Judges 13:19 as a verb when "*the angel* [Messenger] *of the LORD*" ascended to heaven in the flames of the sacrifice to the LORD. This act told Manoah who the Messenger was, for his response in verse 22 was "*We shall surely die, because we have seen God.*" There is no mistake in his understanding as to the identity of the Messenger: He was the LORD. Wood states that by the action of the Messenger, Manoah knew who was speaking to him:

> The Angel described His name as "wonderful," when queried by Manoah on the matter. Then, when the Angel later ascended in the flame of the sacrifice, it is stated that by so doing He did "wonderfully," using the same basic word. The thought is unmistakable that the Angel's description of Himself was thereby proven in demonstration. Manoah thus was given all the evidence He needed to have for knowing the identity of his Visitor.[631]

> Proof that this was the angel of the LORD came when Manoah presented the burnt offering and its accompanying grain offering (v. 19). As the flame rose, the angel ascended in it before the couple's startled eyes (v. 20). This was even more spectacular than the disappearance of the angel who talked with Gideon (6: 21). Manoah's reaction to the miracle, however, matched Gideon's; Manoah too thought he would die as a result of seeing God (vv. 21-22).[632]

---

[629] Wood, *Distressing Days of the Judges,* 306-307.

[630] Keil and Delitzsch, *Commentary on the Old Testament: Judges,* 2:407.

[631] Wood, *Distressing Days of the Judges*, 309.

[632] Herbert Wolf, *The Expositor's Bible Commentary: Judges* (Grand Rapids: Zondervan, 1992), 3:464.

This passage of Scripture concerning Manoah and his wife being introduced to the Messenger (Angel) of the LORD is significant because of the name *"the angel* [Messenger] *of the LORD."* But beyond that was the significance of the term "wonderful" referenced twice. When *"the angel* [Messenger] *of the LORD"* ascended in the flame of fire before the eyes of Manoah and his wife, Manoah's response was that they would die because they had seen God. *"The angel* [Messenger] *of the LORD"* who consistently appeared as God, and twice made reference to the "holy ground" upon which Moses and Joshua stood, continued His appearances as the *Shechinah* glory of God, who spoke and made claims that only God could say and do in His appearances. He spoke as God and yet He obviously was distinct from God. He revealed the will and instruction of the Father as the Second Person of the plural unity of *Elohim*.

The Call of Samuel … 1 Samuel 3:10-14, 21

(10) The LORD came, and stood there, and He called as before: "Samuel! Samuel!" And Samuel answered, "Speak, for Your servant is listening." (11) The LORD said to Samuel: "I am going to do in Israel such a thing that both ears of anyone who hears about it will tingle. (12) In that day I will fulfill against Eli all that I spoke concerning his house, from beginning to end. (13) And I declare to him that I sentence his house to endless punishment for the iniquity he knew about – how his sons committed sacrilege at will – and he did not rebuke them. (14) Assuredly, I swear concerning the house of Eli that the iniquity of the house of Eli will never be expiated by sacrifice or offering.

(21) And the LORD continued to appear at Shiloh: The LORD revealed Himself to Samuel at Shiloh with the word of the LORD.

1 Samuel 3:10-14 deals with the boy Samuel and it does not use the term *"the angel* [Messenger] *of the LORD"* in this context. However, it is still a theophany passage where once again the LORD made His presence known. 1 Samuel 3 stated that the LORD spoke four times. In verse 10 the LORD "stood" by Samuel. Then verse 21 stated that the LORD *"appeared again"* and that *"the LORD revealed Himself to Samuel in Shiloh."* But an unusual phrase is added: *"by the word of the LORD."* Davis and Whitcomb see the Lord speaking to Samuel as an audible call of Samuel.[633] But the text shows more than an audible call with the words "stood" and "appeared" in the biblical narrative.

Twelve times קָרָא [call or called] is used in this narrative between Samuel, Eli, and the LORD. קָרָא is the common word to call a person. It is used four times by the LORD (1 Samuel 3:4, 6, 8, 10). Three times Samuel responded by saying to Eli, *"You called me"* (1 Samuel 3:5, 6, 8), and five times Eli used it as he responded to Samuel (1 Samuel 3:5, 6, 8 twice, 9). In these verses there is a very active narrative going on

---

[633] John J. Davis and John C. Whitcomb, *Israel: A Commentary on Joshua - 2 Kings* (Winona Lake, IN: BMH Books, 2002), 194.

among three persons. Davis and Whitcomb are correct, in that there is an audible call, but this theophany offers far more than that.

This word "to stand" or "stood" (יָצַב) carries with it the idea of taking one's stand, poised to strike, and also appears to be combative.[634] The LORD stood before Samuel because He had a message that would bring aggressive action in the future against the house of Eli. This would be illustrated by His statement in verse 11:

Behold, I will do a thing in Israel, at which both the ears of everyone that heareth it shall tingle.

This word is not the regular word (עָמַד) "to stand" as a simple act of standing, but it carries with it the meaning of a combative aggressive stand.

The word "the LORD appeared" (רָאָה) are the same used in Genesis 12:7; 17:1; 18:1; 26:2 and Exodus 3:2, where God allowed Abraham, Isaac, Jacob, and Moses to actually see Him. The word means "to be seen, appear, make oneself visible;" "cause to see, cause to know, to experience."[635] So in the context of 1 Samuel 3:21 the LORD allowed Samuel to see the LORD, for God had made Himself visible to Samuel as He communicated "by the word of the LORD."

This word, "to be revealed" (גָּלָה) means to "uncover, reveal" and is used in the Hebrew Scriptures to identify God in allowing human eyes to see Him in a form usually as a man.[636] The LORD in 1 Samuel 3:21 appeared and was revealed to Samuel in a form that Samuel could see and communicate with in a personal manner.

One other point that will be studied in chapter 18 of this book concerns the phrase "the word of the LORD" which is used in 1 Samuel 3:7, 21. Samuel would be the last judge and the first of the prophets. Throughout the prophetic writings of the prophets the phrase "the word of the LORD came to" became a common expression used by God when He communicated with the prophets. Some feel this could be just a phrase that God used, or it could be a personification of the Second Person of *Elohim*, whom John in his gospel called the Word, the *Memra*.

Even though 1 Samuel 3 is not a passage that references the Messenger (Angel) of the LORD, it still is a theophany, for *Yahweh* stood by Samuel to communicate His message of judgment against the house of Eli. He clearly appeared and allowed Himself to be revealed to Samuel in the theophany. Once again it has been demonstrated in 1 Samuel 3 that the theophany of God is the Second Person of the plural unity of *Elohim*.

---

[634] VanGemeren, *New International Dictionary of Old Testament Theology & Exegesis,* 2:500.

[635] VanGemeren, *New International Dictionary of Old Testament Theology & Exegesis,* 3:1007.

[636] VanGemeren, *New International Dictionary of Old Testament Theology & Exegesis,* 1:861.

David's Sin of Numbering ...
2 Samuel 24:14-17; 1 Chronicles 21:11-30

(14) David said to Gad, "I am in great distress. Let us fall into the hands of the LORD, for His compassion is great; and let me not fall into the hands of men." (15) The LORD sent a pestilence upon Israel from morning until the set time, and 70,000 of the people died, from Dan to Beer-sheba. (16) But when **the angel** extended his hand against Jerusalem to destroy it, the LORD renounced further punishment and said to **the angel** who was destroying the people, "Enough! Stay your hand!" **The angel of the LORD** was then by the threshing floor of Araunah the Jebusite. (17) When David saw **the angel** who was striking down the people, he said to the LORD, "I alone am guilty, I alone have done wrong; but these poor sheep, what have they done? Let Your hand fall upon me and my father's house!"

(11) Gad came to David and told him, "Thus said the LORD: Select for yourself: (12) a three year famine; or that you be swept away three months before your adversaries with the sword of your enemies overtaking you; or three days of the sword of the LORD, pestilence in the land, **the angel of the LORD** wreaking destruction throughout the territory of Israel. Now consider what reply I shall take back to Him who sent me." (13) David said to Gad, "I am in great distress. Let me fall into the hands of the LORD, for His compassion is very great; and let me not fall into the hands of man." (14) The LORD sent a pestilence upon Israel, and 70,000 men fell in Israel. (15) God sent **an angel** to Jerusalem to destroy it, but as he was about to wreak destruction, the LORD saw and renounced further punishment and said to the destroying angel, "Enough! Stay your hand!" **The angel of the LORD** was then standing by the threshing floor of Ornan the Jebusite.

(16) David looked up and saw the angel of the LORD standing between heaven and earth, with a **drawn sword** in his hand directed against Jerusalem. David and the elders, covered in sackcloth, threw themselves on their faces. (17) David said to God, "Was it not I alone who ordered the numbering of the people? I alone am guilty, and have caused severe harm; but these sheep, what have they done? O LORD my God, let Your hand fall upon me and my father's house, and let not Your people be plagued!" (18) **The angel of the LORD** told Gad to inform David that David should go and set up an altar to the LORD on the threshing floor of Ornan the Jebusite. (19) David went up, following Gad's instructions, which he had delivered in the name of the LORD. (20) Ornan too saw the **angel**; his four sons who were with him hid themselves while Ornan kept on threshing wheat.

(21) David came to Ornan; when Ornan looked up he saw David and came off the threshing floor and bowed low to David, with his face to the ground.

(22) David said to Ornan, "Sell me the site of the threshing floor, that I may build on it an altar to the LORD. Sell it to me at the full price, that the plague against the people will be checked." (23) Ornan said to David, "Take it and let my lord the king do whatever he see fit. See, I donate oxen for burnt offerings, and the threshing boards for wood, as well as wheat for a meal offering – I donate all of it." (24) But King David replied to Ornan, "No, I will buy them at the full price. I cannot make a present to the LORD of what belongs to you, or sacrifice a burnt offering that has cost me nothing." (25) So David paid Ornan for the site 600 shekels' worth of gold.

(26) And David built there an altar to the LORD and sacrificed burnt offerings and offerings of well-being. He invoked the LORD, who answered him with fire from heaven on the altar of burnt offering. (27) The LORD ordered the angel to return his sword to its sheath. (28) At that time, when David saw that the LORD answered him at the threshing floor of Ornan the Jebusite, then he sacrificed there. (29) for the Tabernacle of the LORD, which Moses had made in the wilderness, and the altar of burnt offerings, were at that time in the shrine at Gibeon, (30) and David was unable to go to it to worship God because he was **terrified by the sword of the angel of the LORD**.

In the opening of this passage David has numbered the people against the advice of Joab (2 Samuel 24:3), and *Yahweh* is very angry with David. David's own heart bothers him and he confesses his sin to the LORD (2 Samuel 24:10). Through the prophet Gad (2 Samuel 24:11), David is given three choices of punishment for his sin (2 Samuel 24:13). David chooses the third option, which is *"three days of pestilence."* The LORD sends the pestilence through the hand of *"the angel* [Messenger] *of the LORD"* (24:15). In this plague the Messenger (angel) of the LORD slays 70,000 Israelites. This is the only portion in the Hebrew Scriptures where *"the angel* [Messenger] *of the LORD"* is recorded as bringing an act of judgment against His covenant partners.[637] Normally, He acted as a benevolent intercessor (Genesis 16:7-11; 22:11; 1 Kings 19:5-6) and messenger (Genesis 22:15-18; Judges 2:1-3; 6:11-12; 13:3-21; 2 Kings 1:13-15). However, *"the angel* [Messenger] *of the LORD"* did unsheathe His sword against the false prophet, Balaam (Numbers 22:31) and as the conquest of Jericho loomed near (Joshua 5:13-15). He also acted against the armies of Assyria, killing 185,000 soldiers (2 Kings 19:35; Isaiah 37:36), but the method of that slaughter is not given. Also the *Shechinah* judges Aaron and Miriam. As *"the angel* [Messenger] *of the LORD"* approaches the threshing floor of Ornan the Jebusite, David sees the Messenger (Angel) between heaven and earth with His sword drawn and stretched over Jerusalem. David buys the threshing floor from Ornan and makes an offering to the LORD.

---

[637] Robert Bergen, *The New American Commentary: 1 & 2 Samuel* (Nashville: Broadman, 1996), 478.

Pertaining to "*the angel* [Messenger] *of the LORD*" and His identity, the argument that always surfaces is the one presented by Youngblood, who wants to reference Hebrews 1:3, where he tries to say that "*the angel* [Messenger] *of the LORD*" theophanies seriously weaken the incarnation:

> Although many have taught that the angel was Jesus Christ in a pre-incarnate form (J. Borland, *Christ in the Old Testament* and Reymond, *Jesus Divine Messiah*), such a view severely weakens (1) the uniqueness of the incarnation and (2) the basic argument of Hebrews 1, which goes to great lengths to point out that Jesus is far superior to all of God's angels.

> Since the Hebrew word for "angel" also means "messenger," it is perhaps better to understand the angel of the LORD as a special messenger from the court of heaven who bears all the credentials of the King of heaven and can therefore speak and act on his behalf. He can use the first person pronoun of himself as though he were the sender, or he can use the third person pronoun in reference to the sender (Judg 6:12; 13:3-23 for various titles given to the "angel of the LORD:" "man of God," "angel of God," "man," "God," "the LORD"). In either case, he symbolizes the presence of the King who sends him. Thus when the angel of the LORD appears, the Lord himself is symbolically present.[638]

First of all, it does not weaken the incarnation when these appearances of the Messenger (Angel) of the LORD were not incarnations in the first place. These were very brief appearances of the LORD. The incarnation did not occur until the time appointed by the Father when *Yeshua* took on flesh and confined Himself to a body of flesh for more than 30 years. That is totally different from a very brief appearance of the Messenger (Angel) of the LORD. The second objection relates to Hebrews 1:1-3. Of course, *Yeshua* was superior to the entire heavenly host; He is God, the Creator (Isaiah 48:12-16; Zechariah 12:1, 10). In Hebrews 1:6 the writer quotes from the Septuagint (LXX) and states that all the angels of heaven are to worship the Messenger (Angel), Who is God. God is God, and it is rather petty of Youngblood to tell God that the manner that He chooses to communicate and reveal Himself to mankind weakens His message. God cannot be put in a box. He cannot always be defined by human logic. He is God and will do what He wants to do in the manner that He wants to do it.

Last, the argument about the Messenger (Angel) being symbolic of the LORD just does not take the whole of the subject on "*the angel* [Messenger] *of the LORD*" into account. Isaiah 42:8 ties the identity and plural unity of God together with Exodus 23:20-23. God will not share His Name or His Glory with any created being. No created being in his right mind, with the exception of Satan, is going to take the name of God and apply it to himself and speak as if he were God. All of these passages on the theophanies of God make it impossible to apply such an argument to "*the angel*

---

[638] Ronald F. Youngblood, *The Expositor's Bible Commentary: 1 & 2 Samuel* (12 Vols. Grand Rapids: Zondervan, 1992), 3:1101.

[Messenger] *of the LORD.*" Perhaps you can isolate one reference, but when taking the whole of what God has said and done, it just is not a valid argument to say that theophanies are not God Himself revealing Himself to mankind.

Several points are significant in connection with this theophany and "*the angel* [Messenger] *of the LORD.*" The first thing to be noted is that in these two passages, "*the angel* [Messenger] *of the LORD*" never speaks. God the Father speaks to David through Gad the prophet (2 Samuel 24:11-13). "*The angel* [Messenger] *of the LORD*" is dispatched to spread the pestilence upon Israel. When David finally sees Him, He is between heaven and earth with His sword drawn, executing the judgment on Israel. There are two other times when "*the angel* [Messenger] *of the LORD*" has His sword drawn: once with Balaam to slay him (Numbers 22:31-33), and once in the presence of Joshua, for He is in combat ready to destroy Jericho (Joshua 5:13-15). It is not recorded that David saw the Messenger (Angel) of the LORD with the drawn sword before he saw Him at the threshing floor of Araunah. There is one clue that David did see Him before because he was afraid to go to Gibeon to the tabernacle and make an offering before the LORD (1 Chronicles 21:29-30). If the Messenger (Angel) of the LORD was not visible to David before the threshing floor encounter, He is visible at the threshing floor. The elders of Israel who are in sackcloth with David see Him and fall on their faces. Ornan, the Jebusite, (Araunah) and his four sons also see Him and the four sons hid (1 Chronicles 21:20). One thing is very obvious from the two passages; they saw the destroying Messenger (angel) for He was definitely visible.[639] It is interesting that some authors either do not discuss the issue of "*the angel* [Messenger] *of the LORD*" or only mention it in passing, as do Thompson[640] and Payne.[641]

There is one interesting contrast in 2 Samuel 24:14-17 (1 Chronicles 21:12-20). The destroying angel of the Exodus 12 account and the last plague on Egypt (death of the first-born) is a reversal of roles for "*the angel* [Messenger] *of the LORD.*" He went from judging the Egyptians and protecting the Israelites, to judging the Israelites. Keil and Delitzsch, and Selman note:

And the Angel of the LORD as destroyer (*mashit*) throughout all the borders of Israel: the destroying angel, the *mashit*, occurs in Exod 12:13, 23 as the slayer of the Egyptian firstborn, while sparing those of Israel. Here is a horrifying reversal of the Passover, Israel's foundational act of deliverance (compare the Passover celebrations under Hezekiah and Josiah in 2 Chron 30): the force of destruction is now turned against Israel itself.[642]

---

[639] Keil and Delitzsch, *Commentary on the Old Testament: 2 Samuel,* 2:509.

[640] J. A. Thompson, *New American Commentary: 1 & 2 Chronicles* (Nashville, Broadman, 1994), 162-163.

[641] J. Barton Payne, *The Expositor's Bible Commentary: 1 Kings – Job* (Grand Rapids, Zondervan, 1988), 4:408-409.

[642] William Johnstone, *1 & 2 Chronicles* (Sheffield, England: Sheffield Academic Press, 1997), 232.

In describing him as a 'destroying angel' [1 Chron 21:15] Chronicles, affirms the triple reference of 2 Samuel 24:16-17, but also seems to evoke a deliberate echo of the plague of the firstborn (Exod 12:23).[643]

This story of David and "*the angel* [Messenger] *of the LORD*" is a complete reversal because in the Exodus 12 account, God was judging the Egyptians by the destroying angel, and now He is judging Israel through "*the angel* [Messenger] *of the LORD*" or the destroying Messenger (Angel).

David makes a physical transaction for the purchase of the threshing floor from Ornan, the Jebusite, whereupon David makes a burnt-offering and a peace-offering and calls upon the LORD. The LORD accepts the offerings by sending down fire from heaven upon the altar (1 Chronicles 21:26-27).

Also the location of the threshing floor and "*the angel* [Messenger] *of the LORD*" present a strong argument that this Messenger cannot be a created angel, but the LORD Himself. It is generally accepted that this is the same place where Abraham offered Isaac on Mount Moriah as recorded in Genesis 22. Josephus in his writings ties together the threshing floor with the place that Abraham offered Isaac.[644] But also in the book of Deuteronomy God begins to talk about a place where He will put His Name, which is unique to Deuteronomy.[645] This becomes a central theme in Deuteronomy (12:5, 11-14, 21; 14:23-24) and later throughout the prophets as they refer to the place, Jerusalem, where God put His Name and where Israel defiled His Name. One author points out the significance of God putting His Name in a place:

> In the Book of Deuteronomy, with an eye toward entry into the land of Israel, God speaks of the central shrine in the land as the place I shall select to establish My name. This term is first used in Deuteronomy 12:5, and it appears another 20 times (Deut 12:5, 11-14, 21; 14:23-24; 16:2 (Passover), 6, 11 (Weeks), 15 (Booths); 26:2) throughout the book as the exclusive label for what we term the Temple. In 1 Kings, this nomenclature is likewise employed by Solomon as he constructs the Temple. In his lengthy address to the people at the dedication of the Temple, Solomon refers to the Temple 9 times, exclusively, as the House of God's name. What is implied by a "place," or "house" for "God's name"? The connotation of this term is the key to understanding the transition from Tabernacle to Temple and, indeed, is one of

---

[643] Martin Selman, *Tyndale Old Testament Commentary: 1 Chronicles* (Downers Grove, IL: Inter-Varsity Press, 1994), 207.

[644] Whiston, *Josephus Complete Works,* 167.

[645] Eugene Merrill, *The New American Commentary: Deuteronomy* (Nashville: Broadman, 1994), 252.

the most crucial points for understanding the biblical meaning of the Temple itself.[646]

One of the most interesting passages where God spoke about placing His Name is the section in Deuteronomy 16 where Moses reviews the feasts of the LORD before Israel. Moses specifically speaks about the pilgrim feasts. There are three feasts where God stated that all males were to appear before Him wherever He puts His Name (Deuteronomy 16:16). Those feasts are: The Passover in Deuteronomy 16:2, 6, Shavuot (Weeks or Pentecost) in Deuteronomy 16:11 and Sukkoth (booths or tabernacles) in Deuteronomy 16:15. This place, where God was to put His Name becomes a very important place in the worship and life of Israel from the reign of Solomon and the dedication of the temple onwards (1 Kings 5:5; 8:17-19; 43, 9:3; 14:21; 2 Chronicles 2:1, 4; 6:7-9; Jeremiah 7:3-12; Ezekiel 36:20-23).

David and the Spirit of the LORD ... 2 Samuel 23:2-3

(2) The spirit of the LORD has spoken through me, His message is on my tongue; (3) The God of Israel has spoken, the Rock of Israel said concerning me: "He who rules men justly, He who rules in awe of God."

This reference is not commonly recognized as a theophany, but this passage is unique for in this passage the LORD is called by the name "Rock of Israel." David is using a descriptive term for God that is unique, and he equates the "spirit of the LORD" and "God" as the "Rock" that spoke to him. That is unusual.

I was studying another research subject in reference to a New Covenant passage in Matthew 16:18 and the statement of *Yeshua* in response to Peter's statement of faith on the Messiahship of *Yeshua*. Peter, who would be understood today in terms of being Orthodox in his Jewish faith, responded to *Yeshua*'s question. Then *Yeshua* stated to Peter in response to his statement of faith, "*That thou art Peter, and upon this rock I will build my church....*" The Roman Catholic Church has used this verse to authenticate and establish its teaching that Peter was the first pope in a long line of succession of popes. When the Catholic Church made its interpretation of this verse, they failed to check out the meaning of the word "*rock*" and its established understanding in the Hebrew Scriptures. It is commonly known that the Church became very anti-Semitic, which is an issue for another book.[647] Everything that was Jewish to the Church was viewed heretical and thus interpreted allegorically. So what is the meaning?

---

[646] Joshua Berman, *The Temple: Its Symbolism and Meaning Then and Now* (Northvale, NJ: Jason Aronson, 1995), 58-59.

[647] There are to books good books dealing with the anti-Semitism of the Church: (1) William H. Heinrich, *In the Shame of Jesus: The Hidden Story of Church-Sponsored Anti-Semitism.* (Morgantown, PA: Masthof Press, 2009). Michael L. Brown, *Our Hands are Stained with Blood: The Tragic Story of the "Church" and the Jewish People* (Shippensburg, PA: Destiny Image Publishers, 1990).

The term "Rock" became another name for God. It all started with the two occasions where Moses struck the rock in Exodus 17:6 and Numbers 20:8, 10. Then in Deuteronomy 32, Moses several times referred to God as the "Rock" of Israel. As Scripture progresses, the term "Rock" is used as the name for God by Hannah (1 Samuel 2:2), David (2 Samuel 22:1-2, 32, 47; 23:1-3; Psalm 18:1-2, 31, 46; 28:1; 31:2-3; 61:2; 62:2, 6-7), by Ethan in the court of Solomon (Psalm 89:26) and in many other references in the Psalms (Psalm 42:9; 71:3; 78:35; 81:16; 92:15; 94:22; 95:1). This term "Rock" was also used by Isaiah (8:14; 17:10) and then used also as "Stone" in a messianic context by Daniel (2:34-35, 45). The Apostle Paul used the term "Rock" in the context of Israel's wilderness wanderings in 1 Corinthians 10:4 and applied the term "Rock" from the Exodus and Numbers passages to Messiah *Yeshua*, as the God of Israel.

The Hebrew Scriptures define the term "Rock" as an alternate name for the God of Israel. First of all no thinking, rational, orthodox Jew, like Peter would have accepted the name for God and would have applied it to himself. Secondly, *Yeshua*, knowing the Scriptures, would not have applied it to Peter, a mere mortal. So it is applied to the statement of faith of Peter, not to Peter himself (Matthew 18:16).

The point of this discussion is that when God spoke to or appeared to men of old it was a theophany of God. God spoke through the Second Person of the plural unity of *Elohim* whose responsibility it was to reveal the character, nature and essence of *Elohim* to the nation of Israel. Next David referred to that person, *"the Rock of Israel spake to me."* This passage in 2 Samuel 23:2-3 is a reference to the plurality of *Elohim* because in this passage, the *"Rock"* of Israel and *Yahweh* are mentioned in the same verse. Is it also possible that there is a strong hint at the tri-unity of *Elohim*, with the Holy Spirit, called the Spirit of the LORD, and the LORD, and the *"Rock"* being the tri-unity mentioned by David? This is open to discussion, but the elements are all there.

Yahweh Appears to Solomon … 1 Kings 3:5; 9:2; 11:9

(3:5) At Gibeon the LORD appeared to Solomon in a dream by night; and God said, "Ask, what shall I grant you?"

(9:2) The LORD appeared to Solomon a second time, as He had appeared to him at Gibeon.

(11:9) The LORD was angry with Solomon, because his heart turned away from the LORD, the God of Israel, who had appeared to him twice and had commanded him about this matter, not to follow other gods; he did not obey what the LORD had commanded.

In the life of Solomon the LORD appeared to him twice in dreams and the LORD God referenced to those appearances to Solomon in 1 Kings 11:9 because of His act of judgment on Solomon for his idolatry. The recorder of 1 Kings does not use the same

Hebrew word for "appear" as Moses and other authors of the *Tanakh* as they referenced the visible manifestation of the LORD as recorded about Abraham, Isaac and Jacob. In Genesis 17:1 Moses stated that the "LORD appeared" (וַיֵּרָא יְהוָה) to Abraham. However, in 1 Kings 3:5; 9:2; 11:9 a different word is used. 1 Kings 3:5 states that "the LORD appeared to Solomon in a dream." The words "LORD appeared" are נִרְאָה יְהוָה and convey the meaning that Solomon did see the LORD in his dream, but not with his physical eyes, and there is no description given. The root word is רָאָה and several scholars give descriptive information as to its meaning and usage:

> …its major meaning: 'to show oneself, appear' 'to become visible, appear…'[648]

> … q. see, have visions, see!, look at, see, appear, make oneself visible; pu. To be seen; hi. Cause to see, cause to know, to experience; ho. To be caused to see; hitp. Look at each other, measure one's strength against another.[649]

> Unlike other verbs referring to visual perception, *ra'a* denotes the experience of seeing as a totality, in which sensation and perception merge. The experience of the visual nature of reality has as its content the meaning, character, and nature of images perceived; this experience is the polar opposite of sensation, i.e., the experience of the concrete nature of reality, and experience that conveys the nature and intensity of such sensory data as color, form, and spatial location. The verb *ra'a* refers particularly to the segment of the process that brings the perpetual flux of the visual experience of living reality to the level of conscious recognition – i.e., conscious perception or the act of comprehension.[650]

What is clear is that this word means to "appear," "be seen,"[651] but it also seems to tie together the ability to see with comprehending what is being seen as in a vision. The point is that Solomon saw and communicated with the LORD through the medium of a vision and he comprehended all that the LORD said to him. What is not given in these passages is a clue to the identity of the LORD that is speaking. The term "*the angel of the LORD*" is not present, nor is any other term. But based on what has already been seen throughout this book, when *Yahweh* becomes visible literally or in a vision it is the Second Person of the plurality of *Elohim* whose name is *Yahweh*. This passage would not be of any interest in this study if it were not for the tremendous background of biblical passages already studied. This would not be a major Scripture to substantiate the plurality of God and the Second Person of the plural unity of *Elohim* if it were not for the abundance of Scriptures that already point to that conclusion, along with the many scriptural passages yet to be viewed.

---

[648] Jenni and Westermann, *Theological Lexicon of the Old Testament,* 3:1178.

[649] VanGemeren, *The International Dictionary of Old Testament Theology and Exegesis,* 3:1007.

[650] Botterweck, Ringgren and Fabry, *Theological Dictionary of the Old Testament,* 13:214.

[651] Todd Beall and Banks, *Old Testament Parsing Guide: Genesis – Esther* (2 vols. Chicago: Mood Press, 1986), 1:277.

Elijah and the Angel of the LORD … 1 Kings 19:5-9

(5) He lay down and fell asleep under a broom bush. Suddenly an angel touched him and said to him, "Arise and eat." (6) He looked about; and there, beside his head, was a cake baked on hot stones and a jar of water! He ate and drank and lay down again. (7) The angel of the LORD came a second time and touched him and said, "Arise and eat, or the journey will be too much for you." (8) He arose and ate and drank; and with the strength from the meal he walked forty days and forty nights as far as the mountain of God at Horeb. (9) There he went into a cave, and there he spent the night. Then the word of the LORD came to him. He said to him, "Why are you here, Elijah?"

Numerous authors who were consulted do not even make a statement about the identity of the Messenger (Angel) of the LORD in 1 Kings 19:5-9. However, Hengstenberg is very clear on the identity of this messenger:

> That מלאך יהוה is the angel of the Lord, is very obvious from 1 Kings 19:5, "and behold an angel, מלאך, touched him; compare verse 7, "and the angel of the Lord touched him a second time," – first an angel, then the angel who is already known from what has been mentioned before.[652]

Hengstenberg goes on to express that this messenger is no ordinary messenger but one of exalted dignity and superior in nature. Here in the life of Elijah, "*the angel* [Messenger] *of the LORD*" is active and present in his ministry. The one who is dealing with Elijah in this passage is also called "*the word of the LORD*," and that has connotations that will be discussed in chapter 18. Walvoord refers to this passage as "the thoughtful care" that the Messenger (Angel) of the LORD provided for Elijah.[653]

Elijah, the Angel of the LORD, the Captain of Fifty … 2 Kings 1:9-16

(9) Then he sent to him a captain of fifty with his fifty men. He climbed up to him, and found him sitting at the top of a hill. "Man of God," he said to him, "by order of the king, come down!" (10) Elijah replied to the captain of the fifty, "If I am a man of God, let fire come down from heaven and consume you with your fifty men!" And fire came down from heaven and consumed him and his fifty men. (11) The king then sent to him another captain with his fifty men; and he addressed him as follows: "Man of God, by order of the king, come down at once!" (12) But Elijah answered him, "If I am a man of God, let fire come down from heaven and consume you with your fifty men!" And fire of God came down from heaven and consumed him and his fifty men. (13) Then he sent a third captain of fifty with his fifty men. The third

---

[652] Hengstenberg, *Christology of the Old Testament,* 4:254.
[653] Walvoord, *Jesus Christ Our LORD,* 53.

captain of fifty climbed to the top, knelt before Elijah, and implored him, saying, "Oh, man of God, please have regard for my life and the lives of these fifty servants of yours!

(14) Already fire has come from heaven and consumed the first two captains of fifty and their men; I beg you, have regard for my life!" (15) Then the **angel of the LORD** said to Elijah, "Go down with him, do not be afraid of him." So he rose and went down with him to the king. (16) He said to him, "Because you sent messengers to inquire of Baal-zebub the god of Ekron – as if there were no God in Israel whose word you could seek – assuredly, you shall not rise from the bed which you are lying on; but you shall die."

In 2 Kings 1:9-16 *"the angel* [Messenger] *of the LORD* comforts and instructs Elijah in his time of exhaustion and depression. In this passage, *"the angel* [Messenger] *of the LORD"* instructs Elijah in his controversy with Ahaziah, King of Israel and his judgment on the three groups of fifty soldiers who are ordered to take Elijah to the King.[654] Fire came from heaven and destroyed the first two groups, then the captain of the third group came in humility. Barrett in his book, *Beginning at Moses*, lists 27 passages of theophanies that reveal the plurality of God within the plural unity of *Elohim*. In this and the previous passage *"the angel* [Messenger] *of the LORD"* is definitely viewed as a theophany of God.[655]

The Angel of the Lord instructs Elijah to go and meet with the messengers of the king of Samaria, and He also tells Elijah to go with the 3rd captain of 50.[656]

The Angel of the LORD and 185,000 Assyrian Soldiers … 2 Kings 19:35; Isaiah 37:36; cf 2 Chronicles 32:21

(19:35, 37:36) That night an **angel of the LORD** went out and struck down one hundred and eighty-five thousand in the Assyrian camp, and the following morning they were all dead corpses (2 Kings and Isaiah).

(21) The LORD sent **an angel** who annihilated every mighty warrior, commander, and officer in the army of the king of Assyria, and he returned in disgrace to his land. He entered the house of his god, and there some of his own offspring struck him down by the sword (2 Chronicles).

Both 2 Kings and Isaiah reference *"the angel of the Lord"* and the fact of 185,000 Assyrian soldiers dying in one night. Also, Davis and Whitcomb attribute *"the angel of the Lord"* to be the Second Person of the Godhead.[657] Others like Keil and

---

[654] Walvoord, *Jesus Christ Our LORD,* 53.

[655] Michael P. Barrett, *Beginning at Moses* (Greenville, SC: Ambassador-Emerald Int'l, 2001), 160-163.

[656] Walvoord, *Jesus Christ Our Lord,* 53.

[657] Davis and Whitcomb, *A Commentary on Joshua – 2 Kings*, 457-459.

Delitzsch have connected "*the angel of the LORD*" as the same angel that smote הַמַּשְׁחִית, the firstborn, of Egypt (Exodus 12:23, compared with Exodus 12:12-13) and inflicted the pestilence upon Israel after the numbering of the people by David (2 Samuel 24:15-16).[658]

In the parallel passage of Isaiah 37:36, some only mention "*the angel* [Messenger] *of the LORD*" in passing with no discussion, while others, such as Young, attribute the actions of "*the angel* [Messenger] *of the LORD*" to only those of an ordinary angel.[659] Why an ordinary angel? God, who made a covenant with His vassal kingdom, is actively protecting Judah from the Assyrians. Based on the Deuteronomy context it makes more sense to see Him clearly distinct as "*the angel* [Messenger] *of the LORD*" that has been so prevalent in the Hebrew text:

> Instead of the angel of the LORD it would be more consonant with Old Testament theology to print 'the Angel of the LORD' – That Old Testament personage who is both the Lord and distinct from the Lord (Gen 16:7, 11; Judg 13:21) and who combines in himself divine holiness and divine condescension (Exod 23:20-23).[660]

> The angel of the Lord is a divine figure, at once distinguished from God yet identified with him.[661]

The writer of the Kings and the prophet Isaiah once again use the term Messenger (Angel) of the LORD. The activity of this particular Messenger is consistent throughout the Hebrew Scriptures. It does not belong to just any messenger (angel) in the heavens but to one particular Messenger who is the very likeness of God, part of the plural unity of *Elohim*.

The Angel of the LORD Protects … Psalm 34:7[8]

The angel of the LORD camps around those who fear Him and rescues them.

This psalm deals with that period of time in David's life when he lived with the Philistines as recorded in 1 Samuel 21:10-15. The Messenger of the LORD is also the mighty God who dealt with the patriarchs and was predominant in the Exodus and Wilderness wandering of Israel. But in the psalms He is only mentioned in Psalm 34:7 [8] and in Psalm 35:5-6.[662] "*The angel* [Messenger] *of the LORD*" encircles or camps around those who honor and obey His commandments. That was the promise that the LORD made in the Covenant of Law to the vassal nation, Israel, in Exodus 24.

---

[658] Keil and Delitzsch, *Commentary on the Old Testament: 2 Kings,* 3:457.

[659] Edward J. Young, *The Book of Isaiah* (Grand Rapids: Eerdmans, 1969), 2:504.

[660] J. Alec Motyer, *The Prophecy of Isaiah* (Downers Grove: InterVarsity Press, 1993), 284.

[661] Geoffrey W. Grogan, *The Expositor's Bible Commentary: Isaiah* (Grand Rapids: Zondervan, 1986), 6:233.

[662] Leupold, *Exposition of Psalms,* 280.

Spurgeon equates "*the angel* [Messenger] *of the LORD*" with the "*Captain of the LORD's host*" of Joshua 5. For the covenant messenger, the Messiah camps all around the faithful servants of the LORD.[663]

Keil and Delitzsch make a clear statement as to the identity of the Messenger of the LORD in this passage as they see Him throughout Israel's history:

> The יהוה מַלְאַךְ, is none other than He who was the medium of Jahve's intercourse with the patriarchs, and who accompanied Israel to Canaan. This name is not collective. He, the One, encampeth round about them, in so far as He is the Captain of the host of Jahve (Josh 5:14), and consequently is accompanied by a host of inferior ministering messenger angels; or insofar as He can, as being a spirit not limited by space, furnish protection that covers them on every side.[664]

"*The angel* [Messenger] *of the LORD*" is the one who has been interacting with the patriarchs and giving the protection, guidance, and instruction to Israel in the wilderness and conquest of the Land. He is God ministering to Israel through the Second Person of the plural unity of *Elohim*.

The Angel of the LORD and the Wicked ... Psalm 35:5-6

(5) Let them be as chaff in the wind, the LORD's angel driving them on. (6) Let their path be dark and slippery, with the LORD's angel in pursuit.

In looking at this psalm of David, one thing becomes quite clear. The Messenger that David is referencing is not just any messenger, but one particular Messenger. It is not hard to see him referencing "*the angel* [Messenger] *of the LORD*", even though that exact phrase does not occur in Psalm 35:5-6. This is the Messenger who met with the patriarchs, Moses, and the entire nation of Israel at Mt. Sinai and with others as He spoke and acted as God and yet was distinct from God. Once again He is part of the plural unity of *Elohim*. He is the same Deliverer of the exodus that David is calling to deliver him to safety.[665] Keil and Delitzsch even identify the LORD's Messenger as the One who disabled the chariots of Pharaoh in the midst of the Red Sea.[666]

Isaiah Sees the Lord ... Isaiah 6:1-3

(1) In the year that King Uzziah died, I beheld my Lord seated on a high and lofty throne; and the skirts of His robe filled the Temple. (2) Seraphs stood in attendance on Him. Each of them had six wings: with two he covered his face,

---

[663] Charles H. Spurgeon, *The Treasury of David* (Byron Center, MI: Associated Publishers and Authors, 1970) 1:137.

[664] Keil and Delitzsch, *Commentary on the Old Testament: Psalms,* 5:410.

[665] Leupold, *Exposition of Psalms,* 287.

[666] Keil and Delitzsch, *Commentary on the Old Testament: Psalms,* 5:421.

with two he covered his legs, and with two he would fly. (3) And one would call to the other, "Holy, holy, holy! The LORD of Hosts! His presence fills all the earth!"

Isaiah 6:1 is referenced not because it mentions *"the angel* [Messenger] *of the LORD"*, but because it is a theophany of God and the commissioning of Isaiah the prophet. The question has been raised as to why the commissioning of Isaiah is in chapter 6, and not chapter 1 as in Jeremiah (1:4-10), Ezekiel (1:1-28) and Hosea (1:1-2). God chose to do it this way for His own reasons. By chapter 6, Isaiah has been a prophet for approximately five years (740-735 BCE). So the introductions in Isaiah chapters one through five are his prophecies during the joint reigns of Uzziah and Jotham. Five years before this event in Isaiah 6 at the death of Uzziah, Tiglath-pileser III of Assyria made his ambitions known—to conquer everything between himself and the Nile River. What Isaiah saw and tried to describe in chapter 6 was also at the beginning of the reign of the wicked king of Judah, Ahaz.[667]

What Isaiah saw in chapter 6 is one of the most majestic and awe-inspiring passages on theophanies in the *Tanakh*. He saw the throne of God, with God seated on His throne with the *seraphim* serving the LORD. Is this a contradiction when the Scriptures clearly state that man cannot see God (Exodus 33:20) and live? It is not a contradiction for two reasons: first it was a vision and second because God voluntarily limited part of His nature and essence in order that Isaiah might be able to experience His awesome presence without perishing. God chose to use different methods and ways to reveal Himself to man, whether it was in a human form, *Shechinah*, or audible voice. To Isaiah the Lord manifested Himself as the eternal King enthroned in His holy temple, surrounded by *seraphim* while His glory filled all the earth.[668] Because the nature of a theophany is the revealing of God to man, this is also the Second Person of the plural unity of *Elohim*. Steveson clearly ties this passage to *Yeshua*:

> Isaiah sees the Lord seated upon His throne. This must be a vision of Jesus Christ, the second person of the Trinity. Isaiah sees Him, yet elsewhere the Bible says that no man has seen God; cf. Exodus 33:20; John 1:18, 6:46; 1 Timothy 6:16; 1 John 4:12. The Being here speaks and has a body wearing a robe. Elsewhere God the Father is a spirit, John 4:24; 1 Timothy 1:17; 6:15-16. John 12:40 settles the identity. After referring to this passage, John says that Isaiah saw the glory of the Son of God, John 12:41[669]

Even though these are mostly New Covenant references, the reality of the One Isaiah recorded in the *Tanakh* can be no one else. This One who has been seated on the throne since the days of Adam has been revealing Himself since the days of Adam. He is the Second Person of the plural unity of *Elohim* who consistently throughout the pages of

---

[667] Victor Buksbazen, *The Prophet: Isaiah* (Collinswood, NJ: The Spearhead Press, 1971), 135-137.

[668] Buksbazen, *The Prophet: Isaiah*, 2:135, 138.

[669] Peter A. Steveson, *A Commentary on Isaiah* (Greenville, SC: BJU Press, 2003), 52-53.

the *Tanakh* has "appeared," has revealed and manifested Himself to man, usually as "*the angel* [Messenger] *of the LORD.*"

The Angel of His Presence ... Isaiah 63:9-10

(9) In all their troubles He was troubled, And the angel of His Presence delivered them. In His love and pity He Himself redeemed them, raised them, and exalted them all the days of old. (10) But they rebelled, and grieved His holy spirit; Then He became their enemy, and Himself made war against them.

Isaiah 63:9-10 is a very significant passage as it has been referenced by many authors in their discussion of "*the angel* [Messenger] *of the LORD*" passage from the Torah. However, there is difficulty with a word according to the Masorahs.[670] There are 15 places in the Hebrew text where, according to the Masorahs, the Hebrew word לא meaning "*not*" should be substituted for לו or "to him or it" as referenced by Alexander,[671] and previously by Keil and Delitzsch.[672] It would appear that the word "not" would show God's lack of identity with Israel, but the rest of the verse does not bear that out. God did feel the pain and emotions of His people. Even though He is spirit, He is the creator of feelings and emotions. So He knew them, their feelings of hurt and pain as well as their emotions. Alexander quotes Rabbi Aben Ezra as saying "that in all their distress there was distress to him."[673] Rabbi Aben Ezra is referenced again by Alexander concerning the Messenger (Angel) of His Presence as to His identity. This Messenger of His Presence's identity was that of the Messenger whom God promised to send to Israel in Exodus 23:20-23, whom He did send (Exodus 14:14-15), and who was identified with the presence of *Yahweh* and with *Yahweh* Himself (Exodus 33:12). Alexander summarizes Aben Ezra by saying:

> The combination of these passages determines the sense of the angel of his presence, as denoting the angel whose presence was the presence of Jehovah, or in whom Jehovah was personally present.[674]

The Messenger of His Presence is no ordinary Messenger, for this One reflects the very face or presence of God to whomever He revealed Himself in the Hebrew Scriptures. Steveson ties together the events past with the Messenger (Angel) of His Presence:

> He sent the "angel of his presence" to deliver and sustain them. The phrase "angel of his presence" is similar to "angel of the Lord," e.g., Genesis 16:7-11; 22:11-17, and "angel of God," e.g., Genesis 21:17; Judges 13:6, 9. It refers here

---

[670] *Masorahs* are the rabbis who produced the Hebrew Scriptures that have been in use from the 9th century and were the oldest manuscripts of the Hebrew Scriptures until the Dead Sea Scrolls were found in 1948.

[671] Joseph A. Alexander, *Commentary on Isaiah* (Grand Rapids: Kregel, 1992), 418.

[672] Keil and Delitzsch, *Commentary on the Old Testament: Isaiah,* 7:452-453.

[673] Alexander, *Commentary on Isaiah*, 418.

[674] Alexander, *Commentary on Isaiah*, 419.

to the second person of the Trinity. He "saved" (*yasc*) Israel at such times as the crossing of the Red Sea, Exodus 14:19-20; the guidance through the wilderness, Exodus 33:14-15; and the entrance into Palestine, Joshua 5:14. All these were in "the days of old." He "redeemed them...bare them...carried them." The multiplied description of God's work shows the greatness of His love for the people, [Isaiah 63:9].[675]

The Messenger (Angel) of His Presence is the very presence of *Yahweh* Himself. This Messenger is more than a created being who was very close to God, as the Jewish people try to say in connection to *Metatron*. He is God and manifests Himself through His Messenger, the Second Person of the plural unity of *Elohim*. Victor Buksbazen expresses that clearly:

"The angel of his face" (or Presence) – *malakh panau*. This angel personifies the presence of God with His people to save and protect them. He is the supreme manifestation of God. This angel is mentioned on a number of occasions (Ex 14:19; 23:20-23; 32:12, 14-15). In later rabbinical literature, "The Angel of His Face" became another name for the Messiah.[676]

This passage clearly references the Messenger who embodies the very presence of God for He is God. Likewise Young, in a very clear statement, identifies this Messenger (Angel) as God Himself:

So great was His love toward them that He sent the angel of his face, who saved them from all these afflictions and sufferings. This angel (the word means messenger) God had promised to send to His people (Exod 23:20-23) and actually did send to them (Exod 14:19; Num 20:16). He is the Lord's angel (Exod 13:14-15) and is actually the Lord (Yahweh) Himself (Exod 3:12). The angel of His face is the angel who is His face or in whom His face is made clear. In him the Lord is Himself present.[677]

The Messenger (Angel) of *Yahweh's* face is not the only one present in this passage of Scripture. In Isaiah 63:7-14 the plural unity of *Elohim* is expressed in three verses. In verse 7 *Yahweh* is referenced as well as the Messenger (Angel) of His face, but in addition (verse 10) Israel is told not to rebel against the Holy Spirit. So the tri-unity of God is present in the plural unity of *Elohim*.

Ezekiel's Vision of the LORD ... Ezekiel 1:26-28

(26) Above the expanse over their heads was the semblance of a throne, in appearance like sapphire; and on top, upon this semblance of a throne, **there was the semblance of a human form.** (27) From what appeared as **his** loins

---

[675] Steveson, *A Commentary on Isaiah,* 531.
[676] Buksbazen, *The Prophet Isaiah*, 2:473.
[677] Young, *The Book of Isaiah*, 3:481-482.

up, I saw a gleam as of amber – what looked like a fire encased in a frame; and from what appeared as **his** loin down, I saw what looked like fire. There was radiance all about **him**. (28) Like the appearance of the bow which shines in the clouds on a day of rain, such was the appearance of the surrounding radiance. **That was the appearance of the semblance of the Presence of the LORD.** When I beheld it, I flung myself down on my face. And I heard the voice of someone speaking.

After reading Ezekiel 1:26-28, the description of the throne of God, a person is left speechless. How does one describe something so magnificent? Ezekiel saw it and could not totally express in words what he saw. In reading this passage, the mind immediately travels back in time to Moses at the burning bush and the communication with God on Mt. Sinai with Israel at the foot of the mountain. It also takes a person back to the manifestation of God to Moses, Aaron and his two sons along with the 70 elders who saw God in Exodus 24. The references to the cloud and fire were unmistakably the *Shechinah* glory of God. This indeed was an unusual manifestation of God that Ezekiel received. Wiseman reflects on this unique manifestation of God and then compares it to the Messenger (Angel) of the LORD manifestation:

> Here either his eye or his nerve fails him. Whereas the four living creatures could be described in detail, all he could say of God was that He had human form and the appearance of fire. To say even this, however, was incredibly bold, for was not Yahweh invisible and therefore indescribable? It was an idea deeply written into Israelite thinking that no ordinary person could set eyes on God and live to tell the tale. Hagar, Jacob, Moses, Gideon and Manoah, all had remarkable experiences which proved the rule (Gen 16:13; 32:30; Exod 33:20-23; Judg 6:22; 13:22; cf. Deut 5:24), but in their case they met what at first seemed to be a human being who subsequently turned out to be an angel or some other manifestation of God.[678]

What is recognized by this passage of Scripture is that Ezekiel saw the LORD. This passage presents a theophany, a manifestation of God to the prophet. It is not a vision of *cherubim* or anything else, but it is a vision of God on His throne. All the other things he saw were subordinate issues. The thrust of the text is the throne of God and He that sits on that throne.[679] The net result of what Ezekiel saw was that he fell on his face before the LORD his God. Here before the prophet was a vision of God on His throne. Now the ultimate identification of this Person: The One who has appeared to Ezekiel on the throne was the same member of the plurality of *Elohim* who had already made Himself visible in the past. Once again it is needful to understand a theophany; God chooses to reveal Himself to mankind using different forms and methods. What has been seen repeatedly in the theophanies of God is that the Person represented as God is

---

[678] John B. Taylor, *Tyndale Old Testament Commentaries: Ezekiel* (Downers Grove: InterVarsity Press, 1969), 58-59.

[679] A. B. Davidson, *The Book of the Prophet Ezekiel* (London: Cambridge Press, 1916), 13.

God and yet is distinct from God. This has been seen repeatedly throughout the Hebrew Scriptures.

The Scriptures are the verbal, plenary inspired word of God. They are without error and given to man just as God intended them. God is not a man; God is not a creature; but God is spirit. So why is God represented as a man? The reason is very basic; in order to redeem mankind from sin He had to become a perfect man and become the voluntary sacrifice for sin to do for mankind what they were incapable of doing for themselves. However, Rabbinic Judaism is in total disagreement with that statement because it involves the belief in the plurality of God, God taking on flesh in the incarnation, the total depravity of the human race and the need of a mediator. In Genesis 3:15 God laid out the first installment of His redemptive plan when He told Satan that a man would be born of woman, this seed of the woman would destroy Satan. A mere man could not even touch Satan. The man to be born of woman would be the God/man. Fruchtenbaum, reflecting on Genesis 4:1, points out that Eve understood the idea of the God/man from what she heard God say to the serpent. Her theology was correct but her timing was wrong.[680] The Hebrew text of Genesis 4:1 simply reads, "*I have gotten a man, the LORD*," which the prophets spoke of on several occasions (Psalm 110:1-7; Isaiah 9:6-7; 11:1-2; Jeremiah 23:5-6; Micah 5:2; Daniel 9:24-27; Zechariah 12:10; 13:7). That God/man is the Messiah, the Son of David, the King of Israel, who is God revealed to man in the *Tanakh* in human form, or as the *Shechinah*. In the New Covenant He comes as the babe born in Bethlehem that Herod sought to kill. He cleansed the lepers, raised the dead, and healed multitudes of their sicknesses and diseases as He presented Himself as Israel's Messiah with the power and authority to bring in the Kingdom. He is the incarnation of God in human form that God promised in the Garden of Eden.

Fingers of a Human Hand Wrote on the Plaster Wall ... Daniel 5:5

Just then, the fingers of a human hand appeared and wrote on the plaster of the wall of the king's palace opposite the lampstand, so that the king could see the hand as it wrote.

This author believes that this reference is also a theophany of God, when the hand of God wrote on the wall in the banquet hall in Belshazzar's palace. Some background information must be given to lead up to the Daniel reference. Deuteronomy 9:10 (cp. Exodus 31:18; 32:15-16; 34:1) refers to the *Shechinah* of God who wrote the Ten Commandments with "*the finger of God.*" This event was part of the *Shechinah* of God's activities on Mt. Sinai. In the New Covenant "*Jesus stooped down and with his finger wrote on the ground*" (John 8:6). Jesus, the Messiah of Israel and the *Shechinah* of God, was the pre-incarnate Messiah, who now, with His *Shechinah* glory veiled in

---

[680] Fruchtenbaum, *Messianic Christology*, 15.

247

flesh (Mark 9:2-8), did not speak immediately but wrote with His finger, the *"finger of God"* (Deuteronomy 9:10), on the ground. Did He stoop and write the seventh commandment as He wrote with His finger on Mt. Sinai? That will never be known, but the text of John 8:6 does have strong implications. Also in the Greek the word "finger" appears first in the sentence placing the emphasis on the finger and not on what was written on the ground.

The finger of God was mentioned in three other places. One is found in Psalm 8:3 (not a theophany), where David says, *"When I consider Thy heavens, the work of Thy fingers."* The second reference is a metaphor used for God by Pharaoh's magicians as they reacted to the plagues in Exodus 8:19. The third reference is the one now under consideration. More evidence for a theophany is found in Daniel 5:5 where *"suddenly the fingers of a man's hand"* appeared before Belshazzar on the banquet hall wall. This was a theophany, and the reason for this conclusion is that it was a supernatural event. The context involves the temple vessels being defiled by a proud and obstinate king who evidently had learned little from his grandfather, Nebuchadnezzar. It was the hand of God, not a lesser being, who wrote with His finger.

Identity of Man Who Wrestled, Revealed ... Hosea 12:4-5

> (4) In the womb he tried to supplant his brother; grown to manhood, he strove with a divine being, (5) He strove with an angel and prevailed – The other had to weep and implore him. At Bethel [Jacob] would meet him, there to commune with him.

This passage of Scripture in Hosea 12:4-5 is referring back to Genesis 32:23-30 where Jacob wrestled with an unidentified man throughout the night. Much is assumed in the Genesis account, but the tenor of the text leaves the reader under the impression that Jacob knew with Whom he was wrestling. This One changed Jacob's name to Israel. Jacob asked for His name which the "man" refused to give. In verse 31 Jacob called the place Peniel because he had seen God face to face and his life was preserved. Jacob recognized that he had a personal encounter with God. Hosea adds further information that Moses did not know or did not record. Hosea stated that Jacob wanted God's blessing so intensely that he wept and begged the Messenger for a blessing. It is clearer in the King James Version because *The Jewish Study Bible* has toned it down:

> (4) Yea, he had power over the angel, and prevailed; he wept, and made supplication unto him: he found him in Beth-el, and there he spake with us;
> (5) even the LORD God of hosts; the LORD is his memorial.

Hosea 12:4-5 recounts the story of a Man who wrestled with Jacob as an Angel and Jacob would not let go of Him in his earnest desire to be blessed by Him. Jacob wept and begged the Angel to bless him, whereupon the Messenger (Angel) changed his name. Verse 5 gives the identity of the Man or Messenger (Angel), as the LORD God. Jacob met God as a theophany, in human form, as the following two statements assert:

Here מַלְאָךְ, the Angel, corresponds to אֱלֹהִים, God, verse 4, and designates the UNCREATED ANGEL, of whom we read so frequently in the Old Testament, to whom, as here, names distinctive of Deity are ascribed, and who is represented as possessing the divine attributes.[681]

With tears of repentance, in humble faith with God the Angel of the Lord, who fought with him in the form of a man in whom he recognized his God. He persisted in the battle, "had power" over the Angel, obtained the blessing he sought (Gen 32:24-30).[682]

Hosea gives this example of Jacob and his committed desire to be blessed for the benefit of Israel, the northern kingdom. If they would desire the LORD as their father Jacob did, God would be with them and bless them.

However, Jewish scholars and writers attribute to this passage of Scripture two items. One is correct and the other incorrect. In Targum Jonathan on the Torah, it is recorded of Jacob that "an Angel contended with him in the likeness of a man." This is absolutely correct, but it is the identity of the Angel that next comes into question. Targum Jonathan identifies the Angel in the following terms in Genesis 32:24-25:

Michael answered and said, Lord of the world is Thy lot. And on account of these things he (Michael) remained from God at the torrent till the column of the morning was ascending. And he saw that he had not power to hurt him, and he touched the hollow of his thigh, and the hollow of Jakob's thigh was distorted in his contending with him. (The Targum of Jonathan Ben Uzziel on the Torah)[683]

Michael is the Prince that stood for Israel in Daniel 10:13, 21; 12:1, whom they identified with the angel in Genesis and Hosea. Michael is understood by rabbis as the name of the angel in this passage.[684] However, Michael is only mentioned in Daniel, and there is no justification in equating him with the Angel that wrestled with Jacob back in Genesis. This is especially clear since *the angel* [Messenger] *of the LORD*" is the name and title of one particular Messenger (Angel) Who is the Presence of God (Isaiah 63:7) and Who appeared frequently during the times of the Patriarchs, Moses and the Judges. He appeared in human form and as the *Shechinah* of God, who spoke as God and yet was distinct from God, yet part of the plural unity of *Elohim*.

There are four reasons why this cannot be Michael. First, in Genesis 32:28-29 Jacob's name is changed because he had *"power with God and with men."* Here the

---

[681] Ebenezer Henderson, *The Twelve Minor Prophets* (Grand Rapids: Baker, 1980), 72.

[682] Theodore Laetsch, *Bible Commentary: The Minor Prophets* (Saint Louis: Concordia, 1956), 96.

[683] *The Targum of Jonathan Ben Uzziel, Genesis.* On Line: *www.tulane.edu/~ntcs/pj/ pjgen32-36htm.*

[684] Robert Leo Odom, *Israel's Angel Extraordinary* (Bronx, NY: Israelite Heritage Institute, 1985), 47-48.

identity of the celestial being that wrestled with Jacob is the Holy One of Israel Himself. The second reason is that Jacob named the place of his encounter Peniel, meaning "the face of God." There is no question again as to whom Jacob believed he saw. The third reason is that in Genesis 48:16 he references this one as the "*angel who hath redeemed me from all evil.*" The last reason is that Hosea connects God and the Messenger (Angel) together.[685]

One further note on the character of Jacob; Bible scholars have slandered the character of Jacob by constantly raising the issue of Jacob being a supplanter, a trickster, or a deceiver as a constant flaw in his character. It is my belief that they owe Jacob an apology. Jacob did deceive his father Isaac for the blessing. But throughout the life of Jacob he received the brunt of deception on himself, by others, for years on end, by Laban and his own sons in relation to Joseph. This unbiblical position needs to be re-evaluated by New Covenant scholars.

The Angel of the LORD Standing among the Myrtle Trees ... Zechariah 1:8-14

(8) In the night, I had a vision. I saw **a man**, mounted on a bay horse, standing among the myrtles in the Deep, and behind him were bay [red], sorrel [speckled], and white horses. (9) I asked, "What are those, my lord?" And the **angel who talked with me** answered, "I will let you know what they are." (10) Then **the man** who was standing among the myrtles spoke up and said, "These were sent out by the LORD to roam the earth." (11) And in fact, they reported to **the angel of the LORD** who was standing among the myrtles, "We have roamed the earth, and have found all the earth dwelling in tranquility. (12) Thereupon **the angel of the LORD** exclaimed, "O LORD of Hosts! How long will you withhold pardon from Jerusalem and the towns of Judah, which You placed under a curse seventy years ago?" (13) The **LORD replied** with kind, comforting words **to the angel who talked with me**. (14) Then **the angel who talked with me** said to me: "Proclaim! Thus said the LORD of Hosts: I am very jealous for Jerusalem – for Zion.

In this passage of Zechariah messengers (angels) are mentioned in numerous places. Some refer to "*the angel* [Messenger] *of the LORD*", while others refer to ordinary messengers (angels) who are at the service of "*the angel* [Messenger] *of the LORD.*" One of those messengers (angels) is simply referred to as "*the angel that talked with me*" (Zechariah 1:9, 14, 19; 2:3; 4:1, 4-5; 5:5, 10; 6:4). "*The angel* [Messenger] *of the LORD*" is mentioned in chapters 1 (verses 8, 11, 12), 3 (verses 1, 3, 5-7), and 12

---

[685] Odom, *Israel's Angel Extraordinary*, 48-49.

250

(verse 8).[686] What is seen here is other messengers (angels) responding to *"the angel* [Messenger] *of the LORD,"* as well as interacting with Him.

Zechariah is a Messianic book dealing with Israel and their Messiah. There is much that can be commented on in these chapters. However, what is being noted here is the usage of the term *"the angel of the LORD."* This is the same person as in the writings of Moses.

The first thing to be noticed is the myrtle trees. Myrtle trees are equated with Israel, but in Nehemiah 8:15 the myrtle branch is one of the four branches mentioned to be used in the building of the *Sukkah* for the Feast of Booths, or Tabernacles, which represents the kingdom.[687]

In Zechariah 1:8 there is a man on a red horse who stands between the myrtle trees. He is referenced again in verse 10 and in verse 11, identified as *"the angel* [Messenger] *of the LORD"*. The other messengers report to *"the angel* [Messenger] *of the LORD"* with the words that the earth, the Gentile nations, is still and at rest. However, the nation of Israel is not at rest or at peace, but burdened down. At this point *"the angel* [Messenger] *of the LORD"* intercedes in prayer for Israel to the LORD. The answer comes immediately to the messenger that was talking to Zechariah in his vision (in verse 13). In this passage there are three groupings of messengers: (1) *"the angel* [Messenger] *of the LORD"*, (2) the messengers (angels) that report back to *"the angel* [Messenger] *of the LORD"*, and (3) the messenger (angel) that is talking with Zechariah. Who is *"the angel* [Messenger] *of the LORD"*? Most authors view *"the angel* [Messenger] *of the LORD"* as the same individual who appeared throughout the *Tanakh* as God taking on a form with whom mankind could see and interact. Merrill Unger views Him as the Messenger (Angel) of His Presence, the LORD and Messiah.[688] Likewise, David Baron sees the same person:

> The "man" as we are told in verse 11, was the *Malakh Yahovah* – the Angel of Jehovah, who is none other than the "Angel of His face," the Divine "Angel of the Covenant," the second person in the Blessed Trinity, whose early manifestations to the patriarchs and prophets, as the "Angel" or Messenger of Jehovah in the form of man, were anticipations of His incarnation and of that incomprehensible humiliation to which He would afterwards condescend for our salvation.[689]

---

[686] Gerald Van Groningen, *Messianic Revelation in the Old Testament* (Grand Rapids: Baker, 1990), 875.

[687] Kenneth L. Baker, *The Expositor's Bible Commentary: Zechariah* (12 vols. Grand Rapids: Zondervan, 1985), 7:611.

[688] Merrill F. Unger, *A Zondervan Commentary: Zechariah: Prophet of Messiah's Glory* (Grand Rapids: Zondervan, 1970), 30.

[689] David Baron, *The Visions and Prophecies of Zechariah* (Jerusalem: Keren Ahvah Meshihit, 2000), 23.

From the study of theophanies it becomes clear that God's name is associated with this Messenger who speaks as *Yahweh* even though He is distinct from *Yahweh*. However, as difficult as this is to understand, that is what the Hebrew text presents in relation to the term the Messenger (Angel) of the LORD. This term references deity as in all the other passages in the Hebrew Scriptures. He is the second Person who can best be described as the Messiah.[690] Another point to show the distinction between "*the angel* [Messenger] *of the LORD*" and other angels or messengers is the fact that He addresses the LORD of hosts in Zechariah 1:12 whereas ordinary angels do not. In verse 13 the LORD of hosts immediately answers "*the angel* [Messenger] *of the LORD*" but gives His response to the messenger (Angel) that talked with Zechariah.[691]

Another interesting fact about the word *mal'akh*, as it is known, is the meaning of messenger. Feinberg says the word by itself is "without reference to the character, position, or nature of the individual."[692] The argument seems to surface that "*the angel* [Messenger] *of the LORD*" does not have a definite article, so he is just a created being. However, the rule in Hebrew grammar is that nouns in the construct do not take the article with proper nouns because they are already definite. An example has been given in the phrase, *beth YHWH*, meaning the house of *Yahweh*. How many houses of *Yahweh* are there? Only one! How many LORDs are there? Only one! How many Messengers (Angels) of the LORD are there? Only one! The Hebrew Scriptures never refer to "*the angel* [Messenger] *of the LORD*" in the plural as they do with messengers (angels) of *Elohim*. It is only in the singular.[693] This is the same Messenger (Angel) of the LORD who identified Himself in Genesis 31:13 (see 28:13-22) as the Messenger (Angel) of *Elohim*. He speaks of the vow that Jacob made with Him and repeats the promise of the Abrahamic Covenant given to his father (Isaac) and grandfather (Abraham). The term is used exclusively of only one person.

The Angel of the LORD and Joshua the High Priest ... Zechariah 3:1-2, 5-8

(1) He further showed me Joshua, the high priest, standing before the **angel of the LORD**, and the Accuser standing at his right to accuse him. (2) But [the angel of] **the LORD** said to the Accuser, "**The LORD** rebuke you, O Accuser; may the LORD who has chosen Jerusalem rebuke you! For this is a brand plucked from the fire."

(5) Then he gave the order, "Let a pure diadem be placed on his head." And they placed the pure diadem on his head and clothed him in [priestly] garments,

---

[690] Groningen, *Messianic Revelation in the Old Testament*, 875-876.

[691] Eugene H. Merrill, *An Exegetical Commentary: Haggai, Zechariah, Malachi* (Chicago: Moody, 1994), 103.

[692] Charles L. Feinberg, *God Remembers: A Study of the Book of Zechariah* (New York: American Board of Missions to the Jews, 1965), 30.

[693] Feinberg, *God Remembers: A Study of the Book of Zechariah*, 30-31.

as the **angel of the LORD** stood by. (6) And the angel of the LORD charged Joshua as follows: (7) "Thus said **the LORD of Hosts**: If you walk in My paths and keep My charge, you in turn will rule **My House** and guard **My courts**, and I will permit you to move about among these attendants. (8) Hearken well, O High Priest Joshua, you and your fellow priests sitting before you! For those men are a sign that I am going to bring **My servant the BRANCH**."

Zechariah 3:1-2, 5-8 is the next to last reference to the Messenger (Angel) of *Yahweh* in the *Tanakh*. In verse 1 the Messenger (Angel) of *Yahweh* is introduced. In verse 2 the NASB (New American Standard Bible) and KJV (King James Version) use the name "*Yahweh*," but the Jewish Tanakh places in brackets the [Messenger or angel of] the LORD.[694] However, the Hebrew text simply says in verse 2, וַיֹּאמֶר יְהֹוָה אֶל,[695] the literal meaning being "and he said-Yahweh-to."[696] The word מַלְאָךְ (angel) simply is not in that sentence of the Hebrew text. So putting in the "angel of" is misleading the passage to say what the passage itself does not say. Remember the terms "verbal" and "plenary inspiration"? God gave the Scriptures just as He wanted them given. It is unbiblical to insert into the text a meaning to fit a bias or agenda. Literally, what is happening here is "*the angel* [Messenger] *of the LORD*" in verse 2 speaks as *Yahweh* Himself. In chapter 1:11-12 the LORD and "*the angel* [Messenger] *of the LORD*" are distinguished from each other, but in 3:1-2 they are identified together as the same.[697] This is what has been illustrated from earlier passages (Genesis 21:17; 22:11-12, 15-16; 31:11-13; Exodus 3:2-10; Judges 6:11-24; 13:15-20), that in a theophany the second member of the plural unity of *Elohim* is the same as, and yet distinct from God. That includes the fact that though He is distinguished from *Yahweh*, He often speaks as *Yahweh*. "*The angel* [Messenger] *of the LORD*" is the LORD as He reveals Himself to human beings. Also the accuser is standing at the right side of Joshua (son of Jehozadak). Satan, or the accuser, is only going to argue his case before God, not a representative of God. This also supports the view that the Messenger (Angel) of the LORD is deity. Also in verse 2 "*the angel* [Messenger] *of the LORD*" spoke as *Yahweh* and rebuked Satan, once again supporting the argument that the Messenger (Angel) of the LORD is indeed *Yahweh* Himself. Another factor is brought out by Hengstenberg, who notes that Joshua, the first High Priest of the restoration, stood before the LORD whom he served; that was the same idea as standing before "*the angel* [Messenger] *of the LORD*":

The expression, "to stand before a person," is never used of the appearance of a defendant before a judge, but always of a servant standing before his Lord, to offer his services and await his commands. [Hengstenberg goes on to cite thirteen passages to prove his point.]....Thus the prophet (Zechariah) sees

---

[694] Berlin and Brettler, *The Jewish Study Bible*, 1253.

[695] Rud Kittel, *Biblia Hebraica* (New York: American Bible Society, 1937), 960.

[696] Kohlenberger, *The Interlinear NIV Hebrew-English Old Testament*, 4:565.

[697] Merrill, *An Exegetical Commentary: Haggai, Zechariah, Malachi*, 131-132.

Joshua, the high priest on the present occasion, engaged as a priest in the service of the angel of the Lord, who is introduced in verse 2 under the name Jehovah, which belongs to God alone, and who attributes to himself in verse four an exclusively divine work, the forgiveness of sins.[698]

There is an argument put forth by others that this is a judicial scene. But Hengstenberg puts forth an excellent argument that Joshua is standing before His Lord and Satan is there to accuse him because Joshua is polluted with sin. Joshua, as the spiritual head of the people, stood before his Lord in dirty, polluted clothing, representing their sins, iniquities and trespasses (Daniel 9:24).

Zechariah 3:3 records that Joshua stood before "*the angel*" which is what is also said in verse 1. Joshua was standing before "*the angel* [Messenger] *of the LORD*". Because of the subject material that is coming up in verse 4, it must be verified who "*the angel*" is in verse 3. The following sources were checked in different Hebrew Bibles, both from Christian and Jewish editions: Gramcord,[699] Alexander Harkavy Version,[700] the Soncino series on the prophets,[701] Biblia Hebraica,[702] and Kohlenberger's Interlinear[703] and they all have "*the angel*," with a definite article הַ before מַלְאָךְ [הַמַּלְאָךְ], the angel. So it is a particular Angel that needed to be verified because many angels are referenced in the book of Zechariah. The Angel is "*the angel* [Messenger] *of the LORD*" who gives instructions in verse 4, as Joshua stood before Him.

Zechariah 3:4 begins with "*and he answered and spake unto those that stood before him*." The pronouns "he" and "him" refer back to verse 3, "the angel" who is the Messenger (Angel) of the LORD in verse 1 and who spoke in verse 2 as *Yahweh* Himself. This Messenger (Angel) has the power to remove the filthy garments from Joshua and then say, "*behold, I have caused thine iniquity to pass from thee, and I will clothe thee with a change of raiment.*" Remember the filthy garments represent the sins, iniquities and trespasses of the people, the nation of Israel, which Joshua as High Priest represents. This Angel, the Angel, one particular Angel, has the authority and the power to remove iniquity, which only God can do. So according to the text, "*the angel*" is none other than *Yahweh* Himself, Who represents Himself through the Second Person of the plural unity of *Elohim*, the Messiah, the Son of David, the Shepherd of Israel, *Yeshua*.

---

[698] Hengstenberg, *Christology of the Old Testament,* 3:284.

[699] Paul Miller, *Hebrew Old Testament* (Vancouver, WA: The Gramcord Institute, n.d.)

[700] Harkavy, *The Twenty-Four Books of the Old Testament,* 2:970.

[701] A. Cohen, *The Soncino Books of the Bible: The Twelve Prophets* (New York: Soncino Press, 1994), 280.

[702] Kittel, *Biblia Hebraica,* 960.

[703] Kohlenberger, *The Interlinear NIV Hebrew-English Old Testament,* 4:565.

Verse 5 in the Jewish Tanakh understands the messenger to be the Messenger (Angel) of *Yahweh*, and that is as the text has it. The one who has been speaking is the same individual and here He is identified as the Messenger (Angel) of the LORD.

In verse 6 the Messenger (Angel) of *Yahweh* charges or admonishes the High Priest, Joshua. But notice that He admonishes Joshua, not on someone else's authority, but on His own authority; He speaks as God.

The first thing to be addressed in Zechariah 3 is the speaker, the LORD of Hosts. That would be the plural unity of *Yahweh* and all His created messengers. The speaker interchanges names used in these seven verses: Verse 1 "*the angel* [Messenger] *of the LORD*," verse 2 LORD or *Yahweh*, verse 3 "*the angel*," verse 4 is a continuation of verse 3, verse 5 the "Messenger (Angel) of the LORD," verse 6 "*the angel* [Messenger] *of the LORD*," and lastly verse 7 the "*LORD of hosts*." These are all the same person speaking, and it is without a doubt, God alone. Yet He has used different names and titles for Himself in expressing His plurality in unity as He speaks His will to Joshua.

Three of the six times that the speaker identified Himself, He used the term "*the angel* [Messenger] *of the LORD*" which Jewish people struggle with in relation to His true identity. If the Messenger of the LORD is not God, then the reader has a problem in relation to the following statement. "*If thou wilt walk in my ways and if thou wilt keep my charge.*" According to Unger, the LORD of hosts gives two conditional particles "if" and states that they are in the emphatic position in the Hebrew.[704] The LORD of hosts who has been speaking as "*the angel* [Messenger] *of the LORD*", as "*the angel*," now says to Joshua, "*walk in my ways*" and "*keep my charge*" or commandments. Once again it would be impossible for a mere created being to make such a bold statement, unless He was God Himself. Merrill illustrates what it meant to walk in His ways:

> This way of describing a godly pattern of life is particularly native to covenant contexts, where "way" (דֶּרֶךְ, *derek*) is a metaphor for covenant fidelity. It is not surprising that the idiom occurs many times in Deuteronomy and the "Deuteronomistic" literature, given the covenant basis of that literature. Deut 8:6 commands Israel to walk in the ways of YHWH, an exhortation coupled with that of fearing Him. In the famous covenant charge of Deut 10:12-22, YHWH lists the requirements of the relationship: to fear Him, walk in His ways, love Him, serve Him, and keep His ordinances and statutes. The verb "keep" (שָׁמַר, *samar*) is the same as that in the second part of the charge to Joshua (Zech 3:7). A third example must suffice, that in Deut 28:9, where YHWH promises to make Israel a holy people (cf. Exod 19:6) if they "keep the Commandments" and "walk in his ways." The charge to Joshua the priest to walk in the ways of YHWH must clearly be seen in a covenant framework.[705]

---

[704] Unger, *A Zondervan Commentary: Zechariah: Prophet of Messiah's Glory*, 63.
[705] Merrill, *An Exegetical Commentary: Haggai, Zechariah, Malachi*, 137-138.

Not only is Joshua to walk in "*My way*", but he is to keep "*My charge,*" and is to judge "*My house*" [or people] and keep "*My courts.*" To keep "*My courts,*" Joshua will have to see to it that he keeps away everything of an idolatrous nature from the House of God and that nothing unclean or defiled would enter into it.[706]

What becomes very obvious is that this is covenant language and the LORD of Hosts Who has identified Himself as the Messenger (Angel) of the LORD three times and "*the angel*" once, is making a very clear claim to divinity. The LORD of Hosts continues by using two more clear words as to His identity. He tells Joshua to "*judge my house*" which probably refers to the temple proper whom Joshua the High Priest represents. Also He states that Joshua was to "*keep my courts,*" which is a reference to the temple and compound area. He uses "*my ways,*" "*my charge,*" "*my house*" and "*my courts.*" Notice all the "My" statements; these are possessive pronouns; they are God's ways, God's charge, God's house and God's court. He is speaking as the God of Israel, not as a created being who is an ordinary messenger of God.

There is one quick observation from Zechariah 3:8. The same speaker, the LORD of Hosts says, "*behold, I will bring forth my servant the BRANCH.*" The LORD of Hosts is speaking as God Who is One. The members of the plural unity of *Elohim*, the LORD, act and speak as one, yet They can act and speak as distinct persons of that plural unity of *echad* (one). The LORD Who has spoken all along is going to send "*my servant the BRANCH.*" That is a messianic title for the Messiah and will be dealt with in chapter 17.

The Messenger (Angel) of *Yahweh* speaks as *Yahweh*, showing not only that He is equal and one with *Yahweh* but also that He is distinct from *Yahweh*. Listed in the footnote are the other passages in the *Tanakh* of the Messenger (Angel) of *Yahweh*.[707]

In that day … Zechariah 12:8

In that day, the LORD will shield the inhabitants of Jerusalem; and the feeblest of them shall be in that day like David, and the House of David like a divine being – like an angel of the LORD – at their head.

Zechariah 12:8 is the last reference to "*the angel* [Messenger] *of the LORD*" in the *Tanakh*. It is not that "*the angel* [Messenger] *of the LORD*" is active or present in this

---

[706] Baron, *The Visions and Prophecies of Zechariah*, 104.

[707] Other references of the Messenger of *Yahweh* are: (a) Gen 16:7, 13 in connection with Hagar. (b) Abraham had visitors in Genesis 18, one of whom was the Messenger of *Yahweh*. (c) Gen 31:11-13; 32:24-30 dealt with two examples with Jacob. (d) Moses with his initial contact with the Messenger of *Yahweh* in Exod 3:2-15 when he is commissioned. (e) Josh 5:14-15 before the battle of Jericho, Joshua is confronted by the Captain of the Host. (f) Gideon is confronted with the Messenger of *Yahweh* in Judges 6:11-24 and (g) Manoah and his wife in Judg 13:2-24. (h) During the time of Hezekiah, the Messenger of *Yahweh* destroyed 185,000 Assyrian soldiers in 2 Kgs 19:35. (i) The last occurrence is in Zech 1:12-14, 3:6-8.

passage, but the inhabitants of Jerusalem will fight as David and the house of David shall be as God, as "*the angel* [Messenger] *of the LORD*" before their enemies. From this passage three things shall be discussed. First, what shall take place will be in "*that day*," a term indicating the last days or "*the Day of the LORD*." Second, three times Zechariah uses the word "as" which is a word of comparison. The remnant will be "as" David, and the house of David will be "as" God. Then the text clarifies itself by saying "as" "*the angel* [Messenger] *of the LORD*." In the days of the exodus and wandering in the wilderness "*the angel* [Messenger] *of the LORD*" protected, guided and instructed them. The striking comparison between *Elohim* and the Messenger of *Yahweh* is that They are the same, equal as is pointedly expressed by these two statements:

> He says He will make the house (dynasty) of David like God....He qualifies His comparison by saying that David's house will resemble the Angel of YHWH, that manifestation of God who was before them, that is who led the people of Israel in bygone days.[708]

> The house of David was to be as God, yet not as God in the abstract, of which no proper conception can be formed, but as God manifested to men in his glorious forthcomings under the ancient dispensation, in the Divine Person of the Son, who went before the children of Israel as their Almighty Leader and Protector, and to whom are vindicated the sum total of the Divine attributes.[709]

The clear conclusion is that "*the angel* [Messenger] *of the LORD*" Who made the Abrahamic Covenant (Judg 2:1), was the Author of the Mosaic Law. This Messenger (Angel) of the LORD also guided, protected, instructed and judged Israel in the wilderness for 40 years. He was also involved in the lives of at least three of the Judges, Gideon, Samson and Samuel, as the God of Israel. He revealed Himself in a personal way by manifesting Himself to mankind so that they could learn of His nature, character and essence, the Holy One of Israel. This one, "*the angel* [Messenger] *of the LORD*" is equal to *Elohim* and is one in the plural unity of *Elohim*, where He also shows forth His plurality.

Melchizedek

Many people as they have read through these chapters on theophanies are saying to themselves, where is the theophany of Melchizedek? The reason why it was not included was because I do not view Melchizedek as a theophany. So in the next pages the case for Melchizedek not being a theophany of God will be laid out.

The name Melchizedek is only mentioned two places in the *Tanakh* and several times in Hebrews 5-7 in the New Covenant (Testament). In Genesis 14:18-20 very little

---

[708] Merrill, *An Exegetical Commentary: Haggai, Zechariah, Malachi*, 316.
[709] Henderson, *Thornapple Commentaries: The Twelve Minor Prophets*, 429.

information about Melchizedek is given, but enough is given to achieve some basic important information. Below is the Scripture passage:

> (18) And King Melchizedek of Salem brought out bread and wine; he was a priest of God Most High. (19) He blessed him [Abraham], saying, "Blessed be Abram of God Most High, Creator of heaven and earth. (20) And blessed be God Most High, Who has delivered your foes into your hand." And [Abram] gave him a tenth of everything.

The second reference to Melchizedek is found in Psalm 110:4 which gives very little information except that he was a priest that was of a different order than the Levites. This passage also shows one very important distinction. The Messiah, the Lord of David, will be a priest, but of a different order than the Levitical order. This shows that the Levitical priesthood was not permanent, for the Son and Lord of David who will be priest after the order of Melchizedek will in the future replace the Levitical order for His order will be eternal (Psalm 110:4; Hebrews 7:1-28).

> The LORD hath sworn, and will not repent, Thou art a priest forever after the order of Melchizedek (Psalm 110:4 KJV).

Those are the only references in the *Tanakh* that mention Melchizedek. The New Covenant in the book of Hebrews mentions Melchizedek eight times (Hebrews 5:6, 10; 6:20; 7:1, 10-11, 15, 17).

Before Melchizedek is actually discussed, a review of what a theophany is would be in order. In chapter 4 it was observed that in a theophany, God became visible in the form of a man, or as the *Shechinah* (glory) of God, or was heard audibly as God spoke to Abraham in Genesis 22. Repeating the eight basic facts to refresh the mind concerning the appearances of God is appropriate at this time. The following is the list that was given back in chapter 4: (1) theophanies are actual appearances and not imaginary; (2) they are initiated by God; (3) they are revelatory, meaning that God's primary purpose was to reveal, at least in a partial manner, something about Himself or His will, to the recipient; (4) they were for individuals; (5) they were intermittent in appearance; (6) they were also temporary; (7) they were audible and visible, and lastly (8) they did vary in form.[710] The points that would raise a flag with Melchizedek would be points 5 and 6. In particular point 6 would go completely against Melchizedek being a theophany. In each of the theophanies that have been covered, except the *Shechinah*, all of the appearances are very temporary or very limited in time exposure. Melchizedek's exposure was not temporary or limited in time. Exposure in Scripture is limited, yes, but exposure on earth, no.

As to the person of Melchizedek, who is he? Most sources reference the Jewish tradition that Melchizedek was Shem, the son of Noah. There is nothing in the biblical

---

[710] Borland, *Christ in the Old Testament*, 21-30.

text that would substantiate that. Currid makes the following statement concerning the issue of Shem:

> Who is Melchizedek: A Midrashic (rabbinic) explanation is that Melchizedek is the patriarch Shem, the son of Noah, who is still alive in Abram's day. Indeed, Shem would have lived thirty-five years after Abram's death if one accepts that there are no gaps in the genealogies of Genesis 11.[711]

Theoretically that could be true, but as mentioned before there is no biblical support to identify Shem as Melchizedek. What does the Torah reveal concerning the identity of Melchizedek? Two very basic things are revealed about him; he is a priest-king from the city of Salem. This is a very important point. Theophanies according to all the other descriptions given are temporary manifestations of Messiah. In order to be a king of a city, an individual must be a permanent human resident on earth. Theophanies do not appear as a human king of a literal city on earth; they do not take on human responsibilities. Melchizedek was a real human being who was a literal king of Salem (Jerusalem).[712]

This would naturally bring another issue to bear. No theophany throughout this study has ever been named! The others were descriptive titles, like *"the angel of the LORD"* or the *"captain of the LORD's host."* Even when asked for His name, as in the case of Manoah in Judges 13:17-18, the *"angel of the LORD"* refused to give him His name.

There is another issue from the Genesis 14 account that also needs to be raised. Salem or Jerusalem was a Canaanite city, settled by the Jebusites (Genesis 15:21; Joshua 9:1-2; 10:3, 5, 23; Judges 1:21; 2 Samuel 5:6).[713] Melchizedek is an old Canaanite name.[714] So that would mean that Melchizedek, a Canaanite, was not even a descendant of Shem, but of Ham. To be more precise, he would have been a descendant of Canaan, son of Ham (Genesis 9:22, 25-26).

Then the question arises, how is it that with the idolatry of the Canaanites one king worshipped the true God? There were other godly men who worshipped the true God besides Abraham. Not only was there Melchizedek, but Job was a recognized contemporary with this man. There is a liberal teaching that monotheism developed out of polytheism. However, as McGee points out, the opposite was true, "that there was monotheism before polytheism. In other words, all men had a knowledge of the living and true God."[715] McGee goes on to remind the reader of Paul's words in the New Covenant book of Romans 1:18-32.

---

[711] Currid, *A Study Commentary on Genesis 1:1-18:25*, 1:286.

[712] Skinner, *The International Critical Commentary: Genesis,* 268.

[713] Morris, *The Genesis Record,* 318.

[714] Currid, *A Study Commentary on Genesis 1:1-18:25*, 1:286.

[715] J. Vernon McGee, *Thru the Bible: Genesis – Deuteronomy* (5 vols. Pasadena, CA: Thru The Bible Radio, 1981), 1:64.

The final issue in the Genesis reference to Melchizedek is the name itself. Melchizedek means "King of Righteousness" [716] (Hebrews 7:2), and he was the king of Salem or the King of Peace. This is the first time the word "shalom" is used in the Scriptures. In Joshua 10:1, 3 there was also a Jebusite king whose name was Adoni-zedek meaning "Lord our Righteousness." Adoni-zedek at the time of the conquest was a pagan king of Jerusalem and one of the confederation kings of the south that was killed in Joshua's conquest of the Promised Land, but the Benjaminites never captured the city (Judges 1:21). Melchizedek, who trusted the true God, and Adoni-zedek were separated by 400 years, but yet used the same dynastic name. Adoni-zedek was not a true worshipper of God but of the pagan gods of the Canaanites. It was strongly suggested that these two names were not names but rather royal titles. [717] The "zedek" of the name or title may very well have been the kingly name of the Jebusites, as Fruchtenbaum points out:

> Melchizedek was a priest-king; he was both priest and king. He was the king of Salem (Psa 76:2), which is also known as Jerusalem. The last part of his name, *zedek*, was a Jebusite dynastic name. Many years later, when Joshua came into the Land, he fought against the King of Jerusalem whose name was Adoni-*zedek* (Josh 10:1). Thus, Melchizedek's name was a Jebusite dynastic name. [718]

"Zedek" was used just as the Egyptians used the term "Pharaoh" for their kings. With the information given in the text of Genesis, and because nothing new is added as to the identity of Melchizedek in Psalm 110, Melchizedek is not a theophany. However, the New Covenant book of Hebrews makes the issue of identity of Melchizedek harder.

On the surface it would appear that the writer of the New Covenant book of Hebrews clouds the issue and makes it more difficult to give a precise answer. In Hebrews 7:3 he makes this statement concerning Melchizedek:

> Without father, without mother, without descent, having neither beginning of days, nor end of life; but made like unto the Son of God; abideth a priest continually.

However, one needs to know and understand the argument that the writer of Hebrews is presenting to the first-century Jewish believers in Messiah. That argument will be viewed here briefly for it involves the broader context of Hebrews than just the text above and the immediate surrounding verses. Two authors will be referenced to substantiate that Melchizedek was a type of Messiah, not the pre-incarnate Messiah. First Bruce expresses his understanding in the following statement:

---

[716] Keil and Delitzsch, *Commentary on the Old Testament in Ten Volumes: Genesis,* 1:208.

[717] Alexander and Baker, *Dictionary of the Old Testament: Pentateuch*, 563.

[718] Arnold G. Fruchtenbaum, *Ariel's Bible Commentary: The Messianic Jewish Epistles* (Tustin, CA: Ariel Ministries Press, 2003), 96.

The words which follow present an outstanding example of the argument from silence in a typological setting. When Melchizedek is described as being "without father, without mother, without genealogy, having neither beginning of days nor end of life," it is not suggested that he was a biological anomaly, or an angel in human guise. Historically Melchizedek appears to have belonged to a dynasty of priest-kings in which he had both predecessors and successors. If this point had been put to our author, he would have agreed at once, no doubt; but this consideration was foreign to his purpose. The important consideration was the account given of Melchizedek in holy writ; to him the silences of Scripture were as much due to divine inspiration as were its statements. In the only record which Scripture provides of Melchizedek – Gen 14:18-20 – nothing is said of his parentage, nothing is said of his ancestry or progeny, nothing is said of his birth, nothing is said of his death. He appears as a living man, king of Salem and priest of God Most High; and as such he disappears. In all this – in the silences as well as in the statements – he is a fitting type of Christ; in fact, the record by the things it says of him and by the things it does not say has assimilated him to the Son of God. It is the eternal being of the Son of God that is here in view; not His human life. Our author has no docetic view of Christ; he knows that "our Lord hath sprung out of Judah" [Hebrews 7:14]. But in His eternal being the Son of God has really, as Melchizedek has typically, "neither beginning of days nor end of life;" and more especially now, exalted at the right hand of God, He "abideth a priest continually." Melchizedek remains a priest continually for the duration of his appearance in the biblical narrative; but in the antitype Christ remains a priest continually without qualification. And it is not the type that determines the antitype, but the antitype that determines the type; Jesus is not portrayed after the pattern of Melchizedek, but Melchizedek is "made like unto the Son of God."[719]

The quote is lengthy, but it was important to get the context of Bruce to better understand the issue of the identity of Melchizedek. The second author can help any student who has difficulty understanding the identity and how Melchizedek and Messiah relate. Arnold Fruchtenbaum has written in his new book on Hebrews a very convincing and thorough argument as to the relationship between Melchizedek and Messiah. First he lists, with two pages of explanation, six comparisons between *Yeshua* and Melchizedek. What he does is relate Melchizedek and Messiah to the context between the Aaronic priesthood and the Melchizedekian priesthood. Secondly, he lists five reasons why Melchizedek cannot be a theophany:

(1) In this text he does not use an adjective that would describe Melchizedek in his being and essence to be like the Son of God; instead, he uses a participle, meaning that Jesus was similar to Melchizedek only in the likeness of the

---

[719] F. F. Bruce, *The New International Commentary on the New Testament: The Epistle to the Hebrews* (Grand Rapids: Eerdmans, 1964), 136-138.

biblical statement. The word used for being made is found only here in the Greek New Testament. (2) He states that Melchizedek was like the Son of God; it does not say that he "was" the Son of God in the Old Testament. (3) The second passage where he is mentioned, Psalm 110:4, distinguishes Melchizedek from the Messiah. (4) According to Hebrews 5:1, one of the pre-requisites for priesthood was that the priest had to be human. Jesus did not become a man until the incarnation when He was conceived by the Holy Spirit in the womb of Mary (Miriam). Before that time, Jesus appeared in the form of a man, but He was not an actual man. (5) Another reason why Melchizedek could not have been a theophany is that, in the Old Testament, theophanies appeared and disappeared; they held no long-term office. The Melchizedek of Genesis 14 was a king of the city-state of Jerusalem, which required a position and a permanent residency. Theophanies never had a position; they were always short and temporary manifestations.[720]

Fruchtenbaum's book is well worth reading. Both Bruce and Fruchtenbaum represent others who see Melchizedek not as a theophany but as a type of Messiah. Melchizedek becomes a very useful type of the Messiah long before the writer of Hebrews penned his words. David in Psalm 110 understood that someday the Levitical priesthood would be laid aside for a priest that would be eternal in the person of the Messiah of Israel, the Son of David, *Yeshua* of Nazareth, and His priesthood would be after the order of Melchizedek. He would not take on the priesthood until after He first fulfilled the purpose of His first coming.

In summary of chapters 5-8, every legitimate theophany of God has been viewed. In all of them the theophanies of God, whether it is *"the angel* [Messenger] *of the LORD,"* My Messenger, *"the captain of the LORD's host"* or an Angel (Messenger) that spoke as God, there is ample evidence in the *Tanakh* of the plurality of *Elohim*. Throughout the Genesis account in all the pre-Sinai theophanies, God revealed Himself to the Fathers. Then to Moses and the nation of Israel as well as to individuals like Gideon or prophets like Samuel or Zechariah, God also revealed Himself to His people, the vassal kingdom that was to serve Him alone. There is more than sufficient evidence to show that these theophanies were distinct from God, yet equal to God, full and equal members of the plural unity of *Elohim*.

---

[720] Fruchtenbaum, *Ariel's Bible Commentary: The Messianic Jewish Epistles*, 97-98.

Chapter 9
SHEMA

Hear, O Israel! The LORD is our God, the LORD alone. You shall love the LORD your God with all your heart and with all your soul and with all your might. Take to heart these instructions with which I charge you this day. Impress them upon your children. Recite them when you stay at home and when you are away, when you lie down and when you get up. Bind them as a sign on your hand and let them serve as a symbol on your forehead; inscribe them on the doorposts of your house and on your gates (Deuteronomy 6:4-9).

The *Shema* provides a statement of unity to both Jewish and Gentile believers of biblical faith. God is one and indivisible. He is Israel's God and their full attention and worship are to be directed to Him alone. The focus of attention is verse 4: "*Hear, O Israel! The LORD is our God, the LORD alone* [is one]." But on occasion the *Shema* of Deuteronomy 6:4 presents conflict and disagreements on the nature of God. Whether *Yahweh* is "one" alone as Rabbinic Judaism believes, or whether *Yahweh* is a plural unity or tri-unity as biblical New Covenant believes, there is much contention in relation to the actual meaning of the word *echad*,[721] which is at the center of the controversy between Rabbinic Judaism and biblical Christianity. Even though true biblical believers accept the belief in the tri-unity of God, many scholars, as documented in this chapter, do not see the plurality or tri-unity of God in Deuteronomy 6:4.

Resolving the difficulty of this text calls for a fivefold analysis: (1) the Jewish view of God and how Rabbinic Judaism views the *Shema* in comparison to the Christian view; (2) Christianity's struggles with the proper meaning of *echad*; (3) comments by Christian authors as to why *echad* should or should not be taken as one alone or as a tri-unity; (4) the significance of *yachid* in relationship to *echad*; and (5) this writer's conclusions and observations on *echad*.

---

[721] *Echad* will be used continuously in this and other chapters; it is translated as meaning "one." Judaism references it in Deuteronomy 6:4 to prove that God is an absolute one. However, the word is used repeatedly by Moses and the Prophets but they never use it in the context of an absolute one, but a one in plurality. This will be dealt with in this chapter and in Appendix Two. So I use it throughout this book when referencing God to affirm Him as a plural unity of one rather than Judaism's unfounded use as an absolute one.

JUDAISM

The *Shema* of Deuteronomy 6:4-9 is the cornerstone of the Jewish faith. In the *Shema*, verse 4 in particular, the word translated "*one*" from the Hebrew אֶחָד (*echad*) must be analyzed. The Jewish concept of the unity of God is grounded on a particular understanding of this word, *echad*, in the *Shema*.

Judaism is emphatic about the unity and oneness of God. God is pure spirit, an incorporeal being who cannot, in any way, become a man. Rabbinic Judaism sees New Covenant believers as Tri-theists, dividing God into three persons or parts, making the incarnation of God as a man totally irreconcilable in their minds. Jacobs, a Jewish author, states the following:

> There is only one God and there are no others. Allied to this is the idea that God in His essence is indivisible. A deity like Baal could be split up, as it were, into various local deities, hence the plural form Baalim and Ashterot found in the Bible when speaking of the pagan gods.[722]

> The polytheistic deities were thought of as separate beings, frequently in conflict with one another, each having a part of the universe for his or her domain. Monotheism denies the existence of such beings.[723]

Gerald Root comments that pagan mythology portrays each god as doing his or her own thing. However, there is no such conflict when there is one God. If there were many gods, there would be no uniformity in the universe, whereas with *Yahweh* there is no such conflict. For example: If *Yahweh* is in charge today, and He has made light to travel at 186,000 miles per second, and if tomorrow another god is in control and he wants light to travel at 50,000 miles per second, the whole universe would be in complete chaos. That is only one example of untold myriads of possible illustrations. God must be God, with no rivals.[724] An interesting passage comes to light in Jeremiah 10:11. This passage in Jeremiah is the only passage in Jeremiah that is in Aramaic, the language of the Babylonians. The verse states the following:

> Thus shall ye say unto them, The gods that have not made the heavens and the earth, even they shall perish from the earth, and from under these heavens.

It is as if Jeremiah were writing directly to the Babylonians who were to conquer Israel, their gods were not gods at all, they did not make heaven and earth (Isaiah 44:9-20). It is the God of Israel who will discipline Israel because they have chased after those gods

---

[722] Jacobs, *A Jewish Theology*, 21.

[723] Jacobs, *A Jewish Theology*, 22.

[724] Gerald Root, "*A Critical Investigation of Deuteronomy 6:4*" (B.D. thesis, Grace Theological Seminary, 1964), 42.

who are not gods. The Babylonian gods created nothing. God in Aramaic is telling Babylon that their gods are nothing and will perish from off the earth.[725]

Jacobs continues to state, along with Weiss-Rosmarin, the perception of Jewish scholars:

For many of them the idea of God's unity embraced the further idea that there is no multiplicity in His Being, that, as they expressed it, His was an "absolute simplicity."[726]

The Unity of God, sacred to Judaism beyond all else, is utterly irreconcilable with the Christian idea of the divisibility of the Divine Being and above all, with the belief in incarnation. According to Jewish belief God is pure spirit, eternally transcendent and divorced from even the slightest vestige of corporeality. Christianity, on the other hand, asserts that God became man in Jesus, a teaching which is contrary to the very spirit of Judaism.[727]

Is not this contrary to all Jewish teachings of God which emphasize and stress that God is not like man and can never become man or even resemble man?[728]

How, then, can the Jewish and Christian ideas of God be reconciled, or how can it be said that the "two religions are truly, basically one"? Is the One and Unique God, the absolute Unity – unknowable, indefinable – really the same as the Christian Trinity which divides the Unity of God into three, namely, God the Father, Jesus the Son and the Holy Spirit? Is the Jewish transcendent and purely spiritual belief in a God in Whom there is no trace of matter and Who can never become corporeal really the same as Christian belief which glories in God "who made man"?[729]

Sometimes true biblical authors such as Erickson make confusing statements that appear to support the Jewish concept of Christianity, that God is divisible, a plurality. Erickson says, "He (God) is an organism, that is, a unity of distinct parts."[730] True biblical New Covenant faith has never embraced God as being three parts of a whole, but most of the medieval church totally confused the issue, making it all but impossible for Jewish people to believe in the trinity or the tri-unity of God. Rabbinic Judaism cannot accept God becoming man, and equally Rabbinic Judaism cannot accept placing upon man divine qualities. This is reflected in Weiss-Rosmarin's statements:

Jewish Monotheism is not only the negation of the many gods but also the rejection of the personification of God on the one hand and of the deification of

---

[725] Feinberg, *Jeremiah*, 93.
[726] Jacobs, *A Jewish Theology*, 27.
[727] Weiss-Rosmarin, *Judaism and Christianity*, 21.
[728] Weiss-Rosmarin, *Judaism and Christianity*, 21.
[729] Weiss-Rosmarin, *Judaism and Christianity*, 21-22.
[730] Erickson, *Introducing Christian Doctrine*, 100.

human beings on the other. Judaism's refusal to worship Jesus is therefore not only due to its repudiation of the doctrine of incarnation, the belief that God became a person, but equally so to its defiant resistance to all and any attempts of according Divine qualities and honors to mere mortals.[731]

Catholicism as well as Protestantism worships persons and the images of persons. However, while Catholicism venerates in addition to Jesus a large and still expanding pantheon of Saints and their relics, besides devoting a special cult to the worship of the "Mother of God."[732]

Generally speaking, Jewish people view Christianity from the theological background of Roman Catholicism because it was the Church under Roman leadership that they primarily had to deal with in the past. It is primarily the Roman Catholic Church's corrupt teaching that has dealt with Jewish people so treacherously over the centuries. But Protestants equally are not free from guilt in the negative treatment of Jewish people. To Rabbinic Judaism, God is a pure spirit being, and it is inconceivable that a man could be God or that God would become man. Rabbinic Judaism holds, with unwavering dogmatism, that man is nothing more than man. True believers would completely agree with their assertion of man but differ in the biblical Christian belief that God can become a man.

To Judaism man is man and God is God and shall remain God in unequalled and eternal majesty.[733]

The man Moses has been its watchword through the ages; thus it has warded off all attempts to enthrone any mortal as God. With equal consistency it has refused to admit the possibility of any man's sharing in God's perfection, or the incarnation of God in any human being.[734]

During the Middle Ages the Jewish assertion of God's unity became an explicit denial of the Christian dogma of the Trinity, a total disavowal of the thesis that God, though one, is somehow at the same time three persons, "co-eternal and co-equal."[735]

These statements reveal the antagonism of Rabbinic Judaism towards the Christian teaching on the Trinity, and rightly so, because of the unbiblical, anti-Semitic positions the Church has held. The Church, through the church fathers, laid the foundation for the anti-Semitism that was practiced against the Jews for well over 1700 years.[736] One long quote suffices to reflect the hatred of the Jew by the Church and even by great men of

---

[731] Weiss-Rosmarin, *Judaism and Christianity*, 23.

[732] Weiss-Rosmarin, *Judaism and Christianity*, 24.

[733] Weiss-Rosmarin, *Judaism and Christianity*, 26.

[734] Weiss-Rosmarin, *Judaism and Christianity*, 27.

[735] Milton Steinberg, *Basic Judaism* (New York: A Harvest/HBJ Book, 1947), 45.

[736] Stan Telchin, *Abandoned* (Grand Rapids, Baker Book House, 1997), 51-72.

the Reformation who themselves were products of the Roman Church. Martin Luther's statement is enough to point out the anti-Semitism of Christendom:

> First, he urged, 'their synagogues should be set on fire, and whatever is left should be buried in dirt so that no one may ever be able to see a stone or cinder of it.' Jewish prayer-books should be destroyed and rabbis forbidden to preach. Then the Jewish people should be dealt with, their homes 'smashed and destroyed' and 'their inmates put under one roof or in a stable like gypsies, to teach them they are not master in our land.' Jews should be banned from the roads and markets, their property seized and then these 'poisonous envenomed worms' should be drafted into forced labour and made to earn their bread 'by the sweat of their noses.'[737]

This is enough to set the tone for the unbiblical attitudes and actions of the Church for centuries. More could be written, but that is not the purpose of this book. The Jewish position, which was firm to begin with, became a granite rock. In summary, God is one to the Jewish people, period! To them, belief in the incarnation is inconceivable.

CHRISTIANITY

Rabbinic Judaism today views Paul, the Hellenized Pharisee, rather than *Yeshua*, as the founder of Christianity. Pryor points out that the New Covenant letters provide impressive evidence that the early first-century believers in the (Jewish) church had the highest Christology.[738] Peter was very clear in his letters that *Yeshua* is God (1 Peter 1:1-25; 2:21-24; 4:11; 2 Peter 1:16, 18) the Saviour, Redeemer and resurrected Lord. James spoke of himself as the "*bond-servant*" of *Yeshua* (James 1:1) and challenged his readers to "*hold your faith in our glorious Lord Jesus Christ*" (2:1). Jude is clear that *Yeshua* is Saviour: "*be glory, majesty, dominion and authority, before all time and now and forever*" (verse 25). John, in the first chapter of both his Gospel and in his First Epistle, clearly states that *Yeshua* is God. The theme of the writer of Hebrews is that *Yeshua* is better than the angels, Moses, priesthood and sacrifices. James, Peter, Jude, John and the writer of Hebrews, who knew Paul, did not just copy Paul's theology, because they rarely saw each other. The early Jewish Church knew who *Yeshua* was by living, teaching, and dying for their belief that *Yeshua* was the Messiah of Israel, the God/man.

The understanding of Deuteronomy 6:4, through the eyes of Christianity, will differ depending on how the tri-unity of God is viewed in the Hebrew Scriptures. *Echad* has become a somewhat difficult word to interpret, or has it been given a narrow restricted definition by Rabbinic Judaism because of the impact of a true witness of biblical believers?

---

[737] Paul Johnson, *A History of the Jews* (New York, HarperPerennial, 1988), 242.
[738] Pryor, "One God and Lord," *Mishkan*, no. 39 (2003), 55.

First, in considering verse 4 of Deuteronomy 6 in the Hebrew the *Shema* revolves around four words — יְהוָה אֱלֹהֵינוּ יְהוָה אֶחָד (LORD our God, LORD is one). There is no problem in belief or interpretation with "*Shema* Israel." Nor is there a problem in belief or interpretation with יְהוָה אֱלֹהֵינוּ ("LORD our God") except the way *Elohenu* is viewed ("our Gods" or "God").[739] *Yahweh* is Israel's personal name for their *Elohim* who is the Creator and Covenant Maker! The major problem lies with יְהוָה אֶחָד ("LORD is one,") that God is "one" in regard to interpretation, which will affect belief. *Yahweh* is One, but the difficulty is what is meant by "one."

Although Herbert Wolf suggests that the lexical and syntactical difficulties of אֶחָד יְהוָה ("LORD is one") are evident in numerous translations, all aspects of the challenge can be represented by four common translations. The "LORD is one" is translated four different ways, each of which incorporates a specific aspect of their interpretation.

The first view of Deuteronomy 6:4 is "the LORD is our God, the LORD alone."[740] Wolf's explanation of his option above is that it has in its favor both the broad and immediate context of the book of Deuteronomy. The *Shema* serves as the introduction to motivate Israel to keep the command to love the LORD (verse 5). This notion suits this command in verse 5 very well because the LORD is Israel's unique God Who stands alone, and Israel's obligation is to love that God.

The second view of Deuteronomy 6:4 expresses the interpretation as LORD our God: LORD is unique (only one).[741] Lohfink and Bergmann state that *echad* should be understood as "only one," or "unique one." This is one God who led them, loved them (Deuteronomy 5:10) and gave them the law. God did it without the help of foreign gods (Deuteronomy 32:12). The *Shema* saw Israel's obligation to respond to this unique God in love by being obedient to the Law, which included the Decalogue. Points one and two seem to be very close in their views.

The third view of Deuteronomy 6:4 in looking at the *Shema* is "the LORD our God, the LORD is one." Jenson points out:

> The syntax of the verbless sentence is disputed, but analogy with other uses of "LORD our God" in Deut. suggests that the traditional syntax should be retained ("The LORD our God, the LORD is One"). [742]

He points out further that "one" is not a title or name of God but an adjective of quality. The correlation between the two halves of Deuteronomy 6:4 suggests that the interpretation of *Shema* is not pointed against the polytheism of the day or to a non-abstract monotheism, but it is a claim to Israel's total obedience to the exclusion of all others.

---

[739] Hayford, *The Trinity*, 16.

[740] Harris, Archer, and Waltke, *Theological Wordbook of the Old Testament*, 1:30.

[741] Botterweck, Ringgren, and Fabry, *Theological Dictionary of the Old Testament*, 1:196.

[742] VanGemeren, *Dictionary of Old Testament Theology and Exegesis,* 1:350.

The last view of Deuteronomy 6:4 says the LORD our God, the LORD, is a unity of one.[743] The essence of oneness is linked to the *Shema*, and the *echad* is a compound or complex unity, a united one. This view not only includes the uniqueness and oneness of God but also the unity of God expressed in three persons. This oneness, yet a compound unity, possesses the summation of all divine attributes and persons which in their essence are undivided. These three persons of the tri-unity do not act independently of one another.

All four of the above positions hold to the basic truth that God is "one alone," "unique one," the only one to be loved and worshipped. The last position agrees with the other three but adds the dimension that all that was said of the other three is true. It adds that God is a compound or complex unity, and the word *echad* expresses that interpretation (Genesis 1:5; 2:24).

McConville gives the same points for possible interpretation but says nothing concerning the unity of God or how the word *echad* is used. However, he does give two additional helpful points in determining how the word is used but again with no conclusions:

Between the other renderings the chief difference concerns whether to translate *echad* as an adjective, "one," or an adverb "alone."

It differs from the First Commandment (Deut 5:7) in that the emphasis falls heavily on the word "one."[744]

McConville states that the problem of how *echad* is to be translated, whether as an adjective or as an adverb, is at the center of the question, but he gives no conclusion. He also admits that the emphasis, the thrust, the focus of the verse is on *echad*. His statements do not include the plural unity of God, but he does reinforce the fact that this word *echad* is the focus of attention by Moses. This author believes the key to understanding the verse is to see just how this word *echad* is used, first by Moses, and then by the rest of the *Tanakh* (See Appendix 2 concerning the usage of *echad* in the Torah.).

In the preceding paragraphs it was observed that *echad* is interpreted four ways. Now the usages of this word will be observed. *Echad* is used 970 times throughout the Hebrew Scriptures.[745] What is meant by this word? Does the word indicate one of unity, one alone, one of uniqueness or one in plurality? Smith says that the precise meaning is unclear.[746] That is seen from the previous paragraph with the four possible usages of *echad*. Do those who believe in the tri-unity read too much into *echad*? The immediate

---

[743] Enns, *The Moody Handbook of Theology*, 199-200.

[744] J. G. McConville, *Apollos Old Testament Commentary: Deuteronomy* (Downer Grove, IL: InterVarsity, 2002), 140-142.

[745] Jenni and Westermann, *Theological Lexicon of the Old Testament,* 1:79.

[746] Ralph L. Smith, *Old Testament Theology: its History, Method, and Message* (Nashville: Broadman and Holman, 1993), 226-227.

context of the word in the book of Deuteronomy requires that *Yahweh* is the one and only God and Israel's personal God.[747] Both Judaism and New Covenant faith of believers would not disagree with this view. Evans has noted that *echad*, which expresses the plural unity of the Godhead, is not simple but compound and is always used to describe a divine unity.[748]

According to Payne the *Shema* teaches that:

This passage does not primarily concern a divine unity of simplicity; that God constitutes a unity within Himself, in contrast, for example, with Baal, who was splintered up so as to exist separately in countless individual plots of ground (hence the plural, the Baalim). It concerns rather the divine unity of singularity; that God constitutes the sole deity, as opposed to others, which is the essence of monotheism.[749]

Verse 5, which says "*Love the LORD thy God with all thine heart*," is only relevant because God is the only one.[750] The *Tanakh*, as it recorded the Prophets and the Writings, affirms the fact of Moses' monotheism. The people, however, as a whole, did not love the Lord because they worshipped other gods and did not worship God alone.

USAGES OF *ECHAD*

Gerald Janzen in his journal article is devoted to the *Shema*, but fails to show the importance of *echad* in the *Shema*. The *Shema* is the most significant verse in which *echad* appears, and the question is how it is interpreted in the *Shema*. Other references to *echad* throughout the *Tanakh* should be analyzed in relation to its immediate context so that the Deuteronomy 6:4 passage can be clearly understood as to whether it is one alone, a one in context of plurality, a compound one or a compound unity. Upon reading Janzen's article, this most important word *echad* is not dealt with in relation to the issue of oneness and/or compound unity as it relates to the *Shema*. He refers to *echad* in several passages in the *Tanakh* without any relationship to the immediate context (Deuteronomy 6:4). He does seem to embrace *echad* as being one "alone." He consistently refers to the broader context of Deuteronomy 6:4-5. Janzen's article lacks evidence of a biblical study of the word *echad* and how it is used in the *Tanakh*, in the *Shema* and elsewhere.[751]

An analysis of the Hebrew Scriptures uncovers three distinct usages of the term "*echad*." The word "*echad*" is first used as a compound unity.[752] It is two separate

---

[747] Botterweck, Ringgren, and Fabry, *Theological Dictionary of the Old Testament*, 1:196.

[748] William Evans, *The Great Doctrines of the Bible* (Chicago: Moody, 1974), 26-27.

[749] Payne, *The Theology of the Older Testament*, 126.

[750] Payne, *The Theology of the Older Testament*, 126.

[751] J. Gerald Janzen, "On The Most Important Word In The Shema (Deuteronomy VI 4-5)," *Vetus Testamentum* 37, 3 (1987): 280-300.

[752] Harris, Archer, and Waltke, *Theological Wordbook of the Old Testament*, 1:30.

persons becoming an *echad*, a unity in Genesis 2:24 which says, "*Therefore shall a man leave his father and his mother, and shall cleave unto his wife; and they shall be one [echad] flesh.*" Genesis 11:1 applies the same concept to language: "*And the whole earth as of one [echad] language, and of one speech.*" All humanity had *echad* speech. The spies, upon returning from Canaan in Numbers 13:23, brought with them a cluster (*echad*) of grapes. Exodus 24:3, Judges 20:1 and Ezra 3:1 picture the nation of Israel answering God with one (*echad*) voice and gathering before the Lord as one (*echad*) man. In Ezekiel 37:17, 19, 22, Ezekiel is told by God to put together two sticks as an *echad* stick, "*And join them one to another into one [echad] stick…even with the stick of Judah, and make them one [echad] stick, … and I will make them one [echad] nation in the land.*" The two sticks represented the houses of Israel and Judah being joined together, in the future, as one *echad* nation. Other references that support two separate units becoming one are found in Genesis 34:22, Exodus 25:36, Numbers 14:15, Joshua 10:42, 1 Samuel 11:7b, 1 Kings 22:13b, 2 Chronicles 5:13, 30:12, Nehemiah 8:1, Proverbs 1:14, Jeremiah 32:39 and Malachi 2:10. In actual reality this "unity" concept of *echad* is used the least amount of times among the three divisions that will be mentioned in this section, yet it has become the focal point in discussions of Deuteronomy 6:4.

A second way *echad* is used is to show things or persons in relationships that do not require a compound unity, as in the first category.[753] However, it is still within a plural context, as in Exodus 17:12:

> "*But Moses' hands were heavy; and they took a stone and put it under him, and he sat thereon; and Aaron and Hur stayed up his hands, the one (echad) on the one side, and the other [echad] on the other side and his hands were steady until the going down of the sun.*"

The same *echad* is also applied to offerings. In Leviticus 12:8, for example, sacrificial animals are considered *echad*: "*And if she be not able to bring a lamb, then she shall bring two turtledoves, or two young pigeons; the one [echad] for the burnt offering and the other [echad] for a sin offering.*" Samson, in Judges 16:29, also uses the context of plurality where it says he "*took hold of the two middle pillars upon which the house stood, and on which it was borne up of the one [echad] with his right hand, and the other [echad] with his left.*" After David's sin with Bathsheba, Nathan comes before David with the story in 2 Samuel 12:1 of two men in a city, "*one [echad] was rich and the other [echad] poor.*" These references all illustrate the context of plurality but not as a compound unity. Other references show the same concept (Genesis 21:15; Exodus 25:19; Numbers 6:11; Deuteronomy 21:15; Josh 4:2; 1 Samuel 1:2; 1 Kings 3:25; 2 Kings 6:5; 1 Chronicles 29:1 and 2 Chronicles 3:17). This usage of *echad* is used more frequently than the other two.

---

[753] VanGemeren, *Dictionary of Old Testament Theology and Exegesis,* 1:349.

A third way *echad* is used is to indicate the separateness and individuality of a thing or person. This division will be reflected in three parts. The first denotes one standing among others.[754] The second, as seen in Joshua, demonstrates a cardinal 'one' as he enumerates the kings one by one (Joshua 12:9-24). The third is used as an ordinal (first or first one) number as seen in Exodus 40:17 when the tabernacle was set up on the *echad* or first day of the first month.[755] Additional passages that demonstrate this third type of *echad* include Genesis 33:13; Exodus 23:29; Leviticus 23:18; Numbers 7:13-82; Deuteronomy 17:6; Joshua 12:9-24; Judges 9:53; 1 Samuel 26:8; 2 Samuel 12:3; 1 Kings 2:16; 11:13; 2 Kings 8:26; 2 Chronicles 18:7. An interesting factor is that even when *echad* is used as an individual one, its context often is dealing with two or more of something. The term is usually referring to a singular object within a larger context of many. In Numbers 7:11-82, *echad* is used 85 times; in Numbers 29:1-38 an additional 24 times; in Joshua 12:9-24; 32 times as a cardinal one, in which is a total of 141 times in an individual sense.

With these three factors in mind, how do scholars interpret *echad* in Deuteronomy 6:4? It seems that the oneness of God is not the question, but the compound unity and plurality of God is the area of discussion.

Comments by Christian Authors on Echad

This section is divided into two parts: those who do not see and those who do see the plurality (or tri-unity) of God in Hebrew Scriptures, and in particular, Deuteronomy 6:4. Christian authors are divided over the interpretation of the term "*echad*," except that Moses affirmed the oneness, uniqueness, and the unity of *Elohim*. Only with a passing notice do they say that *echad* may mean a compound one of unity. Herbert Wolf states that *echad* is singular, but the usage of the word "*echad*" in the *Shema* allows for the New Testament teaching of the Trinity. The doctrine of the Trinity is foreshadowed in the Hebrew Scriptures, but this verse concentrates on the fact that God is one and that Israel owes its exclusive loyalty to Him (Deuteronomy 5:9; 6:5).[756] Wolf merely speaks of compound unity, along with other possible usages of the word.

Echad *not seen as Compound Unity*

Lohfink and Bergman basically say that Deuteronomy 6:4 is to be regarded as a reiteration of the love motif in Deuteronomy 5:10 which states, "*but showing kindness to the thousandth generation of those who love Me and keep My commandments.*"

---

[754] Harris, Archer, and Waltke, *Theological Wordbook of the Old Testament*, 1:30.
[755] VanGemeren, *Dictionary of Old Testament Theology and Exegesis,* 1:350.
[756] Harris, Archer, and Waltke, *Theological Wordbook of the Old Testament*, 1:30.

The demand for love is itself one of the many formulations of the fundamental demand made on Israel to worship *Yahweh* alone and not any of the other gods.[757]

These two scholars continue by saying that Deuteronomy 6:4 can be interpreted as two nominative sentences in sequence. This means that "*Yahweh our God*," is taken and pressed to mean that God, though plural, is to be taken as singular, and the second half of the passage, "*Yahweh is one*" is used to express this God as being one. They also mention that it could be taken as one nominative sentence, with three different possibilities, as to subject and predicate:

> …that Deuteronomy 6:4 contains a 'mono-Yahwistic' statement: a statement made in opposition to dividing *Yahweh* into many local individual *Yahwehs*.[758]

Lohfink and Bergman do not even discuss the possibility of a compound unity. They emphasize only the oneness, uniqueness, and unity of God.

Philip Jenson refers to five usages of *echad* in the Hebrew text. He claims that the *Shema* is not intended to do three things as referenced in the statement below, but that it does affirm monotheism. However, no hint is even given to the placement of the *Shema* into the category of one in the context of plurality or a compound unity in his summary statement:

> The correlation between the two halves of the sentence and the following verses suggests that this is not so much an abstract monotheism as a claim to Israel's total obedience and the exclusion of any other [cf. Deut 5:7]. The immediate context does not suggest that it is directed against polytheism or different ideas of *Yahweh* found in local cults. Nor is this idea used to support the deut. program of the centralization of worship. However, in the broader context of Deut and the OT it can imply unity, uniqueness, and monotheism.[759]

Sauer, in *Theological Lexicon of the Old Testament*, says that Deuteronomy 6:4 may refer to God as a cardinal one. He gives two possible translations to the last phrase: "*is one Yahweh*" or "*Yahweh is one* (alone)." His summary statement says that this passage "most clearly expresses *Yahweh's* unity and exclusivity" and that the statement "is embedded in the commandment to love this unique LORD."[760]

While the authors have helpful information, they do not interact with the relationship between *Yahweh* and *Elohim* or *echad* with *Yahweh* and *Elohim*. They look at *echad* within the larger context of the Hebrew Scriptures to determine its possible usage in Deuteronomy 6:4. They all affirm the unity, oneness and uniqueness of God.

---

[757] Botterweck, Ringgren and Fabry, *Theological Dictionary of the Old Testament*, 1:196.

[758] Botterweck, Ringgren and Fabry, *Theological Dictionary of the Old Testament*, 1:197.

[759] VanGemeren, *Dictionary of Old Testament Theology and Exegesis*, 1:349-350.

[760] Jenni and Westermann, *Theological Lexicon of the Old Testament*, 1:79.

But in the opinion of this author, they do not even give *echad* a look as to the possibility of the plurality of God within their interpretations.

Other authors say little, either pro or con. Enns, as an example, simply states that the essence of God is linked to Deuteronomy 6:4 with *echad* being a compound unity or united one. There is no real explanation of how he arrived at that position.[761]

Peter Craigie speaks to the fact that *echad* can be rendered in a number of different ways, stating that one could be a title or name of God. He affirms the uniqueness and unity of God but says nothing about the possibility of *echad* being a compound one.[762]

Eugene Merrill does not deal with *echad* as a compound unity, but he makes this interesting observation of the text:

> The Divine Name should be construed as a nominative in each case and the terms "our God" and "one" as parallel predicate nominatives.[763]

This statement is saying that "LORD" in both cases, is nominative and "our God" and "one" are the predicates. The predicate describes the LORD as (1) *Elohim* and as (2) one. The two words describe, or are reflective of, the nominative. Merrill drops the statement at that point and does not explain what he was trying to establish. This subject and explanation are again discussed at the end of this chapter.

David Hinson does not deal with *echad* as a compound unity. He simply affirms the concept of God being a unity. However, Hinson raises an interesting question:

> But is there any evidence that people of Old Testament times began to share in thoughts which would gradually lead to the New Testament doctrine of the Trinity? Did God provide them with experiences which would prepare the way for belief in the Trinity? Were they, without full realization, experiencing God the Trinity?[764]

Hinson follows up the previous remarks with three sections on wisdom, the Word of God and the Spirit of God, which provide helpful information. But it was also very disappointing that he does not deal with *Elohim, El, Eloah, Yahweh,* and Lord in their relationship to each other. His defining statement is:

> Some readers may ask why God's revelation of himself in Old Testament times omitted the idea of the Trinity. The answer seems to be that the Jews needed first to grasp the truth about the Unity of God.[765]

---

[761] Enns, *The Moody Handbook of Theology,* 199-200.

[762] P. C. Craigie, *The New International Commentary on the Old Testament: The Book of Deuteronomy* (Grand Rapids: Eerdmans, 1976), 168-169.

[763] Merrill, *The New American Commentary: Deuteronomy,* 4:163.

[764] Hinson, *Theology of the Old Testament,* 50.

[765] Hinson, *Theology of the Old Testament,* 49.

The whole point of the *Tanakh* is that God did not omit the idea of the plurality and tri-unity from the pages of the Hebrew Scriptures.

Reginald Fuller clearly reveals his mockery and unbelief in relationship to the Scriptures. However, he does make one very helpful statement concerning Judaism moving toward recognizing distinctions within the Godhead:

> But already the Judaic tradition was moving to the direction of recognizing distinctions within the activity of God. These activities included creation, revelation/redemption, and in-dwelling presence. It was also moving in the direction of distinctions within the being of God, distinctions corresponding to these activities, ascribing them to the Wisdom of Word (logos) and the Spirit of God. Judaism did not go very far in this direction, but the direction was certainly established. The Christian community was impelled to move much further, though still in the same direction. Thus it eventually developed the doctrine of the Trinity. This development was not a deviation from the Hebrew Scriptures but a continuation of a process already begun. On the other hand, those who remained under the first covenant backtracked from this line of development.[766]

Fuller's comments on Judaic tradition moving in the direction of recognizing distinctions within the activity of God would be an extremely interesting subject to follow through. What did Fuller see in his research that prompted his remarks? That will have to be a future study. The first-century believers in Messiah did clearly see the distinctions in the Godhead.

Marvin Wilson gives some valuable information on the *Shema* and its background from the Inter-testament Period and during the life and times of *Yeshua*. Wilson is strong on the unity of God but not on the compound unity. His defining statement is:

> In the Old Testament *echad* usually refers to a single unit, such as a person. Certain interpreters have insisted, however, that *echad* may also be used to designate a collective unit (Gen. 1:5; 2:24; Num. 13:23), a diversity within unity. Thus some Christian scholars have found room for trinitarian monotheism in the *echad* of Deuteronomy 6:4. So interpreted, God is seen as a complex unity, not simply as numerically one. It must be remembered, however, that the main focus of the *Shema* in its original setting – ancient Near Eastern polytheism – is clearly upon the fact that there is one God. (Deut. 4:39).[767]

It is true that the original setting was clearly to promote monotheism, but to say that it rules out the possibility of a compound or complex unity is unwarranted.

---

[766] Reginald H. Fuller, "The *Vestigia Trinitatis* in the Old Testament," in *The Quest for Context and Meaning* (ed. Craig A. Evans and Shemaryahu Talmon, Leiden, Netherlands: Brill, 1997), 507.

[767] Marvin R. Wilson, *Our Father Abraham* (Grand Rapids: Eerdmans, 1989), 125.

Although Paul House states that *Yahweh* is unique and possesses a unified character, he makes no mention of God being a compound one.[768]

Ernest Wright, in *The Interpreter's Bible*, holds the *Shema* to be a statement of "Israel's exclusive attention, affection, and worship and is not diffused, but single."[769] He affirms the unity and oneness of God.

The *Shema* is of great importance, not just for the Jewish people and the whole discussion of the oneness and plural unity of *Elohim*, but also for believers of biblical faith in discussing the theological impact of this verse, "*Hear, O Israel! The LORD is our God, the LORD is one.*" It is surprising that many Christian scholars do not generally acknowledge as a legitimate argument that *echad* is a compound or complex unity of God. Apparently these scholars deem *echad* and the truth of God being a compound or complex unity as unimportant. Based on their concept of how *Elohim* and the tri-unity of God are treated, in general, Christian scholars do not avoid or shy away from the fact that God is speaking of monotheism, but they do avoid the issue that He has stated that He is a plurality of unity, as has been pointed out earlier in this book.

Echad *seen as Compound Unity*

Some authors do acknowledge that the *Shema* presents God simultaneously as both "one" and a compound unity. A select group of scholars openly acknowledge the fact of the compound unity of God and even state so emphatically, but often without supporting their statements. Gerald Root, in his thesis on Deuteronomy 6:4, makes several statements that only deal with the unity of God.

> The answer is this: the verse emphasizes the unity of God rather than the Trinity, but it does not deny God's Tri-unity. The verse does not concern itself with the question and neither affirms nor denies the Trinity.[770]

> If God is One, in what sense is He One? He is one אֶחָד God but three Persons. The normal usage of this word allows such an interpretation.[771]

In referring to Genesis 2:24, 11:6, and Exodus 24:3 which all deal with *echad* as being a compound unity, he says:

> It is evident that that word cannot be restricted to the sense of only or alone.[772]

---

[768] House, *Old Testament Theology,* 178.

[769] George Arthur Buttrick, *The Interpreter's Bible* (Nashville: Abingdon, 1953), 2:372-373.

[770] Root, "A Critical Investigation of Deuteronomy 6:4," 38.

[771] Root, "A Critical Investigation of Deuteronomy 6:4," 38.

[772] Root, "A Critical Investigation of Deuteronomy 6:4," 39.

Root is not avoiding the compound unity of God, but he does not come out strongly for it, even though he goes much further than the previous texts cited. Here is his statement of summary for his position:

> It was God's choice of the word to lead Israel away from idolatry and emphasize His unity, and yet elastic enough to permit a far greater revelation of Himself at a later time. Nor could the argument be used that this word has not as of this time obtained this particular meaning, for it was used long before and after God's revelation in Deuteronomy 6:4.[773]

Root presents the oneness of God very strongly and the compound unity of God in an open, meaningful manner, but without commitment.

When speaking of *echad*, Thomas A. Thomas strongly presents not just the unity of God, but the compound unity of God. He points out that there are two ways to look at *echad*:

> There are at least two senses in which the word one can be used; namely, first of all, in the sense of a compound unity, or, in the second place, in the sense of a single unit; that is, either more than one object composing a whole, or the whole being made up of only a single object. The question, then, is, in which of these two senses is the word אֶחָד to be taken?[774]

He discusses Genesis 2:24, Numbers 13:23 and Judges 20:1 as examples to support a compound unity. His defining statement is:

> It is clearly the term used to express compound unity. Consequently, then, it is quite possible that when Moses declares in Deuteronomy 6:4 "Hear, O Israel: the Lord our God is one (אֶחָד) Lord" he is using the term in this sense. God is one, it is true, but why not in the sense that a man and his wife are one, and the cluster of grapes is one, or as the whole congregation of Israel is one? There is no internal reason why it could not be so used.[775]

This statement clearly supports the Hebrew word "*echad*" as being a compound or complex "one."

Lewis Sperry Chafer clearly raises the two possible views of *echad*. First, he states that God is One and there is no other. Secondly, he cites Genesis 1:5; 2:24 as a possibility that *echad* is a compound unity.[776] Chafer simply raises the issue and then drops it, without further explanation.

---

[773] Root, "A Critical Investigation of Deuteronomy 6:4," 40.

[774] Thomas A. Thomas, "*The Trinity in the Old Testament*" (Th. M. thesis, Dallas Theological Seminary, 1952), 4-5.

[775] Thomas, "The Trinity in the Old Testament," 7.

[776] Chafer, *Chafer Systematic Theology*, 1:266-267.

Jim Nixon points out that Deuteronomy 6:4 allows for the plurality of God. He further says that it does not teach the tri-unity of God but the plurality of God.[777] His position is that the *Shema* teaches exclusive monotheism as well as being plural, with the total denial of any other god.[778]

Henry Heydt, former president of Lancaster Bible College in Lancaster, PA states very clearly his position on the *Shema* by affirming the oneness and compound oneness with *echad* in the following statement:

> The Jew does not understand the Christian doctrine of the Trinity (tri-unity) because he does not understand the teaching of his own Scriptures on unity. There are two kinds of oneness, absolute oneness and compound oneness, and the Hebrew has two words to express these. The word for absolute oneness is *yachid*[779] (Gen 22:2, 12, 16).

Stan Rosenthal,[780] Louis Goldberg,[781] Arnold Fruchtenbaum[782] and Robert Morris[783] take Deuteronomy 6:4 and show it as a compound unity of God in the Hebrew Scriptures. They see *Elohim* as a plurality of God and *echad* as a complex or compound unity of God.

The next three authors were the only three men who dealt with the issue of the plurality of God in a concrete detailed manner. The others have said, variously, nothing, or only alluded to a compound unity, or made strong statements in its favor. But even those who made strong statements of belief did not give a comprehensive study of *echad*.

In dealing with two Jewish objections to the tri-unity of God, Michael Brown presents Deuteronomy 6:4 in a detailed apologetic format on the plurality and tri-unity of God in conjunction with *echad*.[784] One example shows some of the interpretative problems that come with absolute oneness, which is the rabbinic approach:

> The rabbis spoke much about the *Shekhina*, the Divine Presence, corresponding also to the feminine, motherly aspects of God. They taught that the *Shekhina* went into exile with the Jewish people, suffering with "her" children in foreign lands. According to this concept, God cannot be "whole" again until his people

---

[777] Jim Nixon, "*The Doctrine of the Trinity in the Old Testament*" (Th. M. thesis, Dallas Theological Seminary, 1974), 11-12.

[778] Nixon, "The Doctrine of the Trinity in the Old Testament," 22-23.

[779] Henry Heydt, *Studies in Jewish Evangelism* (New York: American Board to the Jews, 1951), 124.

[780] Rosenthal, *One God or Three?* 17-26.

[781] Goldberg, *Our Jewish Friends*, 80-83.

[782] Fruchtenbaum, *Messianic Christology*, 108.

[783] Morris, *Anti-Missionary Arguments: The Trinity*, 14-16.

[784] Michael Brown, *Answering Jewish Objections: Theological Objections* (Grand Rapids: Baker, 2000), 2:3-37.

return from their physical and spiritual wanderings and the Temple is rebuilt. The rabbis based this idea on verses that spoke of God being with his people (corporately or individually) in their trouble, distress, and exile.[785]

This explanation of the Jewish people says that God is divisible and will not be whole again until Israel, as a nation, is regathered from every nation on earth and re-established in the Land. So much for rabbinic teaching of God being a unity and indivisible! Then if God is not a complex unity, how can He be one when He is divided?

David L. Cooper presents a strong, detailed and comprehensive case for the tri-unity of God in the Hebrew Scriptures and for *echad* being a compound unity. He believes in verbal plenary inspiration. Therefore, he deals with the Hebrew text by letting Scripture interpret Scripture, letting God reveal Himself as He chose. In Cooper's book, *What Men Must Believe*, the chapter on "The Unity of the Divine Personalities," gives a biblical argument for the tri-unity of God, as well as the *Shema*, not only proving monotheism but compound unity as well. Cooper illustrates, with *Elohim*, one of the other words used in Deuteronomy 6:4. Moses knew that *Elohim* is plural, so why didn't he use *El* or *Eloah* instead of *Elohenu* (אֱלֹהֵינוּ), "our Gods"? *Elohim* is grammatically incorrect as it is in many places when it is followed by singular verbs.[786]

Robert Morey compares the Unitarian and Trinitarian viewpoints of the Scriptures in relationship to God. He observes that if God is one, a solitary person, then it would be expected that the authors of Scripture would use the Hebrew word יָחִיד (*yachid*). If that were the case, it would be very damaging to the Trinitarian view. However, what is found is that the word for God is never used with יָחִיד (*yachid*).[787] Instead, what is found is that אֶחָד (*echad*) is used in connection with God. Morey states that אֶחָד is the only available Hebrew word they could use to express the idea of a compound or complex one.[788] So, once again, if the authors of Scripture believed God was a plurality or tri-unity, one would expect to find the usage of אֶחָד (*echad*) to express a multi-personal God over against a God who was one alone.

If, in the *Shema*, Moses was teaching monotheism alone, as Rabbinic Judaism states, then why didn't Moses do one of the following in his presentation of God? (1) Why didn't he use correct grammar by using the correct singular forms for God by using *Yahweh* or *El* or *Eloah*? Was the use of *Elohim* a mistake or was Moses guided by the *Ruach haKodesh* as he penned the *Shema*? (2) Why did Moses choose to use a plural concept for one rather than a singular concept of God?

In this final section on the arguments for the *Shema* reflecting the oneness of God, it should be seen that Moses is also presenting the plurality of *Elohim* in a plural unity

---

[785] Brown, *Answering Jewish Objections: Theological Objections,* 2:12.

[786] Cooper, *What Men Must Believe*, 113.

[787] Morey, *The Trinity: Evidence and Issues*, 88.

[788] Morey, *The Trinity: Evidence and Issues*, 89.

of one. In the following lengthy quote, David Cooper presents the Hebrew word for "our God" in the *Shema* with other passages that use the same word. He shows the inconsistency of the translators who translated it plural when it refers to pagan deities, which was correct, and then treated it as a singular when they deal with the true God. Do not misunderstand this author or Cooper to advocate that God is divisible. He is not. But He did reveal Himself as a plurality in one (*echad*). Always notice when God spoke, He did so in the singular. But when He revealed and interacted with mankind, He did so through that agency of the theophany as being distinct from God and yet equal to God:

> According to all Hebrew grammarians this word [our God] is the construct form of אֱלֹהִים (gods) to which the personal possessive pronoun נוּ "our" in the plural number is added. To show that this form in the plural means "our Gods," only a few illustrations will be necessary.
>
> Now therefore put away the foreign gods which are among you, and incline your heart unto the Lord, the God of Israel. Joshua 24:23
>
> Note the similarity of these expressions: אֱלֹהִים הַנֵּכָר is correctly translated "foreign gods," but the latter is translated "the Lord, God of Israel," though to be faithful to the text one must translate אֱלֹהִים of both expressions in the same way, namely, "Gods of," the former being the gods of the foreigners, whereas the latter is the Gods of Israel. A perfect illustration of אֱלֹהֵינוּ "our Gods," which is, as stated above, the construct form of a plural masculine noun with the plural suffix "our," is found in Deut 5:3 in the word אֲבֹתֵינוּ "our fathers." The singular of this word is אָב, and the plural construct is אֲבֹתֵי. Which form with suffix is אֲבוֹתֵינוּ. Hence it is quite manifest that these words like אֱלֹהֵינוּ is a plural noun with the suffix "our." In Isaiah 53 there appear several examples of this same grammatical construction in verses 4 and 5 [these are as follows][789]:

וַאֲנַחְנוּ חֲשַׁבְנֻהוּ נָגוּעַ	our diseases [yet we-considered-him one-being-stricken]
וּמַכְאֹבֵינוּ	our pains [and-sorrows-of-us]
חֳלָיֵנוּ	our transgressions [infirmities-of-us]
מִפְּשָׁעֵנוּ	our iniquities [for-transgressions-of-us][790]

These Hebrew words have the same suffix as אֱלֹהֵינוּ, which is commonly translated "*our God*" in the English text. However, as can be seen in the above two examples (Deuteronomy 5:3; Isaiah 53:4-5) it is always translated in the plural, "*gods of*

---

[789] Cooper, *The Shepherd of Israel Seeking His Own*, 31. This book is out of print. However, if you can find it, read chapter 4 on "The Unity of God."

[790] John R. Kohlenberger, *The Interlinear NIV Hebrew-English Old Testament,* 108-109.

the foreigners," "*our diseases*," "*our pains*," "*our transgressions*," and "*our iniquities*."
Cooper continues:

> When one reads the entire chapter he can see clearly that the servant of the
> Lord, namely, "my righteous servant" צַדִּיק עַבְדִּי is suffering and is smitten of
> God because of the "diseases, pains, transgressions and iniquities" of those to
> whom Isaiah refers as 'us' i.e., the Hebrew nation. From these examples and
> hundreds of others which might be given, it is very clear that אֱלֹהֵינוּ is in the
> plural construct form and means "our Gods."[791]

Cooper further states that the word אלהיכם "your gods" appears in Joshua 3:3; 23:3;
1 Samuel 6:5; and 1 Kings 18:25. In the first two passages it is translated "your God"
because it applies to the God of Israel. But in the latter two passages the identical word
is translated "your gods" because it applies to heathen deities. A faithful translation of
these words demands that they be translated the same in each instance.[792]

If the *Shema* and *echad* were so foundational in the life of the Hebrew nation to
teach absolute monotheism, then when Israel and Judah fell into idolatry, why did the
prophets never refer to Deuteronomy 6:4? Cooper states:

> Proof which corroborates this interpretation of Israel's Great Confession is
> found in the fact that when the nation lapsed into idolatry and her inspired
> prophets endeavored to win her back to God, they emphasized the truth that
> there is but one God. In all of their utterances concerning the proposition that
> there is but one God, they never did use their great confession. If it means what
> it is usually understood to mean, namely, that God is one in the absolute sense
> of the term, then it is unthinkable that the prophets never did use it in their fight
> against idolatry. Therefore, they understood it to refer to God's unity and not to
> His being One in the absolute sense.[793]

It is indeed interesting to note that the great prophet Isaiah, as he spoke to Judah (and
Hosea to Israel), never made any reference to the *Shema*. Isaiah's ministry ended during
the pinnacle of idolatry during the reign of Manasseh whom God said was past the point
of no return (Jeremiah 15:4; 2 Kings 21; 2 Chronicles 34:22-28). However, he did quote
from Deuteronomy 4:35, 39 but not from 6:4:

> To you it was shown that you might know that the LORD, He is God; there is
> no other beside Him (Deuteronomy 4:35).

> Know therefore today, and take it to your heart, that the LORD, He is God in
> heaven above and on the earth below; there is no other (Deuteronomy 4:39).

---

[791] Cooper, *The Shepherd of Israel Seeking His Own*, 31-32.
[792] Cooper, *The Shepherd of Israel Seeking His Own*, 32.
[793] Cooper, *The Shepherd of Israel Seeking His Own*, 35.

Compare these statements from Isaiah and Hosea as they attempted to turn Judah (Israel) back to their faith:

> Thus says the LORD, the King of Israel and his Redeemer, the LORD of hosts: I am the first and I am the last, and there is no God beside Me (Isaiah 44:6).

> Do not tremble and do not be afraid; Have I not long since announced it to you and declared it? And you are My witnesses. Is there any God besides Me, or is there any Rock? I know of none (Isaiah 44:8).

> I am the LORD, and there is no other; besides Me there is no God. I will gird you, though you have not known Me. That men may know from the rising to the setting of the sun that there is no one besides Me. I am the LORD, and there is no other (Isaiah 45:5-6).

> Declare and set forth your case; indeed, let them consult together. Who has announced this from of old? Who has long since declared it? Is it not I, the LORD? And there is no other God besides Me. A righteous God and a Saviour; there is none except Me. Turn to Me, and be saved, all the ends of the earth; for I am God, and there is no other (Isaiah 45:21-22).

> Yet I have been the LORD your God since the land of Egypt; and you were not to know any god except Me, for there is no savior besides Me (Hosea 13:4).

Where is absolute monotheism and the great Jewish confession, the *Shema*, being quoted? It isn't there. What becomes even more interesting is that Isaiah presents God as one God, monotheism and as a plural and tri-unity of one (Isaiah 9:6-7; 44:6; 48:12-16; 50:1-6; 61:1-2; 63:7-10). Cooper continues with this final thought:

> Since they nowhere used the language of the Great Confession in their hard fight for monotheism (the teaching that there is but one God), it is quite evident that they, who were guided and aided by the Lord, and to whom the Word of the Lord came, understood that it had no bearing on the issue.[794]

All of this is to say that *echad* is a compound unity or minimally always in a plural context and not an absolute one as Rabbinic Judaism states. Next it will be shown one of the reasons how that interpretation of Rabbinic Judaism came about in the word *yachid*.

YACHID – יָחִיד

The differences between *echad* and *yachid* are significant in the *Tanakh*. *Echad* minimally means unity, a unity involving a plurality, whereas the meaning of *yachid* is to express absolute oneness, one standing by itself, alone. *Yachid* suits that purpose very well. *Yachid* [יָחִיד] appears 12 times in the Law, Prophets and Writings of the Hebrew

---

[794] Cooper, *The Shepherd of Israel Seeking His Own*, 37.

text. It is used five times in reference to an only son (Zechariah 12:10), three times in reference to a child (Judges 11:34), twice in reference to being "lonely" (Psalm 68:6), and twice in reference to "your precious life" (Psalm 22:20).[795] Paul Gilchrist says that this word "basically refers to an only child," and its basic meaning is "only begotten son, beloved, with secondary meanings of isolated and lonely."[796] In reference to life, Brown, Driver and Briggs say:

> My only one, for my life, as the one unique and priceless possession which cannot be replaced.[797]

The word *yachid* comes into play because of Moses Maimonides (1135-1204 CE), who is also called Rambam. He was a philosopher and a Torah and Talmud scholar who wrote many commentaries as well as practiced medicine. One of the things that Maimonides wrote was the 13 principles of the Jewish faith.[798] The second principle is as follows:

> I believe with perfect faith that God is one. There is no unity that is in any way like His. He alone is our God – He was, He is, and He will be.[799]

As Maimonides (Rambam) wrote the second principle of faith, he substituted *yachid* for *echad* in Deuteronomy 6:4 of the Hebrew text. He clearly recognized that *yachid* contradicted the true biblical believer's use of *echad* to prove the tri-unity of God. A Jewish believer in Israel reflects on Rambam's thoughts and why he replaced *echad* with *yachid*:

> For Rambam, the term *echad* allowed for elements of personal complexity within the Godhead which he had excluded a prioi for philosophical reasons. As used in the *Tanakh*, *echad* is the word of choice to express the unification of two or more elements to form one entity. Whether it is "the evening and the morning" combining to form "one day" (Genesis 1:5), male and female becoming "one flesh" (Genesis 2:24), or Ezekiel's two sticks becoming "one stick" in his hand (37:17), a compound unity is the result. Thus, by describing the Lord as *echad*, the *Shema* does not exclude complexity within the essential divine unity. As Rambam understood, the term falls far short of asserting an absolute philosophical unity.[800]

It is also important to note Robinson's comment about Maimonides, "that his (Maimonides) attempts to unite Aristotle and Torah had a profound influence on his

---

[795] Kohlenberger and Swanson, *The Hebrew English Concordance to the Old Testament,* 697.

[796] Harris, Archer, and Waltke, *Theological Wordbook of the Old Testament,* 372.

[797] Brown, Driver, and Briggs, *A Hebrew and English Lexicon of the Old Testament,* 402.

[798] Robinson, *Essential Judaism,* 415-421.

[799] Robinson, *Essential Judaism,* 416.

[800] Noam Hendren, "The Divine Unity and the Deity of the Messiah," *Mishkan,* no. 39 (2003), 38.

Christian contemporaries."[801] Did men like Maimonides and Rashi (1040–1105 CE)[802] have an impact on New Covenant belief by obscuring the full significance of *Elohim* and *echad*? It is known that Rashi did change the interpretation of the Suffering Servant and His relationship to the Jewish understanding of Isaiah 53. Today the Jewish position on Deuteronomy 6:4 is that God is *yachid*, an absolute one. If Moses was teaching absolute monotheism, then Deuteronomy 6:4 should have the following reading:

> *Yahweh* our *Eloah* or *El* [God], *Yahweh* is *yachid* (absolute one), instead of *Yahweh* our *Elohenu* [our Gods], *Yahweh* is *echad* (compound unity).

The first part of the statement reflects the meaning taught by Maimonides. The second part of the statement reflects the meaning as taught by Moses. There is quite a difference. Moses was guided by the *Ruach haKodesh* in what he wrote; Maimonides was not! The consequential differences between *echad* and *yachid* are made quite clear by scholars like Chafer,[803] Rosenthal,[804] Heydt,[805] Goldberg,[806] Brown,[807] Fruchtenbaum,[808] Cooper,[809] Benach,[810] and Criswell.[811] As the result of studying the Hebrew language and making *aliyah* to Israel, Moshe Golden shared the invaluable insight that in modern Hebrew today *yachid* is a compound "one" and *echad* is an absolute "one," which is just the opposite of the Hebrew Scriptures.[812] So the true meaning of Scripture is once again obscured from the modern Jewish reader.

Did Moses Maimonides purposely use *yachid* to draw the Jewish people away from the word *echad*? This author cannot judge; Maimonides will have to deal with that issue with his Creator when he stands before his Lord and God. However, the net result is that most Jewish people today look at Deuteronomy 6:4 and the word "one" as *yachid*, and thus view God as an absolute one. Sailhamer clearly states the intent of Moses when he wrote Deuteronomy. In the context of that polytheist world, God was the one and only! But at the same time Moses used the word *echad* instead of *yachid* to express a plural unity and not singleness:

---

[801] Robinson, *Essential Judaism*, 420.

[802] *Rashi* (Rabbi Shelomo Yitzhaki): an extraordinary Torah and Talmudic scholar. He was fluent in many languages, an accomplished poet, and a skilled philologist. He wrote many commentaries on the Torah. Today his commentaries are part of the Talmud itself.

[803] Chafer, *Systematic Theology*, 1:267.

[804] Rosenthal, *One God or Three?* 21.

[805] Heydt, *Studies in Jewish Evangelism*, 125.

[806] Goldberg, *Our Jewish Friends*, 81-82.

[807] Brown, *Answering Jewish Objections: Theological Objections*, 2:4.

[808] Arnold G. Fruchtenbaum, *The Trinity – Manuscript #50*, (Tustin, Cal: Ariel Ministries, 1983), 11-12.

[809] Cooper, *The God of Israel*, 44-57.

[810] Henry Benach, *Go To Learn* (Chattanooga: International Board of Jewish Missions, 1997), 20-22, 48-50.

[811] W. A. Criswell, *The Criswell Study Bible* (Nashville: Nelson, 1979), 233.

[812] *Moshe Golden*: obtained in having a personal conversation with him.

Much discussion has focused on the meaning of the phrase "the LORD is one" in this verse. The sense of the phrase becomes quite clear if read in the light of the strict prohibition of idolatry and polytheism in the present text of Deuteronomy. The intent of the phrase is to give a clear statement of the principle of Monotheism, that is, that there is one God and only one God who exists. It thus has also been translated, "The LORD is our God, the LORD alone (Jewish Tanakh)." It is important to note, however, that the stress on the uniqueness of God over against the worship of false idols is not stated in such a way as to exclude the equally important notion of the divine Trinity. The word used for "one" in this passage does not mean "singleness" but "unity."[813]

To be completely clear as to the nature of the word *echad* and *yachid* and how the latter replaced the former in the minds and hearts of Jewish people as shown by David Cooper, one must consider the following:

The question doubtless has arisen in the mind of the reader: Why, if Israel's confession is to be correctly translated, "Hear, O Israel, the Lord our Gods is the Lord a unity," has Israel throughout the centuries understood it to mean that God is one in the absolute sense instead of a compound unity?

Prior to the days of Moses Maimonides, the unity of God was expressed by אֶחָד which, as has been proved beyond a doubt, has as its primary meaning that of a compound unity. Maimonides, who drafted the thirteen articles of faith, in the second one set forth the unity of God, using the word יָחִיד (only) which in the Tenach is never used to express God's unity. The word occurs in twelve passages that the reader may examine for himself, which investigation will prove conclusively that it carries the idea of absolute oneness (Gen 22:2, 12, 16; Amos 8:10; Jer 6:26; Zech 12:10; Prov 4:3; Judg 11:34; Psa 22:20 [21]; 35:17; 25:16; and 68:6[7]). From these facts it is evident that a new idea was injected into this confession by substituting יָחִיד which in every passage carries the primary idea of oneness in the absolute sense for אֶחָד which primarily means a compound unity. Hence from the day of Maimonides on, an interpretation different from the ancient one was placed upon this most important passage.[814]

Finally, Lindberg lays out the issue and submits it to his Jewish brethren. To whom should the Jewish people look for understanding in relation to the *Shema*, Moses Maimonides or Moses the son of Amram (and Jochebed) the Levite?

The Hebrew word Maimonides used in the Principles of Faith for unity is the word yachid. The word yachid carries the thought of absolute oneness rather than unity. True, yachid always means oneness in the absolute sense. But the appeal of every honest seeker after truth is not to the Thirteen Principles of

---

[813] Sailhamer, *The Pentateuch as Narrative: A Biblical-Theological Commentary*, 439.
[814] Cooper, *The Shepherd of Israel Seeking His Own*, 39-40.

Faith, but to the Hebrew Scriptures, the Tanakh. The seventh of those Principles states: "I believe with perfect faith that the prophecy of Moses our teacher, peace be to him, was true, and that he was the chief of the prophets, both of those that preached and of those that followed him." Therefore, to Moses we turn in Deuteronomy 6:4, and read the Shema and two things will be noted, (1) that Moses did not use yachid but echad to express "one," and (2) to see just how echad is used throughout the writings of Moses.[815]

In the fifth book of Moses in Deuteronomy 6:4, God laid down for His people a principle of faith which is superior to that of Moses Maimonides, inasmuch as it comes from God Himself. This stresses the sense of the word "one" not by using "yachid" as Maimonides does, but in using "echad" as God does, and it does not, under any circumstance, include an absolute one, but minimally a plurality.

AUTHOR'S POSITION ON *ECHAD*

A careful analysis of *echad* in the Hebrew Scriptures clarifies that the term signifies unity in the context of plurality. The context of Deuteronomy and the *Torah*, as a whole, is to present God as one. Yet sprinkled throughout the text of the *Torah* and the *Tanakh*, monotheism is conceptualized as a unity of persons equal in nature and essence but with differing activities. Interwoven throughout the *Tanakh* are clear instances with abundant evidence of the plurality of *Elohim*. Abundant evidence of that plurality is found in repeated instances of the plural word *Elohim*, as well as theophanies, and the Messenger (Angel) of *Yahweh* and the *Shechinah* of God. Included are personal pronouns and plural descriptions that God uses of Himself, which are discussed in the next chapter.

Walter Zimmerli confirms the use of plural unity of the verb *echad* in Ezekiel 21 (16) by stating that the only way this word makes any sense in the context of Ezekiel 21:21 is to see it as a plural compound of unity.[816] He simply says that it "gives no satisfactory sense unless understood from אֶחָד (*echad*).[817] It was noted earlier in the chapter that one possible way of interpreting *Shema* is to see *Yahweh* in Deuteronomy 6:4 as a nominative, while *Elohim* and *echad* are predicates of the nominative, or descriptive of the nominative.[818] If *Elohim* is a plural description of God, then it makes complete sense that *echad*, being a compound unity, also expresses a plurality. The text would look like this:

Monotheism, singular (*Yahweh*) our plurality (*Elohim*), plural Monotheism, singular (*Yahweh*) is a compound one (*echad*), plural

---

[815] Milton B. Lindberg, *In Light of Tenach: The Trinity*, 12.

[816] There is a discrepancy with some translations between finding it in verse 16 or 21.

[817] Walter Zimmerli, *Ezekiel 1* (Philadelphia: Fortress Press, 1979), 430.

[818] Merrill, *The New American Commentary: Deuteronomy*, 4:162-163.

Elohim reflects back to *Yahweh* and *echad* reflects back to *Yahweh*. The God of Israel is a compound unity. This author believes that the *echad* of the *Shema* is a compound unity, but recognizes that there is far stronger evidence to show that *echad* is minimally a plurality (See Appendix 2). Because *Elohim* is never presented as a dual personality, yet still as a plurality, He has to be more than two, but is never more than three. In the Hebrew Scriptures the Father speaks to the Son (Psalm 2:7) and the Son speaks to the Father (Zechariah 1:12).[819] Also the Holy Spirit came upon and filled Bezaleel (Exodus 35:30-31), the spirit of wisdom filled Joshua (Deuteronomy 34:9), the spirit came upon Saul, (1 Samuel 11:6) and left him (1 Samuel 16:14) as well as came upon David when he was anointed by Samuel (1 Samuel 16:13). The Hebrew Scriptures and the New Covenant, together or separately, never present more than three. Although the tri-unity is not explicitly presented in the Hebrew Scriptures until Isaiah, yet it is present.[820] Otherwise, Jesus was making false claims of His divinity to the Jewish nation to whom He was presenting Himself as Messiah and God. Louis Goldberg sums up this issue of the plurality of God in relation to Deuteronomy 6:4 by saying:

> We need to be scriptural even though we may never completely understand the scriptural concept. We see from the wording of Deuteronomy 6:4 that it was not Moses' intent to avoid a composite description of God. Rather, he was led to express God's nature in this way to allow for the future unfolding of the truth it contains.[821]

In the previous chapter in the Joshua 1:6 section it shows another aspect of the plurality of *Elohim*. In Deuteronomy 6:10 as Moses gives the words of *Yahweh*, the passage known as the *Shema* (verses 4-9) we see a link to our understanding of the plurality of *Elohim* even in the *Shema*. In verse 10 the one who has spoken to Moses is also the one who is the covenant maker from Genesis 15 who there is identified as the "*word of the LORD*," and in Judges 2:1 who is identified as "*the angel* [Messenger] *of the LORD*" as the same person known to Israel as the Father, the LORD or *HaShem*. This one as to His description throughout the Torah of Moses is not the Father but the Son who is revealing the Father. The Second Person of the plural unity of *Elohim* is equal to and yet distinct from the Father. He is the member of the Godhead who consistently becomes visible and who communicated to Israel on the behalf of the Father.

---

[819] Geisler, *Systematic Theology*, 2:288-289.
[820] Geisler, *Systematic Theology*, 2:289-290.
[821] Goldberg, *Our Jewish Friends*, 82.

Chapter 10
Plural Descriptions

This chapter focuses on the personal pronouns attributed to God, and other plural descriptions of God. This is a significant area of debate and controversy between biblical faith and Jewish scholars. Initial discussion involves four passages where God refers to Himself by using plural pronouns (Genesis 1:26, 3:22, 11:7; Isaiah 6:8).

PRONOUNS

In the Hebrew text, the plural term for God is *Elohim*. From Genesis 1 through Genesis 2:3 *Elohim* is the only one identified as the one doing the action of creating. God (*Elohim*) chose to reveal Himself by not predominantly using the singular forms for God (*El, Eloah*) which were available for His use. Those who subscribe to verbal plenary inspiration must also affirm that the text's use of a plural descriptive term refers to God as being a plural unity. Therefore, at least two persons are involved in the creation of the world, a fact that makes null and void such counter arguments as "plural of majesty," or "plural of deliberation," remnants of polytheism, "heavenly court" and/or "angels." It is this author's view that these counter arguments, which Jewish and Christian theologians force unnaturally upon the text, do an injustice to God and the way He chose to reveal Himself. Jamieson, Fausset and Brown make clear that all such counter arguments are "contrary to the whole tenor of Scripture."[822]

Understanding the plurality of God references in the early chapters of Genesis, as well as the one in the Isaiah passage, requires a clear grasp of the significance of these seven plural Hebrew pronouns.

All of the verbs are first person common plural forms in the Qal Imperfect tense. The suffixes attached to the prepositions are also first person common plural forms. They indicate a plurality of persons acting and making decisions. The following quotation will not mean much to anyone who has no background in Hebrew, so this is for the Hebrew language student:

---

[822] Jamieson, Fausset and Brown, *A Commentary: Critical, Experimental and Practical on the Old and New Testaments*, 1:8.

Genesis 1:26   נַעֲשֶׂה אָדָם בְּצַלְמֵנוּ כִּדְמוּתֵנוּ

> Let us make man – Verb Qal Impf 1 c p
>
> In image of us – Prep ncms const suffix 1 c p
>
> In likeness of us – Prep ncfs const suffix 1 c p

Genesis 3:22   כְּאַחַד מִמֶּנּוּ

> Like one of
>
> From us – Prep + 1 c p suffix

Genesis 11:7   נֵרְדָה וְנָבְלָה

> Let us go down – Verb Qal Impf 1 c p
>
> And let us confuse – Verb Qal Impf 1 c p

Isaiah 6:8   יֵלֶךְ־לָנוּ

> He will go – for us - Prep + 1 c p suffix[823]

To illustrate, in Genesis 1:26 the verb "make" is an imperfect first person common plural with the pronoun "us" which is also first person common plural. In this passage the person speaking is plural and the verb of action is in agreement. From this point on the English equivalent, "us" and "our" of the Hebrew plural pronouns will be used.

Let US Make Man ... Genesis 1:26

And God said, Let us make man in our image, after our likeness. They shall rule the fish of the sea, the birds of the sky, the cattle, the whole earth, and all the creeping things that creep on the earth.

This passage was discussed in chapter 2 in relation to mankind being the bearers of the "image" and "likeness" of God. Here God uses the word "us" in relationship to Himself. The creation of mankind is distinctly different or separate from the rest of creation. There is a distinct contrast being made for *Elohim*. There are four contrasts listed by Sailhamer:

The creation of humanity is set apart from the previous acts of creation by a series of subtle contrasts with the earlier accounts of God's acts. **First**, in verse 26, the beginning of the creation of humanity is marked by the usual "And God said." However, God's command which follows is not an impersonal (third person) "Let there be," but rather the more personal (first person) "Let us make." **Second**, whereas, throughout the previous account the making of each

---

[823] Taken from Gramcord software and Owens, *Analytical Key to the Old Testament*, 5, 13, 41; Kohlenberger, *The Interlinear NIV Hebrew-English Old Testament*, 1:3, 8, 24, 4:13.

creature is described as "according to its own kind," the account of humankind's creation specifies that the man and the woman were made according to the likeness of God ("in our [God's] image"), not merely "according to his own kind." The human likeness is not simply of himself and herself; they also share a likeness to their Creator. **Third**, the creation of humanity is specifically noted to be a creation of "male and female." The author has not considered gender to be an important feature to stress in his account of the creation of the other forms of life, but for humankind it is of some importance. Thus the narrative stresses that God created humankind as "male and female." **Fourth**, only human beings have been given dominion in God's creation. This dominion is expressly stated to be over all other living creatures: sky, sea, and land creatures.[824]

The ramifications of these four contrasts are very important to understand. In Sailhamer's first point *Elohim* makes a clear statement of intent, "*Let us make man.*" This is a unique statement in two ways. First, throughout this chapter, *Elohim* said, "*Let there be*" (verses 3, 6, 9, 14, 20). Then in verse 26, with the creation of mankind, He says, "*Let us make man.*" Hamilton relates these two phrases this way:

> The shift from the consistent use of the verb in the jussive (e.g., "Let there be") to a cohortative ("Let us make") is enough to prepare the reader for something momentous on this sixth day.[825]

There is a significant difference when the verb on the other days of creation is, "*Let there be*" but on the sixth day the verb "make" is grammatically plural.[826] Indeed, *Elohim* is not going to just create man. He is going to create man uniquely by doing and saying, "*Let us make man in our image, after our likeness.*" *Elohim* used the personal plural pronoun "us," which obviously references two or more persons. The pronoun "us" describes *Elohim* when He is about to create man, in "*our image*" and "*our likeness.*" According to Owens the two Hebrew words כִּדְמוּתֵנוּ and בְּצַלְמֵנוּ translated "*in our image*" — "*in our likeness,*" have plural suffixes.[827] Miller states that the words "image" (*selem*) and "likeness" (*demut*) are in the singular.[828] Clearly, the uniqueness of the plural personal pronouns in Genesis 1:26 draws attention to *Elohim*'s choice of specific words to indicate specific actions. For example, in Genesis 1:1 it is *Elohim* who creates. Because the term *Elohim* is plural, it declares God as plural. The singular verb "created" shows *Elohim*'s unity or oneness. In verse 26 the pronoun "our" is tied to two singular words "image" and "likeness" showing the one speaking as being plural while

---

[824] Sailhamer, *The Pentateuch as Narrative: A Biblical-Theological Commentary*, 94-95.

[825] Hamilton, *The New International Commentary on the Old Testament: The Book of Genesis,* Chapters 1-17, 134.

[826] Mathews, *The New American Commentary: Genesis 1:1-11:26 ,* 1a:161.

[827] John Joseph Owens, *Analytical Key to the Old Testament* (4 vols. Grand Rapids: Baker, 1989), 1:5.

[828] Paul A Miller, *Gramcord* (Vancouver, Wash: Gramcord Institute, 1999), www.gramcord.org.

at the same time confirming His unity. The above observation is important because there is no justification for forcing on the text interpretations like consulting with "heavenly court" or "angels" as Loewen and Towner do in their articles in relation to Genesis 1:26:

> The example that is sometimes given, "let us make man in our image," probably does not refer to a plurality of gods, but rather to some kind of 'heavenly council' with which God is represented as being in consultation.[829]

> We are left, then, with the heavenly council as the only likely way of explaining this use of the plural in verse 1:26. Even in the latest hand to contribute to the final form of the Pentateuch – the Priestly writer – we come smack up against the feeble remnants of polytheism. God is speaking for the entire divine court.[830]

One thing becomes very clear. Mankind was not created in the image of angels. *Elohim* is omnipotent, omnipresent, and omniscient and He does not need to consult angels. The "Our" is not *Elohim* speaking to angels but *Elohim* speaking to equal partners in the Godhead.[831] The comments on "remnants of polytheism" are simply a statement of unbelief in the form of liberal higher criticism. Charles Feinberg clearly states that God communicated with the plural unity of Himself as he gives the following statement:

> To this point the simple, forceful statement was "God said, Let there be ..." Now there is counsel or deliberation in the Godhead. No others can be included here, such as angels, for none has been even intimated thus far in the narrative. Thus the creation of man took place, not by a word alone, but as the result of a divine decree.[832]

Clearly, there is a consultation with a divine council, but that divine council is the plurality [tri-unity] of *Elohim*, which at this point is only reflective of *Elohim*'s plurality. Mathews makes a correct observation that the first hearers did not understand tri-unity but did understand plurality:

> The first audience could not have understood it in the sense of a trinitarian reference. Although the Christian Trinity cannot be derived solely from the use of the plural, a plurality within the unity of the Godhead may be derived from the passage.[833]

Mathews' position on the plurality of *Elohim* is visible in his comments on Genesis 1, but the tri-unity is not visible. The plurality of *Elohim* does leave the door open for the

---

[829] Jacob A. Loewen, "The Names of God in the Old Testament," *The Bible Translator* 35, no. 2 (1984): 201- 207.

[830] Towner, *Westminster Bible Companion: Genesis,* 25.

[831] Morris, *The Genesis Record,* 72.

[832] Charles L. Feinberg, "The Image of God," *Bib Sac* 129:515 (July 1972), 238.

[833] Mathews, *The New American Commentary: Genesis* 1:1-11:26, 1a:163.

progression of revelation to the tri-unity of *Elohim*, but Genesis 1 does not show the tri-unity. Other passages in the Hebrew Scriptures, such as Psalm 2:7, 45:7, 110:1 and Isaiah 48:16 record members of the Godhead speaking to or referencing each other.[834] Cassuto also gives three valuable points on why *Elohim* has no reason to consult angels. He says:

> Against this interpretation it can be contended: (1) that it conflicts with the central thought of the section that God alone created the entire world; (2) that the expression 'Let us make' is not one of consultation; (3) that if the intention was to tell us that God took counsel, the Bible would have explicitly stated whom He consulted, as we are told in the other passages that are usually cited in support of this theory (I Kgs 22:19; Isa 6:2-8; Job 1 and 2).[835]

Cassuto's three points make it evident that *Elohim* did not consult anyone besides Himself. However, Cassuto is not consistent with the Genesis 1:26 text because he improperly applies "plural of exhortation," another product of higher criticism. For example, when a person exhorts himself to do a given task, he uses the plural: "Let us go!" "Let us rise up!" "Let us sit!" and the like.[836] Again, the explanation ignores the plain sense of what *Elohim* said. Leupold dogmatically sees the tri-unity in the Genesis 1 account[837] but only because he has read tri-unity into the text. The tri-unity is not revealed in the Genesis 1 account.[838] *Elohim* did consult with Himself, equal partners of the Godhead before time:

> The Lamb had, in the determination of these councils, been slain before the foundation of the world; the names of the redeemed had been written in His book of life before the foundation of the world; and God called those who were to be saved by His grace, before the world began. (1 Pet 1:20; Rev 17:8; 2 Tim 1:9)[839]

Kac observes that the plural verb "*Let us make*" and the two nouns with plural suffixes make it obligatory to translate the text as saying: "And *Elohim* said, Let Us make man in Our images and Our likenesses." Kac points out that up to verse 26, *Elohim* alone is the Creator, but in verse 26, with the creation of mankind, a double plural appears.[840] There is no need to stretch the word *Elohim* and other personal pronouns to say something *Elohim* did not intend.

The Talmud attempts to answer the plural unity of *Elohim* in Genesis 1:26-27 by going to verse 27 to disprove the plural unity of *Elohim*:

---

[834] Morris, *The Genesis Record*, 72.

[835] U. Cassuto, *A Commentary on the Book of Genesis: Part One* (Jerusalem: Magnes Press, 1961), 54.

[836] Cassuto, *A Commentary on the Book of Genesis: Part One*, 54.

[837] Leupold, *Expositions of Genesis*, 86.

[838] Youngblood, *The Genesis Debate*, 123.

[839] Morris, *The Genesis Record*, 73.

[840] Kac, *The Messiahship of Jesus,* 165.

Rabbi Yohanan said: Wherever heretics find apparent support for their heresy in a Biblical passage, such as their belief in a plurality of divine beings, a refutation of their arguments will be found near by. A heretic might try to show that the Bible refers to many gods by quoting the verse (Gen 1:26) "Let us make mankind in Our image" – the plural term בְּצַלְמֵנוּ "in Our image," suggesting that there is more than one god; but the Torah immediately says (Gen 1:27): "So God created mankind in His own image," using the singular verb וַיִּבְרָא "He created." So, too, the Torah says (Genesis 11:7): "Come, let us go down, but in an earlier verse it had already said (Gen 11:5): "And the Lord came down to see the city and the tower," using the singular expression, וַיֵּרֶד "He came down."[841]

Yes, but *Elohim* always speaks in the singular except for the four passages that are being discussed in this chapter. He also reveals Himself in a plural context and interacts with the other members of the plural unity of *Elohim*. This has been clearly shown throughout this book.

The Talmud also gives a completely fictitious story concerning the creation and man. It refers to a story of God confronting the angels, who themselves were just created, about making mankind in their collective image.

Rav Yehudah said in the name of Rav: When the Holy One, blessed be He, decided to create man, he first created a set of administering angels, and asked them (Gen 1:26): "Shall we make man in our image?" The angels said to Him: "Master of the universe, what will be the deed of this creature that You wish to create?" He said to them "Such-and-such will be his deeds, in accordance with the nature that I will implant within him." The angels said to Him: "Master of the universe, 'What is man, that You are mindful of him? And the son of man, that You visit him?' (Psa 8:5) A creature of that nature is not fit to be created." God then stretched out His little finger among the angels and consumed them in fire. The same thing happened with a second set of administering angels. When God created a third set of angels they said to Him: "Master of the universe, the first two sets of angels who spoke up before You – what did they accomplish? Surely, the entire universe is Yours. Whatever You wish to do in Your universe, do."[842]

There is absolutely no biblical justification for this kind of interpretation of Genesis 1:26. Yet in the Talmud such things are found. This Talmudic account closely resembles Elijah when King Ahaziah sent *"a captain of fifty with his fifty"* and the first two companies were consumed by fire. The third company of 50 came in humility as recorded in 2 Kings 1:9-15. Also why God would use angels just created for advice and then destroy them for not agreeing with His plan, is truly a fictitious rabbinic story.

---

[841] Steinsaltz, *The Talmud: The Steinsaltz Edition*, San 38b, 86.
[842] Steinsaltz, *The Talmud: The Steinsaltz Edition*, San 38b, 82-83.

Another aspect of the plurality and unity of *Elohim* is evident in verse 27. Although *Elohim* makes a statement of intent in verse 26, He immediately follows that through with projected action in verse 27. He uses several singular words in verse 27 to express and emphasize His unity in the creation of man. *Elohim* used "created" three times, which is singular in expressing His creation of mankind. This emphasizes His oneness and unity by stating that "in His (singular) image, the image of God (*Elohim*) He created him (mankind)." While verse 26 clearly pinpoints the plurality of *Elohim*, the singularity of *Elohim* in verse 27 further demonstrates that *Elohim* is a plural unity of one. Mathews confirms that view:

> Our passage describes the result of God's creative act by both plural and singular pronouns: the plural possessive "our image" in v. 26 and the singular pronoun "his image" in v. 27. Here the unity and plurality of God are in view. The plural indicates an intradivine conversation, a plurality in the God-head, between God and his Spirit.[843]

Taking into account all that has been said, it is not difficult to understand that God chose to reveal Himself as *Elohim*, Who is plural. He engaged with the other members of the Godhead to create mankind in Their (His) image. The other lines of reasoning, such as "plural of majesty," "plural of deliberation," "heavenly courts" or "councils," that Christians and Jewish scholars use to interpret the Hebrew Scripture, fall short of the context that *Elohim*, in His wisdom, gave to reveal Himself to mankind. Youngblood clearly and precisely states what the human finite mind on the issue of the triune *Elohim* will not grasp and yet is taught:

> Though a mystery, the uniplurality of God's nature is taught consistently throughout Scripture.[844]

This reality is clearly seen by the remarks of the following rabbi in his personal search for the truth in the plural unity of *Elohim* and that the Word of the LORD is an equal member of that unity. He states the following:

> That this Word is the essential and uncreated Word, one of the תלת רישׁין (the Three Heads), which are One, is evident from His being the Creator of man, as the Jerusalem [Targum] Paraphrase of Jonathan ben Uziel (Gen 1:27) faithfully teaches me, saying; ברא יתהוך וברא מימראדי״י ית אדף בדמיתיה בדמות מן קדם יי ברא י״י זכר וזוניה, i.e, "And the Word of Jehovah created man in His likeness, in the likeness of Jehovah, Jehovah created, male and female created He them." I clearly perceive that the WORD is called Jehovah, and that through Him (the uncreated, self-existing WORD) all things, visible and invisible, were created. Thus I read in the Jerusalem Targum (Exod 3: 14). "And the Word of the Lord said unto Moses: I am He who said unto the world, Be! And it was: and who in the future shall say to it, Be! And it shall be. And

---

[843] Mathews, *The New American Commentary: Genesis 1-11:26*, 1a:163.
[844] Youngblood, *The Book of Genesis*, 30.

He said: Thus thou shalt say to the children of Israel: I Am hath sent me unto you."[845]

The clear testimony of Scripture is that the "Let us" of Genesis 1:26 is the plural unity of *Elohim* who spoke and mankind came into being. As the rabbi clearly states, the triune God spoke through the Second Person of His being in creating man.

They Have Become One of US ... Genesis 3:22

In Genesis 3:22 God again uses the personal plural pronoun "us" in the biblical text. First observe the verse:

> And the LORD God said, "Now that the man has become like one of us knowing good and bad, what if he should stretch out his hand and take also from the tree of life and eat, and live forever!"

In the first half of this verse, we see the words "*LORD God*" (*Yahweh Elohim*), and the phrase "*man has become like one of us.*" God used name distinctions to focus attention on His personal name, essence and plurality. *Yahweh* (singular) and *Elohim* (plural) used the personal plural pronoun "us" to designate Himself. Morris adds some further insight by saying that there is a "heavenly council," so to speak, as was also observed in Genesis 1:26, but that "heavenly council" is the inner council of the tri-unity of *Elohim*:

> Verse 22 gives a brief insight into the inner councils of the triune Godhead. As in Genesis 1:26, such a council was recorded relative to the decision to create man, so now the council decrees his expulsion from the garden and the tree of life. In both passages, the divine unity is stressed ('And the LORD God said') and also the divine plurality ("us.")[846]

Elohim, in His plurality (tri-unity), says that man is like one of "us." How did man become like God? It was only in the sense that now man can know good and evil, not as some who suggest that man was upgraded to become like a divine being or angel. Youngblood makes the point that in some way man is becoming like God:

> That is, man in some sense has become like God. Surely the divine lament is not that man has become like an angel or some other creature.[847]

Only in one regard did man become like God. After the fall man knew good and evil.[848] Man is not and cannot be like divine beings or angels. It would be a promotion to be like an angel. Man became degenerate and enslaved to sin. Youngblood continues his

---

[845] Nassi, *The Great Mystery: or How Can Three Be One?*, 32.

[846] Morris, *The Genesis Record*, 131.

[847] Ronald Youngblood, *The Genesis Debate* (Nashville: Nelson Publishers, 1986), 122.

[848] David A. Hubbard and Glenn W. Barker, *World Biblical Commentary: Genesis 1-15* (52 vols. Waco, TX: Word Books, 1987), 85.

statement with a contrast. The Creator of the universe does not need the assistance of lesser beings.

> Again, it is hardly conceivable that the Lord is invoking the assistance of the angels or anyone else. It is he alone who creates, commands, and judges his creation. It is he alone who speaks and who does so on occasion as a subject described by grammatically plural terminology.[849]

Youngblood is correct. It is inconceivable that God would be comparing man with heavenly beings like angels. As the great I AM, He does not need the assistance of any creature in judging man that He, Himself, had created to serve Him.

In Genesis 3:22 and 1:26 *Elohim* was showing His plurality, along with His unity. However, there is one difference. *Yahweh*, which is singular, shows oneness in unity, while *Elohim* shows plurality in oneness. Youngblood continues in presenting the plurality of *Elohim* against the idea of "plural of majesty:"

> It would seem then that the word 'us' must refer to God Himself, and that God is here declaring that man has now become like Him, in that he knows good and evil. If this is the case, why is the plural used? Why does not the Lord simply say that the man has become like Me? The plural is not a plural of majesty, but, like the similar plural of Genesis 1:26 (let us make man in our image) indicates that in the Speaker there is a plurality of persons.... Only this interpretation does justice to the full and deep meaning of the words. Something more profound is being uttered here than the weak conception that man has become like a higher creature.[850]

Youngblood presents a strong case of the plurality of *Elohim* in Genesis 3:22. One further observation on this passage which continues to show plurality is in these words from Genesis 3:22:

> And the LORD God said, Now that the man has become like one of us, knowing good and bad, what if he should stretch out his hand and take also from the tree of life and eat, and live forever!

In Appendix 2 a detailed chart is given on the word *echad*, meaning one, and how it is used in the Torah or the five books of Moses. The overwhelming conclusion of the study is that *echad* is used within a plural context exclusively by Moses. In Genesis 3:22 God states that man has become like *echad*, "one" of us. Here God uses a plural word (*echad*) to represent Himself, along with the plural personal pronoun "us." The plurality of God is very strong in Genesis 3:22 in the following three words, "LORD God" (*Yahweh Elohim*), "one" (*echad*) and "us." If verbal plenary inspiration is believed, then the only conclusion to this passage is that God is revealing Himself as a plurality.

---

[849] Youngblood, *The Genesis Debate*, 122.
[850] Young, *Genesis 3*, 153.

297

In chapter 2 *Elohim* made mankind in His *"image"* and *"likeness."* Man was made *"male and female"* to reflect the unity and plurality of *Elohim*. Genesis 3:22 gives one way that mankind was not in *Elohim*'s image. Before the fall mankind did not have the capability to know good and evil and in that respect was not like God. But after man sinned they would be like *Elohim* from the perspective that *Elohim* did not want them to have the ability to know good and evil. However, the result of sin was that mankind fell into a continual state of corruption, but they still bore the "image of God" because Genesis 5:1-3; 9:6 both were stated when man and woman were sinners.

Let US Go Down ... Genesis 11:7

> Let us, then, go down and confound their speech there, so that they shall not understand one another's speech.

In Genesis 11:7, *Yahweh*, not *Elohim*, says, *"Let us go down"* to confuse the language of the people. The point in Genesis 1:26 is that *Elohim* says, *"Let us make man,"* but in Genesis 3:22 it is *Yahweh Elohim* saying that *"man has become one [echad] of us."* In Genesis 1:26 *Elohim* (plural) says *"let us,"* whereas in 3:22 Israel's personal name for God, *Yahweh*, is combined with *Elohim* to indicate that these names for God are interchangeable. The name *Yahweh*, which emphasizes unity and oneness, is combined with *Elohim*, which emphasizes plurality. Observe the progression of the names of God in Genesis 11:7. God simply uses His personal name, *Yahweh*, when saying, *"Let Us go down."* The significant shift in the nouns from *Elohim* to *Yahweh* is significant because the plural personal pronoun "us" is used each time to designate the plurality of *Elohim*. Whether God uses *Elohim*, *Yahweh Elohim* or *Yahweh*, it points to the same reality that God is a unity of one, yet plural.

Speiser's argument on "grammatical plural" states that the phrase *"Let us go down"* in 11:7 is "grammatically plural; or this may be a plural of majesty."[851] He emphasizes the fact that even though this passage is grammatically plural, it is to be interpreted in reality as a singular rather than a plural statement. Speiser uses the same explanation of the *"let us"* in Genesis 1:26. This view raises the question of one's priority and methods of interpretation of Scripture. Since the term *"let us"* is grammatically plural, it does not have to be changed to mean singular because plurality does not fit a certain theological perspective. *Elohim*, by inspiration in the very first chapter of His revelation to mankind, does not give the names of the tri-unity. There is no reason to remove, delete, or discount the use of the plural noun and plural pronouns to describe His personhood. Speiser makes this statement to defend his view on grammatical plural being changed in reality to a singular meaning:

> For the singulars "my image, my likeness" Hebrew employs here plural possessives, which most translations reproduce. Yet no other divine being has been mentioned and the very next verse uses the singular throughout. The point

---

[851] E. A. Speiser, *The Anchor Bible: Genesis* (Garden City, NY: Doubleday, 1964), 75.

298

at issue, therefore is one of grammar alone, without direct bearing on the meaning.[852]

Speiser argues that *Elohim* is a grammatical plural because He used singular modifiers.[853] Thus, the singular aspect of grammar would take precedent over the interpretation when God chose to use a personal plural pronoun. If that is Speiser's implication, then the word *Elohim* would simply translate as a singular, which is what all translations do. If that argument is correct, God is a very poor communicator, being completely ineffective with language to convey His essence to mankind.

There is one other observation of the text in Genesis 11:3-4 which in my judgment shows interpretive inconsistency of some scholars. When man uses "*let us*" the phrase is considered plural, but when *Yahweh* uses "*let us*" the same phrase is considered singular. When the people at Babel said, "*Let us make bricks*" and "*let us build for ourselves*," they used plural personal pronouns. This observation about the people in the land of Shinar is never argued. Yet when *Yahweh* used "*Let us go down*," suddenly scholars like Speiser take the same "*let us*" and attempt to say that *Yahweh*, singular, is not speaking in a plural. Another author states:

Here we find the singular and plural mixed again, when the word for God is not *Elohim* but Jehovah.[854]

The grammar in verses 3-4 is the same as verse 7, except man is plural and *Yahweh* is singular. Is Moses giving a parallelism here? Mankind is plural and *Yahweh* who is singular speaks in the plural and man spoke in the plural. All of the usages of "*let us make*" or "*let us go down*" are first person common plural (1 c p). Yet Speiser would make the reference to *Yahweh* (verse 7), which he says is a grammatical plural, to be taken as a singular, but the references to the people are taken literally:

Genesis 11:3   נִלְבְּנָה לְבֵנִים וְנִשְׂרְפָה

> Let us make bricks – Verb Qal Cohortative 1 p
>
> and let us bake - Verb Qal Impf 1 c p

Genesis 11:4   וְנַעֲשֶׂה־לָּנוּ

> So let us make – Verb Qal Impf 1 c p
>
> For us – Prep 1 c p

Genesis 11:7   גֵרְדָה וְנָבְלָה

> Let us go down – Verb Qal Cohortative 1 p
>
> and let us confuse – Verb Qal Cohortative 1 p

---

[852] Speiser, *The Anchor Bible: Genesis*, 7.
[853] See chapter 2, section under *Elohim*.
[854] John Wilkinson, *Israel My Glory* (London: Mildmay Mission to the Jews, 1894), 175.

Morris aptly gives his contrast between Nimrod and God. Nimrod's council meets saying "*let us*" and God's council meets saying "*let us.*" God's council is the equal members of the triune God:

> But as Nimrod and his cohorts had held a council of conspiracy and aggression on earth, so God now called a "council," as it were, in heaven, to institute formal action to prevent the accomplishment of Nimrod's plans. Such a divine council is indicated by the plural pronoun in verse 7, "let us."[855]

Yahweh uses the plural personal pronoun "us," as He refers to His divine council of the Godhead when They went down and confused the language of the people. One other observation deserves attention in Genesis 11:1, 6. As was discussed in chapter 9 (and Appendix 2), *echad* in the *Shema* of Deuteronomy 6:4 minimally has to be viewed within a plural context. In verses 1 and 6 *echad* is used not only in a plural context but in the context of a unity as seen in verses 1 and 6:

> (1) Everyone on earth had the same (*echad*) language and the same (*echad*) words.

> (6) And the LORD said, If as one (*echad*) people with one (*echad*) language for all, this is how they have begun to act...

The whole context of this passage is dealing with plurality, whether it was the plurality of men acting together because they have one language so that they can accomplish their act of rebellion against God, or whether it was God Himself referring to Himself in plurality. When Scripture is taken literally as God intended it to be, there is only one conclusion a student of the Scriptures can come to, and that is that God is a plurality. God is making a statement; He is a plural unity of one, which Jewish sages saw, as reflected upon by Wilkinson:

> They [rabbis] believed that doctrine in ancient times, to which ancient Jewish literature (including the Talmud) bears ample testimony. Even the letter ‬ש‬, shin, the initial letter of the word "Shaddai" (Almighty), was formerly taken by Jews to represent the manner of the Divine existence – three in one, a Trinity – with its three perpendicular strokes, and one horizontal uniting the three.[856]

Who Will Go for US? ... Isaiah 6:8

> Then I heard the voice of my Lord saying, "Whom shall I send? Who will go for us?' And I said, "Here am I; send me."

In this passage *Adonai* uses two personal pronouns ("I" and "us") as He invites Isaiah to his prophetic ministry by saying, "*Whom shall I send? Who will go for us?*" First, Isaiah says that he "*beheld my Lord (Adonai) seated on a high and lofty throne.*"

---

[855] Morris, *The Genesis Record*, 273.
[856] Wilkinson, *Israel My Glory*, 177.

Obviously, *Adonai* in verse 1 is God Almighty. The *seraphim* who minister before God continuously say, "*Holy, Holy, Holy is the LORD (Yahweh) of hosts*" (Isaiah 6:3). Then "*the House* (heavenly temple) *kept filling with smoke,*" which is a reference to the *Shechinah* of God (6:4). Isaiah then spoke of his sinfulness and says, "*My own eyes have beheld the King LORD (Yahweh) of Hosts*" (verse 5). Then Isaiah heard the voice of *Adonai* saying, "*Whom shall I send? Who will go for us?*" (verse 8). *Yahweh* and *Adonai* are used interchangeably with one notable distinction; *Yahweh* is singular and *Adonai* when used of God, is plural.[857]

From the time of Isaiah to the time of *Yeshua*, about 700 years, it is significant that the word *Adonai* (plural) slowly began to replace *Yahweh* (singular) as the name of God. That actually occurred sometime before the end of the second temple period. *Yahweh* and *Adonai* are the same person, and even though the *seraphim* are in the context serving *Yahweh*, it is *Adonai* (plural) who asks the question (verse 8) for the triune God in Isaiah's presence. The major names of God are all used with the personal plural pronoun "us," *Elohim* (Genesis 1:26), *Yahweh Elohim* (Genesis 3:22), *Yahweh* (Genesis 11:7) and *Adonai* (Isaiah 6:8).

Opposition to Plural Pronouns

God is one alone and yet a plurality, for He refers to Himself in the context of plurality by using plural pronouns. God is one; with that no one would disagree. While the Hebrew Scriptures give a plural description, others, both Jewish and Christian theologians, do not see these plural pronouns as referring to the plurality of God. Hasel, in his article, clarifies the extent of the disagreement:

> What does the plural "us" in this enigmatic phrase indicate? Should it be changed to the singular or does it indeed have a plural meaning? If it has a plural meaning, is its intention to express an address between gods, or between God and heavenly beings, or between God and the earth or earthly elements? Is it a plural of majesty, a plural of deliberation, or a plural of fullness? These suggestions and their supporting arguments will receive critical consideration with an attempt to evaluate their cogency.[858]

Christian and Jewish scholars agree that the "us" cannot represent plurality of God. Their views express how the plural "us" should be treated. In the following paragraphs these views will briefly be discussed.

In the Hebrew Scriptures there are four references to plural personal pronouns when God used them of Himself to indicate plurality. Of these four references, three are found in Genesis: in the creation account (Genesis 1:26), the fall of man (Genesis 3:22), and the confusing of the language at the tower of Babel (Genesis 11:7).

---

[857] Neusner and Green, *Dictionary of Judaism in the Biblical Period*, 389. See chapter 2, section under Adonai.

[858] Gerhard F. Hasel, "The Meaning of 'Let U' in Genesis 1:26," *AUSS* 13 (1975): 58-66.

The remaining plural pronoun is found in Isaiah 6:8. These four references to the personal plural pronouns support the plural unity of God. However, it seems that the greatest controversy swirls around the disagreement about the plural pronouns in Genesis 1:26. Often authors refer back to the Genesis 1:26 passage when dealing with the other passages on plural pronouns (Genesis 3:22, 11:7; Isaiah 6:8). These four passages on the plural pronouns will be examined in two ways: from the perspective of (1) Jewish and Christian scholars who oppose them as references to the plurality of God and (2) believing authors who affirm the plurality of God in these passages.

Four common proposals surface to be discussed. Jewish scholars and a number of Christian scholars seek to discredit the plural personal pronouns by using one or more of the four different lines of argument: (a) The first is that when *Elohim* used the words "us" and "our," He was referring to His "heavenly court," which included angels, sons of God, and *seraphim*; (b) the second is "plural of majesty"; (c) the third is the "plural of deliberation" argument; (d) and the fourth is that *Elohim* is referencing the earth which He had just created to assist Him.

Heavenly Court

The **first line of argument** is reflected by the following comments in the Jewish interpretation of the plural personal pronoun "us" in the *Tanakh*. Sarna refers to *Elohim* and the pronoun "us" by saying:

> This is an Israelite version of the polytheistic assemblies of the pantheon monotheized and depaganized.[859]

Sarna gives his resistance to the plural personal pronouns by saying:

> *Elohim* is a comprehensive term for supernatural beings and is often employed for angels.[860]

Sarna asserts that in Genesis 35:7 angels are seen as divine beings.[861] There is another Jewish response by Slotki, in the Soncino series, whose sources of authority are Rabbis Abraham Ibn Ezra (1092-1167) and David Kimchi (1160-1235).[862] Slotki states that the "us" (Isaiah 6:8) represents the angelic host. These interpretations are widely held views in Rabbinic Judaism from both modern and ancient scholars as represented by Sarna and Slotki on how the plural personal pronouns God uses of Himself are interpreted by the Jewish scholars.

Christian authors refer to other Jewish writers to understand their claims, as was just spoken about in connection with the plural personal pronouns of God. Driver

---

[859] Sarna, *The JPS Torah Commentary on Genesis*, 12.
[860] Sarna, *The JPS Torah Commentary on Genesis*, 25.
[861] Sarna, *The JPS Torah Commentary on Genesis*, 241.
[862] I. W. Slotki, *Isaiah* (New York: Soncino Press, 1983), 30.

302

asserts that most Jewish thought is that these reflect God and His "heavenly court" whom He is consulting:

> General Jewish interpretation and some Christians (notably Delitzsch) is that God is represented as including with Himself His celestial court (1 Kings 22:19), and consulting with them before creating the highest of His works, man.[863]

Fruchtenbaum, a Jewish believer, illustrates from Rashi concerning the activity of angels in the creation of mankind. Man was not created by angels nor was he created in the image of angels. According to Rashi, God was being polite or showing good manners and humility by asking permission of the lower beings, angels, to create man in their image.[864] Merrill also references Rashi in a journal article concerning the "let us" of Genesis 1:26 in the following quote:

> We will make man – Although they did not assist Him in forming him and although this [use of the plural] may give the heretics an occasion to rebel, yet the passage does not refrain from teaching proper conduct and the virtue of humbleness, namely, that the greater should consult, and take permission from the smaller; for had it been written, "I shall make man," we could not, then, have learned that He spoke to His judicial council but to Himself. And as a refutation of the heretics it is written immediately after this verse "And God created the man," and it is not written "and they created."[865]

Rashi's whole statement is an assumption that he makes with absolutely no precedent in the *Tanakh* of *Elohim* showing humbleness by consulting the lesser (angels) before He creates man. Ryle, who also references Jewish explanation that God was addressing the inhabitants of heaven, adds this statement in connection to Genesis 1:26 by saying:

> Old Jewish explanation that God is here addressing the inhabitants of heaven. In the thought of the devout Israelite, God was one, but not isolated. He was surrounded by the heavenly host (I Kgs 22:19), attended by the Seraphim (Isa 6:1-6), holding His court with "the sons of God (Job 1:6)."[866]

Ryle echoes what was just quoted in relation to the Jewish interpretation of Genesis 3:22.[867]

---

[863] S. R. Driver, *Westminster Commentaries, the Book of Genesis*, (London: Methuen & Co, 1911), 14.

[864] Arnold G. Fruchtenbaum, *Genesis*, tape 1, chapter 1:26.

[865] Eugene H Merrill, "Rashi, Nicholas De Lyra, and the Christian Exegesis," *WTJ* 38 (1975): 66-79.

[866] Herbert E. Ryle, *Cambridge Bible: The Book of Genesis* (London: Cambridge University, 1914), 19.

[867] Ryle, *Cambridge Bible: The Book of Genesis*, 19.

Among Christian scholars, Hamilton replicates the Jewish argument that the pantheon of gods was replaced by the heavenly court concept:

> In the biblical adaptation of the story the pantheon concept was replaced with the heavenly court concept. Thus, it is not other gods, but to the angelic host, the "sons of God," that God speaks.[868]

Westermann speaks of Genesis 3:22 and states that many modern scholars refer to the heavenly court as polytheistic in intent:

> Namely whether the phrase 'like one of us' means 'the higher spiritual beings,' or the heavenly court (H. Gunkel and the majority of recent interpreters), or whether God includes the other gods with himself, the phrase being actually polytheistic in intent.[869]

Driver uses ancient Babylonian accounts to support his argument that the biblical account rose out of a pantheon of gods in a pre-Israelite background:

> There is force in these considerations; and probably the ultimate explanation has to be sought in a pre-Israelite stage of the tradition (such as is represented by the Babylonian account; where a polytheistic view of man's origin found expression). This would naturally be replaced in a Hebrew recession by the idea of a heavenly council of angels, as in 1 Kings 22; Job 1:38; Daniel 4:14; 7:10.[870]

> It has been regarded as a survival of polytheism, and has been compared with "*Elohim*," a plural word for "God" which some regard as a relic of polytheism.[871]

Some true biblical scholars, such as Davidson, are very clear in their meaning that God's plurality is not represented by pagan polytheism. God is representing Himself as a true plurality in unity as Isaiah 6:8 and Genesis 1:26 affirm:

> There is no vagueness or obscurity in either of the passages referred to. If God, who speaks in these passages, uses the word "us" of Himself, there is a perfectly clear statement to the effect that the Godhead is a Plurality.[872]

Davidson is open to the idea that *Adonai* did include the plurality of *Elohim*. However, he also opens the door to the angels being included:

---

[868] Hamilton, *The New International Commentary on the Old Testament: Genesis*, Chapters 1-17, 133.

[869] Westermann, *Genesis 1-11, A Continental Commentary*, 272-273.

[870] S. R. Driver, *A Critical and Exegetical Commentary on Genesis* (Edinburgh: T & T Clark, 1930), 31.

[871] Ryle, Cambridge Bible: *The Book of Genesis*, 18.

[872] A. B. Davidson, *The Theology of the Old Testament*, 129.

The point, however, is whether the Divine speaker uses the word "us" of Himself, i.e. of the Godhead alone, or whether He does not rather include others, e.g. His heavenly council along with Him. The opinion of most expositors is to the latter effect.[873]

Clearly, Jewish scholars will avoid the plural personal pronouns by referring to polytheism as just stated above of the pantheon of gods, who were monotheized and depaganized at a later time. Jewish scholars will also assert the argument of the "heavenly court" and "angels" being involved in the "us" passages. Driver equates the Genesis 1:26 account with ancient pagan Babylonian accounts of a pantheon of gods. According to this line of argument, the "heavenly host" is one and the same thing with this concept of polytheistic relics of gods that have remained in the biblical text. It will also be noted that some authors intertwine the "heavenly court" and "angels" with pagan origins so that the phrase *"let us"* becomes a relic of polytheism carried over from paganism[874] rather than a clear presentation of God's plurality.

It is clear to this author that when the plain sense of Scripture is used and left to speak for itself, there is no problem with the understanding of these texts. The danger of perverting the text occurs when a person has a preconceived belief and cannot see the plurality of God. As Creator of the universe, God was always a plurality and is understood in the New Covenant as a tri-unity. Scholars, both Jewish and Christian, are taking liberties with the Scripture in an attempt to understand it, but in reality they are perverting it. The reality is that God, in the presentation of His Son to Israel as their Messiah and to mankind as the Saviour from sin, would not present a new doctrine of plurality or tri-unity. God would not, in the middle of His redemptive plan for Israel and the world, present the central figure of Scripture without a foundation being laid in the *Tanakh*. The *Tanakh* minimally presents the plural unity of *Elohim*.

Plural of Majesty

The **second line of argument** is the view of "plural of majesty" (also see chapter 3 under plural of majesty). The "plural of majesty" argument given by both Jewish and Christian scholars contends that God was speaking as a western monarch, as the Queen of England would speak to her subjects.[875] The Haftorah in speaking of Genesis 3:22, refers to the "us" as a "plural of majesty," and as a consequence of the fall, man became "as one of the angels" or "us" is a "plural of majesty."[876] Rabbi Hertz, editor of the Haftorah, follows the logic to its natural conclusion:

---

[873] Davidson, *The Theology of the Old Testament,* 129.

[874] G. Herbert Livingston, *The Pentateuch in Its Cultural Environment* (2nd ed. Grand Rapids: Baker Book House, 1987), 140.

[875] Briscoe, *The Communicator's Commentary: Genesis,* 1:34.

[876] Sarna, *The JPS Torah Commentary on Genesis,* 13.

Man is become as God – omniscient. Man, having through disobedience secured the faculty of unlimited knowledge, there was real danger that his knowledge would outstrip his sense of obedience to Divine Law.[877]

That interpretation of "us" making it a "plural of majesty" puts *Elohim* in the same class of beings that are ministering spirits (angels) to man. The "plural of majesty" is echoed again by Sarna in his commentary on Genesis 11:7.[878] The rabbis say that *Elohim* is speaking like a Western monarch who uses the royal "we."[879] Authors such as Ryle, Hamilton, Westermann, and Skinner, advocate or have cited others who raise the possibility that these arguments of "plural of majesty" and "heavenly court" could be a reference to a pantheon of gods with a polytheistic reference to God. What is notable is that frequently "plural of majesty" and "heavenly court" are linked to a pantheon of gods or a survival of polytheism, as it relates to these four plural personal pronoun texts.

> On the plural, "we will go down," cf. comments on 1:26 and 3:22. One is not to assume as background remnants of polytheistic talk or the idea of the heavenly court (as do many modern exegetes, like G.A. Cooke, F.M. Cross, H. Schmidt).[880]

Westermann points out clearly that these plural personal pronouns in Genesis are not to be understood from a background of polytheism as some modern exegetes do.

Plural of Deliberation

The **third line of reasoning is the argument** of "plural of deliberation," or God thinking something over within Himself, as if saying, "let me or I will make man." "Plural of deliberation" means that the speaker is conferring or consulting with himself. Reyburn and McG. Fry refer to Isaiah 6:8 as an example of God consulting Himself before acting.[881] Westermann uses grammar to further his argument in pressing for "plural of deliberation:"

> The grammatical construction is a plural of deliberation. In favor of a plural of deliberation in 1:26 is the fact that in Isaiah 6:8 the plural and the singular are used in the same sentence with the same meaning; similarly in 2 Samuel 24:14 where it is a question of one and the same conclusion: "...Let us fall into the hand of the Lord... but let me not fall into the hand of man." ... A clear

---

[877] Hertz, *The Pentateuch and Haftorahs*, 13.

[878] Sarna, *The JPS Torah Commentary on Genesis*, 39.

[879] For more information on "plural of majesty" refer back to *Elohim* in chapter 2.

[880] Westermann, *Genesis 1-11, A Continental Commentary*, 552.

[881] William D. Reyburn and Euan McG. Fry, *A Handbook on Genesis* (New York: United Bible Societies, 1997), 50.

example of this type of deliberation occurs in Genesis 11:7; "Come let us go down...," has shown that this usage perseveres right down to the present day.[882]

But Westermann misses the point of his own examples. When David says "us" he means the nation. However, when *Yahweh* (singular) says "let us go down," it is the one God who expresses His plurality. Turner, in his book on Genesis, is in agreement with Westermann that this passage should be treated as a "plural of deliberation."[883] Ryle points out that in Genesis 11:7 God is either announcing His purpose by using a deliberative first person plural, or that He is addressing the powers of heaven that attend to and minister to Him.[884] The Haftorah, which references Genesis 1:26, states that the "Scripture represents God as deliberating over the making of the human species." The phrase "*Let us make man*" is a "Hebrew idiomatic way of expressing deliberation as in 11:7; or, it is the 'plural of majesty,' royal commands, being conveyed in the first person plural."[885] Then Hamilton also states that these plural personal pronouns are *Elohim* deliberating with Himself:

> This verse is a deliberation. God dialogues with himself and observes that man has become "like one of us" in "knowing good and evil."[886]

It is highly improbable that an all-knowing and all-powerful *Yahweh Elohim* would talk with Himself; rather *Elohim* is to be understood minimally as a plurality. Christian scholars seem to be forcing an interpretation on the text that is not there. God is not deliberating with Himself. There is no need to because He is plural, yet a unity of one, indivisible. The "plural of deliberation" is not needed when God is a plurality. Cooper states:

> Such an expression as this, God could not use in speaking to a created being. The language unquestionably implies the equality of the speaker and the ones addressed.[887]

The Earth

The **fourth line of argument** is that *Elohim* is referencing the earth that He had just created. Rabbi Ramban or Nachmanides, a 13th-century rabbi, says of Genesis 1:26 that the phrase "*let us make*" in "*our image*" refers to "the aforementioned earth."[888] Payne Smith refers to 12th-century Rabbi Maimonides' view that God took counsel with the

---

[882] Westermann, *Genesis 1-11, A Continental Commentary*, 145.

[883] Laurence A. Turner, *Genesis* (Sheffield, England: Sheffield Academic Press, 2000), 23.

[884] Ryle, *Cambridge Bible, the Book of Genesis*, 148.

[885] J. H. Hertz, *The Pentateuch and Haftorahs* (London: Soncino Press, 1952), 5.

[886] Hamilton, *The New International Commentary on the Old Testament: Genesis Chapters 1-17*, 208.

[887] Cooper, *The God of Israel*, 28.

[888] Moshe ben Nachman, *Ramban (Nachmanides), Commentary on the Torah – Genesis* (trans. Charles B. Chavel: New York: Shilo Publishing House, Inc., 1999), 52.

earth, for the earth supplied the body of man and *Elohim* provided the soul of man.[889] This point does not show up as a biblical argument, even though the earth is in the context of Genesis 1. Rabbi Moshe Ben Nachman (1195–1270) gives the following reason for the usage of the earth in the creation of man:

> The correct explanation of *na'aseh* (let us make) [which is in the plural form when it should have been in the singular] is as follows: It has been shown to you that G-d created something from nothing only on the first day, and afterwards He formed and made things from those created elements. Thus when He gave the water the power of bringing forth a *living soul*, the command concerning them was *Let the water swarm*. The command concerning cattle was *Let the earth bring forth*. But in the case of man he said, Let us make, that is, I and the afore-mentioned earth, let us make man, the earth to bring forth the body from its elements as it did with the cattle and beasts, as it is written, *and the Eternal G-d formed man of the dust of the ground*, and He, blessed be He, to give the spirit from His mouth, the Supreme One, as it is written, *And He breathed into his nostrils the breath of life*. And He said, *In our image, and after our likeness*, as man will then be similar to both. In the capacity of his body, he will be similar to the earth from which he was taken, and in spirit he will be similar to the higher beings, because it [the spirit] is not a body and will not die. In the second verse [Genesis 1:27], He says, *In the image of G-d He created them*, in order to relate the distinction by which man is distinguished from the rest of created beings.[890]

One of the major problems with his interpretation is that in verses 3, 6, 9, 14, 20 and 24 of Genesis 1 there is not a plural personal pronoun in connection to the "Let the" or "Let there" as on the other days of creation. Only in verse 26, with the creation of man, is there a plural personal pronoun. Nachmanides uses a logical argument except when he includes the earth as a partner in the creation of man. That is not a rational statement. Material things do not have intelligence to understand or emotion to feel, let alone a will to make a choice. The earth is there simply because God placed it there. The only thing that the rabbis can point to is the statement that if they do not obey the Law (Deuteronomy 4:26; 30:19; 31:28), God promises to call heaven and earth to witness against them. In conclusion, Isaiah 40:13 is quite clear that God does not have to be informed by any counselor, whether it be the material earth or created beings.

In summary, arguments are given for both the reality of the plurality of God in the plural personal pronouns in the *Tanakh* and the arguments against these pronouns being understood as plural statements by God. Alan Hauser, who does believe in the tri-unity, in the New Covenant, claims that both Genesis 1 and the *Tanakh*, as a whole, do not present the plurality of God:

---

[889] Payne Smith, *The Handy Commentary: Genesis,* ed. Charles John Ellicott, 79.
[890] Nachman, *Commentary on the Torah – Genesis*, 52-53.

The issue of whether the doctrine of the Trinity is implied in Genesis 1 does not have any substantive impact on the broader issue of the validity of the doctrine.[891]

However, the plurality of God does have an impact on witnessing to Jewish people. Mankind and Jewish people, according to Romans 1, stand before God in judgment, condemned. Jewish people were worshipping the one true God, not idols, but they still missed their Messiah (God incarnate) because they did not recognize the plurality of God in the *Tanakh*. Hauser also makes a strong statement to totally discredit the tri-unity in the *Tanakh*:

> Furthermore, when one looks at the Old Testament it becomes clear that there are no discernible references to the Trinity. Claimed allusions to the Trinity became perceptible by hindsight only after the Church councils had defined the doctrine. Without perspective of the Church councils and the Church Fathers who formulated the creeds, it is inconceivable that we could even speak of a doctrine of the Trinity in the Old Testament. In other words, it would not be possible to state the doctrine even in skeleton form on the basis of passages chosen only from the Old Testament.[892]

God did give ample testimony of His plurality in Genesis 1 of the *Torah*, as well as the rest of the *Tanakh*. Every Jewish person who had contact with *Yeshua* in his day was responsible for rejecting or accepting Him as the God/man. The fact is that Israel, as a nation, rejected Him (Matthew 12:22-42) and turned Him over to the Romans for crucifixion. They also stand condemned because God did affirm His plurality in the *Tanakh*. Contrary to the above quote, the doctrine of the plurality (tri-unity) of God in the *Tanakh* does have substantive impact on the broader issue of God's own revelation of Himself. If the plurality of God had not been given in the *Tanakh*, *Yeshua* would have been taking unjustified liberties with the *Tanakh* when He insisted that the Law, Prophets and Writings spoke of Him (Luke 24:24-26, 44-45; John 5:7, 39, 44). Hauser contends that the development of the doctrine of the tri-unity, after the Church councils, was an act of hindsight. There is one major problem with Hauser's view quoted above. Almost 300 years before the Council of Nicea in 325 CE, the tri-unity of God had already been recognized and was being taught by the first-century church. The first-century believers, such as Matthew, Mark, Luke, John, Paul, James, Peter, Jude and the author of Hebrews, did not need the councils to make creeds (which were made because of error in the church) to have and hold to the tri-unity of God. They were eyewitnesses of the Glory of God. As John says, *"our hands have handled, of the Word of Life"* (1 John 1:1). As stated earlier in this paper, God did not present Messiah in a vacuum. Hauser sums up his writing with this statement of the doctrine of the tri-unity:

---

[891] Youngblood, *The Genesis Debate*, 110.
[892] Youngblood, *The Genesis Debate*, 111-112.

Thus we conclude that these plurals can be understood to refer to the different persons of the Trinity only if that concept is read into the passage and only if the plurals are made to carry meanings and implications that run counter to similar usages elsewhere in the Old Testament.[893]

This author's reaction is that the above quotation is a blatant statement of biblical untruth and cannot under any circumstance be substantiated in the Hebrew Scriptures. Hauser cannot believe in verbal plenary inspiration of the Scriptures and arrive at such false conclusions. Hauser has in fact accused Jesus and the writers of the New Covenant [Testament] of speaking and writing fictitious accounts of the deity of Jesus (*Yeshua*) when they use passages from the *Tanakh*. Hauser in his quote is also stating that God is an unjust God who holds the Jewish people responsible for rejecting the Messiah, when there would have been no way that they could have known His true identity. If believers only had the *Tanakh* to study, the conclusion minimally would be that God is one, but is somehow more complex than the word "one" normally conveys; He is a plurality. Even without any exposure to the New Covenant, the belief in the plurality of God would be a minimal understanding of the Hebrew Scriptures. As was clearly stated in the beginning of this book, its goal is to show the plurality and tri-unity of God in the Hebrew Scriptures.

PLURAL VERBS USED WITH *ELOHIM*

There are other passages in the Scriptures that throw light on the plurality of *Elohim* in the *Tanakh* (Genesis 20:13; 35:7; 2 Samuel 7:23; Psalm 58:11). Hebrew grammar requires that verbs agree with associated nouns in both gender and number. When *Elohim* is used of the true God, these rules are normally broken because the plural noun is almost always followed by a singular verb, except in the four verses cited in the beginning of this paragraph. With the plural noun *Elohim* a singular verb should attract attention. Likewise, the plural verbs that follow *Elohim* should equally attract attention when referring to the true God. Even though the grammar is normal, this is an unusual combination because of its infrequent use in the *Tanakh*. Fruchtenbaum expresses the significance well:

> It is also said that while *Elohim* is plural, the verbs used with it are always singular when applied to the true God, and plural for false gods. The rules of Hebrew grammar require that verbs agree with the associated nouns in both gender and number. When *Elohim* is used for pagan gods, these rules are always followed and a plural verb is always used. When *Elohim* is used of the one true God, however, these rules are normally broken – the plural noun *Elohim* is usually followed by a singular verb. While it is true that this is most often the case, it is not always the case. There are several places in the Hebrew

---

[893] Youngblood, *The Genesis Debate*, 123.

text where *Elohim*, speaking of the God of Israel, is followed by a plural verb.[894]

The following passages are four rare instances where the noun *Elohim* and the verb are plural in reference to the true God.

They Caused Me to Wander ... Genesis 20:13

So when God made me wander from my father's house, I said to her Let this be the kindness that you shall do me: whatever place we come to, say there of me: He is my brother.

Because the plural noun *Elohim* with plural verb "cause (me) to wander" is so unusual in connection to *Elohim*, Reyburn and Driver, as well as the Haftorah, attempt to explain away the plural reference to the true God. For example, Driver concludes that Abraham was adapting the above quoted reference of his speech to a pagan (Abimelech), and was accommodating Abimelech's polytheistic outlook as he states the following:

The verb is plural, perhaps, in conversation with a heathen, from accommodation to a polytheistic point of view. *Elohim*, even when used of the true God, is occasionally construed with a plural, for reasons which cannot always be definitely assigned.[895]

This is the same argument given in the Haftorah.[896] Reyburn's own argument contends that the plural noun *Elohim* and the plural verb wander "is probably best to take the plural usage in a singular sense, since this usage occurs elsewhere."[897] Wenham says that this verse speaks of the true God, but because of the plural verb as seen by Reyburn, *Elohim* should be rendered "gods" instead of "(*Elohim* or God) they caused me to wander," for the interpretation "gods" better accommodates Abimelech's polytheistic outlook.[898] However, because this is considered an anomaly,[899] many scholars want it to read as stated in the quotation above. If this plural verb, with the plural noun *Elohim*, is an anomaly, how is it that in Hebrew grammar it is the norm? The plural noun *Elohim* and the singular verb are the exception and not the grammatical rule. The rule is that all plural Hebrew nouns have plural verbs.[900] The fact that biblical scholars consider the plural noun *Elohim* and plural verb as correct usage, is an anomaly of its own according to Hebrew grammar. God chose to give this

---

[894] Fruchtenbaum, *Messianic Christology*, 103-104.

[895] Driver, *Westminster Commentaries, The Book of Genesis*, 208.

[896] Hertz, *The Pentateuch and Haftorah*, 71.

[897] Reyburn and McG. Fry, *A Handbook on Genesis*, 455.

[898] Gordon Wenham, *Word Biblical Commentary: Genesis 16-50*, 72.

[899] *Anomaly*: a deviation from the common rule, irregular.

[900] There are two other words that would also have this in common with *Elohim*, they are "waters" and "heavens."

representation of Himself, and it does not need to be changed. The reason for changing its interpretation is because it does not meet a prescribed view that God can use a plural verb to affirm His plurality, if He chooses to do so.

Westermann indicates that it is quite unlikely that Abraham adapted to Abimelech's polytheism, because the God of Abraham also spoke to Abimelech and gave him instructions.[901] The context of this passage does not warrant Abraham accommodating a heathen (Genesis 20:1, 17).

Simply stated, according to the biblical text, *Elohim* (they) *caused me to wander* is the literal rendering. Because God chose the wording through inspiration, there is no reason to alter the meaning as Reyburn, Driver and the Haftorah prescribe.

Revealed Themselves ... Genesis 35:7

> There he built an altar and named the site El-bethel, for it was there that God had revealed himself to him when he was fleeing from his brother.

This passage clarifies that upon Jacob's return to Canaan, *Elohim* revealed Themselves to Jacob after he built the altar. True to Hebrew grammar, the plural *Elohim* is followed by a plural verb "revealed," which carries the interpretation that *Elohim* revealed Themselves, and that is God demonstrating His plurality. Westermann uses the same argument as in Genesis 20:13, that even though "revealed" is plural, it should be treated as a singular.[902] Speiser says that the verb "revealed" is plural but that it should be rendered "divine beings."[903] Reyburn discusses the text and includes nothing about a plural verb. Driver points out that the plural verb (revealed) "suggests that the sentence preserves a more polytheistic version of the Bethel-legend than Genesis 28:12."[904]

Hamilton recognizes the plural verb and sees *Elohim* referring to the true God for two reasons. First, *Elohim* should have the same meaning as in verses 1 and 5, where it clearly refers to the true God. Secondly, the text gives no evidence that the messengers (angels) revealed themselves to Jacob.[905] However, since God is the actual author of the infallible, inspired Scriptures, He had Moses record the specific personal pronouns and/or verbs that convey the clear meaning of plurality and/or tri-unity. Therefore, *Elohim* revealed Themselves to Jacob showing the plurality in the Godhead.

Also in the Talmud rabbis attempt to explain the plurality in Genesis 35:7 by referring back to verse 3. They attempt to use verse 3, which references God as El, which is a singular word for God as was expressed in chapter 3 of this book. However, throughout the rest of Genesis 35:1-15, *Elohim* is used in verses 1, 5, 7, 9-11, 13. Jacob

---

[901] Westermann, *Genesis 12-36, A Continental Commentary*, 327.
[902] Westermann, *Genesis 12-36, A Continental Commentary*, 552.
[903] Speiser, *The Anchor Bible: Genesis*, 270.
[904] Driver, *Westminster Commentaries, The Book of Genesis*, 424.
[905] Hamilton, *The New International Commentary on the Old Testament: Genesis 18-50*, 377.

in verse 3 spoke of God as *El*, singular, because he worshipped one God, not a pantheon of gods. He built an altar to *El,* not to gods. The context is clear that Jacob worshipped one *El* who revealed Himself to Jacob as *Elohim*, the plural unity of the one *El*.

> The Torah also says (Gen 35:7): "And he built there an altar, and called the place El Bet El, because there God appeared to him," using the plural term נִגְלוּ, "they appeared," but an earlier verse read (Gen 35:3): And I will make there an altar to God who answers me in the day of my distress," using the singular verb הָעֹנֶה, "who answers." The verse (Deut 4:7), "For what nation is there so great, that has God so near to them, as the Lord our God is in all things that we call upon Him for," uses both a plural term, קְרֹבִים, "near," and a singular term, אֵלָיו, "Him." And similarly, the verse (II Sam 7:23), "And what one nation in the earth is like Your people, like Israel, whom God went to redeem for a people to Himself," uses both a plural term, הָלְכוּ, "went," and a singular term, לוֹ, "to Himself." [906]

As already mentioned in chapter 5 of this book, Genesis 35:9 clearly states that *Elohim* in this passage is also a theophany for He "appeared" to Jacob. This is the same word used in reference to the appearances to Abraham in Genesis 12:7; 17:1; 18:1. Here Jacob states in verse 7 that *Elohim* revealed Themselves to him and in verse 9, *Elohim* is referenced as appearing to Jacob, a theophany. There is absolutely no question as to the plural unity of *Elohim* in this text.

They Went Out and Redeemed ... 2 Samuel 7:23

> And what one nation in the earth is like thy people, even like Israel, whom God went to redeem for a people to himself, and to make him a name, and to do for you great things and terrible, for thy land, before thy people, which thou redeemed to thee from Egypt, from the nations and their gods? (NASB)

This verse is the third example of God using a plural verb (redeemed) with his name (*Elohim*). Kohlenberger translates "they went out and redeemed," as being plural.[907] He shows that the plural reference grammatically clearly refers back to *Elohim*. Gramcord also treats the phrase as a plural referring back to *Elohim*.[908] Keil and Delitzsch state that the plural phrase refers to the true God.[909] Through the use of correct grammar, *Elohim* accomplishes the same result as when He violated correct grammar by bringing attention to His plurality. Hence, this plural verb can literally be translated "whom *Elohim* they went to redeem for Themselves." It has been observed by all the authors investigated that the reverse is never true. No one has addressed the issue of a singular verb with an obvious passage that deals with false gods.

---

[906] Steinsaltz, *The Talmud: The Steinsaltz Edition*, San 38b, 17:86.

[907] Kohlenberger, *The Interlinear NIV Hebrew-English Old Testament: 2 Samuel*, 2:270.

[908] Miller, *Gramcord Institute*, CD Rom.

[909] Keil and Delitzsch, *Commentary on the Old Testament*, 2:352.

They Judge on the Earth ... Psalm 58:11(12)

Men will say, "There is, then, a reward for the righteous; there is, indeed, divine justice on earth."

And men will say, "Surely there is a reward for the righteous; Surely there is a God who judges on earth!" (NASB)

In this verse, *Elohim* and the modifier, "judge," are in the plural. Lange says that this is the same usage as in Genesis 20:13 and 2 Samuel 7:23.[910] Both Beale[911] and Owens[912] identify the word "judge" as being plural. There is not much discussion in commentaries on the plural aspect of the word "judge" with *Elohim*. This verse could be translated literally as "*Elohim* they judge on earth!" Thus, Fruchtenbaum states that this and other "plural verbs in reference to the true God support the idea of plurality in the Godhead."[913]

OTHER PLURAL DESCRIPTIONS

The next eight additional Hebrew Scriptures describe God as plural. Each is significant, but there will only be a very brief statement about each one.

Living God ... Deuteronomy 5:23

For what mortal ever heard the voice of the living God speak out of the fire, as we did and lived?

Weinfeld says that both words in the phrase "living God" are in the plural. *Elohim* is plural for God and "living" is a plural adjective (also found in 1 Samuel 17:26, 36; Jeremiah 10:10; 23:36).[914] As a plural adjective, "living" is a description of *Elohim* that gives added weight to God's plurality. Yet according to Gerleman, there are other passages that are translated "living" but they are in the singular (Joshua 3:10; Hosea 1:10; Psalm 42:3; 2 Kings 19:4, 16 with Isaiah 37:4, 17; 2 Samuel 22:47 with Psalm 18:47).[915] Though this term is not used in every case as a plural adjective, there are five passages cited where *Elohim* uses it as a plural description of Himself.

---

[910] Lange, *Lange's Commentary on the Holy Scriptures*, 5:353.

[911] Beale, Banks, and Colon Smith, *Old Testament Parsing Guide: Job-Malachi*, 2:45.

[912] Owens, *Analytical Key to the Old Testament*, 3:356.

[913] Fruchtenbaum, *Messianic Christology*, 104.

[914] Moshe Weinfeld, *The Anchor Bible: Deuteronomy 1-11* (New York, NY: Doubleday, 1991), 320-321.

[915] Jenni and Westermann, *Theological Lexicon of the Old Testament*, 1:415.

God of gods, Lord of lords ... Deuteronomy 10:17

For the Lord your God is God of gods, and Lord of lords, a great God, a mighty, and a terrible, which regardeth not persons, nor taketh reward.916

Moses uses several different names for the same God, as seen more clearly in the NASB:

For the LORD [*Yahweh*] your God [*Elohim*] is the God [*Elohim*] of gods [*elohim*] and the Lord [*Adonai*] of lords [*adonai*], the great, the mighty, and the awesome God [*El*] who does not show partiality, nor take a bribe. (Brackets are author's inserts.)

This verse could be translated, "For *Yahweh* (singular) your *Elohim* (plural) is the *Elohim* (plural) of *elohim* (plural) and the *Adonais* (plural) of *adonais* (plural),917 the great, the mighty, and the awesome *El* (singular)." Cooper comments not only on the divine personalities of God but also on the polytheistic error that must be avoided:

These expressions echo the plurality of divine personalities of the one Sovereign Being. But to avoid the error of polytheism, He asserts their unity using the word *El*, God, in the singular number. Then He differentiates Himself from idols by asserting His absoluteness in greatness, power and terribleness--He is the almighty sovereign.918

Cooper expresses the cautions that God took in giving a clear picture of His plurality while protecting His unity with the use of *El*.

Holy God ... Joshua 24:19

Joshua, however, said to the people, "You will not be able to serve the LORD, for He is a holy God."

As Joshua gives an unusual speech to Israel at the end of his life, he speaks of *Elohim* as being a "*holy God*" as well as a jealous God. Both Kohlenberger[919] and Miller[920] acknowledge the word "holy" as a plural adjective. Lange says that it is a plural adjective and also cites 1 Samuel 17:26 with Joshua 24:19.[921] Both Cooper[922] and Fruchtenbaum[923] agree that "holy" should be translated "holy Gods." By the inspiration

---

916 Harkavy, *The Twenty-Four Books of the Old Testament*, 1:307.

917 Cooper, *The God of Israel*, 33.

918 Cooper, *The God of Israel*, 33-34.

919 Kohlenberger, *The Interlinear NIV Hebrew English Old Testament*, 70.

920 Miller, *Gramcord Institute*, CD Rom.

921 Lange, *Lange's Commentary on the Holy Scriptures*, 2:185.

922 Cooper, *The God of Israel*, 29.

923 Fruchtenbaum, *Messianic Christology*, 107.

of the Spirit of God, Joshua chose to use another plural descriptive adjective to further add weight in describing the plural unity of *Elohim*.

Creators ... Ecclesiastes 12:1

> Remember also your Creator in the days of your youth, before the evil days come and the years draw near when you will say, "I have no delight in them." (NASB – New American Standard Bible)

In this passage, without the term *Elohim* or God being mentioned, Solomon makes an interesting statement: *"Remember now thy creator in the days of thy youth"* (KJV). There is a range of views on the meaning of "creator" in this passage. Ogden and Zogbo state:

> "Your creator" is the object of the imperative 'remember.' The form here is plural (literally "those who created you").[924]

Ogden and Zogbo recognize it as a plural as does Leupold.

> *Bore'ekha* is the plural form *bore'im* plus a suffix and literally means "creators,"....[925]

Along with these plural affirmations of "creator" it is also unique because this word is a plural adjective, which Kohlenberger translates as "Ones-Creating you."[926] Longman says the difficulty with the word "creator" is that it is plural, meaning that the literal reading is "your creators."[927] However, there is no difficulty because if inspiration of Scripture means anything, God can represent Himself as a plural. Jamieson, Fausset and Brown state that clearly when they say:

> The Hebrew is Creators, plural, implying the plurality of persons, as in Genesis 1:26.[928]

If grammatically "creator" is a plural, why attempt to change what God, in His infinite wisdom, gave in His Word?

However, the Jewish Tanakh replaces "creator" with an alternate interpretation of this word. That version says, "So appreciate your vigor in the days of your youth." [929]

---

[924] Graham S. Ogden and Lynell Zogbo, *A Handbook on Ecclesiastes* (New York: United Bible Societies, 1997), 418.

[925] H. C. Leupold, *Exposition of Ecclesiastes* (Grand Rapids: Baker Book House, 1952), 273.

[926] Kohlenberger, *The Interlinear NIV Hebrew English Old Testament*, 588.

[927] Tremper Longman III, *The New International Commentary on the Old Testament: Ecclesiastes,* 264.

[928] Jamieson, Fausset, and Brown, *A Commentary: Critical, Experimental and Practical on the Old and New Testaments,* 3:541.

[929] Berlin and Brettler, *The Jewish Study Bible,* 1620.

The omission is significant because "creator" appears in the Hebrew Scriptures, and some authors feel that this interpretation is not the best, as one author said:

> Some commentaries think the text as we have it may have been damaged in transmission.[930]

This means there must be alternative readings to the Masoretic Text.[931] So three views[932] have arisen, one of which is reflected in the Jewish Tanakh. The first view is that it has a possible meaning of "your well" which is a metaphoric reference to a man's wife.[933] The second possible meaning is "your grave" or "your pit," which reflects death. The third possible meaning is "your vigor," which reflects man's health and strength.

The Hebrew text tells the reader that man is to remember his "creator" in the days of his youth. Others want to depart from it to an alternate non-Masoretic reading. The fact remains that "creator" is plural; and often in the wisdom literature, God is referred to as Creator. The word "remember" is closely associated with "creator." To remember is more than to acknowledge that *Elohim* is the Creator, but it includes with it acknowledgement to act upon what is remembered. Walter Kaiser makes the following observation:

> When he uses the word "remember," he is not asking for mere mental cognizance, for the biblical term "to remember" means much more than simple recall. Besides reflecting on and pondering the work of God in creating each individual and His world, there is the strong implication of action. For example, when God "remembered" Hannah (1 Sam. 1:19), He did more than say, "Oh yes, Hannah: I almost forgot you." When He remembered her, He acted decisively on her behalf, and she who was barren conceived the child Samuel. So it is in our passage. To remember our Creator calls for decisive action based on recollection and reflection on all that God is and has done for us.[934]

Solomon is asking the reader not only to acknowledge the Creator in his youth but also to act upon that knowledge when he is young. Because the word "creator" is plural, all three members of the plural unity of *Elohim* were involved in creation. We should be remembering that fact in our youth as well. Walvoord points out the plurality of *Elohim* that should be remembered:

---

[930] Ogden and Zogbo, *A Handbook on Ecclesiastes*, 418.

[931] Longman III, *The New International Commentary on the Old Testament: Ecclesiastes,* 267.

[932] James L. Crenshaw, *The Old Testament Library, Ecclesiastes* (Philadelphia: Westminster Press, 1987), 184-185.

[933] Robert Gordis, *Koheleth, The Man and His World, A Study of Ecclesiastes* (New York: Schocken Books, 1968), 340.

[934] Walter Kaiser, *Ecclesiastes Total Life* (Chicago: Moody Press, 1979), 118.

It is Elohim who creates in Genesis 1, and already in Genesis 1:2 the Spirit of God is acting creatively. The Holy Spirit is mentioned frequently in the Old Testament as the Creator (Job 26:13; 33:4; Psa 104:30; Isa 40:12-13). The Father is also mentioned specifically in the New Testament (1 Cor 8:6).[935]

To add further to what Walvoord said is to see the involvement of the Messiah in creation in Isaiah 48:13 where He is the one who called Israel and in Zechariah 12:1 where He speaks as *Yahweh*. So in particular God the Holy Spirit and God the Son are mentioned as Creators in the *Tanakh*. There is no need to always turn to Colossians 1:15-18 or to John 1 in the New Covenant.

Makers … Psalm 149:2

Let Israel rejoice in its maker; let the children of Zion exult in their king.

Israel is to sing a new song to *Yahweh*, and Israel is to "*rejoice in its maker.*" "Maker" in the English is a noun, but in the Hebrew text "maker" in an adjective.[936] "Maker" is a plural adjective in the Hebrew and when literally translated it would say, "Let Israel be glad in his makers." Keil and Delitzsch refer to "Maker" as "The Creator of Israel"[937] in the plural form. Dahood also notes that "Maker" is a plural and even ties it in with Isaiah 54:5.[938] The interesting point is that Owens[939] recognizes "Maker" as a plural adjective but refuses to acknowledge the plurality of God in this passage. However, Kohlenberger in his interlinear translates בְּעֹשָׂיו as "in-Ones-Making-him" as plural.[940] Clearly, with *Elohim* and the "Let Us" personal pronouns of Genesis, as well as other plural descriptive words such as "creator," and "maker," God presents Himself as a plurality by the use of a variety of plural terms for God.

Husband is Your Maker … Isaiah 54:5

For He who made you will espouse you—His name is "LORD of Hosts." The Holy One of Israel will redeem you—He is called "God of all the Earth" (Jewish Tanakh).

For thy Maker is thine husband; the LORD of hosts is his name; and they Redeemer the Holy One of Israel; The God of the whole earth shall he be called (KJV).

The plural descriptions in this verse present some very good images of God's relationship to Israel. There are four words to be noted in this verse: *Yahweh*, *Elohim*,

---

[935] Walvoord, *Jesus Christ Our Lord,* 47.

[936] Fruchtenbaum, *Messianic Christology*, 107.

[937] Keil and Delitzsch, *Commentary on the Old Testament: Psalms,* 5:412.

[938] Mitchell Dahood, *The Anchor Bible: Psalms 101-150* (Garden City, NY: Doubleday, 1970), 357.

[939] Owens, *Analytical Key to the Old Testament,* 3:519.

[940] Kohlenberger III, *The Interlinear NIV Hebrew-English Old Testament,* 511.

"husband" and "maker." First, *Yahweh* is the personal name of Israel's God, in the singular. *Elohim*, being plural, is second and is used to name God and to affirm plurality. And finally there are two words that the Jewish Tanakh omitted, for in the Hebrew "maker" and "husband" are also two plural adjectives, and literally mean that Israel has "Makers" and "Husbands." Keil and Delitzsch confirm this usage and also refer to some of the same passages previously discussed in this chapter (Joshua 24:19; 1 Samuel 17:26; Genesis 20:13; 35:7 and 2 Samuel 7:23).[941] Harman also views these two words as plural.[942] Riddle clearly sees the plurality of "maker" and "husband" when he states:

> The word "maker" is in the plural: He is "the Triune God."…In keeping with the plurality of the word "Maker", the word "husband" is also in the plural. The "Triune God" is both her [Israel's] "Maker" and "husband."[943]

Vine briefly combines "maker" and "husband" with *Elohim*[944] to affirm that *Elohim*, of Genesis 1, is the Creator (Ecclesiastes 12:1) and is Israel's "husband" and "maker" when He made the covenant with them on Mt. Sinai. Both "husband" and "maker" are plural adjectives describing *Yahweh*, which is in the singular. Young basically makes application of this passage to God and the Church rather than to God's relationship to Israel.[945] That raises another theological issue that will not be discussed in this book, which is the difference between Covenant[946] and Dispensational Theology.[947] In Isaiah 54:4-5 Young does recognize the plural adjectives but attributes them to "plural of majesty." However, the impact of Isaiah 54:5 is that Israel has "Makers" and "Husbands" whose name is *Yahweh* of hosts. *Yahweh* is Israel's Redeemer, the Holy One of Israel, who is *Elohim*. Once again, these verses show a plural affirmation of His being.

The LORD Flogged? … Isaiah 50:1, 4-6

> (1) Thus said the LORD:…(4-6) The Lord God gave me a skilled tongue, to know How to speak timely words to the weary. Morning by morning, He

---

[941] Keil and Delitzsch, *Commentary on the Old Testament: Isaiah,* 7:344.

[942] Allen Harman, *Isaiah* (Ross-shire, Scotland: Christian Focus Publications, 2005), 370.

[943] J. M. Riddle, *Ritchie Old Testament Commentaries: What the Bible Teaches: Song of Solomon and Isaiah* (Kilmarnock, Scotland: John Ritchie Ltd, 2005), 534.

[944] Vine, *Isaiah*, 174.

[945] Young, *The Book of Isaiah,* 3:364.

[946] *Covenant Theology:* Teaches that the Church has replaced Israel and that now the Church is the Israel of God. Therefore, because God has no place for Israel in the future, the Church assumes all the promises to Israel. Israel can expect only the cursings. Covenant Theology sees only the dispensation of Grace, which involves all of time from Adam to present.

[947] *Dispensational Theology:* Acknowledges seven dispensations during which salvation is by faith alone. It recognizes Israel and the Church as two distinct groups through which God has chosen to work. During the Dispensation of Grace (Acts 2 through the Rapture of the Church) God is working with the Church, both Jewish and Gentile believers and not the nation of Israel at this time. However, because of His covenant promises to Abraham, God will again establish Israel and the Messiah will reign on the world from Jerusalem.

rouses, He rouses my ear to give heed like disciples. (5) The Lord God opened my ears, and I did not disobey, I did not run away. (6) I offered my back to the floggers, and my cheeks to those who tore out my hair. I did not hide my face from insult and spittle.

Walter Kaiser recognizes these verses as a "Servant of the LORD" passage, along with four other passages (Isaiah 42:1-7; 49:1-6; 50:4-9; and 52:13-53:12) as the pre-incarnate Messiah.[948] There are three basic explanations as to who the "Servant of the LORD" is in these passages.[949] First, Rashi, the renowned rabbi from the Middle Ages, taught that the servant was Israel.[950] The second is from David Kimchi (1160-1235), another renowned rabbi of the 12th and 13th centuries who taught that "the servant is said to be Isaiah himself."[951] Briggs also taught that this is not a reference to the Messiah, and like Kimchi taught that it probably refers to Isaiah.[952] The third basic explanation is that the Servant of the LORD is the Messiah, Jesus.[953]

Arnold Fruchtenbaum observes in this passage the plural unity of *Elohim*, whereas no one else seems to. According to Fruchtenbaum, *Yahweh* (Isaiah 50:1) is the first person of the plurality to be mentioned. However, in verse 4 a second person of the plurality is mentioned in the phrase *"the Lord God hath given me."*[954] The "me" is the speaker identified in verse 1 as *Yahweh*. In verse 4 *Yahweh* speaks of *Adonai Elohim*, who gave Him the tongue of the learned. Who are these personalities of plurality? Verses 5-6 identify the person, not by name, but by the actions He voluntarily receives. The description is a preview of the flogging and mocking of the Messiah (Matthew 27:26, 30-31).[955] In verse 6, Young gives a good insight into the voluntary beatings that the Messiah received before the crucifixion:

> There is majesty in the description, as though the servant were in full control of the situation. He sets himself forth as one who acts. Instead of saying that men beat him he declares that he himself gave his back to those who struck him. He either voluntarily yielded himself to flogging, or he offered himself thereto.[956]

---

[948] Walter C. Kaiser, Jr., *Toward an Old Testament Theology* (Grand Rapids, Zondervan, 1991), 215.

[949] There are several other authors that can be studied as to the three basic views on the Servant of the L-rd passages in Isaiah: (1) Victor Buksbazen, *Isaiah's Messiah* (Bellmawr, NJ: Friends of Israel Gospel Ministry, 2002); (2) David Baron, *The Servant of Jehovah* (Jerusalem: Keren Ahvah Meshihit, 2000); (3) Michael L. Brown, *Answering Jewish Objections to Jesus* (vol. 3. Grand Rapids: Baker, 2003), 40-49.

[950] Slotki, *The Soncino Books of the Bible*, Isaiah, 247.

[951] Slotki, *The Soncino Books of the Bible*, Isaiah, 247.

[952] Charles A Briggs, *Messianic Prophecy* (Peabody, MA: Hendrickson, 1988), 356.

[953] Edward J. Young, *The Book of Isaiah* (Grand Rapids: Eerdmans, 1972), 3:301.

[954] Fruchtenbaum, *Messianic Christology*, 50-51.

[955] Herbert Wolf, *Interpreting Isaiah* (Grand Rapids: Zondervan, 1985), 210.

[956] Young, *Isaiah*, 3:300.

Therefore, verse 4 and following identify the speaker as *Yahweh*, the Servant of the LORD, who refers to the "Father" as *Adonai Elohim*. Here again there are two members of the Godhead present, God the Father and God the Son.

The LORD's Value ... Zechariah 11:4-14

Then I said to them, "If you are satisfied, pay me my wages; if not, don't." So they weighed out my wages, thirty shekels of silver. The noble sum that I was worth in their estimation. The LORD said to me, "Deposit it in the treasury."

And I took the thirty shekels and deposited it in the treasury in the House of the LORD (verses 12-13).

Although this passage shows that the speaker is *Yahweh*, what happened to *Yahweh* never happened to God the Father, but to God the Son. Numerous scholars agree that the identity of *Yahweh* in Zechariah 11:12-13 is *Yeshua* the Messiah of Israel (Keil and Delitzsch,[957] Unger,[958] Merrill,[959] Baron,[960] Kaiser,[961] Smith,[962] Hengstenberg,[963] Feinberg,[964] Henderson,[965] Laetsch,[966] and Fruchtenbaum.[967] It has already been noted that the *Tanakh* records two *Yahwehs* (Genesis 19:24; Isaiah 44:6; Hosea 1:4-7; Zechariah 2:8-9).[968] In this passage the LORD (*Yahweh*) is presented as the Good Shepherd (John 10:11-14) as Zechariah acts out the symbolic action of receiving the LORD's wages from the people.[969]

One thing about verse 12 stands out clearly. The LORD (*Yahweh*) was speaking and used the term "I" repeatedly to reaffirm throughout this passage that it was He who spoke (verses 4, 6-10, 12-14). Verses 4 and 13 identified the LORD (*Yahweh*) as the speaker, whereas in the other verses He uses the first person pronoun "I." In verse 12, *Yahweh* asks for His wages through Zechariah, who was acting out the role of the Good Shepherd. The Good Shepherd's (Messiah) request is not compulsory. The wages that *Yahweh* was looking for were Israel's love, obedience and devotion to God their

---

[957] Keil and Delitzsch, *Commentary on the Old Testament in Ten Volumes: Zechariah*, 10:368.

[958] Unger, *Zechariah: Prophet of Messiah's Glory*, 199.

[959] Merrill, *An Exegetical Commentary: Haggai, Zechariah, Malachi*, 298.

[960] Baron, *The Visions and Prophecies of Zechariah*, 380, 403-407.

[961] Kaiser, *The Communicator's Commentary: Micah – Malachi*, 394.

[962] Smith, *The Promised Messiah,* 444.

[963] Hengstenberg, *Christology of the Old Testament,* 4:35.

[964] Charles L. Feinberg, *The Minor Prophets* (Chicago: Moody, 1952), 328.

[965] Henderson, *Thornapple Commentaries: The Twelve Minor Prophets*, 420.

[966] Theodore Laetsch, *The Minor Prophets*, 474.

[967] Arnold Fruchtenbaum, *The True Shepherd of Zechariah: Study of Zechariah 11:1-17*, Manuscript # 90 (Tustin, CA: Ariel Ministries, 1984), 6-7.

[968] See chapter 2, section entitled *Yahweh.*

[969] Baron, *The Visions and Prophecies of Zechariah*, 380.

Shepherd.[970] However, instead of giving Him the internal or spiritual wage of their repentance, Israel gave Him a monetary wage, which was a deliberate insult.[971] Israel could have refrained from paying wages altogether, but instead insulted the Good Shepherd with 30 pieces of silver, which according to the Law, is the price of a dead slave (Exodus 21:32).[972] Merrill clarifies that *Yahweh*, rather than Zechariah, is the one being appraised as unworthy (Zechariah 12:13).[973] The one who was sold out for 30 pieces of silver was the LORD (*Yahweh*), the personal God of Israel, in this case, the Messiah *Yeshua*. Matthew 23:37 takes on greater meaning when it is understood that *Yeshua* is speaking as God, the LORD (*Yahweh*), from the *Tanakh*:

> O Jerusalem, Jerusalem, thou that killest the prophets, and stonest them which are sent to thee, how often would I have gathered thy children together, even as a hen gathereth her chickens under her wings, and ye would not!

TRI-UNITY IN ISAIAH

Isaiah was an eighth-century prophet, a contemporary with Micah. His presentation of Immanuel (Isaiah 7-12), Servant of the LORD (Isaiah 42, 49, 50, and 53), and the future restoration of Israel (Isaiah 54, 60-66) makes this book one of the greatest treasures in the *Tanakh*. Isaiah prophesied the captivity of Israel and the fall of Babylon to the Medes and Persians, as well as God anointing Cyrus, who would permit the Jewish people to return home, to the land of Israel. Isaiah prophesied the birth of the Messiah, His message, His rejection and His sufferings. Isaiah was a great prophet, a man who received an abundance of prophecies from the Lord concerning His people and His Messiah. Last of all, Isaiah was the first to bring all three members of the plural unity of *Elohim* together in at least three chapters (Isaiah 48:12-16; 61:1; 63:7-14). These chapters provide the best evidence for the tri-unity of *Elohim* in the Hebrew Scriptures.

The Caller of Israel Sent by the Father ... Isaiah 48:12-16

> Listen to Me, O Jacob, Israel, whom I have called: I am He—I am the first, and I am the last as well. My own hand founded the earth, My right hand spread out the skies. I call unto them, let them stand up. (verses 12-13)

> Draw near to Me and hear this: From the beginning, I did not speak in secret; from the time anything existed, I was there. And now the Lord God has sent Me, endowed with His spirit. (verse 16)

The passage begins with a familiar word, *Shema*, the same word used in Deuteronomy 6:4. It becomes obvious that God wants Israel to hear because He uses

---

[970] Feinberg, *The Minor Prophets*, 328.
[971] Hengstenberg, *Christology of the Old Testament,* 4:35.
[972] Smith, *The Promised Messiah,* 444.
[973] Merrill, *An Exegetical Commentary: Haggai, Zechariah, Malachi*, 298.

the term *listen* (*Shema*) in verses 12, 14, and 16. Yet in verse 18 *Yahweh* says that Israel did not hear or obey His commandments. One reason is that the English text just referenced (Jewish Tanakh) has been altered in verse 16 to remove the clearest example of the tri-unity of God in the entire *Tanakh*. In verse 12, the speaker is establishing that He called them by saying, "*Listen* (*Shema*) *to me, O Jacob, Israel, whom I called.*" According to Judges 2:1, the Messenger (Angel) of *Yahweh* called Israel where He references the Abrahamic Covenant in Genesis 15. All three references reflect the same person. *Yahweh* continues speaking by saying, "*I AM He, I AM the first, I AM the last.*" That phrase simply means that *Yahweh* was before time and will be after time is no more. *Yahweh* continues in verse 13 reflecting back to Genesis 1 by identifying Himself as *Elohim* the Creator whose "*own hand founded the earth, My right hand spread out the skies. I call unto them, let them stand up.*" Verses 14 and 15 refer to Cyrus, the Mede, who will judge Babylon and allow Israel to return. In verse 16 it is as if *Yahweh* were calling Israel to come close and hear (*Shema*). He makes one point: "*I did not speak in secret*" nor did He hide His thoughts from them. From the time of their calling, even the calling of Cyrus, He was there. Young accurately states that from the beginning God spoke openly and clearly to His people as He clearly and openly presented the tri-unity of Himself. That plurality and tri-unity He has been revealing from the very beginning:

> *Beginning* refers to the time when God first began to give prophetic revelations. From the moment that God first spoke to man through the prophets He did not speak in secret but openly and clearly.[974]

Up to this point, in these verses there is general agreement among scholars that it is *Yahweh* who is speaking. However, in the last part of verse 16 there is no unanimity among scholars as to who is speaking.

There are two contradictory views concerning the identity of the speaker in Isaiah 48:16c, "*And now the Lord God has sent me, endowed with His spirit.*" A footnote in the Jewish Tanakh says that it literally reads "and His spirit,"[975] The footnote will lead to a clear statement of the tri-unity of God whereas the reference from the text will not. Slotki says that according to Rabbi David Kimchi (1160-1235), the "sent one" was the prophet who was present, and he would be sent with His Spirit within him.[976] According to Slotki, "Bible critics" have come to the conclusion that there are three Isaiah's who wrote the book of Isaiah; the second (Deutero-) Isaiah would be the prophet represented in verse 16.[977] Others in the same frame as Slotki say that there are two Isaiahs. These scholars want to change speakers and insert Isaiah or

---

[974] Young, *The Book of Isaiah*, 3:258.

[975] Berlin and Brettler, *The Jewish Study Bible*, 882.

[976] Slotki, *The Soncino Books of the Bible, Isaiah*, 237.

[977] Slotki, *The Soncino Books of the Bible, Isaiah, Introduction* x.

an anonymous "Second Isaiah."[978] Yet still others believe that the speaker is *Yahweh* Himself. Wolf summarizes the two views as to the speaker:

> The phrase the Sovereign LORD has sent me, with his Spirit, either means that God sent Isaiah to speak these words through the power of the Holy Spirit or that God would send the servant as another of the new things He would perform [Isaiah 48:6].[979]

Webb points out that the speaker in Isaiah 48:16c must be the Servant of the LORD (*Yahweh* the Messiah) due to the context in which the statement is placed. Webb gives his thoughts on the subject that *Yahweh* is speaking before and immediately following the phrase in question. So since *Yahweh* is speaking both before and after the phrase "*And now the Lord God has sent Me, and His spirit*" (KJV), it makes no logical sense to say that someone else is speaking:

> With this issue hanging heavily in the air, the scene is set for the Servant of the LORD to take center stage again in chapter 49. In fact it is more than likely that his voice has already been heard here in chapter 48. For who else can it be who announces his presence in verse 16 with the words, And now the Sovereign LORD has sent me, with his Spirit?

> But the reference to the Spirit pointedly recalls the presentation of the Servant in 42:1, I will put my Spirit on him. And the voice we hear in the Sovereign LORD has sent me sounds remarkably like the voice we are about to hear again in 49:1: before I was born the LORD called Me.[980]

Vine does not even make reference to the comment that there is another speaker in verse 16c. He points to the speaker as being the Messiah. He very clearly states his view:

> The close of verse 16 brings before us a striking instance of the work of the Trinity: and now the Lord God hath sent Me and His Spirit. That Christ is the Speaker, and not the prophet is to be gathered from a comparison with 61:1. His words are undoubtedly a prelude to what He is about to declare of Himself in chapter 49:5-6.[981]

To the contrary, Young points out that the Lord and the speaker are two different persons:

> Who is the speaker in the third clause? Obviously it cannot be the Lord, for a distinction is made between the speaker and the Lord.

---

[978] Barry G. Webb, *The Message of Isaiah* (Downers Grove, IL: Inter-Varsity, 1996), 192.

[979] Wolf, *Interpreting Isaiah*, 204.

[980] Webb, *The Message of Isaiah*, 192.

[981] Vine, *Isaiah*, 139.

The speaker is the Servant par excellence, already introduced in 42:1, and about to be brought more prominently into the picture in chapters forty-nine, fifty, and fifty-three.[982]

The point of this whole discussion is to discover who is in view in verse 16. There are two sides with completely opposing views. If the speaker is not *Yahweh*, minimally the plural unity of *Elohim* is still present with the "*Lord God*" and "*His Spirit*." But if *Yahweh* (Me) is the speaker, from verse 12 onward, the tri-unity of God is present. This is significant, if *Yahweh* is the speaker. The one who called Israel (Abrahamic Covenant), also identified Himself as the I AM (Exodus 3:14), the first and last, and the Creator in Genesis 1. Verse 16c gives three distinct personalities in the Godhead. The reference of "Me" is distinct from the Lord God (*Adonai Elohim*) and is distinct from the Holy Spirit. Simply put, *the Lord God* (Father) *and the Holy Spirit sends Me* (Son). It is not a coincidence that in the Gospel of John over 40 times *Yeshua* refers to the fact that the Father sent Him, which corresponds with Isaiah 48:16 as well as with Zechariah 2:6-11. In Isaiah 48:16 there is a very clear presentation of the tri-unity of *Elohim*, which is supported by Barackman, Strong, and Berkhof. Strong's position is clear when he states that "there are three who are implicitly recognized as God."[983] Berkhof, in referencing the tri-unity of God in Isaiah 48:16, says that in the Hebrew Scriptures God spoke to other members of the Godhead and the Messiah spoke of God the Spirit:

> God is the speaker, and mentions both the Messiah and the Spirit, or the Messiah is the speaker who mentions both God and the Spirit, Isaiah 48:16; 61:1; 63:9, 10. Thus the Old Testament contains a clear anticipation of the fuller revelation of the Trinity in the New Testament.[984]

Likewise, Barackman specifically states that Isaiah 48:16 is a reference to the tri-unity of God in the Hebrew Scriptures:

> That the Trinity consists of more than two Persons is indicated by the plural noun "God" (Heb. Elohim in Gen 1:1) and the plural pronoun "us" (Gen 1:26; 3:22; 11:7; Isa 6:8). The three Persons of the Trinity are seen in Isaiah 48:16 and 61:1, with the Son (the Messiah) speaking in both passages (cp. Isa. 49:8-9 with Luke 4:16-21).[985]

Another interesting observation by Wilkinson concerning the tri-unity and the Hebrew letter שׁ, shin:

> They [Jews] believed that doctrine in ancient times, to which ancient Jewish literature (including the Talmud) bears ample testimony. Even the letter שׁ, shin, the initial letter of the word "Shaddai" (Almighty), was formerly taken by Jews

---

[982] Young, *Isaiah*, 3:258-259.

[983] Strong, *Systematic Theology*, 317-318.

[984] Berkhof, *Systematic Theology*, 86.

[985] Barackman, *Practical Christian Theology*, 63.

to represent the manner of the Divine existence – three in one, a Trinity – with its three perpendicular strokes, and one horizontal uniting the three.[986]

In summary, the evidence is there, from numerous sources, that Isaiah 48:16 is a reference to the triune God of the Hebrew Scriptures.

Nazareth Synagogue ... Isaiah 61:1-2a

(1) The Spirit of the Lord God is upon me, because the LORD has anointed me; He has sent me as a herald of joy to the humble, to bind up the wounded of heart,

(2) to proclaim release to the captives, liberation to the imprisoned; to proclaim a year of the LORD's favor.

This is a well-known passage from the New Covenant because *Yeshua* quoted it when He read from the scroll of Isaiah in the synagogue in Nazareth (Luke 4:16-22). The only thing the Soncino Commentary series has to say about these verses is that the anointing is to be taken metaphorically because only kings and priests were anointed.[987] However, it seems unlikely that *Yeshua* would have been anointed since He was neither an earthly king nor a priest. So how was He anointed? According to Isaiah 11:2 and 42:1, *Yeshua*, by the Holy Spirit, would be anointed for service. Matthew 3:16 says exactly the same thing as Isaiah 61:1, that He was anointed, not with oil, but with the Holy Spirit.

The tri-unity of God is clearly enunciated in Isaiah 61:1. Kaiser speaks to the point by saying:

Yahweh appoints the Servant and the Spirit anoints him, hereby making one of the earliest constructs of the doctrine of the Trinity. Rather than being anointed with oil as many [of] the priests and kings in the OT, this Servant is anointed by the Holy Spirit himself.[988]

Vine states firmly that "this passage speaks of the Trinity."[989] Young echoes that point by saying that Isaiah 61:1 is Trinitarian in content and that the speaker is the Messiah.[990] Berkhof recognizes all three passages as representing the tri-unity of God (Isaiah 48:16; 61:1; 63:7-10).

---

[986] Wilkinson, *Israel My Glory*, 175.

[987] Slotki, *The Soncino Books of the Bible, Isaiah*, 298.

[988] Walter C. Kaiser, *The Messiah in the Old Testament* (Grand Rapids: Zondervan, 1995), 183.

[989] Vine, *Isaiah*, 199.

[990] Young, *The Book of Isaiah*, 3:459.

(7) I will recount the kind acts of the LORD, The praises of the LORD for all that the LORD has wrought for us, The vast bounty to the House of Israel that He bestowed upon them according to His mercy and His great kindness. (8) He thought: Surely they are My people, children who will not play false, so He was their deliverer. (9) In all their troubles He was troubled, and the angel of His Presence delivered them. In His love and pity He Himself redeemed them, raised them and exalted them all the day of old. (10) But they rebelled, and grieved His holy spirit; then He became their enemy, and Himself made war against them.

(11) Then they remembered the ancient days, Him, who pulled His people out [of the water]: "Where is He who brought them up from the Sea along with the shepherd of His flock? Where is He who put in their midst His holy spirit, (12) Who made His glorious arm March at the right hand of Moses, Who Divided the waters before them to make Himself a name for all time, (13) Who led them through the deeps so that they did not stumble as a horse in a desert, (14) Like a beast descending to the plain"? Twas the spirit of the LORD gave them rest; thus did you shepherd your people to win for Yourself a glorious name.

In Isaiah 48:16 and 61:1, Isaiah emphasizes the tri-unity of God. In the previous two references the tri-unity of God was in one verse, but here it is spread out over several verses. Isaiah himself is speaking on behalf of *Yahweh*. He refers to *Yahweh* in verse 7; the "*Angel of His presence*" (Exodus. 23:20-23) in verse 9, who saved Israel from their affliction, was the Messenger (Angel) of *Yahweh* that appeared throughout biblical history in the *Tanakh,* who led Israel out of Egypt, through the wilderness and into the Promised Land, Canaan. Then in chapter 63, verses 10 and 14, Isaiah references the Holy Spirit. Once again, the tri-unity of God is present.

The Tri-unity, or Trinity as many New Covenant believers use the term, is a difficult subject to explain. How should they explain such a subject and not be misunderstood by both Jewish people and also by Moslems who equally reject the concept of the triune God? Norman Geisler the former President of Southern Evangelical Seminary in Charlotte, NC, gives some helpful points in his lengthy statement which is entitled "The Rationality of the Trinity:"

The word "Trinity" may not be used in the Bible, but the concept of one God in three Persons is definitely there from the first to the last. They may then object that the concept of the Trinity does not make logical sense. Refer them to an illustration put together by Norman Geisler who also says that "the doctrine of the Trinity cannot be proven by human reason; it is only known because it is revealed by special revelation (in the Bible). However, just because it is beyond reason does not mean that it goes against reason. It is not irrational or contradictory, as Muslim scholars believe.

Geisler then refers to the law of non-contradiction to demonstrate how the concept of the Trinity is not irrational. The law of non-contradiction basically stipulates that something cannot be both true and false at the same time. For example, in regard to the truth of Islam and Christianity, there can only be three possibilities: either (1) Islam is true and Christianity is false, or Christianity is true and Islam is false, or (3) they are both false. The one possibility that cannot be entertained is to say that both of them are true since they make contradictory statements in reference to Jesus being God.

When we look at the rationality of the concept of the Trinity, it can be seen more easily if we state what it is not. For example, the Trinity is not the belief that God is three persons and only one person at the same time. This would be a contradiction. Nor would it be logical to say that the Trinity is the belief that there are three natures in one nature, or three essences in one essence, for that again would be a contradiction. We could agree with our Muslim friend that either of these conditions would be illogical as a "one in three" formula. However, the belief that God is one nature in three persons may be a mystery, but it is not a logical contradiction. As Geisler put it, "While God is one and many at the same time, he is not one and many in the same sense. He is one in the sense of his essence but many in the sense of his persons. So there is no violation of the law of non-contradiction in the doctrine of the Trinity."[991]

The Tri-unity of *Elohim* may be a difficult subject to explain. However, the reality is that *Elohim* throughout the pages of the *Tanakh* presented Himself as a plurality in unity, yet when He spoke He spoke as one *Elohim*. In only four places did He violate that pattern, one of which is found in the creation of mankind from Genesis 1:26 where mankind is made in the plural image of *Elohim*. Mankind is created in plurality, male and female. Couple that with the fact that each individual person on earth is trichotomous, made up of body, soul and spirit. *Elohim* is not only a plurality in unity but so is mankind a plurality or tri-unity wrapped up into one person. The pages of Scripture do not contradict themselves, even though it is a difficult doctrine to comprehend. Arnold Fruchtenbaum clearly draws the line of distinction when he says:

> The Bible teaches a plurality in the God-head, but it never teaches a plurality of gods, only a plurality of Persons.[992]

---

[991] Daniel Janosik, "Explaining the Trinity to a Muslim," *Christian Apologetics Journal* (volume 4, no. 2, Fall 2005): 81.

[992] Arnold Fruchtenbaum, *The Trinity: Manuscript #50* (Tustin, CA: Ariel Press), 12.

Chapter 11
Holy Spirit in the Tanakh רוּחַ קָדֶשׁ

The men who penned the New Covenant clearly perceived the Holy Spirit to be as much "God" as they did *Yeshua* (Jesus). However, the study of the Holy Spirit in the *Tanakh* is still slightly challenging. People of a Unitarian belief only see the Holy Spirit as an impersonal power or influence of God. Once again, can it be determined from the Hebrew Scriptures alone that the Holy Spirit is indeed God, equal in His nature and essence with God the Father and God the Son? The distinctions – first, second, and third person – are not believed to be a reference to rank because all three persons are equal in power and honor.[993] The New Covenant has abundant references to the person of the Holy Spirit, and because of this abundance, many authors rely heavily on the New Covenant to prove the personality of the Holy Spirit. In dealing with progressive revelation in relationship to Messiah, the Son of God is clearly seen. The Holy Spirit in the *Tanakh* was not as clearly stated as in the New Covenant, but He is there and active. This chapter will substantiate the distinct person of the Holy Spirit in the Hebrew Scriptures.

DIFFICULTIES WITH THE TERM "SPIRIT" רוּחַ

One of the difficulties with the Holy Spirit is how to determine if He is distinct from God the Father because the Father is also spirit. Erickson states the problem of understanding the term "Spirit" as it relates to God:

> It is often difficult to identify the Holy Spirit within the Old Testament, for it reflects the earliest stages of progressive revelation. In fact, the term "Holy Spirit" is rarely employed here. Rather, the usual expression is "the Spirit of God."[994]

Louis Goldberg, a Jewish believer in Messiah, draws attention to a basic understanding scholars must have as they deal with the distinction between God, who is a spirit, and the Holy Spirit. He states the following:

> Of course, our Jewish friends do not acknowledge the Spirit as One in the tri-unity of God; the term Spirit is recognized as a synonym for God.[995]

---

[993] Leon J. Wood, *The Holy Spirit in the Old Testament* (Eugene, OR: Wipf and Stock Publishers, 1998), 13.

[994] Erickson, *Christian Theology*, 2nd Ed, 881.

[995] Goldberg, *Our Jewish Friends,* 83.

John Feinberg also expresses the difficulty of determining whether a certain text is speaking of the Father's spirit or the Holy Spirit:

> The OT also frequently refers to the Spirit of God. Though in some passages such as Gen 6:3 ("My spirit shall not strive") and Ps 139:7 (the psalmist asks God, "Where can I go from thy Spirit?") it is not entirely clear whether the Spirit is a distinct personage or rather a reference to God the Father's Spirit, there are many passages in which the Spirit is distinct.[996]

As Goldberg and Feinberg have observed, verses that refer to the Spirit of God are difficult to prove the distinction between the Father and the Holy Spirit. Hildebrandt echoes Feinberg's explanation that the Hebrew Scriptures reveal the "Spirit" but that the focus is different than in the New Covenant when he says:

> But the main difficulty in presenting the personhood of the Spirit in the OT is due to the OT focus on the deeds of the Spirit in relation to humankind. Thus, non-personal words and phrases are used to describe the Spirit as divine energy, as a wind and fire, as light and space.[997]

Some authors, such as Erickson, see clearly the Third Person of the Godhead in the Hebrew Scriptures but also recognize the difficulties in distinguishing His person. Erickson points out that the words "spirit" and "God" are two nouns and that many times the reader cannot distinguish between the two different persons, as he shows in the following quote:

> Most Old Testament references to the Third Person of the trinity consist of the two nouns *Spirit* and *God*. It is not apparent from this construction that a separate person is involved. The expression "Spirit of God" could well be understood as being simply a reference to the will, mind, or activity of God. There are however, some cases where the New Testament makes it clear that an Old Testament reference to the "Spirit of God" is a reference to the Holy Spirit. One of the most prominent of these New Testament passages is Acts 2:16-21, where Peter explains that what is occurring at Pentecost is the fulfillment of the prophet Joel's statement, "I will pour out my Spirit on all people" (2:17).[998]

These authors express the same concerns that this author has on how the term "spirit" is used in connection with God. However, T. S. Caulley goes too far when he makes a definite statement that the Holy Spirit is not mentioned, as a person, in the Hebrew Scriptures. He states:

> The OT does not contain an idea of a semi-independent divine entity, the Holy Spirit. Rather, we find special expressions of God's activity with and through

---

[996] John S. Feinberg, *No One Like Him* (Wheaton, IL: Crossway Books, 2001), 454.

[997] Wilf Hildebrandt, *An Old Testament Theology of the Spirit of God* (Peabody, MA: Hendrickson, 1995), 89.

[998] Erickson, *Christian Theology*, 2nd Ed, 882.

men. God's spirit is holy in the same way his word and his name are holy; they are all forms of his revelation and, as such, are set in antithesis to all things human or material.[999]

Caulley leaves the impression that the Holy Spirit is not a separate entity from the other members of the Godhead. He further confirms that impression when he states:

Holy Spirit: In the NT, the third person of the Trinity; in the OT, God's power. In the OT the spirit of the Lord is generally an expression for God's power, the extension of himself whereby he carries out many of his mighty deeds.[1000]

Caulley seems to deny the personality of the Holy Spirit in the *Tanakh*. J. H. Raven is quoted by Erickson who reflects the same view as Caulley, when he states the following:

There is here no distinction of persons in the God-head. The Spirit of God in the Old Testament is God himself exercising active influence.[1001]

That statement is not acceptable, as will be seen later in this chapter, because the *Tanakh* does make a distinction between "God" and the "Spirit." God, as the greatest communicator in the universe who reveals Himself as a plurality in the Hebrew Scriptures, would not reveal His nature and essence in an incomplete manner. The writers of the New Covenant completely understood the concept of the plurality of *Elohim*, including the Holy Spirit, as the third person of the Godhead. How did they come to understand that concept? It was through the *Tanakh*! Some scholars do not see the Holy Spirit in verses that speak of the spirit, which admittedly are sometimes difficult or hard to interpret. Consequently, only the verses that show, without question, that the Holy Spirit is a person, will be dealt with in this chapter.

The Use of the Term "Spirit"

The basic idea of *ruah* (Gr. *Pneuma*) is "air in motion" from air which cannot come between a crocodile's scales (Job 41:16) to the blast of a storm (Isaiah 25:4; Habakkuk 1:11). The Hebrew word רוּחַ or *ruah* is used 387 times in the Hebrew Scriptures.[1002] Wood says that *ruah* is used in a noun or verb form 388 times. Wood further states that it is used in the following ways:

---

[999] Elwell, *Evangelical Dictionary of Theology*, 521-522.

[1000] Elwell, *Evangelical Dictionary of Theology*, 521.

[1001] Erickson, *Christian Theology*, 2nd Ed, 882. Erickson quotes J.H. Raven from his work *The History of the Religion of Israel* (Grand Rapids, MI: Baker, 1979), 164.

[1002] VanGemeren, *Dictionary of Old Testament and Exegesis*, 3:1073.

It is used to designate the human spirit, God's Holy Spirit, and several other entities such as "wind," "breath," "odor," and "space." Surprisingly, its most basic meaning seems to have been "wind."[1003]

Ruah [spirit] is used in all portions of the *Tanakh* as Hildebrandt gives the divisions of each section of the Hebrew Scriptures. It is used 38 times in the Torah (Law), while in the Prophets 201 times (47 in former Prophets and 154 in the latter Prophets), 139 times in the Writings, and in the Aramaic portions of Daniel 11 times.[1004] Of the 387 times that *ruah* is used, 136 times the term is applied to God and 129 times to man or animals. The basic meaning is physical "wind" or "breath."[1005]

Ruah has different uses for spirit as expressed in emotions of aggressiveness (Isaiah 25:4) or anger (Judges 8:3; Proverbs 29:11). *Ruah* or breath is further used to signify activity and life (Job 17:1), a "second wind," and he "revives" (Judges 15:19; 1 Samuel 30:12; Genesis 45:27). The breath of mankind is in the hands of God (Job 12:10; Isaiah 42:5). Also, *ruah* is used of angelic beings as in "a spirit from God."[1006] Other examples of this usage of *ruah* include the wind that shakes the trees (Isaiah 7:2), in the cool of the day (Genesis 3:8), or as the breath which the Lord gives to the people (Isaiah 42:5), or even as bad breath (odor) as in Job 19:17 where the literal rendering is "my breath is strange to my wife."[1007] In the *Dictionary of Old Testament Theology and Exegesis*, it is divided into six areas (wind, compass point, breath, disposition, seat of cognition, volition and spirit) to help show the usage of *ruah*.

1. *Ruah* is used to refer to the force of nature, commonly known as wind (Exod 10:13; Num 11:31; 1 Kgs 18:45; 2 Kgs 3:17; Psa 48:7 [8]; Isa 7:2; 41:16; Jer 18:17; Ezek 17:10; Hos 13:15; Jonah 4:8).

2. *Ruah* was used as four compass points, as in "every wind" or as in every direction (Ezek 5:10-12; 12:14; 17:21; Jer 49:36; Ezek 37:9; Zech 2:6 [10]; Dan 7:2).

3. *Ruah* is also rendered as breath, which is similar to wind, in that both denote the movement of air. It is used to "refer to the life-sustaining function called breathing or breath. This breath is the essence of life (Gen 6:17; Job 12:10; Isa 38:16; 42:5; Ezek 37:5-14; Mal 2:15-16)."

4. *Ruah* is used to show "a person's or group's disposition, attitude, mood, inclination, as an approximate synonym of *nepel*, appetite, disposition, person (Gen 26:35; Exod 6:9; 1 Kgs 21:5; Job 21:4; Prov 14:29; Isa 19:3; Ezek 3:14)."

[1003] Wood, *The Holy Spirit in the Old Testament*, 16.

[1004] Hildebrandt, *An Old Testament Theology of the Spirit of God*, 2.

[1005] Dyrness, *Themes in Old Testament Theology*, 86.

[1006] Harris, Archer, and Waltke, *Theological Wordbook of the Old Testament*, 836.

[1007] Dyrness, *Themes in Old Testament Theology*, 86.

5. *Ruah* denotes the seat of cognition and volition, those activities involved in thinking, aptitude, and decision-making. The knowledge and ability to perform a particular task is one clear example of this use of *ruah* (I Chr 28:12; Isa 29:24; Ezek 11:5-6; 20:32; 38:10).

6. Lastly, in the *Tanakh* the most significant usage of *ruah* involves its representation of the metaphysical or numinous, specifically the "Spirit of God/ the LORD." The expression "Spirit of God" actually appears only 11 times (Gen 1:2; Psa 104:29; Job 33:4), "Spirit of the LORD" 25 times (Judg 9:23; 1 Sam 16:14-16, 23; 18:10; 19:9), and Holy Spirit 3 times (Psa 51:11 [13]; Isa 63:10-11).[1008]

PERSONALITY AND WORK OF THE HOLY SPIRIT IN THE *TANAKH*

Many Scriptures deal with *ruah* in a non-personal manner, but the focus of this paper is on the ways in which the term reflects the personality of the Holy Spirit and that He is distinct from the Father and the Son. The Holy Spirit did operate in the New Covenant as a person, but it is different in the *Tanakh* in that He did his work in the form of acts without using a personal description of Himself.

The Holy Spirit Is a Person

If the plurality of *Elohim* is true and can stand on its own in the *Tanakh* without the well documented New Covenant, the tri-unity of the New Covenant should also be able to stand on its own in the Hebrew Scriptures, in relation to the Holy Spirit. Morey uses the same logic to argue that whatever biblical evidence is used to show the Son must be taken the same way in relation to the Holy Spirit:

The Biblical evidence that convinced us that the Father and the Son are Persons, is the exact same kind of evidence that demonstrates that the Spirit is a Person. Thus, to deny the evidence when we apply it to the Spirit, but to accept it when we apply it to the Father or to the Son is sheer hypocrisy as well as being self-refuting. If the evidence is valid for One, then it is valid for all Three.[1009]

Passages that affirm the Holy Spirit's personality will be examined first. Both David Cooper and Robert Morey express this point:

Turning back to our original passage, Isaiah 63:8-10, we see God who becomes the Saviour of Israel (vs. 8). In verse 9 the angel of His presence saved her [Israel] in that He carried out the actual plan of the Almighty. Then in verse 10

[1008] VanGemeren, *Dictionary of Old Testament and Exegesis*, 3:1073-1076.

[1009] Morey, *The Trinity: Evidence and Issues*, 188.

we note the Holy Spirit whom she grieved and against whom she rebelled. Thus in these three verses we see three divine personalities.[1010]

First, Isaiah says that רוּחַ קָדְשׁוֹ "His Holy Spirit" was וְעִצְּבוּ "grieved to the point of being provoked." The word וְעִצְּבוּ is a waw consecutive participle of עָצַב and means to feel profound hurt, pain, and grief. For example, the word עָצַב was used to describe the inward pain felt by David when he heard that his son Absalom was dead (2 Sam 19:1-2). His weeping reveals how deeply he felt the pain. It was even used of God in Gen 6:6, where we are told, "He was grieved in His heart." Secondly, only a Person can be grieved by מָרוּ "rebellion" against Him. Thus, the Holy Spirit is a Person and not an impersonal force.[1011]

Walvoord agrees with Cooper and Morey that the Isaiah 63:10 passage expresses the personality of the Holy Spirit.[1012] Here the Holy Spirit is not only recognized as a person but as a distinct person from the other members of the tri-unity.

In Micah 2:7 the author expresses the fact that the Holy Spirit is capable of being impatient. Being impatient is a quality of a person. A wind or force does not have the personal capacity to be annoyed or be impatient. Morey states that fact:

The word [verb] translated "impatient" is הֲקָצַר which is a qal perfect of the word קָצַר which means to be impatient. It is used in this sense in such places as Num 21:4; Judg 10:16; 16:16, etc. The question, "Is the Spirit of the LORD impatient?" reveals that the Jews believed that the Holy Spirit was a Person capable of becoming annoyed with the sin of man.[1013]

Further statements on the personality of the Holy Spirit are given by Payne in referring to Moses. Payne states that God said to Moses, "the" Spirit, not "My" Spirit, which would not indicate the Spirit of the Father, but the Spirit who is distinct from Himself:

The personality of the Spirit was first revealed to Moses. Specifically, God informed Moses relative to the seventy elders who were to assist him in government: "I will take of the Spirit who is upon you and I will place [Him] upon them, so they may bear the burden of the people with thee" (Num 11:17).This statement indicates that the Spirit is distinct from *Yahweh*, that He is personal (giving judicial advice), and that He is divine (guiding Israel).[1014]

Payne's statement shows the distinctness between two members of the tri-unity. It also shows that the Holy Spirit will guide, which is something that a person does, as He

---

[1010] Cooper, *The God of Israel*, 80.

[1011] Morey, *The Trinity: Evidence and Issues*, 189.

[1012] John Walvoord, *The Holy Spirit* (Findlay, OH: Dunham Publishing, 1958), 7.

[1013] Morey, *The Trinity: Evidence and Issues*, 190.

[1014] Payne, *The Theology of the Older Testament*, 173.

guides the 70 elders in administering judicial advice to the people of Israel. Payne also references Isaiah 48:16 ("and the Lord God has sent Me and His Spirit") and shows the Holy Spirit to be a personality that is distinct from the Father.[1015] Kirkpatrick also affirms the personality of the Holy Spirit in referencing some of the same passages already cited:

> Passages like these which imply that the spirit of Jehovah personally acts, prepare the way for the New Testament revelation concerning Him, and can be used in the fullest Christian sense.[1016]

A further confirmation on the personality of the Holy Spirit is seen in creation with the act of intelligence in relation to creation of the world. To be involved in the creation of the universe and the creation of man shows a tremendously complex mind far beyond human understanding. Ryrie refers to Job 26:13 and 33:4 where Job references the Spirit of God as the Creator.[1017] In Psalm 104:30 the psalmist says: *Thou dost send forth Thy Spirit, they are created; and Thou dost renew the face of the ground.*" Lockyer states the following in relation to this verse:

> It is evident from the immediate context that the "all" and the "they" refer to the living creatures of the whole world, and to beasts, birds, and fish in particular.[1018]

Enns expresses the personality of the Holy Spirit in showing His omnipotence and omnipresence in Job 33:4 and Psalm 139:7-10.[1019]

Not only does the "Spirit" guide and show intelligence, but in 2 Samuel 23:1 David, when on his deathbed, makes a very fascinating statement when he says that the Holy Spirit spoke by him, which is another act of personality:

> These are the last words of David: The utterance of David the son of Jesse, the utterance of the man set on high, the anointed of the God of Jacob, the favorite of the Songs of Israel: The spirit of the LORD has spoken through me, His message is on my tongue.

How much of the tri-unity of *Elohim* did David understand? That may never be known, but this text and others clarify that David minimally understood the plurality of *Elohim*. Morey makes a summary statement in relation to the Holy Spirit as a person speaking through David:

> The personhood of the Spirit is as certain as the inspiration of the Psalms of David. Notice that it is the Spirit's word which is the word of God. Only a

---

[1015] Payne, *The Theology of the Older Testament*, 173.

[1016] A. F. Kirkpatrick, *The Book of Psalms* (Cambridge: The University Press, 1914), 2:293.

[1017] Charles C. Ryrie, *The Holy Spirit* (Chicago, IL: Moody, 1965), 31.

[1018] Herb Lockyer, *All About the Holy Spirit* (Peabody, MA: Hendrickson, 1995), 46.

[1019] Enns, *The Moody Handbook of Theology*, 250.

Person can speak the word of God. Only a self-conscious living, person speaks.[1020]

Once again in Nehemiah 9:30 the personality of the Holy Spirit is given in that He testified against rebellious Israel. Morey makes a firm statement that only a person has the capability of "testifying" or giving witness:"

> The word translated "testified against" is וַתָּעַד which is a waw consecutive imperfect and means to bear witness, testify, or protest against someone. It is used of God (Psa 50:7; 81:8) as well as man (Gen 43:3; Deut 8:19). An impersonal force or power cannot bear witness, testify or protest anything.[1021]

Ezekiel gives a very clear example of the personality of the Holy Spirit in Ezekiel 2:2; 8:3; 11:1. Here the Lord God tells Ezekiel to get up, and then the "Spirit entered me [Ezekiel]." In the other two passages the "Spirit lifted me up." This refers to the activity of the Holy Spirit in His act of lifting up Ezekiel.[1022] These verses cited serve as several examples to substantiate the personality of the Holy Spirit. Again, as Morey has stated, if the same evidence to confirm the fact of the personality of the Second Person of the plural unity of *Elohim* is used, the Holy Spirit must be treated in the same manner.

Holy Spirit in Creation

Pache relates that the account of the creation is an allusion to the Trinity and indirectly to the Spirit. In Genesis 1:1 *Elohim*, (discussed in chapter 3 as a plural noun) could be just as easily translated "In the beginning, the Gods created." Included with *Elohim* in verse 1 is verse 26 where *Elohim* shows His plurality by referring to Himself with a plural personal pronoun.[1023] The only other person of *Elohim* that is mentioned is in Genesis 1:2 where Moses says that *Elohim*, the Spirit, hovered, moved or brooded over the face of the waters. Several Jewish and Christian authors attribute the "wind" as being the impersonal force from *Elohim*. Towner makes a statement that "spirit" should not be capitalized because the Priestly (P) writers knew nothing about the Trinity.[1024] Modern scholars using higher criticism have concluded that different authors using different documents composed the Pentateuch. This documentary hypothesis put forth by liberal theologians identified passages by supposed sources into terms known today as Yahwistic (J), Elohistic (E), Deuteronomic (D), and Priestly (P), codes that were combined to form the Pentateuch. Gunkel in his book even divides his table of contents in a way that reflects this view: the primeval History according to J, then primeval

---

[1020] Morey, *The Trinity: Evidence and Issues*, 191.

[1021] Morey, *The Trinity: Evidence and Issues*, 191-192.

[1022] Erickson, *Christian Theology*, 2nd Ed., 882.

[1023] Rene Pache, *The Person and Work of the Holy Spirit* (Chicago, IL: Moody, 1954), 29.

[1024] Towner, *Westminster Bible Companion: Genesis,* 17.

History in P, Abraham Legends of J and E.[1025] These are completely fictitious authors that liberal theologians have concocted to explain the Old Testament in secular terms and remove the supernatural aspect of the inspiration of Scripture. They have lost sight of the fact that God is the author of the Bible and He wrote through the agency of man. His Word was written exactly as He wanted it written, when He wrote it and by whom He said wrote it. The net result is that by 1890 this new secular approach had rejected the Mosaic authorship of the Pentateuch, except by conservative biblical scholars who held to verbal, plenary inspiration of the Scriptures.[1026] It was not the Priestly (P) authors that wrote Genesis 1:2, but God who wrote it through Moses. God knows His own nature, and it is the conclusion of this author that Moses knew His nature. So Towner's comment of the "spirit" to void a reference to the Holy Spirit in creation is not consistent with the Word of God.

In returning to Genesis 1:2 Hildebrandt refers to Rabbi Zlotowitz who states "and the divine presence hovered upon the surface of the water."[1027] Zlotowitz argues that the "Spirit of God" was an impersonal force, not the "Holy Spirit," that was the active one in verse 2. Both Hildebrandt[1028] and Allen Ross[1029] recognize in verse 2 the personality of the Holy Spirit in creation. They refer to Deuteronomy 32:11 in relation to the Spirit who moved upon the waters. Hildebrandt disagrees with the Rabbi Zlotowitz who wants to suppress the thought of the personality of God in Genesis 1:2. Wood makes the following statement in affirming the personality of the Holy Spirit:

> There are several Scripture passages that speak of the Holy Spirit's having had a part in the creative work. The most significant is Genesis 1:2, "And the Spirit of God moved upon the face of the water." The important word here is moved (*merahapeth*). The Hebrew form is a piel participle, connoting continued action. The thought in view is well illustrated in Deuteronomy 32:11, where the only other piel form of the word in the Old Testament is found. In this passage God's care of Israel in the wilderness is likened to an eagle fluttering over her young in providing for them. The idea of the word in Genesis 1:2, then, is that the Holy Spirit "fluttered over," "took care of," "moved upon" the chaotic state of the world in the interest of bringing order and design. Since the indication comes immediately before the description of the six-day creative activity, the implication is that the work of the six days was performed by the Spirit.[1030]

Walvoord states that all the host of heaven was made by the Holy Spirit (Psalm 33:6). He expresses the creative act as a beautiful picture painted of the heavens being garnished by the Holy Spirit (Job 26:13). These heavens that the Holy Spirit has made

---

[1025] Hermann Gunkel, *Mercer Library of Biblical Studies: Genesis* (Macon, GA: Mercer University Press, 1997), contents.

[1026] Alexander and Baker, *Dictionary of the Old Testament Pentateuch*, 61-62.

[1027] Rabbi M. Zlotowitz, *Bereishis: Genesis* (Brooklyn, NY: Mesorah Press, 1986), 1:38.

[1028] Hildebrandt, *An Old Testament Theology of the Spirit of God*, 36.

[1029] Allen P. Ross, *Creation & Blessing: Genesis* (Grand Rapids: Baker, 1988), 107.

[1030] Wood, *The Holy Spirit in the Old Testament*, 30.

"declare the glory of God" (Psalm 19:1). The heavens that the Holy Spirit created have a distinctive characteristic of being designed to bring glory to the Father and Son. It is understood from the New Covenant in John 16:13-14 that the Holy Spirit does not glorify Himself but brings glory to the Son. Walvoord sums up his statement on the Holy Spirit in His active part in creation by saying:

> The work of the Holy Spirit ever bears this characteristic, as it reflects the glory of God, the Holy Spirit not being in the foreground.

> In the work of creation itself, then, the Holy Spirit is revealed to have a distinct character of operation. He brings order to creation; He is the Giver of life; and shapes creation to achieve its significant purpose of bringing all glory to God.[1031]

Walvoord states that even the term *Elohim* implies a work not done by one person but all the members of the triune God.[1032] So when Genesis 1:1 speaks of *Elohim* creating, it involves all the Godhead as the Son is involved in creation in Isaiah 48:13 and Zechariah 12:1. Solomon, in Ecclesiastes 12:1, also implies that all the members of the triune *Elohim* were involved in creation and are to be remembered. Walvoord then proceeds to reference Isaiah 40:12-14 to show that the Spirit is revealed as the Creator by implication:

> The Holy Spirit is described as the untaught, uncounselled, and omnipotent God, who without need of instruction or assistance measured the waters, the heavens, the dust of the earth, and the mountains. His intimate connection with the plan and management of the universe is apparent.[1033]

Since *Elohim* created the universe and the earth, R. A. Torrey continues the argument that the *Elohim* is plural, which includes the Father, Son and Holy Spirit in creation. He states the following in relation to *Elohim*, which adds further information to chapter 2 of this book and implies the Holy Spirit, as well as the Father and Son in creation, was *Elohim*:

> Why did the Hebrews, with their unquestionable and intense monotheism, use a plural name for God? This was the question that puzzled the Hebrew grammarians and lexicographers of the past, and the best explanation that they could arrive at was the plural of God here used was 'the pluralis majestatis,' that is, the plural of majesty. But this explanation is entirely inadequate. To say nothing of the fact that the pluralis majestatis in the Old Testament is a figure of very doubtful occurrence – I have not been able to find any place in the Old Testament where it is clear that the pluralis majestatis is used – but in addition to that, even if it were true that the pluralis majestatis does occur in the Old

---

[1031] Walvoord, *The Holy Spirit*, 42.
[1032] Walvoord, *The Holy Spirit*, 39.
[1033] Walvoord, *The Holy Spirit*, 37-38.

Testament, there is another explanation for the use of a plural name for God that is far nearer at hand and far more adequate and satisfactory, and that is, that the Hebrew inspired writers used a plural name for God, in spite of their intense monotheism, because there is a plurality of person in the one Godhead.[1034]

Even though Torrey does not speak specifically of the Holy Spirit, he is dealing with the whole of the triune God in the word *Elohim*, which includes the Holy Spirit. So whether referring to the passages in Genesis 1:2, 26; Deuteronomy 32:11; Job 26:13; or Psalm 19:1, or with the name of God (*Elohim*), the Holy Spirit was involved in the creation of the world.

Finally, the great evangelist of the 20th century, Billy Graham, states that the Holy Spirit was involved in creation by tying together Job 33:4 with Genesis 2:7:

> When God 'formed man of dust from the ground' (Gen 2:7), the Holy Spirit was involved. We learn this indirectly in Job 33:4, 'The Spirit of God has made me, and the breath of the Almighty gives me life.' A play on words here shows how intimately God's Spirit and our breath are related: both 'Spirit' and breath' are from the same Hebrew word.[1035]

There are numerous references in the *Tanakh* that specifically state, and others that strongly imply, that the Holy Spirit who was involved in creation was a person.

Holy Spirit – Distinct from the Father and Son

In previous chapters it was shown that the Messenger (Angel) of *Yahweh* was distinct from *Yahweh* and yet *Elohim*. The *Shechinah* was distinct from *Yahweh*, and yet His presence was the presence of *Elohim* or *Yahweh*. Also, it was seen that even *Yahweh* was distinct from *Yahweh*! All of these were the representation of the Son being distinct from the Father.

Now the next logical step is to distinguish the Holy Spirit from both the Father and the Son. David, the psalmist, in Psalm 143:10 gave the distinctiveness of the Holy Spirit:

> Teach me to do thy will; for thou art my God: thy spirit is good; lead me into the land of uprightness.

Here David is asking the Spirit to lead him in righteousness as the Spirit indwells and guides him.[1036]

In Haggai 2:1-9, the one who is speaking is *Yahweh*. Yet in verse 5 *Yahweh* speaks as the covenant maker with Israel, whom He brought out of Egypt. He speaks to the fact

---

[1034] R. A. Torrey, *The Holy Spirit* (New York: Revell, 1927), 21-22.

[1035] Billy Graham, *The Holy Spirit* (Waco, TX: Word, 1978), 25.

[1036] Payne, *The Theology of the Older Testament*, 174.

that His Spirit abode among Israel. According to Cooper, the Holy Spirit came and dwelt in Israel when the Lord God, through the angel of His presence, delivered them, making the Holy Spirit distinct from the one who made the covenant with them.[1037]

In Nehemiah 9:20 the Holy Spirit is given to the people by God to instruct them. This verse shows two aspects of His person: first, He is distinct from the Lord, and secondly, He teaches, which only a person can do.

Using Isaiah 48:16, Cooper shows the distinctiveness among all three members of the tri-unity. Cooper makes the following statement:

> Along with the Messiah, God sends His spirit. The latter here is as much a person as the Creator, whom God dispatches to the earth.[1038]

Isaiah 61:1, the passage that *Yeshua* read in the Nazareth synagogue (Luke 4:16-30), also points out that the "Servant" has been anointed by *Yahweh* for a distinct ministry "to preach the good tidings" and that the "Spirit of the LORD" is upon Him. In Isaiah 63:7-10 the distinction of the Holy Spirit from the other members of the tri-unity is clear. In verse 7 the LORD is referenced and the Messenger (Angel) of His Presence is referenced in verse 9. These two personalities are distinct from the Holy Spirit in verse 10. Cooper makes the following observation:

> We must also remember Jehovah made His Holy Spirit to dwell in the midst of Israel and that later she rebelled against Him and grieved Him. Thus the Holy Spirit is recognized as God and as being separate and distinct from the Lord Jehovah.[1039]

The distinction is continued in verse 14 where it says that "*the Spirit of the LORD gave them rest.*" So Isaiah 63 presents the distinction of the personalities of the tri-unity. In concluding this section with statements by Feinberg that show even though the *Tanakh* does not explain how the Godhead is identical and different, it does show the tri-unity of *Elohim*:

> In light of this evidence, it is hard to think that the Spirit of God or Holy Spirit is less than divine. Moreover, several passages cited distinguish him from Yahweh, so the Holy Spirit is somehow both identical and distinct from the Lord. The respects in which he is identical and different are not explained in the OT, but a fairly straightforward reading of the OT about the Spirit of God suggests that there is plurality in the Godhead. Moreover, attributes and actions that could only be true of God are attributed to the Holy Spirit."[1040]

[1037] Cooper, *The God of Israel*, 80.
[1038] Cooper, *The God of Israel*, 117.
[1039] Cooper, *The God of Israel*, 84-85.
[1040] Feinberg, *No One Like Him*, 454-455.

Holy Spirit – Coming Upon and Indwelling

There is a difference and often confusion about the ministry of the Holy Spirit in relation to how He ministered to human beings then and today. What will be observed is that the Holy Spirit functioned differently with Old Testament saints than with New Covenant saints. Several things need to be noted about the ministry of the Holy Spirit under the dispensation of Law. Pache brings out two distinctions: First, "the Spirit is not given to all" and second, "the Spirit was temporarily given, and could be withdrawn."[1041] Ryrie states it a little differently when he gives three divisions that are related to the nature of the Holy Spirit's work. First, "the Spirit was in certain ones," which is illustrated with the Spirit of God in Joseph and Daniel. Second, "the Spirit is said to have come upon many" as illustrated in the book of Judges (chapters 3, 6, 11, 13-15) and 1 Samuel (10). Third, "the Spirit is said to have filled some" as recorded with Bezaleel (Exodus 31:3; 35:31).[1042] Ryrie summarizes his three previous statements:

> What do these examples indicate? Simply that, although the Spirit did indwell men of Old Testament times, it was a selective ministry, both in regard to whom He indwelt and for how long.[1043]

What should be understood is that the Spirit's activity of coming upon, or in, or filling, had nothing to do with the person or his/her spirituality. Walvoord also sees the Holy Spirit in this light when he says:

> "It will be noted, first, that the coming of the Spirit to indwell individuals has no apparent relation to spiritual qualities."[1044]

It is important to understand that the Holy Spirit's ministry was selective as to whom He came upon, in, or filled to accomplish the specific tasks or purposes that He desired. Walvoord and Payne both speak of the Holy Spirit indwelling believers, but Walvoord clarifies it by saying:

> "Only a few were indwelt by the Holy Spirit, and these were known for their distinctive gift, were sought out as leaders and prophets, and were usually marked men."[1045]

David, in his confession of his sin in Psalm 51:11, pleads with the Lord not to remove His Holy Spirit from him. David remembered vividly what happened to Saul. Because of his sin and lack of repentance, the Holy Spirit had been removed from him (1 Samuel 16:14). The fact was that the Holy Spirit could come and leave, totally unlike the ministry of the Holy Spirit in the New Covenant (John 14:17). The Holy Spirit came

---

[1041] Pache, *The Person and Work of the Holy Spirit*, 30.
[1042] Ryrie, *The Holy Spirit*, 41-42.
[1043] Ryrie, *The Holy Spirit,* 42.
[1044] Walvoord, *The Holy Spirit*, 72.
[1045] Walvoord, *The Holy Spirit*, 72.

upon people for specific tasks. Wood states that once that task was completed, He would leave:

> The Spirit came upon the persons involved for the activity concerned and then left them when that activity had been completed.[1046]

The empowering presence of the Holy Spirit upon a person for a specific task was the norm during the Old Testament period.[1047] Different aspects of the Holy Spirit's ministry of empowering will come out clearly as different individuals in the *Tanakh* are viewed.

It appears that the Holy Spirit had a broader ministry than is generally recognized. Walter Kaiser expresses that the Holy Spirit also regenerated people in the Old Testament as referenced in Jesus' conversation with Nicodemus in John 3:3-10.[1048] The Holy Spirit had a ministry among Old Testament saints, but little attention has been given to that aspect of the Holy Spirit's Old Testament ministry.

Holy Spirit's Ministry to Individuals in the Tanakh

In the following examples of the Holy Spirit's ministry to Old Testament believers, it will be observed that the Holy Spirit came upon, filled, indwelt, and left because of sin or the completion of a task. (Those aspects will be shown in bold typeface.)

Bezaleel:

Feinberg points out that in Exodus 31:2-3 God **filled** Bezaleel to do the work of an artisan as he prepared the tabernacle:

> "And I have filled him with the spirit of God, in wisdom, in understanding, and in knowledge and in all craftsmanship, to make artistic designs for work in gold, in silver and in bronze, and in the cutting of stones for setting, and in the carving of wood that he may work in all kinds of craftsmanship" (KJV).

As an artisan in the construction of the tabernacle, Bezaleel was enabled, by the Holy Spirit, to do and complete the task laid out before him. Moses concurs with what God said in Exodus 35:31.[1049]

Unnamed Tailors:

> In Exodus 28:3 God tells Moses that the tailor had been **endowed with the Spirit of wisdom** to make all the High Priestly garments.[1050]

[1046] Wood, *The Holy Spirit in the Old Testament*, 43.

[1047] VanGemeren, *Dictionary of Old Testament Theology and Exegesis,* 3:1076.

[1048] Walter C. Kaiser, *The Christian and the "Old" Testament* (Pasadena, CA: William Carey Library, 1998), 223-224.

[1049] Feinberg, *No One Like Him*, 454.

"And you shall make holy garments for Aaron your brother, for glory and for beauty. And you shall speak to all the skillful persons **whom I have endowed with the Spirit of wisdom**, that they make Aaron's garments to consecrate him, that he may minister as priest to Me. And these are the garments which they shall make: a breast piece and an ephod and a robe and a tunic of checkered work, a turban and a sash, and they shall make holy garments for Aaron your brother and his sons, that he may minister as priest to Me."

Seventy Elders:

In Numbers 11:17, 25 the LORD told Moses that He would take some of the Spirit that he had and place it **upon the seventy elders** so they could bear the burden of the people with him.

> Then I will come down and speak with you there, and I will take of the Spirit who is **upon you**, and will put Him **upon them**; and they shall bear the burden of the people with you, so that you shall not bear it all alone.

> Then the LORD came down in the cloud and spoke to him; and He took of the Spirit who was **upon him** and placed Him **upon the seventy elders**. And it came about that when the Spirit rested upon them, they prophesied.

So Moses gathered the elders together, in obedience to God, for the partial transference of the Spirit to the elders. Hildebrandt gives added information to this movement of the Spirit as some of the Spirit was transferred from Moses to the 70 elders:

> Moses gathers the seventy elders in obedience to *Yahweh's* direction so that *Yahweh* could "take" from the *ruah* on him and bestow some of the *ruah* on each of the elders. The verb *asal* indicates the "withholding" of a portion of the *ruah* that is on Moses for his leadership duties and is then distributed among the elders for their new responsibilities. The term emphasizes the great endowment of Spirit on Moses and is conceived of materially and quantitatively.[1051]

The immediate consequence of the *ruah* resting on the seventy elders was their spontaneous expression of "prophesying." In verse 29 two of the elders continued to prophesy and Joshua objected, but Moses responded by saying he wished all of the Lord's people were prophets and that the LORD would put His Spirit **upon them**. What was immediately apparent was that the Spirit was distinct from *Yahweh*, and that He was personal in giving divine judicial advice in His guidance of Israel.[1052]

[1050] Walvoord, *The Holy Spirit*, 71.

[1051] Hildebrandt, *An Old Testament Theology of the Spirit of God*, 157.

[1052] Payne, *The Theology of the Older Testament,* 173.

Balaam:

There is one non-Israelite example of the Holy Spirit coming upon a false prophet who knew the God of Israel (Numbers 22:8-35). Balaam was from Mesopotamia (Deuteronomy 23:4) and, according to the *Tanakh*, his reputation was that whomever he blessed would be blessed, and whomever he cursed would be cursed (Numbers 22:6). Balak, King of Moab, called for Balaam to curse Israel. In Numbers 23:5 the Scriptures say that the LORD put the words in Balaam's mouth and he could only speak what God put in his mouth. Then in Numbers 24:2 the Scriptures distinctly say, "and the Spirit of God **came upon him**." So Balaam was unable to curse Israel because the Spirit of God came **upon him** and he had to bless Israel.[1053]

> And Balaam lifted up his eyes and saw Israel camping tribe by tribe; and the Spirit of God **came upon him**.

This is a difficult passage in that Balaam was not a genuine prophet but rather a diviner. He knew God but did not follow God. This passage shows God's covenantal protection of Israel in taking over Balaam's mouth.[1054]

Joshua:

> So the LORD said to Moses, take Joshua the son of Nun, a man **in whom is the Spirit**, and lay your hand on him. Numbers 27:18

Joshua was prepared by the Spirit of God to be the successor of Moses and to lead Israel into the Promised Land. He was a man of God, **filled with the Spirit of wisdom** (Deuteronomy 34:9), to do a very difficult job to lead Israel and conquer the Land.

In entering the period of the judges, the Holy Spirit came upon the judges for the purpose of delivering Israel from its oppressors after Israel repented of following other gods. Four judges are specifically mentioned as having the "Spirit of the LORD come upon" them. They were Othniel, Gideon, Jephthah and Samson. Several authors, such as Wood,[1055] Hildebrandt,[1056] Lockyer,[1057] Walvoord,[1058] Erickson,[1059] Butler,[1060] and Enns,[1061] state that the Spirit, as a person, came upon the judges as they delivered Israel.

[1053] Wood, *The Holy Spirit in the Old Testament*, 44.

[1054] Lockyer, *All About the Holy Spirit,* 55.

[1055] Wood, *The Holy Spirit*, 25, 53-55. Also see: Leon J. Wood, *Distressing Days of the Judges* (Grand Rapids, MI: Zondervan, 1975), 161-171, 201-233, 278-340.

[1056] Hildebrandt, *The Holy Spirit in the Old Testament,* 114-117.

[1057] Lockyer, *All About the Holy Spirit,* 55.

[1058] Walvoord, *The Holy Spirit,* 71, 74.

[1059] Erickson, *Christian Theology,* 2nd Ed, 884.

[1060] Butler, *Butler's Bible Work,* 3:179, 210, 230, 237.

[1061] Enns, *The Moody Handbook of Theology,* 260-261.

Morey, in referring to Othniel, states that the Spirit came upon him and instructed him or enabled him. Only a person can instruct or enable judges, not a force or power.[1062]

Othniel:

Othniel the son of Kenaz, Caleb's younger brother. And the Spirit of the LORD **came upon him**, and he judged Israel. Judges 3:9-10

Block, in His discussion on the first judge, Othniel, refers to the Spirit of God, calling Him a member of the Trinity, but at the same time he wants to make Him a power or force rather than a distinct person. However, the above author of Judges distinctly implies the Spirit of God as a person came upon Othniel and enabled him to have victory over the enemy. Block's statement on the personality of the Holy Spirit is confusing because of his statement that the Holy Spirit is an extension of the LORD's personality:

Similarly, the Spirit of God is the agency/agent through which God's will is exercised, whether it be in creation, his dispensing of life, his guidance and providential care, the revelation of his will, his renewal of unregenerate hearts, or his sealing of his covenant people as his own. The Spirit of God is not a self-existent agent operating independently but 'an extension of the LORD's personality,' the third member of the Trinity, by which God exercises influence over the world.[1063]

Block's statement is unclear. Does he see the "Spirit of God" here as a person distinct from the Father, or is he making the "Spirit of God" simply an "extension" of, rather than distinct from, God?

Gideon:

So the **Spirit of the LORD came upon** Gideon; and he blew the trumpet, and the Abiezrites were called together to follow him (Judges 6:34 KJV).

What is significant about Gideon is that he was very hesitant to become the "valiant warrior," as the Messenger (Angel) of *Yahweh* called him in verse 12. He questioned God about the "wondrous deeds" He performed in the past (verse 13). His excuse, in verse 14, showed his reluctance and low position in his father's house. In verse 17 he asked for a sign because of his timidity in pulling down the altar of Baal by night because of the fear of his father's household and the town's people. Then in verse 36 Gideon made the request for the fleece. His faith was not strong, but nestled between all this is the statement in verse 34: "The spirit of the LORD enveloped" or came upon him. The Holy Spirit's personal presence came upon Gideon as He gave him divine

---

[1062] Morey, *The Trinity: Evidence and Issues,* 192.

[1063] Daniel I. Block, *The New American Commentary: Judges, Ruth.* (vol. 6. Nashville: Broadman & Holman, 1999), 6:154-155.

enablement to blow the shofar and begin to muster the men for battle.[1064] Block makes an interesting statement as to the response of the people to Gideon:

> This raises an extremely important question: Why are Gideon's clansmen, tribesmen, and countrymen so ready to respond to him? Are they impressed with his leadership ability or his courage? Do they recognize him as the "valiant warrior," whom the messenger of *Yahweh* had addressed in v. 12? Not if one may judge from the expressed perception of his standing within his own family and tribe (v.15) when God calls him to military leadership or from the trepidation with which he destroyed the Baal cult site in the preceding account (v. 31). From the succeeding narrative of the dew and the fleece (vv. 36-40) it seems that nothing has changed internally or personally. Gideon remains hesitant. Juxtaposed with a text that portrays Gideon doing all he can to avoid a leadership role, the answer must lie in the opening clause of v. 34: the Spirit of *Yahweh* "clothed" Gideon. This idiom expresses in more dramatic form the notion expressed earlier in 3:10: *"The Spirit of the LORD came upon Othniel,"* that is the Spirit took possession of the man.[1065]

What is obvious is that the Spirit of the LORD that came upon him caused him to become the "valiant warrior," and that the people flocked to him to fight the Midianites.

Jephthah:

> Then the **Spirit of the LORD came upon** Jephthah, and he passed over Gilead, and Manasseh, and passed over Mizpah of Gilead, and from Mizpah of Gilead he passed over unto the children of Ammon (Judges 11:29 KJV).

This statement of Scripture is the same as that of Othniel and Gideon. The Spirit of the LORD came upon him, as in this case, upon Jephthah. There seems to be three general ways this passage is viewed by authors: First, some authors such as Grudem,[1066] Wolf,[1067] Keil and Delitzsch,[1068] acknowledge that the Spirit of the LORD did come upon Jephthah, but they did not interact with the passage in relation to the Holy Spirit. Second, others such as Garstang[1069] and Schneider,[1070] do not even refer to the Spirit of the LORD in their discussion of Jephthah. Lastly, some authors, such as

---

[1064] John F. Walvoord and Roy B. Zuck, *The Bible Knowledge Commentary: Old Testament* (Wheaton, IL: Victor Books, 1985), 393.

[1065] Block, *The New American Commentary: Judges, Ruth*, 6:271-272.

[1066] Grudem, *Systematic Theology*, 636.

[1067] Herbert Wolf, *The Expositor's Bible Commentary: Judges* (12 vols. Grand Rapids: Zondervan, 1992), 3:455.

[1068] Keil and Delitzsch, *Commentary on the Old Testament: Judges,* 2:384.

[1069] John Garstang, *The Foundations of Bible History: Joshua, Judges* (Grand Rapids: Kregel, 1978), 329-333.

[1070] Tammi J. Schneider, *Berit Olam: Studies in Hebrew Narrative and Poetry, Judges* (Collegeville, MN: The Liturgical Press, 2000), 169-183.

McCann,[1071] state that Jephthah "looks worse than bad" while Soggin[1072] states that this section of Scripture on Jephthah was a later interpretation so as to make Jephthah a major judge rather than a minor judge. McCann and Soggin both have a tendency to discredit the person and judgeship of Jephthah.

This passage on Jephthah, in reference to the *"Spirit of the LORD,"* is a neglected area by many authors. This author believes the passage is too challenging, thus neglected, so it is passed over due to the Spirit of the LORD coming upon him and the problem with Jephthah's daughter. Yet, God found the events of this judge's life worthy of mention in Hebrews 11:32, even with this problematic passage. The simple question that must be asked is: If the Holy Spirit came upon the others that were previously mentioned in this chapter, wouldn't it be equally true in relationship to Jephthah's judgeship?

Samson:

And the **Spirit of the LORD began to stir** him in Mahaneh-dan, between Zorah and Eshtaol. Judges 13:25 And the **Spirit of the LORD came upon him** mightily, so that he tore him as one tears a kid though he had nothing in his hand; but he did not tell his father and mother what he had done (Judges 14:6).

Then the **Spirit of the LORD came upon him** mightily, and he went down to Ashkelon and killed thirty of them and took their spoil, and gave the changes of clothes to those who told the riddle. And his anger burned, and he went up to his father's house (Judges 14:19).

When he came to Lehi, the Philistines shouted as they met him. **And the Spirit of the LORD came upon him** mightily so that the ropes that were on his arms were as flax that is burned with fire, and his bonds dropped from his hands. And he found a fresh jawbone of a donkey, so he reached out and took it and killed a thousand men with it (Judges 15:14-15).

The ministry of the Holy Spirit in the life of Samson is unique to the judges. Four times the Spirit of the LORD came upon Samson as God used him in judging the Philistines. Only with Gideon (6:11-22) and Samson (13:3-23) was the Messenger (Angel) of *Yahweh* involved in their lives. Only with the promise and birth of Samson was the Messenger (Angel) of *Yahweh* involved with his birth. Each of the four judges mentioned in this section had a special empowerment to carry out God's assigned tasks. Because Samson was designated as a Nazirite (13:14), it seems that the Holy Spirit came upon him until Delilah cut his hair (16:18-20). The Holy Spirit came upon him on several

---

[1071] J. Clinton McCann, *Interpretation: A Bible Commentary for Teaching and Preaching: Judges* (Louisville, KY: John Knox Press, 2002), 85.
[1072] J. Alberto Soggin, *The Old Testament Library: Judges*, (trans. John Bowden; Philadelphia: Westminster, 1981), 206-207.

occasions, with special empowerment, as illustrated by these verses in Judges 13:25; 14:6, 19; 15:14-15.

Samson is also unique among Israel's judges in that God instructed him to fight the Philistines alone rather than to raise an army. On four occasions he received a special enablement for a major display of strength.[1073] *Yahweh's* active participation with Israel is seen with the involvement of the Messenger (Angel) of *Yahweh* as well as the Holy Spirit coming upon these individuals when the nation repented and called for deliverance.[1074]

It should also be noted that respected scholars such as Wood,[1075] Walvoord and Zuck[1076] refer to the Spirit of the LORD as the Holy Spirit. Most authors do not make that specific designation in relationship to the Spirit passages in Judges. This designation of the Holy Spirit is important because the Jewish response is that the Spirit is God's Spirit, not a distinct member of the Godhead. The lack of designation is expressed frequently by Schneider when she says, of the Spirit of the LORD, that He was "moved by the spirit of the deity."[1077]

Elohim specifies and clarifies by showing a distinction in denoting God as a plurality. Hence, when the Hebrew Scriptures refer to the Spirit of *Yahweh*, or the Spirit of God, or by the statement that the Spirit of the LORD came upon an individual, the *Tanakh* is referring to the Holy Spirit, the Third Person of the Godhead of *Elohim*.

One final remark on Samson and the ministry of the Holy Spirit in his life; even though Samson was anointed as a judge, there were periods of godless disobedience in his life. Both the personal and official blessedness of the Spirit were removed. This is not an issue of keeping or losing personal salvation, then or now, but of being anointed for high office or specific skillful tasks.

Saul:

> And the **Spirit of the LORD will come upon thee**, and thou shalt prophesy with them, and shalt be turned into another man (1 Samuel 10:6 KJV).

> When they came to the hill there, behold, a group of prophets met him; and the **Spirit of God came upon him** mightily, so that he prophesied among them (1 Samuel 10:10 KJV).

> And the **Spirit of God came upon Saul** when he heard those tidings, and his anger was kindled greatly (1 Samuel 11:6 KJV).

[1073] Wood, *The Holy Spirit in the Old Testament*, 55.

[1074] Hildebrandt, *An Old Testament Theology of the Spirit of God*, 117.

[1075] Wood, *Distressing Days of the Judges*, 311-312.

[1076] Walvoord and Zuck, *The Bible Knowledge Commentary: Old Testament*, 404.

[1077] Schneider, *Berit Olam: Judges*, 202.

There are four basic passages that speak of the Spirit of God in relationship to Saul. Three references are found in 1 Samuel 10 and 11 and one in chapter 16, which refers to both Saul and David. The first reference is a prophecy by Samuel that the Spirit of the LORD would come upon Saul and make him into a different man. The second reference is the recorded fulfillment of Samuel's words to Saul. Samuel gives Saul three signs that will confirm God's choice of him as king. The last one is the most significant because when the Spirit of God came upon Saul, it caused him to prophesy with a band of prophets. Hildebrandt makes this comment in connection to Saul's prophetic experience and *Yahweh's* confirmation of him as the first king:

> The act of prophesying by Saul and the band of prophets is to be distinguished from that of prophetic inspiration, which conveys a message to the recipient. The ecstatic element indicates an encounter with the *ruah yhwh* that brings about external manifestations in addition to verbal utterances. In this instance, the fulfillment of the three signs would confirm that *Yahweh* is with Saul.[1078]

The Spirit of God came upon Saul, as with the judges, to equip him to fulfill the task of being king. Walvoord and Zuck affirm that the Spirit of God came upon Saul to equip him because he was inexperienced and unlettered and unable to assume kingly responsibilities in much the same way that the judges did before him.[1079] Barber concurs and continues the same idea when he says:

> It seems most likely that God gave to Saul that which he lacked by training and heredity. He provided him with the inner disposition to fulfill the tasks of a king. He equipped him, as He had done the judges, so that Saul would be able to deliver his people from those who sought to oppress them. When the transitory enthusiasm of his meeting with the prophets passed, it left Saul with a certain inner sense that could not be satisfied without further communion with the Lord.[1080]

So the coming of the Spirit of God upon Saul was not only to let him know that God was with him but was also to equip him for his task as king.

One other point that Bergen brings out is the contrast between the use of the terms "*Spirit of God*" and the "*Spirit of the LORD.*" He observes that elsewhere in the *Tanakh*, when the Holy Spirit came upon an individual, it stated that "*the Spirit of the LORD*" came upon them. However, here and only one other place does it say that the "*Spirit of God*" came upon him. Even though both terms refer to the same person of God, the "*Spirit of God*" is used only with one other person, Balaam. The reason for God's choice of words is not clear, but as Balaam was unfaithful to God, Saul was also unfaithful.[1081] Bergen's observation is interesting but not valid. For the "*Spirit of God*"

[1078] Hildebrandt, *An Old Testament Theology of the Spirit of God*, 120.

[1079] Walvoord and Zuck, *The Bible Knowledge Commentary: Old Testament,* 441.

[1080] Cyril J. Barber, *The Books of Samuel* (2 vols. Neptune, NJ: Loizeaux, 1994), 1:116.

[1081] Bergen, *The New American Commentary:1, 2 Samuel,* 7:136.

also came upon others such as Bezaleel in Exodus 31:2-3; Azariah, a prophet, who gave a warning to Asa in 2 Chronicles 15:1; and Zechariah, the priest, in 2 Chronicles 24:20. Bergen's statement is inconclusive because two people acted in disobedience, two people in obedience, and another, an artisan, prepared the tabernacle.

When the Spirit of God came upon Saul it was permanent because of his office. It was temporary with the other judges, because with the possible exception of Samson their ministry was limited in scope. The 1 Samuel passage indicates that if Saul had not sinned with his incomplete obedience (1 Samuel 16) but had remained faithful, the Spirit would have remained with Saul throughout his life as king.[1082] The permanence of the Holy Spirit upon Saul is also noted by McCarter in his remarks on this section:

> Divine spirit follows immediately upon the anointing and remains 'from that day forward.' Moreover, as we are about to discover, *Yahweh's* spirit has departed from Saul (16:14).[1083]

David and Saul:

> (13) Then Samuel took the horn of oil and anointed him in the midst of his brothers; and the **Spirit of the LORD came mightily upon** David from that day forward. And Samuel arose and went to Ramah. (14) Now the **Spirit of the LORD departed from Saul**, and an evil spirit from the LORD terrorized him (1 Samuel 16:13-14).

What is seen here is that the Holy Spirit came upon Saul and was with him up to 1 Samuel 16:14. Then the Lord sent an evil spirit to terrorize him because God had now rejected Saul and had Samuel anoint David to be king. These two events occurred in close sequence to each other. Once the Holy Spirit came upon David, the Holy Spirit left Saul. When the Holy Spirit left Saul, it did not mean that he was unsaved, but rather that the enabling power of God left him and was given to David.[1084]

David:

> The **Spirit of the LORD spoke by me** and his word was on my tongue. The God of Israel said, The Rock of Israel spoke to me (2 Samuel 23:2-3a).

> Do not cast me away from thy presence, and **do not take thy Holy Spirit from me** (Psalm 51:11).

In 1 Samuel 16 it was observed that the Spirit of the LORD came upon David and was with him throughout his lifetime. That is seen by two things: first, the Holy Spirit spoke by David and second, the Holy Spirit's words were on his tongue. In the

---

[1082] Wood, *The Holy Spirit in the Old Testament*, 62.

[1083] P. Kyle McCarter, Jr. *The Anchor Bible: I Samuel* (vol. 8. Garden City, NY: Doubleday, 1980), 8:276.

[1084] Youngblood, *The Expositor's Bible Commentary*, 3:688.

following observation Bergen speaks of David as being in the passive role as the Holy Spirit spoke through him:

> Thus David has now been portrayed throughout the books of Samuel as king, priest, and prophet.… Since David, the first member of Israel's royal messianic line, functioned in these three roles, it seems appropriate that Jesus the Messiah should not only be depicted by the New Testament writers as inheriting these roles but superseding David's accomplishments in them. He did not choose this role but accepted it when 'the Spirit of the Lord spoke through him. David's role was essentially passive in this event. When he spoke, it was the Lord's 'word' not his own that was on his 'tongue.'[1085]

Youngblood makes the observation that as God, He spoke through the mouth of Balaam (Numbers 24:2, 4), and the Spirit of the LORD spoke through David. Youngblood makes the following connection with *Yeshua*:

> That David spoke 'by the Spirit' on another occasion is affirmed by Jesus himself (Matt 22:43), and David's use of the phrase 'spoke through' represents a clear claim to divine inspiration. David was conscious of the fact that the 'word' of the Lord was on his 'tongue' and that the mighty 'Rock of Israel' had spoken to him.[1086]

Youngblood was referring to Psalm 110:1, where David said, "*The LORD said unto my Lord, Sit thou at my right hand, until I make thine enemies thy footstool.*" It is clearly presented by David that the Holy Spirit, who is distinct from *Yahweh*, spoke to and through him.

Also, it can be observed that David pleaded with the Lord (Psalm 51:11) not to take His Holy Spirit from him. David wanted the presence of God with him to guide him and enable him as King of Israel. David also remembered very clearly what happened to Saul because of his sin. David wanted to walk righteously before his God as his Psalms so aptly show.

Micah:

> On the other hand I am **filled** with power – With the Spirit of the LORD (Micah 3:8).

In this verse Micah, a contemporary of Isaiah in the 8th century BCE, spoke of himself as being **filled with the Spirit of the LORD**. He traces the power of his prophetic ministry to the Holy Spirit.[1087] Just as Bezaleel was filled with the Spirit, so was Micah. This filling of the Holy Spirit equipped Micah to deal with the corruption

---

[1085] Bergen, *The New American Commentary: 1, 2 Samuel*, 465-466.
[1086] Youngblood, *The Expositor's Bible Commentary*, 3:1082.
[1087] Walvoord, *The Holy Spirit*, 50.

among the leaders of Israel (3:1-3; 7:1-4) and among the priests and prophets themselves (2:6, 11; 3:5-7).[1088]

Isaiah:

And as for Me, this is My covenant with them, says the LORD: '**My spirit which is upon you**, and My words which I have put in your mouth, shall not depart from your mouth, nor from the mouth of your offspring, nor from the mouth of your offspring's offspring,' says the LORD 'from now and forever' (Isaiah 59:21).

This verse is connected to three themes in the book of Isaiah, as well as Jeremiah and Ezekiel: the New Covenant of Jeremiah, Messiah and the Holy Spirit. Walter Kaiser connects the "My covenant" in the above verse to the New Covenant of Jeremiah 31.[1089]

Motyer also connects the Isaiah 59:21 passage with the ministry of the Servant of the LORD in the servant passages of Isaiah.[1090] Enns connects the fulfillment of the New Covenant to the return of the Messiah and the forgiveness of Israel.[1091] Wolf connects the covenant with the Servant of the Lord and relates it to the New Covenant.[1092]

The fact is that Isaiah 59:21 pertains to Israel's future where the New Covenant is God's future blessing on Israel, even though they grieved His Holy Spirit (Isaiah 63:10). The Holy Spirit was grieved and turned away, but the New Covenant speaks of the pouring out of God's Spirit (Isaiah 44:3). In Jeremiah 31:31-37, which is connected to Isaiah 59:21, is a promise by God, through His New Covenant, that "My spirit" will be upon them and "My words" will be put in their mouths and will not depart from them from generation to generation even "from now and forever." So in Isaiah 59:21 God promises His spirit would come upon them, that His words will be in their mouths, and all will come to pass in the New Covenant and through the Messiah, the Servant of the LORD. Biblical faith recognizes that the New Covenant is the indwelling of the Holy Spirit in the lives of believers, both Jew and Gentile. But this New Covenant will not be totally fulfilled until Israel embraces *Yeshua* as her own personal Messiah and trusts in Him. However, Rabbinic Judaism does not see the New Covenant beginning as a result of the resurrection of *Yeshua* and the outpouring of the Holy Spirit at the Feast of Shavuot or Pentecost, as Levine states:

If the birth of the Christian religion really did introduce the new covenant, then there should no longer be any need for anyone to teach the word of God, "for

---

[1088] Hildebrandt, *An Old Testament Theology of the Spirit of God*, 190-191.

[1089] Kaiser, *Toward an Old Testament Theology*, 231.

[1090] Motyer, *The Prophecy of Isaiah*, 492.

[1091] Enns, *The Moody Handbook of Theology*, 68.

[1092] Wolf, *Interpreting Isaiah*, 235.

they shall know Me." Since, as everyone with eyes can see, the whole world does not yet recognize God, and the Christians are still trying to teach religion to the world, as are others, it is quite clear that [Isaiah 59:21], "they shall teach no more every man, saying, Know the Lord" does not yet apply. In other words, the new covenant has not yet taken place.[1093]

In the studies of the economies (dispensations) of God, one thing becomes very apparent. When a covenant is given by God not every provision of that covenant goes immediately into effect. To illustrate, in Genesis 13:14-17 God told Abraham that the land to the north, south, east and west of him was his personal possession, as well as the possession of his descendants, and that he was to walk the length and breadth of the land. If you use the same logic that Levine uses with Jeremiah 31:31-34, then Abraham who never possessed the land that the Abrahamic Covenant promised to use Levine words, it "does not yet apply." So accordingly the Abrahamic Covenant has never taken effect in Levine's logic. If his logic for Jeremiah 31 does not apply to the New Covenant, then neither does it apply to the Abrahamic Covenant because Abraham has never possessed the Land nor have his descendants possessed all the Land that *Yahweh* promised to them. That would also raise another issue about the integrity of *Yahweh* to keep His word.

Ezekiel:

And as He spoke to me **the Spirit entered me and set me on my feet**; and I heard Him speaking to me (Ezekiel 2:2).

And He stretched out the form of a hand and caught me by a lock of my head; and **the Spirit lifted me up** between earth and heaven and brought me in the visions of God to Jerusalem, to the entrance of the north gate of the inner court, where the seat of the idol of jealousy, which provokes to jealousy, was located (Ezekiel 8:3);

Moreover, **the Spirit lifted me up** and brought me to the east gate of the LORD's house which faced eastward. And behold, there were twenty-five men at the entrance of the gate, and among them I saw Jaazaniah son of Azzur and Pelatiah son of Benaiah, leaders of the people (Ezekiel 11:1).

And the **Spirit lifted me up** and brought me in a **vision by the Spirit of God** to the exiles in Chaldea. So the vision that I had seen left me (Ezekiel 11:24).

The Hand of the LORD was upon me, and He brought me out **by the Spirit** of the LORD and set me down in the middle of the valley; and it was full of bones (Ezekiel 37:1).[1094]

[1093] Samuel Levine, *You Take Jesus, I'll Take God* (Los Angeles: Hamoroh Press, 1980), 15.
[1094] All of the Ezekiel verses are taken from NASB.

Most authors do not interact with the plurality of *Elohim* that is present in these passages. In all these passages there is a plurality of persons involved with Ezekiel and his visions. It is disheartening to notice that scholars, such as Feinberg[1095] and Cooper,[1096] do not interact with the Spirit except in Ezekiel 2:2. In fact, Taylor states that according to Ezekiel 2:2, the Spirit is "spiritual energy" and not a person.[1097] Yet, these passages clearly indicate two members of the Godhead are present. In looking at the description in Ezekiel 1:26, God is appearing in a human form. In fact, Alexander refers to this section of Scripture as a "theophany,"[1098] God appearing in human form. Paralleling these verses highlights the personalities in each of these verses:

Ezekiel 2:2   "a figure with the appearance of a man" (1:26) "Spirit entered me and set me on my feet"

Ezekiel 8:3   "a likeness as the appearance of a man" (8:2) "the Spirit lifted me up between heaven and earth"

Ezekiel 11:1   "And He spoke to the man clothed in linen" (10:2) "the Spirit lifted me up and brought me to the east gate"

Ezekiel 11:24   "Thus says the Lord God" (11:16-17) "And the Spirit lifted me up and brought me in a vision by the Spirit of God"

Ezekiel 37:1   "The hand of the LORD was upon me and He brought me...by the Spirit of the LORD and set me down..."

In each instance and in each verse or immediate context, there are two personalities engaged with Ezekiel. This author believes that the one who was in the appearance of a man is a theophany of the Second Person of the Godhead. The other personality, who is continually called the Spirit, is the Third Person of the Godhead, the Holy Spirit. Cooke makes the following remarks along the same lines:

This was no messenger, no angel. As at the inaugural vision, so now, it is Jehovah Himself in human form, glowing with supernatural splendour, who appears to the prophet, and speaks to him, and announces the hour of visitation.... The distinction between the hand of Jehovah and the spirit seems to be that the one gave the impression of a visible, the other of an invisible agency: the hand appeared to grasp the prophet by the forelock, the spirit impelled his movement.[1099]

[1095] Charles Lee Feinberg, *The Prophecy of Ezekiel: The Glory of the Lord* (Chicago: Moody, 1969), 23, 49,63, 67.

[1096] Lamar Eugene Cooper, Sr. *The New American Commentary: Ezekiel* (vol. 17. Nashville: Broadman and Holman, 1994), 74-75, 119, 139-140, 145.

[1097] John B. Taylor, *Ezekiel* (Downers Grove: InterVarsity, 1974), 61.

[1098] Ralph H. Alexander, *The Expositor's Bible Commentary: Ezekiel* (12 vols. Grand Rapids: Zondervan, 1986), 6:761.

[1099] G. A. Cooke, *The International Critical Commentary: The Book of Ezekiel*, (Edinburgh: T. & T. Clark, 1936), 89-91.

In each of these passages there is a clear distinction between the theophany of God (appearance of a man) and the Spirit of God. These two persons are addressed and treated as being distinct persons.

INSPIRATION OF THE SCRIPTURES

The word "inspiration" comes from the Latin Vulgate Bible in which the verb "inspire" appears in 2 Timothy 3:16 and 2 Peter 1:21. However, the word "inspiration" in the Greek is actually used only once in 2 Timothy to translate the word *theopneustos*. *Theopneustos*, which means "God-breathed," emphasizes the exhalation of God. Inspiration would be more accurate since it emphasizes that Scripture is the product of the breath of God. The Scriptures are not something breathed *into* by God. Rather, the Scriptures have been breathed *out* by God.[1100]

The Greek word that is used for the English word "Scripture" is *graphe*, which simply means "writing."[1101] The written word of God was given by God, and it was recorded in writing as He willed. The writings that He wanted preserved as Scripture have become what is called today *The Bible*.

It is important to understand inspiration and its use in the Hebrew Scriptures, as well as in the New Covenant. Walvoord lays out a clear statement as to the meaning of inspiration:

> That God so supernaturally directed the writers of Scripture that without excluding their human intelligence, their individuality, their literary style, their personal feelings, or any other human factor, His own complete and coherent message to man was recorded in perfect accuracy, the very words of Scripture bearing the authority of divine authorship. Nothing less than a plenary and verbal inspiration will satisfy the demands of the Scripture themselves and give to faith the confidence in the Word of God which is essential to faith and life.[1102]

Geisler also gives the same kind of definition of inspiration as Walvoord:

> Inspiration is the supernatural operation of the Holy Spirit, who through the different personalities and literary styles of the chosen human authors invested the very words of the original books of Holy Scripture, alone and in their entirety, as the very Word of God without error in all that they teach or imply (including history and science), and the Bible is thereby the infallible rule and final authority for faith and practice of all believers.[1103]

[1100] Enns, *The Moody Handbook of Theology*, 160.
[1101] Enns, *The Moody Handbook of Theology*, 153.
[1102] Walvoord, *The Holy Spirit*, 58.
[1103] Geisler, *Systematic Theology*, 1:241.

God worked with individual personalities and literary styles so that when the Word of God was given to human authors, there was an absence of any formal argument to prove the inspiration of their writings because none was deemed necessary. The character of the Scriptures themselves was sufficient evidence for both the authors and the readers.

The term "inspiration" makes other declarations, as expressed by Geisler and Nix.

1. The claim of inspiration has several other characteristics that need to be mentioned. First, inspiration is verbal, meaning that it "extends to the very words of Scripture" (Exod 24:4; Isa 8:1; 30:8).

2. Inspiration makes the Scripture unbreakable or infallible (Psa 82; John 10:35).

3. The Scriptures are irrevocable, meaning that they cannot be changed and will be fulfilled (Matt 5:18; Luke 16:17; 24:44).

4. Inspiration makes the Scriptures the final authority (Matt 4:4, 7, 10). Nothing will supersede the written word of God.

5. Inspiration is plenary, meaning that it is full, complete, extending to every part (2 Tim 3:16).[1104]

There is one thing that needs to be made clear concerning the work of the Holy Spirit in inspiration. The Holy Spirit did not inspire men, but inspired His Word as explained by James Gray when he makes the distinction in the work of the Holy Spirit by saying:

When we speak of the Holy Spirit coming upon the men in order to the composition of the books, it should be further understood that the object is not the inspiration of the men but the books – not the writers but the writings. It terminates upon the record, in other words, and not upon the human instrument who made it.[1105]

The more we think upon it the more we must be convinced that men unaided by the Spirit of God could neither have conceived, nor put together, nor preserved in its integrity that precious deposit known as the Sacred Oracles.[1106]

There are two key verses in the New Covenant that clearly point to the inspiration of the *Tanakh*. Paul states that "all Scripture is given by inspiration of God" in 2 Timothy 3:16 and attributes inspiration of the *Tanakh* to the ministry of the Holy Spirit. Peter affirms in 2 Peter 1:20-21 (to Jewish believers in Messiah who had been scattered in the

---

[1104] Norman L. Geisler and William E. Nix, *A General Introduction to the Bible* (Chicago: Moody, 1968), 48-51.

[1105] R.A. Torrey and A.C. Dixon, *The Fundamentals* (Reprinted without alteration or abridgment from the original four volume edition issued by the Bible Institute of Los Angeles in 1917. Grand Rapids: Baker, 1980), 2:11.

[1106] Torrey, *The Fundamentals*, 2:18-19.

Diaspora) that the writings of the *Tanakh* did not come from the will or intellect of man but "man spake from God, being moved by the Holy Spirit."[1107]

The writers of the *Tanakh*, when referring to the Hebrew Scriptures as the authoritative Word of God, gave their testimony and bore witness to their divine inspiration: the Law (Exodus 20:1; 32:16; Leviticus 27:34; Numbers 36:13) and the Prophets (Joshua 24:26-27; 1 Samuel 3:18-19; Isaiah 1:1-2; Jeremiah 1:1-2; Ezekiel 1:3).[1108]

A valid point needs to be injected here on a particular Jewish consideration of what is inspired. Jewish rabbis treat the Oral Law (Talmud) as equal to Scripture, although they would deny it. The Talmud has become their primary source of interpretation of Scripture. They ignore the Scriptures that refer to Moses writing down all that God gave him (Exodus 24:4; Deuteronomy 31:9, 24; Joshua 24:26).[1109] This Oral Law, and not the written word of God, is the source of all rabbinic authority. The children of Israel did not vow to keep the Oral Law. They made a commitment to *Yahweh* to keep the Written Law of God. Exodus 24:3-7 rules out any possibility of a second fictitious Oral Law being given to Moses, then to Joshua, the Judges, passed on to the Prophets and then to the school of the *Sopherim* as Rabbinic tradition insists. The Oral Law is fictitious because nowhere in the whole of the *Tanakh* is there even a glimmer, let alone a clear statement, of this uniquely Jewish position about the Oral Law (Talmud) having been given by God or as being divinely authoritative. Oral Law has become an "idol" of words instituted by the rabbis for the Jewish people to bow to its authority, rather than the authority of the written word of God (which is what they vowed to keep), that *Elohim* has over and over again confirmed by His Scriptures. The Oral Law has no confirmation by God in the *Tanakh*. Verbal Inspiration deals with the very words of God that He so carefully gave and preserved in His Word (see Appendix 3). The Oral Law is nothing more than the commentaries of the rabbis, their interpretations of the *Tanakh*.

The New Covenant uses the phrase "it is written" over 90 times.[1110] Jesus described this written word as that which "comes out of the mouth of God" (Matthew 4:4). So important were the exact words of God that Jeremiah (26:2) was told:

[1107] Torrey, *The Fundamentals*, 2:20.

[1108] Barackman, *Practical Christian Theology*, 27.

[1109] *Oral Law*: Judaism states that Moses received two laws, one written and one oral. Now Judaism will not call the Oral Law the Word of God, but the authority placed upon the Oral Law practically places the Oral Law on equal or greater footing than the Written Law of God given to Moses. Rabbis will not interpret the Written Law without studying the Oral Law which cannot be substantiated anywhere in the entire *Tanakh*. The actual origin of the Oral Law occurred after the return from captivity. There was a need to read the Word of God in Hebrew (Nehemiah 8:8), then translate it into Aramaic and then apply it to daily life. In the generation after Ezra, they began to expand it by adding manmade rules and regulations to each of the 613 written laws of Moses and giving it equal and greater authority than the Scriptures themselves.

[1110] Geisler, *Systematic Theology*, 1:236.

This is what the LORD says: Stand in the courtyard of the Lord's house and speak to all the people of the towns of Judah who come to worship in the house of the LORD. Tell them everything I command you; do not omit a word."

Another New Covenant testimony of the *Tanakh* comes from *Yeshua* as a witness to divine inspiration.

1. *Yeshua* recognized the whole of the *Tanakh* (John 5:39; Luke 24:44-46) and its three divisions (Mark 7:8-13; Matthew 13:13-14; John 10:34-35).

2. *Yeshua* made reference to 14 books of the *Tanakh*: Genesis (Mark 10:6-8); Exodus (Luke 18:20); Numbers (John 3:14); Leviticus and Deuteronomy (Luke 10:26-28); I Samuel (Mark 2:25); 1 Kings (Matt 12:42); Psalms (Mark 12:10); Isaiah (Luke 4:17-21); Daniel (Matthew 24:15); Hosea (Matthew 9:13); Jonah (Matthew 12:40); Zechariah (Matthew 26:31); and Malachi (Matthew 11:10).

3. *Yeshua* believed in the historicity of persons, such as Abel (Luke 11:51); Noah and the Flood (Matthew 24:37-39); Moses (John 3:14); David (Luke 20:41); Jonah and the fish (Matthew 12:40); God's creation of man and the divine institution of marriage (Matthew 19:4-7); and the prophet Daniel (Matthew 24:15).

4. *Yeshua* submitted Himself to the authority of the Hebrew Scriptures (Matthew 5:17; 26:54; Luke 18:31).

5. *Yeshua* had complete trust in the writings and teachings of the *Tanakh*. This is indicated by His appeal to them for God's will when He was tempted (Matthew 4:4, 7, 10), His referring to God's statement regarding marriage (Matthew 19:4-6), and His argument for the doctrine of the resurrection (Matthew 22:29-32).

6. *Yeshua* declared that the Scriptures could not be broken (John 10:35). In context, the Lord said that the Scriptures (Psalm 82:6), which He identified as the Word of God, could not be annulled as though its declarations were untrue.[1111]

The inspiration of the Holy Spirit is clearly seen in the New Covenant. But how is it seen in the Hebrew Scriptures? In the Hebrew Scriptures there are two phrases that are used literally hundreds of times. These key phrases are: *"Thus saith the Lord"* and *"The Word of the Lord came unto,"* both of which distinctly refer to the inspiration of the Scriptures.[1112] Waterhouse makes the following observation:

Statements from the Law and the Prophets assert not only that the Old Testament is divine revelation, but, more specifically, that the words were at

---

[1111] Barackman, *Practical Christian Theology*, 27.
[1112] Steven W. Waterhouse, *Not By Bread Alone: An Outlined Guide to Bible Doctrine* (Amarillo, TX: Westcliff Press, 2000), 4.

times given by God and at other times guided by God. This is verbal inspiration.[1113]

Waterhouse goes on to quote references from the Hebrew Scriptures to show that God indeed spoke and guided the human authors of Scripture (Deuteronomy 18:18; 34:10; 2 Samuel 23:1-2; Isaiah 8:11, 20; 59:21; Jeremiah 1:9; 15:16; 30:2; Ezekiel 3:1-4).[1114] By closely observing 2 Samuel 23:2 and Isaiah 59:21 respectively, we see that both David and Isaiah express the fact that the Holy Spirit spoke through them:

The Spirit of the LORD spake by me, and his word was in my tongue (KJV).

As for me, this is my covenant with them, saith the LORD; My spirit that is upon thee, and my words which I have put in thy mouth…. (KJV)

Here the Holy Spirit is clearly seen as the one who is speaking through David and Isaiah in the *Tanakh*. Geisler continues by expressing phrases such as *"God said"* (Genesis 1:3, 6) and *"the Word of the LORD came to me"* (Jeremiah 34:1; Ezekiel 30:1), which are found hundreds of times in the Hebrew Scriptures. Geisler states:

These reveal beyond question that the writer is claiming to give the very Word of God. In the book of Leviticus alone there are some 66 occurrences of phrases like "the LORD spoke unto Moses" (1:1; 4:1; 5:14; 6:1, 8, 19; 7:22).[1115]

God used words and expected those words to be used exactly as He instructed. Using them otherwise was a direct violation of verbal inspiration. This simply means that words were inspired, God's Word, not God's thoughts or dynamic equivalents which are so popular today in our modern translations and paraphrases. It is God's Word, rather than inspired thoughts, that man is held accountable for (Exodus 24:3-7; Deuteronomy 18:18; 2 Samuel 23:2; Isaiah 59:21; 2 Chronicles 34:14; Zechariah 7:12). Geisler strongly affirms that Scriptures were not man's words or thoughts, but God's Word:

So it wasn't simply God's message that men were free to state in their words; the very choice of words was from God…. Sometimes we are reminded that even the tense of verbs are stressed by God.[1116]

Inspiration usually has two other descriptive words to help clarify the meaning of inspiration. They are the words "verbal" and "plenary." Here plenary inspiration will be briefly discussed. Inspiration, in being verbal, extends to every word as being inspired. Plenary further defines the term inspiration as "extending to every part of the words and

---

[1113] Waterhouse, *Not By Bread Alone: An Outlined Guide to Bible Doctrine*, 4.
[1114] Waterhouse, *Not By Bread Alone: An Outlined Guide to Bible Doctrine*, 4.
[1115] Geisler, *Systematic Theology*, 1:234.
[1116] Geisler, *Systematic Theology*, 1:236.

all they teach or imply."[1117] Barackman further conveys that "verbal" extends to each word of Scripture and "to the grammatical form of each word," as well as speaking of plenary inspiration as not just the words but the equality of the words:

> Plenary Inspiration means that every part of the sixty-six canonical books of the Bible was a product of divine inspiration to an equal degree (2 Timothy 3:16).[1118]

Plenary inspiration simply means that all Scripture is equally inspired of God. However, in Rabbinic Judaism they deduce from Numbers 12:5-8 three levels of inspiration: The Law (Torah) as the most inspired; then the Prophets, while still inspired, but to a lesser degree than the Torah; and lastly, the Writings, while still inspired but to a lesser degree than the Law and the Prophets.

METHODS OF REVELATION

When speaking of Divine Revelation in connection with the Bible, the word "revelation" is derived from the Greek word *apokalupsis*, which means "disclosure" or "unveiling,"[1119] which signified that God unveiled Himself to mankind through His written Word and through theophanies of Himself. If God did not disclose or unveil Himself to man, without revelation, man would have no idea as to what God is like or how man could interact with Him. Horne gives a clear meaning of revelation in his following comments:

> That act of God whereby he discloses himself or communicates truth to the mind, whereby he makes manifest to his creatures that which could not be known in any other way. The revelation may occur in a single, instantaneous act, or it may extend over a long period of time; and this communication of himself and his truth may be perceived by the human mind in varying degrees of fullness.[1120]

The Holy Spirit is also involved in revelation of God, as expressed in the following statement by Walvoord:

> The most prominent means of revelation is that of the spoken word. "Thus saith Jehovah" is found in hundreds of instances in the Old Testament. A comparison of such passages as Isa 6:1-10 and Acts 8:25 will demonstrate that the Holy Spirit is the person of the Trinity speaking in these instances. While the Old Testament used "Jehovah" and "Lord" as the speaker, the New Testament uses the title, Holy Spirit.[1121]

[1117] Geisler, *Systematic Theology*, 1:236.

[1118] Barackman, *Practical Christian Theology*, 25.

[1119] Enns, *The Moody Handbook of Theology*, 155.

[1120] Thiessen, *Lectures in Systematic Theology*, 7.

[1121] Walvoord, *The Holy Spirit*, 50-51.

In a broader use of the term revelation, God revealed Himself through creation, history, and in the Scriptures and the conscience of man. In general revelation God revealed Himself in history and nature, while in "special" revelation God revealed Himself in the Scriptures and in His Son.[1122]

OLD TESTAMENT AND NEW TESTAMENT COMPARISONS OF THE HOLY SPIRIT

Throughout the Hebrew Scriptures there are times when the reader may not be able to determine that the one speaking is the person of the Holy Spirit. Although this section is not an argument for the personality of the Holy Spirit from the *Tanakh*, this argument does show how the Apostles in the first century C.E. understood the ministry of the Holy Spirit in the *Tanakh*.

Following are five verses from the *Tanakh* that the New Covenant writers understand to refer to the Holy Spirit. These writers are: Matthew and John, who spoke of the statements of *Yeshua*, Peter just before the feast of Succoth (Pentecost), Paul when speaking to the Jewish leadership in Rome and the unknown author of Hebrews who wrote to the suffering Jewish believers who lived in the Land. Each passage will be briefly discussed in supporting the contention that these writers understood the Holy Spirit to be present and active in the Hebrew Scriptures.

Psalm 110:1 with Matthew 22:42-44:

The LORD said to my Lord, 'Sit at My right hand while I make your enemies your footstool.'

While the Pharisees were gathered together, Jesus asked them, saying, what think ye of Christ (Messiah)? Whose son is he? They say unto him, The Son of David. He saith unto them, How then doth David in the spirit call him Lord, Saying, the LORD said unto my Lord, Sit thou on my right hand, till I make thine enemies thy footstool?

Here, according to Ryrie, *Yeshua* asks the Pharisees a question concerning Psalm 110:1. *Yeshua*, at this point, attributes to the Holy Spirit divine authorship of that Psalm of David.[1123] Then Psalm 110:1 is tied in with David's powerful statement of 2 Samuel 23:2-3 where David states that "*the Spirit of the LORD spoke by me*," connecting that with David's statement with Psalm 22, a Messianic Psalm. Walvoord points out from Mark 12:36 the same incident when David spoke by the Holy Spirit, thus attributing inspiration to the Holy Spirit.[1124]

[1122] Tenney, *Zondervan Pictorial Encyclopedia of the Bible*, 5:86.
[1123] Ryrie, *The Holy Spirit*, 36.
[1124] Walvoord, *The Holy Spirit*, 60.

361

Psalm 41:9[10] with Acts 1:16:

My ally in whom I trusted, even he who shares my bread, has been utterly false to me (Psalm 41:9[10]).

Yea, mine own familiar friend, in whom I trusted, which did eat of my bread, Hath lifted up his heel against me (Psalm 41:9 KJV).

Men and brethren, this scripture must need have been fulfilled which the Holy Spirit by the mouth of David spake before concerning Judas, which was guide to them that took Jesus. (Acts 1:16)

Here again Peter gives testimony to the Holy Spirit as the authority of the word of David concerning Judas who betrayed *Yeshua*.

Isaiah 6:9-10 with Acts 28:25-27:

And He said, 'Go, say to that people: Hear, indeed, but do not understand; See, indeed, but do not grasp. Dull that people's mind, stop its ear, and seal its eyes – lest, seeing with its eyes and hearing with its ears, it also grasp with its mind, and repent and save itself.

And when they agreed not among themselves, they departed, after that Paul had spoken one word, Well spake the Holy Spirit by Isaiah the prophet unto our fathers, Saying, Go unto this people, and say, hearing ye shall hear, and shall not understand; and seeing ye shall see, and not perceive: For the heart of this people is waxed gross, and their ears are dull of hearing, and their eyes have they closed; lest they should see with their eyes, and hear with their ears, and understand with their heart, and should be converted, and I should heal them.

In the above passage, Paul ascribes to the Holy Spirit the words of Isaiah, a prophet 700 years before Messiah.

Psalm 95:9-11 with Hebrews 3:7-11:

When your fathers put Me to the test, tried Me, though they had seen My deeds. Forty years I was provoked by that generation; I thought, 'they are a senseless people; they would not know My ways.' Concerning them I swore in anger, 'they shall never come to My resting-place!'

Wherefore as the Holy Spirit saith, today if ye will hear his voice, harden not your hearts, as in the provocation, in the day of temptation in the wilderness: When your fathers tempted me, proved me, and saw my works forty years. Wherefore I was grieved with that generation, and said, they do always err in their heart; and they have not known my ways. So I sware in my wrath, they shall not enter into my rest.

Here again the unknown author of Hebrews relates to his brethren concerning the hearts of the wilderness generation and attributes the words of the psalmist to the Holy Spirit.

Jeremiah 31:33 with Hebrews 10:15-16:

> But such is the covenant I will make with the House of Israel after these days – Declares the LORD: I will put My teaching into their inmost being and inscribe it upon their hearts. Then I will be their God, and they shall be My people.

> Whereof the Holy Spirit also is a witness to us: for after that he had said before, This is the covenant that I will make with them after those days, saith the LORD, I will put my laws into their hearts, and in their minds will I write them.

Once again the unknown Jewish believer takes the New Covenant reference in Jeremiah 31 and ascribes the New Covenant that was given as being authored by the Holy Spirit.

These references of the Holy Spirit do not come from the *Tanakh*. The New Covenant writers understood that the Holy Spirit was responsible for the inspiration of the Hebrew Scriptures.

NEW COVENANT

The Holy Spirit has a role in the New Covenant of Jeremiah 31, as can be seen in several assorted verses from the *Tanakh*, which clarify the Holy Spirit's involvement. Pache, in using these verses, makes four points in relation to the Holy Spirit coming upon mankind.

1. The Holy Spirit will be poured out upon all flesh according to Joel 2:28-29. We see the beginnings of that in Acts 2:16-17 when the Holy Spirit was poured out on the 120 in the upper room.[1125] Even though the fulfillment of this prophecy on the coming of the Holy Spirit is still future, it is a reference from the *Tanakh*. This is also a reference to the pouring out of the Holy Spirit in Isaiah 44:3 and Ezekiel 39:29. All three of these verses relate to the same event when His Spirit is poured out upon Israel.

2. The Holy Spirit that is given in the New Covenant, according to Isaiah 59:21, will remain forever.

3. In Ezekiel 36:26-27; 37:14 it is very clear that the Holy Spirit will be placed within Israel. God through the Holy Spirit will give them a new heart, the stony heart will be removed and they will be placed in the Land. Tie that together with 1 Corinthians 3:16 where the indwelling Holy Spirit makes us a temple to the living God.

[1125] *Joel 2:28-29*: See Manuscript #134 by Dr. Arnold Fruchtenbaum called "*How the New Testament Quotes the Old Testament*. See *www.Ariel.org* for Ariel Ministries in Tustin, CA.

4. It is clear that the Holy Spirit will rest upon the Messiah without measure as Isa 11:2; 42:1; 61:1 indicate.[1126]

Enns addresses another vital issue that *Yeshua*, in all likelihood, was referring to John 3:10 in connection to Ezekiel 36. Enns continues by saying that the Holy Spirit, in Ezekiel 11:19 and 36:25-27 is a promise by God to regenerate Israel during the Millennium.[1127] These passages from the *Tanakh* and *Yeshua*'s discussion with Nicodemus suggest that the Old Testament believers should have been aware of the work of regeneration by the Holy Spirit.

If the New Covenant were to be used, it would be very simple to substantiate the personality of the Holy Spirit because Matthew, Mark, Luke, John, Paul, and Peter's writings are full of references to the Holy Spirit. In the Hebrew Scriptures alone, it must be remembered, as with the Second Person of the Godhead, Scripture is progressive revelation. God did not choose to reveal everything about Himself at the start. That is equally true of the Third Person of the Godhead. At the beginning of this chapter it was expressed that it is difficult to distinguish between the two because God Himself is pure Spirit. So how does one make a distinction between God the Father's Spirit and the Holy Spirit? This chapter began with this very question. In the New Covenant the personality of the Holy Spirit is clearly expressed by the authors. His person is clearly defined and separated from the other members of the triune God. But in the *Tanakh* that pattern is not followed. Rarely is there an expression that relates directly to the Holy Spirit as a person. However, what is clearly seen in the *Tanakh* is the action or movement of the Holy Spirit, which makes it difficult to show His personhood. This means that the personhood of the Holy Spirit has been seen, but only to a limited degree in the *Tanakh*. The Spirit, in the Hebrew Scriptures, can be grieved (Genesis 6:3; Isaiah 63:10) and is distinct from God the Father and God the Son (Isaiah 48:16). The *Tanakh* implies the personhood of the Holy Spirit, but the New Covenant fully lays out the personality of the Third Person of the Godhead.

[1126] Pache, *The Person and Work of the Holy Spirit,* 34-35.
[1127] Enns, *The Moody Handbook of Theology,* 260.

Chapter 12
Messiah Divine

In the *Tanakh* there are Scriptures written by Moses, David, Isaiah, Micah, Zechariah and the unknown author(s) of Samuel and Chronicles that clearly present the Messiah, the Son of David, as God! However, in Rabbinic Judaism there are several views concerning the Messiah. Two of the most prominent will be addressed, concerning who the Messiah is, God or man.

First Reform and Conservative Judaism as well as secular Jews do not believe that Messiah is a person, but that a Messianic age will evolve and universal peace will come. A Messianic believer in Messiah reflects on that ideal:

> Messianism, which in the Bible is described as God's mighty interposition in human history, has become debased by contemporary Jewish spokesmen in something of a socio-economic program to be achieved by man alone by way of progressive, evolutionary fulfillment. The prophetic teachings concerning the day of judgment in which God will put an end to history as we know it are completely disregarded.[1128]

As can be clearly seen, there is no personal Messiah involved at all in secular and Reform and Conservative Judaism's ideology.

Secondly, Orthodox (rabbinic) Judaism clearly believes that the Messiah is a person, but does not regard that person as God.[1129] Ultra-orthodox Hasidim believe that, in the future, two Messiahs will come, due to the obvious portions of Scripture that point to two types of Messiahs. They identify the two as Messiah ben Joseph, who will come, suffer, and die (the Suffering Servant), and secondly, Messiah ben David, who will come and reign physically as king in Jerusalem (Reigning Messiah).[1130] A Jewish believer in *Yeshua*, the Messiah, related the following incident after being in an Orthodox Hasidic home in Brooklyn for Shabbat.[1131] The men sitting around the table were pounding their fists while singing songs with the words, "We want *Mashiach* now, we want *Mashiach* now." They were obviously acting out their fervent desire for the Messiah to come and fulfill the promise of God to Abraham. They obviously did not

---

[1128] Kac, *The Spiritual Dilemma of the Jewish People; Its Cause and Cure*, 26-27.

[1129] Jacobs, *A Jewish Theology*, 293.

[1130] Joseph Klausner, *The Messianic Idea in Israel* (New York: Macmillan, 1955), 11, 519-531.

[1131] *Shabbat* is the evening meal on the Sabbath day which occurs on Friday evenings, remembering the Jewish Sabbath beginning the evening before the day of sabbath.

believe that the Messiah had already come in the person of Jesus (*Yeshua*) Christ (*ha Mashiach* or Messiah).

The term *Moshiach*, a Hebrew word meaning "anointed one," denotes two ideas of consecration and endowment of any object or person. The term appears 39 times in the Hebrew Scriptures and originally was used of the "anointed priest" (Leviticus 4:3, 4) and of kings when God referred to them as "my anointed" (1 Samuel 2:35), "your anointed" (Psalm 84:9), and "his anointed" (1 Samuel 12:3, 5). By the time of the exile and post-exilic period, *Moshiach* had narrowed its meaning to the one who would fulfill the promises to Abraham, bring in the Kingdom and fulfill the covenant to David. So *Moshiach*,[1132] or Messiah, became the term for the long awaited promised one who would bring in the Kingdom spoken of by the Prophets.[1133] In Daniel 9:26 the Scripture says that before the destruction of the city (Jerusalem) occurs, the "anointed" (מָשִׁיחַ) will be cut off. That verse uses the term Messiah [or *Mashiach*] and history acknowledges that *Yeshua* was put to death 40 years prior to the destruction of the "city" and the "sanctuary," fulfilling Daniel's prophecy of the Messiah dying before the destruction of the "city" and the "sanctuary."

There are several factors that need to be reviewed concerning Jewish belief in the Messiah or *Moshiach*, as Orthodox Judaism prefers to use. Three questions will be examined about Rabbinic Judaism in relationship to *Moshiach*. First, what does the term Messiah or *Moshiach* mean and what doesn't it mean? Second, what will Messiah or *Moshiach* do when he comes, and who is he? Third, what kind of Messiah is Judaism looking for, and who is considered a better example of the Messiah than Jesus (*Yeshua*)?

In answering the first question, one fact stands out; orthodox Rabbinic Judaism is looking for a king and a saviour politically and not as a sacrifice from sin:

> The term "moshiach" literally means "the anointed one," and refers to the ancient practice of anointing kings with oil when they took the throne. The moshiach is the one who will be anointed as king in the End of Days.

> The word "moshiach" does not mean "savior." The notion of an innocent, divine or semi-divine being who will sacrifice himself to save us from the consequences of our own sins is a purely Christian concept that has no basis in Jewish thought. Unfortunately, this Christian concept has become so deeply ingrained in the English word "messiah" that this English word can no longer be used to refer to the Jewish concept. The word "moshiach" will be used throughout these pages.[1134]

[1132] *Mashiach* and *Moshiach* are two different spelling for the English Messiah.

[1133] Smith, *The Promised Messiah,* 1-4.

[1134] *www.jewfaq.org/moshiach.htm*

366

First of all, Rabbinic Judaism is correct in saying that "*moshiach*" does not mean "savior." But the reality of the *Tanakh* is that the *Moshiach* will save Israel and the world spiritually and physically. That will be seen in the passages observed in this chapter and the following three chapters. However, by their own admission Rabbinic Judaism sees two *Moshiachs*, Messiah ben Joseph who will suffer and die and Messiah ben David who will reign. To say that a "savior" will "sacrifice himself to save us from the consequences of our own sins" is clearly taught in the *Tanakh*, as will be borne out in the remaining chapters of this book. One prime evidence that the *Moshiach* will be sacrificed is found in Isaiah 53 (see Appendix 4). Rabbinic Judaism fails to understand that before *Moshiach* can come to restore Israel and reign on the throne of David, the promise of the Redeemer from Genesis 3:15 and the payment for the very thing that separates mankind from God must be dealt with. Sin that separated mankind from God must be mended first before the fulfillment of the Abrahamic Covenant and the restoration of the promised kingdom that the prophets clearly spoke of. Rabbinic Judaism totally fails to see the holiness of God in relationship to their sins. God, who is completely holy, cannot tolerate sin of any kind in His presence. Even though *Moshiach* does not mean saviour, God has wrapped up in the word *Moshiach* concepts of a saviour from sin and the political restorer of Israel with the reign of the *Moshiach* on David's throne. The following chapters will substantiate that the Saviour, the *Moshiach,* is divine as well as human.

What will the *Moshiach* have to do to substantiate in the eyes of Rabbinic Judaism that he is their *Moshiach*?:

> The moshiach will be a great political leader descended from King David (Jeremiah 23:5). The moshiach is often referred to as "moshiach ben David" (moshiach, son of David). He will be well versed in Jewish law, and observant of its commandments (Isaiah 11:2-5). He will be a charismatic leader, inspiring others to follow his example. He will be a great military leader, who will win battles for Israel. He will be a great judge, who makes righteous decisions (Jeremiah 33:15). But above all, he will be a human being, not a god, demi-god or other supernatural being.[1135]

Yes, *Moshiach* will be a great political leader, but several other things also come into play. The Scriptures referenced in Jeremiah 23:5-6 state that the *Moshiach* will be God in a human body. The other question is, does the rabbinic *moshiach* have a genealogical record back to David to prove that he is a descendant from David? This proof is absolutely essential and impossible to obtain since in the destruction of the temple in 70 CE all genealogical records of the families and tribes of Israel were destroyed. Rabbinic Judaism has an unbiblical insistence that the *Moshiach* will not be God. But as will be demonstrated in the following chapters, there are many more references to the deity of *Moshiach* than rabbis want to acknowledge. Modern day rabbis will return to a limited sacrificial system with the third temple. But why sacrifice, in a new temple, if

---

[1135] *www.jewfaq.org/moshiach.htm*

Jewish people (from their perspective) are not sinners and have no need of a saviour or a mediator? They do not understand that the fulfillment of Genesis 3:15 must occur first. Someone must deal with the sin issue before an absolutely holy God can inaugurate the Kingdom. The sacrifices are a picture to the Jewish nation of what must be done, not with a temporary sacrifice but with a sacrifice that will deal with the sin issue forever. That can only be done by the *Moshiach*, the Redeemer, the Saviour of Israel, Who would become the substitutionary sacrifice for sin. Then the *Moshiach* could be that great political leader Who literally would rule the world.

Rabbinic Judaism believes that since the *Tanakh* was given to them, they are the ones who should be able to interpret it correctly. Yes, that should be true, but reality is that Jewish belief is at odds with *Yahweh* because of their historic disobedience to the Law and the curses of Deuteronomy 28 which are still happening to them today. The sacrificial system has been removed by *Yahweh* so that sin cannot be dealt with from the Mosaic Law. Rabbinic Judaism has replaced it by saying that sacrifice is no longer necessary because now they are to use prayer, repentance and good works instead.[1136] Yet *Yahweh* has never changed the status quo except in relation to the *Moshiach's* vicarious offering for sin on Passover. Rabbinic Judaism is quick to accuse New Covenant believers of changing the status quo in relation to the biblical interpretation of Messiah, but obviously something is wrong because the *Moshiach* from their perspective has not come. Following is an example of their accusations:

> As you know, the Jews were in Israel for around 1000 years before Jesus appeared. They had a definite concept of what the Messiah would be like – there was a status quo regarding the nature of the Messiah. The Christians appeared and introduced an entirely different picture of what the Messiah would be like (son of God, God incarnate, born of virgin, two comings, etc.). Thus, the Christians changed the status quo concept of the Messiah.[1137]

The point is that the status quo that they claim is not what you see from a literal, historical-grammatical method of interpretation. After the captivity, the scribes and the people did not want to experience the captivity again. Their worship of idols and disobedience of the Written Law had brought about that first captivity. In their zeal not to worship other gods, they failed to see and understand the plural unity of their monotheistic God. As a result, when they came across passages that pointed to the plurality of God, and being what they truly believed was loyalty to the LORD, they simply said that there must be another answer to this verse(s). So today as in the first century CE the plurality of *Yahweh* has been consistently rejected, and in doing so they have rejected their God who revealed Himself to them throughout their history and they will someday mourn bitterly over Him (Zechariah 12:10); when they realize who He is, they will be shocked! In reality Rabbinic Judaism, and not true biblical faith, has

---

[1136] Picker, "Make Us A God!" *A Jewish Response to Hebrew Christianity: A Survival Manual For Jews,* 94.

[1137] Levine, *You Take Jesus, I'll Take God,* 12.

changed the status quo with the introduction of the Oral Law which has absolutely no biblical foundation. Rabbis after Ezra began to change their authority basis from the Written Law to a manmade Oral Law, the interpretations of the rabbis. Rabbi ben Zakkai took that foundation to the next level by creating a Judaism that would survive without the priesthood and temple after the 70 CE destruction by placing the basis of study on the interpretations of rabbis instead of what *Yahweh* literally said and taught in the *Tanakh*. Today we see the outgrowth of those decisions made centuries ago which changed the status quo that *Yahweh* laid out in His Written Word.

Rabbinic Judaism teaches presently that Jesus (*Yeshua*) could not be the *Moshiach* because He did not fulfill the mission of the *Moshiach*. So the last issue is for Rabbinic Judaism to offer who they present as the best illustration of what the *Moshiach* will be like. Following is a comparison of *Yeshua* as *Moshiach* to a well known false *moshiach*:

> Jews do not believe that Jesus was the moshiach. Assuming that he existed, and assuming that Christian scriptures are accurate in describing him (both matters that are debatable), he simply did not fulfill the mission of the moshiach as it is described in the biblical passages .... Jesus did not do any of these things that the scriptures said the messiah would do.

> On the contrary, another Jew born about a century later came far closer to fulfilling the messianic ideal than Jesus did. His name was Shimeon ben Kosiba, known as Bar Kochba (son of a star), and he was a charismatic, brilliant, but brutal warlord. Rabbi Akiba, one of the greatest scholars in Jewish history, believed that Bar Kochba was the moshiach. Bar Kochba fought a war against the Roman Empire, catching the Tenth Legion by surprise and retaking Jerusalem. He resumed sacrifices at the site of the Temple and made plans to rebuild the Temple. He established a provisional government and began to issue coins in its name. This is what the Jewish people were looking for in a moshiach; Jesus clearly does not fit into this mold. Ultimately, however, the Roman Empire crushed his revolt and killed Bar Kochba. After his death, all acknowledged that he was not the moshiach.[1138]

[1138] *www.jewfaq.org/moshiach.htm* The following is taken directly from the Judaism 101 website as a sampling of their comments: "The moshiach will be a great political leader descended from King David (Jeremiah 23:5). The moshiach is often referred to as "moshiach ben David" (moshiach, son of David). He will be well-versed in Jewish law, and observant of its commandments (Isaiah 11:2-5). He will be a charismatic leader, inspiring others to follow his example. He will be a great military leader, who will win battles for Israel. He will be a great judge, who makes righteous decisions (Jeremiah 33:15). But above all, he will be a human king, not a god, demi-god or other supernatural being. The moshiach will bring about the political and spiritual redemption of the Jewish people by bringing us back to Israel and restoring Jerusalem (Isaiah 11:11-12; Jeremiah 23:8; 30:3; Hosea 3:4-5). He will establish a government in Israel that will be the center of all world government, both for Jews and Gentiles (Isaiah 2:2-4; 11:10; 42:1). He will rebuild the Temple and re-establish its worship (Jeremiah 33:18). He will restore

Their first comment is ludicrous; history does substantiate the existence of *Yeshua*. Both the Talmud and other secular authors verify His existence. As to the fact that *Yeshua* does not fulfill the passages that relate to the *Moshiach*, which passages has He not fulfilled? By their own admission there are two groups of passages that speak of the *Moshiach*: one dealing with a suffering *Moshiach* (ben Joseph) and the other dealing with a reigning *Moshiach* (ben David). They have deceived themselves by only looking at the reigning passages of *Moshiach* and not interacting with the suffering passages of *Moshiach* and the purpose of the Messiah suffering. They reject the whole idea that *Moshiach* will be rejected by the Jewish people as the following comment states:

There is not the slightest hint of Messiah's rejection by Israel.[1139]

"There is not the slightest hint," reveals blind ignorance to the many passages of Scripture that point in that direction, passages such as Psalm 22, Isaiah 53, Hosea 5:15, Zechariah 11:4-14, 12:10 and numerous others. They simply did not want to see these passages as relating to their *Moshiach*. There are 2000 years of pride that must be swallowed. They must acknowledge that their fathers and fathers' fathers not only missed Him, but then tampered with the Scriptures by adding the Oral Law to cover their rejection.

So if they focus only on the reigning passages, of course *Yeshua* did not fulfill those passages in His first coming. But if they would look at both sets of passages, they could understand one *Moshiach* coming twice instead of two *moshiach*s. They would see that sin had to be dealt with first before the Kingdom could come. However, their doctrine of sin and salvation is faulty.

In one area the rabbis are correct. Jesus (*Yeshua*) did not fulfill what they were looking for, because they were looking for the wrong thing in the *Moshiach*. *Yeshua* had to deal with priorities; He had to deal with the sin issue that separated mankind from God before He could set up the Kingdom. He had to first remedy the area that separates all of mankind from God – sin! He is the "*seed of the woman*" (Genesis 3:15) promised to Satan in the hearing of Adam and Eve back in the garden of Eden. *Yeshua* came as the servant, to suffer and die as *Moshiach* ben Joseph, not the Joseph of Ephraim as Rabbinic Judaism teaches, but the suffering "Servant of the LORD." But before He could reign and give to Israel and the world a Kingdom of universal peace, sin had to be dealt with. The character of God is holiness, righteousness and justice and mankind falls completely short of all that God is. Question, dear rabbi: How can there be universal peace, without the heart being changed from either overt or covert acts of rebellion? Dear rabbi, you have missed the first and most important point; it is not just the fulfillment of the Covenants, but the fact that mankind must once again have spiritual union with his Creator. For Israel to focus on their restoration without dealing

---

the religious court system of Israel and establish Jewish law as the law of the land (Jeremiah 33:15)."

[1139] Picker, "Make Us A God!" *A Jewish Response to Hebrew Christianity: A Survival Manual For Jews,* 59.

370

with the core issue of sin, or as Moses and Jeremiah referenced it as an "uncircumcised heart" (Deuteronomy 10:16; Jeremiah 4:4) is self serving. Israel's long recorded history is one of sin and separation from their God, *Yahweh*. As Jewish people, you should know by experience that the whole concept of mankind being born with an inclination to do either good or evil is a completely inadequate way of describing sin. Let me get you some personal examples as to the sin nature of mankind which has been committed against mankind, and against you His chosen people and ultimately against God Himself. Over the centuries you have been persecuted, herded as cattle into regions of countries, you have been murdered, beaten, raped, hated, lost all civil rights, and had all kinds of slander against you. I do not need to remind you of the acts of wickedness perpetrated upon the Jewish people through the Crusades, the Inquisition, the Pogroms and the Holocaust. Look at the world around you; you are universally hated and the world will not even let you be at rest in your home land. You feel secure in the United States of America, but when *Moshiach* takes all His true believers home to heaven (Rapture of the Church) or when America becomes completely secularized or paganized (whichever comes first) you will have lost your last friend and ally. Go back to the *Tanakh* and look at what God says about the human heart (Job 5:7; Psalm 53:2-3; Ecclesiastes 7:20; Isaiah 59:2; 64:6; Jeremiah 17:9). Does this author believe in the Covenants? ABSOLUTELY! But until the Jewish Nation says "בָּרוּךְ הַבָּא בְּשֵׁם יְהוָה" or "*Blessed is He who comes in the Name of the LORD,*" and Israel acknowledges its sin against its God, redemption will not come to Israel.

Much of what will be studied in the coming chapters needs to be clearly understood and depends upon the interpretation of two important Hebrew words: (1) עוֹלָם or *olam* and (2) עַד or *'ad*.[1140] Both of these words are translated in the English text as "eternal," "eternity," "everlasting," "forever," "ever and ever," "age" or "ancient."[1141] In English such terms project beyond the end of time. However, in the Hebrew there is no word that expresses the English concept of "eternal." Therefore, to understand the term in English, a reader needs to know what the word meant in the Hebrew language then and how it was used.

OLAM עוֹלָם

The first word, *olam* (עוֹלָם), means "long duration, antiquity, futurity."[1142] The meaning of *olam* is divided into two groups with numerous sub-sections. It deals with time in the past, as well as indefinite futurity with many sub-headings. However, the majority of references deal with man's life, a dynasty, laws that are no longer in use such as the Mosaic Law. The term *olam* deals with families and relationships with

---

[1140] Botterweck, Ringgren, and Fabry, *Theological Dictionary of the Old Testament*, 10:456, 530.

[1141] Young, *Analytical Concordance to the Bible,* 310-312.

[1142] Brown, Driver and Briggs, *A Hebrew and English Lexicon of the Old Testament,* 761-763.

nations or an age. What is obvious is that the term *olam* in the *Tanakh* is confined to time, except when it relates to God who is outside of time. So *olam*, when used in connection with God, indicates that eternity is to be understood. Schoonhoven expresses it this way:

> The OT has no special term for "eternity" that can be contrasted with a term denoting "temporality." The Hebrew word most often used to express "eternity" is *olam*. It is the same word that expresses duration of time, and it designates eternity only in such statements as "from *olam*" and "until *olam*" (Psa 90:2).[1143]

The term *olam* is a very elastic term for time, stretching from a portion of time in man's life, to his whole life right through to a period of time that could be to the end of an age or time period. Schoonhoven's explanation is that:

> When viewed from the vantage point of the Bible, eternity is a term that includes temporal relations. Eternity is time stretching endlessly forward and backward, with the result that time itself must be regarded as a segment of eternity.[1144]

Because God is outside of time, He is not governed by time. So *olam* refers to man's relationship to other men, nations, or to God for a period of time, whether that time is a man's lifetime or an age. The exception is when the reference is to God, as He is not bound by time. Below are some passages of how *olam* is used "generally to point to something that seems long ago, but rarely, if ever, refers to a limitless past:"

Genesis 6:4	"Those were the mighty men who were of old" written from Moses' point in time.
Deuteronomy 32:7	to the time of one's elder
1 Samuel 27:8	"ancient times"
Isaiah 51:9	"days of old, the generations of long ago"
Isaiah 58:12	Rebuild the "ancient ruins," a future prophecy, what they will do in relationship to their past
Isaiah 63:9	"carried them all the days of old"
Jeremiah 6:16	"ancient paths" where the good way is and walk in it
Jeremiah 18:15	"ancient paths" they (Israel) have forgotten me and do not walk in my paths
Jeremiah 28:8	prophets before me and you, from "ancient times"
Ezekiel 36:2	"ancient high places" (ASV)

[1143] Bromiley, *The International Standard Bible Encyclopedia,* 2:162.
[1144] Bromiley, *The International Standard Bible Encyclopedia,* 2:163.

Micah 7:14	"as in the days of old"
Malachi 3:4	"as in the days of old and as in former years"
Job 22:15	"ancient path" which wicked men trod
Proverbs 22:28	"ancient boundary" that your fathers have set
Ezra 4:15	[Aramaic] "have incited revolt within it in past days"
Ezra 4:19	[Aramaic] "that the city has risen up against the kings in past days"[1145]

Although *olam* is sometimes used of the past, the majority of the time it is used of some future period. It refers to a future of limited duration or conditions that will exist continuously throughout a limited period of time, often a single lifetime. The following two examples express that position:

"as long as one lives" (a slave for life) Exod 21:16 (Deut 15:17; I Sam 27:12)

"May my lord King David live forever" 1 Kgs 1:31 (Neh 2:3; Dan 2:4)[1146]

Arnold Fruchtenbaum, speaking in relation to the Sabbath being kept "forever," states that the word is used within time:

While the English term tends to carry concepts of eternity, this is not the meaning of the Hebrew words themselves. Classical Hebrew had no word that actually meant "eternal." [First] the Hebrew term for "forever" (*olam*) means "long duration," "antiquity," or "futurity." The Hebrew terms basically mean "until the end of a period of time." What that period of time is must be determined by the context of related passages. The period of time may have been to the end of a man's life, or an age, or dispensation, but not "forever" in the sense of eternity.

Second, there are two Hebrew forms of *olam*. One is *le-olam*, which means "unto an age." The second form is *ad-olam*, which means "until an age." However, neither of these forms carry the English meaning of "forever." Though it was translated that way in English, the Hebrew does not carry the concept of eternity as the English word "forever" does.

Third, the word *olam*, *le olam* or *ad-olam*, sometimes means only up to the end of a man's life. For example, it is used in Exodus 14:13 of someone's lifetime. It is used in Exodus 21:6, Leviticus 25:46, and Deuteronomy 15:17 of a slave's life. In 1 Samuel 1:22 and 2:35, it is used of Samuel's life. First Samuel 20:23 speaks of the lifetime of David and Jonathan. First Samuel 27:12; 28:2 and 1 Chronicles 28:4 uses [sic] the word of David's lifetime. While the English

---

[1145] Harris, Archer, and Waltke, *Theological Wordbook of the Old Testament*, 2:672-673.

[1146] Botterweck, Ringgren, and Fabry. *Theological Dictionary of the Old Testament*, 10:535-536.

reads, "forever," obviously from the context it does not mean forever in the sense of eternity, but only forever up to the end of the person's life.

Fourth, *olam* sometimes means only an age or dispensation. For example, Deuteronomy 23:3 uses the term "forever," but it limits the term "forever" as only ten generations long. It obviously carries the concept of an age here. In 2 Chronicles 7:16 it is used only for the period of the first temple. So, again, the word "forever" in Hebrew does not mean eternal, it means up to the end of a period of time which could either be a man's life or an age or a dispensation.

Fifth, the same word for "forever" is used of certain ceremonial facets of the Mosaic Law which everyone agrees has ended with the coming of Christ. For example, the same word "forever" is used of the kindling of the tabernacle lamp stands (Exodus 27:20; Leviticus 24:3): it is used of the ceremony of the showbread (Leviticus 24:8); it is used of the service of the brazen laver (Exodus 30:21); is used of the Levitical priesthood and Levitical garments (Exodus 28:43; 40:15; Leviticus 6:18; 10:9; Numbers 10:8; 18:23; 25:13; Deuteronomy 18:5; 1 Chronicles 15:2; 23:13); it is used of the sacrificial system, including the sacrifices and offerings (Exodus 29:28; Leviticus 7:34, 36; 10:15; Numbers 15:15; 18:8, 11, 19; 19:10); it is used of the Day of Atonement sacrifice (Lev 16:34); and, it is used of the red heifer offering (Numbers 19:10). It is used of all of these ceremonial facets that everybody agrees has been done away with in Christ. [1147]

Within all these references to the term *olam*, eternity is conceptualized from the perspective of man—not God, who according to the prophets, dwells in heaven and is outside of time and unlimited by space as pointed out by Vos. God, with the character of immutability, is outside of time, separated from time and not governed by time. Vos states:

> That the prophets represent God as dwelling in heaven, Unlimited by space, and yet they also say that He dwells in Zion and that Canaan is His land....The same relation applied as between Jehovah and time. In popular language, such as the prophets use, eternity can only be expressed in terms of time, although in reality it lies altogether above time."[1148]

In his book *On the Eternity of God*, Charnock does not use the Hebrew word *olam* to lay out the differences between time and eternity, for eternity is before and after time:

> Time hath a continual succession....We must conceive of eternity contrary to the notion of time; as the nature of time consists in the succession of parts, so the nature of eternity in an infinite immutable duration....So eternity is the

---

[1147] Fruchtenbaum, *The Sabbath: Manuscript #176*, 18-19.

[1148] Geerhardus Vos, *Biblical Theology, Old and New Testaments* (Grand Rapids: Eerdmans, 1948), 263.

duration of his essence; and when we say God is eternal, we exclude from him all possibility of beginning and ending, all flux and change. As the essence of God cannot be bound by any place, so it is not to be limited by any time; as it is his immensity to be everywhere, so it is his eternity to be always.... His duration is as endless as his essence is boundless: he always was and always will be, and will no more have an end than he had a beginning; and this is an excellency belonging to the Supreme Being.... Time began with the foundation of the world; but God being before time, could have no beginning in time. Before the beginning of creation, and the beginning of time, there could be nothing but eternity;...for as between the Creator and creatures there is no medium, so between time and eternity there is no medium.[1149]

Charnock's whole chapter on the eternity of God is very worthwhile reading and meditating upon. Several other authors, such as Botterweck,[1150] VanGemeren,[1151] and Harris[1152] also lay out some excellent material on the word *olam*.

So what is the conclusion in relation to the word *olam* and how is it to be understood in the *Tanakh*? Fruchtenbaum gives the clearest and simplest answer when he states that the context determines just how *olam* is to be understood;[1153] the understanding of *olam*, in reference to man and/or to God, will be determined by its context. That context will determine whether *olam* is in the framework of time or whether *olam* is in relation to God and His nature, essence and character as being outside of time, eternal. The following are two examples of *olam* being used in reference to God and carries with it the English concept of eternity:

(19) No longer shall you need the sun for light by day, nor the shining of the moon for radiance [by night]; for the LORD shall be your light everlasting, your God shall be your glory. (20) Your sun shall set no more, your moon no more withdraw; for the LORD shall be a light to you forever, and your days of mourning shall be ended. Isaiah 60:19-20

In this passage Isaiah states that there will be no more need for the sun and moon for the *Shechinah* of God will be their light. Webb,[1154] Wolf,[1155] and Young[1156] refer to Revelation 21:23 (22:5) where John (*Yochanan*) states that after the destruction of the heavens and earth, and the new heavens and earth are in place, God's glory will be their

---

[1149] Steven Charnock, *Existence and Attributes of God* (Grand Rapids: Baker, 1996), 1:280-282. For some additional information see: L. Thomas Holdcroft, *The Doctrine of God* (Oakland, CA: Western Book Company, 1960), 21-23.

[1150] Botterweck, Ringgren and Fabry, *Theological Dictionary of the Old Testament*, 10:531-545.

[1151] VanGemeren, *Dictionary of Old Testament Theology & Exegesis,* 3:345-350.

[1152] Harris, Archer and Waltke, *Theological Wordbook of the Old Testament*, 2:672-673.

[1153] Fruchtenbaum, *The Sabbath: Manuscript #176*, 18.

[1154] Webb, *The Message of Isaiah*, 231.

[1155] Wolf, *Interpreting Isaiah*, 238.

[1156] Young, *The Book of Isaiah*, 3:455.

light. Here something beyond the physical earth and time are in view in connection with God's *Shechinah* light. Psalm 119:89 states, "*the LORD exists forever; your word stands firm in heaven*," meaning that the Word of God is settled in heaven, a place outside of the limits of earth and time. This verse declares that the Word of God is in the eternal heavens. According to Leupold, the Word of God which comes from the eternal Lord of the heavens has its abiding resting place and will, like them, endure forever.[1157]

While *olam* is predominantly used in the context of time, it is also used outside of time in reference to God. So where *olam* is used of man and his relationship to others, whether other people or nations, it has a time context. Yet throughout the *Tanakh*, *olam*, when in context with God, has an eternal perspective beyond time.

AD - עַד

The second word for eternity is עַד [or *ad*] which means "perpetuity."[1158] The word perpetuity reflects both time and eternity. This Hebrew word refers to "past time" and "future time." In past time it is referenced only twice as the "ancient mountains" in Habakkuk 3:6 and in relation to the wicked in Job 20:4.[1159] The other references refer to future time and deal with things earthbound or time-related, except with reference to God. עַד is used 48 times in the *Tanakh*: 29 times in Psalms, 8 times in Isaiah, twice in each of Micah, Job, and Proverbs and once in Ezekiel 15:18, Amos 1:11, Habakkuk 3:6, Daniel 12:3 and 1 Chronicles 28:9.[1160] In these 48 references *ad* is used 19 times in conjunction with *olam*[1161] as in Isaiah 45:17 (*olam*/everlasting; *ad*/without end), Exodus 15:18 (*olam*/forever; *ad*/ever), and Daniel 12:3 (*olam*/forever; *ad*/ever).

Brown, Driver and Briggs, in reference to עַד or *ad*, have two groupings of usages: (1) past time as reflected in the above paragraph, (2) future time as reflected in "forever" as during a lifetime of a king or of things, or of "the continuous existence of nations" as well as "divine existence."[1162] In the future sense, עַד "always denotes the unforeseeable future," which does not necessarily imply eternity. However, when עַד is applied to God, it does imply eternity or everlasting.[1163] Like *olam*, *ad* must be understood and interpreted within the context in which it is given. It must be understood that time is only a segment of eternity, and God is outside of time.

Since no Hebrew word independently reflects eternity by itself, *olam* and *ad* reflect time, because time is only a part of eternity. God lives outside of time; He made time. Hence, He is not bound by time. But when *olam* and *ad* are used of God, in relation to

---

[1157] Leupold, *Exposition of Psalms,* 842.

[1158] Brown, Driver and Briggs, *A Hebrew and English Lexicon of the Old Testament,* 723.

[1159] Harris, Archer and Waltke, *Theological Wordbook of the Old Testament,* 2:645.

[1160] Jenni and Westermann, *Theological Lexicon of the Old Testament,* 2:837.

[1161] Harris, Archer and Waltke, *Theological Wordbook of the Old Testament,* 2:645.

[1162] Brown, Driver and Briggs, *A Hebrew and English Lexicon of the Old Testament,* 723.

[1163] Harris, Archer and Waltke, *Theological Wordbook of the Old Testament,* 2:645.

His being, they are understood to be a reference to eternity, beyond time. Therefore, interpreting *olam* and *ad* requires the context and related passages to determine whether they are bound by time and whether they reflect eternity.

FIRST COMING MESSIANIC REFERENCES

The English words "eternity," "everlasting" and "forever" play a critical role in the understanding of these first coming Messianic references. But first, in Genesis 12, 13, 15, 17, and 22, God makes a covenant called the Abrahamic Covenant, which is recognized as an eternal covenant.[1164] Deuteronomy 30 is not only a promise of a Land Covenant[1165] to be given to Abraham and to his descendants, (Genesis 15:4-5, 18) but it is also an eternal covenant.[1166] This is critical in understanding the situation today in Israel. God is in the process of regathering Israel, as Deuteronomy 30 and Ezekiel 37 denote, for the fulfilling of His covenant to Abraham. Several years ago this author read a quote that is significant and well worth pondering:

> The most central portion of all Scripture is the Abrahamic Covenant; everything else is commentary on it (source unknown).

Not only did God make an eternal covenant with Abraham and enlarge it to Israel in the Land Covenant, He also made an eternal covenant with David. These three covenants are eternal, and minimally last through future time, or "long duration," until time and history close. The Hebrew Scripture reveals nothing beyond the Messianic Kingdom that is promised to Abraham and to David's eternal Son. Only in the New Covenant, in the book of Revelation, is further revelation given about an eternal state. In the Davidic Covenant there is an extremely strong indication that there is something that has an eternal reference to the end of time into eternity. The coming verses on the Davidic Covenant will show the promises of an eternal God, who is working to fulfill them through the eternal Son, who is the eternal Son of David.

In the next three chapters of this book there are several first coming Messianic references (2 Samuel 7:11-16; 1 Chronicles 17:11-14; Isaiah 9:6-7; Micah 5:2) that use the term *olam* or *ad*. How are these verses to be understood when referring to the *Moshiach*? These verses are very important because Rabbinic Judaism often recognizes them as messianic, even when the messianic person appears to be divine. Yet while rabbis recognize these verses as messianic, they will not embrace the idea that *Moshiach* can be God. To them it is completely inconceivable that God would incarnate Himself as flesh and dwell among men. Following is an example of their belief:

[1164] Fruchtenbaum, *Israelology: The Missing Link in Systematic Theology,* 334.

[1165] *Land Covenant*: Traditionally the Land Covenant has been called the "Palestinian Covenant." But to avoid confusion with the Palestinian Covenant that is in the PLO charter, which calls for the destruction of Israel, Land Covenant is being used to identify the Covenant that God made with Israel in Deuteronomy 30.

[1166] Fruchtenbaum, *Israelology: The Missing Link in Systematic Theology,* 572-581.

The "truth about God" is that he is Infinite – a Spirit-being. To say "God became flesh" is to deny the essential nature of God! God cannot be represented in finite form.… The Creator cannot be confined in created matter! This is the essence of Hebrew Monotheism, as proclaimed throughout Hebrew Scriptures.… The incarnation would confine God in a human body, in denial of His universal presence.[1167]

Moshiach is not super-human or divine. He is a fallible, mortal human being. There is no sacrificial, atoning death.[1168]

On one hand rabbis are correct when they state that He is "Infinite – a Spirit being." But to state that "God cannot be represented in finite form" is to completely ignore passages such as Genesis 18 and Exodus 24, to name only two. If God was an absolute one, then it would indeed limit His presence to a human body and no one would be in charge of the "store," so to speak (review chapter 2 on the Image of God). The most sacred place in all of biblical Judaism was the Holy of Holies, in the tabernacle and later the temple, where God's presence the Shekinah Glory dwelt among the people. Yet here God confined Himself between the *cherubim* above the Mercy Seat from the time of Mt. Sinai through to the time of Ezekiel (8-11). So to say that God could not confine Himself via the incarnation is not a logical argument. What is correct is that "*God is not a man*" as Moses wrote, but He is a plural unity where one person of that plural unity took on flesh while the other members of the plural unity remained in His heavenly abode. How can passages such as Genesis 19:24 or Hosea 1:7 be explained any other way? For in both passages the LORD acts as a separate identity from the LORD.

Despite Rabbinic Judaism's disclaimers, the divinity of the *Moshiach* is clearly indicated in two distinct categories of Hebrew Scriptures. The first involves passages in which *olam* is used. Second are passages that are recognized as Messianic, where *Yahweh* is speaking of Himself, and what happened to Him was experienced only by the Second Person of the plural unity of *Elohim*.

What has been established is that *olam* and *ad* play a significant role in understanding the eternal aspect of the Abrahamic, Land, and Davidic Covenants, as well as the first coming references of the *Moshiach* that have direct bearing on those covenants and promises given by the prophets. But before these verses are discussed, one other observation is in order in relation to Genesis 3:15. This passage is commonly called the protevangelium, meaning that it is the prototype for the Christian gospel.[1169] There is something that must be said about this verse that draws attention to the nature and essence of the seed of the woman as related to the promise given by God to Satan concerning his undoing. First the verse:

[1167] Picker, "Make Us A God!" *A Jewish Response to Hebrew Christianity: A Survival Manual For Jews,* 29-30.

[1168] Picker, "Make Us A God!" *A Jewish Response to Hebrew Christianity: A Survival Manual For Jews,* 55.

[1169] Mathews, *New American Commentary: Genesis 1:1-11:26,* 247.

And I will put enmity between thee and the woman, and between thy seed and her seed; it shall bruise thy head, and thou shalt bruise his heel.

It is commonly recognized that Satan, originally called "Lucifer, son of the morning" (Isaiah 14:12), was most likely a very beautiful creature (Ezekiel 28:13). In Ezekiel 28:14 [16] he is called *the anointed Cherub that covereth.*" Apparently, the *cherubim* were the "guardian and proclaimer of God's glorious presence and holiness."[1170] *Cherubim* seem to be the highest rank among the angels and also the closest to the presence of God.[1171] Unger confirms Shower's statement:

He is the highest and most exalted of heaven's beings, who became Satan when he led a celestial revolt that spread to myriads of the angelic beings."[1172]

Satan, as a covering cherub, may have been one of the most powerful angels that God had created. So if "*the seed of the woman*" were just a man, he could not have touched Satan or his seed (anti-Christ). Genesis 3:15 strongly indicates that the "*seed of the woman*" would have to be equal to, or greater than, Satan himself in order to defeat him. If that were the case, then "*the seed of the woman*" would be the incarnation of God in flesh. It would have been impossible for this prophecy, given to Satan, to be fulfilled without "*the seed of the woman*" minimally being a supernatural person. This passage by itself does not necessarily establish that God, in human flesh, is "*the seed of the woman*" but as Cooper states, it does say something unique:

Nevertheless, since the genealogy of men was always reckoned through the male and never through the female, this expression immediately assumes something very extraordinary and strange about this individual.[1173]

Eve understood it as the God/man in Genesis 4:1. In Targum Jonathan it states the following, "And Adam knew Hava [Eve] his wife, who had desired the Angel; and she conceived, and bare Kain [Cain]; and she said, I have acquired a man, the Angel of the Lord." It can be argued that Eve did not mean that, but by the time the last prophet came on the scene in the Hebrew Scriptures, it is the only possibility. Cooper makes an interesting addition to his point that Eve understood the God/man concept:

Let us translate literally what is in the Hebrew without Supplying any words. The sentence reads thus, "I have gotten a man, even Jehovah." The early Jewish Targum, the Aramaic translation, renders it this way: 'I have gotten a man, even the angel of Jehovah.' These Hebrew scholars supplied the word "angel." In

---

[1170] Dickason, *Angels: Elect and Evil,* 128.

[1171] Showers, *Those Invisible Spirits Called Angels,* 27-28.

[1172] Merrill F. Unger, *Biblical Demonology* (Wheaton: Scripture Press, 1952), 15.

[1173] David L. Cooper, *The 70 Weeks of Daniel* (Los Angeles: Biblical Research Society, 1941), 1-2.

doing this they were nearer the meaning of the original than our translators, who inserted the words as indicated above (*the help of*).[1174]

According to Cooper who quoted the Targum, the Hebrew scholars at that time minimally recognized that she believed her first son to be a supernatural individual.

There are two significant passages to start an examination of the *Moshiach* being divine. Deuteronomy 18:15-19 and 1 Chronicles 17:10-14 (2 Samuel 7:11-16) will be brought into the discussion as we come to them in the Jewish order. However, neither of these passages uses the term *Moshiach*. The following three chapters in this book will deal with the *Moshiach* in the Jewish order in the Hebrew Scriptures, the Law, the Prophets and the Writings. This may be a little different for the Christian, but it is done with the Jewish people in mind. Within the next three chapters the vast majority of references will have the term "messiah" in them. However, as foundational, the Deuteronomy and 1 Chronicles (2 Samuel) passages will be discussed in chapters 13 and 14 respectively.

[1174] Cooper, *The 70 Weeks of Daniel*, 3.

Chapter 13
Messiah Divine In the Law

In the Torah there are three primary passages that deal directly with the Messiah. In the New Covenant book of the Gospel of John, *Yeshua* made an interesting statement. He said that in the *Tanakh* it spoke of Him (John 5:39). He stated a few verses later concerning Moses that "*he wrote of me*" (John 5:46). The logical question is, what did Moses have to say about the Messiah and *Yeshua* in particular. There are more passages than these three to be discussed that deal with the Messiah in the writing of Moses, as we have already seen the activity of the Second Person of the plural unity of *Elohim* in the Books of Moses. However, the three that will be studied are the primary ones in the five books of Moses (Genesis through Deuteronomy) that deal with the *Moshiach* (Messiah). There are also several types such as the tabernacle which will not be addressed in this book. These passages are found in Genesis 49:10; Numbers 24:17 and Deuteronomy 18:15-19, which is the most dramatic passage of the *Moshiach* in all of the Torah.

THE SCEPTER SHALL NOT DEPART ... Genesis 49:10

The scepter shall not depart from Judah, nor a lawgiver from between his feet, until Shiloh come; and unto him shall the gathering of the people be (Leeser Version).

The first thing to be noted is that this verse does not have the word Messiah in its context. However, that does not mean that the Messiah is not in view. There are four parts to this verse, of which only the third part has some difficulties. We will view each phrase separately.

The scepter shall not depart from Judah is the first phrase. It is commonly understood that the scepter is equated with kingship and that Judah will be preeminent among all the tribes of Israel with all government functions among the tribes will be lodged in the tribe of Judah.[1175] It is also to be remembered that the tribe of Judah during the wilderness wanderings had the preeminence in being first as the tribes moved to each new location (Numbers 10:14; Judges 1:1-2).

The second phrase, *nor a lawgiver from between his feet,* is a shadow of the first statement as the king would take the scepter when sitting on the throne and place it

---

[1175] David L. Cooper, *Messiah: His First Coming Scheduled* (Los Angeles: Biblical Research Society, 1939), 137.

between his feet. The scepter which belonged to the lawgiver meant that the governmental authority and power as represented in the chief executive shall continue with the tribe of Judah "*until Shiloh come,*" which is our next phrase. There is another but unlikely view that "between his feet" is a euphemism for sexual parts, meaning sexual potency. Thus the thought is that Judah will always have a royal progeny.[1176] It is more credible to see archaeological evidence in a Persian relief that shows King Darius seated on his throne with a ruler's staff between his feet[1177] than it is for the sexual euphemism.

The third phrase, *until Shiloh come,* is the one phrase which presents some difficulties. Before discussing "*Shiloh*" the word "until" needs to be understood. What it does not mean is that when the Messiah comes Judah will be humbled and disgraced before Messiah, losing its preeminence. The Hebrew word for "until" is עַד and implies that Judah will hold that position until the Messiah comes and will continue to hold it because the Messiah is from the tribe of Judah and of the house of David, even if the tribe of Judah loses tribal identity. One Jewish source expresses this truth:

> Yaakov [Jacob] prophesied about Yehuda [Judah], "From King David's time onwards, the rulership will be yours forever. Even after the destruction of the *Bais Hamikdash* [temple], you will maintain your authority by means of the *Sanhedrin*. In exile you will remain a leader too since even in Bavel [Babylon] all Jews will respect the authority of the *raish galusa* (exilarch) who will be a descendant of your tribe.[1178]

So even though the kingdom was removed, the leadership of the tribe of Judah will be predominant to the coming of the *Moshiach* who is a descendant of Judah.[1179] So Rabbi Weissman sees the *Moshiach* in the term "Shiloh," which will be our next point of discussion.

There is a complete lack of agreement as to the meaning of the word שִׁילֹה which is commonly translated as shiloh. The term "shiloh" is often confused with the first location of the tabernacle, which was at the town called Shiloh in the tribal territory of Ephraim. There are four common views of understanding this word in the Genesis 49:10 passage.[1180] Only two of the four have merit and will be mentioned. The first one is that shiloh is a proper name for the Messiah. The verse does have reference to the Messiah, as is commonly seen by Jewish and Christian scholars. But shiloh is not a proper name for the coming *Moshiach*. Mathews expresses the following for the fourth view:

[1176] Mathews, *The New American Commentary: Genesis 11:27-50:26*, 893.

[1177] Pritchard, James B, *The Ancient Near East in Pictures: Relating to the Old Testament* (Princeton, NJ: Princeton University Press, 1954, ANEP no. 463), 159, 303.

[1178] Rabbi Moshe Weissman, *The Midrash Says: The Book of Beraishis* (Brooklyn: Benei Yakov Publications, 1999), 454-455.

[1179] Weissman, *The Midrash Says: The Book of Beraishis,* 455.

[1180] Mathews, *The New American Commentary: Genesis 11:27-50:26*, 893-895.

Most commendable is the alternate Hebrew textual reading (in Samaritan and MT MSS) *selloh* (or *sello*), meaning "to whom it belongs," thus "until he comes to whom it [scepter] belongs." This reading occurs in the Qumran text 4Q252 and in the chief version (LXX, Syrian Targums.) Many English versions prefer this interpretation of the text (NIV, RSV, REB, NLT). Ezekiel 21:27 [32] is the first known "interpretation" of our text, alluding to [Genesis] 49:10 when referring to the future, rightful successor to the wicked Zedekiah (should be Jeconiah) of Judah. The future ruler envisioned in 49:10 will receive the scepter ("it"), which represents the kingdom.[1181]

Atkinson also speaks of the Septuagint Greek text that the proper reading is "shelloh" instead of Shiloh in the following:

The Septuagint Greek version read the Hebrew as if it was differently pointed and translated 'shelloh' instead of 'Shiloh.' This means 'he to whom it belongs' and is a very proper name for Christ (Ezekiel 21:27). The passage would then mean that royalty would be held in trust by the tribe of Judah until Christ to Whom it belonged came to assume it.[1182]

Today many Messianic passages that have been historically viewed by the rabbis as Messianic are often rejected as being Messianic. Let me quote from Targum of Jonathan ben Uzziel on Genesis 49:10:

Kings shall not cease from the house of Jehuda, nor sapherim teaching the law from his children's children, until the time that the King Meshiha [Messiah] shall come, whose is the kingdom, and to whom all the kingdoms of the earth shall be obedient. How beauteous is the King Meshiha, who is to arise from the house of Jehuda!

This Targum from the first to second century of the Common Era is a testimonial to the fact that Judaism recognized Genesis 49:10 as a Messianic passage. An example of modern rabbinic scholarship in their attempt to remove the Messianic significance is found in the statement from Joseph Klausner in his article called "Allusions to the Messianic idea in the Pentateuch and Former Prophets" that aligns Shiloh with Solomon, for David had conquered all the neighboring countries making all of them obedient to King Solomon.

And since all recent scholars conclude that the blessing of Jacob was not composed before the period of the monarchy, it may be conjectured that it was composed in the time of Solomon. After the brilliant victories of David, which subdued many peoples, "the kingdom was established in the hand of Solomon," according to the witness of Scripture (1 Kings 2:46). He did not have to fight any more; and submission of neighboring people was assured. If we remember

---

[1181] Mathews, *The New American Commentary: Genesis 11:27-50:26*, 895.
[1182] Atkinson, *The Pocket Commentary of the Bible: Genesis*, 430.

the promise of Nathan the prophet, mentioned above, the words in this verse will be understood in their plain meaning; "The scepter shall not depart from Judah, nor the ruler's staff from between his feet, until Shiloh (Solomon) comes, and unto him shall be the obedience (submission) of the people."[1183]

Klausner is violating the *Tanakh* by attributing Genesis 49 of the writings of Moses to someone living during the time of Solomon, 500 years later. This would be Jewish higher criticism that attacks the words recorded by Moses. Others like the esteemed Rabbi Ibn Ezra stated that Shiloh was David who inaugurated the Kingdom of Judah.[1184] However, the rabbi departs from the intent of the verse for "*unto him shall the gatherers of the people be.*" The Targums written far before Ibn Ezra saw the nations of the world submitting to Messiah as reflected in these words: "and to whom all the kingdom of the earth shall be obedient."[1185] Numerous authors such as Cooper,[1186] Kaiser,[1187] Fruchtenbaum,[1188] Waltke,[1189] Feinberg,[1190] and Taylor,[1191] connect Ezekiel 21:27 to the Genesis 49:10 passage as further attributing this to the Son of David, *Yeshua*. Ezekiel references the Genesis passage almost exactly as he speaks of the crown being reserved for the Messiah. Kaiser also connects Zechariah 6:11, that the crown will be held for the Messiah to whom it belongs.[1192]

This opens the door for the discussion on the last phrase "*and unto him shall the gathering of the people be.*" This goes beyond all that David ever conquered. The understanding of the Targums and even the word "people" is plural, being peoples. Even the Peshitta[1193] in Genesis 49:10 gives the understanding of Messiah and His rule over the Gentile nations:

> The scepter shall not depart from Judah, nor a lawgiver from between his feet, until the coming of the One to whom the scepter belongs, to whom the Gentiles shall look forward.

What becomes clear is that Judah will have the scepter and will have its identity as a tribe intact when the Messiah appears on the scene. The crown is not only for the Messiah, but all the peoples of the earth will be in obedience to Him. David Baron lays

---

[1183] Leo Landman, *Messianism in the Talmudic Era* (New York: KTAV Publishing, 1979), 194.

[1184] Ibn Ezra, *Commentary on the Pentateuch: Genesis - Bereshit* (translated by H. Norman Strickman and Arthur M. Silver, New York: Menorah Publishing, 1988), 430-431.

[1185] *Targum of Jonathan Ben Uzziel on Genesis* 49:10.

[1186] Cooper, *Messiah: His Nature and Person,* 48.

[1187] Kaiser, *The Messiah in the Old Testament,* 193.

[1188] Fruchtenbaum, *Messianic Christology,* 21.

[1189] Bruce K. Waltke, *Genesis: A Commentary* (Grand Rapids: Zondervan, 2001), 608.

[1190] Feinberg, *The Prophecy of Ezekiel: The Glory of the Lord,* 123.

[1191] Taylor, *Ezekiel,* 165.

[1192] Kaiser, *The Messiah in the Old Testament,* 215.

[1193] *Peshitta* is the Bible translated from the ancient eastern text (Syrian Text) which was in Aramaic.

out the weight of evidence that the Jewish people in history viewed this verse in one (*echad*) accord, as referring to the Messiah:

> With regard to this prophecy, the first thing I want to point out is that all antiquity agrees in interpreting it of a personal Messiah. This is the view of the LXX version; the Targumin of Onkelos, Yonathan, and Jerusalem; the Talmud; Zohar; the ancient book of 'Bereshith Rabba'; and, among modern commentators, even of Rashi, who says, 'Until Shiloh come, that is King Messiah, Whose is the kingdom.'[1194]

Finally, what is the Messianic interpretation of this verse: What does it say? First it states that Judah will have the scepter [kingship], the authority to rule until the one comes whose right it is and to whom it belongs. Second the tribe of Judah must be identifiable. This passage actually sets a general time table as to the appearance of the Messiah. Two things must be in effect when the Messiah comes, Judah's identity and its governmental rule. Both of them were present when *Yeshua* was born in Bethlehem in the days of Herod the Great. However, two equally important things happened in 70 CE when the Roman armies destroyed the "city" and the "sanctuary:" First the governmental authority of Judah was completely removed and has not existed since; second all of the genealogical records of the tribes of Israel including Judah were also destroyed in the destruction of 70 CE. The net result is that Messiah had to come to His people before 70 CE and before those two things ceased to exist. Also the seed of the woman in Genesis 3:15 had been narrowed down from all of humanity, to Jewish humanity, to the tribe of Judah.

Genesis 49:10, which spoke of the *Moshiach* coming as a king from the tribe of Judah, also states that the scepter of Judah and the tribal identity of Judah will have to be intact when the *Moshiach* comes. Judah lost both the scepter and tribal identity in 70 CE, forty years after the death and resurrection of *Yeshua* the *Moshiach*. Even though these two elements do not exist today, *Yeshua*, the risen Lord of the tribe of Judah and the house of David, is the eternal God who became man and all nations and peoples will submit to Him when He comes to fulfill the Abrahamic and Davidic Covenants at His second coming.

A STAR SHALL COME OUT OF JACOB ... Numbers 24:17

> I shall see him, but not now: I shall behold him, but not nigh: there shall come a star out of Jacob, and a scepter shall rise out of Israel, and shall smite the corners of Moab, and destroy all the children of Sheth (Harkavy Version).

The second passage is found in the oracles of Balaam in Numbers 23-24 and in particular Numbers 24:17. This passage has been viewed across the centuries as a vision of the Messiah, whose birth would be marked by the appearance of a star out of the

---

[1194] David Baron, *Rays of Messiah's Glory* (Jerusalem: Keren Ahvah Meshihit, 2000), 258.

east.[1195] First in verse 14, the term "latter days" was used to describe the end times. In verse 17 Balaam references two significant points concerning the *Moshiach*. He references the fact that "*a star will come from Jacob*" and "*a scepter comes forth from Israel.*" The "scepter" is reflective of Genesis 49:10 and speaks of dominion over Israel and the nations of the earth. The "star" speaks to the imperial greatness and splendour of power that will belong to this king. Franz Delitzsch speaks to this in saying:

> Here first the object of the Old Testament hope is personified, for star and scepter are images of a ruler who, like a star, appears out of Israel, a ruler of earthly extraction and heavenly splendour.[1196]

What the reader may be looking at here in Numbers 24:17 is a veiled statement of the God/man. The man is visible in the term "scepter" who as an earthly king will use his power to subdue the earth. The term "star" may picture His heavenly origin. If the text is not alluding to this, certainly a clear application can be drawn from it. The Jewish rabbis of the past have definitely looked to this as a Messianic passage. The following quotes taken from Hengstenberg will clearly illustrate that point:

> Onkelos translates: "When a King shall rise out of Jacob, and out of Israel Messiah shall be anointed:" Jonathan: "When a valiant King shall rise out of the house of Jacob, and out of Israel, Messiah, and a strong Scepter shall be anointed." The Book of Zohar remarks on the words, "I see him, but now:" "This was in part fulfilled at that time; it will be completely fulfilled in the days of Messiah."[1197]

It is no accident that renowned Rabbi Akiba during the second revolt against Rome in 132-135 CE renamed his false messiah from Shimeon ben Kosiba to Simeon bar Kokhba meaning "son of a star." He was identifying his messiah with the Numbers 24:17 passage.[1198] This oracle of Balaam clearly presents the Messiah as King as the rabbis of old clearly recognized. One final observation is the comments made by Fruchtenbaum in relationship to how this verse was understood by those in Babylon:

> The significance of the closing words of chapter 24 should not be missed. Having completed his work, Balaam the Babylonian astrologer returns to "my people" (verse 14), and to "his place" (verse 25). With him he takes the prophecy of a star announcing the birth of a unique and powerful King who will rule over Israel. As we shall see further on in our study [in Appendix 6 of his book], later generations of Babylonian astrologers recorded these words and

---

[1195] Lauriston J. Du Bois, *Beacon Bible Commentary in Ten Volumes: Numbers* (Kansas City, MO: Beacon Hill Press, 1969), 1:477.

[1196] Franz Delitzsch, *Messianic Prophecies in Historical Succession* (Eugene, OR: Wipf and Stock Publishers, 1998), 68.

[1197] E. G. Hengstenberg, *Christology of the Old Testament: Complete in Four Volumes* (Grand Rapids: Kregel Publications, 1956), 1:99.

[1198] Cole, *The New American Commentary: Numbers*, 426.

kept watch for this star. At it appeared they went and found the new-born King and worshipped Him.[1199]

Fifteen hundred years after the prophecy of Balaam the wise men followed the star from the east, Babylon, and came to Jerusalem to give gifts and worship the Promised King. That visit to Jerusalem lead them to Bethlehem to the One who would be King whose origin was from everlasting, *Yeshua*, the Son of David, Immanuel, the Branch, the Promised One, the God/man.

THE PROPHET ... Deuteronomy 18:15-19

(15) The LORD your God will raise up for you **a prophet** from among your own people, like myself; **him** you shall heed. (16) This is just what you asked of the LORD your God at Horeb, on the day of the Assembly, saying, "Let me not hear the voice of the LORD my God any longer or see this wondrous fire any more, lest I die." (17) Whereupon the LORD said to me, "They have done well in speaking thus. (18) I will raise up **a prophet** for them from among their own people, like yourself: I will put my words in **his** mouth and **he** will speak to them all that I command **him**; (19) and if anybody fails to heed the words **he** speaks in My name, I Myself will call him to account.

Even though the Deuteronomy 18:15-19 passage of Scripture does not have the word Messiah within its text, it has long been held by Jewish scholars as a Messianic passage. And even though this passage has been recognized as Messianic by both biblical faith and Jewish scholars, there are some alternate views by other rabbis. David Baron points out some of the alternate views as to who the prophet is in Deuteronomy 18:15-19:

He points out that rabbis are divided on the identity of the "Prophet" of Deut 18:15-19. He gives three Jewish examples: first Rabbi Abarbanel suggests that Jeremiah was the prophet like unto Moses, and gives fourteen points of resemblance, which however, are not at all distinctive. Second he references Rabbi "Aben Ezra, and Bechai, and others, apply this passage to Joshua," and thirdly Rabbis "Rashi, Kimchi, and Alshech say that the prophet like unto Moses implies a succession of prophets, one after the other. They acknowledge, therefore, that they could not find any individual to whom similarity to Moses could be ascribed."[1200]

Three perspectives are given by the rabbis as Jeremiah, Joshua and a succession of the prophets. While Jeremiah is not discussed much, Joshua receives a little more attention. But as Smith points out, Joshua does not fit the text:

By the time this prophecy was made Joshua had already been raised up (Num 27:18-23). Besides, Deut 34:10-12, which was most likely written in the

---

[1199] Fruchtenbaum, *Messianic Christology*, 27.

[1200] Baron, *Rays of Messiah's Glory*, 182-183. This book was originally published in 1886.

days of Joshua (and possibly by him), explicitly states that no prophet like Moses had arisen. [1201]

That leaves the student of Scripture with the third option, a succession of prophets, which needs to be viewed with more attention. Three natural divisions emerge when studying Deuteronomy 18:15-19. The first gives the initial pronouncement by Moses concerning a prophet like him. In verses 16-17, Moses steps back 38 years as he reviews that time when *Yahweh* spoke to ALL of Israel from Mt. Horeb and the request of the people for God to speak through Moses as the mediator. Two things need to be highlighted in the words "like" and "mediator:" The word "like" resembles an aspect of the original; the word "mediator" is important because the Prophet to come will act as a mediator, just like Moses, in speaking God's words as Keil and Delitzsch show:

> The expression, "like unto me," is explained by what follows in verses 16-18 with regard to the circumstances, under which the Lord had given the promise that he would send a prophet. It was at Sinai; when the people were filled with mortal alarm, after hearing the ten words which God addressed to them out of the fire, and entreated Moses to act as mediator between the Lord and themselves, that God might not speak directly to them any more. At that time the Lord gave the promise that He would raise up a prophet, and put His words in his mouth, that he might speak to the people all that the Lord commanded. The promised prophet, therefore, was to resemble Moses in this respect, that he would act as mediator between Jehovah and the people, and make known the words or the will of the Lord. [1202]

After understanding the context of Deuteronomy 18:15-19, Moses in verses 18-19 who spoke for the LORD, steps into the future with a promise of this Prophet and an obligation for every individual Israelite to obey, or the LORD would require the Prophet's words of them. Notice that Moses speaks with his own authority in verse 15 and then goes to the highest authority in verses 17-18 to give the pronouncement by the ultimate authority in promising this Prophet. This Prophet is to be unique. Hengstenberg deals with the authority issue:

> In the fifteenth verse, Moses had delivered it in his own person. In order to give to it the higher authority, he relates in the following verses, when and in what manner he had received it from God. [1203]

Then Hengstenberg presents three views as to the identity of the Prophet but when taken within its context it is only the second view that properly reflects God's intent:

[1201] Smith, *The Promised Messiah,* 67.
[1202] Keil and Delitzsch, *Commentary on the Old Testament in Ten Volumes; Deuteronomy,* 1:394.
[1203] E. W. Hengstenberg, *Christology of the Old Testament* (Grand Rapids: Kregel, 1970), 54-56.

First several consider the 'prophet' as a collective noun, and understand thereby the prophets of all times. Secondly, Some see in it an exclusive reference to Christ. Thirdly, others have steered a middle course, inasmuch as they consider the 'prophet' to be a collective noun, but, at the same time, maintain that only by the mission of Christ, in whom the idea of the prophetic order was perfectly realized, the promise was completely fulfilled.[1204]

There are those that hold to the first view of the word "prophet" being a collective noun which embraces all the prophets throughout the *Tanakh* just does not do justice to the text of Scripture. As to the "succession of prophets" view Kalland reflects that view in the following words:

> Israelite reliance was to be wholly on the Lord, who would send them prophets like Moses, …. These prophets would be selected by the Lord from their own brothers (v. 18). The Lord would put his words in their mouths, and they were to tell the Israelites what the Lord commanded them to speak. The Lord would call to account anyone who did not listen to the words spoken in the Lord's name (v. 19).[1205]

One aspect is correct; God spoke through the prophets of old to His people Israel. However, there would be only one person who would be a singular "like unto me" [Moses] prophet. It is believed by this author that the identity of the Prophet needs to be taken in the singular as it was given by Moses and should not be considered a collective noun as by others. First, the word "prophet" stands at the beginning of the Hebrew sentence because it is being emphasized as a single individual.[1206] Also notice the words bold typeface in the quotation of the verse at the beginning of this section. Moses refers to the Prophet seven times in the singular and not the plural; take the verse as it is literally written. Hengstenberg gives a grammatical view as to why the term "Prophet" should be identified as a single individual and not plural for a succession of prophets:

> There is also internal evidence of its relation to the Messiah. That Moses designed to designate, principally at least, an individual, and not the collective body of the prophets, appears from this, that the Hebrew word נָבִיא [prophet] employed is always used in the singular, and with singular suffixes, whereas in the case of collective nouns, it is usual to interchange the singular and plural…. Moreover, the words do not occur elsewhere as a collective noun.[1207]

McConville, in his work on Deuteronomy, expresses the fact that "Prophet" is to be viewed as an individual and not collectively. He also lays out the differences between

---

[1204] Hengstenberg, *Christology of the Old Testament,* 104-105.

[1205] Earl S. Kalland, *The Expositor's Bible Commentary: Deuteronomy* (Grand Rapids: Zondervan, 1992), 3:122.

[1206] Smith, *The Promised Messiah,* 67.

[1207] Hengstenberg, *Christology of the Old Testament,* 54-55.

the prophet, priest and king, which is in the broader view of the immediate context in the following comments:

15. The promise is made starkly, with the word 'prophet' placed in the strong initial position (lit. "A prophet from your midst, from your brothers, like me, will the LORD raise up."). The emphasis is on the prophet. It is by this means that Yahweh will speak, not by others. The immediate qualification for the prophet, as of the king, is that he shall be an Israelite (and therefore free from the taint of foreign religion). Only then is he likened to Moses.

16-17. The way in which he is like Moses is the subject of vv. 16-17. As for Yahweh's 'raising up' of the prophet, this contrasts with the 'choosing' of the priest and king (17:15; 18:5). The difference may lie in the type of function. In the case of king and priest, Yahweh affirms his right to choose in relation to official public ceremonies performed by the people. In the case of the prophet, in contrast, it seems that there is no corresponding ceremony of institution; rather, the prophet will be appointed by Yahweh as a need arises; the question of the recognition of the true prophet (20-22) then follows from this.

Verses 16-17 are a commentary on 5:23-27, and explain what is meant by the 'prophet like Moses'. The (lit.) 'day of the assembly' refers to the encounter with Yahweh at Mt Horeb when the covenant was first made (ch. 5). Deut 5:23-27 tells how the people fear they will die because of the sight and sound of God, and therefore demand that Moses act as mediator from 5:24.[1208]

There are two other key verses that have a direct bearing on Deuteronomy 18:15-19. One is found in Deuteronomy 34:10-12 as an epitaph on Moses' life. Smith relates directly to the importance of these verses:

The Scriptures state that no other Old Testament prophet can be compared to Moses (Deut 34:10-12). Therefore, the prophet like Moses must be someone who in some significant way transcends the line of Old Testament prophets.[1209]

That means that not even Elijah, who was also unique, was in the same category as Moses. That also means the great prophets like Isaiah, Jeremiah, Ezekiel, Daniel and Zechariah, in spite of all the revelations they received from the LORD, were not like Moses! As Smith and Sailhamer go on to say:

The main point in this prediction is that the future Prophet will be like Moses in some distinctive way.[1210]

It should be noted that even within the OT itself this passage was taken to refer to a specific individual and not merely to the succession of prophets who were

---

[1208] McConville, *Apollos Old Testament Commentary: Deuteronomy,* 302.
[1209] Smith, *The Promised Messiah,* 65.
[1210] Smith, *The Promised Messiah,* 67.

to arise after Moses. In Deuteronomy 34:10, for example, the final words of the book recall the promise of Moses in 18:18 and look far into the future to a single individual for its fulfillment. Thus by the time the last verses of Deuteronomy were attached to the Pentateuch, these verses in Deuteronomy 18 were already being understood eschatologically and messianically.[1211]

John Sailhamer in his newest book expands what he said here.[1212] In Deuteronomy 33:3b-4 there is a change of authorship. It is no longer Moses who is writing but someone else. Verse 4 states:

They followed in Your steps, accepting Your pronouncements, When Moses charged **us** with the Teaching as the heritage of the congregation of Jacob (Jewish Study Bible – emphasis mine)

The question is who is "us"? Some further observations will be helpful. It could not be Joshua who made the addendum to the Torah or the five books of Moses, because the statement in Deuteronomy 34:10-12 simply does not reflect Joshua as being the author of these two chapters. First the office of prophet did not really begin until Samuel and he is 400 years removed from Moses. Second, Samuel begins a long line of prophets that ends with Malachi as the last prophet in the *Tanakh*. So who is the inspired author of Deuteronomy 33-34? We simply do not know. But we do understand the time period that it was penned. Before going further in our study look at Deuteronomy 34:10-12 which lies at the heart of this passage:

10 Never again did there arise in Israel a prophet like Moses – whom the LORD singled out, face to face, 11 for the various signs and portents that the LORD sent him to display in the land of Egypt, against Pharaoh and all his courtiers and his whole country, 12 and for all the great might and awesome power that Moses displayed before all Israel. (Jewish Study Bible)

Earlier in this chapter 3 Jewish views were presented and why they are inadequate to explain to whom these verses refer. They do not fit Jeremiah or a succession of prophets; none of them come close to the Prophet of Deuteronomy 18 when all their acts are accumulated together. Not even Elijah fits this category as great as he was. So who is the author and to whom is he referring? As was stated before we do not know the name of the author, so it is simply an anonymous author. However this much is understood, the author of Deuteronomy 33 - 34 is tying the Messianic passages of the Torah, the five books of Moses, with the conclusion of the Prophets (*Nevi'im*) and Writing (*Kethuvim*) sections of the *Tanakh*. I strongly present the position that some inspired writer during the post-exile period penned the words as an addendum to the Torah to tie it together with the final statements of the Prophets and Writings in respect to the coming of Messiah, the Prophet. In other words that author is stating now that all

---

[1211] Sailhamer, *The Pentateuch as Narrative: A Biblical-Theological Commentary,* 456.

[1212] John H. Sailhamer, *The Meaning of the Pentateuch.* (Downers Grove, IL: InterVarsity Press, 2009),16-29.

the prophets have come and gone and the Prophet that Moses spoke of had not yet appeared at 300-400 BCE. That is amazing when placed in the context at the end of prophetic period to Israel. In other words the author is saying that from the time of Moses to Malachi there has not risen a prophet like unto Moses, meaning the Prophet, the Messiah, is still yet to come.

How do the *Nevi'im*, the Prophets, and the *Kethuvim*, the Writings end their divisions of the *Tanakh*? Like the end of the Torah there seems to be an addendum as well at the end of Chronicles (*Kethuvim*) in 36:21-23. The author of Chronicles moves from the end of the Jewish Kingdom then skips 70 years of the exile and jumps right to Cyrus and his proclamation to rebuild the House of God in Judah.

> 21 In fulfillment of the word of the LORD spoken by Jeremiah, until the land paid back its sabbaths; as long as it lay desolate it kept sabbath, till seventy years were completed. 22 And in the first year of King Cyrus of Persia, when the word of the LORD spoken by Jeremiah was fulfilled, the LORD roused the spirit of King Cyrus of Persia to issue a proclamation throughout his realm by the word of mouth and in writing, as follows: 23 "Thus said King Cyrus of Persia: The LORD God of Heaven has given me all the kingdoms of the earth, and has charged me with building Him a House in Jerusalem, which is in Judah. Any one of you of all His people, the LORD his God be with him and let him go up."

The last two verses were written after the author of Chronicles by another inspired author. What is this author doing? He is saying that at the end of the collection of books in the *Kethuvim* (Writings) there has not arisen a prophet like unto Moses and it certainly was not Cyrus. The author clearly is tying together the proclamation of Cyrus and the 70 years to Daniel's words in Daniel 9:3 and Gabriel's response in Daniel 9:24-27 which lays out the precise timeline of the coming of the Messiah Who will be the Prophet like unto Moses. Do not miss the connection that the author it making. It is interesting to note that *The Jewish Study Bible* only references the Scriptures concerning the Sabbath Year and does not reference Daniel 9.

The *Nevi'im* (Prophets) division of the *Tanakh*, the last book is Malachi and he also ends his book in 4:22-23 with the view of Elijah the forerunner of the Messiah, the Prophet and a reference back to Moses:

> 22 Be mindful of the Teaching of **My** servant Moses, **whom I charged** at Horeb with laws and rules for all Israel. 23 Lo, **I will** send the prophet Elijah to you before the coming of the awesome, fearful day of the LORD. He shall reconcile parents with children and children with their parents, so that **when I come**, **I do not** strike the whole land with utter destruction. (Jewish Study Bible – emphasis mine)

Notice two things, first it is the LORD who is speaking to Israel and what He is going to do. Moses was **His** servant that **He** charged at Mt. Sinai, **He** is going to send Elijah for when **He** comes **He** will not destroy all the land. Is it possible that the LORD that will come is the Prophet like unto Moses who speaks to God *"face to face"* and who also beholds the very form of God? According to all the Scripture that has been revealed throughout this book, the answer is yes.

Secondly notice that the "I" Who will send Elijah His forerunner is the LORD, Who will personally come as the Messiah the Prophet like Moses.

All three divisions in the ending of the Torah, *Nevi'im* and *Kethuvim* conclude their divisions with an expectation of the coming of the Messiah, the Prophet like unto Moses. There is a central person in all of the *Tanakh* and it is a Person who revealed Himself to the fathers and the prophets. He has been interacting with mankind since the days of Adam and Eve and that Person is the Second Person of *Elohim* who has promised to come to Israel as the Prophet like unto Moses.

Numbers 12:5-8 - Sibling Rivalries

The second passage of great importance in relationship to Deuteronomy 18:15-19 is Numbers 12:5-8 where God was dealing with sibling rivalry among Moses, Aaron and Miriam. God came out with some very clear and unique reasons as to what was so different about Moses from all the other prophets. But God also gave groundwork to understand the nature of the difference. First read carefully Numbers 12:5-8:

> (5) The LORD came down in a pillar of cloud, stopped at the entrance of the Tent, and called out, "Aaron and Miriam!" The two of them came forward; (6) and He said "Hear these My words: When a prophet of the LORD arises among you, I make Myself known to him in a vision, I speak with him in a dream. (7) Not so with My servant Moses; he is trusted throughout My household. (8) With him I speak mouth to mouth, plainly and not in riddles, and he beholds the likeness of the LORD. How then did you not shrink from speaking against My servant Moses!"

These verses give unique characteristics of Moses that no other prophet ever had. Deuteronomy 18:15-19 speaks of Moses and the "Prophet" to come who would be "like" Moses. The following verses show in what way Moses and the "Prophet" are "like." Look at some statements given by Jacob Milgrom in his commentary on Numbers:

> Verse 7. *"Not so"* Here he [Moses] is **set apart from and above prophets** like Aaron and Miriam, although all share the same title. "My household" Moses is the most trusted; he alone has **direct access to the Deity and obtains an audience with Him at will.**

> Verse 8 *"mouth to mouth"* By **direct revelation** (Ibn Ezra) and while fully conscious. This expression is synonymous with "face to face" in Exodus 33:11 and Deuteronomy 34:10. Both expressions imply a dialogue: The prophet is the

intercessor for his people as well as the conveyor of God's word. The image is that of a royal house in which only the most trusted servant has regular access to the monarch. Such ones are called literally "those who see the face of the king" (2 Kings 25:19). "plainly" The **Midrash speaks of Moses seeing through a clear mirror, whereas other prophets see through a murky mirror**. In other words, **Moses' visions do not require any interpretation, but the visions (or dreams, riddles) of other prophets do**. "likeness" The **intangible, yet quasi-sensual manifestation of the Godhead** vouchsafed **to Moses**, as **contrasted with the less distinct manifestation by the vision, or the dream** (v. 6) **which might need interpretation** (v. 8), **granted to other prophets**.[1213]

Not only do the rabbis lift up Moses because of his "*face to face*" dialogues with God and seeing the very form of God, so does God! Moses is unique among the prophets of God. Another author clearly states:

> **God emphasizes the role of Moses as the unique and supreme vehicle of divine revelation**. God does speak through other prophets, but only in the **veiled form of visions and dreams** (I Sam 9:9; Deut 13:7). Moses is different. Moses is God's servant, entrusted with all of God's house (Hebrews 3:1-6).... God speaks with Moses "face to face" (literally in Hebrew "mouth to mouth") and "clearly, not in riddles." Moses "beholds the form of the LORD" (:6-8). Communication between God and Moses is clear, direct, and unmediated. Exodus 33:11 had earlier stated that "the LORD used to speak to Moses face to face, as one speaks to a friend."[1214]

Here is what was at stake; Aaron and Miriam were undermining Moses' authority as he presented God's revelation to Israel. Moses was a unique, one-of-a-kind prophet; Aaron and Miriam were also prophets but not on the same level as Moses, for God clearly laid out the difference between them as the following author expresses:

> God's words ... assert that there are various ways in which the divine word is transmitted. It is not contested that God 'speaks' to a man, who is then esteemed a 'prophet'. If Miriam, as Ex 15:20 asserts, was a 'prophetess', and if her partner Aaron could consider himself as a 'prophet' at least indirectly (ef. Ex 4:16), then they could already claim that God 'spoke' with them. But that did not justify their comparison of themselves with Moses, for Moses received the divine word in another, unique way. Yahweh spoke with a 'prophet' indirectly through 'dreams-visions' which are certainly not real 'words' of God, but yet are, as is said at least indirectly in v. 8a, 'dark speech',

---

[1213] Jacob Milgrom, *The JPS Torah Commentary: Numbers* (Philadelphia: The Jewish Publication Society, 1990), 98.

[1214] Dennis T. Olson, *Interpretation: A Bible Commentary for Teaching and Preaching: Numbers* (Louisville: John Knox Press, 1996), 71.

necessitating an interpretation. With Moses, on the other hand, God spoke directly ('mouth to mouth') as men of equal rank speak with each other.[1215]

All of these quotations speak of Moses as being in a completely different class of prophets than any other prophet in the *Tanakh*. He is completely unique. Not only did Moses speak *"face to face"* but he also saw the very form of God. No other prophet had the intimacy with God that Moses had; no other prophet saw the very form of God in His glory. Not only that, but Moses was called *"My servant"* who had been entrusted with the whole house of Israel, as Wenham states in the following:

> Moses is without peer among holy men.... The lines can be literally rendered: "If there is among you a prophet of the LORD, in a vision to him I make myself known." Whereas ordinary prophets had to be content with receiving God's word through dreams and visions and in riddles, Moses is in a different class. He is God's servant entrusted with looking after all his estate, Israel, and like other men in his position he has immediate access to the owner of the estate. He speaks to God directly *mouth to mouth* and therefore can interpret God's will for Israel with total authority. Other men in the Old Testament, e.g. Abraham, Joshua, David and Elijah (Gen 26:24; Josh 24:29; 2 Sam 7:5; 2 Kgs 10:10), are called God's servants, but only Moses is described as *entrusted* with all my house. Finally he sees the very form of God (8).[1216]

What is clear between the Numbers and Deuteronomy passages is that both Jewish and Christian scholars all clearly recognize the complete uniqueness of Moses and the implications on the Deuteronomy 18 passage are dramatic. There are four unique facets of Moses' ministry: first, he spoke to God intimately, *"face to face"*; secondly, he saw the very form of God in His glory; thirdly, he was the administrator of the whole house of Israel, which was entrusted to him by God Himself; fourthly, he was a unique mediator between the people and God Himself. No other prophet had that kind of prophetic ministry. The Torah, the five books of Moses, are the foundation of all the *Tanakh*. A student of the Hebrew Scriptures cannot have a clear understanding or appreciation of all that is happening throughout the entirety of the *Tanakh* without a complete understanding of the Written Torah of God communicated directly and personally to Moses by God Himself. When the other prophets revealed God's revelation, their ministry was not like Moses'. The prophets in all their writings were trying to get Israel to return to the covenant that they had made with *Yahweh* at Mt. Sinai (Exodus 24:1-11). Likewise the Writings are the words of God but they were not given in the manner that God revealed them to Moses. Aaron and Miriam were jealous of the authority that Moses had as a prophet and before the people. God brought their rebellion against Moses to a complete stop. So in Rabbinic Judaism the Torah, the five books of Moses, are supreme and the other two sections of the *Tanakh* reference back to

---

[1215] Martin Noth, *The Old Testament Library: Numbers* (Philadelphia: Westminster Press, 1968), 95-96.

[1216] Wenham, *Tyndale Old Testament Commentaries: Numbers,* 112-113.

the Torah, thus making them less "sacred" than the writings of Moses. It is important that we not judge Judaism for this, because Christianity does the same thing in its practical treatment of the Old Testament.[1217]

When a student studies the Numbers 12:5-8 passage and he grasps the position that God has given to Moses with complete uniqueness he will also begin to understand the uniqueness of the Prophet. Couple that with the words of Moses in Deuteronomy 18:15-19 when Moses, with the same authority, tells Israel of the Prophet "*like*" him that will come. The comparison is stark and clear. For this Prophet will also have the same three characteristics of His ministry: (1) He will speak to God "*face to face;*" (2) He will behold the very form of God, and He will be entrusted with the whole house of Israel as a servant, (3) for He Himself is the Master of the house of Israel. With this important understanding of the biblical account we can understand better Judaism and their belief on revelation and inspiration.

The LORD lays out before Aaron and Miriam three very important reasons (four to Israel) as to the uniqueness of Moses among all other prophets. Notice, the LORD and Moses had an intimate relationship; they spoke mouth to mouth. Second, Moses beheld the very form of the LORD. Third, Moses was called by God "*My servant*" who was entrusted with the whole house of Israel. This was more than Abraham, Isaac and Jacob saw. It was more than Isaiah and Ezekiel saw in the vision. What Moses saw was not a vision. But he beheld, as much as a human could, the very glory of the LORD. This is unique! Fruchtenbaum and Cooper are absolutely correct when they state:

> Even with great men like Elijah and Isaiah, God did not reveal Himself directly but used dreams, visions, and other methods. Moses is the only man who received direct revelation from God.

[1217] Judaism on a practical level practices levels of revelation, but so does Christianity. In Christianity we believe that both testaments of God's revelation to mankind and all parts of that revelation are equally inspired of God. Yet practically almost all Christian churches will treat the Old Testament as old, out of date, no longer relevant, not applicable to the Church, for the Old Testament is Law and the Church is under Grace. Consequently believers today spend very little time in the Old Testament. In all practicality the Church treats the Old Testament as less inspired than the New Testament. Most believers in the Church spend the majority of time in the New Testament and in particular the Pauline Epistles, while almost completely neglecting the Old Testament as if it belongs to a by-gone era. God wrote 66 books and not just 27. It is all equally His Word, yet we practically treat it as 'less sacred' by lack of attention to what it says. Bible colleges and seminaries are equally guilty of indirectly promoting this concept. When the Old Testament and New Testament are taught, they are presented as being divorced from each other instead of being taught together as gears that mesh together in complete harmony and unity. Jesus did not speak from a vacuum, nor did Paul and the other writers of the New Testament write and speak in a vacuum. They all referenced the Old Testament, for all the theology that is taught to the New Testament Church is rooted and grounded in the Old Testament in what Moses and the Prophets taught to Israel. By treating the Old Testament as 'old,' we are saying that it was inspired for Israel, but is less inspired for the Church because we are not under Law but Grace.

Previously we were told that Messiah would be a King [Gen 49:10; Num 24:17]. Now we are told that He will be a prophet too, and not an ordinary prophet, but One who will speak "mouth to mouth" with God and Who will see the very form of Jehovah.[1218]

According to Numbers 12:1-8, Moses occupied a unique position, which was superior to that which any prophet who succeeded him enjoyed.[1219]

Return to Deuteronomy 18:15-19

A little bit of time needs to be spent on this uniqueness of Moses and just how this "*Prophet*" will be like Moses. The broader context of the Prophet in the Deuteronomy passage reveals information about all three offices that God gave to Israel; prophet (Deuteronomy 18:15-19), priest (Deuteronomy 18:1-8) and king (Deuteronomy 17:14-20). There was a marked division between these offices, as Varner relates:

> There were three administrative offices given by the Lord God to Israel to rule over and guide them – the king, the priest and the prophet. The king ruled over Israel *for* God; the priest represented the people *before* God; and the prophet spoke to the people *from* God.[1220]

Each one of the offices had a function to perform before God and the people of Israel. The king ruled over the people for God, the priest was the mediator between God and the people and the prophet spoke to the people from God. These roles were given to different men in the *Tanakh*, but as a student of Scripture understands, *Yeshua* would fill each of these offices, which is also unique. No king, priest or prophet ever held all three offices before the LORD, as Varner relates:

> While an individual could serve as both a priest and a prophet like Samuel, Jeremiah and Ezekiel, and one person might serve as both king and prophet like David, no Israelite ever combined in his own person the roles of priest and king.[1221]

From the Deuteronomy 18:15-19 passage Varner points to seven characteristics of the prophet that will be like Moses which are as follows:

1. He must be called by God.
2. He must be an Israelite.
3. He must be like Moses.
4. He must have the authority of a prophet.

[1218] Fruchtenbaum, *Messianic Christology*, 28.

[1219] Cooper, *What Men Must Believe,* 40.

[1220] William Varner, *The Messiah: Revealed, Rejected, Received* (Bloomington, IN: AuthorHouse, 2004), 58.

[1221] Varner, *The Messiah: Revealed, Rejected, Received,* 58.

5. He must be obeyed.

6. He must speak only God's Word.

7. He must certify himself by tested prophecies.[1222]

As each student of Scripture compares these characteristics of Moses to the ministry of *Yeshua* in the New Covenant, he will find a striking fulfillment in each one:

> Did Yeshua really qualify as the Prophet promised by Moses? It is striking to note how Yeshua fulfilled all seven of the characteristics of the prophet mentioned in Deuteronomy 18:15-19.
>
> 1. He was called by God – Luke 9:35.
> 2. He was an Israelite – Matthew 1; John 1:49.
> 3. He was a mediator like Moses – 1 Timothy 2:5; Hebrews 1:1,
> 4. He spoke with authority, unlike the teachers of His Day – Matthew 7:28-29.
> 5. His Father declared that His words must be obeyed – Matthew 17:5.
> 6. He spoke the Word of God in God's name – John 12:8-49; 5:45.
> 7. He certified Himself by miracles and prophecies which no one could deny – John 3:2; Acts 2:22.[1223]

What becomes so very fascinating is to understand just how the Jewish leadership of *Yeshua*'s day, as well as the common folk, understood Deuteronomy 18:15-18 in the following references:

> Leadership: John 1:20-21, 25
> Common people: John 4:25; 6:14; 7:40

When everything is put together the "*Prophet*" like unto Moses, is very clear in the pages of Scripture, as Cooper states:

> In the eighteenth chapter of Deuteronomy, verses 15-19, he informed Israel that she did well in requesting the Lord not to speak to her again as He had done at Sinai. In connection with this statement is God's promise that He would raise up a prophet like unto Moses from among the Hebrews, that He would put His words into this prophet's mouth, that this one would speak faithfully His message, and that He would require perfect obedience to Him. When we study the general characteristics of the life of Moses and his official positions of deliverer and lawgiver, we are led to the conclusion that this prophet can be none other than the Hebrew Messiah.[1224]

[1222] Varner, *The Messiah: Revealed, Rejected, Received,* 59-60.
[1223] Varner, *The Messiah: Revealed, Rejected, Received,* 61.
[1224] Cooper, *Messiah: His First Coming Scheduled,* 150.

The LORD promised through Moses a singular *"Prophet"* who was unique like himself. This *"Prophet"* would utter the very words of the LORD and every Israelite citizen would be personally responsible to obey His word. If he did not obey, the LORD would hold each and every Israelite personally responsible. So this was a great promise accompanied by much accountability. God never used such words with any other prophet, as Frey and Cooper point out:

> These words contain a promise, an exhortation, and a threatening; the promises of the prophet like unto Moses, the exhortation is to hear and obey all that the prophet teaches, and the threatening is that the disobedient shall be cut off.[1225]

> Moses foretold that God would raise up from among Israel a prophet like unto himself, and that He would place His words in His mouth and warned them that those who would not be obedient to the divine message, which this prophet would utter, should be held personally responsible for rejecting Him and His words.[1226]

> God will hold personally responsible, regarding any of the prophets of the old economy God never hurled such a threat. It becomes, therefore, a matter of the utmost importance that Israel ascertain whether or not God has raised up this prophet. If He has, then every soul in Israel will be held responsible for not obeying him and rendering homage to him.[1227]

The *"Prophet"* like unto Moses was fulfilled in one individual, the God/man, the Son of David, the King of Israel, the *Moshiach*. But David Klinghoffer tries to deny that the prophets prescribed or predicted a time for *"the Prophet"* to come:

> In this time of religious and political ferment, there was a belief current that Hebrew scripture contained an "oracle" pointing to the imminent coming of a messianic deliverer, a world monarch who would emerge from the holy land. Then again, it might be not a messiah, but a prophet. It is unclear what the oracle actually was – though in Deuteronomy, Moses had promised, "A prophet from your midst, from your brethren, like me, shall the Lord, your God, establish for you – to him shall you hearken." The fact that a deliverer was expected at this time does not mean that anything in the words of the prophets actually pointed to the first century as the foretold moment in history when the Jews would be redeemed.[1228]

This statement is inaccurate because two prophets, Moses and Daniel, pointed to a particular time in history when the *Moshiach* would appear. First of all, Moses gave a general time when the *Moshiach* would come through the words of Jacob in

---

[1225] Frey, *The Messiahship of Jesus,* 143.
[1226] Cooper, *Messiah: His First Coming Scheduled,* 477.
[1227] Cooper, *What Men Must Believe,* 40.
[1228] Klinghoffer, *Why The Jews Rejected Jesus,* 22.

Genesis 49:10. The scepter would not depart from Judah until He comes whose right it is. In 70 CE when the temple was destroyed by the Romans, all the genealogical records of the families and tribes of Israel were lost and Judah lost its leadership over the nation. In chapter 9:24-27 of Daniel, he clearly states that the Messiah would be "*cut off*" before the destruction of the "city" and "sanctuary" (see chapter 14). David Klinghoffer's words clearly are inaccurate.

The five books of Moses open the door for the other two divisions of the *Tanakh* to expound on the Messianic prophecies of Moses by tying them together with the words of the Prophets and Writings concerning the Moshiach. The *Tanakh* truly is a commentary on the *Tanakh* which will be clearly seen in the next two chapters.

INTER-TEXTUAL TESTIMONY WITHIN THE BOOKS OF MOSES: Blessing, Seed and King

Moses, the author of the Torah, did not just randomly write the history of Patriarchs and Israel and record the Law. There is a strategy in the themes that Moses is presenting as he writes the Torah. There are verses that interrelate to each other in inter-textual passages of the Torah that will not be seen unless you study carefully by being alert to how those themes are interwoven together throughout the narrative of the five books of Moses. Such themes as faith, king, promise, and seed were taken by the prophets and expanded upon in some of their rich texts that deal with the coming of the Messiah, the "*seed*" of Abraham, the "*king*" that will come from Judah. It is my purpose here to only begin to draw our attention in a limited manner to these themes (seed) as it relates to the promised "king," the Messiah.

The Hebrew word זֶרַע (zera) is the English word for seed, offspring, or descendant. How does Moses weave this theme of the "*seed*" throughout his writings and then combine them with the future "king" the Messiah? In Numbers 5:28 "*seed*" is used to refer to semen and states "she shall be made pregnant with seed," or able to conceive. It also refers to the flow of semen in Leviticus 15:16, 32 and 22:4.[1229] Genesis 38:8-9 clearly illustrates the use of "*seed*" in the *Tanakh* as it relates to human sexual relationships. Judah's first born son was Er who was slain by the LORD because he was wicked in God's sight. Judah told his second born son Onan to go in unto Er's wife, Tamar, and raise up "*seed*" unto his brother Er. So Onan went in unto her and had sexual intercourse with Tamar and then withdrew and spilled the semen or "seed" on the ground. So "seed" in a sexual sense clearly refers to the physical sexual act of intercourse with conception taking place. The offspring of such a union is to raise up "*seed*" or an offspring. It will be important to understand this as we get into the upcoming texts to see how "*seed*" and the blessing to Abraham is used in relationship to the "*king*" that was promised. The term "*seed*" as it was used in the *Tanakh* can be understood in the singular or in the plural, the context of the passage will determine its

---

[1229] Harris, Archer, and Waltke, *Theological Wordbook of the Old Testament,* 1:252.

usage. Lastly, how does Moses use the term *"seed"* and tie it together with the promised *"king"* as Jacob, Balaam and Hannah understood it?

In Genesis 3:15 the LORD clearly gives to the Serpent a promise of his demise and the tension that would be between the *"seed"* of the woman and the *"seed"* of Satan. This verse presents something that is completely unheard of and completely unique among mankind in the LORD's statement:

> I will put enmity between you and the woman, and between your offspring and hers; **they** shall strike at your head, and you shall strike at **their** heel [emphasis mine].

The Jewish Study Bible uses a plural pronoun "they"; however the Hebrew text uses a second person pronoun "he." The plural word "they," instead of singular word "he" deflects from the original intent of the author. The Hebrew Scriptures clearly record it in the singular.[1230] *The Jewish Study Bible* is implying that Israel is the seed of the woman and will crush the Serpent and the Serpent will strike at Israel but not be able to destroy them. This is a completely inaccurate meaning of the text in Genesis 3:15. The King James Version below is much closer to the Hebrew except for the word "it":

> And I will put enmity between you and the woman, and between your seed and her seed; **it** shall bruise thy head, and thou shalt bruise **his heel**.

In the KJV the term *"it"* is neuter and not masculine. However, the end of the verse gives the intent of *"it"* when it says *"his heel"* referring to the masculine pronoun. This means that it should be translated *"he,"* which is of the *"seed"* of the woman and not an *"it."* Observe as well that the seed mentioned here is singular and not plural; it refers to an individual who would be the *"seed."*

The uniqueness of this verse is that woman does not have seed! The woman cannot produce an offspring without the seed of a man (semen). Yet according to the promise of God a woman in the future will produce an offspring without a man. The meaning of this verse will lie largely dormant until Isaiah 7:14 when it is explained by the promised virgin birth of the Messiah of Israel which again is a singular individual. The next important verse to be observed is Genesis 12:3 that deals with blessing:

> I will bless those who bless you and curse him that curses you; And all the families of the earth shall bless themselves by you.

> And I will bless them that bless you, and curse him that curseth you: And in you shall all families of the earth be blessed (KJV).

This verse is part of a larger context and is the first mention of the Abrahamic Covenant which will be expanded in Genesis 13, 15, 17 and 22. A great nation will come of Abraham and all the families of the earth will be blessed through him, yet Abraham has

---

[1230] Beall and Banks, *Old Testament Parsing Guide,* 1:3.

no *"seed"* or offspring. Those who bless Abraham and his descendants, plural, God will bless, but those who curse will be cursed of God. Yet Israel collectively will not be the blessing to the families of the earth. There is something here that is specific but not yet spelled out. There is, under the surface, a hint at an individual as in the *"seed"* of the woman that all the families and nations of the earth will be blessed, including Abraham's descendants. God promises many descendants and yet Abraham does not even have one individual descendant at this point so he is looking to a servant born in his house to be his heir as Genesis 15:3-5 states. Here in this passage Abram, who has no *"seed,"* is promised by God to have a multitude of descendants, as the stars in heaven.

> 3 Abram said further, "Since You have granted me no offspring, my steward will be my heir." 4 The word of the LORD came to him in reply, "That one shall not be your heir; none but your very own issue shall be your heir." 5 He took him outside and said, "Look toward heaven and count the stars, if you are able to count them." And He added, "So shall your offspring be."

In reading this passage something else becomes clear. The word *"seed,"* offspring or descendant can be used singular or plural, both are acceptable usages. In Genesis 15 Abraham is very concerned about having no descendant, no seed, singular, to carry out the promise of many descendants, plural. So the singular point of *"seed,"* rather than the plural descendants, is what is so very important to Abram at that point in his life. The central point is that the Scriptures are emphasizing both the singular and plural aspects of "seed."

In Genesis 22:18 the promise is made that in Abraham's "seed" all the nations of the earth are to be blessed as stated below:

> All the nations of the earth shall bless themselves by your descendants, because you have obeyed My command.

> And in thy seed shall all the nations of the earth be blessed; because you have obeyed my voice (KJV).

By all surface appearances the word *seed* is plural yet Paul in the New Covenant (Galatians 3:16) views Genesis 22:18 as singular, the Messiah. Does he have precedent to do that? Paul was a student of the Hebrew Scriptures so why would he understand it to be singular and not plural in this case? Remember "seed" can be understood as singular or plural; the text determines its usage. As we proceed through the rest of the passages the singular aspect of the *seed* comes more clearly into view. Genesis 27:29 is a confirmation of the Abrahamic Covenant from Isaac to Jacob stating that all nations will bow down before you, and then Isaac quotes directly from Genesis 12:3 in 27:29:

> Let peoples serve you, and nations bow to you; be master over your brothers,
> And let your mother's sons bow to you, blessed [are] they who bless you.

Let people serve you, and nations bow down to you: be lord over your brethren, and let your mother's sons bow down to thee: cursed be every one that curseth you, and blessed be he that blesseth you (KJV).

There is a cross-referencing, a linking as it were of passages. Here in Genesis 27 Isaac is referencing the Abrahamic Covenant from Genesis 12 and confirming it to Jacob; and then Jacob in Genesis 49:10 passes it on to his sons by linking this *"seed"* concept to the "king" singular that is to come from Judah. The specific "seed" will fulfill the Abrahamic Covenant by the *"seed"* of the woman in Genesis 3:15. Sailhamer makes the following statement:

> Genesis 27:29, for example specifically quotes Genesis 12:3. This is the same kind of cross-referencing we have noted in the poems, though here it connects two promise narrative texts.

> The quotation in Genesis 27:29 of the promise to Abraham in Genesis 12:3 establishes a direct link between the Abrahamic promise (Gen 12:3, 7) and Jacob's blessing in Genesis 27:29.

> The link noted above between Genesis 27:29 and the Abrahamic blessing in Genesis 12 is here extended to the royal figure in Genesis 49:10. The "seed" of Abraham is thus linked directly to the king from Judah.[1231]

The clear observation is that Jacob understood the promise to Abraham, Isaac and to himself, as the blessing of the *"seed"* which he then links to the "king" that will come from Judah, Jacob's son in Genesis 49:8-10 as stated next, quoting verses 8-10.

8 You, O Judah, your brothers shall praise; your hand shall be on the nape of your foes; your father's sons shall bow low to you. 9 Judah is a lion's whelp; on prey, my son, have you grown. He crouches, lies down like a lion, like the king of beasts who dare rouse him? 10 The scepter shall not depart from Judah, Nor the ruler's staff from between his feet; so that tribute shall come to him and the homage of peoples be his.

8 Judah, thou art he whom thy brethren shall praise: thy hand shall be in the neck of thine enemies; thy father's children shall bow down before you. 9 Judah is a lion's whelp: from the prey, my son, thou art gone up: he stooped down, he couched as a lion, and as an old lion; who shall rouse him? 10 The scepter shall not depart from Judah, nor a lawgiver from between his feet, until Shiloh come; and unto him shall the gathering of the people be (KJV).

[1231] John H. Sailhamer, *The Meaning of the Pentateuch* (Downers Grove, IL: InterVarsity Press, 2009), 474-475. [I would strongly recommend this lengthy book to get the complete view on the "seed" and "king" that are woven together into one person, the Messiah.]

This passage was already discussed early in this chapter, so that will not be repeated here. What is important to note is in verses 8-9 Jacob says that all his sons will bow before Judah. Now if you remember historically all of Jacob sons had bowed before Joseph, but here all the sons of Jacob will bow in the future before Judah because Judah will be the tribe to whom the scepter is given, kingship. Now Balaam in his fourth oracle makes another linking of passages. He links Genesis 49:9 in Numbers 24:9a to a king that will arise out of Jacob. It is this king who will come in the future, a singular person, the Messiah who will be that king. Look at these two passages in Numbers 24:9a and 17 and notice the statement of a singular king that will come forth:

> They crouch, they lie down like a lion, like the king of beasts; who dare rouse them?

> What I see for them is not yet, what I behold will not be soon: a star rises from Jacob, a scepter comes forth from Israel; It smashes the brow of Moab, the foundations of all children of Seth.

> I shall see him, but not now: I shall behold him, but not nigh: there shall come a Star out of Jacob, and a scepter shall rise out of Israel, and shall smite the corners of Moab, and destroy all the children of Sheth (KJV).

Observe in Numbers 24:9a that Balaam quotes from Genesis 49:9, but he also quotes from Genesis 12:3 in Numbers 24:9b in identifying this singular king whom he connects to the "seed" of Abraham that will come from Jacob:

> Blessed are they who bless you, accursed they who curse you!

Moses carries the theme of the *seed* throughout the narrative passages of the Torah and weaves them together with the Abrahamic Covenant blessing to a singular "seed" or "king" that is promised to come. Moses was giving the foundation upon which the prophets like Isaiah, Jeremiah, Zechariah would build upon as they revealed more and more of the promised singular *king* that was to come first to suffer and die for the sins of the world as a volunteer vicarious sacrifice (Psalm 16; Isaiah 53) and then fulfill all the promises of the Abrahamic, Land, Davidic and New Covenants in one person, the King, the Messiah.

In Deuteronomy 33:7 the author is someone other than Moses. In verse 4 it references "us" as someone speaking for Israel other than Moses. These last two chapters are an appendix to Moses' writing and the author is unknown although Ezra would be a likely candidate. Here in Deuteronomy 33:7 it speaks of Judah being restored to his people. Judah in history has never been separated from his people, for when Israel went into captivity Judah with his brethren went into captivity, so how could Judah be restored if he was never separated? Not unless the "*voice of Judah*" is the Messiah who was separated from His people by rejection and death will He need to be restored to His people in the future as the accepted and living King of Israel. That is particularly interesting in light of Hosea 5:15-6:3 where the LORD has to return to heaven until Israel confesses their sin. But for now look at Deuteronomy 33:7:

> And this he said of Judah: Hear, O LORD the voice of Judah and **restore him to his people**. Though his own hands strive for him, help him against his foes.

This is prophetic future: Someday this future *"king"* of Israel, from the tribe of Judah will be separated from his people and will need to be restored to them. I am reminded of the words of *Yeshua* at the end of the last week of public ministry when he said *"You shall not see me henceforth, till you shall say, Blessed is he that cometh in the name of the Lord* (Matthew 23:39; Psalm 118:26).

The promised *"seed"* of the Abrahamic Covenant, the future "king" that was promised and longed for is clearly seen is the prayer of Hannah in 1 Samuel 2:10:

> The foes of the LORD shall be shattered; he will thunder against them in the heavens. The LORD will judge the ends of the earth. He will give power to His king, and triumph to His anointed one.

Hannah in her prayer was still living in the period of the Judges and Israel still was a theocracy and not a monarchy ruled by a human representative of God, a king. What was being taught to her and what she understood was that someday a "king" was coming who would be the *"anointed one,"* the Messiah. She understood the writings of Moses concerning the "seed" of promise in the singular, a future *"king,"* the Messiah who would rule.

In the New Covenant book of John *Yeshua* made an interesting statement in John 5:46 as He spoke to the Jewish religious leadership during His second Passover celebration (verse 1) of His ministry in verses 15-47:

> For had you believed Moses, you would have believed me: for he wrote of me.

This is a fascinating statement of *Yeshua*, what did He mean? We normally do not look to the Torah, the five books of Moses, to teach the person of the Messiah in *Yeshua*. Yet *Yeshua* clearly did. *Yeshua* also made another statement that is even more surprising in John 8:56:

> Your father Abraham rejoiced to see my day: and he saw it, and was glad.

Yeshua is not just stating that Abraham saw *Yeshua's* day and rejoiced, but Abraham saw the long awaited fulfillment of the promised "seed" and rejoiced in complete understanding of that day

The Torah, the five books of Moses, are the foundation that the prophets constantly referred back to as they presented and expanded upon all the future realities for Israel in the person of their Messiah. The prophets did not prophecy in a vacuum, for they had the foundational source, the writing of Moses, as they expounded upon the message the coming blessing of the "seed" that would be a blessing to all the families of the earth in the person of the promised "king" that Israel has so longed to see. Truly Moses did teach concerning *Yeshua* in the Torah.

The five books of Moses open the door for the other two divisions of the *Tanakh* to expound on the Messianic prophecies of Moses by tying them together with the words of the Prophets and Writings concerning the Moshiach. The *Tanakh* truly is a commentary on the *Tanakh*, which will be clearly seen in the next two chapters.

Chapter 14
Messiah Divine In the Prophets

In this section on the prophets, all the passages that relate to the *Moshiach* (Messiah) being divine will be investigated. In Isaiah, Micah, Jeremiah, Daniel (even though Daniel was a prophet, he is listed in the Writing portion of the *Tanakh* because his primary occupation was a statesman in Babylon), Zechariah and Malachi, His divinity and humanity will be examined. Remember that Rabbinic Judaism rejects two key areas that these and other passages relate to: first, that God would become flesh (incarnation) through the Virgin Birth; and second, that the *Moshiach* would come two times.

ISAIAH 7-12

This portion of Isaiah is a unit and is called the "Book of Immanuel." Within the "Book of Immanuel," where Immanuel is referenced three times (Isaiah 7:14; 8:8, 10), there are strategic portions of Scripture. Immanuel, a person and not the Land,[1232] is the One born of a virgin as stated in Isaiah 7:14. Isaiah states that this child who would be born would have some unique names as a human being and would reign from his father David's throne in Isaiah 9:6-7. Later Isaiah states that this One would be from the "*stem of Jesse*" noting His humble origin, and that "*the spirit of the LORD*" would rest upon Him in Isaiah 11:1-2. The impact of the "Book of Immanuel" is significant, and that is where our attention needs to be focused.

The person who will be born of a virgin in chapter 7 is called Immanuel, which means "*God with us.*" The virgin will conceive and bear a son who will be "*God with us!*" The Virgin Birth passage does directly state the divinity of the *Moshiach*, for He is clearly identified as the LORD, by name "*Immanuel,*" God with us. Consequently Rabbinic Judaism today has rejected this verse because of its obvious meaning in the context of *Yeshua* being the fulfillment of that passage. A typical argument is given by David Kimchi as follows:

> The Bible exegete David Kimchi comments: "The birth of a son was given by the prophet as a sign to Ahaz, king of Judah, to convince him of God's promise that he had nothing to fear from the alliance of the kings of Ephraim and Syria who were attacking Jerusalem. If it refers to Jesus 700 years later, how could it

---

[1232] A. Cohen, *The Soncino Books of the Bible: Isaiah* (New York: Soncino Press, 1983), 39. *Immanuel*: A name for the land of Judah, as in 7:14 for the prophet's son, indicating the conviction that divine protection will be extended to it (Rashi).

convince Ahaz of the truth of Isaiah's prophecy?" Isaiah 7:14 is introduced by hineh, "behold" which suggests something about to occur (cf. Isa. 38:8; 39:6, 8; Josh 23:14). Isaiah speaks of ha-almah, "the young woman," inferring that the young woman was known to him.[1233]

Kimchi, a great rabbinic teacher, misses the whole point in his argument against the future birth of Immanuel, 700 years later, as being a comfort to Ahaz. In his bias against the New Covenant teaching of the Virgin Birth of Messiah, he misses that actual prophecy and promise of comfort to Ahaz and to the house of David. Here are the two points: First the LORD gave a sign to the whole house of David, of which wicked Ahaz was a part, that the house of David would, in the future, have a King whom the LORD would name Immanuel; Secondly, what Kimchi misses and most authors miss is that the LORD gave two prophecies, one in the distant future, the Virgin Birth (Isaiah 7:13-14). Second a prophecy in the near future concerning Isaiah's own son (Isaiah 7:3) when he was old enough to understand good and evil the threat of the kings of Israel and Syria would be completely gone (Isaiah 7:16), which would have given comfort to Ahaz. The distant promise was to give comfort to the house of David. Rabbis also insist on the removal of the term "virgin" from the biblical text and replace it with the term "young woman" in their attempt to cover up the LORD's promises, as shown below:

> "The young woman." Hebrew *ha'almah* means an adolescent woman, one of marriageable age. The contention that the word must necessarily connote 'virgin' is unwarranted. The Hebrew for 'virgin' is *bethulah* though almah too sometimes bears this meaning. It is difficult to say with certainty who was the young woman referred to. Chronological considerations exclude the mother of Hezekiah (Rashi, ibn Ezra, Kimchi); and the fact that the birth (or the name) of the child was to serve as a sign to convince Ahaz of the certain fulfillment of the prophecy rules out the Christological interpretation that the *young woman* and *son* are identical with persons who lived 700 years later. The wife of Isaiah (Rashi, Iben Ezra), wife of King Ahaz (Kimchi) or a woman of the Royal Family (Abarbanel) may have been the *young woman* of the text.[1234]

Rabbi Cohen's argument is flawed in several areas. First of all *bethulah* [young woman] is not the word in the Hebrew to denote virgin but rather *almah*, which is the opposite of what they say in their arguments. Second, it is flawed as to the identity of the woman. One important factor in the Hebrew Scriptures is that the only references that are found to the parentage of the *Moshiach* is His mother. Not once is there any reference to an earthly father. As in Genesis 3:15, "*seed of the woman*," there is no reference to a father or to his seed. In this passage a virgin is to give birth with no reference to a father. In Psalm 22:10 only the mother's womb is mentioned. Nowhere in the *Tanakh* is there any earthly father mentioned in reference to the *Moshiach*. The

---

[1233] Picker, "Make Us A God!" *A Jewish Response to Hebrew Christianity: A Survival Manual For Jews,* 43.

[1234] A. Cohen, *The Soncino Books of the Bible: Isaiah* (New York: Soncino Press, 1985), 35.

identity of the virgin is important, but the reality is that the virgin in Ahaz's day was unknown. They try to discover who the woman is in the text, but another issue is at stake; the child. Third, it is flawed in their endeavour to discover the identity of the child, for there are two children mentioned in the context. Fourth, it is flawed because there are two prophetic pronouncements given by Isaiah, one for the immediate situation and the other to be fulfilled centuries later. Fifth, it is flawed, because long before this verse became an issue, the translations for the Septuagint (LXX) used a Greek word (παρθένοσ - Parthenos) that very clearly meant virgin. It is interesting to note that in Leviticus 21:13, when God gave instructions to the priests as to whom they could marry, the woman had to be a "virgin." The meaning is clear for even *The Jewish Study Bible* [so does the Harkavy, the Stone Edition of the Chumash and the Masoretic] translates the word בְּתוּלָה and בִּבְתוּלֶיהָ as "virgin" or "in her virginity."[1235] The 70 rabbis who translated the *Tanakh* into Greek seemed to clearly understand the intended meaning of the verse to be a virgin and not a maiden. So rather than Isaiah 7:14 and the "virgin' birth of the Messiah being an invention of Christian missionaries, as the anti-missionaries would have people believe, it is a Jewish problem. The ancient rabbis before this became an issue with *Yeshua* clearly interpreted this word as a "virgin." Yet because of the obvious meaning in Isaiah 7:14, they want to change the interpretation. For a thorough discussion on this section of Scripture, it is strongly advised to see Fruchtenbaum's work on Isaiah 7.[1236] The child to be born is the fulfillment of the promise that God made to Satan in the hearing of Adam and Eve, the "*seed of the woman,*" as Varner expresses:

> The Messiah will be of unique birth – He will be the seed of the woman. Although we should be patient with someone who has difficulty seeing the truth of the virgin birth in these veiled words of God, these words do clearly imply that the deliverer will be of unique origin. Else, why is He called the seed of the woman and not the seed of the man? Second, Messiah will be supernatural – He will defeat Satan, a supernatural being. Only one who has power beyond that of mere man can defeat him who is called "the prince of the power of the air" (Eph 2:2). Thus the Messiah's deity is implied. Third, Messiah will be of the human race – from a woman, not an angel or a visitor from another world. Thus, the ultimate mystery begins to unfold – Messiah will be both God and man – a theme later developed by the prophets (Isa 9:6; Jer 23:5-6; Micah 5:2).[1237]

[1235] The Aramaic translation of the Hebrew Scripture called the Peshitta also translates Isa 7:14 to mean virgin and with Leviticus 21:13, is clearly understood by rabbinic scholars. George M. Lamsa, *The Holy Bible from Ancient Eastern Manuscripts Text,* containing the Old and New Testaments translated from the Peshitta, the Authorized Bible of the Church of the East (Philadelphia: A. J. Holman, 1957).

[1236] Fruchtenbaum, *Messianic Christology*, 32-37.

[1237] Varner, *The Messiah, Revealed, Rejected, Received,* 21.

The last argument that is used comes from Chaim Picker, who states that if the virgin birth is true and Mary was "impregnated" by the Holy Spirit, that would be a violation by the LORD of the sanctity of marriage and would be contrary to the seventh commandment against adultery and that it does not commend holiness on the LORD's part. He then appeals to the heathen pagan belief in the gods cohabiting with women to produce mythological deities, as stated below:

> Mary and Joseph were espoused to each other (Mt. 1:19-20). The "spirit impregnation" of Mary violates the sanctity of marriage (Gen. 2:24; Deut. 22:23-24; Mt. 19:5-6) and is contrary to the seventh commandment against adultery (Exod. 20:14). It is reminiscent of the sexual profligacy of the mythological deities (Gen. 6:2-4). Israel was admonished to imitate God's holiness (Deut. 13:4; Lev. 11:44-45; 19:2; 20:26). The "spirit-impregnation" of Mary does not commend God's holiness.[1238]

Sometimes Chaim Picker conveniently forgets that the LORD is the Creator of the universe and He can do with His creation as He pleases. Jeremiah, at the prompting of the LORD, goes to the house of the potter for a visual lesson as the evil [bad things] that He will do to Judah. In Jeremiah 19 the LORD graphically illustrates what He will do to Judah because of their sin. The LORD is the Creator; Ecclesiastes 3 clearly states that there is a time to do things, and there is a time to judge a nation of people like Israel because of their sin. Think of the human atrocities that nations committed against Israel (Assyria) and Judah (Babylon), which the LORD ordained as judgment against Israel. God also can do good by using faithful people to fulfill His promises to Abraham, Isaac and Jacob by supernaturally speaking the "word" to have Mary become pregnant with the Son of God, the Son of David, the Branch, Immanuel, the God/man. Chaim Picker is appealing to secularistic human reasoning which is wrong; his argument is faulty when he speaks of the Creator dealing with His own creation.

Immanuel is also referenced in Isaiah 8:8, 10, which leads us to another well known passage in Isaiah 9:6-7. Here that virgin-born son, who is "*God with us*," is called names that only the LORD is called ("wonderful" or "pele," "mighty God," and the "everlasting Father"). This Immanuel will be the God/man and will reign, still in the future, on the throne of David, His father, forever because He is eternal, as the Davidic Covenant states in 1 Chronicles 17:10-14.

Unto Us a Child is Born ... Isaiah 9:6-7

> 6 For unto us a child is born, unto us a son is given: and the government shall be upon his shoulder: and his name shall be called Wonderful, Counselor, the mighty God, the everlasting Father, The Prince of Peace.

[1238] Picker, "Make Us A God!" *A Jewish Response to Hebrew Christianity: A Survival Manual For Jews*, 44.

7 Of the increase of his government and peace there shall be no end, upon the throne of David, and upon his kingdom, to order it, and to establish it with judgment and with justice from henceforth even forever. The zeal of the LORD of hosts will perform this (KJV).

There are seven observations about these verses that point to this child being uniquely different from anyone else ever born.

First, the verse makes clear that God and not Christians named the child promised in Isaiah 9:6-7. Human parents name a child because they like the sound of the name. Some parents name a child because of the biblical meaning or because of the biblical character of the person that bore that name, or they name the child after a living or deceased family member. But they have absolutely no idea whether or not their child will live up to that name. Not so with God. When He names a child He does so from His omniscience, knowing that the name He gives will exactly fit the character and purpose of that child.[1239] Therefore, the names given for *Moshiach*, the child promised to be born in Isaiah 9, are a description of His character. Of the five descriptions given to Him, three of them are used only of God.

Some rabbis like Levine raise the issue that *Yeshua* was never called by these names during His earthly ministry, with the implication that *Yeshua* is not the one being referenced in this passage. Levine states that *Yeshua* never claimed to be God Himself,[1240] which means that Levine must be a person who only selects verses from the New Covenant that suit his ends. Other anti-missionaries freely admit that *Yeshua* did claim to be equal with God, meaning God Himself.[1241] Levine has a problem with the fact that *Yeshua* was never called by these names: Wonderful Counselor, mighty God, everlasting Father and the Prince of Peace. First of all God, through Isaiah, prophetically gave the names to a child who would be born, to identify His nature and essence as a member of the plural unity of *Elohim*. He was not called in His first coming by those names in His earthly ministry. To illustrate, I have numerous names, but it depends on who I am with as to the name that I am called. John Byron was the name given to me at birth. However, I have also been called Byron, J.B. and Bruce after the noted Greek scholar from Princeton, and a very close friend calls me a name that is only used in a very close circle of friends. My wife asked before we were married, "What is your name?" and I said, "John." The other names are not my usual names for I'm usually called John, but I have other names depending on the context of friends. Now if God in His will wished to identify the child to be born in Isaiah 9:6-7 in a way that actually deals with His eternal nature and essence, who is Levine to say that

---

[1239] In the New Covenant the word "name" becomes very significant. The Greek word for "name" is used 185 times; *Yeshua's* name is either used or implied 96 times. Of the remaining 89 times the New Covenant refers to God's name 24 more times, meaning that *Yeshua* or God's name is used 120 times out of 185. That is two out of three times it is used of *Yeshua* or of God.

[1240] Levine, *You Take Jesus, I'll Take God,* 53-54.

[1241] Kaplan, *The Real Messiah?,* 17.

because *Yeshua* was not called by those names in His earthly ministry that they are not relevant to Him? *Yeshua*, in His earthly ministry, was not called by these names, because the prophet was speaking of the Messiah's two comings, (1) to suffer and die, and (2) then to reign. That does not mean that the names given in Isaiah 9:6-7 are not *Yeshua's*. Those names relate to the second coming when He will sit on the throne of His father David in the Kingdom, but He had to be born first, suffer and die before He could reign. The fact remains that God gave Him these names and they will be used in a future context to completely describe His eternal nature and essence. When He comes the second time, these names will apply, and the name *Yeshua* will not apply. The two comings of Messiah have two completely distinct and different purposes.

Notice also that in verse 7 this person is directly tied to the throne of David. Who was this child? Jewish scholars teach that the "child" to be born was Hezekiah, a contemporary of Isaiah.[1242] Cohen also argues that unlike his father Ahaz, who was a vassal to Assyria, Hezekiah was not a vassal. But Cohen's reasoning is not even logical. Hezekiah, King of Judah, led a vassal state under the Assyrians until he rebelled. Sennacherib then descended upon Judah and totally destroyed 46 fortified cities as the "Oriental Institute Cylinder" gives the account of Sennacherib's campaign against Judah and Jerusalem, which coincides with the biblical text:

> As for himself (Hezekiah), like a bird in a cage in his royal city Jerusalem, I shut (him) up.[1243]

2 Kings 18-20 makes it clear that Judah was a vassal state under Hezekiah's leadership. In fact, Hezekiah stripped the temple of its gold and silver to try to get Assyria to stop attacking Judah. That does not sound like he could be the "*child*" as Cohen tries to state, or the "*Wonderful*" or the "*Mighty God*," let alone the "*everlasting Father*." Hezekiah, according to biblical history, "*did that which was right in the sight of the LORD, according to all that David his father did*" (2 Kings 18:3), but Hezekiah never measured up to the character of any of these names.

Second, the word "*wonderful*" (Isaiah 9:6) in this passage is פֶּלֶא or *pele*, a variant of the Hebrew root word פָּלָא (*pala*).[1244] Albertz states that the verb occurs 78 times in the *Tanakh* and means "to be wondrous" or "to fulfill" (a vow) or "to separate."[1245] Albertz also states that:

> In the large, major category of its usage,…it indicates an event that a person, judging by the customary and the expected, finds extraordinary, impossible, even wonderful. *Pele* never hinges on the phenomenon as such but includes both the unexpected event as well as one's astonished reaction to it…. The

---

[1242] Cohen, *The Soncino Chumash*, Isaiah, 44.

[1243] Joseph P. Free and Howard F. Vos, *Archaeology and the Bible History* (Grand Rapids: Zondervan, 1992), 180-181.

[1244] Botterweck, Ringgren, and Fabry, *Theological Dictionary of the Old Testament*, 11:534.

[1245] Jenni and Westermann, *Theological Lexicon of the Old Testament,* 2:982.

wonder, the astonishment, includes the recognition of the limits of one's own power to conceptualize and comprehend.[1246]

This word "*wonderful*" is used in the context of something that is beyond human knowledge or ability, as stated by Conrad:

> The texts all deal with extraordinary phenomena, transcending the power of knowledge and imagination…. In fact, the texts do not deal with circumstances presented simply as being extraordinary, but rather with certain goals impossible for humans to attain by their own devices or with actions and events directed toward them or affecting them that they are nevertheless unable to influence. In other words, they deal with acts and effects transcending human knowledge and imagination and hence above all transcending the powers of human agency…. Primarily, the observation is made concerning a line that human beings cannot cross but that can be crossed from the other side. The word group thus also marks the contrast between the finitude of what is possible on one side of the line and infinite range of what is possible on the other side…but for the most part it applies to superhuman forces and powers, especially to God. The texts are concerned above all with the insurmountable contrast between what is possible for human beings and what is possible for God.[1247]

What becomes rather obvious is that, even though *pele* is used of God rather than man, the context of verse 6 definitely links the word to God as well as to a child that will bare all governmental responsibility and will sit on the throne of David. This verse states that a child will be born who will govern from the throne of David, and His name is Wonderful (*pele*), God Himself. It should also be observed that *pele* is used two times in connection with the Messenger (Angel) of *Yahweh*. *Pele* is first used in connection with Abraham in Genesis 18:14 and then with Manoah in Judges 13:18. Clearly, this one in Isaiah 9:6-7 will be God in flesh reigning on the throne of David.

Third, the name "*mighty God*" (Isaiah 9:6) is even more perplexing concerning the Jewish dilemma of its dual reference to God and to a child. Jewish people do not believe the *Moshiach* will be God, and yet here is a child that will be born in order to reign on the throne of David, and "*his name shall be called…the mighty God.*" Yet Jeremiah 32:18 states, "*The Great, the Mighty God, the LORD of hosts, is his name.*" Even *The Jewish Study Bible* does not remove its meaning: "*O Great and mighty God whose name is the LORD of Hosts.*" No Jewish person is going to question or doubt that the statement in Jeremiah is the LORD God Almighty Himself. So how can the same truth be denied in Isaiah 9:6, that speaks of a child who would be born whose name is *El gibbor* (God almighty)? Isaiah 10:21 also refers to Israel returning to the "*mighty*

[1246] Jenni and Westermann, *Theological Lexicon of the Old Testament,* 2:982.

[1247] Botterweck, Ringgren, and Fabry, *Theological Dictionary of the Old Testament,* 11:534-535.

God." God is consistent with His word, even if man is not. It is tremendously inconsistent to say that the Jeremiah 32 and Isaiah 10 passages refer to God and the Isaiah 9:6 passage does not.

Fourth, the *"Everlasting"* as in Everlasting Father in Isaiah 9:6 is the Hebrew word עַד (*ad*) which means duration or perpetuity. This is a reference to God as the Father who is their guardian and protector. Fruchtenbaum notes that Isaiah 9:6 can be compared to Isaiah 63:16 which says; *"thou, O LORD, art our Father; our Redeemer from everlasting is thy name."*[1248] Here the word *olam*, rather than *ad*, is used, but both refer to eternity until the end of time and into eternity when used in reference to God. Also Isaiah 63:16 states that "LORD," *"Father,"* and *"Redeemer"* are from everlasting and so is His name, even as Isaiah 9:6 refers to the child to be born, that His name would be called Everlasting Father. Mark Robinson[1249] a Jewish believer in Messiah, points to Psalm 90:2, where only God is "from everlasting," yet in reading Isaiah 9:6-7, the one born in Bethlehem will be called the *"mighty God"* and the *"everlasting Father."* The one born of *"the virgin,"* who is called *"Immanuel"* and upon whom the *"Spirit of the LORD"* rests, is eternal or everlasting.

Fifth, the description in verse 7 *"no end"* is the Hebrew word אֵין־קֵץ. Although Jenni claims that this word for end is "distributed throughout the entire Old Testament," he makes no reference to Isaiah 9:7.[1250] Also Talmon, writing on the word קֵץ, does not reference Isaiah 9:7, but he does divide the meaning and usage of the word into four groups: (1) end as in lifetime, (2) end as a period of time, (3) end as a historical period and (4) eschatology.[1251] Isaiah states that this child will be born, and of His government there will be *"no end"* to its increase and peace. That seems to be self-explanatory. This usage seems to be unique because the other usages do reference a specific period of time, where "no end" in this passage has something in view beyond time. Hill and Matties show the usage of "end" as theological as in divine judgment (Genesis 6:13), "end of time" and "end of human history" (Daniel 8:17, 19; 11:40; 12:4, 6) and even "end of wrongdoing" (Ezekiel 21:25, 29 [30, 34]). But because of the אֵין ("there is not"), the verse is stating that "a time of peace without end is expected."[1252] So the אֵין gives it the opposite meaning, no ending, as is referenced by Brown, Driver and Briggs.[1253] Coppes very clearly shows that difference with the word אֵין (no) when he states: "Contrariwise, the Messiah's kingdom will know no end."[1254] Clearly this word

---

[1248] Fruchtenbaum, *Messianic Christology*, 40.

[1249] Mark Robinson, *One God or Three?* (brochure, El Cajon, CA: Shalom Outreach Ministries, n.d.), 10-11.

[1250] Jenni and Westermann, *Theological Lexicon of the Old Testament,* 3:1154.

[1251] Botterweck, Ringgren, and Fabry, *Theological Dictionary of the Old Testament*, 13:82-83.

[1252] VanGemeren, *Dictionary of Old Testament Theology & Exegesis,* 3:955.

[1253] Brown, Driver, and Briggs, *A Hebrew and English Lexicon of the Old Testament,* 892.

[1254] Harris, Archer, and Waltke, *Theological Wordbook of the Old Testament,* 2:809.

אֵין ("there is not") is used not in a time frame but in the sense of eternity, and the Messianic Kingdom referenced in Isaiah 9:7 will have no end.

Jewish scholars recognize the enduring kingdom, but do not acknowledge that the *Moshiach* will reign forever, God is reigning forever. The first quotation below is a comparison between Moses and Messiah ben David. Moses brought the people of the Exodus to the entrance of the Promised Land and Messiah ben David will bring them to the kingdom. The following quotes coming from the *Messiah Text* will be viewed in four parts:

> With the death of **Moses, the earthly career of Israel's first Redeemer** comes to an end. In the Other World, of course, he continues to keep a watchful eye on his people, continues to intercede in their behalf. **Messiah ben David, too, nears the end of his ministry with his victory over the armies of Gog and Magog and over their satanic master Armilus, whom he kills with the breath of his mouth.** This latter detail, incidentally, is an eloquent indication of the kind of victory Jewish legend envisaged would be achieved by the Messiah. There was to be first of all, a holocaustal sequence of wars, myriads would be killed in actual combat, or by earthquakes and other great cataclysms, but the greatest of victories, that over Armilus himself, the evil incarnate, would be a spiritual one: his annihilation would be brought about by breath from the pure mouth of the Son of David, the elect of God, the Messiah.[1255]

What is so interesting in this section is that Messiah ben David will bring them into the kingdom, the enemy is defeated, but then Messiah ben David fades away into obscurity. Notice the contradiction in language that is used, first (1) "whom he kills with the breath of his mouth," that is language used of God, yet their messiah is not God but a man by rabbinic teaching. Notice next (2) Moses never won any victory by the "*breath of his mouth.*" If you look at Psalm 33:6 the same phrase is used of *HaShem*, "*By the word of the LORD were the heavens made; and all the host of them by the breath of his mouth.*" *HaShem* can create or destroy by the breath of his mouth. The point is a mere human can only fog up a window with the breath of his mouth. What they are attributing to Messiah can only relate to *HaShem* the Messiah. Lastly notice (3) Armilus is evil incarnate, so why cannot Messiah be righteousness Incarnate, born of a virgin as the Son of David, the promised Messiah, the God/Man. But the rabbis propose the premise as in the Messiah Text that there must be two messiahs, of which neither is divine, rather than seeing one *Moshiach* who comes on two separate occasions who is divine.

> This greatest feat of the Messiah is, at one and the same time, also his last one. Just as Moses had brought the Children of Israel to the threshold of the Promised Land and then died, so the Messiah leads them to victory over Gog

---

[1255] Raphael Patai, *The Messiah Texts* (Detroit: Wayne State University Press, 1979), xxxiii-xxxiv.

and Magog, culminating in the elimination of Armilus, **and then fades away, disappears from the scene. Nothing more is heard about him except some very vague and generalized statements to the effect that he would continue to rule over his people for an indeterminate period.** In all the great events which follow the victory over Armilus, the Messiah plays no role whatsoever.[1256]

To the Jewish rabbis the *Moshiach* fades away into obscurity, while God the Father takes central stage in Jerusalem as the King and rules over the earth as the Son of David. That makes the Scriptures null and void! *Moshiach* must rule over the house of David according to Ethan (Psalm 89:29), Isaiah (9:6-7; 16:5), Micah (5:2), Jeremiah (23:5-6; 33:14-26), Daniel (2:34-35, 44-45; 7:13-14), and Zechariah (12:1, 10; 14:3-4, 16). The throne of David is for *Moshiach* to rule on, NOT God the Father. Is God the Father of the tribe of Judah and of the house of David! The fading away, as it is called, is because the *Moshiach*, Son of David, is God. So His person is blended together (for lack of a better term) into One. He does not fade way for *Moshiach* is the LORD, *Yahweh*, *HaShem* a member of the plural unity of *Elohim*. In the following quotation the one who takes center stage is *Moshiach* the LORD. It is so heartbreaking because of Rabbinic Judaism's blindness in seeing the multiple occasions where God shows Himself as a plurality (tri-unity); they mishandle or misinterpret the *Tanakh* because their premise is faulty.

> We know, or at least we are led to believe, that he is present at the Resurrection of the dead, at the Last Judgment, at the Messianic banquet, at the House of Study of the future in which the new, Messianic, Tora[h] will be taught, but if he is, **no mention is made of his presence and he plays no role at all. In all those great occurrences and processes it is God, the Holy One, blessed be He, who Himself takes the central place on the stage.** It is God who resuscitates the dead, who judges the pious and the wicked, who sits with the saintly at the great feast, who pours wine into their cups, who entertains them by dancing before them, who teaches them the new Tora[h], and who receives the homage of the entire rejuvenated, reformed and sanctified world. Where is the Messiah in all this? **We are told nothing of him**, and were it not that in the earlier phases of the Messianic myth we were assured that he would, after the ultimate victory, reign in Jerusalem as the Prince of Peace, **we would not even suspect that he is present.**[1257]

Their conclusion is that just as Moses is a type of the *Moshiach*, both are redeemers, and neither has a part in the Promised Land or in the Kingdom.

Thus, and in this primarily, the **Messiah proves to be essentially a Moses figure, and Moses to be the accurate prefigureation of the Messiah. Both**

[1256] Patai, *The Messiah Texts*, xxxiv.
[1257] Patai, *The Messiah Texts*, xxxiv-xxxv.

are Redeemers, but neither of them has a part in the great era to whose threshold they lead their people at the price of their lifeblood.[1258]

In both the beginning and ending of this statement from the *Messiah Text*, Moses and *Moshiach* are redeemers who do not enter the Promise. That parallel with Moses does not come from the Torah in Deuteronomy 18:15-18, which speaks of a prophet like Moses. But Moses and Messiah, the Prophet, are not alike, only as God speaks to it in Numbers 12:5-8. Moses could not enter the Promised Land because of sin, according to the *Messiah Text* Messiah is a sinner too because he also most have disobeyed *HaShem* as Moses did, so much for the Messiah bringing righteousness to the world. Where is the justification for that from the *Tanakh*? The middle of the second quote from the *Messiah Text* refers to the *Moshiach* that "fades away," as follows:

> And then fades away, disappears from the scene. Nothing more is heard about him except some very vague and generalized statements to the effect that he would continue to rule over his people for an indeterminate period.

Instead of the *Moshiach* reigning, they see God the Father reigning in Jerusalem. Considering what has been seen in all of the previous chapters of this study, God is a tri-unity. *Yeshua*, who is the *Moshiach*, is the one on record in the *Tanakh* as ruling from Jerusalem during the Kingdom. It has also been seen in previous chapters that, without question, the plurality (tri-unity) of God is in the Hebrew Scriptures. The Scripture makes clear, simple statements about who the *Moshiach* is. But in Rabbinic Judaism, if their basic premise is wrong, that the Messiah cannot be God because God is One, He is missed. He does not fade away, because He is God Almighty who will reign in Jerusalem as was promised to David. God the Father is not a descendant of David, but God the Son is clearly understood from Psalm 110:1, even understood by the Pharisees in *Yeshua*'s day.

The words "*no end*" are very significant in Isaiah 9:7. These words are even more significant when the descriptions of the child to be born in verse 6 are placed alongside the fact that this child's kingdom and peace will have "no end." God's Kingdom will be ruled by God Incarnate in the person of *Moshiach*. Although Isaiah, in 9:6-7 underscores that very powerful statement concerning the person of *Moshiach* who was to be born, he adds even more.

Sixth, the statement "*upon the throne of David*" (Isaiah 9:7) has a direct connection to the Davidic Covenant which was given 300 years earlier. This One, who will be human and yet is "*Wonderful*" (*pele*), the "*mighty God*," and the "*everlasting Father*," has a dual nature, and is the fulfillment of the covenant promises to Abraham and to David. The promises to both will be fulfilled when this One, the God/man, actually reigns from the throne of David in Jerusalem, and His Kingdom will have "*no end*."

[1258] Patai, *The Messiah Texts*, xxxiv-xxxv.

Seventh is the statement concerning the kingdom that says *"henceforth even for ever"* (Isaiah 9:7). The point is that a child would be born who would be God Himself. He would personally fulfill His promise to Abraham, to Israel and to David. As stated previously, His Kingdom will have *"no end."* So how can Messiah "fade away" for it is His throne according to Isaiah 9:6-7 and Jeremiah 23:5-6 and it is His forever. Isaiah re-affirms that the Messianic person will personally reign on the throne as said, from "henceforth even for ever (עוֹלָם – olam)."

A Shoot Shall Grow Out of the Stump of Jesse … Isaiah 11:1-2

> But a shoot shall grow out of the stump of Jesse, A twig shall sprout from his stock. The spirit of the LORD shall alight upon him: A spirit of wisdom and insight, A spirit of counsel and valor, A spirit of devotion and reverence for the LORD.

The Jewish Study Bible uses the word "twig" whereas in the KJV the term used is "branch." Both grow from the stump and root of a tree. This is the second time that Isaiah uses the term; the first was in Isaiah 4:2. Isaiah is the first among the prophets; Jeremiah and Zechariah also use the term "branch" in connection with the *Moshiach*.

In Isaiah 11:1-2 a further description is given of Immanuel or *"God with us."* Verse 1 identifies the humanity of Immanuel, and He is presented through the metaphor of Him coming from the stem of Jesse, a Branch growing out of his roots. At the time when Isaiah spoke, the great tree (kingdom) of David would be reduced to a fallen tree, a stump, indicating that when *Moshiach*, the Branch comes, the house of David would be in humility and poverty. This is exactly the case when *Yeshua* was born, for Joseph and Miriam (Mary), were poor and the great house of David was fallen. This is borne out when Miriam fulfilled her *"days of her purification according to the Law of Moses"* for her sacrifice was the offering of poor people who could not afford anything more (Luke 2:22-24; Leviticus 12:8). Isaiah stated that *"the Branch"* would come when David's house had been reduced to a fallen stump, in poverty as Jesse. Isaiah also used this term earlier (4:2) to identify the Branch as the Branch of *Yahweh*. This passage is echoed by two other prophets, first in Jeremiah 23:5-6 where the Branch is called *"the LORD OUR RIGHTEOUSNESS,"* the Branch is *"God with us"* who is Righteousness in character. Then Zechariah (3:8; 6:12) gives further information as to the Branch's person and nature. For more information on the *Moshiach* being *"the Branch"* see chapter 17 entitled *The Branch*. In Isaiah 61:1 the Messiah is anointed by *"the Spirit of the LORD God,"* and in Isaiah 11:2 *"the spirit of the Lord shall rest upon Him"* in seven different manifestations.

Samuel Levine goes to great lengths in his presentation to show that verses 1-2 could not be *Yeshua* because in verses 6-8 the animals no longer have the desire to attack and kill other animals.[1259] These later verses relate to the Messianic Kingdom

---

[1259] Levine, *You Take Jesus, I'll Take God,* 50-51.

when the curse of sin has been removed from the world. Levine continues to criticize biblical faith for its belief in the two comings of *Moshiach*, yet Rabbinic Judaism sees two messiahs. This concept has been dealt with before in this book and time will not be taken to do so again. Rabbinic Judaism, because it resists the plain sense of Scripture, refuses to acknowledge the plurality of God, the incarnation, the need of a saviour and mediator from sin. Rabbinic Judaism teaches that man can better himself before God, thus making himself acceptable to God without the voluntary sacrifice of the *Moshiach*, the Son of God, the Son of David, Immanuel and "*the Branch*." Consequently because of this passage, along with many others such as Isaiah 61:1-3 and Zechariah 9:9-10, Rabbinic Judaism rejects the first coming dealing with the sin of the world and the second coming to fulfill the promises made to Abraham, Isaac and Jacob, and after which the animal kingdom would be at peace.

The Book of Immanuel has some tremendous portions of Scripture that speak of the One who is "*God with us*" as the God/man who was virgin-born, the Son of David, who is also "*Wonderful,*" "*mighty God,*" "*everlasting Father,*" and "*the Branch.*" What a significant section of Scripture Isaiah 7-12 is as it presents "*God with us.*"

ISAIAH: THE SERVANT PASSAGES

The servant passages of Isaiah are remarkable passages in relationship to Israel and its Messiah, the Servant of the LORD. There are two passages that are important here but they were dealt with in two other chapters. Isaiah 44:6 was dealt with in chapter 3 and Isaiah 48:12-16 was dealt with in chapter 10, so reread those sections that deal with those passages for discussion will not be repeated here. However, there are five other passages that need to be examined to shed light on the divinity of Messiah.

The "Arm" of the LORD

Often we find in the *Tanakh* where God uses anthropomorphism to describe His workings among men in physical terms that we can relate to. This was discussed back in chapter 2 of this book. Here again He uses an anthropomorphism to describe Himself to the nation of Israel. God has used many descriptive terms to present the Messiah of Israel such as "*the angel of the LORD,*" the "*word of the LORD,*" and Captain of the LORD's host, "*Immanuel,*" the "Son of David," the "Messiah" or *Moshiach*. In an upcoming chapter we will also see Him as the "*righteous Branch,*" the "*branch of Yahweh,*" and "*My servant the Branch,*" and the "*man whose name is the BRANCH.*" Isaiah the prophet in the second division of his book picks up a term from Moses and uses it as a sub-theme to further describe the Messiah as "*the arm*" or the Arm of the LORD. Look carefully at these 11 passages and particularly look at the connection that Isaiah makes with the "*arm*" and "*salvation*" as he ties it all into the person of Messiah in Isaiah 53.

40:10-11 … Arm Will Rule and Comfort

In Isaiah 40:10-11 the term *"arm"* is used twice. In verse 10 Isaiah states that the *"arm shall rule."* Isaiah picks up this term from Moses as he references God's "stretched out arm" who took Israel out of Egypt and into the Promised Land in the following passages: Genesis 49:24; Exodus 6:6, 15:16; Deuteronomy 4:34, 5:15, 7:19, 9:29, 11:2, 26:8, 33:27 (1 Kings 8:42, 2 Kings 17:36; 2 Chronicles 6:32; Job 40:9; Psalm 44:3, 77:15; 89:10, 13, 21, 98:1, 136:12; Isaiah 33:2). The *"arm"* symbolizes strength and power. It was the *"angel"* (Exodus 23:20-23) who guided Israel to the Promised Land to fulfill the promises made to Abraham (Judges 2:1) and that same *"arm"* was the *"angel,"* the Angel of the LORD who is the strong *"arm"* of God. So in Isaiah 40:10 it states that His *"arm will rule for him."* There is a clear personification here of the *"arm"* for it is His *"arm"* that will rule for Him. Now in verse 11 *"arm"* is mentioned again but this time it is the motif of a shepherd where the *"arm"* of the Lord God will gather Israel in His *"arm."* Here is a picture of the shepherd of Israel (Psalm 80:1, Zechariah 11:4-14, John 10:9) in his strength gently providing and caring for the flock. In these verses we are told that the *"arm"* by His strength will rule, and by His *"arm"* He will as shepherd comfort and care for Israel in the strength of His *"arm."*

48:14 … Arm of Judgment Against Babylon

The "arm" of the LORD is upon the Babylonians and He has raised up Cyrus and will make him prosperous. In the broader context of this passage the speaker is the one who called Israel, the first and the last (verse 12) and the Creator (verse 13) who is identified in verse 16 as the one who is sent by the Lord God and the Holy Spirit. The speaker and the *"arm"* Who is moving history is the Messiah, the Second Person of the Godhead.

51:5 … Gentiles Will Trust

In chapter 51 the LORD will redeem Israel. The part of the nation that survives the time of Jacob's trouble will be the believing remnant who are called *"my people"* (verse 4). His word to them is to listen to the law, kingdom law shall come from the LORD. The Kingdom Law is different than the Mosaic Law, they are not one in the same, they are different with some similarities. His judgment will be for *"a light for the people* (Gentiles)." His righteousness is near because His salvation is gone out. Before righteousness can be a reality salvation must come first, which is another key issue to understand. Rabbinic Judaism believes that it can atone for its own sins by repentance, charity and good deeds. But what good are these without dealing with what causes the sins issue to begin with. This is justification, declaring a sinner righteous by what the *"arm"* will provide, salvation. Now notice that the term *"arm"* is used twice. His *"arms"* shall judge the people or nations and in His *"arm,"* singular, shall the Gentiles trust. Gentiles will not be trusting in a physical arm, but the *"arm"* of the LORD Who is the Messiah in whom the Gentiles will trust. This is equally important to understand when Isaiah 53 is studied. Rabbinic Judaism presents the idea that Israel also atones for the sins of the Gentiles through its suffering when literally it is the *"arm"* who suffers willingly, vicariously for Israel and the Gentiles.

51:9 ... Arm Will Redeem

Here is a call for the *"arm"* of the LORD to awake as in ancient days when the *"arm"* of the LORD cut and wounded Rahab (Egypt) and its dragon (Pharaoh). This is a reference again to the one who brought Israel out from Egypt to the Promised Land. So the *"arm"* will rule, shepherd, bring judgment, be the object of trust by the Gentiles and the *"arm"* will deliver or redeem Israel.

52:10 ... Arm Will Provide Salvation

Here the LORD will make His *"arm"* bare. He will make His Arm visible and all the Gentile nations with their eyes and the ends of the earth will see his *"salvation"* or *Yeshuah* (John 1:18, 5:37, 5:39, 5:46, 8:58, 10:30, 14:9-10). The LORD will become visible; He will bare His Arm and the nations will see His salvation. Isaiah by using the term *"arm"* to define Himself tells us that His Arm is One (*echad*) with Himself, God becoming visible, this is the incarnation of Messiah. Isaiah takes another step closer to showing the identity of the *"arm"* by showing that now His Arm is salvation and the nations of the world will see the LORD's Arm, who is the Servant of the LORD as is seen in the next usage.

53:1 ... Identity of the Arm – Messiah

Here the *"arm"* of the LORD is revealed and the rest of Isaiah 53 personifies the *"arm"* as the suffering Messiah. All of the pronouns *"he"* *"him"* and *"his"* reflect the substitutionary, vicarious suffering and death of the Servant of the LORD, the Messiah.

59:16 ... His Arm Brought Salvation

In Isaiah 59 you have the sinfulness of Israel and their separation from their God in verses 1-8 announced. The confession of their sins in verses 9-15a is like Isaiah 53, these two passages show that Israel is in need of salvation and not atoning for others salvation. In verses 15b-16 God saw no judgment, no righteousness and no intercession in Israel; therefore His *"arm,"* the Messiah brought *"salvation."* Isaiah has just described Israel as a very sinful nation and not as *"my righteous servant"* (Isaiah 53:11), meaning that Israel is not the Servant of the LORD in Isaiah 53. Notice the connection that Isaiah makes with the term *"arm"* in conjunction with *"salvation"* in these passages.

62:8 ... His Arm Will Provide

When the LORD redeems Israel He is the One who has sworn by His right hand, the *"arm"* of strength, He will provide for Israel. It is again interesting that *"the LORD hath sworn by his right hand by the Arm of His strength."* In Psalm 80:17 it is the man who sits on the LORD's right hand that Israel will call for and Psalm 80:15 also identifies this one as the "*branch*." As Scripture is searched out we find that the Abrahamic Covenant was made by the "*word of the LORD*" in Genesis 15 and the Angel was sent by God to bring Israel to the Promised Land and in Judges 2:1 it is the "*angel of the LORD*" that said He swore to the Fathers. That means that the Second Person of the Godhead became visible and would provide salvation and deliverance to Israel as the Arm, the Messiah.

63:5 ... Arm Gives Deliverance from Israel Enemies

Here at the second coming of the Messiah it is the "*arm*" that brings salvation for Israel from their enemies. Yet Rabbinic Judaism refuses to see the two comings of Messiah. They see the two descriptions of the Messiah comings, suffering (Messiah ben Joseph) and reigning (Messiah ben David). However, they clutch to the view of two different messiahs instead of seeing one Messiah who comes twice. In both cases Messiah comes to provide salvation; first in dealing with the issue of sin and second to provide salvation and deliverance to Israel upon their confession of their sin (Isaiah 53) of rejecting Him when He came the first time. Upon their confession He will return and destroy the armies of the anti-Christ who are about to annihilate them at Petra (*Bozrah*) and then set up the Kingdom that they long for, fulfilling His promise to Abraham, Isaac and Jacob.

63:12 ... Moses and the Arm of Deliverance

This section of verses shows the tri-unity of the Godhead (vs. 9-12). In verse 9 you have the "*angel of his presence*" that saved them. In looking at these verses I see a couple of interesting connections. The one who delivered them is called the "*shepherd of the flock*" in verse 11 and then verse 12 refers to the same shepherd as the "*glorious arm*." The shepherd is the one who led them by Moses' right hand with His glorious Arm. An unusual statement, but again it was the LORD, through the "*angel of His Presence*" that empowered Moses, the "*glorious arm*" of the LORD, the Messiah.

In this sub-theme of the "*arm*" God shows His strength through His "*arm*" that will rule and comfort, fight against and judge the Babylonians, in whom the Gentiles will trust, who will redeem Israel, who will provide salvation in the person of the Messiah, the Suffering Servant. This "*arm*" will bring "*salvation*," will provide for Israel and deliver Israel from all their enemies, just as the Arm did through the ministry of Moses. This is a very interesting study that deserves more time. The "*arm*" of the LORD once again is the visible representation of the Father in the person of the Messiah, the Son of David.

The Servant of the LORD ... Isaiah 42:1-6

Isaiah 42 has been recognized by both Jewish and Christian scholars as referencing the Messiah. Because this is clearly seen as a Messiah passage of Scripture I will only make one observation. The "*my servant*" in verse 1 is referenced as being two things: first He is the one who will be given "*for a covenant*," and that is a reference to the future issuing of the New Covenant in Jeremiah 31 and "*for a light to the Gentiles*." Because Israel failed to be the light to the Gentiles, the Messiah of Israel will be that Light.

The Servant to Restore Israel ... Isaiah 49:1-13

Who is the speaker in Isaiah 49:1 that says, "*Listen (shema), O isles, unto me and hearken?*" If you follow the preceding chapter you begin to see the speaker has not changed since Isaiah 48:12. There it states in verses 12-13, 16c:

> *Hearken unto me, O Jacob and Israel, my called; I am he; I am the first, and I am also the last. Mine hand also hath laid the foundation of the earth, and my right hand hath spanned the heavens: I call unto them, they stand up together. ... and now the Lord God and his Spirit, hath sent me* (KJV).

When you look at these passages in 48:12, 16 and 49:1 you begin to understand that the speaker is the same person. So the one who called Israel (vs. 12), the Creator (vs. 13), who was sent by the Lord God and His Spirit (vs. 16) is also the speaker in 49:1. In verse 1 the speaker states that the LORD called Him from the womb. This has to be a man, yet He is speaking as God. This is not the only time this happens because we will also see the plurality of the God in chapter 50 of Isaiah in reverse. It also states that He was called from the womb of His mother, but where is the mention of the father? There are no references to the Messiah's father, for He has no earthly father just as Isaiah 7:14 states, "*a virgin shall conceive.*"

Continue to look at verse 3; the Lord God is speaking to the called one who is doing the speaking that He is "*my servant, O Israel, in whom I will be glorified.*" This is not referencing Israel but the Messiah of Israel the individual known as the servant of the LORD. Now in verse 6 notice what the Lord God says to the speaker:

> *Is it a light thing that thou shouldest be my servant to raise up the tribes of Jacob, and to restore the preserved of Israel: I will also give thee for a light to the Gentiles, that thou mayest be my salvation (Yeshuah) unto the end of the earth* (KJV).

The Lord God is saying to the speaker, the Servant of the LORD, the Messiah, that He will restore Israel and be a light to the Gentiles. This simply states that Israel has to be restored, so how can Israel justify the Gentiles according to Rashi if they themselves need to be restored? These are tremendous verses to know and understand as we show Jewish people that the Messiah is God the Son, their Messiah.

Yahweh and the Lord God … Isaiah 50:1a, 4-6

This passage will be given first from *The Jewish Study Bible* and then the King James Version. You will find them both clear in their presentation of the Messiah and what He experienced.

> (1) Thus said the Lord: (4) The Lord God gave me a skilled tongue, to know how to speak timely words to the weary. Morning by morning, He rouses, He rouses my ear to give heed like disciples. (5) The Lord God opened my ears, and I did not disobey, I did not run away. (6) I offered my back to the floggers, and my cheeks to those who tore out my hair. I did not hide my face from insult and spittle.

> (1) Thus saith the LORD, …. (4) The Lord God hath given me the tongue of the learned, that I should know how to speak a word in season to him that is weary: he wakeneth morning by morning, he wakeneth mine ear to hear as the learned. (5) The Lord God hath opened mine ear, and I was not rebellious, neither turned away back. (6) I gave my back to the smiters, and my cheeks to them that plucked off the hair: I hid not my face from shame and spitting (KJV).

In relation to this passage and other verses in the *Tanakh*, a valid question can be asked. Who in history does this passage of Scripture describe? There can only be one answer: *Yeshua* of Nazareth. In verse 1 *Yahweh* is speaking, but then in verse 4 *Yahweh* states that the Lord (*Adonai*) God (*Elohim*) gave Him something. Here are two distinct personalities, *Yahweh* and the Lord God. Who is who? The answer comes in verse 6 where *Yahweh* gives a description of something happening to Him:

> I offered my back to the floggers and my cheeks to those who tore out my hair.
> I did not hide my face from insult and spittle.

When did *Yahweh*, in history, give His back to the floggers or smiters? When did *Yahweh*, in history, allow His beard to be pulled from His face? When, in history, did *Yahweh* permit Himself to be shamed and spat upon? Before the answer is given, there are two points to observe. First, there are two personalities represented here as God: *Yahweh* in verse 1 who is the speaker and the Lord God in verse 4 who gave something to *Yahweh*. Here are obviously two members of the plurality of *Elohim* being noted. Second, *Yahweh* who is the speaker from verse 1 through verse 6 has allowed men to afflict Him with such beatings, shame and spitting. Some may say this is a metaphor, but there is nothing in the text to warrant that. The identity of *Yahweh* and what happened to Him is what happened to *Yeshua*, who is the exact image of the Father, at His trial before the Sanhedrin and before the Romans.

Isaiah is clearly presenting that a son will be born of a virgin and He will be "*God with us.*" He will be born from the stem of Jesse of the house of David and He will reign on David's throne forever. This one who is to reign on David's throne forever is named by God "*Wonderful,*" "*almighty God*" and the "*everlasting Father.*" He is introduced as "*the Servant of the Lord*" in chapters 42, 49 and 50 of Isaiah. This is the promised Messiah, the God/man repeatedly promised ever since Genesis 3:15.

The Suffering Messiah … Isaiah 52:13 – 53:12

Isaiah 53 introduces the Suffering Servant. (See Appendix 4 for a complete reading of the passage from *The Jewish Study Bible* and the King James Version.) The identity of the Suffering Servant brings controversy between Jewish and New Covenant adherents. Who is this servant? Some Jewish scholars point to Isaiah, but predominantly to Israel as fulfilling the Suffering Servant passage. In this modern contemporary religious world there are three predominant views among the Jewish people and liberal Christians as quoted below:

> First, this has been the dominant Jewish interpretation since at least the Middle Ages (propounded by Rashi and both David and Jacob Kimchi). Secondly, contemporary mainline Christian scholarship, especially under the rise of historical criticism in the eighteenth and nineteenth centuries, has in large part abandoned the messianic view and has itself recognized the legitimacy of understanding the servant as corporate Israel or as a historic individual such as a "second" Isaiah. Thirdly, the social and political events of the twentieth century have provided overwhelming historical evidence that "Israel" continues to have as its mission the role of God's suffering servant, who through death and resilience remains God's agent for good in the world.[1260]

These three arguments and the reasoning behind the rabbis' changing their historic understanding are brought out by Victor Buksbazen, a Jewish believer in Messiah.[1261] In brief he states that because of the horrible atrocities of the period by the Crusaders and the biblical usage of Isaiah 53 in the missionary endeavors, Rashi and others reinterpreted the passage to mean that Israel is the suffering servant. Even though this view has infiltrated the official Jewish understanding of this passage, if a Jewish person is asked to read Isaiah 53 and to identify the person spoken of, he or she invariably will say that this passage comes from the Christian Bible (New Testament) and that it refers to Jesus. What a surprise it is for them when they realize that this passage comes from their own prophet Isaiah, and they themselves have identified *Yeshua* as the Suffering Servant. To illustrate the point the following comes from an article written by Zvi in the magazine "Israel My Glory," which once again shows the true identity of the Suffering Servant of Isaiah 53:

> They were extremely surprised that we who believe in Christ read the Bible. After a few hours of discussion, several men finally asked, "How did you come to know the Lord, as you say?" I told them it was because I read the Bible only,

---

[1260] Andrew H. Bartelt, "The Identity of the Servant of Isaiah 53." *Mishkan*, Issue 43, (2005): 7-8.

[1261] Buksbazen, *The Prophet Isaiah*, 2:400-404.

not a big stack of other [religious] books. But they were not happy to hear this. They became angry and started shouting that there was no way I could believe in Jesus by reading the Hebrew Scriptures. So I opened my Bible to Isaiah 53 and read it to them. They asked why I was reading to them from the New Testament. I showed them that I was reading from one of the major prophets of Israel. They looked at my Bible and began to read Isaiah 53 for themselves.

"We'll have to ask our rabbis about this," one said. "But you believe in This One who was born in Bethlehem. Isn't He your God? Where is it written that God was to be born in Bethlehem?" If you would believe what is written in the Bible," I told them, "you would not be asking such questions." So I told them to look in my Bible and read Micah 5:2. After they read they all were quiet.[1262]

Isaiah 53 is not a passage of Scripture known by most Jewish people because it is neglected purposely or forbidden by the rabbis to be read, and it is never read in the synagogue services. Rabbis in synagogue services end their reading at Isaiah 52:12 and pick up again at the beginning of Isaiah 54. That was not always the case, as Rabbi Moshe Alshekh of the 16th century states:

[Our] Rabbis with one voice, accept and affirm the opinion that the prophet is speaking of king Messiah.[1263]

There are many things that could be presented in this passage to show that this is *Yeshua*. For a fuller treatment of this passage there are numerous books that deal with each verse in depth as indicated in the footnote below.[1264] One point that needs to be brought out in this passage is to identify *Yeshua* as the Suffering Servant. The identities of the speaker and the one about whom he is speaking must be determined. Rabbi Levine tries to show that this passage of Scripture refers to Isaiah rather than Jesus. He is correct that the people of Israel are spoken of in the plural and in the singular; however it becomes equally as clear that the phrase the "*Servant of the LORD*" sometimes references Israel but other times it refers to an individual.[1265]

In briefly reviewing the "*Servant of the LORD*" passages, what does become evident is that the LORD through the pen of Isaiah, references Israel (collective) as the servant as well as an individual as the "*Servant of the LORD*." Some passages that refer to Israel as the servant are located in Isaiah 41:8-10; 44:1-3, 21; 45:4. Passages that

---

[1262] Zvi Kalisher, *Israel My Glory*, (Bellmawr, NJ: The Friends of Israel Gospel Ministry, May/June 2007 – vol. 65, number 3), 42.

[1263] Rachmiel Frydland, *What the Rabbis Know About the Messiah* (Cincinnati, OH: Messianic Publishing Co, 1991), 53.

[1264] (1) Arnold G. Fruchtenbaum, *Jesus Was a Jew* (Tustin, CA: Ariel Ministries); (2) David Baron, *The Servant of Jehovah* (Jerusalem: Keren Ahvah Meshihit, 2000); (3) Victor Buksbazen, *Isaiah's Messiah* (Bellmawr, NJ: Friends of Israel Gospel Ministry, 2002).

[1265] Levine, *You Take Jesus, I'll Take God*; How To Refute Christian Missionaries, 25.

refer to Messiah as the Servant are found in Isaiah 42:1-4; 49:1-7; 50:1-9; 52:13 – 53:12. In Isaiah 40-53 the term *"servant"* occurs 20 times in the singular.[1266]

Rabbinic Judaism runs into a problem when equating the Servant of the LORD with Israel in Isaiah 53. In Isaiah 49:1-7 what the LORD states to His Servant cannot be to Israel. In verse 3 it states: *"You are My servant, Israel in whom I glory."* But then in verse 5-6 it clearly shows by the Servant's response to the LORD that it cannot be Israel but an individual for the Servant is *"to bring back Jacob to Himself"* and *"It is too little that you should be My servant in that I raise up the tribes of Jacob and restore the survivors of Israel."* Here the Servant and the LORD are having a dialog. The LORD says that His Servant will bring back Jacob or Israel as well as raising up the tribes of Jacob and restoring Israel. The text is obviously speaking of an individual who will save Israel rather than Israel saving herself.

The example in Isaiah 53 gives an individual the title *"Servant of the LORD."* What will be addressed here are the personal pronouns in Isaiah 53 and to whom these pronouns refer. Rabbinic Judaism attempts to use Isaiah 53:8 to substantiate their point as illustrated by the following quote:

> The main question is whether this chapter speaks of an individual, or rather collectively of a nation, Israel. In later Jewish tradition it is emphasized that Isaiah 53 would be best interpreted collectively. The collective understanding is mainly based on verse 8, in which we read, *"He was stricken for the transgression of my people."* The Hebrew phrase for "he," *lamo*, can be understood either as plural, "they," or singular, "he." The whole chapter presents, however, a contrast between him and us: "He was despised and rejected," "he has borne our griefs and carried our sorrow," "he was wounded for our transgressions," and "he was bruised for our iniquities," etc.[1267]

What will become increasingly clear as the pronouns in this passage are viewed later in the chapter is that to translate the "he" in verse 8 as "they" is completely contrary to the whole context of the chapter.

As was stated previously, the most common Jewish interpretation of Isaiah 53 is that it refers to Israel, for the nation of Israel is the servant of the Lord. But among the ultra-orthodox the person is still understood to be *Moshiach* as the following quote illustrates:

> Behold, My servant shall be wise, he shall be exalted and lofty, and shall be very high (Isaiah 52:13). [It is interesting that here the servant is the Messiah and not the nation of Israel, as modern Judaism insists.] His wisdom shall exceed even that of King Solomon; he shall be greater than the patriarchs,

---

[1266] Kaiser, *The Messiah in the Old Testament,* 173-181.

[1267] Risto Santala, "The Despised Messiah and His Despised People," *Mishkan.* Issue 43 (2005), 18-19.

greater than all the prophets after Moses, and in many respects even more exalted than Moses. His stature and honor shall exceed that of all kings before him. He will be an extra-ordinary prophet, second only to Moses, with all the spiritual and mental qualities that are prerequisites to be endowed with the gift of prophecy.[1268] [brackets mine]

But most other rabbis take the interpretation as given by Rashi, an 11th-century rabbi. However, his contemporary, Maimonides, a rabbi from Egypt, took issue with Rashi. This interpretation of the servant being Israel in Isaiah 53 did not become popular until the 1800s when Protestant missionaries began to use it with great success in sharing the Gospel of Messiah with the Jewish people in Europe.[1269] So prior to Rashi, the rabbis of the *talmudic* period in one (echad) voice referred to Isaiah 53 as *Moshiach*, an individual, as Varner states:

In this regard, it is important to examine the matter of what the rabbis say about Isaiah 53. Prior to about 1100 A.D., even the rabbis acknowledged that Isaiah 53 must apply to the Messiah. For example, the Targum Jonathan, written in the second century A.D., says of Isaiah 52:13: "Behold my servant, the Messiah, shall prosper." The rabbis of the Talmudic period always referred to the Servant as the Messiah, even though they did not apply it to Jesus. But around 1100 A.D., a great teacher named Rashi (Rabbi Shlomo Itzake) inaugurated a new interpretation of Isaiah 53 that today has become the general Jewish interpretation of this passage. Rashi said that Isaiah 53 does not refer to Jesus, nor does it even refer to the Jewish Messiah. Rather, it refers to Israel as a nation, as a people despised by the Gentiles, rejected by the Gentiles, and who have suffered at the hands of the Gentiles. Rashi pointed to another passage in Isaiah where the term "servant" does appear to refer to Israel as a people (Isa 44:1).[1270]

That is the background for why today in Judaism it is almost universally accepted as referencing Israel rather than the Messiah as an individual. Goldberg gives a brief explanation to the teaching today on Isaiah 53 by mainstream Judaism:

All the sufferings mentioned in the Isaiah text, "the visage marred," "stricken," "smitten," "afflicted," etc., is made to apply to Israel while the glories described in the Isaiah text, "being exalted," "lifted up," " the seed," "the prolonging of the days," etc., is applied to the Messiah. In the Targum, Israel suffers for its own sins (Isa 53). This is in contrast to what is propounded by modern Jewish thought, namely that Israel is suffering for the sins of the world (see David Baron, *The Servant of Jehovah*). This is a deviation from a Biblical treatment of

[1268] Jacob Immanuel Schochet, *Mashiach: The Principle of Mashiach and the Messianic Era in Jewish Law and Tradition* (Brooklyn: S.I.E., 1992), 42.

[1269] Fruchtenbaum, *Messianic Christology*, 54. This whole section in Fruchtenbaum's book is very interesting and valuable (pp. 53-59).

[1270] Varner, *The Messiah: Revealed, Rejected, Received*, 84-85.

the Isaiah text where the sufferings and glories are plainly ascribed to one and the same person.[1271]

The next two paragraphs will show by examining the pronouns in Isaiah 53:2-7 that to interpret these verses to mean Israel is a grammatical impossibility.

In Isaiah 53:2-7, a large number of pronouns are used. In these verses the pronoun "*he*" (used 12 times), "*him*" (used 7 times), and "*his*" (used 3 times) refer to the person who is the subject of Isaiah 53. These 22 pronouns ("*he*," "*him*" and "*his*"), within the space of six verses, all point to this person and describe him. In the same verses other pronouns "*we*" (8 times), "*our*" (6 times), and "*us*" (once) refer to someone else 15 different times. When totaling all of the pronouns used in these six verses, there are 37 personal pronouns.

A close examination of the text gives strong evidence that these pronouns, "*we*" "*our*" and "*us*" cannot be referring to God, for God is not a sinner who has iniquities. These pronouns refer to Israel because they are sinners with iniquities. The "*he*," "*him*," and "*his*" clearly refer to "*the Servant of the LORD*" who is the *Moshiach* because the description cannot possibly be referring to Israel. If the Suffering Servant were Israel, verse 8 would mean that Israel was "*cut off*," executed or dead. Also if Isaiah 53 refers to Israel, then to whom does the phrase "*for the transgression of my people was he stricken*" refer? It does not fit Israel, even if you attempt to change the meaning by translating the "he" as "they" in Isaiah 53:8 as some try to do. It just does not fit the context! But when the person of *Yeshua* is placed in the context of Isaiah 53, and the sins and iniquities of Israel are laid upon him, that fits the context and the passage. In history, when Isaiah 53 is read, who does this passage fit? The answer is *Yeshua*.

One final point of importance about the term "*servant*" in Isaiah 53; there are several places in the servant passages of Isaiah where "*servant*" has two separate identities. First, it is used at times of the nation of Israel and second, it is also used of an individual who is the "*servant of the LORD*" as Varner expresses:

> How do we respond to that explanation in light of Isaiah 53:4-6? First, while there are some passages in the Book of Isaiah where the term "servant" does apply to Israel, there are other passages where it cannot refer to Israel. For example, consider Isaiah 49:6, "It is too light a thing that you should be my servant to raise up the tribes of Jacob and to bring back the preserved of Israel; I will make you as a light for the nations that my salvation may reach to the end of the earth." In other words, the servant is not identified as Israel in this verse, but as an individual who will bring Israel back to God.[1272]

[1271] Goldberg, *The Deviation of Jewish Thought from an Old Testament Theology in the Intertestamental Period,* 48.

[1272] Varner, *The Messiah: Revealed, Rejected, Received,* 84-85.

Mitch Glaser, a Jewish believer in Messiah, gives five brief statements and summary as to why this passage has to refer to Messiah and not Israel as the Suffering Servant. He states:

> Israel is not an innocent sufferer. Israel is not a silent sufferer. Israel never died. The text points to the suffering of an individual. The language makes it impossible for Israel to be the subject.… Once again, many other arguments can be made to demonstrate that the traditional Jewish interpretation of Isaiah 53 as a reference to the nation of Israel is simply not an accurate interpretation. Rather, it is an interpretation driven by history, culture, and politics, and not by the text.[1273]

This is not a complete discussion on Isaiah 53. But it is enough to demonstrate that Isaiah 53 refers to *Moshiach* and not to the nation of Israel.

Opening … Isaiah 61:1

> The Spirit of the Lord God is upon me; because the LORD hath anointed me to preach good tidings unto the meek; he hath sent me to bind up the brokenhearted, to proclaim liberty to the captives, and the opening of the prison to *them that are* bound (KJV).

Not only does this reflect the tri-unity of God as mentioned in chapter 10, but there is another element here that needs to be looked at. This is a recognized Messianic passage that *Yeshua* read in the synagogue in Nazareth. His reading of Isaiah 61:1-2a so upset the people of Nazareth that they wanted to kill *Yeshua*. This whole passage needs to be studied in light of other related passages that it is connected with. We will only look at one aspect briefly. The Hebrew word פְּקַח־קוֹחַ is translated "opening" in the King James Version while Kohlenberger in his interlinear renders it as "release."[1274]

This word is used in other passages such as Isaiah 42:7 in reference to opening the eyes of the blind as well as opening the ears in Isaiah 42:20. Rabbinic Judaism teaches that mankind does acts of sin, but that mankind does not have a sin nature imputed to them from Adam (see Appendix 1 and Romans 5:12-21). The reality is that the whole world has staggered under the weight of sin and that before Messiah can set up His righteous kingdom, He must first deal with sin that has brought spiritual separation from God, which includes spiritual blindness or darkness into the world. In Isaiah 42:7 it speaks to those who "*sit in darkness*" while back in verse 6 it speaks of the people of the Covenant, Israel, as well as the Gentiles. The following authors give their views on the term "opening" as it relates to this text and Messiah *Yeshua*:

[1273] Mitch Glaser, "The Use of Isaiah 53 in Jewish Evangelism," *Mishkan*, Issue 43 (2005), 40-41. [34-46].

[1274] Kohlenberger, *The Interlinear NIV Hebrew-English Old Testament,* 4:123.

The verbal form *peqakh-qoakh* is found only here, but the root, *pagqkh* normally refers to opening the eyes or ears (42:20), and in 42:7 this is associated with bringing people out of the darkness of prison.[1275]

The phrase rendered "the opening of the prison" should probably read as in the R.V. margin, "opening of the eyes" (as in 35:5; 42:7). There were many who were spiritually imprisoned and blinded by the religions of the Pharisees, Scribes and Sadducees (the Lord remarks upon their blindness in Matt. 23:24).[1276]

Isaiah is not speaking of deliverance from a physical prison but from the spiritual darkness in which the people had been imprisoned. Deliverance from that spiritual darkness is an opening of the eyes, in contrast to the darkness in which the people were.[1277]

For reasons which have been already given, the only natural sense which can be put upon the words is that of spiritual blindness and illumination.[1278]

Rabbinic Judaism does not believe in the two comings of the Messiah. They do see the need of redemption for the nation of Israel but they fail to understand that first there is also a need for the redemption of the people of the world from sin. There can be no righteousness upon the earth until all unrighteousness has been dealt with. In this passage the Messiah claims that righteousness will be given to the Jewish people in the last days.

This has long been recognized as a messianic passage. Why did *Yeshua* do the miracles in His public ministry to Israel, from healing the lame, the blind, and the deaf, cleansing the lepers, raising the dead? He was demonstrating that He had the power to inaugurate the Kingdom. But for that Kingdom to be put in place He had to be embraced by the leadership and the people, not only as Messiah but also as God Incarnate.

PROPHETS MICAH, JEREMIAH AND AMOS

The writings of Isaiah are not the only reference to the Messiah being divine; Micah, a contemporary of Isaiah and the later prophet Jeremiah also speak to the same end as Isaiah that Messiah is divine.

[1275] Larry L. Walker, *Cornerstone Biblical Commentary: Isaiah* (Wheaton, IL: Tyndale House Publishers, 2005), 263.

[1276] Vine, *Isaiah: Prophecies, Promises, Warnings,* 199.

[1277] Young, The *Book of Isaiah: Chapters 40-66,* 3:460.

[1278] Alexander, *Commentary on Isaiah: two volumes in one,* 2:397.

Born in Bethlehem ... Micah 5:2

> But thou, Bethlehem Ephratah, though thou be little among the thousands of Judah, yet out of thee shall he come forth unto me that is to be ruler in Israel; whose goings forth have been from of old, from everlasting (KJV).

This verse is understood among true Bible believers to not only give the birthplace of the *Moshiach* but also show His eternality. Jewish scholars likewise recognize this passage as being Messianic. In fact, "all ancient Jewish interpreters regarded the ruler as the Messiah." [1279] Barker goes on to comment that the Targums also favor the Messianic interpretation of the prophecy. Goldman adds a divisive twist to the interpretation by stating that this passage refers to the house of David that originated in Bethlehem. Goldman quotes David Altschul, who reflects his view:

> Not that the Messiah will be born in Bethlehem, but that his origin of old, through David, will be Bethlehem. [1280]

The above statement is very convenient. The Jewish people today do not know what tribe they are from, let alone a future *moshiach* coming if he could prove he was a descendant from the house of David. The fact is that if the *Moshiach* would appear today, he could not prove that he was from the line of David because the Jewish people do not know their tribal origin. They know only that they are Jewish.

Hengstenberg gives a response to the Jewish authors who argue that *Moshiach* does not have to be born in Bethlehem. It is a convenient belief for them because Jewish people today do not know their tribal ancestry. Today (2010) it is doubtful if any Jewish people even live in Bethlehem:

> The reference to the Messiah was, at all times, not the private opinion of a few scholars, but was publicly received, and acknowledged with perfect unanimity. As respects the time of Christ, this is obvious from Matt 2:5. According to that passage, the whole Sanhedrin, when officially interrogated as to the birthplace of the Messiah, supposed this explanation to be the only correct one. But if this proof required a corroboration, it might be derived from John 7:41-42. In that passage, several who erroneously supposed Christ to be a native of Galilee, objected to His being Messiah on the ground that Scripture says [the Messiah was to be born in Bethlehem.] [1281]

Hengstenberg makes it completely clear that *Moshiach* was to be born in Bethlehem, and that is exactly what the Jewish leadership understood when Herod inquired about the *Moshiach*'s place of birth (Matthew 2:4-8).

[1279] Kenneth L. Barker, *The New American Commentary: Micah* (21 vols. Nashville: Broadman, 1998), 97.

[1280] S. Goldman, *The Soncino Books of the Bible: The Twelve Prophets* (New York: Soncino Press, 1994), 175.

[1281] Hengstenberg, *Christology of the Old Testament,* 1:491.

There are two primary phrases that need to be studied: (1) *"whose goings forth have been from old"* and (2) *"from everlasting."* These are important because Jewish scholars state that *Moshiach* is not eternal, and was created by the Father.[1282] So, do these phrases reflect eternity or just antiquity? Barker points out that there are two possible readings of the text. One says, "whose origins are from of old, from ancient time," which does not necessitate being eternal. He reflects the Jewish understanding, as well as liberal Christian theologians in the following quote:

> Those who prefer the main text that the expression *mime olam* refers to the ancient "origins" of the Messiah in the line of David.... The stress is on the "origins" of the future Davidic ruler in the Davidic town of Bethlehem.... The Davidic roots of the coming ruler are emphasized by the prophet Micah.... Certainly the deity and eternality of the Messiah are still plainly taught in other passages.[1283]

An NIV footnote provides an alternative rendering: *"whose goings out are from of old, from days of eternity."* Many prefer the reading in the NIV footnote rather than the main text because of the use of the word "eternity." Eternity, or *olam*, when used of God has eternity in view, but when used of man has only time in view. Jewish authors would like the main text interpretation because it falls in line with Goldman's argument that Messiah is only eternal in the mind of God:

> *goings forth,* i.e. lineage

> from ancient days. The Midrash (Pirke de Rabbi Eliezer, ch. 3) interprets this phrase as alluding to the doctrine that Messiah existed in the mind of God from time immemorial, as part of the Creator's plan at the inception of the universe."[1284]

If Micah 5:2 were the only Messianic reference, these arguments might carry more weight. But with all the preparation by God to ready His people for the *Moshiach* through the words of Moses and the Prophets, plus all the plural references to God, this view is impossible to accept. In the following statements, the reality of the eternality of the Messiah is more in line with the theme and content of the *Tanakh* and Micah. It was noted at the beginning of this chapter that the word *olam* can carry two concepts, time and eternity. *Olam*, when used in conjunction with God, who is not confined and bound by time and lives outside of space, refers to His eternality. The following author points to two perspectives, one by Jewish and liberal Christian scholars and the other by believers who take this passage with all that the *Tanakh* has to say and conclude that what this reference (Micah 5:2) states is that the *Moshiach* is eternal:

[1282] Patai, *The Messiah Texts*, 16-17, 19.

[1283] Barker, *The New American Commentary: Micah,* 97-98.

[1284] Goldman, *The Soncino Books of the Bible: The Twelve Prophets,* 175.

"Goings forth;" "from of old;" "from everlasting". The Jewish rabbis in the Christian era refer these words either to the naming of the Messiah's name in eternity or to the idea of the Messiah existing in God's mind before the creation of the world. Rationalistic interpreters of the early nineteenth century generally adopted these interpretations. Modern Jewish and Protestant interpreters generally refer "from of old," "from everlasting," to the time of the rise of the Davidic dynasty.[1285]

Here Laetsch points not just to Micah 5:2 but to the many references that would not have special significance for tracing one's lineage back to Abraham or Adam:

Yet a lineage dating back to ancient times could not possibly have served as a special characteristic of the future Ruler. Every descendant of David and even of Abraham and Adam could trace his lineage back to creation. Nor can the words denote "the many preparations made by God from the earliest times in prophecy and history for the founding of the Messianic kingdom." For the words speak not of the founding of a kingdom, nor of the preparations for such a kingdom, nor of the prophecies of the going forth of the Ruler. The prophet here speaks of the goings forth and of the birth of a future Ruler.[1286]

Laetsch presents the Jewish view as well as the modern rationalistic interpretations of Christians. He gives a logical augmentation for viewing *Moshiach* as eternal, before time, but without using the word *olam*. Feinberg, a Jewish believer, makes the following statement that the use of words in verse 2 is the strongest possible for infinite duration and preexistence of the Messiah:

These goings forth were in creation, in His appearances to the patriarchs and throughout the Old Testament history of redemption. The phrases of this text are the strongest possible statement of infinite duration in the Hebrew language (Psa 90:2; Prov 8:22-23). The preexistence of the Messiah is being taught here, as well as His active participation in ancient times in the purposes of God.[1287]

Henderson observes that Micah is speaking of one who is eternal and has been active in the affairs of man in the past:

His goings forth, when he created the world, and appeared to Moses and the patriarchs, and revealed to them the Divine will.[1288]

In discussing the concept that the *Moshiach* is eternal, Hailey considers the verse with the same idea but with a different approach:

[1285] Laetsch, *The Minor Prophets,* 272.
[1286] Laetsch, *The Minor Prophets,* 272.
[1287] Charles Feinberg, *The Minor Prophets*, 173.
[1288] Henderson, *Thornapple Commentaries: The Twelve Minor Prophets,* 249.

From here would come the one through whom the "former dominion" would be restored. "Whose goings forth are from of old, from everlasting" indicates more than that He descends from an ancient lineage; it relates Him to God, the eternal One. His rule reaches back into eternity. The priests and scribes of Herod's day recognized that the Messiah would be born in Bethlehem.[1289]

Barnes points out that the *Moshiach* did not come forth from Bethlehem, but that His going forth was from eternity, and must be the incarnation of an eternal person in Bethlehem:

Whose goings forth have been *from of old, from everlasting*, lit. *from the days of eternity. Going forth* is opposed *to going forth; a going forth out of* Bethlehem, to *a going forth from eternity; a going forth*, which then was still to come, (the Prophet says, shall go forth) to a *going forth* which had been long ago, not from the world but from the beginning, not in the days of time, but *from the days of eternity.*[1290]

Jamison, Fausset and Brown equally state that the phrase *"from the days of eternity"* shows the divinity of the Messiah:

Whose goings forth have been from old, from everlasting – lit., from the days of eternity, or the days of the ages [מִימֵי עוֹלָם]. The plain antithesis of this clause, "come forth out of thee" (from Bethlehem), shows that the eternal generation of the Son is meant. The terms convey the strongest assertion of infinite duration of which the Hebrew language is capable (Psa 110:2; Prov 8:22-23; John 1:1). Messiah's generation as man, coming forth unto God, to do His will on earth, is from Bethlehem; but as Son of God His goings forth are from everlasting[1291]

Throughout the *Tanakh* there is much emphasis on the *Moshiach* and the Kingdom that He will bring. According to Goldberg, what Micah 5:2 does is clearly present the God/man aspect of this child to be born:

There is much emphasis on the Messiah and his kingdom. However, the Messiah was regarded as only human. Micah 5:2 has always been regarded as a Messianic passage; thus, the Messiah is to be a human governor of Israel, born in Bethlehem. But this is only part of the truth. This human governor is also described as one "whose goings forth have been from the days of eternity. (see Goldberg's note on page 116.) Clearly, here is a distinct individual, human and also divine. The divine nature is seen from the fact that God has existed from

---

[1289] Homer Hailey, *The Minor Prophets* (Grand Rapids: Baker, 1972), 209.

[1290] Albert Barnes, *Barnes' Notes: Minor Prophets* (2 vols. Grand Rapids: Baker, 1950), 2:70.

[1291] Jamison, Fausset and Brown, *A Commentary: Critical, Experimental and Practical on the Old and New Testaments,* 4:600.

435

the days of eternity. Therefore, Messiah, from an Old Testament concept, is to be more than just human.[1292]

Lastly, Kaiser refers to the Hebrew word *olam* and the fact that, when used in conjunction with God, it refers to eternity:

> But this Ruler was not a recent creation, for even though He would be born in Bethlehem, He had existed from eternity. When the Hebrew word for "everlasting" olam, is used in connection with God, it can only mean "from eternity on" (Psa 25:6; 90:2). That can be its only meaning here if the Ruler is none other than the Son of God, the Messiah.[1293]

Levine refers to the true believers and their view on Micah 5:2 as "a figment of someone's imagination." Then he moves on to show his complete lack of understanding of the texts that he references. I will personally illustrate the complete lack of biblical scholarship used by some anti-missionaries that I experienced while attending an anti-missionary meeting at a Jewish Community Center in Lancaster, PA. It was disheartening to see that the main presenter did not present biblical evidence for his position but rather used emotional, sentimental dogmatisms while giving biased half-truths and inadequate information to the Jewish community in attendance that did not know any better. Here is one of the statements used by Levine in his discussion on Micah 5:2:

> There is a basic question altogether as to whether or not Jesus came from David in the first place. In Matthew chapter 1, there is an entire genealogy which purports to show that Jesus does indeed come from David. However, there is a very serious problem there, for the genealogy shows that Joseph, the husband of Mary was from David, but he was not the father of Jesus. What is the point of showing that Joseph is from David, if Joseph is not the father of Jesus?[1294]

As is detailed in chapter 17 of this book, Levine shows his complete bias and willful ignorance of the New Testament text in relation to the genealogies of Joseph and Miriam (Mary), which he willfully passes on to an even more naive Jewish community who swallows the teachings of these "professed biblical scholars." Truth is sometimes a premium.

The Branch – THE LORD OUR RIGHTEOUSNESS … Jeremiah 23:5-6

> See, a time is coming, declares the LORD, when I will raise up a true branch of David's line. He shall reign as king and shall prosper, and he shall do what is just and right in the land. In his days Judah shall be delivered and Israel shall

---

[1292] Goldberg, *The Deviation of Jewish Thought from an Old Testament Theology in the Intertestamental Period,* 116.

[1293] Kaiser, *The Communicator's Commentary: Micah-Malachi,* 64.

[1294] Levine, *You Take Jesus, I'll Take God; How to Refute Christian Missionaries,* 35-36.

dwell secure. And this is the name by which he shall be called: The LORD is our Vindicator.

Behold, the days come, saith the LORD, that I will raise unto David a righteous Branch, and a King shall reign and prosper, and shall execute judgment and justice in the earth. In his days Judah shall be saved, and Israel shall dwell safely: and this is his name whereby he shall be called, THE LORD OUR RIGHTEOUSNESS. (KJV)

For this passage it is necessary to understand both the historical and spiritual climate of Judah. To briefly summarize, Judah had had a series of wicked kings (Ahaz, Manasseh, and Amon) whose reigns totaled around 75 years. Their reigns were full of wickedness and apostasy by the kings and the people. In fact, Manasseh reigned for 55 years and was the most wicked of all the kings of Judah (2 Kings 21; 23:26-27; 24:3-4; 2 Chronicles 34:23-25; Jeremiah 15:4). The spiritual condition of Judah was very poor. Assyria was the world power but had a growing concern about the rise of the Babylonians. Josiah was a very righteous king and instituted a revival, but it was only a surface movement, because after Josiah, the righteous king, was killed in 609 BC, each of his three sons and a grandson would reign in turn on the throne. These three sons and grandson were all wicked, and Judah quickly lapsed back into sin and idolatry (Ezekiel 8-11). The common denominator is that these last four kings, who came to the throne in a short span of 20 years, did evil in the sight of the LORD and created an unstable and insecure kingdom of Judah. The spiritual state of Judah was absolute rebellion against God as 2 Kings 23:30 – 25:30; 2 Chronicles 36; Ezekiel 8-11 and other passages bear out. Jeremiah was the prophet of God in Jerusalem during this period through the reign of Josiah and his three sons and grandson. The sons and grandson of Josiah can be confusing so listed below is some personal information on their reigns and order of their reigns.

1. Jaohaz, the middle son of Josiah, was crowned king by Judah at the age of 23. He did evil in the sight of the LORD (2 Kings 23:31-32), and after three months he was deposed by Egypt and taken there in exile.

2. Eliakim, the firstborn, was 25 years old when Pharaoh Necho of Egypt renamed him Jehoiakim and appointed him as king over Judah. He did evil in the sight of the LORD (2 Kings 23:37), reigned for 11 years and died.

3. Jehoiachin, the 18 year old son of Jehoiakim, reigned only 3 months before Nebuchadnezzar conquered rebellious Judah and took them into captivity. He also did evil in the sight of the LORD (2 Kings 24:9).

4. Mattaniah was the third son of Josiah and was 21 when he was appointed king by Nebuchadnezzar. Nebuchadnezzar changed his name to Zedekiah. Zedekiah did evil in the sight of the LORD (2 Kings 24:19) and rebelled against Babylon in his 11th year. So Babylon came again and destroyed

Judah, Jerusalem and the Temple. Zedekiah's sons were put to death before his eyes, and then he was blinded for life.[1295]

With this spiritual and historical background in view, there are two significant portions of Scripture in Jeremiah 22 and 23 which had a direct bearing on Judah, both then and in the distant future, one of judgment and the other of promise. In Jeremiah 22:24-30 *Yahweh* cursed Coniah or Jehoiachin, the grandson of Josiah, the king and his descendants in a dogmatic statement that in the future none of his descendants would again reign on the throne of David.[1296] When Coniah was deposed, his uncle Zedekiah, the third son of Josiah, was made king. The kings of Judah were so wicked, especially Coniah, that God, through the prophet, made a severe statement of judgment against his part of the Davidic line in what appears to be an unalterable decree against Coniah and his descendants. In leading up to Jeremiah 23:5-6 *Yahweh* declares this: "*Woe to the shepherds who are destroying and scattering the sheep of my pasture!*" These evil kings, and the ones before them, have destroyed God's people, and God is about to deal with them and the people for their sins. God's promise in verses 5-6 is not a new promise but a clarification of the Davidic Covenant concerning a good Shepherd. *Yeshua* draws from Ezekiel 34 and Zechariah 11 as He refers to Himself as the Good Shepherd in John 10:11. This was not just an illustration, He was referencing back to the *Tanakh*.[1297]

The first item in verse 5 to draw attention is the phrase "*When I will raise up a true branch of David's line*" and that He will "*reign as king and shall prosper, and he shall do what is just and right in the land.*" Fruchtenbaum states in the following comment that the *Moshiach* will be a descendant of David:

> The kingship of Messiah is yet to come, but this verse clearly speaks of Messiah as a descendent of David and thus stresses His humanity.[1298]

The one thing that rings clear, whether in Judaism or Christianity, in the understanding of this verse it speaks of a human descendant of David that would be king and shepherd over his people Israel. Keil and Delitzsch affirm that the one who is "*raised up*" is "*my servant David*":

> Neither of these sayings can be spoken of a series of kings. Besides, we have the passages Jer 30:9; Ezek 34:23; 37:24, where the servant to be raised up to David by Jehovah is called "my servant David."[1299]

[1295] Leon Wood, *A Survey of Israel's History* (Grand Rapids: Zondervan, 1970), 370-376.

[1296] *Davidic kingly line*: David had several sons, the most famous being Solomon. Solomon's line is the subject of Jeremiah 22:24-30. Another lesser known son was Nathan who was not involved in the curse. Messiah could not come from Solomon's line, but Nathan's line was not involved in the curse of Coniah.

[1297] Robert Davidson, *The Daily Study Bible Series: Jeremiah and Lamentations* (2 vols. Philadelphia: Westminster, 1985), 1:25.

[1298] Fruchtenbaum, *Messianic Christology*, 62.

In the beginning of 23:5, Jeremiah says, *"See, a time is coming."* That phrase is a common expression for the Messianic era as we see in Jeremiah 31:27-34.[1299] Jeremiah proceeds to use that phrase three times, emphasizing the Messianic era (verses 27, 29, 31 – KJV *"Behold, the days come"*). The last usage, Jeremiah 31:31, is the promise of the New Covenant which started at the Feast of *Shavuot*, also known as Pentecost and would not be fulfilled until the end of the tribulation, or the time of Jacob's trouble, and then into the Kingdom when Israel says concerning Messiah *Yeshua, "Blessed is he that cometh in the name of the Lord"* (Psalm 118:26; Matthew 23:39). Clearly, these references verify that the *Moshiach* is a true human being.[1301]

The *Moshiach*, whose human descent is through David's line, will reign in three descriptive ways, righteously, wisely, and justly. The *Moshiach* who will reign this way is in stark contrast to the reign of Coniah and the curse placed upon his descendants in Jeremiah 22:24-30,[1302] as well as to the bad shepherds, the kings, priests and other leaders in Jeremiah 23:1. Both Huey[1303] and Davidson[1304] point out an even sharper contrast between the meaning of Zedekiah's name, *"the Lord our righteousness,"* and his reign, which was unlike the promised reign of the *"righteous Branch"* in the following comment:

> This message was most likely delivered during the reign of King Zedekiah. His name means the Lord is righteous or the Lord is my righteousness. The name of the new ruler was intended as a repudiation of Zedekiah. He will be an exact opposite of rulers such as Zedekiah and Jehoiakim. He will be called "the Lord Our Righteousness." The name of this coming ruler implies that a time will come when all the people will acknowledge the Lord as the only source of righteousness.[1305]

The word for "Branch" is the Hebrew word *"Zemach,"* which is never used to denote a twig but to indicate a sprout growing directly out from the root of the original tree forming a new second tree.[1306] This "Branch" will be righteous by nature, not an acquired righteousness. Feinberg clarifies that this reference to the Branch, which is called *"THE LORD OUR RIGHTEOUSNESS,"* is used symbolically of the *Moshiach*. It is not being used horticulturally but is used as a technical term for the *Moshiach*, as Feinberg explains its usage:

[1299] Keil and Delitzsch, *Commentary on the Old Testament: Jeremiah,* 8:350.

[1300] Laetsch, *Bible Commentary: Jeremiah,* 189.

[1301] Laetsch, *Bible Commentary: Jeremiah,* 190.

[1302] Walvoord and Zuck, *The Bible Knowledge Commentary: Old Testament,* 1158.

[1303] F. B. Huey, *Bible Study Commentary: Jeremiah* (Grand Rapids: Zondervan, 1981), 77.

[1304] Davidson, *The Daily Study Bible Series: Jeremiah and Lamentations,* 1:25.

[1305] F. B. Huey, *The New American Commentary: Jeremiah, Lamentations* (Nashville: Broadman, 1993), 212.

[1306] Laetsch, *Bible Commentary: Jeremiah,* 190.

It is clear that the term "Branch" is symbolic of the Messiah because the adjective modifying it is a quality of persons and not plants. The shoot or sprout is a scion of the stock of David. "Branch" has a collective meaning when used horticulturally but not when used symbolically. "Branch,"…a Technical Term in the Prophets.[1307]

This term, *"the BRANCH,"* in the post-exilic times became a technical term for the expected ideal king as noted by the prophet Zechariah (3:8; 6:12).[1308] Interestingly, Jeremiah was not the first to use the term "Branch," for Isaiah had used it (Isaiah 4:2; 11:1-2) a hundred years before Jeremiah.

All this groundwork from verse 5, as to the humanity and righteousness of the future Son of David, leads up to verse 6. Two items in verse 6 need to be discussed: first *"his name"* and *"whereby he shall be called, THE LORD OUR RIGHTEOUSNESS."* When *Adonai Elohim* states the name of the Son of David, it becomes clear that God is using this name because He knows the nature and essence of the future Son of David, the *Moshiach*:

> We must not overlook the unusual manner in which this name is introduced. The Lord does not merely say: His name is or shall be, nor: Call Him, nor: Call His name, nor: This shall He be called. He uses a phraseology unique in the entire Old Testament, occurring only here. "And this (is) His name which one shall call Him." That is not idle redundancy. Two facts of greatest importance are stressed. The first one: "This (is) His name. Name, as used here by the Lord, is not a mere label or tag, but designates the very nature, the essence and being of the Branch. And secondly, He expresses His will that mankind should know this *Zemach* and acknowledge Him and call Him by that name, given to Him by the Lord God of Hosts, which describes to us His inmost essence, as Jehovah Himself knows and understands it.[1309]

The individual's name in Jeremiah 23:5, *"THE LORD OUR RIGHTEOUSNESS"* is God. This man who will be the *Moshiach*, who will be the Righteous Branch and who will be raised up unto David, is the LORD. This man's name, by the very mouth of *Adonai Elohim*, is *"THE LORD OUR RIGHTEOUSNESS."* This *Moshiach* is the God/man. Fruchtenbaum notes that even sources from rabbinic writings support that conclusion:

> In the Midrash on Proverbs 19:21 (200 – 500 A. D.) it says: "Rabbi Hunah said Eight names are given to the Messiah which are: Yinnon, Shiloh, David, Menachem, Jehovah, Justi de Nostra, Tsemmach, Elias."[1310]

[1307] Charles L. Feinberg, *Jeremiah* (Grand Rapids: Zondervan, 1982), 162.

[1308] J. A. Thompson, *The New International Commentary on the Old Testament: The Book of Jeremiah* (Grand Rapids: Eerdmans, 1980), 489.

[1309] Laetsch, *Bible Commentary: Jeremiah,* 195.

[1310] Fruchtenbaum, *Messianic Christology*, 62.

Yet modern day rabbis basically teach that the Messiah will evolve into righteousness, which is completely contrary to the naming of *"the Branch"* by God Himself. Notice the following statement:

> Mashiach is a human being, born in normal fashion of human parents. The only qualification about his origins is that he is a descendant of King David, through the lineage of his son Solomon. From his birth onwards his righteousness will increase continually, and by virtue of his deeds he will merit sublime levels of spiritual perfection.[1311]

There are several faulty statements by Rabbi Schochet. First the *Moshiach* will be born normally, but His conception is supernatural (Isaiah 7:14; Matthew 1:2-21). Secondly, His righteousness will not increase by virtue of His deeds and merit levels of spiritual perfection, for the LORD says through Jeremiah (23:5-6) that He is Righteousness; it is part of His very nature.

To add to the divine nature of the one who has righteousness inherent within him a Jewish Midrash (rabbinic commentary) on Proverbs 19:21 as previously mentioned makes that following interesting statement:

> Rabbi Hunah said, "Eight names are given to the Messiah which are: Yinnon, Shiloh, David, Menachem, *Jehovah*, Justi de Nostra, *Tzemmach*, Elias."

Notice the fifth name and seventh name from the quote just cited, Jehovah, the name of God which is based on Jeremiah 23:6 and *Tzemmach* or Branch which is based on Jeremiah 23:5. Observe three other references quoted from rabbinic sources:

> In the Midrash on Lamentations 1:16, it says, "What is the name of Messiah?" Rav Ava Ben Kahanna said, "Jehovah is his name and this is proved by, this is his name ... [quoting Jeremiah 23:6]."

Clearly, the name of the *Moshiach* in this Midrash quotation identifies the *Moshiach* as Jehovah *"THE LORD OUR RIGHTEOUSNESS."*

> In the Talmud (Babba Bathra Tractate 75b) it says: Shmuel ben Nachman said in the name of Rabbi Yohanan, "the following three will be named with the name of the Holy One blessed be he – the upright, as it is said, [quotes Isa 43:7], the Messiah, as it is written and this is his name whereby he shall be called THE LORD OUR RIGHTEOUSNESS [quoting Jeremiah 23:6]."

In this tractate of the Talmud, one rabbi using the source authority of another rabbi clearly sees the *Moshiach* as the LORD, for that is His name.

> In the Midrash on Psalm 21:1 it says: God calls King Messiah by his own name, but what is his name? The answer is "Jehovah is a man of war

---

[1311] Schochet, *Mashiach: The Principle of Mashiach and the Messianic Era in Jewish Law and Tradition,* 37-38.

(Exod 15:3)" and concerning Messiah we read "Jehovah our righteousness this is his name."[1312]

Because this passage is used by New Covenant believers in pointing to *Yeshua* many Jewish people stumble over it. Remember, Rabbinic Judaism does not believe in two comings of *Moshiach*, even though the more orthodox see two different messiahs coming once each. Rabbinic Judaism emphatically and categorically denies the whole concept of the second coming. Jeremiah does not deal with the first coming at all except that He would be the God/man, and the Son of David. Levine comments again, because of the second coming issues, that *Yeshua* could not be the one in view in this verse because He did not fulfill any of it. In respect to *Yeshua*'s first coming, that is correct, for it will all be fulfilled in the second coming and that is where Levine's problem lies, as he states:

> This passage, which supposedly refers to Jesus because of the reference to the branch of David, has all the difficulties described in the "proof" mentioned before this one, plus some new ones. This passage has certainly not been fulfilled yet, for this branch of David shall be a reigning king, who shall execute justice, which Jesus did not fulfill. In the days of this branch, Judah and Israel shall be saved and will prosper. However, shortly after the death of Jesus, the second temple and the Jewish state in Israel were destroyed. The name to be given to this branch of David was to be the Lord Our Righteousness, not Jesus, nor Yeshua, etc. The whole passage clearly has not occurred yet, nor does it point exclusively to Jesus, nor was Jesus from David.[1313]

Levine is partly correct; *Yeshua* did not do what Jeremiah 23:5-6 states, because He had to deal with the issue of sin that separates man from God before He would set up His kingdom on the throne of His father David.

Simply speaking, Levine, whether he is speaking of Jeremiah 23:5-6 or of the genealogy of *Moshiach,* lays out old unbiblical falsehoods as they relate to *Yeshua.* Stating that *Yeshua*, because he was not the physical son of Joseph, was not a Son of David at all shows complete lack of understanding of Luke 3. His reasoning is faulty and as far as his discussion on this verse being a theological and historical discussion on the subject, to use his own words, "absurd." It is no wonder that when Jewish people are truly searching out the claims of *Yeshua,* they look upon such arguments as ridiculous and they are actually drawn to *Yeshua* and not repelled.

When all of the factors are laid out from Jeremiah 23:5-6, along with the ancient Jewish commentary on the verse, the *Moshiach*, the Promised One of Israel, is the physical Son of David. God not only shows the humanity of the *Moshiach* but that His name is to be called "*THE LORD OUR RIGHTEOUSNESS*." It is interesting to note that Rabbi Cohen in the Soncino series on Jeremiah totally denies the Righteous Branch

---

[1312] Fruchtenbaum, *Messianic Christology*, 62-63.
[1313] Levine, *You Take Jesus, I'll Take God*: How To Refute Christian Missionaries, 52-53.

as being the LORD our Righteousness.[1314] However, when the passage is taken literally, it leaves no doubt that the *Moshiach* is God Incarnate, who came in the person of *Yeshua* of Nazareth. For additional material on this passage, refer to chapter 17 of this book under the subject of the Branch.

The LORD's God ... Amos 4:11

I have wrought destruction among you as **when God** destroyed Sodom and Gomorrah; You have become like a brand plucked from burning. Yet you have not turned back **to Me – declares the LORD.**

This verse belongs to a larger judgment passage against the northern kingdom called Israel that went into captivity in 722 BCE by the Assyrians. Amos ministered to Israel about 50 years before, during the days of Jeroboam II, who led Israel to its zenith in power. In this chapter Amos gives a series of five judgment warnings which Israel will not heed (verses 1-11) and a reoccurring phase is used by the Lord God as He speaks of coming judgment if they do not repent. Those words are *"Yet have ye not returned unto me"* in verses 6, 8, 9, 10, 11, 12.

In Amos 4 the speaker is identified as the Lord God in verse 2. However as He gives the judgment statements against Israel He speaks as *Yahweh* or the LORD in verses 6, 8, 9, 10, and 11. In verses 11-13 the LORD refers to Himself as *Elohim*. As a quick reminder from chapter 3 of this book, the word *Yahweh* is a singular word and *Elohim* is a plural word, both used for God. In verse 11 *Yahweh* references the historical event of the destruction of Sodom and Gomorrah. Where *Yahweh* used the first person pronoun "I" and He made a distinction between Himself and *Elohim* who destroyed Sodom and Gomorrah. If you reference back to Genesis 19:24 it is not God that destroyed the cities, but the LORD or *Yahweh* who rained down fire and brimstone from the LORD or *Yahweh* in heaven. In Genesis you clearly have the plurality of *Yahweh* referenced by the use of two *Yahwehs* who are separate and distinct from each other and yet one (*echad*). Once again the Almighty is the one communicating His word. If He is one G-d as Rabbinic Judaism states then why didn't He use *El* or *Eloah* which are singular words for God but He did not. What we have here again is a reference to the plurality of God in the book of Amos.

In reading through two dozen commentaries in my library, only two even mention the possibility of the plurality of God. One author mentioned it as a possibility but then discards it in the following statement:

[1314] A. Cohen, *The Soncino Books of the Bible: Jeremiah* (New York: Soncino Press, 1985), 152-153.

The reading "the great overthrow," using Elohim as a superlative, is grammatically possible, but out of harmony with the context.[1315]

As to being out of harmony with the context, it is in reality clearly in harmony with both contexts, Genesis 19:24 and Amos 4:11. In Genesis 19:24 you have a plural context with two LORDs and in the Amos 4:11 context you have the LORD making a clear distinct between Himself and *Elohim*, once again showing plurality, notice the wording "*I have wrought destruction among you as when God [Elohim] destroyed Sodom and Gomorrah.*" Also notice in verse 12 where *Yahweh* says "*Prepare to meet your God, O Israel*" as well as verse 13 the One speaking is the Creator and "*His name is the LORD, the God of Hosts.*" In these two verses *Yahweh* refers to Himself in the plural and not the singular. The second of the two authors that mention plurality is very clear as to what he sees in this statement:

> As Jehovah from Jehovah rained hell out of heaven upon them, Gen 19:24, that is God the Son from God the Father.[1316]

He clearly sees that plurality of God in this passage which is a verse that most everyone has passed over.

ZECHARIAH 11:12-13; 12:10; 13:7

These next three passages are all connected and should be approached as a unit, because two of them present *Yahweh* as experiencing something that only a human being can experience. There are some key words in these passages, and they are tied together around one person, the Messiah: "*Shepherd,*" "*pierced,*" "*My Shepherd*" and "*My Associate.*" In Zechariah 11:12-13, and 12:10, the question is who in history do these passages describe? There is not a lack of material as to the Messianic references to *Yeshua* on these passages. Numerous scholars agree on the God/man aspect and see *Yeshua* as the central person fulfilling these passages: Baron,[1317] Feinberg,[1318] Unger,[1319] Fruchtenbaum,[1320] Brown,[1321] Merrill,[1322] Kaiser,[1323] Hartman,[1324] and Barrett.[1325]

[1315] William Rainey Harper, *A Critical and Exegetical Commentary on Amos and Hosea.* (Edinburgh: T & T Clark, 1994), 101.

[1316] John Trapp, *Commentary or Exposition upon the Twelve Minor Prophets* (Richard D. Dickinson, London, 1867), 196.

[1317] Baron, *The Visions and Prophecies of Zechariah*, 379-380, 403-404, 437-440, 447-449, 474-477.

[1318] Feinberg, *God Remembers: A Study of the Book of Zechariah*, 208-209, 229-231, 244-246.

[1319] Unger, *Zechariah: Prophet of Messiah's Glory*, 199, 216-217, 230-232.

[1320] Fruchtenbaum, *Messianic Christology*, 67-74.

[1321] Brown, *Answering Jewish Objections*, 3:37-38, 149-151.

[1322] Merrill, *An Exegetical Commentary: Haggai, Zechariah, Malachi*, 297-298, 320-321, 335-336.

[1323] Kaiser, *The Communicator's Commentary: Micah – Malachi*, 394-395, 405-406, 413.

444

The Jewish interpretation is to distance themselves from anything that would even hint of *Yeshua* being the fulfillment of these passages because they do not believe in the plural unity or tri-unity of God. Rabbis had to deal with these passages to suppress the obvious prophecies of *Yeshua* the *Moshiach* being *Yahweh*. These will be referenced just a little later as each passage is dealt with separately.

30 Pieces of Silver ... Zechariah 11:12-13

(12) And I said unto them, If ye think good, give me my price; and if not, forbear. So they weighed for my price thirty pieces of silver. (13) And the LORD said unto me, cast it unto the potter: a goodly price that I was apprised at of them. And I took the thirty pieces of silver, and cast them to the potter in the house of the LORD.

Zechariah 11:4-14 speaks of the good Shepherd that ministers to the flock of Israel, but his leadership is not wanted by the "flock" or the people of Israel. First, in 11:4, Zechariah, speaking for *Yahweh*, refers to Him as *Yahweh* my *Elohim* (LORD my God). The first person pronouns (I, my, me) appear 23 times in these verses, three times in verse 6, five times in verse 7, four times in verse 8, twice in verse 9, four times in verse 10, once in verse 11, three times in verse 12 and once in verse 14. The backdrop of this passage is that Zechariah is to act out the part of the shepherd for the LORD. *Yahweh* also took two staves called Beauty (verse 10) and Bands (verse 14) and cut them apart, breaking His covenant with the nations and between Israel and Judah. Because of Israel's rejection of His leadership as the good Shepherd, *Yahweh*, the "Shepherd" asks them for His wages. The significance of the two staves is clearly given by Feinberg in his following statement:

The names of the staves imply the blessings flowing from the ministry of the Shepherd: the favor [beauty] of God toward Israel in keeping their enemies from destroying them, and the bonds [union] whereby He kept brother and brother united within the nations.[1326]

The rejection of the Shepherd of Israel by the leadership of Israel in the days of *Yeshua* became a reality in 70 CE when the LORD who was valued at 30 pieces of silver permitted Rome to destroy Israel, Jerusalem and the Temple Mount from without (favor). Also, the lack of cohesion of the defenders within the walls of Jerusalem was removed (union), brother against brother, on the inside of the walls of Jerusalem. Before the wages issue is dealt with, the identity of the Shepherd needs to be determined in Zechariah. On the surface the Shepherd appears to be *Yahweh* and it is. However, the picture that the Shepherd describes concerning His wages leads to an

---

[1324] Fred Hartman, *Zechariah: Israel's Messenger of the Messiah's Triumph* (Bellmawr, NJ: Friends of Israel Gospel Ministry, 1994), 111-112, 129.

[1325] Barrett, *Beginning at Moses*, 236-237.

[1326] Feinberg, *God Remembers: A Study of the Book of Zechariah*, 205.

445

additional conclusion. David Baron adds some valuable insight as to the identity of the "Shepherd" who is also addressed as *Yahweh*. What is discovered is that *Yahweh* is *Yeshua*:

> But it practically comes to much the same thing, whether we regard the prophet as representing in his actions as shepherd, Jehovah, or more directly the Messiah, for the coming of the Messiah is often spoken of in the Old Testament as the coming of Jehovah. In Ezek 34 for instance, Jehovah Himself is represented, in His capacity as the true Shepherd of Israel, as seeking, saving, strengthening, healing, and satisfying His people; but as we read on in that chapter we become aware that it is not Jehovah directly who is going to do all this, but *immediately* through the Messiah. "*And I will set them up one shepherd over them, and He shall feed them, even My servant David; He shall feed them, and He shall be their shepherd*" (Ezek 34:23) namely, the true David, the Messiah as the Jews themselves have always rightly interpreted this passage.[1327]

The Shepherd is none other than *Yeshua*, the Good Shepherd (John 10:11). This will also be seen shortly as the rest of this passage is studied. The Good Shepherd asked for His wages. He did not give a demand, but asked for a voluntary response: "If you are satisfied, pay me my wages; if not, don't." The Good Shepherd was not looking for money but for spiritual qualities or spiritual fruit. Feinberg and Baron make similar observations concerning the wages that the good Shepherd desired:

> He was requesting of them fruitage from His ministry, such as piety, godly fear, devotion, and love and they gave Him instead that which was far worse than a direct refusal (Matt 21:33-41).[1328]

> The wages which He actually sought from them for all His Shepherd care, was, as the commentators rightly understand, the spiritual fruit of His labours – repentance, faith, true heart piety, humble obedience and grateful love. This is brought out clearly in the Lord's parable of the Vineyard, which is Israel, to whom He first sent His servants, and then His own son, "that He might receive the fruits of it."[1329]

But the Jewish leadership considered *Yahweh's* entire ministry to them as worthless, and what they offered Him was an insult. Their response of 30 pieces of silver was a statement, not just an act of payment for services rendered. Their act of payment for how they viewed His ministry to them was that He was totally unworthy and worthless

---

[1327] Baron, *The Visions and Prophecies of Zechariah*, 380.

[1328] Feinberg, *God Remembers: A Study of the Book of Zechariah*, 209.

[1329] Baron, *The Visions and Prophecies of Zechariah*, 403.

in their sight.[1330] By valuing the Good "Shepherd" at 30 pieces of silver, their statement was that He was worth no more to them than a dead slave (Exodus 21:32).

What needs to be observed is that *Yahweh*, in Zechariah 11:4-14, was valued by the Jewish leadership as nothing more than a dead slave. Neither God the Father nor God the Holy Spirit took on humanity. So they literally could never be betrayed or valued for 30 pieces of silver for Their services to Israel as a Shepherd. Only God the Son, the *Moshiach*, the Son of David, the Branch, and the good Shepherd, was valued for 30 pieces of silver (Matthew 26:14-16; 27:3-10; Mark 14:10; John 18:1-3). These verses show that *Yahweh*, in this passage, must have become a man in order to be betrayed in such a manner. This may not have been evident to the Jewish people before *Yeshua*'s coming, but after the death, burial, resurrection and ascension of *Yeshua* there is only one man in history, the God/man, that fits the description of the good Shepherd.

The Shepherd Pierced … Zechariah 12:10

> And I will pour upon the house of David, and upon the inhabitants of Jerusalem, the spirit of grace and of supplications: and they shall look upon me whom they have pierced, and they shall mourn for him, as one mourneth for his only son, and shall be in bitterness for him, as one that is in bitterness for his firstborn (KJV).

Zechariah 12:10 is another powerful statement because *Yahweh* says that something happened to Him that could only be experienced by human beings; He was pierced. The identity of the person speaking in verse 10 must be verified so that there is no confusion. By paying close attention to these first person pronouns the speaker clarifies the identity of the person in verse 10. In verses 1 and 4 the speaker identifies Himself as *Yahweh* (LORD). Then He uses the first person pronouns in verse 2, "*I will make Jerusalem*;" verse 3, "*In that day will I make*;" verse 4, twice, "*I will smite*;" and "*I will open mine eyes*;" verse 6, "*I will make the governors*;" and verse 9, "*I will seek to destroy*," all referring to the speaker *Yahweh*. Notice also that the speaker from verse 1 claims to be the Creator of the heavens and earth, just as the one who called Jacob, and identified Himself as the first and the last in Isaiah 48:12-13, 16. In Zechariah 12:10, *Yahweh* states, "*I will pour upon the house of David*," and then continues with His powerful statement, "*and they shall look upon me whom they have pierced.*" *Yahweh* is referring to a time when He was physically pierced, but that is impossible because Rabbinic Judaism believes that God is pure spirit and cannot, in any way, become a man. Yet, here *Yahweh* distinctly states that He was pierced, and the text does not indicate it is to be read in a metaphorical sense. The literal sense of the verse is obvious. *Yeshua*, the *Moshiach*, the God/man was pierced on Mt. Calvary, as the atonement (Daniel 9:24-25), the sin offering (Isaiah 53:10) for the sins of the world.

[1330] Hartman, *Zechariah: Israel's Messenger of the Messiah's Triumph*, 111.

The Jewish response is to divert the natural meaning of Zechariah 12:10 away from any possibility of it implying that *Yeshua* could be the God/man promised by God from the very beginning when sin entered the world in Genesis 3:15. Brown references two Jewish interpretations of this text that try to say that the "evil inclination" was pierced, or that the people of Israel would weep over Messiah ben Joseph being slain in the last great war. These interpretations are not consistent with the text; Jewish scholars attempt to avoid having to admit that *Yeshua* is speaking in Zechariah 12:10:

> Zechariah 12:10 is discussed in the Talmud in b. Sukkah 55a. The verse – read with a singular, not plural, subject – is first interpreted to mean that it is the evil inclination (i.e., the sinful tendency in man) that was slain, and the people wept when they saw how easily it could have been overcome. The second interpretation states that the people wept over Messiah son of Joseph who was slain fighting in the last great war (i.e., the last great future war) for his people, after which Messiah Son of David asked God to raise him from the dead, and his request was granted. From this we learn two significant points: (1) The Hebrew was understood to be speaking of an individual person or thing, not of a plural subject (in other words, the one who was pierced through and slain, not those who were pierced through and slain); and (2) there was an ancient Jewish tradition interpreting the text in terms of a Messianic figure who died and then was raised from the dead.[1331]

Brown's point is that the text is speaking of an individual and not something collective as the "evil inclination." Brown's other point is that the text is speaking of the *Moshiach*, but not just a mere man called Messiah ben Joseph. What the Jewish scholars do recognize in their interpretation is that the *Moshiach* will be killed; they just miss identifying who the *Moshiach* is. The text is speaking of an individual and not something collective. Now in the same mental frame of reference, consider the translation given in *The Jewish Study Bible* for Zechariah 12:10 as they divert attention away from the Hebrew text, which clearly states "*and they look upon me whom they have pierced.*" They rephrase it to say that Israel will lament to God for those who are slain:

> But I will fill the House of David and the inhabitants of Jerusalem with a spirit of pity and compassion; and **they shall lament to Me about those who are slain, wailing over them as over a favorite son** and showing bitter grief as over a first-born.

Kaiser also quotes this reference from the *New Jewish Publication Society* as well as from the 1896 Jewish translation in an appendix to the Revised Version which reads as follows. Notice the difference in translation:

[1331] Brown, *Answering Jewish Objections: Messianic Prophecy Objections,* 3:148-149.

448

And they [i.e., the house of David and the inhabitants of Jerusalem] shall look up to Me because of Him whom they [i.e., the nations which came up against Jerusalem] have pierced."[1332]

In the first quote (bold), Jewish scholars have made two changes: First they removed the word "pierced" and inserted "slain." Second, they changed the wording from "*look upon me*" to "lament to me." These changes effectively remove the intent of what Zechariah was saying by removing the meaning in the verse that *Yahweh* was pierced, and that they would look upon Him, whereas, the second quote (immediately above) implies that the nations pierced, in Jewish interpretation, Messiah ben Joseph. If the passage is read naturally without the preconception of the interpreter, then Messiah *Yeshua* is in view.

Another Jewish viewpoint follows on the heels of the previous quote indicating very clearly that Rabbinic Judaism teaches that God cannot be pierced:

Actually this verse is not difficult to understand, if we look at it within the context of Zechariah 12, where we are told that God will defend His people and destroy their enemies. On that day, "they [the nation of Israel, i.e., the house of David and the inhabitants of Jerusalem, mentioned at the beginning of verse 10] shall look to Me [God] whom they [the nations, spoken of in verse 9, that shall come up against Jerusalem] have pierced; then they [Israel] shall mourn for him [the slain of Israel as personified by the leader of the people, the warrior Messiah who will die in battle at this time]."

Of course, God cannot literally be pierced. The idea of piercing God expresses the fact that Israel stands in a very special relationship to God among all the nations of the earth. God identifies with His people to the degree that He takes part figuratively in the nation's destiny. To attack (pierce) Israel is to attack God. That is why God says: "Me whom they have pierced" even though it is the people of Israel and not God who is actually "pierced."[1333]

It is interesting how the rabbis change and add words to deflect the real meaning of the text. The phrase "*in that day*" is the last days before the return of *Moshiach* to defend Jerusalem in verse 9. Then verse 10 states that as Israel and Jerusalem are about to be annihilated (Zechariah 13:7) a remnant escapes to Bozrah (Jeremiah 49:13-14; Matthew 24:15-31), known today as Petra. But before they leave in the middle of the seventieth week, they will be witnessed to by the 144,000 Jewish believers (Revelation 7:1-8) and by the two witnesses (Zechariah 4:2-3; Revelation 11:3-12). Once in Bozrah they will pore over the Scriptures and as they confess their sin (Isaiah 53:1-9), in particular the sin of rejecting their *Moshiach* who came 2000 years ago (Daniel 9:24-27; Hosea 5:15; Jeremiah 3:11-13; Leviticus 26:40-42; Psalm 22),

---

[1332] Kaiser, *The Communicator's Commentary: Micah – Malachi*, 405-406.
[1333] Sigal, *The Jew and the Christian Missionary: A Jewish Response to Missionary Christianity*, 80-81.

they will call on Him whom they pierced and they will weep over Him bitterly (Zechariah 12:10).[1334]

Walter Kaiser points out that grammatically the subject of the verb "look" and "pierced" are the same:

> The subject of the verb "look" and the verb "pierce" is the same in Hebrew. Accordingly, those who pierced the Messiah, the same One who will pour out a spirit of grace and supplication in that day, belong to the same national group that will "look" and "mourn" over the pierced One, as one mourns over the loss of a "firstborn son …."[1335]

Next, the word "pierced," which is the Hebrew word דָּקָרוּ, (daqatu – they pierced) is a powerful word if kept within its context. This word "pierced" or דָּקַר (daqaru) is used 11 times in the Hebrew text (Numbers 25:8; Judges 9:54; 1 Samuel 31:4; 1 Chronicles 10:4; Isaiah 13:15; Jeremiah 37:10; 51:4; Lamentations 4:9; Zechariah 13:3) meaning to "pierce" or "thrust through."[1336] Almost all references to being pierced in *The Jewish Study Bible* are rendered as being "pierced through." So there is no doubt as to the meaning of this word in the text of this passage and its fulfillment in the crucifixion when *Yeshua* was pierced with the Roman spear (John 19:34), which is what Zechariah 12:10 references. Rabbinic Judaism believes that Messiah is not God, so the rabbis speak of two completely human messiahs in the form of Messiah ben Joseph (suffering Messiah) and Messiah ben David (reigning Messiah) to try and avoid the obvious reference in Zechariah 12:10 that the Scriptures present the Moshiach as the God/man. But if the text, as given in Zechariah 12:10, is taken for what it says, two messiahs are not needed, because the same Messiah comes twice with two different purposes. The main issue for Jewish scholars is how to resolve the changing of the pronouns that God used of Himself, from "Me" to "Him" in this passage.[1337] This shift in the pronouns goes from *Yahweh* as first person, "Me," to the one who is mourned for in the third person, as "Him." The lament for *Yahweh* who was pierced through is viewed from *Yahweh's* perspective as "Me," whereas the "Him" is viewed from a future generation of Jewish people who will recognize *Yahweh* as "Him" the one they were responsible for piercing. The answer to the problem of the pronouns is a matter of viewpoint as both Barrett and Merrill express:

[1334] Much has been written in the past as to the future events in the last days. Dr. Arnold G. Fruchtenbaum has written an outstanding prophetic book on Eschatology (Future things). It would be well worth your investment of time to study the Scriptures with this book in hand. Arnold G. Fruchtenbaum, *Footsteps of the Messiah: A Study of the Sequence of Prophetic Events* (Tustin, CA: Ariel Ministries, 2002).

[1335] Kaiser, *The Messiah in the Old Testament,* 224-225.

[1336] Unger, *Zechariah: Prophet of Messiah's Glory,* 216.

[1337] Kaiser, *The Communicator's Commentary: Micah – Malachi,* 406.

The shift in pronouns from the first to the third person testifies to the distinctive association. That God would send His perfect representative, His Son, was the great message of hope.[1338]

From YHWH's viewpoint it is "Me" that is the focus; from the standpoint of the people it is "Him." Such a transition from one person to another is not at all uncommon in Hebrew composition, especially in poetic and prophetic language.[1339]

Yahweh, who is the obvious speaker in this passage, is the *Moshiach*, the One who was physically pierced with a sword, the One for whom Israel will mourn bitterly. Kaiser mentions there is only one possible example of that kind of mourning in the biblical account, which was the death of King Josiah in 2 Kings 23:29 and 2 Chronicles 35:25.[1340] Zechariah 12:10 states that Israel will weep for "Him" bitterly as one mourns for his only son, because to that future generation, *Yahweh* will be recognized as *Yeshua* who came as the *Moshiach* twenty centuries ago. The word "only" is the Hebrew word *yachid* (discussed in chapter 4).

Levine also speaks of Rabbinic Judaism's two messiah issue from a slightly different perspective in this following statement:

Ibn Ezra on Zechariah 9:9 is that Zechariah refers to the Messiah that will be from the house of Joseph (who according to Jewish tradition, will introduce the Messianic Age) and Daniel refers to the Messiah from the house of David. Since the first one will be killed, according to the Talmud, as they explain Zechariah 12:10 (see Talmud Succah 52a), it makes sense to say that both verses of Zechariah refer to the same person. Since his end will be in death, his beginning will be lowly and meek. The other answer is given by the Talmud in Sanhedrin 98a. If the Jews are worthy (i.e., righteous), then the verses of Daniel will apply; if they are not worthy, then the verse in Zechariah 9:9 will apply.[1341]

In this description Levine gives two views as to the Messiah of Zechariah 9:9 and Daniel 7:13-14 in connection with Zechariah 12:10. In the first passage the Messiah ben Joseph will be killed, so he will come meek and lowly as in Zechariah 9:9. But in the second if the Jews are worthy, the verses in Daniel 7:13-14 will apply, where He will come riding on the clouds. The sad truth is that He did come lowly, not as a world conqueror but as an itinerant rabbi presenting the kingdom of God. They rejected His presentation of the Kingdom and His person and so He became "*the Lamb of God*" in dealing with the sin issue before God, the root problem of mankind and of Israel's rebellion before God. He will not come later "if" the Jewish people are worthy but because they will finally recognize who He is both in the past and the present.

[1338] Barrett, *Beginning at Moses,* 237.

[1339] Merrill, *An Exegetical Commentary: Haggai, Zechariah, Malachi,* 320.

[1340] Kaiser, *The Communicator's Commentary: Micah – Malachi,* 407.

[1341] Levine, *You Take Jesus, I'll Take God: How To Refute Christian Missionaries,* 17.

As can be clearly seen in Zechariah 12:10, *Yahweh*, who will pour upon the house of David and Jerusalem the spirit of grace and supplication, will also be the one physically pierced, and Israel will someday mourn for Him greatly. This is one of the most gut-wrenching passages in Scripture, when the Jewish people realize that *Yeshua* was indeed the Messiah, the God of Abraham, Isaac and Jacob Incarnate. They will weep and mourn, for they will then realize that all their fathers before them who worshipped *Yahweh* or *HaShem*[1342] with zeal were literally rejecting the One they said they worshipped. The last public words of *Yeshua* bring together the person Messiah and *Yahweh* in Matthew 23:37 as He speaks as *Yahweh*:

> (37) O Jerusalem, Jerusalem, thou that killest the prophets, and stonest them which are sent unto thee, how often would I have gathered thy children together, even as a hen gathereth her chickens under her wings, and ye would not! (38) Behold, your house is left unto you desolate. (39) For I say unto you, Ye shall not see me henceforth, till ye shall say, Blessed is he that cometh in the name of the Lord.

Yeshua not only speaks as *Yahweh*, but his final public statement in verse 39 is what the Jewish people will have to say before He will return to rescue them at the end of the seventieth week of Daniel which is also known as "the time of Jacob's trouble." Jewish rabbis often speak today of repentance as one of the ingredients for atonement, rather than the shed blood of the offering. Yes, they will have to repent, but that repentance will be concerning their rejection of *Yahweh* who came in the flesh as the Second Person of the plural unity of *Elohim*, who was called *Yeshua* (Leviticus 26:40; Hosea 5:15; Zechariah 12:10).

The Shepherd Smitten … Zechariah 13:7

> Awake, O sword, against my shepherd, and against the man that is my fellow, saith the LORD of hosts: smite the shepherd, and the sheep shall be scattered: and I will turn mine hand upon the little ones.

Finally Zechariah 13:7 is a very potent reference in connection with God the Father and God the Son being equals. There are numerous words such as "*sword*," "*man*," "*My shepherd*" and "*My associate*" in this verse. Each one needs to be dealt with individually, and then within the context to see that *Yahweh* takes complete responsibility for the "*sword*" to be used against His Shepherd and His Associate, the Messiah.

First, the speaker is clearly "*the LORD of hosts*," *Yahweh*. However, in this verse the speaker is not the Messiah as in Zechariah 12:10 and 11:4-14.

[1342] *HaShem*: Simply means "the name." Because of Jewish sensitivity to the use of God's name, many Jewish people will avoid using the name of *Yahweh*, and insert *HaShem* in its place.

The "sword" is told to awaken against "My shepherd." Yahweh, in an act of sovereignty, is telling the sword to awaken against His Shepherd, the good Shepherd of Zechariah 11. The "sword" is a valid personification of the instrument of death and is instructed to move against the Shepherd, who is addressed as being "My shepherd."[1343]

The second term "My shepherd" is the same Shepherd of Zechariah 11:4-14, who is the personal Shepherd of Yahweh, "My shepherd." The term "My Shepherd" also indicates that this is no ordinary shepherd but a particular Shepherd, "My shepherd."

The third and fourth words are "man" who is "My associate" or my equal. The Hebrew word is עָמִית or "amith," which means "associate, fellow, relation,"[1344] and is used in the Tanakh 10 times in Leviticus[1345] and once in Zechariah 13:7.[1346] How does this word "amith" or "associate" relate to man and to Yahweh in this verse? First, the associate is a man, a human being that Yahweh designates as His associate. The word associate, as it is used in Leviticus, is a general term for "fellowman." Unger and Feinberg define it:

The Hebrew word employed, amith, is used to denote persons associated together under common love for the enjoyment of common rights and privileges.[1347]

All the citations in Leviticus have reference to laws concerning injuries committed against near relatives "to show how great a crime it is to injure one who is related both bodily and spiritually by a common descent. It is used interchangeably as being equivalent to brother; a word which is invariably employed in the laws of Moses with reference to a common physical and spiritual descent."[1348]

Varner and then Feinberg as he quotes Keil focus in on the real significance of the phrase "My fellow" as it relates to the LORD:

This word is striking because in every other occurrence in the OT it always refers to a man who is a fellow Israelite with another (Lev 5:21). In other words, it refers to "one who shares the nature of another."

[1343] Kaiser, *The Communicator's Commentary: Micah – Malachi*, 413.

[1344] Harris, Archer and Waltke, *Theological Wordbook of the Old Testament*, 2:675.

[1345] Leviticus 6:2; 5:21; 18:20; 19:11, 15, 17; 24:19; 25:14, 15, 17.

[1346] Kohlenberger III and Swanson, *Hebrew English Concordance to the Old Testament*, 1241-1242.

[1347] Unger, *Zechariah: Prophet of Messiah's Glory*, 232.

[1348] Charles L. Feinberg, "The Shepherd Smitten and the Sheep Scattered," 13:7-9, *Bib Sac* (vol. 103:409, 1946), 37-38.

The implications of this verse are amazing. This shepherd who will be smitten with the sword in what is obviously a death blow will be one who shares in the Divine nature of Yahweh!![1349]

When used in Zechariah it refers to One who is connected with God by a unity of essence. Keil explicitly states it: The idea of nearest one (or fellow) involves not only similarity in vocation, but community of physical or spiritual descent, according to which he whom God calls His neighbour cannot be a mere man, but can only be one who participates in the divine nature, or is essentially divine."[1350]

The Shepherd, My fellow who is a man, shares the same nature as *Yahweh* who calls for the sword to arise and slay the Shepherd. Hengstenberg confirms the words of the preceding authors:

From this it is evident, however, that, when the same term is applied to the relation in which a certain individual stands to God, the individual referred to cannot be a mere man, but must be the same person who has already been referred to in chap[ters] 11 and 12 as connected with the Lord by a mysterious unity of essence. The neighbour or fellow of the Lord is no other than he who says in John 10:30, "I and the Father are one," and who is described in John 1:18 as "the only begotten Son, who is in the bosom of the Father," whose connection with the Father is the closest that can possibly be conceived.[1351]

In Leviticus "*amith*" or "associate" is used as a neighbor who is one's equal. Here in Zechariah, God is calling His Shepherd, His Associate or His Equal. Kaiser expresses that concept in this statement:

This Shepherd is One who is side by side with, or the equal of, the Lord! The term "associate" (or companion) is used to refer to those who are close neighbors or close companions (Lev 6:2; 18:20; 19:15). The equality that such a relationship brings to mind is the equality with God claimed by Jesus in John 10:30 and 14:9. The Shepherd's close association with the Lord strengthens the case for identifying him as the Shepherd of 11:4-14 and the One who was pierced in 12:10.[1352]

What has been established is that *Yahweh* has a man who is His Associate or equal. He then instructs a weapon of death (sword) to be against His Shepherd or Associate. It is no coincidence that Zechariah chapter 11 speaks of a good Shepherd who is paid 30 pieces of silver for His leadership among His people, which was an insult. This Shepherd is the one who was pierced in Zechariah 12:10, and the one whom the nation

---

[1349] Varner, *The Messiah: Revealed, Rejected, Received*, 94.

[1350] Feinberg, "The Shepherd Smitten and the Sheep Scattered," 13:7-9, *Bib Sac* (vol. 103:409, 1946), 37-38.

[1351] Hengstenberg, *Christology of the Old Testament*, 4:98.

[1352] Kaiser, *The Communicator's Commentary: Micah – Malachi*, 413.

of Israel will look to in the future. This Shepherd is a Man, just as other Messianic prophecies predicted. But this Man is also God, as Messianic prophecies also predicted. Now this Shepherd, the Man who is *Yahweh's* equal, has a sword instructed to be against Him.

The last phrase in Zechariah 13:7 states "*smite the shepherd*" or kill the shepherd. Here *Yahweh* is instructing the sword to kill the Shepherd. It is not without significance that a sword is used even as it was on *Yeshua* who was given wages (an insult) for His ministry as the good Shepherd in Zechariah 11:12-13. It is also significant that His death would come by being pierced and that a future generation would mourn for Him as Zechariah 12:10 clearly states. The word for "*pierced*" in Zechariah 12:10 is the same word used in Zechariah 13:3 [וּדְקָרֻהוּ translated "and they will stab him"] where parents of a false prophet are to pierce their son or "*thrust him through.*" This verse shows how all of these passages in Zechariah chapters 11 and 12 are connected together with Zechariah 13 in the same person. Also, it is important not to miss Zechariah 9:9, which *Yeshua* fulfilled on His entrance into Jerusalem four days before Passover, or on the 10th day of the first month of the year as the "Lamb of God" (Exodus 12:3-6; Matthew 21:1-11). All of these verses contain a wealth of information concerning God working with Israel and the Messiah, His Shepherd.

The responsibility for killing Christ or the Messiah needs to be examined. The Jewish people have taken the brunt of this for centuries by being called "Christ Killers" at the hands of a completely unbiblical church. Let's set the record straight from a biblical perspective. The Jewish people were instruments in seeing Messiah killed, but so were the Romans. *Yeshua*, in Matthew 12, spells out very clearly that it was "*that generation,*" and not future generations, that was guilty of personally rejecting Him. All the hideous acts against the Jewish people have been inspired by Satan, who has used ignorant biased "Christians" to keep the Jewish people from receiving the Gospel. Barrett and Kaiser express the same idea in this quote:

> The sword is told, "Strike the Shepherd." This accords with what Isaiah taught: "Yet it pleased the LORD to bruise Him" (Isa 53:10). Thus Jesus was delivered up in accordance with the definite plan of God, although it is the men who did the deed who are culpable for what they did (Acts 2:23).[1353]

> Although Zechariah 12:10 indicates that unbelievers were responsible for piercing the Messiah, 13:7 squelches any notion that Messiah's death was anything other than the eternal purpose of God. Zechariah advances Isaiah's announcement that it was God's pleasure or purpose to bruise the Servant (Isaiah 53:10) by revealing that Christ's execution was God's command.[1354]

This subject of who is responsible for killing Messiah must be dealt with biblically. God the Father takes full responsibility for the death of Messiah and, as Isaiah 53:10

[1353] Kaiser, *The Communicator's Commentary: Micah – Malachi*, 413.
[1354] Barrett, *Beginning at Moses*, 237.

clearly states, "*if he was willing to be the guilt offering.*" The sins of the world were placed on *Yeshua* on the Tree (cross), and that Jewish and Roman generation were free moral agents which committed the act and stand guilty of His death. Jewish people have been persecuted for centuries by "Christians" for "killing Christ." But bear in mind that without His voluntary death, there is no resurrection and no eternal life and the entire human race would be completely helpless and lost in their sins, with absolutely no power to remedy the situation. Yes, the Jewish people and the Romans of the first century were the instruments that God used, yet God takes full responsibility. The Jewish people are no more "Christ Killers" than any other person from among the nations.

MALACHI HAS THE LAST WORD

Yahweh has been speaking throughout the Written Word concerning the divinity of the Messiah. Now the last prophet in the Hebrew Bible has the last word on who the Messenger of the Covenant is.

The Messenger of the Covenant ... Malachi 3:1

> Behold, I will send my messenger, and he shall prepare the way before me: and the Lord, whom ye seek, shall suddenly come to his temple, even the messenger of the covenant, whom ye delight in: behold he shall come, saith the LORD of hosts (KJV).

This verse from the *Tanakh* is part of a wider grouping of verses (Malachi 2:17 - 3:5). It does not stand by itself for there are numerous background issues that will be picked up as the actual text is observed.

In Malachi 2:17 the leadership of Israel is making some serious accusations about God. David Levy, a Jewish believer in Messiah *Yeshua*, expresses in his own words the statements of the people:

- "Every one that doeth evil is good in the sight of the LORD."
- Their viewpoint was that the Lord prospered the wicked and left His own righteous people in poverty. Understand that from a Jewish perspective, material blessing was from the hand of God, so God must love the wicked more than the righteous because He has made so many of them.
- "He delighteth in them."
- God not only prospered the wicked but He took pleasure in doing so.
- "Where is the God of justice?"

456

- With sarcasm they skeptically questioned whether God was even available to take just action against the wicked. [1355]

Although Malachi 3:1-5 records the LORD's answer to Israel's false accusations, verse 1 deserves primary attention. Here, though the word "messiah," does not appear, even Jewish authors acknowledge that the *Moshiach* is in view. In fact they even connect the "My angel" with the "My angel" of Exodus 23:20, even Redak (Rabbi David Kimchi) and Ibn Ezra state that the "My angel" will be the Messiah who is the "the angel [messenger] of the Covenant.[1356] Within verse 1, six personal pronouns are used (I, my, he, me, and his) and two "messengers" are referenced. Therefore, it is important to determine who is in view in this passage and to whom those pronouns refer.

Malachi 3:1 begins with the statement, "*Behold,* **I** *will send* **my** *messenger, and* **he** *shall prepare the way before* **me**." In this first part, three first person pronouns refer to the same person who is the speaker (I, my, and me) and one pronoun references the messenger (he). The messenger is distinct from both the speaker and the second messenger mentioned later. Who are these two personalities? According to the last part of the verse the first person is the "*LORD of hosts.*" Malachi does not give the name of the messenger, but rather, he gives a clue. "*He shall* **prepare a way** *before me;*" Malachi ties this hint to Isaiah 40:3 where Isaiah said "**Prepare ye the way** *of the LORD.*" Walter Kaiser makes the following comparisons and contrasts from these two verses as to the messengers:

> The preparing messenger was "to clear the way before [the Lord]." The striking similarity between this expression (וּפִנָּה דֶרֶךְ לְפָנָה) and that found in Isa 40:3, (פַּנּוּ דֶרֶךְ יהוה) 57:14 and 62:10 is too strong to be accidental. The resemblance between Isaiah and Malachi was drawn out even to the omission of the article from דֶרֶךְ, "way"; the only difference is that in Malachi the messenger is to prepare the way while in Isaiah the servants of the Lord are urged to prepare the road.[1357]

Malachi 3:1 (like Isaiah 40:3) is also closely associated with Malachi 4:5, which directly speaks of Elijah who will come before "*the great and dreadful day of the LORD.*" In Malachi 3:1 this messenger is not given a name as in Isaiah 40:3, but is different from the Malachi 4:5 reference. Arnold Fruchtenbaum expresses at length that the first messenger, or forerunner, was fulfilled by John the Baptist and that the second

---

[1355] David Levy, *Malachi: Messenger of Rebuke and Renewal* (Bellmawr, NJ: Friends of Israel Gospel Ministry, 1992), 63.

[1356] Rabbi A. J. Rosenberg, *The Book of the Twelve Prophets: A New English Translation of the Text, Rashi and a Commentary Digest* (2 vols. New York: The Judaica Press, 1996), 2:413, 476.

[1357] Walter C. Kaiser, "The Promise of the Arrival of Elijah in Malachi and the Gospels." *GJT* 3, no. 2 (1982), 221-234 (225). Four other Hebrew texts were observed and Kaiser's states וּפִנָּה דֶרֶךְ לְפָנַי whereas all the others state וּפִנָּה דֶרֶךְ לְפָנָה.

457

messenger of Malachi 4:5 will be Elijah before the second coming of the Messiah.[1358] The speaker, the LORD of hosts, here states that He will send "my messenger" and "he" (the messenger) will prepare the way for the LORD of hosts. The verb translated prepare is *pana* "in this form (*piel*) means to clear away, remove."[1359] But just how does the messenger prepare the way for the Lord? In ancient days when a king made a state visit to another country, forerunners would precede him to prepare or to remove all obstacles for his arrival. Eugene Merrill states the following:

> In both Isaiah and Malachi this is to be taken metaphorically to speak of the removal of obstacles to His coming.[1360]

However, if it is to be taken metaphorically, what did Isaiah and Malachi mean by their statements? The following comments by three authors express the same thing but do so in different words:

> By clearing away the impediments lying in the road, denotes the removal of all that retards the coming of the Lord to His people, i.e. the taking away of enmity to God and of ungodliness by the preaching of repentance and the conversion of sinners. The announcement of this messenger therefore implied that the nation in its existing moral condition was not yet prepared for the reception of the Lord, and therefore had no ground for murmuring at the delay of the manifestation of the divine glory, but ought rather to murmur at its own sin and estrangement from God.[1361]

> His job was to prepare the people morally and spiritually for the coming of the Messiah.[1362]

> The mission…was to prepare the way before the speaker – me – God himself. As befitting the ultimate concerns of that Coming One,…preparation was moral and spiritual in nature. Repentance is the road which leads men to God and allows him to come to men.[1363]

Malachi 3:1 is not talking about a physical road that needs grading attention for the comfort of the coming head of state. But Malachi does mean by this statement that the hearts of the people of Israel needed to change and prepare for the coming of the LORD. A further observation is that the religious leadership of Israel had put obstacles in the path of the people so that they would study Oral Law (also known as rabbinic law or teaching) instead of studying the *Tanakh* alone as the only authority, which would have led them to Messiah. The Pharisees had raised the Oral Law to equality with the

---

[1358] Fruchtenbaum, *The Footsteps of Messiah*, 132-136.

[1359] Richard A. Taylor, *The New American Commentary: Haggai, Malachi* (vol. 21a. Nashville: Broadman, 2004), 384.

[1360] Merrill, *An Exegetical Commentary: Haggai, Zechariah, Malachi,* 430.

[1361] Keil and Delitzsch, *Commentary on the Old Testament: Minor Prophets,* 10:457-458.

[1362] Kaiser, *The Messiah in the Old Testament,* 228.

[1363] Smith, *The Promised Messiah,* 462.

Tanakh. This practice was not only true in *Yeshua*'s day but has come down to this day as an even greater spiritual obstacle.

Both Malachi and Isaiah speak of *"preparing the way"* for the coming of the Lord, but the difference is twofold. Isaiah refers to the Lord as the Glory of *Yahweh,* whereas Malachi refers to the Lord as the *"messenger of the covenant."* Hengstenberg and Stanton both express the same thing in their statements:

> In Malachi, the messenger of the Lord prepares the way before him; in Isaiah, the servants of the Lord are called upon to prepare the way. The meaning is the same in both. For it is self-evident that it is a moral preparation for the coming of the Lord which is intended.[1364]

> Since both Isaiah and Malachi refer to a messenger preparing the way for the arrival of the Lord, and one refers to the Lord as the Glory of Yahweh, and the other as the Messenger of the covenant, the literal understanding of Isaiah 40:3-5 should be 'the glory of Yahweh will reveal Himself.'[1365]

God says that he will send his messenger. The word "send" is a present participle – am sending – indicates that something is being set in motion and will continue until it is accomplished.[1366]

Who is the *"I will send"* and *"before me,"* for grammatically they must be the same person, the LORD? Malachi 3:1 is divided into two parts grammatically. The LORD states that He will send His messenger to prepare the way for Himself, and then the LORD shifts gears. First He spoke in the first person, and then He changed and spoke in the third person referring to Himself as "his" and "he." In essence the LORD is saying, "I the Lord am sending my messenger to prepare the people before me or before I come. These statements equate the Lord here as the *Moshiach*."[1367] Then the LORD shifts the pronoun usage just as He did in Zechariah 12:10 from speaking personally to speaking of Himself from the perspective of the people in the last part of the verse; *"the Lord whom you seek will come suddenly to His temple,"* and the Lord is the messenger of the covenant, for behold He shall come.

The name or identity of *"my messenger"* is not given in the *Tanakh*, nor is it given in the related passage in Isaiah 40:3. The Gospel writers of the New Covenant revealed this messenger as John the Baptist, the forerunner of *Yeshua*, the *Moshiach* (Matthew 3:1-3; Mark 1:1-3; Luke 3:4). The first messenger and *"he shall prepare the way"* is also the same person who is sent by the LORD personally to prepare the people before the arrival of the LORD.

[1364] Hengstenberg, *Christology of the Old Testament,* 4:162-163.

[1365] R. Todd Stanton, *Numbers 12:6-8, Its Contribution to the Study of Revelation and Theophany in the Old Testament* (Th. M. thesis., Master's Seminary, 2000), 110.

[1366] Smith, *The Promised Messiah,* 461.

[1367] Levy, *Malachi: Messenger of Rebuke and Renewal,* 66.

The Lord they seek that will "*suddenly*" come to "*his temple*" is further defined as "*the messenger of the Covenant.*" The word "*suddenly*" is used 25 times in the *Tanakh*, and in all but one of those instances (2 Chronicles 29:36) it is used in connection with disaster and judgment.[1368] J. Vernon McGee is in agreement with the judgment motif in that the Jewish accusation of God in Malachi 2:17 raises the issue that God is not just to Malachi 3:2 where God states that He will put them through the refiner's fire, so the context is judgment.[1369] McGee continues by arguing:

> This messenger of the covenant is the Lord Jesus, but this passage hasn't anything to do with His first coming. This is His coming not in grace, not as a Redeemer, but as a Judge, as the one who will establish His kingdom and put down the rebellion that is on this earth.[1370]

McGee does not believe that this passage is concerned with *Yeshua*'s first coming but His second coming. However, according to Haggai 2:9, the glory of this latter temple had more glory than the first. Yet the Lord never appeared from a Jewish context in the second temple. So what would be so great about the second temple in relation to the first temple, if there is no glory coming from God? For this reason, Joseph Frey equates the "glory" as coming from the appearance of the *Moshiach* in His first coming, which is in a totally different manner than the glory that appeared in the first temple:

> We observe next, that it is promised that the Messiah should come 'to his temple;' the temple built in the days of Malachi; the second temple; which is peculiarly his temple, for he was to appear in it, to be its glory... . To this temple he should come 'suddenly,' i.e., immediately, after his harbinger appeared and prepared the way before him. We have then the testimony of the Angel Gabriel, of the prophets Daniel, Haggai, and Malachi, that the Messiah was to appear during the standing of the second temple; but the temple has been utterly destroyed more than 1700 years ago; it is, therefore, evident that the Messiah must have come. These arguments are so convincing that the time predicted for the coming of the Messiah is long past, that in their perplexity the Rabbis have pronounced a curse on all that shall attempt the computation of the time.[1371] (Talmud Trat. Sanhedrin)

The reference to His coming to "*His temple,*" the second temple, has with it an interesting meaning. Who dwelt in the tabernacle and Solomon's temple? The LORD, yes, but it was the *Shechinah* of God, which in chapter 7 of this book entitled *Shechinah*, was shown to be the Second Person of the Godhead, *Yeshua*. According to Ezekiel, a literal Ichabod occurred (1 Samuel 4:21-22) when the glory of the LORD departed from the temple in Ezekiel 8-11. When comparing the dedication of the second temple (Ezra 6:16-18) with the dedication of Solomon's temple (1 Kings 8:1-11), the

---

[1368] Levy, *Malachi: Messenger of Rebuke and Renewal*, 66.

[1369] McGee, *Thru the Bible: Proverbs - Malachi*, 3:1016-1017.

[1370] McGee, *Thru the Bible: Proverbs - Malachi*, 3:1016.

[1371] Frey, *The Messiahship of Jesus*, 79.

glory of the LORD is glaringly absent. So the glory of the LORD was not in this temple and the Ark of the Covenant was not present in the Holy of Holies, as the Roman General Pompey noted when he entered the Holy of Holies in 63 BCE and found the room empty.[1372]

This temple (Malachi 3:1) is the second temple about which Ezra, Nehemiah, Zechariah and Haggai wrote. In particular there is one related passage which gives further information concerning Malachi 3:1 found in Haggai 2:9:

> The glory of this latter House shall be greater than that of the former one, saith The LORD of Hosts... .

The mystery of how this temple can be greater than Solomon's temple is best resolved by noting a particular word. The emphasis is not on the word "glory" nor on the word "house" but on the words "latter glory," [1373] which will deal with the personal presence of the LORD.[1374] Admittedly, Herod made the second temple larger, more costly and beautiful than Solomon's temple. Obviously the glory of the Lord was not physically present in the *Shechinah* of God. So if the *Shechinah* was not present, how could it be greater? The answer is that the actual personal presence of the Lord would be coming to the temple. This is not referring to the millennial temple described in Ezekiel 40-48, but the second temple, which was the subject of Ezra, Nehemiah, Haggai and Malachi. So this latter temple would receive more glory because as Malachi 3:1, states the Lord Himself would come to "*His temple*" (Psalm 69:9; John 2:13-17; Haggai 2:9; Matthew 21:12-13) and the Lord was the *Moshiach*.

Next the "*messenger of the covenant*" cannot be understood to be the same messenger as mentioned earlier in this verse. Rabbis Rashi and Kimchi claim that the messenger of the covenant is just a man,[1375] which would coincide with Jacob Schochet's statement. However, Schochet does identify the Lord as the Messiah, but only a human messiah:

> Yet there is an explicit verse in Malachi (3:1) that 'The lord whom you seek (i.e., the king Mashiach) will suddenly come to his palace, and the messenger of the covenant whom you desire (i.e., Elijah the prophet), behold he comes.'[1376]

John Smith, in particular, answers the question as to the identity of the "*messenger of the covenant*" being not just a man but *Yahweh* Himself:

[1372] Sacchi, *The History of the Second Temple Period,* 269-270. Also see Schurer, *A History of the Jewish People in the Time of Jesus Christ,* 1:322.

[1373] Taylor, *The New American Commentary: Haggai, Malachi,* 167.

[1374] Kaiser, *The Communicator's Commentary: Micah – Malachi,* 269.

[1375] Frey, *The Messiahship of Jesus,* 78.

[1376] Schochet, *Mashiach: The Principle of Mashiach and the Messianic Era in Jewish Law and Tradition,* 58.

This "messenger" can hardly be identical with the forerunner, viz. "my messenger," at the opening of the verse; for his coming is here made simultaneous with that of "the Lord," who can hardly be other than *Yahweh* himself, and the coming of "my messenger" is explicitly announced as preceding that of *Yahweh*.[1377]

The identity of the "*messenger of the covenant*" is also dealt with by Watson, who sees the messenger as Jehovah's messenger, *Yeshua* the Messiah. Watson explains in the following statement:

The characters under which the person who is the subject of this prophecy is described, are, the Lord, a sovereign Ruler, the owner of the temple, and therefore a Divine prince or governor, he "shall come to his temple." "The temple," says Bishop Horsley, "in the writings of a Jewish prophet, cannot be otherwise understood, according to the literal meaning, than of the temple at Jerusalem. Of this temple, therefore, the person to come is here expressly called the Lord. The Lord of any temple, in the language of all writers, and in the natural meaning of the phrase, is the divinity to whose worship it is consecrated. To no other divinity the temple of Jerusalem was consecrated than the true and everlasting God, the Lord Jehovah, the Maker of heaven and earth. Here, then, we have the express testimony of Malachi, that the Christ, the Deliverer, whose coming he announces, was no other than the Jehovah of the Old Testament. Jehovah had delivered the Israelites from the Egyptian bondage; and the same Jehovah was to come in person to his temple, to effect the greater and more general deliverance of which the former was but an imperfect type.

The Messenger of the Covenant, therefore, is Jehovah's messenger; if his Messenger, his servant; for a message is a service: it implies a person sending, and a person sent. In the person who sendeth there must be authority to send, submission to that authority in the person sent. The Messenger, therefore, of the covenant, is the servant of the Lord Jehovah: but the same person who is the Messenger, is the Lord Jehovah himself, not the same person with the sender, but bearing the same name; because united in that mysterious nature and undivided substance which the name imports. The same person, therefore, is servant and Lord; and, by uniting these characters in the same person, what does the prophet but describe that great mystery of the Gospel, the union of the nature which governs, and the nature which serves, the union of the Divine and human nature in the person of Christ."[1378]

[1377] John Merlin Powis Smith, *The International Critical Commentary, Malachi* (Edinburgh, Scotland: T & T Clark Ltd, 1999), 31.

[1378] Watson, *Theological Institutes: Or, a View of the Evidences, Doctrines, Morals and Institutions of Christianity,* 1:494.

Smith and Watson are absolutely correct that the Messenger is *Yahweh*, but it has also been determined throughout this study that *Yahweh* could refer to God the Father or God the Son. Even though God's identity is known, as to whether it is God the Father or God the Son, Watson very definitely states that it is the Messiah. Todd Stanton gives an insight by showing that *Yahweh* has used different names and by examining these other names, Stanton shows that *Yahweh* is distinct from these other names and yet the same:

> It has been noted earlier that the narratives often describe His appearances by different titles: the Messenger [Angel] of *Yahweh*, the Pillar of cloud and fire, and the Glory of *Yahweh*.[1379]

It was noted in this study that the Messenger of *Yahweh* in Judges 2:1 was the one who led Israel out of the Egyptian bondage, through the wilderness, and into the Promised Land. The Messenger (Angel) of *Yahweh* also stated from Judges 2:1 by referencing Genesis 15 that He made the Abrahamic Covenant. He is identified in Isaiah 63:9 as the Messenger of His Presence. This one is distinct from *Yahweh* and yet speaks as *Yahweh*. The Messenger (Angel) of the LORD is the "*my angel*" that *Yahweh Elohim* said to Moses would be sent with Israel through the wilderness journey and that His Name was in Him (Ex 23:20-23). Young adds further confirmation that this messenger was *Yahweh* and yet was distinct from *Yahweh*:

> So great was His love toward them that He sent the angel of his face, who saved them from all these afflictions and sufferings. This angel (the word means messenger) God had promised to send to His people (Ex 23:20-23) and actually did send to them (Ex 14:19; Num 20:16). He is the Lord's angel (Ex 33:14-15) and is actually the Lord (*Yahweh*) Himself (Ex 33:12). The angel of His face is the angel who is His face or in whom His face is made clear. In him the Lord is Himself present.[1380]

Keil and Delitzsch further state that it is beyond doubt that "*the Lord*" and "*angel of the covenant*" are the same:

> And He comes as the angel of the covenant, for whom the people are longing. The identity of the angel of the covenant with the "Lord" (*ha adon*) is placed beyond the reach of doubt by the parallelism of the clauses, and the notion is thereby refuted that the "covenant angel" is identical with the person previously mentioned as מַלְאָכִי.[1381]

They clearly see "*the Lord*" and the "*angel of the covenant*" as the same individual. Walter Kaiser expresses the same thought with different words:

[1379] Stanton, *Numbers 12:6-8, Its Contribution to the Study of Revelation and Theophany in the Old Testament,* 106.

[1380] Young, *The Book of Isaiah,* 3:481-482.

[1381] Keil & Delitzsch, *Commentary on the Old Testament: Malachi,* 10:458.

463

Because the word "Lord" (*ha adon*) used in [Malachi] 3:1b is singular and is preceded by the definite article, it is certain that it refers to the divine Lord since *adon* preceded the definite article always denotes divinity (see Ex 23:17; 34:23; Isa 1:24; 3:1; 10:16, 33).[1382]

So the "*messenger of the covenant*" and the other theophanies are the temporary (of very short durations) "incarnations" of *Yahweh* before the people of Israel, in the person of *Yeshua*, the *Moshiach* of Israel who literally came to "*His temple.*" It is clear from the context that the messenger of the covenant is synonymous with the Lord. So the people who waited and sought for the return of the glory of the LORD to "*his temple*" by "*the Lord*" were looking for the coming of God in judgment (Malachi 2:17). In ancient days *Yahweh* manifested Himself by revealing His glory in His Messenger (Angel) in a manner that was perceptible to the senses. In the past He manifested Himself as the Messenger (Angel) of *Yahweh,* who was also known as the "*Messenger (Angel) of Yahweh's presence*" and who is the "*messenger of the covenant.*" When the glory of the Lord returned to the second (His) temple, He did so veiled in flesh in the person of *Yeshua*.

The next question is, if "*the messenger of the covenant*" has been determined to be "*the Lord*" the *Moshiach* of Israel, to what covenant is he referring? There are several views concerning what covenant, from a series of covenants, to the New Covenant, to the covenant with Levi and lastly the Mosaic covenant:

> The covenant referred to here is the single plan of God contained in the succession of covenants that began with the word issued to Eve in Genesis 3:15, continued in the word given to Shem in 9:27, to Abraham in 12:2-3, to David in 2 Samuel 7:12-19, and renewed and enlarged in Jeremiah 31:31-34.[1383]

> The covenant, in relation to which the *Malakh*, who is of one essence with Jehovah, is here called the angel of the covenant, is not the new covenant promised in Jer 31:31, but the covenant of Jehovah with Israel, according to which Jehovah dwells in the midst of Israel, and manifests His gracious presence by blessing the righteous and punishing the ungodly (Ex 25:8; Lev 26:11-12; Deut 4:24; Isa 33:14).[1384]

> In a narrow sense, the covenant that this divine servant messenger would come to administer would be that made with Israel in the wilderness of Sinai, the covenant that promised judgment for unbelief. But in a broad and ultimate sense he would be sealing that covenant that God made with Abraham

---

[1382] Kaiser, *The Communicator's Commentary: Micah - Malachi,* 473.
[1383] Kaiser, *The Messiah in the Old Testament,* 228.
[1384] Keil & Delitzsch, *Commentary on the Old Testament*: Malachi, 10:458-459.

promising vindication to God's people and blessing to all the nations of the earth.[1385]

The phrase "messenger of the covenant" should be understood against the background of ancient Near Eastern covenant negotiations, which were usually carried out through messengers. One might argue that whenever a messenger of God appears in the Old Testament, the covenant between the Lord and Israel is always the issue.[1386]

The Lord is the messenger of the covenant, but again what covenant, some have suggested that it was the covenant the Lord made with the Levites (Mal 2:1-5).[1387]

There is no shortage of opinions as to exactly what the "covenant" is that Malachi is speaking about. The context of the book Malachi does focus on one particular covenant. The first two chapters reference the sins of the people but in particular the sins of the restored priests. In fact, Malachi makes a specific reference to the covenant of God given to the Levites as a result of Phinehas' act of judgment against *Zimri, the son of Salu, a prince of a chief house among the Simeonites*" as given in Numbers 25:10-15. The Levites were the priests of Israel before God; now they were accusing God of injustice (Malachi 2:17). The law of Moses promised blessing for obedience and evil or cursing for disobedience. The restored Levites were clamoring for justice, that justice which relates to the Mosaic Law. Hengstenberg gives further expression of this observation:

The divine messenger is called the messenger of the covenant, because he is sent in the cause of the covenant, and his coming to bless, as well as to punish, is the result of the covenant. The two earthly messengers might have been called the same. But the prophet had a special reason for applying this term to the heavenly messenger, in the fact that his coming had been desired by the murmurers on the grounds of the covenant. "The covenant" does not denote one single act, but the covenant relation of God to Israel, which extends through every age. The violation of this covenant on the part of the people, and especially on that of the priests, was the principal theme of the previous addresses (2:10-11); and the violation of the covenant on the part of God was the principal burden of the complaints of the people. The coming of the covenant angel will prove these charges to be groundless, and demonstrate the reality of the covenant by the punishment of those who despise it.[1388]

[1385] Taylor, *The New American Commentary: Haggai, Malachi,* 386.

[1386] Taylor, *The New American Commentary: Haggai, Malachi,* 386.

[1387] Frey, *The Messiahship of Jesus,* 78.

[1388] Hengstenberg, *Christology of the Old Testament,* 4:169-170.

It is this author's view that the "*messenger of the covenant*" is the one who gave that covenant to Israel through Moses on Mt. Sinai. J. Vernon McGee clearly agrees that the covenant in view here is the Mosaic Covenant:

> When it says "the messenger of the covenant," we need to understand which covenant is meant. A great many have thought that it is the New Covenant in the New Testament. Actually, this has no reference to the first coming of Christ but rather to the covenant which God has made with the people of Israel. This covenant is expressed several places in the Scriptures (Lev 26:9-13; Deut 4:23).[1389]

Once again, in referencing chapter 7 in this book, the LORD on Mt. Sinai was the second person of the Godhead, *Yeshua*. The Levites, or the priests, did not fulfill their God-given responsibilities in the Mosaic Covenant, so He was going to send someone extraordinary to His temple, which the following statement reflects:

> Because the priests did not fulfill their duty as the ordinary ambassadors of God the Lord was about to send an extraordinary messenger.[1390]

That extraordinary messenger was the *Moshiach* who came to His temple in the person of *Yeshua*, the Son of David. It is clearly seen that the messengers are distinct persons in John the Baptist and *Yeshua*. Five of the six pronouns spoke of the Lord and the other was the messenger that prepared the way for the Lord to come to His temple. The Lord can be none other than the incarnation of God in the person of *Yeshua*. The net result of this passage shows that if *Yeshua* is not God Incarnate, then the Lord spoke falsely through the prophet Malachi. The LORD did not come to His temple at any point and time; from its rededication to its destruction in 70 CE by the Romans, and manifest Himself in such a way that Israel knew He had returned. But He did come in flesh to His temple.

All of the passages in this chapter show, without a doubt, that the individual reflected in this passage is God, yet unique from God. Malachi 3:1 clearly shows that this individual is God who entered time and space as a human being for 36 years and presented Himself with authority, and not as the scribes (Matthew 7:29; Mark 1:22; Luke 4:36), because He was and is the God of Israel that led them throughout their history and the God whom they worshipped.

The impact of the tri-unity of God and the purpose of the Messiah's two comings are inseparable in understanding the redemptive purposes of God in two areas: first that the plurality of God is taught throughout the pages of the *Tanakh* and that God would have to become man to redeem mankind from his sins, and second that the Messiah is God and would come twice, once to redeem the world from the curse of sin and again to redeem Israel and fulfill the promises made to Abraham in the future coming for the

---

[1389] McGee, *Thru the Bible: Proverbs – Malachi,* 3:1016.
[1390] Keil & Delitzsch, *Commentary on the Old Testament: Malachi,* 10:457.

Kingdom. The key factor is that God is a tri-unity who revealed Himself through the Messenger of *Yahweh*, and His Holy Spirit's coming upon man is critical in comprehending the ministry of *Moshiach* as given in the *Tanakh*. No one should even pretend to know or understand just how *Elohim* is plural and how He works within His person. What is known is that the *Tanakh*, as well as the New Covenant presents God operating in a triune form.

Finally, Josh McDowell said it was all but mathematically impossible for one "man" to fulfill the major prophecies of the first coming of Messiah. For Jesus Christ to fulfill eight of the major prophecies concerning His first coming was 1 to the 17th power, or 1 to 100,000,000,000,000,000.[1391] The eight prophecies are as follows: (1) Born in Bethlehem – Micah 5:2; (2) Preceded by a messenger – Isaiah 40:3; (3) Entered Jerusalem on a donkey – Zechariah 9:9; (4) Betrayed by a friend – Psalm 41:9 and hands and feet pierced – Psalm 22:16; (5) Sold out for 30 pieces of silver – Zechariah 11:12; (6) Money to be thrown into God's house – Zechariah 11:12 and price given for potter's field – Zechariah 11:13; (7) Dumb before His accusers – Isaiah 53:7; (8) Crucified with thieves – Isaiah 53:12.[1392] The probability that a single man could fulfill 48 of the first coming references is 1 to the 157th power.[1393] That one man could fulfill these prophecies of Messiah's first coming is beyond question an absolute miracle of God. But then again, God is good and does miracles to fulfill His promises and covenants in His word.

This chapter has demonstrated that *Yeshua* is divine. He is the God/man that God promised, from the time of the fall in Genesis 3:15 right up through the prophet Zechariah. The Scriptures are clear that *Yeshua* is both God and man, who will reign on the throne of David, and will fulfill the promises to Abraham, Isaac and Jacob, to the Nation of Israel, and to David, all in the New Covenant of Jeremiah.

This section on the divinity of the *Moshiach* in the Prophets will be followed by the divinity of the *Moshiach* in the Writings.

[1391] Josh McDowell, *Evidence That Demands a Verdict*, (Nashville: Nelson, 1979)1:167.

[1392] McDowell, *Evidence That Demands a Verdict*, 1:141-166.

[1393] McDowell, *Evidence That Demands a Verdict*, 1:167.

Chapter 15
Messiah Divine In the Writings

In the Law and the Prophets numerous passages have been used to show the divinity of the *Moshiach*, the Son of David. In the third division of the Jewish Bible, the Writings also have some very important verses that continue to show the fact that the Messiah will be the God/man promised in the garden of Eden in Genesis 3:15.

THE DAVIDIC COVENANT
... 1 Chronicles 17:10-14 and 2 Samuel 7:11-16

The most significant place to start in the Writings is an examination of the Davidic Covenant given in 1 Chronicles 17:10-14 and 2 Samuel 7:11-16. The significance of this covenant hinges on the direct relationship between the Davidic Covenant and the passages given by the prophets equating this physical Son of David with the Messiah as God. Why are there two references for the Davidic Covenant? They are not totally the same, and yet they have tremendous similarities. Observe the two passages with the personages, differences and similarities involved.

1 Chronicles 17 and 2 Samuel 7

1 Chronicles 17:10-14	2 Samuel 7:11-16
Olam – Eternal House or Dynasty	*Olam* – Eternal House or Dynasty
Olam – Eternal Kingdom	*Olam* - Eternal Kingdom
Olam – Eternal Throne	*Olam* – Eternal Throne
No sin or chastening mentioned	If he sins – chasten
Someone beyond Solomon in view	Solomon in view
Olam – Eternal Son	

Fruchtenbaum makes the following observation of these two passages of Scripture as to the differences and similarities:

> The parallel passage in 1 Chronicles 17:10b-14 is very similar, yet there are significant differences. In 2 Samuel the son is immediate; in 1 Chronicles he is distant. In 2 Samuel the son is a sinner; in 1 Chronicles there is no mention of sin. In 2 Samuel the reference is to Solomon; in 1 Chronicles the reference is to Messiah.

> The three promises of 2 Samuel are repeated here, but a fourth is also added: an eternal son. 'I will settle him in my house forever.' David's line will eventually

culminate in the birth of an eternal Person whose eternality will guarantee David's dynasty, kingdom and throne forever.[1394]

Olam is used four times in 1 Chronicles 17 and three times in the 2 Samuel 7 passage. These passages cannot be read without understanding that God is making a perpetual covenant with David. This covenant will last throughout time and eternity because of the aspect brought out in the 1 Chronicles passage concerning an eternal Son, who is the *Moshiach*.

What Ethan, the Ezrahite, who was in Solomon's court (1 Kings 4:30-31), wrote about David in Psalm 89 is significant. He wrote after the time of David and during Solomon's reign, giving important confirmation and understanding as to the interpretation of the Davidic Covenant. Look at some of the following verses:

> verses 3-4 [4-5] I have made a covenant with My chosen one; I have sworn to My servant David; I will establish your offspring forever, I will confirm your throne for all generations. Selah.

> verse 29 [30] I will establish his line forever, his throne, as long as the heavens last.

> verse 34-37 [35-38] I will not violate My covenant, or change what I have uttered. I have sworn by My holiness, once and for all; I will not be false to David. His line shall continue forever, his throne, as the sun before Me, as the moon, established forever, an enduring witness in the sky. Selah.

> verse 51 [52] How Your enemies, O LORD, have flung abuse, abuse at Your anointed at every step.

These statements of Scripture, by the hand of Ethan the Ezrahite, are clear and unmistakable. This Davidic Covenant is viewed by Ethan under the inspiration of Scripture as being *"forever."* The word *"anointed"* in verse 51 is the Hebrew word *Moshiach*, from which Messiah comes. The connection that Ethan makes between the Davidic Covenant and his use of *Moshiach* is significant.

One other dimension is the Jeremiah 22:24-30 passage, which was looked at in chapter 13, which appeared to threaten the *"forever"* implications of the Davidic Covenant. This passage needs to be brought into view as to its direct relationship between Solomon and his kingly line, which was cursed by God in Jeremiah 22:24-30. *Yeshua*, in the New Covenant, could He get His right to rule from His stepfather, Joseph, because God side stepped the Coniah curse through Shealtiel and his son Zerubbabel? *Yeshua* was of the Davidic line through *Miriam* (Mary), but there were many sons of David in the first century CE. The New Covenant book of Luke gives *Yeshua* the right to rule by God Himself because of the Davidic birth recorded in Luke 1:32:

[1394] Fruchtenbaum, *Messianic Christology*, 79.

He shall be great, and shall be called the Son of the Highest: and the Lord God shall give unto him the throne of his father David.

Nathan told David that his house, throne and kingdom would be secure because one of his sons (future descendants) would be the eternal Son of God, whose incarnation would ultimately place Him physically in the house of David and on his throne forever.

There is another significant verse from the New Covenant that deals directly with the Davidic Covenant. *Yeshua*, near the end of His ministry, asked the Pharisees a question as to who the Messiah would be. But they could not, and would not, answer. The answer was not acceptable to them. In Matthew 22:41-46 *Yeshua* refers to Psalm 110:1:

> While the Pharisees were gathered together, *Yeshua* asked them, saying, What think ye of Messiah? Whose son is he? They say unto him, The Son of David. He saith unto them, how then doth David in spirit call him Lord, saying, The LORD said unto my Lord, sit thou on my right hand, till I make thine enemies thy footstool? If David then called him Lord, how is he his son? And no man was able to answer him a word, neither durst [dare] any man from that day forth ask him any more questions.

The answer to the question, "*If David then called him Lord, how is he his son*," is that this Son of David was obviously God. However, the Pharisees would not answer it. This will be dealt with in more detail from Psalm 110 shortly.

Olam, in the 1 Chronicles account, points out clearly that a son of the sons of David would reign on his throne for *olam*. Once again the context definitely points to *olam* as the end of time. When Ethan, in Psalm 89, adds his understanding to the original passage, it becomes even clearer that the one who is settled by God, in His house and in His kingdom, shall be established and reign on the throne of David beyond the end of time into eternity, forevermore. Lastly, does the curse of Jeremiah 22 totally disqualify any descendant of Solomon through Coniah from ever being king over Israel from the throne of David? This has been briefly discussed in chapter 14 and will be thoroughly dealt with in chapter 17.

THE SUFFERING AND EXALTATION OF THE MESSIAH ... Psalm 22

(1) To the chief musician upon Aijeleth-hashahar, a psalm of David. (2) **My God, my God, why hast thou forsaken me**? Why art thou so far from helping me, and from the words of my roaring? (3) O my God, I cry in the daytime, but thou hearest not; and in the night season, and am not silent. (4) But thou art holy, O thou that inhabitest the praises of Israel. (5) Our fathers trusted in thee: they trusted, and thou didst deliver them.

(6) They cried unto thee, and were delivered: they trusted in thee, and were not confounded. (7) But I am a worm, and not man; a reproach of men, and despised of the people. (8) **All they that see me laugh me to scorn: they shoot out the lip, they shake the head, saying, (9) He trusted on the Lord that he would deliver him: let him deliver him, seeing he delighted in him.** (10) But thou art he that took me out of the womb: thou didst make me hope when I was upon my mother's breasts.

(11) I was cast upon thee from the womb: thou art my God from my mother's belly. (12) Be not far from me; for trouble is near; for there is none to help. (13) Many bulls have compassed me: strong bulls of Bashan have beset me round. (14) They gaped upon me with their mouths, as a ravening and a roaring lion. (15) **I am poured out like water, and all my bones are out of joint: my heart is like wax; it is melted in the midst of my bowels**.

(16) **My strength is dried up like a potsherd; and my tongue cleaveth to my jaws**; and thou hast brought me into the dust of death. (17) For dogs have compassed me: the assembly of the wicked have inclosed me: **they pierced my hands and my feet**. (18) I may tell all my bones: they look and stare upon me. (19) **They part my garments among them, and cast lots upon my vesture**. (20) But be not thou far from me, O Lord: O my strength, haste thee to help me.

(21) Deliver my soul from the sword; my darling from the power of the dog. (22) Save me from the lion's mouth: for thou hast heard me from the horns of the unicorns. (23) I will declare thy name unto my brethren: in the midst of the congregation will I praise thee. (24) Ye that fear the Lord, praise him; all ye the seed of Jacob, glorify him; and fear him, all ye the seed of Israel. (25) For he hath not despised nor abhorred the affliction of the afflicted; neither hath he hid his face from him; but when he cried unto him, he heard.

(26) My praise shall be of thee in the great congregation: I will pay my vows before them that fear him. (27) The meek shall eat and be satisfied: they shall praise the Lord that seek him: your heart shall live for ever. (28) All the ends of the world shall remember and turn unto the Lord: and all the families of the nations shall worship before thee. (29) For the kingdom is the Lord's: and he is the governor among the nations. (30) All they that be fat upon earth shall eat and worship: all they that go down to the dust shall bow before him: and none can keep alive his own soul.

(31) A seed shall serve him; it shall be accounted to the Lord for a generation. (32) They shall come, and shall declare his righteousness unto a people that shall be born, that he hath done this (Harkavy Version).

The shepherd psalms were written by David and include the 22nd through the 24th Psalm. The 22nd Psalm does not have the term Messiah within its verses however, this psalm speaks to the suffering of the Messiah in verses 1-22 and the exaltation of the

472

Messiah in verses 23-32. The interesting point in this psalm is that the description that David gives of his suffering follow prophetically what happened to the greater Son of David at his crucifixion in the Gospel accounts of the New Covenant (Matthew 27:27-50; Mark 15:16-37; Luke 23:27-46 and John 1:37). The emphasis in the Scripture quotation above is parallel to the description of the crucifixion in the Gospel accounts of the New Covenant. These verses do not need to be discussed for they are really self-explanatory.

The main point of disagreement between Judaism and biblical faith is verse 16 or 17 depending upon the version used. The contentious phrase is "*they pierced my hands and feet.*" New Covenant believers teach that David is describing the Roman crucifixion 1000 years before it happened. Because of this interpretation Rabbinic Judaism has reacted very aggressively against this interpretation. In reading through Gerald Sigal's statements concerning this verse he points to the use of the Septuagint by the early church.[1395] Now this was true, the Bible of the early church was the Septuagint, however he conveniently ignores one very important point. The early Christian church did not create the Septuagint! The Septuagint was translated into Greek not by Christians but by 70 Jewish religious scholars in Alexandria, Egypt between the years of 275 – 247 B.C.E. long before this ever became an issue in the first century of the Common Era.[1396]

The point is that because true believers quote a Jewish translation, it is made to look like it is a Christian translation by Jewish anti-Missionaries and that is purposefully being misleading to the reader. The heart of the issue is the Hebrew word כָּאֲרִי translated by Rabbinic Judaism as "as a lion" and by New Covenant believers as "they pierced" and the Greek word "ωρυξαν and the meaning "*they pierced.*" How is it that Jewish and Christian scholars get two completely different meanings. The problem is expressed by Boice:

A translator must always be careful how he or she disagrees with the Masoretic text, particularly when there is no explicit textual variant to base an alternative translation on. Yet in this case there seems to be good reason for doing so. For one thing, the Septuagint (Greek) translation of the Old Testament produced a century or two before the Christian era and therefore an unbiased witness, rendered the word "pierced." Second, the other major versions also translate the Hebrew this way. Third, the meaning "as a lion" has little sense in the context and leaves the phrase in question without an explicit verb (it would have to be supplied from the preceding line). This suggests that the Masoretic text with its vowel pointing is just wrong and that alternative vowel should be supplied. It may even suggest that the Masoretic text was deliberately pointed in the way it

---

[1395] Sigal, *The Jew and The Christian Missionary: A Jewish Response to Missionary Christianity,* 97.

[1396] Thomas O. Figart, *Meaningful Mediations II: Psalm 22-24* (Longwood, FL: Xulon Press, 2007), 60.

was by later Jewish scholars to avoid what otherwise would be a nearly inescapable prophecy of Jesus' crucifixion.[1397]

The Hebrew Scripture is the verbally inspired Word of God. However, the vowel markings are not verbally inspired but were added by the Masoretes for the purpose of knowing the pronunciations and punctuations of the Hebrew words. In other words the vowel points or markings were added well over 1500 years after the Scriptures were penned. Rabbi Cohen of the Soncino series references that there are two viewpoints on this view; one from the Masoretes and the other from the Greek Septuagint in the following statement:

> "*like a lion, they are at my hands and feet*." The Hebrew is difficult, there being nothing to correspond to "they are at." The Targum has, "biting like a lion my hands and my feet." [Authorized Version] and [Revised Version] render "they pierce," adopting the reading of the LXX (the Greek translation of the Old Testament) to accord with the Christological interpretation of the Psalm.

The Septuagint was a Jewish translation of Psalm 22:16 [17], so the issue is of Jewish background and not Christian. Also it is interesting to note that even the Peshitta (the Ancient Eastern Text) renders the word, "*they pierced my hands and feet*." One final source that needs to be looked at is the Dead Sea Scrolls. These are the oldest known Hebrew scrolls of the *Tanakh*, predating the Masoretic text by 1000 years, the following statement is made:

> Psalm 22 is a favorite among Christians since it is often linked in the New Testament with the suffering and death of Jesus. A well-known and controversial reading is found in verse 16, where the Masoretic Text read "Like a lion are my hand and feet," whereas the Septuagint has "They have pierced my hands and feet." Among the scrolls the reading in question is found only in the Psalms scroll found at Nahal Hever (abbreviated 5/6HevPs), which reads "They have pierced my hands and my feet"![1398]

Not only is the phrase "*they pierced my hands and feet*" verifiable, but it really carries the most weight and is the most convincing. Two other ancient Jewish sources, the Septuagint 250 years before the issue and the Dead Sea Scrolls of the Essenes during or before the time of Messiah both completely verify the New Covenant teaching of Psalm 22:16 [17]. According to Fruchtenbaum the Scriptures not only teach that the Messiah's hands and feet were to be pierced, but Psalm 22 also teachings the following concerning the sufferings of the Messiah:

[1397] James Montgomery Boice, *An Expositional Commentary: Psalms* (3 vols. Grand Rapids: Baker Books, 1994), 1:196.

[1398] Martin Abegg Jr, Peter Flint and Eugene Ulrich, *The Dead Sea Scrolls Bible: The Oldest Known Bible Translated for the First Time into English* (San Francisco: HarperCollins Publisher, 1999), 518-519.

In extreme agony, Messiah would cry out for God's help. Messiah would be a despised and rejected individual. In the agony of death, Messiah would be stared at and mocked. The Messiah's bones would all be pulled out of joint. The Messiah's heart would rupture. The Messiah would suffer an extreme degree of thirst. Messiah's hands and feet would be pierced. Messiah's clothing would be divided by the casting of lots. At the point of death, Messiah's trust would be in God the Father. Messiah would be resurrected.[1399]

The term Messiah is not mentioned in this passage but what the Messiah endured for sinful men cannot be argued. Messiah *Yeshua* suffered all these things on the cross for Jewish and Gentile souls.

DAVID'S SON IS HIS LORD
... Psalm 110:1-7

(1) The LORD said unto my Lord, Sit thou at my right hand, until I make thine enemies thy footstool. (2) The LORD shall send the rod of thy strength out of Zion: rule thou in the midst of thine enemies. (3) Thy people shall be willing in the day of thy power, in the beauties of holiness from the womb of the morning: thou hast the dew of thy youth. (4) The LORD hath sworn, and will not repent, Thou art a priest forever after the order of Melchizedek. (5) The Lord at thy right hand shall strike through kings in the day of his wrath. (6) He shall judge among the heathen, he shall fill the places with the dead bodies; he shall wound the heads over many countries. (7) He shall drink of the brook in the way: therefore shall he lift up the head (KJV).

This Psalm is one of the most fascinating Psalms in the *Tanakh* because of the way *Yeshua* used it, and how it relates to the equality of David's Lord with the LORD. There are four observations about this passage that need to be investigated. First, David's son is his Lord. Second, this Lord has enemies. Third, this psalm ties together two positions of priest and king that are forbidden in biblical Judaism. The kings of Israel (Judah) were not to be priests, yet in this psalm the future reigning Son of David is portrayed as a priest *"after the order of Melchizedek."* It is completely unheard of that the Son of David, of the tribe of Judah, would be king and priest. When King Uzziah tried to officiate in a high priestly function, God smote him with leprosy (2 Chronicles 26:16-21). Fourth, this psalm is quoted in the New Covenant more times than any other passage from the Hebrew Scriptures. The Jewish response to Psalm 110:1-4 is very sharp and clear as Rabbi Singer explains why this psalm cannot refer to *Yeshua*:

Psalm 110 represents one of the New Testament's most stunning, yet clever mistranslations of the Jewish Scriptures. Moreover, the confusion created by the Christianization of this verse was further perpetuated and promulgated by numerous Christian translators of the Bible as well.... The story of the church's

---

[1399] Fruchtenbaum, *Messianic Christology*, 86.

tampering with Psalm 110 is so old that it begins in the Christian canon itself.[1400]

Rabbi Singer, an anti-missionary for the Jewish people, makes some serious charges against the biblical interpretation of Psalm 110. However, in Michael Brown's book, it is observed that Singer's problem is not with Christians but with the Jewish translators themselves. When translating the Greek Septuagint (LXX) from the Hebrew Scriptures, the usage of the Greek word for Lord (*kyrios*) lies at the heart of controversy.[1401] A part of this lengthy argument will be discussed later in this chapter.

The Psalm 110 passage is used 14 times by the New Covenant writers more than any other portion of the Hebrew Scriptures. Wilson states that this verse, in each case, refers to *Yeshua*. *Yeshua* uses Psalm 110:1 with authority against the Pharisees, affirming that it was written by David under the inspiration of the Holy Spirit.[1402] Echoing Wilson, Mays asserts that it is used more than any other reference from the *Tanakh* in reference to *Yeshua* (Matthew 22:44; Mark 14:62; 16:19; Luke 22:69; Acts 2:34-35; 7:55; Romans 8:34; Ephesians 1:20; Colossians 3:1; Hebrews 1:3, 13; 8:1; 10:12; 1 Peter 3:22).[1403]

Previously it was mentioned that four areas need to be studied in reference to this passage: (1) David's son is his Lord, (2) this Lord has enemies, (3) this psalm ties together two positions, kingship and the priesthood, (4) and this psalm is referenced in the New Covenant more than any other passage from the *Tanakh*. The fourth point has already been observed and now each of the three remaining will be taken separately and discussed.

In the first argument David writes Psalm 110:1 as being an oracle of *Yahweh*. David states the following: *"The LORD said to my lord."* Philips is correct in seeing God (Lord) as two distinct personalities, but he gives no information as to how he arrived at his conclusion:

Hebrew and Gentile scholars translate it the following way: "God said unto my God." This is very significant and revealing, for it presents two personalities: God number one and God number two. God number one spoke to God number two and said, "Sit thou at my right hand until I make thine enemies thy footstool."[1404]

[1400] Tovia Singer, http://www.OutReachJudaism.org/ psalm110.html.

[1401] Michael Brown, *Answering Jewish Objections to Jesus: Messianic Prophecy Objections*, 3:133-145.

[1402] T. Ernest Wilson, *The Messianic Psalms* (Neptune, NJ: Loizeaux, 1978), 126.

[1403] James L. Mays, *Interpretation, A Bible Commentary for Teaching and Preaching: Psalms* (Louisville: John Knox Press, 1989), 350.

[1404] O. E. Phillips, *Exploring the Messianic Psalms* (Philadelphia: Hebrew Christian Fellowship, 1967), 274.

Hebrew scholars? Phillips cannot mean Jewish Hebrew scholars because no Jewish scholar would make such a rash and abrupt acknowledgement concerning God. Rabbi Singer has a valid point on the words for Lord, to which some versions give misleading translations by using two Lords, as representing two Gods.[1405] Searching eight of nine popular versions confirms that only one of them replicates the emphasis of the original Hebrew. The King James Version uses "LORD" and "Lord" in that order. The problem of how "Lord" is used lies in the Greek Septuagint (LXX). In the Greek, "lord," "Lord," or "LORD" are all *kyrios*, which is translated "lord" or "Lord" in the New Covenant. However, in the Hebrew text the first LORD is Israel's personal name for God, whereas *adon* simply means "lord" or "master," not necessarily referring to God. Johnson states that *adon* is used 334 times (Genesis 18:12; 19:2; Ruth 2:13; 1 Samuel 1:15), 300 of which directly refer to a human lord and master. Only 30 times is the word used "of the divine Lord/Master, as in a divine title (Exodus 34:23; Deuteronomy 10:17)."[1406] If only the first six words of Psalm 110:1 (The LORD said unto my Lord) are considered, it could very easily be seen as *Yahweh* speaking to the Messiah. But those first six words would not necessitate the "lord" (*adon*) being God. However, those six words are not isolated but are connected to "*Sit at My right hand*," and that changes the whole perspective of the verse. That is a personal invitation by *Yahweh* for the *Moshiach* to sit on the very throne of *Yahweh* at His right hand. Fruchtenbaum states that in the ancient Near East in Old Testament times, when a host king entertained a visiting king from another country, he would place him on his right side (1 Kings 2:19). This act of the host king was making a statement that the visiting king was his equal.[1407] Keil and Delitzsch affirm that conclusion:

> The conclusion to be drawn from this Psalm must have been felt by the Pharisees themselves, that the Messiah, being the Son of David and Lord at the same time, was of human and at the same time of superhuman nature; that it was therefore in accordance with Scripture if this Jesus, who represented Himself to be the predicted Christ, should as such profess to be the Son of God and of divine nature.[1408]

Also to sit at the right hand of a king was considered a position of honor or respect. On one occasion Solomon had his mother Bathsheba sit on his right hand, not because she was co-ruler with him. Rather, it indicated Solomon's desire to grant her a position of honor and respect. Aloisi makes a good observation as it relates to *Yahweh*:

> Outside of Psalm 110, no one in the OT is ever said to (or commanded to) sit at the right hand of Yahweh. Even the kings of Israel [and Judah] are never

---

[1405] Tovia Singer, http://*www.OutReachJudaism.org/psalm110.html.*
[1406] VanGemeren, *Dictionary of Old Testament Theology & Exegesis,* 1:257.
[1407] Fruchtenbaum, *Messianic Christology,* 88.
[1408] Keil and Delitzsch, *Commentary on the Old Testament: Psalms.,* 5:185.

described as sitting at God's right hand. This is a unique command. David's Lord is instructed to take a position of unusual honor alongside the deity.[1409]

A mere mortal will never sit on God's right hand, not even Abraham to whom the Talmud refers as sitting at His right hand.[1410] The statement of Levine, an anti-missionary points to Abraham to remove himself from the obvious meaning of the text:

> Now, who is David's master? Could it be someone who was not born yet, such as Jesus? That seems very forced and absurd. Therefore, the Talmud says it refers to Abraham, our forefather, and the Psalm refers to the anxious time before Abraham had to fight the four kings, in Genesis 14. God is telling Abraham not to worry, sit, so to speak, at my side, until I take care of your enemies.... Moreover, it does seem to point directly to someone else, namely, Abraham, who was a master, in some way, to David, who had a relationship to Melchizedek.[1411]

It is indeed "forced and absurd" to make the assertion that Abraham was David's "Lord." Abraham is not even in the context of the Psalm and is not even alluded to nor was he ever invited by the LORD to sit at His right hand. In fact only the *Moshiach* has been invited to sit at the Father's right hand (Psalm 80:17). Because the statement of David is so powerful, they had to find an alternate answer. Yes, the Second Person of the plural unity of *Elohim* had not yet come in the flesh, but that does not mean that He was not David's Lord. As has been seen throughout this book, the Second Person of the plural unity of *Elohim* was very present in the *Tanakh* as "*the angel* [Messenger] *of the LORD,*" the "*captain of the LORD's host,*" *Shechinah* of God, "*the Branch,*" the RIGHTEOUS one, the pre-incarnate *Yeshua.*

Not even angels sit on God's right hand. God Himself is making a statement that this physical seed of David is *Yahweh's* equal. No human father, if he has any pride as a man, would ever call his physical son lord! Yet here *Yahweh* has made an invitation for an earthly monarch to sit on His right hand. To say that this is momentous and even stupendous for the Hebrew mind is an understatement. The invitation between *Yahweh* and this future lord of David "shows an exceptional degree of intimacy between God and this new monarch."[1412] Phillips is correct in his statement that there are two Gods (Lords).

Cooper states that Psalm 110:1-2 has three personalities which are revealed to the reader. There are two Lords (Lord and LORD) and one enemy. Hebrew parallelism shows that the Lord is the ruler and the enemies are the ones that He rules over:

[1409] John Aloisi, "Who is David's Lord? Another Look at Psalm 110:1." *DBSJ* 10, (2005):103-123. (pg 107).

[1410] Steinsaltz, *The Talmud: The Steinsaltz Edition, Sanhedrin 108b,* 21:150.

[1411] Levine, *You Take Jesus, I'll Take God: How to Refute Christian Missionaries,* 38.

[1412] Samuel Terrien, *Critical Eerdmans Commentary: The Psalms* (Grand Rapids: Eerdmans, 2003), 752.

The following verse [110:2] shows very clearly who these enemies are: "The scepter of Thine authority shall the Lord stretch forth from Zion: rule Thou in the midst of Thine enemies." The first part of this Hebrew parallelism shows that the Messiah is to rule in Zion and the latter part points to the inhabitants of same is His enemies; therefore the inhabitants of Zion are His enemies.[1413]

Cooper continues to present the argument for the distinctions in the two Lords, the two comings of the *Moshiach*. The enemy would be hostile to Him in His first coming but in His second coming the enemies will be in subjection:

These two verses [110:1-2], therefore, presuppose that the Messiah comes to Zion and incurs the displeasure of the Hebrew people. When they become hostile to Him, the Lord invites Him, the Messiah, to leave the place of hostility and to sit at His right hand – in heaven. The period during which the Messiah is to remain in heaven with the Lord will be terminated by the latter's subduing the former's enemies. Therefore this passage assumes two comings of the Messiah: at His first coming the Hebrew people reject Him and He returns to the right hand of the throne of God awaiting the time (the length of which is not suggested here) when the Lord shall have brought the Hebrew people, those hostile to His Messiah, into a state of subjection. This conquest having been accomplished, the Messiah returns to Zion as its King and with divine authority and power rules in the very place where He formerly was rejected.[1414]

This whole idea of David's Lord having enemies and the LORD inviting Him to sit on His right hand, draws one's mind to Hosea 5:15 which states:

And I will return to My abode till they realize their guilt. In their distress, they will seek Me and beg for My favor.

The question this verse raises is: When did God leave His abode so that He would have to return to His abode until Israel realized her guilt? The identity of David's Lord and God returning to His abode gives much anxiety to Jewish scholars. Davis adds to the argument but approaches the subject of the identity of David's Lord in the following statement concerning Psalm 110:

This verse introduces the persons mentioned in the psalm – Yahweh, Adoni, and the enemy. Assonance is used to unite the first two cola following the title לַאדֹנִי, "to my Lord," is parallel to לִימִינִי "at My right side". This device binds Yahweh and Adoni together, thereby showing that they are distinct from the enemy.

A second example of assonance begins in verse 1c and carries through verse 3. This is the repetition of the final ך ("Your") which highlights Adoni's ownership of His opponents ("Your enemies," who become "Your footstool,"

[1413] Cooper, *The Shepherd of Israel Seeking His Own,* 88.
[1414] Cooper, *The Shepherd of Israel Seeking His Own,* 88.

v. 1; "Your enemies," v. 2b), His ability to rule ("Your scepter," v. 2a; "Your power," v. 3a), and His relationship to His friends "Your people;" "Your youth," v. 3). A further instance of the ד assonance occurs in verse 3 in the prepositional phrase לְךָ ("to You").[1415]

Psalm 110:1 records a conversation between two members of the Godhead. The only adequate explanation for this conversation between two persons with divine names is that there must be a plurality of personalities within the Godhead – a concept which is consistent with many other passages (Genesis 1:1, 26; 3:22; 11:7; Deuteronomy 6:4; Isaiah 48:16). This verse is also further confirmation that the Messiah would be more than just a great man – He would be God! What is interesting is that the same person "Lord" is addressed as both king and priest as Van Groningen states:

> Vs 1. The term *ne'um* (oracle) is often used of a prophetic pronouncement made in the name of or on behalf of God. Thus, the very first word places this psalm in a prophetic setting. Yahweh was the source of the oracle: Yahweh made the pronouncement; *adoni* (my Lord, i.e., sovereign Master) is addressed. Yahweh addresses the sovereign Master whom David claims as his. Three distinct persons are involved: Yahweh, the sovereign Lord, and David who claims a close relationship with the sovereign Lord.... David makes a clear distinction between Yahweh, his sovereign Lord, and himself.[1416]

> *Seb liminay* (Sit to my right hand) is in the imperative. The right hand is the place of honor, power, and privilege. The command to sit gives the right and authority to occupy that position and the ruling function that accompanies it. It is not only a royal privilege and position that is referred to; it is divine! It is Yahweh who speaks; it is Yahweh's right hand; it is the reign of Yahweh that is transferred to "my Lord".... In fact, David's throne represents the throne of the Son referred to in Psalm 2:6-9.[1417]

Even though the modern day rabbis interpret this verse as not being Messianic, the rabbis of the ancient synagogue clearly interpreted this verse as referring to the Messiah. (See Sanhedrin 108:2 and Midrash Tehillim.)

> In verses 1-3, two commands are issued to Messiah: "Sit" (v. 1) and "Rule" (v. 2). "Sit at my right hand, until I make your enemies your footstool." The first command refers to Messiah's ascension and exaltation to the place of authority (right hand).... The second command ("rule") is found in verse 2: "The LORD sends forth from Zion your mighty scepter. Rule in the midst of your enemies!"[1418]

[1415] Barry C. Davis, "Is Psalm 110 a Messianic Psalm?" *Bibliotheca Sacra* 157, no. 626 (April – June 2000): 163.

[1416] Van Groningen, *Messianic Revelation in the Old Testament,* 391.

[1417] Van Groningen, *Messianic Revelation in the Old Testament,* 393.

[1418] Varner, *The Messiah: Revealed, Rejected, Received,* 68-69.

Verse 4 introduces the center and climax of this Psalm: "The LORD has sworn and will not change his mind, 'You are a priest forever after the order of Melchizedek.'" In all of God's dealings with man, He has resorted to the human custom of oath-taking only twice: once to Abraham (Gen 22:16-18) and once to David (Psa 89:35-36). This statement in Psalm 110:4 is a further elaboration of that oath-promise. In this Psalm, we see that Messiah will be the occupant of David's throne, and that He will rule as a priest. The only way in which He could do this would be if He were in another priestly order, for the Aaronic priests were never to occupy the office of King at the same time. This the Messiah can do, however, because He is a "priest forever after the order of Melchizedek."[1419]

There is simply too much in this verse to explain it away as being David himself or Solomon his son.[1420] As this passage is studied, the only logical meaning is a Messianic interpretation of this passage that David's Lord is not just the Messiah but God Himself. Further insight is given by Van Groningen that as God has given the deity to David's Son, He has also not given any flexibility as to what He means:

> Vs 4. In this verse the second of Yahweh's utterances is recorded. The verb *nisba* (niphal, reflexive use: he has sworn by himself) expresses a strong oath. Yahweh binds himself unalterably to the pronouncement to follow.[1421]

> The text gives interpreters no legitimate alternatives. Yahweh is addressed as adonay (Lord) as in verse 1 (adoni). The sovereign Master, the victorious King, is also addressed as the eternal Priest. In Israel, the functions performed by the three divinely established offices were assumed by specific individuals such as Abraham, Moses, Samuel, and David in unique circumstances. When, however, the priesthood was well established and functioned properly, only the priests officiated; no anointed king did so. Thus, to consider a king in Israel a "priest forever" is entirely contrary to biblical evidence and Israelite practices.[1422]

> The eternal priesthood of the sovereign Master is not Aaronic, that is, a man and his house elected by God to serve in the office from generation to generation within the confines of Israel. The Hebrew phrase *'aldibrati malki-sedek* (according to the order of Melchizedek) denotes a priesthood of another kind.[1423]

Before leaving verses 1-2 there is one other point that needs to be brought to the student's attention. Cooper states that there are three individuals in this passage.

[1419] Varner, *The Messiah: Revealed, Rejected, Received,* 70-71.

[1420] Aloisi, "Who is David's Lord? Another Look at Psalm 110:1." *DBSJ* 10, (2005):103-123.

[1421] Van Groningen, *Messianic Revelation in the Old Testament,* 393.

[1422] Van Groningen, *Messianic Revelation in the Old Testament,* 394.

[1423] Van Groningen, *Messianic Revelation in the Old Testament,* 394-395.

However, there are four individuals, the LORD, *Adonai*, the enemies of *Adonai* and lastly the identity of the person called "my" in this text. The speaker of the psalm is in view with the usage of this word "my." It has been commonly recognized by true believers and it was evidently recognized by the Pharisees (Matthew 22:41-45) that the Psalm was written by David. However, there are some rabbis that attempt to cover up the Davidic authorship by stating that the psalm was written for a priestly choirmaster, as recorded in the following statement:

> Psalm 110 was written for the priestly choirmaster. The Levities, not David, sang the Psalms in the Temple. Thus, when a Levite or Israelite chanted the words "YHVH said to my lord," the second "lord" referred to King David. It has no Christological overtones, as though a divine being were seated in heaven at the literal right-hand of God. The right-hand position denotes favor.[1424]

Notice the attempt to move away from a literal understanding of the text. There is nothing in verse 1 that would lead anyone to think it was anything but a literal statement. It is interesting that rabbis accuse Christians of picking on the "weak" and "vulnerable" within Jewish society to lead them to Messiah. Yet here they do not mind giving to their own fellow Jews, whom they know are uneducated in the *Tanakh,* an interpretation that for many centuries the rabbis taught was a Messianic Psalm written by David himself. Notice the text clearly states that the author's (David) Lord (Messiah) is invited by the LORD to sit at His own right hand. If they do not believe in *Yeshua* as the Messiah, they will alter the interpretation to fit their perspective.

Yahweh gives the second argument when He states, *"while I make your enemies your footstool."* Phillips issues a very valued statement concerning who these enemies of God are and who the Son of David is. When and where did God and His enemies ever have the opportunity to meet each other to become enemies in the first place?

> God number two has some enemies…On further reflection, we realize that the enemies of God number two could not have been His enemies without knowing Him and having had some dealings with Him. The natural thought that comes to us is, who are these enemies? And when did they have an acquaintance with each other, and why did they become enemies?[1425]

When will his enemies become the footstool of a king? When the enemies were defeated, the ancient practice of a victorious king was to symbolically place his foot on the neck of the defeated enemy who was lying on the ground. Smith refers to that very action as the practice of the ancient Near East:

[1424] Picker, "Make Us A God!" *A Jewish Response to Hebrew Christianity: A Survival Manual For Jews,* 68.

[1425] Phillips, *Exploring the Messianic Psalms,* 275.

The allusion is to the custom of conquerors placing their feet upon the necks of the captured enemies as a symbolic token of total victory (Josh 10:24).[1426]

Lay,[1427] Pritchard[1428] and Howard[1429] affirm Smith's statement by also referencing Joshua 10:24 as a biblical example of placing one's foot on the neck of the defeated enemy. *Yahweh* is saying that David's physical Lord, the Messiah, is invited to sit on His right hand because this Son of David is His equal and He is going to make Messiah's enemies His footstool, and He will reign over them. That verse is a powerful statement to show David's Lord is indeed the LORD, equal with the Father and that He will reign from David's throne over all the earth.

The last argument concerns the forbidden area of intertwining the offices of the king and the priesthood. A king could be a prophet but not a high priest (Numbers 16:40; 18:7). A high priest could be a prophet, but not a king. Merrill,[1430] Smith[1431] and Geisler[1432] express that these two offices were never to be combined in the same person, yet Messiah *Yeshua* will be King of Israel and also be Priest. The answer is not complex, for *Yeshua* was born of the house of David, the tribe of Judah, which would disqualify Him from serving in a priestly function under the Law. However, according to Psalm 110:4, this Son of David, the Messiah, will serve as a priest-king even though God forbade that kind of dual role in the Mosaic Law, which means that the Mosaic Law will not be in effect when the Messiah reigns as King and Priest. This Son of David will not be a priest through the tribe of Levi, for David (and the author of the book of Hebrews) compares Him to a different High Priestly order *"after the order of Melchizedek;"* Melchizedek was not Jewish, but Canaanite. The Hebrew Scriptures reveal that the *Moshiach* will hold three offices when He comes and subdues His enemies:

> The Messiah will fill the offices of Prophet, Priest and King as the Tanakh points out. Moses predicted of the Messiah that He would be a Prophet (Deut 18:15-18). The Priesthood was anticipated in David's Psalm (110:4). Jacob and Balaam present Him as the King in Genesis 49:10 and Numbers 24:17. Include with that the Davidic Covenant and all the promises that speak of the Messiah being a king. The prophet Zechariah combines the fact that He will be a priest and a king in Zech 6:13.[1433]

[1426] Smith, *The Promised Messiah,* 187.

[1427] Bromiley, *The International Standard Bible Encyclopedia,* 2:332.

[1428] Pritchard, *The Ancient Near East in Pictures,* 285.

[1429] Howard, *The New American Commentary: Joshua,* 254.

[1430] Eugene H. Merrill, *Kingdom of Priests* (Grand Rapids: Baker, 1987), 377.

[1431] William Smith, *Old Testament History* (Joplin, MO: College Press, 1970), 639.

[1432] Norman L. Geisler, *A Popular Survey of the Old Testament* (Grand Rapids: Baker, 1977), 155.

[1433] Walvoord, *Jesus Christ Our Lord,* 88-89, 136-137.

There is absolutely no way a mere human being of the house of David, of the tribe of Judah, could be a priest or Levite at the same time unless His priestly function came from a different order. The order of Melchizedek is a type of His High Priestly order. While this Son of David is of the tribe of Judah, His origin is eternal; Melchizedek is described in Hebrews 7:1-3 as being *"without father, without mother, without descent, having neither beginning of days, nor end of life"*. Messiah, *"after the order of Melchizedek"* means that the Mosaic Law has been discontinued because the *Moshiach* is both Priest and King. This simply means the Law cannot be in force during the dispensation of Grace and the Kingdom, otherwise known as the church age and the Millennium. Fruchtenbaum gives insight on this situation:

> The Law of Moses laid down that all priests had to be of the tribe of Levi and that kings had to be of the tribe of Judah. In order for this prophecy to be fulfilled, therefore, it is clear that it will be necessary for the Law of Moses and the Levitical Order to be removed.

> The New Testament (Hebrews 7:11-18) clearly teaches that with the death of Jesus, the Law of Moses was rendered inoperative by His fulfillment of it and was replaced with the Law of Christ. Under the new Law of Christ, the Order of Melchizedek is instituted in place of the Levitical Order; therefore, Messiah is indeed a priest and a king. Verse 4 states that Messiah's priesthood and kingship will be eternal.[1434]

These four arguments clarify that Psalm 110 is a unique Psalm that was used by *Yeshua* to silence the Pharisees and for the writers of Scripture to show that He is the Lord of all.

WHO WAS WITH DANIEL IN THE LIONS' DEN?
... Daniel 6:21-22 [22-23]

(21) Daniel then talked with the king, 'O king, live forever! (22) My God sent His angel, who shut the mouths of the lions so that they did not injure me, inasmuch as I was found innocent by Him, nor have I, O king, done you any injury.'

Very few commentaries refer to this verse as a possible reference to *"the angel* (Messenger) *of the LORD."* While that particular name is not in this passage, there are several other interesting clues about the verse that need to be brought to attention. The first one comes from the text of *The Jewish Study Bible* quoted above, which clearly states *"His angel."* Who was this angel is the question one author asks:

> Who was the "angel" who spent the night in the den with Daniel? He may have been a member of the angelic host, but it is more likely that this heavenly being was the divine angelic messenger, the angel of the LORD.... The angel was

---

[1434] Fruchtenbaum, *Messianic Christology*, 89.

484

evidently visible to Daniel, and it is comforting to think of the faithful old prophet spending the night in fellowship with the Lord during his trying ordeal. Hebrews 1:33 alludes to this experience.[1435]

Miller clearly sees the Messenger of the LORD as the one who spent the night with Daniel. This becomes a very interesting phrase. If it was just an ordinary angel, it would have stated such, but the text clearly states "*His angel.*" God the Father sent His personal Messenger to rescue Daniel from the lions. Whether the King James Version (KJV), New American Standard Version (NASV), American Standard Version (ASV) 1901 or the New International Version (NIV) is read, each clearly states "His angel." The Jewish translations such as Leeser, the Harkavy, and the Masoretic text itself, along with *The Jewish Study Bible*, all state "His angel." In fact, *The Jewish Study Bible* and the Masoretic Text also capitalize "His" angel. In the Aramaic text[1436] it is translated "His angel" from the Aramaic מַלְאֲכֵהּ meaning "angel of Him."[1437]

Here is the point of the statement "His angel." This was no ordinary messenger, but it was the Father's own personal messenger. Throughout this book, *Discovering The Mystery of the Unity of God,* many accounts of "*the angel* (Messenger) *of the LORD*" show that this messenger was no regular angel, but one Messenger in particular. He was the Messenger who spoke and acted as God and yet was distinct from God throughout Israel's history, from Abraham through Zechariah the prophet. The word "his" is a possessive pronoun. It is clearly seen in the Aramaic text that it was "His angel," not one of the angels nor an ordinary messenger. The likelihood of this being the Messenger of the LORD is very strong.

One other observation about this text is that Daniel knew that God had sent His Messenger to shut the lions' mouth. How did Daniel know that? There is no reference to any physical appearance of this Messenger. But the language of the verse lends itself very strongly to the fact that this Messenger appeared to Daniel.

THE ANCIENT OF DAYS
... Daniel 7:9-14

(9) As I looked on, thrones were set in place, and the Ancient of Days took His seat. His garment was like white snow, and the hair of His head was like lamb's wool. His throne was tongues of flame; its wheels were blazing fire. (10) A river of fire streamed forth before Him; thousands upon thousands served Him; myriads upon myriads attended Him; the court [judgment] sat and the books

---

[1435] Stephen R. Miller, *The New American Commentary: Daniel* (Nashville: Broadman & Holman Publishers, 2003), 187.

[1436] Leon Wood, *A Commentary on Daniel* (Grand Rapids: Zondervan, 1973), 18. Daniel 2:4 – 7:28 as well as Ezra 4:8 – 6:18; 7:12-26; and Jeremiah 10:11 were written in the Aramaic language.

[1437] Kohlenberger, *The Interlinear NIV Hebrew-English Old Testament,* 461.

were opened. (11) I looked on. Then, because of the arrogant words that the horn spoke, the beast was killed as I looked on; its body was destroyed and it was consigned to the flames. (12) The dominion of the other beasts was taken away, but an extension of life was given to them for a time and season. (13) As I looked on, in the night vision, one like a human being [Son of man] came with the clouds of heaven; he reached the Ancient of Days and was presented to Him. (14) Dominion, glory, and kingship were given to him; all peoples and nations of every language must serve him. His dominion is an everlasting dominion that shall not pass away, and his kingship, one that shall not be destroyed (KJV).

This passage of Scripture does not have the word "Messiah" within the text. Yet this passage has been recognized by both religious systems as being Messianic. The Talmud makes a clear reference to Daniel 7:13, that the "Son of man" is the Messiah:

Rabbi Alexandri said: Rabbi Yehoshua ben Levi raised the following contradiction between two verses dealing with the Messiah's arrival: In one place, the verses state (Daniel 7:13-14): "I saw in the night visions, and, behold, one like a son of man came with the clouds of heaven, and came to the Ancient of Days, and they brought him near before Him." Elsewhere the verse states (Zechariah 9:9) "Rejoice greatly, O daughter of Zion; shout, O daughter of Jerusalem; behold, your king comes to you; he is just, and victorious; humble and riding upon an ass, and upon a colt, the foal of an ass." Rabbi Yehoshua ben Levi explained: If Israel merits it through repentance and good deeds, the Messiah will come speedily "with the clouds of heaven." But if Israel does not merit it, the Messiah will come slowly, "humble, and riding upon an ass."[1438]

The rabbis saw the Messiah in Daniel 7:13, but they do not understand the nature of His coming. Daniel 7:9-14 has three basic sections and each one will be analyzed individually. But first let us look at the overall picture of Daniel 7, before the three basic sections are discussed.

In the beginning of the chapter Daniel gives a list of the four great Gentile world powers that have dominated Israel and the world. "*The Ancient of Days*" has seen them all and will judge. The little horn will be slain and consigned to hell. These kingdoms described in the first part of the chapter are described as beasts,[1439] which is in stark contrast to the one who is "*like the Son of man*" who rules in the last kingdom as He comes to "*the Ancient of Days*" on the clouds of heaven. Unto the "*one like the Son of man*" the Ancient of Days gives dominion, glory and a kingdom. The whole world will serve Him and His dominion and kingdom will not pass away or be destroyed.

[1438] Steinsaltz, *The Talmud: The Steinsaltz Edition, Tractate Sanhedrin 98a*, 21:18-19.

[1439] The beasts of Daniel 7 stand in stark contrast to the image of Nebuchadnezzar in Daniel 2 of gold, silver, bronze and iron. Daniel 2 gives the future kingdoms from man's perspective, gold, silver and bronze and iron whereas in contrast, God gives the same kingdoms as animals in Daniel 7 which is from His perspective as He looks at the future kingdoms of the world.

As this passage is studied, one overriding question lies before the reader: What is the identity of *"the one like the Son of man"*? In the first section, consisting of Daniel 7:9-10, the *"Ancient of Days"* is introduced. First, the *"Ancient of Days"* sits upon one of several thrones that are set up. God in His holiness, righteousness and justice sits upon His throne to preside over the court. God the Father knows the beastly acts of the Gentile world powers for they are all recorded in the book that was opened. An obvious question that arises and is not answered: Who sits on the other thrones? There are some likely scenarios given in the New Covenant portion of the Scriptures.

The second section is recorded in Daniel 7:10-12 where the "horn" that speaks great or arrogant words is judged. It is understood by other passages of Scripture to be the Anti-christ.

The third section in Daniel 7:13-14 introduces the one who is like the *"Son of man."* There are two predominant views as to the identity of the "Son of man." Archer gives the first view in this statement:

> Many liberal scholars take this cloud-borne son of man to be a mere personification of the Jewish people as a holy nation and point to vv. 22, 27 (which speak of the "saints" or "the saints of the Most High" as taking possession of the kingdom.)[1440]

This view cannot be supported because without a king or a kingdom, the saints could take possession of nothing, and if they did, to whom would they report? The second view is that the *"Son of man"* is the *Moshiach*. For it is unto Him that *"the Ancient of Days,"* as recorded in Daniel 9:14, gives dominion, glory and a kingdom and it is He Whom all peoples and languages serve. This passage has a direct relationship to Psalm 110:1-3 where David's Lord will rule over His enemies. David's Lord from Psalm 110 is the Lord God Himself who is also a physical descendant of David.

Daniel 7:13-14 needs to be studied more closely as four predominant aspects of this *"Son of man"* are reviewed. The text does not give the *"Son of man's"* name; His identity must be arrived at through other clues given in verses 13-14, along with all the information that the prophets have given.

As to the identity of the *"Son of man,"* it is known from other passages in the *Tanakh* that it is not King David (Psalm 110:1-3; 1 Chronicles 17:10-14). This one who is presented to the *"Ancient of Days"* is not a man, but like the *"Son of man."* He is not an angel, for no angel was ever given the responsibility from God to rule the earth and to have all men on the earth *"serve him."* Showers makes a clear statement as to the nature of the *"Son of man:"*

> As Daniel continued to watch his dream, a new person appeared in the heavenly scene. This person was "like a Son of Man" and was "coming with the clouds

---

[1440] Gleason L. Archer, *The Expositor's Bible Commentary: Daniel* (12 Vols. Grand Rapids: Zondervan, 1985), 7:90.

of heaven." The expression "a Son of Man" indicated that this person was human, an offspring of man, but the word "like" implied that He was more than just a human. Several Old Testament passages declared that the clouds are the chariot of God (Psa 104:3; Isa 19:1). Thus, the fact that this Son of Man was coming "with the clouds of heaven" indicated that He also was deity. Daniel was seeing a person who was deity incarnated in human form.[1441]

There is ample evidence in the *Tanakh,* not only in Daniel, that points exclusively to Messiah as the ruler during the Kingdom period. Only the Messiah took on flesh and became a man. That is not just New Covenant teaching but teaching from the *Tanakh* itself. One of the best books out today that will give a student of prophecy a clear picture of future events is written by Arnold Fruchtenbaum, entitled *The Footsteps of the Messiah.*

The *"Son of man"* is a way of expressing God in human flesh, whom prophets like Micah and Isaiah presented as God coming in flesh; and "it sets forth the humanity of the Lord."[1442] Here He presents Himself to the *"Ancient of Days"* by coming *"with the clouds of heaven."* Numerous scholars state that the clouds show divinity as well as the mode of transportation that deity uses, as reflected by Miller, Longman and Smith:

> The LXX [Septuagint] has "upon" [*epi*] the clouds, presenting a logical explanation for the clouds. The clouds would naturally serve as a vehicle of transportation. Clouds often were associated with deity in the ancient world, and this being was no mere mortal.[1443]

> This image has an ancient pedigree, of course, extending back into ancient Near Eastern mythological texts that describe the war god, typically a storm god, riding a cloud into battle.... In a number of poetic and prophetic texts, Yahweh is described as riding the cloud into battle (Psa 18:10-13; 68:33; 104:3; Isa 19:1; Nah 1:3).[1444]

> He came with the clouds of heaven. Clouds are frequently associated with the presence of deity in the Old Testament. In Acts 1 the ascension of Christ is described as follows: "While they beheld he was taken up; and a cloud received him out of their sight." The apostles witnessed the beginning of his journey back to glory; Daniel in prophetic vision sees the conclusion of that journey.[1445]

Other authors, such as Wood, clearly describe the *"Son of Man"* as being deity because of His coming on the "clouds of heaven:"

[1441] Renald Showers, *The Most High God* (West Collingswood, NJ: The Friends of Israel Gospel Ministry, 1982), 80.

[1442] Miller, *The New American Commentary: Daniel*, 210.

[1443] Miller, *The New American Commentary: Daniel,* 207.

[1444] Tremper Longman III, *The Messiah in the Old and New Testaments* (Grand Rapids: Eerdmans, 2007), 27.

[1445] Smith, *The Promised Messiah,* 381.

The person called "son of man" here is ascribed the status of deity in being said to come "with the clouds of heaven."

Was coming with the clouds of heaven: The word for "was coming" is a participle depicting Christ, as Daniel looked on, moving into the courtroom before the Ancient of Days. The phrase "with the clouds of heaven," is a mark of divine authority and majesty as noted.[1446]

There are three things that are important to notice as the "*Son of man*" comes before the "*Ancient of Days*" with the clouds of heaven: the direction of His coming, the manner of His coming and the glory of His coming. All of this points to this person being not just a man but God in the flesh. This person is special and unique, as Van Groningen expresses:

The person comes into view transported as deity (on the clouds). He comes into the presence of the eternal One. He does not come as a lowly one, but rather as a royal dignified person. He comes as mankind was before sin entered and affected humanity.... Those who speak of him as an angel or a figure drawn from mythological sources are incorrect; they have not drawn their views and conclusions from the entire biblical account.[1447]

The last part of this statement needs to be highlighted. All conclusions as to the identity of the "*Son of man*" need to take the entire biblical record into account, not just what Daniel saw in his vision, but what Moses, Nathan, Isaiah, Jeremiah, Ezekiel, Micah, and Zechariah wrote concerning this person who would fulfill the promises made to Abraham, in what is commonly called the Abrahamic Covenant, which was given to him by this very same person (Genesis 15; Deuteronomy 6:10; Judges 2:1)!

The second aspect is that the "*Ancient of Days*" gives to the "*Son of man*" three things: dominion, glory, and a kingdom. This is the point and time in the prophetic calendar where God the Father grants to the *Moshiach* the Kingdom. In the prophetic picture this is the Messiah's coronation day as the King of the Kingdom and the fulfillment of the Abrahamic Covenant. Notice how the coronation of the King corresponds with the prophetic words of the prophets concerning the establishment of the Kingdom. The net result is that all people, not just Jewish people, will serve Him. Daniel defines it more by saying all languages – every people group in the world – will serve Him. This is worldwide rule, just as the prophets spoke and even as Daniel himself saw in another vision (Daniel 2:34-35, 44-45) where the stone that is cut out of the mountain without hands will break to pieces all the kingdoms mentioned in Daniel 7:1-8. Walvoord clearly states that this could only be Messiah:

Obviously, the expression the Son of man should be interpreted by the context. In verse 13, He is presented as being near the Ancient of Days, and in verse 14

[1446] Leon Wood, *A Commentary on Daniel* (Grand Rapids: Zondervan, 1973), 193.

[1447] Van Groningen, *Messianic Revelation in the Old Testament,* 815.

given dominion over all peoples and nations. This could not be an angel, nor could it be the body of saints, as it corresponds clearly to other Scriptures which predict that Christ will rule over all nations (Psa 72:11; Rev 19:15-16). Only Christ [Messiah] will come with clouds of heaven, and be the King of kings and Lord of lords over all nations throughout eternity.[1448]

The final aspect to be observed is the longevity and endurance of this Kingdom that is granted to the "*Son of man*" the *Moshiach*. Two key words are used to define this Kingdom. It is "everlasting" and it will not pass away; this Kingdom will not be destroyed. The word for "everlasting" is the Hebrew word *olam*. It had been determined at the beginning of chapter 12 that when this word is used of God, eternity is in view and not a designated number of days or years, as when given in the context of men who live in the framework of time. Van Groningen reflects on this passage by stating:

> Thus the authority, greatness, and grandeur of the God given kingdom will never fade away, be overthrown, or in any way be subdued…. This kingdom was, is, and will be eternal and indestructible.[1449]

It was the quoting of this passage by *Yeshua* as He stood before Caiaphas and members of the Sanhedrin at His Jewish trial that produced such outrage by the High Priest. In the New Covenant book of Matthew 26:64-67, *Yeshua* responded to Caiaphas' demand (verse 63) to declare whether or not He was the Messiah, the Son of God. *Yeshua* responded by saying:

> Thou hast said: nevertheless I say unto you, Hereafter shall ye see the Son of man sitting on the right hand of power, and coming in the clouds of heaven. (Matthew 26:64)

With that the High Priest, a Sadducee, was visibly upset, renting his priestly garment and accusing *Yeshua* of blasphemy. He further stated that *Yeshua* was guilty of death. Notice the statement of *Yeshua* to Caiaphas, how He spoke with authority, reminiscent of Matthew 5, when He said, "*I say*" unto you. He used no other authority but His own. *Yeshua* is the Son of man, a title He used frequently during His earthly ministry. Son of man is the theme of the Gospel of Luke in the New Covenant. Luke most likely drew from Zechariah 6:12 in reference to "*the man whose name is The BRANCH*." This title is significant because the man, a human being, whose name is the BRANCH, correlates man and God together as one (echad) as Baron states:

> In the Gospel of Luke the most prominent feature of our Lord's character is that of the "Son of man," which in the Scriptures means the Man par excellence, the true Man, both the ideal and Representative of the race, the second Adam and the Saviour of men. The chief characteristic of this Gospel is its universality. It

---

[1448] John F. Walvoord, *Daniel: The Key to Prophetic Revelation* (Chicago: Moody, 1971), 168.
[1449] Van Groningen, *Messianic Revelation in the Old Testament,* 816-817.

is a message which ignores all differences of race and class, and appeals to all the children of Adam, who are embraced in the one fallen family of man, to whom it proclaims a common Saviour Who would arise from their midst; and hence the Lord Jesus is presented here, not as in Matthew, as the Son of David, the Messiah of Israel merely, but as the long-looked-for "Seed of the woman," Who, by conquering Satan, should redeem from his power men of all nations, and become the "Light of the Gentiles" as well as "the glory of His people Israel" (Luke 2:32). This is the reason why the Evangelist took upon him the laborious task of tracing the genealogies of Jesus to Adam. In this Gospel "behold the Man Whose name is the Branch."[1450]

SEVENTY WEEKS OF DANIEL
... Daniel 9:24-27

(24) Seventy weeks are determined upon thy people and upon thy holy city to finish the transgression, and to make an end of sins, and to make reconciliation for iniquity, and to bring in everlasting righteousness, and to seal up the vision and prophecy, and to anoint the most holy. (25) Know therefore and understand, *that* from the going forth of the commandment to restore and to build Jerusalem unto the Messiah the Prince *shall be* seven weeks, and threescore and two weeks: the street shall be built again, and the wall, even in troublous times. (26) And after threescore and two weeks shall Messiah be cut off, but not for himself: and the people of the prince that shall come shall destroy the city and the sanctuary; and the end thereof *shall be* with a flood, and unto the end of the war desolations are determined. (27) And he shall confirm the covenant with many for one week: and in the midst of the week he shall cause the sacrifice and the oblation to cease, and for the over-spreading of abominations he shall make it desolate, even until the consummation, and that determined shall be poured upon the desolate (KJV).

In a personal conversation this author had with a Jewish believer, she stated that her rabbi said it was forbidden to study this passage. She resented that, and as a result she read and studied it and God opened her eyes to see that if the Messiah is in this passage, He had already come. The result of her investigation of this passage, and other passages, brought her to a saving knowledge of her Messiah *Yeshua*. What is so powerful and convincing about this passage that rabbis do not want Jewish people to study it? Here are several rabbinic comments:

Maimonides, also acknowledges, "that the period of time revealed to Daniel by Gabriel, relates to the Messiah; but that the Rabbins of blessed memory have said, 'let the bones of him rot who attempts to compute the end;' and the reason they assigned is, that because the common people, finding the end is come, i.e.,

---

[1450] Baron, *Rays of Messiah's Glory,* 74-75.

the time specified is elapsed, might be led into an error to think that the Messiah has come already." Iggereth Hatteman, fol. 125: c. 4. [1451]

Because the time appointed by God in Daniel 9:24-27 had come and gone and they were not willing to proclaim *Yeshua* as Messiah, the rabbis pronounced a curse on anyone trying to understand the meaning:

> Besides, our Rabbins themselves acknowledge that the time for the Messiah's advent was determined and foretold; but, convinced that the period is elapsed, and unwilling to acknowledge Jesus Christ, although he came at the exact time, they have pronounced a curse upon every one that attempts to compute the end. [1452]

Add to that, if people understood that the time had passed, discouragement would ensue. So the rabbis in the Talmud say that those who would calculate the time of the Messiah's coming are under a curse:

> Rabbi Shmuel bar Nahmani said in the name of Rabbi Yohanan: May those who calculate the end and offer a date for the Messiah's arrival be cursed, for they say: Since the time that we thought had been designated for the Messiah's arrival has already passed, and still he has not come, he will not come at all. Rather, the proper approach is to wait for him patiently, as the end of the aforementioned verse[Habakkuk 2:3] states: 'Though it tarry, wait for it.' [1453]

The rabbi's statement is a problem; why wait for the Messiah instead of studying the *Tanakh* to see why they missed it, instead of laying the missed appointment on God? God does not miss divine appointments! If the time had passed, it would be strange that God, who gave precise time tables in the past for things of lesser importance, would not give the time table of the Redeemer of the world and the *Moshiach* of Israel. Frey, a Jewish believer of the 19th century, speaks to the issue:

> That God had determined and revealed that exact period for Messiah's advent, we might reasonably expect; for we know that he revealed the times of various other events, of much less importance, and which have been verified at the exact predicted period. He informed Noah how many years would pass from the time he spake to him of the flood until it should come; and at the end of that period the flood came (Gen. 6:3). He told Abraham how many years his posterity should be in bondage in Egypt, and at the end of that period he delivered them (Gen. 15:13). By the prophet Ezekiel, he made known the number of years from the revolt of the ten tribes to the destruction of the first temple, which accordingly came to pass (Ezek 4:5-8) and the period of seventy years of the Babylonish captivity, foretold by Jeremiah, was exactly fulfilled.

[1451] Frey, *The Messiahship of Jesus*, 68.

[1452] Frey, *The Messiahship of Jesus*, 52-53.

[1453] Steinsaltz, *The Talmud: The Steinsaltz Edition: Tractate Sanhedrin Part VII, 97b*, 21:11.

Now is it credible that the Spirit of God, who predicted those several events, should not have foretold what time the Messiah should come? Christ, the end and scope of the law and the prophets, the hope of the church, and the joy of the patriarchs? He to whom the nations were to gather, and from whom they expected an everlasting redemption? Is it credible, I say, that a prefixed time, more necessary than all the former events, should have been omitted? No, my dear brother, God has revealed, at sundry times, and in divers manners, the exact period for the Messiah's advent.[1454]

The fact is that God did lay out the appointed time of the Messiah's coming, so how did they miss Him? First the Jewish people missed Him because of their failure to understand that absolute monotheism was inaccurate. Monotheism was correct, but not as an absolute one; He is a plural unity of one (*echad*). So when *Yeshua*, the Second Person of the plural unity of *Elohim*, came as a man (Deuteronomy 18:15-18; Isaiah 7:14; 9:6-7; 50:1-6; Jeremiah 23:5-6; Micah 5:2), they could not embrace Him. The second reason is that *Yeshua*, who was the God of Israel that became visible, interacted with Israel as the author of the law of Moses (Exodus 3:3-14; 24:1-11) as well as being the covenant-making God with Abraham (Genesis 15:1, 4, 7; Judges 2:1). When *Yeshua* came, He did the same thing as the prophets to bring Israel back to the obedience of the Written Law of God which the Pharisees were in the process of supplanting with the Oral Law. So *Yeshua* irritated the Pharisees and neither the leadership nor the people understood the two comings of the *Moshiach*, that He had to die for the sins of the world in His first coming before He could come and bring righteousness to the world and reign on the throne of David in His second coming. This biblical belief is totally rejected by Rabbinic Judaism from *Yeshua*'s day through the 21st century.

The Disillusionment: The Result of Rejecting Daniel 9:24-27

To review, the arrival time of the *Moshiach* has been a very important issue for Judaism for 21 centuries. To understand the outworking of missing the Messiah by the Jewish people, two important points need to be understood. The Jewish people down through the years have embraced 46 false messiahs and the disillusionment of the Jewish people has occurred for 20 centuries to this present time. As was mentioned previously, the LORD had given to Israel time tables for events of less significance than the coming of the Messiah; it would be completely out of character for God not to give them the time of the Messiah's coming. In Daniel 9:24-27, God gave to Daniel the timetable of *Moshiach*'s coming and historically the Jewish people of the first century understood that it was time for Him to appear. The rabbis over the centuries since they missed *Yeshua* have gone to numerous passages in Daniel and Genesis to calculate the time of the Messiah's coming, but at the same time avoided Daniel 9:24-27 because of what it clearly teaches. After the "*city*" (Jerusalem) and the "*sanctuary*" (temple) were

---

[1454] Frey, *The Messiahship of Jesus,* 52-53.

destroyed by the Romans in 70 CE, the longing for the Messiah became great. In 132 CE Rabbi Akiva proclaimed bar Kochba as the Messiah, but in 135 CE both were dead and Israel was in total devastation. So the rabbis began to speculate and calculate when the Messiah was to come, as the follow quote states:

> Following the collapse of this rebellion, the date of the coming of the Messiah was pushed forward – it was estimated that it would occur 400 years after the destruction of Judah. This figure was naturally assumed because it corresponds to the period of Egyptian exile as recorded in Scripture. Hence Rabbi Dosa maintained that the Messiah will come in the fifth century this calculation was based on a comparison between Psalm 90:15 and Genesis 15:13 (Sanhedrin 99a). A similar view was expressed by Judah ha-Nasi who maintained that the coming of the Messiah will take place 365 years after the destruction of Jerusalem; this number corresponds to the days of the solar year and is based on Isaiah 63:4 (Sanhedrin 99a). Similarly, Rabbi Hanina believed that the Messiah would come 400 years after the fall of Jerusalem.[1455]

The result of these predictions was that a pseudo-messiah appeared around 448 CE in Crete who was called Moses, who would lead the people through the Mediterranean on dry ground, like Moses led the Israelites through the Red Sea. It did not happen. The longing for the Messiah continued down through the centuries. The rabbis used different scriptural passages to calculate the coming of Messiah, passages such as Genesis 15:9; Exodus 3:20; Daniel 12:6-7, 11-12 all to no avail. Some very noted rabbis were engaged in the calculations of the Messiah's coming: Rashi pointed to 1352 CE; Nahmanides said 1290 CE; even Maimonides set a date. In reading the history of the false messiahs the Jewish people longed for the arrival of the Messiah, but as each false messiah came and went, all hopes were dashed through each of the 46 false messiahs over 20 centuries.[1456] Time after time, century after century the hope for the Messiah was only dashed to the ground. It is heart wrenching to see a people who for 20 centuries hoped to see the Messiah come, when He had already come and been rejected. They do not refer to Daniel 9:24-27 but to other passages in Daniel and Genesis which have absolutely nothing to do with the coming of the Messiah. Today much of Conservative and Reform Judaism has abandoned the belief in a personal return of a Messiah. Nineteen hundred years of disappointments have led them to say that they must make the world better themselves, they must take it into their own hands to survive this world, they will do good works, charity and repentance to achieve their own atonement. Yet Daniel 9:24-27 clearly states that the Messiah will be cut off before the destruction of "*the city*" and "*the sanctuary*." What makes it even more of a heartache is that Zechariah 12:10 states that they "*shall mourn for Him, as one mourneth for his only son.*" Some day in the future they will call for Him that sits at the right hand of the Father because they have come to realize and understand that it is

---

[1455] Cohn-Sherbok, "The Jewish Messiah," 84; Singer, *The Jewish Encyclopedia*, 10:252.

[1456] Read Rabbi Dan Cohn-Sherbok's book *The Jewish Messiah*, chapters 5-9, for a good review of the Jewish dating and longing for the coming of the Messiah.

Yeshua. What agony of heart and soul as they finally realize that the God they worshipped and were so zealous for had already come and He is *Yeshua* of Nazareth!

The net result of all this has been disillusionment. Today except for the Orthodox and ultra-orthodox groups such as the Hasidim, Lubavitch and Satmar, Conservative and Reform Judaism has given up on the literal coming of the Messiah. Most Jewish people have no real knowledge of the Scriptures. The rabbis moved away from the Scriptures; now 50% or more of Jewish people have moved away from the rabbis into secular humanism. (See Appendix 7.) Rabbi Cohn-Sherbok makes the following summary statements on where Judaism is today:

> Instead of declaring that God uniquely disclosed his word to the Jewish people in the Hebrew Bible as well as through the teaching of rabbinic sages, Jews should recognize that their Scriptures are simply one record among many others. Both the Written and the Oral Torah have particular significance for Jewry, but this does not imply that these writings contain a uniquely true and superior divine revelation. Instead, the Torah as well as rabbinic literature should be conceived as a record of the spiritual experiences of the nation and testimony of its religious quest. (pages 183-184)

> Despite the centrality of messianic belief in the history of the nation, the modern period has witnessed the disintegration of this doctrine. Increasingly Jews have found it difficult, if not impossible, to believe in the advent of messianic redemption. (page 186)

> A second factor which has brought about the eclipse of Jewish theism is the fact of evil. For many Jews today, the existence of human suffering makes the idea of an all-good and all powerful God utterly implausible: after the events of the Holocaust, the traditional belief that God is a loving father who watches over his chosen people has become impossible to sustain. In modern society, faith in such a Deity has been overshadowed by an overwhelming sense that the universe is devoid of a divine presence. (page 187)

> Similarly, for Humanistic Jews it no longer makes sense to believe in a God who saves. Rather than subscribe to traditional notions of divine deliverance through a messianic agent, Humanistic Judaism asserts that Jews must rely on themselves. (page 189)

> The Jewish people are thus on the verge of a new awakening as the twentieth century reaches its climax: rather than rely on the miraculous intervention of a messianic redeemer who will inaugurate a time of earthly bliss and bring about the consummation of human history, Jews are coming to accept that the burden of creating a better world rests ultimately with themselves. Out of the ashes of the past then, the vision of a human-centered Judaism has emerged: this is not a

fatal tragedy for the nation, but rather a challenge to reflection and action on the threshold of a new millennium. (page 190)[1457]

Overall today Judaism is secular and humanistic in its approach to the Messiah and His deliverance as well as its approach to both the Written and Oral Torah. Rabbinic Judaism is worried about evangelistic believers reaching Jewish people for Messiah *Yeshua*. Their concern is an even bigger problem; they do not have a grasp on the reality of the end result of the choice they made in rejecting *Yeshua* as Messiah centuries ago. Jews have left the faith of their fathers in droves. Rabbis removed themselves from the authority of the Scriptures to their own authority and now Jewish people have in practice rejected all that is Rabbinic Judaism for Humanism. Yet there remains Daniel 9:24-27 for those Jewish people who wish to see what God said about the appointed time of Messiah's coming, for He came and was rejected 40 years before the destruction of the "city" and "sanctuary."

RETURN TO DANIEL … 9:24-27

Because it has been a while since Daniel 9:24-27 was read, it needs to be looked at again before we move on to other aspects of this passage.

(24) Seventy weeks are determined upon thy people and upon thy holy city to finish the transgression, and to make an end of sins, and to make reconciliation for iniquity, and to bring in everlasting righteousness, and to seal up the vision and prophecy, and to anoint the most holy. (25) Know therefore and understand, *that* from the going forth of the commandment to restore and to build Jerusalem unto the Messiah the Prince *shall be* seven weeks, and threescore and two weeks: the street shall be built again, and the wall, even in troublous times. (26) And after threescore and two weeks shall Messiah be cut off, but not for himself: and the people of the prince that shall come shall destroy the city and the sanctuary; and the end thereof *shall be* with a flood, and unto the end of the war desolations are determined. (27) And he shall confirm the covenant with many for one week: and in the midst of the week he shall cause the sacrifice and the oblation to cease, and for the over-spreading of abominations he shall make it desolate, even until the consummation, and that determined shall be poured upon the desolate (KJV).

But today even some Christian scholars, mostly liberals, see this passage on Daniel 9:24-27 differently than is historically understood. Authors such as Goldingay,[1458] Charles,[1459] and Towner,[1460] state that this passage was fulfilled during the time of the

---

[1457] Cohn-Sherbok, *The Jewish Messiah*, 183-184, 186,187, 189, 190.

[1458] John E. Goldingay, *Word Biblical Commentary: Daniel* (Dallas: Word Books, 1989), 30:266-268.

[1459] R. H. Charles, *A Critical and Exegetical Commentary on the Book of Daniel* (Oxford: Clarendon Press, 1929), 246-247.

[1460] W. Sibley Towner, *Interpretation: Daniel* (Atlanta: John Knox Press, 1984), 140-144.

Maccabees (171 - 164 BCE). One problem with this view is that they believe that Onias III was the *"anointed one"* who was cut off. [1461] He was the legitimate High Priest at the time when the Greek Seleucids from Syria, namely Antiochus IV, took over Israel from the Greek Ptolemies of Egypt, but Onias III had no spiritual impact on Judah at that time. By subtracting the 69 "weeks" or 483 years from 444 BC as the starting date, the cutting off of the Messiah would be approximately 30 CE, and that is almost 200 years after the Maccabean Revolt. If the starting date of the 483 years was the return in 536 BCE of Israel from Babylon, that would give a date of approximately 50 BCE. The point is that the Messiah had to appear before the destruction of Jerusalem and the temple. *Yeshua* easily fits in that window of time. However, to those scholars this passage is not to be understood as the promise of the coming of the Messiah to Israel as in *Yeshua*, who was put to death or *"cut off."* Nor do those same scholars see it as referring to the destruction of the city of Jerusalem and the temple. This is liberal higher criticism at its "best." The biggest problem between the position that liberal higher critics take and the historical position concerns when the seventy weeks begin? Was the starting date 536 BCE at the time of Cyrus or was it 445 BCE with the decree of Artaxerxes the King of the Mede-Persian Empire? The purpose of this book is to substantiate the plural unity of God (as well as the tri-unity of God), and in this particular passage, to examine the place of the Messiah in prophetic history, not to spend a multitude of pages showing why fundamental New Covenant scholars hold to 445 BCE date. Sir Robert Anderson has written a whole book just dealing with this 445 BCE dating of this prophecy and its fulfillment in *Yeshua*. [1462] His writing does not need to be duplicated. Again, the bottom line is that whether the 536 or 445 BCE dates are used, the Messiah must appear and be *"cut off"* before the destruction of *"the city"* and *"the sanctuary"* and *Yeshua* is the only one who fulfills that promise of God through the angel Gabriel to Daniel.

There are two things that need to be observed concerning Daniel 9:24-27. First, Jewish scholars today generally do not view this text as referencing the first century and especially not referring to *Yeshua*. Second, it is to show that this prophecy of Messiah, the destruction of Jerusalem and the temple had a direct bearing on the deity of the Messiah from the standpoint of true Bible believers.

Michael Brown quotes portions of Rashi, the respected Rabbi (1040-1105 CE) of the 11th century from northern France[1463] whose commentaries are included in the Talmud. To summarize Rashi's understanding and interpretation of Daniel 9:24-27, Brown makes the following comments from Rashi: that the *"anointed one"* was the Judean King Agrippa, who was ruling at the time of the rebellion and destruction of Jerusalem and the temple. Rashi interprets the *"prince"* as Titus, the Roman general, who flooded the Land with Roman legions. What Rashi does is place the *"anointed one"* in the first century before the destruction, the same century as *Yeshua*. Rashi ultimately does point to the Messiah and His reign, but his identification is misplaced to

---

[1461] Towner, *Interpretation: Daniel*, 144.
[1462] Sir Robert Anderson, *The Coming Prince* (Grand Rapids: Kregel, 1967), 1-304.
[1463] Rob inson, *Essential Judaism*, 300-301.

the wrong person. In terms of God's purposes, the death of King Agrippa had absolutely no impact on His people Israel.[1464] As far as the identification of the *"prince"* as being General Titus, that is impossible. Titus never made a seven year (seventieth week of Daniel) covenant with rebellious Israel, plus grammatically the *"he"* in verse 27 does not refer to Messiah but to a future "prince" that will come offering Israel a seven year covenant, as Fruchtenbaum explains:

> The pronoun 'he" in verse 27 goes back to its nearest antecedent in verse 26, which is not the Messiah but "the prince who is to come." This "prince" has been a topic of Daniel's earlier prophecies in chapters 7-8. This political leader is better known to Christians as the Antichrist.[1465]

So the *"prince"* is neither General Titus nor the Messiah, but the future anti-Christ. That reality has startled more than one Jewish person. Who is the *"prince?"* According to Cooper, this *"prince"* must be of only one nationality:

> All historians say that the Romans did it and that Titus was the general who finally destroyed the city. Since the Romans were the ones who captured Jerusalem, we may be certain that the prince to whom reference is made is to be a Roman.[1466]

Beyond that point of identification it cannot be known who he is, except that according to Genesis 3:15, he will be the *"seed"* of the serpent. Now it can be fairly asked, could a person today or in the future appear who would have the same credentials and be Israel's Messiah? William Varner answers that question clearly:

> But someone may ask, *Could a Jewish person appear in the future who would have these same credentials and be Israel's Messiah*? No, he could not, because there are no records available to substantiate such a claim. When the Romans destroyed Jerusalem in 70 A.D., the Temple, with all of its treasures and archives, was completely destroyed as well. One of the treasures of the Temple were the records necessary to validate the family and tribal genealogies. Since that fateful day, no Jewish person has been able to prove by written records his or her ancient genealogy.[1467]

[1464] Brown, *Answering Jewish Objections: Messianic Prophecy Objections*, 3:86-92.

[1465] Fruchtenbaum, *Messianic Christology*, 98. Also see Cooper, "One writer objects to this interpretation upon the basis that the pronoun *he* does not appear in the original Hebrew text but is included in the verb stem. This statement is correct. There is no pronoun in this verse separate and apart from the verb. Everyone who knows Hebrew is aware of the fact that the person of a verb is expressed by its ending. This verb is in the third person, singular number, and definitely must be rendered *he, she,* or *it* when there is no noun or pronoun expressed. The context alone determines what is intended." David L. Cooper, *The 70 Weeks of Daniel* (Los Angeles: Biblical Research Society, 1941), 60-61.

[1466] Cooper, *The 70 Weeks of Daniel*, 57.

[1467] Varner, *The Messiah: Revealed, Rejected, Received*, 39.

Some Jewish people have searched Daniel 9:24-27 and have come to the only conclusion possible as given in the following example. Rachmiel Frydland was a young orthodox man who was confronted with the Messiah, by a German missionary in pre-World War II Poland, using Daniel 9:24-27. He states that as he looked through rabbinic commentaries, they were saying the same thing that Rashi stated centuries before.[1468]

The reason why the rabbis have forbidden the reading and studying of Daniel 9:24-27 is because after the rejection of *Yeshua* as Messiah, rabbis over the centuries have tried to figure out the time of the Messiah's coming and in the process have accepted many false messiahs, as stated by Frydland:

> The Jewish people rarely study the Book of Daniel because many rabbinic Jews were misled attempting to interpret Daniel's cryptic "time." Some were led so far astray that they came to believe in false messiahs, and therefore Talmudic Jews frowned on students who studied Daniel with a view of finding out the time of the Messiah. However, religious Jews knew that this book revealed more about Messiah than any other book.[1469]

His statement is absolutely true, for the Jewish people over the centuries, in trying to determine the time of the Messiah's coming, have followed 46 false messiahs.[1470]

Levine tries in vain to deflect *Yeshua* from being the Messiah in this text. He spends four pages in his book only to say that true believers have a view that is a "very forced explanation, born of desperation." In short, his interpretation is that Cyrus is the Messiah spoken of in Daniel 9:26.[1471] Levine disagrees with the great Rabbi Rashi who misplaced the identity of the Messiah, but does place it in the first century CE. Levine is not on the same level as Rashi, whose writings are included in the Talmud. In reviewing the text McClain explains that there are two significant dates in the *Tanakh* that relate to Jerusalem and the temple, one of which Daniel understood.

First Daniel understood through the prophecy of Jeremiah that Israel would be in captivity for 70 years. Daniel looked forward to the restoration of Israel as a nation and kingdom for the year 536 BCE was the seventieth year. McClain states the following:

> Daniel also knew that the very length of the Babylonian captivity had been based on Jewish violation of the divine law of the Sabbatic year. Since according to 2 Chron 36:21 (also see Jer 25:9-12; 29:10 with Dan 9:2) the Jews had been removed off the land in order that it might rest for seventy years, it

---

[1468] Rachmiel Frydland, *When Being Jewish Was a Crime* (Nashville: Nelson, 1978), 72-73.

[1469] Frydland, *When Being Jewish Was a Crime,* 72.

[1470] Smith, *The Promised Messiah,* 470-474.

[1471] Levine, *You Take Jesus, I'll Take God: How to Refute Christian Missionaries,* 31.

should be evident that the Sabbatic year had been violated for 490 years, or exactly seventy "sevens" of years.[1472]

It was the seventy sevens of years that Daniel did not understand. It is needful to understand what the messenger (angel) Gabriel told Daniel. When looking at the Hebrew text of Ezra (1:1-2; 4:1-5; 6:1-5) it becomes absolutely clear that the only return which granted permission to rebuild the temple and the city was in 536 BCE. There was no permission granted to rebuild the walls and gates of the city of Jerusalem. There was no decree from Cyrus that would fulfill Daniel 9:25-26 at that time. It was not until Nehemiah came on the scene that he learned of the status of the city, whereupon he sat down and wept and mourned over the city many days. The language of Nehemiah 1:1-4 and 2:1-8 is very clear that the decree given here was to rebuild the walls and gates of the city of Jerusalem in 445 BCE, which starts God's prophetic time clock for the coming of the Messiah, the "*seventy* [sevens of] *weeks*" of Daniel 9:24. Contrary to Levine's argument that Cyrus is the Messiah of Daniel 9, his view completely lacks biblical support. To borrow Levine's own phrase, it is he who has a "very forced explanation, born of desperation" to get away from the reality of the Messiah being *Yeshua* who was "*cut off*" after 483 years or 69 "[sevens of] *weeks*" in Daniel 9:26, whether the 536 or 445 BCE date is used.

The impact of the seventy weeks of Daniel 9:24-27 in determining whether they reference the Messiah as divine will also be studied. These four verses will be observed in connection to the subject at hand. In verse 24 the seventy weeks that are determined need to be understood because of the confusion that has arisen over the centuries as to the meaning of the term "weeks":

> Many English versions have translated the phrase to read seventy "weeks." But this translation is not totally accurate and has caused some confusion about the meaning of the passage. Most Jews know the Hebrew for "weeks" because of the observance of the Feast of Weeks, and that Hebrew word is *Shavuot*. However, the word that appears here in the Hebrew text is *shavuim*, which means "sevens." This word refers to a "seven" of anything with the context determining the content of the "seven." It is similar to the English word "dozen," which means twelve of anything based upon the context.[1473]

Also in dealing with this issue David L. Cooper lays out an extensive study on understanding what is meant by the term "*weeks*."[1474]

The second item to be observed is the word "people." God's message is being relayed through Gabriel to Daniel to the Jewish people, not the church. These three

---

[1472] Alva J. McClain, *Daniel's Prophecy of the 70 Weeks* (Winona Lake, IN: BMH Books, 2007), 19.

[1473] Fruchtenbaum, *Messianic Christology*, 94-95.

[1474] Cooper, *The 70 Weeks of Daniel*, 19-23.

authors, Fruchtenbaum,[1475] Lang[1476] and Feinberg,[1477] among many others, identify six things in verse 24 that are determined upon "*your people and your holy city.*" Feinberg lists them as follows:

> During those seventy weeks of years, the great works to be accomplished were: first, "to finish the transgression;" second, "to make an end of sin;" third, "to make atonement for iniquity;" fourth, "to bring in everlasting righteousness;" fifth, "to seal up vision and prophecy;" and sixth, "to anoint the most holy place."[1478]

These six areas are divided into two classes. The first three are concerned with the removal of sin, and the second three deal with bringing in righteousness. Walvoord points out that the first group of three all deal with sin named three ways: transgression, sin and iniquity.[1479] Each one of these phrases needs to be looked at individually. Fruchtenbaum states that in the **first phrase** "*to finish the transgression*," the words "*to finish,*" mean "to restrain firmly," "to restrain completely," or "to bring to completion," while the word "transgression" is a very strong word for sin and means literally "to rebel." Also, in the Hebrew this word has a definite article: "*the transgression*" or "the rebellion" indicates that some specific singular act of rebellion is finally going to be finished:

> The point is that some specific act of rebellion is finally going to be completely restrained and brought to an end. This act of rebellion or transgression is to come under complete control so that it will no longer flourish. Israel's apostasy is now to be firmly restrained in keeping with a similar prediction in Isa 59:20. Specifically, this is the rejection of the Messiah as dealt with in Isa 52:13-53:12.[1480]

This understanding of "*the transgression*" lends credence to Renald Showers' assertion that Israel has committed a particular transgression:

> With the word "the" in this context, it refers to the Jew's specific sin of rebellion against the rule of God. This rebellion was the root sin which prompted all of Israel's other sins. Gabriel was saying that Israel would not stop its rebellion against God's rule until these 490 years would run their course. In agreement with this, other scriptures indicate that Israel will not repent, turn to

---

[1475] Fruchtenbaum, *Messianic Christology*, 95-96.

[1476] G. H. Lang, *The Histories and Prophecies of Daniel* (Grand Rapids: Kregel, 1940), 130-131.

[1477] Charles Lee Feinberg, *Daniel: The Kingdom of the Lord* (Winona Lake, IN: BMH Books, 1981), 127.

[1478] Feinberg, *Daniel: The Kingdom of the Lord,* 127.

[1479] Walvoord, *Daniel: The Key to Prophetic Revelation,* 221.

[1480] Fruchtenbaum, *Messianic Christology,* 95.

God and be saved until the second coming of Christ at the end of these 490 years (Zech 12:10-13:1; Rom 11:25-27).[1481]

Showers clearly established the fact, with scriptural references, that Israel has been in a state of rebellion against God and against His Messiah, and will continue to be so until they confess their sin (Isaiah 53:1-9) and repent; then and only then will the Messiah come the second time and redeem and physically rescue Israel. As was seen in the previous chapters in this study, *Yeshua* was very active as the God of Israel, and He was the ultimate Theophany of God in flesh evidenced in such passages as Isaiah 9:6-7; 48:12-16; 50:1-7; Micah 5:2. In other words, Walvoord adds to Showers' argument by stating that Israel's rebellion will only come to an end when "*the transgression*" is finished:

> The expression is derived from the *piel* verb form of the root *kala* meaning "to finish" in the sense of bringing to an end.[1482]

However, Fruchtenbaum interprets the phrase "*the transgression*" as a singular act of rebellion, being the future rejection of their own God, when He became flesh and "*dwelt among us*," the Messiah, the Messenger of the LORD, the Branch, the Son of God, the Son of David, Immanuel. As the Hebrew Scriptures are reviewed, it was He that made the Abraham Covenant, who spoke to Moses on Mt. Sinai and spoke to the people through the prophets.

The **second phrase of the six** in Daniel 9:24 is "to make an end of sins." This phrase for sin is a more general word for transgressions that Israel has and is committing toward their God. The word "sin" also carries the idea of "missing the mark," as an arrow would miss its intended mark. Miller discusses the word and concept as follows:

> "To put an end to sin" may either be translated *tamam*, "be complete, come to an end, finish," or *hatam*, "to seal, affix a seal, or seal up." Either translation would make sense and have basically the same meaning, for "sealing up" sin would be tantamount to putting an end to it. Yet "to put an end to" would fit the context better, a reading most scholars and translations accept.[1483]

Accordingly, the transgression of Israel as they rebelled against *Yahweh* and His *Moshiach* at His coming, all of these and future individual acts of sins will be sealed up, come to an end or be finished. The way God intends to deal with the sins and transgression of Israel will be through atonement.

The **third phrase of the six** in Daniel 9:24 is "*to make atonement for iniquity*." The Hebrew word translated "*to make atonement*" is *kaphar*. This word has the same root meaning as the word *kippur*, as in Yom Kippur, the Day of Atonement. In fact, this

---

[1481] Showers, *The Most High God*, 118.

[1482] Walvoord, *Daniel: The Key to Prophetic Revelation*, 221.

[1483] Miller, *The New American Commentary: Daniel,* 260.

atonement is the means that God will use "*to finish the transgression*" and "*to make an end of sins*." The word "*iniquity*" refers to the inward sin or what biblical believers term the "sin nature." But that term "sin nature" would not be known or accepted in Judaism today. The phrase that would be known to them is *yetzer hara* — "the evil inclination."[1484] Fruchtenbaum expresses the purpose of atonement and how the nation of Israel will be reconciled with their God:

> The third purpose of the Seventy Sevens is: to make reconciliation for iniquity. The Hebrew word for reconciliation is a word that means "to make an atonement." This is the means by which the first and second purposes will be accomplished. The means by which Israel's national sin of rejecting the Messiah will be removed and the means by which her daily sins will be removed is by an atonement.
>
> The third purpose is to make atonement specifically for iniquity. The word iniquity refers to the sin nature. The program of the Seventy Sevens is a cleansing of Israel that will include the removal of all three things; first, the national sin of rejecting His Messiahship; second, sinning daily; and third, dealing with the sin nature itself.[1485]

Miller states in a brief summary of Daniel 9:24 that sin will be ended and transgression finished, for this would all be accomplished through *Yeshua*'s atonement for humanity's sin by the Messiah's substitutionary death upon the cross at Calvary. His blood was to be the atonement, or the covering for sin, reflected in this verse.[1486]

> These three purposes – "*to finish the transgression,*" "*make an end of sins,*" and "*make reconciliation for iniquity*" – will deal with sin and the cleansing of Israel, who is today in a state of rebellion. Lang further states that this atonement for iniquity will be expiated by sacrifice.[1487] These same three purposes mentioned at the beginning of this paragraph will bring about the three other remaining purposes. God will deal with the sin issue of Israel, as well as all of mankind, through the *Moshiach*.

The **fourth phrase of the six purposes** (first of the second group) will be to "*bring in everlasting righteousness.*" Feinberg expresses that the atonement will be necessary to bring righteousness to Israel:

> He would first provide a basis on which men can become righteous, and then He will set up on earth an eternal kingdom of righteousness. Salvation and righteousness are in fact, the chief characteristics of Messiah's coming rule on earth (Isa 45:17; 51:6-8; Jer 33:14-16).[1488]

[1484] Fruchtenbaum, *Messianic Christology*, 96.

[1485] Fruchtenbaum, *The Footsteps of the Messiah*, 192.

[1486] Miller, *The New American Commentary: Daniel*, 260.

[1487] Lang, *The Histories and Prophecies of Daniel*, 131.

[1488] Feinberg, *Daniel: The Kingdom of the Lord*, 127.

This is a significant point because Rabbinic Judaism today does not grasp the concept of the two comings of Messiah: first to deal with the sin issue and second with the sin issue removed to establish righteousness. The Kingdom (Millennium) cannot come into being without the sin issue being dealt with. Orthodox Rabbinic Judaism believes that righteousness will simply come when their strictly human messiah comes. That is not biblical reality, nor will it ever be a human reality. This subject of righteousness has been dealt with in detail in chapters 14 as well 16 of this book. Showers illustrates that in the past, Israel had revivals but fell again into sin. That righteousness was only temporary, but this future righteousness will be permanent:

> In the past, as the result of periodic revivals, Israel had experienced righteousness. However, that righteousness was temporary, for eventually the nation rebelled against God again. But when Israel repents and believes in Jesus Christ at His second coming, they will never rebel against God again (Jer 31:31-34; Ezek 36:22-32). It will be given righteousness that will last forever.[1489]

This righteousness will be permanent, but when does this future righteousness come? The first three purposes (Daniel 9:24a) and the atonement for transgression, sin and iniquity are tied to sacrifice, and that atoning sacrifice which has been accomplished will bring in righteousness, but not until the Jewish nation embraces *Yeshua*. That Messianic person bringing in righteousness is the "*righteous BRANCH*" of Jeremiah 23:5-6 who is called "*the LORD OUR RIGHTEOUSNESS*." In Daniel 9:24, one of the purposes of the Seventy Sevens is "*to bring in everlasting righteousness*." Fruchtenbaum states that the word translated "everlasting" is the word *olam* and should be understood as being "age" and not "eternity."

> This could be more literally translated "to bring in an age of righteousness," since the Hebrew *olam* is better translated as "age" rather than as "everlasting." This age of righteousness is to be the Messianic Kingdom spoken of in the Prophets (Isa 1:26; 11:2-5; 32:17; Jer 23:5-6; 33:15-18). It is this very age that Daniel had been expecting to see established after the 70 years of captivity, but now he is told that that will only be after the 490 year period of the Seventy Sevens.[1490]

The phrase "*to bring in everlasting righteousness*" is connected in the immediate context to the Messianic Kingdom and not in the context of eternity. The Book of Revelation in the New Covenant states that after this righteousness is brought in for the Messianic Kingdom, it will then go into the new order of the New Heavens, New Earth and the New Jerusalem for eternity (Revelation 21-22), but the immediate context in Daniel only has the Kingdom in view.

[1489] Showers, *The Most High God*, 118-119.
[1490] Fruchtenbaum, *Messianic Christology*, 96.

The **fifth phrase of the six** is "*to seal up vision and prophecy*" (Daniel 9:24). In Genesis 3 when sin came into the world, prophecy was introduced by God Himself in verse 15 as the method that He would use to reveal His plan of redemption from sin. Sin will be removed from Israel as referenced in the first half of Daniel 9:24. There will be no further need for prophecy and visions for sin will no longer be an issue.[1491] Hence, "*vision and prophecy*" will be sealed up and removed in the future Messianic Kingdom. The actual Hebrew word *hatam* means to "seal, affix seal, seal up."[1492] Showers adds some additional insights as to the future completion of the "*seal*[ing] *up* [of the] *vision and prophecy*":

> The thrust of this phrase seems to be as follows: revelation that comes through vision or prophecy no longer has to be of concern to people once that revelation has been fulfilled. The vision of prophecy can be sealed up in the sense of being laid aside from the realm of active concern. The word translated "to seal up" is the same word which was translated "to make an end" in the phrase "to make an end of sins" earlier in this verse. It would appear that there is an intended relationship between the two phrases. That relationship is as follows: when Israel will make an end of its daily sins at the end of the 490 years, then all revelation that came through vision and prophecy concerning God's chastening of Israel can be sealed up. The people of Israel will no longer have to be concerned about that revelation, for all the foretold chastening will have been fulfilled. Since their sins which caused chastening will have ended, there will be no further need for chastening.[1493]

When transgression, sin and iniquity are removed (Leviticus 26:40-42; Jeremiah 3:11-18; Hosea 5:15) by the atoning work of *Moshiach* (Isaiah 53), and the Jewish nation calls on Him (Psalm 80:1, 15-17; Daniel 7:13 with Matthew 26:64) and believes on Him, the second coming will occur (Psalm 118:26; Matthew 23:39). According to the New Covenant of Jeremiah 31 and Ezekiel 36, there will be no need for visions and prophecy because Israel will be saved and walking in His statutes.

The **last phrase of the six** is "*to anoint the most Holy* [place]." This is the anointing of the millennial temple (Ezekiel 40-48). In other words, after transgression, sin and iniquity are removed by the anointing sacrifice of the Messiah and all sin, as it relates to Israel, is put away, the millennial temple will be anointed.[1494] The term "*anointed*" here is *Masah*, "*to anoint,*" which means "to consecrate for religious service."[1495]

Daniel 9:24 clearly shows that something supernatural will happen in regard to Israel and their sin in relationship to their God. That relationship between God and Israel is connected by two opposites: first, Israel's sin which keeps them in the state of

---

[1491] Lang, *The Histories and Prophecies of Daniel,* 132.

[1492] Miller, *The New American Commentary: Daniel,* 261.

[1493] Showers, *The Most High God,* 119.

[1494] Feinberg, *Daniel: The Kingdom of the Lord,* 128.

[1495] Miller, *The New American Commentary: Daniel,* 261.

rebellion, and second, in making reconciliation for iniquity, the sacrifice for sin will bring righteousness; visions and prophecy will come to an end and the temple consecrated, all culminating in the Messiah Himself. The Messiah is interwoven throughout verse 24, as well as verses 25-27. In verse 26 only two words will be analyzed because of the impact they have on *Yeshua* in His first coming: "*Messiah*" and being "*cut off.*"

The term "*Messiah*" in the *Tanakh* denotes two ideas, one of consecration and endowment of either an individual, such as with Saul, David and priests, or an object such as the tabernacle, the altar and laver. Messiah in Daniel 9:26 (מָשִׁיחַ - Anointed-one) comes from the Hebrew word משׁח, is pronounced *moshiach* "anointed one," and occurs 39 times[1496] in the Hebrew Scriptures.[1497] Smith does not place the Daniel passage in with the listing of references, but *Young's Concordance* does,[1498] as well as Oswalt, who states that the term "*Messiah*" developed in its understanding to focus in a person:

> This existence of the concept of "The Anointed One" in its own right, over and above the more narrowly prescribed historical functions of prophet, priest, and king, undoubtedly contributed to the rise of the concept of the eschatological Anointed One, the Messiah. Within the canon of the OT there are only two unambiguous references to this figure, both in Dan 9:25, 26. Here Daniel predicts a time in the future when the Anointed One, who may well be the Most Holy who is anointed in 9:24, will appear and then be cut off with nothing.[1499]

This term Messiah developed into the understanding of a Messianic person in Jewish thinking from very early times, especially during the exile and post-exilic period. Oswalt expresses the fact that these two references in Daniel 9:25-26 are without a doubt a reference to the Messiah. The Jewish rabbis, from the post-exilic period into the time of *Yeshua*, had good reason to see Daniel 9 as a reference and a time table for the coming of the Messianic person. In the following statement Rabbi Silver agrees that the Messianic expectation was very high during the second quarter of the first century CE:

> Prior to the First Century (C.E.) the messianic interest was not excessive.... The First Century, however, especially the generation before the destruction [of the Second Temple] witnessed a remarkable outburst of Messianic emotionalism. This is to be attributed, as we shall see, not to an intensification of Roman persecution, but to the prevalent belief induced by the popular

---

[1496] **Saul** - 1 Sam 12:3, 5; 24:6, 10; 26:9, 11, 16, 23; 2 Sam 1:14, 16, 21; **David** – 2 Sam 19:21; 22:51; 23:1; Ps 18:51; 20:6; 28:8; **Priest** – Lev 4:3, 5, 16; 6:22; **Reigning King** – Lam 4:20; Ps 84:9; 89:38; **Patriarchs** – Ps 105:15; 1 Chron 16:22; **Solomon** – 2 Chron 6:42; **Prospective King** – 1 Sam 16:6; **Cyrus** – Isa 45:1; **Messiah** – 1 Sam 2:10, 35; Ps 2:2; 89:51; 132:10; Hab 3:13 and Dan 9:25-26.
[1497] Smith, *The Promised Messiah,* 1-3.
[1498] Robert Young, 's *Analytical Concordance to the Bible,* 39.
[1499] VanGemeren, *Dictionary of Old Testament & Exegesis,* 2:1126.

chronology of that day that the age was on the threshold of the Millennium…
When Jesus came into Galilee, spreading the gospel of the Kingdom of God
and saying the 'time is fulfilled' and the Kingdom of God is at hand, he was
voicing the opinion universally held that … the chronological fact which
inflamed the Messianic hope rather than the Roman persecutions … Jesus
appeared in the procuratorship of Pontius Pilate (26-36 C.E.) … It seems likely,
therefore, that in the mind of the people the Millennium was to begin around
the year 30 C.E. Be it remembered that it is not the Messiah who brings about
the Millennium. It is the inevitable advent of the Millennium which carries
along with it the Messiah and his appointed activities. The Messiah was
expected around the second quarter of the First Century C.E. because the
Millennium was at hand. Prior to that time he was not expected, because
according to the chronology of the day the Millennium was still considerably
removed.[1500]

It is significant that a rabbi would acknowledge the time of the coming of the expected
Messiah, even recognize *Yeshua*'s presence historically, and yet miss *Yeshua* as the
promised Messiah. These verses in Daniel 9:25-26 are very significant, powerful and
forceful in unambiguously pinpointing the time of the Messiah's coming. Even Moses,
in a more general sense, spoke of the time of the Messiah in Genesis 49:10. The words
"scepter will not depart from Judah until" he comes whose right it is,[1501] clearly show
that Messiah's tribal identity must be present. Judah and all the other tribes lost their
tribal identity when the Romans destroyed the temple in 70 CE. This simply means that
in order for the Jewish people to identify the Messiah, and even identify the tribal
identity, the Messiah had to come before the destruction of the temple because the
genealogical records of the families and tribes were kept in the temple. Both Moses and
Daniel predicted the time of the coming of the Messiah, but Daniel was more precise in
regard to time and purpose of the Messiah's coming. This one, the Messiah, would deal
with the transgressions, sin and iniquity of the people by His sacrifice or anointing work
at Calvary.

The last word to be discussed in Daniel 9:26 is מָשִׁיחַ [Messiah]. The Hebrew word
יִכָּרֵת is translated *"Messiah be cut off"* or simply *"cut off."* Examples of the term *"cut
off"* are defined as follows: (1) as cutting off part of the body as the head or hands,
(2) or the cutting off of the foreskin in the act of circumcision, (3) or the cutting down
of trees, idols, to cut out or to eliminate, to kill or to cut (make) a covenant.[1502] The
Messiah, in the context of Daniel 9, is viewed as being killed in the prophetic future. A
violent death is seen by Walvoord,[1503] Miller,[1504] Showers,[1505] Fruchtenbaum[1506] and

---

[1500] Rabbi Abba Hillel Silver, *A History of Messianic Speculation in Israel*, (New York:
Macmillan, 1927), 5-7.

[1501] Kaiser, *The Christian and the "Old" Testament*, 161. Compare the words in Genesis
49:10 with Ezekiel 21:27. [Shiloh is not in the Genesis text.]

[1502] Harris, Archer, and Waltke, *Theological Wordbook of the Old Testament*, 1:456.

[1503] Walvoord, *Daniel: The Key to Prophetic Revelation,* 229.

Lang,[1507] Walvoord states the verb rendered "*to cut off*" means "to destroy, to kill" and makes reference to Genesis 9:11, Deuteronomy 20:20, Jeremiah 11:19, and Psalm 37:9. Miller relates the phrase "*cut off*" to the crucifixion of *Yeshua*. Lang relates the phrase "*cut off*" to the Passover sacrifice in the month of Nisan. Although Lang and Feinberg[1508] suggest that Artaxerxes issued the decree in 445 under Nehemiah to rebuild the walls of Jerusalem in the month of Nisan, neither one has it documented. Showers connects the words "*cut off*" with the death penalty (Leviticus 7:20, 21, 25, 27) and with reference to a violent death (1 Samuel 17:51; Obadiah 9; Nahum 3:15). Being "*cut off*" is obviously a separation of body parts, foreskin, or the severing of a tree from its trunk. But it is also used in reference to death, a violent death. The context of Daniel 9:24-27 would lend itself very strongly to a death by execution, as the Romans did on their crosses.

This passage in Daniel 9 becomes quite powerful in that Israel will be reconciled from its transgression, sin, and iniquity against the LORD. Israel will experience real righteousness for the first time through Jeremiah's New Covenant (Jeremiah 31:31-34). The Millennial temple is anointed, and there is an end to Israel's sins. Therefore, there is no further need for vision and prophecy, because all of the elements in Daniel 9:24-27 are focused in the Messiah, who was "*cut off*" in death as the substitutionary sacrifice for sin and was literally the "anointed one" who would and did come 483 years after the decree of Artaxerxes. A tremendous amount of power and time is compressed into four verses. Finally, Cooper makes a statement worth noting concerning the six items in verses 24-25:

> ... at the end of the seventieth week of this period, the six things mentioned in Daniel 9:24 will be accomplished.[1509]

In the last four chapters, the whole subject of the divinity of the Messiah has been looked at in the Law, the Prophets and now the Writings, the threefold Jewish division of the *Tanakh*. What has been clearly seen is that if the Hebrew Scriptures are taken in a literal style, the divinity of the *Moshiach* becomes very apparent. This Messiah is referred to as being eternal, beyond time and space. He is the One who has interacted with Israel from the time of Abraham. Through theophanies He has revealed Himself consistently as "*echad*" God Who is a plurality in unity. He was also "*the captain of the LORD's host*," the "*son of David*," "*Immanuel*," the virgin born one from Bethlehem who will sit upon the throne of His father David as long as the sun and the moon. He is "*the righteous Branch*" who will come as the Servant of the LORD to die for the sins of mankind and then later, after He is finally embraced by a repentant Israel, will come

---

[1504] Miller, *New American Commentary: Daniel*, 267.

[1505] Showers, *The Most High God*, 125.

[1506] Fruchtenbaum, *Messianic Christology*, 97.

[1507] Lang, *The Histories and Prophecies of Daniel*, 134.

[1508] Feinberg, *Daniel: The Kingdom of the Lord*, 130.

[1509] Cooper, *The 70 Weeks of Daniel*, 56.

and inaugurate the Kingdom and rule in Jerusalem over the entire world. When all of these references are piled one upon the other, the sheer weight of evidence should be so compelling that Jewish people will recognize that their rabbis have led them astray, for they have lifted up the Talmud in the place of *Moshiach,* the God/man. This weight will continue to become so heavy as the final three chapters in this book continue to show that the Hebrew Scriptures have clearly revealed the Second Person of the unity of *Elohim* as God incarnate.

Chapter 16
God Has a Son!

The term *"son of God,"* as it relates to Messiah, is used frequently in the New Covenant. Was this term used in the *Tanakh* and if so, how was it used by the writers of Scripture and how was it to be understood? In the *Tanakh* the term *"son of David"* is used very frequently and in this book it refers to the promised coming of the *Moshiach* who will be that Son of David. To those who hold to the biblical faith and the Jewish people this Son of David will be the one that the prophets had promised. This one will come and restore to Israel the Kingdom, set up the temple, as well as the temple worship, and regather all the sons and daughters of Abraham from around the world to Israel. This one will institute the long awaited peace that the Jewish people long for.

Judaism and New Covenant believers would agree on this. However, on one point Judaism and those who hold to biblical faith are at opposite ends of the issue. True New Testament believers believe that Messiah is the God/man who came 2000 years ago, born of the "virgin" and was rejected by His brethren. He died on the cross for the sins of Israel and the world and returned to Heaven (Hosea 5:15) where He presently sits at the right hand of the Father (Psalm 80:17). He will come back the second time and restore all things that the Jewish faithful look for. However, Rabbinic Judaism does not believe in the plural unity of *Elohim* or that *Elohim* has a Son who is equal to Him who will accomplish these longed for promises. Simply put, orthodox and ultra-orthodox Judaism believes that Messiah will be the son of David, but he is nothing more than a man; he is not the God/man. The issue and controversy over the humanity and divinity of the Messiah have been discussed at length in chapters 12 through 15 of this book, and the *Tanakh* supports the belief that the Son of David will be the promised God/man. But does the *Tanakh* also support the belief that God has a Son?

In the opening pages of the New Covenant in the Gospel of Luke a Jewish reader comes almost immediately face to face with the term *"Son of God"* (Luke 1:32) as it relates to *Yeshua*, Son of David. The Jewish writer of the Gospel of Matthew records, in addition to the Luke account, that an angel came to the "virgin" named Miriam (Mary) living in Nazareth and announced to her that she was going to bare a son, and that this son would be Immanuel, meaning *"God with us"* (Matthew 1:23; Isaiah 7-12). The immediate Jewish response was that God does not have a son and that the Messiah is not God! The purpose of this section is to view the *Tanakh* and see what the Hebrew Scriptures do or do not say.[1510] The question at the heart of the issue is: Does the

---

[1510] Wilkinson, *Israel My Glory*, 180-186.

511

Tanakh reference a divine Son? Son of God or the son of anyone gives the idea of birth and human generations. Milton Lindberg states clearly the issue that is at stake:

> Does the Tanakh indicate how a divine eternal personality can be a Son? Is this not a great problem, since being a son suggests the idea of generation and birth? The divine solution: deity becomes a Son by way of incarnation, God taking upon himself humanity. Hear the words of the prophet Isaiah (9:6-7).[1511]

Lindberg's statement is significant and prompts further discussions among Christian theologians. Was Jesus the son eternally or was He designated the eternal son after His incarnation? It is the belief of this author that He was given the title of Son as it related to the incarnation and His resurrection and His future ministry. For example, the passages of Scripture that relate to His Sonship all deal with Him from the time of His incarnation and not before. Another example, in the 1 Chronicles passage on the Davidic Covenant (17:10-14) He is the eternal Son in the future when He reigns on the throne of David. The Psalm 2 passage that will be studied in this chapter also relates to Him being the Son during the Millennial Kingdom. For New Covenant believers at *Yeshua*'s baptism (Matthew 3:17) the Father states, *"This is my beloved Son, in whom I am well pleased."* The second New Covenant passage states almost the same thing from the Father concerning *Yeshua* at His transfiguration (Matthew 17:5) when He said, *"This is my beloved Son, in whom I am well pleased, hear ye him."* In the mind of the Father from eternity past *Yeshua* would be given the title of Son, but not until His incarnation. The author, Lindberg, clearly lays to rest the belief that the title of "Son" was not given to Him until the Second Person of the plural unity of *Elohim* became a man at His incarnation. In this chapter that very issue of the *"Son of God"* will be discussed and primarily three passages will be studied: Psalm 2, 72 and Proverbs 30:4 along with referencing a few other passages.

PSALM 2

> (1) Why do nations assemble, and peoples plot vain things; (2) kings of the earth take their stand, and regents intrigue together against the LORD and against His anointed? (3) "Let us break the cords of their yoke, shake off their ropes from us!" (4) He who is enthroned in heaven laughs; the Lord mocks at them. (5) Then He speaks to them in anger, terrifying them in His rage, (6) "But I have installed My king on Zion, My holy mountain!" (7) Let me tell of the decree: the LORD said to me, "You are My son, I have fathered you this day. (8) Ask it of Me, and I will make the nations your domain; your estate, the limits of the earth. (9) You can smash them with an iron mace, shatter them like potter's ware." (10) So now, O kings, be prudent; accept discipline, you rulers of the earth! (11) Serve the LORD in awe; tremble with fright, (12) pay homage

---

[1511] Lindberg, *In Light of Tenach: The Trinity*, 7-8.

in good faith, lest He be angered, and your way be doomed in the mere flash of His anger. Happy are all who take refuge in Him.

Psalm 2 has been commonly looked upon from beginning to end as an out-and-out prophecy of the Messiah.[1512] This psalm (Acts 4:24-28; 13:33; Hebrews 1:5; 5:5; Revelation 2:27; 12:5; 19:15) along with Psalm 110 is the most quoted psalm in the New Covenant. All of these references are applied to the Messiah, giving the New Covenant the authority it needs to call it a Messianic Psalm. This psalm is also one of the greatest of the Messianic Psalms. It is one of the very few Old Testament passages, and the only one in the Psalms, that refers to the Second Person of the plural unity of *Elohim* by the name Son of God (verses 7 and 12).[1513]

This psalm has been recognized by rabbis as a Messianic Psalm, but they also have a tendency to ascribe the psalm to David because of its use by true biblical believers. But the point is that rabbis, such as Rashi and Kimchi, saw it as a Messianic Psalm as noted:

> The ancient Jewish commentators describe the Messianic interpretation of this psalm as a common one. Kimchi says, "Some interpret this psalm of Gog and Magog, and the anointed is King Messiah: but it is more natural to suppose that David spake it concerning himself." Rashi makes a similar statement, but adds with singular candour: "In order to keep to the literal sense and answer the heretics (Christians), it is better to explain it of David himself." [1514]

It seems to be a matter of who uses and interprets it as to how the rabbis understand it. If within the rabbinic context it is viewed as messianic, but true believers use it to substantiate *Yeshua* as the Messiah, the rabbis will interpret it as referring to David. But that is not being honest or consistent.

There are some authors who believe that Psalms 1 and 2 were once tied together as one psalm. Two reasons for this thinking are that Psalm 1 begins with *"Blessed is the man,"* which deals with the individual decision to either walk in righteousness or to walk in the counsel of wicked men. The second reason is that Psalm 2 ends with the words, *"Blessed are all they that put their trust in him"* indicating that you are blessed if you trust in the "Son" and worship Him rather than putting your lot in with the kings of the earth who are vainly plotting to overthrow the LORD's Anointed King and Son, as the following two authors reflect:

> Like Psalm 1, but unlike almost every other psalm of Book 1 (Psa 1-41), this one has no superscription. Psalm 1 opens with a blessing and Psalm 2 closes

---

[1512] Leupold, *Exposition of Psalms,* 41.

[1513] Henry M. Morris, *Treasures in the Psalms* (Green Forest, AR: Master Books, 2001), 26-27.

[1514] G. H. S. Johnson, C. J. Elliott and F. C. Cook, *The Book of Psalms with an Explanatory and Critical Commentary* (London: John Murray, Albemarle Street, 1880), 3.

with a blessing, which may indicate that this pair is meant to be read together as an introduction to the final collection of the Psalter.[1515]

This throws light on how Psalm 2 should be taken. For if the psalm is messianic, and if it was originally linked with Psalm 1, then the doctrine of the two ways introduced in Psalm 1 is here carried forward but at a higher pitch, On the one hand, the way of sinners in Psalm 1 now becomes a cosmic revolt of the nations against God and his Anointed. It becomes an unfolding of the wrong path and its consequences. On the other hand, the righteous man of the opening psalm is now explicitly seen to be God's Son, the Lord Jesus Christ, which I suggested at the close of the previous chapter. It is by taking refuge in Jesus that the judgment awaiting the wicked can be avoided by them.[1516]

These authors have some interesting and logical views. However, there is no way of knowing if these two psalms were combined in the past. But this much is certain; their application of the two psalms is correct.

There are four official Messianic titles for the Messiah in each section of this psalm, one for each stanza: the "Anointed" in verse 2; "My King" in verse 6; "My Son" in verse 7; and the "lord" in verse 11.[1517] David is the commonly recognized author of the psalm. Although it has no superscription, this psalm is ascribed to David in Acts 4:25, and is identified as 'the second psalm' in Acts 13:33.[1518] Wilson points out that this psalm is not only attributed to David, but clearly gives the authorship to him as well as its placement in the Psalms:

The second psalm is unique among the psalms in three interesting respects. It is actually referred to by number in the New Testament (Acts 13:33), a fact which indicates that the chapter divisions were present in the Book of Psalms right from the start. Secondly, its Davidic authorship is confirmed in the New Testament (Acts 4:25), even though the heading of the psalm itself, contrary to the usual situation, does not say who the author is.[1519]

Some have disputed the authorship of David, but rather attribute it to the Psalter who could be, but is not necessarily David:

The Psalm is anonymous. For this very reason we may not assign it to David nor to Solomon; for nothing is to be inferred from Acts 4:25, since in the New

---

[1515] Craig Broyles, *New International Biblical Commentary: Psalms* (Peabody, MA: Hendrickson, 1999), 44.

[1516] James Montgomery Boice, *An Expositional Commentary: Psalms* (3 vols. Grand Rapids: Baker, 1994), 1:22.

[1517] Wilson, *The Messianic Psalms,* 12.

[1518] Derek Kidner, *Tyndale Old Testament Commentaries: Psalms 1-72* (Downers Grove, IL: InterVarsity Press, 1979), 49-50.

[1519] Morris, *Treasures in the Psalms,* 26.

Testament "hymn of David" and "psalm" are co-ordinate ideas, and it is always far more hazardous to ascribe an anonymous Psalm to David or Solomon,....[1520]

Yet Acts 4:25 is explicitly clear concerning the authorship when it states that by the inspiration of the Holy Spirit this psalm was given: "by *the mouth of thy servant David hast said.*" Acts 4:25 leaves no doubt as to the authorship of Psalm 2.

Psalm 2 is divided into four parts or four strophes as is reflected by these two authors:

Vs. 1-3	deals with the rebellion of the nations and their kings against the dominion of the LORD and his anointed.
Vs. 4-6	involves the scorn and wrath of the LORD and his installation of his own king on his holy mount.
Vs. 7-9	reports the content of a decree that records the identity and dominion that the LORD has granted His King, His Son which He has promised universal dominion and power to achieve it.
Vs. 10-12	The rulers of the earth reexhorted to submit to the LORD's king.[1521]

The first strophe describes the bitter opposition of the enemies of the Lord's anointed. The second describes the calm assurance of the Lord Himself in the face of this opposition. The third presents the glorious divine ordinance appointed for the Lord's anointed. The last consists of an exhortation to the rebels to submit discreetly to Him who is their Lord.[1522]

Others divide this psalm into four sections, each with three verses, and state there are four speakers, one for each section:

1. The voice of rebellion – man in revolt (verses 1-3).
2. The reply of Jehovah – God in His wrath (verses 4-6).
3. The revelation of the Son (verses 7-9).
4. The Spirit's call to reconciliation (verses 10-12).[1523]

Some have tried to insert the tri-unity of God in Psalm 2 with the Father speaking in verses 4-6, God the Son speaking in verses 7-9 and the Holy Spirit speaking in verses 10-12. This author sees no good reason to attribute the last strophe of verses to the Holy Spirit. It is a stretch at best. Wilson alludes to that point, but Morris and Allen are more specific about their opinion when they state:

[1520] Keil and Delitzsch, *Commentary on the Old Testament in Ten Volumes: Psalms,* 5:89-90.
[1521] Mays, Interpretation, A *Bible Commentary for Teaching and Preaching: Psalms,* 45.
[1522] Leupold, *Exposition of Psalms,* 41.
[1523] Wilson, *The Messianic Psalms,* 13.

The final stanza is a testimony which most appropriately would come from God, the Holy Spirit.[1524]

It is not a matter of it being "appropriate," but it is a matter of it being biblical and there is no biblical evidence within Psalm 2 to attribute this final strophe to the Holy Spirit.

This Psalm is remarkable in terms of the speakers as well. In the first strophe, the speaker is David as he reflects on the irrational evil of rulers and world leaders (vv. 1-3). In the second strophe, the speaker is God the Father. All heaven rocks with His laughter at the arrogance of wicked men (vv. 4-6). In the third strophe we hear the words of the son (each king, the ideal king, and the final King), who is ultimately the Son of God Himself and who reports the words of the Father on His behalf (vv. 7-9). In the fourth strophe (vv. 10-12) we hear the words of the Spirit in solemn warning to all earthly leaders of the reality of the rule of God, both in the present and in the future. The rule on earth of the heavenly King is coming. None shall stand against Him, not one![1525]

It sounds good to put the Holy Spirit in the last stanza, but again there is no internal evidence within the psalm to attribute this stanza or any stanza in the psalm to the Holy Spirit.

This psalm has been recognized as a Messianic Psalm by both Jews and New Covenant believers alike, however they differ as to the person to whom it applies. Before entering into a study of this psalm, there are four very important phrases found in four different verses within this psalm. These focus the eyes of the student of Scripture on the Son of God as they are laid out simply below:

Psalm 2:2   "עַל־יְהֹוָה וְעַל־מְשִׁיחוֹ" "against Jehovah, and against His Anointed (Messiah)."

Psalm 2:6   Jehovah calls Him "My King."

Psalm 2:7   The Messiah says, "Jehovah hath said unto Me, בְּנִי אַתָּה is literally translated " Son of Me, You" or "My Son Thou art."

Psalm 2:12   In the last verse; referring to the same Person, we have the exhortation "Kiss the Son, lest He be angry, and ye perish … Blessed are all they that put their trust in Him."

These phrases or words clearly present the fact "that the Son of God is also the Messiah, and also a Divine Person, for a blessing is pronounced on all who trust in Him."[1526] This second psalm is a poetic speech concerning the sonship of the Messiah.

[1524] Morris, *Treasures in the Psalms,* 26-27.
[1525] Allen, *Rediscovering Prophecy: A New Song for a New Kingdom,* 168.
[1526] Wilkinson, *Israel My Glory,* 183.

It is the only text in the *Tanakh* that speaks of God's King, Messiah, and Son in one place.[1527]

A close study of Psalm 2 will show the true seeker that the Messiah referred to in verse 3 [2] is clearly the same as "My King" in verse 6. Likewise the speaker of verses 7-9 who claims that God addressed Him as "My Son" and Who is to have universal dominion over the nations of the earth is the One referred to as מְשִׁיחוֹ "His anointed" and מַלְכִּי "My King." Hence the Messiah is both human and divine – God's Son. These facts being true, one is not surprised to read in the Septuagint version, translated around 250 BC, that the Hebrew translators used the same Greek word κυριοσ (lord) in translating both the word יְהוָה (LORD – Yahweh) and אֲדֹנִי (Lord - Adonai). This proves conclusively that the Hebrew scholars who translated the Greek version understood that the One to Whom God spoke was likewise divine. With this information laid out, look at each of the four stanzas individually.

First Stanza ... Verses 1-3:

> (1) Why do nations assemble, and peoples plot vain things; (2) kings of the earth take their stand, and regents intrigue together against the LORD and against His anointed? (3) "Let us break the cords of their yoke, shake off their ropes from us!"

In these verses David is describing a staged rebellion of the world leaders against *Yahweh* and His Anointed. This description of the *"kings of the earth"* conspiring together against *Yahweh* and His Anointed King simply does not fit anything in recorded Scripture, especially as it related to David or Solomon. This is brought out by Weiser when he states:

> We shall look in vain for a situation in the course of the history of Israel and Judah in which an Israelite king would in reality have ruled the whole world as is implied in the psalm. Nor can it be assumed that the poet would call the princes of the small neighboring peoples, which had been temporarily subjugated by Israel 'kings of the earth' or 'judges of the earth' (v. 10) which would have been an unjustified and extravagant exaggeration.[1528]

The Gentile nations and their kings are imagining in vain if they think that they can consult together and unite against the Creator of the universe and get away with it. It is absurd to even imagine or think for a moment that they could succeed. Yet they rebel, knowing full well what they are doing, as the following author expresses:

> The first word *lama* (for what purpose? Why?) expresses surprise and registers an expression of incomprehension. Reference is made to the *goyim* (nations)

[1527] Mays, *Interpretation, A Bible Commentary for Teaching and Preaching: Psalms,* 44.

[1528] Artur Weiser, *The Old Testament Library: The Psalms* (trans. by Herbert Hartwell. Philadelphia: Westminster Press, 1962), 110.

who *ragesu* (are thronging tumultuously); Mitchell Dahood correctly translated this as "foregathering." The national leaders or kings (cf. vv. 2-3) are disturbed, they are raising a tumult as they gather their forces, count their troops, and form an alliance *yityassebu* (take a stand, and/or form a solid front). They are well aware of what they are doing: *nosedu* (from *sod*, niphal perfect, hence reflexive: they counsel together, they form a conclave with each other). As they counsel they exhort one another to rebellion against Yahweh and his *masiah* (anointed king on Mount Zion). They acknowledge they are under bondage; they plan rebellion to have their freedom. To be noted particularly here is reference to the close relationship between Yahweh and his anointed one. To resist the One is to resist the other.[1529]

David and Solomon, the two greatest kings of Israel, never encountered this kind of opposition, nor did the other kings of Judah. The King James Version is even more blunt when it says, "*Why do the heathen rage*." A literal rendering of *rage* is a "tumultuous assembly." Imagine the kings of the earth sitting down to develop a plan against God, coming together to consult each other on how to orchestrate a rebellion, throw off His yoke and free themselves against the LORD and His Anointed. These kings of the earth who collectively come together to overthrow the LORD and His Anointed view the LORD's leadership as a yoke. They wish to break away from His righteous rule over them, as reflected by the following quote:

> The rebellious kings and rulers propose to set themselves free from the dominion of Yahweh and the king of Israel. The bonds and cords are figures for "rule" and "control."[1530]

The futile attempt of the creature to break away from his Creator is simply senseless. Yet because "*man's heart is deceitful above all things and desperately wicked*" (Jeremiah 17:9) man deceives himself into thinking he can succeed in his vanity, as stated below:

> **Why ... in vain**? Its senselessness is simple; it cannot succeed. The enforcer of the Israelite empire is none other than "the LORD, the One enthroned in heaven" (v 4), who has given **his Anointed One** a decree promising him, "I will make the nations your inheritance" (v. 8). We must keep in mind that **chains** and **fetters** are part of a quotation from **the kings of the earth**. This is how they characterize Yahweh's rule over them;[1531]

Only one other attempt of the nations to accomplish such a rebellion was carried out by Nimrod and his compatriots in Genesis 11. That met with aggressive action by the LORD. There has simply not been any rebellion of such magnitude in the history of the

---

[1529] Van Groningen, *Messianic Revelation in the Old Testament,* 336-337.

[1530] Robert G. Bratcher and William D. Reyburn, *A Handbook on Psalms* (New York: United Bible Societies, 1991), 25.

[1531] Broyles, *New International Biblical Commentary: Psalms,* 45.

world against the LORD and His Anointed. What is interesting is that Peter in Acts 4:25-28 applied this psalm to the Sanhedrin and to Rome through the procurator Pilate in the trial and crucifixion of *Yeshua,* as VanGemeren points out:

> The first-century church applied the second psalm to the Messiah as an explanation of the crucifixion of Christ by the rulers (Herod and Pontius Pilate), the nations, and Israel (the priests, scribes, and Pharisees). They had conspired together against the Messiah of God (Acts 4:25-28). Paul applied it to Jesus' ministry: His sonship, resurrection, and ascension to glory, which confirmed God's promises in Jesus as the Messiah (Acts 13:32-33).[1532]

Peter states that Herod and Pontius Pilate, with the Gentiles and the people of Israel, were gathered together. This could hardly be the fulfillment of Psalm 2. That rebellion was small and insignificant in relationship to what David describes in Psalm 2. To be specific, the crucifixion simply does not fit the picture that David paints. Morris and Phillips express a more correct, but still incomplete understanding of this psalm and Peter's word by these statements:

> The prophecy was fulfilled in a precursive way at the trial of Christ. After quoting this very verse, the Early Church then applied it thus: "For of a truth against thy holy child Jesus, whom thou hast anointed, both Herod and Pontius Pilate with the Gentiles, and the people of Israel, were gathered together (Acts 4:27)." The ultimate fulfillment, however, will no doubt be at the very end of the age, in the last great rebellion against God, of both men and devils.[1533]

> In the case of the Second Psalm, the New Testament portrays "A" fulfillment at the trial and crucifixion of Jesus. Part of the Psalm is quoted in Acts 4:25-28.

> Pontius Pilate, Herod, the Sanhedrin and most of the leaders of Israel fulfilled in a small way that which the world will fulfill in the near future.... .[1534]

So why did Peter reference this verse if it was not a fulfillment of Psalm 2? Arnold Fruchtenbaum gives a very helpful section in his book *Messianic Christology.* Appendix 7 entitled "How the New Testament quotes the Old Testament"[1535] is a very helpful study. Using Matthew 2 he illustrates four ways that the New Covenant writers quoted the *Tanakh.* First, there was a literal prophecy with literal fulfillment; second was literal prophecy plus typical fulfillment; third was literal prophecy plus application; and last was summation. In Acts 4 Peter was using the literal prophecy plus application method. It was not a literal fulfillment, nor was it typology or a summation of all that

---

[1532] Willem VanGemeren, *The Expositors Bible Commentary: Psalms* (Grand Rapids: Zondervan, 1991), 65.

[1533] Morris, *Treasures in the Psalms,* 27-28.

[1534] Phillips, *Exploring the Messianic Psalms,* 23-24.

[1535] Fruchtenbaum, *Messianic Christology,* 146-152.

the prophets said about this issue. That helps to clarify and answer the issue about how Peter was interpreting Psalm 2.

In studying this psalm, I do not believe that this portion of Psalm 2 literally relates to *Yeshua*'s rejection by the leadership of Israel and the Romans. This psalm makes no reference to the suffering of the Messiah, but only to the combined attempt by world leaders to rebel against the LORD and His Anointed. It is treated by the psalmist as prophetic future, to the last uprising at the end of the Millennium Reign. Yet the application of the prophecy of the rejection of *Yeshua* lingers in the mind because of other passages such as Psalm 110, where David's Lord is invited by the LORD to "*Sit thou at my right hand, until I make thine enemies thy footstool*" and that connected with Israel's rejection of Him. Even though *Yeshua* was rejected by Israel at His first coming it is not the fulfillment of Psalm 2. Fulfillment comes at the end of His Millennial Reign when the nations of the world consult together to revolt against Him. Chapter 2 in Psalms pictures the Anointed King already being on His throne when the world rulers revolt against Him. In *Yeshua*'s first coming He was not seated upon the throne of David. The following author misplaces Israel's rejection of the Anointed King by connecting it with Isaiah 53; the rest of the quote is accurate. That rejection has nothing to do with the passage in Psalm 2. The rejection of Israel and the revolt of the world leaders in Psalm 2 are separated by at least 3000 years:

> Psalm 2 affirms the Davidic ruler's special status as God's chosen king. He is God's very own "son" and is given the nations as his inheritance (vv. 7-8). (389) This passage (Isa 53), one of the best known in the Bible, depicts a suffering servant who plays a key role in God's redemptive program for His people and the nations. (391)

> They confess that one whom they rejected and wrote off as an object of divine wrath is really their savior and destined to be their king. Israel (1) first expresses shock and surprise at what they have heard (vs. 1-3). Then in verses 4-6 reflection replaces shock, as they realize appearances can be deceiving. Israel essentially says, "when we saw this servant suffering, we assumed he was being punished by God for his own sin. But we were only partially correct. He was being punished by God, but for our sins, not his own sins." Israel's reflection continues in verses 7-10. They remember how the servant silently endured harsh treatment. At this point God speaks again (vv. 11-12), and the song ends as it began, with God announcing that the servant will be exalted and rewarded for his obedience.[1536]

The previous quote is good because it pictures Israel's identification of *Yeshua* and their confession against the Servant of the LORD, the Messiah. To this author, these first three verses of Psalm 2 give a picture of the future rebellion of the Gentile nations and

---

[1536] Robert B. Chisholm Jr., "The Christological Fulfillment of Isaiah's Servant Songs," *Bibliotheca Sacra* (Vol. 163, number 652, October-December 2006): 387-404.

the final rebellion of Satan after being released from his prison where he was confined for 1000 years during the Millennial Reign of the Messiah (Revelation 20:7-9). A second picture of worldwide rebellion, but less likely is that world at the time of the battle of Armageddon (Revelation 19:17-19). Also at the time of Armageddon the Messiah is not yet reigning physically on the throne of His father David in Jerusalem. This is not likely because the nations under the Anti-Christ are gathered together to destroy Israel. There is nothing, even at the highest point of David's military exploits where he subdued only his immediate neighbors (2 Samuel 8:1-18; cf. 22:41-46; Psalm 18:43-45). David never exercised power over the kings of the earth that would have prompted such an act of rebellion by the Gentile nations of the earth against the LORD's Anointed, the Messiah.[1537]

The important thing here is to have a proper focus on who man is as God views him. God is the Creator and man is the creature. God is so holy that His glory would completely consume man. Yet here is man plotting to overthrow God. Here is God's perspective from Isaiah 40:

(15) Behold, the nations are as a drop in a bucket, and are counted as the small dust of the balance: behold, he taketh up the isles as a very little thing.... (17) All nations before him are as nothing; and they are counted to him less than nothing, and vanity. (22) It is he that sitteth upon the circle of the earth, and the inhabitants thereof are as grasshoppers; that stretcheth out the heavens as a curtain, and spreadeth them out as a tent to dwell in. (25) To whom then will ye liken me, or shall I be equal? saith the Holy One. (26) Lift up your eyes on high, and behold who hath created these things, that bringeth out their host by number: he calleth them all by names by the greatness of his might, for that is strong in power; not one faileth.

Man who sits on his ant hill thinks he is mighty while God looks at him as nothing. When that perspective is taken, it is easy to understand the reaction God has to man's futile attempt to overthrow Him. God breaks out in laughter as described in the next stanza of Psalm 2. Charles Haddon Spurgeon has rightly said:

We have, in these first three verses, a description of the hatred of human nature against the Christ of God."[1538]

The last point to be made is the last part of verse 2. The term *"anointed"* was a term used to anoint a king or a priest to his office in the priesthood or a prophet. But the word *"anointed"* in this passage is the word for *"moshiach"* from which Messiah

---

[1537] Terrien, *Eerdmans Critical Commentary: The Psalm,* 82.
[1538] Charles Haddon Spurgeon, *The Treasury of David* (3 vols. Mclean, VA: MacDonald Publication, n.d.), 1:10.

comes.[1539] As this chapter unfolds it becomes very obvious that this "*anointed*" one is no ordinary person.

Second Stanza ... Verses 4-6:

> (4) He who is enthroned in heaven laughs; the Lord mocks at them. (5) Then He speaks to them in anger, terrifying them in His rage, (6) "But I have installed My king on Zion, My holy mountain!"

This is one of the most unusual passages in Scripture. Here the LORD, who is the Creator of the universe, enthroned in heaven, laughs at the little insignificant man of earth as he lifts his collective fist in the air in rebellion and defiance of his Creator. Allen and Leupold reflect on the defiance of man and on the laughter of the LORD:

> For the first time since the building of the tower of Babel, rulers of the world and their subjects will be united in defying the Almighty.... Here is a laugh of sarcastic scorn – a dreadful, mocking laugh.[1540]

> In a bold figure the Lord is represented as being amused at the foolish endeavors of His enemies: He "laughs," He "derides" them. He has not been moved even to rise from His throne.... The expression naturally involves the thought of the calm and serene dignity that characterizes Him who is so infinitely removed from the frailty and littleness of man.[1541]

In the previous strophe the world rises up against the LORD's Anointed who in verse 6 the Father identifies as "*my king*" whom He has set in Zion (Jerusalem). The Father looks at these puny humans and breaks into laughter, the kind of laughter that, when He stops, causes Him to judge with awesome, terrifying power. The pronoun "I" in the Hebrew is emphatic, for He has placed His "*Anointed*," whom He identifies as "*my king*" in Zion, against whom the world attempts to rebel. In the next strophe (verses 7-9) the LORD identifies the King as "*My Son*" (verse 7) who is His representative (verses 11-12) on earth.[1542] Van Groningen states the following in relationship to the first person pronoun "I" in the biblical text:

> *Ani*, the emphatic form of the first personal pronoun, sets the speaker in the forefront. The conjunction *wa* (and) preceding the pronoun also adds emphasis; it is meant to stress that the I, in spite of what opponents plan or wish to do, will have and continue to carry out the decree he has made known.[1543]

[1539] Morris, *Treasures in the Psalms*, 27-28.

[1540] Allen, *Rediscovering Prophecy: A New Song for a New Kingdom*, 164.

[1541] Leupold, *Exposition of Psalms*, 48.

[1542] J. J. Stewart Perowne, *The Book of Psalms* (2 vols. Grand Rapids: Zondervan, 1966), 1:116.

[1543] Van Groningen, *Messianic Revelation in the Old Testament*, 335.

The LORD has installed His "*Anointed*" (verse 2), whom He refers to as "*my king*" (verse 6) and states it with an emphatic "I," meaning that this will be done regardless of what the rebellious kings of the earth think. Van Groningen continues with the following statement:

> The "I" of verse 6 is identified in these two preceding verses. *Yoseb* (the one sitting, dwelling, and firmly settled) in the heavens is none other than Yahweh, who is God, Creator, Owner, and Ruler of all things in heaven and on earth. Thus, the One enthroned on high – above and over all – is the One who placed his king on the throne on Zion. This sovereignly enthroned One maintains his enthroned one, and efforts to dislodge or overthrow him move Yahweh *yishaq* (to laugh; cf. Gen 21:1-6). This laugh is qualified by the parallel statement: *adonay yilag* (mocks, make sport of them [Dahood], derides) and after he laughs he speaks in his anger and in his wrath *yebahalemo* (he terrifies them). Yahweh, having installed his chosen One, made his attitude known to his opponents: he will not tolerate opposition because of his decree. It is best to understand the King on Mount Zion speaking about his enthroned King or king who rules over all nations.[1544]

Another author states that His installment of His King is a divine act of *Yahweh*, for it is a sacred inauguration of His King:

> The basic assertion is that the king's installation is a divine act. The entire process of his designation and inauguration was a sacred enactment of the choice of the LORD who had installed him on the holy mount.[1545]

It is clear that God has installed His Anointed, His King on the Throne in Zion and absolutely no one can dislodge Him. It should be made equally clear that when the LORD states that He sits in heaven, it literally means to reign, or rule as king. It does not just indicate that the Lord is sitting in heaven rather than standing.[1546] Even though the kings of the earth wish to dislodge the "*Anointed*" "*King*," they will fail. Regardless of what the Gentile world thinks of Him, His rule is absolute and will take place as King states:

> This is God's answer in person to his enemies. The "I" is emphatic. Men make plots, princes may conspire, the nations may oppose, but I, the Almighty, the Sovereign of heaven and earth, have set my anointed King, my Son. Upon the throne, I have done it, and no power on earth can annul or set aside my action. Christ is King. Our Christ is the anointed, the enthroned of God. He may be despised and rejected of men; he may come to his own and his own perceive him not; he may be scourged and spit upon, crowned with thorns, and robed in mock purple; he may be crucified, and classed with thieves, and covered with

---

[1544] Van Groningen, *Messianic Revelation in the Old Testament*, 335-336.
[1545] Mays, *Interpretation, A Bible Commentary for Teaching and Preaching: Psalms*, 47.
[1546] Bratcher and Reyburn, *A Handbook on Psalms*, 26.

dishonor in the eyes of the world, his kingly authority laughed to scorn and his royal claims treated with contempt; yet God says, I have exalted him to the throne of the universe. "I have set him upon my holy hill of Zion."[1547]

In summary, these first two strophes speak of the "*kings of the earth*" in collective rebellion and consultation with each other to throw off the yoke of rulership of the LORD and His Anointed. When the LORD looks at their ridiculously futile attempt to throw off the leadership of His Anointed, His King, He breaks into mocking sarcastic laughter. He will speak to them in judgment and wrath, for any move on the part of the collective powers of the "*kings of the earth*" against the one He has set as King in Jerusalem will be met first with laughter and then wrath.

There is absolutely nothing in Israelite history with any monarch, from David to Zedekiah, which encompasses all the kings of Israel/Judah that have sat on the throne of David that reflects in any way the magnitude of the rebellion of the "*kings of the earth*." The LORD gets very personal by His use of the first person pronoun in verse 6. But in verse 2 He also uses a personal pronoun "*his anointed*" and in verse 6 with "*his anointed*" being identified as "*my king*." What has become evident is that this King, the Anointed of the LORD, is someone who is a man but who also must be the God/man promised in Genesis 3:15 to rule all the nations of the earth.

What is completely illogical in some Christian theological systems, such as Amillennialism, is the belief that this world will evolve into a messianic millennial period of peace among nations. They totally disregard the corrupted nature of mankind. Equally illogical on the part of Rabbinic Judaism is the belief that a sinful Messiah ben David could rule the entire world. (See Appendix 6 to get a fuller understanding of Judaism's belief system by Jakob Jocz as he relates Jewish development of belief to Man, Sin, Mediator, Messiah, and Salvation.) What the *Tanakh* teaches is that this Messiah will reign in righteousness because His essence is Righteousness. If Rabbinic Judaism were only minimally aware of human history, they would know that that scenario is not even possible. Just look at David, called by God a man after His own heart; yet he was a murderer, an adulterer, a poor father in dealing with his own children, and one who disobeyed the law of Moses outright by numbering the people, which resulted in the LORD's judging Israel with the death of 70,000 Israelite citizens. Rabbinic Judaism needs to challenge itself to look at the completely illogical possibilities of a human sinful Messiah ben David ruling a corrupted world in righteousness when he himself has been corrupted by sin. Those are two concepts at opposite ends to each other. It is as illogical as in this psalm to even imagine that the "*kings of the earth*" could overthrow the LORD's Anointed, His King.

[1547] Henry Melville King, *The Messiah in the Psalms* (Philadelphia: American Baptist Publication Society, 1899), 14-15.

Third Stanza ... Verses 7-9:

(7) Let me tell of the decree: the LORD said to me, "You are My son, I have fathered you this day. (8) Ask it of Me, and I will make the nations your domain; your estate, the limits of the earth. (9) You can smash them with an iron mace, shatter them like potter's ware."

In this third strophe, the Anointed (verse 2) King (verse 6) is now specified by the Father as "*My Son*" for "*this day have I begotten thee.*" Review the whole picture that has been laid out by the psalmist to this point. The world, "*the kings of the earth,*" will be in complete rebellion against the Anointed of the LORD, who is further identified as "*My King*" and now "*My Son.*" This is a worldwide action by the kings of the earth, not a local or regional rebellion against the LORD's Anointed. Also, review the fact that no ruler of the earth in the history of man, no matter how good, could rule the earth in righteousness, not even Messiah ben David, for he, like every other human being, is corrupted by sin to the very core of his being. Look at these following Scriptures from the *Tanakh*:

(6) Know, then, that it is not for any virtue of yours that the LORD your God is giving you this land to possess; for you are a stiff-necked people. (7) Remember, never forget, how you provoked the LORD your God to anger in the wilderness: from the day that you left the land of Egypt until you reached this place, you have continued defiant toward the LORD. (8) At Horeb you so provoked the LORD that the LORD was angry enough with you to have destroyed you. (13) The LORD further said to me [Moses], "I see that this is a stiff-necked people. (14) Let Me alone and I will destroy them and blot out their name from under heaven, and I will make you a nation far more numerous than they" (Deut 9:6-8, 13-14).

Most devious is the heart; It is perverse – who can fathom it? (Jeremiah 17:9)

For man is born to [do] mischief, Just as sparks fly upward (Job 5:7).

Indeed I was born in iniquity; with sin my mother conceived me (Psalm 51:5 [7])

For there is not a just man upon earth, that doeth good, and sinneth not (Ecclesiastes 7:20 KJV).

Flesh, whether Jewish or Gentile, is sinful and separated from God. Look how Moses had to intercede for Israel just to keep *HaShem* from destroying your fathers. At man's best his heart is deceitful or perverse; man is born to trouble even as the sparks of a fire fly upward. David even said that he was born in sin and Solomon stated simply that there is no man that does not sin. Oh, Jewish reader, understand your own *Tanakh*. You and all of mankind are sinners separated from a holy G-d, whose glory would consume us because of our sin. You needed a mediator in the past, the priests to whom your fathers took their sacrifices. You and your fathers' sin required death of an animal instead of your death. Any future Messiah ben David is plagued with the same unrighteousness as every human being that has ever lived! Messiah ben David would have to be completely righteous in and of himself, as Jeremiah clearly stated (Jeremiah 23:5-6).

What becomes very obvious is that this Son is personally connected to *Yahweh* and He will be given dominion over the earth from His throne on Zion (Jerusalem). Also notice carefully that the time period that is being referenced here is prophetic future. In this strophe *Yahweh* declares the Son as begotten (future title) by Himself, but the Son is also a physical Son of David, as Mays reflects on this passage:

> This Psalm speaks of the LORD's king, Son as having dominion over the earth and the universe. "You are my son" in verse 7 is the only appearance of "son" as title of the Davidic king in the psalms.[1548]

Notice the connection between the Davidic son and the Son of God in this psalm. The fact of the Anointed King being the very Son of God has nothing to do with procreation, like the Mormons teach. However, it has everything to do with the plural unity of *Elohim* in designating the Second Person of the plurality of *Elohim* and His voluntary submission to the Father in relationship to His dealing with mankind in the prophetic future. Also observe that the divine grant of a worldwide rule to the King stands in stark contrast to the reality of Israel's history. This Son of David, the Son begotten by God is ranked by *Yahweh* as the only one to whom He will (future) grant the rule of the nations that have been promised to Him on the throne of David in Jerusalem. There are authors who simply wish to make this a coronation psalm that was used by each of Israel's or Judah's kings, but there is no biblical justification for this, as the following author states:

> Scholars who see Psalm 2 chiefly as a psalm of coronation for a Davidic king take the words "You are my Son; today I have become your Father" (v. 7) as a formula for the symbolic adoption of the Jewish king by God at the time of his inauguration. But aside from the fact that nothing like this is ever said or suggested in the Old Testament, the Bible's own handling of the words is always in regard to Jesus. The words "You are my Son" and "This is my beloved Son" were spoken of Jesus by the Father twice during his earthly ministry: once at his baptism and once at the transfiguration. At the baptism a voice from heaven said, "This is my Son, whom I love; with him I am well pleased" (Matthew 3:17; cf. Mark 1:11; Luke 3:22). At the transfiguration God said, "This is my Son, whom I love; with him I am well pleased. Listen to him!" (Matthew 17:5; cf. Mark 9:7; Luke 9:35).[1549]

[1548] Mays, *Interpretation, A Bible Commentary for Teaching and Preaching: Psalms,* 47.
[1549] Boice, *An Expositional Commentary: Psalms*, 1:25.

We have already discussed throughout this book the connection of these positions: Son of God and Son of David into one person, the God/man, *Yeshua* the Messiah. These two positions are placed together in many passages of the *Tanakh* where the Son of David is attributed the character of God, the eternality of God and the very Name of *Yahweh* Himself, as seen in the following list:

The Righteous Branch – Jeremiah 23:5-6

The child who will rule is described as God – Isaiah 9:6-7

The eternal Son of David – I Chronicles 17:10-14

He will be Immanuel – Isaiah chapters 7-12

Whose goings forth have been from of old, from everlasting – Micah 5:2

These are only a few of the passages that come into view when the future title, Son of God in Psalm 2, is connected to the Son of David throughout the Hebrew Scriptures. It becomes quite obvious in the *Tanakh* that this Son of David is more than a human descendant of David; He becomes God in the flesh. It becomes apparent that what is attributed to "*My son*" in Psalm 2 could not even begin to pertain to any of the sons of David that have reigned on his throne in the past. This expresses a unique relationship between the LORD and the "Son," as is stated below:

Messiah, without preface, takes up the word of Jehovah, "I will tell," He says, "of a decree, an eternal, immutable decree, by which I reign. Jehovah said unto Me, Thou art My Son; not as all the Israelites (Ex 4:22-23; Deut 14:1) are sons, or as any king of Israel is a son; but My only Son, the Inheritor of my Sovereign dominion."[1550]

In chapter 12 of this book, where Psalm 110 is discussed, it is clearly seen from David's own words that *Yahweh* spoke to his Lord and gave Him, his Lord, the earth and made Him a Priest after the order of Melchizedek; this is still future. Another interesting factor is that this Son of David, the Son of God, will rule in Jerusalem forever. That hardly could be speaking of a mere sinful human being. According to Psalm 2, in what way is the Son begotten by *Yahweh*? One author states that it was on the day *Yahweh* declared and manifested the Second Person of the plural unity of *Elohim* as His Son, and then connected it to the incarnation and the resurrection of the Messiah from the dead (Romans 1:3-4):

The expression, "I this day have begotten thee," can only mean, This day have I declared and manifested thee to be my Son, by investing thee with thy kingly dignity, and placing thee on thy throne. St. Paul teaches us to see the fulfillment of these words in Christ's resurrection from the dead. It was by *that* that He was

---

[1550] Johnson, Elliott and Cook, *The Book of Psalms with an Explanatory and Critical Commentary*, 4.

declared to be (marked out as, in a distinct and peculiar sense,) the Son of God. (Rom 1:4; cf. Acts 13:33.) The day of Christ's coronation was the day of His resurrection. From henceforth He sits at the right hand of the Father, waiting till His enemies be made His footstool.[1551]

This author not only ties in the resurrection of the Messiah, but he connects Him to the One who is presently sitting at the right hand of the Father, waiting for His enemies to be made His footstool, as David spoke of his Lord in Psalm 110. Van Groningen adds some additional pertinent insights to this third strophe of Psalm 2:

> The speaker of these words is the one who has been installed on the throne of Zion by Yahweh: " 'asappera (let me recount) the *hog* (decree) of Yahweh." The decree is the inscribed statute; it is the unalterable declaration of Yahweh's purpose in regard to the king who is reciting what Yahweh has said. The king quotes what was said about David and his son(s) (2 Sam 7:14 KJV): "I will be his father, and he shall be my son." He made the statement emphatic: *beni'atta* (my son, You!). The emphatic form of the first personal pronoun (I), adds to Yahweh's decree. Yahweh is the source and powerful performer in the establishing of the throne and the relationship between the King on the heavenly throne and the king on the throne on Mount Zion. The Hebrew term *hayyom* (today) has led some scholars to think that this is proof of all successive kings making this statement during their coronation ritual; that would mean that the relationship commenced at the time of the anointing of each king. Reference, however, is to Yahweh's covenanting act with David when the promises were made and the father-king and son-king relationships were established. *Yelidtika* (I have given existence to you, from *yalad*, to bear, give birth) qualifies the adverbial phrase in that it was an act of origination which had continuous effect. Once given existence, it continued; once king, kingship continued. Thus the son-king proclaims assurance not only in regard to relationship between the King and the king, but also of its continuity 'ad-'olam (to perpetuity; cf. 2 Sam 7:13, 16). This continuity is elaborated in verses 8 and 9 in which the king repeats the promises of a universal kingdom which would include other nations as *nahalateka* (your lasting possession or inheritance). In addition, complete victory is assured in the picturesque language of a potter smashing useless pottery. Before considering the warning, the actions of these nations, which by Yahweh's decree are to be subservient, are described.[1552]

Van Groningen gave some very valuable insight into this third strophe of Psalm 2. This author would make only one change to what Van Groningen stated and that is to use 1 Chronicles 17:10-14 instead of 2 Samuel 7:12-16 to refer to the future Son of David. For as was already shown in this book, the Chronicles passage deals with a Son of

---

[1551] Perowne, *The Book of Psalms*, 1:117.

[1552] Van Groningen, *Messianic Revelation in the Old Testament,* 336.

David that is beyond the sons of David to an eternal Son who will sit on David's eternal dynasty, house and kingdom while the 2 Samuel reference refers to David's immediate son, Solomon.

Rabbi Tzvi Nassi, who began to study the Scriptures and the Zohar as he searched to understand the nature of God clearly relates that the Messiah is not only in view but that the Messiah is the *Metatron* and the Son of God:

> Having penetrated thus far the mystery of the nature of God, and seen what the faith of my fathers had been at that time when the candlestick was burning in all its effulgent glory in the sanctuary, I took up the second Psalm, which speaks of no other than of Metatron, the Son of God.[1553]

What this section of Psalm 2 does is make the connection that "*My Son*" and the "*Son of David*" are one and the same. None of this could ever refer to a past Son of David. This "Son" of God is obviously not Israel and/or a past reigning Son of David, but a future "Son" who will rule all the earth.

Fourth Stanza ... Verses 10-12:

> (10) So now, O kings, be prudent; accept discipline, you rulers of the earth! (11) Serve the LORD in awe; tremble with fright, (12) pay homage in good faith, lest He be angered, and your way be doomed in the mere flash of His anger. Happy are all who take refuge in Him.

The speaker from the first stanza challenges, encourages and exhorts by giving a warning and an invitation to the kings and judges of the earth to understand that obedience is better than rebellion. Showing reverence to the King is far better than imagining in vain that mankind could resist and escape from God's rule over them. It is far better to pay homage to the "Son" or to "Kiss the Son." The Jewish version tampers with the text to avoid the use of the word "Son" for in the Hebrew the word is "Son" and not just "pay homage in good faith." In verse 12 the "Son" is the same "Son" that the LORD has placed on the throne of David in Jerusalem in verse 6. He should be feared; even rejoicing should be done with trembling. This is the only "Son" in view, the "*Son of David*" who is also designated as the "*Son of God*" in this psalm. No one else could fill the shoes of the one described in this psalm, as is noted by the quotation below:

> The introduction of the Son in v. 7 makes a recurrence to His separate dignity to be expected: and the propitiation of Jehovah in v. 11 leads naturally to a mention of some homage to be paid to the Son. The absence of the article in the original is emphatic. "A Son," as if none could doubt what Son and Whose Son is intended. So v. 7, Heb., "a decree," as if none could doubt what decree. If this translation be adopted, it is unnatural to introduce, in vv. 11-12 any subject

---

[1553] Nassi (Hirsch Prinz), *The Great Mystery or, How Can Three Be One*, 69.

except the Son: it is He that may be angry; it is His wrath that is sometimes kindled; they are blessed that take refuge in Him.[1554]

In verse 12 the psalm ends with a potential blessing for those who choose to obey the "Son" rather than rebel. It simply says that the obedient ones will be blessed as they trust in Him. What is interesting, mankind has always been disappointed by man, yet the instructions here are that the kings of the earth will be blessed when they trust in Him. That cannot refer to any mere man or ordinary Son of David. It can only refer to God or in this case His "Anointed," "King," and "Son" who is God Incarnate, "*the Messiah, the Son of the living God*" (Matthew 16:16). In the benediction of this psalm, He is the Sovereign Lord:

> It should be noticed, also, that the benediction at the end of the psalm, "Blessed are all they that put their trust in Him," is a benediction which in the Scriptures is used only of God or the Son of God, and is a very strong proof that the psalm could be understood of no earthly sovereign.[1555]

Summary

What stands out in the psalm is the names ascribed to the One who is the subject of this psalm, who is called the LORD's "*Anointed*," "*my king*" and lastly is described by the LORD as "*my Son*." Another outstanding description of the One described is the universality of His rule in righteousness. That simply cannot apply to a mere mortal. To rule in righteousness, He must be divine.

Numerous authors such as King,[1556] MacDonald,[1557] Gaebelein[1558] and Johnson[1559] have expressed that this is a prophetic passage during which time the rulers of the earth will vainly imagine that they can overthrow the LORD's Anointed King and Son. The Church will no longer be present on the earth, for it will be a time when the kings of the earth either attempt to stop His coming or more likely the time that immediately follows the millennial period when the nations revolt against the LORD's Son whom He Anointed as His personal King.

[1554] Johnson, Elliott and Cook, *The Book of Psalms with an Explanatory and Critical Commentary*, 5.

[1555] King, *The Messiah in the Psalms*, 6.

[1556] King, *The Messiah in the Psalms*, 6.

[1557] William MacDonald, *Enjoying the Psalms: Vol. 1* (Kansas City: Walterick Publications, 1976), 15-16.

[1558] Arno Clemens Gaebelein, *The Book of Psalms* (New York: "Our Hope" Publications, 1939), 22-24.

[1559] Johnson, Elliott and Cook, *The Book of Psalms with an Explanatory and Critical Commentary*, 5.

PSALM 72 Of Solomon

(1) O God, endow the king with Your judgments, the king's son with Your righteousness; (2) that he may judge Your people rightly, Your lowly ones, justly. (3) Let the mountains produce well-being for the people, the hills, the reward of justice. (4) Let him champion the lowly among the people, deliver the needy folk, and crush those who wrong them. (5) Let them fear You as long as the sun shines, while the moon lasts, generations on end.

(6) Let him be like rain that falls on a mown field, like a downpour of rain on the ground, (7) that the righteous may flourish in his time, and well-being abound, till the moon is no more. (8) Let him rule from sea to sea, from the river to the ends of the earth. (9) Let desert-dwellers kneel before him, and his enemies lick the dust. (10) Let kings of Tarshish and the islands pay tribute, kings of Sheba and Seba offer gifts.

(11) Let all kings bow to him, and all nations serve him. (12) For he saves the needy who cry out, the lowly who have no helper. (13) He cares about the poor and the needy; He brings the needy deliverance. (14) He redeems them from fraud and lawlessness; the shedding of their blood weighs heavily upon him. (15) So let him live, and receive gold of Sheba; let prayers for him be said always, blessings on him invoked at all times.

(16) Let abundant grain be in the land, to the tops of the mountains; let his men sprout up in towns like country grass. (17) May his name be eternal; while the sun lasts, may his name endure, let men invoke his blessedness upon themselves; let all nations count him happy. (18) Blessed is the LORD God, God of Israel, who alone does wondrous things; (19) Blessed is His glorious name forever; His glory fills the whole world. Amen and Amen. (20) End of the prayers of David son of Jesse.

This psalm, though never mentioned in the New Covenant, speaks of an exalted King and the blessings of His reign as the psalmist gathers together in one person the glorious aspects of the Messianic reign of the Son of David and the Son of God from Psalm 2. There are three immediate points that become quickly apparent in this psalm. First, it is addressed as a psalm of Solomon. Rather the expression *"of Solomon"* it would be better understood in the last verse as a psalm for Solomon, for it states that it is the *"end of the prayers of David son of Jesse."* It is likely that it is reflective of 2 Samuel 23:1-3, which is speaking of the Messiah, as presented by Wilkinson, Kidner and Morris:

> But the Person spoken of is a King's Son, and Jehovah is King; and the description given does not fit any mere earthly king or king's son.[1560]

[1560] Wilkinson, *Israel My Glory*, 182.

As a royal psalm it prayed for the reigning king, and was a strong reminder of his high calling; yet it exalted this so far beyond the humanly attainable (e.g. in speaking of his reign as endless) as to suggest for its fulfillment no less a person than the Messiah, not only to Christian thinking but to Jewish.[1561]

Its promises were not, and indeed could not, have been fulfilled in Solomon. These promises clearly point to the glorious future millennial reign of Christ when He comes again to set up His earthly kingdom of peace and righteousness on earth...[1562]

Solomon was not really the one intended because the language of the psalm points to someone beyond Solomon's capabilities. Kidner expresses that Solomon never attained to the heights that this psalm proclaims, so it has to be future in context, as Van Groningen and Kidner state:

Psalm 72 has been considered the outstanding messianic royal psalm.... It is, however, very close to Isaiah 11:1-5; 60-62. The reign that is described is humanly unattainable because it is described as endless (72:5).[1563]

The New Testament nowhere quotes it as Messianic, but this picture of the king and his realm is so close to the prophecies of Isaiah 11:1-5 and Isaiah 60-62 that if those passages are Messianic, so is this.[1564]

Not only do they see someone greater than Solomon in view, but both of these men tie together Isaiah 11:1-5 and Isaiah 60-62, which describe the millennial reign of the Messiah, Son of David, Son of God in the future. There are numerous other points that these passages have in common, but only one will be mentioned. Psalm 72 and Isaiah 11 and 60-62 use the term "righteousness" for the son's and King's character. In Psalm 72 the psalmist asks that the LORD's righteousness be upon the king's son and Isaiah 11:5 states that "*righteousness shall be the girdle of his loins.*" This fact is pointed out because, no matter how good mere mortal man is or how hard he tries, he cannot rule the world in righteousness for he himself is not righteous. This "Son" and "King" must be righteous in Himself, which is exactly how Jeremiah refers to Him:

(5) Behold, the days come, saith the LORD, that I will raise unto David a righteous Branch, and a King shall reign and prosper, and shall execute judgment and justice in the earth. (6) In his days Judah shall be saved, and Israel shall dwell safely: and this is his name whereby he shall be called, THE LORD OUR RIGHTEOUSNESS (Jeremiah 23:5-6 KJV)

Morris states that this psalm, just as Psalm 2, presents a universal and everlasting kingdom, which can only be accomplished by the Redeemer of the world as promised

---

[1561] Kidner, *Tyndale Old Testament Commentaries: Psalms 1-72*, 254.
[1562] Morris, *Treasures in the Psalms,* 305.
[1563] Van Groningen, *Messianic Revelation in the Old Testament,* 379.
[1564] Kidner, *Tyndale Old Testament Commentaries: Psalms 1-72*, 254.

in Genesis 3:15 and understood by Lamech in Genesis 5:29. Hodge presents the universal and eternal aspect of this future king and sees Him as being divine:

> The seventy-second Psalm contains a description of an exalted king, and of the blessings of his reign. These blessings are of such a nature as to prove that the subject of the psalm must be a divine person. (1) His kingdom is to be everlasting. (2) universal. (3) It secures perfect peace with God and goodwill among men. (4) All men are to be brought to submit to him through love. (5) In him all the nations of the earth are to be blessed.... . The subject of this psalm is, therefore, the Redeemer of the world.[1565]

This Messianic psalm is then divided by different authors into stanzas with each one presenting aspects of the future reign of the king over the whole earth. Wilson, Van Groningen and Kidner point out the themes they see in this psalm:

1. The judgment of the King and the King's Son (verses 1-7)
2. The universal extent of the kingdom (verses 8-11)
3. The impartial justice of His reign (verses 12-15)
4. The effect on nature. The curse removed (verse 16)
5. The fulfillment of the promise to Abraham (verses 17-19)
6. The answer to David's prayers (verse 20)[1566]

The structure of Psalm 72 has, as a rule, been seen as consisting of five unequal parts:

verses 1-7	the king and the people;
verses 8-11	universal homage for the king;
verses 12-14	the king and the needy;
verses 15-17	the king's welfare; and
verses 18-19	the doxology.

This general outline, however, does not give proper expression to the manner in which the covenant themes are emphasized.[1567]

Kidner entitles Psalm 72 as the Perfect King and divides the chapter up into sections:

verses 1-4	Royal righteousness
verses 5-7	Endless reign
verses 8-11	Boundless realm
verses 12-14	Compassionate king

[1565] Hodge, *Systematic Theology*, 1:491-492.
[1566] Wilson, *The Messianic Psalms*, 152.
[1567] Van Groningen, *Messianic Revelation in the Old Testament,* 379.

| verses 15-17 | Endless blessing |
| verses 18-20 | Doxology and conclusion[1568] |

Even though these men come up with slightly different stanzas for Psalm 72, they all see the common threads that run through the psalm, as the king and his judgment and righteousness, the universal and endlessness of His reign. They see the compassion of the king meeting the needs of the needy and poor. They also see the blessings being fulfilled through the king's son as the blessing of the Abrahamic Covenant on the inhabitants of the earth. Psalm 72 gives a beautiful word picture of the coming kingdom that the earth groans for (Romans 8:21-23). Psalm 72 is a unique tribute by David to the promised Messiah, Son of David, Son of God, and the Anointed King in this prophetic word picture of the coming millennial kingdom.

There are several pronouns that tie together all the descriptions of the character of the person who is the king's son, namely righteousness, and His eternality as mentioned in the previous paragraph. The personal pronouns "*he*," "*his*," and "*him*" that are continually used (10 times, 4 times and 7 times respectively) and relate to all aspects of the description given of the "king's son." They make Him a very literal person as righteousness, judgment and eternity are wrapped around Him by the psalmist.

This psalm has been seen as a messianic psalm not just by those holding to biblical faith but by the Jewish sages that wrote the Targums, as reflected in the following two quotations:

> The Targum paraphrases the first verse of the psalm in this manner: "O God, give the knowledge of thy judgments to the King Messiah, and thy justice to the son of King David." And the Midrash Tehillim says of the king here spoken of, "This is the King Messiah."[1569]

> The messianic notes that are heard in the LXX are unmistakable in the Targums to Psalms. The opening petition in v. 1 says: "O God, give your ordinances to the king messiah." And v. 17 has this Messiah explicitly existing even before the sun, that is, from the creation of the world: "His name will be remembered forever and ever, and before the sun existed his name was already determined."[1570]

So the *Targums*, which were used by the Jewish people both before and after the time of *Yeshua*, saw in this psalm the Messiah. Other authors have also observed the Targum on this passage as referring to the Messiah.[1571]

[1568] Kidner, *Tyndale Old Testament Commentaries: Psalms 1-72* , 253-257.

[1569] King, *The Messiah in the Psalms*, 103.

[1570] Frank-Lothar Hossfeld and Erich Zenger, *Psalms 2: A Commentary on Psalms 51-100* (trans. Linda M. Maloney, Minneapolis: Augsburg Fortress Press, 2005), 220.

[1571] Kidner, *Tyndale Old Testament Commentaries: Psalms 1-72*, 254.

In proceeding through Psalm 72, only certain points will be highlighted as they relate to the nature, character and reign of the king's son. I will use the six-point theme or stanzas that Kidner used above.

First Stanza ... Verses 1-4:

(1) O God, endow the king with Your judgments, the king's son with Your righteousness; (2) that he may judge Your people rightly, Your lowly ones, justly. (3) Let the mountains produce well-being for the people, the hills, the reward of justice. (4) Let him champion the lowly among the people, deliver the needy folk, and crush those who wrong them.

In the first three verses of this stanza righteousness is used three times as the key word which is attributed to the king and then to the king's son. This theme of righteousness pervades the entire psalm with the king's son being introduced. There are 21 personal pronouns that reference His nature, character and eternality. They also define who the king and the king's son are, for the king's son is the Son of God. The righteousness, justice and eternality of the king's son make all the sons of David, of history past, fade into insignificance in comparison with this future king:

> In the first four verses is set forth the righteous and peaceful character of the coming kingdom of the Messiah. How appropriate the language as applied to David's greater Son, before whose glory all other descendants disappear and are forgotten. His throne shall be established in righteousness, which is the foundation of all good government, human or divine.... The last word [righteousness] qualifies both members of the sentence. It is peace by righteousness.[1572]

Not only do the sons of David pale in significance to this son of the king, but it is a fact that His righteousness is not a human characteristic; it is a divine characteristic which will only be seen in the God/man, the Messiah, Son of David and Son of God, as Weiser points out:

> Righteousness is ultimately not a relative human requirement of 'humanitarianism,' but a divine, and for that reason absolute, requirement of a religiously binding character. For behind the reign of the earthly king is God's rule as King; the righteousness of the king is a function and the mirror-image of the righteousness of God....[1573]

The righteousness of the king's son sets the stage for the rest of the psalm as His reign and the eternality of His reign unfold. Isaiah 32:17 brings forth an interesting principle: peace comes only as a result of righteousness. A Messianic Age will not come upon the earth because man has not learned to live in righteousness by overcoming his evil

---

[1572] King, *The Messiah in the Psalms*, 106-107.
[1573] Weiser, *The Old Testament Library: The Psalms,* 503.

inclination or his sin nature. History has not taught that, and as man stands at the beginning of the 21st century, he sees on every side mankind living in complete wickedness, both Jew and Gentile. The earth stands ready to devour itself in its personal biases, hatred, violence and corruption. The righteousness of the King will bring peace to the world because He alone is righteous. Isaiah 32:17-18 in the *Tanakh* clearly states that peace will only come when righteousness comes first and that first phase of peace was obtained by the first coming of the *"righteous Branch"* (Jeremiah 23:5-6) who made peace by dealing with the sin issue that grips the world (Isaiah 52:13-53:12). Until the sin issue, which separates man from God, is dealt with (Genesis 3:15) by the *"Prince of Peace,"* the world will not and cannot have peace; that which corrupts the heart of man (Jeremiah 17:9) must be dealt with. David Baron brings this out as it directly relates to the Jewish people and their rejection of Messiah *Yeshua*:

> Just now the Jews object to the doctrine of the Messiah's Divinity, but it is mostly because they have not yet learned the real object of the Messiah's mission on the earth. When once they are brought by the Spirit of God fully to learn and believe that Messiah's work on earth is nothing less than the deliverance of mankind from the bondage of sin and Satan they will be convinced that if He is to be the Redeemer of all, He must needs be Divine; for if He were mere man, He could not possibly turn away "ungodliness from Jacob" (Isa 49:20),[1574] "redeem Israel from all his iniquities" (Psa 130:8), seeing every man, even the righteous, appears sinful in the sight of God, so that He would Himself need redemption. Has not God Himself declared (Jer 30:15), that, because of the multitude of his iniquity, and because his sins are increased, Israel's wound is absolutely "incurable" as far as any human means is concerned? (Jer 2:12; 3:22-23; Isa 1:5-6; 44:6-7; 59:16-17).[1575]

Not only will there be no peace in the heart of man, Jerusalem will know no peace (Zechariah 12:1-3) until the *"Prince of Peace,"* the *"righteous Branch"* the Son of David and the Son of God comes the second time. That is why Messiah ben Joseph (rabbinic name), the Son of David, the Son of God, the Messiah of Israel, had to suffer and die for the sins of the world (Psalm 22; Isaiah 50:1, 4-6 and Isaiah 53). Gaebelein also reflects on this same issue in the following statement:

> Righteousness and peace are mentioned in verses 2 and 3. The One who comes is the true Melchizedek, the King-Priest, the King of Righteousness and the King of Peace. Scripture never puts peace before righteousness, but always after, because the work of righteousness is peace and the effect of righteousness quietness and assurance forever (Isa 32:17). His work of righteousness which He worked not in His life, but in His death on the cross, has secured peace. It is peace now for all who trust in Him and are justified by Faith (Rom 5:1). And

---

[1574] Reference in quote is incorrect in the original, should be Isaiah 59:20, also see Roman 11:26.
[1575] Baron, *Rays of Messiah's Glory*, 91.

when He comes and begins His Kingly rule of righteousness He is going to judge in righteousness, …[1576]

Boice continues the theme as he reflects on the ramifications that righteousness will have on the inhabitants of the earth when he states:

> The first four verses of the psalm lift up the essential character of the kingdom being described. It is righteousness, a word that occurs three times (vv. 1, 2, and 3). Verse 1 asks that the king might be endowed with righteousness. Verse 2 predicts that, so endowed, the king will judge the people in righteousness. Verse 3 speaks of the fruit of righteous judgment, which is prosperity, a theme to be developed more fully in stanza five.[1577]

Verse 2 begins with a series of statements "*He shall*" in verses 2, 4, 6, 8, 12-15, 17 where the text speaks of the King in the manner that "He shall" do certain things as a statement of fact.[1578] The king "*shall judge thy people with righteousness*" (verse 2), "*shall judge the poor of the people and shall save the children*" (verse 4), "*shall come down like rain*" (verse 6), "*shall have dominion also from sea to sea, and from the river unto the ends of the earth*" (verse 8), "*shall deliver the needy…and the poor*" (verse 12), "*shall spare the poor and needy*" (verse 13), "*shall redeem their soul*" (verse 14), "*shall live*" (verse 15), and lastly "*his name shall endure forever*" (verse 17). These "*shall*" statements of things that the king's son will do are enveloped with the 21 personal pronouns that relate to all the king's son will do.

Second Stanza … Verses 5-7:

> (5) Let them fear You as long as the sun shines, while the moon lasts, generations on end. (6) Let him be like rain that falls on a mown field, like a downpour of rain on the ground, (7) that the righteous may flourish in his time, and well-being abound, till the moon is no more.

This stanza speaks of the endless reign of the king's son with two key words describing the time of His reign. The endless righteous reign on the earth shall cause the righteous on earth to flourish and have peace in abundance. The following two authors express the endless reign of the king's son in relationship to what humanity has grown accustomed to:

> The next three verses set forth the endless duration of the kingdom of the Messiah, and at the same time its rapid and beneficent growth and its blessed effect upon the people.… The sun and moon are mentioned here, it has been said, as witnesses to an everlasting order, and, as it were, figures of eternity compared with the fleeting, dying generations of men. So long as the solar

---

[1576] Gaebelein, *The Book of Psalms*, 281.
[1577] Boice, *An Expositional Commentary: Psalms*, 2:601.
[1578] MacDonald, *Enjoying the Psalms*, 1:320.

system stands, so long as sun shall rise and set, so long as moons shall wax and wane, so long as the generations of the human race shall survive, the name of Christ shall be reverenced.[1579]

The stanza describes the duration of the king's reign as eternal. Kings live and reign and then die one after another. They all pass on their kingdom to another. All kings are imperfect rulers even when they are good rulers. However, the king and his kingdom in this passage is eternal, enduring as long as the sun and moon endure (verses 5, 7, 17).[1580]

What is abundantly clear is that the King's son is completely unique from all other earthly rulers for His dominion and reign will last as long as the sun and moon remain in the sky. There will be no future descendants of this king who will reign, for He will personally reign *"throughout all generations"* *"as long as the sun and moon endure."*

If David were writing a psalm about Solomon or if Solomon were himself the author of the psalm, he did not live up to the righteousness nor the endlessness of the reign described of him or by him in this psalm. First Kings 3 and 9 point out that Solomon, early in his reign, started out well but then departed from the Lord by allowing his wives to turn his heart from the LORD. Both David and Solomon died and left the kingdom to another. Boice states further that Solomon laid a heavy tax on the 10 northern tribes because of all his building projects (1 Kings 10:14-29), which caused them to split later from Judah when Rehoboam became king (1 Kings 12:1-15).[1581] So there was ill feeling that was building up because of the sinful heart on the part of the 10 tribes and for the lack of judgment on the part of Solomon; righteousness was not exhibited.

Third Stanza … Verses 8-11:

(8) Let him rule from sea to sea, from the river to the ends of the earth. (9) Let desert-dwellers kneel before him, and his enemies lick the dust. (10) Let kings of Tarshish and the islands pay tribute, kings of Sheba and Seba offer gifts. (11) Let all kings bow to him, and all nations serve him.

The previous stanza dealt with the endurance or eternality of the reign of the King's Son. This stanza deals with dominion or His worldwide rule as King over the entire earth. Hand in hand with His rule is the honor, reverence and worship that is given to the King on a worldwide basis. Connect this with the previous stanza, the endless righteous reign, the reign of the King's son will not only be eternal, but notice the honor, reverence and worship given to Him. According to Van Groningen the reign of the King's son will include every sphere of human relationships:

[1579] King, *The Messiah in the Psalms*, 108.
[1580] Boice, *An Expositional Commentary: Psalms*, 2:602.
[1581] Boice, *An Expositional Commentary: Psalms*, 2:601.

Weyerd (and he will rule) with *waw* here indicates continuity of concepts. The reign, that act of exercising dominion, by the just and righteous king will extend:

1. geographically – from sea to sea, that is, the entire world;
2. militarily – his foes and enemies will all be defeated and humiliated;
3. economically – tribute and gifts will be brought by the richest of the world's kings; and
4. politically – all kings will be under his rule and will render him service.[1582]

This clearly has not been fulfilled by David or Solomon or any other king of Judah in the history of Israel. This psalm definitely relates to a future king, the Messiah, the Son of David, the Son of God who will physically reign on a literal throne in Jerusalem over all the nations of the earth. Also notice the Son of David will reign, not God the Father. The Father is not of Judah, nor is He a Jew. But the *Moshiach*, the Son of David will be God and man. He will rule on a literal throne in Jerusalem.

In verse 8 there is a very strong allusion to the Abrahamic Covenant taken from Genesis 15:18 which speaks of the immediate boundaries of the nation of Israel that were given to Abraham and repeated to the wilderness generation (Deuteronomy 1:7-8; 11:24; Joshua 1:4), as is stated in the following quotation:

> The formulas in v. 8 that address the universal expansion of the realm of the king's rule first adopt the promise made to Abraham in Gen 15:18: "To your descendants I give this land, from the river of Egypt to the great river, the river Euphrates" (cf also 1 Kgs 5:1). That the promises to Abraham are in view here is confirmed also by v. 17c-d, where there is an allusion to the promises of blessing given to Abraham in Gen 12:1-3; 22:18; 28:14. With this, the fundamental horizon of this royal rule is established: through the actions of this king the history of Israel and of the nations, begun in and with Abraham, will become a divinely effected reality, a history of blessing of salvation.[1583]

The psalmist in Psalm 72:8 and 17 definitely had in mind the Abrahamic Covenant as he laid out the extent of the worldwide breadth and the eternality of its length already seen in the preceding stanza. Before speaking about the peace that the King brings, it needs to be noted that the King does have enemies (Psalm 110:1-2) for verse 9 says that those who dwell in the wilderness shall bow and *"his enemies shall lick the dust."* This is a figurative statement speaking of submission and homage in the political world (Micah 7:17).[1584]

It was previously mentioned in the first stanza that peace is a result of the righteousness that the King has, before peace can come to the earth itself. Verse 8 has a definite connection with Zechariah 9:9-10. Zechariah 9:9 is understood to refer to the

---

[1582] Van Groningen, *Messianic Revelation in the Old Testament,* 383.
[1583] Hossfeld and Zenger, *Psalms 2: A Commentary on Psalms 51-100,* 215.
[1584] Hossfeld and Zenger, *Psalms 2: A Commentary on Psalms 51-100,* 216.

first coming of the Messiah Son of David when He entered Jerusalem on the 10th day of Nisan, first month of the year (Exodus 12:3), riding on a colt of a donkey, just before Passover on the 14th day. However, there is a gap of time between Messiah the King being *"cut off"* (Daniel 9:26) and the final restoration of Israel before the Messiah returns (Hosea 5:15) to establish the long awaited fulfillment of the Abrahamic Covenant and the promise of the Kingdom where He will reign in righteousness and peace. Zechariah 9:10 reflects much of the same language as Psalm 72:8, as the following author brings out:

> At the same time, v. 8 has an inter-textual reference to the promise of the "messianic" king of peace in Zech 9:9-10. This promise sketches the picture of a king who "shall command peace to the nations; his dominion shall be from sea to sea and from the river [Euphrates] to the ends of the earth." It is decisive that this king of peace from Zech 9:9-10 on the one hand precisely fits the description of the office in Psa 72:2-4 and that on the other hand it is clear in Zech 9:9-10 why he can fulfill his commission:[1585]

The kings of the earth shall come and pay tribute to the King's son reigning in Jerusalem. The kings of Tarshish were from the farthest known world of the day, the west coast of Spain; "coasts" were a synonym for the farthest outreaches of the earth, as stated by the following:

> The isles or coastlands were synonymous with the ends of the earth (Isa 42:10).[1586]

> Tarshish and the isles represent the west, of which vague but impressive accounts were brought to Palestine by the Phoenicians, whose commerce at that time extended to the south west of England. Sheba, in Arabia, and Seba (i.e. Meroe, according to Josephus, 'antt.' II. X. 2), represents the nations of Asia and Africa. Cf. 1 Kgs 10:1, and note on Gen 10:7.[1587]

The realm of the King's son is unlimited; it is boundless; His dominion is worldwide. Those in the outreaches of the earth, as well as the enemies of the King, will be subdued and will submit to the King and shall bow before Him. In addition, all the economic powers of the earth will come to the King in Jerusalem and *"offer gifts"* to Him. Verse 11 is all inclusive: *"Yea, all kings"* shall fall before Him and serve Him. The character of the psalm reflects His righteousness, not military campaigns. However, verse 9 gives an allusion to the military power and might of the King when the psalmist references the fact that *"his enemies shall lick the dust"* as is noted by the following statement:

[1585] Hossfeld and Zenger, *Psalms 2: A Commentary on Psalms 51-100*, 215-216.

[1586] Kidner, *Tyndale Old Testament Commentaries: Psalms 1-72*, 256.

[1587] Johnson, Elliott and Cook, *The Book of Psalms: Explanatory and Critical Commentary*, 160.

Psalm 72 does not provide a comprehensive portrait of the king's/messiah's government. It does make clear, however, that militarism is not the defining characteristic of his government, an impression one might infer from other royal psalms, especially Psalms 2 and 110. It becomes clear that, when faced with violent opponents, he will exercise force. Psalm 72 itself makes brief mention of this in verse 9.[1588]

One further point before moving on to the next stanza is the descriptive words used by the psalmist to describe the ends of the earth. Verse 8 expresses the extent of the kingdom of the King's son. Psalm 72:8 states that "*He shall have dominion also from sea to sea, and from the river unto the ends of the earth.*" The two seas mentioned in this verse are most likely the Mediterranean Sea in the west and possibly the Dead Sea or the Sea of Galilee in the east. The identity of the second sea is uncertain from a biblical context.[1589] The psalmist then mentions the river as another point of reference. This dominion not only uses the seas as a boundary point but "*the river*" connects this passage to the promise to Abraham (Genesis 15:18). The dominion of the King going beyond the river Euphrates unto the ends of the earth is worldwide. Verses 8-11 indicate that Messiah will be Monarch of the world. This "*dominion*" will actually be global, for Psalm 2:8 states that the Father had promised His Son "*the uttermost parts of the earth for thy possession.*" Psalm 72:11 states: "*Yea, all kings shall fall down before Him, all nations shall serve Him.*" This kingdom of the Messiah, the Son, will reach to every king of every nation. They will worship Him and serve Him. This reality is expressed by the following author:

> The YHVH-king of Psalm 72 thus imposes his world dominion neither with an iron club (cf. 2:9) nor in battle (cf. 110:5-7). In vv. 9-11 the psalm apparently imagines the universal acknowledgement of this royal dominion according to the model of the pilgrimage of the nations and the people's homage (cf. Isa 2:1-4; Mic 4:1-4); the world is fascinated by this "king of justice," and so they all come, the "inhabitants of the desert" and "those who dwell on the sea," that is the kings and people of all regions, to the ends of the inhabitable earth, to do homage to this king, to bring him gifts and tribute, and thus to enter into the service of his (peaceful) rule – in order that they too may share in the "justice" of YHVH. That here it is ultimately and properly a question of the integration of the nations and their kings into YHVH's royal dominion is subtly indicated by our psalm through the allusions in v. 9 to Isa 49:23; Mic 7:14-17 and in v. 10 to Isa 60:9-11 (cf. also Isa 49:7, 23).[1590]

[1588] Broyles, *New International Biblical Commentary: Psalms*, 298.

[1589] The only other alternatives would be the Black Sea on the northern border of Asia Minor (Turkey), or the Caspian Sea which lies between the ancient Babylonian and Mede-Persian empires on their immediate south and on the north of the Arabian Peninsula in the south. The only other sea would be the Red Sea.

[1590] Hossfeld and Zenger, *Psalms 2: A Commentary on Psalms 51-100*, 216.

Fourth Stanza ... Verses 12-14:

(12) For he saves the needy who cry out, the lowly who have no helper. (13) He cares about the poor and the needy; He brings the needy deliverance. (14) He redeems them from fraud and lawlessness; the shedding of their blood weighs heavily upon him.

This stanza, more than any other, shows the concern and passion of the King's son who dispenses righteousness and justice for the poor and the needy of His realm. The psalmist picks up the thought from verse 4 and expands upon it. What is interesting is that in or under any government of men, no matter how good the intention, the poor and the needy usually fall between the cracks and their lot does not improve. But here the King's son shall "*deliver*," "*spare*," "*save*" and "*redeem*" the poor and needy because they are precious in His sight.

Fifth Stanza ... Verses 15-17:

(15) So let him live, and receive gold of Sheba; let prayers for him be said always, blessings on him invoked at all times. (16) Let abundant grain be in the land, to the tops of the mountains; let his men sprout up in towns like country grass. (17) May his name be eternal; while the sun lasts, may his name endure, let men invoke his blessedness upon themselves; let all nations count him happy.

Verse 17 is the predominant verse in this stanza. The stanza starts with the King's son being given gold. Prayer is made for Him continually, and He shall be praised daily. His blessing shall cover the earth, as presented in verse 16. This is reflected in the following statement:

This remnant will presumably, therefore, constitute the "handful of corn," in their city on the "top of the mountains" – that is, Mount Zion – which in that day will be "beautiful for situation, the joy of the whole earth...on the sides of the north, the city of the great King" (Psa 48:2).

Israel has actually been symbolized occasionally in the Bible by corn (e.g., Amos 9:9 – "as corn sifted in a sieve"), and this handful of corn will rapidly multiply into a great nation, the leading nation of earth during the Millennium. "It shall come to pass in the last days that the mountains of the LORD's house shall be established in the top of the mountains, and shall be exalted above the hills; and all nations shall flow unto it" (Isa 2:2).[1591]

Two times verse 17 states "*his name*," shall endure forever, comparing it further with the sun and moon which will endure, so will His name. This psalm is reflective as an accumulative statement. Not only will His Name endure, but so will His righteousness,

---

[1591] Morris, *Treasures in the Psalms*, 308.

justice and peace endure because He endures. That is the context of the psalm and is the theme captured in the following statements:

> The response of fear is appropriate worship before the mighty King and His kingdom of peace. Such worship is to continue as long as creation lasts, "as long as the sun and moon endure, throughout all generations." Note the eschatological thrust here. No human king can receive perpetual worship. Only God's Son, the Messiah, can fulfill this promise down through all the generations of earth.[1592]

> His reign shall not be terminated by his death. His dynasty shall be without end. He shall have no successor on his throne. The tribute of the world shall be forever laid at his feet.[1593]

The second half of verse 17 is equally significant because it has a very strong allusion to the blessing aspect of the Abrahamic Covenant in Genesis 12:1-3, particularly verse 3. All the blessing that will be dispensed on Israel and on the nations of the earth comes from the "*seed*" (Genesis 22:18; Galatians 3:16) of Abraham, the focus of the blessing here in Psalm 72, as stated in the following quotation:

> Verse 17b echoes the Abrahamic or patriarchal promise of blessing to the nations (Gen 12:3, etc.), but Psalm 72 here departs from the rest of the OT and ties it directly to the monarchy.[1594]

The observation by Broyles should not be missed; the "seed" of Abraham, the Son of David, the Messiah, the Son of God is, according to Psalms 2 and 72, directly related to the monarchy of a personal literal king reigning on a physical literal throne in Jerusalem. This is important to note because after David died, his kingdom corrupted itself, the people were later taken into a long period of captivity and then later into the Diaspora. This is important to grasp because this King of righteousness, justice and peace will be eternal, according to the text, rule with those characteristics here and in other places, as reflected in the following:

> This is necessary because even the greatest of Israel's leaders is fallible. Moses dies outside the Promised Land and David's kingdom disintegrates within a generation. Human disappointment, however, continually points Israel beyond history to the God of history.[1595]

> It should be stressed again that the Messiah, though He is the Son of God, is also the rightful heir to the throne of David, because God has intervened, and by His own will He has given Him a human body through a virgin of Israel,

---

[1592] Donald Williams, *Mastering the Old Testament: Psalms 1-72* (Dallas: Word, 1986), 488.

[1593] King, *The Messiah in the Psalms*, 111.

[1594] Broyles, *New International Biblical Commentary: Psalms*, 298.

[1595] Williams, *Mastering the Old Testament: Psalms 1-72*, 485.

"Therefore the LORD himself shall give you a sign; Behold, a virgin shall conceive, and bear a son, and shall call his name Immanuel" (Isa 7:14).[1596]

The king is associated with the promise given to Abraham, in order that he may be the mediator of blessing not only for his posterity, but for all the tribes and nations of the earth (cf. Gen 12:1-3; 22:18; 28:14).[1597]

One of the fascinating themes of the *Tanakh* is how prophet after prophet spoke of a redeemer, a king and a priest who would be the physical Son of David, the Messiah. Yet uniquely He was also to be the Son of God who would restore Israel and bring righteousness, justice and peace to the whole world and not just to Israel. Whether the promises were given to Abraham, Moses, David, Isaiah, Jeremiah or Zechariah, they all agree and yet enlarge the ramifications of the Promised One. One element that Psalms 2 and 72 do not present is the aspect of redeemer of the earth. Everyone understands that mankind and the world need to be redeemed from itself. The curse of sin came upon this world when it first entered the garden of Eden and consequently the whole world needs a redeemer. The *Tanakh* runs two parallel themes of redemption. One comes from the fact that God says that He will redeem the world and rule and reign, and the second from the *Tanakh* which presents the great hope given by the prophets in the coming of the Messiah, Son of David, who will rule and reign. The following author shows how these two themes come together in one:

> The Redeemer of the world is Jahve [Jehovah]. The appearing of Jahve [Jehovah] is the centre of the Old Testament proclaimation of salvation.... In this Night there rise in opposite directions two stars of Promise. The one describes its path from above downwards: it is the promise of Jahve [Jehovah] who is about to come. The other describes its path from below upwards: it is the hope which rests on the seed of David, the prophecy of the Son of David, which at the outset assumes a thoroughly human, and merely earthly character. These two stars meet at last, they blend together into one star; the Night vanishes and it is Day. This one Star is Jesus Christ, Jahve [Jehovah] and the Son of David in one person, the King of Israel and at the same time the Redeemer of the world, – in one word, the God-man.[1598]

That all focuses on Isaiah 7:14, which all of Judaism and liberal Christianity have rejected as the promised God/man to this corrupted planet. Here the *Tanakh* focuses on the birth of a son from the "*virgin*." This "*son*" will have the same character as the Father, righteousness, holiness and justice. Here God chooses to enter humanity to fulfill both sides of the prophecies in the Hebrew Scriptures. God will redeem and rule the world by voluntarily submitting Himself to be born of the "*virgin*" so that He can also completely fulfill the Davidic Covenant.

[1596] Phillips, *Exploring the Messianic Psalms*, 173.
[1597] Hossfeld and Zenger, *Psalm 2: A Commentary on Psalms 51-100*, 218.
[1598] Keil and Delitzsch, *Commentary on the Old Testament in Ten Volumes: Psalms*, 5:300.

Sixth Stanza ... Verses 18-20:

> (18) Blessed is the LORD God, God of Israel, who alone does wondrous things; (19) Blessed is His glorious name forever; His glory fills the whole world. Amen and Amen. (20) End of the prayers of David son of Jesse.

This final stanza of Psalm 72 has been called the doxology of the psalm. This stanza can be understood two ways, but the context of the psalm lends more weight to the second understanding. Verses 18-19 could be read as the author digresses from the King's son back to the LORD God of Israel. Within the context of the psalm, the King's son has the righteousness of God and exercises it in judgment and compassion. The King's son will reign as long as there is a sun or moon. The realm of the King's son will be worldwide with the kings of the earth bowing before Him and giving gifts to Him. The name of the King's son will endure as long as the sun and the moon. What is already present in the text is the eternality of the King's son. The usage of the term "eternal" by the psalmist simply means that He always was in eternal past and will be in eternal future. He is the I AM that spoke to Moses on Mt. Sinai (Exodus 3:14). When the prophets are studied together, it quickly becomes apparent that the LORD and all these theophanies of the LORD are God yet distinct from God.

Even if the psalmist is referring back to the LORD and not to the King's son, the Messiah, the character of the Son is the same as the character of the LORD. In verse 18 the psalmist used a technical word that refers only to the LORD Himself. It is the word translated "wonderful," which comes from the Hebrew verb פָּלָא (to be wonderful – pala). This word has been discussed before in chapter 12 under the section on Isaiah 9:5-6 and in chapter 5 under the section on Genesis 18. It is a term used only of God Himself. It is used only about a work that He Himself could perform.

Verse 19 restates that the glorious name of the LORD will be blessed forever and that the whole earth will be filled with His glory. In chapter 7 on theophanies it was observed that when the LORD's glory appeared, it was the Second Person of the plural unity of *Elohim*.

In summary of Psalm 72, along with Psalm 2, when the descriptive language about the ruler is combined and examined, it reveals a ruler who is more than human. It may have been written by the psalmist for the coronation of a son of David, but none of David's sons, or even David himself, ever came close to the fulfillment of these passages. Human sinful nature being what it is, it is evident that no mere human son of David could fulfill the language in this psalm. Coupled with Psalm 2, which has similar language, adding the descriptive terms of the monarch that will rule over the earth, such as "*His Anointed*" (verse 2), "*My King*" (verse 6), "*My Son*" (verse 7) and then "*Kiss the son*" or do homage to the Son, leads the student to only one conclusion: this "Son" must be divine. He is the physical offspring of David, the promised Son of David, the Messiah, but He has also been chosen or designated by the LORD Himself as His Son. The following authors express the same sentiments:

The psalm is too large to be accepted as the description of the little glory and pomp of any historic reality. Its language is too spiritual, too grand, too lofty, too far-reaching, to be limited to the proudest empire that the world has ever seen or that the annals of history have preserved any record of. The portrait of the king is glorious beyond any human original. The beneficence of his reign and the happy and prosperous condition of his subjects find no counterpart this side of the predicted millennium. The extent and the duration of his dominion are as wide as the universe and lasting as eternity.[1599]

But it is the character of the psalm itself, its remarkable language, its wonderful description of the coming king and his kingdom, its beautiful imagery as to the beneficence and universal extent of his reign that determines its reference and application.[1600]

Psalm 72 is a witness in history to the end of history. As a prophetic psalm in the full sense of the word, it describes the ideal King and His universal reign (vv. 8-11). This reign also has more than a hint that it is eternal (v. 17). None of Israel's kings could come near the praise and expectations offered here. If this psalm were used in some coronation or enthronement liturgy, the ceremony it scripted would be dwarfed by its vision.[1601]

This Psalm starts out as a prayer for an earthly monarch, possibly Solomon, but before long we realize that the writer is looking beyond Solomon to the glories of the reign of the Lord Jesus Christ. It will be a wonderful time for this weary, warring world. The golden era for which mankind has yearned will then be ushered in. Creation's groan will be hushed, and peace and prosperity will flourish.[1602]

Psalms 2 and 72 both present God's "*anointed*," "*My Son*," "*My king*" who will reign on a literal throne in Jerusalem. His reign will be eternal, characterized by righteousness. These psalms blend together the divinity and humanity of the Son of God into one person, the Son of David, the *Moshiach*.

PROVERBS 30:4

Who has ascended into heaven and come down? Who has gathered up the wind in the hollow of his hand? Who has wrapped the waters in his garments? Who has established all the extremities of the earth? What is his name or his son's name, if you know it?

[1599] King, *The Messiah in the Psalms*, 105.
[1600] King, *The Messiah in the Psalms*, 105.
[1601] Williams, *Mastering the Old Testament: Psalms 1-72*, 485-486.
[1602] MacDonald, *Enjoying the Psalms*, 1:320.

Proverbs 30:4 asks one of the most unusual, difficult and perplexing questions in the Scriptures. Agur, the author of Proverbs 30, asks a series of four rhetorical questions with the common assumption being that Israel would know the answers through the first half of the fifth question. However, it is the answer to the second half of that question that causes at this point in Scripture a blank in the mind of the readers. The point is, why did Agur, speaking through inspiration, ask that second half of the fifth question? Each one of these six questions [and answers] will be dealt with individually. Fruchtenbaum reflects on this verse in the following statement:

> Amongst the sayings of Agur in Proverbs 30 is a riddle. The riddle consists of six questions, the first four of which are rhetorical. The answers to these questions are obvious since only God Himself could accomplish these things. The fifth question is also easy since the name of God was revealed to men long before the Book of Proverbs was written.[1603]

It is easily seen that every Jewish reader, upon reading this verse would have said yes, we know His name for it is the LORD or *Yahweh*. That would give no problem to any Jewish student of the *Tanakh*. However, to answer the second half of the fifth question was impossible, as Fruchtenbaum continues:

> What is not revealed, however, is the name of that son, hence the teasing "if you know." At this stage of progressive revelation, no one could know His name.[1604]

The goal in the rest of this section is to discover if the LORD has a son, and if He does, who that son is. When one reads this verse, it is reminiscent of the words of the LORD to Job in chapters 38-39 of the book that carries his name. In particular the words of Job 38:8-11 are quite similar to the words of Agur in Proverbs 30:4.

In the notes of *The Jewish Study Bible* on verse 4, they answer the first half of question five and then ignore the second half:

> These provocative questions may be answered in different ways: (1) God, and He alone, has done these things. As in Job chapters 38-41, human wisdom consists in recognizing God's infinite and incomparable powers. (2) No one – no human, that is – has done them. Either way, the point is that God is infinitely powerful and wise and man lowly and limited. Human intellect, therefore, must bow before God's word.[1605]

The notes at the bottom of the page of *The Jewish Study Bible* are absolutely correct as far as they go. In fact, if only the rabbis would follow these words ("Either way, the point is that God is infinitely powerful and wise, and man is lowly and limited. Human intellect, therefore, must bow before God's word."), they would not put so much

---

[1603] Fruchtenbaum, *Messianic Christology*, 90.
[1604] Fruchtenbaum, *Messianic Christology*, 90.
[1605] Berlin and Brettler, *The Jewish Study Bible*, 1494-1495.

authority on Oral Torah, which is an invention of the rabbis, for the Scriptures themselves do not support it.

Briefly, each question will be dealt with so that the student of Scripture has a complete understanding of the questions that Agur is asking under the inspiration of God.

Question One: Who has ascended into heaven and descended?

The answer to this question is completely unknowable. Even if man could ascend into heaven, where is heaven, the dwelling place of God, for no human being knows of the place of God's abode. Even if man knew the location, how would he transport himself there and, once he was there, how would he return? From the pages of the *Tanakh* two men ascended into heaven, Enoch and Elijah, but they never returned. Also it is known that angels have ascended and descended (Genesis 28:10-22). But being only messengers of God, they only speak in relationship to the commission given to them by God. It has already been noted in chapters 4-8 of this book, where the theophanies of God were discussed, that the Messenger (Angel) of the LORD has ascended. This Messenger (Angel) of the LORD is distinct from the LORD and yet speaks as the LORD Himself. He is the Second Person of the plural unity of *Elohim*. One example of the LORD descending and ascending was when He appeared to Abraham in Genesis 17:1 and then ascended into the heavens as found in Genesis 17:22 even as the following Jewish Bibles reflect. Notice the words in bold typeface:

And he left off talking with him, and God **went up** from Abraham.[1606]

And when He had finished speaking with him, God **ascended** from upon Abraham.[1607]

And He left off talking with him, and God **went up** from Abraham.[1608]

And He ceased speaking with him; and the Glory of the Lord **ascended** from Abraham.[1609]

And when he had left off talking with him God **went up** from Abraham.[1610]

And when He was done speaking with him, God **was gone** from Abraham.[1611]

The Hebrew word in the text is וַיַּעַל and Kohlenberger translates it as "then he went up"[1612] from the presence of Abraham, not from upon Abraham as in the Stone

---

[1606] Harkavy, *The Holy Scriptures*, 20.

[1607] Scherman, *The Stone Edition: The Chumash, The Torah: Haftaros and Five Megillos*, 77.

[1608] Hertz, *The Pentateuch and Haftorahs*, 60.

[1609] Jonathan Ben Uzziel, *The Targum Palestine: Genesis*, 8.

[1610] Isaac Leeser, *The Twenty-Four Books of the Holy Bible: Hebrew and English* (New York: Hebrew Publishing, 1916), 7.

[1611] Berlin and Brettler, *The Jewish Study Bible*, 38.

Edition, which tries to cover it up (footnote #1605). It is equally clear in the following statement from a lexicon that they see God appearing and then He "returns to his heavenly dwelling:"

> Admittedly, statements with *lh* occur rather infrequently. The priestly documents use *lh meal* for God's departure after an encounter with one of the patriarchs (Gen 17:22; 35:13; his appearance is expressed in each case by *rh ni* "to appear," (Gen 17:1; 35:9): God returns to his heavenly dwelling. Accordingly, the ascension of Yahweh's messenger, i.e., his manifestation, in the flames is mentioned (Judg 13:20); that the flames ascended "from the altar to heaven" is explicitly stated here.[1613]

It is interesting that the lexicon makes three references to God not only ascending but that He, in the first place, made a physical appearance (theophany) before Abraham and Jacob as well as referring to the Messenger (Angel) of the LORD who appeared to Manoah. In each case the Hebrew word וַיַּעַל is used to show that the LORD ascended.

> This verb is used 900 times in the *Tanakh* and a common usage is to "go up, climb, ascend."[1614]

> The question begins from earth and asks who has gone up and come down. The answer is, "No human being." God may be said to come down from heaven (or better yet, his is in heaven as well as on earth – Psa 139:8), and certainly the angels come down and go back up, as Jacob's dream at Bethel describes (Gen 28:10-22). But this question presupposes that wisdom and knowledge of the Holy One is in heaven, which is not the source of human beings.[1615]

So simply put, the answer to the first question is God for He alone is able to descend and ascend back to His abode in heaven. Mankind simply has never had that capability in the past or in the present and will not in the future until the eternal order is in place, then man will be able to.

Question Two: Who has gathered up the wind in the hollow of his hand?

Likewise, this question demands the answer that no human being can do such a thing. Man is incapable of controlling the winds that race across the surface of the earth. Only God can gather the winds in His fists and control them as the following Scripture references demonstrate: Genesis 8:1; Exodus 10:13, 19; 14:21; 15:10; Numbers 11:31; Psalm 135:7; Amos 4:13; Mark 4:39; and Luke 8:24-25.

[1612] Kohlenberger, *The Interlinear NIV Hebrew-English Old Testament,* 38.

[1613] Jenni and Westermann, *Theological Lexicon of the Old Testament,* 2:890.

[1614] Harris, Archer and Waltke, *Theological Wordbook of the Old Testament,* 2:666.

[1615] Longman III, Baker, *Commentary on the Old Testament Wisdom and Psalms,* 522-523.

Question Three: Who has wrapped the waters in his garments?

This question demands the same answer; only God can do this mighty act. Man once again is incapable of holding the water in his garment. Yet God does; even as Job states (26:8), He uses the thick clouds to hold the waters: "*He wrapped up the waters in His clouds.*"

Question Four: Who has established all the extremities of the earth?

Man had absolutely nothing to do with the establishment of the earth. *Elohim* alone created the heavens and the earth (Genesis 1:1) and introduced man to the created order of the universe and the earth.

All four of these questions clearly make the point that God is in control of all things in relation to this earth as well as the universe. Wardlaw in his statement on this verse gives a clear and persuasive answer to the questions of Proverbs 30:4:

> Such is the lesson of these words now before us: "Who hath ascended up into heaven" — that is, to see the glories of the Invisible, — to learn the secrets of the world unknown, — to read the books of providence, and grace, and judgment? And who hath "descended?" — that is, to bring down and to communicate the discoveries He has made? No man has mounted to the third heaven and explored their hidden wonders, and received a commission to carry back the revelation of what he has seen and heard to the sons of men — the children of earth. If such a man there be, "What is his name, and what is his son's name, if thou canst tell? (323)…The language clearly conveys the sentiment, that no one but a being who himself possesses the perfections, and exercises the powers, and performs the works of God, can be capable of comprehending God. (324)[1616]

Man in his rebellion against God has tried to explain it all away by the use of natural means, citing evolution as the agent. But man in his unwillingness to place himself under the hand of God seeks to replace God with the natural. God is the only answer to these questions. Man is incapable, and only in his corrupted mind does he futilely try to replace God as the Creator and sustainer of the world and universe. The focus of these questions comes back to God, as stated below:

> In a series of rhetorical questions (v. 4), he first challenges the reader to admit that no one has achieved direct understanding of the world and the truth behind the world. To "go up to heaven and come back down" is to attain and bring direct knowledge of eternal truth. Then, with three questions that allude to the

---

[1616] J. S. Wardlaw, *Lectures on the Book of Proverbs* (Minneapolis: Klock & Klock Christian Publishers, 1982), 323-324 (originally published in 1861).

creative power of God (and human lack of that power), he implies that no one can explain the metaphysical powers behind the visible creation.[1617]

It is just as impossible for men, without divine illumination, to discover God, and to reveal him to their fellow-creatures, as to ascend into heaven, or descend from it; to bind up the waters in a garment, or to gather the winds in his fists, or to establish all the ends of the earth. Has any man ever been able to achieve such wonders? Where did he live? What is his name? Or what is the name of any man that has the honour to spring from such a wonderful ancestor? If you can tell me the name of such a man as this, or his son, then I will confess that he is possessed of treasures of wisdom sufficient to supply all your wants, and to satisfy all your desires of knowledge.[1618]

The point is, there is no mere man who can give a positive answer to these four rhetorical questions. Only God can be the answer to these questions. In Isaiah 40:12-14 the prophet, speaking for God, also asks questions that can only be answered with one word, God:

(12) Who measured the waters with the hollow of His hand, and gauged the skies with a span, and meted earth's dust with a measure, and weighted the mountains with a scale and the hills with a balance? (13) Who has plumbed the mind of the LORD, What man could tell Him His plan? (14) Whom did He consult, and who taught Him, guided Him in the way of right?

Who guided Him in knowledge and showed Him the path of wisdom?

To give the answer is to be completely redundant for no man can do such things; only God can be the answer.

Question Five: *What is his name or his son's name, if you know it?*

God answers the question with a riddle, with sarcasm as it were, to tease or even taunt the readers of this verse. The first answer to this question Jewish people would give one (echad) voice, the LORD or *Yahweh*. The answer to the second half of question five at the time of the writing of this proverb, was unknowable.

Before attempting to answer the second half of the fifth question, another issue must be discussed. Just how is the term "son" used in the *Tanakh*? Both the Hebrew word בֵּן (ben) and the Aramaic word בַּר (bar) are translated as son. These two words are used and understood as being interchangeable; they mean the same thing.[1619] However, a student of Scripture will also observe that the term "son" can have either a

---

[1617] Duane A. Garrett, *The New American Commentary: Proverbs* (Nashville: Broadman, 1993), 236-237.

[1618] George Lawson, *Exposition of Proverbs* (Grand Rapids: Kregel, 1980), 835-836.

[1619] Botterweck and Ringgren, *Theological Dictionary of the Old Testament*, 2:149-153.

literal or a metaphorical meaning. Here are five brief summary examples of how "son" is used in Scripture:

1. It can mean literal offspring, as well as a metaphorical offspring such as the "sons of the prophets" (1 Kings 20:35).

2. It is also applied to the Israelite king and it means "son" by divine adoption (2 Samuel 7:14).

3. This term is also applied to the people of Israel as a whole who were specially called God's son, His firstborn (Exodus 4:22-23).

4. Obedient children of Israel as individuals were called "sons of the living God" (Hosea 1:10).

5. Angels (messengers) are called "sons of God" because they share with God, both partaking of heavenliest, both having

6. a spirit nature as opposed to the earthly, flesh nature of humans.[1620]

In point three Israel is the LORD's son according to Exodus 4:22: "*Israel is my son, my first born.*" If Israel is God's son, then cannot God also have an eternal son chosen from the plural unity of *Elohim*? Even the LXX (Septuagint) attempts to cover the intended meaning, which reads "his son" making it plural, "*his children,*" apparently interpreting "*his son*" as "*the children of Israel.*"[1621] That reading in the LXX is not the context nor is it the intent of Proverbs 30:4. These usages are easily understood. God can have a son of whomever He chooses. Jewish people would never argue against the fact that Israelites as a whole and obedient individual Jewish people were called in Scripture the "*son*" or "*sons*" of God. Did God give physical birth to Israel? No. So the Messiah of God can be designated by God His son as well. But this does not answer the question as to whether or not the designated "son of God" is divine.

In the first four rhetorical questions the expected answer is God. Then an additional question is asked: "*What is his son's name?*" Wilkinson demonstrates clearly that the term "*sons of God*" cannot mean angels. In this passage four rhetorical questions are asked: (1) "Who hath ascended up into heaven, and descended? (2) Who hath gathered the wind in His fists? (3) Who hath bound the waters in His garment? (4) Who hath established all the ends of the earth? Then he asks for this one's name which answers the first four questions. Every Jewish person would respond "The Lord God of Israel." Then the most perplexing question is asked, "*What is His Son's name, if thou knowest?*" The question is asked in such a way that automatically presumes that God does have a Son, and surely they know His Name. However, it is fair to ask, if that means that the "Son of God" has to be divine, and with that the Scriptures do refer to angels as the

---

[1620] Brown, *Answering Jewish Objection to Jesus: Theological Objections*, 2:38-39. The whole of Michael Brown's section on the "Son of God" is well worth reading (pgs 38-48).

[1621] Bruce K. Waltke, *The New International Commentary on the Old Testament: The Book of Proverbs, Chapters 15-31* (Grand Rapids: Eerdmans, 2005), 474.

sons of God. This Son of God will also be the Son of David so He can't be a mere angel.[1622]

There is a word in the fifth question that stands out and cannot be avoided. It is the word "*name*." Gerry Berry, in his comments on the verse, confirms the observation that Wilkinson made in this statement:

> The second phrase, "And what is his son's name," is probably used in the former meaning, it is a request to designate the individual who can be called the Son of God. What is meant by this? The meaning of the word "son" in relation to God in the Old Testament is well established. In the early history of Israel it was used as a designation of the nation of Israel. Later the thought is narrowed to that of the Davidic king, so called as God's representative, standing in an especially intimate relation with him. The beginning of this usage is the promise made by God to David, recorded in 2 Sam 7:14 [1 Chron 17]. This promise is definitely alluded to in the words of Psa 2:7.[1623]

Notice the connection that he makes. If the king of Israel is the adopted son of God and is the figure through whom God was to rule Israel, why is it so difficult for the physical Son of David to be the "son of God"? What needs to be determined is not if God has a son, but whether the son is divine.

Now the word "name" comes into play. "Name" needs to be discussed, and it must be established what the term "name" means. When the *Tanakh* says, "*what is his name*" the intent of the question is to refer to a person who is God. It then goes on and asks "*what is his son's name?*" The question places the LORD and the Son on equal status. To have the name of God is to know Him personally, as referred to in the following quote:

> "Name" stands for character. To know the name, especially the covenant name "Yahweh" is to know the person of God as Creator and Redeemer (Exodus 3:13-14).[1624]

What Agur is doing is placing on equal status the one named in the first half of the fifth question with the "son" in the second half of the question. As was stated previously, as God progressively revealed Himself to mankind, more things could be learned by later writers of Scripture. There was absolutely no way that Jewish people at the writing of this proverb could have known the name of the "*son*" of the LORD. But as time progressed so did the understanding and knowledge of the student of Scripture as more of God's Word was revealed by God.

[1622] Wilkinson, *Israel My Glory*, 183-184.

[1623] George R. Berry, *The Book of Proverbs* (Philadelphia: American Baptist Publication Society, 1904), 94.

[1624] David A Hubbard, *The Communicator's Commentary: Proverbs* (Dallas: Word, 1989), 459.

Focus on the word "name." As the great prophets of God, such as Isaiah and Jeremiah come upon the scene further information is given. In Psalm 2 it was learned that God had a Son and in both Psalm 2 and Psalm 72 this Son will have a worldwide rule upon the earth. He is a physical Son of David, but to be a worldwide ruler and to rule in complete justice and righteousness, that ruler must be more than a human being; He must also be God. As was said, "name" stands for character, and when God names a person He names them according to their character. In Isaiah 7:14 the child to be born was to have the name "Immanuel" meaning that God Himself personally is with us. Isaiah 9:6 states "*His name shall be called*" and He is given four names, three of which can only refer to God Himself. Yet in verse 6 His human side is given when it says, "*For unto us a child is born.*" Then the next phrase gives the divine side by saying "*unto us a son is given,*" God's Son, the Son of David. His names are Wonderful Counselor, the Mighty God, the everlasting Father. These names are attributed to God alone. Notice also He will be the Prince of Peace. When that true peace comes, it will be accompanied first by true righteousness (Isaiah 32:17). Only God has that righteousness. Jeremiah, a century later, refines the peace aspect further by stating in Jeremiah 23:5-6 that He will be a righteous Branch, referring to the physical Son of David. Later in verse 6 this Son of David is named again as "*The LORD our righteousness.*" Once more Isaiah 49:6 says the "*my servant*" the servant of the LORD, He will be salvation unto the ends of the earth.

What is interesting is that the Hebrew word for salvation here is יְשׁוּעָתִי (*yeshuati*), which is a noun. Seven centuries later the messenger (Gabriel) appeared to a man named Joseph who was engaged to a virgin named Miriam (Mary) and told him to name her firstborn son *Yeshua*, which is taking *yeshuati* and making it a proper noun, a name. Gabriel quotes from Isaiah 7:14 about a "virgin" who would give birth to a son whose name is Immanuel. Gabriel stated further to Miriam (Mary) that this child would be the "Son of the highest" and would reign upon the throne of His father David. This all can be found in the New Covenant books in Matthew 1:18-25 and Luke 1:26-38. In the New Covenant the Jewish people met Him in person, but because He was not what they expected and because He challenged the Pharisees and the Oral Law, the very person of God was rejected by His own:

> It was not until New Testament times that the name of God's Son was finally revealed. The angel said to Joseph, "Thou shalt call his name Jesus: for he shall save his people from their sins" (Matt 1:21). The Jehovah of the Old Testament is the Jesus of the New Testament – and that name is the greatest and most glorious of all the names for God.[1625]

It has not been the habit of this author to quote from the New Covenant, but here one passage will be quoted from the Gospel of Matthew 23:37-39:

[1625] John Phillips, *Exploring Proverbs* (Neptune, NJ: Loizeaux, 1996), 546.

(37) O Jerusalem, Jerusalem, thou that killest the prophets and stonest them which are sent unto thee, how often would I have gathered thy children together, even as a hen gathereth her chickens under her wings, and ye would not! (38) Behold, your house is left unto you desolate. (39) For I say unto you, Ye shall not see me henceforth, till ye shall say, Blessed is he that cometh in the name of the Lord.

This was the last public statement given by *Yeshua* to the children of Israel before He was taken and crucified. Notice in these verses He clearly equates Himself as *HaShem*, and He speaks of the desolation that would be Israel's 40 years later. He also clearly states that He, the Messiah, will not come again until the nation says to Him, "*Blessed is He that cometh in the Name of the LORD*" (Matthew 23:39). Wilkinson refers to Isaiah 7:14 and the name Immanuel, plus Isaiah 9:6-7 where this person is obviously human and divine; thus he makes the connection as to the identity of the "*Son of God*" in the following statement:

> These terms could not with any propriety be applied to any mere man, but can only be applied to a Person who is Divine as well as human, and most appropriately to Jesus as the Messiah, the Son of David and the Son of God."[1626]

The context of these verses (Isaiah 9:6-7) is not open to just any one of the possible usages for "son" for rabbis will attempt to interpret it to mean Israel as God's first born son. The question asked and the names requested are tied together. Did Israel ever ascend or descend? Did Israel ever hold the winds in her fist? Did Israel ever bind the waters in her garment or establish the ends of the earth? No is the resounding answer. Even the Soncino series clearly states that the name of God is the answer to the first half of the fifth question, as stated in the following:

> The purpose of the series of questions is to point out the impossibility of any man having this knowledge, because to do so, he must be able to ascend to heaven (Job 38:4). "And Descended," Only God has done that (e.g. Gen 11:7; Exod 19:18), although it is related that Elijah had ascended. "Gathered the wind," An act of God (Amos 4:13; Psa 135:7). "Bound...garment," Defined in Job 26:8, "He bindeth up the waters in His thick clouds." It is God Who arranges for the store of waters to provide the rain without which existence is impossible. "Established...earth," That it rotate on its axis, suspended in space. "What is his name?" A sarcastic question: if you assert that any man possessed these qualifications, who is he? (Rashi). "What is his son's name? More sarcasm: should you claim that such a person has existed, let me test your

---

[1626] Wilkinson, *Israel My Glory*, 185.

knowledge of him; if you give me his name, what more do you know of him? What was his son called? (Rashi).[1627]

Israel, as a nation, was the servant of the LORD chosen to reveal the LORD to the Gentile nations, but failed. Instead Israel took on the gods of the Gentiles and paid a steep price for their sins. So God has promised to raise up a *"righteous Branch"*, the Son of David, the Messiah, who is also the God of Israel. He came first as a servant to suffer and redeem man (Isaiah 40, 42, 49, 50, 53 and 61) so that righteousness could be established and then peace would come. Keil and Delitzsch made an interesting comment that reflects on this when they stated concerning Messiah's work, "Redemption is the beginning and the judgment the end of His work."[1628]

Summary

What stands out in Psalms 2 and 72 and Proverbs 30:4 is the fact that God does have a son in this case and it not Israel, not just any earthly descendant of David, but one who is in every way the God of the *Tanakh*, the God of Israel. It is not just Psalms 2 and 72 with Proverbs 30:4 that spoke of the Sonship of the Messiah to the student of Scripture. It is all the other references of the plural unity of *Elohim* which, when coupled with these three passages, confirm the reality that *Yeshua*, before His incarnation, was the one who dealt with Israel from the call of Abraham through the close of the canon of the Hebrew Scripture. A casual devotional reading of the *Tanakh* does not reveal the identity of the Second Person of the plural unity of *Elohim*; it must be studied comparing Scripture with Scripture. The Messenger of the LORD; the *Shechinah* glory; the Captain of the LORD's Host; the personal pronouns that *Elohim* and *Yahweh* used of themselves; the plural descriptions of the Lord God; plus the multiple places in the *Tanakh* when the LORD describes something being done to Him that only happened to *Yeshua*, God the Son. Knowing and understanding all of these terms that relate to the Messiah are the fruits of studying God's Word rather than the writings and laws of man.

Another key aspect of these passages is the word "righteousness" that the Son of God possesses. Psalms 2 and 72 are so clear on this issue, but they are not the only places that point to the righteous Son, who is both the Son of David and by the incarnation of the Second Person of the plural unity of *Elohim,* also becomes the Son of God. These passages clearly demonstrate the Sonship of *Yeshua,* who is also the God of Israel.

[1627] A. Cohen, *The Soncino Books of the Bible: Proverbs* (New York: The Soncino Press, 1985), 201.
[1628] Keil and Delitzsch, *Commentary on the Old Testament in Ten Volumes: Psalms,* 5:91.

Chapter 17
The Branch

As the study of the plurality in unity of *Elohim* and the identity of the Messiah unfolds in the *Tanakh*, another Hebrew specialized or technical word comes into view. It is the word translated as *"branch," "shoot"* or *"sprout."* There are two Hebrew words that are used in the Hebrew Scriptures that draw the attention of the serious student of God's Word.

The first Hebrew word for *"branch"* or *"sprout"* is צֶמַח [*semach*] and is used in the *Tanakh* 32 times in the verb form and 12 times as a noun. [1629] Seven of those times it is used literally as a shoot or growth from a tree.[1630] The noun is used the remaining five times as a messianic term in Isaiah 4:2; Jeremiah 23:5; 33:15; Zechariah 2:8 and 6:12. The second Hebrew word נֵצֶר [*netser*], is translated also as *"branch"* in Isaiah 11:1 (Isaiah 14:19; 60:21; Daniel 11:7), also a messianic portion of Scripture. The word comes from a root that is not used in the verb form in Hebrew. However, its meaning is constant: "shoot, blossom, branch, scion." Wagner gives the following description of its usage:

> In extension of this basic botanical meaning, the word is applied to historical situations: branch or shoot of a clan, offshoot of the rootstock of a family. This meaning appears in the well-known oracle of salvation Isa. 11:1-11, which declares that a shoot (netser) shall come out from the stump of Jesse,...The image of a new king as netser may be compared to the similar usage of צֶמַח [semach].[1631]

Both of these Hebrew words are used in reference to the Messiah and are translated as *"branch," "shoot"* or *"sprout."* The purpose of this chapter is to show that these two words are used not only of David, but also of the *"son of David"* who will reign on the throne of David in the future. Within their context they are used to identify this *"son of David"* as someone who is much greater than an ordinary son of Jesse, who was born under sin. The *Tanakh* does not teach an inclination to do good or evil but the fact that mankind is born with a nature to sin. These verses will act as more pieces of the puzzle in identifying the true nature, essence and character or that One who is called *"Messiah,"* who is presented in the *Tanakh* as the LORD Himself.

[1629] Harris, Archer and Waltke, *Theological Wordbook of the Old Testament,* 2:769.

[1630] VanGemeren, *New International Dictionary of Old Testament Theology & Exegesis,* 3:816.

[1631] Botterweck, Ringgren and Fabry, *Theological Dictionary of the Old Testament,* 9:549-550.

THE BRANCH OF *YAHWEH*
Isaiah 4:2

> In that day, the radiance of the LORD will lend beauty and glory, and the splendor of the land [will give] dignity and majesty, to the survivors of Israel.

This verse comes from *The Jewish Study Bible*, which deflects the reader from the true meaning of the Hebrew text. However, in the footnotes they state the following:

> Radiance…splendor, lit. "branch…fruit." The former term alludes to the royal line, as indicated by its use elsewhere in the Bible (Jer 23:5; 33:15; Zech 3:8; 6:12)…. Following this sense, the Targum translates it as "Messiah." Some rabbinic commentators interpret it as a reference to King Hezekiah.[1632]

If the student did not read the footnotes, he would never know that some rabbis did relate this verse to the Messiah. It is also interesting to see that some Jewish scholars wish to tie in Hezekiah with some of these references. This is another illustration of stretching the text to get away from the intended meaning of the text. Once again, in reviewing the passages of Scripture that pertain to Hezekiah (2 Kings 18-20; 2 Chronicles 29-32; Isaiah 36-39), it can quickly be established that he was a godly king who brought about a revival in the Land. But Hezekiah was a vassal king under the king of Assyria, and when he rebelled against the Assyrians they devastated the Land and only Jerusalem survived. It is simply impractical and impossible to implicate Hezekiah as the "*branch*" with the description that Isaiah gives concerning the "*branch*."

Isaiah 4:2 is not an isolated verse but belongs to a larger context of verses going back to Isaiah 2:6 and running through Isaiah 4:6. In this section of Isaiah, God is announcing, through His prophet, His judgments on Israel (Judah) for their sins against Him. There is a key phrase that helps the student of Scripture place these verses in God's calendar of events. The phrase "*in that day*" is referencing the time when God will judge Israel (Judah) for their sins in preparation for the reign of the *Moshiach*. This phrase would mean the same as "*the day of the LORD*" or the "*time of Jacob's trouble*" recorded in other places in the *Tanakh* (Isaiah 2:12; 13:6, 9; Jeremiah 30:7; Ezekiel 13:5; 30:3; Joel 1:15; 2:1, 11, 31; 3:14; Amos 5:18, 20; Obadiah 15; Zephaniah 1:7, 14; Zechariah 14:1; Malachi 4:5). It is at the end of this section on judgment that God makes a promise of Israel's restoration. Isaiah 4:2 begins that section and it ends with verse 6. The following authors speak to the issue of the judgments and the ensuing time of restoration:

> As a warning, Isaiah turns to the heavenly judgments. God will judge the wicked and their idols, 2:6-11; the wicked leaders of the land, 2:22-3:15; and the proud women, 3:15-4:1…. In contrast to the judgment that falls upon the wicked nation, the Lord will establish this kingdom for those who trust Him.

[1632] Berlin and Brettler, *The Jewish Study Bible*, 792.

The phrase "in that day" occurs widely in Isaiah. In the previous six times it occurs (2:11, 17, 20; 3:7, 18; 4:1), it refers to the Day of Judgment. For the first time, the phrase now refers to the kingdom era.[1633]

Isaiah 4:2 initiates a shift in 4:2-6 to a description of a future time of restoration and relief.… Elsewhere, "branch of the LORD" is a messianic title indicating the royal and priestly roles of the Messiah.[1634]

There is a problem of interpretation in this verse, however, but the problem is not with the time period. That period refers to the Kingdom otherwise known as the Millennial Kingdom of Messiah and the 7 years of God's preparation of Israel for their Messiah known as the tribulation, also known as the seventieth week of Daniel 9. That preparatory period, the tribulation, will end with the Battle of Armageddon, which then culminates with the beginning of the Millennial Kingdom. As this verse is written, it gives parallel descriptions of the Kingdom period. Victor Buksbazen is very clear as to the meaning of this section of Scripture from Isaiah 2:6 – 4:6:

After a severe indictment of the sins of his people and a prediction of divine judgment, the prophet now completes his message with a glorious vision of Israel's redemption, after the time of her punishment and purging is completed. Israel's redemption will come through "the branch of the LORD," in Hebrew "*Tsemah Jehovah*," or sometimes "*Tsemah David.*" "*Tsemah*" means growth or vegetation in general, or a sprout, a plant, a branch. When used in conjunction with Jehovah or David, it has a Messianic connotation, and refers to the Messianic King who is a branch of the stem of Jesse (11:1).[1635]

This quotation summarizes the whole section in a brief way but also captures the thrust of what Isaiah is saying. However, the two parallel phrases, "*the branch of the LORD*" and "*the fruit of the earth*," evoke several different viewpoints as to the meaning of these two phrases. There is not a consensus among scholars as to how these two phrases are to be understood. "*Branch*" in this verse does not distinctly reflect an individual, as in Jeremiah 23:5. Some believe that "*branch*" is referring to a literal "*branch*" because the parallel "*fruit*" must be referring to literal fruit of the earth, for an individual called Messiah is not present. Below an author reflects on other possible views and their possible interpretations of this passage:

However, in Isa 4:2, the reference is not to a "sprout" of David but rather, a "Sprout of Yahweh." In 11:1, Isaiah speaks about a "shoot from the stump of Jesse," a "sprig from his roots." This shows that he also was able to speak about a צמח (sprout) from the family line of David, but hardly about a צמח יהוה (sprout of Yahweh).… And yet, a most compelling argument against taking this

[1633] Steveson, *A Commentary on Isaiah*, 38-39.

[1634] Walker, *Tyndale Cornerstone Biblical Commentary: Isaiah, Jeremiah & Lamentations*, 30.

[1635] Buksbazen, *The Prophet Isaiah*, 1:125-126.

passage in a messianic sense can be found in the parallel in v. 2b: פרי הארץ (fruit of the land). There is no possible way that it could be understood as a designation for the Messiah. Vitringa's opinion, that the sprouts from Yahweh and the fruit from the earth pointed to the divine and human nature of the Messiah, certainly cannot be read in between the lines of this particular text. Interpreting "fruit of the earth" as referring to the pious ones in Israel (Raschi), and possibly seeing in the offspring of Yahweh a reference to the holy remnant (Mauchline) falter as an explanation, since "the fruit of the land" is supposed to be provided for the redeemed of Israel. There is no other explanation left, except the one which is closest at hand, that the פרי הארץ refers to the fruits which the land will bring forth (Deut 1:25, and often elsewhere). The expression has the same meaning as what is otherwise referred to in the expression טוב הארץ (good gifts of the land) (Isa 1:19; Jer. 2:7) but most explicitly means the same as פרי האדמה (fruit of the ground) (Gen 4:3, and often elsewhere, especially in the promises of blessing in Deuteronomy, e.g., 28: 4, 11, and often elsewhere).[1636]

As can be seen, there is no shortage of ideas as to how this verse should be understood. Below are several authors' statements that this verse does not refer to a personal Messiah but to the abundance of fruit that will be available during the Kingdom period.

Many deny that Isaiah is referring to the Messiah when he speaks of "the Branch or Shoot of Yahweh" because it is paralleled by the expression "the fruit of the earth." Therefore, 4:2 is simply a reference to the agricultural prosperity of the land. [1637]

The word *branch* has been interpreted [and]…refers to the righteous remnant that will emerge from the impending judgment. A[nother view is the] possibility that this word (tsemach), whose literal meaning is "that which sprouts," should be rendered "the growth of the Lord." According to those who favor a literal interpretation of the term, therefore, it refers neither to the Messiah nor to a righteous remnant, but to the fertility of the land in the eschatological age. This would make it parallel to the fruit of the land in the latter half of the verse. Those who advocate this viewpoint out that one of the recurring themes in Old Testament eschatology is the miraculous transformation of nature, resulting in the return of the earth to a paradisiacal state (cf. 11:6-9; Hos 2:21-23; Amos 9:13-15).[1638]

Modern critics have been quick to point out the exegetical problems involved in this rendering. First, in the above "messianic" (Jer 23:5; 33:15; Zech 3:8; 6:12) passages the "branch" is related to a scion of David, and not to Yahweh as in

---

[1636] Hans Wildberger, *Isaiah 1-12: A Commentary* (Minneapolis: Fortress Press, 1991), 166.

[1637] Harris, Archer and Waltke, *Theological Wordbook of the Old Testament*, 2:770.

[1638] Page Kelley, *The Broadman Bible Commentary: Proverbs – Isaiah* (Nashville: Broadman, 1971), 5:202.

4:2. Second, if the Messiah is the branch, who is the paralleled "fruit of the land?" As a consequence the great majority of scholars (also Delitzsch) interpret the verse to mean that Yahweh promises to renew fertility to the land, which will spring forth in the new period of Zion's redemption.[1639]

These arguments are logical conclusions but this author believes that another perspective that relates to this passage regarding the Messiah is more compelling. This perspective will be investigated shortly. However, one of the other arguments to be discussed is that this verse presents the divine and human nature of the Messiah. That is not a satisfactory response to this author. One author briefly expresses it below:

> However, the difficulty that this interpretation creates in this instance is that the next statement, "fruit of the earth," constitutes a strange parallel to the Messiah. Some attempt then to make this second expression to be a description of the human origin or nature of the Christ. [1640]

> The first phrase stresses Christ's relation to the Father, the second His relation to the earth. It is reasonable to understand "branch of the Lord" as referring to the deity of the Lord. The "fruit of the earth" refers to the humanity of Christ...."[1641]

While recognizing that as a legitimate argument and that there is a connection between the "*branch*" and the "*fruit of the earth*," this author does not see the divine and human nature of Messiah as seen by some scholars. Leupold also expresses his disapproval in seeing the human side of the Messiah in the phrase "*the fruit of the earth*," as he expresses in the following statement:

> This leads us to the consideration of the second interpretation, which is much more to the point. This is the interpretation which says that tsemach is none other than the Messiah himself, an interpretation found already in the Jewish Targum on the passage. What lends special weight to this interpretation is the fact in later passages tsemach clearly becomes a sort of title for the Messiah (Jer 23:5; 33:15; Zech 3:8; 6:12). However, the difficulty that this interpretation creates in this instance is that the next statement, "fruit of the earth," constitutes a strange parallel to the Messiah. Some attempt then to make this second expression to be a description of the human origin or nature of the Christ. But to make "fruit of the earth" bear such a meaning is far-fetched in any case. So the truth of the matter appears to be that, where in the earlier instance of the use of the term *tsemach*, it covers the whole work of God, later on in prophecy it specifically and appropriately describes the Christ himself, who is the greatest branch, or sprout, or shoot, that God's providence ever brought forth. Therefore

---

[1639] Brevard S. Child, *The Old Testament Library: Isaiah* (Louisville, KY: Westminster John Knox, 2001), 35-36.

[1640] H. C. Leupold, *Exposition of Isaiah* (2 Vols. Grand Rapids: Baker, 1968), 1:104.

[1641] Steveson, A Commentary on Isaiah, 38-39.

we conclude that in this instance the whole of the saving work of God is meant by the term.[1642]

Leupold only offers a very general explanation for the meaning of the phrase "*the fruit of the earth*." However, what is obvious is that the impact of the "*branch of Yahweh*" when He comes has a very definite effect. But what this author does see is twofold: First the Messiah is "*the branch of Yahweh*," showing His divinity and not the branch of David as seen in the other references that will be studied. What Jeremiah (23:5-6) did is put both the "*branch of Yahweh*" and the "Branch of David" together, as Motyer expresses in the following statement:

> Only here do we have 'the LORD's branch.' The Messiah springs from a dual ancestry as he belongs in the 'family tree' of both David and the Lord.[1643]

Motyer goes on by connecting the branch of David with the metaphor "*the fruit of the land/earth*" which I do not see unless Jeremiah 23:5-6 is connected to it. Second, this author sees the phrase "*the fruit of the earth*" as being a possible reference to the lifting of the curse when Messiah comes, the curse that was placed on the earth in Genesis 3 when mankind first sinned. Isaiah says that the animal kingdom will be at peace with itself (11:6-9; Amos 9:13-15). Mankind will live 1000 years during this period, and Paul, in Romans 8:22, references that all of creation groans for its redemption. The Messiah "*the branch of Yahweh*" when He comes will remove the curse from the earth so that the thorns and thistles (Genesis 3:17b-18) will no longer be a hazard to the growth of "*the fruit of the earth*."

In the first half of Isaiah 4:2 the "*branch*" is called "*the branch of Yahweh*." This branch is not the branch of David or Jesse but "*the branch of Yahweh*." As David was the son of Jesse, so the Messiah will be the "*son of David*." But this verse adds an additional dimension by saying the "*branch*" will be the Son of *Yahweh* (Psalm 2:7; Psalm 110:1; Proverbs 30:4) as well as the "*son of David*" in the other "*branch*" passages. Is that too much to assume? A further study of this passage will reveal several additional points that need to be investigated. Isaiah is making a reference back to the words of David in 2 Samuel 23:5 and possibly Psalm 132:17.

David makes an interesting statement in 2 Samuel 23:5. What must be asked is what David knew and understood concerning the truth that relates directly to the "*branch*." What is the subject of discussion by David in 2 Samuel 23:5? David, in his last words, speaks of the covenant that the LORD made with him in 2 Samuel 7:12-17 (1 Chronicles 17:10-14). As David reflects on the everlasting covenant, which Nathan previously announced to him, he asks rhetorically: "*Will not God cause all my salvation and all my desire to sprout?*" (II Samuel 23:5). The later biblical writers take up this theme and answer, as did the writer of one of the Psalms of Ascent (132:17), with a "yes!" In Jerusalem God will cause the horn of David to sprout up. In fact, it will spring

---

[1642] Leupold, *Exposition of Isaiah*, 1:104.
[1643] Motyer, *The Prophecy of Isaiah*, 65.

forth for the whole house of Israel (Ezekiel 29:21),[1644] meaning that Isaiah was not the first to use the *"branch"* concept, for here David himself mentions it almost 250 years before Isaiah. Keil and Delitzsch make the following statement in relationship to the covenant that the LORD made with David:

> Each of the two clauses [in verse 5] contains a distinct thought. That of the first is, "Does not my house stand in such a relation to God, that the righteous ruler will spring from it?" This is then explained in the second: "for He hath made an everlasting covenant with me." David calls the promise in chapter 7:12 sqq., that God would establish his kingdom to his seed forever, a covenant, because it involved a reciprocal relation, — namely, that Jehovah would first of all found for David a permanent house, and then that the seed of David was to build the house of the Lord.[1645]

The word for *"grow"* in verse 5 is the Hebrew word *"sprout."* God was going to do a work for David and he knew that God would raise up from his seed, from his sons, a *"branch"* or *"sprout"* where all the promises to David (and Abraham) would come together in one person. Two other authors add to what David said in 2 Samuel 23:5 in the following quotations:

> In Psa 132:17, it is said: "There I cause a horn to sprout to David," and already in the fundamental passage, 2 Sam 23:5, which contains the first germ of our passage, David says: "For all my salvation and all my pleasure should He not make it to sprout forth." As the words "Sprout of the Lord" denote the heavenly origin of the Redeemer,...[1646]

> The germinal thought from which this and the other "branch" passages are developed is 2 Sam 23:5. כִּי־לֹא יַצְמִיחַ "Although he maketh it not to grow." As was noted in the discussion of David's swan song it is fashioned after the model of Balaam's predictions, especially the last one (Num 24:15f). Our study of those passages revealed the fact that the subject of discussion was the Ruler who comes out of Jacob and from the house of David. Isaiah's use of the noun shows clearly that it is but the development of the embryonic idea expressed in the verb צָמַח [semach] used by David. Balaam's original oracle foretold the coming of the star out of Jacob, this king of kings, in the remote future. The Davidic passage reiterates this thought but expresses it under the figure of a sprouting seed or plant. Hence, in order to indicate the fact that the rise of this king was in the distant future, he declared that the Lord was not then causing this plant to shoot forth. In vision, however, he did see Him come forth, for he said that all his salvation and delight were in this coming one.[1647]

[1644] Harris, Archer and Waltke, *Theological Wordbook of the Old Testament,* 2:769-770.
[1645] Keil and Delitzsch, *Commentary on the Old Testament: 2 Samuel,* 2:489.
[1646] Hengstenberg, *Christology of the Old Testament,* 2:15.
[1647] Cooper, *Messiah: His Nature and Person,* 204.

Psalm 132:17 is the 13th Psalm of Ascent.[1648] It was written by an unknown psalmist concerning David, probably shortly after the death of David. From verses 11 to 17 it alludes to the Davidic Covenant. Here David's horn will bud or sprout, referring to a future king. The following author clearly sees this passage as a reference to the Messiah, the Son of David:

> There is another reference that seems to lie behind this great theme of the Branch. Psalm 132:7 says, "Here I will make a horn grow for David...." The NIV renders the word *grow*, but it is a growing which means 'to branch out' or 'to sprout:' *tsemah*. David is called the 'horn' which symbolizes the power of an animal. God says, "I will make a horn to sprout – to branch out – from David...." So here we have the concept of horn, Messiah, and branch all brought together within the scope of one verse, through verbal ideas, certainly in Psalm 132:17. Then God continues, "I set up a lamp for my anointed one." Lamp, horn, anointed one, and Branch: four metaphors for the Messiah brought together in the scope of one verse.[1649]

Both 2 Samuel 23:5 and Psalm 132:17 are precursors to Isaiah 4:2. David, at least 250 years before Isaiah (4:2; 11:1), 370 years before Jeremiah (23:5; 33:15) and 440 years before Zechariah (3:8; 6:12), used the embryo of the branch passages which were used in later years to reveal the nature of the Branch. It is no different than God in Genesis 3:15 referencing the *"seed of the woman"* and Isaiah picking up that embryonic truth and using it to reveal the virgin birth of Immanuel in Isaiah 7:14. Would it be any different from the passage in Genesis 3:21 where God makes coats to clothe Adam and Eve from the skins of animals that were used by God in the first sacrifice for sins? This would be later developed in the giving of the sacrificial code in the law of Moses, which would be a picture of the ultimate sacrifice for sins by the Messiah on the Tree. One of the reasons that some scholars do not accept this is that they say the term *"branch"* had not been established yet. However, was sacrifice established before the

---

[1648] The Psalms of Ascent are 15 in number and are Psalms 120-134. In the Temple there were 15 steps leading from the Court of Israel to the Court of the Women. During the Feast of Tabernacles the priests would have a procession from the Temple Mount down to the Pool of Siloam, fill their pitchers and then have a procession back to the Temple Mount. Upon reaching the 15 steps of Ascent they would sing Psalm 120 on step one, sing Psalm 121 on step two in that manner until all 15 steps and psalms were completed. Then they would pour out the water on the southwest corner of the Altar of Sacrifice, which was followed by great rejoicing. The rabbis equated the pouring out of the water to symbolize the outpouring of the Holy Spirit on Israel in the last days. The rabbis said that if you have not seen and heard the rejoicing of the pouring out of the water you have never heard rejoicing. To see a complete description of this, see the following sources: Arnold G. Fruchtenbaum, The Feast of Tabernacles: Manuscript #120 (Tustin, CA: Ariel Press, 1987), 9-10; Arnold G. Fruchtenbaum, The Feasts of Israel: Manuscript #62 (Tustin, CA: Ariel Press, 1984), 25. Rabbis Nosson Scherman and Meir Zlotowitz, Tehillim: Psalms (Brooklyn: Mesorah Publications, ltd, 1983), 5:1501.

[1649] Kaiser, *The Christian and the "Old" Testament*, 215.

law of Moses? Is the seed of the woman held in doubt? If not, then the *"Branch of Yahweh"* should not be held in doubt. Another author states:

> Furthermore, they overlook the progressive nature of Revelation, for certainly 2 Sam 23:5 and perhaps Psa 132:17 are controlling ideas when we come to the eighth century B.C. Thus the "Sprout of Yahweh" (or as clarified by the cognate studies, "the son of Yahwe") is an obvious reference to the divine nature of the semah."[1650]

The progressive nature of revelation is so very important to understand. God did not unload everything all at once on mankind as He revealed Himself and His prophetic messages to mankind in one generation. Rather He revealed it in stages, sometimes with hundreds or thousands of years between revelations.

Isaiah 4:2 is a unique verse, even though the Messiah is not presented as a person as in Jeremiah 23:5; 33:15; Zechariah 3:8; 6:12. This fact is illustrated by the following author as he shows the uniqueness and importance of this verse:

> Mention is made of the branch of the LORD being beautiful. The same word for branch (Heb. *tsemach*) is later used as a royal title in Jeremiah 23:5; 33:15 and Zechariah 3:8; 6:12. Many therefore take the title 'branch' here to have messianic significance, but all the later references identify the title with an individual, which is not done here. Jeremiah goes even further and links the title with the Davidic family. But that is not so in Isaiah 4:2.[1651]

As progressive revelation is given, Isaiah presents the *"branch"* concept that David referenced in 2 Samuel 23:5 and the unknown psalmist in Psalm 132:17 and uses it to present the *"branch of Yahweh."* This *"branch"* comes forth from *Yahweh* Himself, thus making the *"branch"* deity. David Baron makes a connection between the *"branch of Yahweh"* and the *"Son of God"* in the Gospel of John who was sent by the Father:

> John presents the Messiah as the "Son of God." In the Gospel of John, the light that shines most transcendently throughout is His Divine Sonship, that glory which He had with the Father from all eternity; hence His genealogy is not, as in Matthew, taken back to Abraham, for He of Whom it speaks was before Abraham (John 8:58), nor yet as in Luke, to Adam, because John deals not here with the Son of Adam, but with the Son of God in Whose image Adam was created. He therefore traces not his human, but Divine pedigree, and shows us that, although He "became flesh and dwelt among us" (John 1:14), He that did thus tabernacle with the children of men was none other than "the only begotten of the Father, full of grace and truth;" and that, although "the Light" had only then just shone upon the darkness of this world, He that in grace and mercy had thus become the Light and Life of this dark and dead world was none other than

---

[1650] Harris, Archer and Waltke, *Theological Wordbook of the Old Testament*, 2:770.
[1651] Harman, *Isaiah*, 60.

He "Whose goings forth have been from of old, even from the days of eternity" (Micah 5:2), "Who in the very beginning was with God and Himself was God" (John 1:1). Here then is the "Branch of Jehovah," Whose glory and beauty Isaiah sang (Isa 4:2).[1652]

One of the interesting observations is that each Gospel of the New Covenant carries a theme throughout its gospel story of *Yeshua*. In the Gospel of John, *Yeshua*, the Son of God, is presented as divine as John picks up Isaiah's *"branch of Yahweh"* and demonstrates that *Yeshua* is God who was sent to the earth by *Yahweh* Himself (Isaiah 48:16; Zechariah 2:8). David Baron saw the same thing. The *"branch of Yahweh"* is clearly the Messiah in this passage, as this author states:

> The *branch of the Lord* is not Hezekiah, nor in general the blessings of the Messiah, but Messiah Himself. He is also called *branch* in Jeremiah 23:5; 33:15; Zechariah 3:8; 6:12…. At His first coming, there was neither form nor comeliness that Israel should have desired Him. After His return, He will not only be beautiful and glorious but also Israel's beauty and glory. Obviously, the prophet points to these glorious attributes of King Messiah in contrast to the whorish adornments he enumerated in the preceding chapter…. The name fruit of the earth also refers to Christ. The first name indicated Him as the Son of God, who has branched forth from Jehovah. The second name refers to Him as the true man who has come forth from mankind; He has become one with mankind for the benefit of mankind.[1653]

Did Isaiah understand the significance of the term *"branch"* that he used in 4:2? The answer is in the affirmative as Isaiah spoke of the *"branch"* in chapter 11:1. There he also used the technical term *"branch"* in his presentation of *"Immanuel"* who would be virgin born (Isaiah 7:14), and this virgin born child would be named by God Himself with the very names of God, and whose reign upon the throne of David would have no end (Isaiah 9:6-7). This *"branch"* called *"Immanuel"* would be given a full measure of the Spirit (Isaiah 11:2). According to the information given in Isaiah 1:1 and 6:1 "The Book of Immanuel" which is embedded in the book of Isaiah was written in the early years of the ministry of Isaiah.

When all the information on the *"branch"* of Isaiah 4:2 is put together with David's references in 2 Samuel 23:5 and Psalm 132:17 and Isaiah's understanding of *"Immanuel,"* it becomes abundantly obvious that Isaiah understood what and of whom he was writing about when he used the phrase *"the branch of Yahweh."* This *"branch of the LORD"* has its origin in the LORD, as Walter Kaiser states:

> The Branch of the LORD that appears in Isa 4:2 to be a Genitive of source, the Branch that is from the LORD. It is of the LORD: of, in the sense of source, from which he comes. So this is his name: The LORD Our Righteousness. We

---

[1652] Baron, *Rays of Messiah's Glory*, 75-76.
[1653] Harry Bultema, *Commentary on Isaiah* (Grand Rapids: Kregel, 1981), 74.

can also see it treated later on in Jeremiah for Jeremiah 23:5-6 is not the only passage where we see this name. In Jeremiah 33:14-15, he uses this same name once again.[1654]

THE BRANCH
Isaiah 11:1

But a shoot shall grow out of the stump of Jesse, a twig [branch] shall sprout from his stock [roots].

Chapter divisions in the Scriptures are not always helpful in studying a passage, for often the student will start at verse 1, as in Isaiah 11, and not understand that there is a larger context that must be considered. In chapter 10 the proud, arrogant nation of Assyria is likened to a forest that is fallen never to arise again,[1655] which was indeed the case. Assyria disappeared from history until only recently when archaeologists uncovered Nineveh. Then Judah is compared to Assyria, for Judah had one lone tree that was reduced to a stump (Isaiah 11:1). This prophecy may also be in the context of Ahaz when the Davidic dynasty was still in existence but was being threatened from the north by Syria and Israel (Isaiah 7).[1656] The dynasty of King David would continue for 130 -140 years before it would be reduced to a stump. Any significance that the Davidic dynasty had appeared to have been lost.

There are three words in Isaiah that need to be reviewed. The first one used by Isaiah is חֹטֶר [choter – "shoot"] translated as "rod." The second word used was וְנֵצֶר [netser] which is translated as "branch." The final word used was מִשָּׁרָשָׁיו [sheh-resh] which is translated "from roots of him." One of the key and unexpected words is יִשַׁי [Jesse] in referring to the dynasty of David.

What is amazing is that before the Davidic Dynasty was cut down to only a stump, Isaiah prophesied that such would be the case. All seeming possibilities of a kingdom being restored to David appear to have been dashed against the face of reality. Yet Isaiah stated that the dynasty of David would be so poor and remote that he did not even refer to it as the stump of David, but went back to the very humble beginning of that dynasty, back to Jesse the father of David, and back to Bethlehem, which was *"little among the thousands of Judah"* (Micah 5:2). While the Assyrian *"forest"* is fallen never to arise, David's single tree would be cut off and by all appearances was dead, lying dormant for years. But life is in the roots and a *"branch"* sprouts forth from its roots. Two authors express the situation of David's dynasty at the time when the *"branch"* would appear:

[1654] Kaiser, *The Christian and the "Old" Testament*, 215-216.
[1655] Cohen, *The Soncino Books of the Bible: Isaiah*, 56.
[1656] Van Groningen, *Messianic Revelation in the Old Testament*, 556-557.

The origin of King Messiah was very humble. We see a bare, withered tree stump, robbed of its trunk and top, and it looks as though the stump will never bear any fruit any more. But, a small shoot sprouts from the root of this dry stump which is the Davidic dynasty. Because of its unsightliness and misery, it is not named after David but after his father. When Christ was born, there was nothing royal about the dynasty. But a new shoot sprang from this old stem. Christ was born in Bethlehem, and a heavenly messenger said of Him that He would sit on the throne of His father David and reign over the house of Jacob forever (Luke 1:33). This image of the Shoot does not point to His divinity but to His human nature and origin.[1657]

The preceding chapter had depicted the downfall of the Assyrian military strength in terms of the cutting down of a mighty forest. After the axe of divine judgment had crashed in among the trees, nothing but stumps were left standing all over the vast mountainside. So the imposing might of empire collapses. But God's way of working his purpose is to use the small, the weak, and the insignificant. But, adhering to the same general pattern just employed, there will be an insignificant stump in Israel, the house of David, or Jesse, fallen upon evil days and become very unimportant. This stump God will enable to bring forth a live shoot, which will develop into a tree actually bearing fruit. This tree of lowly beginnings is the Christ of God. In other words, that which is imposing collapses; that which is insignificant is capable of producing the greatest possible results.[1658]

The tree of David's dynasty was cut down because of the sin of Judah and their unwillingness to repent and turn back to the God of their fathers. They worshipped *Yahweh*, but they also worshipped other deities even in the temple of the LORD as Ezekiel 8-11 reveals. This "rod" and "branch" reveal the humanity of the Messiah. But Isaiah did not give just this verse in a vacuum in reference to the Messiah. In chapters 7 through 12 Isaiah the prophet revealed that Immanuel would be virgin born and Immanuel's kingdom would have "*no end*" for He was named by the LORD "*wonderful counselor*," "*mighty God*," "*everlasting Father*" and the "*prince of peace*." Isaiah revealed both the human and divine side of Immanuel, the "*branch*" that would come from the "*root of Jesse*," within the pages of the "Book of Immanuel." Isaiah stated that the "*branch*" would come from Jesse, which tied him directly into the Davidic Dynasty. But another interesting view has been pointed out concerning the uniqueness of this "*branch*:"

One of the most striking features of this remarkable passage is the dual title of the coming King as both the *shoot* (1) and the *Root* (10) *of Jesse*. The reference to *Jesse* indicates that the *shoot* is not just another king in David's line but rather another David (Jer 30:9; Ezek 34:23-24; Hos 3:5). In the book of Kings,

[1657] Bultema, *Commentary on Isaiah*, 141-142.
[1658] Leupold, *Exposition of Isaiah*, 1:215.

successive kings were assessed by comparison with 'their father David' (e.g. 2 Kgs 18:3) but no king is called 'David' or 'son of Jesse.' Among the kings, David alone was 'the son of Jesse' (1 Sam 20:27-33; 1 Kings 12:16), and the unexpected reference to Jesse here has tremendous force: when Jesse produces a shoot it must be David.... *Shoot* (*hoter*) is only found here and at Proverbs 14:3 and means 'young growth' or 'twig.' For *stump* (*geza*) see [Isa] 40:24 and Job 14:8. *Branch* (*neser*) is from the verb 'to grow green' and hence means 'a sapling.' It is not the word used in 4:2 but is the same metaphor, the 'family tree,' referring here to the human ancestry of Messiah.[1659]

The references above in Jeremiah, Ezekiel and Hosea definitely point to the Messiah being called David, who is not only an ancestor of Jesse or David, but this *"David"* is not the same David of First and Second Samuel. It is David's greater son (Psalm 80:1, 15-17; 110:1) who is *"the man of thy right hand"* of the LORD.

Isaiah 11:2 says that the Holy Spirit will rest upon the one who is the *"branch"* from the *"root of Jesse."* Here is the ministry of the Holy Spirit of God who is described as gifting the *"branch"* in three areas. First, the Holy Spirit bestows upon the *"branch"* wisdom and understanding so that the *"branch"* can make the right decisions. The second area of gifting by the Holy Spirit is in the area of administration by giving Him counsel and might. The third area of gifting by the Holy Spirit is the spiritual insights of knowledge and fear of the LORD. Not only do these verses express the personality of the Third Person of the plural unity of *Elohim*, they also show that the *"branch"* has a full measure of the Spirit of *Elohim* to accomplish His task of ruling over the earth. These three areas of attributes, intellectual, administrative and spiritual, are seen by authors such as Smith,[1660] Young,[1661] Van Groningen,[1662] Cohen,[1663] and Keil & Delitzsch.[1664] Two other authors express their perspective on this passage in the following statements:

Isaiah arranges the final six names in three groups of two names each. In each case, the first characteristic is the source from which the second characteristic flows. The first group, "the spirit of wisdom and understanding," relates to the intellect of the Holy Spirit. He has "wisdom," the practical ability to apply knowledge. This gives Him "understanding," the ability to discern the differences, particularly the rightness or wrongness, in various situation and matters. As a consequence of this, the Holy Spirit is omniscient. The second group relates to the practice of the Holy Spirit. He has "counsel," the ability to form right conclusions. This gives Him "might," the ability to carry out His

---

[1659] Motyer, *The Prophecy of Isaiah*, 121-122.
[1660] Smith, *The Promised Messiah*, 268-269.
[1661] Young, *The Book of Isaiah*, 1:381-382.
[1662] Van Groningen, *Messianic Revelation in the Old Testament*, 557-558.
[1663] Cohen, *The Soncino Books of the Bible: Isaiah*, 56.
[1664] Keil and Delitzsch, *Commentary on the Old Testament in Ten Volumes: Isaiah*, 7:282.

plans since He bases them on right plans. As a consequence of this, the Holy Spirit is omnipotent. The final group relates to the deity of the Holy Spirit. He has "knowledge." By virtue of the grammatical construction, this is the "knowledge of the Lord." We may say that the Spirit possesses the full knowledge of God. This leads to the conclusion that the Spirit is God: cf. 1 Cor 2:11. He has the "fear of the Lord," a reverence for the things that concern God.[1665]

Isaiah notes three pairs of gifts for this shoot. (1) He will have the intellectual gifts of wisdom and understanding. He will know what decisions to make and his appraisal of all situations will be correct. (2) He will have administrative gifts. Rather than attaching to his government a string of advisors and handlers, he will not need such services. He can formulate his own plans for the future and has the power and authority to make them happen and to bring them into fruition. (3) He will possess spiritual gifts.[1666]

In chapter 11 of this book the plural unity of the Third Person of *Elohim* was discussed. Isaiah 11:2 is another place that points to the personality of the Holy Spirit. The emphasis in the Hebrew Scriptures on the Holy Spirit is the work that He does and not necessarily His personality as He comes upon certain individuals within the pages of the *Tanakh*. This not only points out the personality of the Second Person of the plural unity of *Elohim*, but also the Third Person of the plural unity of *Elohim*, as Young points out:

> Upon this Messiah the Spirit of Yahweh is to rest. Not the spirit of prophecy, not a mere influence is this Spirit, but rather the Spirit that belongs to Yahweh, and who works for Yahweh. He is therefore a person. Furthermore, He is distinct from the Messiah. Isaiah is not speaking of the human spirit of the Messiah, but of the Spirit which comes from Yahweh. This Spirit had already wrought good and blessing in Israel. A portion of the Spirit had been placed upon the elders who assisted Moses; the Spirit of the Lord was to come upon Saul in order that he might be changed into another man; and at his anointing the Spirit of the Lord came upon David. Assyria's ruler had boasted of his own wisdom; but the Branch receives His gifts from the Spirit.[1667]

One final point before moving on to Jeremiah 23:5. Rabbinic Judaism sees this passage as a Messianic passage referring to the coming *"branch"* of David. However, the rabbis do not want to see *Yeshua* as the Messiah in this text. Rabbinic Judaism presupposes that *Yeshua* did not fulfill this passage because the verses that follow refer to the animal kingdom being at peace. They also like to point to the Gospel of Matthew in the New Covenant to show that *Yeshua* was not a descendant of Joseph nor from David's line, so

---

[1665] Steveson, *A Commentary on Isaiah*, 99-100.

[1666] Kaiser, *The Messiah in the Old Testament,* 165.

[1667] Young, *The Book of Isaiah*, 1:380-381.

He could not be the Messiah.[1668] Their reasoning is faulty on at least two counts. First, it is well understood in the Hebrew Scriptures that there can be gaps of time between phrases in a verse or between verses. Jeremiah presents the two comings of Messiah without identifying a time period between the two comings. This passage primarily speaks to the second coming of the Messiah. However, Jeremiah spoke of the Messiah first as being born as the "*son of David*" and then without hesitation moves right into the second coming without identifying an interval of time. Isaiah uses the same procedure again in 61:1-3. Zechariah does the same thing in 9:9-10. Rabbinic Judaism is not willing to acknowledge that there is a gap of time between the two comings as they argue against *Yeshua* here being the "*branch.*"

To digress for a moment, I would like to ask a question directly to the rabbis as it relates to gaps of time in prophetic fulfillment. When Abraham received the promises of the Land as his own personal possession (Genesis 13:17), did he receive it in his lifetime (Genesis 25:9-10)? The answer is no. Did his descendants ever occupy all the Land that was promised to Abraham's descendants? Again the answer is no. They did not occupy all of it, as Judges 1 clearly states, nor did David and Solomon possess all the Land promised. The Abrahamic Covenant was unfulfilled, or it was fulfilled at different times with a gap of years between fulfillments. Arnold Fruchtenbaum clearly demonstrates that it was fulfilled with gaps of time involved. Look at his statement:

> As stated earlier, while a covenant may be signed and sealed at a specific point of time, this does not mean that every provision goes immediately into effect. Three things happen. Some go into effect immediately, such as the changing of Abram's and Sarai's names and circumcision. Some go into effect in the near future, such as the birth of Isaac (25 years) and the Egyptian sojourn, enslavement, and the Exodus (400 years). Some go into effect in the distant future, such as the possession of all of the Promised Land by the patriarchs and their descendants.[1669]

Why then, if that is the case with the Abrahamic Covenant, can that not also be true in the two comings of *Moshiach*? You already believe erroneously that there are two separate messiahs, because you see a suffering messiah and a reigning messiah. Why can't these passages that relate the first and second coming of Messiah also have a gap in years as Daniel 9:26 so clearly shows between the sixty-ninth and seventieth week? There is clearly a gap of time in the fulfillment of the Abrahamic Covenant: Why can there not be a gap of time between Isaiah 9:6-7, Zechariah 9:9-10, and Isaiah 61:1-3? So yes, *Yeshua* has not fulfilled Jeremiah 23:5-6 yet because He has not returned to set up the Kingdom, but He was born in the family and kingly line of David.

The second point is the rabbis' insistence on using Matthew 1 as a proof text against *Yeshua* being a descendant of David. They will even say that Miriam's (Mary's)

[1668] Levine, *You Take Jesus, I'll Take God*, 50-51.
[1669] Fruchtenbaum, *Israelology: The Missing Link in Systematic Theology*, 581.

genealogy in Luke 3 is not her genealogy. It is true that a woman's genealogy is not written down in the Scriptures. But every woman has a father, so her genealogy is traced back through her father's genealogy, which is exactly what Luke does in the third chapter of his Gospel. Luke follows Miriam's (Mary's) father's line, which runs through Nathan, another son of David. So Miriam (Mary) is a descendant of David and so is *Yeshua*. Joseph was also the legitimate heir to the throne of David because God bypassed the curse He placed on Coniah in Jeremiah 22:24-30 through Zerubbabel. This will be discussed in length a little later in this chapter.

Rabbinic Judaism has a complete misunderstanding as to the purpose of the coming of the Messiah. They are very selfish in that the Messiah is only for them, so that Israel will control the nations of the world. David Baron, as a believer in *Yeshua*, states the following concerning the lack of spiritual understanding and the inability to see the need for the two comings of the Messiah:

> Just now the Jews object to the doctrine of the Messiah's Divinity, but it is mostly because they have not yet learned the real object of the Messiah's mission on the earth. When once they are brought by the Spirit of God fully to learn and believe that Messiah's work on earth is nothing less than the deliverance of mankind from the bondage of sin and Satan they will be convinced that if He is to be the Redeemer at all, He must needs be Divine; for if He were mere man, He could not possibly turn away "ungodliness from Jacob" (Isa 49:20), or "redeem Israel from all his iniquities."[1670]

In summary, to this point Isaiah 4:2 presented the "*branch of Yahweh*" in relation to the future restoration of Israel. Isaiah keys in on David's own statement in 2 Samuel 23:5 and Psalm 132:17 and in the process showed that the "*branch of Yahweh*" is divine. Isaiah, in his lengthy section on Immanuel, revealed the human side of the Messiah (7:14; 9:6) while at the same time showing the divine side of the Messiah (9:7). This is also the theme that the Apostle John picked up as he wrote the fourth gospel, the Gospel of John, which presents Messiah as the Son of God being divine. In Isaiah 11:1 the "*branch*" was presented as arising out of the ashes of the dynasty of David. The possibility is so hopeless that he refers not to David but to the root of Jesse. Yet with God nothing is hopeless when His word is at stake; He will bring it to fruition.

THE RIGHTEOUS BRANCH
Jeremiah 23:5-6

> (5) Behold, the days come, saith the Lord, that I will raise unto David a righteous sprout, and he shall reign as king and prosper, and shall execute judgment and justice in the earth. (6) In his days Judah shall be saved, and Israel shall dwell safely: and this is his name whereby he shall be called, The Lord *is* our righteousness. (Harkavy Version)

[1670] Baron, *Rays of Messiah's Glory*, 91-92.

These verses come from the Harkavy Version, which is a Jewish version of the *Tanakh*. Both this version and *The Jewish Study Bible* add a word that changes the whole understanding of theses verses. The word is "is," a form of the verb "to be." We will discuss later why this verb to be ("is") is not in the original text. For now, it is significant to know that its proper translation is "THE LORD OUR RIGHTEOUSNESS." *The Jewish Study Bible* also attempts to further obscure the meaning of צֶמַח [Branch] as Vindicator, when Kohlenberger[1671] and Gramcord[1672] both interpret the word as Branch.

As is often the case, these two verses stand within a larger context that needs to be reviewed so that the full impact of Jeremiah 23:5-6 can be clearly seen by the reader. There is a larger section of verses that will be divided into two smaller sections as the text is discussed. Jeremiah 22:24-30 and 23:1-8 are the two main sections that have a direct bearing on Jeremiah 23:5-6.

Josiah, who died in 609 BC, was probably the most righteous king to rule on the throne since David, for Josiah walked with the LORD in obedience, and had instituted many reforms and brought about a revival. However, these were only surface reforms and revival in the heart and lives of the people and the leadership. His three sons and grandson followed in a few short years and they all did *"evil in the sight of the LORD."* Two of them play a part in these upcoming verses, Jehoiachin in Jeremiah 22:24-30 and Zedekiah in Jeremiah 23:1-4. Jehoiachin, the son of Jehoiakim, the son of Josiah, reigned for only three months, until he surrendered to the Babylonians and was taken prisoner to Babylon with the queen mother and many other officials.

In Jeremiah 22:24-27 the LORD presents an oath, *"As I live, saith the LORD."* *Yahweh* is about to make an unexpected statement to the Jewish people. He tells Coniah or Jehoiachin, the grandson of Josiah, that if he was a signet ring on His own finger He would *"pluck"* it off His hand. The king was to be the direct representative of *Yahweh* in governing the people; he was the signet ring on God's hand. The signet ring with the king's seal was very valuable, for it represented the only source of authority for sealing documents with the impression of his seal. However, Coniah would be plucked off *Yahweh's* hand and be *"thrown"* or *"hurled"* from Jerusalem and Judah into the hand of Nebuchadnezzar King of Babylon, never to return, for he would die there. Several authors comment on Coniah and the statement of intent by *Yahweh*:

> This segment consists of two oracles (vv. 24-27, 28-30), both of which are announcements of judgment against Jehoiachin.... The first oracle, in prose, is cast in the form of a divine oath ("as I live,"); it is thus identified as having a special stature.... God would tear the ring off his own finger, deprive him of his authority as king, and give him into the hands of Nebuchadnezzar to be exiled. In fact, God will "hurl" them into a country that is not their own.... The second

---

[1671] Kohlenberger, *The Interlinear NIV Hebrew-English Old Testament,* 4:193.
[1672] Paul Miller, *Gramcord.*

oracle (vv. 28-30), in poetry, reinforces the point of vv. 24-27 from the perspective of Jehoiachin in exile.[1673]

Coniah (the name occurs only in Jer 22:24, 28; 37:1) is the abbreviated form of Jeconiah and alternate form of Jehoiachin, which is probably his throne name. The son and successor of Jehoiakim (v. 24), Jehoiachin was exiled in 597 B.C. (cf. 2 Kgs 24:8-17; 25:27-30). After a reign of three months over Judea, he was imprisoned for thirty-seven years in Babylon.... In him the royal line became extinct.[1674]

Other sources say that he was released from prison in 561 BC by Nebuchadnezzar's successor, Amel-Marduk (Evil-Merodach of Jeremiah 52:31-34) but remained and died in Babylon.[1675] With this first oracle *Yahweh* is setting the stage for the second oracle in verses 28-30. In this passage *Yahweh* gives a harsh, dogmatic statement that not only would Coniah go to Babylon, but the dynasty of David which lasted for 400 years would come to an end, an abrupt end with no apparent hope for the immediate future. The question is whether *Yahweh* has canceled His covenant with David, for no son of David has ruled in Israel since the days of Coniah the last king. God makes no effort to protect the royal line in reigning over Judah as He did in Isaiah 7 with Ahaz. There is no statement in relation to the defeat of the enemy as seen in Isaiah 7. But rather *Yahweh* gives judgments on Judah with the promise of captivity and complete victory for Babylon who will conquer and destroy Jerusalem and Judah.

In verses 28-30, Coniah is referred to by *Yahweh* as a despised broken vessel that is cast out, he and his seed, into a foreign land. Then in verses 29-30 *Yahweh* adds to His dogmatic statement that no one from Coniah's seed shall ever reign on the throne of David again. *Yahweh* states "*Write ye this man childless*" for no one will prosper on the throne of David from his seed again; *Yahweh* is finished with it. Does this mean that God has canceled His covenant with David? The following author develops that thought in this statement:

That epitaph doubles as an obituary for the house and line of David. With the exile to Babylon, Israel seems to have come to the end of the legitimate monarchy. How can that be? The Lord had promised David, "Your house and your kingdom will endure forever before me; your throne will be established forever" (2 Sam 7:16). Did the Lord break his promise? Did he foreclose on his pledge to his people? Had the covenant and kingdom come to an end? How

---

[1673] Terence E. Fretheim, *Smyth & Helwys Bible Commentary: Jeremiah* (Macon, GA: Smyth & Helwys Publishing, 2002), 322.

[1674] Feinberg, *Jeremiah: A Commentary*, 159-160.

[1675] Huey, *Bible Study Commentary: Jeremiah*, 76.

could God say that "none" of Jehoiachin's offspring would ever prosper or sit on the throne of David?[1676]

Jeremiah was not the only prophet to speak of the corruption of Coniah and his uncles, for Ezekiel, a contemporary of Jeremiah who had already been exiled to Babylon (Ezekiel 1:1), also speaks to the removal of the kingship and Judah in Ezekiel 21:25-27 [30-32] into captivity:

> (25) And to you, O dishonored wicked prince of Israel, whose day has come – the time set for your punishment – (26) Thus said the Lord God: Remove the turban and lift off the crown! This shall not remain as it is; exalt the low and abase the high. (27) Ruin, and utter ruin I will make it. It shall be no more until he comes to whom it rightfully belongs; and I will give it to him.

This passage clearly references the kings of that period of Judah's history. As Jeremiah speaks judgment against Judah and the house of David, so also Ezekiel speaks to the same issue, but Ezekiel gave a word of hope when he stated that the crown would be given to someone in the future to whom it belongs. Even as Jeremiah gave the promise of the righteous Branch in 23:5-6, so Ezekiel declared that the kingship would be removed until "*he comes to whom it rightfully belongs*" (Ezekiel 21:25-27 [30-32]; Genesis 49:10), the Messiah of Israel. Ryken reflects upon the comparison of the two prophets when he states the following:

> In this case, Ezekiel makes the meaning clear. Like Jeremiah, Ezekiel prophesied that the monarchy would come to an end: "O profane and wicked prince of Israel, whose day has come, whose time of punishment has reached its climax, this is what the Sovereign LORD says: "Take off the turban, remove the crown" (Ezek 21:25-26). Yet Ezekiel warned that the crown should not be thrown away! A king was still coming, the rightful heir to the throne of David. The crown would "not be restored until he comes to whom it rightfully belongs; to him I [God] will give it" (v. 27). God was saving the crown for Christ.[1677]

What is definitely known is that Coniah, according to Jeremiah, was to be childless whereas Ezekiel only stated that the crown would be removed until he comes to whom it belongs. However, it appears that Coniah adopted the sons of Neri (Luke 3:27; Matthew 1:12) or he had a daughter that married Neri, for Scripture records that he had seven sons (1 Chronicles 3:17). The following statement from the Babylonian cuneiform tablet spoke of him and five of his (adopted) sons:

> Write this man down as childless: According to 1 Chr 3:17 Jehoiachin had seven sons, and Babylonian cuneiform tablets, published in 1939, list the ration

---

[1676] Philip Graham Ryken, *Jeremiah and Lamentations: From Sorrow to Hope* (Wheaton, IL: Crossway Books, 2001), 331.

[1677] Ryken, *Jeremiah and Lamentations: From Sorrow to Hope*, 331-332.

of oil allowed to *Iaukin*, king of *Iakuda* and his five sons. This would probably be in 592 B. C. (ANET, p. 308).[1678]

Not only did Coniah have seven sons, but five of them were living at the time of the recording of the Babylonian cuneiform tablet. One of his grandsons was Zerubbabel who became a governor under the authority of the Mede-Persian Empire over Judah, but was never king. Thus it is to be recorded that Coniah would be childless, for no one from his line would reign on the throne:

> The command to "record" relates to a register of citizens (cf. Isa 4:3); the figure is that of a census list.... Zerubbabel, grandson of Jehoiachin, though governor of Judah in 520 B.C. never ruled as king, nor did any other descendant of his.[1679]

There is a difference of understanding concerning the pronouncement that *Yahweh* made in stating that none of Coniah's immediate family would reign. First, some teach that the line of Coniah was not just cursed for the immediate future in relationship to his sons, but also that the line was permanently cursed to the time of Joseph the stepfather of *Yeshua*, thus making Joseph ineligible and not the legitimate heir, because of the curse, to reign on the throne of David. Even though he was a direct descendant from David, through Solomon, he was ineligible, thus making *Yeshua*, the adopted or legal son of Joseph, ineligible to someday reign on the throne of David, as the following author states:

> This is a very significant verse, for it means the end of the Solomonic line of succession. Up to this time, all the kings of Judah had been descendents of King Solomon, son of David. But with this man, that line of succession ended. No more was any man of that line allowed to rule on the throne of Judah. This affects the story of Jesus in the New Testament, for when you trace the genealogy of Joseph, the stepfather of Jesus, you discover that Joseph was the son of David through this man Coniah, or Jehoiachin, and thus had lost the right to sit on the throne of Judah.[1680]

The argument goes that *Yeshua* did not receive His right to rule through Joseph but received it from Miriam (Mary), who is also a direct descendant from David through Nathan the brother of Solomon, as is reflected below:

[1678] Douglas Rawlinson Jones, *The New Century Bible Commentary: Jeremiah* (Grand Rapids: Eerdmans, 1992), 295-296. James B. Pritchard, *The Ancient Near East: An Anthology of Text and Pictures*. (2 Vols. Princeton, NJ: Princeton University Press. 1958), 1:205.

[1679] Feinberg, *Jeremiah: A Commentary*, 160.

[1680] Ray C. Stedman, *Death of a Nation: Jeremiah* (Waco, TX: Word Books, 1976), 123-124.

But because he was the son of Mary, who was likewise a descendant of David through Nathan, a brother of Solomon, Jesus therefore had the right to the throne of David.[1681]

Arnold Fruchtenbaum goes to considerable lengths to prove this point in one of his books.[1682] The second line of argument is that the curse only refers to the immediate descendants of Coniah. This argument states that *Yeshua*, a descendant 14 generations later, does have the right to rule, as the following author implies:

When Jeremiah said that none of Jehoiachin's children would sit on the throne of David (22:30), he was talking about his immediate offspring. True, Jehoiachin's sons did not rule the people of God in Jerusalem (cf. 1 Chr 3:17-18). But the family line continued, and the rightful king did come to reign.[1683]

Both of these views have some positive features as well as some negative. The rest of the argument will be presented later when Zechariah 3:8 is discussed. That passage and a related Haggai passage present some very important information concerning Zerubbabel. In relationship to this passage, and in particular Matthew 1, they completely discount *Yeshua* as a Son of David for they say:

Considering the fact that Jesus did none of these, and considering the fact that Matthew 1 says that Jesus was not from Joseph, and therefore not from David, it becomes almost incredible that one could accept Jesus as the Messiah.[1684]

Their hatred for *Yeshua* blurs their judgment. They discount Miriam's (Mary's) genealogy in Luke 3 as nothing for as they said, women in Judaism do not carry genealogies. That is true, but what they totally ignore is the fact that the genealogy of Luke 3 is Miriam's (Mary's) father's genealogy, which made him a direct descendant of David, which makes Miriam (Mary) a direct descendant and makes *Yeshua* a legitimate heir and descendant to the throne, as a son of David. In observing Zechariah 12:10 this becomes even more dynamic, for indeed they will weep bitterly for *Yahweh* who is speaking (verse 1) as the one whom they pierced! Historically, that can only fit one person, *Yeshua*.

One further point, if *Yeshua*, being virgin born was to receive His right to rule from the Matthew 1 account, commonly called Joseph's genealogy, and if the curse on Coniah was only to his immediate sons as some state, then why did not God have Miriam (Mary) be born of Jacob (Matthew 1:16) instead of Heli (Luke 3:23) making *Yeshua* a direct descendant of the "royal line" from which the kings came? Realizing that this question is hypothetical and cannot be answered, we retain the thought of whether God had to avoid the "royal line" of Coniah. Why did God not have Mary born

---

[1681] Stedman, *Death of a Nation: Jeremiah*, 123-124.

[1682] Fruchtenbaum, *Messianic Christology*, 135-139.

[1683] Ryken, *Jeremiah and Lamentations: From Sorrow to Hope*, 331.

[1684] Levine, *You Take Jesus, I'll Take God: How To Refute Christian Missionaries,* 53.

in that "royal line" be the virgin spoken of in Isaiah 7:14? This issue will be answered later in this chapter as the Zechariah passages on the "*branch*" are discussed.

"*Write this man childless*" means he would have no children for his reign and the ruling Davidic Dynasty would be at this time in history finished. The word "*write*" is used for the official records as the following author presents:

> Record/write is used in relation to drawing up an official register of citizens (Num 11:26; 1 Chron 4:41; Psa 87:6; cf. Ezra 2:2-62; Neh 7:5-64).[1685]

Coniah did "*evil in the sight of the LORD.*" That is the epitaph and his legacy to Judah. *Yahweh* was finished with their wickedness. Since the days of King Manasseh all the kings of Judah had the same legacy; they did "*evil in the sight of the LORD.*" Only in the reign of Josiah was there a righteous, godly king who was a true example of a signet ring on the hand of *Yahweh*. Laetsch gives a brief statement as to the true character of Coniah in the following statement:

> Against Jehoiachin, here called Coniah. A young, lecherous prince, ruled by his passions, entirely unfit to be the ruler of God's people. "Signet ring," used for sealing important documents, very highly valued and guarded against possible loss. Even if Jehoiachin had been so valuable an instrument, God would have rejected him (vv. 24-27).[1686]

Coniah was not fit to rule because he was corrupt and because of the ungodly leadership that went back to the days of Manasseh when the people were also corrupted. Brueggemann states that "biblical tradition" dealt with Coniah two ways:

> Jehoiachin receives two distinct treatments in Biblical tradition. On the one hand, he bears the hopes of this people and keeps the thread of the royal promise alive; on the other, he is clearly helpless and historically impotent, as he has no chance to act on the hopes he embodies. In this passage Jehoiachin is not a figure of hope. He is only an object of deep pity.[1687]

The first half of Brueggemann's statement raises one final issue before we move into Jeremiah 23. There were other "prophets" besides Jeremiah that were speaking to the people, but they were false prophets speaking in *Yahweh's* name. Jehoiachin or Coniah carried with him the hopes and dreams of the kingdom being re-established. In the fourth year of the reign of Zedekiah, the uncle of Jeconiah, the false prophet Hananiah, the son of Azur from Gibeon (Jeremiah 28:1), prophesied in the name of *Yahweh* that *Yahweh* had broken the yoke of Babylon and that two primary things would happen within two years. First, in verse 3 he states that the vessels from the temple that had been taken by

---

[1685] John L. Mackay, *Jeremiah: A Mentor Commentary* (2 vols. Ross-shire, Scotland: Christian Focus Publications, 2004), 2:45.

[1686] Theo Laetsch, *Bible Commentary: Jeremiah* (St Louis: Concordia, 1952), 187.

[1687] Walter Brueggemann, *A Commentary on Jeremiah: Exile and Homecoming* (Grand Rapids: Eerdmans, 1998), 203.

Nebuchadnezzar would be returned. Secondly, in verse 4 Jeconiah himself would be returned with the captives. The rest of Jeremiah 28 involves the dialog between Hananiah and Jeremiah, as well as the LORD speaking to Jeremiah. Was there a precedent for the words of Hananiah and the hopes of the people in history that would give rise to the false prophet's words? The answer is yes. In 2 Chronicles 33:10-13 the following is recorded:

> (10) The LORD spoke to Manasseh and his people, but they would not pay heed, (11) So the LORD brought against them the officers of the army of the king of Assyria, who took Manasseh captive in (with) manacles (hooks), bound him in fetters, and led him off to Babylon. (12) In his distress, he entreated the LORD his God and humbled himself greatly before the God of his fathers. (13) He prayed to Him, and He granted his prayer, heard his plea, and returned him to Jerusalem to his kingdom. Then Manasseh knew that the LORD alone was God.

Manasseh was the great, great, great grandfather of Jeconiah, and here is the historical precedent for the hopes of the people and for the words of Hananiah. Notice Manasseh was carried off to Assyria as a captive, released and restored to his kingdom (2 Chronicles 33:1-20). However, much had changed since the days of Manasseh. First of all Manasseh repented; the sons and grandson of Josiah did not, at least there is no biblical record. A casual reading of Jeremiah will show the complete wickedness of the people, but in Jeremiah 15:4 *Yahweh* states the core reason for the complete destruction of Jerusalem and Judah with no hope of a return for King Jeconiah:

> And I will cause them to be removed into all kingdoms of the earth, because of Manasseh the son of Hezekiah king of Judah, for that which he did in Jerusalem (King James Version).

On a surface reading it appears that *Yahweh* has cursed Coniah from any future ruling of the kingdom either by his sons or their descendants. This particular line of David has been canceled, but the covenant of David has not been canceled. In Jeremiah 23:1-2 *Yahweh* moved to a more general condemnation of the leadership of Judah. In these verses the leadership, other than the king, is brought into view; they were corrupt (Ezekiel 34:1-6) and *Yahweh* would visit upon them their sins. The following author describes the situation:

> The "shepherds" on whom Jeremiah pronounced woe are not only kings but all the leaders of Judah (v. 1). They were the civil leaders and also the spiritual leaders, the prophets and priests.... In Zedekiah's reign the court officials exercised inordinate influence on policy because of his weakness (cf. 38:5). The leaders were guilty of gross dereliction of duty. By oppression and shedding innocent blood, they destroyed the flock; those who were not destroyed were scattered to wander without protection. So the leaders were guilty of the very things the shepherds are charged with preventing. By leading the nation into idolatry and so into the Babylonian captivity, the leaders had scattered the

people. Moreover, contrary to the duty of shepherds to lead and feed the flock, they had driven the flock away. The doom on the people would not leave their leaders unscathed. By a play on words, Jeremiah uses the double sense of the Hebrew word *paqad* ("to care for," "to chastise"): the shepherds had "not bestowed care on" the flock; God would "bestow punishment on" them in judgment (v. 2).[1688]

A parallel passage for these two verses comes from a contemporary of Jeremiah, Ezekiel, who was taken into captivity in Babylon. Ezekiel (34:1-6) lays out in more detail the sins of the shepherds of Judah. Notice in Jeremiah 23:2 that the LORD has a personal interest and attachment to the people of Israel, for they are very special to Him; He refers to them as "*my people*," and "*my flock.*" Because the shepherds have scattered the flock, now *Yahweh* Himself will drive them away, but God's love for them is still very evident in His language as this author states:

> Not so surprisingly, God is now the one who is said to have driven Israel away. God will gather "my flock" (see 29:14; 31:8, 10; 32:37). Note God's repeated language for the people: "my flock" (vv. 2-3; see 13:17); "my people" (v. 2; over forty times in Jeremiah!); and "the sheep of my pasture" (v. 1; see the divine "my" in 12:7-14). The personalism of these references demonstrates a special relationship between God and people; God claims these people as God's own.[1689]

Because of His love for the flock, He is requiring accountability of the shepherds for their scattering of the flock of God. Not only had the king done evil in the sight of the LORD, but the political and religious leaders were just as guilty, and the LORD would require accountability of them. The leadership were the shepherds and the people were the sheep. In Jeremiah 23:3 after the evil shepherds have scattered the sheep, the LORD God states, "*I will gather*" that which was scattered. He will gather as a shepherd the people, as the following author states:

> The verb "gather" is a precise resolution of "scatter" in verses 1-2a, and stays with the metaphor of sheep.[1690]

It is also noteworthy to observe that the literal scattering of the people took place. Just as there is to be a literal regathering of the people back to the same land that was given to them in Abraham, contrary to the replacement theologians, it is Israel that is regathered and not the Church. Now God Himself will gather the people and be their shepherd as Feinberg states:

[1688] Feinberg, *Jeremiah: A Commentary*, 161.

[1689] Fretheim, *Smyth & Helwys Bible Commentary: Jeremiah*, 325.

[1690] Walter Brueggemann, *A Commentary on Jeremiah: Exile and Homecoming* (Grand Rapid: Eerdmans, 1998), 206.

Just as the scattering of the people was literal, so will the regathering be (v.3). The promise of restoration presupposes the Exile. The return from dispersion had already been announced in 3:15-18. Now it is God himself who does the work of the true shepherd, regathering the sheep from all countries. Here a worldwide dispersion is in view, not just in Assyria and Babylon. What the shepherds did in driving the people away is now attributed to the Lord because he ultimately carried out the penalty brought on the people by their own sins and by the sins of their leaders (shepherds). The people will be returned to their own pasture. Moreover, God will replace the faithless shepherds with faithful ones (v.4).[1691]

Coniah is an unworthy king for the nation of Judah (Israel) and now Jeremiah proclaims the sin and incompetence of the "shepherds" with the very serious word "woe." In verses 3-4 after the flock is gathered, the LORD will place his shepherds over the flock of Israel and will feed them, and they will fear no more, neither will they lack anything. All this sets the context for the verses to be studied in Jeremiah 23:5-6.

The first word in Jeremiah 23:5 is the word הִנֵּה or *behold*. Here the LORD is asking for the attention of the people for He has something to say to them, something for them to see or understand. It carries the idea of demanding attention, to look at or to see in emphasizing information.[1692] The next phrase is equally important in that "*the days are coming.*" *Yahweh* is making a declaration, and He wants them to take notice that in contrast to the time of Zedekiah there are days coming, the days of Messiah,[1693] that will be totally different than the days of Zedekiah (sin and unrighteousness) and the destruction of Jerusalem and Judah. Jeremiah uses a play on words with his description of the "*righteous Branch*" on one hand and the meaning of Zedekiah on the other hand. *Zedekiah* means "*Yahweh* is righteousness." A future king will be righteous in character while Zedekiah was not righteous is character. *Yahweh* will raise up unto David a righteous Branch. Bear in mind the line of David from Coniah on has just been cursed by the LORD and now *Yahweh* is going to raise up unto David a righteous Branch which the following author points out is different:

> The fact that Jeremiah has predicted that no son of Jehoiachin shall inherit the throne, means there must be another growth from the royal tree, or, as we should say, another 'branch.' The fact that Jehoiakim was condemned for not doing justice and righteousness, means that the prophet looks for a guardian and exemplification of righteousness. Crown prince – maybe – but a Branch who is the embodiment of righteousness.[1694]

Since Coniah's line is cursed, *Yahweh* is going to cause to sprout from the royal line a branch which has an altogether different character. That is something completely

---

[1691] Feinberg, *Jeremiah: A Commentary*, 161.

[1692] Harris, Archer, Jr. and Waltke, *Theological Wordbook of the Old Testament*, 1:220.

[1693] Kaiser, *The Messiah in the Old Testament*, 188.

[1694] Jones, *The New Century Bible Commentary: Jeremiah*, 299.

different for *Yahweh* has just spent 22 chapters telling Judah of their sin, unrighteousness, corruption and idolatry. In Isaiah 4:2 the "*branch*" is of *Yahweh* and not David. Here in Jeremiah 23:5-6 the "*branch*" is of David, but His character is righteousness. Somehow God is going to bypass the curse of Coniah so that He can "*raise unto David a righteous Branch.*" Here the "*Branch*" is united by Jeremiah 23:5-6 into both divine and human as will be seen shortly in verse 6. In Matthew's gospel he presents Messiah as the Son of David. Matthew wrote to the Jewish people where he presents to them a Jewish man from the line of David. There is a problem because of Coniah but that has already been partially answered. The rest of the answer will be given later in the chapter when Zechariah 3:8 is discussed. The Gospel of Matthew was aimed at a Jewish audience and it stressed Messiah's Davidic roots. Jeremiah's presentation of the Branch, the King of Righteousness, as both human and divine is presented by Frey:

> That this prediction belongs to the Messiah we have already seen. Now, in respect of his humanity, he is affirmed to be a branch raised up unto David; for, as man he was of the tribe of Judah, and of the household of David; but, with respect to his divinity, he is called Jehovah.[1695]

So the "*behold*" is for them to listen to what *Yahweh* is going to do in future days as He ties together the promises in the uniqueness of this "*Branch*" Who is both God and man. The following author connects this verse to the picture that God is painting from Genesis onward:

> "Behold!" A noteworthy event is being announced. "The days come," a common expression for the Messianic era, see Jer. 31:27-34, quoted in Heb 8:8-12; 10:16-17. This message is "an oracle of the LORD," the Covenant God, the God of the Amen (Isa 65:16; Rev 3:14), who will keep His word (2 Cor 1:20). This oracle points back to the promise given to David (2 Sam 7:3-5, 11-16, cp. 1 Chron 17:1-15). The promised Woman's Seed (Gen 3:15), the Seed of Abraham (Gen 22:18), was to be an offspring of David, a true human being, in order to be our substitute (Isa 53; Gal 4:4-5; Phil 2:6-8; Heb 2:9-18; 4:15; 5:7 9).[1696]

When this "*righteous Branch*" comes, Judah will be saved and Israel will dwell safely. After the captivity in post-exilic times the word "*Branch*" became a technical term used for the coming Son of David:

> In postexilic times the term [branch] became the classic technical one for the expected ideal king (Zech 3:8; 6:12).[1697]

[1695] Frey, *The Messiahship of Jesus,* 117.

[1696] Laetsch, *Bible Commentary: Jeremiah,* 189-190.

[1697] Thompson, *The New International Commentary on the Old Testament: The Book of Jeremiah,* 489.

What also became abundantly clear is that the *"Branch"* is symbolic of the Messiah because here the *"Branch"* is modifying the quality of a person and not of plants.[1698] So the net result is that Israel and Judah will be reunited into one nation, under one Whose reign will bring salvation, peace and security as Feinberg observes:

> Now Jeremiah dilates on the benefits that will come to Messiah's people from his reign. First, he will rule over a reunited nation; both Judah and Israel will be restored (cf. Ezek 37:19). Second, he will bring salvation to his people. The verb "saved" (*yasa*) denotes spiritual not physical deliverance (cf. same verb in Isa 45:22). Third, peace and security will characterize Messiah's righteous rule.[1699]

This *"righteous Branch"* will rule and reign and shall prosper, and He shall execute judgment and justice in the earth. That phrase implies that He will not do all of this only in Israel, but in the entire earth or all the Gentile nations. Jeremiah 23:6, is going to further define his statement by giving the people the name of this One, who has righteousness residing in Him, for this is what the people needed. Ryken points out that the *"righteous Branch"* would be a just king, safe king, righteous king. That is what the people needed, a righteous king, for neither their kings nor they themselves were righteous.[1700] This king or *"Branch"* is unique for no one among mankind has ever had righteousness as his character. Also the significance of *Yahweh* stating that name by which He will be called *"THE LORD OUR RIGHTEOUSNESS"* is completely unique to mankind, as was pointed out by a Jewish believer in the 17ᵗʰ century:

> "and this is the name wherewith he *fhall* be called, the Lord our *Righteoufnefs*." Well, ye know, my Hebrew Brethern, that this name of Jehovah, that is יהוה Lord, can not be given nor is it ever given, nor is it found written, but for the proper divine *effence*....yet when this name is written with this word יהוה Jehovah, it cannot be *allow'd otherwife* than Sacred, Holy and for Divine *Effence itfelf*. Then if the *Mefsiah* is called with this title of יהוה Jehovah, he *muft* be God *himfelf*, and not an ordinary man.... I *obferve alfo*, Brethren, that the prophet *Ifaiah fpeaking* of the *Mefsiah*, and of the names by which he is to be called, "wonderful, *Counfellor*, the mighty God, the *everlafting* Father, the Prince of peace. O grand titles among the *reft* אל נביר the mighty God, *fpirituality* אל God, & Humanity *conjoyn'd* נביר (deriving from the name rbn which *fignifies* Man.) *Obferve* that ye *fhall* not find in all the *facred* Scriptures any particular *perfon* intituled אל God (with this word) only the *Mefsias*, which was to come, for whom had been *fpoken* all the Prophecies which have been in him fulfilled; thus then the *Mefsias* is not only to be

---

[1698] Feinberg, *Jeremiah: A Commentary,* 162.

[1699] Feinberg, *Jeremiah: A Commentary*, 162-163.

[1700] Ryken, *Jeremiah and Lamentations: From Sorrow to Hope*, 341.

corporeal, as ye believe, but corporeal and *fpiritual* both, God and man. [1701]
[This is old English, where the *"f" is an "s"*].

This one is not just a man as Rabbi Scialitti points out, He is the God/man. There is another reason why the people needed a *"righteous Branch;"* for 22 chapters Jeremiah laid out meticulously their sin and unrighteousness, as shown in this next statement:

There is another reason the people of God needed a Righteous Branch. True, their king was unrighteous. But they also needed a righteous king because they were unrighteous. For twenty-two chapters Jeremiah has documented the sins of God's people in careful dctail. They weie no more righteous than their kings were. They broke every one of God's commandments.

Back in chapter [Jer] 5, God promised that he would forgive his people if Jeremiah could find just one good man. The prophet searched high and low. He walked up the streets and down the alleys, but he could not find even one man to be righteous for the people. [1702]

Some more liberal Christian scholars have translated or interpreted the phrase "THE LORD OUR RIGHTEOUSNESS" as "The LORD is Our Righteousness," even as the Harkavy version and *The Jewish Study Bible* state. That changes the whole complexion of this phrase. It changes it from being the name and character of the *"Branch"* to being a mere description of the LORD. The following author uses it as a description of the LORD:

This king will embody righteousness, to which his very name will attest. It is perhaps intentional and ironic that the "real king" anticipated is called "Yahweh is our righteousness" (*Yahweh tsidqenu*), while the last king of the line up to 587 is Zedekiah ("Yahweh is righteous"). The coming king will be genuine "righteousness" (*tsedaqah*), whereas the remembered King Zedekiah is not at all an embodiment of righteousness. The king bore the name; the coming king will embody the reality. [1703]

Other authors are more pointed about this interpretation. *The Jewish Study Bible*, the Harkavy Version, the Leeser Version and the English translation of the Masoretic text all use the verb "is" to get away from the intended interpretation of the passage. The fact is *Yahweh* is righteous, but what Jeremiah is stating is that the promised Branch, the Messiah, Son of David is the very embodiment of righteousness, for He is the God/man. Walter Kaiser shows that the verb "to be" should not be used:

Now let's examine Jeremiah 23 in particular, for the Branch here is given a distinctive name, and that name is just plain outright a divine name: "The LORD Our Righteousness." It is not "The LORD is Our Righteousness," for it

---

[1701] Rabbi Mofes Scialitti, *A Letter Written to the Jewes* (London: Thom Tanner, 1663), 6-7.
[1702] Ryken, *Jeremiah and Lamentations: From Sorrow to Hope*, 342.
[1703] Brueggemann, *A Commentary on Jeremiah: Exile and Homecoming*, 207.

does not have the verb "to be" in the middle there. Instead, this is the name he will be called: "The LORD Our Righteousness." I would understand this to mean that his name refers to his character; to speak of his name is to speak of his character and the nature by which he will be known. The nature and character of the Branch, who will be born in the line of seed of Abraham, Isaac, Jacob, and David, will be divine. For he will be called "The LORD Our Righteousness." Yahweh, Jehovah, LORD (spelled with capital letters) denotes his divine nature; 'Our Righteousness' denotes his divine work on our behalf. In this name we have both his divine nature and his divine work: The LORD Our Righteousness.[1704]

Rabbis, with some Christian scholars, try to avoid the intended meaning by inserting the "to be" verb, thus making it a statement about God rather than the coming "Branch," the Messiah. Kaiser continues by giving a three pronged argument in substantiating the reading of Jeremiah 23:6, saying it needs to be translated THE LORD OUR RIGHTEOUSNESS. He appeals to the Isaiah 4:2 passage, the fact that God names Him, and that the Hebrew Masoretic text does not have the verb "to be":

1. The "righteous Branch" (*semah saddiq*) promised by Jeremiah was already promised by Isaiah 4:2 as the "Branch of the LORD" (*semah YHVH*), a genitive of source or origin that declares his divine roots. Since what lies behind the idea of "branch" or "sprout" also appeared in 2 Samuel 23:5 ("Will not God cause to sprout [*yasmiah*] all my salvation and all [my] desire? – pers. Tr. and emphasis) and in Psalm 132:17 ("I will make a horn sprout [*asmiah*] for David; I will set up a lamp for my Messiah" – pers. Tr), Jeremiah is certainly developing an accepted concept, not a new one.

2. The one speaking here is not an ordinary human being, as is true when other symbolic names are given in the OT, but this is Yahweh himself. In addition, note that the introductory formulas that lead up to the name are unique. Rather than saying, "Call his name" (cf. Gen 16:11, 13; 21:3; 22:14; Ex 17:15), or "Call him" (cf. Gen 16:14; 33:20; 35:7; Judg 6:24), or even "His name will be" (cf. Gen 17:5b; Ezek 48:35), the text of Jeremiah 23:6 states two things: "This is [his] name (i.e., his name will describe the very nature and essence of the "Branch"), and "This is the name by which he will be called" (i.e., the name is given to him *by the Lord God himself*).

3. Finally, the tradition of the Masoretes indicates that the best translation is, "The LORD Our Righteousness," because the conjunctive accent called a *meraka* under Yahweh connects the word with *sidqenu* ("our righteousness") without interjecting the verb "is" between the two nouns. Moreover, the dividing line (*paseq*) in the Masoretic punctuation after Yahweh indicates that "our righteousness" should not be regarded as a predicate of Yahweh (i.e., "The Lord *is* our righteousness"); instead, "Our

---

[1704] Kaiser, *The Christian and the "Old" Testament*, 215.

Righteousness" is a second name. Yahweh then denotes his nature; Our Righteousness signifies his work. This Masoretic reading is all the more remarkable when one remembers that the Christian Church had been appealing to this passage to demonstrate the deity of Jesus for centuries.[1705]

Here Kaiser connects the name of the Branch of David with the Branch of *Yahweh* in Isaiah 4:2 where he also draws upon the words of David in 2 Samuel 23:5 and the psalmist in Psalm 132:17. *Yahweh* Himself calls this *"Branch"* by this name, *"THE LORD OUR RIGHTEOUSNESS."* But perhaps his most significant observation is that the Masoretic in the Hebrew text (not the English) does not have the "to be" verb in the passage. This makes this passage very unique, for all of David's descendants had to confess their sinfulness, with David, as Laetsch observes:

> "A Righteous Branch." All other descendants of David had to confess with him Psa 51:5, and plead Psa 143:2. This Branch is righteous; as already the Lord had called Him "the Righteous One, My Servant (Isa 53:11), because He was sinless (Isa 53:9; cp Matt 3:17; 17:5; John 8:46; I Pet 1:19; 2:22; I John 3:5; Heb 7:26). This was not merely an acquired righteousness. God raised Him as a Righteous Branch. Righteousness is His very essence, His nature and being.[1706]

The next two verses in Jeremiah reference an annual event that has been practiced by the Jewish people for over 3500 years (Exodus 12:14, 24). It is the Passover Seder celebration when they are to remember their deliverance from Egypt and the Exodus many centuries ago. God did many supernatural acts to obtain Israel's freedom from Egypt and throughout the wilderness journey of 40 years. Yet in these verses *Yahweh* uses the word *"Behold"* so they will remember how the LORD regathered them from the nations of the earth. The Exodus will pale into insignificance in comparison to this future return under the leadership of the *"righteous Branch"* as Feinberg expresses:

> The future restoration of the people will exceed anything in the past. It will surpass the deliverance from Egypt. The Exodus (v. 7) will pale into insignificance in comparison with the future ingathering of the nation from world-wide dispersion (v. 8). The inauguration of the new Exodus cannot be equated with the return of Israel under Cyrus in the last decades of the sixth century B.C. (cf. Isa 11:11-12).[1707]

In Deuteronomy 18:15-18 the LORD said through Moses that there will be a prophet *"like"* Moses who will come, and Israel is to obey Him and give Him their utmost attention. For indeed this One will be *"like"* Moses in that He will lead Israel to redemption and freedom to the Promised Land. The uniqueness of Moses (Numbers 12:5-8) was that he spoke to the LORD face to face and beheld the very form of God. This Righteous Branch is the One who is *"like"* Moses, for He embodies

---

[1705] Kaiser, *The Messiah in the Old Testament,* 187-188.

[1706] Laetsch, *Bible Commentary: Jeremiah,* 190.

[1707] Feinberg, *Jeremiah: A Commentary,* 163.

RIGHTEOUSNESS in His very character, being and essence. He, as the Second Person of the plural unity of *Elohim*, has from eternity past spoken with the Father face to face and has beheld the Father's glory, because the Father's glory is also His own. He will deliver and redeem Israel from the nations of the earth. This one who is the "*Branch*," who is Himself RIGHTEOUSNESS, will come first to deal with the sin of mankind on the "Tree," for as Isaiah said, "the work of righteousness shall be peace" (Isaiah 32:17). Sin had to be dealt with before He, as the "*righteous Branch*," could come and fulfill the Abrahamic and Davidic Covenants. However, Rabbinic Judaism has for 2000 years rejected the "*son of David*" Who is the "*righteous Branch.*"

The Jewish people today ask, "If *Yeshua* is the Messiah, where is the peace?" First, there must be peace with *Yahweh*, for sin has separated mankind from Him since Adam and Eve fell into sin in the garden of Eden (Genesis 3) which separated a holy God from sinful human race; that must be dealt with first! That reconciliation of mankind is the purpose of the suffering passages of the Messiah like Isaiah 53 that Jewish people reject with "*echad*" (one) voice. To use rabbinic terms "Messiah ben Joseph" is not the first of two messiahs.' Those suffering passages relate to the first of two comings when Messiah will come to first bring peace with God and then a second time the same Messiah Who is now called "Messiah ben David" will come to restore Israel. But that second coming will only come upon Israel's confession of their sin against rejecting Him when He came the first time (Leviticus 26:40-42; Hosea 5:15; Matthew 23:39). This Righteous Branch is the one spoken of in Psalms 2 and 72. When righteousness reigns, prosperity in the Land will come, but prosperity will not come until Israel as a nation repents for the sin of rejecting the "*seed of the woman*," the "*prophet like unto Moses*," the "*son of David*" sent to her as Messiah *Yeshua*.

THE BRANCH OF DAVID'S LINE
Jeremiah 33:15-18

(15) In those days and at that time, I will raise up a true branch of David's line, and he shall do what is just and right in the land. (16) In those days Judah shall be delivered and Israel shall dwell secure. And this is what she shall be called: "The LORD is our Vindicator [Righteousness]." (17) For thus said the LORD: There shall never be an end to **men** of David's line who sit upon the throne of the House of Israel. (18) Nor shall there ever be an end to the line of the Levitical priests before Me, of those who present burnt offerings and turn the meal offering to smoke and perform sacrifices.

In verse 14 Jeremiah states "*Behold, the days come*" and in verse 15 "*In those days*," which all relate to the time of Israel's salvation, deliverance and restoration, when the Messiah, the Righteous Branch will come. This passage also repeats the promise of the LORD concerning the Righteous Branch from 23:5. However, verse 17 in the Jewish Bible quoted above has one very important word mistranslated to remove the intended meaning. The passage above states that David's line will never lack men, but that is not what the Hebrew states. The Hebrew used אִישׁ, means man, not men. אִישׁ in the Hebrew text is in the singular, not in the plural. David's throne will never lack a man, singular, for the *"righteous Branch,"* the *"Branch"* of David, is also the *"branch of Yahweh"* (Isaiah 4:2) who is the incarnation of the Second Person of the plural unity of *Elohim*. There is only one Branch of Righteousness, not many. The word is also used to differentiate, from a sexual distinction, between man and woman.

This passage reveals more information, for not only will the throne of David never lack a man, but verse 18 says that neither the Levites nor priests will lack a אִישׁ [man]. This is not the idea of singular or plural but that of sexual distinction, for women never served as priests. In these promises of *Yahweh* He also refers to day and night as continuing; so will *Yahweh's* covenant continue as Kaiser states:

> The prediction in Jeremiah 33:15-16 repeats 23:5-6, which we have already treated. But this repetition adds a good deal more to what the earlier text reported. For just as David will never lack a man to sit on his throne forever, so the priests and the Levites, who serve at the altar and in God's house of worship, will never be without a representative to fulfill this function (33:17). So certain is God of this promise that it can only be broken if God's covenant with day and night can be broken (vv. 20-21, 25-26). However, all one has to do is to look outside. If one can see day or night coming and going in their normal rotation, then one had better believe that God is still maintaining his covenant with David, the priests, and the Levites.

> Thus, the royal line and the priestly role will continue in the coming days when the Messiah himself appears. God's covenant with David first appeared in 2 Samuel 7:12-16, whereas his covenant with Levi was probably first made with Phinehas, the grandson of Aaron, in Numbers 25:13 and was repeated in Malachi 2:4-5, 8.[1708]

This passage on the Righteous Branch references two covenants of God, the Davidic Covenant and the Abrahamic Covenant from which it comes. Coupled with that is the covenant that God had also made with the priests and the Levites. Jeremiah 33:14-26 ties together these covenants and the fulfillment of them with the Branch of Righteousness. This *"Branch"* is the fulfillment of God's promises to Abraham and David in one person, the Messiah.

Before moving on to passages in Zechariah, one other issue that has troubled some scholars is that in verse 16 the city of Jerusalem is also called *"The LORD Our righteousness."* In the text of verse 16 Jeremiah used תִּוָּשֵׁעַ, meaning *"she will be saved,"* using a verb to speak directly of Jerusalem in the third-person feminine. Jerusalem here is called *"The LORD our righteousness"* because of its king of Righteousness; she will embody righteousness because the Messiah, the Branch, The LORD OUR RIGHTEOUSNESS bestows it on her. For the first time in history,

---

[1708] Kaiser, *The Messiah in the Old Testament,* 191.

Jerusalem will be known as the City of Righteousness which goes along with her name City of Peace. Jerusalem will only be the great city of peace when the Righteous Branch takes the throne of David as *THE LORD OUR RIGHTEOUSNESS*. The view of the name of Jerusalem is reflected in the statements of the following two authors:

> The title is transferred from the Messiah to the city of Jerusalem. The significance of this is variously assessed. But if the title referred to the fact that the Messianic king would be the very embodiment of the truth that the LORD is the one who provides and constitutes all that is involved in righteousness for his people, then the restored and renewed city of Jerusalem embodies that truth as well. The city is renamed because the character of the ruler who is provided for her by the LORD conveys a new status to the city as his capital. Such a variation in what Jerusalem will be called is a device that is frequently employed to bring out the change that will occur when the LORD looks on her with favour once more ([Jer] 3:17; Isa 62:2-4; Ezek 48:35; Zech 8:3).[1709]

> Salvation and safety are in store for Judah and Jerusalem because of the presence of justice and righteousness personified. The name given the Messiah in [Jer] 23:6 is here given to Jerusalem.... Most scholars agree that the name "THE LORD OUR RIGHTEOUSNESS" refers to Jerusalem. She can have the same name as the Messiah because she reflects that righteousness the Messiah bestows on her. Jerusalem will then be the embodiment of the nation's ideal in the Messiah. The city will be marked by righteousness (cf. 2 Cor 5:21).... Jerusalem will be called by his name because she will partake of his nature, which has been graciously imparted to her. She has the same name as Messiah because of the mystical oneness between them.[1710]

The summary of these two sections (Jeremiah 22:24-30; 23:1-8) of verses emphasize two aspects of the words of the LORD in relation to the Branch. First, in Jeremiah 23:5 the humanity of the Son of David is emphasized; and secondly, His divinity is referenced as none other than THE LORD OUR RIGHTEOUSNESS. The Righteous Branch is the personification of the LORD Himself, the Second Person of the plural unity of *Elohim*. This is the one who appeared to Abraham, Jacob, Moses, Joshua and Gideon as the Messenger of the LORD. He also is the *Shechinah* that appeared to Israel in the wilderness and Who resided in the Holy of Holies in the tabernacle and later the temple, as well as the "angel" that went with them (Exodus 23:20; 32:34). This *"righteous Branch"* will be the "son of David" who will save Judah and Israel for His very essence is righteousness. That is why in Psalms 2 and 72 He can rule upon Zion in righteousness for He Himself is the personification of righteousness. He is not given a name that He could not live up to as was Zedekiah whose name meant *"the LORD is righteousness."* This Branch is Righteousness.

[1709] Mackay, *Jeremiah: A Mentor Commentary*, 2:278.
[1710] Feinberg, *Jeremiah: A Commentary*, 235-236.

MY SERVANT THE BRANCH
Zechariah 3:8

Hearken well, O High Priest Joshua, you and your fellow priests sitting before you! For those men are a sign that I am going to bring My servant the Branch.

In studying this text it became apparent that there are two views on this verse as to the identity of the *"Branch."* One view looks to the time period of Zechariah for the identity of the *"Branch"* and the other looks to a person who will fulfill it in the future. One very important element in this discussion will be the discussion from Jeremiah 22 and 23. What was learned there is that not one of Jeconiah's descendants would sit upon the throne of David. But *Yahweh* would raise up to David a *"righteous Branch"* and His name, His character, His essence is THE LORD OUR RIGHTEOUSNESS.

What some authors have attempted to do is to identify the *"Branch"* in Zechariah 3:8 as Zerubbabel, which means "seed of Babylon." Zerubbabel's name was Babylonian and he was the new Jewish governor of the returned captives under the leadership of Ezra. Zerubbabel was the grandson of Jeconiah but, as will be seen, he was not a physical descendant of Jeconiah. So for him to be the *"Branch"* puts an unbearable burden on Scripture. All recent Jewish scholars, that is from the last several hundred years, and some Christian scholars refer to *"My servant the BRANCH"* as Zerubbabel as stated in the following:

> In Zechariah's time, hopes for the culmination of such a promise rested with one person, the returned Davidic heir, Zerubbabel. This sentiment is also attested in Hag 2:23, a text that emphasizes the political future of the Davidic scion. [1711]

One thing is true; the hopes of the people would have been with Zerubbabel since he was an immediate heir, although not the physical heir to the throne of David. However, if Zerubbabel was the *"Branch,"* it conflicts with the other *"Branch"* passages in Isaiah 4:2 (2 Samuel 23:5; Psalm 132:17); Jeremiah 23:5-6; 33:15, for he never became the king, just a governor, nor did he fulfill the *"Branch"* passages. After that the royal line of David disappears from the *Tanakh* and does not resurface until the New Covenant in Matthew 1. The following author refers to the "sign" issue of verse 8 and the difficulty that some have concerning the two crowns that Zechariah was asked to make (Zechariah 6:11):

> Haggai, the messenger of the LORD, Zechariah, a messenger of the LORD, and potentially Joshua, the high priest, are a sign that the LORD is about to bring the Branch whom the LORD calls, 'my servant.' The high priest, Joshua, is about to be joined by the civil authority, the Branch (Zerubbabel), who will be the subject of the next scene. Haggai, the messenger of the LORD, has already

---

[1711] David L. Peterson, *The Old Testament Library: Haggai and Zechariah 1-8* (Philadelphia: Westminster Press, 1984), 209-210.

referred to Zerubbabel as 'my servant' (2:23). Furthermore, there seems to be a play on words in relation to Zerubbabel's name 'seed of Babylon' and 'branch,' which can also be translated 'shoot' or 'sprout.' What the LORD is about to bring is the governor, 'the seed of Babylon,' who is about to shoot or sprout as the governor of Judah. That Zerubbabel appears nowhere in the scenes as a character in Zechariah's world [sic]. He is only about to come and to begin growth as governor. Although 'branch' is used for a future Davidic monarch in some texts outside the Twelve (e.g. Jer 23:5), Haggai always designates Zerubbabel by the Persian term of 'governor' (1:1, 14; 2:2, 21).[1712]

The text of Zechariah 3:8 gave Joshua, the High Priest and the priests seated before him as a sign, not Haggai and Zechariah! Nor is the civil authority (Zerubbabel) about to join the religious authority (Joshua) in the text. The reason for scholars seeing two authorities coming together is because of the fact the Zechariah was instructed by the LORD to make two crowns (Zechariah 6:11); this will be addressed when the Zechariah 6:12 passage is discussed. Also, to stretch Zerubbabel, a Babylonian name, as the *"seed," "shoot," "sprout"* as the biblical Hebraic *"Branch"* is completely improper. The LORD used the historical context of the building of the second temple as a backdrop to speak of *"My servant the Branch"* as a future *"son of David"* who would come. One more quotation on the alleged combination of civil and religious authorities:

> The high priest and his fellows were typical of the righteous Branch to come. This is the first introduction of the Branch by Zechariah. Both Isaiah (4:2; 11:1-10) and Jeremiah (23:5; 33:15) had introduced the Branch who was to come. He would be a descendant of David and a servant of Jehovah. In Him the priesthood and kingship through Zerubbabel (Hag 2:23) would be combined and made complete.[1713]

If Hailey had said "Messiah, the Branch," instead of "Zerubbabel," his statement would have been accurate. At this point it is needful to go to a contemporary of Zechariah, the prophet Haggai, who made a prophecy which implicates Zerubbabel as the civil leader being understood by some as the Branch, with the signet ring being restored to him and the Davidic line being brought back in favour with the LORD. The passage is Haggai 2:23:

> On that day – declares the LORD of Hosts – I will take you, O My servant Zerubbabel son of Shealtiel – declares the LORD – and make you as a signet; for I have chosen you – declares the LORD of Hosts.

This passage is not without its problems, as it is a difficult passage. But the problems are not insurmountable. What is clearly recognizable is that the time period that Haggai spoke of would be the time of the coming of the Messiah, as Kaiser states:

[1712] Edgar W. Conrad, *Zechariah* (Sheffield, England: Sheffield Academic Press, 1999), 95.

[1713] Hailey, *A Commentary on the Minor Prophets*, 336.

For the second time on December 18, 520 B.C., God spoke to His servant. Using the language of 2:6-9, Zerubbabel was warned that "[God] will shake heaven and earth" (2:21). This shake-up did not refer to any impending revolt that would disrupt the Persian empire; disruptive revolts had occurred in 521 B.C., and order had already been restored by the time this message came to God's people. No, this shake-up was to be an eschatological one to occur in connection with the coming of the Lord.[1714]

Arnold Fruchtenbaum, in his tape series on the Minor Prophets, reflects the same conclusion on this passage in Haggai 2:20-23.[1715] The timing is not the problem. The problem comes because Haggai appears to address Zerubbabel directly and he also makes reference to the signet ring. Before dealing with the signet ring, another issue needs to be addressed. Pausing here as students of the *Tanakh*, we must explain an important issue in relationship to the genealogy of *Yeshua*, the Messiah. This issue that becomes very important in answering objections of anti-missionaries is that *Yeshua* is not the rightful heir to the throne of David.

Genealogical Record of Messiah

In reviewing all the Scriptures (1 Chronicles 3:17-19; Matthew 1:12-13; Luke 3:27) that relate to the generation before and after Zerubbabel, there seems to be a crossover between the lines of Nathan and Solomon, both sons of David, with Zerubbabel being that crossover point. It was quickly noted that numerous authors avoid the discussion of the curse of Coniah and Zerubbabel as a grandson of Jeconiah. However, several authors offer explanations that avoid the curse of Coniah and yet open the door for Zerubbabel to be the link, the direct heir to both lines of *Yeshua*'s genealogical line, from Miriam (Mary) and His stepfather Joseph. Walter Kaiser briefly shows how Zerubbabel is the link, yet avoids the curse by involving a possible adoption. Although adoption is not likely, Levirate Marriage law will bring about the answer below:

> Jehoiachin adopted the seven sons of Neri, a descendant of David from David's son Nathan. So it was that the line of David through Solomon terminated with Jehoiachin, but continued through Neri's son Shealtiel. But Shealtiel also died childless, so his brother Pediah had to perform the duty of Levirate Marriage (Deut 25:5-10) out of which Zerubbabel was born. Hence, Zerubbabel was the legal son of Shealtiel, but the actual son of Pediah, a descendant of King David.[1716]

What is so very interesting is that this fits if adoption was used. The line of Coniah is cursed, but Coniah adopts the seven sons of Neri, whose father and mother were probably killed in the destruction of Jerusalem. However, one of those sons, Shealtiel,

---

[1714] Kaiser, *The Communicator's Commentary: Micah – Malachi*, 279.

[1715] Arnold G. Fruchtenbaum, *Minor Prophets* (Tustin, CA: Ariel Press, n.d.), tape 12.

[1716] Kaiser, *The Communicator's Commentary: Micah – Malachi*, 253.

is childless at death and his brother Pediah performs the Levirate Marriage for his deceased brother Shealtiel by raising up a son named Zerubbabel to his brother Shealtiel. The New Covenant book of Luke (3:27), records from his [Luke's] research of temple records that Neri and his sons were descendants of Nathan, the brother of Solomon. So a crossover of family lines between Nathan and Solomon occurred with the birth of Zerubbabel. Upon Zerubbabel lay the hopes of the Jewish people who returned from the captivity, for here God, through Cyrus, designated Zerubbabel who is associated by adoption and Levirate Marriage laws to the kings of Judah. God has effectively bypassed the Coniah curse by using Zerubbabel, a legitimate heir to the throne of David and by making him governor of the province of Judah. Also Keil and Delitzsch have a similar explanation to answer the problem of Zerubbabel being a grandson of Jeconiah in this following lengthy quote:

> According to 1 Chron 3:19, Zerubbabel was a son of Pedaiah, a brother of Shealtiel. And…according to the genealogy in Luke 3:27, Shealtiel was not a son of either Assir or Jeconiah, but of Neri, a descendent of David through his son Nathan. These three divergent accounts, according to which Zerubbabel was (1) a son of Shealtiel, (2) a son of Pedaiah, the brother of Shealtiel, and a grandson of Assir or Jeconiah, (3) a son of Shealtiel and grandson of Neri, may be brought into harmony by means of the following combinations, if we bear in mind the prophecy of Jeremiah (22:30), that Jeconiah would be childless, and not be blessed with having one of his seed sitting upon the throne of David and ruling over Judah. Since this prophecy of Jeremiah was fulfilled, according to the genealogical table given by Luke, inasmuch as Shealtiel's father there is not Assir or Jeconiah, a descendent of David in the line of Solomon, but Neri, a descendent of David's son Nathan, it follows, that neither of the sons of Jeconiah mentioned in 1 Chron 3:17-18 (Zedekiah and Assir) had a son, but that the latter had only a daughter, who married a man of the family of her father's tribe, according to the law of the heiresses, Num 27:8; 36:8-9 – namely Neri, who belonged to the tribe of Judah and family of David. From this marriage sprang Shealtiel, Malkiram, Pedaiah, and others. The eldest of these took possession of the property of his maternal grandfather, and was regarded in laws as his (legitimate) son. Hence he is described in 1 Chron 3:17 as the son of Assir the son of Jeconiah, whereas in Luke he is described, according to his lineal descent, as the son of Neri. But Shealtiel also appears to have died without posterity, and simply to have left a widow, which necessitated a Levirate marriage on the part of one of the brothers (Deut 25:5-10; Matt 22:24-28). Shealtiel's second brother Pedaiah appears to have performed his duty, and to have begotten Zerubbabel and Shimei by this sister-in-law (1 Chron 3:19), the former of whom, Zerubbabel, was entered in the family register of the

deceased uncle Shealtiel, passing as his (lawful) son and heir, and continuing his family.[1717]

Keil and Delitzsch, along with Kaiser, present very similar accounts of the possible scenario to the genealogical question. A very good friend of mine, a Jewish believer, raised two objections. First, adoption was not a common practice in Judaism of the time, which is true. However, this is where Keil and Delitzsch's account would fit. Jeconiah possibly had a daughter (no sons) who married Neri who was a direct descendant of Nathan. However, that still does not account for the Babylonian cuneiform tablets that reference the five sons of Jeconiah.[1718] So the adoption scenario or the daughter of Jeconiah are the most likely possibilities. Secondly, my friend also said you have to be sure that the Zerubbabel mentioned in the Matthew and Luke accounts is the same Zerubbabel of Zechariah. I would question it if there was a difference between the Zerubbabel of the Zechariah account and the Matthew and Luke account. However, it is highly unlikely that there are two Zerubbabels because in both the Matthew and Luke account, Zerubbabel in both genealogies had the same father, Shealtiel, and the Hebrew text of Zechariah and Haggai numerous times when speaking of Zerubbabel also refers to Shealtiel as his father.

One further matter of importance is in reference to the arguments of the anti-missionaries in Rabbinic Judaism. They attempt to say that the birth record of *Yeshua* is not there and thus He cannot be the Messiah of Israel that was to come from the family of David. It is difficult to believe that anti-missionaries would even use this faulty argument, but then again the vast majority of Jewish people would not know the difference. Here is an argument from Chaim Picker,[1719] who knows better:

> To authenticate Jesus' Messiahship, his ancestry is traced to King David, through Joseph (Luke 1:27; 2:4). But this genealogy is invalid since Joseph was not Jesus' biological father. Some have attempted to reconcile this by suggesting that Joseph adopted Jesus. But Jewish law makes no provision for legal adoption nor can there be any substitution for the biological father in matters of descent. **Moreover, since Jesus was supposedly the "son of God," there could be no paternal line. The genealogy of Mary is not given because Hebrew royal lineage was paternal.** Paul likens Jesus to Melchizedek who was "without father or mother or genealogy" (Heb 7:3). **Is Paul** attempting to de-emphasize Jesus' genealogy? (Note: Mary's kinswoman Elizabeth is "of the daughters of Aaron" — a Levite (Luke 1:5, 36). **But of Mary's tribal origin**

[1717] Keil and Delitzsch, *Commentary on the Old Testament in Ten Volumes: Haggai,* 10:175-176.

[1718] James B. Pritchard, *The Ancient Near East: An Anthology of Text and Pictures* (2 vols. Princeton, NJ: Princeton University Press, 1958), 1:205.

[1719] Chaim Picker, grandson of an Orthodox cantor, left Judaism at an early age and embraced Christianity, subsequently presiding over a congregation. At the age of 30, he returned to the faith of his ancestors, becoming a Jewish educator and cantor. This statement comes from the back cover of his book "Make Us A God!"

we know nothing! For Jesus to descend from David, Mary would have to be of the tribe of Judah.[1720]

Before interacting with Chaim Picker's statement, look at one other response from another anti-missionary, Samuel Levine, as he references Micah 5:2 about the birth of *Yeshua*:

> There is a basic question altogether as to whether or not Jesus came from David in the first place. In Matthew chapter 1, there is an entire genealogy which purports to show that Jesus does indeed come from David. However, there is a very serious problem there, for the genealogy shows that Joseph, the husband of Mary was from David, but he was not the father of Jesus. What is the point of showing that Joseph is from David, if Joseph is not the father of Jesus?
>
> In fact, the genealogy of the New Testament proves that Jesus was not from David. Jesus is considered by the New Testament to be a child of God, who is not from the tribe of Judah, nor any other tribe. Jesus is therefore not the subject of Micah 5:1 or 2.[1721]

Both Levine and Picker are stating the same thing: *Yeshua* cannot be of David because Joseph was not His father; that Mary has no recorded genealogy, and God, *Yeshua*'s Father, is not of any of the tribes of Israel. The reason for the genealogy of Joseph is to clear up the Coniah problem (Jeremiah 22:24-30), which is dealt with in this chapter. For Levine to state that if *Yeshua* was a child of God and not of his father David and thus was not from the tribe of Judah is an absolutely absurd biased statement. *Yeshua*'s tribal and family descent comes from Miriam (Mary) His mother. Before this is discussed further an offensive statement by Levine is made:

> Now, one may or may not wish to believe that God had sex with Mary, but one thing is certain – Joseph was not the father of Jesus, according to Matthew.[1722]

This is a slanderous statement, pure and simple. True Bible believers never believed any such thing. But anti-missionaries are bent on the fact that the tri-unity of God comes from the early church, compromising their faith with the faith of pagan Gentile worshipers who believed that the gods had sex with women and had children born to them. Levine's statement is offensive to all denominations and branches of Christianity[1723] except for Mormons who are not Christians anyway but part of a cult. Levine continues his argument:

[1720] Picker, "*Make Us A God!*" *A Jewish Response to Hebrew Christianity: A Survival Manual For Jews,* 45.

[1721] Levine, *You Take Jesus, I'll Take God,* 35-36.

[1722] Levine, *You Take Jesus, I'll Take God,* 78.

[1723] Mormons are continually attempting to make themselves look like an denomination of Christianity. However, they are a cult riddled with false unbiblical doctrine. One of those false beliefs is that God had sex with Mary and Jesus was the result.

595

So the question remains – how could Jesus be the Messiah, which the Christians claim that he is, if his father was not from the descendents of David? God is not a descendent of David, and yet God was supposedly his father, so how could Jesus be the Messiah? After all, even the Christians agree that the Messiah must be from the family of David. Some Christians have answered this question in a most unusual fashion – they claim that Mary was from David! Of course, this answer is terrible, because there is no source for that.[1724]

If Levine and Picker would have done unbiased research, they both would not have made such unscholarly false statements. Luke 3 is the genealogy of Mary (Miriam) for her father's name is Heli. If the two genealogies of Matthew and Luke are compared, it becomes quickly apparent that they are distinctly different. Two separate family lines are given, which both go back to King David; Matthew 1 was Joseph's and Luke 3 was Miriam's. So in human descent, *Yeshua* received His tribal and family identity from Miriam the daughter of Heli (Luke 3:23). Arnold Fruchtenbaum deals with this issue clearly in his tape series on "The Life of Messiah" as well as in his manuscript (#25) called "Christ's Right to David's Throne" where he states the following:

> The question is suppose someone like Luke was doing research and picked a genealogical tablet or scroll, how could he tell by reading it whether the genealogy is that of the husband or of the wife, because both genealogies have the Husband's name. The answer is not difficult but the problem lays in English grammar. It is considered bad English to use a definite article before a proper name. You would not go around saying, the Sharon, the Patty, the George, or the John and so on. This is not considered good English. However, in the Hebrew it was permissible. In the Greek text of Matthew and Luke before every name you have the definite article in front of it. So as the Jewish custom of the day, Joseph's name does not have the definite article, which means that his name is replacing Mary's name. This is the wife's genealogy and not the husband's.[1725]

Although most versions translate Luke 3:23 as follows "Being the son (as was supposed) of Joseph, the son of Heli…." That same Greek phrase could easily be translated in a different way. While all the names of Luke's genealogy are preceded with the Greek definite article, the name of Joseph is not. Because of this grammatical point that same verse could be translated as follows: "Being the son (as was supposed of Joseph) the son of Heli…" In other words, the final parenthesis could be expanded so that the verse reads that although Jesus was "supposed" or assumed to be the descendant of Joseph, He was really the descendant of Heli. The absence of Mary's name is quite in keeping with the

[1724] Levine, *You Take Jesus, I'll Take God*, 78-79.
[1725] Arnold G. Fruchtenbaum, *The Life of the Messiah* (Tape series. Tustin, CA: Ariel Ministries, n.d.), tape 1. A. T. Robertson, *A Harmony of the Gospels* (New York: Harper Collins, 1950), 259-261.

Jewish practices on genealogies, and it was not unusual for a son-in-law to be listed in his wife's genealogy.[1726]

On top of that even the Talmud mentions that Mary (Miriam) is the daughter of Heli, as Fruchtenbaum references:

> The Talmud itself refers to Mary as the daughter of Heli (Jerusalem-Hagigah 2:4; Jerusalem-Sanhedrin 23:3; Babylonian Sanhedrin 44). It is obvious, then that in longstanding Jewish tradition, Mary was recognized to be the daughter of Heli as mentioned in Luke 3:23.[1727]

So it was clearly recognized that *Yeshua* was the son of Miriam who was of the line of David through Heli her father. This then would make *Yeshua* the grandson of Heli, of the tribe of Judah, of the house of David through Nathan the son of David. Before going further, the two genealogies of Matthew and Luke need to be clearly viewed so that the reader can see without difficulty what has been previously stated concerning the genealogy of Miriam and Joseph. The names in the **bold print** are the same names in both genealogies at the same period of time, thus the intertwining of lines. Following is a simple chart of the two family lines from David. The asterisks (*) in the Matthew genealogy indicate the names that Matthew deleted from his list to keep the numeric 14 in his genealogy. Also the names in parentheses are the English names as they are translated from the Hebrew to Greek and into English.

Matthew Genealogy of Joseph	**Luke Genealogy of Miriam**
David son of Jesse	David son of Jesse
Solomon son of David	Nathan son of David
Rehoboam (Roboam)	Mattatha
Abijam (Abia)	Menan
Asa	Melea
Jehoshaphat (Josaphat)	Eliakim
Jehoram (Joram)	Jonan
*Joash	Joseph
*Amaziah	Juda
Uzziah (Ozias)	Simeon
Jotham (Joatham)	Levi
Ahaz (Achaz)	Matthat
Hezekiah (Ezekias)	Eliezer
Manasseh (Manasses)	Er
Amon	Elmodam
Josiah (Josias)	Addi
**Jehoahaz	Melchi
**Jehoiakim (father of Jechonias)	Neri

[1726] Arnold G. Fruchtenbaum, *Christ's Right to David's Throne: Manuscript #25* (Tustin, CA: Ariel Ministries, 1983), 4.

[1727] Arnold G. Fruchtenbaum, "Messiah's Right to David's Throne," *Voice: An Independent Church Journal* (Vol. 86 no. 6, Nov/Dec 2007): 34.

Jehoiachin (Jechonias)	**Shealtiel (Salathiel)**
**Zedekiah	**Zerubbabel - Zorobabel**
Shealtiel (Salathiel)	Rhesa
Zerubbabel – Zorobabel	Joanna
Abiud	Juda
Eliakim	Joseph
Azor	Semei
Sadoc	Mattathias
Achim	Maath
Eliud	Nagge
Eleazar	Esli
Matthan	Naum
Jacob	Amos
Joseph, the husband of Miriam	Mattathias
	Joseph
	Janna
	Melchi,
	Levi,
	Matthat
	Heli – father-in-law to Joseph

As can be clearly seen even by a casual observer, these two genealogies cannot both belong to Joseph. The answer to this problem has been dealt with in previous paragraphs. Also it is clearly visible that the names Neri, Shealtiel and Zerubbabel are the names spoken of in the other references made; they are also in the proper order of birth.

As for children receiving their Jewishness from their mother, the following information needs to be brought to light. Up until the time of the crusades children were Jewish because they were born of a Jewish father, which is biblical. However, because so many Jewish women were raped and had children from crusader men, the rabbis changed the biblical mandate meaning that today if a child is born of a Jewish woman, the child is Jewish, and if the father is Jewish and not a Jewish mother they are not recognized as Jewish.[1728] That is Jewish teaching today, so if a Jewish mother has a child, the child is Jewish in every sense of the word. Isn't it a double standard for Levine to say that because Mary was the mother and God was the father that *Yeshua* was not a descendant from David? He also states that there is no source to support that

---

[1728] In the first century if a Jewish woman was married to a Gentile, in order for the son to be declared Jewish without any question, he had to declare his Jewishness. In Acts 16:1-3 Paul, understanding the situation, took Timothy, whose mother was Jewish and whose father was Greek, and had him circumcised so that there would be no question as to his Jewish identity. The point is that *Yeshua* did not have an earthly father but as Luke 2:21 points out clearly, on the 8th day *Yeshua* was circumcised and named *Yeshua*.

Mary was of the tribe of Judah.[1729] The genealogy of Luke 3 is the family record of Miriam (Mary) traced from her father Heli all the way back to Nathan the son of David. Levine should know better, but perhaps he is appealing to his Jewish readers to mislead them as the anti-missionary did in the meeting that I attended at the Jewish Community Center in Lancaster, PA.

My Signet Zerubbabel ... Haggai 2:23

Look back to the Haggai 2:23 passage which is couched in the context of the last days; Zerubbabel is spoken to literally and prophetically. The point is that *Yahweh* is speaking to Zerubbabel prophetically and symbolically because Zerubbabel is a legitimate representative as a son of David and is called "*My servant*" because (among other things) he is the crossover point of two lines of David. He represents the future messianic king, while bypassing Coniah. Also *Yahweh* states that Zerubbabel will be made as a signet as in a signet ring. That signet ring was taken from the hand of Jeconiah and now has been replaced in Zerubbabel who represents family lines from his own sons, and the future Messiah. In Luke 3:27 Rhesa is named as Zerubbabel's son, which leads down to Heli the father of Miriam (Mary), whereas, in Matthew 1:13 Abuid is named as Zerubbabel's son which leads down to Jacob the father of Joseph (Abuid is omitted from the genealogy of 1 Chronicles 3:19). The naming of Zerubbabel in the New Covenant books of Matthew and Luke and two different sons is not just an accident but was in the plan of God to guarantee *Yeshua*'s title to the throne of David, as Gaebelein states:

> That Zerubbabel is named in both New Testament genealogies of Christ (Mt 1:12; Lk 3:27) proves his place in the royal line that guaranteed our Lord's title to the Davidic throne.[1730]

Zerubbabel is thus honored by *Yahweh* by being called "*My servant*" prophetically and symbolically for he is also the hope and key to his people by God making him a signet or a seal, guaranteeing to Israel that God has not forgotten His promises to David as Laetsch and Kaiser state:

> He also established him as a signet, as a seal guaranteeing to His people the fulfillment of God's promise given to David (2 Sam 7:12-16). As such he was "chosen" not by the people, nor by the powerful emperor Cyrus (cp. Ezra 1:8-11). This petty prince of Judah (Ezra 1:8), a small impoverished nation under foreign dominion, was honored by the supreme Ruler of the world..., the Lord

---

[1729] When Paul took Timothy as his apprentice he had him circumcised because his father was an Greek (Acts 16:1-3). So Timothy's Jewishness was declared by his being circumcised. Equally so Miriam, *Yeshua*'s mother, and Joseph, *Yeshua*'s stepfather had Him circumcised on the 8th day according to the law of Moses, thus removing any question as to His Jewishness; it was confirmed by His circumcision.

[1730] Frank E. Gaebelein, *Four Minor Prophets; Obadiah, Jonah, Habakkuk, and Haggai* (Chicago: Moody, 1970), 241-242.

of Hosts, to be a prominent link in that illustrious chain of ancestors (Matt 1:1ff., 6ff., 12; Luke 3:23ff., 27), extending from King David to Jesus Christ, the God-Man, King of Kings, and Lord of Lords (Rev 17:14; 19:16; cp. Eph 1:20f.; Phil 2:9ff.).[1731]

The fact that Zerubbabel emerged at this time in the life of the struggling nation was just another sign that God had not forgotten His promises to Abraham and David.[1732]

According to this, the signet has been reissued to Zerubbabel as he faithfully leads the captives back to Jerusalem to restore the city and the temple. As Pusey states, God reverses to Zerubbabel the sentence on Jeconiah for his impiety.[1733]

The next question to be asked according to Haggai 2:20-23; is whether the promises stated to Zerubbabel were fulfilled in his time. The obvious answer to this is no. This little helpless province of the Persian Empire and the appointed governor of that province did not see *Yahweh "shake the heavens and the earth."* Nor did they see *Yahweh "overthrow the throne of kingdoms"* and *"destroy the strength of the kingdoms of the heathen"* as prophesied in Haggai 2:21-22. What Zerubbabel had been told did not come to pass. So, did the prophecy of Haggai, who had spoken *"the word of the LORD,"* fall to the ground unfulfilled? No. *Yahweh* spoke to Zerubbabel using him as a symbol for the future Son of David who would fulfill that promise of the one who would actually wear that signet ring. The following two authors show that *Yahweh* had spoken of the future using Zerubbabel's name as *Yahweh* used David's name:

The magnitude of these promises to Zerubbabel poses an exegetical problem. Were these pronouncements actually fulfilled in Zerubbabel? Did he usher in a restoration of Israelite monarchy that was accompanied by the overthrow of Gentile nations in the fashion that Haggai describes? The history of this period provides no evidence that he did so. Haggai's promises did not come to fruition in the person of Zerubbabel. On the contrary, not long after this prophecy was given, Zerubbabel dropped into obscurity and passed off the scene. History is silent about what became of him or under what conditions he concluded his life. Whether he was removed from office by the Persians out of concern over possible insurrection in Judah, or died while in office, or continued to govern for a period of time is unknown. What is clear is that Zerubbabel did not usher in a triumphant period of rule such as vv. 20-23 describe.... A better understanding of this matter lies in viewing Zerubbabel as a representative figure. Just as the name David could carry associations of a royal figure who is

[1731] Laetsch, *Bible Commentary: The Minor Prophets*, 401-402.

[1732] Kaiser, *The Communicator's Commentary: Micah – Malachi*, 281.

[1733] E. B. Pusey, *The Minor Prophets* (Grand Rapids: Baker, 1957), 2:320.

in the Davidic line but who transcends the historical figure of David, so it is with Zerubbabel.[1734]

Zerubbabel was (Persian) governor in Judah, and had no doubt been selected for this office because he was prince of Judah (Ezra 1:8), and as a son of Shealtiel was a descendant of the family of David. Consequently the sovereignty of David in its existing condition of humiliation, under the sovereignty of the imperial power, was represented and preserved in his appointment as prince and governor of Judah, so that the fulfillment of the divine promise of the eternal perpetuation of the seed of David and his kingdom was then associated with Zerubbabel, and rested upon the preservation of his family. Hence the promise points to the fact, that at the time when Jehovah would overthrow the heathen kingdoms, He would maintain and take good care of the sovereignty of David in the person of Zerubbabel. For Jehovah had chosen Zerubbabel as His servant. With these words the Messianic promise made to David was transferred to Zerubbabel and his family among David's descendants, and would be fulfilled in this person in just the same way as the promise given to David, that God would make him the highest among the kings of the earth (Psa 89:27). The fulfillment culminates in Jesus Christ, the Son of David and descendant of Zerubbabel (Matthew 1:12; Luke 3:27), in whom Zerubbabel was made the signet ring of Jehovah.[1735]

RETURN TO ZECHARIAH 3:8

Now with this important background laid out before us, the study in Haggai and related verses becomes very significant in returning to the Zechariah 3:8 passage. In verse 1 of Zechariah 3, Joshua, the High Priest, is standing before the *"angel of the LORD"* and Satan is standing at Joshua's right hand to accuse him. However, in verse 2 the Messenger (Angel) of the LORD as the judge in a court room rebukes Satan. Joshua as a representative for the people is clothed with filthy, detestable garments which symbolize his iniquity. Satan, in accusing Joshua, is probably correct in speaking of Joshua's iniquity. However, the LORD, the *"angel of the LORD"* before them, orders Joshua a new, clean set of garments illustrating that the iniquity that Joshua represents has been removed (verse 4). This scene also pictures the Messenger (Angel) of the LORD as *Yahweh*, as Boice observes:

We see the deity of the "angel of the LORD" clearer here even than in the previous chapter. It is he who speaks to Satan, saying, "The LORD rebuke

---

[1734] Taylor, *The New American Commentary: Haggai, Malachi,* 198-200.

[1735] Keil and Delitzsch, *Commentary on the Old Testament in Ten Volumes: Haggai,* 10:214-215.

you!" but he is himself called the Lord: "The LORD said to Satan, 'The LORD rebuke you!'"[1736]

The companions or the other priests that were seated before Joshua are together a sign of *Yahweh's* servant the Branch. These priests are not active in the vision; they are just seated there as the following author states:

> The companions of Joshua were the ordinary priests, who were associated with him for the purpose of carrying on the service of the temple. They are represented as "sitting before" him, not at the time the words are addressed to him, for they are spoken of in the third person, but usually, when consulting together about religious matters.[1737]

Yahweh uses Joshua and the priests who were servants of the LORD as His backdrop to introduce His future servant that He calls *"My servant* [the] *BRANCH."* Up until this time in the biblical text, the BRANCH was not given a name. However, here Zechariah has given him a proper name *"My servant* [the] *BRANCH."* Pusey expresses the following concerning the proper name the servant is given:

> The Branch had now become, or Zechariah made it, a proper name. Isaiah had prophesied, *in that day shall the Branch of the Lord be beautiful and glorious for the escaped of Israel*; and, in reference to the low estate of him who should come, *There shall come forth a rod out of the stump of Jesse, and a Branch shall grow out of his roots*; and Jeremiah, *Behold the day come, saith the Lord, that I will raise unto David a righteous Branch, and a king shall reign and prosper, and shall execute judgment and justice in the earth, and this is the name whereby he shall be called, The Lord our Righteousness*; and, *in those days and at that time, will I cause the Branch of righteousness to grow up unto David, and he shall execute judgment and righteousness in the land.* Of him Zechariah afterward spoke as, *a man whose name is the Branch.* Here Zechariah names him simply, as a proper name, *My servant* [the] *Branch*, as Ezekiel prophesied of *My servant David.* The *title* My servant, which is Isaiah's chiefest title of the Messiah, occurs in connection with the same image of His youth's lowly *estate*, and of His atoning Death.[1738]

This *"Branch"* that Isaiah, Jeremiah and now Zechariah have been revealing to the student of the *Tanakh* has many characteristics, but the two most predominant are the humanity of the *"Branch"* and the divinity of the *"Branch."* It will also be noticed that in the Hebrew text of Zechariah 3:8 it is simply translated *"My servant Branch."* There is no definite article (ה) before the proper name *"Branch."* This makes *"My servant"* [the] *Branch"* a strong statement, as reflected by the following author:

[1736] James M. Boice, *An Expositional Commentary: The Minor Prophets; Micah – Malachi* (Grand Rapids: Baker, 1986), 2:501-502.

[1737] Henderson, *Thornapple Commentaries: The Twelve Minor Prophets*, 381-382.

[1738] Pusey, *The Minor Prophets: Micah –Malachi*, 2:356-357.

Zechariah uses the name Branch without the article and in apposition to (my servant) as a proper name, it being a well-known prophetic epithet of the coming Messiah from the days of Isaiah and Jeremiah, and if it had not already become a proper name Zechariah made it so, as Pusey observes.[1739]

This name the "*Branch*" also has a number of other points that need to be expressed to receive a full and complete idea as to the full ramifications of the term "*Branch*" used by Isaiah, Jeremiah and Zechariah.

The name Zemach (a proper noun in our text) conveys several truths. First, it brings out the lowliness and humiliation of the Messiah (Isa 11:1), second, it reveals His eminence (Isa 53:2). He grows up before the Lord Himself. Third, it directs our attention to His humanity. He is connected with the earth, and more particularly the land of Palestine (Zech 6:12). Fourth, it relates Him to the Davidic dynasty (Jer 3:5-6). Fifth, it focuses our thought upon the deity of the Branch (Isa 4:2). Sixth, it conveys the truth of His fruitfulness in comparison with the barrenness of all others (Isa 11:1; 53:10). Seventh, it speaks of his priestly work and character; for being touched with the feeling of our infirmities, He is a becoming and fit High Priest for sinful men (Zech 6:12).[1740]

Not only is the name "*Branch*" significant, but here in Zechariah 3:8 it is coupled with the term "*My servant*," which was used repeatedly and is the most frequently used title for the coming Messiah. It is even more frequently used than the term "*Moshiach*" itself. A large number of the twenty appearances of the title "*servant*" in Isaiah 41-53 refer to the Messiah.[1741] It is also true in reference to Jewish arguments that God used this term frequently throughout the *Tanakh*, but there is a uniqueness about this "*My servant*," as Wilkinson states:

It is true that God speaks of Abraham as "My servant," and "My servant Moses," "My servant Caleb," "My servant David," "My servant Job," "My servant Isaiah," "My servant Eliakim," "Israel My servant," "Jacob My servant" and even "Nebuchadnezzar My servant" but when He speaks of the messiah as "My Servant," the Branch of David and Branch of Jehovah, stand alone. He is so high above all other servants of Jehovah, that He needs no description beyond "My Servant." So in Isa 62:1, we have "Behold, My Servant, whom I uphold, My chosen, in whom My soul delighteth."[1742]

This "*My Servant*" is a distinctly and uniquely different Messiah. He is higher than any other servant of God as attested to by the way God speaks of Him.

[1739] Unger, *A Zondervan Commentary: Zechariah*, 65-66.
[1740] Feinberg, *God Remembers: A Study of the Book Zechariah*, 64.
[1741] Kaiser, *The Communicator's Commentary: Micah – Malachi*, 324-325.
[1742] Wilkinson, *Israel My Glory*, 197.

Two prophetic and symbolical passages are used by the LORD in presenting His future role for the Messiah. Haggai presented Zerubbabel as the signet and LORD through whom the Messiah would come. Zechariah presented Joshua, the High Priest, symbolically as "*My servant* [the] *Branch*." Here the "*My servant* [the] *Branch*," the Messiah will wear the kingly crown as well as a priestly crown, which represents the two crowns that *Yahweh* asks Zechariah to prepare and which have been misunderstood as the uniting of the priestly and civil authorities of Zerubbabel and Joshua. Rather, these two symbols are used of the Messiah's two offices, King and Priest. He is the Son of David, the "Branch," as well as a priest after the order of Melchizedek (Psalm 110:4) which will be a different priestly office taken on by Him. In His first coming as the "*servant*" the Son of David would be rejected (Psalm 22; Isaiah 53; Zechariah 11:4-14). Then at His second coming He comes as the Righteous Branch, the promised King who will restore Israel and rule over the whole earth after the time of "*Jacob's trouble*" and Israel's repentance of their sin in rejecting Him in His first coming as the Servant-Branch. He will also be the priest after the order of Melchizedek. Unger reflects on these two aspects of the Messiah:

> This great Messianic prediction introduces my servant the Branch. The Lord's servant the Branch, presents messiah in the aspect of His first advent in humiliation and rejection, obedient unto death (Isa 52:13-53:12; Phil 2:5-8), purchasing that redemption on the cross which will be the basis of Israel's future conversion and restoration as a priestly nation at the second advent (Isa 42:1-7; 49:1-7). The gospel of Mark presents "the Lord's Servant the Branch."[1743]

That is not all that Zechariah presents concerning the Messiah, for in [Zechariah chapter 3] verse 9 he continues by equating the Messiah as "*the stone*." Here the "*Branch*" is also called "*the stone*." He is "*My servant* [the] *Branch*" showing His humanity, which parallels the Messiah's first coming as the Servant. This also happens to be the theme of the Gospel of Mark in the New Covenant. "*My servant* [the] *Branch*" looks to the first coming of the Messiah whereas the "*stone*," which also can be tied into Daniel 2:34-35, looks toward the deity of the Messiah.[1744] In that passage the "*stone*" which is cut out of the mountain that crushes the image in Daniel 2, is the Messiah and His kingdom that will rule the entire earth will correspond with the second coming of Messiah as King. The "*stone*" has an obvious messianic context, as Kaiser states:

> The "*stone*" ([Zech 3] v. 9) was set before Joshua. The stone had seven eyes and this inscription: "*And I will remove the iniquity of that land in one day*" (v. 9d). The stone must be the same one that Isaiah talked about: "Behold I lay in Zion a stone for a foundation, a tried stone, a precious cornerstone, a sure foundation; whoever believes will not act hastily" (Isa 28:16). Again, Psalm 118:22 declares,

---

[1743] Unger, *A Zondervan Commentary: Zechariah*, 65.

[1744] Kaiser, *Toward an Old Testament Theology*, 254.

"The stone which the builders rejected has become the chief cornerstone." This stone is also reminiscent of the "stone" in Daniel 2:44-45.

The number seven, in the reference to the seven eyes, may be used here because seven is the number of completeness, or it may be a deliberate reference to the sevenfold fullness of the one Spirit of Yahweh given to Messiah (Isa 11:2).[1745]

The emphasis in verse 8 is the Servant-Branch, showing the humanity of the Servant-Branch, while the emphasis in verse 9 centers on the deity of the "*Branch*" also as the "*stone.*" However, Unger states that these two verses also speak of the first and second advents of the Messiah:

The reason two figures are used, one the Servant-Branch, the other the single stone, is because one applies specifically to the first advent and the other centers in the second advent.[1746]

This would be another clear reference to the two comings of the Messiah with no textual indication that there is a gap of time between His comings. Zechariah 3:8 speaks to His first coming whereas verse 9 speaks to His second coming (Isaiah 61:1-3; Zechariah 9:9-10). In verse 9 this "*Stone*" has seven eyes, which refer to the infinite intelligence and the all seeing or omnipresence as well as omniscience of God (Ezekiel 1:18; 10:12). This is the stone that the builders rejected (Psalm 118:22; Isaiah 8:14; Acts 4:11) spoken of by Isaiah and Peter.[1747] This "*Stone*" of stumbling and offense is the "*stone*" that "*was cut out of the mountain without hands*" (Daniel 2:45) that will break the image to pieces; this stone "*shall stand forever*" (Daniel 2:44). This "*Stone*" the Messiah that Zechariah speaks of is the divine nature of the Messiah that will come and destroy the kingdom of darkness, as Unger continues:

[1745] Kaiser, *The Communicator's Commentary: Micah-Malachi*, 325.

[1746] Unger, *A Zondervan Commentary: Zechariah*, 66.

[1747] The "Stone" passages that relate to the Messiah are important passages. However, there is another related term that needs to be mentioned. This term has been greatly abused by the Catholic Church as it tries to find biblical support for the office of the pope. In Matthew 16:13-18 *Yeshua* in speaking to Peter supposedly refers to him as the "Rock" on which the Church is built. However, nothing else in the New Covenant substantiates that premise. Throughout the Gospels, *Yeshua* and the New Covenant writers did not give that kind of supremacy to Peter. The writings of the Apostles, including Peter himself, did not give any support to the idea that Peter was the Chief Apostle. It is even more important to understand the definition of the term "Rock" that was already defined in the *Tanakh*. Remember that the Gospels were not written in a vacuum. If a person studied the usages of the word "Rock" as used by Moses, Hannah, David and the psalmists, he would quickly discover that the term "Rock" was defined as the God of Israel. The understanding of the term in the Hebrew Scriptures was that it was a name for God and referenced Him alone. So Peter, being an orthodox Jew, would never have accepted the title of God. The whole idea would have been completely repulsive to Him (Deut 32; 1 Sam 2:2; 2 Sam 22:1-2, 32, 47; 23:1-3; Psa 18:1-2, 31, 46; 28:1; 31:2-3; 61:2; 62:2, 6-7; 42:9; 78:35; 81:16; 89:26; 71:3; 92:15; 94:22; 95:1; Isa 8:14; 17:10).

605

For behold the Stone which I set [or "will set" (prophetic perfect)] before Joshua does not mean that the Stone was placed at Joshua's feet as his ward. It simply means that "Messiah, the Stone" was held out to Joshua in prophetic prospect (cf. "set before," 1 Kings 9:6) as the Stone cut without hands which will smite the kingdoms of the nations symbolized by Daniel's colossus and become a "great mountain" (the millennial kingdom) to fill "the whole earth" (Daniel 2:34-35). It is precisely by this destruction of the Satanic world system that the establishment of the kingdom is brought about, which in turn makes possible the restoration of Israel as a high-priestly nation of which Joshua and his priest colleagues are men of predictive portent.[1748]

According to Feinberg the "*stone*" was unanimously understood by early expositors as the name of the Messiah:

We see in the stone another well-known name for the Messiah. Early expositors were almost unanimous in assigning this name to the Messiah.[1749]

Even in the Zohar, an old Jewish book of mysticism, the "*stone*" was equated with the *Shechinah* of God as Pusey relates:

The Shechinah is called the stone, through which the world subsisteth; of which it is said, 'A stone of seven eyes, and, the stone which the builders refused.'[1750]

Even three of the major Jewish translations of the *Tanakh* all see the "*Branch*" as the Messiah. *The Jewish Study Bible* uses "*Branch*" while the Harkavy version uses "*Sprout*" and the Leeser translation uses "*Zemach*" or "*the Sprout.*" However, some rabbis only want to see Zerubbabel because if this passage is the Messiah, then the Zechariah 6:12 passage also must be the Messiah. The following author reflects why some rabbis only want to see Zerubbabel:

Some eminent Jewish commentators see here only a promise to Zerubbabel. In support of the Messianic interpretation, however, the following points can be made: 1.The oldest Jewish commentators see here and in Zechariah 6 a reference to the Messiah. [Rashi and Kimchi. To acknowledge the Shoot here as Messiah would require a similar identification in 6:12. This would necessitate an admission that the Messiah would be priest as well as king.] 2. The passage uses the title "Shoot" which is elsewhere (Jer 23:5-6; Isa 4:2) used of Messiah. 3. The focus here is on one who would come in the future, not Zerubbabel or some other contemporary of the prophet: "I will bring my Servant, the Shoot." 4. The notation that God would remove the iniquity of the

---

[1748] Unger, *A Zondervan Commentary: Zechariah*, 66-67.

[1749] Feinberg, *God Remembers: A Study of the Book Zechariah*, 65.

[1750] Feinberg, *God Remembers: A Study of the Book Zechariah*, 65. E. B. Pusey, *The Minor Prophets: Micah –Malachi*, 2:357-358.

land in one day. This statement would be hard to reconcile with any interpretation other than the Messianic.[1751]

The branch and the stone are two pictures of the Messiah, speaking of His humanity and His deity. One other point that indicates the deity of the stone; the LORD *"will remove the iniquity of that land in one day"* and *"all Israel shall be saved"* (Romans 11:26). What day is that? The next verse uses a technical term or phrase, *"in that day"* which is understood as the time of *"Jacob's Trouble"* the seventieth week of Daniel, the tribulation when Israel embraces *Yeshua* as the Messiah at the end of that period, then they shall *"look on me whom they pierced"* (Zechariah 12:10) as is pointed out by Kaiser:

> The "one day" promised here is "that day" of Zechariah 9-14, i.e., the "day" of Israel's national repentance when her people will look on Him whom they have pierced (Zech 12:10).[1752]

A summary of this section adds much more material in connection to the term *"Branch."* By using the literal method of interpretation, once again it can clearly be seen that the Messiah is both human and divine. It also answers all the questions of the anti-missionaries who deny at their own spiritual peril the birth and legal connections that show *Yeshua*'s right to rule and that He is a legitimate son of David.

THE MAN WHO IS THE BRANCH
Zechariah 6:12-13

> (12) And speak unto him, saying, Thus speaketh the Lord of hosts, saying, Behold the man whose name is the Sprout [Branch]; and he shall grow up out of his place, and he shall build the temple of the Lord: (13) Even he shall build the temple of the Lord: and he shall bear the glory, and shall sit and rule upon his throne; and he shall be a priest upon his throne: and the counsel of peace shall be between them both. (Harkavy Version)

This passage of Scripture has a larger context than just these two verses. In verse 9 the *"word of the LORD came"* unto Zechariah. Verses 10-15 are the words that the LORD spoke to Zechariah. Notice that the context of these verses could in no way refer to Joshua personally. In verse 11 Zechariah is told to make *"crowns"* of silver and gold and set them upon the head of Joshua the High Priest. This verse has been an area of stumbling for numerous scholars as they try to understand the plural *"crowns"* and its connection to Joshua. There is not only a plurality of *"crowns,"* but there is also a mixture of priestly and kingly functions. Some scholars try to insert Zerubbabel into the passage when only Joshua is addressed, as reflected in the following two quotations:

[1751] Smith, *The Promised Messiah*, 413.
[1752] Kaiser, *The Communicator's Commentary: Micah – Malachi*, 326.

In the Hebrew text the word for "crown" (*'ataroth*) is plural. That has led some liberal scholars to imagine that two crowns are being discussed and to insert the words "and on the head of Zerubbabel the governor." This is not only an unjustified interpolation – a vice of which liberal scholars are all too often guilty – it also completely misses the point. In Israel the priestly and kingly office were kept separate. The priest never wore a crown or sat upon a throne. The king never performed the priestly functions. Yet here a crown is placed upon the head of *Joshua*, not Zerubbabel, pointing forward to the one who should be both king and priest. It is said that "he will be a priest on his throne" (v. 13).[1753]

Modern liberal scholars change the text by substituting "Zerubbabel, the son of Shealtiel, the governor," for "Joshua," etc. (See J.M.P. Smith in The Complete Bible, p. 873.) They have invented the fable that Haggai and Zechariah regarded Zerubbabel as the promised Messiah.[1754]

If Zerubbabel is not involved, what is the meaning of this passage? First, the BRANCH is designated as the "*man*" speaking to the humanity of the BRANCH. Secondly, there are several significant ingredients that help in determining the identity of this BRANCH. This "*man*" the BRANCH will "*build the temple*," he will "*bear its glory*," he "*shall sit and rule upon his throne*," and he will be "*priest upon the throne*." It is clearly recognized in the *Tanakh* that a king belonging to the tribe of Judah cannot function as priest from the tribe of Levi in the temple. Reading in the *Torah* (Law) one quickly becomes aware that the priests were to function in the temple, fulfilling all the responsibilities that belonged to them alone, not to the civil authority or the king (Exodus 30:7-8) as Sailhamer[1755] and Merrill[1756] clearly point out. One only needs to remember what happened to Uzziah when he tried to function as a priest (2 Chronicles 26:16-21). This passage is a prophecy concerning the Messiah whereby God used Joshua the High Priest symbolically, just as God used Zerubbabel symbolically. Here the emphasis is on the priestly office and the "*man*" the "*BRANCH*" who will sit on the throne of David and rule, not Joshua. To no priest, whether in Zechariah's day or any day before or after that, has such an event happened. Laetsch clearly states what is at stake:

Joshua was not to be pronounced king of Jerusalem. Such a transference of the royal crown from the tribe of Judah and the house of David to the tribe of Levi would have been not only obnoxious to the Jews, but also have voided all the promises of the Lord to the tribe of Judah (Gen 49:10 ff.) and to the house of David (2 Sam 7:12ff). The Lord would have contradicted Himself; or the

---

[1753] Boice, *An Expositional Commentary: The Minor Prophets: Micah – Malachi*, 2:514.
[1754] Laetsch, *Bible Commentary: The Minor Prophets*, 439.
[1755] John Sailhamer, *Everyman's Bible Commentary: First & Second Chronicles* (Chicago: Moody, 1983), 103.
[1756] Walvoord and Zuck, *The Bible Knowledge Commentary: Old Testament*, 640.

prophet, the high priest, and the governor would have been guilty of a despicable, blasphemous deception.[1757]

Hengstenberg makes the following comments to show that Joshua was a symbolic figure used by the LORD to bring home the point that the "BRANCH" was going to function also as a priest, not as a Levite, but after the order of Melchizedek:

> The prophecy is placed by the side of the symbolical action as if it was independent of it, though the meaning is precisely the same. הִנֵּה [here] points to the Messiah as if he were present, and calls to Joshua, who represented him in name as well as office, to fix his mental eye upon him. The manner in which the word צֶמַח [semach – branch] is introduced here, viz. as a proper name of the Messiah, though with a direct allusion to its literal meaning as is apparent from what follows, points back to earlier prophecies, in which the Messiah is represented as a Sprout of David to be raised up by the Lord, and particularly to that of Jeremiah.[1758]

Yes, the "*BRANCH*" will function as a priest and he will reign upon the throne of David. Notice again the words, "*and he shall be a priest on his throne,*" not as a Levite, but after the order of Melchizedek, as Boice expresses:

> Four Hebrew words, rendered "He will be a priest on his throne," portray all that the prophets had spoken about the Messiah's person and work. "Here is the true Melchizedek, who is at the same time King of Righteousness, King of Salem which is the King of Peace, and the great High Priest, whose period, unlike the Aaronic, abideth 'forever.'"[1759]

This simply is not a difficult thing to understand when it is seen prophetically and symbolically. The "*BRANCH*" will sit upon the throne of David as both king and priest, thus the meaning and purpose of the two crowns. This, within a biblical and Jewish context, is absolutely an amazing statement by Zechariah. He was a lone voice in combining two offices (priestly and kingly offices) into one person, the BRANCH as is reflected by David Baron:

> This is one of the most remarkable and precious Messianic prophecies, and there is no plainer prophetic utterance in the whole Old Testament as to the Person of the promised Redeemer, the office He was to fill, and the mission He was to accomplish.[1760]

This was a unique statement made by Zechariah, for these offices simply were not mixed. It just would not be acceptable for Zerubbabel to be priest, nor was it possible

---

[1757] Laetsch, *Bible Commentary: The Minor Prophets*, 439.

[1758] Hengstenberg, *Christology of the Old Testament,* 3:316.

[1759] Boice, *The Minor Prophets: Micah – Malachi*, 2:515.

[1760] Baron, *The Visions and Prophecies of Zechariah*, 190-191.

for Joshua to sit on the throne. These would be like polar opposites; each would repel the other as is clearly presented by Feinberg:

> The speaker in [Zech 6] verse 12 is Zechariah and the one addressed is Joshua in particular. No high priest of the Old Testament ever needed to be told that the kingly and priestly offices were kept apart in Israel. The regal office was irrevocably lodged in the house of David (see 2 Sam 7; Psa 89), while the sacerdotal office was given to the tribe of Levi. We have only to recall the awful visitation from God that befell Uzziah when he essayed to offer incense, to realize that God meant these offices and functions to be kept separate (2 Chron 26). This being so, Zerubbabel had no right to perform any priestly functions (and he did not), nor could Joshua, as a priest, wear a crown, then sit and rule upon the throne. But this is precisely what is pictured here of Joshua. Then it must be in a typical sense, and such it is. Joshua is here a type of Christ who is the true Melchizedek, both King and Priest. Cf. Hebrews 7:1-3 with Psalm 110:4. Joshua, being already high priest, had the kingly dignity added to him in type; so with Christ: His kingly office is grounded in His high priestly work for us, on the Cross and then at the right hand of the Father.[1761]

God uses words that should not be missed or counted as insignificant. When He calls the BRANCH a servant when speaking to Joshua, He is referring to the basic ministry of the priest. The priest was a servant of the LORD who mediated between the people and their God. These two passages in Zechariah 3:8 and 6:12-13 are extremely important in understanding the full ministry of the BRANCH, as understood from Isaiah, Jeremiah and now Zechariah. I am trying not to be redundant, but this cannot be missed. This Servant-Branch will uphold two offices in one person, as both Kaiser and Van Groningen affirm:

> The "Branch" or "Sprout" of 3:8 and 6:12 was another proper name for the last Davidite, who would arise out of obscurity, already known from Isaiah 4:2 and Jeremiah 23:5-6. The fact that He appears as the "Servant" in connection with the priesthood cannot be a mere coincidence. It is here made plain that the "Branch" and "Servant" will not only be David's successor but also Joshua's. As Isaiah had declared that the Servant would give His life as an atonement for others and thereby remove their iniquity, so Zechariah 3:9 promised that the Messiah would do so in "one day."[1762]

Yahweh commands Zechariah to perform an unusual deed which will bring together various prophecies concerning the Messiah, his position, roles, and work. In this one symbolic act of placing a royal crown on the high priest's head, Zechariah makes a declaration concerning the Messiah who had been referred to as both human and divine by previous prophets (Zech 1:12-13; 3:1-

---

[1761] Feinberg, *God Remembers: A Study of the Book of Zechariah*, 102-103.
[1762] Kaiser, *Toward an Old Testament Theology*, 254.

2; 6:12; Jer 23:5-6; Isa 52:13-53:12; 9:6-7; Psa 2, 110). Zechariah, by placing the royal crown on the high priest's head, demonstrates the unity of the messianic offices and roles. This had been indicated before, but this unity and mutual interaction are now declared as never before. There is thus a progression in the revelation of this fact.[1763]

Some respected rabbis such as Rashi and Kimchi[1764] departed from the older interpretation of the text. For instance, in Targum of Jonathan it states: "Behold the Man; Messiah is His Name. He will be revealed, and He will become great and build the Temple of God." They wish to see Zerubbabel instead of the Messiah because of the obvious impact of Zechariah's prophetic words. Even the Septuagint, because of the obvious conflict of offices, tries to soften the impact of Zechariah 6:13, as Walter Kaiser points out:

> "So He shall be a priest on His throne, and the counsel of peace shall be between them both" (v. 13d, e). This is the greatest Old Testament passage on the fact that the coming Messiah will be both a Davidic king and a Priest (cf. Heb 7). So amazing is this prediction that it has troubled many a commentator. Was it likely that a "priest" would "sit upon His throne?" The Greek Septuagint translation attempts to soften this prediction by substituting "at His right hand" for "on His throne." But as we know from the royal Psalms (e.g., Psa 110:4), the Anointed One would exercise an everlasting priesthood in addition to His royal and prophetic offices. Thus, Zechariah daringly combines the priestly and kingly offices into one person, "the Branch."[1765]

The One who sits on the throne as priest will build the temple. It is commonly known that Solomon built the first temple and Zerubbabel built the second temple. But who will build the temple during the Kingdom described in Ezekiel 40-48? It is the Servant-Branch, the Messiah described by Isaiah, Jeremiah and Zechariah. He is the one who will build that final temple, as expressed by Cooper:

> This One in whom the dynasty culminates is the One who is to build the Temple of God. Solomon is the one who built the First Temple, which was destroyed by the Babylonians, but rebuilt on a much smaller scale by Zerubbabel at the time of the restoration from Babylonian captivity. The Second Temple was destroyed by Titus, the Roman general, in the catastrophe of A.D. 70. It is to be rebuilt in the kingdom age. Who then will build it? The answer to this question appears in Zechariah 6:12, 13.... The term branch, occurring four times in the prophetic word, has a definite technical meaning. It

---

[1763] Van Groningen, *Messianic Revelation in the Old Testament,* 890.
[1764] Baron, *The Visions and Prophecies of Zechariah,* 191.

[1765] Kaiser, *The Communicator's Commentary: Micah – Malachi,* 346.

611

is one of the names of Messiah – as many of the sages of Israel have recognized.[1766]

In summary, the Branch is presented by Isaiah as the "*Branch of Yahweh*" and by Jeremiah the Branch is the LORD OUR RIGHTEOUSNESS who will physically sit on the throne of David. Zechariah presents the Branch as the Servant-Branch and the "*Man*" who will rule and reign upon the throne of David as both king and priest. These three prophets of the Hebrew Scriptures present a fourfold picture of the Branch, the Messiah as presented by Cooper and Kaiser:

> To many scholars the two passages in Jeremiah furnish the theme of the Gospel of Matthew. Zechariah 3:8, which speaks of "my servant the Branch," seems to be the theme of Mark, who wrote the second record of the Gospel. Zechariah 6:12, which speaks of "the man...the Branch," furnished the theme for the writer of the third Gospel, who presented Jesus of Nazareth as the ideal man. Isaiah 4:2, which speaks of "the branch of Jehovah," may well be considered as the theme of the fourth writer of the Gospel.[1767]

> These prophetic promises give four presentations of the Branch that correspond to the four presentations of Christ in the four gospels. They are: (1) The Branch as Royal King. "I will raise to David a Branch of righteousness" (Jer 23:5); "Behold your King" (corresponds to the presentation of the Messiah in Matthew). (2) The Branch as Servant. "My Servant the Branch" (Zech 3:8); "Behold the Servant" (corresponds to the presentation of the Messiah in Mark). (3) The Branch as Fully Man. "The Man whose name is the Branch" (Zech 6:12); "Behold the Man (corresponds to the presentation of the Messiah in Luke). (4) The Branch as Fully God. "The Branch of the LORD" (Isa 4:2); "Behold the Son of God" (corresponds to the presentation of the Messiah in John).[1768]

Furthermore, Levy points out that this passage presents six things that illustrate the Branch to be the Messiah who will be a man but will also be the LORD Himself, who will be both King and Priest, the God/Man. Below is a summary of Levy's statements:

1. This Branch will be a "*tender plant, and as a root out of dry ground*" (Isaiah 53:2) in His first coming, but will shoot upward into a strong, fast-growing plant in His second coming.

2. Messiah, the Branch, "*shall build the Temple of the LORD*" (Zechariah 6:12). This does not refer to Zerubbabel's construction of the second temple in 516 BCE but to the Millennial Temple at Messiah's second coming.

[1766] David L. Cooper, *Messiah: His Historical Appearance* (Los Angeles: Biblical Research Society, 1961), 165.

[1767] Cooper, *Messiah: His Historical Appearance*, 165.

[1768] Kaiser, *The Communicator's Commentary: Micah – Malachi*, 325.

3. Messiah, the Branch, is to *"bear* [carry] *the glory"* (Zechariah 6:13). The word "glory" refers to the majesty and splendor of God, which will become a reality when the Messiah reigns as both King and Priest on the throne of David His father.

4. Messiah, the Branch, will *"sit and rule on His throne"* in the city of Jerusalem (Zechariah 6:13). Messiah, earth's Creator-Redeemer will reclaim the earth, lost by man in Genesis 3 to Satan.

5. Messiah, the Branch, will also rule upon the throne as a priest, not as a Levitical priest, but as a priest after the order of Melchizedek (Psalm 110:4; Hebrews 7).

6. Messiah, the Branch, will build the Temple by the gifts from righteous Gentiles, as it states (Zechariah 6:15), *"Even those from afar shall come and build the temple of the LORD."*[1769]

One final important observation before leaving this passage of Zechariah 6:9-15. In verse 15 Zechariah states, *"and ye shall know that the LORD of hosts hath sent me unto you."* Who is the "me" that was sent? Is it Zechariah or someone else? Verse 9 gives the identity of "me." It states *"the word of the LORD came unto me,"* the "me" here in verse 9 is Zechariah. Zechariah is relaying the *"word of the LORD"* meaning that the "me" of verse 15 is *"the word of the LORD,"* the *Metatron*, the Messiah, the Branch, the Son of David, the King-Priest of Israel. Verse 15 also substantiates the plural unity of the LORD. The *"word of the LORD"* who is speaking in verse 9 is sent by the *"LORD of hosts"* in verse 15. Once again, there are two LORDs involved in the transmitting of this passage through Zechariah to Israel on the Man, the Branch.

[1769] David Levy, "Messiah's Coronation and Reign," *Israel My Glory*, vol. 63, no. 2 (March/April, 2005) Bellmawr, NJ: Friends of Israel Gospel Ministry, 31.

Chapter 18
"The Word of the Lord Came"

Judaism's view of monotheism in the first century C.E. is a very important issue and has two primary views. The question is, could *Yeshua* fit into the monotheism of Judaism of that day? The first view of Second Temple Judaism was characterized by a strict monotheism that would have made it impossible to attribute deity to any figure other than God the Father Himself. It would not leave the door open in any way for *Yeshua* to be considered divine. The second view was that Second Temple Judaism struggled with an absolute monotheism because the Hebrew Scriptures seem to portray various kinds of intermediary figures, namely angels and exalted humans. For example, Enoch is said to be elevated to the high angel called *Metatron*, as shown below:

> Such views usually focus on various kinds of intermediary figures – principal angels, exalted humans, personified divine attributes or functions – who are understood to occupy a subordinate divine or semi-divine status, so that the distinction between the one God and all other reality was by no means absolute in the Judaism of this period, it is claimed.[1770]

The reality is that portions of both these views are correct. It has already been noted in chapter 4 of this book that *Metatron* was a puzzling figure to the ancient rabbis and some of them considered making him a second-class *Yahweh* because of his character and position. *Metatron* is not discussed much today in modern Rabbinic Judaism. *Metatron* would be the equivalent to the Christian understanding of *"the angel (Messenger) of the LORD."* Since that has already been discussed, it will not be repeated here. The issue of heavenly being speaking as God was discussed and debated by rabbis of the past, but they all came around to the uniform teaching on the absolute monotheism that is prevalent today. What will be studied in this chapter is the identity of *"the Word of the LORD"* as revealed within the *Tanakh*. This whole book has been dedicated to understanding that issue as it relates to the plural unity of *Elohim*, which all of Judaism has systematically rejected.

In the New Testament, the Apostle John in his gospel states that *Yeshua* was the Word of the LORD, the agent of revelation, the means whereby God became visible, the Creator and the one who spoke the universe into existence, as stated in John 1:1-5, 9-14, 18:

[1770] Richard Bauckham, *God Crucified: Monotheism & Christology in the New Testament* (Grand Rapids: Eerdmans, 1998), 2.

(1) In the beginning was the Word, and the Word was with God, and the Word was God. (2) The same was in the beginning with God. (3) All things were made by him; and without him was not any thing made that was made. (4) In him was life; and the life was the light of men. (5) And the light shineth in darkness; and the darkness comprehended it not.

(9) That was the true Light, which lighteth every man that cometh into the world. (10) He was in the world, and the world was made by him, and the world knew him not. (11) He came unto his own, and his own received him not. (12) But as many as received him, to them gave he power to become the sons of God, even to them that believe on his name. (13) Which were born, not of blood, nor of the will of the flesh, nor of the will of man, but of God. (14) And the Word was made flesh, and dwelt among us, (and we beheld his glory, the glory as of the only begotten of the Father,) full of grace and truth.

(18) No man hath seen God at any time; the only begotten Son, which is in the bosom of the Father, he hath declared him (King James Version).

Of course true biblical faith views these verses from the New Covenant as the personification of the Word of the LORD who took on flesh. However, Judaism as a whole does not embrace this teaching and aggressively rejects it. So can anything be learned from the *Tanakh* that would substantiate John's declaration of *Yeshua* as the very Word of God, the Creator who was with God, and one (*echad*) with God at the very beginning of time who took on flesh and dwelt among men? That will be the goal of this chapter.

The following quotation Rabbi Louis Jacobs gives some pertinent information on the history and background of the Word from a rabbinic perspective:

Word: In Jewish thought much is said about the power of the word, whether it be the creative word of God or the word in human speech. In Philo the Logos represents the means by which God creates. The Targum of Onkelos often uses the Aramaic memra ('word') as a means of softening the biblical anthropomorphisms so that instead of the Hebrew in which it is stated that God does this or that it is the memra from God that is active. Although the influence of Greek thought is evident in all this, the Hebrew prophets also trace their message to the word or oracle of God. It goes without saying that the identification of the Logos with Jesus in the Gospel of John (1:14) introduces a notion completely foreign to any version of the Jewish religion. On the contrary, Philo and the Targum are at pains to use the Word in order to distance man from the direct action of the Deity. In Judaism the 'Word' is never 'made flesh'.[1771]

[1771] Jacobs, *A Concise Companion to the Jewish Religion*, 301.

The fact that Jacobs says that the concept of Jesus being the *Logos* (*Davar* in Hebrew and *Memra* in Aramaic) is foreign to all of Judaism will be the central issue that this author wishes to reveal in this chapter. It is frustrating that Christian authors focus on the Greek *Logos* instead of what was intended by John in the opening chapter of his gospel. Although John was writing in Greek, he was first and foremost a Jew who was interested in focusing on the Jewish theology as it related to Messiah from the *Tanakh* with his emphasis on the Aramaic word *memra* or the Hebrew word *davar* as used in his day.

For the first 50 years of this author's life, only the term *Logos* from John 1:1 was known to him. However, in the last 14 years he has discovered that John was not referencing *Logos* as much as he was referencing the Aramaic word *Memra* [meaning "word"] or the Hebrew word *Davar* (which also means "word"). Being taught the Greek emphasis of *Logos* which implies "reason" (the idea of God) and "speech" (the expression of God) was not necessarily wrong, just inadequate as it came from the wrong source. John was not using Greek for the purpose of spreading Greek Hellenized philosophy, but as a Hebrew fisherman he was emphasizing Hebrew theology from a Jewish perspective. He was putting together (John 1:1-18) at least five and perhaps six things that the rabbis had been emphasizing in John's day.

> First, the *Memra* [Word] was recognized as God yet was distinct from God (John 1:1-2; Genesis 18; Exodus 21). However, they did not go very far with this, but they did see it. Secondly, the *Memra* [Word] was the agent of creation (John 1:3, 10; Psalm 33:6; Isaiah 48:12-16; Zechariah 12:1, 10). The third was the *Memra* [Word] the agent of salvation (John 1:12). Fourth, the *Memra* [Word] was the means whereby God became visible (John 1:14; Exodus 3:1-5 and 24:9-11; Joshua 5:14-15). Lastly, the *Memra* [Word] was the agent of revelation (John 1:18; Hebrews 1:1-2; I Samuel 3:19-21; 1 Kings 17:2, 8; 18:1; 21:17; Jeremiah 1:1; Ezekiel 1:3; Hosea 1:1; Joel 1:1; Jonah 1:1; Micah 1:1; Zephaniah 1:1; Haggai 1:1; Zechariah 1:1; Malachi 1:1).[1772]

So John is making a concerted effort to tie together theological teaching of the *Tanakh* that the rabbis of his day were emphasizing and connecting it to *Yeshua* as the incarnation, not only as God (plural unity of *Elohim*) but as the Word (*Memra*) of the LORD who was God and yet distinct from God.

This chapter will discuss three aspects as they relate to this Word: first, *Logos* and its relationship to Philo and Greek Hellenism; second, the use of the Word from the *Tanakh* and third, how Word was used in the Targums, the Aramaic paraphrase of the *Tanakh*. This study will only begin to introduce uncharted biblical research basically untouched today on this subject for students of the Scriptures. It needs to be thoroughly

---

[1772] Arnold Fruchtenbaum, *Life of Messiah: from a Jewish Perspective* (San Antonio, TX: Ariel Ministries), MP3 – Paragraph #2.

studied with someone writing a book on the relationship of the Word as a distinct person from the Father in the Hebrew Scriptures.

LOGOS

This author will be very quick to state that his knowledge of Greek philosophy is not his strong point and will defer to others as this section is opened. Philo and his understanding of the Hebrew text was greatly influenced by the Stoics and Platonism. Stoicism began around 300 BC. One of its main teachings was that the universe was ordered by a principle called the *logos* (commonly translated "word," but also meaning "thought" or "reason"). In other words, there is logic and reason to the cosmos, and the highest good for mankind was to live in harmony with that natural order. They were materialists and did not believe that mankind lived beyond death, whereas Plato believed that each person possesses a spirit which was liberated from the body at death. The Stoics also believed that people were not to show emotion or be emotional; hence, unbridled passion was deemed inconsistent with logic or reason. Because people were naturally social creatures, the Stoics maintained very high moral and ethical standards.[1773] Beyond that the Stoics believed that God was distant from His creation and when He chose to communicate with mankind, He used intermediaries as the following author states:

> Greek philosophical thought maintained that the god (whoever they conceived that ultimate being to be) was quite remote from the universe and generally impersonal. How could the creator of all things interact with mere humans? How could the "unmoved mover" be moved by human pain? Some speculated that God, as perfect spirit, couldn't interact with matter at all, or he would become imperfect. So they posited that if God interacted with the world, it would be through intermediaries, like the *logos* ("word" or "logical principle") of the Stoics. To the philosophers, the god of the Bible was simply too "human" to be divine.[1774]

Philo, in his writings, took this Greek Hellenism from Plato and the Stoics and combined it with the Scriptures in order to reconcile Hellenism with the Scriptures. He also employed allegory as his method of interpretation of the Scriptures which, by the way, was later introduced to the Church through Origen. The following author confirms that Philo used this method of interpretation:

> But the foundations of his philosophical-theological system were the Scriptures and his Jewish faith. In order to reconcile Greek philosophical concepts with the Scriptures, Philo employed the method of allegorical interpretation. In this

---

[1773] Anthony J. Tomasino, *Judaism Before Jesus* (Downers Grove, IL: InterVarsity, 2003), 216.

[1774] Tomasino, *Judaism Before Jesus*, 239.

method each element of a story or narrative is understood to have some symbolic significance that points to a greater truth.[1775]

Not only was Philo attempting to reconcile Hellenism with the Scriptures, but he was also dealing with the anthropomorphisms of God in the Hebrew text. Judaism, during the Second Temple period, was struggling with the biblical expressions that could lead an unlearned student of Scripture into believing that God was like a human with arms, legs, hands, eyes, and one who walked and talked with people. Later the church fathers took the writings of Philo and used them to help prove that *Yeshua*, the Messiah, was the very Word of God instead of going back to the *Tanakh* to prove it, which is what John was doing in the first chapter of his gospel.

Gerald Sigal has responded negatively to *Logos* by tying together *Logos* and the paganism of Greek Hellenism to which it is connected. His approach is to say that the early church fathers took the writings of Philo, twisting and distorting what he said in his metaphorical use of the term *Logos* (Word) as expressed below.

> The Christian doctrine of the Logos, "Word," has its origins in the writings of Philo. The Philonic Logos is the result of an attempt to harmonize the Greek Logos and certain Jewish ideas concerning the nature and role of God in the universe. This was to deeply influence early Christian theologians, who paganized and distorted the meaning of the Logos in Philo's writings. The metaphorical phrases employed by Philo to explain his concept of the Logos were taken literally by the early Christian Church, still under pagan influence.[1776]

Philo was a Hellenized Jew who was interpreting the *Tanakh* from a Greek Hellenized understanding. Judaism today states the Church took Philo's writings on *Logos* and applied them to *Yeshua*. Judaism in the first and second centuries CE was not about to accept lesser deities or incorporate a "human" as a deity. The Greeks did that and the charge from Judaism is that Christianity incorporated and Hellenized the Greek view of their gods into Christianity. Sad to say, there is some truth to Sigal's statement. However, one point is missed by Sigal: John was not referencing Philo but the prophets of old who used the term "*word*" or "*the Memra of the LORD*" as his point of connection. It is consistent with the other writers of the New Covenant to present *Yeshua* as one with the Father. To John and to Judaism God is unique and cannot be compared to the Greek concept of God, as stated below:

> The typical-Hellenistic view was that worship is a matter of degree because divinity is a matter of degree. Lesser divinities are worthy of appropriate degrees of worship.... Jews understood their practice of monolatry to be justified, indeed required, because the unique identity of YHVH was so

---

[1775] Tomasino, *Judaism Before Jesus*, 238.

[1776] Sigal, *The Jew and the Christian Missionary: A Jewish Response to Missionary Christianity*, 145.

619

understood as to place him not merely at the summit of a hierarchy of divinity, but in an absolutely unique category, beyond comparison with anything else.[1777]

Fundamental biblical faith would have to agree with that God cannot be compared with any other god, for there are no other gods. Yet true Bible believers, as they view the *Tanakh*, state that God had revealed Himself as a plural unity of *Elohim* who is one (*echad*) and when He spoke He spoke only as one (*echad*) God. The apostles and early believers in *Yeshua* did not believe they were violating Judaism's position on monotheism as shown below:

> I shall be arguing what will seem to anyone familiar with the study of New Testament Christology, the inclusion of Jesus in the unique divine identity, was central to the faith of the early church even before any of the New Testament writings were written, since it occurs in all of them .... The New Testament writers did not see their Jewish monotheistic heritage as in any way an obstacle to the inclusion of Jesus in the divine identity.[1778]

What the early believers in *Yeshua* came to recognize was that the God of Israel, who is *echad* (one in plurality), with whom their fathers interacted in centuries past, was none other than "*the angel* (Messenger) *of the LORD*" and the promised righteous Branch, Immanuel, the Son of David who was born of the virgin whom *Yahweh* would name in the future "*the LORD our Righteousness*" and also as El-gibbor (God Almighty). They did not view this belief as alien to the faith of their fathers, as expressed below:

> Such a revelation could not leave the early Christian understanding of God unaffected, but at the same time the God whose identity the New Testament writers understood to be now defined by the history of Jesus was undoubtedly the God of Israel. His identity in Jesus must be consistent with his identity in the Hebrew Scriptures.[1779]

The church of later centuries did, perhaps in their eagerness, take the words of Philo and use them in reference to Messiah *Yeshua*. Even if they took the metaphorical use of Philo's *Logos* and applied it literally to *Yeshua*, they still came up with correct theology. What the church failed to do was to connect the Word of John 1:1 with *memra* (Aramaic) or *davar* (Hebrew) in the Hebrew text. Instead they based everything around *Logos* and Hellenism. The Hebrew Scriptures clearly revealed the "*Word of the LORD*" as a person, who was also the *Metatron* [*the angel of the LORD*], who was God and yet was distinct from the Father, contrary to Sigal's response:

> Philo portrays the Logos as the instrument of God's creation and revelation, and of His activity in the universe. This conception of the Logos is derived not from the biblical text, but from Hellenistic sources. It is primarily from the

---

[1777] Bauckham, *God Crucified: Monotheism & Christology in the New Testament*, 15.

[1778] Bauckham, *God Crucified: Monotheism & Christology in the New Testament*, 27.

[1779] Bauckham, *God Crucified: Monotheism & Christology in the New Testament*, 46-47.

latter sources that Philo developed the concept of the Logos as mediator between God and the world in the Reason of Greek philosophers (Logos in Greek means both "word" and "reason") with the Aramaic term memra' ("the Word").[1780]

There is another thought that could be true of John's intentions and is mentioned next by two parallel thoughts applying to both the Jewish and Gentile world. First, in John's gospel he was presenting the Messiah of Israel as divine to the Jewish people by focusing on the Word of God in the *Tanakh* using the term *Logos*. Second, by using the same familiar term (*Logos*) John was also introducing his Hebrew theology in relation to the Word (*davar* or *memra*) to the Roman-Greek world of the west, and by using the Hebrew understanding of the Word (*davar* and *memra*) he tied them together with the Greek word *Logos* which would overlap into the Hellenized world. John very possibly was stating to the Hellenized world that the *Logos* of the God of Israel was far more than reason, thought or logic of the Hellenized world. John was endeavoring to show the Greek world that *Logos* is the God of Israel, the Creator of the universe, implying that the Greek-Roman world should worship Him as the only God instead of a multiplicity or degrees of gods and semi-gods. John could have been doing the same thing that Paul did on Mars Hill when he spoke to the Greek religious world concerning the "Unknown God" (Acts 17:22-34). The following statement supports this possibility:

> The use of logos implies that John was endeavoring to bring out the full significance of the Incarnation to the Gentile world as well as to the Jewish people. He does not adopt the Greek concept in its entirety, but he uses this term to indicate that Jesus had universal rather than local significance and that he spoke with ultimate authority. He was preexistent, involved in the act of creation, and therefore superior to all created beings. This presentation lifted Christ above the materialistic, pagan concept of deities just as the Incarnation brings the Hebrew concept of God into everyday life.[1781]

So from John's Jewish theological background he may have been speaking to both the Jewish and Hellenized world, because neither of them were unfamiliar with the term *Logos*.

Throughout this book it has been clearly presented that if you take the Hebrew Scriptures literally, they become the primary source with abundant evidences from the biblical text that substantiate the plurality in unity of *Elohim*. The Second Person of that plural unity of *Elohim* was the mediator between Himself and the Father and with mankind when dealing with man and his sin. Nonetheless, scholars debate the meaning of John's *Logos*:

[1780] Sigal, *The Jew and the Christian Missionary: A Jewish Response to Missionary Christianity*, 146.

[1781] Merrill C. Tenney, *The Expositor's Bible Commentary: John and Acts* (12 vols. Grand Rapids: Zondervan, 1981), 9:28.

There's been a great deal of speculation on whether or not his teachings inspired the theology of John 1, where Jesus is identified as the preexistent Word of God. But there are some significant differences between Philo's Word and John's Word. Philo carefully avoided identifying the *logos* with God, but that identification is the basis of John's Christology (doctrine of Christ): "In the beginning was the Word, and the Word was with God, and the Word was God" (Jn 1:1). Philo's Hellenistic theology wouldn't have countenanced the notion of the Word becoming flesh, which is the climax of John's hymn to the *logos* (Jn 1:14). So it seems more likely that John developed his thoughts on the Word of God independent of Philo, both men drawing on the same Old Testament traditions and their own unique insights. Nonetheless, Philo's ideas were profound, and later Christian theologians found them extremely useful.[1782]

Tomasino is absolutely correct. The Apostle John did receive his material independent of Philo and the Hellenization of the period; he received it from the written word of God. In the upcoming section of this chapter the term *Logos*, or the Word, will be our focus, not from the Hellenized Jew, Philo, but from the writing of the *Tanakh* and *Targums* themselves in substantiating the personification of the Word of the LORD as *Yeshua*.

Some New Testament scholars recognize the distinction between the Greek *logos* and the *Logos* of John. The following author draws a sharp distinction between the two by stating what John's *Logos* is not:

> Philo's and the Jewish-Alexandrian doctrine of a *logos* near the time of Christ has nothing to do with the *Logos* of John. Philo's *logos* is in no sense a person but the impersonal reason or "idea" of God, a sort of link between the transcendent God and the world, like a mental model which an artist forms in his thought and then proceeds to work out in some kind of material. This *logos*, formed in God's mind, is wholly subordinate to him, and though it is personified at times when speaking of it, it is never a person as is the Son of God and could not possibly become flesh and be born a man. Whether John knew of this philosophy it is impossible for us to say; he himself betrays no such knowledge.[1783]

Lenski clearly points to the fact that Philo's *logos* is completely different than the *Logos* of John that is the Word of God Himself who spoke the world into existence. Philo's *logos* is based on Greek philosophy of reason, not on the "*Thus saith the LORD*" of the *Tanakh*.

There was a trend in Second Temple Judaism even with the teaching of absolute oneness to personify the Word of the LORD with the Father. This trend was already

---

[1782] Tomasino, *Judaism Before Jesus*, 241.

[1783] R. C. H. Lenski, *The Interpretation of St. John's Gospel* (Minneapolis, MN: Augsburg Publishing House, 1963), 29.

noticeable in the *Tanakh* as it fused together the Word of the LORD with the Father as one (*echad*) yet being distinct from each other, as the following author illustrates:

> Philo's point of departure was the growing trend in popular Jewish literature to personify the Word of the Lord. The seeds of this trend were already present in the Old Testament. The book of Isaiah sometimes seems to "hypostatize" (attribute independent existence to) God's word, as in Isaiah 9:8: "*The Lord has sent a word against Jacob, and it fell on Israel*" (see also Isa 55:11). Similar images appear in Psalm 33:6, which speaks of the word of the Lord creating the cosmos, and Proverbs 8, where "wisdom" is personified and made God's "partner" in creation.[1784]

These verses definitely make a distinction between the Word and the LORD and the Father, but they also present them as one (*echad*). However, the Apocryphal books of "Ben Sirach," "Wisdom of Solomon," and "4 Ezra" took the distinctions between the Word of the LORD and the Father to even stronger statements, as the following author describes:

> In Hellenistic times some Jewish authors went further still. Ben Sirach personified wisdom, who comes from the mouth of the "Most High" and sits on a heavenly throne (Sir. 24:3-4). He also apparently hypostatized the Word of God, stating that the Word of the Lord goes forth to perform God's work (Sir. 42:15). Similar ideas can be found in the first century A.D. apocalypse 4 Ezra, which makes God's word the creator of heaven and earth (4 Ezra 6:38). But the most striking personification of God's Word in this era comes from the Wisdom of Solomon (a book of the Apocrypha probably written in the first century A.D.), which says that God's "all-powerful Word" leaped from the throne of heaven to carry God's commands to earth (Wis. 8:15). It was in this tradition that Philo stood, and he took the logical step of identifying the personified Word with the *logos* of the Stoics. For Philo, the *logos* was a literal intermediary between God and creation. He was divine, but not God, and so an appropriate mediator between the immutable God and the very mutable natural world.[1785]

Even in Second Temple Judaism where monotheism was strictly held, there were still those within it that promoted the Word as a mediator between the Father and humanity. In fact, the Word of God was at times presenting Him, the Word, as equal to God. There definitely was a struggle in understanding the complexity of the unity of God as Judaism would use the term. Today all of Judaism is uniform in viewing absolute monotheism as the only response that Jewish people can have in their worship and as they understand their statement of faith in the *Shema*. However, the need for a mediator truly does fly in the face of overwhelming testimony in the *Tanakh*. God always used a

---

[1784] Tomasino, *Judaism Before Jesus*, 239-240.
[1785] Tomasino, *Judaism Before Jesus*, 241.

mediator with the people, which is illustrated by Moses, the Levites, the high priest and the prophets. God, when dealing with the sins of the people, uniformly required someone to mediate between Himself and the sinner. The best example would be the high priest who took the blood of the goat as the guilt offering behind the veil and sprinkled it upon and before the Mercy Seat in the Holy of Holies on Yom Kippur (Leviticus 16). This biblical mandate is contrary to what I personally heard in an Orthodox synagogue in Washington D.C. It is also contrary to the statements made by Sigal and others who try to present the issue that the Jewish people always had access to the Father without a mediator. Sigal clearly presents a rabbinic concept that is different than the biblical procedure given by God in the law of Moses that there is no need for a mediator today. Sigal completely misses the point. A Jewish person was always free to come before God in prayer and know that he would be heard. However, when dealing with sin, God consistently used a mediator. That is the picture God has given over and over again in the *Tanakh*. However, it is denied by Judaism, as shown by Sigal:

> Even the Torah was received through an intermediary (Moses); the Scriptures teach us, however, that at no time is God inaccessible to direct contact. The biblical record teaches that there is never a gap between God and man: "the Lord is near to all who call upon Him, to all who call upon Him in truth" (Psalms 145:18). The conception of the Logos as a second god, a divine being higher than the ordinary angels, runs counter to the absolute monotheism of the biblically based Jewish religion. Many of Philo's concepts and conclusions have no roots in Judaism, as they contain many alien admixtures.[1786]

Sigal's statements are flawed in two ways. There is a gap between God and man (sin) which does limit man's approaching God. The second area that Sigal uses is that absolute monotheism is based on a biblical Jewish religion. That is a false statement because absolute monotheism is based not on the Scriptures but on the Oral Law that Rabbinic Judaism, without biblical justification, has elevated to greater authority than the actual Written Word of God. Yes, in the economy of God in the *Tanakh*, *Yahweh* was always accessible to those who came to Him. But when they came to Him to deal with their sin, God always used intermediaries to act between the sinner and Himself as the Holy God. The *Memra* was not a second god but the God of Israel to whom they must confess their sin of rejecting Him before He would come and redeem them (Isaiah 53). So in the following pages the personification of the Word of the LORD in the *Tanakh* will be examined.

There is one final point before going on. Jewish translators have used words to soften the anthropomorphic references of God in the *Tanakh*. This was done to separate or to make God distinct from appearing as a man. The translators have not changed the Hebrew text to read differently, but they have changed it in the English translation of the Aramaic text as well as the English from the Hebrew text to keep God from

---

[1786] Sigal, *The Jew and the Christian Missionary: A Jewish Response to Missionary Christianity*, 149.

appearing to have human characteristics. This is brought out in the following statement by Tomasino:

> And like Philo the rabbis found the concept of the *"word of the Lord"* a useful one for distancing God from creation. In rabbinic texts the word of the Lord isn't called the logos but the dabar elohim (Hebrew) or memra (Aramaic). In some of the Targumin (the Aramaic translations of the Old Testament), biblical passages that depict God interacting with creation are consistently altered or "glossed" by inserting the phrase "the word of the Lord" in place of *"the Lord."* So in Genesis 2:2, it wasn't *"the Lord"* who completed the heavens and the earth but "the word of the Lord." It wasn't *"the Lord"* who spoke to Adam and Eve or visited with Abraham or delivered Israel from Egypt; it was "the word of the Lord" who did all of those things. God himself somehow stayed aloof from the cosmos.[1787]

The reality is whether they were softening the anthropomorphisms of God or interacting with intermediate persons. Judaism in their own writings have acknowledged a plurality of divine or semi-divine persons. In trying to protect God, they have unwittingly opened the door for the plural unity of *Elohim* within their own rabbinic writings, while at the same time denying it. The next section will investigate the testimony of the written word of God itself as it builds on all the previous chapters that have been discussed up to this point.

TESTIMONY OF THE WRITTEN WORD – TANAKH

The testimony of the Written Word to the personification of the Word in the Second Person of the plural unity of *Elohim* is an extremely neglected area of study by fundamental biblical scholars and others. This is uncharted waters for this author. The difficulty is not the understanding of the biblical New Covenant perspective. The difficulty lies in the lack of study done on the *Tanakh* and in confirming the Jewish Scriptures as presenting the Second Person of the plural unity of *Elohim* as the Word.

In the Hebrew Scriptures the word דבר *dabar* (meaning word) is used almost 2600 times. It is translated in the noun form as "word" or "words" דָּבָר and its verb form דָּבַר as "said," "speak," "spoken," "spoke," or "speaking." It is used as a noun or nominative about 1455 times in the phrase *"the word of the LORD came unto."* It is used as a verb another 1140 times as in *"God said,"* or *"and the LORD spoke unto."* It is the same word and its usage is determined by the sentence in which it is found. But there is more involved in this study than the word *davar*, although the focus of the study will ultimately return to *davar*.

The next predominant word used in the *Tanakh* is אמר. The Hebrew word for "said" [אמר – amar] is used in the Hebrew text 5,282 times, making it the most

---

[1787] Tomasino, *Judaism Before Jesus*, 242.

frequently used verb in the *Tanakh*; it is commonly translated "to say" or to "speak."[1788] אמר is a word used in the Hebrew Scriptures as a verb of communication and declaration. It is used by God in speaking to mankind, as well as for mankind speaking to other human beings and to God. It is most often used by God or man in the form of direct speech and is rarely used in indirect speech. אמר is also the word that appears in the common phrase "*thus saith the LORD.*" This word is used of God when He speaks with authority or judgment and at other times is used to issue hope or deliverance.[1789]

In Genesis 1 אמר (said) is the word used by Moses to express what God said when He gave the command by the Word of His mouth to create the heavens and the earth in six literal days. In chapter 3 of this book the term *Elohim* was discussed and shown to be a plural word describing the plural unity of *Elohim*. It does not *per se* state tri-unity but it does state plurality in *Elohim*. All the members of the plurality of *Elohim* were involved in creation as Ecclesiastes 12:1 indicates. However, two prophets of *Yahweh*, Isaiah (48:12-16) and Zechariah (12:1, 10) speak concerning who was involved as the agent of creation, and His identity is found within the context of those passages. Rather than repeating all that information, go back to chapters 10 and 14 of this book respectively to receive the larger review.[1790] What was discovered is that in Isaiah 48:12-16, the Sent One was the Creator and He was also the one who called Israel. He was sent by the Father and the Holy Spirit. The Zechariah 12:1 and 10 passage reviews that the Creator is the one who was "pierced" that the Jewish nation at the end of the tribulation (time of Jacob's Trouble) will mourn over. So in brief, according to the *Tanakh*, the Creator of the universe was the Second Person of the plural unity of *Elohim*, *Yeshua ha Mashiach*. This strongly implies that the God who spoke on day one through day six was the same God who in Genesis 1:26, when creating man, said, "*let us.*" It could very easily be said that *Yeshua*, as the agent of creation in Genesis 1:26, said to the other members of the plural unity of *Elohim*, "come," and "*let us make man in our image and after our likeness.*" He was the one who spoke the world and universe into existence; He is the literal Word of God of whom John the apostle spoke.

Genesis 1 establishes, with references to parallel passages in the *Tanakh*, that the Creator of the universe was the Sent One and the one who was pierced by His own people. He is one in unity with the other members of the plural unity of *Elohim* according to the "Preacher" (Solomon in Ecclesiastes), who are the creators (Ecclesiastes 12:1), plural, of mankind. Now move on to the term "*davar*" the Hebrew for "word." The first recorded reference of "*the word of the LORD came unto*" is found in Genesis 15:1, 4. Here *davar* is used twice and it will be shown that "*the word of the LORD*" was the same member of the plural unity of *Elohim* that made the covenant with Abraham. He was also

---

[1788] Jenni and Westermann, *Theological Lexicon of the Old Testament,* 1:160.

[1789] VanGemeren, *New International Dictionary of Old Testament Theology and Exegesis,* 1:444.

[1790] Review the passages in Isaiah 48:12-16 in chapter 10 of this book and Zechariah 12:1, 10 in chapter 14 of this book. Also Genesis 1:26 may be reviewed in chapter 10 of this book.

"*the word of the LORD*" personified and later is known as Y*eshua* the Son of David, the Righteous Branch, Immanuel, the God/man. In Genesis 15 the Word that spoke to Abraham in confirming the Abrahamic Covenant was also the Word that said of Eliezer of Damascus that he would not be Abraham's heir. Below are the two references where "*the word of the LORD*" spoke to Abraham:

Genesis 15:1, 4

(1) After these things the **word of the LORD** came unto Abram in a vision, saying, Fear not, Abram: I am thy shield, and thy exceeding great reward.

(4) And, behold, the **word of the LORD** *came* unto him, saying, This shall not be thine heir; but he that shall come forth out of thine own bowels shall be thine heir. (Bold lettering is mine)[1791]

It becomes obvious that Abram, in this vision according to verse 2, addresses "*the word of the LORD*" as *Yahweh Elohim*. How is it that "*the word of the LORD*" here in this passage could be identified with *Yeshua*? There is a reference point in the *Tanakh* that speaks to this event in Genesis 15. In chapter 8 of this book, the post-Sinai theophanies were explored and "*the angel* [Messenger] *of the LORD*" in Judges 2:1 was studied. In that passage "*the angel* [Messenger] *of the LORD*" states that He "*made you to go up out of Egypt, and have brought you unto the Land which I sware unto your fathers.*" In this statement two important things are determined. First, "*the angel of the LORD*" took Israel from point A (Egypt) to point B (the Promised Land), a journey which included all the events of the wilderness wanderings or journey. An illustration of that point is the Exodus 24 account where God appeared literally before 74 men to confirm the newly given Mosaic Covenant that was being instituted at that time. Second, Judges 2:1 shows that "*the angel* [Messenger] *of the LORD*" was fulfilling His covenant or promise with Abraham, Isaac and Jacob, the fathers of the Nation of Israel. This part of "*the angel* [Messenger] *of the LORD's*" statement connects Himself with "*the word of the LORD*" that confirmed the covenant to Abram back in Genesis 15. As the theophanies were studied in chapters 4 through 8 of this book, it became abundantly clear that when *HaShem* (LORD) manifested Himself in a form that mankind could hear, see, or both, it was the Second Person of the plural unity of *Elohim* that revealed Himself as the LORD (*HaShem*) of Israel. So "*the word of the Lord*" in Genesis 15, who made the covenant with Abraham, was the manifestation of the Second Person of the plural unity of *Elohim* known in later history through the incarnation as *Yeshua*.

The last passage and the one about to be studied also double as passages that are clear theophanies of God. In 1 Samuel 3 the child Samuel is introduced in the pages of the *Tanakh* as ministering before Eli the High Priest up until his early ministry to Israel as a judge and prophet. There are three key passages in 1 Samuel 3 that use the phrase "*the word of the LORD*," but the one in 1 Samuel 3:21 is the most significant. It clearly

---

[1791] All bold emphasis is mine unless otherwise stated.

distinguishes "*the word of the LORD*" from *HaShem* (LORD). The first passage to be discussed is given below from 1 Samuel 3:7:

> Now Samuel did not yet know the LORD, neither was **the word of the LORD** yet *revealed* unto him.

In this passage it simply states that Samuel did not know the LORD in a personal way for God had not yet communicated with him. There is a distinction in verse 7 between the LORD or *HaShem* who was not yet made known to him and "*the word of the LORD*" who had not yet revealed Himself to Samuel. In the verses that precede and follow this verse, the LORD calls for Samuel three times. In verses 4, 6, 8, and 11 *HaShem* or *Yahweh* calls for Samuel, but in verse 7 the LORD is distinct from "*the word of the LORD.*" "*The word of the LORD*" (verse 7) that speaks to Samuel is also the LORD or *HaShem*. It is commonly purported by Jewish rabbis that these theophanies of God were created beings that acted on behalf of God. Yet each one of the theophanies mentioned in chapters 4 through 8 of this book speak as God Himself and not as a representative in the place of God. These are passages in which *HaShem* (LORD) personally communicated and acted on the behalf of mankind, with the two persons being distinct yet equal. "*The word of the LORD*" is God and yet is distinct from God just as other referenced theophanies are.

The most significant verse is found in 1 Samuel 3:21 after "*the word of the LORD*" has spoken to Samuel. In verses 19-21 the writer gives a brief spiritual summary of the very early years of Samuel's ministry to Israel. First Samuel 3 was mentioned in chapter 8 of this book in the post-Sinai Wilderness theophanies as an appearance of the LORD to Samuel. However, here there is another facet of verse 21 that needs attention. The complete verse is as follows:

> And the LORD **appeared** again in Shiloh: for the LORD **revealed** himself to Samuel in Shiloh by **the word of the LORD**. (1 Samuel 3:21)

In this verse the LORD has appeared and revealed Himself to Samuel at Shiloh. These verses speak of a manifestation that Samuel both saw and heard from the LORD. However, the last phrase of verse 21 states that these appearances and revealings of the LORD to Samuel at Shiloh were by or through "*the word of the LORD.*" In looking through other Jewish versions, such as the Masoretic, Harkavy and Leeser translations, they all word the verse exactly as the King James Version. Kohlenberger, in his Hebrew interlinear, also uses the same phrase. The Lord appeared and revealed Himself to Samuel by "*the word of the LORD.*" Here "*the word of the LORD*" is a person who is distinct from the LORD Himself.

In the next passage in 1 Samuel "*the word of the LORD*" again speaks to Samuel in chapter 15 verses 10-11. Here "*the word of the LORD*" specifically states that "*it repenteth me that I have set up Saul to be King*" as the verses state below:

Then came **the word of the LORD** unto Samuel, saying, it repenteth **me that I have set up Saul to be king**: for he is turned back from **following me**, and hath not performed **my commandments**. And it grieved Samuel; and he cried unto the LORD all night.

Here the personification of "*the word of the LORD*" is open for all to read as He spoke to Samuel concerning Saul's sin. Notice in each of the references used to this point "*the word of the LORD*" is speaking, thinking, and acting as a person distinct from the LORD or *HaShem*. "*The word of the LORD*" specifically states He repented that He had set up Saul, for he had not followed Him and had not kept His commandments. Obviously the speaker here is the Word of the LORD and He is not speaking on behalf of the LORD. He is speaking as the LORD.

The next two passages both relate to the same incident concerning Nathan the prophet returning to David and telling him that he could not build the temple he desired to build, but that "*the word of the LORD*" would instead make a house for David. This passage has been commonly called the Davidic Covenant. Notice the two accounts from 2 Samuel 7:4 and 1 Chronicles 17:3 below:

And it came to pass that night, that the **word of the LORD** came unto Nathan, saying, Go and tell my servant David, Thus saith the LORD, …

And it came to pass that same night, that **the word of God** came to Nathan, saying, Go and tell my servant David, Thus saith the LORD….

In these passages "*the word of the LORD*" that came to Nathan identifies Himself as the LORD. Yet in verse 6 "*the word of the LORD*" said that He had dwelt "*in a tent and in a tabernacle.*" Here again "*the word of the LORD*" spoke as *HaShem* (LORD) to Nathan as the one who led Israel through the period of the wilderness wanderings and the judges. He also stated in verse 8 that it was He who called and took David from being a shepherd of sheep into being the shepherd "*over my people, over Israel.*"

Someone may say that it is the LORD speaking using a descriptive term for Himself and that it is not another member of the plural unity of *Elohim*. There is a principle at work here. The passages that relate to "*the angel* [Messenger] *of the LORD*" (referred to in chapters 4 to 8 of this book), He spoke as the LORD, and yet was distinct and equal to Him. If "*the angel* [Messenger] *of the Lord*" is viewed as God, then "*the word of the LORD*" must be viewed the same way for in principle they are the same; whether it is "*the angel* [Messenger] *of the LORD*" or "*the word of the LORD*" they are both to be viewed as the LORD and yet distinct from the LORD. Review a couple of references: In Genesis 22 "*the angel* [Messenger] *of the LORD*" who spoke with Abraham also is referred to as the LORD in verses 15-16:

The angel of the LORD called to Abraham a second time from heaven, and said, "By Myself I swear, the LORD declares: because you have done this and have not withheld your son, your favored one."

629

The clear statement of Scripture equates *"the angel* [Messenger] *of the LORD"* and the LORD as two distinct, yet equal, individuals. The context is very powerful. Yet another reference is seen in Exodus 3, where Moses meets the LORD for the first time. Here again it is *"the angel* [Messenger] *of the LORD"* who appeared to Moses. Compare verse 2 with *"the angel* [Messenger] *of the LORD,"* and verse 4 *"when the LORD saw that he turned aside to look, God called unto him out of the bush."* Two other terms were used in reference to *"the angel* [Messenger] *of the LORD,"* first as LORD and second as God. Then in verse 6 *"the angel* [Messenger] *of the LORD"* identified Himself as the *"God of your fathers, the God of Abraham, the God of Isaac, and the God of Jacob."* There is one final reference in Judges 6, where *"the angel* [Messenger] *of the LORD"* is identified as the LORD, distinct from the LORD yet equal. So when comparing these accounts of *"the angel* [Messenger] *of the LORD"* with the accounts of *"the word of the LORD"* speaking in passages such as Genesis 15:1, 4; 1 Samuel 3 and 2 Samuel 7 (1 Chronicles 17), He is speaking as the LORD or *HaShem*, while being distinct from *HaShem*, yet equal. It is not consistent to view *"the angel* [Messenger] *of the LORD"* passages with the Second Person of the plural unity of *Elohim* and not also view *"the word of the LORD"* as the Second Person of the plural unity of *Elohim* who communicated with Abraham, Samuel, and Nathan, as well as David, who shall be viewed next.

As David calls Solomon to instruct him in becoming king of Israel, he uses very clear references to *"the word of the LORD."* In 1 Chronicles 22:8-9 David references a time when *"the word of the LORD"* said to him, instructing him that because he was a man of blood, he would not be permitted to build the temple. But he also mentions that *"the word of the LORD"* prophetically references Solomon, his son, who would build the temple in Jerusalem:

> But the **word of the LORD** came to me [David], saying, You have shed much blood and fought great battles; you shall not build a House for **My name** for you have shed much blood on the earth in My sight. But you will have a son who will be a man at rest, for **I will give him rest** from all his enemies on all sides: Solomon will be his name and **I shall confer peace** and quiet on Israel in his time.

Notice the personal pronouns that David used when he referenced what *"the Word of the LORD"* told him; *"My name"* and *"I will give him rest"* and *"I shall confer peace."* As David passed this information on to Solomon, he referenced *"the word of the LORD"* with the phrase *"My name"* and *"I will's"* two times. David is pointing to the fact that *"the word of the LORD"* spoke to him and he understood it not to be the words of an agent of God but of the LORD (*HaShem*) Himself.

There is one final illustration from Scripture that points to *"the word of the LORD"* being a person distinct from and yet equal to *Yahweh*; it occurs when He speaks to Elijah.

630

The *Tanakh* has often been called the Law and the Prophets. Two central figures are usually identified with these two sections of Scripture, Moses and Elijah. In 1 Kings 19:9-10 the writer of Kings gives a dialog of interaction between "*the word of the LORD*" and Elijah. Elijah references the one to whom he is speaking as the one whose covenants Israel has forsaken as the following verses show:

> There he went into a cave, and there he spent the night. Then **the word of the LORD** came to Him. He said to him "Why are you here, Elijah?" He replied, "I am moved by zeal for the LORD, the God of Hosts, for the Israelites have forsaken **Your covenant**, torn down **Your altars**, and put **Your prophets** to the sword. I alone am left, and they are out to take my life."

Here "*the word of the LORD*" is not only speaking to Elijah but is having a conversation with Elijah. Elijah speaks to Him as the Sovereign of Israel that they have forsaken. Elijah responds by using personal pronouns when he rehearses before "*the word of the LORD*" that Israel has torn down "*Your altars*" and has put "*Your prophets*" to the sword. Elijah is obviously speaking to the LORD God of Israel. Notice that *The Jewish Study Bible* even capitalizes "*Your*" twice because it refers directly to "*the word of the LORD*." It is obvious that in this passage "*the word of the LORD*" is a person who speaks with equality with *HaShem* (LORD) but is also a distinct personality from *HaShem* (LORD). This is a powerful verse to demonstrate the personhood of "*the word of the LORD*" and to show that as a theophany, He is also the Second Person of the plural unity of *Elohim*.

Although there are numerous other references concerning "*the word of the LORD*" in the life of Israel in the *Tanakh*, only one more verse will be studied. This verse connects Genesis 1 and related passages discussed early in this chapter, with "*the word of the LORD*" who created with the breath of His mouth. In Psalm 33:4-6 the psalmist equates "*the word of the Lord*" not only with the Creator but also with the LORD Himself. Notice the reference to His creation acts and through whom He created:

> For **the word of the LORD** is right; **His** every deed is faithful. **He** loves what is right and just; the earth is full of the LORD's faithful care. By **the word of the LORD** were the heavens made, by the breath of **his** mouth, all their host.

Notice in these verses first that the earth is full of the LORD's faithful care, which makes a distinction and equality between the LORD and "*the word of the LORD*." In these verses notice the personal pronouns "*He*" and "*His*" which point to the personality of "*the word of the LORD*" and the fact that His every deed is faithful and He loves that which is right and just. This is attributed to "*the word of the LORD*" as if He is the LORD, and He is! Also notice in verse 6 the LORD's faithful care demonstrated "*by the word of the LORD,*" making a clear distinction between *HaShem* (LORD) and the person called "*the word of the LORD*." The word "by" would indicate that when the plural unity of *Elohim* decided to create, They (the plural unity of *Elohim*) did so by the means of His Word. In connection with Genesis 1, verse 9 of Psalm 33 states that "*For*

631

He spoke, and it was; He commanded, and it endured." Who spoke in Genesis 1; *Elohim*, as a plural unity? He spoke, but other related verses in the *Tanakh* make it clear that the Creator was the Second Person of the plural unity of *Elohim* (Isaiah 48:12-16; Zechariah 12:1, 10).

These verses all help to show the personality of the Word, His deeds and His interaction with mankind. The Word is far more than the Greek philosophic word *Logos* of Reason (logic) and Speech; He is the literal Word of the LORD who spoke and interacted with Israel and the prophets throughout the pages of the *Tanakh*.

"*The word of the LORD came unto*" other individuals in the *Tanakh*. This was not an uncommon event in the lives of God's chosen vessels. The following list of references and persons will show a thread of the Word communicating (speaking) with people as He relates to them the will of the LORD. The messenger from the LORD who is also "*the word of the LORD*" speaks. "*The word of the LORD*" is distinct and yet one with the plural unity of *Elohim*. The passages listed below are not discussed, but are worthy of studying:

2 Sam 24:11	… the **word of the LORD** came unto the prophet Gad,
1 Kgs 6:11	And the **word of the LORD** came to Solomon, saying,
1 Kgs 12:22	But the **word of God** came unto Shemaiah the man of God, saying, …
1 Kgs 13:1-2	And behold, there came a man of God out of Judah by the **word of the LORD** unto Bethel: and Jeroboam stood by the altar to burn incense. And he cried against the altar in the **word of the LORD**, and said, …
1 Kgs 16:1	Then the **word of the LORD** came to Jehu the son of Hanani against Baasha, saying….
1 Kgs 17:2, 8	And the **word of the LORD** came unto him [Elijah],
1 Kgs 18:1	And the **word of the LORD** came unto him [Elijah],
1 Kgs 21:17, 28	And the **word of the LORD** came to Elijah the Tishbite, saying,
2 Kgs 20:4	And it came to pass, afore Isaiah was gone out into the middle court, that the **word of the LORD** came to him, saying, ….
2 Chron 11:2	But the **word of the LORD** came to Shemaiah the man of God, saying,
2 Chron 12:7	… the **word of the LORD** came to Shemaiah, saying,
Hosea 1:1-2	The **word of the LORD** that came unto Hosea, the son of Beeri, … and in the days of Jeroboam the son of Joash,

632

king of Israel. The beginning of the **word of the LORD** by Hosea. And the LORD said to Hosea, ...

Joel 1:1	The **word of the LORD** that came to Joel the son of Pethuel
Jonah 1:1	Now the **word of the LORD** came unto Jonah ...
Jonah 3:1	And the **word of the LORD** came unto Jonah the second time, saying,
Micah 1:1	The **word of the LORD** that came to Micah the Morasthite ...
Zeph 1:1-2	The **word of the LORD** which came unto Zephaniah the son of Cushi,
Haggai 1:3	Then came the **word of the LORD** by Haggai the
Haggai 2:5	... came the **word of the LORD** by Haggai
Haggai 2:20	And again the **word of the LORD** came unto Haggai in the four and twentieth day of the month, saying, ...
Zech 1:1	... came the **word of the LORD** unto Zechariah, the son of Berechiah, the son of Iddo the prophet saying,
Zech 1:7	... came the **word of the LORD** unto Zechariah, the son of Berechiah, the son of Iddo the prophet saying, ...
Zech 4:8	Moreover the **word of the LORD** came unto me,
Zech 6:9	And the **word of the LORD** came unto me, saying, ...
Zech 7:1	... the **word of the LORD** came unto Zechariah ...
Zech 7:4	Then came the **word of the LORD** of hosts unto me,
Zech 7:8	And the **word of the LORD** came unto Zechariah,
Zech 8:1	Again the **word of the LORD** of hosts came, saying,
Zech 8:18	And the **word of the LORD** of hosts came unto me,
Zech 2:1	The burden of the **word of the LORD** for Israel, saith the LORD
Mal 1:1	The burden of the **word of the LORD** to Israel by Malachi.

In this next section of Scripture there are simply too many references to deal with directly or individually. So they are simply listed for the reference of the student of the Scripture. In all of these references the word *davar* is used. The very words of God are given as spoken to the intended individuals. The emphasis again is that "the *word of the LORD*" is far more than the Greek logos. They are the very words, the speech of God

633

given to Moses and the prophets as they ministered before the people of God. These verses are different than the preceding passages, for most of these references concerning the Word of God were transmitted to Israel with the emphasis on the word spoken and *"the word of the LORD"* who gave the revelation. The problem with the majority of these verses is that it is not the purpose of these statements of *"the word of the LORD"* to reveal His Person as much as it is to reveal His revelation to mankind. So being able to point to these verses to prove distinction and personhood of the Word of God is not the purpose of Jeremiah and Ezekiel and some of the other references listed. The following author expresses the problem:

> This does not of itself settle the question in favour of symbolic perception as distinct from the pictorial vision, because the **phrase emphasizes the revelatory nature of the experience, rather than reflecting on its mode.**[1792]

These verses are revelatory in nature, for *Yahweh* is presenting His Word, or revealing His revelation to His people. So throughout the following references in this chapter *HaShem* (LORD) is revealing His Word through *"the word of the LORD"* and not *"the word of the LORD"* acting distinctly and independently of the plural unity of *Elohim*, but rather in unity with *Elohim*. In the Written Torah of Moses, the following verses reflect the words of the LORD that *Yahweh* gave to Israel, ending with three verses relating to the prophet Jeremiah that state *"the word of the LORD"* came to him.

Exod 4:28	And Moses told Aaron **all the words** of the LORD ….
Exod 4:30	And Aaron **spake all the words** which the LORD had spoken unto Moses …
Exod 20:1-2	And God **spake all these words**, saying, I am the LORD thy God
Exod 24:3	And Moses came and **told the people all the words of the LORD,**
Exod 24:4	And Moses **wrote all the words of the LORD**
Num 11:24	And Moses went out, and **told the people the words of the LORD,**
Num 12:6	And he [LORD] said, **Hear now my words:** ….
Num 15:31	Because he hath **despised the word of the LORD,** ….
Deut 5:5	I stood between the LORD and you at that time, to **shew you the word of the LORD:** ….
Deut 5:22	**These words the LORD spake** unto all your assembly in the mount out of the midst of the fire, of the cloud, and of the thick darkness.

[1792] Mackay, *Jeremiah: A Mentor Commentary*, 1:106.

Josh 3:7, 9	And the LORD said unto Joshua, … And **hear the words of the LORD** your God.
Judg 2:4	And it came to pass, when the **angel of the LORD spake these word**s unto all the children of Israel, that the people lifted up their voice, and wept.
1 Sam 15:23, 26	Because thou hast **rejected the word of the LORD.**
1 Kgs 12:24	They **hearkened therefore to the word of the LORD,**
Ezra 1:1	… that **the word of the LORD** by the mouth of Jeremiah ….
Isaiah 38:4	**Then came the word of the LORD** to Isaiah, saying,
Daniel 9:2	… whereof **the word of the LORD** came to Jeremiah the prophet,

The last remaining sections are from Jeremiah and Ezekiel where, by far, most usages of the Hebrew word "*davar*" appear. In these two books the phrase "*the word of the LORD*" is used more than in all the other books in the *Tanakh*. In Jeremiah the phrase "*the word of the LORD came unto*" [25 times] and the "*word that came to Jeremiah from the LORD*" [17] are used 42 times. After all these references there are still more phrases such as "*thus saith the LORD*" or "*saith the LORD*" or "*saith the LORD of host*" which are used an additional 294 times. In these instances it is the Hebrew word אָמַר [*amar*] meaning "to say" or "to speak." Several times the Hebrew *amar* is connected with "*the word of the LORD*" as He speaks. All of these references and phrases are interlocked to continue to demonstrate that "*the word of the LORD*" is God Himself. The grammatical structure of this phrase "*the word of the LORD came to*" is a noun. The statement of the LORD where the word "saying" is used as a verb in the sentence emphasizes the Word as the speaker, a person distinct from the LORD Himself. Below you will find the following references to "*the word of the LORD*" in Jeremiah:

Jer 1:2	To whom [Jeremiah] the **word of the LORD came** in the days of Josiah,
Jer 1:4	Then the **word of the LORD came** unto me saying, ….
Jer 1:11	Moreover the **word of the LORD came** unto me, saying, Jeremiah, …
Jer 1:13	And the **word of the LORD came** unto me the second time, saying, …
Jer 2:1	Moreover the **word of the LORD came** to me, saying,
Jer 7:1	The **word that came to Jeremiah from** the LORD,
Jer 10:1	Hear ye the **word which the LORD** speaketh unto you,
Jer 11:1	The **word that came to Jeremiah from** the LORD,

Jer 13:3	And the **word of the LORD came** unto me the second time, saying, ….
Jer 13:8	Then the **word of the LORD came** unto me, saying,
Jer 14:1	The **word of the LORD came** to Jeremiah concerning the dearth.
Jer 16:1	The **word of the LORD came** also unto me, saying,
Jer 17:20	Hear ye **the word of the LORD**, ye kings of Judah, …
Jer 18:1	The **word which came to Jeremiah from** the LORD,
Jer 18:5	Then the **word of the LORD came** to me, saying, …
Jer 19:3	And say, **Hear ye the word of the LORD**, O kings of Judah, …
Jer 20:8	… because the **word of the LORD** was made a reproach unto me
Jer 21:1	The **word which came unto Jeremiah from** the LORD, …
Jer 22:2	And say, **Hear the word of the LORD**, O king of Judah,
Jer 24:4	Again the **word of the LORD came** unto me, saying,
Jer 25:1	The **word that came to** Jeremiah concerning all the people of Judah ….
Jer 25:3	..the **word of the LORD hath come** unto me, and I have spoken unto you,
Jer 26:1	In the beginning of the reign of Jehoiakim the son of Josiah king of Judah **came this word from the LORD,**
Jer 27:1	In the beginning of the reign of Jehoiakim the son of Josiah king of Judah **came this word unto Jeremiah** from the LORD, saying, …
Jer 28:12	Then the **word of the LORD came** unto Jeremiah….
Jer 29:20	Hear ye therefore the **word of the LORD**, all ye of the captivity,…
Jer 29:30	Then **came the word of the LORD unto** Jeremiah,
Jer 30:1	The **word that came** to Jeremiah from the LORD,
Jer 31:10	Hear the **word of the LORD**, O ye nations, …
Jer 32:1	The **word that came to** Jeremiah from the LORD …
Jer 32:6	And Jeremiah said, The **word of the LORD came unto** me, saying, ….

Jer 32:26	Then **came the word of the LORD unto** Jeremiah,
Jer 33:1	Moreover **the word of the LORD came unto** Jeremiah the second time,
Jer 33:19	And the **word of the LORD came** unto Jeremiah
Jer 33:23	Moreover the **word of the LORD came** to Jeremiah,
Jer 34:1	The **word which came unto Jeremiah from** the LORD, ….
Jer 34:4	Yet hear **the word of the LORD**, O Zedekiah king of Judah;
Jer 34:8	This is the **word that came unto** Jeremiah from the LORD, ….
Jer 34:12	Therefore **the word of the LORD came** to Jeremiah from the LORD, saying, ….
Jer 35:1	The **word which came unto Jeremiah from** the LORD in the days …
Jer 35:12	Then **came the word of the LORD** unto Jeremiah,
Jer 36:1	And it came to pass in the 4th year of Jehoiakim the son of Josiah king of Judah, that **this word came unto** Jeremiah from the LORD, saying, …
Jer 36:27	Then **the word of the LORD came** to Jeremiah, ….
Jer 37:2	But neither he, nor his servants, nor the people of the land, did hearken unto **the words of the LORD**, which he spake by the prophet Jeremiah.
Jer 37:6	Then **came the word of the LORD** unto the prophet Jeremiah, saying,…
Jer 39:15	Now the **word of the LORD** came unto Jeremiah, …
Jer 40:1	The **word that came to Jeremiah from** the LORD, …
Jer 42:7	… that the **word of the LORD came** unto Jeremiah.
Jer 42:15	… now therefore **hear the word the LORD**, ye remnant of Judah;
Jer 43:1	… all **the words of the LORD** their God, ….
Jer 43:8	Then came the word of the LORD unto Jeremiah in Tahpanhes, saying,
Jer 44:1	The **word that came to Jeremiah** concerning all the Jews
Jer 44:24	Hear the **word of the LORD**, all Judah that are in the land of Egypt: …

Jer 44:26	Therefore hear ye **the word of the LORD**, all Judah that dwell in
Jer 46:1	The **word of the LORD which came** to Jeremiah the prophet against the Gentiles; ...
Jer 46:13	The **word that the LORD spake** to Jeremiah the
Jer 47:1	The **word of the LORD that came** to Jeremiah the prophet against ...
Jer 49:34	The **word of the LORD that came** to Jeremiah the prophet against ...
Jer 50:1	The **word that the LORD spake** against Babylon ...

There is a wealth of study in these references as each one is taken and studied in relation to the personification of *"the word of the LORD."* The next large grouping of the phrase *"the word of the LORD came unto"* is found in Ezekiel and used 48 times. The other phrase of *"thus saith the LORD"* is used another 199 times. But there are many more such as *"you shall know that I am the LORD"* or *"I am the LORD"* or *"I the LORD have spoken it"* and lastly *"the LORD said."* If all these were added to the *"thus saith the LORD"* expressions, the total references to the LORD speaking would be well over 300. Below are *"the word of the LORD"* references in Ezekiel:

Ezek 1:3	The **word of the LORD came** expressly unto Ezekiel the priest,
Ezek 3:16	... that the **word of the LORD came** unto me, saying,
Ezek 6:1	And the **word of the LORD came** unto me, saying, ...
Ezek 7:1	Moreover the **word of the LORD came** unto me,
Ezek 11:14	Again the **word of the LORD came** unto me, saying,
Ezek 12:1	The **word of the LORD also came** unto me, saying, ...
Ezek 12:8	And in the morning **came the word of the LORD** unto me, saying, ...
Ezek 12:17	Moreover the **word of the LORD came** to me, saying,
Ezek 12:21	And the **word of the LORD came** unto me saying, ...
Ezek 12:26	Again the **word of the LORD came** to me, saying, ...
Ezek 13:1	And the **word of the LORD came** unto me, saying, ...
Ezek 14:2	And the **word of the LORD came** unto me, saying, ...
Ezek 14:12	The **word of the LORD came** again to me, saying, ...
Ezek 15:1	The **word of the LORD came** unto me, saying, ...

Ezek 16:1	Again the **word of the LORD came** unto me, saying,
Ezek 17:1	And the **word of the LORD came** unto me, saying, …
Ezek 17:11	Moreover the **word of the LORD came** unto me,
Ezek 18:1	The **word of the LORD came** unto me again, saying,
Ezek 20:2	Then came the **word of the LORD** unto me, saying, …
Ezek 20:45	Moreover the **word of the LORD came** unto me
Ezek 21:1	And the **word of the LORD came** unto me, saying, ….
Ezek 21:8	Again the **word of the LORD came** unto me, saying,
Ezek 21:18	The **word of the LORD came** unto me again, saying,
Ezek 22:1	Moreover the **word of the LORD came** unto me,
Ezek 22:17	And the **word of the LORD came** unto me, saying, ….
Ezek 22:23	And the **word of the LORD came** unto me, saying, ….
Ezek 23:1	The **word of the LORD came** again unto me, saying,
Ezek 24:1	… the **word of the LORD came** unto me, saying, ….
Ezek 24:15	Also the **word of the LORD came** unto me, saying, ….
Ezek 24:20	Then I answered them, The **word of the LORD came** unto me, saying,
Ezek 25:1	The **word of the LORD came** again unto me, saying,
Ezek 26:1	… the **word of the LORD came** unto me, saying, ….
Ezek 27:1	The **word of the LORD came** again unto me, saying,
Ezek 28:1	The **word of the LORD came** again unto me, saying,
Ezek 28:11	Moreover the **word of the LORD came** unto me,
Ezek 28:20	Again the **word of the LORD came** unto me, saying,
Ezek 29:1	… the **word of the LORD came** unto me, saying, ….
Ezek 29:17	… the **word of the LORD came** unto me, saying, ….
Ezek 30:1	The **word of the LORD came** again unto me, saying,
Ezek 30:20	… the **word of the LORD came** unto me, saying, ….
Ezek 31:1	… the **word of the LORD came** unto me, saying, ….
Ezek 32:1	… the **word of the LORD came** unto me, saying, ….
Ezek 32:17	… the **word of the LORD came** unto me, saying, ….
Ezek 33:1	Again the **word of the LORD came** unto me, saying,

Ezek 33:23	Then the **word of the LORD came** unto me, saying,
Ezek 33:30	… and hear what is the **word that cometh forth from the LORD.**
Ezek 34:1	And the **word of the LORD came** unto me, saying, ….
Ezek 35:1	Moreover the **word of the LORD came** unto me,
Ezek 36:16	Moreover the **word of the LORD came** unto me,
Ezek 37:15	The **word of the LORD came** again unto me, saying,
Ezek 38:1	And the **word of the LORD came** unto me, saying, ….

All of this becomes a formidable weight of evidence to the personification of *"the word of the LORD."* In Jeremiah and Ezekiel, whenever *Yahweh* begins a new subject or repeats it for the sake of emphasis, He commonly states *"the word of the LORD came unto"* and the text then proceeds to give what the LORD said. What it clearly demonstrates is that the *"word of the LORD"* is a separate, distinct person within the plural unity of *Elohim* who also, when He speaks, speaks as *HaShem* (LORD).

TESTIMONY FROM THE TARGUMS

This section on the Targums contains mixed blessings. There are two other components that need to be introduced before getting into this section in relation to the Targums and their use of the phrase *"the word of the LORD."*

First, Rabbinic Judaism had issues with God using references to Himself in human terms, anthropomorphisms such as God's eyes, arms, feet and mouth. Rabbinic Judaism shied away from those terms because people might equate God with humanlike appearances and make graven images of Him. The Targums and even the Septuagint softened those terms so that they could not be misunderstood and emphasized the fact that God is an incorporeal spirit, meaning He is pure spirit and does not have a body or body parts. True followers of *Yeshua* would completely agree with Judaism on that issue. Believers in *Yeshua*'s problem is that Rabbinic Judaism changes that literal meaning of the Hebrew when translating to a sort of dynamic equivalent. In doing so Rabbinic Judaism often removed the intended language impact that God Himself used when revealing Himself to them. The bottom line on this issue is that God had no problem using anthropomorphisms in revealing Himself to mankind.

The second issue is that Rabbinic Judaism took passages that spoke of God doing this or that and changes the translated text to an intermediate person like *Metatron* or *"the word of the LORD"* who in turn does this or that to fulfill the will of God for He is acting for God in His behalf. Here is part of a quote from Rabbi Louis Jacobs expressing that:

The Targum of Onkelos often uses the Aramaic memra ('word') as a means of softening the biblical anthropomorphisms so that instead of the Hebrew in which it is stated that God does this or that it is the memra from God that is active.[1793]

Notice closely that Rabbi Jacobs states that the Word (*memra*, Aramaic – word) is active in the place of God Himself. As this section on the use of the phrase *"the word of the LORD"* unfolds, Rabbinic Judaism of that day was not saying that God is a plurality of persons. Rabbinic Judaism had softened the anthropomorphisms and the active engagement of God in the affairs of men. However, one clear fact remains. In the Hebrew Scriptures God was the one who was active in the affairs of men. True biblical faith believes, from the *Tanakh*, that the plurality of God is an unquestioned biblical reality and that one member of plural unity of *Elohim* revealed Himself and was personally involved in the affairs of men. He was not an intermediary or an agent of God; He, the Word, was God Himself.

Also, what this whole subject points to is that within Rabbinic Judaism they were struggling with Scripture and the personal interaction that God was having with His creation. Unwittingly in their attempt to soften the anthropomorphisms and with the rejection or refusal to believe the plurality in unity of *Elohim*, they have been, in essence, teaching the plurality of *Elohim* by presenting what God said or did to an intermediary agent who was actually God Himself! God did present Himself in different ways to His people, but because they insist on using *echad* as an absolute one, they have taken those plural references and applied them to *Metatron, Shechinah*, the *word of the LORD* and numerous other intermediary agents. What they have actually done in the Targums is to help authenticate the plurality of *Elohim* by making the intermediary person who does the speaking and acting as God, the same as God. Biblically, there is no intermediary agent in those passages because the one who is speaking and acting is the Second Person of the plural unity of *Elohim*. The members of the plural unity of God are equal and yet they are also distinct.

The Targums were written approximately in the first century BCE into the first or second century of the Common Era (CE) also reflect the ideas and the theological conceptions of the Synagogue.[1794] The origin of the Targums first appears in Nehemiah 8:8 when the people returned from captivity and could not read or understand Hebrew. Nehemiah and the scribes would read the Torah and then translate it into Aramaic *"and they gave the sense so that they understood the reading."* This section in Nehemiah will point out clearly that John, in his gospel, was not drawing from the Hellenized Greek philosophy of *logos*. Rather it was the rabbis themselves as they inadvertently pointed to the Second Person of the plural unity of *Elohim,* who revealed Himself through the theophanies and His revealed Word (*Memra*) in the *Tanakh*. In the *Tanakh* He is known as God, LORD, *the angel of the LORD, Shechinah,*

[1793] Jacobs, *A Concise Companion to the Jewish Religion*, 301.
[1794] Cooper, *The God of Israel*, 89.

the Branch, Immanuel, the Servant of the LORD, Son of David who was the one born of "*the virgin*" in Bethlehem as the legitimate Son of David, the Promised one to Israel, the God/man of the New Covenant who is the only one who can bring true and genuine righteousness and peace to this world, *Yeshua ha Mashiach*.

In an investigation of the Targums, notice carefully that most of these passages were clearly identified as theophanies in chapters 4 to 8 of this book, and Targums have replaced them with the phrase "*the Word of the LORD.*" This process will be repeated over and over again as "*the Word of the LORD*" is presented as a person who is carrying out the will of the LORD. These verses are repeated as the same theophanies already discussed, but the difference is the Targums have attributed the character and qualities of God to what they believe are intermediaries. The following passages will be quoted directly from the Targum Palestine and the Jerusalem Targum. Numerous ones will be quoted and set in bold typeface to draw attention to the Word as a separate person of the plural unity of *Elohim*. Comments will be made after the verses are quoted:

> Gen 1:27   And the **Word of Jehovah created man in his likeness**, in the likeness of Jehovah, Jehovah created, male and female created he them.
>
> Gen 3:8   And they [Adam and Eve] heard **the voice of the word of the Lord God walking** in the garden.
>
> Gen 3:9   And the **Word of the Lord God called** to Adam.
>
> Gen 3:10   The **voice of thy Word** heard I in the garden, ...
>
> Gen 4:1   Adam knew Hava [Eve] his wife, who had desired **the Angel**; and she conceived, and bore Kain [Cain]; and she said, **I have acquired a man, the Angel of the Lord.**
>
> Gen 5:24   ... and he ascended to the firmament **by the Word before the Lord**, and **his name** [Enoch] **was called Metatron** the Great Saphra.
>
> Gen 6:3   An the **Lord said by His Word,**
>
> Gen 6:6   And **it repented the Lord in His Word** that He had made man upon the earth; and **He passed judgment upon them by His Word**.
>
> Gen 6: 7   the Lord said, I will abolish **by My Word** man, whom I have created upon the face of the earth, ... because **I have repented in My Word** that I have made them.
>
> Gen 7:16   and **the Word of the Lord** covered over the door of the ark ....
>
> Gen 8:1   And **the Lord in His Word** remembered Noah, ...

Gen 8:21	the **Lord said in His Word**, I will not add again to curse the earth on account of the sin of the children of men;
Gen 9:9	And the Lord said, This is the sign of the covenant which **I establish between My Word and between you** and every living soul that is with you, ….
Gen 9:11	And **I will remember My covenant** which is between **My Word and between you and every living soul** of all flesh, ….
Gen 9: 13	And bow shall be in the cloud, and **I will** look upon it, to remember the everlasting covenant **between the Word of the Lord and every living soul of all flesh** that is upon the earth.
Gen 11:1	…while their hearts erred afterwards **from the Word of Him who spoke,**
Gen 11:7	And **the Word of the Lord** was revealed against the city,

These verses of the Targums literally equate the Word [*Memra*] with the LORD and make the Word equal to the LORD. The Word [*Memra*] is the LORD, the Second Person of the plural unity of *Elohim*. In these pre-Abrahamic references "*the Word of the Lord*," is identified as the *Memra*, and were used in the following ways:

The **Word of the Lord** Created Man;

The **voice of the Word of the Lord** walked in the garden;

The **Word of the Lord called** Adam;

Enoch ascended to heaven by the Word before the Lord; in the flood narrative the Lord spoke **by His Word**; the Lord repented **in His Word**;

The Lord passed judgment **by His Word**;

The Lord will destroy man **by His Word**;

The **Word of the Lord closed** the door of the ark;

The Lord remembered Noah **by His Word**;

The Noahic Covenant was established **by His Word**;

In the Tower of Babel context the people erred **by the Word of Him** who spoke; and the **Word of the Lord was revealed** to the people of the city.

In all these references the Targum capitalizes the "Word" and the pronouns "His" and "My." Without question, what is being presented here is that the Targum attributes a personality to the "Word" or *Memra* who acts and talks on behalf of the LORD. He has the character and essence of the LORD and carries out judgment on sin. The Targums have the "Word" involved with creating mankind, confronting Adam and Eve when they sinned, in the ascension of Enoch, as well as working with Noah and making the Noahic Covenant and judging the generation at the Tower of Babel. The Targums were doing this not because they believed in the plurality of *Elohim*, but because they did see plurality and attributed it to intermediaries like angels.

In Genesis 4:1 an understanding of Eve's theology is very revealing as she listened to what God said to Satan in the Genesis 3:15 account. Look at the description and the understanding of the rabbis who paraphrased the Hebrew text:

> And Adam knew Hava [Eve] his wife, who had desired **the Angel**; and she conceived, and bore Kain [Cain]; and she said, **I have acquired a man, the Angel of the Lord.**

Eve understood clearly what the LORD God said to Satan, that there would be a man born who was more than a man. He would also be God incarnate who "*dwelt among us.*"

Because there are so many times that the Targums use *Word* or *Memra* in reference to God, only a sampling of passages will be reviewed. When reading the Targums, one finds much that is fictional in nature and has absolutely no authority based on the *Tanakh* to be even part of the Targums. But such fictions are there in abundance in the Torah passages of the Targums that this author read and compared with the Hebrew Scriptures. In the following verses notice that the term "Word" or "*Memra*" is used as a synonym for the LORD God and that the *Memra* or "Word" is worshipped by people like Hagar, Abraham and Moses. It is also used to show a distinction between the Lord and the Word [*Memra*] yet equal with *Elohim*. One other point is that the Targums were sanctioned by the rabbis and placed alongside Scripture, as the following quotation points out:

> We may with confidence, then, come to the Targums and see reflected therein quite accurately the teachings of the great masters in Israel. Especially can we draw this conclusion with regard to the two Targums about which we have been studying, since they are the ones that appear along with the Hebrew text in the Bible edited by the rabbis. This fact gives official sanction, in a general way at least, to these Targums.[1795]

The Targums should be looked upon as adding valuable insights to the understanding of the rabbis of that era. This section will be opened with reviewing Genesis 15:6, and noting carefully as verses from Targums of the *Tanakh* are discussed:

Genesis 15:6

And he believed in the Lord, and had faith in the (*Memra*) Word of the Lord, and He reckoned it to him for righteousness.

[1795] Cooper, *The God of Israel*, 89.

The context of the passage on "*the Word of the LORD*" is the ratification of the Abrahamic Covenant by the God of Israel. However, verses 1 and 4 and then verse 6 in the Targum stated "*the Word of the LORD came unto*" Abraham and he believed in "*the Word of the LORD*" and "*the Word of the LORD*" accounted it to Abraham for righteousness. Notice that his faith was in the *Memra*, the Word, as stated in the Targum. In order for the *Memra* to declare Abraham righteous, the "*Lord*" and "*the Word of the Lord*" in the Targums must also be God. The Targums clearly makes a distinction of persons, yet they both speak as God.

Genesis 16:13

And she gave thanks before the Lord whose Word spake to her, … For., behold, here is **revealed the glory of the Shekina of the Lord** after a vision. (Jerusalem Targum) And Hagar gave thanks, and **prayed in the Name of the Word of the Lord**, who had been manifested to her, ….

The Targums and the *Tanakh* both use the term "*the angel of the LORD*" for the one interacting with Hagar. However, here in the Targums in verse 13 the Angel of the LORD is connected to the glory of the *Shekinah* and in the Jerusalem Targum Hagar gives thanks and prays in the name of the Word of the Lord. Angels do not receive prayers nor are angels prayed to. But this Angel (Messenger) is the Second Person of the plural unity of *Elohim* discussed back in chapter 5 of this book. The Targums and the *Tanakh* teach that not only was the Word of the Lord prayed to, Hagar prayed in His Name. If there is absolute unity as Rabbinic Judaism states, why did the Angel of the LORD receive Hagar's prayer to Him unless there is a plurality of persons in *Elohim*? One additional point needs to be made. In Isaiah 42:8 the glory of the LORD belongs to Him and to Him alone. It will not be given to an agent or angel of God, for His glory belongs solely to Him. Here the Targum refers to the glory of the LORD who then can only refer to God Himself in the Second Person of the plural unity of *Elohim*. This will show up in other verses in the Targum, so keep this in mind. The Glory of God is His and His alone; it cannot be used by any other being but the LORD Himself, according to Isaiah 42:8.

Genesis 17:7

And I have established **My covenant between My Word** and thee, and thy sons after thee.

In Genesis 17 in the Targums the phrase "My covenant between My Word and thee" is used four times to express that the LORD made the Abrahamic Covenant through the Word of the LORD. In Judges 2:1 "*the angel of the LORD*" states that He made the covenant and swore to Abraham, Isaac and Jacob that He would fulfill it. Chapters 17 through 19 of Genesis in the Hebrew Scriptures are closely related. In Genesis 17:22 the LORD promises the Covenant will be established with Isaac and then the Lord, or as the Targum has it, the Glory of the Lord, ascended from before Abraham, as stated:

Genesis 17:22

But My COVENANT will I establish with Izhak (Isaac), whom Sarah shall bear to thee at this time in the year after. And He ceased speaking with him; and the **Glory of the Lord ascended from** Abraham.

In the Hebrew text there is no reference to the glory of the LORD appearing to Abraham. It simply states in the Hebrew Scriptures that *"the LORD appeared to Abram."* It has to be a physical appearance of some kind because the LORD *"went up from Abraham"* in verse 22. The covenant that was established by "My Word" that was spoken to Abraham ascended from before him. Rabbinic Judaism's attempt is to negate the personal interaction of the LORD and go through an intermediary agent, a heavenly being, but not God. The LORD does go through His Word but as it has been seen already, the Word is a person who is equal to and yet distinct from the LORD. He is the one who, after appearing and speaking to Abraham, ascended. He is the Second Person of the plural unity of *Elohim*.

The Targum stated that "the glory of the Lord" was revealed to Abraham, but notice that in the biblical text there is no reference to God's glory appearing. This "glory," according to the Targum, was revealed as three angels. Abraham then asked the three angels, if he has found favour, that "the glory of Thy shekina may not now ascend from Thy Servant" as stated in the next two verses:

Genesis 18:1

And the **glory of the Lord** was revealed to him in the valley of Mamre; ....

Genesis 18:3 And he said, I beseech, by the mercies (that are) before Thee, O Lord, if now I have found favour before thee, that the **glory of Thy shekina may not now ascend from Thy servant**, until I have set forth provisions under the tree.

In the Targum there is confusion between what "the glory of the Lord" is and the "three angels" that appeared. In this chapter of the Targum there is lots of fanciful material added that has no biblical merit. In verse 3 Abraham refers to the three angels as Lord, so there is a recognition that one of these "Angels" is the LORD Himself, which is exactly what the biblical text says. Even in the Targum it is clearly seen that one of the men before Abraham is the LORD, because of the following comments: "before the Lord;" "the Lord said;" "before Me;" "now, I have begun to speak before the Lord;" "the Lord of all the world;" and finally "And the majesty of the Lord went up when He had ceased to speak with Abraham; and Abraham returned to his place." If the angels who looked like men are mere servants of God, the language of the Targum betrays Judaism in not comprehending the plural unity of *Elohim*. In verse 17 in the Targum there is a reference to "the Lord, with His Word," which once again identifies the Lord and the Word as two distinct individuals.

Genesis 19:24

And **the Word of the Lord** had caused showers …. There are now sent down upon them sulphur and fire **from before the Word of the Lord from Heaven.**

The verse above has much fictional material. The beginning of the verse states that "the Word of the Lord" sent the destruction on Sedom (Sodom) and Amorah (Gomorrah), then that it came "from before the Word of the Lord in Heaven." The Targum attributes the act against "Sedom" and "Amorah" as coming from "the Word of the Lord." However, in the Hebrew text it is the LORD who was standing with Abraham and sent the fire and brimstone upon Sodom and Gomorrah from the LORD in Heaven. In the Targum "the Word of the Lord" was the person judging, but in the *Tanakh* it was the LORD who revealed His plurality in the biblical text. The following is an interesting testimony of a rabbi who honestly studied the Scriptures and came to understand the great mystery of the plurality of *Elohim*:

> Our God has declared by the Prophet Isaiah (42:8), "I am the Lord: that is my name: and my glory will I not give to another." What a stream of light was poured into my mind, when investigating the mystery contained in these words, "Then the Lord rained upon Sodom and upon Gomorrah brimstone and fire from the Lord out of heaven" (Genesis 19:24). My teacher Jonathan ben Uziel, taught me, by his Jerusalem [Targum] Paraphrase, that the Lord (יחוה) mentioned in this passage of Scripture, is the Word of the Lord. "And the Word of the Lord caused to descend upon the people of Sodom and Gomorrah, brimstone and fire from the Lord from heaven."[1796]

The reference to Isaiah 42:8 is a wonderful insight, for God's glory belongs to Him alone. No angel or intermediate being can have His glory. Because the Word of the LORD is the Second Person of the plurality of *Elohim*, He was the one speaking to Abraham, and He was the one who consistently revealed Himself to His people.

Genesis 22:1, 7-8, 15-16

(1) These words were heard before the Lord of the world, and the Word of the Lord at once tried Abraham, and said to him (7-8) (Jerusalem Targum) And Abraham said, **The Word of the Lord will prepare for me a lamb**, and if not, then thou art the offering, my son! And the **Angel** of the Lord called to him from the heavens, and said to him, Abraham! … for now it is manifest before **Me** that thou fearest the Lord; neither hast thou withheld thy son the only begotten from **Me**. (15-16) And the **Angel** of the Lord called to Abraham the second time from the heavens, and said, **By My Word have I sworn**, saith the Lord, ….

[1796] Nassi (Hirsch Prinz), *The Great Mystery: Or How Can Three Be One?*, 31.

In the story of Abraham offering up Isaac before the LORD, as written in the Targum, there are three names that apply to the same person who is tempting Abraham, "the Lord of the world," "the Word of the Lord," and *the angel of the LORD*." Notice that it is "the Word of the Lord" who spoke to Abraham, and when Isaac asked where the lamb was Abraham replied "the Word of the Lord" would provide. In verse 11 of the Hebrew text and the Targum presents "the Word of the LORD" as the Angel of the LORD in calling Abraham to stop his act of slaying his son Isaac. Also, in verse 11 the Targum equates *the angel of the LORD*" as God in the Targum. Twice in the verse the speaker uses the personal pronoun "Me:" "before Me" and "withheld thy son the only begotten from Me." Then in verses 15-16 the Angel of the Lord states that "By My Word have I sworn, saith the Lord." Also, in the Targum it is interesting that the Angel of the Lord is used twice; each time it is capitalized and several times the personal pronouns are used such as "My Word" and "Me." It is this author's understanding that you do not capitalize pronouns like this unless you are referring to God Himself.

Genesis 24:1, 3

(1) And Abraham was old with days, and **the Word of the Lord had blessed** Abraham with every kind of blessing. (3) And swear to me **in the name of the Word of the Lord God**, whose **habitation is in heaven on high, the God whose dominion is over the earth**, that thou wilt not take a wife for my son from the daughters of ….

Genesis 24 is the story of Abraham obtaining a bride for his son Isaac. In verse 1 it clearly states that Abraham was blessed by the Word of the LORD, and that blessing was the fulfillment to Abraham personally of the promise he received in Genesis 12:1-3 that he would be blessed and a blessing to others. Then Abraham had his servant, who was probably Eliezer of Damascus, swear by the name of the Word of the LORD. Look at Abraham's description of the Word of the LORD; His habitation is in heaven and He is God who has dominion over all the earth. The LORD has never given that kind of authority to an angel or an agent of Himself. He alone reserves that authority to Himself, the Word of God.

Genesis 28:20-21

(Targum Onkelos) And Jacob vowed a vow, saying, If **the Word of Jehovah** will be my support, and will keep me in the way that I go, and will give me bread to eat, and raiment to put on, so that I come again to my father's house in peace; **then shall the Word of Jehovah be my God**.

From this quotation we see that Onkelos understood that one of the divine beings is called the Word of Jehovah.[1797] Look at this verse in the Targum closely. At the end of the verse Jacob said that the Word of Jehovah would be his God. Jacob is claiming the Word as his God. Even though some things in the Targum are fictional, they are correct

---

[1797] Cooper, *The God of Israel*, 90.

in connecting "the Word of the LORD" with the "Almighty God" as *HaShem*. They also present "the Word of the LORD," the "LORD" and the "Almighty God" as distinct individuals within the plural unity of *Elohim*.

Genesis 32:24

(24) And Jakob remained alone beyond the Jubeka; and **an Angel** [Michael] contended with him in the likeness of a man.

As mentioned before, there are fictitious elements in the Targums. A good example of that is the verse above. Michael the archangel is not mentioned in the biblical text until Daniel references him. Between this passage and Hosea 12:3-4, it is clearly seen that the One who wrestled with Jacob was the (angel) Messenger of the LORD, Who had appeared many times in the biblical text, and was identified as the Second Person of the plural unity of *Elohim*. Also, notice "Angel" is capitalized, which would normally mean that the Angel is God, but then later in the text of the Targum he is called Michael, who is a created being and not God.

Genesis 35:1, 3, 9

(1) And the **Lord said** to Jakob, Arise, go up to Bethel and dwell there, and **make there an altar unto Eloha** (Elohim), **who revealed Himself** to thee in thy flight from before Esau thy brother. (3)… who heard my prayer in the day when I was afflicted, and **whose Word was my helper** in the way that I went. (9) And the **Lord revealed Himself** to Jakob again on this return from Padan of Aram, and **the Lord blessed him by the name of His Word**, after the death of his mother. (Targum Jerusalem) And **the Word of the Lord blessed them**, and the **Word of the Lord said to them,** Be strong and multiply, and fill the earth and subdue it. He hath taught us to visit the afflicted, from our father Abraham the Righteous, **when He revealed Himself to him** in the plain of Vision, … and **the Word of the Lord revealed Himself to him** in the plain of Vision.… for He revealed Himself to him on his coming from Padan of Aram, … The **Word of the Lord revealed Himself unto Jakob** the second time on his coming from Padan Aram, and blessed him.

These passages are also covered in chapter 5 of this book where a clear theophany of God appeared to Jacob. In this passage the Targum very clearly presents the plurality of *Elohim* where the LORD tells Jacob to build an altar to *Elohim* who revealed Himself to him. Then the LORD blesses Abraham by the name of His Word. If the Word is not the LORD, then why is the LORD blessing Abraham in the name of the Word? Once again, the Targum presents the plurality of *Elohim* and points to the Second Person of the plural unity of *Elohim*, the Word of God.

Genesis 48:9

And Joseph answered his father, They are my sons which the **Word of the Lord gave me** according to this writing, ….

Here Joseph has spoken to his father Jacob, presenting his sons (Ephraim and Manasseh) that the Word of the LORD has given to him. Joseph is not saying his sons were given to him by angels or intermediary agents, but by the Word of God Himself, who is equal with the LORD in His essence and character, yet as a person is distinct.

Exodus 3:2, 4, 8, 14

(2) And **Zagnugael, the angel of the Lord, appeared** ....

(4) ... the **Lord called to him from the midst of the bush** and said, ...

(7) And I have revealed Myself to thee this day, that **by My Word they** may be delivered from the hand of the Mizraee [Egyptians], ...

(14) (Jerusalem Targum) And **the Word of the Lord said** to Mosheh, **He** who spake to the world, **Be**, and it was; and who will speak to it, Be, and it will be. **And he said,** Thus shalt thou speak to the sons of Israel **EHEYEH [I AM] hath sent me unto you.**

The name Zagnugael only appears in the Targums and it is another name for *Metatron*,[1798] the Messenger of the LORD, who appeared to Moses in the burning bush. It is clearly seen when reading the *Tanakh* or the Targums that "*the angel of the LORD*" that spoke to Moses was the LORD God. In the Targum He refers to Himself as "My Word" who told Moses to remove his shoes because he was standing on holy ground. Even if an ordinary angel or messenger of God spoke the words of God, he would not request the recipient (Moses in this case) to remove his shoes because the ground on which he was standing was holy. That ground was holy because the very presence and person of God was there in the person of the Second Person of the plural unity of *Elohim*. Verse 14 is incredible: "the Word of the LORD" spoke to Moses telling him that He was the Creator by the Word of His Mouth. Then He told Moses to tell Israel the "I AM" had sent him unto them. Cooper references this passage by saying:

> Here again the one who is called the "angel of Jehovah" and also Jehovah himself, who spoke to Moses out of the burning bush, is called in this translation "The Word of Jehovah." Here, as in the passages just mentioned, one of the divine personalities is called the Word of Jehovah.[1799]

Exodus 14:31

And Israel saw the power of the mighty hand by which the Lord had wrought the miracles in Mizraim; and the people feared before the Lord, **and believed in the name of the Word of the Lord**, and in the prophecies of Mosheh [Moses] His servant.

[1798] Neusner and Green, *Dictionary of Judaism in the Biblical Period*, 686.
[1799] Cooper, *The God of Israel*, 89-90.

Notice who the people of Israel feared and believed in, "the Name of the Word of the LORD" the God of Israel. Once again notice what is capitalized and the deity status given to "the Word of the LORD." and they believed in His Name.

Exodus 19:7-9

(7) And Mosheh [Moses] came and called the sages of Israel and set in order before them **all these words which the Word of the Lord had commanded him**. (8) And all the people answered together in the fullness of their heart, and said, **All that the Word of the Lord hath spoken, we will do.** And Mosheh returned the words of the people in prayer before the Lord, (9) And **the Word of the Lord said to Mosheh**, Behold, **My Word will be revealed to thee in the thickness of the cloud**, that the people may hear while I speak with thee, and may also believe for ever in the words of the prophecy of thee, My servant Mosheh.

Notice throughout these verses who spoke to Moses: "the Word of the LORD." The LORD told Moses that "My Word" would be revealed. In the following verse the description of the mountain and the people was given. "The Word of the LORD" spoke to Moses as God Himself and not as an intermediary agent. Once again, according to Isaiah 42:8, it was the glory of *HaShem* that appeared on the mountain and spoke to Moses. Moses was communicating with a person, "the Word of the LORD," the Second Person of the plural unity of *Elohim*.

Exodus 20:1, 7

(1) And the Lord spake all these words, saying: (Jerusalem Targum) And the **Word of the Lord spake all the excellency of these words saying:** The first word, as it **came forth from the mouth of the Holy One, whose Name be blessed**, …. The second word which came **from the mouth of the Holy One, whose name be blessed**, …. (7) My people of the house of Israel, **Let no one of you swear by the name of the Word of the Lord your God** in vain; ….

In Exodus 20 there is no change of persons, and Moses gives the people what the Targums call the "Ten Words" or the Ten Commandments. The description of the LORD or "the Word of the LORD," for His words come "from the mouth of the Holy One, whose Name be blessed." It is His Name that is not to be taken in vain: *"the word of the LORD your God."* There is no mistaking the identity of the Word of the LORD, for He is *HaShem*, the LORD, the Second Person of the plural unity of *Elohim*. This was clearly seen by Rabbi Tzvi Nassi as he spoke concerning his understanding of Exodus 20:1 where he saw the WORD of the LORD as distinct from the LORD:

The ancient faith of my nation was, that the WORD of the Lord, was the Lawgiver. That no other than, the WORD of Jehovah, has been their Lawgiver, is proved from the words of the Jerusalem Targum, on Exodus 20:1, in which we read as follows: "And the WORD of the Lord spake all these glorious words."[1800]

What this rabbi sees is that the WORD of the Lord is the giver of the Law to Moses, a separate and distinct person from the Father. The connection here with the Messenger of the LORD and the *Shechinah* of God and now the WORD of the Lord should not be missed.

Numbers 10:35-36

(Jerusalem Targum) It was when the ark went forward. Mosheh stood, with hands (outstretched) in prayer, and said, **Arise now, O Word of the Lord**, in the power of thy might, and let the adversaries of Thy people be scattered, and make Thine enemies flee before Thee. But when the ark rested, Mosheh lifted his hands in prayer, **and said O Word of the Lord**, turn from the strength of Thy anger, and return unto us in the goodness of Thy mercy, and bless the myriads and multiply the thousands of the children of Israel.

Moses is addressing *HaShem*, the LORD God of Israel, and calls Him "the Word of the Lord." With consistency the Targums make the LORD and "the Word of the LORD" two distinct yet equal persons in character and essence, but the Targums, along with the *Tanakh*, also show the plurality and individuality of the persons of the plural unity of *Elohim*.

Deuteronomy 6:13

(Jerusalem Targum)… but fear the Lord your God, and worship before Him, and **swear by the Name of the Word of the Lord in truth**.

In Deuteronomy when Moses rehearsed the Law to the generation that was about to enter the land of Canaan, he told them to fear the LORD their God, to worship Him and to swear "by the Name of the Word of the LORD." Individuality and unity were expressed by Moses to this new generation.

Deuteronomy 6:21-22

We were servants to Pharaoh in Mizraim, **and the Word of the Lord brought us out of Mizraim with a mighty hand; and the Word of the Lord wrought signs, great wonders, and sore plagues on Mizraim and on Pharaoh** and all the men of his house, ….

Who brought Israel out from the land of Egypt? It was "the Word of the LORD" with great signs and wonders. In the *Tanakh*, according to Judges 2:1, "*the angel of the LORD*" brought Israel out of bondage into the Promised Land. He had sworn to the Fathers as the covenant maker to Abraham (Genesis 15). In the *Tanakh*, according to Deuteronomy 6:21-22, who brought Israel out of Egypt? It was *HaShem*, the LORD.

[1800] Nassi, *The Great Mystery: or How Can Three Be One?*, 34.

According to the testimony of the *Tanakh* and the Targums, it was the LORD, "*the angel* [Messenger] *of the LORD*" and "the Word of the LORD," a great mystery, a plurality in unity.

Deuteronomy 32:39, 43

> 39 When **the Word of the Lord shall reveal Himself to redeem His people, He will say** to all the nations: Behold now, **that I am He who Am and Was, and Will Be**, and there is no other God beside Me: ....43 Rejoice, ye nations, ye people of Beth Israel; for the blood of His servants which was shed, He hath avenged. He hath kept (in mind) and returned just vengeance upon His adversaries, and **by His Word will He make Atonement for His land, and for His people.**

These two verses speak of redemption and atonement. In verse 39 "the Word of the LORD" will redeem His people. A couple of questions come to mind: How will He redeem them? Would a mere intermediary agent of *HaShem* refer to Israel as His people? The answer is that He personally, at His incarnation, will redeem His people from their sins, and because of their rejection of Him He will, at His second coming, fulfill the Abrahamic Covenant, bringing in righteousness and peace and the physical redemption of Israel. But when did *HaShem* become a man? When did *HaShem* die? When He took on flesh and dwelt among us (Psalm 22; Isaiah 52:13-53:12; Zechariah 12:10), that is when *HaShem* died. The prophets spoke about His incarnation when He took on flesh and was born according to Isaiah 7:14; 9:6-7; Micah 5:2; and John simply connected the dots in his gospel in John 1:1-14.

Secondly, in verse 43, how will the Word of God make atonement for His Land and His people? Atonement is a technical term going back to Leviticus 16. Leviticus 17:11 is very clear on the meaning, interpretation and purpose of blood sacrifice, as quoted from the *Tanakh* and Targum:

> For the life of the flesh is in the blood: and I have given it to you upon the altar to make an atonement for your souls: **for it is the blood that maketh an atonement for the soul.**

> Because the subsistence of the life of all flesh is in the blood, and I have given it to you for a decree, **that you shall bring the blood of the victim unto the altar to make atonement for the blood of your lives, because the blood of the victim is to atone for the guilt of the soul**.

Sinful man cannot atone for his own sin, let alone the sins of another. That is why the prophet Isaiah said in Isaiah 53:10 that the Messiah would be the guilt offering for sins. See the interesting references from the Harkavy and Leeser translations:

> But it pleased the Lord to bruise him; he hath put *him* to grief: if **his soul shall consider it a recompense for guilt**, he shall see *his* seed, he shall prolong *his* days, and the pleasure of the Lord shall prosper in his hand (Harkavy Version).

But the Lord was pleased to crush him **through disease**: when (now) **his soul hath brought the trespass-offering**, then shall he see (his) seed. Live many days, and the pleasure of the Lord shall prosper in his hand (Leeser Version).

The Hebrew text does not have the words "through disease" in the original text. Both versions state that the "Servant of the LORD" will suffer and die by the words "a recompense for guilt" and as a "trespass-offering." The "servant of the LORD," collectively was Israel, was never offered as a trespass-offering. However, an individual who is called the "Servant of the LORD" (*Yeshua ha Mashiach*), did become that offering for the sins of the world. Only one who was not infected with the cancer of sin could be that atonement Moses spoke of in Deuteronomy 32:43. Throughout the Targums the Word of the LORD is equated with the LORD or *HaShem* as being equal yet there is a distinction of persons. When the Word is to be worshipped, obeyed and feared and speaks as the Almighty God, there is no question that "the Word of the LORD" is distinct from the LORD, yet He is God.

All of these references were not only from the *Tanakh*, but from the foundation of the Scripture and Judaism itself, the Torah, the five books of Moses. This by itself bears a tremendous weight of evidence, for the Prophets and the Writings of the *Tanakh* do not stand by themselves but are themselves based on the Torah. The following three verses from Joshua and Isaiah are only a few of many that refer to the Word of the LORD as God.

Joshua 2:12

(Targum Jonathan) Now therefore **swear unto Me by the Word of the Lord**, since I have shewed you kindness, that ye will also shew kindness unto my father's house, and give me a true token.

According to the Scriptures the Jewish people were not to swear by any name but only to the LORD, and not to swear falsely, thus profaning God's name as Leviticus 19:12 states (Exodus 20:7). Here Rahab spoke to the two spies she harbored in Jericho and asked them to swear by the LORD that they would show kindness to her father's house. In the Targum Rahab is to have said, "swear unto me by the Word of the Lord." This was a binding agreement between two parties whereas in the case of the spies, they swore in "the Name of the Word of the LORD." Once again "the Word of the LORD" is equal to the LORD Himself.

Joshua 9:19

But all the princes said unto all the congregation, We have sworn unto them **by the Word of the Lord, the God of Israel**; and now, therefore, we dare not injure them."

In this passage the leaders or princes of Israel told the people that even though they were deceived by the Gibeonites, they had sworn "by the Word of the Lord" and so were still duty bound to keep that oath. Also notice that in the Targum "the Word of the

LORD" is clearly called the God of Israel by the leadership of Israel. David Cooper makes the following observation:

> Quotations could be multiplied very greatly which show that the translators of the Targums in differentiating Jehovah from Jehovah often called on the Word of Jehovah and at the same time attributed the divine nature to Him who was thus designated.[1801]

Cooper's point is very well taken. The Targum actually helps to prove the plurality of God in the *Tanakh*. Couple the Targum with the passages discussed in the *Tanakh* and there is a formidable weight of evidence to substantiate the plurality of *Elohim* in the Hebrew Scriptures.

The last two passages come from Isaiah.

Isaiah 6:8

And **I heard the voice of the Memra [Word] of the Lord [Adonai] which said,** Whom shall I send to prophesy, and who will go to teach?

In Isaiah 6 the prophet sees a vision of *Adonai* (Lord) with verses 1-7 describing what he saw. In verse 8 Isaiah hears the *Memra* or Word of the Lord (*Adonai*) asking a question in the singular, only to have the *Memra* or *Adonai* as He continues to speak ask a follow-up question in the plural. There is no question that God is speaking here in the singular and in the plural. After Isaiah responds that he should be sent, *Adonai* speaks to him through the next couple of verses. However, in verse 12, with no indication of the speaker changing, *Adonai* is identified as the LORD. In this passage the Hebrew Scriptures open with *Adonai* speaking as one (*echad*) *Elohim*, yet He spoke of Himself in the singular and plural within the same context. Rabbis wish to include the angel's presence to accommodate the plural reference. However, the angels are not addressed and the vision is for the express purpose of commissioning Isaiah in the prophetic ministry. Based on what has already been studied on the subject of theophanies, it is clearly understood that the Second Person of the plural unity of the *echad* (one) *Elohim* is speaking. That speaker is identified in the Targum of Isaiah as the *Memra* or Word of the Lord.[1802]

Isaiah 63:8-10

(8) And he said, Surely, they are my people, children who will not deal falsely; and **his Memra was their saviour.** (9) Whensoever they transgressed before him, so as to bring affliction upon them, he did not afflict them, but **an angel sent from before him** delivered them; in his mercy and in his pity for them he rescued them, and bare them, and carried them all the days of old. (10) But they rebelled and provoked to anger **against the word [Memra] of his holy**

[1801] Cooper, *The God of Israel*, 91-92.
[1802] Stenning, *The Targum of Isaiah*, 22.

prophets, and **his Memra was turned to be an enemy** and he himself waged war against them.

This passage was dealt with in chapter 10 of this book, so we will not go into detail here. Two things need to be observed: First, the phrase "an angel sent from before him" is a lot different in the Targum than in the *Tanakh* which states, "*And the angel of His Presence delivered them.*" The *Tanakh* gives a completely different understanding than the Targum. This Messenger of His Presence is not just any messenger of God. He is one particular Messenger, a unique Messenger. This one was the Messenger (Angel) of the LORD who is distinct from the Father and yet equal to the Father. The second thing to be noticed is the use of *Memra*; the Word (*Memra*) is Israel's Saviour. Israel rebelled against the *Memra* that the prophets gave and the *Memra* turned against them to be their enemy. The *Memra* in the Targums is treated as a Person.

SUMMARY

What becomes clear as the issue of "the Word of the LORD" is viewed from the *Tanakh* and the Targums is that Moses and the Prophets spoke of the Word as a divine person, a member of the plurality of *Elohim*. Yes, many times the term is used in the context of the revelatory nature of the Scriptures and the personality of the Word is not clearly seen, but at other times it is clearly seen as a person, a member of the plurality of *Elohim*. Whether reading the Hebrew Scriptures or the Aramaic (or English translation) Targums, the identity of the Word of God is the personification of the Word as the Second Person of the plural unity of *Elohim* before His incarnation in Bethlehem.

What becomes equally clear is that John was not referencing Greek Hellenistic *logos* in the opening chapter of his gospel. He had something else in mind when he wrote those verses, as this author reflects:

> In John 1:1-5, in what appears to be a midrashic interpretation of Genesis 1:1-5, the pre-incarnate Jesus is called "the Word" and identified with God. The claim that this Word is the means whereby the universe was created (John 1:3) appears to be a development of the notion that the heavens were created "by the word of God" (Heb 11:3; 2 Pet 3:5), that is by the command of God. In 1 John 1:1 (probably an interpretation of John 1:1-3), the incarnate Jesus is designated "the Word of life."[1803]

Even though Jacob Neusner is not a believer in *Yeshua*, his honest evaluation of the origin of John's material is close to being correct. This author would not give Midrash the credit, for John predates the Midrashic literature. John's original material came from the *Tanakh*, the Targums which were very popular at that time, and from the oral teachings of the rabbis in the first century C.E. The simple conclusion is that the Word of God spoke, acted and interacted with individuals throughout the *Tanakh*. The Word

---

[1803] Neusner and Green, *Dictionary of Judaism in the Biblical Period*, 676.

of the LORD as John expressed in his gospel is God, and even today His own people do not yet know Him.

Chapter 19
Summary

This author recognizes that above everything else "*all scripture is given by inspiration of God*." The utmost point to be advanced is that the Scriptures, including both the *Tanakh* and New Covenant, are God's revelation of Himself. God had authors, such as Moses, use words to best describe His nature and character to human beings who could not have known Him at all unless He revealed Himself to them.

The purpose of this study was to analyze the teachings of Rabbinic Judaism that state that the plurality of God is not inherent in the Hebrew Scriptures. Therefore, research was confined to the context of the *Tanakh*. As a believer in Messiah *Yeshua* I am committed to the plural unity and tri-unity of God. It was my goal to determine whether it is possible to substantiate that doctrine solely from the Hebrew Scriptures. After nine years of intensive study and analysis, the conclusion is that the plurality (tri-unity) of God is unquestionably presented in the *Tanakh*. That conclusion is possible because, as Paul asserts, the *Tanakh* is the inspired Word of God (2 Timothy 3:16), used to reveal Himself to mankind through human authors.

Chapter 2 clearly points out that God can be one, as Deuteronomy 6:4 states, and yet be a plural unity of one. The key to understanding the Person of God is Genesis 1:26 and the phrase "*let us make man in our likeness and our image*." Man and woman are the earthly expression of the plural unity of *Elohim*, because mankind is a plural unity of one who reflects the "*likeness*" and "*image*" of our Creator(s) (Ecclesiastes 12:1; Isaiah 48:12-16; Zechariah 12:1, 10; Genesis 1:2). Even beyond that point each human being, whether male or female, reflects the triune nature of *Elohim*, because we ourselves as persons are also triune in our personhood. Men and women are body, soul and spirit, yet each is one. Each one of these aspects of mankind reflects the Person of *Elohim* who is Himself triune in one. God in His wisdom made mankind one part visible and two parts invisible. We become the exact representation of *Elohim* for in His revelation of Himself, two persons of the Godhead are invisible and one is the visible manifestation of God as the theophanies discussed in chapters 4 through 8 reveal. Finally the ultimate revelation of God was in the Messiah of Israel by the incarnation of Himself through the virgin. We are plural and yet one as we are the reflection of the plural God who is One (*echad*).

As demonstrated in chapter 3, God's names reflect His character and nature, unlike human beings who cannot look down through the life of their children when they are born and know their character. Names are chosen that sound good, or parents name their child envisioning what they would like their child's character to be. But whether the name and character of the child is compatible to his future life is totally unforeseen to earthly parents. However, God knows His nature, character and who He is. Michael Barrett expresses the practice of naming children well, asserting that God is capable of doing so with perfect knowledge of Himself:

> The point is that we use names without necessarily thinking about what the name means. That, however, was not the case for the writers of Scriptures. Names, particularly and especially the names of God, were never used haphazardly or casually in the Scripture. Names conveyed something about the nature or character of the one so named. "Thou shalt call his name JESUS: for he shall save his people from their sins" (Matt 1:21). That "Jesus" means "Jehovah saves" is certainly a significant statement given the purpose of the Savior's being born. What God called Himself was always an important means of His revealing Himself.[1804]

When God used terms such as *Elohim, Eloah, Elah, El, Adonai* and *Yahweh* to describe Himself, He did so with an intended meaning for the reader. God consistently chose to violate Hebrew grammar by using the plural noun "*Elohim*" with a singular verb "create" in Genesis 1:1. This was so readers would recognize that God revealed Himself as one God (which the singular verb would affirm), but also to show Himself as a plurality (which the plural noun would affirm). God's use of *Elohim* 2,350 times to refer to Himself in the plural was not a mistake. God who is one and a plurality is not the author of confusion. Why then are the very people He has revealed Himself to so unable to see the multitude of plural references He has made? This author believes that if God were one, then He would have used *El, Elah*, or *Eloah* in the singular so that mankind would not be confused. However, if God is a tri-unity, then the plural noun *Elohim* makes absolutely logical sense.

The fact remains that God did use the plural noun *Elohim* with singular verbs. Coupled with that God used, on several occasions, His personal name *YHVH* (*Yahweh* – LORD), which is a singular noun, not plural, in the *Tanakh* to refer to two *Yahwehs*, which again reveals plurality. God chose words to describe Himself in the plural which is what confuses readers. As human beings, singular-plural beings, readers are still confused by God referring to Himself in both singular and plural ways and sometimes with a singular-plural combination of names as *Elohim* (plural) and *Yahweh* (singular). Added to that, God Himself and others refer to Him as Lord (*Adonai*), which again is a plural description of Him. Rabbinic Judaism has taken that plural form (*Adonai*) and used it to replace the personal name for God, which is singular. God shows Himself to be a plural compound unity, while at the same time confirming the fact that He is "one." All of these facts and references to *Elohim, Yahweh* and *Adonai* show a significant number of times that God chose to represent Himself as plural while being "one," as discussed in this book. Here is a brief summary: (1) Uses of *Elohim* as the true God – 2,350 times; (2) two *Yahwehs* – 4 times; (3) uses of Lord when used with God – 449

[1804] Barrett, *Beginning At Moses*, 24.

660

times; (4) combination of *Elohim* and *Yahweh* – 930 times; (5) uses of two *Elohims* – 1 time. Those usages of God, which He prompted the writers of Scripture to use of Himself, should not be overlooked or interpreted in ways that God by inspiration did not intend. Those usages amount to a significant number of plural references in the Hebrew Scriptures.

In chapters 4 through 8 of this book, the theophanies of God, of the Messenger (angel) of *Yahweh* and the *Shechinah* Glory of God, further build the case for the plurality of God. The Messenger (angel) of *Yahweh* and the *Shechinah* of God are, without question, God, yet are distinct from God. However, the fact and presence of these theophanies of God give great difficulty to Jewish scholars who attempt to explain away the significance of these passages throughout the *Tanakh*. If these theophanies were not God appearing to mankind, then why didn't God who is the great communicator clearly use terms such as, "one of the angels of God" appeared, and so on. But God did not. These appearances of God before man were a precursor to the incarnation of God in the New Covenant. These passages are generally held in common by those of biblical faith to be the pre-incarnate Messiah, the Second Person of the Godhead. Barrett alone lists 25 references to the Messenger (angel) of *Yahweh*.[1805] Here again is a substantial number of references that lay a strong foundation for the plurality (or tri-unity) of God.

In chapter 9 we saw that the term *echad* in the *Shema* makes the point that God is "one" but also that oneness is made up as a compound or complex unity. The word *echad* is used 970 times throughout the *Tanakh*. Minimally, this word for "one" is in a plural context of others being involved. Some of these references relate specifically to a compound or complex unity. If Jewish scholars want to use *echad* to show oneness as to only one, their usage of *echad* does not accomplish that.

Chapter 10 dealt with passages which have four types of plural descriptions of God and as a group are difficult to ignore. First, there are the plural personal pronouns in Genesis and Isaiah, where God uses all His significant names of Himself, affirming plurality. Second, there are plural verbs with the plural noun *Elohim* that also point to the plurality of God. This is important because usually God uses the plural noun (*Elohim*) and a singular verb to show plurality and unity or oneness whereas in the four references cited, God has chosen to use the plural noun with plural verbs. On the one hand, the plural noun with the singular verb departs from the pattern of Hebrew grammar. On the other hand, the plural noun and plural verb are in harmony with Hebrew grammar. Once again God affirms that He is one God in a plurality of persons. Third, plural descriptions of Him by the writers of Scripture affirm His plurality with plural modifiers of God. Fourth, there are three references in Isaiah that show not only plurality, but also the tri-unity of God. Since God cannot make mistakes in the writing of His revelation of Himself to man, this is another significant number of passages that show not only His plurality but the tri-unity of God in the *Tanakh*. One or two passages

---

[1805] Barrett, *Beginning At Moses*, 160-162.

in the *Tanakh* would prove absolutely nothing, but the number of references cited in this study becomes an overwhelming weight to affirm God's plurality.

In chapter 11 the tri-unity of God becomes visible in the pages of the Hebrew Scriptures when the person of the Holy Spirit is included in the plurality of God in the *Tanakh*. As was demonstrated, the Holy Spirit is not as visible in the *Tanakh* as in the New Covenant. It is harder to see Him in the Hebrew Scriptures because in the *Tanakh*, the Holy Spirit works as the active power of God. However, it was also seen from other passages that His personality is not removed from the pages of the *Tanakh*. He is never really given a name in either testament, but His personality, character and ministry are present in the *Tanakh*.

The Hebrew Scriptures do reveal the personality of the Holy Spirit by Him being involved in creation, being grieved, or being impatient, and saying that He can testify or give witness against rebellious Israel. All these aspects of His personality have been borne out in chapter 11. Also His ministry has been seen to be different in the *Tanakh* than in the New Covenant, for in the *Tanakh* He came upon people to guide them, as with Saul and David, and to equip artisans, to accomplish specific tasks in the making of the tabernacle and high priestly garments. He came upon others like the judges to deliver the people. Isaiah alone is the prophet who couples together all three members of the tri-unity in the Godhead as three distinct persons (Isaiah 42:1; 48:16; 61:1; 63:7-14), all operating as God throughout the *Tanakh*.

So once again the Hebrew Scriptures add more evidence to strengthen support for the plural unity of a triune God. Even though it is the deeds of the Holy Spirit that are predominant, personality still comes through, confirming Him as part of the unity of God, the triune God.

Chapters 12 through 15 give unquestioned evidence to the fact that the Messiah is divine. It has been substantiated that the Messiah is God and not just a man. The understanding of the English terms "forever," "everlasting," and "eternity" is very helpful in understanding the usage of *olam* in connection with the Messiah. His divinity becomes very clear in passages such as 1 Chronicles 17; Isaiah 9; Micah 5:2; Jeremiah 23:5-6; Psalm 110:1; Daniel 9:24-27; Zechariah 11:4-14; 12:1, 10. As these passages are added to the evidence already accumulated on the triune nature of God, it continues to build an insurmountable weight of evidence as we substantiate the tri-unity of God in the *Tanakh*.

Chapter 16 presented documented proof from the *Tanakh* that God has a Son. The New Covenant has many references to *Yeshua* being the Son of God. However, in the *Tanakh* there are only two references to the fact of God having a unique son other than Israel, God's first born. In the Hebrew Scriptures, except for Psalm 2 and Proverbs 30:4, most of the emphasis is placed on the plural unity of *Elohim* and not on God having a Son. These two references speak clearly to the fact that God has a Son.

As was presented in the previous chapters, the Messiah has a dual nature, fully God and fully man.

Chapter 17 presented the God/man relationship of the Messiah as He is portrayed as the Branch. Each one of the references in Isaiah, Jeremiah and Zechariah present Him as the Branch of *Yahweh*, Righteous Branch, My servant the Branch, and the man who is called the Branch. These passages continue to demonstrate the plural unity of *Elohim* and that the Second Person of that unity, in this case called the Branch, is the Messiah of Israel, the God/Man.

Chapter 18 on the Word of God becomes more fascinating the deeper it is studied. In the *Tanakh* it is clear that the Word of the LORD acted in unison with the Father but also as a separate distinct person within the plural unity of *Elohim*. On top of that, the Aramaic Targums present a brighter and even clearer picture to the personality of the Word of the LORD and the clear distinction that is made in the text of the Aramaic Targums between the LORD and the Word of the LORD. This is a very powerful argument for the plurality of *Elohim* that has been sadly neglected.

When all of this material is correlated, the weight of evidence is tremendous; it cannot be ignored. This is a neglected study in Christian circles and completely ignored by rabbis because of a belief in absolute monotheism based on a false interpretation of *echad* in the *Shema*.

On pages four and five of this book, Rabbi Greenberg was quoted. He compared Judaism's and Christianity's belief in the oneness of God and found them incompatible with each other. He spoke of the "overwhelming testimony" of the Bible that speaks only of a monotheistic God, and that whatever Christians call monotheism is not the monotheism of Judaism. After going through all the Hebrew Scriptures and analyzing a multitude of passages, it becomes clear that the *Tanakh* points, without question, to the plurality (tri-unity) of God. In summarizing Rabbi Greenberg's words in comparison to the context of the *Tanakh*, the testimony of the Hebrew Bible on the plural unity of God "flies in the face" of Rabbinic Judaism to explain that God is not a plurality or triune God.

The whole tone of Scripture, when read as God gave it, clearly supports the plurality and tri-unity of God. It is only when man entangles himself with the liberal, humanistic thought that liberal Christian scholars attempt to rewrite Scripture to suit their personal, humanistic philosophy or pseudo-Christian bias. Throughout this study, the question has been asked: Have Christian scholars abandoned the doctrine of the triune God in the Hebrew Scriptures to rabbinic thought? The reality is that Christian scholars have abandoned this doctrine but not because of rabbinic teaching, rather because of the secular humanism that has infiltrated the Church over the last 300 years. Wilson points out that the church, up until modern times (the 1700s), saw the plurality and tri-unity of God in the Hebrew Scriptures.[1806] What made the difference? It is this

---

[1806] Wilson, *Our Father Abraham*, 54-55.

author's opinion that secular humanistic thought could not accept the supernatural aspect of the Word of God. Modern humanistic thinkers had to find natural ways to get around the obvious intent of Scripture. Erickson speaks of this humanism as modernism:

> Basically, modernism retained the conception of the world but removed its supernatural or at least extra-natural basis. Thus, the vertical dualism was replaced by a horizontal dualism, in which the meaning or cause was found within or behind the natural world, rather than beyond or above it. The pattern of history is to be found within it rather than beyond it. Events are explained in terms of the social realities that cause them, rather than in terms of the purpose of a transcendent God.

> Modernism has been essentially humanistic. The human being is the center of reality, and in a sense everything exists for the sake of the human. In an earlier period, God had been thought of as the central and supreme object of value.[1807]

A good example of humanism, or modern thinking, is expressed by Parkes. Even though he has some very valuable insights into the Jewish world of Paul's day, he does not see anything trinitarian in Paul or the *Tanakh*:

> His double experience of the atonement compelled him to think of Jesus Christ as more than human. But into what category was he then to place him? For as a Jew he recognized only one being to whom the category divine was fully applicable, and that was God himself. Paul was not a trinitarian; he had not the resources which were to be made available by several centuries of hammering on the anvil of both experience and philosophic thought. For him Jesus was never equal to God; whatever of divinity was to be ascribed to him was to be so ascribed because God had willed and planned it thus.[1808]

> Undoubtedly the early Church was puzzled as to who Jesus was.... The experience which they had undergone was an emotional and not an intellectual one.... It is only as we understand this that we can appreciate the profound bewilderment which the Christian message caused in Jewish circles, and even among Jewish adherents of the new faith.[1809]

As a scholar Parkes has some very interesting information on the early first-century Jewish church which was surrounded by Rabbinic Judaism's beliefs and concepts. It seems strange that anyone would say that Paul was not a trinitarian, but that is the context of Parkes' statement. He does not refer or allude to Paul before his salvation, but only after his conversion experience on the Damascus Road. This author's view is

---

[1807] Millard J. Erickson, *Christian Theology* (2nd ed. Grand Rapids, Baker Books, 1998), 161, 163.

[1808] James Parkes, *The Foundations of Judaism and Christianity* (Chicago: Quadrangle Books, 1960), 219-220.

[1809] Parkes, *The Foundations of Judaism and Christianity*, 215.

that Parkes' views are not consistent with the teachings of Scripture and that he and many others have succumbed to the teaching that the tri-unity was an invention of the Church as well as following the lead of higher criticism and anti-missionary teachings. This humanistic modern thought sounds just like many rabbis who, not from humanistic reasons but for religious reasons, reject the plurality of God. Modern humanistic thought has infected many New Covenant scholars to not accept God's Word but find humanistic reasons that leave out God and the supernatural. However, contrary to Parkes, Paul and all the other New Covenant writers clearly taught and understood the triune God from the *Tanakh* long before it was hammered out by experience and philosophic thought in the Nicean Council in 325 CE. A careful observation of first-century Jewish believers in Messiah *Yeshua* clarifies one basic concept. These believers had no problem moving from the plural monotheism presented in the *Tanakh* to monotheism with three persons making up that unity of God as a complex unity in the New Covenant. Buswell expresses it clearly:

> In the section in which we called attention to the unity of God as taught in the New Testament, several passages were cited in which the divine unity is strongly affirmed, in direct conjunction with equally strong references to the deity of Jesus Christ. These passages are remarkable in that they contain no hint that the New Testament writers were at all conscious of any problem in the conjunction of these two ideas. That one God is complex in His being, and so subsists that there are personal distinctions within the Godhead, was no problem for the first century Christians.[1810]

It appears that many Christian scholars have abandoned the doctrine of the tri-unity of the Godhead in the Hebrew Scriptures not primarily because of the unbelief of rabbinic scholars, but because of the unbelief of humanistic "Christian" secularists who use the unbelief of "higher criticism" to reinterpret God.

This author sees three valuable benefits in having an understanding of the character and nature of God in the Hebrew Scriptures as shown in the plurality of the Godhead. With a clear, practical and balanced understanding of the character and nature of God in the *Tanakh*, the Church today would be better equipped for living and witnessing for their Saviour and Lord. First, having a practical understanding of the plurality of God in the *Tanakh* will impact the Church by grasping the full nature and essence of the God of Israel who is the Incarnate Messiah. It is important to couple both testaments together so that the character and essence of the Second Person of the plural unity of *Elohim* can be fully grasped. It can be life changing. The Church today primarily has a New Testament understanding of the character and nature of God and shies away from the *Tanakh* because God is not so much demonstrating love as He is His holiness, righteousness and justice. Second, this material on the plurality of God in the Hebrew Scriptures is not only valuable in witnessing to Jewish people, but also in witnessing to anyone who deprecates Christ, including Moslems. Islam has the same issue with

---

[1810] Buswell, *A Systematic Theology of the Christian Religion*, 120.

believing in absolute monotheism as Rabbinic Judaism, as do others such as the "Christian" cults such as Jehovah Witnesses. Third, it produces a better understanding of the Second Person of the Godhead as to His character of holiness, righteousness and justice, demonstrated in the Hebrew Scriptures. Understanding the plurality of God from the *Tanakh* is important because the Church teaches that God is immutable (Malachi 3:6), and as a consequence has done Jesus a disservice by presenting a lopsided view in relation to the character of God. The Church has depressed the holiness, righteousness and justice of Jesus, who was very active in the Hebrew Scriptures as the Second Person of *Elohim*. At the same time, the Church has elevated the love of God totally out of proportion to the other characteristics of Jesus. *Yeshua* demonstrated His love by coming as the "Servant of the LORD" (Isaiah 42; 49; 53) and becoming the Lamb that God would provide (Genesis 22:8), the substitutionary sacrifice for the sins of the world. Thus, the Church today has an imbalanced view of the person of Christ, lacking fear, reverence, awe and commitment to the Almighty God who is the active sustainer of the universe (Colossians 1:18).

At the beginning and in the summary of this book I quoted a statement by Rabbi Greenberg concerning Rabbinic Judaism's teaching on the trinity or tri-unity of God. That issue has been answered in the pages of this book. But there was another valid question raised by a Jewish believer, Milton B. Lindberg. Let me quote again his statement from page 11 of this book:

> Although it may be granted that the Christian's New Testament teaches that the term God may be applied to God the Father, to God the Son, and to God the Holy Spirit, the Christian should cease to claim that he worships the God of Abraham, Isaac, and Jacob, the God of Moses and the prophets, the God of the Torah, the Nevi'im, and the Ketuvim, unless there is found in the Tanakh, indisputable evidence that God exists in more than one personality.[1811]

The clear answer to Lindberg's statement is that there is indisputable evidence from the *Tanakh* that God exists in more than one personality. In fact, that evidence is overwhelming. One very big observation needs to be made that biblical believers as well of Jewish people completely over look. Evidence is not only overwhelming for the plurality of God in the *Tanakh*, but just who is the God of Israel that they worshipped? When we understand that the Second Person of the Godhead was the one who became visual to mankind and that He is the one who spoke to Moses, the Judges and to both the writing and non-writing prophets, we begin to see which member of the Godhead was active in the lives of patriarchs, Moses and the prophets. The two aspects of the visual and audio appearances of this Second Person of the plural unity of *Elohim* is that He is not God the Father, but rather God the Son. It is He who spoke and appeared to mankind on behalf of the Father. What does that mean? I have grown up in the Church all my life and I have always heard and still do that it is God the Father who was active

---

[1811] Milton B. Lindberg, *In the Light of the Tenach: The Trinity* (Brochure, Lansing, MI: AMF International, 1992), 1-2.

and worshipped in the *Tanakh*. May I submit to you that it was not God the Father but God the Son as His representative who communicated to Israel on behalf of the Father. So the God of the Hebrews Scriptures is God the Son, the Messiah of Israel, who is known in the flesh by New Covenant believers as *Yeshua*. In other words He is the God of Abraham, Isaac and Jacob that we worship. I am not depreciating the Father. All three members of the Godhead were active in the Hebrew Scriptures, but it was the Second Person who communicated with Israel and revealed Himself to Israel as the God of Israel. He was the one they were worshipping along with the Father and They are the *echad* or one we as New Covenant believers worship. We pray to the Father in the name of the *Yeshua*, He is our access to the Father. So Israel's God that interacted with them was God the Son.

For New Covenant believers this is easy to see as you look in the Gospel of John at words of *Yeshua* in John 5:37. His clear statement to the religious leaders lets us see, without question, who had been communicating to Israel in the *Tanakh*. John 5:37, 39, and 46 quoted below all clearly show by *Yeshua*'s own words which member of the Godhead was active in the *Tanakh*:

> And the **Father** himself, which hath **sent me**, hath borne witness of me. **Ye have neither heard his voice at any time, or seen his shape.**

> Search **the Scriptures**; for in them ye think ye have eternal life: and they are they which **testify of me**.

> **For had ye believed Moses, ye would have believed me: for he wrote of me**.

These verses powerfully demonstrate that it is *Yeshua* that God the Father sent. It was *Yeshua* as the Second Person of the Plural unity of *Elohim* that spoke (voice) and appeared (his shape) in the *Tanakh* as the LORD (YHVH). The testimony of the *Tanakh* is upon *Yeshua* for even Moses wrote of Him.

However, this lack of understanding as to the plurality (and tri-unity) of God in the *Tanakh* and His identity has negatively impacted the evangelizing of Jewish people by discouraging them and keeping them from recognizing *Yeshua* as their Messiah (Hosea 5:15; Matthew 23:39). Ultimately they must believe the plurality (and tri-unity) of God and embrace that plural unity. Without believing in the oneness and plurality of God, that Jesus is God, they will continue to reject Him as their Messiah and remain lost in their sins. Zechariah 12:10 is one of the most gut-wrenching verses in Scripture: *"They shall mourn for him, as one mourneth for his only son."* When the Jewish nation calls for the one sitting on the Father's right hand (Psalm 80:17) because they have come to understand and realize that He is *Yeshua* (Jesus), the Messiah whom they rejected almost 2000 years earlier, they will weep bitterly. Why? Because they and their fathers and their fathers' fathers had been rejecting the very one in whom they said they trusted, the *Yeshua* who is the God of Israel.

In closing, in Matthew 23:39 *Yeshua* made His last public statement to the Jewish nation, that they will not see Him again until they say the following words, "*Blessed is he that cometh in the name of the Lord.*" The rabbis say that when the Messiah comes they are to greet Him with these words. In fact, only four days earlier (Matthew 21:9) many used these words as He entered Jerusalem riding on the donkey (Zechariah 9:9). But their statement was not accepted because the nation had already rejected Him by attributing all the works He had done by the power of the Holy Spirit to Beelzebub, the prince of the devils (Matthew 12:23-24). So the unpardonable sin, which was a national or corporate sin of the Jewish nation of *Yeshua*'s generation, was committed and until He is recognized for who He is by Jewish people of a future generation as God Incarnate, the Messiah of Israel, the Suffering Servant, the King of Kings, the Son of David, Immanuel, the Branch and they call for Him to come, the Jewish nation will not see His face. *Yeshua* withdrew the offer of the kingdom from that "*evil generation*" so that the kingdom can be offered to a future generation of Jewish people who will embrace Him at the end of the time of "Jacob's Trouble" otherwise known as the tribulation or the seventieth week of Daniel. The plurality of God is at the heart of Jewish evangelism, and being able to defend it from the Hebrew Scriptures is essential.

One final encouragement to biblical believers: God has given the responsibility to each believer to share the gospel of Messiah with the world. The believing Church sends thousands of missionaries to every corner of the earth and to as many unreached people groups as possible and that is commendable and necessary. However, many believers, and most mission agencies, have forgotten about God's chosen people, through whom every believer traces their spiritual heritage. The Church in history has been the biggest obstacle to Jewish people coming to faith in Messiah Jesus. The Church over the span of 1800 years has been the largest anti-Semitic group in the world. Because of the church's unbiblical treatment of Jewish people, they have become harder and more resistant to the Gospel of Messiah. Keep in mind the Abrahamic Covenant: If Israel is blessed, the one who blesses Israel will be blessed. It is the conviction of this author that worldwide missions would see more fruit for its labor if mission agencies and individual believers would revisit the Jewish people and once again share the Gospel with the Jew first. Stan Telchin, a Jewish believer in Messiah, has said that the greatest act of anti-Semitism that the Church could commit is to withhold the Gospel of Messiah from the Jewish people.[1812]

[1812] Telchin, *Messiah Judaism IS NOT Christianity*, 137.

Epilogue
A Special Word to the Covenant
People of Israel

As a true New Testament believer in Jesus who believes that the Jewish people are the elect and chosen people of God and as a Christian Zionist, I recognize that the topic of this book is rejected by rabbis and Jewish people alike. Without one bit of hesitation I believe Israel's best days are ahead. The Abrahamic Covenant that God made with your father Abraham is an eternal covenant. It is the kind of covenant that if God does not fulfill it for all the faithful believing Jewish people, past, present and future, then God is not God at all and the Bible is worthless. The whole picture of the Hebrew Scriptures and the New Testament is that God chose Israel to be His instrument to reveal Himself to the Gentiles. Israel, because of sin against Him, caused God to bring His judgment upon the nation of Israel. However, the promise of God given by God to the prophets through the centuries remains. His love will once again be poured out on you as a nation, and Israel will rule over the nations by the hand of Messiah. However, if you have studied the *Tanakh*, you understand that the "*day of the LORD*" or "*the time of Jacob's trouble*" will occur before the Kingdom is realized by Israel. I believe the rabbis of the past referred to it as the "birth pangs of the Messiah."

What I am about to ask you to read has to do with those days called "the birth pangs of the Messiah" that Israel will experience before they are redeemed by *HaShem*. For you, as Jewish people, it has been 2400 years since the last prophet spoke to Israel. For true New Testament believers it has been 1900 years since the final words of John the Apostle recorded the words in the book called "Revelation." I would like to lay out for you a very general chronology of events, so that when they happen you will recognize them clearly and understand that the redemption of Israel is very near.

These events as they are laid out may overlap or may have one event happening a short time before or after what I have written down. In other words, some of these events may occur very close together. I will simply go through it point by point:

1. In 1948 Israel was formed as a nation for the first time in 1878 years. Ezekiel 37 states that Israel will return to the land in unbelief.

2. It is believed by many conservative New Testament believers and scholars that "the birth pangs of Messiah" began in 1914 with the beginning of World War I (WWI). Remember that history commonly recognizes WWI and WWII as the same war with a 20-year pause between conflicts.

669

3. The Christian church today is largely an apostate body; they are not true believers in Jesus the Messiah as their Saviour. Being Gentiles we are true New Testament believers not because we are born with or baptized into Church as a baby. That is NOT biblical Christianity. True genuine believers who have made a personal decision to embrace Jesus as their Saviour and Lord are the true Church, known as the Body of Christ (Messiah). We believe that Jesus will return and take all believers out of this world to be with Him in heaven (1 Thessalonians 4:13-18) before *"the day of the LORD."* So someday in your future you will receive news reports, reported worldwide, that true New Testament believers in Jesus have suddenly disappeared; it is called the rapture, or the catching up of the Church. At that point in time Israel will have lost its best and only friend. There is no biblical date or time given, but it is believed that this will happen before the 7-year period known as the seventieth week of Daniel, the Great Tribulation, the time of Jacob's trouble (Daniel 9:24-27; Revelation 4-19).

4. The following scenario is very possible although the exact timing of the following events may vary slightly. Sometime closely associated to the beginning of the 7-year covenant signed by Israel a world leader, probably from Western Europe, or perhaps the Moslem world, Russia, Iran, and some other Islamic nations will attack Israel according to Ezekiel 38-39. What Ezekiel states is that there will be no one who will come to Israel's aid, which means that the United States of America will not defend Israel. The reason for that is unknown. Ezekiel states that God will step in personally and not only defend Israel, but miraculously, supernaturally destroy Israel's enemies. This will result in two major changes: (1) It will cause a resurgence in Jewish people to return to their God, the God Abraham, Isaac and Jacob, the God of Israel. Jewish people will, in effect, say to themselves, God did not die in the Holocaust. (2) It will shatter the Islamic world when they realize that Allah (Arabic word for God) did not fight for them but against them on Israel's side. That will cause great disillusionment among Islamic peoples who will realize what they have been taught for centuries was not true and that the God of Israel, He is God alone. Not only does *HaShem* destroy the armies, but He also destroys parts of their countries. Ezekiel also states that there will be earthquakes. Will that be the method *HaShem* uses to destroy the Dome of the Rock in Jerusalem? With Islam shattered, Israel would be free to build the third Temple in Jerusalem.

5. Israel will sign a 7-year peace pact with a leader of the western nations or an Islamic leader to provide safety and security for Israel (Daniel 9:26-27; Matthew 24:15-31). As true New Testament believers understand this leader will be the anti-Christ, a person indwelt and empowered by Satan himself.

6.   This will begin the period known as the seventieth week of Daniel recorded in Daniel 9:24-27. During this worldwide destruction and loss of life will be staggering, for half the world's population will perish during this time (Revelation 4-19).

7.   Also somewhere around this time of the signing of the covenant, Israel will begin and complete construction on their third temple. The New Testament book of Revelation also states that God will seal 144,000 Jews at that time who will recognize what is going on and that Jesus or *Yeshua* is indeed the Messiah of Israel (Revelation 7:1-8). Also at this time there will be two men who are simply called "two witnesses" who will do their ministry in Jerusalem (Revelation 11:3-12; Zechariah 4:1-7). In the middle of the seventieth week they will finally be killed and the whole world will rejoice at their death. Their bodies will lie in the streets of Jerusalem for three and a half days and then they will come back to life, be resurrected, and ascend into heaven as the whole world beholds.

8.   In the middle of the seventieth week, when the leader of the western nations comes to defend Israel, he will make his move to proclaim himself as god by setting himself up as god in the new temple just built in Jerusalem (Matthew 24:15; Daniel 9:27; 7:8).

9.   Israel is told in Scripture to flee (Matthew 24:16-22; Revelation 11:2) for the anti-Christ will unleash his fury upon Israel in what could be called the "Holocaust II." He will be bent on the complete destruction of every Jewish person in the world and Zechariah 13:8-9 tells us that two-thirds of the Jewish population will be killed during that time and only one-third will survive.

10. It is believed that Israel will flee to Petra in Jordan (Micah 2:12-13; Isaiah 34:1-8; 63:1-6; Habakkuk 3:3).

11. As the anti-Christ destroys Jerusalem and Israel, he will proceed in his goal to kill the remnant of Jewish people hiding at Petra (Bozrah).

12. During this time the rabbis will be searching the Scriptures and they will come to the realization that Jesus, or *Yeshua*, was indeed the Son of God, the Son of David, the Messiah and will call for His return (Psalm 80:17; Daniel 7:13-14; Hosea 5:15-6:3; Matthew 23:37-39). Because of Israel's repentance, faith and confession of their sin to *HaShem* concerning Yeshua the Messiah (Isaiah 53:1-9) Israel will be saved (Isaiah 59:20-21; Romans 11:26-27).

13. Messiah will return and personally destroy the anti-Christ and all his armies as He fights His way from Petra back to Jerusalem. In the Valley of Jehoshaphat He will judge the nations for how they treated Israel (Matthew 25:31-46).

14. Within a matter of 75 days after the seventieth week, He will set up the Messianic Kingdom and rule and reign over the world from the throne of

David in Jerusalem and establish righteousness and peace for 1000 years. At that point in time Jerusalem, the 4th temple will be built, as described in Ezekiel 40-48.

For your interest and future study I would like to recommend to you four books that deal with Israel, its covenants and its prophetic future:

1. *Israelology: The Missing Link in Systematic Theology.* Written by Dr. Arnold G. Fruchtenbaum and published by Ariel Ministries in 1994 (revised), now located in San Antonio, TX, *www.Ariel.org* (ISBN: 0-914863-5-3)

2. *The Footsteps of Messiah: A Study of the Sequence of Prophetic Events.* Written by Dr. Arnold G. Fruchtenbaum and published by Ariel Ministries in 2003 (revised), *www.Ariel.org* (ISBN: 0-914863-9-6)

3. *Things to Come: A Study in Biblical Eschatology.* Written by Dr. Dwight Pentecost and published by Zondervan Press in 1958 (ISBN: 0-310-30890-9)

4. *Epicenter: Why the Current Rumblings in the Middle East Will Change Your Future.* Written by Joel Rosenberg and published by Tyndale House Publishers (ISBN: 1-4143-1135-4).

Because I know and understand the beliefs of Judaism, I realize you may even laugh at all this, but keep it on hand, for the day will come when a large body of people from all nations of the earth will suddenly disappear and you will find this book and the others referenced very important as "Holocaust II" descends on the Jewish people. I am writing to you now because I love Israel and the God of Israel.

Rev. John B. Metzger, M.A.

Appendices

Appendix 1 How to Become One with G-d to be Reconciled to G-d

It is my prayer that upon reading this book your heart has been stirred as you recognized Jesus of Nazareth as the incarnation of G-d; He is *HaShem*. It has been demonstrated throughout this book that He is G-d Almighty, *Yahweh*, the Messenger (Angel) of *Yahweh*, the Son of David who sits at the right hand of G-d, the One for whom the Father will make His enemies His footstool (Psalm 110:1). The vast majority have lost hope in the future reality of the literal coming of *Moshiach* and rightfully so, for He came 2000 years ago and was rejected because He did not come in the manner they expected Him to come.

Later there will be a group of verses referred to as the Jerusalem Road to lead you into embracing the *Moshiach*, the Son of David, *Yeshua*, as your Saviour from sin. I know you do not consider yourself a great sinner. But consider in your *Tanakh* the G-d of your fathers Abraham, Isaac and Jacob, Who is absolutely Holy, Righteous, Just, and totally separated from sin. Open your Scripture and study His character and how He originally gave to you His covenant people, your fathers, sacrifices and priests to mediate between them and Himself, your fathers needed a mediator. What was the need for the sacrifices and why did your fathers need a mediator to act on their behalf before *HaShem* in His temple? It is because they were sinners and there was nothing they could do to merit themselves before a sinless Holy Righteous G-d. Israel needed a substitute to take *HaShem's* wrath for their sins. That is what the sacrificial system was all about.

To sin against *HaShem* is simply man's disobedience against His Law and against *HaShem* Himself. You may call it the "evil inclination," but whatever you call it, it is simply missing the mark of His holiness. In *HaShem*'s eyes little acts of sin are just as much sin as murder for they are sin equally before a Holy G-d. Sinful things that you think or hide in your heart, even if you do not do them physically, are sins in *HaShem*'s eyes. If you in your mind or your heart have lusted after a woman, you have committed adultery in your heart before *HaShem*. You have not broken the letter of the Law, but you have revealed the sinfulness of your heart and have broken the spirit of the Law. Ladies, if you coveted something that is your neighbor's, and want it to the point that you will obtain it at most any cost, *HaShem* judges that as sin. Notice that in neither of these examples was the act literally committed, yet *HaShem* views your hearts from

673

which wrong, evil, or sin comes. Listen to the words of *Yeshua* from the New Testament:

> (18) But those things which proceed out of the mouth come forth from the heart; and they defile the man. (19) For out of the heart proceed evil thoughts, murders, adulteries, fornication, thefts, false witness, blasphemies. (Matthew 15:18-19)

Also the New Testament book that was written to Jewish believers in Messiah in the first century of the Common Era reflects the penetration of the Word of *HaShem*:

> (12) For the word of God is quick, and powerful, and sharper than any two-edged sword, piercing even to the dividing asunder of the soul and spirit, and of the joints and marrow, and is a discerner of the thoughts and intents of the heart.

> (13) Neither is there any creature that is not manifest in his sight: but all things are naked and open unto the eyes of him with whom we have to do. (Hebrews 4:12-13)

That verse is simply stating that the Scriptures are like a double edged sword and can pierce into the spiritual part of man (soul and spirit), as well as the physical part of man (joints and marrow). It can even discern the very thoughts you think and the motivation behind them before you ever do them.

Nearly 2000 years ago *HaShem* allowed Rome to destroy the Holy City and the Holy Temple, just as He allowed Babylon centuries before to destroy Jerusalem and Solomon's temple. When *HaShem* destroyed Jerusalem the first time, He gave Israel prophets, like Jeremiah, Ezekiel, and Daniel. He also gave them prophets after the return, like Haggai, Zephaniah, Zechariah, and Malachi. *HaShem* destroyed Jerusalem because of the sin of His covenant people, Israel. Notice that there has not been from Judaism's perspective a prophet to Israel since Malachi who lived 2400 years ago. Now if the sacrificial system was *HaShem*'s picture of His Holy demands and man's complete inability to keep His laws, why did *HaShem* remove the sacrificial system which was absolutely necessary, and why did He not replace it or even give a prophet with a word from Himself? Or did He give a prophet (Deuteronomy 18:15-18) in the person of His Son (Psalm 2:7-12; Proverbs 30:4), the Suffering Servant of Isaiah 53, the Servant of the LORD? The disciples on the Emmaus Road had problems understanding the shameful death of *Yeshua*. Because of the teaching they had received from the Pharisees, they looked for a military leader to liberate them from Rome. Their lack of understanding was their problem; they had a wrong Jewish expectation. *Yeshua* never denied His coming to restore Israel. He first had to come and suffer and die. In Rabbinic Judaism today, how do you get rid of your sins biblically? Back in Genesis 3:15, before there were Jewish people, before Abraham and the Covenant, *HaShem* spoke to Adam and Eve and promised a spiritual deliverer who would restore that paradise lost. *HaShem* must first deal with the curse of sin that all of mankind is plagued with. So before Israel can be restored and the promise fulfilled to Abraham, *HaShem* must fulfill His promise to Adam and Eve to restore the creation and mankind back to their original place. That meant that the "seed of the woman" would first deliver mankind spiritually by removing the sin that separated *HaShem* from mankind before Israel could be restored by the very same "*seed of the woman*." According to your own commentators in Bereshit Rabba 23, a rabbinic commentary on Genesis:

> Eve had respect to the seed which is coming from another place. And who is this? This is Messiah the King.[1813]

So the Scriptures actually had prophesied that *Moshiach* would be rejected (Psalm 22; Isaiah 52:13-53:12) and would die a shameful death before His glorification.[1814] You well know the Scriptures that relate to the person you call Messiah ben Joseph. But rabbis have made substitutions, not on *HaShem*'s authority, only on theirs. Since your eternal destiny is at stake, whose word is more important, the rabbis' or *HaShem* Himself through His Word? That is a question you must ask yourself: Who is my spiritual authority, rabbis or *HaShem*? *HaShem* loves you with an everlasting love and you are inscribed on the palm of His hands!

> The LORD did not set his love upon you, nor choose you, because ye were more in number than any people; for ye were the fewest of all people: But because the LORD loved you, and because he would keep the oath which he had sworn unto your fathers (Deuteronomy 7:7-8).

> For thus says the LORD of hosts, "After glory He has sent me against the nations which plunder you, for he who touches YOU, touches the apple of His eye (Zechariah 2:12).

Search the Scriptures, ask the G-d of your fathers to show you what He has written in His Word that your prophets recorded for Him concerning His Son, your *Moshiach*, the Son of David, the King of Israel, and your substitutionary sacrifice for your sin. Most of the Scripture verses quoted below come from the *Tanakh* Harkavy Version published by the Hebrew Publishing Company unless otherwise noted.

The Jerusalem Road

1. *"There is none without sin"*

- Psalm 14:3

[1813] Varner, *The Messiah: Revealed, Rejected, Received,* 21.
[1814] Varner, *The Messiah: Revealed, Rejected, Received,* 3.

They are all gone aside, they are all together become filthy: there is none that doeth good, no, not one.

- Psalm 51:7 [5]

  Behold, I was shapen in iniquity; and in sin did my mother conceive me.

- Isaiah 53:6

  All we like sheep have gone astray; we have turned every one to his own way; and the LORD hath caused the iniquity of us all to fall upon him.

- Jeremiah 17:9

  The heart is deceitful above all things, and desperately sick: who can know it?

- Isaiah 59:1-2

  Behold, the LORD's hand is not shortened, that it cannot save; neither his ear heavy, that it cannot hear: But your iniquities have separated between you and your God, and your sins have hid his face from you, that he will not hear.

- Ecclesiastes 7:20

  For there is not a just man upon earth, that doeth good, and sinneth not.

2. Good deeds cannot purify

- Isaiah 64:6

  But we are all as an unclean thing, and all our righteousness is as a filthy garment; and we all do fade as a leaf; and our iniquities, like the wind, have taken us away.

- Habakkuk 2:4

  Behold, his soul is haughty, it is not upright in him: but the just shall live by his faith.

- Jeremiah 18:20

  Shall evil be recompensed for good? For they have digged a pit for my soul. Remember that I stood before thee to speak good for them, and to turn away their wrath from them.

3. God requires a blood sacrifice

- Leviticus 17:11

  For the life of the flesh is in the blood: and I have given it to you upon the altar to make an atonement for your souls: for it is the blood that maketh an atonement for the soul.

4. Apply the blood of the Messiah

- Exodus 12:21-23

  Then Moses called for all the elders of Israel, and said unto them, Draw out and take you a lamb according to your families and kill the Passover. And ye shall take a bunch of hyssop, and dip it in the blood that is in the basin and strike the lintel and the two side posts with the blood that is in the basin; and none of you shall go out at the door of his house until morning. For the LORD will pass through to smite the Egyptians; and when he seeth the blood upon the lintel, and on the two side posts, the LORD will Passover the door, and will not suffer the destroyer to come in unto your houses to smite you.

- Leviticus 16:15-19

  Then shall he kill the goat of the sin-offering, that is for the people, and bring his blood within the vail, and do with that blood as he did with the blood of the bullock, and sprinkle it upon the mercy seat, and before the mercy seat: And he shall make an atonement for the holy place, because of the uncleanness of the children of Israel, and because of their transgressions in all their sins: and so shall he do for the tabernacle of the congregation, that remaineth among them in the midst of their uncleanness. And there shall be no man in the tabernacle of the congregation when he goeth in to make an atonement in the holy place, until he come out, and have made an atonement for himself, and for his household, and for all the congregation of Israel. And he shall go out unto the altar that is before the LORD, and make an atonement for it; and shall take of the blood of the bullock, and of the blood of the goat, and put it upon the horns of the altar round about. And he shall sprinkle of the blood upon it with his finger seven times, and cleanse it, and hallow it from the uncleanness of the children of Israel.

- Daniel 9:26

  And after threescore and two weeks shall Messiah be cut off, but not for himself: and the people of the prince that shall come shall destroy the city and the sanctuary; and the end thereof shall be with a flood, and unto the end of the war desolations are determined.

- Hebrews 9:12

  Neither by the blood of goats and calves, but by his own blood he entered in once into the holy place, having obtained eternal redemption for us.

- Psalm 2:12

  Kiss the Son, lest he be angry, and ye perish from the way, when his wrath is kindled but a little. Blessed are all they that put their trust in him (KJV).

- Psalm 51:15 [13]

  Then will I teach transgressors thy ways; and sinners shall be converted unto thee.

"Who Is this Messiah?"

- He was born of a virgin – Isaiah 7:14

  Therefore the Lord himself shall give you a sign; Behold, a virgin [young woman] shall conceive, and bear a son, and shall call his name Immanuel.

- Born in Bethlehem – Micah 5:1 [2]

  But thou, Bethlehem Ephratah, though thou be little among the thousands of Judah, yet out of thee shall one come forth unto me that is to be ruler in Israel; whose goings forth have been from of old, from everlasting.

- Slain for our sins – Isaiah 53:5-6

  But he was wounded for our transgressions, he was bruised for our iniquities: the chastisement of our peace was upon him; and with his stripes (wounds) we are healed. All we like sheep have gone astray; we have turned every one to his own way; and the LORD hath caused the iniquity of us all to fall upon him.

- Resurrected – Psalm 16:10, Daniel 12:2

  For thou will not leave my soul in the grave; neither wilt thou suffer thine Holy (pious) One to see corruption.

  And many of them that sleep in the dust of the earth shall awake, some to everlasting life, and some to shame and everlasting contempt.

Isaiah Avenue

1. *Sinners Before God – Isaiah 64:5-6*

   But we are all as an unclean thing, and all our righteousness is as a filthy garment; and we all do fade as a leaf; and our iniquities, like the wind, have taken us away. And there is none that calleth upon thy name, that stirreth up himself to take hold of thee: for thou hast hid thy face from us, and hast consumed us, because of our iniquities.

2. *Separation from God – Isaiah 59:1-2*

   Behold, the Lord's hand is not shortened, that it cannot save, neither his ear heavy, that it cannot hear: But your iniquities have separated between you and your God, and your sins have hid his face from you, that he will not hear.

3. *Salvation in God – Isaiah 53:6*

   All we like sheep have gone astray; we have turned every one to his own way; and the Lord hath caused the iniquity of us all to fall upon him.

4. *Saviour Is God – Isaiah 9:5-6*

   For unto us a child is born, unto us a son is given: and the government is upon his shoulder: and his name shall be called Wonderful, Counsellor of the Mighty God, of the everlasting Father, Prince of Peace. Of the increase of his government and peace there shall be no end, upon the throne of David, and upon his kingdom, to order it, and to establish it with judgment and with justice from henceforth even forever. The zeal of the Lord of hosts will perform this.

5. *Stayed Upon God – Isaiah 26:3*

   Thou wilt keep him in perfect peace, whose mind is stayed on thee: because he trusteth in thee.

All Men Are Sinners

1 Kings 8:46

If they sin against you (for there is no man that sinneth not,) and thou be angry with them and deliver them to the enemy, so that they carry them away captives unto the land of the enemy, far or near.

Job 5:7

But man is born unto trouble, as sure as the sparks fly upward. For man is born to [do] mischief, just as sparks fly upward. (Jewish Study Bible)

Ecclesiastes 7:20

For there is not a just man upon earth, that doeth good, and sinneth not.

Psalm 14:1-3

The fool hath said in his heart, there is no God. They are corrupt, they have done abominable works, there is none that doeth good. The LORD looked down from heaven upon the children of men, to see if there were any that did understand, and seek God. They are all gone aside, they are all together become filthy: there is none that doeth Good, no, not one.

Psalm 53:1-4

The fool hath said in his heart, There is no God. Corrupt are they, and have done abominable iniquity: there is none that doeth good. God looked down from heaven upon the children of men, to see if there were any that did understand, that did seek God. Every one of them is gone back: they are altogether become filthy; there is none that docth good, no, not one.

Psalm 130:3

If thou, LORD, shouldest mark iniquities, O Lord, who shall stand?

Isaiah 64:5

But we are all as an unclean thing, and all our righteousness is as a filthy garment; and we all do fade as a leaf; and our iniquities, like the wind, have taken us away.

We have all become like an unclean thing, and all our virtues like a filthy rag. We are all withering like leaves, and our iniquities, like a wind, carry us off (Jewish Study Bible).

Jeremiah 17:9

The heart is deceitful above all things, and desperately sick: who can know it?
Most devious is the heart; It is perverse – who can fathom it? (Jewish Study Bible)

Sin Separates Us from G-d

Job 15:14-16

What is man, that he should be clean? And he which is born of a woman, that he should be righteous? Behold, he putteth no trust in his saints; yea, the heavens are not clean in his sight. How much more abominable and filthy is man, which drinketh iniquity like water? (KJV)

What is man that he can be cleared of guilt, one born of woman, that he be in the right? He puts no trust in His holy ones; the heavens are not guiltless in His sight; what then of one loathsome and foul, man, who drink wrongdoing like water! (Jewish Tanakh)

Isaiah 59:2

But your iniquities have separated between you and your God, and your sins have hid his face from you, that he will not hear.

But your iniquities have been a barrier between you and your God, your sins have made Him turn His face away and refuse to hear you. (Jewish Study Bible)

The Penalty of Sin Is Death

Jeremiah 31:29

But every one shall die for his own iniquity.

v. 30 But every one shall die for his own sins (Jewish Study Bible).

Ezekiel 18:4, 20

(4) Behold, all souls are mine; as the soul of the father, so also the soul of the son is mine: the soul that sinneth, it shall die.

(20) The soul that sinneth, it shall die. The son shall not bear the iniquity of the father, neither shall the father bear the iniquity of the son: the righteousness of the righteous shall be upon him, and the wickedness of the wicked shall be upon him. Consider, all lives are Mine; and life of the parent and the life of the child are both Mine. The person who sins, only he shall die (KJV).

(20) The person who sins, he alone shall die. A child shall not share the burden of a parent's guilt, nor shall a parent share the burden of a child's guilt; the righteousness of the righteous shall be accounted to him alone, and the wickedness of the wicked shall be accounted to him alone (Jewish Tanakh).

Daniel 12:2

And many of them that sleep in the dust of the earth shall awake, some to everlasting life, and some to shame and everlasting contempt.

Many of those that sleep in the dust of the earth will awake, some to eternal life, others to reproaches, to everlasting abhorrence (Jewish Tanakh).

G-d Punishes for Disobedience

Jeremiah 6:19-20

Hear, O earth: behold, I will bring evil upon this people, *even the fruit of their thoughts*, because they have not hearkened unto my words, nor to my law, but rejected it. (Italics added for emphasis) To what purpose cometh there to me incense from Shcba, and the sweet cane from a far country? Your burnt offerings are not acceptable, nor your sacrifices sweet unto me.

Hear, O earth! I am going to bring disaster upon this people, the outcome of their own schemes; for they would not hearken to My words, and they rejected My Instruction. What need have I of frankincense that come from Sheba, or fragrant cane from a distant land? Your burnt offerings are not acceptable and your sacrifices are not pleasing to Me (Jewish Tanakh).

Results of Disobedience

Jeremiah 5

(read this lengthy section)

Joshua 23:14-16

And, behold, this day I am going the way of all the earth: and ye know in all your hearts and in all your souls, that not one thing hath failed of all the good things which the LORD your God spake concerning you; all are come to pass unto you, and not one thing hath failed thereof. Therefore it shall come to pass, that as all good things are come upon you, which the LORD your God promised you; so shall the LORD bring upon you all evil things, until he has destroyed you from off this good land which the LORD your God hath given you. When ye have transgressed the covenant of the LORD your God, which he commanded you, and have gone and served other gods, and bowed yourselves to them; then shall the anger of the LORD be kindled against you, and ye shall perish quickly from off the good land which he hath given unto you.

Deuteronomy 4:23-40

Deuteronomy 28

Men Must Turn from Sin

Ezekiel 33:10-11

Therefore, O thou son of man, speak unto the house of Israel; Thus ye speak, saying, If our transgressions and our sins be upon us, and we pine (rotting) away in them, how should we then live (survive)? Say unto them, As I live, saith the Lord God, I have no pleasure in the death of the wicked; but that the wicked turn from his way and live: turn ye, turn ye from your evil ways; for why will ye die, O house of Israel?

Hosea 14:2

Return, O Israel, unto the Lord thy God; for thou hast stumbled in thine iniquity.

Inability to Redeem or Cleanse Our Hearts

Psalm 49:8

None of them can by any means redeem his brother, nor give to God a ransom for him.

Proverbs 20:9

Who can say, I have made my heart clean, I am pure from my sin?

Jeremiah 2:22

Though you wash with natron, and use much lye (soap), your guilt is ingrained before Me – declares the Lord God.

We Need a Mediator and Redeemer

Isaiah 59:16, 20

And he saw that there was no man, and wondered that there was no intercessor: therefore his arm brought salvation unto them; and his righteousness, it sustained him. And the Redeemer shall come to Zion, and unto them that turn from transgression in Jacob, saith the LORD.

Blood Is Needed for Remission of Sin

Exodus 12:13

And the blood shall be to you for a token upon the houses where ye are; and when I see the blood, I will pass over you, and the plague shall not be upon you to make an atonement for your souls; for it is the blood that maketh an atonement for the soul.

Leviticus 17:11

For the life of the flesh is in the blood; and I have given it to you upon the altar to make an atonement for your souls; for it is the blood that maketh an atonement for the soul.

A Circumcised Heart Is Needed

Deuteronomy 10:12-17

And now, Israel, what doth the LORD thy God require of thee, but to fear the LORD thy God, to walk in all his ways, and to love him, and to serve the LORD they God with all thy heart and with all thy soul, To keep the commandments of the LORD, and his statutes, which I command thee this day for thy good? Behold, the heaven and the heaven of heavens is the LORD's thy God, the earth also, with all that therein is. Only the LORD had a delight in thy fathers to love them, and he chose their seed after them, even you above all people, as it is this day. Circumcise therefore the foreskin of your heart, and be no more stiff-necked. For the LORD your God is God of gods, and Lord of lords, a great God, a mighty, and a terrible, which regardeth not persons, nor taketh reward.

Deuteronomy 30:6

And the Lord thy God will circumcise thine heart, and the heart of thy seed, to love the Lord thy God with all thine heart, and with all thy soul, that thou mayest live.

Leviticus 26:40-42

If they shall confess their iniquity and the iniquity of their fathers, with their trespass which they trespassed against me, and that also they have walked contrary unto me; and that I also have walked contrary unto them and have brought them into the land of their enemies; if then their uncircumcised hearts be humbled, and they then accept of the punishment of their iniquity: Then will I remember my covenant with Jacob, and also my covenant with Isaac, and also my covenant with Abraham will I remember; And I will remember the land.

Jeremiah 4:4

Circumcise yourselves to the Lord, and take away the foreskin of your heart, ye men of Judah and inhabitants of Jerusalem: lest my fury come forth like fire, and burn that none can quench it, because of the evil of your doings.

Jeremiah 6:9-10

Thus saith the Lord of hosts, they shall thoroughly glean the remnant of Israel as a vine: turn back thine hand as a grape gathered in the baskets. To whom shall I speak, and give warning, that they may hear? Behold their ear is uncircumcised, and they cannot hearken: behold, the word of the Lord is unto them a reproach; they have no delight in it.

Jeremiah 9:25

Egypt, and Judah, and Edom, and the children of Ammon, and Moab, and all that are in the utmost corners, that dwell in the wilderness: for all these nations are uncircumcised, and all the house of Israel are uncircumcised in the heart.

You Must Turn Back to G-d

Psalm 51:15

I will teach transgressors Your ways; that sinners may return to You (Jewish Tanakh).

Isaiah 6:10

Make the heart of this people fat, and make their ears heavy, and shut their eyes; lest they see with their eyes, and hear with their ears, and understand with their hearts, and convert, and be healed.

There Will Be a Resurrection

Daniel 12:2

And many of them that sleep in the dust of the earth shall awaken, some to everlasting life and some to shame and everlasting contempt.

Job 19:25-26

For I know that my Redeemer liveth, and that he shall stand at the latter day upon the earth, and after they have thus destroyed my skin yet from my flesh shall I see God.

Psalm 49:16

But God will redeem my soul from the power of the grave: for he shall revive me.

Isaiah 25:8

He [Messiah] will destroy death forever and the Lord God will wipe away from off all faces; and the rebuke of his people shall he take away from off all the earth, for the Lord hath spoken it.

Isaiah 26:19

Thy dead men shall live, together with my dead body shall they rise.

Hosea 13:14

I will ransom them from the power of the grave; I will redeem them from death: O death, where are thy plagues? O grave, where is thy destruction?

Personal Invitation

Both the Hebrew Scriptures and the New Covenant (Testament) present Jesus (*Yeshua*) as being equal with the Father (John 10:30). He became flesh and dwelt among us (John 1:14) and according to the Father's plan, His Son, the *Moshiach*, the Son of David was the final sacrifice for our sins, which took place on the Feast of Passover. He was the perfect Unleavened Bread that came down from heaven (John 6:28-51). He then arose from the dead on the Feast of First Fruits (John 20:1) on the first day of the week becoming the first fruits of the resurrection (1 Corinthians 15:20-26). He ascended and was seated on the Father's right hand to make intercession for us and will return in the future to restore Israel and fulfill the promises to Abraham, Isaac and Jacob. Go to the Father and confess that you're a sinner, separated from Him, and acknowledge that Jesus is your Saviour from sin, your Redeemer. Ask Him to come into your heart and life as your Messiah and Lord.

John 1:12

But as many as received him (*Yeshua*), to them gave he the power to become the sons of God, even to them that believe on his name.

John 3:16-17, 36

For God so loved the world, that he gave his only begotten Son, that whosoever believeth in him should not perish, but have everlasting life. For God sent not his Son into the world to condemn the world; but that the world through him might be saved.

He that believeth on the Son hath everlasting life: and he that believeth not the Son shall not see life; but the wrath of God abideth on him.

Acts 4:12

Neither is there salvation in any other: for there is none other name under heaven given among men, whereby we must be saved.

Romans 3:23

For all have sinned, and come short of the glory of God

Romans 5:8

But God commendeth his love toward us, in that while we were yet sinners, Messiah died for us.

Romans 6:23

For the wages of sin is death; but the gift of God is eternal life through *Yeshua* Messiah our Lord.

Philippians 2:5-11

Let this mind be in you, which was also in Messiah *Yeshua*: Who, being in the form of God, thought it not robbery to be equal with God: But made of himself of no reputation, and took upon him the form of a servant, and was made in the likeness of men: And being found in fashion as a man, he humbled himself, and became obedient unto death, even the death of the cross. Wherefore God also hath highly exalted him, and given him a name which is above every name: That at the name of *Yeshua* every knee should bow, of things in heaven, and things in the earth, and things under the earth; And that every tongue should confess that *Yeshua* Messiah is Lord, to the glory of God the Father.

Colossians 2:9-11

For in him dwelleth all the fullness of the Godhead bodily. And ye are complete in him, which is the head of all principality and power: In whom also ye are circumcised with the circumcision made without hands, in putting off the body of sins of the flesh by the circumcision of Messiah:

Hebrews 1:1-3

God, who at sundry times and in different manners spake in time past unto the fathers by the prophets, Hath in these last days spoken unto us by his Son, whom he hath appointed heir of all things, by whom also he made the worlds; Who being the brightness of his glory, and the express image of his person, and upholding all things by the word of his power, when he had by himself purged our sins, sat down on the right hand of the Majesty on high.

Hebrews 10:10-18

By the which will we are sanctified through the offering of the body of *Yeshua* Messiah once for all. And every priest standeth daily ministering and offering oftentimes the same sacrifices, which can never take away sins: But this man, after he had offered one sacrifice for sin forever, sat down on the right hand of God; From henceforth expecting till his enemies be made his footstool. For by one offering he hath perfected forever them that are sanctified. Whereof the Holy Spirit also is a witness to us: for after that he had said before, This is the covenant that I will make with them after those days, saith the Lord, I will put my laws into their hearts, and in their minds will I write them; And their sins and iniquities will I remember no more. Now where remission of these is, there is no more offering for sin.

I completely understand what the rabbis have taught for 2000 years, making repentance, good works and prayer as the replacement for the Atonement. Repentance is essential, but what is the subject of the repentance? Whom does it concern? You are some of the most gifted and intelligent people on the earth. Look into the Written Word and to *HaShem* and compare what He said and what your rabbis said; there is a difference.

Appendix 2
References to *Echad* in the Torah

This section will demonstrate the plurality of *echad* as Moses used it in the Torah. There are 382 references scattered throughout his writings. The Hebrew word *echad* is translated as "one." There are three ways that scholars say *echad* is used: (1) *echad* used as a unity, more than two things coming together in a plural unity of one, (2) *echad* used in relationship to other things or persons but not as a compound unity, (3) *echad* used to indicate the separateness or individuality of a person or thing. The third grouping is then divided into three parts: (a) first part denotes one standing among others as going into a flock to obtain one for sacrifice, (b) second part, called a "cardinal one" as Joshua enumerates the kings that he defeated in conquering the Land, (c) and an ordinal number expressed by the first day of the week or month as in Exodus 40:17. It is never used as one standing alone as the only one.

Jewish rabbis believe that the *echad* in the *Shema* of Deuteronomy 6:4 (see chapter 4), refers to *HaShem* being an absolute one with absolutely no suggestion or hint of a plurality. In order to demonstrate the usage of *echad*, all the references of *echad* listed below show how this word was used and understood by Moses. It is my desire that Jewish people understand that the *echad* within the *Shema*, which is the cornerstone of their faith, is consistently used in a plural context in all three divisions listed above.

As a New Covenant believer, this author was surprised to discover that the word for "one" in the *Shema* was not always a "one of unity." Forced by the evidence that has been observed, this author has revised his understanding of *echad*. The first division above, the unity of more than one thing, is the least frequently used (34 times) of any of the other usages of the word *echad*. The second usage appears quite frequently (172 times). That usage is a context of plurality, not necessarily unity. It was also observed in the third section that even though a particular "one" is being referenced (176 times), it is also used in the context of plurality. It is never used as an absolute one like *yachid*, which is only "one" with absolutely no reference to plurality. Moses in his usage of *echad* used this word exclusively within a plural context. G-d is viewed in Rabbinic Judaism as "one" alone, and they would have people believe that *echad* is only "one," but that just does not fit the context of *echad* and how Moses, the teacher of blessed memory, used it.

Notice on the following chart, in the first column are the scriptural references, in the second column are the quotations in which *echad* is found, and the third column shows the three areas of the third section mentioned above: (a) First *echad* denotes unity of one, (b) second denotes one in the context of plurality and (c) third, one as an individual one among others. In these quotations *echad* is italicized as well as in bold print, and if the *echad* is translated with another word besides one, that is italicized as well.

After going through all 382 references, there is only one conclusion that a student of the Scriptures can come to: *echad* is not generally used as a unity of one, but in all instances it is used in the context of plurality. Clearly, Deuteronomy 6:4 evidences a plural context: *"Hear, O Israel, the LORD our God, LORD is one."* The plural context is *elohenu* which is translated *"our God*(s)." *Elohim* is the plural form for G-d as was discussed in chapter 3, and *elohenu* is translated *"our God*(s)." Moses was stating that *Yahweh* was their G-d(s), emphasizing G-d as a one of unity and as one within a plurality. Moses knew that at his disposal were the singular forms for G-d, like *El* or *Eloah* (*Elah* was not used until the time of the exile and post-exilic period), and yet he chose to use the plural form. According to rabbis, if *Yahweh* is "one," then Moses surely confused the issue when he used *echad* in Deuteronomy 6:4 to describe God. But if G-d chose to represent Himself as a plurality — as He did so frequently throughout the *Tanakh* — then the plural word *elohim* is correct, and the plural usage of *echad* is also correct.

In using the Hebrew Scriptures published by assorted Jewish publishers, it should be noted that most often they treat *echad* the same way as translated in the King James Version or the New American Standard Version. Even passages that view *echad* within a plural context are viewed in a plural context in their translations. So Rabbinic Judaism does understand that in Deuteronomy 6:4 *echad* is not an absolute one because Jewish scholars also translate *echad* as one in a plural context.

In investigating the usage of *echad* in different Jewish translations to see how they viewed *echad* in the Torah, the observation can clearly be seen that *echad* is used the same way as in the Christian Bibles. The chart that follows this section this author has checked in the following copies of the Hebrew Scriptures: *The Jewish Study Bible*,[1815] The Soncino Chumash,[1816] The Harkavy Version,[1817] The Pentateuch and Haftorahs,[1818] Friedman's Commentary on the Torah,[1819] The Holy Scriptures according to the Masoretic Text,[1820] and the Isaac Leeser Version.[1821] In going through the references of *echad* in all the Hebrew/English editions listed above, *echad* was used consistently the same way as in the King James Version and the New American Standard Version.

It is quite apparent that *echad* is primarily used in a plural context throughout the writings of Moses. That plural usage implies that *echad* is a unity of one, but even more so a plurality and not an absolute one.

[1815] Berlin and Brettler, *The Jewish Study Bible*.

[1816] Cohen, *The Soncino Chumash: The Five Books of Moses with Haphtaroth*.

[1817] Harkavy, *The Twenty-Four Books of the Old Testament*.

[1818] Hertz, *The Pentateuch and Haftorahs*.

[1819] Friedman, *Commentary on the Torah* (San Francisco: Harper Collins Publishers, 2001).

[1820] The Jewish Publication Society, *The Holy Scriptures: According to the Masoretic Text* (Philadelphia: Jewish Publication Society, 1917).

[1821] Leeser, *The Twenty-Four Books of the Holy Bible*.

References of *Echad* in the Torah

1 = compound unity 2 = one as plurality 3 = one among others	1	2	3
GENESIS			
Gen 1:5 — And the evening and the morning were the ***echad-first*** day.	✓		
Gen 1:9 — God said, Let the waters under the heaven to be gathered unto ***echad*** place,			✓
Gen 2:11 — The name of the ***echad-first*** is the Pishon;		✓	
Gen 2:21 — and he slept: and he took ***echad*** of his ribs, and closed up the		✓	
Gen 2:24 — and shall cleave unto his wife: and they shall be ***echad*** flesh.	✓		
Gen 3:22 — Behold, the man is become as ***echad*** of us, to know good and evil:	✓		
Gen 4:19 — the name of the ***echad*** (was) Adah, and the name of the other Zillah		✓	
Gen 8:5 — on the ***echad-first*** (day) of the month,			✓
Gen 8:13 — And it came to pass in the six hundredth and ***echad-first*** year,			✓
Gen 8:13 — in the ***echad-first*** month,			✓
Gen 10:25 — And unto Eber were born two sons: the name of ***echad*** (was) Peleg		✓	
Gen 11:1 — And the whole earth was of ***echad*** language,	✓		
Gen 11:1 — and of ***echad*** speech.	✓		
Gen 11:6 — Behold, the people (is) ***echad***,	✓		
Gen 11:6 — and they have all ***echad*** language;	✓		
Gen 19:9 — This ***echad*** came in to sojourn, and he will needs be a judge:			✓
Gen 21:15 — and she cast the child under ***echad*** of the shrubs.		✓	
Gen 22:2 — a burnt-offering upon ***echad*** of the mountains which I will tell thee of.		✓	
Gen 26:10 — ***echad*** of the people might lightly have lien with thy wife,		✓	
Gen 27:38 — Hast thou but ***echad*** blessing, my father?			✓
Gen 27:45 — why should I be deprived also of you both in ***echad*** day?		✓	
Gen 32:8 — If Esau come to the ***echad*** company, and smite it,			✓
Gen 33:13 — and if men should overdrive them ***echad*** day, all the flock will die.		✓	
Gen 34:16 — and we will dwell with you, and we will become ***echad*** people.	✓		
Gen 34:22 — to be ***echad*** people, if every male among us be circumcised,	✓		
Gen 37:20 — and let us slay him, and cast him into ***echad-some*** pit,		✓	
Gen 40:5 — each man his dream in ***echad*** night,		✓	
Gen 41:5 — and behold, seven ears of corn came up upon ***echad*** stalk,	✓		
Gen 41:11 — And we dreamed a dream in ***echad*** night, I and he;		✓	
Gen 41:22 — and behold, seven ears came up in ***echad*** stalk, full and good:	✓		
Gen 41:25 — The dream of Pharaoh (is) ***echad***: God hath shewed Pharaoh	✓		
Gen 41:26 — and the seven good ears (are) seven years: the dream (is) ***echad.***	✓		
Gen 42:11 — We (are) all ***echad*** man's sons: we (are) true (men),	✓		
Gen 42:13 — twelve brethren, the sons of ***echad*** man in the land of Canaan;	✓		
Gen 42:13 — the youngest is this day with our father, and ***echad*** is not.		✓	
Gen 42:16 — Send ***echad*** of you, and let him fetch your brother		✓	

References of *Echad* in the Torah		1	2	3
1 = compound unity **2 = one as plurality** **3 = one among others**				
Gen 42:19	If ye (be) true (men), let *echad* of your brethren be bound in the house		✓	
Gen 42:27	And as *echad* of them opened his sack to give his ass		✓	
Gen 42:32	We (be) twelve brethren, sons of our father; *echad* (is) not,		✓	
Gen 42:33	leave *echad* of your brethren (here) with me		✓	
Gen 44:28	And the *echad* went out from me, and I said,		✓	
Gen 48:22	Moreover I have given to thee *echad* portion above thy brethren,		✓	
Gen 49:16	Dan shall judge his people, as *echad* of the tribes of Israel.		✓	
EXODUS				
Ex 1:15	Hebrew midwives, of which the name of the *echad* (was) Shiphrah		✓	
Ex 8:31	removed the swarms of (flies) from Pharaoh,…Remained not *echad*		✓	
Ex 9:6	but of the cattle of the children of Israel died not *echad*.		✓	
Ex 9:7	And Pharaoh sent, and, behold, there was not *echad* of the cattle		✓	
Ex 10:19	there remained not *echad* locust in all the coasts of Egypt.		✓	
Ex 11:1	Yet will I bring *echad* plague more upon Pharaoh,		✓	
Ex 12:18	until the *echad* and twentieth day of the month at even,			✓
Ex 12:46	In *echad* house shall it be eaten; thou shalt not carry forth		✓	
Ex 12:49	*Echad* law shall be to him that is homeborn,	✓		
Ex 14:28	there remained not so much as *echad* of them.	✓		
Ex 16:22	they gathered twice as much bread, two omers for *echad* (man)	✓		
Ex 16:33	Take *echad-a* pot, and put a omer full of manna therein,		✓	
Ex 17:12	and Aaron and Hur stayed up his hands, the *echad* on the *echad* side		✓	
Ex 17:12	the *echad* on the *echad* side, and the other on the other side;		✓	
Ex 18:3	of which the name of the *echad* (was) Gershom;		✓	
Ex 18:4	And the name of the *other-echad* (was) Eliezer;		✓	
Ex 23:29	I will not drive them out from before thee in *echad* year;			✓
Ex 24:3	and all the people answered with *echad* voice,	✓		
Ex 25:12	and two rings shall be in the *echad* side of it,		✓	
Ex 25:19	And make *echad* cherub on the *echad* end,		✓	
Ex 25:19	and the *echad-other* cherub on the other end:		✓	
Ex 25:32	three branches of the candlestick out of the *echad* side,		✓	
Ex 25:33	with a knop and a flower in *echad* branch;		✓	
Ex 25:33	and three bowls made like almonds in the *echad-other* branch,		✓	
Ex 25:36	all it (shall be) *echad* beaten work (of) pure gold.	✓		
Ex 26:2	The length of *echad* curtain shall be eight and twenty cubits,		✓	
Ex 26:2	and the breadth of *echad* curtain four cubits:		✓	
Ex 26:2	and every *echad* of the curtains shall have echad measure		✓	
Ex 26:2	and every echad of the curtains shall have *echad* measure	✓		

References of *Echad* in the Torah ||||		
1 = compound unity 2 = one as plurality 3 = one among others		1	2	3
Ex 26:4	And thou shalt make loops of blue upon the edge of the ***echad*** curtain		✓	
Ex 26:5	Fifty loops shalt thou make in the ***echad*** curtain,		✓	
Ex 26:8	The length of ***echad*** curtain (shall be) thirty cubits,		✓	
Ex 26:8	and the breadth of ***echad*** curtain four cubits:		✓	
Ex 26:8	and the eleven curtains (shall be all) of ***echad*** measure.	✓		
Ex 26:10	And thou shalt make fifty loops on the edge of the ***echad*** curtain		✓	
Ex 26:11	and couple the tent together, that it may be ***echad***.	✓		
Ex 26:16	and a cubit and a half (shall be) the breadth of ***echad*** board.		✓	
Ex 26:17	Two tenons (shall there be) in ***echad*** board,		✓	
Ex 26:19	two sockets under ***echad*** board for his two tenons,		✓	
Ex 26:21	And their forty sockets of silver; two sockets under ***echad*** board,		✓	
Ex 26:24	they shall be coupled together above the head of it unto ***echad*** ring	✓		
Ex 26:25	sixteen sockets; two sockets under ***echad*** board,		✓	
Ex 26:26	five for the boards of the ***echad*** side of the tabernacle,		✓	
Ex 27:9	the court of (fine) twined linen of a hundred cubits long for ***echad*** side:		✓	
Ex 28:10	Six of their names on ***echad*** stone		✓	
Ex 28:17	(even) four rows of stones: the ***echad-first*** shall be a sardius,		✓	
Ex 29:1	Take ***echad*** young bullock, and two rams without blemish,			✓
Ex 29:3	and thou shalt put them into ***echad*** basket,	✓		
Ex 29:15	Thou shalt also take ***echad*** ram;		✓	
Ex 29:23	And ***echad*** loaf of bread		✓	
Ex 29:23	and ***echad*** cake of oiled bread,		✓	
Ex 29:23	and ***echad*** wafer out of the basket of the unleavened bread		✓	
Ex 29:39	The ***echad*** lamb thou shalt offer in the morning		✓	
Ex 29:40	And with the ***echad*** lamb a tenth deal of flour mingled with		✓	
Ex 30:10	***echad-once*** in a year with the blood of the sin-offering of atonements:			✓
Ex 30:10	***echad-once*** in the year shall he make atonement upon it			✓
Ex 36:9	The length of ***echad*** curtain was twenty and eight cubits		✓	
Ex 36:9	and the breadth of ***echad*** curtain four cubits:		✓	
Ex 36:10	And he coupled the five curtains ***echad*** unto another;		✓	
Ex 36:11	And he made loops of blue on the edge of ***echad*** curtain		✓	
Ex 36:12	Fifty loops made he in ***echad*** curtain,		✓	
Ex 36:12	the loops held ***echad*** curtain to another.		✓	
Ex 36:13	fifty taches of gold, and coupled the curtains ***echad*** unto another		✓	
Ex 36:13	so it became ***echad*** tabernacle.	✓		
Ex 36:15	The length of ***echad*** curtain was thirty cubits,		✓	
Ex 36:15	and four cubits (was) the breadth of ***echad*** curtain:		✓	

References of *Echad* in the Torah

1 = compound unity 2 = one as plurality 3 = one among others	1	2	3
Ex 36:15 — the eleven curtains (were) of **echad** size.	✓		
Ex 36:18 — to couple the tent together, that it might be **echad**	✓		
Ex 36:21 — and the breadth of a board **echad** cubit and a half		✓	
Ex 36:22 — **Echad** board had two tenons,		✓	
Ex 36:22 — equally distant **echad** from another:		✓	
Ex 36:24 — two sockets under **echad** board for his two tenons,		✓	
Ex 36:24 — and two sockets under **echad-another** board for his two tenons.		✓	
Ex 36:26 — And their forty sockets of silver; two sockets under **echad** board,		✓	
Ex 36:26 — and two sockets under **echad-another** board.		✓	
Ex 36:29 — and coupled together at the head thereof, to **echad** ring:		✓	
Ex 36:30 — their sockets (were) 16 sockets of silver, under **echad-every** board		✓	
Ex 36:31 — five for the boards of the **echad** side of the tabernacle,		✓	
Ex 37:3 — even two rings upon the **echad** side of it,		✓	
Ex 37:8 — **Echad** cherub on the end on this side,		✓	
Ex 37:8 — and **echad-another** cherub on the (other) end on that side:		✓	
Ex 37:18 — three branches of the candlestick out of the **echad** side thereof,		✓	
Ex 37:19 — Three bowls made after the fashion of almonds in **echad** branch,		✓	
Ex 37:19 — and three bowls made like almonds in **echad-another** branch,		✓	
Ex 37:22 — all of it (was) **echad** beaten work (of) pure gold.	✓		
Ex 39:10 — And they set in it four rows of stones: the **echad** (first) row		✓	
Ex 40:2 — On the **echad-first** day of the first month thou shalt set up			✓
Ex 40:17 — on the **echad-first** day of the month, the tabernacle was reared up			✓

LEVITICUS

Lev 4:2 — Speak unto the children of Israel, saying, If **echad-a** soul shall sin		✓	
Lev 4:2 — If echad-a soul shall sin through ignorance against **echad-any** of the		✓	
Lev 4:2 — commandments…and shall do against **echad-any** of them.		✓	
Lev 4:13 — and they have done (somewhat agaist) **echad-any** of the commandments		✓	
Lev 4:22 — When a ruler hath sinned, and done through ignorance (against) **echad-any**		✓	
Lev 4:27 — And if **echad** of the common people sin through ignorance,		✓	
Lev 4:27 — while he doeth (somewhat against) **echad-any** of the commandments of the		✓	
Lev 5:4 — then he shall be guilty in **echad** of these		✓	
Lev 5:5 — And it shall be, when he shall be guilty in **echad** of these (things),		✓	
Lev 5:7 — unto the LORD, **echad** for a sin-offering		✓	
Lev 5:7 — and the **echad-other** for a burnt-offering.		✓	
Lev 5:13 — In this way the priest will make atonement for him for **echad-any** of these		✓	

694

References of *Echad* in the Torah

1 = compound unity 2 = one as plurality 3 = one among others		1	2	3
Lev 7:7	As their sin-offering (is), so is the trespass-offering: there is **echad** law	✓		
Lev 7:14	And of it he shall offer **echad** out of the whole oblation		✓	
Lev 8:26	he took **echad** unleavened cake			✓
Lev 8:26	and **echad-a** cake of oiled bread,			✓
Lev 8:26	and **echad** wafer, and put (them) on the fat			✓
Lev 12:8	the **echad** burnt-offering,		✓	
Lev 12:8	and the **echad-other** for a sin-offering;		✓	
Lev 13:2	then he shall be brought unto Aaron the priest, or unto **echad** of his sons		✓	
Lev 14:5	And the priest shall command that **echad** of the birds be killed		✓	
Lev 14:10	and **echad** ewe lamb of the year without blemish,			✓
Lev 14:10	mingled with oil, and **echad** log of oil.			✓
Lev 14:21	then he shall take **echad** lamb (for) a trespass-offering to be waved,			✓
Lev 14:21	to make an atonement for him, and **echad** tenth deal of fine flour		✓	
Lev 14:22	and the **echad** shall be a sin-offering		✓	
Lev 14:22	and the **echad-other** a burnt-offering.		✓	
Lev 14:30	And he shall offer the **echad** of the turtledoves,		✓	
Lev 14:31	the **echad** (for) a sin-offering,		✓	
Lev 14:31	and the **echad-other** (for) a brunt-offering		✓	
Lev 14:50	And he shall kill the **echad** of the birds in an earthen vessel		✓	
Lev 15:15	the **echad** (for) a sin-offering,		✓	
Lev 15:15	and the **echad-other** (for) a burnt-offering;		✓	
Lev 15:30	And the priest shall offer the **echad** (for) a sin-offering,		✓	
Lev 15:30	and the **echad-other** (for) a burnt-offering;		✓	
Lev 16:5	two kids of the goats for a sin-offering, and **echad** ram for a burnt-offering			✓
Lev 16:8	And Aaron shall cast lots upon the two goats: **echad** lot for the LORD,		✓	
Lev 16:8	and the **echad-other** lot for the scapegoat.		✓	
Lev 16:34	make an atonement for the children of Israel for all their sins **echad** a year,			✓
Lev 22:28	ye shall not kill it and her young both in **echad** day.			✓
Lev 23:18	seven lambs without blemish of the first year, the **echad** young bullock,			✓
Lev 23:19	Then ye shall sacrifice **echad** kid of the goats for a sin-offering,		✓	
Lev 23:24	In the seventh month, in the **echad** (day) of the month,			✓
Lev 24:5	two tenth deals shall be in **echad** cake.		✓	
Lev 24:22	Ye shall have **echad** manner of law, as well for the stranger,		✓	
Lev 25:48	After that he is sold he may be redeemed again, **echad** of his brethren		✓	

References of *Echad* in the Torah			
1 = compound unity 2 = one as plurality 3 = one among others	1	2	3
Lev 26:26	ten women shall bake your bread in **echad** oven,			✓

NUMBERS

		1	2	3
Num 1:1	on the **echad** (day) of the second month, in the second year			✓
Num 1:18	And they assembled all the congregation together on the **echad** (day) of the			✓
Num 1:41	of the tribe of Asher, (were) forty and **echad** thousand and five hundred			✓
Num 1:44	(being) twelve men: each **echad** was for the house of his fathers.		✓	
Num 2:16	in the camp of Reuben (were) an 100,000 and 50 and **echad** thousand and			✓
Num 2:28	and those that were numbered of them, (were) 40 and **echad** thousand			✓
Num 6:11	And the priest shall offer the **echad** for a sin-offering,		✓	
Num 6:11	and the **echad-other** for a burnt-offering,		✓	
Num 6:14	he shall offer his offering unto the LORD, **echad** he lamb of the first year			✓
Num 6:14	without blemish for a burnt-offering, and **echad** ewe lamb of the first year			✓
Num 6:14	without blemish for a sin-offering, and **echad** ram without blemish			✓
Num 6:19	and **echad** unleavened cake out of the basket			✓
Num 6:19	and **echad** unleavened wafer,			✓
Num 7:3	and twelve oxen; a wagon for two of the princes, and for each **echad** an ox:		✓	
Num 7:11	They shall offer their offering, **echad-each** prince on this day,		✓	
Num 7:13	And his offering (was) **echad** silver charger,			✓
Num 7:13	**echad** silver bowl of seventy shekels,			✓
Num 7:14	**Echad** spoon of ten (shekels) of gold, full of incense:			✓
Num 7:15	**Echad** young bullock			✓
Num 7:15	**echad** ram,			✓
Num 7:15	**echad** lamb of the first year, for a burnt-offering:			✓
Num 7:16	**Echad** kid of the goats for a sin-offering:			✓
Num 7:19	He offered (for) his offering **echad** silver charger,			✓
Num 7:19	**echad** silver bowl of seventy shekels, after the shekel of the sanctuary;			✓
Num 7:20	**Echad** spoon of gold of ten (shekels), full of incense:			✓
Num 7:21	**Echad** young bullock,			✓
Num 7:21	**echad** ram,			✓
Num 7:21	**echad** lamb of the first year, for a burnt-offering:			✓
Num 7:22	**Echad** kid of the goats for a sin-offering:			✓
Num 7:25	His offering (was) **echad** silver charger, the weight whereof			✓
Num 7:25	**Echad** silver bowl of seventy shekels,			✓

References of *Echad* in the Torah			
1 = compound unity 2 = one as plurality 3 = one among others	**1**	**2**	**3**
Num 7:26	**Echad** golden spoon of ten (shekels), full of incense:			✓
Num 7:27	**Echad** young bullock			✓
Num 7:27	**echad** ram,			✓
Num 7:27	**echad** lamb of the first year, for a burnt-offering:			✓
Num 7:28	**Echad** kid of the goats for a sin-offering:			✓
Num 7:31	His offering (was) **echad** silver charger, the weight whereof			✓
Num 7:31	**echad** silver bowl of seventy shekels, after the shekel of the sanctuary;			✓
Num 7:32	**Echad** golden spoon of ten (shekels), full of incense:			✓
Num 7:33	**Echad** young bullock,			✓
Num 7:33	**echad** ram,			✓
Num 7:33	**echad** lamb of the first year, for a burnt-offering:			✓
Num 7:34	**Echad** kid of the goats for a sin-offering:			✓
Num 7:37	His offering (was) **echad** silver charger, the weight whereof			✓
Num 7:37	**echad** silver bowl of seventy shekels,			✓
Num 7:38	**Echad** golden spoon of ten (shekels), full of incense:			✓
Num 7:39	**Echad** young bullock			✓
Num 7:39	**echad** ram,			✓
Num 7:39	**echad** lamb of the first year, for a burnt-offering:			✓
Num 7:40	**Echad** kid of the goats for a sin-offering:			✓
Num 7:43	His offering (was) **echad** silver charger, the weight whereof			✓
Num 7:43	**echad** silver bowl of seventy shekels, after the shekel of the sanctuary;			✓
Num 7:44	**Echad** golden spoon of ten (shekels), full of incense:			✓
Num 7:45	**Echad** young bullock			✓
Num 7:45	**echad** ram,			✓
Num 7:45	**echad** lamb of the first year, for a burnt-offering:			✓
Num 7:46	**Echad** kid of the goats for a sin-offering:			✓
Num 7:49	His offering (was) **echad** silver charger, the weight whereof			✓
Num 7:49	**echad** silver bowl of seventy shekels, after the shekel of the sanctuary;			✓
Num 7:50	**Echad** golden spoon of ten (shekels), full of incense:			✓
Num 7:51	**Echad** young bullock			✓
Num 7:51	**echad** ram,			✓
Num 7:51	**echad** lamb of the first year, for a burnt-offering:			✓
Num 7:52	**Echad** kid of the goats for a sin-offering:			✓
Num 7:55	His offering (was) **echad** silver charger, the weight whereof			✓
Num 7:55	**echad** silver bowl of seventy shekels, after the shekel of the sanctuary;			✓
Num 7:56	**Echad** golden spoon of ten (shekels), full of incense:			✓
Num 7:57	**Echad** young bullock			✓

References of *Echad* in the Torah

1 = compound unity 2 = one as plurality 3 = one among others		1	2	3
Num 7:57	*echad* ram,			✓
Num 7:57	*echad* lamb of the first year, for a burnt-offering:			✓
Num 7:58	*Echad* kid of the goats for a sin-offering:			✓
Num 7:61	His offering (was) *echad* silver charger, the weight whereof			✓
Num 7:61	*echad* silver bowl of seventy shekels, after the shekel of the sanctuary;			✓
Num 7:62	*Echad* golden spoon of ten (shekels), full of incense:			✓
Num 7:63	*Echad* young bullock			✓
Num 7:63	*echad* ram,			✓
Num 7:63	*echad* lamb of the first year, for a burnt-offering:			✓
Num 7:64	*Echad* kid of the goats for a sin-offering:			✓
Num 7:67	His offering (was) *echad* silver charger, the weight whereof			✓
Num 7:67	*echad* silver bowl of seventy shekels, after the shekel of the sanctuary;			✓
Num 7:68	*Echad* golden spoon of ten (shekels), full of incense:			✓
Num 7:69	*Echad* young bullock			✓
Num 7:69	*echad* ram,			✓
Num 7:69	*echad* lamb of the first year, for a burnt-offering:			✓
Num 7:70	*Echad* kid of the goats for a sin-offering:			✓
Num 7:73	His offering (was) *echad* silver charger, the weight whereof			✓
Num 7:73	*echad* silver bowl of seventy shekels, after the shekel of the sanctuary;			✓
Num 7:74	*Echad* golden spoon of ten (shekels), full of incense:			✓
Num 7:75	*Echad* young bullock			✓
Num 7:75	*echad* ram,			✓
Num 7:75	*echad* lamb of the first year, for a burnt-offering:			✓
Num 7:76	*Echad* kid of the goats for a sin-offering:			✓
Num 7:79	His offering (was) *echad* silver charger, the weight whereof			✓
Num 7:79	*echad* silver bowl of seventy shekels, after the shekel of the sanctuary;			✓
Num 7:80	*Echad* golden spoon of ten (shekels), full of incense:			✓
Num 7:81	*Echad* young bullock			✓
Num 7:81	*echad* ram,			✓
Num 7:81	*echad* lamb of the first year, for a burnt-offering:			✓
Num 7:82	*Echad* kid of the goats for a sin-offering:			✓
Num 7:85	His offering (was) *echad* silver charger, the weight whereof			✓
Num 7:85	*echad* silver bowl of seventy shekels, after the shekel of the sanctuary;			✓
Num 8:12	and thou shalt offer the *echad* (for) a sin-offering,		✓	
Num 8:12	and the *echad-other* for a burnt-offering, unto the LORD		✓	
Num 9:14	ye shall have *echad* ordinance, both for the stranger,	✓		

References of *Echad* in the Torah

1 = compound unity 2 = one as plurality 3 = one among others		1	2	3
Num 10:4	And if they blow (but) with *echad* (trumpet), then the princes,			✓
Num 11:19	Ye shall not eat *echad* day, nor two days, nor five days, neither ten days,			✓
Num 11:26	and the name of the *echad* (was) Eldad, and the name of the other Medad:		✓	
Num 13:2	of every tribe of their fathers shall ye send *echad-a* man,		✓	
Num 13:2	every *echad* a ruler among them.		✓	
Num 13:23	and cut down from thence a branch with *echad* cluster of grapes,	✓		
Num 14:15	Now (if) thou shalt kill (all) this people as *echad* man,	✓		
Num 15:5	with a burnt-offering or sacrifice, for *echad* lamb.			✓
Num 15:11	Thus shall it be done for *echad* bullock,			✓
Num 15:11	or for *echad* ram,			✓
Num 15:11	or for *echad-a* lamb,			✓
Num 15:11	or *echad-a* kid.			✓
Num 15:12	According to the number that ye shall prepare, so shall ye do to every *echad*		✓	
Num 15:15	*Echad* ordinance (shall be both) for you of the congregation,	✓		
Num 15:16	*Echad* law and *echad* manner shall be for you,		✓	
Num 15:16	*Echad* law and *echad* manner shall be for you,		✓	
Num 15:24	that all the congregation shall offer *echad* bullock for a burnt-offering,		✓	
Num 15:24	according to the manner, and *echad* kid of the goats for a sin-offering.		✓	
Num 15:27	And if *echad-any* soul sin through ignorance,		✓	
Num 15:29	Ye shall have *echad* law for him that sinneth through ignorance,		✓	
Num 16:15	I have not taken *echad* ass from them, neither have I hurt echad of them.		✓	
Num 16:15	I have not taken echad ass from them, neither have I hurt *echad* of them.		✓	
Num 16:22	O God, the God of the spirits of all flesh, shall *echad* man sin,		✓	
Num 17:3	for *echad* rod (shall be) for the head of the house of their fathers.		✓	
Num 17:6	and every *echad* of their princes gave him a rod apiece,		✓	
Num 17:6	each prince *echad*, according to their fathers' houses, (even) twelve rods:		✓	
Num 28:4	the *echad* lamb shalt thou offer in the morning		✓	
Num 28:7	drink-offering thereof (shall be) the fourth (part) of an hin for the *echad* lamb			✓
Num 28:11	two young bullocks, and *echad* ram, seven lambs of the first year without			✓
Num 28:12	mingled with oil, the *echad* bullock;			✓
Num 28:12	mingled with oil, for *echad* ram;			✓
Num 28:13	flour mingled with oil (for) a meat-offering unto *echad* lamb;			✓

References of *Echad* in the Torah

1 = compound unity 2 = one as plurality 3 = one among others		1	2	3
Num 28:15	And ***echad*** kid of the goats for a sin-offering unto the LORD shall be offered,			✓
Num 28:19	two bullocks, and ***echad*** ram, and seven lambs of the first year:			✓
Num 28:21	A several tenth deal shalt thou offer for ***echad-every*** lamb,			✓
Num 28:22	and ***echad*** goat (for) a sin-offering, to make an atonement for you.			✓
Num 28:27	two young bullocks, ***echad*** ram, seven lambs of the first year;			✓
Num 28:28	three tenth deals unto ***echad*** bullock, two tenth deals unto echad ram,			✓
Num 28:28	three tenth deals unto echad bullock, two tenth deals unto ***echad*** ram,			✓
Num 28:29	A several tenth deal unto ***echad*** lamb, throughout the seven lambs;			✓
Num 28:30	(And) ***echad*** kid of the goats, to make an atonement for you.			✓
Num 29:1	And in the seventh month, on the ***echad-first*** (day) of the month,			✓
Num 29:2	***echad*** young bullock, echad ram, (and) seven lambs of the first year			✓
Num 29:2	***echad*** young bullock, ***echad*** ram, (and) seven lambs of the first year			✓
Num 29:4	And ***echad*** tenth deal for echad lamb, throughout the seven lambs;		✓	
Num 29:4	And echad tenth deal for ***echad*** lamb, throughout the seven lambs;			✓
Num 29:5	And ***echad*** kid of the goats (for) a sin-offering, to make an atonement for			✓
Num 29:8	***echad*** young bullock, echad ram, (and) seven lambs of the first year			✓
Num 29:8	echad young bullock, ***echad*** ram, (and) seven lambs of the first year			✓
Num 29:9	three tenth deals unto ***echad*** bullock, two tenth deals unto echad ram,			✓
Num 29:9	three tenth deals unto echad bullock, two tenth deals unto ***echad*** ram,			✓
Num 29:10	three tenth deals unto echad bullock, two tenth deals unto ***echad*** ram,			✓
Num 29:11	***Echad*** kid of the goats for a sin-offering:			✓
Num 29:14	three tenth deals unto ***echad-every*** bullock of the thirteen bullocks,		✓	
Num 29:14	two tenth deals to ***echad-each*** ram of the two rams.		✓	
Num 29:15	And a several tenth to ***echad-each*** lamb of the fourteen lambs:		✓	
Num 29:16	And ***echad*** kid of the goats (for) a sin-offering,			✓
Num 29:19	And ***echad*** kid of the goats (for) a sin-offering;			✓
Num 29:22	And ***echad*** goat (for) a sin-offering, beside the continual burnt-offering,			✓
Num 29:25	And ***echad*** kid of the goats (for) a sin-offering, beside the continual			✓
Num 29:28	And ***echad*** goat (for) a sin-offering, beside the continual burnt-			✓

References of *Echad* in the Torah

1 = compound unity 2 = one as plurality 3 = one among others		1	2	3
	offering,			
Num 29:31	And ***echad*** goat (for) a sin-offering, beside the continual burnt-offering,			✓
Num 29:34	And ***echad*** goat (for) a sin-offering, beside the continual burnt-offering,			✓
Num 29:36	***echad*** bullock, echad ram, seven lambs of the first year without blemish:			✓
Num 29:36	echad bullock, ***echad*** ram, seven lambs of the first year without blemish:			✓
Num 29:38	And ***echad*** goat (for) a sin-offering, beside the continual burnt-offering,			✓
Num 31:28	***echad*** soul of five hundred, (both) of the persons, and of the beeves,		✓	
Num 31:30	thou shalt take ***echad*** portion of fifty, of the persons, of the beeves,		✓	
Num 31:47	Moses took ***echad*** portion of fifty, (both) of man and of beast,		✓	
Num 33:38	in the ***echad-first*** (day) of the fifth month.			✓
Num 34:18	ye shall take ***echad*** prince of every tribe, to divide the land by inheritance.		✓	
Num 34:18	Any ye shall take echad prince of ***echad-every*** tribe, to divide the land by		✓	
Num 35:30	but ***echad*** witness shall not testify against any person (to cause him) to die.			✓
Num 36:3	And if they be married to any of the sons of the ***echad*** tribes of the children		✓	
Num 36:8	shall be wife unto ***echad*** of the family of the tribe of her father,		✓	
DEUTERONOMY				
Deut 1:3	in the fortieth year, in the eleventh month, on the ***echad-first*** (day) of the			✓
Deut 1:23	and I took twelve men of you ***echad*** of a tribe:			✓
Deut 4:42	and that fleeing unto ***echad*** of these cities he might live:			✓
Deut 6:4	Hear, O Israel: the LORD our God (is) ***echad*** LORD.	✓		
Deut 12:14	But in the place which the LORD shall choose in ***echad*** of thy tribes,		✓	
Deut 13:12	If thou shalt hear (say) in ***echad*** of thy cities,		✓	
Deut 15:7	If there be among you a poor man of ***echad*** of thy brethren		✓	
Deut 15:7	within ***echad-any*** of thy gates in thy land,		✓	
Deut 16:5	Thou mayest not sacrifice the passover with ***echad-any*** of thy gates,		✓	
Deut 17:2	If there be found among you, within ***echad-any*** of thy gates		✓	
Deut 17:6	(but) at the mouth of ***echad*** witness he shall not be put to death.			✓
Deut 18:6	And if a Levite come from ***echad-any*** of thy gates out of all Israel,		✓	

References of *Echad* in the Torah				
1 = compound unity 2 = one as plurality 3 = one among others		**1**	**2**	**3**
Deut 19:11	and smite him mortally that he die, and fleeth into ***echad*** of these cities:		✓	
Deut 19:15	***Echad*** witness shall not rise up again a man for any iniquity,			✓
Deut 21:15	If a man have two wives, ***echad*** beloved,		✓	
Deut 21:15	and ***echad-another*** hated, and they have born him children,		✓	
Deut 23:16	(even) among you, in that place which he shall choose in ***echad*** of thy gates,		✓	
Deut 24:5	(but) he shall be free at home ***echad*** year, and shall cheer up his wife			✓
Deut 25:5	If brethren dwell together, and ***echad*** of them die, and have no child,		✓	
Deut 25:11	men strive together one with another, and the wife of the ***echad*** draweth		✓	
Deut 28:7	they shall come out against thee ***echad*** way, and flee before thee seven			✓
Deut 28:25	thou shalt go out ***echad*** way against them, and flee seven ways before			✓
Deut 28:55	So that he will not give to ***echad-any*** of them of the flesh of his children		✓	
Deut 32:30	How should ***echad*** chase a thousand, and two put ten thousand to flight,			✓
Totals for individual columns:		34	172	176
Grand total of *echad* references in the five books of Moses:				382

Appendix 3
The Word: Verbal Plenary Inspiration

The subject of verbal plenary inspiration could easily fill a book. However, here in this context only one aspect will be viewed in relation to the spoken or written word of God. Inspiration is defined in this book with two other terms "verbal" and "plenary" so there is no need to address it again. This is a challenge to both Christian and Jewish adherents to take another look at the doctrine of Inspiration.

The two purposes of this appendix are first to draw attention to the Hebrew word(s) for the expression "*the word of the Lord*," or similar expressions like "*it is written*," that deal with the words of God that were penned by human authors and written in the Hebrew Scriptures. Based on the Written Word as the only inspired authority for faith, life and practice, it will be the second purpose to draw the attention of biblical believers as to how they interpret the Word of God and to Jewish people concerning the validity of the Oral Law verses the Written Law. The Oral Law versus the Written Word will be dealt with a little latter in this appendix.

The first purpose is to express the dire need in the 21st century for pastors and teachers to re-examine the Doctrine of Inspiration as to how it is being presented in the church today. The believing church is quickly losing its biblical bearings in three basic ways: (1) liberal scholars (higher criticism), and (2) evangelicals disguising themselves with "Open Theism," "Seeker Sensitive" and the "Emergent Church" have infected evangelical and some so-called fundamental authors and translators who, as a result, are chipping away at this doctrine and (3) the charismatic movement that has introduced feelings, emotions and extra-biblical revelation as authority. They are aggressively flooding the "Christian" market place with books that reinterpret what God says into what they think God meant. They give the dynamic equivalent to the words in the Bible (NIV, Living Bible, Good News, TNIV, etc.) instead of what God literally said in an unbiblical attempt to make the Scriptures more readable and more understandable. It is true that words and cultures change, so the word can be translated in the vernacular of the day. But to change Scripture to make it more acceptable to the culture is totally unwarranted. God's Word is inspired for any and every culture; it does not under any circumstance need to be brought up to date by dynamic equivalents.

During a conversation with my writing coach,[1822] she expressed that the humanistic secular academic approach to all writings — including Scripture — is not the same today, in the postmodern world, as it was in previous years. She explained the new perspective: "The meaning lies – not in the text – but in the interpretation of the text." Fundamental Bible believers bristle at that statement because it undercuts their firmly held belief in verbal plenary inspiration of Scriptures. The core of that postmodern

---

[1822] In a private conversation with Dr. Elaine Huber. I owe a great debt of gratitude to her for all her help and advice in writing this book.

perspective is a frontal attack on the very words that God used. Their implication is that all literature — including the Scriptures — is to be given over to the fallible mind of the humanistic secular person; some are disguised as evangelicals who want to interpret all literature – including the Scriptures – the same way. Many contemporary Evangelical authors have adopted that view in relation to Scripture, even though they claim a belief in the Inspiration of Scripture. Also Rabbinic Judaism has adopted the method of re-interpreting the Scriptures to avoid the deity of Messiah as illustrated by Louis Goldberg:

> Can Passover have a meaning **without** a paschal lamb? Of course, the Jewish religious leader will be quick to point out that there is no temple standing today; There is no opportunity today to make any such sacrifices. So, to circumvent this, the Talmud, based on Mishnah and Gemarah, indicates that substitutes can be made for the paschal lamb. Authority for this procedure is based on the assertion that Judaism, as a way of life, is a living, moving faith, and that Torah must be interpreted in the light of ever-changing conditions.[1823]

Robert Wilkin expresses deep concern that some evangelicals are broadening their view of Inspiration:

> He [Wallace of Dallas Theological Seminary] suggested that the authors of the NT did not approach the reporting of history in the same way that current historians do. In order to interpret the NT correctly, we must be aware of this different approach. Practically speaking this brings into question the NT author's concern about historical accuracy in terms of the speaker, the location, the date, and the precise content of what was said.[1824]

As Wilkin later points out, it is ludicrous to claim that the New Testament can contain historical inaccuracies and still be God-breathed, without error. God, who is the author, used words, precise words, to express His nature and His person to mankind. It is troubling to see evangelical authors saying and implying that the Scriptures can't be trusted with the facts in history and science. History has demonstrated that it is finite man who cannot be trusted when he moves away from what God said and reinterprets what God said.

Today those who have been known as Evangelical believers in the past are now in the beginning stages of a new movement called "The Emergent Church" that claims that what the authors of Scripture wrote in their day was correct and appropriate for that generation. However, they clearly say that it is not accurate for today and needs to be updated and made relevant for the 21st-century culture. This is apostasy, a complete denial of the Scripture and most naïve unlearned Christians today do not have the

---

[1823] Goldberg, *The Deviation of Jewish Thought from an Old Testament Theology in the Inter-testamental Period*, 3.

[1824] Robert N. Wilkin, "Toward a Narrow View of Ipsissima Vox," *JOTGES* 14, no. 26 (Spring 2001), 3-8.

biblical wherewithal to discern what is being presented to them by their pastor and leaders.[1825] This could be the great apostasy before the return of Messiah for His Church.

In the process evangelicals move believers away from *"Thus saith the LORD"* as the absolute final authority of Scripture. In their attempt to make the Scripture more readable for people, scholars have sacrificed one of the foundational doctrines of Scripture — Inspiration. Unfortunately, 21st-century evangelicals have taken it upon themselves to correct God's Word into what they think God meant. That is ludicrous — that an unreliable, fallible man, a creature made by infallible God, would take it upon himself to correct the Creator and Author of His own word.

The second purpose is to invite rabbis and Jewish people at large to reinvestigate the claims of *HaShem* and His inspired word, which He gave to Moses and the prophets to write ALL of it down. His Word is supreme, not the writings of fallible men in their interpretations of the *Tanakh* in Talmud and other rabbinic commentaries. This next statement may be viewed as a harsh statement, but it is meant to be taken in love and to be thought through logically within the context of this book. Rabbinic Judaism has been the instrument to cause Jewish people to prostrate themselves before an idol, the god of the Oral Law, the one and only authoritative pillar of Rabbinic Judaism.

Oral Law

Judaism has two Torahs, the written Torah, which is found in the first five books of the Hebrew Bible and the Oral Torah, which cannot be found in the Hebrew Bible. It will be seen that the Oral Torah in practice carries more importance in Rabbinic Judaism than the written words of God in the *Tanakh*. The rabbis contend that God revealed two laws to Moses at Mt. Sinai, a written law and an oral law. The written law was recorded by Moses, whereas the oral law was memorized and communicated orally for over 1500 years before it was written down around 220 CE. However, history shows that the Oral Torah began with the generation of scribes (*Sopherim*) after Ezra, who began to build up the traditions and regulations of the rabbis so as to build a fence around the Law of God with the express purpose of preventing the people from disobeying God's law so that there would not be a another expulsion from the Land. Please notice very carefully in the following statement the emphasis that rabbis place upon the Oral Law and its purpose. In these first two quotations Goldberg states the order of the revelation of God from a rabbinic perspective to Israel with the purpose of gaining merit before God:

> As regards the oral Torah, the Holy One revealed himself on Sinai to give the Torah to Israel, He delivered it to Moses in order, Scripture, Mishnah, Talmud,

---

[1825] It is strongly recommended to obtain material to learn about "The Emergent Church" and "The Emerging Church" that Gary Gilley speaks and writes about. His ministry is called "Think on These Things Ministries" and his website is *www.tottministries.org*.

and Haggadah. But there has already been an answer to the giving of the oral law on Mt. Sinai. The Midrash goes on to say why two Toroth were given. God gave Israel the written Torah in which were 613 commandments in order to fill them with precepts whereby they could earn merit. He gave Israel the oral Torah to set Israel apart (Numbers Rabba 14:10).[1826]

The study of Torah is emphasized always to gain merit, to control the evil impulse, and to earn eternal life. But then again, Torah includes all of tradition as well as the Scriptures; Torah sees tradition above the Scriptures.[1827]

As Goldberg points, out the word "torah" is a very elastic term. It can mean one teaching point and can go far beyond the five books of Moses to encompass all rabbinic literature. The Oral Torah is to gain merit before God and that is works based salvation. But then again Rabbinic Judaism is completely built on a works system. In Rabbinic Judaism by the use of repentance, prayer and good works you can acquire atonement for your sins, which is not a biblical teaching. Rabbinic Judaism fails to understand that salvation is not based on works, but by faith in the LORD God. The Jewish person was to demonstrate his faith by being obedient to the Written Law of God. The "righteous" works of a Jewish person does not give them salvation. Rather the *Tanakh* teaches salvation by faith in the LORD God of Israel who then gives them eternal life. Goldberg continues as he expresses that Rabbinic Judaism gave interpretations of the Written Law and then gave those interpretations (oral law) scriptural status as a living faith. But this new "faith" kept the Jewish people from seeing *Yeshua* as the Messiah of Israel in fulfillment of the prophets:

> Thus, this was the inception and development of mainstream Judaism. It was mainly an interpretation of the meaning of the Mosaic Law and its application in the daily life of the Jew. Interpretations and re-interpretations made the Talmud a deviation from the Old Testament. It is recognized that much of it is good and the producer of the steadfastness and moral dignity of the Jewish person. But at the same time it must be recognized that the build-up of this thought eventually countered the claims of Jesus of Nazareth. The greatest Prophet Israel ever had was born under the Law, was reared under the Law, and lived under the Law. The written Law was sacred to him, even to the jot and tittle. His whole ministry was an effort to turn Judaism of his day, with all of its halakoth and haggadoth, back to the written Torah. He wanted to impress upon the people of his day that real spirit of the Old Testament. In so doing, it would not have been difficult then to recognize in Jesus of Nazareth the Messiah of Israel. Those Jewish people of his day who did indeed go back to the very basis for the reason for their existence, the written Torah, found and recognized their

---

[1826] Goldberg, *The Deviation of Jewish Thought from an Old Testament Theology in the Intertestamental Period*, 75.

[1827] Goldberg, *The deviation of Jewish Thought from an Old Testament Theology in the Intertestamental Period*, 118.

redeemer and Saviour. They found and recognized what an oral Torah, that only represented at best the traditions and thoughts of men, had stifled and hid from the people of Israel. Thus, the deviation of Jewish thought in the mainstream Judaism from an Old Testament theology in the intertestamental period laid the ground work for the national rejection of the claims of Jesus of Nazareth.[1828]

Another author states that both laws were equal as sacred books to the Jewish people, the written as the foundation and the oral as a supplement to it, but also sacred as the following statement clearly shows:

> The whole revelation of God was not comprised in the sacred books. By the side of Scripture there had always gone an unwritten tradition, in part interpreting and applying the written Torah, in part supplementing it.[1829]

It is important to explain the Jewish concept of the written word of God and the Oral Law known primarily as the Talmud and Midrash writings today. Even though this is not directly related to the study of the plurality of God in the *Tanakh*, it has a great bearing on how rabbis interpret and study the *Tanakh*, which presents the basis for the rejection of the incarnation of God, coming as the promised Son of David to first provide salvation through His vicarious sacrifice on the Tree and then restore the kingdom and fulfill the Abrahamic Covenant at His second coming.

In several of Rambam's writings he teaches what appears to be a high view of Scripture as quoted by Rabbi Nosson Scherman:

> In several of his writings, Rambam sets forth at much greater length the unanimously held view that every letter and word of the Torah was given to Moses by God; that it has not been and cannot be changed; and that nothing was ever or can ever be added to it. Indeed, the Talmud states emphatically that if one questions the Divine origin of even a single letter or traditionally accepted interpretation of the Torah, it is tantamount to denial of the entire Torah (Sanhedrin 9a).

> Throughout history, Jews have maintained the absolute Integrity of their Torah scrolls, zealously avoiding any change, even of a letter that would not change the meaning of a word. They knew that their Torah was not merely a 'sacred book,' it was the word of God, and as such it had to remain unchanged.[1830]

So here Rabbi Scherman seems to relate a high view of Scripture; nothing can be added or taken away. When he uses "torah" he may be implying written and oral revelation.

[1828] Goldberg, *The Deviation of Jewish Thought from an Old Testament Theology in the Intertestamental Period*, 118-119.

[1829] George Foot Moore, *Judaism* (2 vol. Peabody: Hendrickson, 1997), 251.

[1830] Scherman, *The Chumash* (Brooklyn: Mesorah Publications, 2004), xix-xx.

However, in the following statements Rabbi Scherman contradicts the previous statement by lifting the Oral Law equal to or greater than the written word of God:

> The Talmud goes further. One who denies that the Rabbinic tradition, what is commonly called the Oral Torah, was given by God to Moses is castigated as someone who "despises the word of God" (Sanhedrin 99a), and Rambam labels such a person a heretic (Hilchos Teshuvah 3:8).[1831]

Here the rabbi lifts the Oral Torah to the status of equal and even greater than the Written Word and quotes Rambam as an authority that a person who does not lift up that Oral Torah is a heretic. Following are the words of Rambam, also known as Moses Maimonides:

> The Rambam, **Moses Maimonides, taught in his introduction to the Mishnah that the rabbinic traditions were to be followed even if they contradicted the plain, grammatical sense of the Torah and even if a prophet of God confirmed that the plain, grammatical sense of the Torah was correct** (using Deut 25:11-12 as his example). So, the written Word, confirmed by a prophet, has less authority than the rabbinic traditions! Add to this the Talmudic teaching in B. Bava Metzia 59b that states that even divine miracles and a voice from heaven cannot overrule the majority opinion of the rabbis, you realize just how extreme this position really is.[1832]

Observe even if the plain grammatical sense of the Torah is not sufficient, the Oral Law will override it. That is a recipe for biblical apostasy. David Klinghoffer states that "no idea is more strenuously emphasized than the binding nature of the commandment"[1833] and then quotes twice from Deuteronomy to prove his point. Yet conveniently they detour the clear statements of Moses to interact with the Oral Law, which is not just adding a "word" but many volumes of "words" to depreciate the Written Law and authenticate the teachings of Rabbinic Judaism by Oral Law:

> The covenant would stand unchanged in all its details: 'You shall not add to the word that I command you, nor shall you subtract from it' (Deut 4:2). 'You shall not add to it and you shall not subtract from it' (Deut 13:1) [12:32].

Isn't it deceptive to say that nothing is to be added or subtracted from the Written Law and then hold up the volumes of Oral Law as greater than the Written?

Next Rabbi Scherman makes an unbiblical assumption concerning the Oral Torah. He will insist from Deuteronomy 4:2 and 13:1 [12:32] that nothing is to be added or subtracted from the Law, but Klinghoffer (and Judaism) then violate it when he states:

[1831] Scherman, *The Chumash* (Brooklyn: Mesorah Publications, 2004), xix-xx.

[1832] Michael L. Brown, "Rabbinic Objections" *The Chosen People* (vol. XII, issue 9, special edition), 7. Chosen People Ministries, NY.

[1833] Klinghoffer, *Why the Jews Rejected Jesus*, 29.

Even a cursory reading of the Torah proves that such a tradition had to exist, that there is much more to the Torah than its written text. The implication ... **is clear beyond a doubt**: there is a companion to the Written Torah, and Oral Law פֶּה תּוֹרָה שֶׁבְּעַלְפֶּה without which the Written Torah can be twisted and misinterpreted beyond recognition, as indeed it has been by the ignorant down through the centuries.[1834] (Emphasis mine)

The question has to be asked, "Where, Rabbi Scherman, is it stated 'clearly beyond a doubt' that the Oral Torah was given to Moses as an oral companion equal to the Written Law?" Rabbi Scherman has just jumped off a cliff without a parachute, so to speak! First even in a cursory reading of the Torah, there is nothing to substantiate the existence of an Oral Torah. Second, as far as twisting the Written Torah, yes, people have been unfaithful to the Written Word. However, the rabbis equally have twisted the Written Torah or the Written Word by attaching an unbiblical Oral Torah to the Scriptures and placing equal or greater importance to the Oral Torah. Some rabbis go as far as to say that what truly makes Judaism unique is the Oral Torah, for the Hebrew Scriptures are shared with Roman Catholicism and the Protestant faith as is related by Dr. Immanuel Jakobovitz, former Chief Rabbi of the United Kingdom in the following statement:

> When our Sages asserted that "the Holy One, blessed be He, did not make His covenant with Israel except by virtue of the Oral Law" (Gittin 60b), they not only propounded a cardinal Jewish belief, they also expressed a truth as evident today as it was in Talmudic times. The true character of Judaism cannot be appreciated except by an intimate acquaintance with the Oral Law. The Written Law, that is, the five books of Moses, and even the rest of the Hebrew Bible, we share with other faiths. What makes us and our faith distinct and unique is the oral tradition as the authentic key to an understanding of the written text we call the Torah.[1835]

In the *Tanakh* it was not Oral Torah that made Israel unique or distinct. Their uniqueness was the fact that they worshipped the one and only God, the Creator of the Universe, and obeyed all the 613 Laws of Moses. With this testimony and God's abundant blessing upon them they were to interact with the pagan nations around them to draw them to the God of Israel. But they have replaced God's uniqueness with manmade uniqueness, which God never authorized.

There is no question that this is a very difficult concept for rabbis to handle for they have been taught it in their yeshivas and seminaries for centuries. Not only did the *Sopherim*, the generation of scribes after Ezra the scribe, start all this, but Rabbi ben Zakkai took that foundation when he went to Yavne (near to Joppa) in 70 CE to retool

---

[1834] Scherman, *The Chumash* (Brooklyn: Mesorah Publications, 2004), xxiii.
[1835] Immanuel Jakobovitz, *The Oral Law: A Study of the Rabbinic Contribution to Torah She-be-al-Peh* (2nd , rev. ed.; New York: Feldheim, 1996), Foreword.

Judaism to survive without a temple and sacrificial system. That should have raised flags to begin with. If Judaism needed to be retooled to survive without a temple and sacrificial system, hasn't Judaism missed something when *Yahweh* divinely judged Judea and Jerusalem in 70 CE and as both *Yeshua* (Luke 21:6, 20-21) and Daniel (9:26) said? If only they would study the Written Word, they would find that there is absolutely no justification for an Oral Torah. Next the rabbi ties the two laws (Written and Oral Torah's) together as being "indivisible part of a sacred whole" in this statement:

> In more recent times, when blasphemers raised their heads against the sanctity of the Oral Torah, such commentaries as Malbim, R' Samson Raphael Hirsch, Haamek Davar, and Ha'Ksav V'haKabbalah demonstrated how the Written and the Oral Torah are indivisible part of a sacred whole.[1836]

To the rabbis who control the minds of the Jewish people, the Oral Torah is sacred and so in the yeshiva schools young men are taught Oral Law because that is where their authority lies. Just look at the emphasis that rabbis place on the Oral Law:

> R. Yochanan said: The greater part of the Torah is oral tradition; the lesser, written, as it says "It is through [literally, 'by the mouth of'] these words that I have made a covenant with you" (Gittin 60a).[1837]

There is no question as to where the authority lies; the rabbis have supplanted the Written Law of God, which they had committed themselves to obey (Exodus 24:3-8) with another law, the Oral Law, and to that they submit themselves.

> The Torah – the written part as mediated by the oral …. God's means for man's regeneration is set forth in the Torah of Sinai, in oral and written traditions.[1838]

Nowhere in the Written Torah or even the entire *Tanakh* does God say that regeneration comes from obedience to the Law. Regeneration comes by faith; how that faith was lived out was by obedience to the Written Law, the law of Moses. That kind of statement makes fertile ground for the teaching of Dual Covenant theology which is held by Judaism and liberal apostate Christianity (see Appendix 5). Two more quotes that follow continue to demonstrate the superior position that rabbis place on the Oral Torah:

> When we turn to the Talmud of the land of Israel, we find an explicit claim that not just episodic rules or sayings but something constitutive of the Torah, namely, the Oral Torah, possessed by the sages and transmitted in the master-disciple-relationship, takes priority over the Written Torah.

[1836] Scherman, *The Chumash*, xxv.

[1837] Finkel, *The Torah Revealed*, 142.

[1838] Bruce D. Chilton and Jacob Neusner, *Classical Christianity and Rabbinic Judaism* (Grand Rapids: Baker, 2004), 42-43.

The Rabbinic sages took the position that the Oral Torah not only was authentic, revealed Torah of Sinai, but indeed superior in value to the written part of the Torah that Christians possessed along with Israel.[1839]

As regards to the oral Torah, the Holy One revealed himself on Sinai to give the Torah to Israel, He delivered it to Moses in order, Scripture, Mishnah, Talmud, and Haggadah. But there has already been an answer to the giving of the oral law on Mt. Sinai. The Midrash goes on to say why two Torahs were given. God gave Israel the written Torah in which were 613 commandments in order to fill them with precepts whereby they could earn merit. He gave Israel the oral Torah to set Israel apart (Numbers Rabba 14:10).[1840]

Here is a blatant statement that the Oral Torah takes priority and superiority over the Written Law of God, and that is heresy! Unbiblical Rabbinic Judaism today has the spiritual destiny of Jewish souls wrapped up in a myth that has negative eternal consequences. Israel is a unique nation, not because of the Oral Torah, but because of the Abrahamic Covenant and because they were called of God to be a *"kingdom of priests"* to the Gentile nations that surrounded them. They were to live out the Written Law by faith in the living God before the nations and with God's abundant blessing (Deuteronomy 28) they would draw the Gentiles to the God of Israel as is illustrated by the testimony of Rahab the Canaanite (Joshua 2:9-11) and Naaman the Syrian (2 Kings 5:15). It was not the Oral Torah (Law) that made Israel unique, but the Written Law given to them by God through Moses on Mt. Sinai. Yet rabbis will continue to propagate heresy against *Yahweh* as is seen next:

What makes Israel unique is its possession of the oral part of Torah…. The very conception of an oral tradition in addition to Scripture now is broadened. Revelation itself is not limited to the exact words of the Written Torah, augmented by formulas considered to this point.[1841]

Not providing for the oral Torah is a mark of heresy Qiddushin 3:10-11.III. 13/66a-b).[1842]

Oral Torah is supreme over the Written Torah, and yet one author states that they do not have some of the Oral Torah because it was lost in the first generation after Moses and it was never reclaimed:

Many which were delivered by Moses to his contemporaries were forgotten even in the first generation…. Joshua himself forgot three hundred as a punishment for his self-sufficiency, and neither was he nor were the priests and

---

[1839] Jacob Neusner, *Judaism When Christianity Began* (Louisville, KY: Westminster John Know Press, 2002), 107.

[1840] Goldberg, *The Deviation of Jewish Thought from an Old Testament Theology in the Intertestamental Period*, 75.

[1841] Neusner, *Judaism When Christianity Began*, 112.

[1842] Neusner, *Judaism When Christianity Began*, 115.

prophets who came after him able to restore them. Many hundreds of exegetical proofs were also forgotten, ...[1843]

Here, from the Rabbinic Judaism perspective, some valuable teaching and exegetical proofs were lost forever. Here again is Rabbinic Judaism at its creative, imaginative "best." For what sin was Joshua punished that he forgot three hundred teaching points from Oral Torah, and how do they know that it was three hundred? This quote is puzzling for if they were lost and yet later rabbis write in the Talmud words considered to be revelation from God to Moses at Sinai, how were they lost? If they were valuable, why did not God reveal the lost commands to them as He revealed other things to the prophets? The next quotation makes a pointed statement that the Oral Torah is supreme to the written word of God:

> Hence the Written Torah does not stand in judgment of the Oral Torah; what governs is **the sages; own reason** (Menahot 3:7.II.5/29b). While it is forbidden to write down what is meant to be handed on in memory, if it is necessary to do so in order to preserve the tradition, it is permitted to violate the law (Temurah 2:1.III.1/14a, b).[1844]

> It is not Scripture alone that God sets forth but truth that takes shape and reaches us in oral form, that is, Torah in the medium of memory.[1845]

The sages' own reason is better than the Written Torah, that is absolutely heresy! These references should give enough information to show that Rabbinic Judaism is not biblical, and is not the genuine spiritual heritage of the Jewish people. But a false system of worship, a "golden calf" religion (Exodus 32:1-6; 1 Kings 12:28-29) that has been raised up just as their forefathers had done. Goldberg's summary should be convicting to Jewish rabbis:

> ...but enough has been indicated to show how far men's traditions have drifted from God's revelation in spite of the protest that the oral law comes from the written Torah.[1846]

Yet rabbis lament that Jewish people do not attend synagogue, nor do most of them observe any law, written or oral. Mixed marriages, Jews marrying non-Jews, among secular Jews is at epidemic proportion with some reports stating 50%. Rabbinic Judaism has itself to blame, because of its focus on Oral Torah instead of the Written Torah as Kac maintains:

> ...if it be also true, as the 'Perplexed Rabbi' maintains, that at the basis of the present crisis of the Jewish religion lies the lack of faith on the part of both

---

[1843] Moore, *Judaism*, 256.

[1844] Neusner, *Judaism When Christianity Began*, 116.

[1845] Neusner, *Judaism When Christianity Began*, 17.

[1846] Goldberg, *The Deviation of Jewish Thought from an Old Testament Theology in the Intertestamental Period*, 119.

Jewish clergy and laity in the Divine origin of the Bible, it is the Talmud which, having relegated the Hebrew Bible to a relatively unimportant place in Jewish life, has contributed heavily to Jewish unbelief.[1847]

In a free and open society where anti-Semitism is not restricting the Jewish people, they have escaped their "ghettos" for the secular world. For them their faith has no appeal; they maintain their Jewishness, but have cast off their Jewish religion.

Neusner makes an interesting observation about Jesus and Moses, but his conclusion reflects the opposition of Rabbinic Judaism to the Messiahship of *Yeshua*:

> In making these statements, Jesus represents himself not as a sage in a chain of tradition but as an "I," that is, a unique figure, a new Moses, standing on the mount as Moses had stood on Sinai. That view sages never adopted of themselves or granted to anyone else.[1848]

Neusner is absolutely correct in this statement: *Yeshua* was another Moses; He was the "prophet" that Moses promised to the people in Deuteronomy 18:15-18 that would be "*like*" him. Jesus used the "I" because He was God, He was the author of the Written Law, He was the one who gave it to Moses as has been clearly pointed out in this book. Neusner states that the language of *Yeshua* was strikingly different from that of Moses: *Yeshua* spoke in His own name "*as one having authority*"; whereas, Moses spoke in God's name. In other words, to Neusner, *Yeshua* was speaking as God:

> On the mountain, Jesus use of language, "You have heard that it was said …but I say to you…" contrasts strikingly with Moses' language at Mount Sinai. Sages, we saw, say things in their own names but without claiming to improve on the Torah, to which they aspire to contribute. The prophet, Moses, speaks not in his own name but in God's name, saying what God has told him to say. Jesus speaks not as a sage nor as a prophet. Note, when Moses turns to the people at Mount Sinai, he merely cites what God has said then he always starts with these words:[1849]

Yeshua as God understood that the Oral Law (Mishnah) would be an ever widening spiritual wedge that would keep His people from embracing Him not only as the Messiah, the Son of David, but as the God of Israel.

But the sages were so concerned about *Yeshua* making Himself the authority, that in reality they collectively lifted their human wisdom above the wisdom of the Creator of the universe in instituting the Oral Law equal to and superior to the Written Law. They have become the "I" that stands against the Written Law, which has given no justification for an Oral Law as the following statement reflects:

[1847] Arthur Kac, *The Rebirth of the State of Israel* (London: Marshall, Morgan, and Scott, 1958), 133-134.

[1848] Neusner, *Judaism When Christianity Began*, 24-25.

[1849] Neusner, *Judaism When Christianity Began*, 24-25

Rabbinic Jews followed the teaching of their Pharisaic predecessors, who propounded the idea of Oral Torah as the primary framework for expanding the written words of Scripture. They considered their oral traditions to be part of the continuous revelation that God had given Moses at Sinai (M. Avot 1:1).[1850]

The Pharisees opposed Jesus for his rejection of the oral law.[1851]

What *Yeshua* was attempting to do was to remove the Oral Torah and at that point the Jewish people would have had a better opportunity to recognize Him as Messiah and the God of Israel as Goldberg states:

Yeshua's "whole ministry was an effort to turn the Judaism of his day, with all of its halakoth[1852] and haggadoth, back to the written Torah. He wanted to impress upon the people of his day the real spirit of the Old Testament. In so doing, it would not have been difficult then to recognize in Jesus of Nazareth the Messiah of Israel. These Jewish people of his day who did indeed go back to the very basis for the reason for their existence, the written Torah, found and recognized their Redeemer and Saviour. They found and recognized what an oral Torah, that only represented at best the traditions and thoughts of men, had stifled and hid from the people of Israel. Thus, the deviation of Jewish thought in the mainstream Judaism from an Old Testament theology in the intertestamental period laid the ground work for the national rejection of the claims of Jesus of Nazareth.[1853]

The actual formation of the Oral Torah was not at Mt. Sinai but after the time of Ezra in the school of the *Sopherim* as stated:

The groundwork for this literature was laid in the Intertestamental period. In fact, some Jewish conception posit (to assume or affirm the existence of) out that all tradition is based on an oral Law received simultaneously with the written revelation on Mt. Sinai by Moses; however, Strack points out that an oral Law from the pre-exile times is contradicted by quite certain conclusions of sound Pentateuchal criticism since nothing in the Old Testament points in that direction with compelling force. The cultural pattern and background that

---

[1850] Frymer-Kensky, Novak, Ochs, Sandmel, *Christianity in Jewish Terms*, 89.

[1851] Varner, *The Messiah: Revealed, Rejected, Received*, 124.

[1852] *Halachah*: The entire body of Jewish law is known as Halachah, and it is this law that guides observant Jews through life, indicating what should be done at any given time or in given situation as well as what should not be done and what is not acceptable. In other words, Halachah indicates patterns for behavior and for life in general. The root of the word Halachah means "to go" or "to walk," and Halachah can be thought of as a person's "path through life." Halachah, therefore, is a set of codes based on the Talmud that regulates family relationships, legal matter, education, diet, and personal and religious observances. Robert Schoen, *What I Wish My Christian Friends Knew about Judaism* (Chicago: Loyola Press, 2004), 36.

[1853] Louis Goldberg, *The Deviation of Jewish Thought from an Old Testament Theology in the Intertestamental Period*, 118-119.

forms the basis of an oral Law does not fit in with that of the pre-exile historical pattern of the Old Testament.[1854] (2) [Point 1 & 2 are by H. Strack, *Introduction to the Talmud and Midrash* (Philadelphia: Jewish Publication Society, 1945), 3-6].

When all is studied from a biblical groundwork, the Oral Torah is the vehicle used by the enemy of Israel to keep them from embracing the truth of the *Tanakh* and the New Covenant.

Next in several statements, mostly written by Jewish authors, is the human rationale that is used to give authority to the Oral Torah by the rabbis as they seek to give validity to the myth of an Oral Law that God gave to Moses at Mt. Sinai:

> In the scheme developed in Rabbinic Judaism there is a Written Torah, the Pentateuch, and an Oral Torah. The doctrine runs that Moses received at Sinai a detailed elaboration of the laws and doctrines contained in the Written Torah and this is the Oral Torah. But the term denotes much more than the original revelation. **All the later teachings of the sages and teachers of Israel are embraced by the Oral Torah, seen as a continuous process.** The Mishnah and the Talmud are thus the great depositories of the Oral Torah.[1855] (Emphasis mine)

The bold portion distinctly states that the teachings of the sages have been embraced as the continuation of the Law of God given to Moses as part of the full revelation of God. Below is a statement by Louis Jacobs that freely admits to the addition of laws:

> Religious laws introduced by the Talmudic Rabbis and other early sages in order to create, as it is put in Ethics of the Fathers, **a 'fence around the Torah', that is, to add restrictions, over and above those found in the Bible**, so as to keep people away from any risk of infringing biblical law. For instance, according to biblical law, it is forbidden to saw wood on the Sabbath but there is no prohibition against handling a saw or other such tools. This is forbidden by Rabbinic law on the principle that if one is not allowed even to handle tools on the Sabbath, there is less risk that the tools will be used.[1856]

David Klinghoffer makes an extremely direct statement that the Oral Torah was given in "every word" to Moses as it would eventually be written by the sages centuries later. Notice the direct attack on the Word of God by attempting to get around the precise statements of Scripture:

[1854] Louis Goldberg, *The Deviation of Jewish Thought from an Old Testament Theology in the Intertestamental Period*, 4.

[1855] Jacobs, *A Concise Companion to the Jewish Religion*, 172.

[1856] Jacobs, *A Concise Companion to the Jewish Religion*, 132.

The important *tannaitic* text called *Sifra, a Midrash* on the book of Leviticus, taught that **all the commandments were revealed from Sinai, in every detail, whether in written or oral form. Not only that, but God spoke to Moses every word that would be recorded in the ancient rabbinic sources, no matter in whose name any given teaching might be reported, no matter when it happened to be first written down.** Oral Torah was a special bond between God and the Jewish people, a secret link untrammeled by outsiders.[1857]

As will be pointed out in later paragraphs, God makes it very clear that the very words that He gave to Moses, which he repeated to Israel, were "all" the words and "all" the words were written down. It was on the basis of those very words that God gave Israel who agreed to obey and the covenant was made or ratified by blood in Exodus 24. It becomes very convenient for rabbis to read into the passage teachings and laws that simply did not exist in the days of Moses, Joshua, Samuel, David, Elijah, Isaiah, Jeremiah, Ezekiel, Daniel or even in the days of Ezra the scribe.

Samuel Levine refers to Deuteronomy 17:8-13 as the basis for the Oral Law.[1858] He attempts to say that if there is an issue that comes up that the Written Law does not deal with, it is to be taken to the Elders for a judgment. He (and Rabbinic Judaism) then leaps to the conclusion that all future generations are obligated to obey that decision. Other rabbis put together the Elders the Sanhedrin making the point that all of the Jewish people are obligated to obey the decisions of Sanhedrin. It is these decisions that Klinghoffer quotes from the *Sifre* which say that all of these teachings and laws were given to Moses by God in unwritten form. How convenient!

Louis Goldberg, a Jewish believer in *Yeshua*, states that the only law given to Moses was the very words that God gave to Moses and he is very precisely states that he wrote down all the words. Goldberg distinctly states that the Oral Torah came into existence after the Babylonian captivity:

> More plausible is the assertion that the Law found in the Torah or Moses was the only written Law which the Jews possessed after their return from the Babylonian exile but because of ever-changing conditions of life, new ordinances and laws were felt to be necessary by the religious leaders. This was spurred on first by the Sopherim, then Hasidim, and eventually the Pharisees.[1859] [comes from H. Graetz, History of the Jews, Vol. I & II (Philadelphia: Jewish Publication Society of American 1893.]

The teaching of the rabbis that the Oral Torah is God given is a myth, an assumption that is made without any biblical foundation.

[1857] Klinghoffer, *Why the Jews Rejected Jesus*, 25.

[1858] Levine, *You Take Jesus, I'll Take God: How to Refute Christian Missionaries*, 22.

[1859] Louis Goldberg, *The Deviation of Jewish Thought from an Old Testament Theology in the Intertestamental Period*, 29.

The Hebrew Scriptures lift up the Word of the LORD as being final to any opinion, theory or teaching of men. Nowhere in the Hebrew Scriptures did God even hint at another law, the Oral Law, running parallel to the Written Law. Judaism, before the time of the destruction of Jerusalem and the temple, has prefabricated the myth that *HaShem* gave two laws to Moses, the written and oral law. Nowhere in the writings of Moses or the prophets is there even a shred of evidence that *HaShem* did such a thing. The only possible reference to oral anything in the Hebrew Scriptures is when the written law was read orally as Ezra did to the people (Nehemiah 8:1-8).

This is a challenge to any Jewish rabbi or Jewish person to investigate for themselves the claims that *HaShem* makes concerning His own word. Your eternal destiny hinges on what *HaShem* said versus what the rabbis say that *HaShem* said. The two are different and even contradictory. Stop accepting the words of the rabbis blindly. You are the most intelligent, blessed people of the world, which is a byproduct of the Abrahamic Covenant. Investigate *HaShem*'s word for yourself with the minds that *HaShem* gave you and open your minds and hearts to what *HaShem* said in HIS Written Word.

Moses, the prophets and other unknown writers of the *Tanakh* used several words to express the concept of words and writing:

אֱמֶר	emer (50)	words[1860]
אִמְרָה	imra (36)	word, words, utterance[1861]
דָבַר	dabar – v (1140)	said, speak, spoken, spoke, speaking, tell[1862]
דָּבָר	dabar – nm (1455)	word, words[1863]
כָּתַב	katab – v (223)	written, write, wrote[1864]
מִכְתָּב	miktab – nm (9)	writing[1865]
פֶּה	peh – nm (498)	mouth[1866]

These Hebrew words which are generally translated as indicated in English word(s) refer to "words" that were spoken by *HaShem* directly or by *HaShem* through a human agent and "written down" by those human agents. These Hebrew words also refer to "words" spoken between mankind as well as directed from man to *HaShem*. "Writing" refers to several things: (1) "writing down" the very "words" that *HaShem* wanted in a book or scroll by the human agent, whether *HaShem* to man, man to man, or man to *HaShem*, (2) *HaShem* personally has used "writing" as He wrote down the Ten Commandments with His finger, and (3) the word "mouth" refers to the "words" that

---

[1860] Botterweck, Ringgren and Fabry, *Theological Dictionary of the Old Testament*, 1:343.

[1861] Harris, Archer, and Waltke, *Theological Wordbook of the Old Testament*, 1:55.

[1862] VanGemeren, *Dictionary of Old Testament Theology & Exegesis,* 1:912.

[1863] VanGemeren, *Dictionary of Old Testament Theology & Exegesis,* 1:913.

[1864] Botterweck, Ringgren and Fabry, *Theological Dictionary of the Old Testament,* 7:373.

[1865] Harris, Archer, and Waltke, *Theological Wordbook of the Old Testament*, 1:458.

[1866] Harris, Archer, and Waltke, *Theological Wordbook of the Old Testament*, 2:718.

come from the mouth, where they are formed and spoken. What is to be observed is that *HaShem* used "words" and directed Moses and the Prophets to "write down" the "words." *HaShem* did not give divine thoughts and leave it to the human agent to decide how to say or write His word. God the *Ruah HaKodesh* (Holy Spirit), so guided the authors of the "words" in such a way that *HaShem*'s "words" were spoken or "written down" without violating the personality and style of that particular human agent. If there is a conflict with some of the words that *HaShem* used, it is our lack of understanding, not *HaShem*'s inability to convey His word to us.

Next is a chart with references concerning the "word," "words" or all the words "written" by God or *HaShem*. In the first column is a scriptural reference and in the second column is an actual quote. This is not a complete list, but a sampling from the Hebrew Scriptures. The list is intended to demonstrate that words used of God or man mean just that, God used words to express Himself to His people. Words make up phrases and sentences to express what God wants the reader to understand. Words that *HaShem* used point out strongly that His words were *written down*. In fact, Moses is very clear that he wrote down "*all*" the words of *HaShem*. The Scriptures are the verbal plenary inspired word of God, and man should not be tampering with or altering His word, to suit their personal bias or to meet "Christian" marketing needs.

"The Word" Verbal Plenary Inspiration

Genesis

Gen 15:1	After these things the **word** of the LORD came unto Abram in a vision,	dabar		
Gen 15:4	And, behold, the **word** of the LORD came unto him, saying	dabar		

Exodus

Exod 17:14	And the LORD said unto Moses, **Write** this for a memorial in a book,		katab	
Exod 19:6	These are the **words** which thou shalt speak unto the children of	dabar		
Exod 19:7	and laid before their faces all these **words** which the LORD commanded him.	dabar		
Exod 19:8	All that the LORD hath spoken we will do. And Moses returned the **words** of the people	dabar		
Exod 20:1	And God spake all these **words**, saying	dabar		
Exod 24:3	And Moses came and told the people **all the words** of the LORD…and said **all the words** which the LORD hath said will we do.	dabar		
Exod 24:4	And Moses **wrote all the words** of the LORD		katab	
Exod 24:8	behold the blood of the covenant, which the LORD hath made with you concerning **all the words**	dabar		
Exod 31:18	two tables of testimony, tables of stone, **written** with the finger of God	katab	katab	
Exod 32:16	tables were the work of God, and the **writing** was the **writing** of God,			miktab
Exod 33:4	And when the people heard these evil **tidings-words,**	dabar		
Exod 34:1	Hew thee two tables of stone like unto the first: and I will **write** upon these tables the **words** that were that were in the first tables	dabar	katab	
Exod 34:27	And the LORD said unto Moses, **Write** thou these words: for after the tenor of these words I have made a covenant with thee and with Israel	dabar	katab	
Exod 34:28	And he **wrote** upon the tables the **words** of the covenant, the ten commandments	dabar	katab	
Exod 35:1	These are the **words** which the LORD hath commanded,	dabar		
Exod 39:30	And they made the plate of the holy crown of pure gold, and **wrote** upon it a **writing,**		katab	miktab

Numbers

Num 3:16	And Moses numbered them according to the **word** of the Lord,			peh
Num 3:51	according to the **word** of the LORD, as the LORD commanded			peh
Num 5:23	And the priest shall **write** these curses in a book,		katab	

Num 12:6	Hear now my **words**: If there be a prophet among you, I the LORD	dabar			
Num 15:31	Because he hath despised the **word** of the LORD, and hath broken his commandments	dabar			
Num 24:4	He hath said, which heard the **words** of God,			emer	
Num 24:16	He hath said, which heard the **words** of God, and knew the knowledge of the most High,			emer	
Num 33:2	And Moses **wrote** their goings out according to their journeys				peh

Deuteronomy

Deut 1:1	These be the **words** which Moss spake unto all Israel on this side	dabar			
Deut 4:10	and I will make them hear my **words**, that they may learn to fear	dabar			
Deut 4:13	ten commandments and he **wrote** them upon two tables of stone		katab		
Deut 4:36	Out of heaven he made thee to hear his voice,…and thou heardest his **words** out of the midst of the fire	dabar			
Deut 5:5	I stood between the LORD and you at that time, to shew you the **word** of the LORD	dabar			
Deut 5:22	These **words** the LORD spake unto all the assembly in the mount out of the midst of the fire, of the cloud, and of the thick darkness, with a great voice and he added no more, and he **wrote** them in two tables of stone and delivered them unto me.	dabar	katab		
Deut 8:3	but by every **word** that preceedeth out of the **mouth** of the LORD doth man live.				peh
Deut 9:23	then ye rebelled against the **commandment** of the LORD your God				peh
Deut 10:4	And he **wrote** on the tables, according to the first **writing,** the ten commandments,		katab		miktab
Deut 11:18	Therefore shall ye lay up these my **words** in your heart and in your soul, and bind them for a sign upon your hand,	dabar			
Deut 11:20	And thou shalt **write** them upon the door posts of thine house,		katab		
Deut 17:18	And it shall be, when he sitteth upon the throne of his kingdom, that he shall **write** him a copy of this law in a book		katab		
Deut 17:19	that he may learn to fear the LORD his God, to keep all the **words** of this law and these statutes, to do them.	dabar			
Deut 18:18	and I will put my **words** in his **mouth** and he shall speak unto them	dabar			peh
Deut 18:19	And it shall come to pass, that whosoever will not hearken unto my **words** which he shall speak in my name, I will require it of him.	dabar			
Deut 24:1	then let him **write** her a bill of divorcement,		katab		

Deut 24:3	if the latter husband hate her, and **write** her a bill of divorcement,		katab	
Deut 27:3	And thou shalt **write** upon them all the **words** of this law,	dabar	katab	
Deut 27:8	shalt **write** upon the stones all the **words** of this law very plainly.	dabar	katab	
Deut 27:26	Cursed be he that confirmeth not all the **words** of this law	dabar		
Deut 28:58	If thou wilt not observe to do **all the words** of this law that are **written** in this book	dabar	katab	
Deut 28:61	Also every sickness, and every plague, which is not **written** in the book of this law,		katab	
Deut 29:20	and all the curses that are **written** in this book shall lie upon him,		katab	
Deut 29:21	curses of the covenant that are **written** in this book of the law		katab	
Deut 29:27	to bring upon it all the curses that are **written** in this book		katab	
Deut 29:29	that we may do **all the words** of this law.	dabar		
Deut 30:10	to keep his commandments and his statutes which are **written** in this book of the law and his statutes which are **written** in this book		katab	
Deut 31:1	And Moses went and spake these **words** unto all Israel	dabar		
Deut 31:9	And Moses **wrote** this law, and delivered it unto the priests		katab	
Deut 31:12	that they may hear, and that they may learn, and fear the LORD your God, and observe to do **all the words** of this law.	dabar		
Deut 31:19	Now therefore **write** ye this song for you and teach it		katab	
Deut 31:22	Moses therefore **wrote** this song the same day, and taught it the children of Israel.		katab	
Deut 31:24	when Moses had made an end of **writing** the **words** of this law in a book, until they were finished	dabar	katab	
Deut 31:30	And Moses spake in the ears of all the congregation of Israel the **words** of this song	dabar		
Deut 32:1	Give ear, O ye heavens, and I will **speak;** and hear, O earth, the **words** of my **mouth**	dabar	Emer	peh
Deut 32:46	And he said unto them, Set your hearts unto all the **words** which I testify among you this day, which ye shall command your children to observe to do, all the **words** of this law.	dabar		
Joshua				
Josh 1:8	This **book of the law** shall not depart out of thy **mouth,**...that thou mayest observe to do according to all that is **written** therein		katab	peh
Josh 1:13	Remember the **word** which Moses the servant of the LORD	dabar		

721

Josh 1:18	Whosoever he be that doth rebel against thy **commandment,** and will not hearken unto thy **words** in all that thou commandest him,	dabar			peh
Josh 3:9	And Joshua said unto the children of Israel, Come hither, and hear the **words** of the LORD your God.	dabar			
Josh 6:10	Ye shall not shout, nor make any noise with your voice, neither shall any **word** proceed	dabar			
Josh 8:31	As Moses the servant of the LORD commanded the children of Israel, as it is **written** in **the book of the law** of Moses,		katab		
Josh 8:32	And he **wrote** there upon the stone a copy of the law of Moses, which he **wrote** in the presence of the children of Israel.		katab		
Josh 8:34	And afterward he read all the **words** of the law, the blessings and cursings, according to all that is **written in the book of the law**	dabar	katab		
Josh 8:35	There was not a **word** of all that Moses commanded, which Joshua read not before all the congregation of Israel,	dabar			
Josh 10:13	Is not this **written** in the book of Jasher		katab		
Josh 18:6	Ye shall therefore **describe-written** the land into seven parts saying go and walk through the land, and **describe-write** it and come again		katab		
Josh 18:9	And the men went and passed through the land, and **described-wrote** it by cities into seven parts in a book		katab		
Josh 23:6	Be ye therefore very courageous to keep and to do all that is **written in the book of the law** of Moses		katab		
Josh 24:26	And Joshua **wrote** these **words** i**n the book of the law** of God,	dabar	katab		
Josh 24:27	for it hath heard all the **words** of the LORD which he spake unto us:				emer
Judges					
Judg 11:11	and Jephthah uttered all his **words** before the LORD in Mizpeh	dabar			
1 Samuel					
1 Sam 3:1	And the **word** of the LORD was precious in those days;	dabar			
1 Sam 3:7	neither was the **word** of the LORD yet revealed unto him.	dabar			
1 Sam 10:25	Then Samuel told the people the manner of the kingdom, and **wrote** it in a book,		katab		
1 Sam 15:10	Then came the **word** of the LORD unto Samuel, saying	dabar			
1 Sam 15:23	Because thou hast rejected the **word** of the LORD, he hath also rejected thee	dabar			
2 Samuel					
2 Sam 1:18	behold, it is **written** in the book of Jasher		katab		

722

2 Sam 7:4	that the **word** of the LORD came unto Nathan,	dabar		
2 Sam 7:17	According to all these **words,** and according to all this vision,	dabar		
2 Sam 11:14	And it came to pass in the morning that David **wrote** a letter to Joab,		katab	
2 Sam 11:15	And he **wrote** in the letter, saying, Set ye Uriah in the forefront of the hottest battle,		katab	
2 Sam 12:9	Wherefore hast thou despised the **commandment-word** of the LORD	dabar		
2 Sam 22:31	As for God, his way is perfect; the **word** of the LORD is tried: he is a buckler to all them			imra
2 Sam 24:11	when David was up in the morning, the **word** of the LORD came unto the prophet Gad	dabar		

1 Kings

1 Kgs 2:3	And keep the charge of the LORD thy God…as it is **written** in the law of Moses,		katab	
1 Kgs 6:11	And the **word** of the LORD came to Solomon, saying	dabar		
1 Kgs 11:41	his wisdom, are they not **written** in the book of the acts of Solomon.		katab	
1 Kgs 12:22	But the **word** of God came unto Shemaiah the man of God, saying,	dabar		
1 Kgs 13:1	there came a man of God out of Judah by the **word** of the LORD	dabar		
1 Kgs 13:2	And he cried against the altar in the **word** of the LORD	dabar		
1 Kgs 13:5	the sign which the man of God had given by the **word** of the LORD	dabar		
1 Kgs 13:9	For so was it charged me by the **word** of the LORD, saying	dabar		
1 Kgs 13:17	For it was said to me by the **word** of the LORD	dabar		
1 Kgs 13:20	as they sat at the table, that the **word** of the LORD came unto	dabar		
1 Kgs 13:26	the man of God, who was disobedient unto the **word** of the LORD:			peh
1 Kgs 13:32	For the saying which he cried by the **word** of the LORD against the altar in Beth-el	dabar		
1 Kgs 14:19	behold, they are **written** in the book of the chronicles of the kings		katab	
1 Kgs 14:29	are they not **written** in the book of the chronicles of the kings of		katab	
1 Kgs 15:29	according unto the **saying-word** of the LORD	dabar		
1 Kgs 16:1	Then the **word** of the LORD came to Jehu the son of Hanani	dabar		
1 Kgs 16:34	according to the **word** of the LORD, which he spake by Joshua	dabar		
1 Kgs 17:2	And the **word** of the LORD came unto him (Elijah), saying	dabar		

1 Kgs 18:1	that the *word* of the LORD came to Elijah	dabar		
1 Kgs 22:19	and he said (Micaiah), Hear thou therefore the *word* of the LORD	dabar		

2 Kings

2 Kgs 15:12	This was the *word* of the LORD which he spake unto Jehu	dabar		
2 Kgs 22:11	when the king had heard the *words* of the book of the law,	dabar		
2 Kgs 22:13	concerning the *words* of this book that is found:…because our fathers have not hearkened unto the *words* of this book to do according unto all that which is *written* concerning us.	dabar	katab	
2 Kgs 22:16	even all the *words* of the book which the king of Judah hath read:	dabar		
2 Kgs 22:18	As touching the *words* which thou hast heard:	dabar		
2 Kgs 23:2	and he read in their ears all the *words* of the book of the covenant which was found in the house of the LORD	dabar		
2 Kgs 23:16	and polluted it, according to the *word* of the LORD which the man of God proclaimed, who proclaimed these *words*.	dabar		
2 Kgs 24:2	according to the *word* of the LORD, which he spake by his servant the prophets	dabar		

1 Chronicles

1 Chr 10:13	even against the *word* of the LORD, which he kept not,	dabar		
1 Chr 15:15	as Moses commanded according to the *word* of the LORD.	dabar		
1 Chr 16:15	Be ye mindful always of his covenant; the *word* which he commanded to a	dabar		
1 Chr 16:40	and to do according to all that is *written* in the law of the LORD, which he commanded		katab	
1 Chr 17:3	that the *word* of God came to Nathan, saying	dabar		

2 Chronicles

2 Chr 6:17	Now then, O LORD God of Israel, let thy *word* be verified, which thou hast spoken	dabar		
2 Chr 10:15	for the cause was of God, that the LORD might perform his *word*, which he spake by the hand of Ahigah	dabar		
2 Chr 11:2	But the *word* of the LORD came to Shemaiah the man of God,	dabar		
2 Chr 11:4	And they obeyed the *words* of the LORD, and returned from going	dabar		
2 Chr 12:7	And when the LORD saw that they humbled themselves, the *word* of the Lord	dabar		
2 Chr 21:12	And there came a *writing* to him from Elijah the prophet,			miktab

2 Chr 23:18	as it is **written** in the law of Moses, with rejoicing and with singing,		katab	
2 Chr 25:4	But he slew not their children, but did as it is **written** in the law in the book of Moses		katab	
2 Chr 29:15	according to the commandment of the king, by the **words** of the LORD, to cleanse	dabar		
2 Chr 30:12	one heart to do the commandment of the king…the princes by the **word** of the LORD	dabar		
2 Chr 31:3	as it is **written** in the law of the LORD		katab	
2 Chr 33:18	and the **words** of the seers that spake to him in the name of the LORD God of Israel behold, they are **written** in the book of the kings	dabar	katab	
2 Chr 34:19	when the king had heard the **words** of the law, that he rent his	dabar		
2 Chr 34:21	concerning the **words** of the book that is found…Because our fathers have not kept the **word** of the LORD, to do after all that is **written** in this book.	dabar	katab	
2 Chr 34:26	Thus saith the LORD God of Israel concerning the **words** which thou hast heard	dabar		
2 Chr 34:30	and he read in the ears all the **words** of the book of the covenant that was found in the	dabar		
2 Chr 34:31	to perform the **words** of the covenant which are **written** in this book.	dabar	katab	
2 Chr 35:4	according to the **writing** of David king of Israel, and according to the **writing** of Solomon		katab	miktab
2 Chr 35:12	to offer unto the LORD, as it is **written** in the book of Moses.		katab	
2 Chr 35:26	according to that which was **written** in the law of the LORD		katab	
2 Chr 36:16	But they mocked the messengers of God, and despised his **words,**	dabar		
2 Chr 36:21	To fulfill the **word** of the LORD by the **mouth** of Jeremiah,	dabar		peh
2 Chr 36:22	that the **word** of the LORD spoken by the **mouth** of Jeremiah might be accomplished,…the spirit of Cyrus king of Persia, that he made a proclamation throughout all his kingdom, and put it also in **writing**,	dabar	Peh	miktab

Ezra				
Ezra 1:1	the first year of Cyrus king of Persia, that the **word** of the LORD by the **mouth** of Jeremiah might be fulfilled, and put it also in **writing**,	dabar	peh	miktab
Ezra 3:2	as it is **written** in the law of Moses the man of God		katab	
Ezra 3:4	They kept also the Feast of Tabernacles, as it is **written,**		katab	
Ezra 9:4	Then were assembled unto me every one that trembled at the **words** of the God of Israel	dabar		

Nehemiah

Neh 8:9	For all the people wept, when they heard the **words** of the law.	dabar			
Neh 8:12	because they had understood the **words** that were declared unto	dabar			
Neh 8:13	unto Ezra the scribe, even to understand the **words** of the law.	dabar			
Neh 8:14	And they found **written** in the law which the LORD had commanded		katab		
Neh 10:34	to burn the altar of the LORD our God, as it is **written** in the law		katab		
Neh 10:36	the firstborn of our sons, and of our cattle, as it is **written** in the law,		katab		

Psalms

Psa 12:6	The **words** of the LORD are pure **words:** as silver tried in a furnace				imra
Psa 19:14	Let the **words** of my **mouth,** and the meditation of my heart,			emer	peh
Psa 33:4	For the **word** of the LORD is right and all his works are done in truth.	dabar			
Psa 33:6	By the **word** of the LORD were the heavens made;	dabar			
Psa 107:11	Because they rebelled against the **words** of God,				emer
Psa 119:9	by taking heed thereto according to thy **word.**	dabar			
Psa 119:13	With my lips have I declared all the judgments of thy **mouth.**				peh

Isaiah

Isa 1:1	Hear the **word** of the LORD, ye rulers of Sodom;	dabar			
Isa 1:20	devoured with the sword: for the **mouth** of the LORD hath spoken it.				peh
Isa 2:3	and the **word** of the LORD from Jerusalem.	dabar			
Isa 5:24	and despised the **word** of the Holy One of Israel.				imra
Isa 8:1	Take thee a great scroll, and **write** in it with a man's pen		katab		
Isa 30:8	Now go, **write** it before them in a table, and note it in a book,		katab		
Isa 38:4	Then the **word** of the LORD came to Isaiah:	dabar			
Isa 38:9	The **writing** of Hezekiah king of Judah, when he had been sick,				miktab
Isa 41:26	there is none that declareth,...that heareth your **words.**				emer
Isa 58:14	for the **mouth** of the LORD hath spoken it.				peh
Isa 66:5	Hear the **word** of the LORD, ye that tremble at his **word;**	dabar			

Jeremiah

Jer 1:2	To whom the **word** of the LORD came in the days of Josiah	dabar			

Jer 1:9	the LORD said unto me, Behold, I have put my **words** in thy **mouth.**	dabar		peh
Jer 2:1	Moreover the **word** of the LORD came to me, saying,	dabar		
Jer 6:10	behold, the **word** of the LORD is unto them a reproach;	dabar		
Jer 21:1	The **word** which came unto Jeremiah from the LORD,	dabar		
Jer 30:2	Thus speaketh the LORD God of Israel saying, **Write** thee all the **words** that I have spoken unto thee in a book	dabar	katab	
Jer 31:33	I will put my law in their inward parts, and **write** it in their hearts,		katab	
Jer 36:2	Take thee a scroll of a book, and **write** therein all the **words** that I	dabar	katab	
Jer 36:4	Baruch **wrote** from the mouth of Jeremiah all the **words** of the LORD	dabar	katab	
Jer 36:6	Therefore go thou, and read in the roll, which thou hast **written** from my mouth, the **words** of the LORD in the ears of the people	dabar	Katab	
Jer 36:16	when they had heard all the **words,** they were afraid both one and other, and said…, We will surely tell the king of all these **words**.	dabar		
Jer 36:17	Tell us now, How didst thou **write** all these **words** at his mouth?	dabar	katab	
Jer 36:18	He pronounced all these **words** unto me with his mouth and I **wrote** them with ink	dabar	katab	
Jer 36:27	and the **words** which Baruch **wrote** at the mouth of Jeremiah,	dabar	katab	
Jer 45:1	The **word** that Jeremiah the prophet spake unto Baruch the son of Neriah, when he had **written** these **words** in a book	dabar	katab	

Lamentations

Lam 2:17	he hath fulfilled his **word** that he had commanded in the days of old:			imra
Lam 3:38	Out of the **mouth** of the most High proceedeth not evil and good?			peh

Ezekiel

Ezek 1:3	The **word** of the LORD came expressly unto Ezekiel the priest,	dabar		
Ezek 2:10	And he spread it before me; and it was **written** within and without; all my wo**rds** that I shall speak unto thee receive in thine heart,	dabar	katab	
Ezek 6:1	And the **word** of the LORD came unto me, saying	dabar		
Ezek 7:1	Moreover the **word** of the LORD came unto me, saying,	dabar		
Ezek 12:1	The **word** of the LORD also came unto me, saying	dabar		
Ezek 37:4	and say unto them, O ye dry bones, hear the **word** of the LORD	dabar		

Ezek 38:1	And the **word** of the LORD came unto me, saying,	dabar			

Daniel

Dan 9:2	whereof the **word** of the LORD came to Jeremiah the prophet,	dabar			
Dan 9:11	and the oath that is **written** in the law of Moses the servant of God		katab		
Dan 9:13	As it is **written** in the law of Moses,		katab		

Hosea

Hos 1:1	The **word** of the LORD that came unto Hosea, the son of Beeri,	dabar			
Hos 6:5	I have slain them by the **words** of my **mouth:**			emer	peh

Joel

Joel 1:1	The **word** of the LORD that came to Joel the son of Pethuel.	dabar			

Amos

Amos 3:1	Hear this **word** that the LORD hath spoken against you, O Children of	dabar			

Jonah

Jonah 1:1	Now the **word** of the LORD came unto Jonah the son of Amittai,	dabar			

Micah

Micah 1:1	The **word** of the LORD that came to Micah the Morasthite	dabar			
Micah 4:4	for the mouth of the LORD of hosts hath **spoken** it.				peh

Zephaniah

Zeph 1:1	The **word** of the LORD which came unto Zephaniah the son	dabar			

Haggai

Hag 1:1	came the **word** of the LORD by Haggai the prophet unto	dabar			

Zechariah

Zech 1:1	second year of Darius, came the **word** of the LORD unto Zechariah,	dabar			
Zech 8:18	And the **word** of the LORD of hosts came unto me, saying	dabar			
Zech 12:1	The burden of the **word** of the LORD for Israel, saith the LORD,	dabar			

Malachi

Mal 1:1	The burden of the **word** of the LORD to Israel by Malachi	dabar			

Appendix 4
The Servant of the LORD

Below are some passages of Scripture from two different versions. Yet they both say the same thing. The Jewish Tanakh is clear that the Servant of the LORD will suffer and die for the transgressions of His people. Once again check the pronouns; there is no possible way that this passage could be referring to the nation of Israel.

Isaiah 52:13 - 53:12

Jewish Tanakh

(13) Indeed, My servant shall prosper, Be exalted and raised to great heights. (14) Just as the many were appalled at him, so marred was his appearance, unlike that of man, His form, beyond human semblance, (15) Just so he shall startle many nations. Kings shall be silenced because of him, for they shall see what has not been told them, shall behold what they never have heard.

(1) Who can believe what we have heard? Upon whom has the arm of the LORD been revealed? (2) For he has grown, by His favor, like a tree crown, like a tree trunk out of arid ground. He had no form or beauty, that we should look at him: No charm, that we should find him pleasing. (3) He was despised, shunned by men, A man of suffering, familiar with disease. As one who hid his face from us, he was despised, we held him of no account. (4) Yet it was our sickness that he was bearing, Our suffering that he endured. We accounted him plagued, smitten and afflicted by God; (5) But he was wounded because of our sins, crushed because of our iniquities. He bore the chastisement that made us whole, and by his bruises we were healed. (6) We all went astray like sheep, each going his own way; and the LORD visited upon him the guilt of all of us.

(7) He was maltreated, yet he was submissive, he did not open his mouth; Like a sheep being led to slaughter, like a ewe, dumb before those who shear her, he did not open his mouth. (8) By oppressive judgment he was taken away, who could describe his abode? For he was cut off from the land of the living through the sin of my people, who deserved the punishment. (9) And his grave was set among the wicked, and with the rich, in his death, though he had done no injustice and had spoken no falsehood. (10) But the LORD chose to crush him by disease, that if he made himself an offering for guilt, he might see offspring and have long life, and that through him the LORD's purpose might prosper. (11) Out of his anguish he shall see it; he shall enjoy it to the full through his devotion. "My righteous servant makes the many righteous, it is their punishment that he bears; (12) Assuredly, I will give him the many as his portion, he shall receive the multitude as his spoil. For he exposed himself to death and was numbered among the sinners, whereas he bore the guilt of the many and made intercession for sinners.

Isaiah 52:13 – 53:12

King James Version

(13) Behold, my servant shall deal prudently, he shall be exalted and extolled, and be very high. (14) As many were astonished at thee; his visage was so marred more than any man, and his form more than the sons of men: (15) So shall he sprinkle many nations; the kings shall shut their mouths at him: for that which had not been told them shall they see; and that which they had not heard shall they consider.

(1) Who hath believed our report? And to whom is the arm of the LORD revealed? (2) For he shall grow up before him as a tender plant, and as a root out of a dry ground: he hath no form nor comeliness; and when we shall see him, *there* is no beauty that we should desire him. (3) He is despised and rejected of men; a man of sorrows, and acquainted with grief: and we hid as it were *our* faces from him; he was despised, and we esteemed him not. (4) Surely he hath borne our griefs and carried our sorrows: yet we did esteem him stricken, smitten of G-d and afflicted. (5) But he *was* wounded for our transgressions, *he was* bruised for our iniquities: the chastisement of our peace *was* upon him: and with his stripes we are healed. (6) All we like sheep have gone astray; we have turned every one to his own way; and the LORD hath laid on him the iniquity of us all.

(7) He was oppressed, and he was afflicted, yet he opened not his mouth: he is brought as a lamb to the slaughter, and as a sheep before her shearers is dumb, so he openeth not his mouth. (8) He was taken from prison and from judgment: and who shall declare his generation? For he was cut off out of the land of the living: for the transgression of my people was he stricken. (9) And he made his grave with the wicked, and with the rich in his death; because he had done no violence, neither *was any* deceit in his mouth. (10) Yet it pleased the LORD to bruise him; he hath put *him* to grief: when thou shalt make his soul an offering for sin, he shall see *his* seed, he shall prolong his days, and the pleasure of the LORD shall prosper in his hand. (11) He shall see of the travail of his soul, *and* shall be satisfied: by his knowledge shall my righteous servant justify many; for he shall bear their iniquities. (12) Therefore will I divide him *a portion* with the great, and he shall divide the spoil with the strong; because he hath poured out his soul unto death: and he was numbered with the transgressors; and he bare the sin of many, and made intercession for the transgressors.

Appendix 5
Dual Covenant Theology: Inclusivism

This has become the "new" heresy of the late 20th and the beginning of this new century. Inclusivism in relation to Soteriology (salvation) says that as long as a person lives and believes in faith to the light that he has received, he will go to heaven, whether he is Jewish, Moslem, Hindu, Mormon or Roman Catholic. But that is totally contrary to the *Tanakh* and the New Covenant (Testament). To be blunt, if a person does not come God's way, he just will not make it to heaven (Isaiah 43:10-11; John 14:6; Acts 4:12).

Look briefly at the beginning of what is called Inclusivism. Because Christendom has taken an earlier Jewish teaching of Dual Covenant Theology, and simply has expanded it to include any religious person from any religion on the earth, who can then be saved without ever seeing or hearing about the way of salvation God provided in *Yeshua*. The earlier teaching of Dual Covenant was espoused by Franz Rosenzweig in 1919 while he was serving in the German army during WWI.[1867] This theory basically stated that God made a covenant with Israel (Mosaic Law), and if they obey that covenant, they have eternal life through the law of Moses and do not need to accept *Yeshua* as the Jewish Messiah. Jewish people have their way of salvation through the Law and Christians have their way of salvation through Jesus. Goldberg summaries Rosenzweig's theory which after the Holocaust was endorsed by Jewish rabbis and Christian leaders alike:

> The Christian is different from the Jews. At a certain point in the life of every individual from the nations, when he comes to the miracle of rebirth, he or she "is made, not born." Every non-Jew who accepts Jesus becomes a Christian and is reborn. But God deals with a Jew differently. A Jew is a Jew because he is already a part of his people as soon as he is born. We can see therefore why Rosenzweig insists that a Jewish person never needs to become a Christian because he is already a part of the covenant people. The Jew is not the one who has the pagan background.[1868]

But those who endorse this teaching fail to take into account what God said about the whole issue. Consequently if a Jewish person attempts to gain salvation because he is a son of Abraham or because he keeps the law of Moses or rabbinic law he is just as lost as pagan Gentiles.

There are three basic views that attempt to broaden the narrow gate to salvation that *Yeshua* spoke of in Matthew 7:13-14. These views are: (1) Universalism which states that all men will be saved in the end, (2) Eschatological Evangelism states that all will

---

[1867] Louis Goldberg, *Are There Two Ways of Atonement?* (Baltimore: Lederer Publication, 1990), 5.

[1868] Goldberg, *Are There Two Ways of Atonement?* 9.

hear the gospel at or following death. Finally, (3) Inclusivism states that at least some will be saved by Messiah without knowing Him specifically.[1869] The third one is the one that will be discussed here. John Sanders expresses this view in the following quotation:

> Salvation for the unevangelized is made possible only by the redemptive work of Jesus, but God applies that work even to those who are ignorant of the atonement. God does this as people respond in trusting faith to the revelation they have. In other words, unevangelized persons may be saved on the basis of Christ's work if they respond in faith to the God who created them.[1870]

In response to Sanders, where in the *Tanakh* or the New Covenant did God ever say that He would save anyone who is ignorant of the atonement? This view has absolutely no biblical merit whatsoever! Anyone who believes or makes such a statement shows their complete ignorance of the nature and character of God Himself as well as His written word.

This third position is a subtle perversion of a biblical truth. Inclusivism, while not denying the centrality of the atonement of *Yeshua* on the cross (which the first two positions do), broadens the requirements of conscious faith in the atonement of *Yeshua* which God Himself never gave. The danger of Messianic pastors and Gentile Christians who love Israel is to see Jewish people being saved apart from the name of *Yeshua* throughout time and so find it unnecessary to present the gospel of Messiah to the Jewish people. Leman again expresses two concerns that need to be given here:

> Yet I think it fair to observe that Inclusivism is a doctrine especially appealing to those of us who love Israel. Having found much truth and beauty in rabbinic forms, who has not wondered if at least some practitioners of Rabbinic Judaism are saved apart from faith in Messiah? The same impulse applies to Jewish thought which sometimes comes very close to New Testament truth. Who has not wondered if Levinas or Heschel might have been close enough to the truth without Messiah to be accepted by God?
>
> Not only is Inclusivism antithetical to the scriptures, but it is also a great de-motivator to our task of making Messiah known to our Jewish brothers.[1871]

The spiritual dangers are real when it is understood what God gave as His requirement for salvation. Jewish people are deceiving themselves by believing that being born Jewish or observing the Mosaic Law or rabbinic law is sufficient for salvation. If Jewish people are close enough as Inclusivism teaches, then why present *Yeshua* as the Messiah, Creator, Righteous Branch, the angel of the LORD, the Servant of the LORD and the God/man to them? Inclusivism would encourage Jewish reliance on community

---

[1869] Derek Leman, "Inclusivism and the Task of Making Jewish Disciples," *Mishkan* (issue 42, 2005), 39.

[1870] John Sanders, *What About Those Who Never Heard?* (Downers Grove: IVP, 1995), 36.

[1871] Leman, "Inclusivism and the Task of Making Jewish Disciples." *Mishkan* (issue 42, 2005), 40-41.

prayer, charity, and good deeds for atonement, which completely misses the point of numerous passages from the Law and Prophets. A modern day proponent of Dual Covenant Theology would be John Hagee. Many people are carried away by his Zionism, but his Zionism is a political Zionism and completely lacks or withholds the presentation of the Gospel from Jewish people. David Brickner of Jews for Jesus makes the following statement:

> In one of Hagee's latest books, "In Defense of Israel: The Bible's Mandate for Supporting the Jewish State" (2007), he contends that the Jewish people as a whole did not reject Jesus as Messiah, Jesus did not come to earth to be the Messiah. Jesus refused by word and deed to be the Messiah. And the Jews cannot be blamed for not accepting what was never offered.[1872]

John Hagee has withheld the Gospel from Jewish people because he has deceived himself into believing that Jewish people have not rejected the Messiahship of *Yeshua* and thus are not guilty of rejecting Him. So according to Hagee, Jewish people will be saved by obedience to the Law or responding to the light that they have. Peter was so very clear in Acts 4:12 where it says to a completely Jewish audience:

> Neither is there salvation in any other: for there is none other name under heaven given among men, whereby we must be saved.

Jewish people have had more light than any other people on earth. And to say that they are not responsible for rejection *Yeshua* as their Messiah is being biblically illiterate beyond description. The Jewish people have the entire *Tanakh* that stands against them. Hagee has denied believing in Dual Covenant Theology, but here are some excerpts from his book "In Defense of Israel:"

> If God intended for Jesus to be the Messiah of Israel, why didn't he authorize Jesus to use supernatural signs to prove he was God's Messiah, just as Moses had done. (pg 137)

> Jesus refused to produce a sign ... because it was not the Father's will, nor his, to be Messiah. (pg 138)

> If Jesus wanted to be Messiah, why did he repeatedly tell his disciples and followers to "tell no one" about his supernatural accomplishments? (pg 139)

> The Jews were not rejecting Jesus as Messiah; it was Jesus who was refusing to be the Messiah to the Jews. (pg 140)

> They wanted him to be their Messiah, but he flatly refused. (pg 141)

> He refused to be their Messiah, choosing instead to be the Savior of the world. (pg 143)

[1872] David Brickner, "How Christian is Christian Zionism?" *Mishkan* (issue 60, 2009, 75-76.

Jesus rejected to the last detail the role of Messiah in word or deed. (pg 145).[1873]

One who has studied the Scriptures can readily see from Hagee's statements that he is irresponsible and lacks biblical competence.

Leman, who writes in Mishkan, continues the argument that Jewish people have had more light than any other people on the earth and they are personally responsible:

How can it be said that Jewish people rejecting *Yeshua* have responded to the light they have?[1874]

Jewish people have been given more light than any people on the planet, and the writings of Moses and the Prophets are very clear. Salvation is by faith alone in *Yahweh*. As has been pointed out throughout this book, *Yeshua* speaks frequently throughout the pages of the *Tanakh* as *Yahweh*. Why do the new Jewish believers at the end of the seventieth week of Daniel weep bitterly as stated in Zechariah 12:10? Because they suddenly realize that they, their fathers, and their fathers' fathers have been rejecting the very God they said they worshipped. So much for responding to the light they had; they rejected that Light.

The danger of Inclusivism is a very real issue that has the eternal destiny of Jewish souls at stake. But that danger is equally as real to Gentiles of the Islamic, Hindu, Roman Catholic or any other faith. Numerous people have presented Inclusivism to the point where it is being heard more and more from national religious leaders, both from Catholic and Protestant adherents. One of the most well known people of the 20th century who has great respect around the world is Billy Graham. He has become the best known and respected evangelist maybe of all time. What this author is about to say is difficult, for it was through his preaching in December 1960 at the National Teen Convention (Youth for Christ) in Washington D. C. that I dedicated my life to serve the Lord. This author does not like to criticize the Lord's servants, but when something is this important I must be faithful to the Lord and exposure error like this.

The following are excerpts taken from a television interview of Billy Graham by Robert Schuller of the Crystal Cathedral on May 31, 1997:

Graham: God's purpose for this age is to call out a people for His name. And that's what God is doing today, He's calling people out of the world for His name, whether they come from the Muslim world, or the Buddhist world or the Christian world or the non-believing world, they are members of the Body of Christ because they've been called by God. They may not even know the name of Jesus but they know in their hearts that they need something that they don't have, and they turn to the only light that they have, and I think that they are saved, and that they're going to be with us in heaven.

[1873] John Hagee, *In Depense of Israel* (Lake Mary, FL: Frontline Publishers, 2007), 137-145.
[1874] Leman, "Inclusivism and the Task of Making Jewish Disciples," *Mishkan* (issue 42, 2005), 41.

Schuller: What, what I hear you saying, that it's possible for Jesus Christ to come into human hearts and soul and life even if they've been born in darkness and have never had exposure to the Bible. Is that a correct interpretation of what you're saying?

Graham: Yes, it is, because I believe that. I've met people in various parts of the world in tribal situations that have never seen a Bible or heard about a Bible, and never heard of Jesus, but they've believed in their hearts that there was a God, and they tried to live a life that was quite apart from the surrounding community in which they lived.[1875]

As can be clearly seen, Billy Graham is proposing that people from the Muslim, Buddhist, Hindu, as well as non-believing world (pagan) will be in heaven if they turn to the light that they have without ever having seen a Bible or heard the gospel message of salvation. Lest someone think that Graham's statement was an isolated one, nineteen years earlier in an interview with McCall's magazine, he is quoted as giving the following statement:

Graham confesses that he has taken a more modest view of his own role in God's plan for man. 'I used to play God,' he acknowledged, 'but I can't do that any more. I used to believe that pagans in far-off countries were lost – were going to hell – if they did not have the Gospel of Jesus Christ preached to them. I no longer believe that,' he said carefully. 'I believe that there are other ways of recognizing the existence of God – through nature, for instance – and plenty of other opportunities, therefore, of saying yes to God.'[1876]

That is heresy and false teaching that the Apostle Paul warned the church at large about (Romans 16:17; 2 Corinthians 11:3-4; Galatians 1:6; Ephesians 4:14; Colossians 2:4; 1 Timothy 1:7; 4:1) and the Apostle Peter reminded Jewish believers in Messiah that there would come from our own ranks people who would teach false doctrine, and it has (2 Peter 2:1-2). Paul warned the elders of the Ephesus Church that "*grievous wolves* [would] *enter in among you, not sparing the flock*," and "*of your own selves shall men arise, speaking perverse things, to draw away disciples after them*" (Acts 20:29-30). Leman has a good insight that rebukes Graham's statement:

Inclusivism should be evidenced in the mission field. If Inclusivism is true, and there are in fact, numbers of people who have come to saving faith in the true God without knowing Messiah, then why aren't these people turning up in world missions? Why aren't missionaries to pioneer fields meeting Buddhists and Hindus who say, 'This faith you proclaim is what I have believed all along. Now I know who the God is I was trying to serve.' Why in Jewish outreach are

---

[1875] Robert E. Kofahl, "Graham Believes Men Can be Saved Apart from the Name of Christ," *Foundation Magazine* (May-June 1997).

[1876] James Michael Beam, "I Can't Play God Any More," *McCall's* (Jan 1978): 156, 158.

we not finding faithful religious people who say, 'This Yeshua is the one I have been serving without realizing it?'[1877]

The fact is that what Graham said is not happening. When missionaries go to a foreign field to pagans, they do know that there is a God, but they serve demons. As for other religions Peter in Acts 4:12 was very clear:

> Neither is there salvation in any other: for there is none other name under heaven given among men, whereby we must be saved.

Dual Covenant or Inclusivism has never been taught by the Scriptures, but it is taught by Catholicism, liberal and some evangelical Protestants. Acts 4:12 was given within a Jewish context, as Peter and John stood before the Jewish religious leaders (Sanhedrin) who had rejected the light they had.

This is of utmost importance today in the modern culture of the "Christianized" world with its philosophy of pluralism and tolerance. Believers must stand firm with the truth of the gospel that was first delivered to the prophets and apostles. For the truth of the gospel will become increasingly unpopular as America (and the world) continue to corrupt themselves.

[1877] Leman, "Inclusivism and the Task of Making Jewish Disciples," *Mishkan* (issue 42, 2005), 42.

Appendix 6
Judaism and Christianity

Taken from Jakob Jocz's book
The Jewish People and Jesus Christ
Chapter VII

We have already had occasion to notice that the controversy between the Church and the Synagogue centers in the person of Jesus Christ. The problem for the Jew is, What place can be assigned to Jesus in Jewish thought without endangering the fundamental principles of Judaism? It has become increasingly obvious to Jewish thinkers that the traditional attitude of aloofness is not only impossible in modern conditions of life but also harmful to the cause of Judaism. Yet room for the Master of Nazareth within the structure of Jewish thought is only possible on the condition of a clear distinction between the Christ of the Christian dogma and Jesus the *Jew*. Jesus can enter the sanctuary of the Jewish heart only divested of all his supernatural glory. Is such a distinction possible? Jewish writers say, yes. It is not only possible, but absolutely essential for the sake of Divine truth. The Christian perception of Jesus in terms of the Holy Trinity to them rests upon a tragic misunderstanding. Such differentiation between the historic Jesus and the Christian Christ is a modern development, and was made possible by the influence of advanced scholarship. The rehabilitation of the "historic Jesus" at the expense of the orthodox Son of God is the logical answer on the part of progressive Jewish writers, after critical study had reduced the Divine Saviour to the plebeian position of a Jewish Rabbi. But what need is there, one would ask, to attach so much importance to the restoration to a place of honour of a man thus reduced to insignificance? It is just to satisfy the modern Jewish craving to reaffirm the Jewish origin of important personages?

John Cournos, an enthusiastic champion of the reclamation of Jesus by the Jews, has no real answer to that question. He holds that for a Jew to deny Jesus is "to reject the Jewish heritage, to betray what was best in Israel." But, we would ask, is it not possible to claim that heritage, minus Jesus? Has not Judaism assimilated the teaching of the Prophets without paying special attention to the Prophets themselves? To Judaism there can be no religious significance attached to any historic person. It is not the man who brings the message but the message which he brings that is decisive. So far, our study has clearly shown that Jewish scholars are unable to discover in all honesty any objective truth by which Judaism could have been enriched by Jesus. Cournos tells us that "Christ's essential Jewishness has been admitted by Jewish scholars and divines." But in the light of our investigation this sentence requires careful examination. "The Jewishness of Jesus" admitted by Jewish scholars refers to the background of Jesus' life, which existed in its self-sufficiency *before* Jesus and remained essentially *unaffected* after his coming. Jesus owes a debt to Judaism, but

Judaism owes *no* debt to Jesus. Such is the general view of Jewish scholarship. It is obvious that the Jesus whom Cournos has stripped of all theological and dogmatic significance, in order to make him acceptable to the Jewish taste, has simultaneously lost all his peculiar uniqueness, which both attracts and repels the Jew. Jesus, secularized and divested of all his religious meaning, ceases to be important. Rabbi Enelow and John Cournos thus defeat their own ends: a Jesus whom the Jews do no reject need not be reclaimed! The controversy regarding Jesus left on the plane of humanitarian idealism inevitably works itself to a standstill. It ends in the resolve to admit the Man of Nazareth to the venerable assembly of the geniuses belonging to the Jewish race. Such admittance entails no obligations and makes no demands.

The *real* controversy regarding Jesus takes place, not on the plane of secularized idealism but on the plane of religious truth. It is essentially a *theological* controversy which can only be carried on in its full significance between the Synagogue and the Church. The nature of their mutual relationship, their historic interdependence, their common hope, their profound divergence, and their deep rooted opposition to each other, make them, and them only, legitimate partners in the discussion. The dialogue which has taken and still takes place between *Synagogue* and Church is more than mere theological quibbling; it is a *necessity* upon which their life depends. In juxtaposition to each other, they learn the meaning of their own existence. Confronting each other in question and answer, they perpetuate their decision and affirm their faith.

The divergence between the Church and the Synagogue is fundamental and covers the whole sphere of human-Divine relationship. At no point do these two divergent circles intersect. It is only a vague and diluted Christian theology which imagines it possible to come to terms with Judaism. In reality, there is no understanding between the two faiths: they possess no common denominator which could form the basis for a "bridge theology." They can only compromise by surrender: either the Church becomes the Synagogue or the Synagogue the Church. But in their separateness their only legitimate relationship is that of continuous interrogation. They can, nay, they *must* question each other until the end of time. Their existence side by side puts both simultaneously under a question mark. The theme of their conversation is thus as to the why and wherefore of their separate life. The answer to this question leads to the person of Jesus Christ. Between Church and Synagogue stands the Crucified. Church and Synagogue derive their existence from their attitude to Him. The Synagogue perpetuates her existence in her continued negation, and the Church in her continued affirmation of the claims which Jesus made.

THEOLOGICAL ISSUES

Mr. Montefiore has hinted at the possibility of an understanding between liberal Judaism and Christianity on the basis of the Sermon on the Mount. He even went one step further. In his book *The Old Testament and After* he makes a remark which has been severely criticized on the Jewish side. His words are: "It will be needful for the

738

liberal Jewish theologians to consider the new modern interpretation of the doctrine of the Trinity;" and: "Nor does it follow that because the doctrine has been, and even is, in frequent danger of degeneration into Tri-theism, or has often so degenerated, it is therefore not true." But whatever opinions Montefiore may hold about the philosophical significance of the Trinitarian doctrine, it has no bearing upon the person of Jesus. Not even in its diluted Unitarian form is the Christian emphasis upon the importance of Jesus acceptable to a liberal Jew. An approach to the Church is therefore made impossible for any form of Judaism as long as the Christian faith has Jesus at the centre. That Montefiore is well aware of the difficulty can be seen from an earlier remark: "The centre of the teaching of the historic Jesus is God: the centre of the teaching of the Church is he" (i.e. Jesus himself). It is this peculiar attitude to Jesus which divides for ever the Church from the Synagogue. By working out the implication of faith in Jesus Christ, we automatically draw the demarcation line which divides Judaism from Christianity. But because we are writing from the Christian point of view, we will reverse the process by stating primarily the Jewish position.

(a) The Unity of God

The essence of Judaism is the doctrine of the absolute and unmodified unity of God. Prof. Moore's masterly definition of the Jewish conception of that unity can hardly be surpassed. He calls it, "the numerically exclusive and uncompromisingly personal monotheism." With it, Judaism stands and falls. Indeed, the absolute unity of the God of Israel together with the Torah, i.e. the revelation of this one and only God, form the heart and essence of Judaism. The rest of Jewish thought and practice is of secondary importance when compared with these two fundamental truths. Though liberal Judaism has only retained the first pillar upon which the Synagogue rests and has substituted for the unchangeable Torah a progressive conception of revelation commensurate with reason, yet in its emphasis upon absolute monotheism and in its conception of Law it is still in spirit and essence Judaism.

This characteristic emphasis upon the oneness of God, which forms the basis of the Ten Commandments and has found its classic expression in the Old Testament literature, differentiates the Synagogue from all other religions. But the Rabbinic interpretation of the Old Testament conception of the unity of God is such that it runs contrary to the Christian conception of the Messiah. This most vital tenet, as conceived by orthodox and liberal Judaism alike, stands thus in direct opposition to the Trinitarian doctrine of the Christian Church. It is at this point that the gulf between the Church and the Synagogue opens before us in all its depth and significance. On this issue, Judaism has never faltered. It still speaks with one united voice. Dr. J. H. Hertz, an orthodox Jew, and Kaufmann Kohler, a liberal, unequivocably say the same thing. The teaching of the divinity of Jesus Christ is an unpardonable offence in the eyes of Judaism. It is for this reason that Judaism could never proclaim whole heartedly the Christians to be

Monotheists; at best they were looked upon as "semi-proselytes;" while Mohammedanism was always regarded as more closely related to the mind of Judaism.

The puzzle which confronts the historian in his study of the inner causes which led to the division between the early Christian Church and the Synagogue, resolves itself into a simple question when viewed from this fundamental theological aspect. Did the disciples in Jerusalem, *i.e.* Jews upon Jewish soil, claim for Jesus divinity? This question is difficult to answer, and we have seen that even Bousset hesitates. But there can be little doubt that the first believers in Jesus claimed for the Master a unique importance which gradually lifted him out of the ranks of mere humanity. Against this, Judaism could not but protest with all its strength. Even the suggestion that Jesus' position was unique amongst men, a claim which was upheld by every shade of Hebrew Christianity, no matter how it differed in every other respect, could not be anything else but an offence to the Synagogue. Such an admission would inevitably break the closed ranks of humanity and set Jesus upon a plane outside history. It is for this reason that Judaism can admit neither the authority, the uniqueness, nor the perfection of Jesus. It consequently rejects even the Unitarian point of view.

Fredinand Weber has shown that the Synagogue's conception of the unity of God underwent a change under the influence of Christianity. He maintains that the conception of God in the older Targums is more closely related to that of the Old Testament. But even there he finds "a certain monism and transcendentalism which renders it incapable of conceiving the inter-divine movement of life (innergottliche Lebensbewegung) underlying the Trinitarian conception of God, incapable also of doing justice to the entry of God into history as it is demonstrated by the Old Testament." Such criticism, however, may appear to overlook the great tradition of Jewish piety and the strongly developed Jewish awareness of God's interference in human life. So much may be said in defence of Judaism. But it will be noticed that an appeal to *experience* removes the discussion from the theological plane on to empiricism. Philosophically, however, and theologically the Jewish conception of *ahdut elohim* (unity of God) reveals an abstract monism and a cold transcendentalism which strangely contrasts with the indwelling richness of the Christian view. We have already referred to Montefiore's remark regarding the Christian conception of the Trinity, which goes to show that he was aware of that fact. But Judaism as long as it confronts the Christian Church is irrevocably committed to such a position. The slightest retraction from rigid monotheism makes room for the Christian conception of the Christ. But such a conception runs directly contrary to the whole structure of Jewish thought. This can be seen from Husik's comments on Maimonides' conception of the Godhead. He says: "God is conceived as absolutely transcendent and unknowable. No positive predicate can apply to him so as to indicate his essence. We can say only what he is not, we cannot say what he is. There is not the faintest resemblance between him and his creatures. And yet he is the cause of the world and of all its happenings. Positive attributes (e.g. life, power, knowledge) signify that God is the cause of the experience denoted by the attributes in question." From this description it can be clearly recognized wherein lies the difference between the Christian and the Jewish conceptions of God. The God of Jewish theology, especially under Maimonides' influence, is reduced to a philosophical principle. The active and intervening God of Old Testament Scriptures assumes here the form of the *First Cause*. His absolute otherness removes him entirely from the world of his Creation. But while the infinite difference between man and God is also the starting-point of Christian thinking, God's transcendence is overcome not by the arbitrary act of human piety but by the self-chosen and self willed manifestation of God in the person of Jesus Christ; in Judaism it is overcome by *man himself*. This is the most significant difference between Church and Synagogue.

Closely connected with the unity of God is the Jewish conception of man. Here it is well to remember that philosophical and theological thinking is never suspended in the abstract air of pure logic, but has a generic relationship to the *concrete* facts of life. It is a remarkable fact that the Jews, a small people, living for centuries in most difficult circumstances, exhibit a positivism to life and an optimism about man which is peculiarly their own. There is an interesting connexion between the Jewish outlook and the actual historical experience of the Jewish people.

It seems to us that Jewish life, which for centuries has entailed humiliation and suffering, has coloured Jewish thought in a peculiar way. The natural result of oppression is the development of an inferiority complex. But by way of compensation that sense of inferiority has been turned into a positive tendency to assertiveness. In Jewish thought this expresses itself in an exaggerated emphasis upon the importance of Israel in particular and of man in general.

We hold that there is an inner connexion between the Jewish conception of man and the Synagogue's attitude to the Christian concept of the Messiah; we will thus turn to consider Jewish anthropology.

(b) The Jewish Conception of Man

Dr. Dienemann has seen aright when he said that the most characteristic difference between Judaism and Christianity "is the doctrine about man, the view concerning his nature and essence." This is by no means an exaggeration. At first sight, it would seem that the fundamental difference between Judaism and Christianity lies in their respective conceptions of God. But this is not so. Man's conception about God reflects his view about himself. Feuerbach's contention that the idea of the Godhead is a projection of the human mind undeniably contains some truth. The starting-point of man's thinking is man himself. It cannot be otherwise. Thus, the genesis of the division between Church and Synagogue is of an anthropological nature. Because the Church and the Synagogue radically differ on this point, they differ on all other points.

What is man? Upon the answer to this question depends the philosophical outlook and ultimately the theological direction of both faiths. Needless to say, both Synagogue and Church try to answer this question in the light of Scripture. Their difference lies in the emphasis, but it is a difference of far-reaching consequences. The Synagogue emphasizes the *Imago Dei* in man; the Church stresses man's fall. The result is that the Synagogue offers a lofty humanism which is essentially idealistic and optimistic in its outlook. The Church, on the other hand, by emphasizing the depravity of human nature and the impotence of man to save himself presents a negative, ascetic attitude to the world. It is thus in direct opposition to the frame of mind of which humanism is the expression.

There have naturally been attempts to combine the two views in a synthesis, as both apparently contain elements of truth, and on the surface seem to supplement each other. Indeed, the history of Christian thought, viewed from this angle, reveals repeated attempts in one form or another to find a compromise. But in reality a synthesis is impossible. The *Imago Dei* concept, which ultimately dispenses with the need for man's restoration, or adoption, as Paul would call it, destroys the most central fact of the Christian faith, namely the incarnation. If man is essentially good, then the difference between him and Jesus is only a difference of degrees in the scale of perfection. Then there is no *actual* difference between him and us. He only *is* what we *shall* be. Upon the ladder of human perfection Jesus merely occupies a higher rung. He has attained while we are still striving. But even such a relativization between Jesus and the rest of humanity is unbearable to Judaism. As Montefiore puts it: "There have been many men who were very good and very wise; there never has been, and there never can be, a man who was perfectly good and perfectly wise." Here we meet with the inexorable logic of Judaism. To admit perfection on the part of one man means to detach him from the rest of the human race, and thus to break the closed circle of humanity. In essence it amounts to the deification of one man. The only other alternative is to assume that so perfect a man is not *man* in the ordinary sense of the word. But against such an assumption, Judaism revolts, for underlying it is the thought of human impotence. If God revealed himself in history through his Son, as the Christian Church claims, then his appearing amongst us is an indication of human helplessness; it is the greatest crisis in the history of man. Such a crisis Judaism cannot admit, for in the light of the *Imago Dei* concept the line between God and man is not really broken; it is only marred. It is still within the power of man to ascend heavenwards. It is for these reasons that Judaism is able to accept, without restriction or qualification, the doctrine of the Fatherhood of God and from it the deduction of the brotherhood of man. The equality of men is thus a logical corollary to the Jewish outlook. Hence the democracy of the Synagogue. It is a democracy with a positive sign.

It is at this point that the bridge is built between the transcendental and eternal God and finite man. God's transcendence is not overcome by God himself, in that he condescends to dwell amongst men, but by man, in that he reaches out God-wards. Thus, the barrier which divides man from God is broken down not by an act of God, as the Christian believes, but by the self-sufficiency of man. Buber has admirably defined the position, by contrasting Judaism with Christianity: Judaism, he said is based upon the belief that there is a way from earth to heaven, from below, upwards. It is the faith that struggling man, in his mortal effort, can climb the steep hill which leads to God. Christianity, on the other hand, holds the opposite view. It is based upon the belief that there is no way from earth to heaven, from man to God. Unless God in his mercy stretches out his hand from above, man can never reach him. Hence the incarnation, which teaches that in the person of Jesus Christ God came from heaven to earth to find and to save mankind.

Judaism is built upon the assumption of man's unlimited resources to attain to the highest. "If you wish to stand under the special protection of special Providence," says Rabbi Wise, "you must exert your energies to rise, to climb, to ascend and come as near to your God as you can." But what if man cannot? The Synagogue does not admit such a possibility: Judaism is essentially a religion for those who can. We quote Dr. Wise again: "To rise to self-conscious immortality and happiness is in man's power exclusively; it depends on no circumstances and no outer influences. Man is to all intents and purposes a free and independent being."

It is obvious that the Fall of man, which occupies a central position in Christian theology, reverses the picture which Judaism draws. The corollary of the Fall is that the original relation between man and God is broken. Henceforth man stands before God not as a child before the father but as a creature before the Creator, as guilty before a Judge.

The Church thus speaks in terms of unredeemed humanity. Without this fact, the incarnation becomes superfluous. The Cross, which in the eyes of the Church is the symbol of Salvation, otherwise becomes a mere tragedy and the Christian Faith the result of a misunderstanding.

Indeed, the Church also knows about the Fatherhood of God, but this is conditioned by an act of adoption on the part of God of which Jesus Christ is the pledge and token. For man to claim relationship with God, without the Cross, without forgiveness, is to overlook the grim fact of sin; it is an act of supreme presumption.

(c) Free Will

From what has been said already about Jewish anthropology, it is an easy inference that the teaching of free will is an important element in the whole conception. Indeed, Jewish thinkers from the earliest times invariably assert the absolute freedom of the human will. This is already implied in the well-known sentence: *ha-kol bide shamayim huz miyirat shamayim*. The meaning of this adage is, that though God, by virtue of his position, controls the affairs of man, his control is not such as to override human choice. The assumption being that man is capable of choosing for himself and choosing aright.

743

The doctrine of free will plays a prominent part in Jewish thought. It is constantly asserted by Jewish divines and has been claimed to be a fundamental principle of Judaism. Husik says: "So fundamental has it seemed for Judaism to maintain the freedom of the will that no one hitherto (*i.e.* till Crescas, *circa* 1340-1412) had ventured to doubt it. Maimonides no less than Judah Halevi, and with equal emphasis Gersonides, insist that the individual is not determined in his conduct. This seemed to be the only way to vindicate God's justice in reward and punishment." But in actual fact, the insistence upon human freedom has deeper reasons than the vindication of divine justice. The whole concept about man and his relationship to God makes freedom of will a logical necessity for Judaism. Husik is well aware of this. The main difficulty which Jewish thinkers have felt was that the idea of human freedom clashes with the doctrine of God's omniscience. They have been thus forced either to restrict human freedom or God's omniscience; or else, as in the case of Maimonides, evade the problem by a reference to God's transcendence. Crescas' position is exceptional for Judaism. But even in his case the tension is lessened by a dialectical distinction between determinism and fatalism. On the whole, it may be said that the natural trend in Jewish theology is towards an emphasis upon the human side. But while medieval thinkers still restricted human freedom so as to relate it to God's sovereignty, moderns assert unqualified freedom of will.

Judah Halevi explained that free will, which by its nature belongs to the class of intermediary causes, is linked up with other causes "which reduce it, chain like, to the Prime Cause." Human action is thus, in one way or another, related to God's omniscience. The final choice, however, is not compulsory, but *potential*: "the mind wavers between an opinion and its opposite, being permitted to turn where it chooses. The result is praise or blame for the choice." This may be contrasted with the advanced views of modern writers. Rabbi Dienemann, pointing out the Christian conception of grace which man requires not only in order to abstain from evil, but also to do good, observes: "Jewish ideology (Anschauung) holds tenaciously to the thought of the complete *independence* of the moral personality." But Dienemann actually goes further than this. In the interests of ethics, on the grounds that "moral renewal must grow out of one's own strength," and that man in himself must therefore carry the sources of moral regeneration, he does not hesitate to place man *opposite* God: "Next to the grandeur and limitless grace of God stands as an equally important religious value, the dignity of Man," The Jewish conception of man and the characteristic emphasis upon human action provide the background for this sentence. It is the logical conclusion of a theology which is essentially anthropocentric. That Dienemann by no means occupies an isolated position may be judged from the words of another writer, who represents a somewhat different school of thought. The leader of the Neo-Kantian school in Judaism, Hermann Cohen, explaining the connexion between freewill and ethics, says: "Man's task is to choose the good. Freedom of choice is the basic condition of moral judgment (*Vernunft*). For it, for the freedom of the human as the moral will, there can be no limitation in God. The Will of God, the Essence of God demands the freedom of the human will." At the point, the borderline between Judaism and Christianity becomes visible. Whatever *freedom* the Christian assigns to himself, whatever worth he ascribes to human personality, in view of the Cross he stands incapacitated, *i.e.* he cannot save *himself*. Salvation is a gift from God: in the last resort, man undergoes salvation; he does not attain to it. But such is not the Jewish view. God indeed acts, but his action is conditioned by human behaviour. Israel's redemption depends on Israel's repentance: R. Eliezer said: "If Israel repent, they will be redeemed; if not, they will not be redeemed. R. Joshua said to him, If they do not repent they will not be redeemed. But the Holy One, blessed be he, will set up a king over them, whose decrees shall be as cruel as Haman's whereby Israel shall engage in repentance, and he will thus bring them back to the right path." Against this may be put the words of the Apostle, which by contrast reveal in a remarkable way the profound difference between the Christian and the Jewish idea of redemption: "While we were yet sinners, Christ died for us" (Romans 5:8).

The whole idea of salvation in the Christian sense is foreign to Judaism: and naturally so. The Synagogue knows of two kinds of redemption; national redemption *i.e.* the redemption of Israel, and the redemption from sin. Israel's redemption depends on Israel's repentance; redemption from sin is understood in terms of forgiveness: it is God's prerogative to save man from sin. This he does by an act of forgiveness. Hermann Cohen thus makes forgiveness of sin "the particular speciality of God's goodness." Judaism, therefore, emphasizes not Salvation but Atonement. The Day of Atonement occupies a central place in the calendar of the Synagogue. Characteristically enough, Hermann Cohen's great book on Judaism (*Die Religion der Vernunft*) has a chapter on Atonement (*Versohnung*), but no chapter on Salvation. Wherever Salvation is referred to, its meaning is that of Atonement.

The prerequisite to Atonement is repentance. The rabbis had an extraordinary estimation of repentance. The Mishnah teaches that repentance atones for lesser transgressions of the Law, while the punishment for greater transgressions is, thanks to repentance, suspended until the Day of Atonement. But in later Rabbinical writings the importance of repentance is even more magnified. A fine example of the place *teshubah* occupies in Rabbinic thought is offered by Pesikta de Rab Kahana, where one section deals exclusively with repentance (*Piska* XXV). R. Juda Nishraja said in the name of R. Juda bar Simon: "When a man shoots an arrow, how far does it go? The length of a field (required) for the sowing of one cor of corn, or two fields (required) for the sowing of one cor of corn. But great is the power of repentance, for it reaches to the throne of Glory." There is no crime for which repentance cannot atone. Even Cain's sin was forgiven because he repented. Kaufman Kohler says: "Repentance occupies a very prominent position in all the ethical writing of the Middle Ages." It is still the cornerstone of Jewish piety.

Montefiore seems to be in agreement with Delitzsch's estimate of the difference between Jewish and Christian conception of repentance. "According to the Jewish doctrine," says Delitzsch, "God lets himself be reconciled through repentance; according to the Christian doctrine, he is reconciled (*versohnt*) through the mediation

745

(*Mittlerwerk*) of Christ, and the individual man is reconciled to God (*versohnt*) when in faith and repentance he accepts the mediation, which is common and general for all mankind. The New Testament method of salvation (*Heilsordnung*) has the same sound as (*lautet auch wie*) *jer. Maccoth* 1.6: *ya`aseh teshubah we-yitkaper lo* ('let him repent and receive atonement'), but repentance is not the factor which atones (*das Suhnende selbst*), but only the way to receive atonement (*der Weg zur Versohnung*)." It seems to us that in this subtle distinction lies the whole difference between the Church and the Synagogue with regard to human freedom and divine grace. For the main point under discussion is not what is intended by repentance (on this Church and Synagogue are agreed) but the question what efficacy we ascribe to the act. In the estimation of Judaism, forgiveness is conditioned by repentance; according to the Church, forgiveness has its foundation in the Cross. The centre of gravity is thus for Judaism on the human side, and for Christianity on God's action which precedes repentance.

We restate the case: according to Judaism, it is man who takes the first step towards reconciliation, and not God; hence the utter importance of repentance. In the act of contrition, man expresses his willingness to amend his life and to ask for forgiveness. That God will forgive is taken for granted. It is on these grounds that Maimonides can pronounce without hesitation: "Now in our days, when the house of the Sanctuary exists no longer, and when we have no atoning altar…repentance atones for all transgressions." This actually goes beyond the Mishnah, where forgiveness is still to a certain degree tied to the efficacy of the Day of Atonement. But even in the Mishnah, the reference to the Day of Atonement does not lessen the importance of repentance: "death and the Day of Atonement effect atonement if there is repentance." It is therefore quite true to the spirit of Judaism when Leo Baeck says, "Atonement too is ours, our task and our way." Dr. Dienemann has not over accentuated the Jewish position by differentiating between the Christian conception of Salvation and the Jewish conception of Atonement: the Jew stands in no need of Salvation, all he requires is Atonement (*Versohnung*): "*in the act of Atonement,*" however, "*both God and man co-operate.… but in the forefront stands the work of man accomplished by his own strength.*" Klausner explains that Paul's doctrine of predestination, which he calls a "mystico-religious determinism," puts man in a position where the chance to determine his own fate is taken from him. Such a doctrine is unacceptable to Judaism, which is characterized by profound faith in life and a strong optimism. In the Jewish view, human dignity requires that man be free, with an absolute freedom, for only thus can he be held responsible for his deeds. It is for this reason that in the Jewish conception sin does not totally affect human nature; man only sins, but is *not sinful*.

746

(d) The Jewish Conception of Sin

Closely related to the problem of free will is the problem of evil. Judaism, with its characteristic emphasis upon morality and law, is naturally conscious of the fact of evil. The Synagogue knows of sin and human depravity. It often speaks of the *yezer tob* and *yezer ha-ra`* fighting for supremacy within the human heart. But the Jewish conception of *yezer ha-ra`* is totally different from the Christian conception of sin. The difference is logically connected with the doctrine of free will.

Evil and good are ever-present potentialities in human life. Man is constantly put to the test by being offered the choice between right and wrong. He carries in his bosom the tension between two dispositions. But his human dignity requires that he be free to tip the balance in either direction. The final decision is with him. Deuteronomy 30:19 plays an important part in Jewish thinking: "I have set before thee life and death, blessing and cursing; therefore choose life that thou mayest live." Dr. J. H. Hertz comments on this text: "Jewish ethics is rooted in the doctrine of human responsibility, that is, *freedom of will*." Dr. Hertz, however, knows that the human will is conditioned by heredity and environment; nevertheless, he holds that "in the moral universe, man ever remains his own master." This is an axiom to Judaism; on it depends its whole structure. Maimonides rightly regarded the doctrine of free will as the pillar of the Law and the Commandments. The enacting of Commandments postulates the possibility of keeping them; they presuppose human freedom. I. M. Wise puts it: "The Sinaic revelation is the proof for the immortal and God-like nature of man." It is then obvious that for Judaism there can only be sins, but no sin in the Christian sense. Its main concern is with *`aberot*, trespasses and the safeguarding of the Law, but not with the redemption of sinners as the Church understands it.

Original sin was unknown to the old Synagogue and it is of no consequence in the teaching of Judaism. The rabbis taught that man at his birth is given by God a pure and holy soul; and though man possesses that latent possibility towards evil or good, the inclination towards good is stronger than the inclination towards evil. Thus, man at the outset starts with a *plus* and not with a *minus*. Dienemann has shown that the existence of evil is not a postulate of Judaism. It is not something that man finds already present on entering the world, but is of his own creation. Judaism denies the a *priori* character of evil. "And if thou wilt now ask," says a Midrash, "why did then God create the yezer ha-ra`, God replies: 'Who makes him a yezer ha-ra? Only thou thyself.'" Sin is therefore not an inherent characteristic of human nature, it is only acquired. To quote Dienemann again: "Sin is according to Jewish teaching therefore no necessity, nothing that is inborn in man and inseparable from him." Hence, sinfulness to Judaism is not a state to which man is confined, but rather "a transient and passing repression (Hemmung)." Or, as Rabbi Wise puts it: "A sin, according to Rabbinical definition, must be an action."

If we understand Hermann Cohen's difficult discourse on the origin of evil aright, sin is essentially a means for the individual to develop into an Ego and thus to find his completion. Cohen guards himself against the thought that there is an inherent inclination (Anlage) within man towards evil. On the contrary, man carries in his bosom the holy spirit. Man by nature, however, is bound up socially with the rest of humanity: he is, therefore, only an individual, but not an Ego. Sin serves as a medium by which man develops into a self-conscious "I." Cohen strongly differentiates between social sin and sin before God. Religious sin, *i.e.* sin before God, is the refusal on the part of man to rise to the state of isolated existence as an Ego. To use his own words for the sake of clarity: "Only this kind of sin of the individual do we acknowledge as sin before God by means of which the human individual is lifted up to the human Ego." Sin thus understood serves a *positive* end. It becomes a ladder which leads man to his highest existence. It is not something from which man must be *saved*, it is something which man is called upon to *overcome*. Without it, man is deprived of the means of attaining his highest end: "Sin before God," Hermann Cohen explains, "leads us to man as Ego. Sin before God leads us to redemption by God. Redemption by God leads us to man's atonement with himself. And this in the last instance to the atonement of the Ego with God. It is the atonement with God however that finally brings the individual to maturity as an Ego."

The involved philosophical reasoning of H. Cohen need not obscure the fact that his structure is built upon the foundations of Judaism. The whole Jewish outlook is marked by a deep seated optimism. Judaism is fundamentally at peace with the world. It affirms life and existence and is determinately opposed to every form of otherworldliness. '*Olam Ha-ba*, which plays such an important part in Rabbinic thought, is not the expression of renunciation of *this* world, but the longing for an improved form of present existence. Leo Baeck rightly regards this inveterate affirmation of life as a peculiarity of Judaism, which he calls "the religion of ethical optimism." Not that Judaism is unaware of the wrongs and tragedies of human existence. A denial of evil is impossible in face of the accumulation of Jewish experience. But Jewish optimism is founded upon the belief that evil is not a necessary prerequisite of life, but only a deficiency which man has the power to remedy. "The optimism of Judaism," says Baeck, "consists in a *belief in the good* which *wills* the good. It is the belief in God, and consequently the belief *in man*, in God through whom the good finds reality, and in man who is able to realize the good. All the ideas of Judaism can be traced back to it."

Now, in the opinion of some Christian writers, "the other-worldly aspect of Christianity needs to be balanced by the incorrigible optimism of the Jews with regard to this world." That may be so. Pessimism which expresses itself in retreat and seclusion is alien to the Christian spirit. Christianity is also essentially optimistic. But its optimism springs from a different source. The basic note of the Easter message is victory, but not man's victory; it is God's victory. God's victory, however, is man's defeat. Not so to Judaism: here, man's victory is God's victory; it is man who helps

God to triumph. It cannot be otherwise; any other position for Judaism would mean the denial of its fundamental proposition – the inherent self-sufficiency of man.

The difference here between Judaism and Christianity is fundamental. While to Judaism sin is only a latent disposition or an acquirement easily corrected, to Christianity sin is an all pervading principle of life. It has cosmic significance and expresses itself in the human attitude of inward rebellion against God: *Eritis sicut Deus* (Gen 3:5). In the Christian view, man stands as a usurper of God's glory and a rival to his power; he is thus guilty of high treason. Sin is a power which enslaves man, incapacitates his will, pushes him irresistibly towards evil, and puts him in a state of utter helplessness. To the Church man is sinful before he has yet done anything; to the Synagogue, man is sinful when he is full of sins. Consequently, in the eyes of the Church even the best of men needs salvation; in the view of the Synagogue, the transgressor needs only amendment of life. Hence, Christianity speaks in terms of regeneration, Judaism in terms of moral conduct. What Strack-Billerbeck say about the old Synagogue well applies to Judaism in general: "The old Jewish religion is thus completely a religion of self-salvation; it has no room for a Saviour-Redeemer who dies for the sins of the world."

(e) Mediation

The concept of sin determines the question as to the human approach to God. To Judaism, man's access entirely depends upon his moral integrity (cf. Psalm 24:3ff). "The essence of Judaism is ethics." Or, as Baeck puts it: "It is the right deed alone which always places man in the presence of God." The attention of the Synagogue is arrested upon man in his moral endeavour. It is for this reason that Judaism is unable to accept the doctrine of the incarnation, for such a doctrine implies the need for mediation. Mediation, however, implies the inadequacy of the human effort to reach out Godwards. Judaism is founded on the premise that man is capable by virtue of his moral effort of approaching God. Hence, God's coming to man's aid not only becomes superfluous, but actually interferes with the progress of human development.

To Judaism the way from man to God is open. All that man needs is to amend his ways and return to God: "If he has sinned he is always able to become different, he is able to find his way back…he can hallow and purify himself again, he can make atonement." This possibility is not only a Jewish prerogative: "The righteous of all nations have a share in the world to come." Jewish writers are proud of this sentence and quote it frequently. The meaning of it is that not faith but works decide. God judges man according to his deeds. Though man transgress and fall away from God he never can fall so as not to be able to stand up again. The guarantee for his ability to rise is the Imago Dei, which man has imprinted upon his soul. Thus "the covenant of God with man is never broken;" contact between God and man is always possible: "Everybody can draw near to his God, and a way to God proceeds from every soul." It is no exaggeration to say, that the Synagogue's motto is: *man is able*.

This almost unlimited confidence in human ability pervades the whole Jewish outlook. There is an interesting passage in (Talmud) Sanhedrin 97b: "Rab said: 'All predestined dates (for Messiah's coming) have passed, and the matter (now) depends only on repentance and good deeds.' But Samuel maintained: 'It is sufficient for a mourner to keep his (period of) mourning.'" H. Friedman explains Samuel's words to mean: "Israel's sufferings in the *Galuth* in themselves sufficiently warrant their redemption, regardless of repentance." But to both rabbis Israel himself is the decisive factor. Mediation, therefore, is foreign to the spirit of Judaism. Kaufmann Kohler rightly says: "Judaism recognizes in principle no mediatorship between God and man." This directness of approach is a definite departure from the Old Testament position. It is here, if nowhere else, that we recognize the difference between the Synagogue and the Old Testament religion.

Mediation in the Old Testament plays an important part in religion. The priest, the prophet, the angels who act as messengers of God – they all stand between sinful man and the Lord of Hosts. The Torah itself was received by Israel '*al-yede-sarsor* (through a mediator). This was still the view of the Old Synagogue. Philo's *Logos*, which assumes such importance in his conception of God, has its root not only in Greek philosophy but also in the Old Testament. It rests upon the principle that between God and man there is a gap. Judaism, however, with its characteristic predisposition towards the unitary view of life and its emphasis upon human action, has gradually departed from the doctrine of mediation. An important factor will have been opposition to the teaching of the Church, which made mediation an absolute necessity. There is a characteristic remake by Abraham ibn Ezra which singularly well describes the Jewish tendency: "The angel that mediates between man and God is reason." Behind these words lies concealed the thought that man, by virtue of his God-given faculties, is able to bridge the gulf which divides him from his Creator. The whole trend of modern Jewish thought is in this direction.

How then does sinful man, we ask, find approach to the holy and invisible God? "First," says Rabbi Wise, he must "find and understand the loftiest and surest standard of rectitude." This standard Judaism finds in the Torah. The second step is exemplified in the words Israel spake at Sinai: *na'aseh we-nishm'a*, "we will do and obey." In this manner man returns to God, and in doing so he "obliterates his own sins…he changes and reforms his character…he rises to the dignity of manhood." Communication between man and God is made possible by the fact that man participates in God's spirit. The unity between them is therefore never broken. The Holy Spirit belongs as much to man as to God: "The Holy Spirit can neither be altogether God nor man, even less God and man at the same time, but an attribute of the two conceptions or rather the union of both." In other words, the Holy Spirit is conceived not in the sense of Hypostasis but in terms of *function*; it is the result of the meeting between God and man. Cohen calls it "the uniting link of correlation." Relationship between God and man does not so much

750

postulate the existence of the Holy Spirit as the equality of partnership. The spirit comes into evidence not only when God speaks to man, but also when man speaks to God. It is the self same spirit indwelling in both. The reason for declaring the spirit a *function* is obvious. The purpose is to exclude every form of mediation. "Union precludes mediation," says Cohen.

Man occupies a position in the Jewish view which makes mediation not only superfluous but unbearable. It is an intrusion which violates man's rights and injures his dignity. Righteousness, to Judaism, cannot be imputed, it must be attained. "Righteousness," says Rabbi Wise, "is the ability or state of man to live and act in exact conformity with the highest standard of rectitude within his reach." Judaism does not require the impossible of man; what it requires is within the sphere of human ability. Man is able to stand by himself; herein lies his dignity. "Nobody stands between him and God; no mediator or past event, no redeemer and no sacrament." The whole idea of vicarious atonement, Rabbi Wise declares, is a "product of the Christianity of history." Neither in Scripture nor in philosophy can he see the reason for it. The whole conception is directly opposed to Jewish thinking. "What need have I of a God-Man when I myself have God within me?"

The gulf which divides man from God is of man's creation. Thus, only he himself can restore the divine-human relationship. By virtue of the *Imago Dei* dwelling in him, he is able to do so, if he wills. "Every man," says Miss Lazarus, "has to bridge the gulf for himself;" nobody can do it for him. Man must do it himself by means of his moral endeavour. Here the divergence between Judaism and Christianity becomes very clear. These are two worlds diametrically opposed to each other. The XIIIth of the thirty-nine Articles of the Church of England provides a classical example of the wide divergence between the two faiths: "Works done before the grace of Christ and the inspiration of his Spirit are not pleasant to God, for as much as they spring not of faith in Jesus Christ.... Yea rather, for that they are not done as God willed and commanded them to be done, we doubt not but they have the nature of sin (*peccati rationem habere non dubitamus*)."

In the Christian view nothing therefore, no human endeavour, no good deeds, can restore man to sonship. Sin is so grave that atonement can only be made by God himself. Jesus Christ stands as Mediator between man and God by virtue of his sacrificial death. The believer through faith identifies himself with the Crucified Saviour. There is no *direct* approach to God, it leads over Calvary. In Christ Jesus God has stretched out his hand to save mankind. Underneath the Cross man stands condemned and pardoned; in it is revealed human helplessness and God's power, human sinfulness and God's eternal Love.

(f) The Messiah

From the preceding remarks, it is obvious that the Jewish conception of the Messiah must differ fundamentally from that of the Church.

To start with, it is well to remember that faith in a personal Messiah does not belong to the fundamental tenets of Judaism. This is the more curious when we consider that Maimonides has included it in the Creed which is still in use in our day, and that Jewish hopes were for centuries associated with the coming of Messiah. No doubt in the old Synagogue the Messianic hope was adhered to with great fervour, though Bousset has shown that in the pre-Christian era the Messiah did not occupy as central a position as is usually assumed. It appears to us, however, that the apocalyptic literature must not be solely relied upon for our judgment concerning the Messianic views of that period. But even that literature contains enough evidence to show the place the Messiah occupied in Jewish thinking. At a later period, especially after the decline of the Hasmonean dynasty, the Messianic hope came to new life again. In the post-Christian era, it became the subject for many speculations, and Rabbinic literature is full of references to the Messianic age and the person of the Messiah. There are reasons, however, why the person of the Messiah was never emancipated so as to occupy a central place in Judaism. The first is an external reason, and is connected with the appearance of Christianity. Some Rabbinic sayings, like that of Johanan b. Torta, addressed to Akiba on his proclaiming Bar Cochba the Messiah, "Akiba, grass will sprout through your cheeks ere the Son of David comes," may have been prompted by its rise. The context, however, makes this doubtful. A more likely case is that of Rabbi Hillel, who declared: "There shall be no Messiah for Israel, because they have already enjoyed him in the days of Hezekiah." This strange remark has been sometimes connected with the story recorded by Epiphanius about Hillel the Patriarch, who is supposed to have accepted baptism before his death. But it seems to us that Rabbi S. Mendelsohn's explanation is more plausible. He suggests that Hillel "may have been prompted to this declaration by Origen's professed discovery in the Old Testament of Messianic passages referring to the founder of Christianity." In later times, Jewish views concerning the Messiah's functions have been greatly modified. This can be seen from Rashi's remark that the Almighty himself will redeem Israel and reign over him. This can also be seen from Maimonides' utmost caution in describing the position of the Messiah: "The king who is to arise out of the seed of David will be wiser than Solomon and he will be a great prophet near (*karob*) unto Moses our Rabbi." The second reason is of an internal nature. The hegemony of the Law conflicts with the idea of a Messiah who may command supreme authority. Even the Messiah can *only* occupy a place *near* Moses and is under obligation to obey and keep the commandments. The Targum already conveys this idea plainly. The rabbis spoke of the *torato shel mashiah*, but the Messiah's Torah was essentially Moses' Torah. The abrogation of the Torah by the Messiah is totally alien to the Rabbinic view. Strack-Billerbeck observe: "Such an assumption is excluded from the beginning by the firmly established doctrine

(Glaubenssatz) that just as the Torah of Moses pre-existed in eternity, so it was given to Israel for all eternity and nobody has the right to add anything to it or subtract from it." The Messiah not only obeys the Torah, but also studies it and expounds it. In the days of the Messiah, the Torah will assume new significance and will be universally obeyed, the theatres and circuses of Edom will be turned into schools of study. Thus, the centrality of the Torah in Jewish thought has forced the Messiah into the background. This has already been recognized by Albo. "Faith in the Messiah, according to Albo, would prejudice the redemptive significance (Heilsbedeutung) of the Law." "The nomistic principle," as Weber calls it, determined Jewish Christology. The supremacy and the immutability of the Torah, which is fundamental for Rabbinic thinking, has necessarily forced Jewish theology to assign to the Messiah a secondary place.

Nevertheless, hope in the Messiah's coming and the establishment of a Messianic age played an important part in Jewish life and worship and still sways the imagination of Jewry. It forms the backbone of Jewish eschatology. It must be remembered, however, that the rabbis have never worked out a consistent and systematic theory concerning the Messiah, his person, his coming, and his reign. Their ideas are confused, often contradictory and vague. On the whole, it may be said that Rabbinic notions connected with the coming of the Messiah show more signs of the play of imagination than of serious theological thinking. Against modern liberal views, however, it may be safely affirmed that the rabbis never detached the Messianic age from the person of the Messiah. The two were inseparable. They conceived the Messiah not as an ideal but as a real historical person. The Messianic function, however, was conceived to be primarily political. His chief mission was to free Israel from bondage. Klausner's description well states the case: "The Jewish Messiah," he says, "is above all a redeemer of his nation from subservience to foreign rulers." That this was the case can be seen from Akiba's behaviour towards Bar Cochba. It is, however, noteworthy that not all the rabbis shared Akiba's enthusiasm. No doubt the Synagogue expected more than political leadership from the Messiah. Even Klausner admits so much.

Dr. S. Schechter has worked out four main points under which the Rabbinic ideas concerning the Messianic age can be summarized; these notions reveal their view concerning the person of Messiah himself. All the other features attached to the Messiah by various rabbis are only of secondary importance. They are of a mystical nature (like the pre-existence of the Messiah, the creation of his name before the creation of the world, etc.), and have never seriously affected Judaism. Dr. A. Cohen rightly remarks: "The Talmud nowhere indicates a belief in a superhuman Deliverer as the Messiah." Dr. Schechter's points are: (1) The Messiah is a descendent of the house of David and his purpose is to restore the kingdom of Israel and extend it over the whole world. (2) In a last terrible battle the enemies of God will be defeated and destroyed. (3) The establishment of the Messiah's kingdom "will be followed by the spiritual hegemony of Israel, when all nations will accept the belief in the unity of God, acknowledge his kingdom and seek instruction from the law." (4) The Messianic age will bring material and spiritual happiness, death will disappear and the dead will rise.

For the sake of clarity, however, it must be added that the Messianic concept of the rabbis contains other important elements. One of the most striking is that of suffering. The passages referring to the suffering Messiah have been studiously collected by Strack and Billerbeck in their great Commentary. The most striking of these, which show remarkable likeness to the Christian conception of vicarious suffering, come from the *Pesikta Rabbati*. But three things must be borne in mind: (1) Though the rabbis were acquainted with the thought of sacrificing one's life "whether voluntarily or involuntarily for the sake and benefit of others," *vicarious* suffering on the part of the Messiah was unknown to them. (2) The occasional allusions to the suffering Messiah have a definite nationalistic colouring. It is Strack's and Billerback's opinion that "only Israel's sin is atoned by the Messiah. The thought that the Messiah carries the sins of the world, therefore also those of non-Israelites (John 1:29), we meet nowhere in old Rabbinical literature." With this statement Mr. Montefiore is inclined to agree. (3) The Messianic kingdom of the future is, according to Rabbinic views, essentially this worldly. It is a kingdom within history and time and is ultimately superseded by the final end.

We see, then, that whatever similarity there might be between the Jewish and the Christian conceptions of the Messiah and the Messianic age, on three most vital points they totally differ. The Christian faith is founded upon the belief in the vicarious suffering of the Messiah; this suffering benefits *all* nations; the Messianic kingdom, though conceived to take place upon *earth*, is not *totally* of this world; it brings history to an abrupt conclusion and starts a New Order. But there is a further point of even greater importance. In Christian faith the Messiah occupies a central position. He commands obedience, he makes claims upon loyalty, he forgives sin, he mediates between man and God, he redeems men, he renews their spirit, he reveals God and His love. And furthermore, this Messiah is identified with a *historical* person whose name is Jesus of Nazareth.

The divergence between liberal Judaism and orthodox Christianity is even greater. Liberal Jewish theology has completely abandoned the idea of a personal Messiah. Leo Baeck, a typical representative of liberal thinking, interprets the prophetic conception of the Messiah as a symbolic form of speech. He explains that Hebrew genius, being averse to the abstract form of expression, invested the Messianic ideal in a concrete person. But later, Judaism shifted the emphasis from a *person* upon the *time*: it began to speak more of "the days of the Messiah" and of "the kingdom of God" than of the Messiah himself. Thus, liberal Judaism has completed the process of evolution. It detached the Messianic ideal from the person of the Messiah, and looks forward to the realization of the Messianic age. "The future man," says Rabbi I. M. Wise, "will need no Messiah." To liberal Judaism the kingdom of God is no gift from Heaven; it is the result of the slow but steady progress of humanity. It is brought about by "the uninterrupted work of humanity upon itself." The establishment of the kingdom depends on the final triumph of human reason and the highest human aspirations; "it is not given, but achieved." The kingdom of God is not God's kingdom, but man's kingdom where God has been made King.

It is obvious that though the orthodox and liberal conceptions regarding the Messianic age appear to differ on a vital point, in essence they are agreed. With the Messiah or without the Messiah, to Judaism the kingdom of God is in our hands; it is for us to *establish* it upon this earth. The idea that Israel himself is the Messiah is not far removed from the Jewish mind. Dr. K. Kohler's view will meet with approval from many on the orthodox side that the kingdom of God is not the work of an individual Messiah but of Israel as a whole. Kohler says, "Deutero-Isaiah stated it for all time, Israel, the servant of God, the Messiah of the nations, working amid woe and suffering," will ultimately bring "the divine kingdom of righteousness and peace on earth."

(g) The Torah

Felix Perles in a short essay on *Die Autonomie der sittlichkeit im udischen Schrifttum* points out that the importance of Hermann Cohen's work lies in showing that the concept of moral autonomy stands in opposition to religion, and therefore also to Judaism. The writer traces the anomaly to the Philonian influence upon Rabbinic thinking. He holds that the rabbis did not realize the existing contradiction "between Philo's teaching of the autonomy of ethics and the Jewish conception (Anschauung) of God as the only Law-giver:" a contradiction which, when thought out to the last consequences, destroys the very basis of religious faith. Naively enough, Perles thinks that rabbis could not have been aware of this fact before Kant had explained the meaning of "autonomy." But to regard this phenomenon as a mere result of faulty thinking appears to us to overlook the whole nature of Judaism. The autonomy of ethics in Jewish thinking has its roots not in speculative metaphysics but in the concrete conception of man. The absolute validity of the moral act *vis a` vis* God postulates freedom on the part of man and therefore the autonomy of ethics. The whole structure of Jewish religious thinking depends upon it. The depreciation of the validity of moral action strikes at the foundations of Judaism, underlying which is the conception of law and justice.

Jewish scholars have rightly protested against the erroneous view that "Torah" and "Law" are synonyms. Torah is a much wider and more comprehensive conception than the word noVmos conveys. "The legalistic element," says Dr. S. Schechter, "which might rightly be called the Law, represents only one side of the Torah." Torah itself covers the whole sphere of Judaism, as it expresses itself both in doctrine and practice. Torah, then, is the norm against which Jewish life is measured, and it fulfills, in a sense, the purpose the dogmas do in the Church. But here lies a significant difference. H. Loewe has with fine insight recognized that the difference between Judaism and

Christianity expresses itself in that the former insists upon *orthopraxy* and the latter upon *orthodoxy*. Behind this fact lies concealed the gulf which divides the two faiths.

Jewish scholars often dwell upon the peculiarity of the Church in that it insists upon orthodoxy, *i.e.* the adherence to a creed and to dogmas. That Judaism, however, has no dogmas is a view which has been repudiated by Dr. S. Schechter. There is, however, a good deal of truth in H. Loewe's statement. The main emphasis in Judaism is upon the *right deed*. Leo Baeck hardly exaggerates when he says: "Judaism too has its Word, but it is one word only – 'to do'; hence the multiplicity of commandments. They all pursue the same end – the guiding of human life into the channel of *right* action. It is through the medium of the moral act that the Jew finds his approach to God." Indeed, Baeck goes so far as to say that obedience to the law of God is prior to any comprehension of God himself. It is only when men become "conscious of the *moral unity*" that they can "comprehend the *unity of God*." It is from such insistence upon the right deed that the Law is put in its proper perspective.

The significance of Torah as Law and Commandment is the most characteristic feature of Judaism. It is for this reason that Moses occupies a unique position in Rabbinic thought, and that the Pentateuch stands above the rest of the canon. What Weber says about the Scriptures in general applies primarily to the *torat Mosheh*; it is the *norma normans* of all Rabbinic thinking. The Torah is looked upon as the greatest and most perfect gift that God has bestowed upon Israel. In it is embodied "the will and purpose of the perfect God – perfect in wisdom, perfect in righteousness, perfect in loving-kindness." It forms the sure guide under all conditions of life and its purpose is the purification and the sanctification of man. Israel, therefore, owes his loyalty to the Torah, and he expresses his obedience by keeping the Commandments. By doing so he ratifies the covenant established at Mount Sinai between the chosen people and the God of Israel. Thus, the Torah occupies a central place in the Jewish faith.

The late Chief Rabbi, Dr. Hertz, in a speech said with great emphasis that the second fundamental principle of Judaism (the first being the Unity of God) was morality and law. "It proclaimed the divine origin of the moral law; that there was an everlasting distinction between right and wrong, an absolute 'Thou shalt' and 'Thou shalt not' in human life, a categorical imperative in religion." This connexion between moral action and faith in God is upheld by Christianity as well as by Judaism. St. Paul's antinomy between faith and works has never been understood by the Church as a dispensation from the human obligation to do right. It seems to us that Schoeps mis[re]presented St. Paul's position when he implied that the Apostle misunderstood the purpose of the Law, namely the sanctification of the *will* of God. Schoeps' well-chosen passages to show that the rabbis too knew of the value and greatness of faith have nothing to do with the main issue. The Apostle would have been the last to deny to the Synagogue the claim to the possession of faith. There is also no hint in the Epistles of St. Paul to show that he repudiated the right of the Law to make demands upon men. On the contrary, he affirms the divine origin and the justice of the Law; to him the Law is the law of God. He too knows that not the hearers but the *doers* of the Law shall be justified.

The extent of the misunderstanding on the Jewish side can be gathered from Montefiore's suggestion that the antinomy between the Jewish emphasis upon works and the Christian emphasis upon faith may be combined in a synthesis, for "we need them both: each possesses its measure of truth." Montefiore continues: "I cannot help believing that this old point of difference between Judaism and Christianity may gradually be done away with. Each will recognize that the fuller truth lies in a combination of doctrines hitherto thought opposed and alien to each other. To this we might ask: did the Apostle Paul ever oppose and does the Church oppose *faith* to *work* in the sense that one excludes the other? Such an allegation we would emphatically deny. There is no antinomy between faith and works; this is made impossible by the fact that in the Christian view they both belong to different *spheres*. In Christian thought faith and work are held separate, the one relating to God, the other to human relationship. Herein lies the duality at the heart of Christian thinking to which Benzion Kellerman draws attention. Such *duality* is conditioned by the singular position which Jesus Christ occupies in the Church.

Man's relationship to God depends, in the Christian view, not upon right *action* but upon a right attitude to *Jesus Christ*. This is the meaning of faith in the Pauline epistles; a striking example is offered by the strange phrase in Galatians 3:23 and 25: πρὸ τοῦ δὲ ἐλθειν τὴν πίστιν …. ἐλθούσησ δὲ τῆσ πίστεωσ…Paul does not mean to imply that *before* the appearance of Christ there was no faith, but that faith *now* centres in the person of the Messiah. Herein lies the reason for the characteristic emphasis upon the creed, which Kohler calls the *condition sine qua non* of the Christian Church. The creed, as the intellectual deposit of faith, is the only criterion, whether a man affirms or denies the claims the Church makes for Jesus of Nazareth.

But there is still one further point to be considered. Montefiore severely criticizes Christian theologians for presenting Judaism as a religion of external Law observance and Lohnsucht (passion for merit). This mistaken view has arisen from the position which the Law occupies in Judaism. Montefiore himself agrees with Weber that the Law forms the centre of the Jewish religion: "All radiates out from the Law, and from it all depends." The supremacy of the Law goes right through the whole history of Judaism. Even in Hermann Cohen's religious philosophy the emancipation of religion from ethics has not taken place. Cohen was not able to overcome the supremacy of the Law as completely as Felix Perles seems to imply. Faith and Law, religion and ethics are intertwined to a degree which makes any attempt at separation impossible. This utter dependence of religion upon ethics puts man in a position of independence *vis a vis* God which in the Christian view is nothing else but rebellion, for it ultimately implies that man is *able* to stand before God on his own merits. This the Church categorically denies.

757

Schoeps rightly regards St. Paul's assumption that man is unable of himself to keep the Law as alien to the spirit of Judaism. "Every Jew," says Dienemann, "is convinced that 'faith in the moral power of man' and 'Law,' upon the fulfillment of which that faith depends, are both inseparably connected." It is here that the difference reveals itself. The discussion, as throughout, turns round man's position *before* God. To the Synagogue, man appears as an independent agent capable of holding his own: "Thou canst" is its constant cry. Pauline theology, on the other hand, begins with the assumption that man is *unable* to keep the Law; he thus stands condemned before God. God in His mercy, however – and herein lies the meaning of the Gospel – sent His Son to die for sinners: "While we were yet sinners, Christ died for us" (Romans 5:8). It is thus that God becomes the Justifier of the ungodly (Romans 4:5). Romans 10:4, τέλοσ γαρ νόμου Χριστὸσ εἰσ δλκαιοσύνην ..., does not imply, therefore, arbitrary abrogation of the Law on the part of the Apostle. The end of the Law is in its completion, in the fact that God has accomplished on behalf of man what man was unable to do for himself. The "righteousness" of the believer is not his *own*; he owes it to God through the Messiah. Kohler says that loyalty to the Torah is an "all-penetrating principle of the Synagogue." What the Jew owes to the Torah, the Christian owes to Jesus Christ. But the difference lies not merely between loyalty to a *person* and loyalty to a *code*. Underneath the Cross man stands in the position of crisis, asking for grace; under the Scrolls of the Law, man stands in a position of self-assertiveness, giving *his* best. Thus the difference between Judaism and Christianity lies in the difference of *attitude*.

(h) Revelation

The connexion between Torah and revelation is obvious. Traditional Judaism has always claimed faith in revelation as a fundamental tenet of the Synagogue. The inference from the principle of revelation is the immutability of the Law. Maimonides, Hasdai, Albo, and others regard this as an essential belief of Judaism. The rigidity which such a tenet would inevitably impose upon Jewish thinking has been remedied by the conception of tradition. Next to the written Law (*torah she-beketab*) is the oral Law (*torah she-beal peh*), in the orthodox view both originating from Moses and enjoying equal sanctity. This principle of oral tradition accompanying the written Law provides Judaism with the possibility of growth and adaptability to circumstances. The rational tendency and the idea of progress are thus organically connected with the concept of revelation. This wide conception of Torah is already present in the teaching of the old Synagogue. When two schools of thought, like that of Hillel and Shammai, differed on a vital point, both claiming the right to *halakah*, the Talmud simply declared both right: "All words come from the same shepherd." The rabbis worked on the principle that the words of the Torah "are fruitful and multiply." Torah thus assumes a much wider meaning than the principle of immutability would imply. Indeed, the rabbis went so far as to maintain that all which was to be taught in the future was already communicated to Moses on Mount Sinai: "The doctrines of the Rabbis were the harvest from the seed which was sown at the time of the original Revelation."

This fluid and broad conception of revelation lends to Judaism a unique power of adjustment to the ever changing concepts in human development. All manifestations of the human spirit – all wisdom, all philosophy, all science – become thus, as it were, a diffusion of Torah, being related to the revelation of God. Once again we meet here the underlying principle of unity between God and the world. The totalitarian tendency of Judaism to extend religion to all spheres of life springs from this source. The division between the secular and the holy, the material and the spiritual is thus reduced to a minimum. The connexion between Spinoza's philosophy and the Jewish conception of revelation becomes evident. There is an undeniable pantheistic strain in Judaism which manifests itself in the narrow margin separating God from man. Hermann Cohen, who is determined to draw a clear dividing line between his ethical monotheism and Spinoza's pantheism, is only able to establish his case within the sphere of ethics. There is no denying that Spinoza's *amor intellectualis* and the categorical imperative derived from the law of Moses differ both in intensity and quality. But it is significant that the dividing-line appears most prominently within the sphere of ethics as nowhere else. The reason for this lies deeply embedded in the fibre of Judaism.

It is true that Judaism is deeply aware of God's transcendence; it is equally true that the Immanence of God is a vital element of Jewish piety. "Resting on this twofold anchorage," says Abelson, "Rabbinical Judaism was saved from destruction. Its outwardness and its inwardness were both necessary for its preservation." But the vital question which concerns us is, by what *means* does the transcendent God become immanent? In other words, under what conditions does the finite meet with the Infinite? To this Judaism has only one answer: *man* creates those conditions himself. By his piety, by his earnest endeavour, by his striving upwards he reduces the distance which divides him from the Holy One. The immanence of God is thus obtained by intrusion: it is left to man to break down the barrier which keeps him separate from God.

Here we come upon the internal connexion between Spinoza's philosophy and the Jewish conception of revelation. The great philosopher in his *Short Treatise on God, Man and his Well-being* asks the important question: how can God make himself known to man? Does it happen by means of the spoken word or by direct communication through himself? To this he answers: "We consider it to be unnecessary that it should happen through any other thing than the mere essence of God and the understanding of man; for, as the Understanding is that in us which must know God, and as it stands in such immediate union with him that it can neither be nor be understood without him, it is incontrovertibly evident from this that no things can ever come into such close touch with the Understanding as God himself can." Spinoza's point is that the affinity between the human and the divine Spirit is such that any intermediary instrument is not only unnecessary, but impossible: "Because we can never attain to the knowledge of God through any other thing (i.e. words, miracles or any other created thing), the nature of which is necessarily finite…for how is it possible that we should infer an infinite and limitless thing from a finite and limited thing?" Only on the assumption, therefore, that man and God partake of the same infinity is revelation possible. The process itself takes place within the soul of man. With this we should like to compare the statement made by the great Jewish theologian Kaufmann Kohler. In his article on "Revelation" in the Jewish Encyclopedia he describes the process as "the gradual unfolding of the divine powers in man." The difference between Israel and the other nations lies in that the Jewish race "has been endowed with peculiar religious powers that fitted it for the divine revelation." In view of these two statements it is difficult to see how Dr. Kohler can assert that the essential feature of revelation "is not merely a psychological process in which the human imagination or mental faculty constitutes the main factor." Can the "divine powers in man," we would ask, be legitimately segregated from the intellectual life of any individual? That Kohler's conception of revelation is a purely subjective one, and this in spite of his remark "that man is but the instrument upon which a superhuman force exerts its power" can be judged from his concluding remark. He finishes the article by saying: "Whether 'Torah' has not frequently a far broader and deeper meaning in the prophetic and other inspired books – denoting rather the universal law of human conduct, the Law of God as far as it is written upon the heart of man in order to render him a true son of God – is a question at issue between orthodoxy and reform.

The difference, however, between the orthodox and reformed conception of Torah is only a *formal* one. It turns round the position of the written Law within the wider concept of revealed Truth. While orthodoxy relates all truth in some way or another, to the Mosaic Law, liberal Judaism does not hesitate to brush the Law aside when it conflicts with reason. Montefiore thus bluntly declares: "Liberal Judaism no longer teaches a progressive religion, a progressive apprehension and unfolding of the will of God." But, strange as it may seem, there is no essential difference between the liberal and orthodox view. We shall find this affirmed by the example of H. Loewe, who describes himself as orthodox, but not as a "fundamentalist."

In his introduction to the Rabbinic Anthology he dwells upon the subject of revelation. "Judaism," Mr. Loewe explains, "whether orthodox or liberal, old or modern, teaches that God's Law is universal as well as immutable. What is true in nature is true in religion; what is false in science cannot be true in religion. Truth is one and indivisible. God is bound by his own laws." Between Torah and the laws of nature there is then no essential difference. Not only the Holy Scriptures, say Mr. Loewe, but also history and archaeology "have been vouchsafed to us by revelation." Revelation, he thus concludes, "is the silent imperceptible manifestation of God in history;" or to be more precise, "God in history is the definition of Revelation." If we ask in what relation then stands the Torah to this concept of revelation, Mr. Loewe has a twofold answer: (1) "Judaism regards the Torah as capable of expansion." He provides proof from Rabbinic literature to show that this is by no means a novel view. According to the rabbis "God's word," we are told, "is not an antiquated diatavgma, but one which is ever new, which men run to read. The Torah is 'your life,' and like life, it grows."

(2) Side by side with the doctrine of the immutability of the Torah "there is in Judaism a basic principle of the most potent mutability, the doctrine of progress."

It is clear to us that Mr. Loewe has sufficiently demonstrated the essential unity between the orthodox and the liberal view. On this subject, to use his own words again, "there is no difference between liberal and orthodox Jew." This fact is of the utmost importance, as it warns us from drawing too clear a line of demarcation between the two schools of thought.

It is evident then that between the Jewish and the Christian concept of revelation is a deep cleavage. The cleft appears not in the question as to the primacy of the Bible or value of biblical criticism, but over the problem of history. In the Jewish view history is essentially the manifestation of unfolding of God's will. It is on these grounds that revelation and history can be linked up in one straight line. "In Judaism," say Leo Baech, "the Kingdom of God is not a kingdom above the world, or opposed to it, or even side by side with it. It is rather the answer to the world…the reconciliation of its finiteness with its infiniteness." Between the kingdom of God and this world there is no qualitative difference, but only a difference of degree. Human history progressively unfolds God's purpose. All that happens within the experience of man serves a higher end. History becomes thus the supreme test of good and evil. What survives is good, what is unable to survive is evil. It is for this reason that thinkers like Rosenzweig, Buber, Schoeps, and others have included Christianity within the general scheme of salvation. It withstood the test of history; it thus proved its value and is therefore God-willed.

The Christian position, however, is diametrically opposed to such a view. Revelation, to the Christian Church, is not something that runs alongside the world, and certainly not something that merges with it; it is something that stands *opposed* to it. The word of God is primarily a word of judgment, a condemnation of history. Between God and the world stands the Cross of Jesus Christ. The meaning of the incarnation is that the continuity of history has been broken at a definite point. Whatever progress can mean for mankind, it *cannot* mean that man is able to advance to a position *beyond* the place where Jesus Christ stood. In the Christian view revelation is thus concentrated in his person. The value of the Bible is that it points to him. It is for this reason that the Church could maintain the unity between the Old and the New Testament. The very fact that the Old and New Testaments were knit together into one whole refutes the view of a progressive unfolding of God in history. The idea of endless evolution is excluded not merely by the fact of the Canon but by the position which Jesus Christ occupies in the Christian Faith.

The existence of a *new* Testament never meant to the Church that the *old* one had been outgrown, but that it had reached its culminating point in the Messiah. In the words of Luther: "*Christus universae scripturae scopus est.*" Schleiermacher's opinion, therefore, that Christianity is a new and different religion, detached from the Old Testament, does not represent the view of the historic Church. Mr. Davies' *via media*:

761

Christianity grew out of Judaism, but "in the marvelous personality, life and teaching of Jesus, we have a new beginning," also fails to understand the Christian point of view. His underlying principle is the idea of evolution, which extends not only in the sphere of human existence, but to God's dealing with man. The view the Church has taken is perhaps best expressed in Prof. Macmurray's words: "Jesus is at once the culmination of Jewish prophecy and the source of Christianity. These are not two different aspects of the life of Jesus. They are the same things referred backwards into the past and forward into the future."

Revelation, as far as God's dealing with man is concerned, the Church finds not outside but *inside* the Canon. The Canon forms, as it were, the periphery of revelation, its centre being Jesus Christ. This unique position assigned to the Messiah runs contrary to the whole Jewish conception. "That word from the burning bush," says Buber, "'I will be present as the one who will be present' (*i.e.* as the one I am ever present), makes it for us impossible to accept something that happened but once as the final revelation of God."

The reasons for objecting to the singling out of one person and attaching to him revelational significance are not difficult to find: (1) Jewish anthropology demands absolute equality of the human race. All men stand basically in the same relation to God. At no point may the chain of humanity be broken. (2) The superiority of the Torah and Israel's unique position in the process of revelation cannot admit revelation to be vested in an individual person. (3) The concept of revelation understood in terms of continuous growth contradicts all claims to finality: "The richness of the religion is not contained in a single one.… The whole content of Judaism truly lies in its unended and unending history."

Modern Jewish thought, deeply impressed by the idea of evolution, inevitably tends to deny absolute validity to religious values. The Christian emphasis upon the historical, the concrete, the individual, clashes with the basic principle of evolution. Herein modern Judaism differs vitally from the old Hebrew attitude to history. A-historical thinking in terms of the general and the abstract is alien to the Bible. It always speaks in terms of *concrete* events. To regard the concrete individual case as a mere manifestation of the general and the abstract, a mere fraction of the pattern which is to evolve by way of endless evolution, is Greek and not Hebrew. It is for this reason that Greece had no real sense for the historical; instead of concrete history it developed an abstract mythology, where the heroes of history became shadows or symbols of an idea.

Christianity, by its very nature, is anchored in history. The Christian Messiah is not a mythological abstraction but a historical person. He lived, taught, died at a definite moment in history. It is on behalf of a historical person that the Church makes stupendous claims. These claims have the nature of finality: there will never be a person to bring to mankind a more complete revelation or a greater truth. It is on this issue that Judaism and Christianity part.[1878]

[1878] Jakob Jocz. *The Jewish People and Jesus Christ: A Study in the Controversy Between Church and Synagogue* (London: S.P.C.K., 1954), 262-296.

Appendix 7
Anti-Missionary Teaching Against Biblical Faith

It is commonly said that Judaism is not a religion of creeds but deeds. If Judaism has a creed, it is the 13 Articles of Faith penned by Moses Maimonides in the 12th century. Judaism holds closely to the Articles of Faith particularly in the Orthodox and ultra-Orthodox communities. Articles 2 and 12 are of the most interest to Christians concerned with witnessing to Jewish people. In reading through these Articles of Faith remember that these statements largely are a statement against Christianity in what they believe positively.

Maimonides Articles of Faith

1. I believe with perfect faith that the creator, blessed be his name, is the author and guide of everything that has been created, and that he alone has made, does make, and will make all things.

2. I believe with perfect faith that the creator, blessed be his name, is a unity, and that there is no unity in any manner like unto his, and that he alone is our God, who was, is, and will be.

3. I believe with perfect faith that the creator, blessed be his name, is not a body, and that he is free from all the accidents of matter, and that he has not any form whatsoever.

4. I believe with perfect faith that the creator, blessed be his name, is the first and the last.

5. I believe with perfect faith that the creator, blessed be his name, and to him alone it is right to pray, and that it is not right to pray to any being besides him.

6. I believe with perfect faith that all words of the prophets are true.

7. I believe with perfect faith that the prophecy of Moses our teacher, peace be unto him, was true, and that he was the chief of the prophets, both of those who preceded and of those that followed him.

8. I believe with perfect faith the whole law, now in our possession, is the same that was given to Moses our teacher, peace be unto him.

9. I believe with perfect faith that this law will not be changed, and that there will never be any other law from the creator, blessed be his name.

10. I believe with perfect faith that the creator, blessed be his name, knows every deed of the children of men, and all their thoughts, as it is said, it is he that fashioneth the hearts of them all, that giveth heed to all their deeds (Psalm 33:15).

11. I believe with perfect faith that the creator, blessed be his name, rewards those that keep his commandments, and punishes those that transgress them.

12. I believe with perfect faith in the coming of the Messiah, and though he tarry, I will wait daily for his coming.

13. I believe with perfect faith that there will be a resurrection of the dead at the time when it shall please the creator, blessed be his name, and exalted be the remembrance of him for ever and ever.[1879]

Maimonides rejected the tri-unity of God as idolatrous, or at best tri-theism (the worship of three gods), which would eliminate from their perspective all the messianic passages that deal with the Messiah being God and the redeemer of the world. Since they have rejected *Yeshua* as the Messiah and have embraced 45 other false messiahs the teaching is that "though he tarry, I will wait daily for his coming."

Anti-Missionary Arguments
Against Nature of the Messiah and His Coming

This section will give a sampling of quotations of these anti-missionaries and how they look at the doctrines of the Tri-unity of God, the Virgin Birth and the incarnation of Messiah, the genealogy of *Yeshua*, *Yeshua* being the Mediator between God and man, and the second coming of Messiah *Yeshua*. We will also look at such doctrines as Original Sin and its close connection to their teaching on the Evil Inclination, Redemption or Atonement. Their teaching on the New Testament being anti-Semitic will be addressed to help New Covenant believers understand the perspective and response from Jewish people when they are approached by those holding to biblical faith. Sometimes many of the doctrines will not come to the surface in a discussion with a Jewish person, but their thinking would still relate to what they have been taught. Also another factor is that well over 50% of Jewish people today are secular, meaning that they are completely ignorant of their Scriptures and know nothing about these doctrines except for some vague ideas. In listening to a lecture given by an anti-missionary, it was amazing to see how little content was given to the Jewish audience and how much emotion and hype were used to speak negatively of what Christians teach. It was very sad to realize as I looked around at the Jewish audience, that probably all of them were completely ignorant of what the Hebrew Scripture teaches; they were like putty in anti-missionaries' hands. One thing is sure, whether you are speaking to an ultra-Orthodox or secular Jewish people the following two statements will be given in one fashion or another: "You cannot believe in Jesus and be Jewish," or "I was born a Jew and I will die a Jew."

[1879] Cohn-Sherbok, *The Jewish Messiah*, 181-182. An in-depth book on the 13 Articles of Faith by J. David Bleich, *With Perfect Faith: The Foundation of Jewish Belief* (New York: KTAV Publishing House, 1983).

The format of this appendix is that first the comments of the anti-missionaries will be given and then at the end they will be responded to. Certain sections will be set in bold typeface or italics to draw your attention to statements that you need to grasp. First we start out with a quotation which accuses the Christians of changing the picture of the Messiah that Rabbinic Judaism believes the *Tanakh* presented:

> As you know, the Jews were in Israel for around 1000 years [actually 1500] before Jesus appeared. They had a definite concept of what the Messiah would be like – there was a status quo regarding the nature of the Messiah. The Christians appeared and introduced an entirely different picture of what the Messiah would be like (son of God, God incarnate, born of virgin, two comings, etc.). Thus, the Christians changed the status quo concept of the Messiah, and so the full burden of proof rests upon them.[1880]

The full burden of proof rests on Rabbinic Judaism and not New Covenant believers for they elevated the Oral Law over the Written Law of God as well as their absolute refusal to recognize the plurality of God which is in abundance in the *Tanakh*. Yes, from the days of the Pharisees before and after Jesus' birth up to today Rabbinic Judaism has a prescribed view of the Messiah, His character and military ability to restore the Kingdom of David. However, what they did was ignore the passages that spoke of the Messiah being Divine because of their belief in absolute monotheism which leaves no room for the promised "Son of David" being the God/man. Naturally then, their status quo was disturbed because their own Scriptures speak against their prescribed bias and misconception of Messiah and the very nature of God. That was the whole purpose of this book: to demonstrate from the Hebrew Scripture alone that God did present Himself to His people in plurality of unity.

Now sit back and read these comments with utter amazement for the lack of scholarship and the falsehoods leveled against biblical faith and the absolute denial of biblical truths.

Anti-Missionaries: Tri-unity (Trinity)

There are three core issues that Judaism rejects concerning Jesus and Christianity: they are the Trinity, the Incarnation and Mediation. Though not a complete list, these are issues Judaism uses in its attempt to disprove New Covenant faith before a Jewish readership. That Jewish readership has never studied the *Tanakh* on their own and are very vulnerable to the teaching of these anti-missionaries:

> Worship of any **three-part god by a Jew is nothing less than a form of idolatry. The three-part God of Christianity is not the G-d of Judaism.** Therefore, in the Jewish view, **Christianity may very well be a variation of idolatry**. Although Christianity began among Jews, it was rapidly adopted by

---

[1880] Levine, *You Take Jesus, I'll Take God: How to Refute Christian Missionaries,* 12.

the pagans of the ancient world. **These pagans believed in an entire pantheon of gods. It was just too much for them to give up all these gods in favor of the One True G-d. So early Christian missionaries compromised with these pagans by introducing the Trinity, a sort of three-in-one god.** Even many **contemporary Christian scholars** see the Trinity as the result of pagan influence on Christianity.[1881]

Yet the Christians feel that there can be **three separate gods** who are really one. This is not a matter of theological profundity, but rather, illogical thinking which no thinking person should accept.[1882]

Israel progressed from image-worship to one, invisible God, Christianity regressed when an intercessor became necessary to approach God.[1883]

Since the whole book *Discovering the Mystery of the Unity of God* was dedicated to show that God did reveal Himself to Israel as a plural unity of one, the time will not be taken for a lengthy rebuttal of these statements. But just a couple of short comments will suffice. Since the Protestant Reformation we have parted company with the Roman Catholic Church. Not being raised Catholic I cannot speak for them. However, this much I know: When the early church in 325 CE at the Council of Nicea dealt with the issue of the "Trinity," they affirmed and confirmed that the Scriptures, both the Hebrew Scriptures and the New Testament clearly saw the plural unity of *Elohim*. It is true that in the following centuries the Catholic Church compromised many issues for the benefit of the pagans. But the Tri-unity of God was settled long before all that took place. As you well know, true biblical faith has never accepted "three gods in one." As to contemporary Christian scholars, understand they are referring to liberal scholars who reject most of the Bible and we as fundamental Bible believers in *Yeshua* parted company with them back in the 1920-'40s. As to Chaim Picker's statement, it becomes clear that he does not even understand the Scriptures he says that he is defending. Israel from the beginning worshipped *Echad* (ONE) invisible God who revealed Himself through theophanies to His people. The reality is that Scripture shows that it was Israel who "regressed" and not true biblical faith, to worship many gods, except for the faithful remnant.

The next section deals with the Incarnation and the Virgin Birth. Their comments show their complete lack of understanding in the nature of God. They really try to confine God and put Him in their theological box. Two things God will not do; one He will not sin for He is completely holy and righteous and second, He will not force His will on anyone. If God chooses to reveal Himself in a physical form as He did in the past, He can do that. If God chooses to come as a man and live among men He is all powerful and can do that as well. Judaism reacts because of their past problems of

---

[1881] Kaplan, *The Real Messiah? A Jewish Response to Missionaries,* 15.

[1882] Levine, *You Take Jesus, I'll Take God: How to Refute Christian Missionaries,* 77.

[1883] Picker, "Make Us A God!" *A Jewish Response to Hebrew Christianity: A Survival Manual for Jews,* 98.

"regressing" back to paganism and now have swung to the opposite extreme by saying that the Virgin Birth and Incarnation are impossible.

Anti-Missionaries: Virgin Birth and the Incarnation

Nowhere does the Bible predict that the Messiah will be born to a virgin. In fact, virgins never give birth anywhere in the Bible. This idea is to be found only in pagan mythology. **To the Jewish mind, the very idea that G-d would plant a seed in a woman is unnecessary and unnatural. After all, – what is accomplished by this claim? What positive purpose does it serve**?

Judaism believes that G-d is eternal, above and beyond time, G-d **cannot** be born, He **cannot** die, He **cannot** suffer, He **cannot** "become flesh", **nor can** He be divided into sections ("Father, Son, and Holy Ghost"). These are pagan notions.[1884]

Judaism says: Nowhere does our Bible say that the Messiah would be a god or G-d like. The very idea that G-d would take on human form is **repulsive to Jews** because it contradicts our concept of G-d as being above and beyond the limitations of the human body and situation. **Jews believe that G-d alone is to be worshipped, not a being who is His creation, be he angel, saint, or even the Messiah himself**.[1885]

God is the Ultimate, the Infinite, the All Powerful Creator of all things. **To say that any man was G-d is, to the Jew, the height of absurdity**.[1886]

In the first quotation I want to answer "what is accomplished by this claim." First of all Judaism does not believe in someone who saves them from sin. They believe their sins can be atoned for by repentance, prayer and good deeds, which will be seen later. Having said that, sinful man cannot atone for his own sin or anyone else's. However, if God who is spirit chooses to be born from the womb of a virgin by speaking the word, cannot God do that? The answer is a resounding yes, He is all powerful. At that point the God/man that is born is fully God and fully man, and being both He can be born, He can die, He can suffer, He can take on flesh, and He is still indivisible as a member of the plural unity of *Elohim*.

The Hebrew Bible clearly sets forth a clear presentation of the Messiah, Son of David, the Righteous Branch, Immanuel, that He is indeed God as has been pointed out in numerous places in this book. But if they refuse to see the multitude of plural references that God makes of Himself, for the Bible is His word, then their preset bias is faulty. The Bible teaches that a man cannot be god, unless God chooses to take on "flesh" and dwell among men as the God/man.

[1884] Aryeh Kaplan, *The Real Messiah? A Jewish Response to Missionaries*, 52-61.

[1885] Aryeh Kaplan, *The Real Messiah? A Jewish Response to Missionaries,* 52.

[1886] Aryeh Kaplan, *The Real Messiah? A Jewish Response to Missionaries,* 18.

In the next section the subject of the need of a Mediator to take the sin of mankind on Himself and die for them is not acceptable in Judaism. Man needs a Mediator between himself and a Holy God. The animal sacrifices only provided a covering for sin. It was to prepare the Jewish people for the time when He would come as that Mediator, not to cover sin but to remove it completely so that man could have immediate access to God in life and upon death.

Anti-Missionaries and a Mediator

When G-d says "Before Me," He is stressing that you should not believe in any other deity, even if You believe in G-d as well. **One who sets up a mediator between G-d and man is guilty of violating this Commandment.** (Exod 20:3)

If a man believes in G-d, then why should he need any **other deity?** But a person might think that G-d is so high as to be unapproachable without a mediator. The opening statement of the Ten Commandments teaches us that this is also idolatry.

G-d is infinite and all-knowing. To say that He needs a mediator to hear our prayers is to deny His infinite wisdom.

If Jesus actually made these statements recorded in the Gospel (John 14:6; cf. 1 Tim 2:5), **then he was advocating idolatry, with himself as the deity.**[1887]

...the Israelite personally entreated God's forgiveness – without a mediator! Israel did not need a mediator; God was present with his people.[1888]

The fundamental problem with their statements are the two words "other deity." New Covenant believers in Messiah *Yeshua* do not believe Him to be another deity, but they do believe that God in the person of His Son who gave the 10 commandments in Exodus 20 is a plural unity of *echad* [one] *Elohim*. Are you breaking the commandment when that mediator is God Himself? New Covenant believers do not pray to *Yeshua* but pray to the Father in the name of *Yeshua*. Why? Because He by becoming the believer's sin-bearer is the access for a sinful man to approach a Holy God. Israel always had a mediator, the priests and the High Priest were human mediators for the people. They prepared and offered the sacrifice for the individual sinner who brought the live lamb to the altar. The High Priest with the blood of the lamb, and I repeat with the blood of the Lamb, went behind the veil into the presence of God to have their sins atoned for. But that atonement only lasted one year, because the same thing had to be repeated the

---

[1887] Kaplan, *The Real Messiah? A Jewish Response to Missionaries*, 19.

[1888] Picker, "Make Us A God!" *A Jewish Response to Hebrew Christianity: A Survival Manuel tor Jews*, 97-98.

following year, year after year. If there was no mediator in the *Tanakh* in the person of the High Priest, their sins were not atoned for. If anyone else tried to go beyond the veil with blood besides the High Priest, God would strike him dead on the spot. Israel needed and had mediators all through the tabernacle and temple periods. So they are completely inaccurate when they say Israel never had a mediator. Mankind needs a mediator and that Mediator is the God/man who came the first time to suffer and die to be the ultimate atonement for sin.

The next area that they reject with almost equal fervour is the whole concept of the two comings of the Messiah. They embrace two messiahs coming one after the other, but not a Messiah who comes and dies and then waits 2000 and more plus years before He comes again to restore the kingdom.

Anti-Missionaries: The Second Coming

Nowhere does the Jewish Bible say that the Messiah would come once, be killed, and return again in a "second coming." The idea of a second coming is a pure rationalization of Jesus' failure to function in any way as a messiah, or to fulfill any of the prophecies of the Torah or the Prophets. The idea is purely a Christian invention, with no foundation in the Bible.[1889]

In this section the subject will be dealt with more individually. The Jewish Bible has been shown throughout and it does maintain that the Messiah does come first and will be rejected by His own people. God will not impose Himself on a nation that does not want Him. What is interesting about God is that He could force Himself upon Israel as the Messiah, but He wants to be freely accepted by an act of the will of the nation of Israel. They, by an act of their will, rejected Him and He will only come the second time when Israel finally turns to Him, and freely, by an act of their will, will believe that *Yeshua* is God who is seated at the right hand of the Father and accept Him. Then He will return in the clouds of glory. This they will do near the end of Holocaust II, biblically known as "*the Day of the LORD*" or "*the Time of Jacob's Trouble.*" This is not a Christian invention, it is a Jewish denial.

The Jewish Messiah is expected to return the Jews to their land. Jesus was born while the Jews still lived in their land, before they had gone into exile. **He could not restore them to their land because they were still living in it.**

Judaism says that *Yeshua* was not the Messiah because the Jewish people were in the Land when He was there. They propose that He could not have regathered Israel to the Land if they were already in it. It is historically accurate to state that when *Yeshua* lived on the earth, there were then as today more Jewish people living outside the land of Israel than in it. The majority of Israel lived in the Roman Empire which included

---

[1889] Kaplan, *The Real Messiah? A Jewish Response to Missionaries*, 55.

Egypt and the rest of North Africa, Spain, Italy, Greece, Asia Minor (Turkey) and that does not even include the multitudes of Jewish people living in the ancient lands of Assyria, Babylon and Persia. It was also known that Jewish people lived in Ethiopia, India, and the Saudi Arabian Peninsula, which includes Yemen. Jewish people may have even made their way to China by that time as well as France, Germany, the Balticans etc. So it is paramount that true and reliable facts be presented to Jewish people.

The true Messiah is to rebuild the Temple in Jerusalem – but Jesus lived while the Temple was still standing.

The Jewish Bible says that the Messiah will redeem Israel. In the case of Jesus, the very opposite took place. Not long after his death, the Holy Temple in Jerusalem was destroyed, Jerusalem was laid to waste, and the Jews went into exile to begin a 1900 year long night of persecution, – largely at the hands of the followers of this self-styled "Messiah"!

The Prophets in the Bible foretold that when the Messiah comes, **all the nations of the world will unite to acknowledge and worship the one true G-d**.

If *Yeshua* would have been accepted by the nation of Israel as their Messiah, which the Prophets said would not happen, when He first presented Himself, *Yeshua* would have been proclaimed the King of Israel by the nation. The Romans would have taken that as a direct revolt against them, they would have taken *Yeshua* and crucified him and as a result the "city" and the "sanctuary" would also have still been destroyed. *Yeshua* had to first fulfill the promise made to Satan (Genesis 3:15) in the hearing of Adam and Eve that he (Satan) would be destroyed and sin that has cursed this whole earth in every area of life; human, animal, earthquakes, floods, disease, and agriculture, to name only a few, would be reversed to the way it originally was in the garden of Eden. *Yeshua* then would have been raised from the dead victorious. He then would have destroyed the Roman Empire and fulfilled the covenant to Abraham first and redeemed Israel. In the process of all that, the people would be regathered, with no long exile of 1900 years, from all the nations of the earth and the temple described in Ezekiel 40-48 would be built. That would be the likely scenario if Israel had accepted Him. At that time Messiah *Yeshua* would reign over all the nations of the earth from His throne in rebuilt Jerusalem, and all those nations would come up to Jerusalem to worship Him there. But that was not reality, nor was that what the prophets said. Judaism presented the (first) Messiah as being killed in the battle with Gog and Magog, but biblical prophecy and history clearly shows and states that His own people would reject Him and turn Him over to the Romans to be crucified, and that is history. The "long night of persecution" will be dealt with in the last part of this section.

The Jews never had the concept of a second coming, and since it was the Jews themselves who first taught the notion of a Messiah, via the **Jewish prophets**, it seems quite **reasonable to respect their opinion more than anyone else's.**[1890]

The reality of this statement is that New Covenant believers do "respect their [prophets'] opinion more than anyone else's." It is a shame that Rabbinic Judaism does not "respect their opinion more than anyone else's," but they value their own opinion over the prophets' by the elevation of oral tradition over the prophets.

> Judaism does not envisage a world-wide destruction like the flood (Gen. 8:21; 9:11). Society is redeemable (Gen. 4:7) and Messiah's coming is hastened by man's efforts to improve the world. Man is a participant in history not a spectator in a cosmic drama.[1891]

Yes, Rabbinic Judaism does envision a worldwide destruction not like the flood where only 8 people survived. Well over 3 billion people during "the Time of Jacob's Trouble" will die worldwide, and that is destruction. Here are some quotations from a rabbi as to the conditions at the time of the coming of *Moshiach*:

> The time appointed by G-d for the Messianic redemptions a closely guarded secret (*Pesachim* 54b; *Midrash Tehilim* 9:2. See *Zohar Chadash, Bereishit*, 8a). Nonetheless, we are offered many hints to recognize its proximity: when certain conditions come about, await the imminent coming of *Moshiach*. Most of these conditions are quite disturbing, clearly is playing a situation of the very "bottom of the pit" (*Midrash Tehilim* 45:3. See *Ma'amarei Admur Hazaken-Ethalech*, p. 103f.; and *Besha'ah Shehikdimu*-5672, vol. I: p. 551; relating this to the principle [*Midrash Tehilim* 22:4; *Zohar* II:46a] that the darkest moments of the night are immediately before daybreak). One major source describes the world-condition in those days as follows: increase in insolence and impudence; oppressing inflation; unbridled irresponsibility on the part of authorities; centers of learning will turn into bawdy houses; wars; many destitutes begging, with none to pity them; wisdom shall be putrid; the pious shall be despised; truth will be abandoned; the young will insult the old; family-breakup with mutual recriminations; impudent leadership (*Sotab* 49b).

> Other sources add: lack of scholars; succession of troubles and evil decrees; famines; mutual denunciations; epidemics of terrible diseases; poverty and scarcity; cursing and blaspheming; international confrontations – nations provoking and fighting each other (*Sanhedrin* 97a; *Shir Rabba* 2:29). In short, it will be a time of suffering that will make it look as if G-d were asleep. These

---

[1890] Levine, *You Take Jesus, I'll Take God: How to Refute Christian Missionaries,* 23.
[1891] Picker, "Make Us A God!" *A Jewish Response to Hebrew Christianity: A Survival Manual for Jews,* 126.

773

are the birthpangs of Mashiach, bearable only in anticipation of the bliss that follows them.[1892]

This quotation from an Orthodox rabbi clearly presents that Judaism is expecting some very hard days ahead, which is the exact opposite of what Chaim Picker, anti-missionary, stated. Now also to be evenly balanced, the rabbi goes on to present the view that this does not have to be:

> The troubles and agony of *chevlei Mashiach* (birthpangs of Mashiach), however, are not unavoidable: "What is man to do to be spared the pangs of Mashiach"? Let him engage in Torah and acts of loving-kindness (Sanhedrin 98b).[1893]

With this Rabbi Schochet seems to agree with Chaim Picker. The author does not want to minimize "acts of loving-kindness" and the study of the Scriptures. However, by the word Torah that is not what Rabbi Schochet is implying. In his statement to "engage in Torah," he is referencing the study of all rabbinic literature and not the Scriptures alone. Notice the underlying faulty premise that man can better the world. That is completely anti-biblical. Man has made many wonderful technological improvements for the human race, but the basic nature of man remains and will continue to remain unchanged. Only Messiah can change the nature of man. Man cannot make the world morally better and free from sin, for man himself is born in sin.

> The belief in the coming of Mashiach and the Messianic redemption is one of the fundamental principles of the Jewish faith. Every Jew must believe that Mashiach will arise and restore the kingdom of David to its original state and sovereignty, rebuild the *Bet Hamikdash* (Holy Temple of Jerusalem), gather the dispersed of Israel, and in his days all the laws of the Torah shall be reinstituted as they had been aforetimes.[1894]

The first part of this quote has been dealt with earlier; however, all the laws of Torah being reinstituted as before the destruction of the second temple is not biblically accurate, for Ezekiel 40-48 clearly presents a different picture.

> Any time is a potential time for the coming of Mashiach. This does not mean, however, that at the appropriate time he will suddenly emerge from Heaven to

---

[1892] Schochet, *Mashiach: The Principle of Mashiach and the Messianic Era in Jewish Law and Tradition*, 34-36.

[1893] Schochet, *Mashiach: The Principle of Mashiach and the Messianic Era in Jewish Law and Tradition*, 36.

[1894] Schochet, *Mashiach: The Principle of Mashiach and the Messianic Era in Jewish Law and Tradition*, 17.

appear on earth. On the contrary Mashiach is already on earth, a human being of great saintly status (a *tzadik*) appearing and existing in every generation.[1895]

In Orthodox Judaism a potential Messiah is always there and in the future God will have the "unique pre-existing soul of Mashiach – 'stored' in Ga[rde]n [of] Eden from aforetimes – will descend and be bestowed upon the *tzadik"[1896]* [or righteous man] which is described below:

> With respect to his arising, he will not be known beforehand until it is declared to him … a man, unknown prior to his manifestation, shall rise, and the signs and wonders that will come about through him will be the proof for the authenticity of his claim and pedigree…[1897]

In Rabbinic Judaism the Messiah is not the God/man, one individual for one time in history to come be the sacrifice for sin and the same individual to come and restore Israel. To them that potential messiah is living in each generation and will be revealed at God's timing.

> The actual date of the Messianic redemption is a guarded mystery unknown to man. It will happen "in its time" (Isa 60:22), predetermined from the beginning of creation…. Even so, the wording of Isa 60:22 seems to display a contradiction by stating "in its time I will hasten it": "in its time" means a set date; "*I will hasten it*" means that it may occur earlier, *before* "its time." The contradiction is resolved as follows: "If they are worthy — 'I will hasten it:' if not — 'in its time.'"[1898]

They continue to give two guides to hasten the coming of *Moshiach*, first is special *Mitzvot* with four things listed: *Teshuvah, Shabbat, Torah-study* and *Tzedakah*.[1899] The second is the unity of Israel. They reference Micah 2:12-13 that if Israel has internally and external unity the *Moshiach* will come. The following example is given:

[1895] Schochet, *Mashiach: The Principle of Mashiach and the Messianic Era in Jewish Law and Tradition*, 38.

[1896] Schochet, *Mashiach: The Principle of Mashiach and the Messianic Era in Jewish Law and Tradition*, 39.

[1897] Schochet, *Mashiach: The Principle of Mashiach and the Messianic Era in Jewish Law and Tradition*, 39.

[1898] Schochet, *Mashiach: The Principle of Mashiach and the Messianic Era in Jewish Law and Tradition*, 45.

[1899] Schochet, *Mashiach: The Principle of Mashiach and the Messianic Era in Jewish Law and Tradition*, 48-50. *Teshuvah* will bring about an immediate redemption, "Today, if you will listen to His voice" (Psa 95:7). This comprehensive principle of submission to G-d and His will, thus is the most obvious means to bring about the immediate coming of Mashiach. *Shabbat*; if Israel will keep just one Shabbat properly, Mashiach will come immediately. *Torah-study* is equivalent to all [the *mitzvot*]. *Tzedakah*, too, is equivalent to all the *mitzvot*. Our compassion for the needy and downcast evokes a reciprocal compassion from Heaven, thus hastening the day of the scion of David (Mashiach) and the days of our redemption.

Notwithstanding the idyllic *ritual* observance in the days of the Second Temple, dissension, gratuitous hatred and divisiveness, caused the destruction of the *Bet Hamikdash* and the present *galut* (Yoma 9b; and see also Tossefta, Menachot 13:22). Rectification of this condition will bring about the restoration of the *Bet Hamikdash* and the Messianic redemption.[1900]

This is what they attribute the destruction of the second temple and Jerusalem to, not to the rejection of the Messiah after the end of the 69th week of Daniel. They reject the two comings of the Messiah, first to be the vicarious sacrifice for the sins of the world and then the second time to set up the Kingdom fulfilling the promises made to Abraham, Isaac and Jacob as well as to all those Jewish people who lived and walked out their belief in faith.

Anti-Missionaries: *Yeshua's* Genealogy

The genealogy of the New Testament proves that Jesus was not from David. Jesus is considered by the New Testament to be a child of God, who is not from the tribe of Judah, nor any other tribe. Jesus is therefore not the subject of Micah 5:1 or 2.[1901]

Some Christians have answered this question in a most unusual fashion – they claim that Mary was from David! Of course, this answer is terrible, because there is no source for that.[1902]

The Bible says that the Messiah would be descended in a direct line from King David. However, if G-d was Jesus' "father," is it not somewhat ridiculous to claim that he is descended from King David on his father's side?[1903]

Jews reckoned legal descent through the father. But the genealogies of Jesus in Matthew and Luke, which trace Jesus' lineage through Joseph, are irrelevant; Joseph was not Jesus' biological father. Mary's genealogy is missing.[1904]

This material will not be dealt with again for it was handled clearly in chapter 17 of this book, entitled the Branch.

The next two sections have to be dealt with together because in Judaism they are inseparably linked together: the complete denial of original sin and what they replace it with, the inclination towards good and evil.

[1900] Schochet, *Mashiach: The Principle of Mashiach and the Messianic Era in Jewish Law and Tradition*, 53.

[1901] Levine, *You Take Jesus, I'll Take God: How to Refute Christian Missionaries,* 36.

[1902] Levine, *You Take Jesus, I'll Take God: How to Refute Christian Missionaries,* 79.

[1903] Kaplan, *The Real Messiah? A Jewish Response to Missionaries,* 55.

[1904] Picker, "Make Us A God!" *A Jewish Response to Hebrew Christianity: A Survival Manual for Jews,* 59.

Anti-Missionaries: Original Sin

> Being created from the dust implies mortality, perishability. What comes from the earth must eventually decompose and revert to its essential elements. Morality is man's natural and intended state; it is not due to Eden's transgression. The penalty for eating the forbidden fruit was not mortality – or the loss of immortality – but premature death.[1905]

Genesis 1 teaches that God created the heavens and the earth in six literal days. Man was created from the dust (ground) of the earth but that does not necessitate perishability. Man physically became perishable after his rebellion from God. Up until that time there was no death; that means no fossils, no pre-Adamic race, for until sin came into the world there was no death. Clearly man was created as an eternal being. It is not mandatory that the physical body must decompose, but sin brought separation (death) from God; a dead body will decompose. God purposely removed Adam and Eve from the Garden. Why? Lest they would eat of the tree of life and live forever as sinful people. Mankind was created to have fellowship with his Creator forever. Absolutely nothing in the *Tanakh* would indicate that the natural state of man was morality.

> Death is not necessarily due to sin; the "righteous" die as well.[1906]

This is almost not worthy of an answer. Of course the "righteous" die, they are sinners too! In the Hebrew Scriptures the "righteous" were righteous by faith and because they made the required sacrifice in the tabernacle or temple to deal with the sin they committed.

> God warned Adam: "In the day you eat of it you shall surely die." … God was telling Adam, "When you eat of it you shall surely die." But Adam lived 930 years! God mercifully rescinded his decree, as evidenced by his provision of skin-garments for Adam and Eve.[1907]

> Jesus provides "eternal, heavenly life." But such was not lost by Adam; he did not have it in the first place.[1908]

There is again no reference in the Scriptures that God rescinded His decree. You cannot teach what the Scriptures do not deal with. The key phrase in Genesis 5 are the words "and he died." God gave immortality to mankind, but when they sinned against God, He said that they would die. There is not even a hint that God created man to be only

---

[1905] Picker, "Make Us A God!" *A Jewish Response to Hebrew Christianity: A Survival Manuel for Jews,* 81.

[1906] Picker, "Make Us A God!" *A Jewish Response to Hebrew Christianity: A Survival Manuel for Jews,* 81.

[1907] Picker, "Make Us A God!" *A Jewish Response to Hebrew Christianity: A Survival Manuel for Jews,* 81.

[1908] Picker, "Make Us A God!" *A Jewish Response to Hebrew Christianity: A Survival Manuel for Jews,* 82.

mortal. Mankind lives forever, his body, soul, and spirit. What is death? It literally means separation. Man because of sin on a human level will be separated from family members, along with his soul and spirit, man is not annihilated; spiritually because of sin man is separated from God in his body, soul and spirit. When God clothed Adam and Eve with skins of animals, what is implied is that God made the first sacrifice of a lamb to show man that a perfect lamb was required to take the place for his sinful act, thus restoring fellowship with God. But the blood sacrifice did not remove the sin, it only covered that sin until the ultimate sacrifice would come and die. If man believes with his heart, not just with a religious act, he will in the future either live with God in heaven or ultimately be separated from God in Hell forever. This the Hebrew Scriptures teach, however Rabbinic Judaism does not.

> David's statement of being "conceived in sin and iniquity," is not a reference to *all* human birth, as though all are born in sin. David is not talking about sin as a "state" but as an individual *act*.[1909]

> [Eccl 7:20] "There is not a righteous person on earth who does good and sins not." This does not preclude the existence of righteous persons. Indeed, there are righteous persons, but they are not perfect.

> Jeremiah 17:9-10] "The heart is deceitful above all things, and desperately corrupt; who can understand it…. I YHVH search the mind and try the heart, to give to every man according to his way, according to the fruit of his doings." Adam is not blamed; the deceitful heart is in man's nature. Judgment is based on individual merit. The good inclination can overcome the evil and God rewards accordingly.[1910]

In all of these verses quoted from the *Tanakh*, Chaim Picker attempts to remove mankind from the obvious teaching by God that man is born a sinner and is separated from Himself. At the end of the last statement quoted the term "good and evil inclination" is used. It will be discussed in the next section, but what they do is attempt to replace sin with the evil inclination. It is not man's fault that he sins; it is God's according to the rabbis because God created the evil inclination.

> The Psalmist knows nothing of "original sin." There is universal sinfulness but not hereditary guilt. The evil inclination was created in Adam, not caused by his sin. Otherwise, he could not have been tempted.[1911]

> Sin is conquerable; its antidote is the Torah, the "Tree of Life." **We are responsible for our own sins**. Life and death, good and evil are in our hands.

[1909] Picker, "Make Us A God!" *A Jewish Response To Hebrew Christianity: A Survival Manuel For Jews,* 83.

[1910] Picker, "Make Us A God!" *A Jewish Response To Hebrew Christianity: A Survival Manuel For Jews,* 86

[1911] Picker, "Make Us A God!" *A Jewish Response To Hebrew Christianity: A Survival Manuel For Jews,* 87.

The world is not hostile, with an ever present "devil-tempter." Nor is it doomed and soon to pass away. Holiness is not through self-denial but through acts of loving kindness.[1912]

There is no doctrine of original sin. There is no teaching in any literature that man is morally depraved and cannot of his own accord satisfy a righteous God. This does not mean that sin is minimized. Sin is spelled out in detail and all of the literature deals with descriptions of sin in every aspect. The noncomformists saw almost everything and everyone outside of their groups as suspect. But, in every case, no man is considered so morally depraved that he cannot make the right choices and thereby obtain the good graces of God.[1913]

One fact among the falsehoods is true: "We are responsible for our own sins." Contrary to Rabbinic Judaism God requires a blood sacrifice; it was pictured for centuries in the blood sacrifice of a lamb offering by the priests in the temple. The ultimate lamb, the Lamb of God, came as the voluntary sacrifice that all the other sacrifices looked toward. Man is incapable of meriting anything before a holy righteous God, but Judaism teaches that man can earn merit from God and that is completely contrary to the Hebrew Bible. Judaism teaches that there is no original sin, thus man does not need a Saviour or Mediator to save him from his sins. Obedience to the law of Moses, both Oral and Written, with prayer, repentance and good works are sufficient to make them righteous in the eyes of God. There is only one problem: God never taught that man could lift himself up to God by his own boot straps.

Good and Evil Inclinations

Judaism believes that mankind is born with an inclination for good or evil. If mankind yields to the good inclination, he is okay before God. He may still do acts of sin but his good works, prayer and repentance will redeem him. Judaism does not believe, as was noted in the previous section, in original sin. To Judaism sin originated with Adam's sin but because man was given a free moral will, he was created with the ability to choose. God in Judaism created a good and evil inclination and mankind has the responsibility to choose good over evil. They do not say that God created sin, but that God created the good inclination (*yetzer ha-tov*) and evil inclination (*yetzer ha-ra*), so that mankind does not have a sin nature, but that he was created with an inclination to do either good or to do evil. In other words we are not bad (evil) people, we just need to learn to choose the good over the evil. In the following quotes different aspects of Judaism and their belief on the "evil inclination" are made:

[1912] Picker, "Make Us A God!" *A Jewish Response To Hebrew Christianity: A Survival Manuel For Jews,* 128.

[1913] Goldberg, *The Deviation of Jewish Thought from an Old Testament Theology in the Intertestamental Period,* 332-333.

We are created with a "good inclination" and an "evil inclination." This should not seem strange since everything in creation is attributed to God: "**I make peace and create evil: I, YHVH, do all these things**" (Isa 45:7; cf. Deut 32:39). **The evil inclination" is innate; it is not due to Adam's transgression** (Gen 8:20-21; Psa 103:13-14). **The "good inclination" can overcome the "evil inclination"** (Gen 4:7; Psa 119:33). This is not mankind in a "pre-sin" state but is an ongoing condition! The Psalmist takes no account of the "Eden transgression" and Jesus never mentions the "Fall of Adam." **Hebrew Scripture does not present a "depraved, sin-laden" man.**[1914]

There is no contradiction. **Although the yetzer ha-ra, the "evil inclination" is operative, we can be righteous. Human sinfulness is not connected to Adam. Repentance, not "vicarious atonement," erases sin-guilt**.[1915]

In Judaism, it is not the "flesh" that is sinful but man. Man is good or evil: "The soul that sins, it shall die" (Ezek 18:4). "Carnal," meaning "evil," (Rom 7:14; 1 Cor. 3:1, 3) and "worldly," meaning "ungodly," (Titus 2:12; 1 Jn. 2:16) are foreign to Judaism. **Good works atone for sin and the antidote for sin is God's law** (Prov. 3:18). Christianity emphasizes creed – "You shall believe"; Judaism emphasizes deed – "You shall do."[1916]

Sin is conquerable; its antidote is the Torah, the "Tree of Life." We are responsible for our own sins. Life and death, good and evil are in our hands. The world is not hostile, with an ever present "devil-tempter." Nor is it doomed and soon to pass away. **Holiness is not through self-denial but through acts of loving kindness**.[1917]

I want to make two points out of these quotations: First is the misuse of Isaiah 45:7 where they attempt to lay at God's "feet" that He created evil in order to remove the sin nature or evil inclination from man's shoulders to God's. This verse does not teach that God created evil, but that God can bring evil things upon a disobedient nation like drought, earthquakes, invasion of foreign armies and insects to destroy the Land, etc.

The second point is that the Hebrew Scriptures do not present a "depraved sin-laden" man. Look at the picture the Scripture and history itself paint of man's depravity. Genesis 5 is dedicated to death because of the sin in Genesis 3. In Genesis 6 God sees so much wickedness on the earth that He destroys the world by a flood saving only eight people. In the period of the patriarchs it is clearly seen that mankind had

---

[1914] Picker, "Make Us A God!" *A Jewish Response to Hebrew Christianity: A Survival Manuel for Jews,* 83

[1915] Picker, "Make Us A God!" *A Jewish Response to Hebrew Christianity: A Survival Manuel for Jews,* 85

[1916] Picker, "Make Us A God!" *A Jewish Response to Hebrew Christianity: A Survival Manuel for Jews,* 124.

[1917] Picker, "Make Us A God!" *A Jewish Response to Hebrew Christianity: A Survival Manuel for Jews,* 128.

completely degenerated into pagan polytheism worshipping sticks, stones, the stars, sea creatures, and themselves. They practiced religious prostitution, homosexuality, and the offering of humans to their gods. God told Abraham that He would have mercy on the Amorites for 400 more years because *"the iniquity of the Amorites is not yet full"* (Genesis 15:16) and then He would destroy them. Israel, even within the very presence of God, made a "golden calf" and constantly rebelled against God to provoke Him to enough anger to destroy them throughout the wilderness wanderings. The book of the Judges tells us that Israel went through the cycles of rebellion (sin) in the Land by prostrating themselves before Baal and other gods until finally God judged them, but they finally called upon the Lord for a deliverer and He would then send a deliverer. The story continues through Samuel, Kings and Chronicles as the prophets challenged the people to return to the God of their Fathers (Abraham, Isaac and Jacob). God finally sent the Assyrians to remove Israel and the Babylonians to remove Judah from the Land because of this "sin-laden" nation. But it continues throughout the post-exile period.

Don't forget the Greeks that ruled over the nation, and all the Jews that were Hellenized, all the gods of Greece and Rome, the Romans with their harassment of the people of the Land, and the slaughters and crucifixions and eventual destruction of the "city" and "sanctuary" as God promised would happen (Daniel 9:26-27). Have you, the Jewish people, forgotten what it was like being unwanted in so-called "Christian" nations? Have you forgotten the Crusades when your women, husbands, wives and mothers lay dead or raped? Have you forgotten the false accusations of blood libel, host desolation, all the banishments from nations or regions of countries, the ghettos, the black plague, the inquisition, the pogroms, and the Holocaust? Have you forgotten the signs that said in America "No Jews permitted," "No Jews and Blacks" and the coffin ships filled with your people trying to escape Nazi Germany only as some who sat in New York harbor in sight of the Statue of Liberty being refused entry only to have to return to Nazi Germany and die in the death camps? Most of this generation has lived through the bloodiest generation of all time, the 20th century. Men like Stalin, Hitler, Chairman Mao and many others are responsible for all the crimes that have been committed against you as Jews, as well as against all the Gentiles who died as well. Yet Rabbinic Judaism is going to make the world better?? I am amazed at the lack of mental awareness to connect point A to point B. In going over this list of things, only the very surface of the sinfulness of mankind was mentioned. Have you forgotten the barbaric attacks on your own people by a religion bent on Jihad to destroy you, whether by military confrontation, suicide bombs, or by infiltration and over-population, or now the real threat of nuclear annihilation?

Please show me the goodness of man. Yes, there are people who live peaceful, law-abiding lives, but their hearts are corrupted by sin. Job stated that *"man is born unto trouble, as the sparks fly upward"* because they still think, meditate and plan sinful acts against other people. This could go on and on, for Jewish secular leaders in the secular world promote for profit sin and immorality. Rabbinic Judaism thinks and theorizes they can make the world better. But it is a fairy tale. An unholy messiah who is just a man lacks the ability to be righteous or holy because he is a sinner, separated from God. The Messiah who is the God/man is Holy not by acts, but by attribute, essence and character; He is the Holy God of Israel.

> There is no doctrine of original sin. **There is no teaching in any literature that man is morally depraved and cannot of his own accord satisfy a righteous God**.

> This does not mean that sin is minimized. Sin is spelled out in detail and all of the literature deals with descriptions of sin in every aspect. The nonconformists saw almost everything and everyone outside of their groups as suspect. But, in every case, **no man is considered so morally depraved that he cannot make the right choices and thereby obtain the good graces of God**.[1918]

Not only does history refute their arguments against the doctrine of original sin, but more importantly so do the Scriptures. Dr. Louis Goldberg summarizes the topic of these two inclinations from a Jewish point of view:

> God created two impulses, one good and the other evil (Berakoth 61a). The good impulse controls the righteous, the evil impulse controls the wicked, and both impulses are present in the average person (Berakoth 61b). The evil impulse is thirteen years older than the good impulse while the good impulse is born at thirteen years of age and is identified with moral consciousness. The general prevailing opinion is that the evil impulse is just the disposition of the human being with his natural instincts, especially in the area of sex desire. It is recognized that God created all things very good and even the evil impulse is good for without it a man would not build a house, marry a wife, beget children, or conduct business affairs (Genesis Rabba 10:7). So the evil desire is evil only in so far as it is liable to be misused. Furthermore, this evil impulse is looked upon as the instrument to lead a man to become a moral being. By constantly making the right choices, choices between evil and good, he develops and begins to perceive goodness. The evil impulse is strong. In temptation, it is described first as like a spider's web, but in the end it is strong like cart ropes (Succah 52a). In temptation again, it is first like a passerby, then like a lodger, and finally like the master of the house (Succah 52b). A man conquers this evil impulse by occupying himself with Torah. If this doesn't work, then he should recite the night prayer, and finally if the previous two procedures do not work, he should reflect concerning the day of his death (Makkoth 10b).[1919]

[1918] Goldberg, *The Deviation of Jewish Thought from an Old Testament Theology in the Intertestamental Period,* 332-333.
   [1919] Goldberg, *The Deviation of Jewish Thought from an Old Testament Theology in the Intertestamental Period,* 69-70.

Judaism has a preoccupation with the thought that man can be righteous. Man can be righteous but not because he does good works. The question is not what man can do for himself to be righteous, but what has been done for him that righteousness can be imputed to him. Judaism states that the law or Torah, the tree of life, is the antidote for sin. In the *Tanakh*, a faithful Jewish believer knew he was a sinner and he went to the temple to offer the prescribed sacrifice so that his sin could be "atoned," which means to be covered, not removed, but covered, for no offering in the Hebrew Scriptures removed sin. It was the act of a faithful believer acting in faith that God would see the blood and forgive him of his sins. All the sacrifices of the first and second temple period foreshadowed the ultimate sacrifice that God Himself would provide to permanently remove the sins of the faithful believer. The flaw in Judaism is that righteousness cannot be obtained by good works, but by an act of God. Judaism has an earthly view of holiness and of righteousness. To think that a sinful person can obtain or merit righteousness from God based on his own works is a wishful imagination on their part as this statement prescribes, "no man is considered so morally depraved that he cannot make the right choices and thereby obtain the good graces of God."

Anti-Missionaries: Atonement (Redemption)

The Scriptures implicitly state that there is no atonement or redemption without the shedding of the blood of a perfect lamb. Yet Judaism has added and altered the meaning and descriptions of atonement and redemption. The first quotation is an example of adding something that God never gave as a method of atonement:

> **Our sages teach us that keeping the Sabbath is particularly effective for such atonement.**[1920]

> The **sacrificial system was temporary, intended to wean Israel from pagan human sacrifice**. God's plan for man is not static. For example, at first man was vegetarian; then meat was permitted (Gen 1:29; 9:4). Animal sacrifice was replaced by prayer, repentance, and good works. (Psa 51:14-17; 40:6; 50:13-14, 23; 69:30-31; Prov 21:3; 1 Sam 15:22; Hos 6:6; Micah 6:6-8)[1921]

In looking at the verses from the quote, one common error is made in all of them. They used these verses to state that God does not want sacrifices by "good deeds." Look at the first reference in 1 Samuel 15:22, but also look at verses 19-21 that precede verse 22, which they use to set the pace for the rest of the other verses:

> "Why did you disobey the LORD and swoop down on the spoil in defiance of the LORD's will?" Saul said to Samuel, "But I did obey the LORD! I performed the mission on which the LORD sent me: I captured King Agag of Amalek, and I proscribed Amalek, and the troops took from the spoil some

---

[1920] Kaplan, *The Real Messiah? A Jewish Response to Missionaries,* 24.
[1921] Picker, *"Make Us A God!" A Jewish Response To Hebrew Christianity: A Survival Manuel For Jews,* 94.

783

sheep, oxen – the best of what had been proscribed – to sacrifice to the LORD your God at Gilgal." But Samuel said: "Does the LORD delight in burnt offering and sacrifices as much as in obedience to the LORD's command? Surely, obedience is better than sacrifice, compliance than the fat of rams."

No verse stands alone, but must be taken within its context. Remember that parts of Exodus and Numbers and all of Leviticus dealt with the sacrificial system laid out very clearly for the nation of Israel to obey. Now all of a sudden you have a couple verses used by Rabbinic Judaism that cancels out all the instructions that the LORD gave meticulously through Moses for the people to obey. By the way, this is the Law of God that they are canceling. Notice the context: God through the prophet Samuel told Saul to completely destroy the Amalekites and all their flocks. What does Saul do in disobedience to God? He kills all the people and most of the animals except for King Agag and the best of the sheep. This chapter has been called the "incomplete obedience of Saul." Notice incomplete, Saul was only partially obedient. Now because of that disobedience God has rejected Saul from being king (1 Samuel 15:26). Then verse 22 comes into play. Saul would have been better off to obey Samuel's word, which was received from the LORD than to use sacrifice as a means to disobey God's word. Then see Samuel's continued statement to Saul, *"for rebellion is as the sin of witchcraft, and stubbornness is as iniquity and idolatry."* So when looking at the whole context, the rabbis have picked a poor verse to use.

The other verses also are within a larger context and teach the same thing that Samuel said to Saul, *"Behold to obey is better than sacrifice."* Is God rescinding His Law? God was always interested in complete obedience, obedience from the heart and not from just actions. Rabbinic Judaism does the same thing with other passage such as Psalm 51:16-17; Hosea 6:6; and Micah 6:6-8. They have ripped these Scriptures out of the larger context of the Written Law of God as a diversion because today there is no temple or sacrificial system nor has there been since 70 AD. This is why Rabbi ben Zakkai retooled Judaism so it would survive without a temple and sacrifice. They had to go this way because the means that God gave in the Mosaic Law cannot be accomplished. So they read into the text because they have no other answer, especially since they have rejected the vicarious sacrifice of Messiah *Yeshua* on the Tree as the sin offering, so that sin can now be removed and not covered as in the days of the temple and Levitical system.

This quotation is Rabbinical Judaism's attempt to nullify the very commands of God to suit Judaism. God has cut off the continuation of the temple and sacrificial system because of their outward compliance like Saul, but lacked the inward obedience of the heart by embracing Messiah *Yeshua* who was the fulfillment of all that the Law and the Prophets spoke. Sacrifices 40 years before the destruction of the temple became null and void because God had already made the ultimate sacrifice for sin, His Son. Also where in the *Tanakh* was it stated that the sacrificial system was temporary for the expressed reason to wean Israel from pagan animal sacrifices? Their logic is astonishing in the negative. The sacrificial system was temporary until the fulfillment of what all the sacrifices pictured in the Hebrew Scripture, the perfect *"Lamb of God"* who would come

784

and be the final sacrifice for sin. They have continued to this day abusing Scripture by artificially substituting repentance, prayer and good works as a way to replace sacrifice and say that they have atonement. Those verses in the *Tanakh* do not express the removal of the sacrificial system but that Israel would first obey the law and live justly and act justly before their family, friends, business acquaintances, the poor and the widows. In these verses God is pleading with a sinful nation not to bring sacrifices but to observe the Law; first *"love your neighbor as yourself"* (Leviticus 19:18) and then bring the sacrifices. It is not a command to stop the sacrifices. If Rabbinic Judaism has the correct interpretation, then why were the Jewish people for hundreds of years disobeying the Pharisees by offering sacrifices if Hosea and Micah and the Psalms said the method of atonement had changed? The anti-missionaries are not being very consistent!

> The first man was not created perfect; otherwise he could not have sinned. God does not demand sinlessness from imperfect man; He demands only righteousness. **With no condemnation for innate sinfulness, there is no need for a "Ransom Sacrifice." Repentance and good deeds atone**.[1922]

Just look at the previous statement. No condemnation for innate sinfulness, no need for a "ransom sacrifice," but only repent and do good deeds and atonement is received. Judaism does not have a biblical view of sin, mediation, holiness or righteousness. To them you are okay, just be good. The whole issue is summed up by this statement written by a Jewish believer in Messiah *Yeshua*:

> All false religions teach basically the same thing – we reach God by doing good deeds. Rabbinical Judaism today teaches that good deeds give us access to God. But Jewish prophets taught that we are all sinners and deserve to die. We can come into the presence of a just God only when the death penalty has been paid. "For the life of the flesh is in the blood, and I have given it to you on the altar to make atonement for your souls; for it is the blood by reason of the life that makes atonement" (Lev. 17:11).[1923]

Anti-Missionaries and Anti-Semitism of the Church

The anti-Semitism of the largely apostate Church is used as a club against the believing Church, that their kind of love for God and for Israel is hypocritical. As to its purpose, it is intended to make believers feel guilty about the church's bad history in relationship to the Jewish people so that they will not be witnessed to by true biblical Christians. They are completely correct when they speak of the Church's being anti-Semitic, and it truly is a dark, depressing history as it relates to the Jewish people.

[1922] Picker, "Make Us A God!" *A Jewish Response to Hebrew Christianity: A Survival Manuel for Jews,* 95

[1923] Shira Sorko-Ram, *Israel's Call: What Jews and Christians Should Understand About Each Other* (Grand Prairie, TX: Moaz Israel Ministries, 2006), 31-32.

True New Covenant believers, who are Christians, but not of the same kind that persecuted the Jewish people, are accused of killing Jewish souls and being worse than the Nazis who only could kill the body. To defend the historic apostate Church is pointless. It is guilty of anti-Semitism in a big way and many of the Church Fathers added to the persecutions of the Jewish people through bad theology. However, the anti-missionaries also attempt to silence the believing Church by stating that the New Testament is anti-Semitic. Chaim Picker attempts to use the New Testament to show that it has the origins of anti-Semitism and he spends seven pages giving illustrations to prove his point from the Gospels, from Luke who wrote Acts and from the Apostle Paul. He summarizes his statements with the following:

> But, some may protest, the prophet castigated ancient Israel! But the spirit is altogether different. The prophets did not criticize Israel as "outsiders" [*the writers of the New Testament were hardly outsiders*]. Moreover, their criticisms invariably concluded with consolation and assurances of God's forgiveness for sincere repentance: "As a man chastens his son, so YHVH your God chastens you (Deut 8:5). We have but to compare the Christian Scripture' censure of the Jews with its censure of wayward Christians to note the different in spirit. As for anti-Semitism – the prophets address their censure toward ancient Israel. Modern readers of these accounts do not associate the Israelites with the Jews. We believe, therefore, that the seeds of anti-Semitism are to be found not in the pages of the Hebrew Scriptures, but in the Christian Scriptures[1924] (italics mine).

Two points need to be discussed in relation to these accusations concerning the New Testament. The first point is that the Gospel writers who recorded the words of *Yeshua* along with the words of Peter and Paul said some hard things to and about the leadership of the Jewish people but never taught anti-Semitism. *Yeshua* was the prophesied reality of what the prophets taught and the harshness that comes from *Yeshua* is because of Who He is and Who they were rejecting. However, *Yeshua* never, never, never taught vengeance against Jewish people for their rejection of Him. The second point is that the New Covenant never, under any circumstances, taught the repression, hatred, persecution, or of making Jewish people social outcasts from the "Christian" majority. Nor did the New Covenant authorize slander, lies, forced conversions, physical violence, banishment or murder of Jewish people. *Yeshua* in His own words taught His disciples to love their enemies. Jewish people are not the enemy of the New Testament Church; whether in rebellion to God or not, they are still His Covenant People.

The sadness is that this has to even be discussed. The Church became predominantly Gentile believers after the first century. Because of bad teaching from the early church fathers who were Gentiles, much was said and done that gave rise to

---

[1924] Picker, "Make Us A God!" *A Jewish Response to Hebrew Christianity: A Survival Manuel for Jews,* 135.

anti-Semitism. It was no longer "we" as Jews, but "they" as Jews. The writers of the New Testament Scriptures were not anti-Semitic, but several generations down the road the hatred and animosity against the Jewish people began and the ramifications of that are still with us today. The writers of the New Testament did proclaim the restoration of Israel and the fulfillment of the Abrahamic Covenant. The spirit of the New Testament was not different; the Church as it moved away from its Jewish roots became anti-Semitic and used and abused the Hebrew Scripture and the New Testament as a source book for the anti-Semitic heart.

True believers in Messiah must acknowledge to Jewish people the injustices done to them over the centuries. Remember: Those injustices were often carried out in the name of Christ with the cross raised high. It was not only shameful, it was the greatest sin that the Church has ever committed outside of the bad doctrine that it took on which was also responsible for much of the abuse against the Jewish people.

Jesus and the New Testament writers put the blame of the rejection and betrayal of the Messiah squarely at the feet of the Sanhedrin and other Jewish leaders. But that does not make them any more anti-Semitic than Moses, Isaiah, Jeremiah, Ezekiel, Hosea, Micah and the other prophets of the *Tanakh*. The prophets of the Hebrew Scriptures also laid the rejection of Israel in regards to God personally and His Law at the feet of the kings, priests and leaders of that day. Jewish leaders today can truly say that the history of the Church has been deplorable, but they cannot honestly place the term "anti-Semitic" against the New Testament. The New Testament has been greatly abused by the Church but that does not mean the New Testament is guilty or caused the deplorable reaction of the Church to Jewish people.

Summary

In summary of the Jewish "doctrinal" responses to true biblical believers, they have not been consistent and faithful to the interpretation of the *Tanakh* to themselves and to the Jewish people in general. They are teaching their people incorrect biblical and historical data as it relates to the message of the Messiah as presented by God in the Hebrew Scriptures. To illustrate the vulnerability of the general Jewish population, this author went to observe a meeting that the anti-missionaries were holding at the Jewish Community Center in Lancaster, PA. In almost disbelief this author listened to the speaker as he dogmatically and emotionally twisted the beliefs of true believers into half truths in relation to his teaching as to what biblical faith teaches concerning God and Jesus. With emotional speech and self-induced tears, he used the Holocaust, Crusades, Inquisition and other issues to speak of Christian missionaries being worse than Hitler because Christian missionaries kill Jewish souls by seeking to evangelize them. From there they went on using emotion to twist what the biblical faith truly teaches. This author was completely disappointed in the lack of content in the anti-missionaries' arguments. In presenting facts and data, truth should be used so that the audience can make an informed decision pro or con about the claims of biblical Christianity.

In the beginning of this appendix the 13 Articles of Faith of Maimonides were given. Here at the end of the chapter is another article on the lack of faith by many Jewish people today. This has largely been brought about by secularism and the Jewish disappointment of 45 false messiahs and the many laws, rules made up by Rabbinic Judaism, the Oral Torah and all the literature that goes with it. They are tired of being persecuted because they are Jewish, and they are tired of looking Jewish and sticking out as different from everyone else. The Jewish people have been strung along by the rabbis for over 1900 in waiting patiently for the Messiah. They have largely lost faith and do not view the Hebrew Scriptures with any trust; they have new articles of faith.

A Post-Messiah Credo

1. I believe that in biblical times the belief in the Messiah sustained the ancient Israelites through the destruction of both the Northern and Southern Kingdoms. With the fall of Jerusalem in 70 C.E., the messianic hope served as a utopian ideal which enabled the Jewish people to remain faithful to God. Assured of divine deliverance and ultimate redemption in the World to Come, the Jewish community was able to face persecution, tragedy and death.

2. I believe that, despite the significance of the process of messianic redemption in the life of the Jewish nation, it must be recognized that Jewish eschatological beliefs are human in origin. Paralleling the development of religious doctrines in other faiths, the messianic idea was elaborated by sages and scholars to provide an explanation for God's dealing with his chosen people.

3. I believe that the attempt of Jewish scholars in previous centuries to determine the date of the advent of the Messiah was a pious, though misguided quest.

4. I believe that the various Jewish messianic figures of the past were all pseudo-Messiahs; despite the sincerity of their followers, these messianic pretenders suffered from a delusion about their messianic role.

5. I believe that, given the subjective character of messianic belief, it makes more sense for Jews today to set aside the hope for final deliverance and redemption through a divine agent who will usher in a period of peace and harmony and bring about the end of history.

6. I believe that, with the demise of the messianic hope, the Jewish people must look to themselves for survival. It is only through the actions of the nation on its own behalf that a Jewish future can be secured. After the destruction of six million Jews in the Holocaust, it has become clear that Jewry must remain ever vigilant to protect itself from its enemies.

7. I believe that the State of Israel, as a symbol of Jewish vitality in a post-Holocaust world, is of central importance for the Jewish community.

Now established in its ancient homeland, the Jewish people has a means to safeguard itself from destruction. Modern Zionism – as a conscious rejection of the messianic promise of return from exile – has brought to the Jewish people renewed hope for the future.

8. I believe that the humanistic values of the Jewish heritage should serve as guiding principles for regulating national affairs within the Jewish State. Israel's political policies should not be determined solely on the basis of *realpolitik*; instead ethical ideals rooted in the tradition should be at the forefront of the nation's decision-making.

9. I believe that Jews in the diaspora have the responsibility to engage in social action; the quest to create a better world through human endeavour is at the heart of the Jewish faith. Jews today must actively engage in this process rather than wait for a miraculous divine intervention to bring about peace and harmony on earth.

10. I believe that in the struggle to ameliorate society Jews should look beyond their own community. Together with members of other faiths, they should strive to improve the lives of all human beings and the world they live in.[1925]

[1925] Cohn-Sherbok, *The Jewish Messiah*, 197-199.

Appendix 8
Jesus Before the Sanhedrin

Jesus Before the Sanhedrin
by Julius Magath
1911

Chapter Three

Details Of The Trial (Night Session)

Two distinct sessions were occupied in the trial. The first was held on the night of the fourteenth of Nisan (March). Accounts of it are given by John, Matthew, and Mark. The second took place on the morning of the same day. The latter session is mentioned by both Matthew and Mark, and its proceedings are related in detail by Luke.

The Sanhedrin is once more assembled, but this time it lays aside the mask of secrecy; for Jesus is to be judged publicly. We emphasize the word, "Sanhedrin," for it is the veritable body that was composed of the three principal orders of the Hebrew people the priests, the scribes, and the elders. "And they that had laid hold on Jesus led Him away to Caiaphas the high priest…and with Him WERE ASSEMBLED ALL THE CHIEF PRIESTS AND THE ELDERS AND THE SCRIBES." (Matthew 26:57; Mark 14:53.)

"It was night," says John, "Judas having received a band of men and of officers from the chief priests and Pharisees, cometh thither with lanterns and torches and weapons…. Then the band and the captain and officers of the Jews took Jesus, and bound Him, and led Him away." (John 13:30, 18:3, 12, 13.)

The **FIRST IRREGULARITY** that we shall notice in the proceedings of the trial is the violation of the Jewish law that prohibited the transaction of legal business at night: *"Let a capital offense be tried during the day, but suspend it at night."* (Mishnah, *Sanhedrin*, and Chapter. 4. 1).

Its being held before the evening sacrifice is the **SECOND IRREGULARITY**. *"The Sanhedrin sat from the close of the morning sacrifice to the time of the evening sacrifice,* (Talmud, *Jerusalem, Sanhedrin*," Chapter. 1, fol. 19).

The **THIRD IRREGULARITY** is to be found in the fact of its being the first day of the feast of unleavened bread and the eve of the Passover. *"They shall not judge on the eve of the Sabbath-day nor on that of any festival."* (Mishnah, *Sanhedrin*, C. 4.1).

First Interrogatory Put to Jesus by Caiaphas

"The high priest then asked Jesus..." (John 18:19.) It is Caiaphas, be it remembered, who interrogates the same man who, a short time before, in a general assembly of the Sanhedrin held in his own palace on the occasion of the resurrection of Lazarus, had declared that the public welfare imperatively demanded that Jesus of Nazareth be put to death. What! an *accuser* act as *judge?* In this case he is even more than a judge, for he is *president* of an assembly of judges. Here we have a **FOURTH IRREGULARITY** – an irregularity too glaring to escape the notice of even a casual observer for it is a well-known fact that no legislative body ever allowed an accuser to act as judge. "If a...witness rise up against any man...then both the men, between whom the controversy is, shall stand before the Lord, before the priests and the judges, which shall be in those days." (Deuteronomy 19:16, 17.) From this passage we see that the accuser and the judge were to be two distinct persons; but here Caiaphas, who was accuser yesterday, is judge today! This unprecedented monstrosity is especially pointed out by John. He says: "Caiaphas was he, which gave counsel to the Jews that it was expedient that one man should die for the people." (John 18:14.)

"The high priest then asked Jesus of His disciples and of His doctrine." (John 18:19.) Caiaphas, the judge and accuser, instead of opening the proceedings by reading the indictments and producing the witnesses, in accordance with the requirements of the Jewish law, proceeds as prosecuting attorney. "If there be found among you...a man or woman, that hath wrought wickedness in the sight of the Lord thy God...and thou hast heard of it, and inquired diligently, and, behold, it be true...at the mouth of two witnesses or three witnesses...." (Deuteronomy 17:2-6.) Caiaphas, as we have said, begins with a captious question, in order to criminate Jesus on His own confession. This mode of procedure constitutes a **FIFTH IRREGULARITY**; for what could be more inconsistent than to arraign a man against whom no formal accusation had been presented, or to interrogate him regarding his own affairs without confronting him with his legally constituted accusers?

"Jesus answered him, I spake openly to the world; I ever taught in the synagogue, and in the Temple, whither the Jews always resort; and in secret have I said nothing. Why askest thou me? Ask them which heard me, what I have said unto them: behold, they know what I said." (John 18:20, 21). This answer of Jesus brings out clearly the illegality committed by Caiaphas in opening the trial without previously preparing a bill of indictment and specifications against the accused a preliminary necessary to legalize the decisions of every court of justice.

Why do you ask me? That is to say, do you wish me to become my own accuser? Have you any specific charge to bring against me? If so, it is your duty formally to state it, that I may assert my innocence or plead my guilt; but if you know nothing against me, and there are no witnesses to testify against me or my doctrines, how can you expect me to become my own accuser? Do you not see that by your endeavors to extort from me a confession of guilt you legally declare my innocence? *We have it as a fundamental principle of our jurisprudence that no one can bring an accusation against himself.* (Mishnah, *Sanhedrin*, and Chapter. 4.2).

"And when He had thus spoken, one of the officers which stood by struck Jesus with the palm of his hand, saying, Answerest thou the high priest so?" (John 18:22.)

In this unprecedented act of brutality we find a **SIXTH IRREGULARITY**, reflecting as it does upon the humanity and sense of justice of the judges in permitting a deed so shameful in their presence. Every prisoner is entitled to the fullest protection of the law, and is to be considered innocent until his guilt be proved; but here the silence observed by the judges in allowing the dastardly act to go unpunished and unreproved shows clearly that the insult was sanctioned by the entire body. The chief blame, of course, rested upon the judges, especially upon him who presided over the assembly. For if both the Bible and the Mishnah enjoin upon the judges the use of terms expressive of humanity and kindness in addressing a prisoner as, "My son, confess your sin;"…"My very dear daughter, what is the cause of your sin?" (Joshua 7:19; Mishnah, *Sotah*, Chap. 1.4) – much more do they prohibit the tolerance on the part of the judges of any act of violence or brutality perpetrated against the prisoner.

"Jesus answered him, If I have spoken evil, bear witness of the evil: but if well, why smitest thou me?" (John 18:23.)

This answer might be paraphrased thus: "If I have spoken evil against the truth or against the high priest, testify to my guilt, or show wherein I have erred; but if you cannot prove that I have said anything against either, why do you insult me thus? I only claim the right to which, as a prisoner, the law entitles me." The truth is, Jesus would have been justified in using even stronger language, not only to the insolent servant, but even to the high priest who tacitly authorized so manifest a violation of the law. "If He did it not, it was because He was unwilling to dishonor the high priesthood in the person holding that sacred office. His defense, however, was none the less forcible, nor His protestations of innocence less dignified on account of the mildness of His language." (St. Cyprien, *Epist.*, 4. *ad Corn.*, p. 114).

Deposition of the Witnesses

"Now the chief priests, and elders, and all the council, sought false witness against Jesus, to put Him to death; but found none: yea, though many false witnesses came, yet found they none" (Matthew 26:59, 60; Mark 14:55.)

Jesus having demanded that the charges alleged against Him be adduced and supported by the testimony of witnesses, it was found impossible to effect His condemnation without producing some witnesses against Him. Now see the next step taken by the Sanhedrin. Messengers are actually sent out promiscuously among the crowd to summon men as witnesses, with orders to offer them bribes for bearing testimony against the accused. In this iniquitous proceeding, together with the miserable

793

pretense of an examination given by the judges to the naturally conflicting reports of the fraudulent witnesses, we find the **SEVENTH IRREGULARITY**. "*And the judges shall make diligent inquisition, and, behold, if the witness.*" (Deuteronomy 19:18.) But this is not all. They commit an **EIGHTH IRREGULARITY** in violating the fundamental law enjoining the judge, before hearing the testimony of a witness, to administer to him an oath binding him to absolute truthfulness in all his statements. "Remember that a heavy responsibility rests on you...." (Mishnah, *Sanhedrin*, and Chapter 4.5). It is but natural that these humane and righteous judges, having themselves assented to the suborning of the witnesses, should have shrunk from the inconsistency of holding them responsible for their perjury, thus involving themselves in a new difficulty, which is nothing less than a breach of the law demanding the prompt punishment of false witnesses. "Behold, if the witness be a false witness...then shall ye do unto him as he had thought to do unto his brother...life shall go for life, eye for eye, tooth for tooth, hand for hand, foot for foot." (Deuteronomy 19:18-21.)

This constitutes the **NINTH IRREGULARITY**. In truth, these men are no longer judges, but a band of murderers clamoring for the blood of a guiltless man. To the strange scenes enacted in the Sanhedrin hall on this memorable occasion history furnishes no parallel, except one be found in that mockery of a trial which, by order of the wicked Jezebel, was to result in the condemnation of the innocent Naboth. She wrote letters in Ahab's name, and sealed them with his seal, and sent the letters unto the elders and to the nobles that were in his city, dwelling with Naboth. "And she wrote in the letters, saying, proclaim a fast, and set Naboth on high among the people: and set two men, sons of Belial, before him, to bear witness against him, saying, Thou didst blaspheme God and the king. And then carry him out and stone him, that he may die. And the men of his city, even the elders and the nobles who were the inhabitants in his city, did as Jezebel had sent unto them...and the men of Belial witnessed against...Naboth in the presence of the people, saying, Naboth did blaspheme God and the king. Then they carried him forth out of the city, and stoned him with stones, that he died." (1 Kings 21:8-14.)

But let us continue with the deposition of the witnesses.

"For many bare false witness against Him, but their witness agreed not together. At the last came two false witnesses, and said, This fellow said, I am able to destroy the temple of God, and to build it in three days."

"I will destroy this temple that is made with hands, and within three days I will build another made without hands."

"But neither so did their witness agree together." (Mark 14:56-59; Matthew 26:60.)

Before noticing the discrepancies in the testimony of these two witnesses, we observe a **TENTH IRREGULARITY**, consisting in the fact of their being examined simultaneously and in the presence of each other, when the law required that only one witness should be admitted for examination at a time. "Separate them, and I will examine them." (Apocrypha.)

In the testimony quoted above, the enormity of the charges is obvious. For it is a well-known fact that the Jews were always very jealous of the glory of their temple; so much so that Jeremiah narrowly escaped stoning by the priests and the people for having dared to prophesy that God would one day reduce the temple to the condition of Shiloh, and convert it into a desert (Jeremiah 26:6). It was only through the intervention of the lords at court that his life was spared. We can understand, therefore, that the charges brought against Jesus by the two witnesses were of the gravest importance, and must have produced a profound impression upon the entire assembly, inspiring them with the hope of at last finding a legal pretext for the conviction and condemnation of their defenseless victim; and so it might have been but for the falseness and incongruity apparent in the testimony. But what about the law that so rigorously demanded an absolute agreement in the statements of witnesses, not only as regarded facts and events but even their minutest details?

We shall now proceed to show that the testimony was *false*.

1. The language imputed to Jesus was not the same that He actually used. He did not say, "*I can destroy*" or "*I will destroy*," but DESTROY! "Destroy this temple, and in three days I will raise it up." (John 2:19.) This speech being merely hypothetical, since it signified *supposing you destroy this temple*…was not sufficient to constitute a serious charge; but the witnesses, well remunerated for their services, observing in the judges signs of increasing impatience and determination, were by no means loath to bring the business to a close by distorting the words of Jesus into a treasonable threat that would inevitably insure His condemnation.

2. The testimony given by these two witnesses was clearly a misinterpretation of the words of Jesus, who, in uttering them, had made no allusion to the material temple at Jerusalem, but referred to the living temple of His body. This is affirmed by the apostle John, in whose presence the words had been spoken: "He spake of the temple of His body." (John 2:21.) For further corroboration of our assertion, let us notice the terms actually used by Jesus. To make it obvious to His hearers that He intended to speak of His own body, He made use of an expression corresponding to the Latin word "solvite," which instead of "destroy" really signifies "break, or dissolve" – expression very appropriate as applied to an animated body, a living temple, the members of which can be broken or dissolved by death; but not so in connection with a material edifice, an inanimate temple. But a final proof that such was the sense in which these remarkable words were uttered, we find in the latter clause of the sentence, "And in three days I will RAISE IT UP" – i.e., *revive* it not "I will *rebuild* it." If Jesus had referred to the temple at Jerusalem, he would have used the words *destroy* and *rebuild;* but since He had in view none other than a mystical temple His own body He employed the terms *break* or *dissolve the members*, and *revive or resuscitate*. With regard, then, to the two

witnesses who had so grossly perverted the words of Christ, we must conclude one of these two things:

Either they failed to understand the words, as did those other Jews who, present on the same occasion, exclaimed on hearing them, "Forty and six years was this Temple in building, and wilt thou rear it up in three days?" or, while perfectly apprehending the idea thus figuratively expressed, they designedly and maliciously put upon the language a false construction. In the latter case they were false witnesses in a twofold degree: not only imputing to Christ words that He had not used i.e., I can destroy, I will destroy but applying those words to the temple at Jerusalem when they bore to it no reference whatever. Thus they falsified both the letter and the spirit of these utterances of Christ.

Be it further noticed, that if the witnesses had spoken the truth, and if Christ had really spoken the words which they imputed to Him, their evidence could not have been legally accepted for the following reason: According to the Hebraic law, it was necessary to the validity of the testimony that *all the witnesses should agree upon the same fact in all its parts,* (Mishnah, *Sanhedrin*, Chap. 5.2). *For instance, if one witness were to testify to having seen an Israelite in the act of worshiping the sun, and another to have seen the same man worship the moon, yet, although each of the two facts proves clearly that the man had been guilty of the horrible crime of idolatry, the discrepancy in the statements of the witnesses invalidates their testimony, and the accused is free,* (Maimonides, *Sanhedrin*, Chapter 20).

The first witness, in testifying that Jesus had said, *I will destroy this temple that is made with hands,* charged Him with the serious crime of uttering threats against a religious and national institution; while the second, in imputing to Him the words, *I am able to destroy the Temple of God*, only makes Him out a swaggerer and a braggart. Now, the acceptance by the council of these incongruous (Mark 14:59) statements constitutes the **ELEVENTH IRREGULARITY**; for by the law above quoted the testimony should have been declared null, and the prisoner released.

Second Interrogatory Put to Jesus by Caiaphas

Caiaphas, instead of refusing to receive the testimony of the false witnesses, as he was duty bound to do, made it the basis of a second interrogatory. "And the high priest stood up in the midst, and asked Jesus, saying, Answerest thou nothing? What is it which these witness against thee?" (Mark 14:60.) That is to say, Do you not hear the overwhelming charges which these witnesses bring against You? Why are You silent? Speak! Caiaphas, by drawing the attention of Jesus to the danger of His position, hoped to evoke from Him such replies in explanation of the statements imputed to Him as would implicate Him, and make Him appear guilty in the eyes of the people.

"But He held His speech, and answered nothing." (Mark 14:61.)

The cause of Christ needed no defense nor palliation, nor did the statement constituting the principal charge against Him require any explication beyond a faithful rendering by the witnesses. Besides, His refusal to answer the questions put to Him by the crafty Caiaphas was doubtless meant to show not only His interrogator, but the whole assembly, that He perfectly understood the motives that had prompted them. His silence was indeed an eloquent rebuke, and at this period of the trial was fulfilled the prophecy of David: "They also that seek after My life lay snares for Me; and they that seek My hurt speak mischievous things, and imagine deceits all the day long. But I, as a deaf man, heard not; and I was as a dumb man that openeth not his mouth. (Psalm 38:12, 13.)

It is indeed astonishing that this calm and majestic silence, so unnatural to men under impending death, should not have opened the eyes of His judges. True, a few hours later, Pilate, pagan as he was, was so impressed by the grand solemnity of the silent figure before him that, under the uneasiness of mind awakened by the sight, he would have released the defenseless victim. But Caiaphas and the Sanhedrin, far from recognizing in the silent attitude of Jesus the fulfillment of the prophecy by Isaiah. "He was afflicted, yet He opened not His mouth: He is brought as a lamb to the slaughter, and as a sheep before her shearers is dumb, so He openeth not His mouth." (Isaiah 53:7) – were only exasperated by it the more; for they saw in that silence an accusation against themselves that confused and overwhelmed them. An issue! They must have an issue to dispatch the business at once! Caiaphas very soon found one.

Third Interrogatory Put to Jesus by Caiaphas

"Again the high priest asked Him, and said unto Him, I adjure Thee by the living God, that Thou tell us whether Thou be the Christ, the Son of God." (Mark 14:61; Matthew 26:63.)

It is very important to notice the sudden change in the manner of the accusation. There is, in fact, no longer any question either as regards the witnesses or their testimony. Caiaphas, so to speak, now throws all the evidence into the wastebasket, and declares the testimony that had been so dishonorably obtained and shamelessly given, insufficient, of itself, to condemn the accused. Furthermore, the fact of Caiaphas being driven, as a last resource, to interrogating the prisoner in the hope of extorting from Him a confession of guilt, or in some way inducing Him to criminate Himself, is in itself an involuntary admission that nothing has been found in Him worthy of death. Why, then, is He still retained as a criminal?

The witnesses and their depositions having been put aside, the scene changes, and Caiaphas, judge and president of the tribunal, becomes a self-constituted witness and accuser. But in thus actively arraying himself against Jesus, he openly violates his official obligations, and in so doing, commits a **TWELFTH IRREGULARITY**. (See Deuteronomy 19:16, 17.)

797

A **THIRTEENTH IRREGULARITY** is found in the oath that he proffered to Jesus: "*I adjure Thee by the living God, that Thou tell us whether Thou be the Christ, the Son of God.*" The law required that this awful adjuration should be addressed to the witnesses: "Remember that a heavy responsibility rests upon you.... If you cause the accused to be unjustly condemned, God will require an account of you, even as He did of Cain for the blood of Abel." (Mishna, *Sanhedrin*, Chap iv. 5.) But it was in all cases the witnesses alone who were required to take a preliminary oath of the character; for to administer it to the accused would be to place Him in the alternative of committing perjury or of criminating himself. "We have it as a principle of our jurisprudence that no one is to bring an accusation against himself." (Mishnah, *Sanhedrin*, and Chapter. 6.2). But in this iniquitous trial an oath is required not of the witnesses but of the accused! This serious infraction of the moral and civil law had been predicted and stigmatized by a prophetic voice: "For they speak against Thee wickedly, and Thine enemies take thy name in vain." (Psalm 139:20.)

As to the interrogatory itself, it was a snare set by Caiaphas. In adjuring Jesus, in the name of the living God, to declare whether He was the Son of God or not, He foresaw that whatever His answer might be, His doom was fixed. Should He answer any question in the negative thus He must have reasoned with Himself. He will be condemned as an impostor, for such He has certainly claimed to be; if in the affirmative, He will be condemned as a blasphemer. Thus, a denial was to be treated as no less a crime than an avowal.

"And Jesus said, 'I am'" (Mark 14:61, 62). Jesus respects on the lips of the high priest the majesty of the name of God. He replies to the question, despite the malice which prompted it, on account of the sacred language in which it was clothed. He is not deceived by the dissimulation of the high priest far from it but He is ready to do homage to the divine name, although knowing that in this instance it was basely employed to entrap Him.

Condemnation Pronounced by the Sanhedrin

"Then the high priest rent his clothes, saying, He hath spoken blasphemy; what further need have we of witnesses?...What think ye?" (Matthew 26:65, 66.)

The denouement is precipitated, and irregularities are heaped one upon another.

The high priest tears his clothes that is to say, gives way to anger. In this act we have a **FOURTEENTH IRREGULARITY**, since it is not only a violation of the law enjoining the judge to comport himself toward the prisoner with gentleness and respect using in addressing him such terms as these: "My son, confess your fault." "My very dear daughter, what is the cause of your sin?" (Joshua 7:19; Mishnah, *Sotah*, 1.4) but it is also a breach of the religious law, which strictly prohibits the high priests tearing his garments even as a sign of mourning. Any ordinary Israelite could, as an emblem of bereavement, tear his garments, but to the high priest it was forbidden, because his vestments, being made after the express orders of God, were figurative of his office. "And he that is the high priest among his brethren, upon whose head the anointing oil was poured, and that is consecrated to put on the garments, shall not uncover his head, nor rend his clothes." (Leviticus 21:10.) Tear thy garments, O Caiaphas! Before the day closes, the veil of the temple shall also be torn in twain, to signify that the Aaronic priesthood and the sacrifices of the Mosaic Law have been abolished to make place for the eternal priesthood of the high priest of the new covenant.

"He hath spoken blasphemy!" In this exclamation of the chief priest we notice two irregularities:

The **FIFTHTEENTH IRREGULARITY** consists in the fact of his pronouncing against the accused the charge of blasphemy without having duly inquired into the reasonableness of the declaration contained in the response to the high priests question. Caiaphas had demanded that Jesus should say whether or not He was the Son of God. Jesus had answered, "I am." Simple justice required that this bold avowal, presumptuous and even blasphemous though it may have appeared, should have been examined into with the utmost care. Order the holy books to be brought in, O Caiaphas! Open them on your tribunal. Read from their sacred pages the various names and attributes ascribed to the Messiah and Saviour of the world; and above all, find out from the same source whether He is to be the Son of God. This done, see if such names and attributes could be appropriately applied to the person before you claiming to be the Son of God. If, of all the characteristics and conditions ascribed by the prophets to the Messiah, a single one be wanting in Him, then proclaim loudly and fearlessly that He has blasphemed. But to pronounce Him a blasphemer without having given the statement contained in His answer so much as even a superficial investigation, what iniquity! Here we find a violation of the simplest obligations belonging to the office of the president of the Sanhedrin council. The law says, "The judges shall make diligent inquisition" (Deuteronomy 19:8); but in this case, there was not even a simple examination! The Mishnah adds: "The judges shall weigh [the matter] in the sincerity of their conscience" (Mishnah *Sanhedrin*, Chap. 4.5); but here the conscience itself is stifled!

The next or **SIXTEENTH IRREGULARITY** committed by Caiaphas in the unwarrantable exclamation, "He has blasphemed!" is that he virtually forestalls the decision of the other judges. In declaring the answer of Jesus blasphemous, he deprives the subordinate judges of the freedom of suffrage. According to the Mishnah, the formula of his vote, as well as of each of the other judges, should have been expressed simply, *I absolve*, or *I condemn*, (*Sanhedrin*, Chap. 5.5). But in his vehement utterance of a decision prompted not by justice but by malice, he precludes the possibility of his colleagues differing from him in the character of their votes; for it is a well-known fact that the decision of the high priest was considered infallible authority among the Jews.

"What further need have we of witnesses?" Here we have a speech fully as iniquitous as the other. What! A judge dare deny the necessity for witnesses, when the law expressly and absolutely demanded them! For the impartial administration of justice, the judge was required to make a careful and minute examination of every witness, putting to them one at a time the following seven questions: "Was it in a year of jubilee? Was it in an ordinary year? In what month? On what day of the month? At what hour? In what place? Do you identify the accused?" (Mishnah, *Sanhedrin*, Chap. 5.1). But Caiaphas, thirsting for the blood of his victim, tramples under foot all prescribed forms in his eagerness to reach a speedy termination of the trial, even proposing to dispense with the calling and hearing of witnesses. Thus we find him guilty of a **SEVENTEENTH IRREGULARITY**.

"What think ye?" This question forms the **EIGHTEENTH IRREGULARITY**; for nothing could have been more irregular than the calling for a public and general vote. The Mishnah says expressly, "Let the judges, each in his turn, absolve or condemn" (*Sanhedrin*, 15.5); but Caiaphas, to end the matter, would have them vote *en masse*. And through the whole proceeding, what bitter derision is manifest in the conduct of Caiaphas! He tears his garments as a mark of the profoundest horror, and in so doing impresses all present with a religious awe; he proclaims Jesus guilty of the most horrible blasphemy; he declares that there is no need of further proofs or witnesses; and after all this, he demands of the other judges an expression of their opinion!

The response of the Sanhedrin was exactly what Caiaphas had anticipated.

"They answered and said, He is guilty [worthy] of death." (Matthew 26:66; Mark 14:64.)

In this one sentence we find several irregularities. The first, or the **NINETEENTH** in order, is seen in the precipitate assent of the other judges to Caiaphas accusation of blasphemy, instead of first deliberating among themselves, as the law directs. "Having deferred the trial to the next day, the judges reassemble by twos, and proceed to reexamine the whole case." (Mishnah, *Sanhedrin*, and Chapter 5.5).

The next or **TWENTIETH IRREGULARITY** is as follows: the sentence was pronounced on the same day the trial began; whereas, according to law, it should have been deferred to the next day at least. "A criminal case resulting in the acquittal of the accused may terminate the same day the trial began; *but if a sentence of death is to be pronounced, it cannot be concluded before the following day*." (Mishnah, *Sanhedrin*, 4.1).

Again, as the judges did not vote one at a time and in order, it is obvious that the votes could not have been recorded by the two scribes appointed for that purpose another irregularity (the **TWENTY-FIRST**); for says the Mishnah: "At each extremity [of the semicircle] a secretary was placed, whose business it was to record the votes. One of these secretaries recorded the votes in favor of the accused, the other those against him." (*Sanhedrin*, Chapter 4.3).

Such was the night session, prophetically described by David: "The assembly of the wicked have enclosed Me." (Psalm 22:16.) Twenty-one irregularities were then committed; and not one of the judges arose to enter a protest against them. The evangelist says, "They" – that is, all of them "said, He is worthy of death!" In this sententious exclamation we perceive some expression of the shame and wonder that filled the minds of the gospel narrators in contemplating the fact that among the seventy-one members composing the council of the Sanhedrin there was not a single one conscientious and brave enough to protest against proceedings so vile and unprecedented. We must remember; however, that all who took part in this trial were creatures of Caiaphas, and no less corrupt than himself.

The Jewish law permitted any spectator at a public trial to speak a word in defense of the accused. To do so was even considered a pious and meritorious act; but on this memorable night, not a voice from all that crowd of lookers-on was raised in His behalf. The only two persons who would have been likely to offer a favorable word for Jesus were members of the Sanhedrin, but not present on that occasion. These were Joseph of Arimathea and Nicodemus, who refused to attend an irregular session held on the solemn night of the Passover. Remembering how at a former session of the trial the protestations of Nicodemus against the condemnation of Jesus were disdainfully set aside, (John 7:52) they knew that nothing they could say on this occasion would carry any weight with the fierce and determined Caiaphas; and so they purposely absented themselves. Referring to Joseph of Arimathea, the evangelist says, "He had not consented to the counsel and deed of them." (Luke 23:51.) And from the courage formerly displayed by Nicodemus in defense of Jesus, we may safely infer that he too was unwilling to take part in a trial so illegally conducted.

We then see Jesus before his accusers defenseless and alone. When the eleven sons of Jacob concerted to put Joseph to death, two of them, Reuben and Judah, struck with remorse, made some feeble protests against the murder of their innocent brother: "Come, and let us sell him to the Ishmaelites, and let not our hand be upon him; for he is our brother and our flesh." (Genesis 37:27.) When the treacherous Ahithophel would have persuaded the council to pursue and put to death the lawful King David, a stranger (Hushai, the Archite) took up the defense of the unfortunate monarch, who was on the point of being betrayed by his subjects into the hands of his rebellious son (II Samuel 15:32, 17:1-25). But no compassionate voice is raised in defense of Him who is greater than Joseph, and who is a King and a Father in a higher sense than David.

The members of the Sanhedrin having unanimously ratified the death sentence passed by Caiaphas upon Jesus, a signal was given the soldiers in attendance to seize and guard him for the rest of the night.

A strange scene was then enacted: "Then did they spit in His face, and buffeted Him; and others smote Him with the palms of their hands, saying, Prophesy unto us, thou Christ, Who is he that smote Thee?" (Matthew 26:67, 68; Mark 14:65.)

Thus after His condemnation, Jesus was delivered to soldiers and menials, who were left free to perpetrate upon His person all possible outrages. Some authors have regarded that night of torture as the most cruel scene in the drama of the Passion. And, indeed, for barbarity and diabolism it stands without a parallel in history. Among all civilized nations a prisoner, whatever may be his guilt, is under the protection of the law until the arrival of the time for the execution of his sentence, and nowhere do we find judges tolerating the commission by their soldiers and servants of excessive cruelties upon a prisoner under their charge.

As these brutalities were committed after the adjournment of the night session, we shall not add them to the list of irregularities under enumeration; but we would emphasize the shamefully culpable weakness of Caiaphas, who, in permitting such atrocities under his own roof displayed a cowardice equal to that of the Philistines in their treatment of Samson. Like Samson, Jesus was surrounded by those who, basely taking advantage of His misfortunes, heaped upon Him the vilest raillery and insult. Such was the cruel fulfillment of prophecy.

Chapter Four
Details of the Trial (Morning Session)

Reason for Holding a Second Session

"And straightway in the morning the chief priests held a consultation with the elders and scribes and the whole council against Jesus to put Him to death." (Mark 15:1; Luke 22:66; Matthew 27:1.)

Caiaphas and the other members of the Sanhedrin were exceedingly anxious lest the sentence resulting from the manifestly illegal proceedings of the night before should be annulled. That their apprehensions were not without foundation is evident, if we bear in mind the number of revolting irregularities then committed. What would be more natural than for the people, under the excitement of the occasion, to open upon them a volley of embarrassing questionings and protests? What answer, for instance, could they give to the question of the necessity of holding a session of the council of the Sanhedrin at night, contrary to established custom? What about the non-agreement of the witnesses, and the precipitate pronouncing of the sentence? To avoid all these difficulties, the entire body of the Sanhedrin assembles early in the morning *to hold a council against Jesus to put Him to death.*

We here call attention to the fact that the present session of the Sanhedrin is by no means held for the purpose of revising the sentence pronounced on the previous night. The condemnation of Jesus remains the same. His doom is irrevocably sealed. The only point that concerns that body now is the necessity for giving to the irregular proceedings just enacted an appearance of legality in the eyes of the people. But in their efforts to that end we shall show that irregularities were committed quite as gross as those that marked the events of the preceding session.

"And as soon as it was day, the elders of the people and the chief priests and the scribes came together, and led Him into their council." (Mark 15; Luke 22:66)

The assembling before the time of day prescribed by law constitutes the **TWENTY-SECOND IRREGULARITY**. It was forbidden to convene the Sanhedrin before the celebration of the morning sacrifice. "They shall sit from after the morning sacrifice until the sacrifice of the evening." (Talmud, *Jerusalem Sanhedrin*, C. 1., fol. 19). But in assembling thus early,[1926] they could not have waited for the consummation of the morning sacrifice, for the preparation for the morning sacrifice began at break of day, and one hour at least was required in the slaying and offering up of the victim, which was consumed amid the usual prayers. We see, then, that the Sanhedrin must have convened just one hour in advance of the time prescribed by law.

Besides, it is now the great day of the Feast of the Passover, when to sit in judgment was strictly prohibited. "They shall not judge on the Sabbath day, nor on a feast day." (Mishnah, *Betzah*, C. 5.2). The violation of this law forms the **TWENTY-THIRD IRREGULARITY.** Origen, one of the most eminent Bible commentators, commenting on the passage in Isaiah, "*Your new moons and your appointed feasts My soul hateth*," Isaiah 1:14, says, "It was prophetically that God declared His hatred for the feasts of the synagogue, for in delivering Jesus to be executed on the very day of Passover, the Jews committed a great crime." (Origen, *Commentary on Isaiah*).

Renewal of the Cross-Examination of Jesus

"And [they] led Him into their council, saying, Art thou the Christ? Tell us." (Luke 22:66-67.)

We would call attention to the fact that the original method of conducting the trial is entirely abandoned. Efforts are no longer made for the securing or the producing of false witnesses; neither are the declarations made by Jesus Himself used against Him. All these things had been tried without success on the previous evening, and the members of the Sanhedrin knew too well that a repetition of the selfsame order of procedure would be subject to the same difficulty that embarrassed their efforts before the possibility of a protest on the part of the people. To secure themselves against such a frustration of their designs, they resolved to do away with witnesses and interrogate

---

[1926] (Respecting the hours for the offering of the daily sacrifice, the Bible says simply, One lamb thou shalt offer in the morning, and the other lamb thou shalt offer at even." (Exodus 29:38-39.) But Josephus indicates the exact time for the offering of these sacrifices: The law requires that at the public expense a lamb of the first year be killed every day, at the beginning and ending of the day, (Jos. *Ant.*, 3.10.1)

Jesus as to His claims to divinity, knowing full well that His reply would be received as blasphemy by the people, who would thereupon yield a ready assent to His condemnation.

"Jesus said unto them, If I tell you, ye will not believe: and if I also ask [i.e., question] you, ye will not answer me, nor let me go. Hereafter shall the Son of man sit on the right-hand of the power of God" (Luke 22:67-69). This answer shows that Jesus understood clearly enough the sinister designs underlying this renewal of His cross-examination. Nevertheless, He hesitated not in His reply. Hereafter that is, when you shall have exercised all the power given to you, and shall have put Me to death I shall go to sit on the throne of the Almighty, at the right hand of God. "Then said they all, Art thou then the Son of God?" (Luke 22:70)

The conclusion implied in the above question was logically correct, for the expression, "to sit at the right-hand of God" could not be applied to a human being; and His judges knew perfectly well that in speaking thus of Himself, He attributed to His own person the same honor, the same power, the same majesty, and consequently the same nature as of God Himself.

"And He [Jesus] said unto them, Ye say that I am." (Luke 22:70.)

Jesus repeats in the same terms, and with the same solemnity, the declaration which He made during the night session. Caiaphas had then asked Him, "Art thou the Christ, the Son of God?" His answer was, "I am." And now, when the same question is put to Him by the entire body of the Sanhedrin, His reply is still the same.

Sentence Again Passed Upon Jesus by the Sanhedrin

"And they said, What need we any further witness? For we ourselves have heard of His own mouth." (Luke 22:71.) Thus the second general assembly confirms the sentence pronounced by the first. The united voices of all the members pass sentence of death upon Jesus, and the judges, in their eagerness for the execution of the sentence, declare the proceedings at an end; and from their decision there is no appeal. But the trial has not reached its conclusion, without a further increase to the list of irregularities we have been enumerating.

The **TWENTY-FOURTH IRREGULARITY** is found in the fact that, as on the previous evening, the sentence, contrary to law, was pronounced *en masse*. The Mishnah says expressly, "Every one *in his* turn shall absolve or condemn." (*Sanhedrin*, C. 5.5).

The answer of Jesus to the question, "Art thou the Son of God?" ought to have been minutely examined under the following heads: 1. Was the Messiah to have been the Son of God? 2. Was Jesus the Son of God? Their failure to scrutinize the question constitutes a **TWENTY-FIFTH IRREGULARITY**.

Again, the passing of the sentence should have been deferred to the next day. Without invalidating the trial, the sentence could not have been passed before Saturday morning. The proceedings began on Thursday night, which was really counted as Friday, for among the Hebrews the days were reckoned from one setting of the sun to another, (Leviticus 23:32.) The first day of the trial, then, was from Thursday evening to Friday evening; but, as we have seen, an interval of one night was required between the trial itself and the pronouncing of the sentence. (See Mishnah, *Sanhedrin*, C. 4.1.) It is clear, then, that the sentence could not have been legally pronounced earlier than Saturday morning. So, in the premature passing of the sentence we find a **TWENTY-SIXTH IRREGULARITY.**

Finally, the sentence against Jesus was invalid because it was pronounced in a place prohibited by the law the house of Caiaphas, instead of the Hall of Hewn Stones, which was the only place where a criminal sentence could be legally passed. "A sentence of death can be pronounced only so long as the Sanhedrin holds its sessions in the appointed place." (Talmud, Babylonian, *Abodah Zarah*, or *of Idolatry* C. 1, fol. 8; Maimonides, *Sanhedrin*, C. 14). This is the **TWENTY-SEVENTH** and last **IRREGULARITY.**

The authors of the Talmud so well understood the seriousness of the last irregularity that they have endeavored, in spite of historical assertions to the contrary, to prove that Jesus was both judged and condemned in the Hall of Hewn Stones. Thus we read in the *Thosephthoth*, or *Additions to the Talmud, Babylonian, Sanhedrin*, C. iv. fol. 37, recto: "It is important to notice that every time the necessities of the case so required, the Sanhedrin returned to the Hall Gazith, or of Hewn Stones, as in the case of Jesus, and others."

This, however, is a ridiculous statement, invented by some rabbi six centuries after the great event. For the truth, as recorded by the evangelists, and confirmed by eyewitnesses, is that Jesus was brought, judged, and condemned in the house of Caiaphas. In the terse language of St. John, "Then led they Jesus from Caiaphas unto the hall of judgment" (the pretorium of Pilate).

And now it is finished. Jesus is condemned! The priests, the scribes, and the elders, precipitately leaving their seats, bind the victim and hasten tumultuously to Pilate, clamoring for his ratification of their sentence, and his assent to its speedy execution. (Luke 23:1; Mark 15:1; Matthew 27:2; John 18:28.)

At this juncture, we might call attention to the part taken by the people at the instigation of the priests and scribes in this affair. But we will reserve that subject for a future treatise. Our object in the present work is to hold up to view the enormous outrages committed by the Sanhedrin itself, upon which body the responsibility of our Lords condemnation chiefly rests. The house of Caiaphas was the vile den from whence proceeded the full depth of the cruelty and injustice that subsequently marked the proceedings at the pretorium, and found their culmination on the hill of Calvary.

BIBLIOGRAPHY

Abegg, Martin. Peter Flint and Eugene Ulrich. *The Dead Sea Scrolls Bible: The Oldest Known Bible Translated for the First Time into English*, 1999.

Alexander, Joseph A. *Commentary on Isaiah*. Grand Rapids: Kregel, 1992.

Alexander, Ralph H. *The Expositor's Bible Commentary: Ezekiel*. 12 vols. Grand Rapids: Zondervan, 1986.

Alexander, T. Desmond and David W. Baker. *Dictionary of the Old Testament Pentateuch*. Downers Grove, Ill: InterVarsity, 2003.

Allen, Ronald B. *Rediscovering Prophecy: A New Son for the Kingdom*. Portland, OR: Multnomah Press, 1983.

Anderson, Sir Robert. *The Coming Prince*. Grand Rapids: Kregel, 1967.

Ankerberg, John and John Weldon. *Fast Facts on Islam*. Eugene, OR: Harvest House Publishers, 2001.

Archer, Gleason L. *The Expositor's Bible Commentary: Daniel*. 12 vols. Grand Rapids: Zondervan, 1985.

Atkinson, Basil R. C. *The Pocket Commentary of the Bible: Genesis*. Chicago: Moody, 1957.

Baker, Charles F. *A Dispensational Theology*. Grand Rapids: Grace Bible Publications, 1971.

Baker, Kenneth L. *The Expositor's Bible Commentary: Zechariah*. 12 vols. Grand Rapid: Zondervan, 1985.

Bancroft, Emery H. *Christian Theology*. Grand Rapids: Zondervan, 1964.

Barackman, Floyd H. *Practical Christian Theology*. 4th ed. Grand Rapids: Kregel, 1998.

Barber, Cyril J. *The Books of Samuel*. 2 Vols. Neptune, NJ: Loizeaux, 1994.

Barker, Kenneth. *The New American Commentary: Micah*. 21 vols. Nashville: Broadman, 1998.

Barnes, Albert. *Barnes' Notes: Minor Prophets*. 2 vols. Grand Rapids: Baker, 1950.

Baron, David. *Rays of Messiah's Glory*. Jerusalem: Keren Ahvah Meshihit, 2000.

Baron, David. *The Servant of Jehovah*. Jerusalem: Keren Ahvah Meshihit, 2000.

Baron, David. *The Visions and Prophecies of Zechariah*. Jerusalem: Keren Ahvah Meshihit, 2000.

Barrett, Michael P.V. *Beginning at Moses*. 2nd ed. Greenville, SC: Ambassador-Emerald International, 2001.

Bauckham, Richard. *God Crucified: Monotheism & Christology in the New Testament*. Grand Rapids: Eerdmans, 1998.

Beall, Todd S. and William A. Banks. *Old Testament Parsing Guide: Genesis-Esther*. 2 vols. Chicago: Moody Press, 1986.

Benach, Henry. *Go to Learn*. Chattanooga: International Board of Jewish Missions, 1997.

Berger, David. *The Rebbe, The Messiah and the Scandal of Orthodox Indifference*. Portland: The Littman Library of Jewish Civilization, 2001.

Bergen, Robert D. *The New American Commentary: 1 and 2 Samuel*. 21 vols. Nashville: Broadman, 2002.

Berkhof, L. *Systematic Theology*. Grand Rapids: Eerdmans, 1941.

Berlin, Adele, and Marc Zvi Brettler. *The Jewish Study Bible*. New York: Oxford University, 2004.

Berman, Joshua. *The Temple: Its Symbolism and Meaning Then and Now*. Northvale, NJ: Jason Aronson, 1995.

Berry, George R. *The Book of Proverbs*. Philadelphia: American Baptist Publication Society, 1904.

Bleich, J. David. *With Perfect Faith: The Foundation of Jewish Belief*. New York: KTAV Publishing House, 1983.

Block, Daniel I. *The New American Commentary: Judges, Ruth*. Nashville: Broadman, 1999.

Boice, James Montgomery. *An Expositional Commentary: Psalms*. 3 vols. Grand Rapids: Baker, 1994.

Boice, James Montgomery. *An Expositional Commentary: The Minor Prophets: Micah-Malachi*. Grand Rapids: Baker, 1986.

Borland, James. *Christ in the Old Testament*. Ross-shire, Great Britain: Christian Focus Publications, 1999.

Botterweck, G. Johannes, Helmer Ringgren and Heinz-Josef Fabry. *Theological Dictionary of the Old Testament*. Grand Rapids: Eerdmans, 1977.

Bratcher, Robert G. and William D. Reyburn. *A Handbook on Psalms*. New York: United Bible Societies, 1991.

Brenton, Sir Lancelot C. L. *The Septuagint with the Apocrypha: Greek and English*. Grand Rapids: Zondervan, 1980.

Briggs, Charles A. *Messianic Prophecy*. Peabody, MA: Hendrickson, 1988.

Briscoe, Stuart. *The Communicator's Commentary: Genesis*. Waco, TX: Word Books, 1987.

Bromiley, Geoffrey W. *The International Standard Bible Encyclopedia*. 4 vols. Grand Rapids: Eerdmans, 1988.

Brown, Francis, S. R. Driver and Charles A. Briggs. *A Hebrew and English Lexicon of the Old Testament*, Oxford: Clarendon, n.d.

Brown, Michael L. *Answering Jewish Objections to Jesus: Theological Objections.* Vol. 2. Grand Rapids: Baker Books, 2000.

Brown, Michael L. *Answering Jewish Objections to Jesus: Messianic Prophecy Objections.* Vol. 3. Grand Rapids: Baker Books, 2003.

Brown, Michael L. *Our Hands are Stained with Blood: The Tragic Story of the "Church" and the Jewish People.* Shippensburg, PA: Destiny Image Publishers, 1990.

Broyles, Craig. *New International Biblical Commentary: Psalms.* Peabody, MA: Hendrickson, 1999.

Bruce, F. F. *The New International Commentary on the New Testament: The Epistles to the Hebrews.* 18 vols. Grand Rapids: Eerdmans 1964.

Brueggemann, Walter. *A Commentary on Jeremiah: Exile and Homecoming.* Grand Rapids: Eerdmans, 1998.

Brueggemann, Walter. *Interpretation, A Bible Commentary for Teaching and Preaching: Genesis.* Atlanta: John Knox Press, 1982.

Brueggemann, Walter. *Theology of the Old Testament.* Minneapolis: Fortress Press, 1997.

Buksbazen, Victor. *Israel's Messiah.* Bellmawr, NJ: Friends of Israel Gospel Ministry, 2002.

Buksbazen, Victor. *The Prophet Isaiah.* 2 vols. Collingswood, NJ: Spearhead Press, 1971.

Bultema, Harry. *Commentary on Isaiah.* Grand Rapids: Kregel, 1981.

Bush, George. *Exodus.* Minneapolis: Klock & Klock Christian Publishers, 1981.

Buswell, James Oliver. *A Systematic Theology of the Christian Religion.* Grand Rapids: Zondervan, 1962.

Butler, J. Glentworth. *Butler's Bible Work.* 6 vols. New York: Funk & Wagnalls, 1889.

Buttrick, George Arthur. *The Interpreter's Bible.* Nashville: Abingdon, 1953.

Cassuto, U. *A Commentary on the Book of Exodus.* Jerusalem: Magnes Press, 1967.

Cassuto, U. *A Commentary on the Book of Genesis: Part One.* Jerusalem: Magnes, 1961.

Chafer, Lewis Sperry. *Systematic Theology.* 8 vols. Dallas: Dallas Seminary Press, 1964.

Charles, R. H. *A Critical and Exegetical Commentary on the Book of Daniel.* Oxford: Clarendon Press, 1929.

Charnock, Steven. *Existence and Attributes of God.* Grand Rapids: Baker, 1979.

Child, Brevard S. *The Old Testament Library: Isaiah*. Louisville, KY: Westminster John Knox, 2001.

Chilton, Bruce D. and Jacob Neusner, *Classical Christianity and Rabbinic Judaism*. Grand Rapids: Baker, 2004.

Cohen, A. *The Soncino Chumash, Isaiah*. New York: The Soncino Press, 1983.

Cohen, A. *The Soncino Books of the Bible: Jeremiah*. New York: Soncino Press, 1985.

Cohen, A. *The Soncino Books of the Bible: Proverbs*. New York: Soncino Press, 1985.

Cohen, A. *The Soncino Chumash, The Five Books of Moses with Haphtaroth*. New York: The Soncino Press, 1993.

Cohen, A. *The Soncino Books of the Bible: The Psalms*. New York: Soncino Press, 1980.

Cohen, A. *The Soncino Chumash, The Twelve Prophets*. New York: Soncino Press, 1994.

Cohn-Sherbok, Rabbi Dan. *The Jewish Messiah*. Edinburgh, Scotland: T & T Clark, 1997.

Cole, R. Alan. *Tyndale Old Testament Commentaries: Exodus*. Downers Grove: InterVarsity, 1973.

Cole, R. Dennis. *The New American Commentary: Numbers*. 21 vols. Nashville: Broadman, 2000.

Conrad, Edgar W. *Zechariah*. Sheffield, England: Sheffield Academic Press, 1999.

Cooke, G. A. *The International Critical Commentary: The Book of Ezekiel*. Edinburgh: T & T Clark, 1936.

Cooper, David L. *God's Gracious Provision for Man*. Los Angeles: Biblical Research Society, 1953.

Cooper, David L. *Messiah: His First Coming Scheduled*. Los Angeles: Biblical Research Society, 1939.

Cooper, David L. *Messiah: His Historical Appearance*. Los Angeles: Biblical Research Society, 1961.

Cooper, David L. *Messiah: His Nature and Person*. Los Angeles: Biblical Research Society, 1933.

Cooper, David L. *The 70 Weeks of Daniel*. Los Angeles: Biblical Research Society, 1941.

Cooper, David L. *The God of Israel*. Los Angeles: Biblical Research Society, 1945.

Cooper, David L. *The Shepherd of Israel Seeking His Own*. Los Angeles: Biblical Research Society, 1962.

Cooper, David L. *What Men Must Believe*. Los Angeles: Biblical Research Society, 1943.

Cooper, Lamar Eugene. *The New American Commentary: Ezekiel*. 17 vols. Nashville: Broadman and Holman, 1994.

Craigie, P. C. *The New International Commentary on the Old Testament, The Book of Deuteronomy*. Grand Rapids: Eerdmans, 1976.

Crenshaw, James. *The Old Testament Library, Ecclesiastes*. Philadelphia: Westminster Press, 1987.

Criswell, W.A. *The Criswell Study Bible*. Nashville: Nelson, 1979.

Currid, John D. *A Study Commentary: Genesis*. 2 vols. Webster, NY: Evangelical Press, 2003.

Currid, John D. *A Study Commentary on Exodus*. 2 vols. Auburn, MA: Evangelical Press, 2000.

Dahood, Mitchell. *The Anchor Bible: Psalms 101-150*. Garden City, NY: Doubleday, 1970.

Davidson, A. B. *The Book of the Prophet Ezekiel*. London: Cambridge Press, 1916.

Davidson, A. B. *The Theology of the Old Testament*. Edinburgh: T & T Clark, 1955.

Davidson, Robert. *The Daily Study Bible Series: Jeremiah and Lamentations*. 2 vols. Philadelphia: Westminster Press, 1985.

Davis, John J. and John C. Whitcomb. *Israel: A Commentary on Joshua – 2 Kings*. Winona Lake, IN: BMH Books, 2002.

Davis, John J. *Moses and the Gods of Egypt: Studies in Exodus*. Winona Lake, IN: BHM Books, 2003.

DeHaan, Richard W. *The Living God*. Grand Rapids: Zondervan, 1967.

Delitzsch, Franz. *Messianic Prophecies in Historical Succession*. Eugene, OR: Wipf and Stock Publishers, 1998.

Dickason, C. Fred. *Angels: Elect and Evil*. Chicago: Moody, 1975.

Driver, S. R. *Westminster Commentaries, the Book of Genesis*. London: Methuen & Co. 1911.

Driver, S. R., A Plummer and C. A. Briggs, eds. *The International Critical Commentary: Genesis*. Edinburgh: T & T Clark. 1930.

Du Bois, Lauriston J. *Beacon Bible Commentary in Ten Volumes: Numbers*. Kansas City: Beacon Hill Press, 1969.

Dunnam, Maxie D. *The Communicator's Commentary: Exodus*. Waco: Word, 1967.

Dyrness, William. *Themes in Old Testament Theology*. Downers Grove: InterVarsity, 1977.

Edersheim, Alfred. *The Exodus and the Wandering in the Wilderness*. London: The Religious Tract Society, 1876.

Elwell, Walter A. *Evangelical Dictionary of Theology*. Grand Rapids: Baker Book House, 1984.

Enns, Paul. *The Moody Handbook of Theology*. Chicago: Moody Press, 1989.

Epstein, Rabbi I. *The Babylonian Talmud*. London: The Soncino Press, 1938.

Erickson, Millard J. *Christian Theology*. 2nd ed. Grand Rapids: Baker Books, 1998.

Erickson, Millard J. *Introducing Christian Doctrine*. Grand Rapids: Baker, 1992.

Evans, William. *The Great Doctrines of the Bible*. Chicago: Moody, 1974.

Feinberg, Charles L. *God Remembers, A Study of the Book of Zechariah*. New York: American Board of Missions to the Jews, 1965.

Feinberg, Charles L. *Daniel: The Kingdom of the Lord*. Winona Lake, IN: BMH Books, 1981.

Feinberg, Charles L. *Jeremiah*. Grand Rapids: Zondervan, 1982.

Feinberg, Charles L. *The Minor Prophets*. Chicago: Moody, 1951.

Feinberg, Charles L. *The Prophecy of Ezekiel: The Glory of the Lord*. Chicago: Moody, 1969.

Feinberg, John S. *No One Like Him*. Wheaton: Crossway Books, 2001.

Figart, Thomas O. *Meaningful Mediators II: Psalms 22-24*. Lakewood, FL: Xulon Press, 2007.

Finkel, Avraham Yaakov. *The Torah Revealed*. San Francisco: Jossey-Bass, 2004.

Frame, John M. *The Doctrine of God*. Phillipsburg, NJ: P & R Publishers, 2002.

Free, Joseph P. and Howard F. Vos. *Archaeology and the Bible History*. Grand Rapids: Zondervan, 1992.

Fretheim, Terence E. *Smyth & Helwys Bible Commentary: Jeremiah*. Macon, GA: Smyth & Helwys Publishing, 2002.

Frey, Joseph Samuel C. F. *The Messiahship of Jesus*. Philadelphia: American Baptist Publication Society, 1850.

Fruchtenbaum, Arnold. *Ariel's Bible Commentary: The Messianic Jewish Epistles*. Tustin, CA: Ariel Ministries, 2003.

Fruchtenbaum, Arnold. *Christ's Right to David's Throne, Manuscript #25*. Tustin, CA: Ariel Ministries, 1983.

Fruchtenbaum, Arnold. *Footsteps of Messiah*. Tustin, CA: Ariel Ministers, 2002.

Fruchtenbaum, Arnold. *Genesis*. Tapes. Tustin, CA: Ariel Ministries, n.d.

Fruchtenbaum, Arnold. *How the New Testament Quotes the Old Testament. Manuscript #134*. Tustin, CA: Ariel Ministries, 1991.

Fruchtenbaum, Arnold. *Israelology, the Missing Link in Systematic Theology*. Tustin, CA: Ariel Ministries, 1993.

Fruchtenbaum, Arnold. *Jesus Was a Jew*. Tustin, CA: Ariel Ministries, 1981.

Fruchtenbaum, Arnold. *Messianic Christology*. Tustin, CA: Ariel Ministries, 1998.

Fruchtenbaum, Arnold. *Minor Prophets. Tapes.* Tustin, CA: Ariel Press, n.d.

Fruchtenbaum, Arnold G. *The Feasts of Israel.* Manuscript #62. Tustin, CA: Ariel Press, 1984.

Fruchtenbaum, Arnold G. *The Feast of Tabernacles.* Manuscript #120. Tustin, CA: Ariel Press, 1987.

Fruchtenbaum, Arnold. *The Footsteps of Messiah.* Tustin, CA: Ariel Ministries, 2003.

Fruchtenbaum, Arnold. *The Life of the Messiah. Tape Series.* Tustin, CA: Ariel Ministries, n.d.

Fruchtenbaum, Arnold. *The Sabbath, Manuscript #176.* Tustin, CA: Ariel Ministries, 1991.

Fruchtenbaum, Arnold. *The Trinity – Manuscript #50.* Tustin, CA: Ariel Ministries, 1983.

Fruchtenbaum, Arnold. *The True Shepherd of Zechariah: A Study of Zechariah 11:1-17,* Manuscript #90. Tustin, CA: Ariel Ministries, 1984.

Frydland, Rachmiel. *What the Rabbis Know About the Messiah.* Cincinnati, OH: Messianic Publishing Co, 1991.

Frydland, Rachmiel. *When Being Jewish Was a Crime.* Nashville: Nelson, 1978.

Frymer-Kensky, Tikva, David Novak, Peter Ochs, David Fox Sandmel and Michael A. Signer, *Christianity in Jewish Terms.* Boulder, CO: Westview Press, 2000.

Fuchs, Daniel. *Israel's Holy Days.* Neptune, NJ: Loizeaux Brothers, 1985.

Fuller, Reginald H. "The *Vestigia Trinitatis* in the Old Testament." Page 507 in *The Quest for Context and Meaning.* Edited by Craig A. Evans and Shemaryahu Talmon. Leiden, Netherlands: Brill, 1997.

Gaebelein, Arno Clemens. *The Angels of God.* Grand Rapids: Baker, 1969.

Gaebelein, Arno Clemens. *The Book of Psalms.* New York: "Our Hope" Publications, 1939.

Gaebelein, Frank. *Four Minor Prophets: Obadiah, Jonah, Habakkuk, and Haggai.* Chicago: Moody, 1970.

Garrett, Duane A. *The New American Commentary: Proverbs.* Nashville: Broadman, 1993.

Garstang, John. *Joshua – Judges: Foundations of Bible History.* Grand Rapids: Kregel, 1978.

Geerhardus, Vos. *Biblical Theology, Old and New Testaments.* Grand Rapids: Eerdmans, 1948.

Geisler, Norman L and William E. Nix. *A General Introduction to the Bible.* Chicago, IL: Moody Press, 1968.

Geisler, Norman L. *A Popular Survey of the Old Testament.* Grand Rapids: Baker, 1977.

Geisler, Norman. *Systematic Theology*. 4 vols. Minneapolis: Bethany House, 2003.

Goldberg, Louis. *Our Jewish Friends*. Neptune, NJ: Loizeaux Brothers, 1983.

Goldberg, Louis. "The Deviation of Jewish Thought from an Old Testament Theology in the Inter-testamental Period." Doctor of Theology. diss., Winona Lake, IN: Grace Theological Seminary,1963).

Goldingay, John E., *Word Biblical Commentary: Daniel*. 32 vols. Dallas: Word, 1989.

Goldman, S. *The Soncino Books of the Bible: The Twelve Prophets*. New York: Soncino Press, 1994.

Gordis, Robert. *Koheleth, The Man and His World, A Study of Ecclesiastes*. New York: Schocken Books, 1968.

Graham, Billy. *The Holy Spirit*. Waco: Word, 1978.

Greenberg, Moshe. *The Heritage of Biblical Israel: Understanding Exodus*. New York: Behrman House, 1969.

Greenstein, Howard R. *Judaism: An Eternal Covenant*. Philadelphia: Fortress Press, 1983.

Grogan, Geoffrey W. *The Expositor's Bible Commentary: Isaiah*. 12 vols. Grand Rapids: Zondervan, 1986.

Groningen, Gerald Van. *Messianic Revelation in the Old Testament*. Grand Rapids: Baker, 1990.

Grudem, Wayne. *Evangelical Feminism & Biblical Truth*. Sisters, OR: Multnomah Publishers, 2004.

Grudem, Wayne. *Systematic Theology*. Grand Rapids: Zondervan, 1994.

Gunkel, Hermann. *Mercer Library of Biblical Studies: Genesis*. Macon, GA: Mercer University Press, 1997.

Hagee, John. In Defense of Israel, Lake Mary, FL: Frontline Publishers, 2007

Hailey, Homer. *The Minor Prophets*. Grand Rapids: Baker, 1972.

Hamilton, Victor P. *The New International Commentary on the Old Testament: Genesis Chapters 1-17*. Grand Rapids: Eerdmans, 1990.

Hamilton, Victor P. *The New International Commentary on the Old Testament: Genesis Chapters 18-50*. Grand Rapids: Eerdmans, 1990.

Harkavy, Alexander. *The Twenty-Four Books of the Old Testament*. 2 vols. New York: Hebrew Publishing Co, 1916.

Harman, Allen. *Isaiah*. Ross-shire, Scotland: Christian Focus Publications, 2005.

Harper, William Rainey, *A Critical and Exegetical Commentary on Amos and Hosea*. Edinburgh: T & T Clark, 1994.

Harris, R. Laird., Gleason L. Archer, Jr., and Bruce K. Waltke, eds., *Theological Wordbook of the Old Testament,* Chicago: Moody, 1981.

Hartman, Fred. *Zechariah: Israel's Messenger of the Messiah's Triumph*. Bellmawr, NJ: Friends of Israel Gospel Ministry, 1994.

Hayford, Jack. *The Trinity*. Grand Rapids: Chosen Books, 2003.

Heinrich, William. *In the Shame of Jesus: The Hidden Story of Church-Sponsored Anti-Semitism*. Morgantown, PA: Masthof Press, 2009.

Heinze, E. Charles. *Trinity & Triunity*. Dale City, VA: Epaphras Press, 1995.

Henderson, Ebenezer. *Thornapple Commentaries: The Twelve Minor Prophets*. Grand Rapids: Baker, 1980.

Hengstenberg, E.W. *Christology of the Old Testament*. 4 vols. Grand Rapids: Kregel, 1956.

Hengstenberg, E.W. *Christology of the Old Testament*. Grand Rapids: Kregel, 1970.

Hertz, J.H. *Pentateuch and Haftorahs*. London: Soncino Press, 1952.

Heydt, Henry J. *Studies in Jewish Evangelism*. New York: American Board to the Jews, 1951.

Hildebrandt, Wilf. *An Old Testament Theology of the Spirit of God*. Peabody, MA: Hendrickson, 1995.

Hill, Andrew E. and John H. Walton. *A Survey of the Old Testament*, Grand Rapids: Zondervan, 1991.

Hinson, David F. *Theology of the Old Testament*. London: Society for Promoting Christian Knowledge, 2001.

Hodge, Charles. *Systematic Theology*. 3 vols. Grand Rapids: Eerdmans, 1970.

Hoekema, Anthony A. *The Four Major Cults*. Grand Rapids: Eerdmans, 1963.

Holdcroft, L. Thomas. *The Doctrine of God*. Oakland, CA: Western Book Company, 1960.

Hossfeld, Frank-Lothar and Erich Zenger. *Psalms 2: A Commentary on Psalms 51-100*. Translated by Linda M. Maloney. Minneapolis: Augsburg Fortress Press, 2005.

House, Paul. *Old Testament Theology*. Downers Grove: InterVarsity, 1998.

Houtman, Cornelis. *Historical Commentary on the Old Testament: Exodus*. 3 vols. Kampen, Netherlands: Kok Publishing House, 1993.

Howard, Jr., David M. *The New American Commentary: Joshua*. 21 vols. Nashville: Broadman, 1998.

Hubbard, David A. *The Communicator's Commentary: Proverbs*. 21 vols. Dallas: Word, 1989.

Hubbard, David A. and Glenn W. Barker. *Word Biblical Commentary: Genesis 1-15*. 52 vols. Waco, Tex: Word Books, 1987.

Huey, F. B. *Bible Study Commentary: Jeremiah*. Grand Rapids: Zondervan, 1981.

Huey, F. B. *The New American Commentary: Jeremiah, Lamentations*. 21 vols. Nashville: Broadman, 1993.

Jacob, Benno. *The Second Book of the Bible: Exodus*. Translated by Walter Jacob. Hoboken, NJ: KTAV Publishing, 1992.

Jacob, Rabbi Ernest I. *The First Book of the Bible: Genesis*. New York: KTAV Publishing, 1974.

Jacobs, Louis. *A Concise Companion to the Jewish Religion*. Oxford, England: Oxford University Press, 1999.

Jacobs, Louis. *A Jewish Theology*. West Orange, NJ: Behrman House, Inc. 1973.

Jakobovitz, Immanuel. *The Oral Law: A Study of the Rabbinic Contribution to Torah She-be-al-Peh*. 2nd rev. ed.; New York: Feldheim, 1996.

Jamieson, Robert, A. R. Fausset and David Brown. *A Commentary: Critical Experimental and Practical on the Old and New Testaments*. 6 vols. Grand Rapids: Eerdmans, 1945.

Jenni, Ernest and Claus Westermann. *Theological Lexicon of Old Testament*, Peabody, MA: Hendrickson, 1997.

Jocz, Jakob. *The Jewish People and Jesus Christ: A Study in the Controversy Between Church and Synagogue*. London: S.P.C.K., 1954.

Johnson, G. H. S. *The Book of Psalms with an Explanatory and Critical Commentary*. London: John Murray, 1880.

Johnson, Paul. *A History of the Jews*. New York: Harper Perennial, 1988.

Johnstone, Patrick and Jason Mandryk, Eds. *Operation World*. Waynesboro, GA: Paternoster USA, 2001.

Johnstone, William. *1 & 2 Chronicles*. Sheffield, England: Sheffield Academic Press, 1997.

Jones, Douglas Rawlinson. *The New Century Bible Commentary: Jeremiah*. Grand Rapids: Eerdmans, 1992.

Jukes, Andrew. *The Names of God*. Grand Rapids: Kregel, 1980.

Julien, Tom. *Studies in Exodus: Spiritual Greatness*. Winona Lake, IN: BMH Books, 1979.

Kac, Arthur W. *The Messiahship of Jesus*. Grand Rapids: Baker Book House, 1986.

Kac, Arthur. *The Rebirth of the State of Israel*. London: Marshall, Morgan, and Scott, 1958.

Kac, Arthur W. *The Spiritual Dilemma of the Jewish People: Its Cause and Cure*. Grand Rapids: Baker, 1983.

Kaiser, Walter C. *Ecclesiastes Total Life*. Chicago: Moody Press, 1979.

Kaiser, Walter C. *The Christian and the "Old" Testament*. Pasadena, CA: William Carey Library, 1998.

Kaiser, Walter C. *The Communicator's Commentary: Micah – Malachi*. 21 vols. Waco, TX: Word Books, 1992.

Kaiser, Walter C. *The Expositor's Bible Commentary: Exodus*. 12 vols. Grand Rapids: Zondervan, 1990.

Kaiser, Walter C. *The Messiah in the Old Testament*. Grand Rapids: Zondervan, 1995.

Kaiser, Walter C. *Toward an Old Testament Theology*. Grand Rapids: Zondervan, 1991.

Kalland, Earl S. *The Expositor's Bible Commentary: Deuteronomy*. 12 vols. Grand Rapids: Eerdmans, 1992.

Kaplan, Aryeh. *The Real Messiah? A Jewish Response to Missionaries*. New York: National Conference of Synagogues, 1985.

Keil, C. F. and F. Delitzsch. *Commentary on the Old Testament*. Translated by James Martin. 10 vols. Grand Rapids: Eerdmans, 1973.

Kelley, Page H. *Biblical Hebrew: An Introductory Grammar*. Grand Rapids: Eerdmans, 1992.

Kelley, Page H. *The Broadman Bible Commentary: Proverbs – Isaiah*. Nashville: Broadman, 1971.

Kidner, Derek. *Tyndale Old Testament Commentaries: Psalms 1-72*. Downers Grove, IL: Inter-Varsity Press, 1979.

King, Henry Melville. *The Messiah in the Psalms* (Philadelphia: American Baptist Publication Society, 1899.

Kirkpatrick, A. F. *The Book of Psalms*. Cambridge: The University Press, 1914.

Kittel, Rud. *Biblia Hebraica*. New York: American Bible Society, 1937.

Klausner, Joseph. *The Messianic Idea In Israel*. New York: Macmillan, 1955.

Klinghoffer, David. *Why the Jews Rejected Jesus*. New York: Three Leaves Press: Doubleday, 2005.

Knight, George A. F. *A Christian Theology of the Old Testament*. Carlisle, UK: Paternoster Publishing, 1998.

Kohlenberger, John R., III. *The Interlinear NIV Hebrew-English Old Testament*. Grand Rapids: Zondervan, 1987.

Kohlenberger, John R., III. and James A Swanson. *The Hebrew English Concordance to the Old Testament*. Grand Rapids: Zondervan, 1998.

Kolatch, Alfred J. *Inside Judaism: The Concepts, Customs, and Celebrations of the Jewish People*, Middle Village, NY: Jonathan David Publishers, Inc. 2006.

Laetsch, Theodore. *Commentary: Jeremiah*. St. Louis: Concordia, 1965.

Laetsch, Theodore. *The Minor Prophets*. St. Louis: Concordia, 1956.

Lamsa, George M. *The Holy Bible from Ancient Eastern Manuscripts*. Philadelphia: A. J. Holman, 1957.

Landman, Leo. *Messianism in the Talmudic Era.* New York: KTAV Publishing, 1979.

Lang, G. H. *The Histories and Prophecies of Daniel.* Grand Rapids: Kregel, 1940.

Lange, John Peter. *Lange's Commentary on the Holy Scriptures.* Translated by Philip Schaff. 12 vols. Grand Rapids: Zondervan, 1960.

Lawson, George. *Exposition of Proverbs.* Grand Rapids: Kregel, 1980.

Leeser, Isaac. *The Twenty-Four Books of the Holy Bible.* New York: Hebrew Publishing, 1916.

Lenski, R. C. H. *The Interpretation of St. John's Gospel.* Minneapolis, MN: Augsburg Publishing, 1963.

Leupold, H. C. *Exposition of Ecclesiastes.* Columbus, OH: Wartburg Press, 1952.

Leupold, H. C. *Exposition of Genesis.* Grand Rapids: Baker Book House, 1942.

Leupold, H. C. *Exposition of Isaiah.* 2 vols. Grand Rapids: Baker, 1968.

Leupold, H. C. *Exposition of the Psalms.* Grand Rapids: Baker Book House, 1959.

Levine, Samuel. *You Take Jesus, I'll Take God.* Los Angeles: Hamoroh Press, 1980.

Levy, David. *Malachi: Messenger of Rebuke and Renewal.* Bellmawr, NJ: Friends of Israel Gospel Ministry, 1992.

Livingston, G. Herbert. *The Pentateuch in Its Cultural Environment.* 2nd ed. Grand Rapids: Baker Book House, 1987.

Lockyer, Herbert. *All About the Holy Spirit.* Peabody: Hendrickson, 1995.

Lockyer, Herbert. *All the Divine Names and Titles in the Bible.* Grand Rapids: Zondervan, 1975.

Longman III, Tremper. *The Messiah in the Old and New Testaments.* Grand Rapids: Eerdmans, 2007

Longman III, Tremper. *The New International Commentary on the Old Testament: Ecclesiastes.* Grand Rapids: Eerdmans, 1998.

MacDonald, William. *Enjoying the Psalms*: Vol. 1. Kansas City: Walterick Publications, 1976.

Mackay, John L. *A Mentor Commentary: Exodus.* Fearn, Ross-shire, Great Britain: Mentor, 2001.

Mackay, John L. *A Mentor Commentary: Jeremiah.* Fearn, Ross-shire, Great Britain: Mentor, 2004.

McCann, J. Clinton. *Interpretation, A Bible Commentary for Teaching and Preaching: Judges.* Louisville, KY: John Knox Press, 2002.

McCarter, P. Kyle, Jr. *The Anchor Bible: I Samuel.* Vol. 8. Garden City, NY: Doubleday, 1980.

McClain, Alva J. *Daniel's Prophecy of the 70 Weeks.* Winona Lake, IN: BMH Books, 2007.

McConville, J. G. *Apollos Old Testament Commentary: Deuteronomy*. Downers Grove, IL, 2002.

McDowell, Josh. *Evidence that Demands a Verdict*. 2 vols. Nashville: Nelson, 1993.

McGee, J. Vernon. *Thru the Bible: Genesis-Deuteronomy*. 5 vols. Pasadena, CA: Thru The Bible Radio, 1981.

Madvig, Donald. *The Expositor's Bible Commentary: Joshua*. 12 vols. Grand Rapids: Zondervan, 1992.

Mathews, Kenneth. *The New American Commentary: Genesis 1:1-11:26*. 21 vols. Nashville: Broadman & Holman Publishers, 1996.

Mathews, Kenneth. *The New American Commentary: Genesis 11:27-50:26*. 21 vols. Nashville: Broadman & Holman Publishers, 2005.

Mays, James L. *Interpretation, A Bible Commentary for Teaching and Preaching: Psalms*. Louisville: John Knox Press, 1989.

Merrill, Eugene H. *An Exegetical Commentary: Haggai, Zechariah, Malachi*. Chicago: Moody, 1994.

Merrill, Eugene H. *Kingdom of Priests*. Grand Rapids: Baker, 1987.

Merrill, Eugene H. *The New American Commentary: Deuteronomy*. 21 vols. Nashville: Broadman & Holman Publishers, 1994.

Milgrom, Jacob. *The JPS Torah Commentary: Numbers*. Philadelphia: The Jewish Publication Society, 1990.

Miller, H. S. *General Biblical Introduction*. Houghton, NY: Word Bearers, 1960.

Miller, Paul. *The Gramcord Institute*. Vancouver, WA: Gramcord, 1999.

Miller, Stephen. *The New American Commentary: Daniel*. 21 vols. Nashville: Broadman & Holman, 1994.

Moeller, Henry R. *The Legacy of Zion*. Grand Rapids: Baker, 1977.

Moore, George F. *International Critical Commentary: Judges*. New York: Charles Scribner's, 1903.

Moore, George Foot. *Judaism*. 2 vol. Peabody: Hendrickson, 1997.

Morey, Robert. *The Trinity: Evidence and Issues*. Grand Rapids: Word Publishers, 1996.

Morris, Henry M. *The Genesis Record*. Grand Rapids: Baker Book House, 1980.

Morris, Henry M. *Treasures in the Psalms*. Green Forest, AR: Master Books, 2001.

Morris, Robert. *Anti-Missionary Arguments, the Trinity*. Irvine, CA: HaDavar Messianic Ministries, n. d.

Motyer, J. Alec. *The Prophecy of Isaiah*. Downers Grove, IL: InterVarsity, 1993.

Nachman, Moshe ben. *Ramban (Nachmanides), Commentary on the Torah – Genesis*. Translated by Chavel. New York: Shilo Publishing Inc.

819

Nadler, Sam. *The Messianic Answer Book*. Charlotte: Word of Messiah Ministries, 2005.

Nassi, Rabbi Tzvi. *The Great Mystery or, How Can Three Be One*? Cincinnati, OH: M. L. O. n.d.

Neusner, Jacob. *An Introduction to Judaism*. Louisville: Westminster/John Knox Press, 1991.

Neusner, Jacob and William Scott Green. *Dictionary of Judaism in the Biblical Period*. Peabody, MA: Hendrickson, 1999.

Neusner, Jacob. *Judaism When Christianity Began*. Louisville, KY: Westminster John Knox Press, 2002.

Niehaus, Jeffrey J. *God At Sinai*. Grand Rapids: Zondervan, 1995.

Nixon, Jim. "The Doctrine of the Trinity in the Old Testament." Th.M. diss., Dallas Theological Seminary, 1974.

Noth, Martin. *The Old Testament Library: Numbers*. Philadelphia: Westminster, 1968.

Odom, Robert Leo. *Israel's Angel Extraordinary*. Bronx, NY: Israelite Heritage Institute, 1985.

Oehler, Gustave Friedrich. *Theology of the Old Testament*. Grand Rapids: Zondervan, 1883.

Ogden, Graham and Lynell Zogbo. *A Handbook on Ecclesiastes*. New York: United Bible Societies, 1997.

Olson, Dennis T. *Interpretation: A Bible Commentary for Teaching and Preaching, Numbers*. Louisville, John Knox Press, 1996.

Orlov, Andrei A. *The Enoch-Metatron Tradition: Texts and Studies in Ancient Judaism 107*. Tubingen, Germany: Gulde-Druck, 2005.

Orr, James. *The International Standard Bible Encyclopedia*. 5 vols. Grand Rapids: Eerdmans, 1939.

Owens, John Joseph. *Analytical Key to the Old Testament*. Grand Rapids: Baker, 1989.

Pache, Rene. *The Person and Work of the Holy Spirit*. Chicago: Moody, 1954.

Parkes, James. *The Foundations of Judaism and Christianity*. Chicago: Quadrangle Books, 1960.

Patai, Raphael. *The Messiah Texts*. Detroit: Wayne State University Press, 1979.

Payne, J. Barton. *The Expositors Bible Commentary: 1 Kings– Job*. 12 vols. Grand Rapids: Zondervan, 1988.

Payne, J. Barton. *The Theology of the Older Testament*. Grand Rapids: Zondervan, 1962.

Perowne, J. J. Stewart. *The Book of Psalms*. 2 vols. Grand Rapids: Zondervan, 1966.

Peterson, David L. *The Old Testament Library: Haggai & Zechariah 1-8*. Philadelphia: Westminster Press, 1984.

Pfeiffer, Charles F. *Old Testament History*. Grand Rapids: Baker, 1973.

Phillips, John. *Exploring Genesis*. Chicago: Moody, 1980.

Phillips, John. *Exploring Proverbs*. Neptune, NJ: Loizeaux, 1996.

Phillips, O. E. *Exploring the Messianic Psalms* Philadelphia: Hebrew Christian Fellowship, 1967.

Picker, Chaim. "*Make Us A God!*" *A Jewish Response to Hebrew Christianity: A Survival Manual for Jews*. New York: iUniverse Press, 2005.

Pressler, Carolyn. *Joshua, Judges and Ruth*. Louisville: Westminster John Knox Press, 2002.

Preuss, Horst Dietrich. *Old Testament Theology*. 2 vols. Translated by Leo G. Perdue. Louisville: Westminster John Knox, 1995.

Pritchard, James B. *The Ancient Near East: An Anthology of Text and Pictures*. 2 vols. Princeton, NJ: Princeton University Press. 1958.

Pritchard, James B. *The Ancient Near East in Pictures*. Princeton, NJ: Princeton University Press, 1954.

Pusey, E. B. *The Minor Prophets*. Grand Rapids: Baker, 1957.

Reyburn, William D. and Euan McG. Fry. *A Handbook on Genesis*. New York: United Bible Societies, 1997.

Reymond, Robert L. *Jesus: Divine Messiah*. Ross-shire, Scotland: Mentor Imprint, 2003.

Reznick, Leibel. *The Holy Temple Revisited*. Northvale, NJ: Jason Aronson, Inc. 1993.

Riddle, J. M. *The Ritchie Old Testament Commentary: What the Bible Teaches, Song of Solomon, Isaiah*. Kilmarnock, Scotland: John Ritchie Ltd. 2005.

Robertson, A. T. *A Harmony of the Gospels*. New York: Harper Collins, 1950.

Robinson, George. *Essential Judaism*. New York: Pocket Books, 2000.

Root, Gerald. "A Critical Investigation of Deuteronomy 6:4." B.D. thesis., Grace Theological Seminary, 1964.

Rosenberg, A.J. *The Book of the Twelve Prophets: A New Translation of the Text, Rashi and a Commentary Digest*. New York: The Judaica Press, 1996.

Rosenthal, Stanley. *One God or Three?* Bellmawr, NJ: Friends of Israel Gospel Ministry, 1978.

Ross, Allen P. *Creation & Blessing: Genesis*. Grand Rapids: Baker, 1988.

Ross, Allen P. *Introducing Biblical Hebrew*. Grand Rapids: Baker Academics, 2001.

Runes, Dagobert D. *Concise Dictionary of Judaism*. New York: Philosophical Library, 1966.

Ryken, Philip Graham. *Jeremiah and Lamentations: From Sorrow to Hope*. Wheaton: Crossway Books, 2001.

Ryle, Herbert E. *Cambridge Bible, the Book of Genesis*. London: Cambridge University Press, 1914.

Ryrie, Charles Caldwell. *The Holy Spirit*. Chicago: Moody, 1965.

Sacchi, Paolo. *The History of the Second Temple Period*. Sheffield, England: Sheffield Academic Press, 2000.

Sailhamer, John. *Everyman's Commentary: First & Second Chronicles*. Chicago: Moody, 1983.

Sailhamer, John H. *The Expositor's Bible Commentary: Genesis*. 12 vols. Grand Rapids: Zondervan, 1990.

Sailhamer, John H. *The Pentateuch as Narrative: A Biblical-Theological Commentary*. Grand Rapids: Zondervan, 1992.

Sanders, John. *What About Those Who Never Heard?* Downers Grove: IVP, 1995.

Sarna, Nahum M. *The JPS Torah Commentary, Genesis*. Philadelphia: The Jewish Publication Society, 1989.

Saucy, Robert L. *The Church in God's Program*. Chicago: Moody, 1972.

Scherman, Rabbi Nosson. *The Chumash: The Stone Edition*. Brooklyn: Mesorah Publications, 1993.

Schneider, Tammi J. *Berit Olam: Judges*. Collegeville, MN: Liturgical Press, 2000.

Schochet, Jacob Immanuel. *Mashiach: The Principle of Mashiach and the Messianic Era in Jewish Law and Tradition*. Brooklyn: S.I.E., 1992.

Schoen, Robert. *What I Wish My Christian Friends Knew About Judaism*. Chicago: Loyola Press, 2004.

Scholem, Gershom G. *Major Trends in Jewish Mysticism*. London: Thames and Hudson, 1955.

Schurer, Emil. *A History of the Jewish People in the Time of Jesus Christ*. 5 vols. Trans. by John Macpherson. Peabody, MA: Hendrickson, 2003.

Scialitti, Rabbi Mofes. *A Letter Written to the Jewes*. London: Thom Tanner, 1663.

Schiffman, Michael. *Return of the Remnant*. Baltimore: Lederer, 1992.

Schultz, Samuel J. *The Old Testament Speaks*. New York: Harper & Row, 1970.

Scott, J. Julius. *Jewish Backgrounds of the New Testament*. Grand Rapids: Baker Books, 1995.

Selman, Martin. *Tyndale Old Testament Commentary: 1 Chronicles*. Downers Grove: InterVarsity Press, 1994.

Shorrosh, Anis A. *Islam Revealed: A Christian Arab's View of Islam*. Nashville: Nelson, 1988.

Showers, Renald E. *The Most High God: Daniel*. West Collingswood, NJ: The Friends of Israel Gospel Ministry, 1982.

Showers, Renald E. *There Really Is a Difference!* Bellmawr, NJ: Friends of Israel Gospel Ministry, 1990.

Showers, Renald E. *Those Invisible Spirits Called Angels.* Bellmawr, NJ: Friends of Israel Gospel Ministry, 1997.

Sigal, Gerald. *The Jew and the Christian Missionary: A Jewish Response to Missionary Christianity.* New York: KTAV Publishing House, 1981.

Silver, Rabbi Abba Hillel. *A History of Messianic Speculation in Israel.* New York: Macmillan, 1927.

Singer, Isidore. *The Jewish Encyclopedia.* New York: Funk and Wagnalls Co. 1906.

Skinner, John. *The International Critical Commentary: A Critical and Exegetical Commentary on Genesis.* Edinburgh: T & T Clark, 1969.

Sloan, W. W. *Between the Testaments.* Paterson, NJ: Littlefield, Adams & Co. 1964.

Slotki, I. W. A. *Isaiah.* New York: The Soncino Press, 1983.

Smith, Henry Preserved. *The Religion of Israel.* New York: Charles Scribner's Sons, 1914.

Smith, James E. *The Promised Messiah.* Nashville: Thomas Nelson, 1993.

Smith, John Merlin Powis. *The International Critical Commentary: Malachi.* Edinburgh, Scotland: T & T Clark, 1999.

Smith, Payne. *Handy Commentary: Genesis,* ed. Charles John Ellicott, , London: Cassell & Co, n.d.

Smith, Ralph L. *Old Testament Theology, Its History, Method, and Message.* Nashville: Broadman, 1993.

Smith, William. *Dictionary of the Bible.* 3 vols. Boston: Little, Brown, and Company, 1863.

Smith, William. *Old Testament History.* Joplin, MO: College Press, 1970.

Soggin, J. Alberto. *The Old Testament Library: Judges.* Translated by John Bowden. Philadelphia: Westminster, 1981.

Sorko-Ram, Shira. *Israel's Call: What Jews and Christians Should Understand About Each Other.* Grand Prairie, TX: Moaz Israel Ministries, 2006.

Speiser, E. A. *The Anchor Bible: Genesis.* Garden City, NY: Doubleday & Company, 1964.

Spurgeon, Charles H. *The Treasury of David.* Byron Center, MI: Associated Publishers and Authors, 1970.

Spurgeon, Charles H. *The Treasury of David.* 3 vols. Mclean, VA: MacDonald Publications, n.d.

Stanton, R. Todd. "Numbers 12:6-8, Its Contribution to the Study of Revelation and Theophany in the Old Testament". Th. M. diss. Sun Valley, CA: Master's Seminary, 2000.

Stedman, Ray C. *Death of a Nation: Jeremiah*. Waco, TX: Word Books, 1976.

Steinberg, Milton. *Basic Judaism*. New York: Harvest/HBJ Book, 1947.

Steinsaltz, Rabbi Adin. *The Talmud: The Steinsaltz*. 21 vols. Trans. by Rabbi David Strauss. New York: Random House, 1998.

Stenning, J. F. *The Targum of Isaiah*. London: Oxford University Press, 1953.

Steveson, Peter A. *A Commentary on Isaiah*. Greenville, SC: BJU Press, 2003.

Stone, Nathan. *Names of God*. Chicago: Moody, 1944.

Strickman, H. Norman and Arthur M. Silver. *Ibn Ezra's Commentary on the Pentateuch*. New York: Menorah Publishing, 1988.

Strong, Augustus H. *Systematic Theology*, Westwood, NJ: Revell, 1907.

Talbot, Gordon. *A Study of the Book of Genesis*. Harrisburg, PA: Christian Publications, 1981.

Talmage, James E. *A Study of the Articles of Faith*. Salt Lake City: The Church of Jesus Christ of Latter-day Saints, 1982.

Tanenbaum, Marc H., Marvin R. Wilson, and A. James Rudin. *Evangelicals and Jews in Conversation on Scripture, Theology, and History*. Grand Rapids: Baker, 1978.

Taylor, John B. *Tyndale Old Testament Commentary: Ezekiel*. Downers Grove: InterVarsity, 1974.

Taylor, Richard A. *The New American Commentary: Haggai Malachi*. 21 vols. Nashville: Broadman & Holman, 2004.

Telchin, Stanley. *Abandoned*. Grand Rapids: Baker Book House, 1997.

Telchin, Stan. *Messianic Judaism IS NOT Christianity*. Grand Rapids: Chosen Books, 2004.

Tenney, Merrill C. *The Expositor's Bible Commentary: John and Acts*. 12 vols. Grand Rapids: Zondervan, 1981.

Tenney, Merrill C. *The Zondervan Pictorial Encyclopedia of the Bible*. 5 vols. Grand Rapids: Zondervan Publishing House, 1975.

Terrien, Samuel. *Critical Eerdmans Commentary: The Psalms*. Grand Rapids: Eerdmans, 2003.

Thiessen, Henry C. *Lectures in Systematic Theology*. Grand Rapids: Eerdmans, 1979.

Thomas, Thomas A. "The Trinity in the Old Testament." Th.M. diss., Dallas Theological Seminary, 1952.

Thompson, J. A. *New American Commentary: 1 & 2 Chronicles. 21 vols*. Nashville: Broadman Press, 1994.

Thompson, J. A. *The New International Commentary on the Old Testament: The Book of Jeremiah*. Grand Rapids: Eerdmans, 1980.

Tomasino, Anthony J. *Judaism Before Jesus*. Downers Grove, IL: InterVarsity, 2003.

Torrey, R. A. *The Holy Spirit*. New York: Revell, 1927.

Torrey, R. A. and A. C. Dixon. *The Fundamentals*. Grand Rapids: Baker, 1980.

Towner, W. Sibley. *Interpretation: Daniel*. Atlanta: John Knox Press, 1984.

Towner, W. Sibley. *Westminster Bible Companion: Genesis* (Louisville, KY: Westminster John Knox Press, 2001.

Trapp, John. *Commentary or Exposition upon the Twelve Minor Prophets*. Vol. 4. Richard D. Dickinson, London, 1867.

Tregelles, Samuel Prideaux. *Gesenius' Hebrew and Chaldee Lexicon to the Old Testament Scriptures*. Grand Rapids: Eerdmans, 1957.

Turner, Laurence A. *Genesis*. Sheffield, England: Sheffield Academic Press, 2000.

Unger, Merrill F. *A Zondervan Commentary: Zechariah; Prophet of Messiah's Glory*. Grand Rapids: Zondervan, 1970.

Unger, Merrill F. *Biblical Demonology*. Wheaton: Scripture Press, 1952.

Unger, Merrill F. *Unger's Bible Dictionary*, Chicago: Moody Press, 1961.

Uzziel, Jonathan Ben. *The Targum Palestine*: Genesis, 8.

VanGemeren, Willem A. *New International Dictionary of Old Testament Theology & Exegesis*, Grand Rapids: Zondervan, 1997.

VanGemeren, Willem. *The Expositor's Bible Commentary: Psalms*. Grand Rapids: Zondervan, 1991.

Van Groningen, Gerard. *Messianic Revelation in the Old Testament*. Grand Rapids: Baker, 1990.

Van Rad, Gerhard. *The Old Testament Library: Genesis*. Philadelphia: Westminster, 1961.

Varner, William. *The Messiah: Revealed, Rejected, Received*. Bloomington, IN: AuthorHouse, 2004.

Vine, W. E. *Isaiah*. Grand Rapids: Zondervan, 1946.

Vos, Geerhardus. *Biblical Theology, Old and New Testament*. Grand Rapids: Eerdmans, 1948.

Vriezen, Th. C. *An Outline of Old Testament Theology*. Newton, MA: Charles T. Branford Company, 1970.

Walker, Larry L. *Tyndale Cornerstone Biblical Commentary: Isaiah, Jeremiah & Lamentations*. Wheaton: Tyndale, 2005.

Waltke, Bruce K. *Genesis: A Commentary*. Grand Rapids: Zondervan, 2001.

Waltke, Bruce K. The *New International Commentary on the Old Testament: The Book of Proverbs, Chapters 15-31*. Grand Rapids: Eerdmans, 2005.

Walvoord, John F. *Daniel: The Key to Prophetic Revelation*. Chicago: Moody, 1971.

Walvoord, John F. *Jesus Christ Our Lord*. Chicago: Moody Press, 1969.

Walvoord, John F. *The Holy Spirit*. Findlay, OH: Dunham Publishing, 1958.

Walvoord, John F. and Roy B. Zuck. *The Bible Knowledge Commentary: Old Testament*. Wheaton: Victor Books, 1985.

Wardlaw, J. S. *Lectures on the Book of Proverbs*. Minneapolis: Klock & Klock Christian Publishers, 1982.

Warfield, Benjamin Breckinridge. *Biblical and Theological Studies*. Philadelphia: Presbyterian and Reformed Publishing, 1968.

Waterhouse, Steven W. *Not By Bread Alone: An Outlined Guide to Bible Doctrine*. Amarillo, TX: Westcliff Press, 2000.

Watson, Richard. *Theological Institutes: Or, a View of the Evidences, Doctrines, Morals, and Institutions of Christianity*. New York: Phillips & Hunt, 1850.

Webb, Barry G. *The Message of Isaiah*. Downers Grove, IL: Inter-Varsity, 1996.

Weinfeld, Moshe. *The Anchor Bible: Deuteronomy 1-11*. New York: Doubleday, 1991.

Weiser, Artur. *The Old Testament Library: The Psalms*. Trans. by Herbert Hartwell. Philadelphia: Westminster Press 1962.

Weissman, Moshe. *The Midrash Says: The Book of Beraishis*. Brooklyn: Benei Yakov Publications, 1999.

Weiss-Rosmarin, Trude. *Judaism and Christianity, the Differences*. Middle Village: Jonathan David Publishers, Inc, 1997.

Wenham, Gordon. *Tyndale Old Testament Commentaries: Numbers*. Downers Grove, IL: Inter-Varsity Press, 1981.

Wenham, Gordon. *Word Biblical Commentary: Genesis 16-50*. 32 vols. Waco: Word, 1994.

Westermann, Claus. *Genesis 1-11: A Continental Commentary*. Trans. by John J. Scullion. Minneapolis: Fortress Press, 1995.

Westermann, Claus. *Genesis 12-36: A Continental Commentary*. Trans. by John J. Scullion. Minneapolis: Fortress Press, 1994.

Whiston, William. *Josephus' Complete Works*. Grand Rapids: Kregel, 1978.

Wigram, George V. *The Englishman's Hebrew Concordance of the Old Testament*. Peabody, MA: Hendrickson Publishers, 1996.

Wilcock, Michael. *The Bible Speaks Today: The Message of Judges*. Downers Grove: InterVarsity Press, 1992.

Wildberger, Hans. *Isaiah 1-12: A Commentary*. Minneapolis: Fortress Press, 1991.

Wilkinson, John. *Israel My Glory*. London: Mildmay Mission to the Jews, 1894.

Williams, Donald. *Mastering the Old Testament: Psalms 1-72*. Dallas: Word, 1986.

Wilson, Marvin R. *Our Father Abraham*. Grand Rapids: Eerdmans, 1989.

Wilson, T. Ernest. *The Messianic Psalms*. Neptune, NJ: Loizeaux, 1978.

Wolf, Herbert M. *Interpreting Isaiah*. Grand Rapids: Baker, 1985.

Wolf, Hebert M. *The Expositor's Bible Commentary: Judges*. 12 vol. Grand Rapids: Zondervan, 1992.

Wood, Leon J. *A Commentary on Daniel*. Grand Rapids: Zondervan, 1973.

Wood, Leon J. *A Survey of Israel's History*. Grand Rapids: Zondervan, 1970.

Wood, Leon J. *Distressing Days of the Judges*. Grand Rapids: Zondervan, 1975.

Wood, Leon J. *The Holy Spirit in the Old Testament*. Eugene, OR: Wipf and Stock, 1998.

Woudstra, M. H. *The New International Commentary on the Old Testament: The Book of Joshua*. Grand Rapids: Eerdmans, 1981.

Young, Edward. *Genesis 3*. London: The Banner of Truth, 1966.

Young, Edward. *The Book of Isaiah*. 3 vols. Grand Rapids: Eerdmans, 1972.

Young, Robert. *Analytical Concordance to the Bible*. Grand Rapids: Eerdmans, 1955.

Youngblood, Ronald F. *New Illustrated Bible Dictionary*. Nashville: Nelson Publishers, 1995.

Youngblood, Ronald F. *The Book of Genesis*. 2nd ed. Eugene, OR: Wipf and Stock, 1999.

Youngblood, Ronald F. *The Expositor's Bible Commentary: 1 & 2 Samuel*. 12 vols. Grand Rapids: Zondervan, 1992.

Youngblood, Ronald. *The Genesis Debate*. Nashville: Nelsons, 1986.

Zimmerli, Walter. *Ezekiel 1*. Philadelphia: Fortress, 1979.

Zlotowitz, Meir. *The Family Chumash Bereishis: Genesis*. Brooklyn: Mesorah Press, 1986.

Journal

Aloisi, John. "Who is David's Lord? Another Look at Psalm 110:1." *DBSJ* 10, (2005):103-123.

Bartelt, Andrew H. "The Identity of the Servant of Isaiah 53." *Mishkan*, issue 43 (2005), 6-15.

Black, M. "The Origin of the Name Metatron," *Vetus Testamentum*, vol. 1 (1951), 216-219.

Brickner, David. "How Christian is Christian Zionism?" *Mishkan* issue 60 (2009): 69-80.

Chisholm, Jr. Robert B. "The Christological Fulfillment of Isaiah's Servant Songs." *Bibliotheca Sacra* 163:652 (October-December, 2006): 387-404.

Davis, Barry C. "Is Psalm 110 a Messianic Psalm?" *Bibliotheca Sacra* 157:626 (April – June 2000): 160-173.

Dockery, David S. *Biblical Illustrator, Monotheism in the Scriptures.* Nashville, TN: Sunday School Board of the Southern Baptist Convention, 1991.

Feinberg, Charles L. "The Image of God." *Bibliotheca Sacra* 129:515 (July 1972): 235-246.

Feinberg, Charles L. "The Shepherd Smitten and the Sheep Scattered." *Bibliotheca Sacra* 103:409, (January 1946): 28-38.

Fischer, John. "Yeshua: The Deity Debate." *Mishkan* issue 39 (2003): 20-28.

Glaser, Mitch. "The Use of Isaiah 53 in Jewish Evangelism." *Mishkan* issue 43 (2005): 34-46.

Harvey, Richard. "Jesus the Messiah in Messianic Jewish Thought: Emerging Christologies." *Mishkan,* issue 39, (2003): 4-19.

Hasel, Gerhard F. "The Meaning of "Let Us" in Genesis 1:26." *Andrews University Seminary Studies* 13 Spring (1975) 58-66.

Hendren, Noam. "The Divine Unity and the Deity of Messiah." *Mishkan,* issue 39, (2003): 36-47.

Janosik, Daniel. "Explaining the Trinity to a Muslim," *Christian Apologetics Journal* (volume 4, no. 2, Fall 2005): 73-85.

Janzen, J. Gerald. "On the Most Important Word In The Shema (Deut VI 4-5)." *Vetus Testamentum* 37, no. 3 (1987): 280-300.

Jocz, Jacob. "The Invisibility of God and the Incarnation." *Canadian Journal of Theology* (1958): 179-186.

Johnson, John J. "A New Testament Understanding of the Jewish Rejection of Jesus: Four Theologians on the Salvation of Israel." *Journal of the Evangelical Theological Society* (2000): 229-246.

Kaiser, Walter C. "The Promise of the Arrival of Elijah in Malachi and the Gospels." *GJT* 3, no. 2 (1982).

Leman, Derek. "Inclusivism and the Task of Making Jewish Disciples," *Mishkan,* issue 42, (2005).

Loewen, Jacob A. "The Names of God in the Old Testament." *The Bible Translator* 35, no. 2 (1984): 201-207.

Merrill, Eugene H. "Rashi, Nicholas de Lyra, and Christian Exegesis." *Westminster Theological Journal 38,* (Fall 1975): 66-79.

Moore, George Foot. "Intermediaries in Jewish Theology: Memra, Shekinah, Metatron," *Harvard Theological Review* 15, (1922): 41-85.

Niehaus, Jeffrey J. "In the Wind of the Storm: Another Look at Genesis 3:8", *Vetus Testamentum* v. 44 no. 2, (1994), 263-268.

Orlov, Andrei A. "Titles of Enoch-Metatron in 2 Enoch," *Journal for the Study of the Pseudepigrapha*, (vol. 18, 1998), 71-86.

Pryor, Dwight A. "One God and Lord." *Mishkan* (issue 39, 2003): 48-58.

Rendsburg, Gary. "Dual Personal Pronouns and Dual Verbs in Hebrew." *Jewish Quarterly Review* 73, no. 1 (July 1982): 38-58.

Santala, Risto. "The Despised Messiah and His Despised People." *Mishkan,* issue 43 (2005), 16-24.

Wilkin, Robert N. "Toward a Narrow View of Ipsissima Vox." *JOTGES* 14, no 26 (Spring 2001): 3-8.

Young, Edward. "The Call of Moses." *WTJ* 30, (1967-68).

Magazines

Beam, James Michael. "I Can't Play God Any More," *McCall's* (Jan 1978).

Brown, Michael L. "Rabbinic Objections" *The Chosen People* (vol. XII, issue 9, special edition), 7. Chosen People Ministries, NY.

Fruchtenbaum, Arnold, "Messiah's Right to David's Throne." *Voice* 86:6 (Nov/Dec 2007): 33-34.

Gitlin, M. "The Divine Veil," *Message to Israel*. Vol. 65 (May-August, 2000):

Kalisher, Zvi. "ZVI," *Israel My Glory*. Vol. 65, no. 3, (May-June 2007), 42.

Kofahl, Robert E. "Graham Believes Men Can be Saved Apart from the Name of Christ," *Foundation Magazine* (May-June 1997).

Levy, David. "Messiah's Coronation and Reign," *Israel My Glory*. Vol. 63, no. 2 (March/April, 2005).

Wood, B. G. "Prophecy of Balaam Found In Jordan." *Bible and Spade* 6 (Autumn 1977): 121-124.

Paper Presented at a Professional Society

Keiser, Thomas A. The Divine Plural Contextual Presentation of Plurality in the Godhead. Paper presented at the Evangelical Theological Society Southwest Region. Fort Worth, TX. March 24, 2006.

Newspapers

MacDonald, Jeffrey G. "Christian Scholars: Jews Don't Need Jesus." *Press Republican*. Plattsburgh, NY. September 13, 2002, A7.

Brochures and Booklets

Goldberg, Louis. *Are There Two Ways of Atonement?* Baltimore: Lederer Publication, 1990.

Lindberg, Milton B. *In the Light of the Tenach: The Trinity* (Brochure), Lansing, MI: AMF International, 1992.

Robinson, Mark. *One God or Three?* Brochure. El Cajon, CA: Shalom Outreach Ministries, n.d.

The Book of Mormon; Doctrine and Covenants; The Pearl of Great Price. Salt Lake City: The Church of Jesus Christ of the Latter-day Saints, 1983.

Glossary of Terms
for Christians and for Jewish People

-A-

Abraham

The ancient Semite called out of ancient Babylon to serve the one God, and become the father of the nation of Israel.

Abrahamic Covenant

The contract (or "promise") God made with Abraham as recorded in Genesis 12, 13, 15, 17, 19, 22 in which He unconditionally promised to make of Abraham a great nation with the promise extending to his descendants.

Adonai

Adonai means "Lord" or "Master" usually referring to the God of Israel. Since they do not like to use any words referring to God they will often use the following, G-d or L-rd. Since the Hebrew name of God, YHVH is not used by Jewish people because it is too holy to pronounce, they dropped the vowels probably before the time of Messiah, only leaving the consonants. So the word that is translated LORD, Jehovah, or Yahweh in our English Bible is only an attempt to pronounce God's name. Orthodox Jewish people will often use the term "*HaShem*," meaning "the Name," in place of God or Lord.

Aggadah or Haggadah

(lit. "telling"). Non-halakhic matter in Talmud and Midrash; includes folklore, legend, theology/theosophy, scriptural interpretations, biography, etc.; also spelled Haggadah, not to be confused, however, with the text of the Passover Seder, which is also called "the Haggadah."

Akiba ben Joseph

Akiba (45-135 CE) was a well respected Rabbi and in the year 132 he announced that Simeon bar Kokhba was the Jewish Messiah. Bar Kokhba led the second Jewish revolt against Rome in 132-135 CE and was defeated and killed along with Akiba in 135 CE.

Aliyah

Aliyah means "going up" or ascension; thus making emigration to Eretz Yisrael (land of Israel); a pilgrimage.

Amillennialism

Amillennialism is a system of theology that was established by Augustine in the 6th century. He built on the foundation formed by Origen in the 3rd century, that the interpretation of the Scriptures are to be from an allegorical (or spiritualized) method of interpretation. Basically it teaches that the Church is the kingdom of God promised to Abraham and that the Millennial Reign of Christ is present now through the Church. It teaches that the Kingdom started at Christ's first coming and that there is no literal 1000 year reign of Christ on the throne of David as promised to David in the Davidic Covenant. This teaching became the official position of the Roman Catholic Church and it also affected the end time views of the Protestant Reformers.

Anti-Semitism

Attitudes and actions directed against the Jewish people. This has plagued the Jewish people through the centuries by some of these well know actions of the "Christian Church," the Crusades, the Inquisition, Host Desecration, the Black plague, Pogroms of Eastern Europe and Russia, and the Holocaust of Nazis Germany. This only names a few of the atrocities done against the Jewish people, as there is much, much more that history records.

Arabs

Arabs are the descendants of Ishmael, basically from the Arabian Peninsula. Syrians, Egyptians, Iraqis and Iranians, for example, are not Arab, but Syrian, Egyptians, Chaldaeans and Persians. What they share in common is the religion of Islam and the Arabic language.

Aramaic

A Semitic language that is closely related to Hebrew, in which some of the biblical text like Daniel was written; but most notably the Talmud, both Babylonian and Palestinian, were written in Aramaic. It was also used in the writings of the Targums, which are an Aramaic paraphrase of the *Tanakh*.

Ashkenazi

Ashkenazi Jewish people are from Eastern and Central European descent (Poland, Russia, Germany, France). Also see Sephardic.

Atonement

Reconciliation with God through the expiation of sin. (See Yom Kippur and Leviticus 16.)

-B-

Bar

The Aramaic word meaning "son."

Baruch

Baruch means "blessing."

Bar Mitzvah

Son of the Commandments is a boy who has reached the age of religious maturity, age 13, culminating in a special ceremony. This is not biblical but tradition.

Bat Mitzvah

Daughter of the Commandments is a girl who has reached the age of maturity, at age 13, also culminating in a special ceremony. This was originated in the 20th Century by the Jewish Reform movement.

BCE

Meaning **B**efore the **C**ommon **E**ra or the Christian period. It replaced the Christian use of B.C. or Before Christ.

Ben

The Hebrew word meaning "son."

Bereshit

Hebrew name for the book of Genesis taken from the opening word of the book.

Bet Knesset

Meaning literally the "house of assembly" or a Synagogue. It is also used in modern Israel for the government building like our capital building; they call it the Knesset.

B'nai B'rith

Means "sons of the covenant;" a Jewish fraternal organization founded in 1843.

Born Again

Was a first-century rabbinic term used by *Yeshua* in the 3rd chapter of the Gospel of John in the New Testament (John 3:3). *Yeshua* gave it a new meaning which was to receive salvation by trusting in Jesus, and being spiritually born again. (see Edersheim's Life and Times of Jesus Christ – vol. 1, page 381-388)

Bris

Covenant of circumcision which is performed on a male child on the 8th day of birth.

Brit

This is the Hebrew word for Covenant.

Brit ha-Hadashah

Hebrew for "the New Covenant" or New Testament, a phrase used by the prophet Jeremiah (Jeremiah 31:31). That which is also called the New Covenant by Christians is the 27 books of the New Testament.

-C-

Cantor

In Judaism it is a reciter and chanter/singer of liturgical materials in the synagogue.

CE

Common Era. Judaism prefers this to A.D., Anno Domini, which is Latin for "year of Our Lord."

Challah – see Hallah

Christ

Christ comes from "Christos," the Greek equivalent of the Hebrew term "Messiah" or *Moshiach*. Both words literally mean "Anointed One." This was the word used in the Septuagint, an ancient Greek translation of the Hebrew Scriptures as prepared by Jewish translators three centuries before the time of Jesus. Early Christians believed they had found their Messiah and naturally referred to him as "the Christ." When Christian say "Jesus Christ" they are actually saying "Jesus the Messiah."

Christian

According to the New Testament, this term was first used at Antioch (of Syria) to describe the Jewish faction that believed they had found the "Christ" (Messiah) in Jesus (*Yeshua*). Today it means anyone who trusts in Christ as their personal Saviour from

834

sin. According to Jewish interpretation, a Christian is someone who is born into a Christian home. Gentiles in general are considered Christian. If you are not Jewish, you are Christian.

Christian Zionism

This is Christian Zionism activism on the part of Christians toward the establishment and support of a homeland for the Jewish people.

Church

(1) An assembly of Christian believers. (2) All Christians believer everywhere. A Christian is one who has personally trusted by faith in Jesus, believing that His death on the cross is their substitute for sin, and Saviour from the penalty and power of sin, and that He was buried and rose again from the grave the third day. (3) A Christian is NOT someone who has been born into a "Christian" family and raised in a "Christian" home. It is an individual personal choice that every individual must make for himself. (4) The Church is not a building, but the people who assemble together.

Conservative Judaism

In Judaism you have three basic branches: First is the Orthodox which is the original; second is Reform, which was a reaction to the Orthodox. They wanted to be religious by not holding to orthodoxy, which developed in the 18th century. Thirdly you have the conservative branch which is of American origin who reacted against the liberal Reform branch and moved back toward Orthodox, but did not want to be Orthodox. Conservative Judaism attempted to retain a clearer link to classical Jewish Law while at the same time adapting it to modern situation. Its scholarly center in the U.S. is the Jewish Theological Seminary in Manhattan, New York.

Covenant

Covenant is a legal agreement between two people. But God made four covenants by Himself and not with another person. The Mosaic Covenant is an example of a covenant obligating two parties. But the Abrahamic, Land, Davidic and New Covenant are examples made for others by God, hence making them unconditional. The second party who is the recipient of the covenant does not have to do anything for the benefits of the covenant.

Crusades

Military campaigns on the part of "Christian" Europe to liberate Palestine from the hands of the Moslem between the years of 1096-1271. The fervor against the "infidel" Moslems easily spread to Anti-Jewish sentiments. Jewish monies were confiscated to help defray the expenses of the Crusades. Jewish communities had to buy "protection" from their "Christian" overlords. The "Christian" armies while going through Europe, buried, murdered, and destroyed whole Jewish communities as well as raping the women and stealing anything of value.

-D-

Days of Awe

Ten days from Rosh Hashanah to Yom Kippur, a time for introspection and considering the sins of the previous year.

Decalogue

A Greek term referring to the Ten Commandments (*aseret hadibrot*) received by Moses on Mount Sinai according to the Jewish Scriptures (Exodus 20:1-17; Deuteronomy 5:1-21).

Denominations (Christian)

Christianity can be divided up into four major divisions: Roman Catholicism, Greek Orthodox, Russian Orthodox and Protestant Christianity. The first three have added many traditions and writings of the Church Fathers which carry more weight than the written Word of God. They have largely become ritualistic and apostate.

Protestants can be divided into many groups such as Anglican (Episcopal), Baptist, Lutheran, Methodist, Presbyterian and Reform. But because of liberalism most of these denominations have also become apostate. Before liberalism entered into the picture these denominations agreed on the basic doctrines of Christianity, but they disagreed on how to implement them. They are not separate religions. The true believers in Christ today come primarily from Independent Baptist and Bible Churches, Westminster Presbyterian, Wesleyan, Nazarene and the Missouri Synod of Lutheran Churches. They would make up the conservative Bible believers that look to the Scriptures alone for faith and practice.

There are many Christian cults that are not recognized by any branch of Christianity as being true to the faith. Some of them are: Christian Science, Jehovah Witnesses, Moonies, Mormons, and a multitude of other usually very small groups.

Devarim

The Hebrew word for the Book of Deuteronomy

Diaspora

(lit. "the scattering of seed") The "scattering of the Jewish people across the earth initially through the Assyrian, Babylonian Empires and throughout the Roman provinces. It continued as the Jewish people were scattered to the four corners of the earth. It refers to all Jews living outside of Israel. It is also referred to as the "Exile."

Dispensationalism

A theological view of the end times as held by many conservative evangelicals and fundamentalist Christians, which divides the history of mankind into period called dispensations, according to the ways God related to man in each period.

Dual Covenant

This is a pluralistic belief that Judaism and Christianity have their separate ways to God. The Jewish people use it to tell Christians to stop evangelizing them. They will get to heaven by being good Jews, and Christians by being good Christians. The system became popular among liberal Christians and Rabbinic Judaism after the Holocaust. It is a belief system that is in total contradiction to the Bible.

-E-

El – Elah – Eloah

These are all singular words used in the Hebrew Scriptures for God.

Eliezer Ben Yehuda

He is the father of modern Hebrew. He was born in Lithuania in 1858.

Elohim

This is a plural word used in the Hebrew Scriptures for God. It is used 2600 times far more then the singular words for God. It also is used of pagan deities 250 of the 2600 times used.

Eretz Israel

Hebrew for "the Land of Israel" – The Promised Land as promised and given to Israel by God.

Evangelical

The word "evangelical" comes from the word "euangelion," which means "Good News," or "Gospel." Briefly stated, an evangelical is a Christian who believes, lives and wants to share the gospel message with the world. However, in recent years evangelicals have been moving away, or apostatizing, from their original position.

-F-

Feast of Hanukkah

This is not one of the seven Feasts of the LORD given to Israel in Leviticus 23. This feast began during the intertestament time when the Maccabees revolted against the

Syrian Greeks that dominated Israel in 165 BCE. This feast is also called the Feast of Dedication for it originated when the temple was rededicated. Jesus, in His earthly ministry, also celebrated this feast as recorded in the Gospel of John. One of the ways that it is celebrated today is that a Jewish home will for eight days light a candle every night on a 9-branch menorah.

-G-

Gemara

(lit. "Completion") A compilation of rabbinical commentaries from the 3rd to the 5th centuries on the Mishnah, which is the core of the Talmud written down by CE 500. Also see Talmud.

Ghetto

A portion of a city in which Jews were required to live separately from the general populace. The most well known ghetto was the Warsaw Ghetto in Poland during World War II.

Gospel

(Lit. "good news," a literal translation of the Greek word "euangelion.") The story of Jesus (*Yeshua*) who "died for our sins according to the Scriptures, and … was buried and … rose again the third day according to the Scriptures" (1 Corinthians 15:3, 4). The gospel will display those three elements that people must believe to have everlasting life with the Father and His Son in heaven.

Goy, Goyim

Gentile(s), non-Jews. The plural form "goyim" is used in the Hebrew Bible of "nations" in general, non-Jewish. Later came to mean all other nations (besides Israel), and thence to individuals outside the fold of Israel.

-H-

Hadassah

Jewish women's Zionist organization in the United States.

Haftorah

Specific section of the biblical prophets read in synagogue services immediately after the corresponding Torah (Pentateuch) section called the *parashah*.

Haggadah

Haggadah means, "the telling" of the Passover story. Also the ritual manual used for the Passover Seder meals.

Halakhah

Means "the way" or "walk;" tradition, practice, rule in Judaism. A general term for the proscriptive material in the Talmud.

Hallah

A special sweet, braided bread served in pairs of loaves and traditional for the Sabbath.

Hallel Psalms

Psalm 113-118, recited at the end of morning services at festivals.

Hamas

Terrorist group founded in 1987 as an outgrowth of the Palestinian branch of the Muslim Brotherhood. Principal political rival was Arafat's Fatah (PLO) organization now headed by Abbas. Has tens of thousands of Palestinian supporters and sympathizers, but the number of hardcore terrorists is unknown. In the early 2000s Hamas was able to take over the Gaza area and as well has many supporters in the West Bank.

Hanukkah

An eight-day holiday commemorating the rededication of the Jewish temple in BCE 165 where a candle is lit on a 9-branch menorah for 8 days. (See Feast of Hanukkah)

Har ha-Bayit

Hebrew for Hill of the House, the Temple Mount

Haroset

One of the dishes featured in the Passover Seder, typically made with apples, nuts, honey, cinnamon, lemon juice, and wine to represent the mortar used by the Jewish slaves in Egypt.

HaShem

"The Name," Hebrew alternative for the divine Name, LORD (YHVH).

Hasid

Hasidim (plural); means "pious one;" follower of Hasidism.

Hasidism

(1) A Jewish sect of the second century BC opposed to Antiochus Epiphanes and his Hellenism and were devoted to strict observance of ritual law; (2) To the pietists in the 13th century, known as the Ashkenazi Hasidim, and (3) followers of the movement of Hasidism founded in the first half of the 18th century by Israel Baal Shem Tov in opposition to rationalism and ritual laxity. On the streets of Brooklyn the casual observers can identify them with their side curls, black coat and hats.

Hatikvab

"The Hope;" Israel's national anthem.

Hebrew

This can have two meanings: first the ancient and modern language of the Jewish people used in the past and in modern Israel today. Secondly, it also can designate a Jewish person as an Israelite.

Hebrews

Is an ethnicity of people who are descendants of Abraham, Isaac, and Jacob. It is also the name of a book in the New Testament (Brit ha-Hadashah), addressed to Jewish believers in Jesus (*Yeshua*) in the first century BCE.

Hezbollah

An umbrella terrorist organization of various radical Shiite groups, formed following the 1982 Peace for Galilee War conducted under Ariel Sharon to force the PLO, another terrorist organization, out of Lebanon. The war succeeded only in part. On Israel's departure from Lebanon (under foreign pressure), they maintained, at the request of the southern Lebanese, a buffer zone south of the Litani River in Lebanon to protect the panhandle of Israel and the civilian population living there. That buffer zone was patrolled by the Israeli army and the South Lebanese forces, loyal to Israel. Roadside bombs and other attacks were conducted against the Israeli and Southern Lebanese forces in this zone. In 2000 the Israel army pulled out of Lebanon and it quickly fell into the hands of the Hezbollah. The Hezbollah is funded and supported by Syria and Iran.

Holocaust

Holocaust comes from the Greek term for a burnt offering. The systematic Nazi destruction of six million European Jewry which began in 1933 when Adolph Hitler was appointed chancellor of Germany. This tragic event reduced the world's Jewish population by one-third.

Huppah

Bridal canopy (sometimes a large Tallit is used) denoting God's presence in the new home and of the temple in Jerusalem; symbolic of God's dwelling place with man. The Huppah can be held by four men holding poles at each of the four corners.

-I-

Ibn Ezra, Abraham

Among the great Bible commentators, Ibn Ezra's (1092-1167 CE) popularity is exceeded only by Rashi's (Rabbi Shelomo Yitzkhaki – 1040-1105), Abraham Ibn Ezra was a man of many talents, a poet, biblical commentator, grammarian and philologist, scientific writer and doctor.

Inquisition

A tribunal once set up by the Roman Catholic Church, intended to weed out heresy from the realms of Christendom. Many Jews lost their homes, livelihoods and their lives in this age of intolerance, as did many Gentile believer who did not confess to the official doctrines of the Roman Church. For the Jewish people this resulted in the expulsion of the entire Jewish populace from Spain in 1492 and Portugal in 1496. Many of the Jewish people evicted from Spain went to the new world; however, the inquisition followed them there.

Isaiah 53

A chapter of the Hebrew Bible which refers to the Messiah that is not read in the synagogues by the rabbis.

-J-

Jehovah or Yahweh

Jehovah is a mechanical attempt to represent the special name for the God of Israel, YHVH, the Tetragrammaton.

Jerusalem

In Hebrew it is *Yerushalayim*. The capital of Israel since it was taken from the Jebusites by King David (2 Samuel 5:6-10).

Jesus

The name of a Jew from first century CE, during the Second Temple Period known more fully as *Yeshua* ben Yosef ha-Notzri, the stepson of a carpenter from Nazareth, and the son of a the virgin Mary (Miriam) who was hailed by His followers as the promised Jewish Messiah spoken of in the Hebrew Bible, otherwise known as the Law, Prophets and Writings. He came offering the Kingdom, was rejected and crucified, becoming the Saviour of the world from their sins that separate them from God.

Jew

From Greek "Ioudaios," meaning someone from Judea or "Judah;" later used of anyone descended from Israel. In modern usage, according to halakhah, one is a Jew if one has Jewish parents (at least a Jewish mother), or has undergone conversion in accordance with Jewish law.

Josephus, Flavius

Josephus was a first-century Jewish historian. His works are one of the principle extra-biblical historical sources of information for the Second Temple/New Testament period. Josephus was present and witnessed the destruction of Jerusalem and the temple by the Romans in 70 CE.

Judah

Hebrew is pronounced *Yehudah*. It can refer to several things: (1) One of the 12 sons of Jacob; (2) The tribe that descended from the 4th son of Jacob, Judah; (3) The tribal allotment in the Promised Land; (4) After the political division of the country following Solomon's reign, the southern kingdom, consisting of Benjamin and Judah.

Judah Ha-Nasi

Lived from 138-220 CE who collected and codified the Mishnah in 220 CE which until this time was orally transmitted.

Judaism

The religious system of the Jewish people, centered on the belief in one God, absolute monotheism, and his covenants with the Jewish people as described in the Torah. Today Judaism is divided into several identities with all holding to the Oral Law, traditions of the sages more than the Written Law of God. The only exception to this would be secular Jewish people who are ethical Jewish, but religiously they are secular.

Judaizers

Judaizers were first-century believers in Jesus as the Messiah of Israel. They were Christians and believers as much as the Apostles Paul and Peter. These people were saved from the sect known as the Pharisees. They believed you must accept *Yeshua* (Jesus), the Messiah as your Saviour but you must also observe the Mosaic Law. Judaizers came into play as they attempted to convince Gentile believers to also keep the Mosaic Law. Paul dealt with their error in Galatians and the first Church Council in Jerusalem which is the primary issue of Acts 15.

Judenfrage (German)

The "Jewish Question," How was non-Jewish society to deal with the newly emancipated Jews?

-K-

Kabbalah

Means "to receive;" literally, "the received or traditional lore" (see Cabala). This is an esoteric or mystic doctrine concerning God and the universe, asserted to have come down as a revelation to elect saints from the remote past and preserved only by a privileged few. It can be said that this is Jewish Mysticism.

Kaddish

Prayer that extols the greatness of God. Best known as the mourners' prayer. Kaddish is said at other times during Jewish liturgy.

Kapparah

Ritual of atonement performed just before Yom Kippur, involving the swinging of a live chicken (now often replaced by a handkerchief containing money) as a surrogate for ones sins. It is still practiced by the ultra-orthodox in New York City, a hen for the female and a rooster for the male. There is also a prayer that is still used at this time: "This is my substitute, this is my exchange, this is my atonement, this fowl will go to its death and I will go into a good and long life and peace."

Karaites

The word *Karaite* was derived from Hebrew *kara*, meaning "a reader of Scripture." Jewish sect of the middle ages which accepted the Hebrew Bible and its Law and rejected the Talmud and Rabbinic Law. In other words they were in opposition to Rabbinism. At one time they were a real threat to Rabbinic Judaism, but today there are only a handful left.

Kashrut

Dietary Laws

Kethuvim

The division of the Hebrew Scriptures called the Writings (Psalms, Proverbs, Job, Song of Songs, Ruth Lamentations, Ecclesiastes, Daniel, Ezra, Nehemiah, and 1 & 2 Chronicles).

Kibbutz

A (usually) rural community in Israel based on communal property in which members have no private property but share the work and the profits of some collective enterprise, typically agricultural but sometimes also industrial and hotels for tourist.

Kiddush

Prayer of sanctification recited over wine sanctifying the Sabbath or a holiday.

Kimkhi, David

David Kimkhi (1160-1235 CE) is known as Radak, who was and is very respected in Judaism for he wrote many commentaries.

Kippah

Hebrew name for the skull cap worn by observant Jewish males, also known by its Yiddish name, yarmulke. This is a rabbinic custom started around the 10th century. Today, Orthodox and many Conservative Jews believe that covering the head is an expression of *yirat Shama'yim* ("Fear of God" or "reverence for God").

Kittel

Special white garment worn on special occasions such as Pesach (Passover) or Yom Kippur (Day of Atonement), reminiscent of the garment the priest would have worn in temple times.

Kosher

Clean, acceptable food in accordance with Jewish law, especially excluding pork and shellfish (Deuteronomy 14:3-21). Kosher is that which is biblically kosher, but it also includes that which is rabbinic kosher, such as the rabbinic laws on the separation of meat and dairy products by at least four hours.

-L-

Ladino

The colloquial language of Sephardic Jews based primarily on Spanish with word taken from Hebrew, Arabic and other language, and written in the Hebrew alphabet.

Latkes

Potato pancakes traditionally eaten during Hanukkah.

Law of Return

Israeli law that permits Jews to make *aliyah* to Israel, receiving automatic citizenship.

L'Chayim

Means: "to life" or "to health" (a toast or salute).

Lord's Day

The first day of the week (Sunday), as the day Lord *Yeshua* was raised from the dead. The first Lord's Day was on the Feast of Firstfruits and it became by tradition the day of worship for Christians.

-M-

Magen David

Literal meaning is the "shield of David." This familiar six-pointed star has become the universal sign of Judaism and the nation of Israel which is also featured on the modern Israeli flag.

Marranos

An old Spanish term meaning "swine," used to execrate Medieval Spanish Jews who converted to Christianity but secretly kept their Judaism.

Masoretes, Masoretic text

Derived from *masorah*, meaning "tradition:" The Masoretes were the rabbis in 9th-century Palestine who sought to preserve the traditional text of the Bible (hence called the Masoretic text), which is still used in contemporary synagogues. The Masoretes were scholars who encourage Bible study and attempted to achieve uniformity by establishing rules for correcting the text in matters of spelling, grammar, and pronunciation.

Matzah, Matzoh

Flat, unleavened bread used during the Passover.

Mazel Tov

Meaning "Good luck" or "congratulations."

Megillah

Literally it means "scroll." Refers to one of the five scrolls read on special holidays: Sukkot / Ecclesiastes; Purim / Esther; Pesakh (Passover) / Song of Songs; Shavuot / Ruth; Tisha b'Av / Lamentations.

Menorah

A candelabrum; usually refers to the 9-branch candelabrum used to hold the Hanukkah candles (more properly called a *hanukiyah*). Can also refer to the 7-branch candelabrum used in the temple.

Meshiach, Moshiach, Mashiach

Means "anointed one;" Messiah. It was used of kings, priests, and prophets when they were anointed by God. But after the captivity it became a technical term for the one who the Jewish people believe will be the "Meshiach," their deliverer, who will also bring in the Kingdom and peace.

Meshugenah

A person by their speech or actions that is not quite normal. Crazy.

Meshumad

Literally "one deserving of extinction." One who "converts" to Christianity. A heretic and traitor to Judaism.

Messiah

Messiah is the long-awaited deliverer of the Jewish people, as was foretold by the Hebrew prophets. Jewish Orthodox people believe in two different and distinct Messiahs coming two different times. They call them Messiah ben Joseph, the Suffering Servant, and Messiah ben David, the reigning King who will bring peace to the world. Reform Judaism believes only in a Messianic age, not a personal Messiah at all. No one in Judaism believes that the Messiah is divine or God; they consider that to be idolatry. In Christianity we believe the Messiah is one person who will come twice. We also believe that Jesus of Nazareth is the Messiah of Israel and fulfilled all the first coming references of Messiah in His suffering and death as our substitute on the cross. He will come again in the second coming to rescue Israel from doom at the hands of the anti-Christ, but only when Jewish people repent and call on Him to come, will He come.

Messiah ben David

(see Messiah ben Joseph)

Messiah ben Joseph

Because the rabbis of old saw the passages that dealt with a suffering Messiah and the passages that dealt with a reigning Messiah, they came up with this view. Messiah ben Joseph would come first and fight the battles for freedom and peace but would suffer and die, then would come Messiah ben David who would usher in the promised kingdom. They did then and do now view two separate Messiah's. In Christianity Jesus is viewed as one Messiah who comes twice, once to suffer and die and later to reign upon the throne of His father David.

Messianic

Messianic pertains to the person or concept of "Messiah." Jewish people who believe *Yeshua* to be the Messiah usually use this term to describe their particular kind of faith. It is the etymological equivalent of the word "Christian," which is derived from *Christos*, the word used by ancient Greek-speaking Jews for Messiah. So hence today you will find Jewish believers in Messiah *Yeshua* (Jesus) calling themselves Messianic believers, who attend Messianic congregations or synagogues on the Sabbath and belong to the Messianic movement.

Messianic Age

A time of peace and prosperity that was foretold by the Hebrew prophets. Traditional thinking is that Messiah will bring this about. Reform Judaism holds this to be an ideal to be reached through human endeavor, and does not expect a personal Messiah at all. Orthodox and most Conservative Jews believe the Messiah to be a person, but not divine. We who believe in Him believe that *Yeshua ha-Mashiach* will usher in the Messianic Age when He returns at the second coming to set up the Millennial Kingdom.

Mezuzah

In the Hebrew it means "doorpost." A small, elongated decorative box, usually of metal or ceramic attached to the exterior doorframe (at the right side of the entrance) of a Jewish home. Sometimes it will be found on the interior doorposts of rooms particularly in Orthodox homes. Inside the mezuzah is a tiny handwritten scroll on which are written Deuteronomy 6:4-9; 11:13-21; Exodus 13:1-10, 11-16. These passages are the writings of the precepts of God on the doorposts. The word *Shaddai* (almighty) or the letter *shin* (שׁ) usually is inscribed on the mezuzah. The mezuzah is a way of fulfilling this literally.

Midrash

Rabbinical Commentary on the Torah.

Mikvah

Mean "immerse," ritual bath of spiritual purification. It is used primarily in conversion rituals and after a woman's menstrual cycles. But many Hasidim immerse themselves in the mikvah regularly for general spiritual purification. This is self immersion and Christian baptism originated in this Jewish practice by the first followers of Messiah *Yeshua*.

Millennium

A Latin based word literally meaning a period of a thousand years. This will be the period of time for the "thousand year" physical reign of Messiah on the throne of David in Jerusalem. It will be a time of peace and prosperity on the earth that was promised to Israel by the prophets.

Minyan

Quorum needed for any religious service, ten men who are 13 years old or older.

Miryam

Miriam

Miriam

This is the name of Mary the mother of Jesus. Miriam's name is Mary in the New Testament because if you move from Hebrew to Greek to Latin and English it changes.

Mishnah

During the years between the two Testaments a group of Jewish men called *Sophrim* (scribes) developed rules on how to observe the Law of God. Later in the 1st and 2nd centuries another group of men called the *Tannim* continued the process until it was written down in 220 CE by Rabbi Yehuda ha Nasi. This compilation of the rabbinical oral laws or traditions is also known as the Oral Law. This Oral Law was the authoritative source of *halacha* or Jewish law, supposedly second only to the Bible itself. But in actuality the Mishnah is revered more highly by Rabbinic Judaism then the Written Law of God.

Mitzvah

Command; commonly used to mean "a good deed."

Moshe ben Maimon

A rabbi of the 12th century (1135-1204) living in Egypt during the time of the Crusades. It is said, "From Moses to Moses there was none like Moses." This statement means that Maimonides is to be regarded as the greatest figure in Jewish history since the man who delivered the Ten Commandments to the Jewish people. In fact, the spiritual development of Judaism up to the present age is incomprehensible without taking account of Maimonides; activities as a codifier, judge and commentator of the Bible and the Talmud. He also is the author of the 13 Articles of Faith, which are theological statements directed against Christianity.

Mohel

A person who performs religious circumcisions on baby boys eight days after birth.

-N-

Nachmanides

Moses ben Nakhman Gerondi (1194-1270 CE) also known as Nachmanides or Ramban was a native of Spain and also a well respected rabbi and commentator on Scripture.

Nevi'im

The second division of the Hebrew Scriptures called the prophets (Joshua, Judges, 1 & 2 Samuel, 1 & 2 Kings, Isaiah, Jeremiah, Ezekiel, Hosea, Joel, Amos, Obadiah, Jonah, Micah, Nahum, Habakkuk, Zephaniah, Haggai, Zechariah, Malachi).

New Covenant

The prophet Jeremiah predicted a time when God would make a "New Covenant" with Israel, unlike the first covenant (Mosaic Law) made at Mt. Sinai.

New Testament

A collection of documents composed in the first century CE. They comprised the four Gospels, (biographies of *Yeshua* and His ministry), a history of the early church (book of Acts), several letters from the apostles addressed to various churches, pastors and believers in general (Pauline and General Epistles), and the book of John's vision of the things to come (Revelation). These documents compose the teachings of *Yeshua* and the Apostles of Messiah for the Church.

-O-

Oral Law

Oral instruction beyond the written Torah, which was written down in the Mishnah (core of the Talmud) and is considered by Jewish people as authoritative, equal to the Scriptures. The rabbinic authorities use this argument to substantiate the Oral Law being as weighty as Scripture. They teach that Moses received more from God than the Written Torah on Mt. Sinai. He also received the Oral Law which was memorized, taught to Joshua, who taught it to the Judges, who then taught it to the Prophets and finally to the Sophim. This Oral Law is the central reason why *Yeshua* and the Pharisees were at odds.

-P-

Palestine

A name given to Israel by the Romans after the second Jewish revolt in 135 CE. It is derived from the word "Philistines," a people who had occupied the coastal areas of the land in ancient times, but who had long since passed from history.

Passover

Is a celebration on the 14th of Nisan (March/April) of the liberation of the Jewish people from their bondage in Egypt as described in the book of Exodus (see Exodus 12). This has been celebrated around the world in Jewish homes for over 3500 years.

Pentateuch

Originated from the Greek for "five books/scroll." The five books attributed to Moses; Genesis / Bereishit, Exodus / Shemot, Leviticus / Vayikra, Numbers / Bamidbar, and Deuteronomy / Devarim; known in Jewish tradition as *Torat Mosheh* (the teaching of Moses), or simply the Torah.

Pesach

Hebrew for "Passover."

Peshat

Interpretative method of reading the Torah based on the "plain" meaning of the text.

Phylacteries

See Tefillin

Pilgrim Festivals

The three of the seven Feasts of the LORD required a pilgrimage to Jerusalem by all males who were able to present themselves before the LORD and worship. These three feasts were: Passover, Shavuot (Pentecost) and Succoth (tabernacles or booths).

Pilpul

Dialectical **rational** method of studying Jewish Oral Law as codified in the Talmud, usually identified with the Tosafists.

PLO

Palestinian Authority was a terrorist organization that finally settled on the West Bank and that government was headed up by a terrorist Yasser Arafat. It has commonly been called the Palestinian Liberation Organization, set up to liberate what they called Palestine (Israel) from all Jewish authority.

Pogroms

Organized massacres of Jewish communities carried out in the 19th century in Poland, Russian and Ukraine by the government, sanctioned by the Church and sometimes led by Orthodox priest with the "Christian" cross held high. Thousands of Jewish people immigrated to America and settled in New York City.

Pre-millennialism

The view within early Christianity and today that the Rapture or catching up of the Church will occur before the second coming of Christ and before the Millennial reign of Christ.

Purim

The Jewish holiday is not one of the 7 Feasts of the LORD given in Leviticus 23. It was observed each year on the 14th of Adar (February/March), celebrating the deliverance of the Jewish people from the wicked Haman in the days of Queen Esther of Persia, as described in the book of Esther.

Pushke

A box in the home or the synagogue used to collect money for donation to charity.

-Q-

Quiet Time

A term used among conservative evangelicals and fundamentalists to denote a time set aside for personal meditation and communion with God.

-R-

Rabbinic Judaism

Rabbinic Judaism is different from biblical Judaism. Much of the teaching and customs of the Jewish people today are not biblical but Rabbinic. Rabbinic Judaism has been a process that has been going on since the inter-testament period, 400 BCE through 600 CE, with the rabbis adding to what has become known as the Talmud with thousands of rules and regulations being added by these ancient rabbis which has supplanted the authority of the Hebrew Bible.

Rambam

See Moshe ben Maimon

Rapture

The supernatural "catching up" of all believers into the air to meet Jesus (*Yeshua*) when He comes for His church, as taught in 1 & 2 Thessalonians (1 Thessalonians 4:17). There are three positions taken on when this event occurs: (1) Pre-Tribulational rapture; (2) Mid-Tribulational rapture; and the (3) Post-Tribulational rapture.

Rashi

This is a term used for Shelomo Yitzkhaki of the 11th century (1040-1105) who lived in northern France who is called the world's greatest commentator; his notes on the Bible are recorded in the Talmud in virtually every part of the text.

Rebbe

The title of the spiritual leader of the Hasidim.

Rebbetzin

(Yiddish) the wife of a rabbi.

Reconstructionist Judaism

This is a lesser known branch of Judaism. Founded by Mordecai M. Kaplan (1881-1982), this represents a recent development in American Judaism and attempts to focus on Judaism as a civilization and culture constantly adapting to ensure survival in a natural social process.

Reform Judaism

One of the three major branches of Judaism and the most liberal.

Rosh Hashana

The Jewish secular or civil New Year celebrated on the First of Tishri (September/October), the same as what the Bible calls the "Feast of Trumpets" (Leviticus 23:23-25; Numbers 29:1-6).

Ruach haKodesh

The Holy Spirit

-S-

Sabbath

The Sabbath is the seventh day of the week, holy to the Jewish people by the commandment of God (Exodus 20:8-11; Deuteronomy 5:12-15).

Second Temple Period

This period is from the rebuilding of the temple after the return from captivity in Babylon in 516 BCE through to the destruction of Herod's temple in 70 CE by the Romans.

Seder

Hebrew word for "order." A ceremonial meal eaten at Passover.

Sephardic

This word is the ancient biblical name "Sepharad," which came to be associated with Spain. It pertains to Jews whose ancestors came from Spain and Portugal before the expulsion of the Jews from those lands in 1492 and 1496 respectively. They mostly immigrated to North Africa and to the new world in South America.

Septuagint – LXX

Strictly speaking, this refers to the ancient Greek translation of the Hebrew Pentateuch, probably made during the reign of Ptolemy II, Greek ruler of Egypt around 250 BCE. Subsequently, Greek translations of other portions of the Jewish Scriptures came to be added to the corpus, and the term Septuagint was applied to the entire collection. Such served as the "Scriptures" for Greek-speaking Jews and Christians.

Shabbat

Hebrew for "Sabbath."

Shabbles/Shabbos

Yiddish for "Sabbath."

Shaddai

Means almighty as in El Shaddai or God Almighty.

Shalom

Hebrew word for peace used as a greeting like Hello, and Goodbye.

Shalom Alechem

"Peace be unto you"

Shavuot

One of the three Pilgrim Feasts required in the Torah when all able males are to appear before the LORD in Jerusalem. Also known as the Feast of Weeks and Pentecost, celebrated seven weeks plus one day after Passover.

Shekhitah

Kosher ritual slaughtering

Shem HaMeforash

"The Forbidden Name," the Tetragrammaton.

Shema, Sh'ma

Sh'ma is a Jewish affirmation of faith (Deuteronomy 6:4), recited morning and evening by religious Jews and during all worship services. In Rabbinic Judaism it emphases the absolute oneness of God.

Shemonehesreh

In the Hebrew it is called the "eighteen." The main section of Jewish prayers recited in a standing position and containing 19 "benedictions:" (1) praise to God of the fathers / patriarchs, (2) God's power and (3) holiness; (4) prayer for knowledge, (5) repentance, (6) forgiveness, (7) redemption, (8) healing sick persons, (9) agricultural prosperity, (10) ingathering the diaspora, (11) righteous judgment, (12) punishment of wicked and heretics (Birkat Haminim), (13) reward of pious, (14) rebuilding Jerusalem, (15) restoration of royal house of David, (16) acceptance of prayers, (17) thanks to God, (18) restoration of temple worship, and (19) peace.

Sheol

Place of departed dead.

Shoah

In the Hebrew is means "whirlwind" and it refers to the Holocaust.

Shofar

Shofar is a ram's horn which makes a very impressive noise and has been used since ancient times to summon troops to battle or the people to assemble; also used to mark the approach of Sabbath and other Holy Days, especially associated with Rosh Hashana, biblical known at the Feast of Trumpets.

Shokhet or Schochet

A kosher ritual slaughterer.

Shuklin

It is a Yiddish word for swaying or rocking during prayer.

Shule

Another word for an Orthodox or Chasidic Synagogue, from the German word for "School;" it indicates that the chief purpose of the synagogue is for the study of the Law.

Simcha

Joyous occasions

Simchat Torah

Rejoicing over the Law. Marks the conclusion of the public reading of the Torah in the Synagogue each year.

Siddur

Jewish prayer book which contains prayers, Scripture and order of services.

Sophrim

After the return from captivity in Babylon, Ezra the Scribe set up what was known as the School of the Sophrim. This was to teach the scribes the Law so they could teach the people so they would know the Law and obey it. However, the generation that followed Ezra began to teach that they must build a fence around the Law of rules and regulations, the thought being that the people might then break the fence about the Law but not break the Law itself. When all the scribes and later rabbis agreed on a new rule or regulation, it became binding. After the Sophrim came the Tannim in the first century CE; they did the same thing but added one point. All that preceded them that was done by the Sophrim was made equal in authority to the Hebrew Scriptures. Then later the Gemara added hundreds of new laws, rule and regulations. This later became known as the Talmud. One illustration is of what they did with the 613 Laws of God. There is one that says, "Thou shalt keep the Sabbath day holy," meaning that no work was to be done on the Sabbath. Over the course of those years as the fence was built around that Law, in the Talmud, they added 1500 new laws, rules and regulations to God's one law. They did this with all 613 Laws of Moses given to him at Mt. Sinai.

855

Sukkah

A temporary "booth" or shelter made for the holiday of the Feast of Sukkoth (or booths or tabernacles). It is used to eat meals and for sleeping and so on during the feast.

Sukkoth

Literally means "booths." One of the three Pilgrim Festivals marked by the building of makeshift shelters called "Succoth" to commemorate the wandering of the Israelites in the wilderness on the way to the Promised Land. In the Hebrew Scriptures it is known as the Feast of Tabernacles.

Synagogue

Means "assembly;" this word usually indicates either Orthodox or Conservative Judaism.

-T-

Tabernacle

From the Latin word *tabernaculum*, "tent." The word is used in many English translations of the Torah for the Tent of Meeting, the portable forerunner of the temple, which God commanded Moses to build when the Israelites were wandering in the Wilderness. This word is also used for *Sukkah*, a temporary structure built yearly for the holiday of *Sukkoth*, which is called the Feast of Tabernacles.

Tallit, or Tallis

The prayer shawl is a large shawl with fringes and special knots at the extremities, worn by Jewish men during prayer in the synagogue or at home. The fringes, according to the Bible (Numbers 15:38-39), remind the worshiper of God's commandments.

Talmud

Means "study;" the oral traditions, discussions and instruction of the great rabbis and scholars of Judaism. Written in two divisions, the Mishnah and Gemara taken together equal the Talmud. This system of comments when completed became more important than the Scriptures upon which it was based – thus began Talmudic or Rabbinic Judaism, culminating in what we call Orthodox Judaism.

Tanakh

The Jewish Scriptures are exactly the same as the Protestant "Old Testament." The Hebrew term *Tanakh* is an acronym derived from the Hebrew words "**T**orah," "**N**evi'im," and "**K**ethuvim;" or the Law, the Prophets and the Writings (poetry and wisdom literature).

Targums

Aramaic paraphrases from the first century BCE and the first century of the CE of the Hebrew Scriptures.

Tefillin or Phylacteries

Small boxes containing verses of Scripture which religious Jewish males bind to the left arm next to the heart and another around the forehead by means of leather straps, in obedience to Exodus 13:9, 16 and Deuteronomy 6:8; 11:18.

Temple

The holy place of worship in Jerusalem, which replaced Moses' wilderness tabernacle on land purchased for it by King David, and originally built by Solomon. In Reform Judaism they often name their synagogues using the term temple, such as Temple Bethel.

Temple Mount

The artificially expanded hill by Herod in Jerusalem on which the first and second temples stood, now occupied by the Muslim Dome of the Rock.

Teshuvah

The Hebrew word for "repentance," which literally means "turning" away from sin, towards the good.

Tetragrammaton

Greek for the four-letter "forbidden name" of God. The four letters are YHVH and is translated in the King James Version of the Bible as LORD.

Tish'a b'Av

The "Ninth of Av." A Jewish holy day commemorating the destruction of the first temple built by Solomon in 586 BCE by Nebuchadnezzar King of Babylon (Zechariah 7:5; 8:19). According to tradition, it was on this same date in 70 CE that the Romans under Titus destroyed the second temple known as Herod's temple. Many other national disasters have been associated with this date, including the Spanish inquisition and the Holocaust. So Tish'a b'Av has come to stand for national calamity in general.

Torah

The Pentateuch. The first five books of the Bible; literally "teaching" or "instruction" or "guidance." Often translated "the Law" in English Bibles, as in "the Law of the LORD is perfect" (Psalm 19:7 [8]). This is also an elastic term, which can also mean a single point of teaching to the whole of the Hebrew Bible, and the Oral Law.

Tosefta

Tosefta is a generation of Talmudic interpreters after Rashi, best known as exponents of Pilpul, hair-splitting dialectical exegesis of Talmud.

Treyfe

Treyfe is a Yiddish word meaning unacceptable food, non-kosher, not in accordance with God's food laws.

Tzitzit

The fringe attached to the four corners of the Tallit (prayer shawl) or to the four corners of the garments of Orthodox Jews, which is based on the Torah passages of Numbers 15:37-41 and Deuteronomy 22:12.

-W-

Wailing Wall – see Western Wall

Western Wall

Western wall or the Wailing Wall is a portion of the western retaining wall built by Herod when he renovated the Temple Mount. It is regarded by the Jewish people as a holy place owing to its proximity to the site of the Holy of Holies on the platform above it.

-X-

Xenophobia

Xenophobia is the irrational fear of strangers or of persons different from yourself. One of the roots of anti-Semitism.

-Y-

Yad

Hand-shaped pointer used while reading from Torah scrolls in the synagogue.

Yarmulke

A Yiddish word for the skull-cup worn by observant Jewish males (see Kippah).

Yavneh

This was the first location of the first Great Rabbinic Academy. It is located 25 miles west of Jerusalem on the Mediterranean coast near present day Joppa and Tel Aviv. It was established by Yochanan ben Zakkai who escaped from Jerusalem about 69 CE and received permission from Vespasian, the Roman general who had Jerusalem under siege, to establish a school to study Torah. With the loss of Jerusalem and the temple Rabbi Zakkai retooled Judaism to survive without a temple and sacrifice. He is most responsible for the establishment of Rabbinic Judaism and the complete authority of the Oral Law over the Written Law.

Yerushalayim

The Hebrew name of the city of Jerusalem.

Yeshiva

An orthodox religious school of higher learning for the study of the Talmud.

Yeshua

Meaning "Jesus" and comes from the Hebrew root word for "salvation."

Yeshua ha-Mashiach

Hebrew for "Jesus the Messiah."

Yetzer Hara

The inclination to do evil

Yetzer hatov

The inclination to do good.

YHVH (Yahweh)

YHVH, the sacred name of God in Jewish Scriptures and tradition is also known as the Tetragrammaton. Since Hebrew was written without vowels in ancient times, the four consonants YHVH contain no clue to their original pronunciation. They are generally rendered "Yahweh" in contemporary scholarship. In traditional Judaism, the name is not pronounced, but Adonai, "Our Lord" or something similar is substituted. In most English versions of the Bible the Tetragrammaton is represented by "LORD" and less frequently, "Jehovah."

Yiddish

Yiddish is a language which was widely spoken and written by Jews from Germany, Poland and Russia. It used middle high German, incorporating some Hebrew words and local idioms. Hebrew print and script were used. It has been in decline for years but in recent years with the growth of ultra-orthodox groups like the Hasidim, it has been on the increase in the New York area. People who use it as their mother tongue or first language are on the increase today.

Yochanan

The Hebrew name for John

Yom Ha'Atzmaut

Israeli Independence Day

Yom Ha-Shoah

Holocaust Remembrance Day

Yom Ha-Zikkaron

Israeli Memorial Day

Yom Kippur

The Day of Atonement. The holiest and most solemn day in the Jewish calendar. In temple times, this was the day the High Priest would approach the throne of God in the Holy of Holies to seek atonement for the sins of the people (Leviticus 16). Today it is marked by fasting and abstinence from marital relations and use of cosmetics and toiletries.

Yom Yerushalayim

Holiday celebrating the reunification of Jerusalem in the hands of the modern state of Israel.

Yosef

Hebrew name for Joseph

-Z-

Zakkai, Rabbi Yochanan ben

See Yavneh

Zion

Originally another name for Mt. Moriah, the hill just north of David's Jerusalem, which he purchased from Araunah the Jebusite as the site for the first temple as built by Solomon. By extension, the name is used of Jerusalem, and by further extension, the land of Israel.

Zionism

The movement to restore the Jewish people to a sovereign homeland of their own.

Zionist

A supporter of the Jewish State, namely, Israel.

Zohar

Zohar is the basic work of Kabbalah, mystical Aramaic commentary on the book of Moses, ascribed to Simeon ben Johai of the second century, but probably written by Moses de Leon of the 13th century.

AUTHOR INDEX

Butler, J. Glentworth, 59, 148, 344, 809
Buttrick, George Arthur, 276, 809

C

Cassuto, Umberto, 187, 293, 809
Chafer, Lewis Sperry, 23, 90, 102, 110, 277, 284, 809
Charles, Robert Henry, 496, 809
Charnock, Steven, 374, 375, 809
Child, Brevard, 810
Chilton, Bruce D., 710, 810
Chisholm, Jr., Robert B., 520, 827
Cohen, Hermann, 744, 745, 748, 755, 757, 759
Cohen, Rabbi A., 408, 412, 442, 474, 569, 753, 810
Cohn-Sherbok, Rabbi Dan, 4, 494, 495, 496, 766, 789, 810
Cole, R. Alan, 175, 810
Cole, R. Dennis, 199, 386, 810
Conrad, Edgar W., 413, 591, 810
Cook, F.C., 513, 527
Cooke, G.A., 306, 354, 810
Cooper, David L., 12, 13, 60, 71, 76, 80, 81, 83, 84, 86, 89, 94, 121, 122, 123, 124, 158, 279, 280, 281, 282, 284, 285, 307, 315, 333, 334, 340, 354, 379, 380, 381, 384, 396, 397, 398, 399, 478, 479, 481, 498, 500, 508, 563, 611, 612, 641, 644, 648, 650, 655, 810
Cooper, Lamar Eugene, 354, 811
Cornelis, 815
Craigie, P. C., 274, 811
Crenshaw, James, 317, 811
Criswell, W. A., 284, 811
Currid, John D., 130, 132, 137, 142, 144, 145, 150, 152, 156, 160, 164, 167, 168, 169, 182, 183, 184, 187, 188, 192, 259, 811

D

Dahood, Mitchell, 318, 518, 523, 811
Davidson, A. B., 175, 304, 811
Davidson, Robert, 439, 811
Davis, Barry C., 480, 828
Davis, John J., 177, 179, 186, 229, 230, 240, 479, 811
DeHaan, Richard W., 64, 811
Delitzsch, Franz, 60, 131, 136, 138, 139, 147, 151, 152, 157, 162, 166, 169, 170, 181, 188, 196, 197, 198, 199, 207, 227,

228, 234, 240, 241, 242, 244, 260, 303, 313, 318, 319, 321, 346, 386, 388, 438, 439, 458, 463, 464, 466, 477, 515, 544, 556, 561, 563, 569, 593, 594, 601, 745, 811, 817
Dickason, C. Fred, 120, 379, 811
Dixon, A. C., 356, 825
Dockery, David S., 20, 828
Driver, Samuel R., 50, 170, 175, 192, 283, 302, 303, 304, 305, 311, 312, 371, 376, 414, 809, 811
Du Bois, Lauriston J., 386, 811
Dunnam, Maxie D., 176, 811
Dyrness, William, 86, 332, 811

E

Edersheim, Alfred, 97, 180, 184, 188, 811, 834
Ellicott, C. J., 151, 162, 167, 823
Elwell, Walter A., 90, 99, 208, 331, 811
Enns, Paul, 3, 90, 99, 214, 269, 274, 335, 344, 352, 355, 360, 364, 812
Epstein, Rabbi I, 114, 812
Erickson, Millard J., 20, 79, 265, 329, 330, 331, 336, 344, 664, 812
Evans, William, 270, 275, 812, 813
Ezra, 384

F

Fabry, Heinz-Josef, 35, 60, 88, 89, 206, 238, 268, 270, 273, 371, 373, 375, 412, 413, 414, 557, 717, 808
Fausset, A. R., 199, 289, 316, 435, 816
Feinberg, Charles, 35, 97, 252, 265, 292, 321, 322, 342, 354, 384, 434, 439, 440, 444, 445, 446, 453, 454, 501, 503, 505, 508, 574, 576, 580, 581, 583, 586, 589, 603, 606, 610, 812, 828
Feinberg, John, 330, 340, 342
Feinberg, John S., 330
Figart, Thomas, ix, 473, 812
Finkel, Avraham Yaakov, 153, 194, 710, 812
Fischer, John, 18, 19, 828
Frame, John M., 49, 50, 51, 202, 812
Free, Joseph P., 412, 812
Fretheim, Terence E., 574, 580, 812
Frey, Joseph Samuel C. F., 134, 185, 399, 460, 461, 465, 492, 493, 582, 812
Fruchtenbaum, Arnold G., xi, xxi, xxv, 17, 22, 23, 24, 35, 66, 67, 71, 78, 88, 93, 97,

Janzen, J. Gerald, 270, 828

Jenni, Ernest, 38, 60, 64, 88, 125, 148, 238, 269, 273, 314, 376, 412, 413, 414, 549, 626, 816

Jocz, Jacob, 10, 763

Jocz, Jakob, iv, 10, 97, 524, 737, 816, 828

John J., 828

Johnson, Gordon, 477

Johnson, Gordon H. S., 23, 267, 477, 513, 527, 530, 540, 816

Johnson, John J., 23

Johnstone, Patrick, 31, 816

Johnstone, William, 234, 816

Jones, Douglas Rawlinson, 576, 581, 816

Jukes, Andrew, 26, 816

Julien, Tom, 192, 816

K

Kac, Arthur W., 8, 97, 293, 712, 816

Kaiser, Walter C., 94, 177, 181, 182, 184, 186, 192, 193, 196, 317, 320, 321, 326, 342, 352, 384, 427, 436, 444, 448, 449, 450, 451, 453, 454, 455, 457, 458, 461, 463, 464, 507, 564, 566, 567, 570, 581, 584, 585, 586, 588, 591, 592, 594, 599, 600, 603, 604, 605, 607, 610, 611, 612, 816, 817, 828

Kalisher, Zvi, 426, 829

Kalland, Earl S., 389, 817

Kaplan, Aryeh, 5, 9, 52, 411, 768, 769, 770, 771, 776, 783, 817, 852

Keil, C. F., 60, 109, 131, 136, 138, 139, 147, 151, 152, 157, 162, 166, 169, 170, 181, 188, 195, 196, 197, 198, 199, 207, 227, 228, 234, 240, 241, 242, 244, 260, 313, 318, 319, 321, 346, 388, 438, 439, 453, 454, 458, 463, 464, 466, 477, 515, 544, 556, 563, 569, 593, 594, 601, 817

Keiser, Thomas A., 41, 43, 45, 829

Kelle, Page, 77, 79, 560, 817

Kelley, Page, 77

Kidner, Derek, 514, 531, 532, 533, 534, 535, 540, 817

King, Henry Melville, 530, 817

Kirkpatrick, A. F., 335, 817

Kittel, Rud, 253, 254, 817, 844

Klausner, Joseph, 365, 383, 384, 746, 753, 817

Klinghoffer, David, 7, 10, 13, 399, 400, 708, 715, 716, 817

Knight, George A. F., 72, 77, 817

Kofahl, Robert E., 735, 829

Kohlenberger, John R, III, 50, 58, 131, 132, 133, 134, 136, 161, 167, 170, 253, 254, 280, 283, 290, 313, 315, 316, 318, 430, 453, 485, 548, 549, 573, 628, 817

Kolatch, Alfred, 143, 817

L

Laetsch, Theodore, 249, 321, 434, 439, 440, 578, 582, 586, 599, 600, 608, 609, 817

Lamsa, George M., 409, 817

Landman, Leo, 384, 818

Lang, G. H., 501, 503, 505, 508, 818

Lange, John Peter, 198, 199, 314, 315, 818

Lawson, George, 818

Leeser, Isaac, 66, 122, 381, 485, 548, 584, 606, 628, 653, 654, 690, 818

Leman, Derek, 732, 734, 735, 736, 828

Lenski, R. C. H., 622, 818

Leupold, H. C., 60, 108, 109, 131, 139, 157, 159, 165, 167, 241, 242, 293, 316, 376, 513, 515, 522, 561, 562, 568, 818

Levine, Samuel, 20, 352, 353, 368, 411, 418, 419, 426, 436, 442, 451, 478, 499, 500, 571, 577, 595, 596, 598, 599, 716, 767, 768, 773, 776, 818

Levy, David, 97, 456, 457, 459, 460, 612, 613, 818, 829

Lindberg, Milton G., 9, 285, 286, 512, 666, 830

Livingston, 818

Livingston, G. Herbert, 305

Lockyer, Herbert, 26, 61, 335, 344, 818

Loewen, Jacob A., 292, 828

Longman, Tremper, III, 316, 317, 488, 549, 818

M

MacDonald, G. Jeffrey, 22

MacDonald, Jeffrey G., 829

MacDonald, William, 530, 537, 546, 818

Mackay, John L., 175, 183, 185, 187, 191, 196, 578, 589, 634, 818

Madvig, Donald, 215, 819

Mandryk, Jason, 31, 816

Mathews, Kenneth, 44, 66, 67, 131, 138, 143, 149, 151, 162, 291, 292, 295, 378, 382, 383, 819

Mays, James L., 476, 515, 517, 523, 526, 819

McCann, J. Clinton, 347, 818

McCarter, P. Kyle, Jr., 350, 818

McClain, Alva J., 499, 500, 818
McConville, 269, 389, 390, 819
McDowell, Josh, 467, 819
McG. Fry, Euan, 306, 311, 821
McGee, J. Vernon, 259, 460, 466, 819
Merrill, Eugene H., 125, 235, 251, 252, 253, 255, 257, 274, 286, 303, 321, 322, 379, 444, 450, 451, 458, 483, 608, 819, 828
Milgrom, Jacob, 393, 394, 819
Miller, H. S., 11
Miller, Paul, 50, 254, 291, 313, 315, 573
Miller, Stephen, 485, 488, 502, 503, 505, 508
Moeller, Henry R., 211, 819
Moore, George Foot, 48, 218, 225, 707, 712, 739, 819, 828
Morey, Robert, 15, 16, 100, 101, 102, 104, 218, 279, 333, 334, 335, 336, 345, 819
Morris, Henry, 71, 74, 93, 94, 130, 137, 142, 144, 146, 157, 160, 163, 166, 170, 259, 278, 292, 293, 296, 300, 513, 514, 515, 516, 519, 522, 531, 532, 542, 819
Morris, Robert, 72, 74, 94
Motyer, J. Alec, 241, 352, 562, 569, 819

N

Nachman, Moshe ben, 307, 308, 441, 819
Nadler, Sam, 17, 94, 95, 97, 820
Nassi, Rabbi Tzvi, 93, 296, 529, 647, 651, 652, 820
Neusner, Jacob, 14, 28, 88, 89, 115, 201, 211, 301, 650, 656, 710, 711, 712, 713, 810, 820
Niehaus, Jeffrey J., 87, 128, 129, 130, 133, 134, 204, 208, 209, 210, 820, 828
Nix, William E., 356, 813
Nixon, Jim, 278, 820
Noth, Martin, 395, 820
Novak, David, 56, 714, 813

O

Ochs, Peter, 56, 714, 813
Odom, Robert Leo, 249, 250, 820
Oehler, Gustave Friedrich, 57, 107, 820
Ogden, Graham, 316, 317, 820
Olson, Dennis T., 394, 820
Orlov, Andrei, 113, 117, 820, 829
Orr, James, 125, 820
Owens, John Joseph, 290, 291, 314, 318, 820

P

Pache, Pache, 336, 341, 363, 364, 820
Parkes, James, 664, 665, 820
Patai, Raphael, 415, 416, 417, 433, 820
Paul, 816
Payne, J. Barton, 26, 27, 58, 63, 69, 86, 103, 110, 234, 270, 334, 335, 339, 341, 343, 820
Perowne, J. J. Stewart, 522, 528, 820
Peterson, David L., 590, 820
Pfeiffer, Charles, 211, 821
Phillips, John, 36, 554
Phillips, O. E., 35, 36, 476, 477, 478, 482, 519, 544, 821, 826
Picker, Chaim, 52, 96, 368, 370, 378, 408, 410, 482, 594, 595, 596, 768, 770, 773, 774, 776, 777, 778, 779, 780, 783, 785, 786, 821
Pressler, Carolyn, 216
Preuss, Horst Dietrich, 57, 69, 821
Pritchard, James B., 382, 483, 576, 594, 821
Pryor, Dwight A., 18, 267, 829
Pusey, E. B., 600, 602, 603, 606, 821

R

Rendsburg, Gary, 83, 829
Reyburn, William D., 306, 311, 312, 518, 523, 808, 821
Reymond, Robert, 103, 233, 821
Reznick, Leibel, 23, 821
Riddle, 319, 821
Riddle, J. M., 319
Ringgren, Heimer, 35, 60, 88, 89, 206, 238, 268, 270, 273, 371, 373, 375, 412, 413, 414, 551, 557, 717, 808
Robertson, A. T., 596, 821
Robinson, George, 283, 821
Robinson, Mark, 97, 414, 830
Root, 276
Root, Gerald, 264, 276, 277, 821
Rosenberg, A. J., 457, 821
Rosenberg, David, 41
Rosenberg, Joel, 672
Rosenthal, Stanley, 72, 97, 278, 284, 821
Ross, Allen P., 83, 99, 103, 175, 319, 337, 578, 808, 814, 818, 821
Rudin, James A., 824
Runes, Dagobert D., 112, 821
Ryken, Philip Graham, 575, 577, 583, 584, 821
Ryle, Herbert E., 303, 304, 306, 307, 822

Ryrie, Charles Caldwell, 335, 341, 361, 822

S

Sacchi, Paolo, 211, 461, 822
Sailhamer, John, 42, 43, 44, 82, 133, 147, 148, 150, 151, 152, 169, 179, 188, 192, 284, 285, 290, 291, 390, 391, 403, 608, 822
Sanders, John, 732, 822
Sandmel, David Fox, 56, 714, 813
Santala, Risto, 427, 829
Sarna, Nahum, 64, 66, 69, 302, 305, 306, 822
Saucy, Robert L., 21, 822
Scherman, Rabbi Nosson, 137, 143, 153, 154, 155, 179, 189, 193, 194, 208, 548, 564, 707, 708, 709, 710, 822
Schiffman, Michael, 18, 65, 80, 822
Schneider, Tammi J., 346, 348, 822
Schochet, Jacob Immanuel, 428, 441, 461, 774, 775, 776, 822
Schoen, Robert, 15, 714, 822
Scholem, Gershom G., 117, 822
Schultz, Samuel, 57, 822
Schurer, Emil, 14, 211, 461, 822
Scialitti, Rabbi Mofes, 584, 822
Scott, J. Julius, 822
Scott, Jack, 63, 65, 77, 87
Scott, William, 201
Selman, Martin, 234, 235, 822
Shorrosh, Anis A., 84, 822
Showers, Renald E., 70, 487, 501, 502, 504, 505, 507, 508, 822, 823
Sigal, Gerald, 449, 473, 619, 620, 621, 624, 823
Signer, Michael A., 56, 813
Silver, Arthur M., 824
Silver, Rabbi Abba Hillel, 506, 823
Singer, Isidore, 113, 114, 123, 125, 210, 211, 494, 823
Singer, Rabbi Abba Hillel, 475, 476, 477
Singer, Tovia, 476, 477
Skinner, John, 38, 259, 306, 823
Sloan, W. W., 211, 823
Slotki, I. W., 302, 320, 323, 326, 823
Smith, Colon, 314
Smith, Henrey Preserved Smith, 73
Smith, Henry, 73
Smith, Henry Preserved, 73, 823
Smith, James E., 21, 57, 321, 322, 366, 387, 388, 389, 390, 458, 459, 482, 483, 488, 499, 506, 569, 607, 823

Smith, John Merlin Powis, 461, 463, 608, 823
Smith, John Merlin Powis., 462
Smith, Payne, 142, 151, 167, 307, 308, 823
Smith, Ralph L., 269, 823
Smith, William, 89, 148, 483, 823
Soggin, J. Alberto, 347, 823
Sorko-Ram, Shira, 785, 823
Speiser, E. A., 298, 299, 312, 823
Spurgeon, Charles H., 242, 521, 823
Stanton, R. Todd, 459, 463, 823
Stedman, Ray C., 576, 577, 824
Steinberg, Milton, 266, 824
Steinsaltz, Rabbi Adin, 116, 156, 294, 313, 478, 486, 492, 824
Stenning, J. F., 70, 71, 194, 655, 824
Steveson, Peter A., 243, 244, 245, 559, 561, 570, 824
Stone, Nathan, 73, 824
Strickman, H. Norman, 384, 824
Strong, Augustus, 325, 824
Swanson, James A., 58, 132, 134, 170, 283, 453, 817

T

Talbot, Gordon, 40, 41, 89, 145, 152, 169, 824
Talmage, James E., 34, 824
Tanenbaum, Marc H., 14, 824
Taylor, John B., 246, 354, 384, 824
Taylor, Richard A., 458, 461, 465, 601, 824
Telchin, Stan, 266, 668, 824
Tenney, Merrill C., 99, 101, 111, 183, 201, 361, 621, 824
Terrien, Samuel, 478, 521, 824
Thiessen, Henry C., 87, 360, 824
Thomas, Thomas A., 277, 824
Thompson, J. A., 234, 440, 582, 824
Tomasino, Anthony J., 618, 619, 622, 623, 625, 825
Torrey, R. A., 338, 339, 356, 357, 825
Towner, W. Sibley, 73, 74, 292, 336, 337, 496, 497, 825
Trapp, John, 444, 825
Tregelles, Samuel Prideaux, 61, 825
Turner, Laurence A., 307, 825

U

Unger, Merrill, 251, 255, 321, 379, 444, 453, 604, 605, 825
Unger, Merrill., 825

SCRIPTURE INDEX

TORAH – LAW

HISTORICAL BOOKS

Joshua

MAJOR PROPHETS

MINOR PROPHETS —The Twelve

NEW TESTAMENT —GOSPELS

Matthew

HISTORICAL—Acts of Apostles

Acts

PAULINE EPISTLES

GENERAL EPISTLES

PROPHETIC